BLACK MUSIC IN AMERICA:
a bibliography

by
JoAnn Skowronski

The Scarecrow Press, Inc.
Metuchen, N.J., & London
1981

Library of Congress Cataloging in Publication Data

Skowronski, JoAnn.
  Black music in America.

  Includes index.
  1. Afro-Americans--Music--History and criticism--
Bibliography. 2. Afro-American musicians--Bibliog-
raphy. 3. Music--United States--Bibliography.
  I. Title.
ML128.B45S6   016.7817'296073   81-5609
ISBN 0-8108-1443-9   AACR2

This book is dedicated
to my husband, Ray,
for his assistance in the
preparation of this book.

CONTENTS

INTRODUCTION

This bibliography is designed as a reference work with which to locate books and articles about black music and black musicians in the United States from Colonial times through 1979. It is divided into three sections: Selected Musicians and Singers, General References, and Reference Works.

Section One, Selected Musicians and Singers, includes representative artists from various fields of music, such as jazz, opera, and popular music. All were either born in the United States or, if born elsewhere, had a definite influence on American music. Individuals were included who principally gave concerts and recorded their material. Several musicians were selected from each musical style in an effort to provide a balanced treatment. Fame was not used as a decisive criterion, therefore some well-known musicians have been included as well as some lesser-known musicians.

Extensive material was available on some of the musicians listed, such as Louis Armstrong and Count Basie, but relatively little material was available on others. Occasionally it was found that there was more than one musician with the same name, such as Billy Taylor and Joe Turner. Access to all the references found was not possible, so it could not always be determined which reference referred to which individual. Consequently, names such as these were eliminated to prevent confusion.

Many of the listed musicians were active in jazz. This is one of the areas in which black musicians had considerable impact on the development of American music. In contrast, country music has few active black musicians. If a reference discusses several musicians, it is listed under each musician's name provided the name is included in Selected Musicians and Singers.

The second section, General References, includes books and articles that examine various aspects of black music, such as general history.   Exceptions include entries on more specific subjects such as the Fisk Jubilee Singers, Opera/South (a black opera company), and selected dissertations that analyze various black musicians' styles.

Reference Works, the third section, emphasizes material such as bibliographies, indexes, and encyclopedias that contain a significant amount of information on black music or black musicians.   An Index to authors' names keyed to entry numbers completes the book.

Entries consist chiefly of books and journal articles.   Musical compositions, phonograph records, films, and most newspaper articles are excluded.   However, reviews of these items are included.   Books written for young people are listed and noted as juvenile literature to assist the researcher in ascertaining the intellectual level of material.   Books and articles in foreign languages are included.   However, if an English translation of a book is available, that is the only version listed.   Books and articles that contain musical notation are included only when important historical literature is present as well.

Entries are numbered consecutively throughout the book. The references are listed chronologically by publication date from the earliest to the most recent time within each section and under each musician's name.   The longest period of time appears first. Therefore, an entry that contains only a year in its publication date is filed before one that includes both a month and a year. Following these are entries that contain day, month, and year. A reprint edition is filed in its appropriate section by its original publication date.   However, the entry also carries the most recent information about the current publisher.   Only the latest edition of a book is listed when it has been revised.

When more than one entry has the same publication date, the entries are arranged alphabetically by author, or by title if there is no author.   Names beginning with "Mac" and "Mc" are

listed together as if they were all spelled "Mac." Multiple sur-
names are listed as if there were no hyphens or spaces between the
names. For example, Le Bris is alphabetized as Lebris.

Several large university and public libraries in the Los Angeles area were utilized in this research. Some of the bibliographic sources used in compiling this work include Music Index, Index
to Periodical Articles By and About Negroes, Readers' Guide, National Union Catalog, Cumulative Book Index, Books in Print, Popular Music Periodicals Index, Music Article Guide, RILM Abstracts
of Music Literature, and Cumulated Magazine Subject Index.

PUBLISHER'S NOTE

The selection of black musicians and singers for this bibliography was necessarily limited in order to keep the cost and size of the volume within reason.   The publisher plans to issue a supplement and would appreciate receiving names of people whom our readers would like to see included.   Please send your suggestions to

Scarecrow Press, Inc.
Box 656, 52 Liberty St.
Metuchen, N. J.   08840

I. SELECTED MUSICIANS AND SINGERS

ALLEN, BETTY (Mrs. R. Edward Lee).

1 "Betty Allen." Musical Courier 146:38, December 1, 1952; 150:30, September 1954.

2 "Hillis Conducts Honegger's Judith." Musical America 77:185, February 1957.

3 "Betty Allen." Musical Courier 155:25, March 1, 1957.

4 Craig, M. "The Cinderella Girl." Musical Courier 155:13, April 1957.

5 "Betty Allen." Musical America 78:27, January 15, 1958; Musical Courier 157:16, February 1958. Review of her recital at Town Hall, New York.

6 "Mozart-Hindemith List by New York Chamber Soloists." Musical Courier 161:24, June 1960.

7 Sabin, R. "Betty Allen." Musical America 80:62-63, November 1960.

8 "Betty Allen." Musical Courier 162:34, December 1960.

9 "Revolucion!" Musical America 81:34 September 1961.

10 Manzer, C. "Three Young Men Pianists Heard in Recitals on Berkeley Campus." Music of the West 17:20, March 1962.

11 "SAIs in Active Roles in American Music." Pan Pipes 55:33, no. 2, 1963.

12 ["Recital, New York."] Musical America 83:40, November 1963.

13 Allen, Betty. "Music--a Religious Expression." Music Journal 22:32-33, May 1964.

14 _____. "2 Part Invention." Music Journal 23:86-87, February 1965.

15 Smith, P. J. "From France: Classic and Romantic." High Fidelity/Musical America 15:115, June 1965.

16 Wallace, K. D. "Cabrillo Report." High Fidelity/Musical America 16:MA25, November 1966.

17 Madden, J. "Mourning Cuts Audience; Archbishop at Concert; Betty Allen Scores." Variety 250:55, April 10, 1968.

18 Hemming, Roy. "Lively Arts." Senior Scholastic 94:21-22, May 2,
    1969. Allen discusses the problems that American black singers en-
    counter in finding operatic roles.

19 ["Recital, New York."] High Fidelity/Musical America 19:MA16, June
    1969.

20 Mayer, M. "Recordings." Esquire 72:32, November 1969.

21 Zakariasen, W. "Gypsy." Opera News 35:13, January 23, 1971. In-
    terview with Allen.

22 "Betty Allen." Detroit Symphony Program Notes p. 422, March 2, 1972.

23 Merkling, F. "New York." Opera News 37:34, May 1973.

24 "Names, Dates and Places." Opera News 39:15, October 1974.

25 Jones, R. T. "Betty Allen, Mezzo." High Fidelity/Musical America
    25:MA30, June 1975. Allen participated in the series "Divas and Di-
    versions," presented at Hunter College, New York.

26 Fleming, S. "Scott Joplin's Treemonisha." High Fidelity/Musical Amer-
    ica 25:MA32-33, September 1975.

27 Belt, B. "American Composers--Serendipitous Find." Music Journal
    34:8-9, March 1976.

28 "Betty Allen: 'Sing Out, America.'" High Fidelity/Musical America
    26:MA28, May 1976.

ANDERSON, IVIE (IVY) MARY (Mrs. Walter Collins), 1904-1949.

29 "Obituary." Variety 177:290, January 4, 1950.

30 "Death of Ellington Singer." Melody Maker 26:7, January 7, 1950.

31 "Obituary." Billboard 62:42, January 7, 1950.

32 "Thrush Ivy Anderson Dies in Los Angeles." Billboard 62:41, January
    14, 1950.

33 "Singing the Blues." Melody Maker 26:6, January 28, 1950.

34 "Ivie Anderson." Metronome 66:13, February 1950.

35 Grut, H. "Ivie Anderson Död." Orkester Journalen 18:9, February
    1950.

36 "Wrangle over Estate of Late Ivie Anderson." down beat 17:12, February
    10, 1950.

37 "Set Ivie's Estate at over 50G's." down beat 17:1, February 24, 1950.

38 Short, Bobby. "I Remember Ivie." Saturday Review 54:50-51, February
    27, 1971. An excerpt from Short's book Black and White Baby.

39 Wilson, J. S. "Presenting Ivie Anderson." High Fidelity/Musical America 23:92, November 1973. Discussion of her recording by Columbia.

40 Bellerby, V. "Random Reflections in D." Jazz Journal 27:12, July 1974.

ANDERSON, MARIAN, 1902- .

41 "New York Endorses Europe's Opinion of a Negro Contralto." News Week 7:28, January 11, 1936.

42 "Colored Contralto." Time 27:35-36, January 13, 1936.

43 Waters, C. "Singing for Your Supper." Independent Woman 15:106-8, April 1936.

44 "Headliners in American Affairs." Scholastic 30:11, May 15, 1937.

45 "Singer's Flame." Literary Digest 123:29-30, May 22, 1937.

46 Davenport, M. "Music Will Out." Collier's 102:17, December 3, 1938.

47 "Ex-choir Singer." Newsweek 12:24-25, December 19, 1938.

48 Wood, V. "Little Hymn Singer; Marian Anderson." Missionary Review of the World 62:98, February 1939.

49 "Jim Crow Concert Hall." Time 33:38, March 6, 1939.

50 "Washington Color Line." Newsweek 13:33, March 6, 1939.

51 "Anderson Affair." Time 33:23, April 17, 1939.

52 Heylbut, R. "Some Reflections on Singing." Etude 57:631-632, October 1939.

53 Sedgwick, R. W. "Over Jordan; Story of a Voice." Christian Century 57:245-247, February 21, 1940; abridged in Reader's Digest 36:26-30, March 1940.

54 Vehanen, Kosti. Marian Anderson, a Portrait. Westport, Conn.: Greenwood Press, 1970, c1941.

55 "Marian Anderson to Sing in D. A. R. Hall." Christian Century 59:1245, October 14, 1942.

56 Baker, G. "Interview." Scholastic 41:17, December 14, 1942.

57 "Marian Anderson at Last Sings in D. A. R.'s Hall." Life 14:102, January 25, 1943.

58 Bronson, A. "Marian Anderson." American Mercury 61:282-288, September 1945.

59 "In Egypt Land." Time 48:59-60, December 30, 1946.

60 Albus, Harry James. The "Deep River" Girl; the Life of Marian Anderson in Story Form. Grand Rapids, Mich.: W. B. Eerdmans Pub.

Co., 1949.

61 Piquion, René, and Jean F. Brierre. Marian Anderson. Port-au-
       Prince: Henri Deschamps, 1950.

62 "Faith Is the Dynamo." Opera 15:18, February 1950.

63 "Marian Anderson." Musical America 70:272, February 1950.

64 Goldberg, A. "Marian Anderson Retains Spell over Audience."
       Voice 6:15, March-April 1950.

65 "Marian Anderson." Music News 43:14, March 1951; Musical America
       71:18, April 1, 1951.

66 "Of Men and Music." Ebony 6:49-50, May 1951. Anderson's career
       is shown in a music film series.

67 "Anderson Awards Announced for 1951." Musical America 71:13, No-
       vember 15, 1951.

68 "Marian Anderson." Cincinnati Symphony Orchestra Program Notes
       p. 323, January 11, 1952.

69 "Marian Anderson's TV Debut." Our World 7:22-24, August 1952.

70 "Americans in Scandinavia." Billboard 64:24, September 27, 1952.

71 "My People Pray." Coronet 32:131-138, October 1952.

72 "Marian Anderson Returns to Wash." Billboard 65:18, March 14, 1953.

73 "Marian Anderson Steps in for Ailing Horowitz in Mpls.; Only 8 Ask
       Out." Variety 190:56, March 18, 1953.

74 "Japan Sees Marian Anderson." Our World 8:27-31, November 1953.

75 "Anderson in Baltimore." Musical America 73:12, November 15, 1953.
       Anderson was the first black permitted to perform at Baltimore's
       Lyric Theatre.

76 "Marian Anderson Free to Play Lyric, Balto; Board in Facesaver."
       Variety 192:73, November 18, 1953.

77 "At Home with Marian Anderson." Ebony 9:52-59, February 1954.

78 "Now One Is Speechless." Time 64:87, October 18, 1954. Anderson
       performs at Metropolitan Opera.

79 "Opera's Gain." Newsweek 44:96, October 18, 1954. Anderson is the
       first black singer to be under contract to the Metropolitan Opera.

80 "Anderson to Sing at Met." Scholastic 65:19, October 20, 1954.

81 "A Barrier Is Broken." Musical America 74:4, November 1, 1954.
       Anderson broke the racial barrier at the Metropolitan Opera by per-
       forming an important role in Verdi's A Masked Ball.

82 "Marian Anderson." Musical Courier 150:36, November 1, 1954.

83 "Anderson 'Ball' Hottest Ticket." Variety 197:52, December 29, 1954.

84 De los Ronderos, M. F.   "Sevilla y Su II Festival de Musica y Dan-
    za." Musica 5:149-150, no. 12-13, 1955.

85 De Montsalvatge, X. "La Actividad Musical en Barcelona." Musica
    5:105, no. 12-13, 1955.

86 Dowdy, D., and R. Devries. "Chicago." Musical Courier 151:24,
    January 1, 1955.

87 "Marian Anderson." Cincinnati Symphony Program Notes p. 319, Jan-
    uary 8, 1954.

88 Bronson, A. "Marian Anderson's Sock Met Debut in Historic 'Ball'
    Seen as Trailblazer." Variety 197:72, January 12, 1955.

89 "Absent Friend." Musical America 75:9, January 15, 1955.

90 "Un Ballo in Maschera." Musical Courier 151:15-16, January 15,
    1955. Anderson is the first black singer to appear on the Metro-
    politan Opera roster.

91 Eyer, R. "Anderson Debut in Masked Ball Makes Metropolitan His-
    tory." Musical America 75:3, January 15, 1955.

92 Sargeant, W. "Anderson at the Met." New Yorker 30:89, January
    15, 1955.

93 "Debut." Time 65:68, January 17, 1955.

94 "Stranger at 'the Met'." Newsweek 45:50, January 17, 1955.

95 "Anderson Due Back at Met Next Season; Off Soon on Her First Tour
    of Israel." Variety 197:71, January 19, 1955.

96 Kolodin, I. "Miss Anderson Makes History." Saturday Review 38:46,
    January 22, 1955.

97 "Triumph at the Metropolitan." America 92:416, January 22, 1955.

98 "Marian Anderson Sings Second Time at White House." Musical Amer-
    ica 75:186, February 15, 1955.

99 "Anderson Repeats Metropolitan Success in Philadelphia." Musical
    America 75:18, March 1955.

100 Redewill, F. H. "San Francisco." Musical Courier 151:33; March
     1955.

101 Hinton, J. "America." Opera 6:240-242, April 1955.

102 Schabas, E. "Toronto." Musical Courier 151:34, April, 1955.

103 White, A. "Triumph of Marian Anderson." Our World 10:60-67, April
     1955.

104 Gradenwitz, P. "Israel." Musical Courier 151:28, June 1955.

105   "Carnegie Hall Recital." Musical America 75:28, November 15, 1955.

106   "Miss Anderson's Witchcraft." Opera News 20:15, December 5, 1955.

107   "Marian Anderson." Musical Courier 152:12, December 15, 1955.

108   Anderson, Marian. My Lord, What a Morning; An Autobiography.
      New York: Viking Press, 1956. "A condensed version ... ap-
      peared in serial form in the Woman's Home Companion."

109   "Stronger than Death." Saturday Review 39:29, March 24, 1956.

110   Dowdy, D., and R. Devries. "Chicago." Musical Courier 154:9,
      August 1956.

111   Hickman, C. S. "Los Angeles." Musical Courier 154:14, August
      1956.

112   Anderson, Marian. "My Lord, What a Morning." Woman's Home
      Companion 83:33-35, October 1956; 83:58-59, November 1956.
      These articles are extended in her book with the same name.

113   Van Vechten, C. "Soft Voice of Feeling." Saturday Review 39:22,
      November 3, 1956.

114   "Marian Anderson." Musical Opinion 80:135-136, December 1956.

115   "Recitals." London Musical Events 11:68, December 1956.

116   "Marian Anderson Tells Her Story." Musical America 76:28, Decem-
      ber 1, 1956.

117   "Grace Rainey Rogers Auditorium Recital." Musical America 77:37,
      March 1957.

118   "Marian Anderson's ANTA Global Tour as 'See It Now' Seg." Variety
      207:23, August 28, 1956.

119   "Secret Weapon." Newsweek 50:63, December 30, 1957.

120   "CBS-TVs 'See It Now' on Marian Anderson an RCA Victor Pkge."
      Variety 209:37, January 1, 1958.

121   "Marian Anderson as America's 'Secret Weapon' in TV Triumph."
      Variety 209:27, January 1, 1958.

122   "Marian Anderson Feted by Philly; Murrow There." Variety 209:2,
      January 1, 1958.

123   "Philadelphia Lady." Musical America 78:18, January 15, 1958.

124   Shayon, R. L. "The Lady from Philadelphia." Saturday Review
      41:57, January 18, 1958.

125   "Bigger Audience." Newsweek 51:46, January 20, 1958.

126   "Lady from Philadelphia; Marian Anderson's Far East Trip Is Tele-
      vision's Finest Hour." Ebony 13:31-32, March 1958.

127 Wald, R. C. "How to Live with a Famous Wife; Architect Describes Life with Marian Anderson." Ebony 13:53-54, August 1958.

128 "A Well-bestowed Honor." Musical America 77:4, August 1958. Anderson received an appointment to membership in the United Nations General Assembly.

129 "A Newer Voice." down beat 25:9, September 4, 1958. Anderson becomes a UN General Assembly delegate.

130 "Marian Anderson New Delegate to UN." Musical Courier 158:5, October 1958.

131 Hemming, R. "Voice of the Century at the U.N." Senior Scholastic 73:16, October 31, 1958.

132 "Marian Anderson." Musical America 78:11, November 1, 1958.

133 "Marian Anderson Given Award." Sepia 6:70, December 1958.

134 Hughes, A. "Something Eternal." Musical America 79:13, February 1959.

135 Zegrí, A. "Song and Statesmanship." Américas 11:28-31, February 1959.

136 "Diplomat Role for Marian Anderson, U.N. Delegate." Pan Pipes 51:4, March 1959.

137 "Marian Anderson." Musical America 79:40, April 1959.

138 Kolodin, I. "Music to My Ears." Saturday Review 42:51, April 11, 1959.

139 "Marian Anderson." Musical Courier 159:16, May 1959.

140 Dreis, I. "Anderson Hailed in Virgin Islands." Musical America 79:35, July 1959.

141 "Famed Singer Now with United Nations." Sepia 7:67, August 1959.

142 Anderson, Marian. "Cios." Ruch Muzyczny 4:14-16, March 15, 1960. Excerpt from her book entitled My Lord, What a Morning.

143 Crawford, M. "Should Marian Anderson Retire?" Ebony 15:77-78, June 1960.

144 Kimbrough, E., ed. "My Life in a White World." Ladies Home Journal 77:54-55, September 1960.

145 "Boston University." Negro History Bulletin 24:20, October 1960.

146 "Awards and Honors." Musical Courier 162:41, December 1960.

147 "Marian Anderson Receives SAI [Sigma Alpha Iota] Certificate of Merit." Pan Pipes 54:10-11, no. 1, 1961.

148 Confer, G. B. "How Marian Anderson Blessed My Life." Negro Digest 11:37-40, February 1962.

149   "Sydney." Canon 15:27, June 1962.

150   Winters, L. "Honolulu: Week of New Music." Music Magazine
      164:26, July 1962.

151   Brunet, F. "Le Drame de Marian Anderson." Musica no. 102:25-30,
      September 1962.

152   "Marian Anderson Texas Dates All Unsegregated; Asks Churches to
      Help." Variety 228:1, September 26, 1962.

153   Roy, J. H. "Pin Point Portrait of Marian Anderson." Negro History
      Bulletin 26:104, November 1962.

154   "23d Honarary Degree to Marian Anderson." Variety 229:2, December
      19, 1962.

155   Spivey, Lenore. Singing Heart; A Story Based on the Life of Marian
      Anderson. Largo, Fla.: Community Service Foundation, 1963.

156   Stevenson, Janet. Marian Anderson; Singing to the World. Chicago:
      Encyclopaedia Britannica Press, 1963.

157   "Anderson OK Aids in Breakdown of Inn Segregation." Variety 229:21,
      January 23, 1963.

158   Hawkins, W. "Marian Anderson Says Farewell." Musical America
      84:8-11, September 1964; High Fidelity 14:51, October 1964.

159   Newman, Shirles Petkin. Marian Anderson: Lady from Philadelphia.
      Philadelphia: Westminster Press, 1965.

160   Sterne, Emma Gelders. I Have a Dream. New York: Knopf, 1965.
      The first chapter is "Lift Every Voice and Sing: Marian Anderson."

161   Hawkins, W. "Marian Anderson Says Farewell." Negro Digest 14:93-
      95, March 1965.

162   Landry, R. J. "Marian Anderson--a Symbol." Variety 238:64, April
      21, 1965.

163   "Beacon." Newsweek 65:87-88, April 26, 1965. Many of the first in
      Anderson's career are related, including her appearance at the Met-
      ropolitan Opera.

164   "Lady from Philadelphia; Editorial." Crisis 72:281, May 1965.

165   Kolodin, I. "Music to My Ears." Saturday Review 48:32, May 1,
      1965. Discussion of Anderson's final concerts before retirement.

166   "Farewell, Marian Anderson." Ebony 20:39-40, June 1965. Farewell
      concert tour.

167   "RCA Victor's Farewell Recital of Marian Anderson." Negro Digest
      14:82, June 1965.

168   Lawrence, R. ["Recital, New York."] High Fidelity/Musical America
      15:106, July 1965.

169 Madden, J. "Mourning Cuts Audience; Archibishop at Concert; Betty Allen Scores." Variety 250:55, April 10, 1968.

170 "My Deepest Ties to People." Redbook 132:48-49, December 1968.

171 "Marian Anderson to Top New World Symph's Gala." Variety 254:59, April 23, 1969.

172 ["Marian Anderson Scholarship Fund."] Music Journal 28:73, January 1970.

173 Novak, B. J. "Opening Doors in Music." Negro History Bulletin 34:1-14, January 1971.

174 Dobrin, Arnold. Voices of Joy, Voices of Freedom: Ethel Waters, Sammy Davis, Jr., Marian Anderson, Paul Robeson, Lena Horne. New York: Coward, McCann & Geoghegan, 1972.

175 Tobias, Tobi. Marian Anderson. New York: Crowell, 1972. Juvenile literature.

176 Timokhin, V. "Ee Stikhiya--Vozvyshennaya Lirika." Soviet Muzyka 36:117-119, May 1972.

177 "Miss Anderson Inducted in Birmingham Hall of Fame." Jet 42:62, June 15, 1972.

178 "Three Black Women Earn Place in New Hall of Fame." Jet 44:7, September 13, 1973.

179 "Marian Anderson Honored by Pennsylvania Glee Club." Jet 45:74, November 8, 1973.

180 Hill, R. "Fannie Douglass Reminiscences of Yesteryear." Black Perspective in Music 2:54-62, no. 1, 1974.

181 "Marian Anderson." Music Journal 32:35, December 1974. She received the honorary doctor of humane letters degree from Duke University.

182 Truman, Margaret. "Triumph of Marian Anderson." McCalls 103:114, April 1976. This is an excerpt from Truman's book Women of Courage.

183 "Tribute and Medal to Marian Anderson." Pan Pipes 69:15, no. 4, 1977.

184 Klaw, B. "Voice One Hears Once in a Hundred Years." American Heritage 28:50-57, February 1977. Anderson is interviewed about her career.

185 "Honor Marian Anderson." Variety 286:2, March 16, 1977.

186 "Marian Anderson Given Unique Awards During 75th Birthday Bash in N.Y." Jet 51:12, March 17, 1977.

ARMSTRONG, LIL (LILLIAN) HARDIN (Mrs. Louis Armstrong), 1902-1971.

187 "Do You Remember ... Lil Armstrong?" Negro Digest 8:69-70, July
     1950.

188 Armstrong, Lil. "Lil Tells of 1st Time She Met Louis." down beat
     17:18, July 14, 1950.

189 _____. "Lil Armstrong Reminisces About Early Chicago Days."
     down beat 18:12, June 1, 1951. Lil and Louis Armstrong played
     in the New Orleans Creole Jazz Band.

190 "Mezz and Peanuts Hit Paris in U.S. Jazz Convoy." Melody Maker
     28:7, October 11, 1952.

191 Jones, M. "Lil Armstrong." Melody Maker 29:8, January 17, 1953.

192 "Lil Armstrong--'I'll Be Back'--Is Hopping Mad About London." Mel-
     ody Maker 29:7, January 31, 1953.

193 "German Critic Horst H. Lange Discinterviews Lil Armstrong." Mel-
     ody Maker 29:13, October 17, 1953.

194 "Lil Loves Paris." Melody Maker 30:1, September 11, 1954.

195 Gara, L. "The Baby Dodds Story." Jazz Journal 8:8-10, July 1955.

196 "Lil, the Forgotten Armstrong." Sepia 14:54-58, September 1965.

197 "Penny Farthing, Tor'nto." Variety 240:59, September 8, 1965.

198 Jones, M. "Lil Armstrong, Royalties and the Old Songs." Melody
     Maker 42:8, April 8, 1967.

199 Armstrong, Lil. "Louis par Lil." Jazz Hot no. 263:10, Summer
     1970.

200 Affeldt, P. E. "Paul's Piece." Jazz Report 7:6, no. 6, 1971.

201 Hodes, A. "Passing Through Much Too Fast." Jazz Report 7:5-6,
     no. 6, 1971. A discussion of Lil Armstrong's last musical per-
     formance.

202 "Lil Hardin Dies at Louis Memorial Concert." Footnote 3:10, no. 1,
     1971.

203 Mitchell, B. "Lillian Hardin Armstrong--an Appreciation." Jazz Re-
     port 7:34, no. 6, 1971.

204 ["Obituary."] Second Line 25:33, Fall 1971; Variety 264:63, September
     1, 1971.

205 Atterton, J. "Lucille Says Thanks." Melody Maker 46:6, September
     4, 1971.

206 Chilton, J. "Lil--Louis' Second Lady." Melody Maker 46:21, Sep-
     tember 4, 1971.

207 "Tribute to Satchmo Proves to Be Fatal for His Former Wife, Pianist Lil Armstrong." Jet 4:56-58, September 16, 1971.

208 Albertson, C. "Lil Hardin Armstrong, a Fond Remembrance." Saturday Review 54:66-67, September 25, 1971.

209 ["Obituary."] International Musician 70:12, October 1971; Jazz Hot no. 276:28, October 1971; Orkester Journalen 39:5, October 1971.

210 Choice, H. "Lil's Last Stand." down beat 38:11, October 28, 1971.

211 ["Obituary."] down beat 38:9-10, October 28, 1971.

212 Englund, B. "Lil Hardin Armstrong." Orkester Journalen 39:10-11, November 1971; 39:22-23, December 1971.

213 ["Obituary."] Jazz Forum no. 16:43, March-April 1972; Black Perspective in Music 1:197, no. 2, 1973.

214 Hopf, R. "Lil Hardin-Armstrong." Jazz Podium 22:18-19, September 1973.

215 Shultz, H. L. "Oh, Play That Thing, Louis! And He Did." Second Line 28:33-35, Spring 1976. Reprinted from Panorama Magazine, November 8, 1975.

216 "Records in Brief--Reissues: Black and White Masters." Coda no. 156:24, July-August 1977.

ARMSTRONG, DANIEL LOUIS (Satchmo), 1900-1971.

217 Armstrong, Louis. Swing That Music. London, New York: Longmans, Green, 1936.

218 "Reverend Satchelmouth." Time 47:47, April 29, 1946.

219 Goffin, Robert. Horn of Plenty; The Story of Louis Armstrong. New York: Allen, Towne & Heath, 1947. English edition translated from the French by James F. Bezon.

220 "Satchmo Comes Back." Time 50:32, September 1, 1947.

221 "Louis the First." Time 53:52-56, February 21, 1949.

222 "Inside Orchestras--Music." Variety 173:40, February 23, 1949.

223 Liuzza, T. "Satchmo a Natch in N.O. Mardi Gras." Variety 173:1, March 9, 1949.

224 "'Satchmo' Hailed as King of Zulus at N.O. Mardi Gras." Billboard 61:23, March 12, 1949.

225 Feather, L. "Louis: King of the Zulus." Melody Maker 25:3, March 26, 1949.

226 Gagliano, N. "King Louis' Triumph Tempered." down beat 16:18, April 8, 1949.

227 Wolff, D. L. "Bop Nowhere, Armstrong Just a Myth, Says Wolff."
     down beat 16:1, June 17, 1949.

228 Levin, M. "Wolff's Article Is Garbage--Mike." down beat 16:1,
     July 1, 1949.

229 "Overseas Trip for Louis Unit." down beat 16:1, July 1, 1949.

230 "Teagarden Plans to Quit Armstrong." down beat 16:17, August 26,
     1949.

231 Feather, L. "Lombardo Grooves Louis!" Metronome 65:18, Septem-
     ber 1949.

232 "Armstrong's Nostalgia Envelops Bop City." Billboard 61:14, Septem-
     ber 3, 1949.

233 "Bop City, New York." Billboard 61:38, September 3, 1949.

234 "L. Armstrong Combo Takes Off Sept. 30 on New European Route."
     Variety 176:42, September 21, 1949.

235 Feather, L. "Pops Pops Top on Sloppy Bop." Metronome 65:18, Oc-
     tober 1949.

236 Simon, G. T. "Armstrong, Commercialism and Music." Metronome
     65:38, October 1949.

237 "Armstrong Sellout in Stockholm Bow." Variety 176:35, October 5,
     1949.

238 "Louis Armstrong in Scandinavia." Melody Maker 25:3, October 15,
     1949.

239 "Satchmo Sock in Sweden: Italian Tour Mapped." Variety 176:43, Oc-
     tober 19, 1949.

240 "Louis Group Tours Europe." down beat 16:2, October 21, 1949.

241 "Satchmo Europe Trip Successful: Plans 2d Tour." Billboard 61:13,
     October 22, 1949.

242 "With Louis on the Danish Air." Melody Maker 25:9, October 22,
     1949.

243 "My Biggest Break." Negro Digest 8:75-76, November 1949.

244 Zwonicek, E., and C. Dumont. "Armstrong in Switzerland." Melody
     Maker 25:9, November 5, 1949.

245 "Welcome." Time 54:44-46, November 7, 1949.

246 "Satchmo Hottest Package to Hit Europe in Years." Variety 176:2,
     November 9, 1949.

247 "Armstrong Tops the NFJO Poll." Melody Maker 25:9, November 12,
     1949.

248   Kahn, H. "Bebop? One Long Search for the Right Note, Says Louis
      Armstrong." Melody Maker 25:3, November 12, 1949.

249   Traill, S. "Armstrong Completes His Half-Century of European Con-
      cert." Melody Maker 25:2, November 12, 1949.

250   Jones, M., and S. Traill. "Corner Scoops World on 1930 Armstrong
      Disc." Melody Maker 25:9, November 19, 1949.

251   "Armstrong in Italian Movie." down beat 16:3, December 2, 1949.

252   "Satchmo Booked 12 Weeks on the Coast." Variety 177:40, December
      21, 1949.

253   Wilson, J. S. "Armstrong Explains Stand Against Bop." down beat
      16:3, December 30, 1949.

254   De Radzitzky, C. "Louis Armstrong in Europe." Jazz Journal 3:6,
      January 1950.

255   Race, S. "Louis Armstrong's Description of Bop." Jazz Journal
      3:6-7, January 1950.

256   "Louis Armstrong and His Hot Seven." Melody Maker 26:9, January
      7, 1950.

257   "Louis Armstrong All-Star Orchestra Has Not Been Approved by Min-
      istry of Labour." Melody Maker 26:9, February 4, 1950.

258   "The Old-Time Stars Are Trying to Forget It!" Melody Maker 26:4,
      February 18, 1950.

259   Gleason, R. J. "Louis Bash Doesn't Blow up Storm." down beat
      17:18, February 24, 1950.

260   "Louis Armstrong and Bebop." Melody Maker 26:6, February 25,
      1950.

261   "Armstrong Reigns as King of the Zulus Back Home." Playback
      2:3-4, March 1949.

262   Levin, F. "The American Jazz Scene." Jazz Journal 3:18-19, April
      1950.

263   "National Memorial Week of the Music of Thomas 'Fats' Waller."
      Jazz Journal 3:1, May 1950.

264   Torme, M. "Of Singing and Singers." Metronome 66:22, May 1950.

265   "Roxy, N.Y." Variety 178:54, May 3, 1950.

266   "Louis Writes Life Story." down beat 17:1, May 5, 1950.

267   "Europe, with Kicks." Holiday 7:8-12, June 1950.

268   Taubman, H. "Half Century with Satchmo." Negro Digest 8:23-28,
      June 1950.

269 Traill, S. "Louis the Great--1925." Melody Maker 26:9, June 3,
     1950.

270 "Bop City, N.Y." Variety 179:44, June 21, 1950.

271 "Armstrong May Go Under Knife for Ulcer Removal." down beat 17:1,
     June 30, 1950.

272 Armstrong, Louis. "Bunk Didn't Teach Me." Record Changer 9:30,
     July-August 1950.

273 _____. "Joe Oliver Is Still King." Record Changer 9:10-11, July-
     August 1950.

274 _____. "Louis' Favorite Dish." Record Changer 9:18, July-August
     1950.

275 Avakian, G. "I Mean the Jeebies." Record Changer 9:22, July-Au-
     gust 1950.

276 Blesh, R. "On the Riverboats." Record Changer 9:9, July-August
     1950.

277 Drew, P. "The Professional Viewpoint." Record Changer 9:31, July-
     August 1950.

278 "Editorial." Record Changer 9:6, July-August 1950.

279 "From Louis' Photo Album." Record Changer 9:28-29, July-August
     1950.

280 Grauer, B. "Louis Today." Record Changer 9:27, July-August 1950.

281 Henderson, F. "He Made the Band Swing." Record Changer 9:15-16,
     July-August 1950.

282 "In Praise of Satchmo." Record Changer 9:12-13, July-August 1950.

283 Keepnews, O. "The Big Band Period." Record Changer 9:25-26,
     July-August 1950.

284 Koenig, L. "The Hot Five Sessions, by Kid Ory." Record Changer
     9:17, July-August 1950.

285 "Louis on the Spot; an Interview." Record Changer 9:23-24, July-
     August 1950.

286 McCarthy, A. J. "Discography." Record Changer 9:36-42, July-Au-
     gust 1950.

287 Merriam, A. P., and R. J. Benford. "Bibliography." Record Chang-
     er 9:33-35, July-August 1950.

288 Moon, B. "The Horn Behind the Blues." Record Changer 9:14, July-
     August 1950.

289 Smith, C. E. "The Making of a King." Record Changer 9:19-21,
     July-August 1950.

290 Thompson, K. C. "Louis and the Waif's Home." Record Changer 9:8, July-August 1950.

291 Simon, G. T. "L." Metronome 66:15, July 1950.

292 Armstrong, Lil. "Lil Tells of 1st Time She Met Louis." down beat 17:18, July 14, 1950.

293 Armstrong, Louis. "Ulceratedly Yours." down beat 17:1, July 14, 1950.

294 Bankhead, T. "Louis the End--and Beginning." down beat 17:1, July 14, 1950.

295 Bushkin, J. "Ole Satchmo, the Gourmet." down beat 17:12, July 14, 1950.

296 Garroway, D. "Everyone Owes Debt to Louis." down beat 17:1, July 14, 1950.

297 "Happy Birthday, Louis." down beat 17:2-3, July 14, 1950.

298 Hobson, W. "Louis Always Has Golden Song to Offer." down beat 17:1, July 14, 1950.

299 Hoefer, G. "Louis Armstrong Discography." down beat 17:14-15, July 14, 1950.

300 _____. "Will the Louis Sides on Cylinder Ever Turn Up?" down beat 17:11, July 14, 1950.

301 "Louis, Babe Ruth Go Hand in Hand." down beat 17:10, July 14, 1950.

302 Murray, K. "Louis, Bix Had Most Influence on der Bingle." down beat 17:16, July 14, 1950.

303 "'My Idol' None but Bunk Johnson." down beat 17:11, July 14, 1950.

304 Ory, K. "Louis Was Just a Little Kid in Knee-Pants." down beat 17:8, July 14, 1950.

305 Shaw, B. "Satchmo Knows the Secret of Grosses." down beat 17:16, July 14, 1950.

306 Singleton, Z. "Zutty First Saw Louis in Amateur Tent Show." down beat 17:6, July 14, 1950.

307 Spanier, M. "Louis My Idol and Inspiration." down beat 17:4, July 14, 1950.

308 "Years Rest Lightly on Louis' Head, but Give Him Stomach Ache." down beat 17:6, July 14, 1950.

309 Borneman, E. "Louis Armstrong Half a Century Old." Melody Maker 26:2, July 15, 1950.

310 "Satchmo at 50." Newsweek 36:76, July 17, 1950.

311   Hoefer, G. "Louis Armstrong Discography." down beat 17:18-19,
         July 28, 1950.

312   Tanner, P. "Armstrong, Shearing at Bop City." Melody Maker 26:11,
         July 22, 1950.

313   "In Person." Metronome 66:18-19, August 1950.

314   Hoefer, G. "Louis Armstrong Discography." down beat 17:16, Au-
         gust 11, 1950; 17:19, August 25, 1950.

315   "'Satchmo' Armstrong; Old Man with a Horn." Our World 5:35-37,
         September 1950.

316   Hoefer, G. "Louis Armstrong Discography." down beat 17:14, Sep-
         tember 8, 1950.

317   Bankhead, T. "An Appreciation of Louis Armstrong." Flair 1:36-37,
         November 1950.

318   "Armstrong to Make Another Europe Trip." down beat 17:3, Novem-
         ber 3, 1950.

319   "Amerikanskt Stjarnalbum--Louis Armstrong." Orkester Journalen
         18:7-8, December 1950.

320   Ulanov, B. "History of Jazz." Metronome 66:14-15, December 1950.

321   "Wows 'em on Seine; Duke, Mezz Popular." Billboard 62:2, Decem-
         ber 23, 1950.

322   "Armstrong Still King." International Musician 49:14, February 1951.

323   Goffin, R. "Horn of Plenty." Jazz Journal 4:4, February 1951.

324   Hobson, W. "Mr. Armstrong's Earlier Works." Saturday Review of
         Literature 34:52-53, April 28, 1951.

325   "Louis Wins Again; All-Time All Star No. 1." Record Changer 10:3,
         May 1951.

326   Grauer, W. "Letter to Louis." Record Changer 10:5, June 1951.

327   Freeman, D. "Have to Learn Your Horn, Says Armstrong." down
         beat 18:18, June 1, 1951.

328   "Louis: 1925-1947." Metronome 67:18-19, August 1951.

329   Armstrong, Louis. "They'll Never Come Back--the Good Old Days."
         Melody Maker 27:3, September 15, 1951.

330   "'Butterbeans' Armstrong." Jazz Journal 4:18, October 1951.

331   "Ole Satchmo; the Cat-Man of Jazz." Our World 6:20-23, October
         1951.

332   Whiston, H. F. "Soon I'll Be Leaving Louis to Record with My Own
         Band ... Says Earl Hines." Melody Maker 27:3, October 6, 1951.

333 Armstrong, Louis. "Jazz on a High Note." Esquire 36:85-61, De-
      cember 1951. Recordings of Armstrong are discussed, as "Strut-
      tin' with Some Barbeque."

334 Traill, S. "Requiem for the All Stars." Jazz Journal 4:1-2, Decem-
      ber 1951.

335 Emge, C. "Louis Pleased with Role in MGM's 'Glory Alley.'" down
      beat 18:11, December 28, 1951.

336 Harper, Mr. "Bix and Louis." Harper's Magazine 204:100-102, Feb-
      ruary 1952.

337 "Col. Records, Armstrong File Suit in First Action Against Bootleg-
      ging." Variety 185:46, February 6, 1952.

338 "Louis Armstrong Doing Two-Year World Tour." Variety 185:1, Feb-
      ruary 6, 1952.

339 "Columbia Files Suit Against 'Jolly Roger.'" Billboard 64:21, Febru-
      ary 9, 1952.

340 Anderson, J. L. "Evolution of Jazz." down beat 19:18, February 22,
      1952.

341 Freeman, D. "We'll Get Along Without Hines' Ego, Says Armstrong."
      down beat 19:3, February 22, 1952.

342 "Bootlegging Dead! Armstrong-Columbia Suit Scares Pirates Out."
      Record Changer 11:3, March 1952.

343 Anderson, J. L. "Evolution of Jazz." down beat 19:18, March 7,
      1952.

344 "Columbia Starts Action to Break Bootleggers' Backs." down beat
      19:3, March 7, 1952.

345 Anderson, J. L. "Evolution of Jazz." down beat 19:18, March 21,
      1952.

346 "Armstrong to Make Round-World Jaunt." down beat 19:1, March 21,
      1952.

347 "Never Had Any Hassels with Louis, Says Hines." down beat 19:3,
      March 21, 1952.

348 Lucas, J. "Bix or Louis." Record Changer 11:3, April 1952.

349 "Armstrong Scores Triumph in Honolulu Concert Dates." down beat
      19:1, April 4, 1952.

350 Gleason, R. J. "Going Back to Hawaii Every Year, Says Satch."
      down beat 19:5, April 18, 1952.

351 "Glory Alley." Ebony 7:100-102, May 1952. Armstrong will have a
      role in a movie set in New Orleans.

352 "Armstrong's Alter Ego." Metronome 68:16, June 1952.

353   "Armstrong Still Hot After Disking 30 Years." Variety 186:1, June
       4, 1952.

354   "Armstrong's Wax Activity, on Numerical Count, Ranks Below Several
       Oldtimers." Variety 187:45-46, June 18, 1952.

355   Anderson, E. "Background to the Book." Melody Maker 28:9, June
       28, 1952.

356   Armstrong, Louis. "My Kicks in Europe." Melody Maker 28:9, June
       28, 1952.

357   "Louis Armstrong--the Genius of Jazz." Melody Maker 28:9, June
       28, 1952.

358   "What They Say About Louis." Melody Maker 28:9, June 28, 1952.

359   Armstrong, Louis. "There Were Three Encores to that Spaghetti!"
       Melody Maker 28:9, July 5, 1952.

360   Armstrong, Louis. "My Kicks in Europe." Melody Maker 28:9, July
       12, 1952; 28:9, July 19, 1952; 28:9, July 26, 1952; 28:9, August
       2, 1952.

361   "Ministry of Labour Kills Plan to Star Armstrong in British Variety."
       Melody Maker 28:1, August 2, 1952.

362   Armstrong, Louis. "My Kicks in Europe." Melody Maker 28:9, Au-
       gust 9, 1952.

363   "They Talk About Louis and Dizzy in the Same Breath." Melody Mak-
       er 28:9, August 9, 1952.

364   Armstrong, Louis. "My Kicks in Europe." Melody Maker 28:9, Au-
       gust 16, 1952; 28:9, August 23, 1952; 28:9, August 30, 1952.

365   Tanner, P. "And Satchmo Slayed Them!" Melody Maker 28:3, Sep-
       tember 20, 1952.

366   "Armstrong och Wilson Här." Orkester Journalen 20:6, October 1952.

367   "Satchmo Toots Horn for LP's as Best Jazz Hypo." Variety 188:56,
       October 8, 1952.

368   "At 52, He Is Artistically at His Peak." Melody Maker 28:12, Oc-
       tober 11, 1952.

369   "French Impresarios Battle for Armstrong." Melody Maker 28:12,
       October 11, 1952.

370   "Police Called to Quell Louis Fans." Melody Maker 28:12, October
       11, 1952. Armstrong fans became unruly during his concerts in
       Sweden.

371   "Satchmo Wows 'em in Copenhagen, Jams Hall 3 Times." Billboard
       64:50, October 11, 1952.

372   "Armstrong Wows Swedes in Concert." Billboard 64:50, October 18,
       1952.

373 McCarthy, A. "Louis Armstrong on Transcriptions." Melody Maker
     28:8, October 25, 1952.

374 Noakes, G. "Louis Rejects 'Gabriel and Jericho' Offer from Behind
     Iron Curtain." Melody Maker 28:7, October 25, 1952.

375 "Satchmo Ends Scandia Tour." Billboard 64:26, October 25, 1952.

376 "Armstrong-Feber i Tyskland." Orkester Journalen 20:7, November
     1952.

377 "In Person." Metronome 68:11, November 1952.

378 Lindgren, C. E. "... Och Hans Fall var Stort; Armstrong Glömde
     Jazzmusiken." Orkester Journalen 20:16-17, November 1952.

379 McCarthy, A. "Louis Armstrong on Transcriptions." Melody Maker
     28:8, November 1, 1952.

380 "Louis Tells Warring Fans: 'Shut Up!'" Melody Maker 28:1, Novem-
     ber 15, 1952.

381 "Satchmo and Troupe Beaucoup SRO in Paris." Variety 188:43, No-
     vember 19, 1952.

382 "Wild Crowds, Broken Records Greet Armstrong Abroad Again." down
     beat 19:1, November 19, 1952.

383 Jones, M., and S. Traill. "Collectors' Corner." Melody Maker
     28:8, November 29, 1952.

384 Bankhead, T., and J. James. "World's Greatest Musician." Ebony
     8:103, December 1952.

385 Lindgren, C. E. "Pa Luffen med Louis." Orkester Journalen 20:22-
     23, December 1952.

386 "'Beat' Readers Elect Louis to Hall of Fame." down beat 19:1, De-
     cember 31, 1952.

387 Sypniewski, Jan. Louis Armstrong; Zehn Monographische Studien, by
     Jan Slawe [pseud.]. Basel: Papillons-Verlag, 1953.

388 Friedländer, W. "Armstrong und Seine Hörer." Musikleben 6:30,
     January 1953. Reprinted from the Frankfurter Allgemeinen Zei-
     tung.

389 Armstrong, Louis. "A Toast to Mezzrow and Joe Oliver." Melody
     Maker 29:3, January 10, 1953.

390 "Satchmo Storms Boston; Gets Plaque, Scroll, Etc." down beat 20:3,
     January 28, 1953.

391 "All-Star Unit to Join Armstrong on Tour." Billboard 65:17, Febru-
     ary 7, 1953.

392 Feather, L. "Feather's Nest." down beat 20:21, February 11, 1953.
     Feather relates the legend of Louis Armstrong.

393 Dankworth, J. "Where Joe Loss and Louis Share Jazz Honours."
     Melody Maker 29:3, March 21, 1953.

394 Schoenfeld, H. "Goodman-Armstrong 'Flashback' to '38 Jazz Idiom
     Dimmed by Time." Variety 190:43, April 22, 1953.

395 "Crowds Jam Carnegie Hall to Hear BG--Armstrong." Billboard
     65:45, April 25, 1953.

396 Anderson, E. "This Jazz Was Dazzling--Even for Armstrong!" Mel-
     ody Maker 29:3, May 9, 1953.

397 Feather, L. "BG--Louis Tour Is Cited as Bitterest Jazz Hassel
     Ever." down beat 20:1, June 3, 1953.

398 "Big Rift." Metronome 69:5, July 1953.

399 Moon, B. "Louis and the Blues." Record Changer 12:9, September
     1953.

400 "Satchmo Socko over in Tokyo." Variety 193:39, December 23, 1953.

401 Armstrong, Louis. Satchmo; My Life in New Orleans. New York:
     Prentice-Hall, 1954.

402 Browne, C. "That's Our Louis--in 6 Japanese Words!" Melody Mak-
     er 30:3, January 15, 1954. Armstrong's nickname, "Satchmo," is
     discussed.

403 "Honolulu Ban Put on Satchmo." Variety 193:45, January 20, 1954.

404 "Pops Japan Tour a Smash." down beat 21:1, January 27, 1954.

405 "Basin Street, N.Y." Variety 194:53, March 17, 1954.

406 Ackerman, P. "Satchmo Does NY Club Date, 1st Since '49." Bill-
     board 66:13, March 27, 1954.

407 "Oh, Didn't They Ramble?" New Yorker 30:54, April 24, 1954.

408 "'Recording Artists' Roster." down beat 21:86, June 30, 1954.

409 Armstrong, Louis, and J. James. "It's Tough to Top a Million."
     Our World 9:22-25, August 1954.

410 "Why I Like Dark Women." Ebony 9:61-62, August 1954.

411 Feather, L. "Satch Mellows a Little on Bop, but Only a Bit." down
     beat 21:15, August 11, 1954.

412 _____. "Louis Still Lauds Guy, Digs Turk but Not Bird." down
     beat 21:17, August 25, 1954.

413 Lowe, W. "The Jazz Jester?" Jazz Journal 7:7, September 1954.

414 "Sands, Las Vegas." Variety 196:60, September 22, 1954.

415 "Publishers Get Armstrong Disc Banned: 'In Bad Taste'" Melody

Maker 30:16, October 9, 1954. Armstrong's rendition of "The Whiffenpoof Song" was considered unacceptable to the publishers.

416 "Way Down Yonder." Newsweek 44:96, October 18, 1954.

417 "Satchmo Setting Marks in Australia Openers." Variety 196:51, November 3, 1954.

418 Balliett, W. "Good King Louis." Saturday Review 37:54, November 27, 1954.

419 Lucas, J. "Satchmo or Pops." Jazz Journal 7:7-9, December 1954.

420 "In the Kitchen with the Red Bean Experts." Melody Maker 30:iv-v, December 11, 1954 Supplement.

421 Hobson, W. "A Is for Armstrong." Saturday Review 37:40, December 25, 1954. A review of Armstrong recordings.

422 Eaton, Jeanette. Trumpeter's Tale; The Story of Young Louis Armstrong. New York: Morrow, 1955.

423 "Authenticity and Artistry." Jazz Journal 8:4, January 1955. Recording reviews.

424 "Crescendo, Hollywood." Variety 197:62, January 12, 1955.

425 "Satchmo to Bow Basin St. Revamp." Variety 197:48, January 26, 1955.

426 "Jazz Evolution." Negro History Bulletin 18:115, February 1955.

427 Jepsen, J. G. "Jazzens Instrumentalister: Trumpeten." Orkester Journalen 23:10, February 1955.

428 Gleason, R. J. "Perspectives." down beat 22:14, February 9, 1954.

429 "Nu Är Det Dags Igen!" Orkester Journalen 23:14, March 1955.

430 "Basin Street, N.Y." Variety 198:69, April 13, 1955.

431 Gara, L. "The Baby Dodds Story." Jazz Journal 8:4-6, June 1955.

432 "Lightly and Politely." Jazz Journal 8:26-27, June 1955. Recording reviews.

433 "Satchmo Is a Smash on the Gold Coast." Life 40:38-39, June 11, 1955.

434 Gara, L. "The Baby Dodds Story." Jazz Journal 8:8-10, July 1955.

435 "Basin Street, N.Y." Variety 199:54, July 6, 1955.

436 "Is Pops Weakening?" down beat 22:7, August 24, 1955. Discussion of Armstrong's feelings about bebop.

437 Gara, L. "The Baby Dodds Story." Jazz Journal 8:26-27, October 1955.

438   "Satchmo Hänryckte Jazzungdomen Med Enkel och Frisk Jazz." Or-
      kester Journalen 23:6-7, October 1955.

439   "Satchmo Is Set for German One-Niters." Variety 200:58, October
      12, 1955.

440   Nevard, M. "Tickets for Louis? Not a Chance!" Melody Maker
      31:3, October 15, 1955.

441   "Satchmo Socko in Smorgasbord Concert Swing." Variety 200:44, Oc-
      tober 19, 1955. Discussion of Armstrong's European tour.

442   Kahn, H. "Satchmo Fans Riot at Hamburg Jazz Show." Melody Mak-
      er 31:9, October 22, 1955.

443   "Armstrong Wows Danes." Variety 200:44, October 26, 1955.

444   "Germany." Melody Maker 31:8, October 29, 1955. Armstrong's per-
      formance in Hamburg is marred by rioting fans.

445   Gottschick, A. M. "Ost und West und die Mitte." Hausmusik 19:198-
      199, November-December 1955.

446   "Armstrong Dansk Student." Orkester Journalen 23:18, November
      1955.

447   Leslie, P. "He's a Giant All the Same." Melody Maker 31:7, No-
      vember 5, 1955.

448   _____. "What's Happened to Louis?" Melody Maker 31:3, Novem-
      ber 5, 1955.

449   "Satchmo Sells Out Berlin's 7,000-Seater." Variety 200:40, Novem-
      ber 9, 1955.

450   "Louis Runs the Gauntlet." Melody Maker 31:5, November 12, 1955.
      Fans riot after Armstrong's performance in France.

451   Jones, M., and S. Traill. "A Guide for Armstrong's 'Paris' Fans."
      Melody Maker 31:8, November 19, 1955.

452   "Satchmo Paris Crowd Calls for Riot Squad." Variety 200:44, Novem-
      ber 23, 1955.

453   Jones, M. "Louis Still the King!" Melody Maker 31:6, November
      26, 1955.

454   Armstrong, Louis. "They Cross Iron Curtain to Hear American
      Jazz." U.S. News and World Report 39:54-60, December 2, 1955.

455   Hutton, J. "15 Minutes with Louis." Melody Maker 31:3, December
      3, 1955.

456   "Jazz in the Cold War." Commonweal 63:274, December 16, 1955.

457   "This Trumpet Madness." Newsweek 46:48, December 19, 1955. Re-
      port on Armstrong's concerts in Paris.

458 "Louis & Wagner at the Milan Opera House." Melody Maker 31:3,
     December 24, 1955. Reprinted from U.S. News and World Report.

459 "Satchmo Extending Click European Tour; Still Eyes USSR Trek." Va-
     riety 201:43, December 28, 1955.

460 "Armstrong to Lead the Way in Musical Cultural Invasion?" down
     beat 23:7, January 11, 1956.

461 Fulbright, T. "Ma Rainey and I." Jazz Journal 9:1-2, March 1956.

462 "Satchmo, Randall in New British-U.S. Band Swap Setup." Variety
     202:47, March 28, 1956.

463 Jepsen, J. G. "Jazzens Instrumentalister: Manliga Vokalister."
     Orkester Journalen 24:12, April 1956.

464 "Lose Weight the 'Satchmo Way.'" Ebony 11:35-37, April 1956.

465 "Bands Across the Sea: Louis Follows Heath, Stan." down beat
     23:5, April 4, 1956.

466 Jones, M. "Louis at the Crescendo." Melody Maker 31:15, April
     14, 1956.

467 Cerulli, D. "Louis, Herd Break It Up." down beat 23:12, April 18,
     1956.

468 "Editorial." Jazz Journal 9:9, May 1956.

469 "Louis Armstrong on Stage." Jazz Journal 9:10-11, May 1956.

470 Panassie, H. and M. Gautier. "Louis Armstrong Off Stage." Jazz
     Journal 9:1, May 1956.

471 "Mezz on Satch." Melody Maker 31:6, May 5, 1956.

472 Silverman, S. "Satchmo Returns to Brit. After 21-Year Gap; See
     $4.25 Top 'Troublesome.'" Variety 202:2, May 9, 1956.

473 "Louis at the Empress Hall." Melody Maker 31:3, May 12, 1956.

474 "Mezz on Satch." Melody Maker 31:17, May 12, 1956.

475 "Union Vetoes Armstrong Disc." Melody Maker 31:1, May 19, 1956.

476 Jones, M., and S. Traill. "No More Revolving Bandstands--Please!"
     Melody Maker 31:6, May 26, 1956.

477 "Armstrong 'too high.'" Variety 202:43, May 30, 1956.

478 "Near East Click Cues Woo of Dizzy in Latin Lands; Satchmo's O'seas
     Coin." Variety 202:43, May 30, 1956.

479 Padmore, G. "Holiday Honored 'Satchmo' Armstrong." Crisis 63:341-
     342, June-July 1956.

480 "A Band There to Greet Us, Old Friends to Meet Us." Jazz Journal

9:10-11, June 1956. A report on Armstrong's recent trip to London.

481 "Editorial." Jazz Journal 9:6, June 1956. Comments on Armstrong's concerts in London.

482 Nicholls, B. "A Jazzman's Diary." Jazz Journal 9:31, June 1956.

483 Stewart-Baxter, D. "Satchmo." Jazz Journal 9:5, June 1956.

484 Wilkinson, G. "Oscar, Ella and Louis." Jazz Journal 9:1, June 1956. Discussion of the music of Oscar Peterson, Ella Fitzgerald, and Louis Armstrong.

485 Wilson, J. S. "New Orleans Jazz." High Fidelity 6:75-76, June 1956.

486 "Good Will with Horns." Newsweek 47:50, June 4, 1956. Concerts by Armstrong and Dizzy Gillespie in Europe are related.

487 "Just Very." Time 67:63, June 4, 1956.

488 "Satchmo Is a Smash on the Gold Coast." Life 40:38-39, June 11, 1956.

489 "Lightly and Politely." Jazz Journal 9:27-28, July 1956. Comments on Armstrong's London concerts.

490 Lovette, H. "Louis Armstrong, Is He an Immature Jazz Fan?" Metronome 72:10-11, August 1956.

491 "Sands, Las Vegas." Variety 203:55, August 1, 1956.

492 "Real Gone Ambassador." America 95:434, August 11, 1956.

493 "London Symphony Offers to Armstrong." Melody Maker 31:1, August 18, 1956.

494 Hague, D. "Satchmo." Jazz Journal 9:9-10, September 1956.

495 "Satchmo Goes 'Back Home'; Famed Jazz Star Scores Big Triumph in First African Visit." Ebony 11:31-33, September 1956.

496 "Mr. Jazz." Look 20:10-12, September 4, 1956.

497 "Louis Denies He Was Undisturbed by Racial Barrier." down beat 23:28, September 5, 1956.

498 "Editorial." Jazz Journal 9:14, October 1956.

499 Jones, M. , and S. Traill. "Louis." Melody Maker 31:6, October 20, 1956.

500 "Chez Paree, Chi." Variety 204:53, November 7, 1956.

501 "Satchmo Returning for Hungary Relief." Melody Maker 31:1, November 24, 1956.

502 Glaser, J. "Satchmo Says." Melody Maker 31:12, December 15,
     1956.

503 Jones, M. "Storm at Armstrong Relief Fund Concert." Melody Maker
     31:1, December 22, 1956.

504 "A Bom Ahead." Newsweek 48:58, December 31, 1956. The Royal
     Philharmonic Orchestra has Armstrong as a featured performer.

505 "Ambassador Called 'Satchmo.'" Color 11:7-10, January 1957.

506 "The Press and Louis." Melody Maker 32:6, January 5, 1957.

507 "Cat Among the Pigeons." Jazz Journal 10:12, February 1957.

508 "Satch's Saga." down beat 24:19, February 20, 1957.

509 Wood, B. "Don't Blame Louis." Jazz Journal 10:13, April 1957.

510 Halberstam, D. "Day with Satchmo." Reporter 16:37-40, May 2,
     1957.

511 Simon, B. "Dizzy Attacks Louis." Melody Maker 32:5, May 18,
     1957. Gillespie criticizes Armstrong in "Jazz Is Too Good for
     Americans," published in Esquire.

512 "Armstrong--Künstlerisch Wertvoll?" Neue Zeitschrift für Musik
     118:378, June 1957.

513 "Louis Armstrong and the Modernists." Metronome 74:15, June 1957.

514 "Louis Packin' His Satchmo for S. American Bow." Variety 207:55,
     June 19, 1957.

515 "Moulin Rouge, L. A." Variety 207:69, June 19, 1957.

516 Millstein, G. "Ambassador with a Horn." Reader's Digest 71:93-96,
     July 1957.

517 "State Dept. Pipes Up with 'Satchmo for the Soviets.'" Variety 207:1,
     July 31, 1957.

518 Halberstam, D. "A Day with Satchmo." Jazz Journal 10:1, August
     1957.

519 "Newport Jazz Festival." down beat 24:11, August 8, 1957.

520 "Satchmo's Symph Stint at Hollywood Bowl as Prelude to Teleshow."
     Variety 207:43, August 21, 1957.

521 Wood, B. "American Jazz Scene." Jazz Journal 10:10, September
     1957.

522 "'Satchmo the Great,' Documentary Film about Louis Armstrong."
     Variety 208:26, September 11, 1957.

523 "Ike Swipe May Cost Satchmo Edsel Spec; Others 'Penalized.'" Va-
     riety 208:1, September 25, 1957.

524   Feather, L.   "Satchmo Blitzes Governor Faubus."   Melody Maker
      32:6, September 28, 1957.

525   Hentoff, N.   "'Satchmo' Fullface."   Saturday Review 40:107-109, Sep-
      tember 28, 1957.

526   Shipman, J.   "The Newport Jazz Festival."   Jazz Journal 10:6-8, Oc-
      tober 1957.

527   "'They're Crucifying Pops.'"   Melody Maker 32:5, October 5, 1957.

528   Nelms, C.   "Louis Doesn't Swing."   Melody Maker 32:17, October
      12, 1957.

529   Voce, S.   "Louis Is Not an Uncle Tom; Interview with Max Kamin-
      sky."   Melody Maker 32:5, October 12, 1957.

530   "Satchmo Safari in S. Amer. Gets Pre-Ole in B.A."   Variety 208:77,
      October 30, 1957.

531   "Satch Speaks Twice."   down beat 24:10, October 31, 1957.

532   Coss, B.   "Louis Armstrong on Decca: 57 Years Later."   Metro-
      nome 74:14-17, November 1957.

533   Lardner, J.   "Air."   New Yorker 33:114, November 2, 1957.

534   "Latin Blowout for Louis."   Life 43:169-170, November 25, 1957.   Re-
      view of Armstrong's concerts in Buenos Aires.

535   "Satchmo Swamps Sputnik in South Am."   Variety 209:1, December 4,
      1957.

536   Lucraft, H.   "Editor in New Satchmo Film."   Melody Maker 32:8-9,
      December 21, 1957.

537   Joensen, Bendt.   Louis Armstrong.   København: Gyldendal, 1958.

538   "Armstrong, Great American Boy."   Variety 209:65, January 22, 1958.

539   Feather, L.   "The Trumpet in Jazz."   down beat 25:15, January 23,
      1958.

540   "Ambassador Satch Sounds Off."   Variety 209:49, January 29, 1958.

541   Norris, J.   "A Musical Autobiography of Louis Armstrong."   Jazz
      Journal 11:24-26, February 1958.

542   Gleason, R. J.   "Perspectives."   down beat 25:33, February 6, 1958.
      The integration of Little Rock, Arkansas schools is noted.

543   Lyttelton, H.   "Louis Is Not Finished ... This Album Proves It."
      Melody Maker 32:2, February 22, 1958.

544   Graham, C.   "He Tapes It All!"   High Fidelity/Musical America
      5:42-3, March 1958.

545   Houlden, D.   "All Stars, Past and Present."   Jazz Journal 11:3-4,
      March 1958.

546 Bernstein, B. "'Satchmo the Great' Is No Less." Billboard 70:9, March 3, 1958.

547 Hague, D. "Louis Plays the State House." Jazz Journal 11:5-6, April 1958. A performance by Armstrong in Boston.

548 Lyttelton, H. "A Feast of Nostalgia." Melody Maker 33:4, April 26, 1958. Review of "Satchmo the Great" film.

549 "Satchmo the Great." Jazz Journal 11:10, May 1958.

550 "Satchmo Only Skips Tibet in '59 World Tour." Variety 211:2, August 27, 1958.

551 Race, S. "Louis--the Immortal." Melody Maker 33:5-6, September 27, 1958. The Hot Seven recording of "Melancholy Blues."

552 "Heard in Person." down beat 25:38, October 30, 1958.

553 "'Collector's Items' and 'My Musical Autobiography.'" Jazz Review 1:30-32, December 1958.

554 McCarthy, Albert J. Louis Armstrong. New York: Barnes, 1959.

555 "Satchmo Revisited." down beat 26:14-15, January 8, 1959.

556 Jones, M. "Forever Armstrong." Melody Maker 34:11, January 24, 1959.

557 "Armstrong Still Going Strong." Orkester Journalen 27:7, February 1959.

558 Green, B. "His Name ... a Household Word?" Jazz Review 2:19, February 1959.

559 "Lewis, Basie and Satch." Jazz Journal 12:1, February 1959.

560 "Buying Extra Insurance for German Theatres as Satchmo Goes Marching In." Variety 213:51, February 18, 1959.

561 "Basin Street, Berlin." Newsweek 53:52, February 23, 1959.

562 "It's Louis--He's Back." Melody Maker 34:3, February 28, 1959.

563 "Satch & Co." Jazz Journal 12:1, March 1959.

564 Jones, M., et al. "Four Views of the Louis Armstrong Band--Now Touring Britain." Melody Maker 34:3, March 7, 1959.

565 "Satchmo & Co. Repeating in Brit. on Good Friday After Romp at Kilburn." Variety 214:57, March 11, 1959.

566 Hutton, J. "Louis Is Supreme!" Melody Maker 34:13, March 14, 1959.

567 Jones, M. "There Will Never Be Another Armstrong." Melody Maker 34:13, March 14, 1959.

568   "Yugo B. O.   SRO via Word-of-Satchmouth."   <u>Variety</u> 214:57, March
      25, 1959.

569   Wilson, J. S.   The Jazz Panorama."   <u>High Fidelity Review</u> 2:73-76,
      April 1959.

570   "Satchmovic Just a Slav to Fans in Hot & Hectic Flying Yugoslav
      Tour."   <u>Variety</u> 214:1, April 15, 1959.

571   Schmidt-Garre, H.   "Louis Armstrongs Deutschland-Tournee."   <u>Neue</u>
      <u>Zeitschrift für Musik</u> 120:281, May 1959.

572   Lambert, G. E.   "Louis Armstrong Today."   <u>Jazz Monthly</u> 5:10-11,
      June 1959.

573   "How to Do the Impossible...."   <u>down beat</u> 26:14, June 25, 1959.

574   "Happy Birthday Louis."   <u>Second Line</u> 10:5, July-August 1959.

575   Tenot, F.   "Satchmo en Gross Forme."   <u>Jazz Magazine</u> 5:30-31, July
      1959.

576   "That Man on the Trumpet."   <u>Newsweek</u> 54:80, July 6, 1959.

577   "Lewisohn Stadium's Satchmo Surprise."   <u>Variety</u> 215:72, July 8, 1959.

578   "Louis Armstrong, Gueri, Regagne les Etats-Unis."   <u>Jazz Magazine</u>
      5:13, August-September 1959.

579   Edey, M.   "Reconsiderations."   <u>Jazz Review</u> 2:28-29, August 1959.
      "Young Louis Armstrong" recording is analyzed.

580   Lyttelton, H.   "Where Are Today's Giants of Jazz?"   <u>Melody Maker</u>
      34:11, August 15, 1959.

581   Feather, L.   "The Three Armstrongs."   <u>Melody Maker</u> 34:2-3, Au-
      gust 22, 1959.

582   "The Daniel Louis Satchmo Armstrong."   <u>Music U.S.A.</u> 76:13, Sep-
      tember 1959.

583   Gaspard, J. J.   "Louis Armstrong."   <u>Musica</u> no. 66:20, September
      1959.

584   Feather, L.   "Satchmo Le Grand."   <u>Jazz Magazine</u> 5:26-29, October
      1959.

585   "Chi Chi, Palm Springs."   <u>Variety</u> 216:73, October 21, 1959.

586   "Satchmo to Cairo Re Israel: It's All Greek."   <u>Variety</u> 216:69, No-
      vember 18, 1959.

587   "Sayings of Satchmo."   <u>Ebony</u> 15:85-88, December 1959.

588   "Louis Blasts Jim Crow."   <u>Melody Maker</u> 34:11, December 12, 1959.

589   O'Brien, Ralph.   <u>Armstrong.</u>   Mit Texten von Louis Armstrong, Sid-
      ney Bechet, Mezz Mezzrow, Bunk Johnson.   Zürich: Sanssouci,
      1960.

590 "Louis and New Orleans." down beat 27:15-16, January 7, 1960.

591 "Louis Armstrong and Dinah Shore Win Favorite Male and Female
     Musical Personalities for 1959 in Annual Survey of International
     Fan Club of America." Jet p. 60, January 7, 1960.

592 Morgenstern, D. "Three Giants." Jazz Journal 13:15-16, February
     1960.

593 "Soliloquy by Satch." down beat 27:14, February 18, 1960.

594 Patruno, L., J. Russo, and L. Mango. "Louis e Fletcher." Musica
     Jazz 16:20-22, April 1960.

595 Dachs, D. "Daddy, How the Country Has Changed." Ebony 16:81-90,
     May 1960.

596 "Satchmo's Summer Stomping." Variety 219:49, June 22, 1960.

597 Armstrong, Louis. "Scanning the History of Jazz." Jazz Review
     3:6-9, July 1960.

598 Jones, M. "At 60, Louis Is Still Swinging." Melody Maker 35:9,
     July 9, 1960.

599 "Louis Armstrong." Neue Zeitschrift für Musik 121:277-278, August
     1960.

600 "Satchmo to Hit Spots in Africa for Pepsi-Cola; State Dept. Rep in
     Congo." Variety 220:1, September 21, 1960.

601 "Crescendo, Hollywood." Variety 220:68, October 5, 1960.

602 "Akwaaba, Satchmo." Time 76:78, October 31, 1960.

603 Hentoff, N. "The King Meets the Dukes." High Fidelity Review
     5:57-60, November 1960.

604 "Louis Armstrong Is Guest Star on 'An Hour with Danny Kaye.'" Jet
     p. 57, November 17, 1960.

605 "Armstrong's Akwaaba in Ghana." down beat 27:12, November 24,
     1960.

606 "Armstrong, Louis." Metronome 77:44, December 1960.

607 "Le Dernier Miracle de Satchmo." Jazz Magazine 6:32-35, December
     1960.

608 "On the Road with Louis Armstrong." Metronome 77:13-17, Decem-
     ber 1960.

609 "Diplomat with a Horn." Newsweek 56:84, December 19, 1960.

610 Da Cunha, M. "Louis Armstrong e Os Meninos Bem Educados."
     Gazeta Musical e de Todas as Artes 10:219, no. 120, 1961.

611 Ginibre, J. L. "Louis Armstrong à la Conquete de Hollywood." Jazz
     Magazine 7:36-39, January 1961.

612   Jones, M. "With Duke and Louis in Paris." Melody Maker 36:2-3,
           January 7, 1961. Armstrong receives the American Legion Medal
           of Merit as a result of his promotion of U.S. relations with France
           through his concerts.

613   Destombes, A. "Toujours Louis." Jazz Hot no. 162:32-33, Febru-
           ary 1961.

614   Armstrong, Louis. "How Jazz Came to Life." Music Journal 19:13,
           March 1961.

615   Traill, S. "With Duke and Louis in Paris." Jazz Journal 14:1,
           March 1961.

616   Lyttelton, H. "Louis Changed the Face of Jazz!" Melody Maker
           36:5, March 18, 1961.

617   Traill, S. "'Paris Blues.'" Metronome 78:16-17, April 1961.

618   "The Beautiful Americans." Jazz Journal 14:19, May 1961.

619   Dachs, D. "Daddy, How the Country Has Changed." Ebony 16:81-82,
           May 1961.

620   "Russians Want Satchmo for 30-City Autumn Tour." Melody Maker
           36:1, May 20, 1961.

621   Rolontz, B. "Louis Armstrong Sings 'em All." Billboard Music
           Week 73:6, May 29, 1961.

622   Destombes, A. "Sur 13 Microsillons de Louis Armstrong." Jazz Hot
           no. 166:28-29, June 1961.

623   Morgenstern, D. "Rotating with Satchmo & Mingus." Metronome
           78:19-21, June 1961.

624   "Satchmo et Duke Face à Face." Jazz Magazine 7:15, June 1961.

625   "Count et Duke dos à dos." Jazz Magazine 7:16, September 1961.

626   Panassie, H. "Louis Armstrong: His Records; His Influence." Met-
           ronome 78:8-13, October 1961.

627   Steiner, J. "Beyond the Impression." Record Research no. 38:4,
           October 1961.

628   "Nominate Satchmo for Congress' Accolade." Variety 224:1, October
           11, 1961.

629   McRae, B. "Louis Armstrong--Big Band Trumpeter." Jazz Journal
           14:10-11, December 1961.

630   "Minsky's $11,500,000 Suit Versus Satchmo." Variety 225:53, De-
           cember 13, 1961.

631   "Basin St. East, N.Y." Variety 225:46, December 27, 1961.

632   "King's Scepter Is Enshrined." Second Line 13:3, no. 5-6, 1962. The

New Orleans Jazz Museum has added a trumpet of Armstrong's to its collection.

633   Winkler, Hans Jürgen. Louis Armstrong; ein Porträt. Wetzlar: Pegasus, 1962.

634   Feather, L. "Satchmo--Then and Now." International Musician 60:22-23, January 1962.

635   "Louis and Others Sued for 11½ Million Dollars." down beat 29:15, January 18, 1962.

636   "Fairmont, S. F." Variety 225:59, January 31, 1962.

637   "Ageless Man with the Magic Horn: Louis Armstrong." Sepia 11:38-41, February 1962.

638   Feather, L. "Jazz Records." Show 2:103, February 1962.

639   Pilon, G. "Louis Daniel 'Satchmo' Armstrong." St. Cecilia 11:35-37, March 1962.

640   Feather, L. "There's a Lot in Me the Public Hasn't Heard! Interview with Louis Armstrong." Melody Maker 37:8-9, April 28, 1962.

641   Morgenstern, D. "Pops in Perspective." Jazz Journal 15:4-8, May 1962.

642   Traill, S. "Armstrong ... V.S.O.P. [Very Special Old Phonography]." Jazz Journal 15:3, May 1962.

643   _____. "Editorial." Jazz Journal 15:1, May 1962.

644   Williams, M. "A Note on Louis Armstrong and Jazz Rhythm." Jazz Journal 15:9-10, May 1962.

645   Dawbarn, B. "Louis on Short Ration." Melody Maker 37:10, May 5, 1962.

646   "Jazz Museum Gets Original Satchmo Horn." down beat 29:14, May 24, 1962.

647   "Une Attraction Royale." Jazz Magazine 8:25-26, June 1962.

648   Capasso, R. "Louis Armstrong à Roma." Musica Jazz 18:12-13, June 1962.

649   "Louis Armstrong--His Greatest Years." Jazz Monthly 8:26-27, June 1962.

650   "The King of Jazz." Norsk Musikerblad 51:3, June 1962.

651   "Round About Satch." Jazz Hot no. 177:10, June 1962.

652   "Living Room, Chi." Variety 227:52, June 27, 1962.

653   Rosenkrantz, T. "Reflections on Louis Armstrong." down beat 29:50, July 19, 1962.

654 "Du caoutchouc au celluloid." Jazz Magazine 8:15, September 1962.
     The dedication of a film to Louis Armstrong entitled "Goodyear of
     Jazz."

655 "Hamp Set for Japan, Louis to Go 'Down Under.'" down beat 29:11,
     September 13, 1962. Concerts scheduled for Lionel Hampton and
     Armstrong in Australia.

656 Dutton, F. "Satchmo--a Musical Autobiography." Matrix no. 43:10,
     October 1962.

657 Graham, C. "Listening with Louis." Jazz 1:22, October 1962.

658 Williams, M. "Louis Armstrong and Jazz Rhythm." American Rec-
     ord Guide 29:207-209, November 1962.

659 Spivey, V. "The Louis Armstrong That I Know." Record Research
     no. 48:3, January 1963.

660 "Cocoanut Grove, L.A." Variety 229:44, January 2, 1963.

661 "Louis Armstrong Says He Will Retire--Again." down beat 30:15,
     February 14, 1963.

662 "Louis Deserves a Monument!" Melody Maker 38:7, July 27, 1963.

663 "Riviera, Las Vegas." Variety 231:58, August 14, 1963.

664 Jones, M. "50 Years of Satchmo!" Melody Maker 38:12-13, Septem-
     ber 14, 1963.

665 "A Pile of Ashes." Second Line 15:8, no. 7-8, 1964.

666 Williams, M. "Louis Armstrong." Jazz 3:12, January-February
     1964.

667 Armstrong, Louis. "Jazz Is a Lan'guage." Music Journal 22:16, Jan-
     uary 1964.

668 "Duke Ellington's 'My People.'" Jazz 3:21-23, February 1964.

669 "Riviera, Las Vegas." Variety 234:77, April 8, 1964.

670 "Satch Suffers Inflamed Veins, No Heart Attack, as Rumored." down
     beat 31:13, April 23, 1964.

671 "Up Among the Beatles." Newsweek 63:103-104, April 27, 1964.

672 "Satchmo's 'Dolly' Topples Beatles." Variety 234:169, April 29, 1964.

673 "Louis Armstrong Show." Variety 234:77, May 6, 1964.

674 Jones, M. "Hello Dolly!" Melody Maker 39:3, May 23, 1964.

675 "Armstrong's Birthplace Center of Confusion." down beat 31:12, July
     16, 1964.

676 "Deadline Passes; Armstrong Birthplace Torn Down." down beat
     31:10, July 30, 1964.

677 Robertson, S. "Jazz World." Sepia 13:40, October 1964.

678 Williams, M. "Les Lumieres du Couchant." Jazz Hot no. 202:30-
     33, October 1964.

679 _____. "Armstrong Before 'Dolly.'" Saturday Review 47:77, Oc-
     tober 17, 1964.

680 Sanders, C. L. "Louis Armstrong--the Reluctant Millionaire." Eb-
     ony 20:136-146, November 1964.

681 Feather, L. "Retire? I've Too Many Bookings--Louis." Melody
     Maker 39:8, November 28, 1964.

682 Hilbert, B. "Louis Armstrong Research." Record Research no.
     65:5, December 1964.

683 "U. of Alabama Bars Satchmo." Variety 237:49, December 9, 1964.

684 Feather, L. "It's Crazy to Fight Louis Ban." Melody Maker 39:5,
     December 12, 1964.

685 "Apartheid Cancels Satchmo." Variety 237:1, December 23, 1964.

686 Macha, Z. "Louis Armstrong Potvrzena Legenda." Hudebni Rozh-
     ledy 18:295, no. 7, 1965.

687 "Set Satchmo for Iron Curtain Tour." Variety 237:4, January 6, 1965.

688 "Things Popping for Pops." down beat 32:12, February 11, 1965.

689 "Louis Armstrong and His All Stars in Memphis." Second Line 16:34,
     March-April 1965.

690 "A Visit with Satchmo." Second Line 16:35-37, March-April 1965.

691 "With or Without a Party Badge, East Berlin Cats Dig Satchmo's Con-
     certs." Variety 238:56, March 31, 1965.

692 "Armstrong Speaks Out on Racial Injustice." down beat 32:14-15,
     April 22, 1965.

693 "Armstrong Derrière le Rideau." Jazz Magazine no. 118:15, May
     1965.

694 Feather, L. "Pensionären Satchmo i Högform." Orkester Journalen
     33:6, May 1965.

695 Hilbert, B. "Armstrong Research Project." Record Research no.
     68:10, May 1965.

696 Leahu, A. "Oaspeti." Muzica 15:41-42, May 1965.

697 Dahlgren, R. "Armstrong Alltid Lika Välkommen." Orkester Jour-
     nalen 33:8, June 1965.

698 Feather, Louis. "Louis e Tornato a Casa." Musica Jazz 21:27-28,
     June 1965.

699   Williams, M.   "Satchmo & the Soloist."   Jazz Journal 18:4-6, June
      1965.

700   "Sen. Javits Asks That Armstrong Receive Medal of Freedom."   down
      beat 32:8, June 3, 1965.

701   Dawbarn, B., and M. Jones.   "Hello, Louis!"   Melody Maker 40:6,
      June 5, 1965.

702   Godwin, H. E.   "Getting to Know Satch."   Second Line 16:101-102,
      July-August 1965.

703   Haeggloef, G.   "Samtal med Satchmo."   Orkester Journalen 33:8-9
      July-August 1965.

704   Koechlin, P.   "Louis le Grand."   Jazz Hot no. 211:20-23, July-Au-
      gust 1965.

705   "Limericks for Louie."   Second Line 16:97, July-August 1965.

706   "Louis Armstrong 1915-1965."   Second Line 16:99-100, July-August
      1965.

707   Watson, C.   "50 Golden Years."   Second Line 16:88-91, July-August
      1965.

708   Carles, P.   "Louis au Palais."   Jazz Magazine no. 120:15-16, July
      1965.

709   Lambert, G. E.   "Jazz in Britain."   Jazz Journal 18:6, July 1965.

710   Morgenstern, D.   "Yesterday, Today, and Tomorrow."   down beat
      32:15-18, July 15, 1965.

711   Stewart, R.   "Boy Meets King."   down beat 32:23-27, July 15, 1965.

712   "USSR, Germany, Hungary, and Hollywood Focus on Armstrong."
      down beat 32:8, July 29, 1955.

713   Dance, S.   "Kansas City Perspective."   Saturday Review 48:36-37,
      July 31, 1965.

714   Arlt, H.   "Satch Eager for Visit Home."   Second Line 16:115-117,
      September-October 1965.

715   Hildebrand, B. J.   "New Orleans Night in Hollywood."   Second Line
      16:128-129, September-October 1965.

716   Koechlin, P.   "Armstrong 65."   Musica no. 138:54-55, September
      1965.

717   Williams, M.   "Last Trip Up the River."   Jazz Journal 18:6-7, Oc-
      tober 1965.   Reprinted from the Saturday Review.

718   Barker, D.   "The 'King' Comes to Town."   Second Line 16:138-140,
      November-December 1965.

719   "The 'King' Is Crowned."   Second Line 16:140-143, November-Decem-
      ber 1965.

720 "Red Letter Day: A Compendium." Second Line 16:150-154, Novem-
     ber-December 1965.

721 Elsner, J. "Gedanken zu Jazzveranstaltungen in Leipzig und Berlin."
     Musik und Gesellschaft 15:765-768, November 1965.

722 "Satchmo Goes Home." Newsweek 66:98, November 8, 1965.

723 Kopkind, A. "Satchmo Returns to His Home Town, Briefly." New
     Republic 153:10-11, November 13, 1965.

724 "AGVA and NYC to Honor Louis Armstrong." down beat 32:10, De-
     cember 2, 1965.

725 "New Orleans Hails Conquering Hero Pops." down beat 32:10, Decem-
     ber 16, 1965.

726 "Harolds, Reno." Variety 241:58, December 22, 1965.

727 Failows, J. R. "Louis Armstrong and Guy Lombardo." Jazz 5:16-
     21, no. 9, 1966.

728 Whistle, P. "Red Letter Day Finale." Second Line 17:17-19, Jan-
     uary-February 1966.

729 Balliett, W. "Jazz Records." New Yorker 41:108, January 15, 1966.

730 Meryman, R. "An Authentic American Genius." Life 60:92-102,
     April 15, 1966. Interview which was translated into French as
     "Satchmo Se Penche sur Son Passe" in Jazz Magazine no. 180:18-
     23, July-August 1970.

731 Feather, L. "Louis: Swinging Again with the King of Corn." Mel-
     ody Maker 41:6, April 23, 1966.

732 "Si Louis Revenait ... ; un Ouvrage sur le Ghana ou Louis Armstrong
     Est Evoque." Jazz Magazine no. 130:17, May 1966.

733 "Unit Reviews." Variety 243:66, June 15, 1966.

734 "Indestructible Louis Armstrong." Sepia 15:44-49, August 1966.

735 "Harolds, Reno." Variety 244:59, November 16, 1966.

736 Napoleon, A. "Mr. Strong; An Appreciation." Jazz Journal 19:14-16,
     December 1966.

737 Richards, Kenneth G. Louis Armstrong. Chicago: Childrens Press,
     1967. Juvenile literature.

738 "Riviera, Las Vegas." Variety 245:52, February 15, 1967.

739 "Satchmo Illness Cancels 10 Concerts and $67,000." Variety 246:64,
     May 3, 1967.

740 Morgenstern, D. "Caught in the Act." down beat 34:27, August 10,
     1967.

741 Hennessey, M. "Armstrong's Musical Magic Conquers Antibes Jazz
     Fest." Billboard 79:58, August 12, 1967.

742 "Editorial." Jazz Journal 20:3, September 1967. Review of a Dublin
     concert.

743 Laverdure, M. "Louis Armstrong." Jazz Magazine no. 146:18-20,
     September 1967.

744 Locke, D. "The Jazz Vocal." Jazz Monthly 13:6-7, September 1967.

745 "Harolds, Reno." Variety 248:67, September 13, 1967.

746 "'Satchmo' Illness Hurts 'Dixieland at Disneyland.'" Variety 248:51,
     October 4, 1967.

747 Hennessey, M. "Caught in the Act." down beat 34:36-37, October
     5, 1967.

748 King, L. L. "Everybody's Louie." Harper's Magazine 235:61-69,
     November 1967.

749 "Louis Malade." Jazz Magazine no. 148:17, November 1967.

750 King, L. L. "Everybody's Louie." ASCAP 2:20-23, no. 3, 1968.
     Reprinted from King's book And Other Dirty Stories.

751 Romary, F. "Struttin' with Some Louie." Storyville no. 15:4-8, Feb-
     ruary-March 1968.

752 "Satchmo Scats in Eye-talian." Second Line 19:27, March-April 1968.

753 Adler, P. "Viva Louis!" Melody Maker 43:20, March 2, 1968.

754 Kennedy, S. "When Louis Played on the Boat." Saturday Review
     51:52, March 9, 1968.

755 Walsh, A. "Tell Them Satchmo Is Feeling Great, Looking Pretty and
     Blowin' Great!" Melody Maker 43:5, April 13, 1968.

756 "Latin Quarter, N.Y." Variety 250:67, April 24, 1968.

757 McRae, B. "A B Basics; A Column for the Newcomer to Jazz."
     Jazz Journal 21:11, May 1968.

758 "Embassy, Toronto." Variety 251:51, May 29, 1968.

759 Hutton, J. "Satchmo: Still the Great Entertainer." Melody Maker
     43:10, June 22, 1968.

760 Jones, M. "Wonderful World of Louis Armstrong." Melody Maker
     43:13, June 29, 1968; 43:12-13, July 6, 1968.

761 _____. "Satch Says Thanks for the Thrill." Melody Maker 43:9,
     July 13, 1968.

762 McCarthy, A. "Louis Armstrong in London." Jazz Monthly 14:18,
     August 1968.

763 Traill, S. "Editorial." Jazz Journal 21:1, August 1968.

764 "Harolds, Reno." Variety 251:48, August 7, 1968.

765 Voce, S. "Hello Skinny." Jazz Journal 21:14, September 1968.

766 "Pop Goes the Trumpet." Melody Maker 43:12, September 7, 1968.

767 Kumm, B. "Louis Armstrong; Reflections on King Oliver and the
     Cotton Club." Storyville no. 19:9-11, October-November 1968.

768 "En Bref ..." Jazz Hot no. 243:31, October 1968.

769 "Armstrong's British Visit Is Cancelled--Still in Hospital." Melody
     Maker 43:1, October 19, 1968.

770 "Dieting and Hard Work Bad Mixture for Satch." down beat 35:10,
     October 31, 1968.

771 Williams, M. "Henderson, Armstrong, and Noone." Saturday Review
     57:87, November 16, 1968.

772 Schonfield, V. "Second Opinion." Melody Maker 43:10, November
     30, 1968.

773 Albertson, C., et al. "Record Reviews." down beat 36:20, February
     20, 1969.

774 Haeggloef, G. "Snatches of Satch." Orkester Journalen 37:7, May
     1969.

775 Feather, L. "Man of Many Faces." down beat 36:8, July 24, 1969.

776 "Glaser's $3-Mil. Estate to Staff; Also to Satchmo." Variety 256:2,
     September 24, 1969.

777 Walsh, A. "Satchmo '69." Melody Maker 44:16-17, September 27,
     1969.

778 "Editorial." Jazz Journal 22:1, October 1969. Discussion of the fund
     for a Louis Armstrong Statue.

779 Walsh, A. "Satchmo '69." Melody Maker 44:11, October 4, 1969;
     44:11, October 11, 1969.

780 "Back to Work for Louis." Melody Maker 44:4, November 29, 1969.

781 "The Saga of a Wayward Bus; or, a Fund Is Created in Old N.O."
     Second Line 23:248-250, December 1969.

782 "Planning Monument to Satchmo in New Orleans." Variety 257:1, De-
     cember 10, 1969.

783 Feather, L. "A Fund to Honour Louis." Melody Maker 44:14, De-
     cember 13, 1969.

784 "Armstrong-Jahr." Musikhandel 21:56, no. 2, 1970.

785 "Hello Louis!" Jazz Report 7:5, no. 3, 1970.

786   Jones, Max, John Chilton, and Leonard Feather. Salute to Satchmo.
        London: I. P. C. Specialist & Professional Press, 1970.

787   Scully, A. "The Building Nobody Wanted." Jazz Journal 23:12-13,
        January 1970. The story of the Coloured Waifs Home where Arm-
        strong spent part of his childhood and learned to play the trumpet
        in New Orleans. Reprinted in Second Line 23:349-351, July-August
        1970.

788   "Satchmo Statue Fund Raising Drive Is On." down beat 37:7, January
        8, 1970.

789   "Une Statue pour Satchmo." Jazz Hot no. 258:9, February 1970.

790   "Record Reviews: Louis in Los Angeles--1930." Jazz Journal 23:24,
        May 1970.

791   Wilmer, V. "Chords & Discords: Statues Vs. Playgrounds." down
        beat 37:8, May 18, 1970.

792   Armstrong, Lil Hardin. "Louis par Lil." Jazz Hot no. 263:10, Sum-
        mer 1970.

793   "Biographie." Jazz Hot no. 263:26, Summer 1970.

794   Cullaz, M. "Maurice Andre: Louis Armstrong." Jazz Hot no. 263:22,
        Summer 1970.

795   _____. "Satchmo." Jazz Hot no. 263:24-25, Summer 1970.

796   Delaunay, C., et al. "Filmographie." Jazz Hot no. 263:29, Summer
        1970.

797   _____. "Pop's Music." Jazz Hot no. 263:8-9, Summer 1970.

798   "Discographie Francaise." Jazz Hot no. 263:28, Summer 1970.

799   "Disques 'Pirates.'" Jazz Hot no. 263:27-28, Summer 1970.

800   Lafitte, G. "Un Ange Passe." Jazz Hot no. 263:23, Summer 1970.

801   Mialy, L. V. "Barney Bigard: Me and Brother Satch." Jazz Hot
        no. 263:16-18, Summer 1970.

802   Morh, S. H. "A Monday Date par Earl 'Fatha' Hines. Jazz Hot no.
        263:12-15, Summer 1970.

803   Pernet, R., and C. G. Mecklenburg. "Bibliographie." Jazz Hot no.
        263:30, Summer 1970.

804   "[Quatre] Trompettistes parlent d'Armstrong." Jazz Hot no. 263:19-
        21, Summer 1970. The four trumpet players discussing Armstrong
        are: C. Bellest, I. Davrichevy, R. Guerin, and Y. Jullien.

805   "Selection Discographique." Jazz Hot no. 263: 26-27, Summer 1970.

806   Vian, B. "Louis Armstrong--une Sante!" Jazz Hot no. 263:7, Sum-
        mer 1970.

807 "Record Reviews: Louis in Los Angeles--1930." Storyville no. 29:196, June-July 1970.

808 Zwicky, T. "Louis--and Some West Coast Friends." Storyville no. 29:176-184, June-July 1970.

809 "Louis: 70 Ans." Jazz Magazine no. 179:18-19, June 1970.

810 McCarthy, A. "Record Reviews: Louis and the Big Bands 1928-1930." Jazz Monthly no. 184:19-20, June 1970.

811 "Reeditions: The Great Reunion." Jazz Magazine no. 179:49, June 1970.

812 Bostwick, F. "Hello Louis!" Second Line 23:247-248, July-August 1970.

813 Dove, I. "Armstrong Enregistre pour Flying Dutchman." Jazz Magazine no. 180:16-17, July-August 1970.

814 "Reeditions: Louis Armstrong and the All Stars." Jazz Magazine no. 180:48-49, July-August 1970.

815 "Satchmo Saluteras paa 70-Aarsdagen." Orkester Journalen 38:8-9, July-August 1970.

816 Dance, S. "Boy from New Orleans." Jazz Journal 23:10-11, July 1970. Armstrong has a London recording session for RCA.

817 Traill, S. "Back o' Louis." Jazz Journal 23:24-25, July 1970.

818 _____. "Editorial." Jazz Journal 23:2-3, July 1970.

819 Dance, S. "Louis Armstrong, American Original." Saturday Review 53:13-14, July 4, 1970.

820 Freeman, D., and I. Kolodin. "The Father and His Flock." Saturday Review 53:15-17, July 4, 1970.

821 Gabler, M. "My Thousand-Year Man." Saturday Review 53:18-19, July 4, 1970.

822 "Salute to Satchmo." Melody Maker 45:23-27, July 4, 1970.

823 "Trumpet Fanfare." Saturday Review 53:19, July 4, 1970. Trumpet players Billy Butterfield, Ray Nance, and Clark Terry discuss Armstrong.

824 "Blow Riffs for Satchmo's 70th." Variety 259:51, July 8, 1970.

825 Aronowitz, A. "You Learn How to Defend Your Style." Rolling Stone no. 62:12, July 9, 1970.

826 Ellington, D., et al. "Roses for Satchmo." down beat 37:14-19, July 9, 1970.

827 Feather, L. "Satchmo Remembered." down beat 37:21, July 9, 1970.

828 Morgenstern, D. "Basic Louis." down beat 37:28-29, July 9, 1970.

829   "Satchmo News: Salute, Record Date, New Book." down beat 37:11,
      July 9, 1970. A gala event held at the Shrine Auditorium, Los
      Angeles to celebrate Armstrong's birthday, a notable occurrence.

830   "Satchmo's down beat Scrapbook." down beat 37:20, July 9, 1970.

831   Williams, M. "For Louis Armstrong at 70." down beat 37:22-23,
      July 9, 1970.

832   "Salute to Satchmo." Melody Maker 45:8, July 11, 1970.

833   Feather, L. "Louis' Birthday Party." Melody Maker 45:29, July 18,
      1970.

834   Suber, C. "Chords & Discords: Statuary Reap." down beat 37:10,
      July 23, 1970.

835   Pleasants, H. What Jazz Is All About." Music and Musicians 18:26,
      August 1970.

836   _____ . "What Louis Armstrong and Jazz Are All About." Stereo
      Review 25:98, August 1970.

837   "Salute to Satchmo." Jazz Journal 23:24, August 1970.

838   "Satchmo at 70." International Musician 69:13, August 1970.

839   "Tribute for Louis." Jazz and Pop 9:12, August 1970.

840   Siders, H. "Los Angeles Love-in for Louis." down beat 37:21, Au-
      gust 20, 1970.

841   "Louis Blows Again." Melody Maker 45:3, August 22, 1970.

842   Cullaz, M. "La Chronique des Disques: The Good Book; Louis Arm-
      strong Sings the Blues." Jazz Hot no. 264:36-37, September 1970.

843   Dance, S. "Jazz." Music Journal 28:38, September 1970.

844   Dove, H. "Louis Armstrong: Give Peace a Chance." Jazz and Pop
      9:26-27, September 1970.

845   Feather, L. "Newport sans Grise." Jazz Magazine no. 181:22, Sep-
      tember 1970.

846   "It's 70 for Satch." Ebony 25:80-82, September 1970.

847   Mialy, L. V. "A Hollywood: Hello Louie." Jazz Hot no. 264:13,
      September 1970.

848   Jones, M. "Beryl--on a New York Walkabout." Melody Maker 45:30,
      September 12, 1970.

849   "International, Las Vegas." Variety 260:80, September 16, 1970.

850   Feather, L. "Louis Plays Again." Melody Maker 45:31, September
      19, 1970.

851   "Hello Louis!" Jazz Journal 23:14-15, October 1970.

852 "Col. Wein Huddling on LP on Satchmo Salute." Billboard 82:12, Oc-
     tober 24, 1970.

853 "Last Time in Britain for Louis?" Melody Maker 45:5, October 24,
     1970.

854 "Louis Show Shock." Melody Maker 45:1, October 31, 1970.

855 Feather, L. "Louis Souffle Encore." Jazz Magazine no. 183:9, No-
     vember 1970.

856 Niquet, B. "La Chronique des Disques: The Great Reunion." Jazz
     Hot no. 266:39, November 1970.

857 "Record Reviews: Louis Armstrong and His Friends." Jazz and Pop
     9:46, November 1970.

858 Jones, M. "Armstrong the Unstoppable." Melody Maker 45:19, No-
     vember 7, 1970.

859 Allen, W. C. "Louis Armstrong 1930-32." Matrix no. 90:6-7, De-
     cember 1970.

860 "Disques du Mois: Louis Armstrong and His Friends." Jazz Maga-
     zine no. 184:50, December 1970.

861 Tercinet, A. "La Chronique des Disques: The Great Louis Arm-
     strong." Jazz Hot no. 267:43, December 1970.

862 Traill, S. "Editorial." Jazz Journal 23:3, December 1970.

863 _____. "Record Reviews: Satchmo at Pasadena; Satchmo at Sym-
     phony Hall." Jazz Journal 23:28, December 1970.

864 McDonough, J. "Record Reviews: The Definitive Album by Louis
     Armstrong." down beat 37:22, December 24, 1970.

865 Affeldt, P. ["Obituary."] Jazz Report 7:37, no. 5, 1971.

866 Armstrong, Louis. Louis Armstrong--a Self-portrait. The interview
     by Richard Meryman. New York: Eakins Press, 1971.

867 Barrell, A. "Long Live the King: A Tribute to Louis Armstrong."
     Footnote 2:18-20, no. 6, 1971.

868 Blesh, Rudi. Combo: USA; Eight Lives in Jazz. Philadelphia: Chil-
     ton Book Co., 1971. Includes Armstrong, Sidney Bechet, Eubie
     Blake, Charlie Christian, Billie Holiday, Gene Krupa, Jack Tea-
     garden, and Lester Young.

869 "Clarence Muse Recalls Satchmo." ASCAP 5:28, no. 2, 1971.

870 "The Genius of Louis Armstrong, Vol. 1: 1923-1933." Jazz Report
     7:23, no. 6, 1971.

871 Jones, Max, and John Chilton. Louis: The Louis Armstrong Story,
     1900-1971. 1st American ed. Boston: Little, Brown, 1971.

872   Kostal, A. "In Memoriam Louise Armstronga." Hudebni Rozhledy
      24:401-402, no. 9, 1971.

873   "Louis Armstrong Ist Tot." Musikhandel 22:216, no. 5, 1971.

874   "Louis Armstrong, 1900-1971." Coda 10:41, no. 2, 1971.

875   "Louis Armstrong Town Hall Concert Album." Footnote 2:9-11, no.
      4, 1971.

876   "Louis 'Satchmo' Armstrong Is Dead." Hip 10:1, no. 3, 1971.

877   ["Obituary."] American Symphony Orchestra League Newsletter 22:29,
      no. 4, 1971; Music and Artists 4:44, no. 4, 1971.

878   Panassie, H. Louis Armstrong. Photograph collection by Jack Brad-
      ley. New York: Da Capo Press, 1979. Reprint of the 1971 edi-
      tion published by C. Scribner's Sons, New York.

879   "Record Reviews: Louis Armstrong." Footnote 2:30, no. 6, 1971.

880   "'Satchmo' Silenced at 71." ASCAP Today 5:17, no. 2, 1971.

881   Wilson, J. S. "Louie 1900-1971." Educator 4:4-5, no. 1, 1971.
      Reprinted from International Musician.

882   Zondek, S. "Wspomnienie o Louisie Armstrongu." Ruch Muzycany
      15:17, no. 19, 1971.

883   Brown, R. "Record Reviews: Louis Armstrong and His Friends."
      Jazz Journal 24:30, January 1971.

884   Gerber, A. "Salute to Satchmo." Jazz Magazine no. 185:17, Jan-
      uary 1971.

885   "Reeditions: Satchmo, a Musical Autobiography of Louis Armstrong."
      Jazz Magazine no. 186:40, February 1971.

886   Gerber, A. "Reeditions: Rare Recordings of the Twenties." Jazz
      Magazine no. 187:45, March 1971.

887   "Satchmo Doing OK but Still in N.Y. Hospital." Variety 262:75,
      March 24, 1971.

888   "The Louis Legend." Melody Maker 46:6, March 27, 1971.

889   "Ailing Satchmo, Waring and Carmen Lombardo Stir Concern in Music
      Trade." Variety 262:1, April 7, 1971.

890   "Satchmo, in Absentia, Kid Ory, 84, Highlight New Orleans Jazz
      Fest." Variety 262:59, April 28, 1971.

891   "Louis Armstrong in Hospital." Rolling Stone no. 81:10, April 29,
      1971.

892   Gerber, A., et al. "Reeditions: Louis Armstrong--Satchmo's Great-
      est--Vol. 1, 1932-1933." Jazz Magazine no. 189:50, May 1971.

893 Goddet, L. "Chronique des Disques: Satchmo's Greatest, Vol. 1,
     1932-1933." Jazz Hot no. 272:29, May 1971.

894 Niquet, B. "Chronique des Disques: Rare Recording of the Twen-
     ties." Jazz Hot no. 272:29, May 1971.

895 Traill, S. "Editorial." Jazz Journal 24:1, May 1971.

896 Arlt, H. "Memories of You--Old Satchmo." Second Line 25:13,
     Summer 1971.

897 Kay, G. "Goodbye, Louis, We Will Never Forget You." Second
     Line 25:10-11, Summer 1971.

898 Levin, F. "Move over Gabriel!" Second Line 25:17-19, Summer
     1971.

899 "Louis Armstrong Statue Fund Progress Report." Second Line 25:15,
     Summer 1971.

900 Morris, B. "Sleepy Time Up North." Second Line 25:4-9, Summer
     1971. Discussion of Armstrong funeral.

901 Traill, S. "Record Reviews: Louis Armstrong and the Good Book."
     Jazz Journal 24:32, June 1971.

902 "A Toast to Louis at 71." Melody Maker 46:14, June 26, 1971.

903 ["Obituary."] Musik und Bildung 3:378, July-August 1971.

904 Traill, S. "Record Reviews: The Definitive Album." Jazz Journal
     24:30, July 1971.

905 "Louis Armstrong, Global Symbol of U.S. Jazz, Dies at 71 in New
     York." Variety 263:37, July 7, 1971.

906 "'Satchmo' Ist Tot." Musik in der Schule 22:408-409, no. 10, 1971.
     Reprinted from Neues Deutschland, July 8, 1971.

907 Chilton, J. "A Brief History of Louis." Melody Maker 46:49, July
     10, 1971.

908 Jones, M. "The First Genius of Jazz." Melody Maker 46:49, July
     10, 1971.

909 "Satchmo Is Dead." Melody Maker 46:1, July 10, 1971.

910 "Satchmo Left Jazz Disk Treasury; Ranges from Early '20s to Recent
     LP." Variety 263:1, July 14, 1971.

911 "Satchmo Rites Draw Big Name Contingent." Variety 263:45, July 14,
     1971.

912 Meryman, R. "Parting Shots: Satchmo, the Greatest of All, Is
     Gone." Life 71:70-71, July 16, 1971.

913 "Louis Armstrong Funeral Service." Melody Maker 46:3, July 17,
     1971.

914 "The Louis Legend." Melody Maker 46:23-26, July 17, 1971.

915 ["Obituary."] New Yorker 47:21, July 17, 1971.

916 "Satchmo Dies at 71; Causes Disk Flurry." Billboard 83:3, July 17, 1971.

917 "Last Trumpet for the First Trumpeter." Time 98:34-35, July 19, 1971.

918 Saal, H. "Good-by, Louis." Newsweek 78:76, July 19, 1971.

919 "New Orleans Not Final Resting Place for Satchmo, Some Disappointed." Jet 4:1478, July 22, 1971.

920 ["Obituary."] America 125:24-25, July 24, 1971.

921 Thompson, C., and P. Garland. "Satchmo's Funeral 'White and Dead,' in New York, but 'Black, Alive and Swinging' in New Orleans." Jet 4:58-63, July 29, 1971.

922 Conover, W. "The Funeral of Louis Armstrong." Saturday Review 54:43, July 31, 1971.

923 Jones, M. "Jazz Records: The Melody Maker Tribute to Louis Armstrong, Vols. 1, 2, and 3." Melody Maker 46:26, July 31, 1971.

924 Dance, S. "Lightly & Politely." Jazz Journal 24:16, August 1971.

925 Elsdon, A., et al. ["Obituary."] Crescendo International 10:1-2, August 1971.

926 James, B. "Louis Armstrong--the Lucky Guy." Jazz Journal 24:2-3, August 1971.

927 Laverdure, M. "Louis Armstrong 1900-1971." Jazz Magazine no. 191:11-23, August 1971.

928 "Louis Armstrong, 1900-1971." Instrumentalist 26:86, August 1971.

929 "Louis Blues." Jazz Magazine no. 191:42-46, August 1971. Armstrong's funeral.

930 Massin, J. R. "Portrait d'un Grand Homme." Jazz Magazine no. 191:24-31, August 1971.

931 Napoleon, A. "At Dinnertime--a Belgian Vignette." Jazz Journal 24:12, August 1971.

932 ["Obituary."] Music Trades 119:98, August 1971; Neue Zeitschrift fuer Musik 132:447, August 1971.

933 "'Round About Satchmo." Jazz Magazine no. 191:38-41, August 1971. Musicians talk about Armstrong's performances.

934 Rust, B. ["Obituary."] Gramophone 49:309, August 1971.

935 "Satchmo à Hollywood." Jazz Magazine no. 191:34-37, August 1971.

936 "Stele pour Satchmo." Jazz Magazine no. 191:32-33, August 1971.

937 Townley, E. "Remembering Louis; A Personal Tribute." Jazz Journal 24:29, August 1971.

938 Traill, S. "Editorial." Jazz Journal 23:1, August 1971.

939 Voce, S. "It Don't Mean a Thing." Jazz Journal 24:4-6, August 1971.

940 Wilson, J. S. "Louis Armstrong 1900-1971." International Musician 70:7, August 1971.

941 Gleason, R. J. "God Bless Louis Armstrong." Rolling Stone no. 88:26-33, August 5, 1971.

942 Jones, M. "Jazz Records: Memorial: Record 1 and 2." Melody Maker 46:30, August 21, 1971.

943 Balliett, W. "Musical Events." New Yorker 47:75-77, August 28, 1971.

944 Feather, L. "Stars in the Park--for Louis." Melody Maker 46:26, August 28, 1971.

945 ["Obituary."] Nuova Rivista Musicale Italiana 5:933, September-October 1971.

946 "An Episode Ends in American Music." Music Educators Journal 58:52-53, September 1971.

947 Garland, P. "Taps for Satchmo--Life Ends for America's Most Famous Jazz Musician." Ebony 27:31-34, September 1971.

948 Haeggloef, G. "Satchmo." Orkester Journalen 39:8-9, September 1971.

949 Lindenberger, H. "Personifizierter Jazz; Aum Tode des Trompeters Louis Armstrong." Hifi-Stereophonie 10:763-764, September 1971.

950 "Louis Armstrong." Entire issue of Record Research no. 112, September 1971.

951 Garland, P. ["Obituary."] Ebony 26:31-34, September 1971.

952 ["Obituary."] Orchester 19:453, September 1971.

953 Olsson, J. "Armstrong Doed i Radio och TV." Orkester Journalen 39:21, September 1971.

954 Von Konow, A. "Armstrong paa Skiva." Orkester Journalen 39:10-11, September 1971.

955 Morgenstern, D., et al. "Louis Armstrong: 1900-1971." down beat 38:12-14, September 16, 1971.

956 _____. "Record Reviews: Louis Armstrong, July 4, 1900-July 6, 1971." down beat 38:23, September 16, 1971.

957   Suber, C. "The First Chorus." down beat 38:5, September 16, 1971.

958   "Tribute to Satchmo Proves to be Fatal for His Former Wife, Pianist Lil Armstrong." Jet 4:56-58, September 16, 1971.

959   Jones, M. "Jazz Records: The Best of Louis Armstrong." Melody Maker 46:28, September 25, 1971.

960   Dance, S. "Jazz." Music Journal 29:54-56, October 1971.

961   Gonda, J. "Armstrong." Muzsika 14:22-24, October 1971.

962   Haeggloef, G. "Louis." Orkester Journalen 39:8-9, October 1971.

963   Joseph, D. V. "A Tribute to Louis 'Satchmo' Armstrong." School Musician 43:24, October 1971.

964   Mellers, W. "And the Trumpets Sounded." Music and Musicians 20:24-25, October 1971.

965   ["Obituary."] High Fidelity/Musical America 21:MA22, October 1971; Negro History Bulletin 34:139, October 1971.

966   Traill, S. "Record Reviews: Louis Armstrong, Vol. 1." Jazz Journal 24:28, October 1971.

967   "Satchmo Loved Pot, Disdained Liquor, His New Book Reveals, Portrait." Jet 41:52, October 21, 1971.

968   Feather, L. "Los Angeles: Memorial for Satchmo." Jazz Magazine no. 194:44-45, November 1971.

969   Goddet, L. "Chronique des Disques: Satchmo's Greatest, Vol. 2, 1933." Jazz Hot no. 277:33, November 1971.

970   Goodfriend, J. "Louis Armstrong: Two New Memorial Albums." Stereo Review 27:134-135, November 1971.

971   Gros-Claude, P. "Disques du Mois: Memorial Album." Jazz Magazine no. 194:32, November 1971.

972   Haeggloef, G. "Pops." Orkester Journalen 39:14-15, November 1971.

973   Napoleon, A. "Record Reviews: Memorial." Jazz Journal 24:26, November 1971.

974   Pereverzev, L. "Glavnoe--Eto Zhit' Dlya Publiki...." Sovetskaya Muzyka 35:136-137, November 1971.

975   Armstrong, Louis. "Scanning the History of Jazz." Esquire 76:184-187, December 1971.

976   Daubresse, J. P. "La Chronique des Disques: Satchmo's Greatest, Vol. 3, 1933-1946." Jazz Hot no. 278:33, December 1971.

977   Glenn, T. "Unforgettable Satchmo." Reader's Digest 99:81-85, December 1971.

978 "Record Reviews: Louis in the 1970's." Jazz Journal 24:34-35, December 1971.

979 "Record Reviews: The Best of Louis Armstrong." Jazz Journal 24:35, December 1971.

980 "Scanning the History of Jazz." Esquire 76:184-187, December 1971.

981 Cornell, Jean Gay. Louis Armstrong, Ambassador Satchmo. Champaign, Ill.: Garrand Pub. Co., 1972. Juvenile literature.

982 Kisielewski, S. "A Few Words on Armstrong." Jazz Forum no. 15:14, 1972.

983 "Record Reviews: Greatest Hits Recorded Live." Coda 10:28, no. 6, 1972.

984 "Record Reviews: Louis Armstrong; An Early Portrait." Footnote 3:34, no. 5, 1972.

985 "Record Reviews: Louis Armstrong and Luis Russell." Coad 10:16, no. 8, 1972.

986 "La Chronique des Disques: Satchmo's Greatest, Vol. 4: 1946-47; Vol. 5: 1947-1956." Jazz Hot no. 279:29, January 1972.

987 "Disques du Mois: Satchmo's Greatest, Vol. 2 (1933); Jazz Spectrum, Vol. 2." Jazz Magazine no. 196:24-25, January 1972.

988 "Record Reviews: Immortal Sessions--Louis Armstrong, Vol. 1." Jazz & Blues 1:21, January 1972.

989 Viera, J. "Louis Armstrong." Neue Zeitschrift fuer Musik 133:16-17, January 1972. Reprinted in Orchester 20:79-80, February 1972.

990 "Schallplattenbesprechungen: Louis Armstrong." Jazz Podium 21:53, February 1972.

991 Morgenstern, D. "Night of Pride for Jazz Interactions." down beat 39:9-10, February 17, 1972. The "Suite for Pops" is a memorial for Armstrong by Thad Jones.

992 "Swinging News: Louis Armstrong." Jazz Forum no. 16:29, March-April 1972.

993 Niquet, B. "Handful of Records: Greatest Hits Recorded Live." Points du Jazz, no. 6:121-122, March 1972.

994 Terjanian, L. "Handful of Records: Integrale en 5 Volumes des Enregistrements de Louis Armstrong sur RCA Disponible Separement ou en un Coffret Memorial." Points du Jazz no. 6:122-125, March 1972.

995 "Blacks Win 17 Grammy Awards, but Miles Davis, Motown, etc. Walk Out." Jet 42:58, March 3, 1972.

996 "Chronique des Disques: Louis Armstrong and the Good Book." Jazz Hot no. 282:24, April 1972.

997   "Disques du Mois: Satchmo's Greatest, Vols. 4 and 5." Jazz Maga-
      zine no. 199:31, April 1972.

998   "Record Reviews: Louis and the Blues Singers 1925-1929." Jazz &
      Blues 2:24, April 1972.

999   "Record Reviews: Satchmo's Greatest, Vols. 1-5." Jazz & Blues
      2:22, April 1972.

1000 "USC Memorial to Louis Armstrong Recaps Career of a Great Tal-
      ent." Variety 266:2, April 12, 1972.

1001 "Jazz Records: The Genius of Louis Armstrong." Melody Maker
      47:36, April 15, 1972.

1002 "Schallplattenbesprechungen: Memorial Album, 'Edition Integral.'"
      Jazz Podium 21:166, May 1972.

1003 Mares, J., et al. "Tribute to Satchmo!" Second Line 24:4-9, Sum-
      mer 1972.

1004 Cholinski, H. "Collector's Corner: Louis Armstrong on LP's."
      Jazz Forum no. 17:82-84, June 1972.

1005 "Collectors' Armstrong." Jazz & Blues 2:29, June 1972.

1006 Lee, R. M. "Live Performances: A Tribute to Louis Armstrong,
      Odeon, Edinburg." Jazz Forum no. 17:77-78, June 1972.

1007 "Record Reviews: Hines '65; My Tribute to Louis." down beat
      39:20-21, June 8, 1972.

1008 "Record Reviews: The Beautiful Americans." Jazz & Blues 2:28,
      July 1972.

1009 Jones, M. "Louis: The Legend Lives on and His Latest Reissues."
      Melody Maker 47:36, July 8, 1972.

1010 "Jazz Records: I Remember Louis." Melody Maker 47:36, July 15,
      1972.

1011 Cholinski, H. "Louis Armstrong on LP's." Jazz Forum no. 18:66-
      71, August 1972.

1012 "Jazz im Film: In Memoriam Mahalia Jackson und Louis Armstrong."
      Jazz Podium 21:21-22, August 1972.

1013 Traill, S. "Editorial." Jazz Journal 25:3, August 1972.   New Or-
      leans' Congo Square becomes Louis Armstrong Park.

1014 "Bank Selling Satchmo Medal." Billboard 84:66, August 12, 1972.

1015 "New York Names Stadium after Louis Armstrong." Jet 43:54, Oc-
      tober 19, 1972.

1016 "Satchmo Pub Launched in Dover." Jazz Forum no. 19:31, October 1972.

1017 Sebastiani, M. "Louis Armstrong." Points du Jazz no. 7:106-111,
      October 1972.

1018 "Record Reviews: The Best of Louis Armstrong." Jazz & Blues
      1:26-27, February 1972.

1019 "Satchmo Armstrong Leaves $300,000 Estate to His Wife." Jet
      43:29, December 14, 1972.

1020 "The Jazz Photographer." Coda 11:12-14, no. 2, 1973.

1021 Jepsen, Jorgen Grunnet. A Discography of Louis Armstrong, 1923-
      1971. Copenhagen NV: Karl Emil Knudsen, 1973.

1022 ["Obituary."] Black Perspectives in Music 1:97, no. 2, 1973.

1023 "Record Reviews: Louis Armstrong with Fletcher Henderson." Foot-
      note 4:28, no. 6, 1973.

1024 Schawlow, A. "Joe Muranyi." Coda 10:5-6, no. 12, 1973.

1025 "Special Issue Celebrating the Genius of Louis Armstrong." entire
      issue of Coda vol. 11, no. 2, 1973.

1026 Wayne, Bennett. 3 Jazz Greats. Champaign, Ill.: Garrard Pub.
      Co., 1973. Juvenile literature on Armstrong, Duke Ellington, and
      William C. Handy.

1027 Suber, C. "The First Chorus." down beat 40:4, February 1, 1973.
      A tribute to Armstrong by David Baker: "Louis Armstrong in
      Memoriam."

1028 Lyttelton, H. "The Lessons of 'Lessons of Nice.'" Jazz Journal
      26:18-20, May 1973. Reprinted from Jazz Music.

1029 Bolton, C. "When Satchmo Was Zulu." Second Line 25:21-25, Sum-
      mer 1973.

1030 "Benny, Louis Take Off!" Metronome 69:13, June 1953.

1031 "Satchmo Memorial Showcases Roster of Major Jazz Names." Vari-
      ety 271:52, July 11, 1973.

1032 "Speed Multi-Million $ Armstrong Memorial Park in New Orleans."
      Variety 271:44, August 1, 1973.

1033 Hammond, M. "Louis and 'Swiss Kriss.'" Second Line 25:25-26,
      Fall 1973.

1034 "On Record: The Great Soloists." Jazz & Blues 3:14, September
      1973.

1035 "Jazz Records: Armstrong-Henderson 1924-25." Melody Maker
      48:42, September 1, 1973.

1036 Traill, S. "Editorial." Jazz Journal 26:1, October 1973. Dis-
      cussion of the fund for the statue in honor of Louis Arm-
      strong.

1037 "Heard and Seen." Coda 12:34-35, no. 1, 1974. An anniversary
      concert in honor of Armstrong.

1038   Record Reviews: A Chronological Study, 1935-1945; Paris Session
       1934 and Rare Films." Coda 11:14-15, no. 12, 1974.

1039   Colombe, G. M. "How Do They Age So Well?--Louis' Last Half-
       Dozen." Jazz Journal 27:22-23, January 1974.

1040   Allen, W. C. "Satchmo Kommt!" Jazz Podium 23:32, February
       1974. An excerpt from Allen's book Hendersonia, the Music of
       Fletcher Henderson and His Musicians.

1041   "Colored Waifs' Home." Second Line 26:8, Spring 1974. A letter
       written by Armstrong when he lived at the home in 1937.

1042   Kay, G. W. "The Milne Boys and Colored Waifs and Little Louis."
       Second Line 26:9-11, Spring 1974.

1043   "Louis Armstrong Jazz Award." Instrumentalist 28:28, March 1974.

1044   Tanner, P., and M. Gerow. "Louis Armstrong." Instrumentalist
       28:39-41, April 1974.

1045   "Jazz Records: Tootin' Through the Roof, Vol. 2." Melody Maker
       49:54, May 11, 1974.

1046   "Armstrong Anniversary." Melody Maker 49:27, July 13, 1974.

1047   Stenbeck, L. "Louis Armstrong Memorial Concert." Orkester Jour-
       nalen 42:7, September 1974.

1048   Goldstein, R. "Sound." Mademoiselle 80:58, December 1974.

1049   "Satchmo Bust." Jazz Forum no. 32:15, December 1974.

1050   Caffey, H. D. "The Musical Style of Louis Armstrong, 1925-1929."
       Journal of Jazz Studies 3:72-96, no. 1, 1975.

1051   Englund, B. "A Louis Armstrong Filmography." Coda 12:5-6, no.
       3, 1975.

1052   Gleason, Ralph J. Celebrating the Duke, and Louis, Bessie, Billie,
       Bird, Carmen, Miles, Dizzy, and Other Heroes. Boston: Little,
       Brown, 1975.

1053   Levin, F. "The Current Status of the Louis Armstrong Statue."
       Jazz Report 9:15-16, no. 1, 1975.

1054   Poe, G. D. "An Examination of Four Selected Solos Recorded by
       Louis Armstrong Between 1925-1928." NACWPI Journal 24:3-9,
       no. 1, 1975.

1055   Stratemann, K. "Letters: Armstrong Filmography--Addition/Correc-
       tions." Coda 12:32-33, no. 4, 1975.

1056   "Records: Great Early Vocals." Crawdaddy no. 44:78-79, January
       1975.

1057   Erskine, G. M. "'Everybody Loves My Baby': Bix and Louis, New
       York City, Fall 1924." Second Line 27:10-14, Spring 1975.

1058 Williams, M. "Tout Vient d'Armstrong." Jazz Hot no. 314:16-17, March 1975.

1059 Levin, F. "About the Statue--and the Sculptor." Second Line 27:9-10, Summer 1975.

1060 Morris, R. J. "The Louis Armstrong Legend." Second Line 27:3-9, Summer 1975.

1061 Feather, L. "Armstrong Faar Aentligen Staty: Amerikanska Nyheter." Orkester Journalen 43:6-7, June 1975.

1062 "Louis Armstrong 75." Musik und Gesellschaft 25:444, July 1975.

1063 "Caught in the Act." Melody Maker 50:44, July 12, 1975. A concert held in London in honor of Louis Armstrong's date of birth.

1064 Shultz, H. L. "Oh, Play That Thing, Louis! And He Did." Second Line 28:33-35, Spring 1976. Reprinted from Panorama November 8, p. 9, 1975.

1065 Daubresse, J. P., and D. Nevers. "Chicago." Jazz Hot no. 322:22-23, December 1975.

1066 Boujut, Michel. Pour Armstrong. Paris: Filipacchi, 1976. Includes bibliography, discography, and filmography.

1067 Iverson, Genie. Louis Armstrong. New York: Crowell, 1976. Juvenile literature.

1068 Koch, L. "Notes and Comments: 'Potato Head Blues': Structure and Harmonies." Journal of Jazz Studies 3:89-90, no. 2, 1976.

1069 "Notes." Jazz Magazine (U.S.) 1:12, 1976.

1070 "Record Reviews: the All-Stars in Philadelphia 1948-9." Coda no. 144:20-21, January-February 1976.

1071 Albertson, C. "Anthony Braxton: Improvisations as Liberated and Fresh as Louis Armstrong's." Stereo Review 36:76, February 1976.

1072 Feather, L. "New Orleans Awaits Satchmo Statue." Second Line 28:19-21, Spring 1976. Reprinted from the Los Angeles Times February 15, 1976.

1073 _____. "Satchmo Lives Again." Melody Maker 51:48, February 21, 1976.

1074 Erskine, G. M. "Countin' the Blues--a Survey of the Recordings of Louis Armstrong Accompanying Singers in the 1920s." Second Line 28:10-19, Spring 1976. Also lists Armstrong discography arranged chronologically.

1075 Dance, S. "The Terrors of Television." Jazz Journal 29:11, March 1976.

1976 Feather, L. "Letters: Leonard Feather on Satchmo." Radio Free Jazz 17:2, March 1976.

1077   "Satch Honored Twice." down beat 43:9, March 11, 1976.

1078   Wilson, J. S. "From the Smithsonian: Perspective on King Oliver,
       Hines, and Satchmo." High Fidelity/Musical America 26:140, April
       1976.

1079   "Armstrong Memorial." down beat 43:10, April 22, 1976.

1080   "Satchmo Benefit at Beacon Theatre Flops at $12.50 Top." Variety
       282:62, April 28, 1976.

1081   "Record Reviews: Armstrong and Hines, 1928." down beat 43:30-
       31, May 20, 1976.

1082   Kay, G. W. "Louis Armstrong's Letter to His 'Daddy'--Forward."
       Second Line 28:12-15, Summer 1976.

1083   Dexter, D. "Armstrong Statue's Unveiling in Doubt." Billboard
       88:34, June 5, 1976.

1084   _____. "Acts Toil to Hike Armstrong Statue $." Billboard
       88:14, June 26, 1976.

1085   Levin, F. "Louis' Giant Memorial." Melody Maker 51:41, July 10,
       1976.

1086   "Record Reviews: V.S.O.P. Vols. 1-8." Jazz Journal 29:32, Au-
       gust 1976.

1087   Vance, J. "The 1928 Collaborations of Louis Armstrong and Earl
       Hines." Stereo Review 37:88, August 1976.

1088   "Louis Statue Erected." Melody Maker 51:22, August 7, 1976.

1089   Levin, F. "New Orleans--July 4, 1976." Second Line 28:16-19,
       Fall 1976. The Armstrong statue ceremonies were held.

1090   Stenbeck, L. "Paa Kurs med John LaPorta Louis Armstrong Mem-
       orial Concert." Orkester Journalen 44:16, September 1976.

1091   "A Jazzman on Lombardo." Variety 284:80, September 8, 1976. A
       reprint of a letter which appeared in the Sept. 28, 1949 issue of
       Variety.

1092   "Records: Louis Armstrong and Earl Hines--1928." Creem 8:71,
       October 1976.

1093   "Waxing On: Porgy and Bess." down beat 43:30-32, November 18,
       1976.

1094   "Record Reviews: Louis Armstrong and Earl Hines." Coda no.
       152:21-22, December 1976.

1095   Wilson, J. S. "Louis and Ella and Ray and Cleo." High Fidelity/
       Musical America 26:95, December 1976. Recordings of "Porgy
       and Bess."

1096   Faber, Anne. Louis Armstrong. Hamburg: Dressler, 1977.

1097 Reda, J. "Armstrong et la Question du Coffret." Jazz Magazine no. 252:18-19, February-March 1977.

1098 Wiggs, J. "Wiggs--Self-Explained." Second Line 30:4, Spring 1977.

1099 Hentoff, N. "Indigenous Music." Nation 224:414, April 2, 1977.

1100 Balliett, W. "Jazz: New York Notes." New Yorker 53:84-90, April 4, 1977. RCA has reissued some of Armstrong's early recordings.

1101 "Caught in the Act." Melody Maker 52:42, May 21, 1977.

1102 Stenbeck, L. "Armstrong Memorial." Orkester Journalen 45:17, September 1977.

1103 "Waxing on: 1932-1933." down beat 44:36, October 6, 1977.

1104 Hoberman, J. "If Youse a Viper: Pot Luck Behind the Bandstand." Crawdaddy no. 79:18, December 1977.

1105 "Caught in the Act." Melody Maker 52:14, December 3, 1977.

1106 McDonough, J. "Roy Eldridge: Legendary Lip in the Golden Years." down beat 44:24-25, December 15, 1977.

1107 "Jazz Live!" Jazz Journal International 31:33, March 1978.

1108 Berry, J. "Jazz Literature: Through a Rhythm, Joyously." Village Voice 23:61, May 8, 1978.

1109 "Records: Louis Armstrong and the Dukes of Dixieland: The Great Alternates." down beat 45:29-30, June 1, 1978.

1110 Sandner, W. W. "Louis Armstrong in Memoriam." Jazz Podium 27:18-19, July 1978.

1111 "Caught in the Act." Melody Maker 53:19, July 15, 1978.

1112 Crouch, S. "Laughin' Louis." Village Voice 23:45, August 14, 1978. Notes on Armstrong and a review of the RCA reissue of "Young Louis Armstrong."

1113 "Jazz Albums: Rare Louis Armstrong Vol. 3: The Big Band 1943-1944." Melody Maker 53:21, August 26, 1978.

1114 "Jazz Albums: And the All Stars." Melody Maker 53:26, September 30, 1978.

1115 Lucas, J. "Music of the Mississippi." Second Line 30:24-25, Winter 1978.

1116 Rene, L. "Sleepytime Down South." Second Line 30:56-59, Winter 1978.

ARMSTRONG, MRS. LOUIS see ARMSTRONG, LIL HARDIN

BAKER, DAVE (David Nathaniel, Jr.), 1931- .

1117 "David Baker." Musical Courier 143:25, March 1, 1951.

1118 Schuller, G. "Indiana Renaissance." Jazz Revue 2:48-50, September 1959.

1119 "David Baker, Tenor, in De Breville Novelties." Musical Courier 161:25, June 1960.

1120 "Dave Baker and the Dues." down beat 28:11-12, September 14, 1961.

1121 DeMicheal, D. "Vortex; The Dave Baker Story." down beat 31:14-18, December 17, 1964.

1122 Baker, Dave. "Jazz: The Academy's Neglected Stepchild." down beat 32:29-32, September 23, 1965.

1123 "Dave Baker Named I. U. Jazz Head." down beat 33:16, September 22, 1966.

1124 Caswell, A. B. "Caught in the Act." down beat 35:35, July 11, 1968. Performance of Baker's "Black America."

1125 "David Baker." Musart 21:44, no. 4, 1969.

1126 "Come Summer." Variety 253:70, January 29, 1969.

1127 "Shows on Broadway." Variety 254:92, March 26, 1969. Performances of "Come Summer."

1128 "Baker's Book--Newman's Bag." down beat 36:14, May 29, 1969.

1129 Bourne, M. "Defining Black Music." down beat 36:14-15, September 18, 1969.

1130 Baker, Dave. "The String Player in Jazz." down beat 37:37-39, April 30, 1970.

1131 "Premieres." BMI p. 15-16, May 1970.

1132 "Professor Plays Jazz." Ebony 25:1-4-106, May 1970.

1133 Baker, Dave. "The String Player in Jazz." down beat 37:34-35, May 28, 1970.

1134 "Premieres." BMI p. 17, June 1970; Music Journal 28:14, June 1970. Performances of Baker's "Concerto for Violin and Jazz Band."

1135 "Premieres." BMI p. 20, October 1970. Performances of Baker's "Five Songs to the Survival of Black Children."

1136 Keating, Sister M. T. "Jazz--a Tanglewood Conversation." Music Educators' Journal 57:55-56, March 1971.

1137 Caswell, A. B. "David Baker; A Wise and Powerful Voice." down beat 38:18, October 14, 1971.

1138   Baker, Dave. "Jazz Improvisation--the Weak Link." Instrumentalist
       26:21-24, November 1971.

1139   "Premieres." BMI p. 21, December 1971. Performances of sever-
       al Baker works: "Concerto for Flute and Jazz Band," "Evening Song,"
       "Reve," "A Salute to Beethoven," "A Song of Mankind," and "Songs."

1140   Suber, C. "The First Chorus." down beat 40:4, February 1, 1973.

1141   DeRhen, A. "Composers String Quartet." High Fidelity/Musical
       America 23:MA22-23, March 1973.

1142   Solothurnmann, J. "The Diverse David Baker." Jazz Forum no.
       25:46-50, October 1973.

1143   "Jazz Versus Academia: The Battle for Legitimacy." Black World
       23:20-27, November 1973.

1144   Ammann, B., et al. "Five Questions, Fifty Answers." Composer
       (U.S.) 5:71-79, no. 2, 1974.

1145   "News Nuggets." International Musician 72:11, February 1974; 72:14,
       March 1974. Performances of Baker's "Concerto for Double Bass
       and Jazz Ensemble" and "Sonata for Violoncello and Piano, D Min-
       or," respectively.

1146   Baker, Dave. "How to Use Strings in Jazz." down beat 41:38, April
       25, 1974.

1147   Solothunmann, J. "Jazz in Theorie und Praxis--das Beispiel des
       Musikers, Komponisten, Lehrers und Autoren David Baker." Jazz
       Podium 23:26-9, May 1974.

1148   "Janos Starker." High Fidelity/Musical America 24:MA31, June 1974.

1149   Fowler, W. L., et al. "How to Bone Up on Slip-Horn Changes."
       down beat 41:28, December 5, 1974.

1150   "Happenings." Symphony News 27:24, no. 2, 1976. Performance of
       "Kosbro."

1151   "Dave Baker's 'Sonata for Tuba and String Quartet' for Harvey Phil-
       lips." down beat 43:43, October 7, 1976.

1152   Humanities Through the Black Experience [by] David N. Baker, et al.
       Edited by Phyllis Rauch Klotman. Dubuque, Iowa: Kendall/Hunt
       Pub. Co., 1977.

1153   "Premiers." Musical Journal 35:28, December 1977. Performance
       of "Singers of Songs, Weavers of Dreams."

1154   "Record Reviews: A New Approach to Jazz Improvisation, Volumes
       VII-X." down beat 44:26, December 1, 1977.

1155   Schneckloth, T. "Guardians of the Musical Future." down beat
       44:16-17, December 1, 1977.

1156   Kerner, L. "Music: To Hell with Transitions." Village Voice
       22:69-70, December 5, 1977.

1157   Everett, T. "A Survey of Studio and Big Band Bass Trombonists."
       Newsletter of the International Trombone Association 5:9, no. 3,
       1978.

1158   "Baker/Starker Premier." down beat 45:15, February 23, 1978.

BASIE, COUNT (William James), 1904- .

1159   Basie, Count. "Critics in the Doghouse." down beat 39:25, July 20,
       1972. Reprinted from down beat July 1939.

1160   "Basie Set to Reopen Florentine Gardens." Billboard 61:20, January
       15, 1949.

1161   "Count Basie Orch." Variety 175:22, July 6, 1949.

1162   "Count Basie." Billboard 61:41, September 10, 1949.

1163   Tracy, J. "Basie Best of What's Left?" down beat 17:21, January
       13, 1950.

1164   "Band Reviews." Variety 177:42, March 8, 1950.

1165   "Basie Works with Combo." down beat 17:17, March 10, 1950.

1166   Harris, P. "Woody, Basie Work with Small Units, Explain Why."
       down beat 17:5, March 24, 1950.

1167   Hoefer, G. "Basie Led the Greatest Rhythm Machine in Jazz."
       down beat 17:11, March 24, 1950.

1168   "Count Basie." Metronome 66:26, May 1950.

1169   "From Count Basie." Jazz Journal 3:1, May 1950.

1170   "Orpheum, L.A." Variety 179:55, August 30, 1950.

1171   "Basie Discography." down beat 17:14, November 17, 1950.

1172   Gleason, R. J. "Basie Will Always Have a Swinging Band." down
       beat 17:1, November 17: 1950.

1173   Whiston, H. "The Count Still Counts!" Melody Maker 27:3, March
       10, 1951.

1174   "N.Y. Swing Revival Is Like Old Times." Billboard 63:10, May 12,
       1951.

1175   Borneman, E. "One Night Stand." Melody Maker 27:3, October 13,
       1951.

1176   _____. "What Basie Had to Do with the Beginning of Bop." Mel-
       ody Maker 27:3, October 20, 1951. Borneman examined Basie's
       contributions to bop in a series of articles on jazz in Kansas City.

1177   "Basie at Savoy with Big Band." down beat 18:1, November 30, 1951.

1178 Hammond, J. "Two Kings and a Joe." down beat 19:7, June 4,
      1952.

1179 Feather, L. "The Count Jumps for Everything." down beat 19:12,
      June 18, 1952.

1180 "Bill Basie Again Has Best Band for Beat, Excitement." down beat
      19:2, August 27, 1952.

1181 Hammond, J. "Basie Band Best in Biz." down beat 19:7, Septem-
      ber 10, 1952.

1182 "Eckstine-Shearing-Basie Combo Pulls 18½G in L.A. Teeoff of 80
      Concerts." Variety 188:50, September 17, 1952.

1183 Sippel, J. "On the Stand." Billboard 64:22, September 27, 1952.

1184 Linde, U. "Basie--Basie--Basie--Basie." Orkester Journalen 21:9,
      January 1953.

1185 "In Person." Metronome 69:17, March 1953.

1186 Ulanov, B. "Count Basie at the Bandbox." Metronome 69:18, June
      1953.

1187 _____. "Up for the Count." Metronome 69:13-14, July 1953.

1188 "Big-Band Jazz." Time 63:52, January 11, 1954.

1189 "Allt Klart med Basie." Orkester Journalen 22:4, February 1954.

1190 "Nu Kommer Count Basie." Orkester Journalen 22:6-7, February
      1954.

1191 "Swinging the Blues." Jazz Journal 7:4, February 1954.

1192 "Basie's Band Termed 'Best.'" down beat 21:7, February 10, 1954.

1193 "Count Basie, Bandbuilder." down beat 21:2, February 24, 1954.

1194 "Basie with a B-e-a-t." Melody Maker 30:7, March 20, 1954.

1195 "Who's Who in the Basie Band." Melody Maker 30:9, March 27,
      1954.

1196 Lindgren, C. E. "Down for the Count; Ner för Räkning Under Basie-
      Konserterna." Orkester Journalen 22:6-8, April 1954.

1197 "Pa Rundtur med Basie." Orkester Journalen 22:9, April 1954.

1198 Feather, L. "More Gen on Basie's Men." Melody Maker 30:13,
      April 3, 1954.

1199 "Count." Melody Maker 30:3, April 10, 1954.

1200 Jones, M. "Basie and Byas." Melody Maker 30:9, April 17, 1954.

1201 "Birdland, N.Y." Variety 194:54, May 5, 1954.

1202   Dance, S. "Basie in Paris." Jazz Journal 7:1-2, June 1954.

1203   "Two Views of Europe, as Seen by Basie, Sideman." down beat
       21:3, June 16, 1954.

1204   "'Recording Artists' Roster." down beat 21:89, June 30, 1954.

1205   Gleason, R. J. "Perspectives." down beat 21:4, August 11, 1954.

1206   Hobson, W. "Iron Bands and Iron Bandsmen." Saturday Review
       37:60, August 28, 1954.

1207   "Ernie Wilkins Epitomizes Spirit of Blues-Swinging Basie Band."
       down beat 21:25, September 8, 1954.

1208   "Basie, Sarah Wail, but Some Others Suffer an Off Night." down
       beat 21:20, November 3, 1954.

1209   "Show Biz Bash for Basie's 20th Anni." Variety 196:48, November
       3, 1954.

1210   Feather, L. "Basie--20 Years a Leader: Still Going Strong." Mel-
       ody Maker 30:3, November 20, 1954.

1211   "Basie Bashes." Metronome 70:5, December 1954.

1212   "Basie Band Re-formed at Fete." down beat 21:6, December 15,
       1954.

1213   "In Person." Metronome 71:27, April 1955.

1214   Traill, S. "Jazz Records." Melody Maker 31:7, April 9, 1955.

1215   Basie, Count. "Hit the Road, Men." down beat 22:9, April 20,
       1955.

1216   "Want to Buy a Band?" down beat 22:43, April 20, 1955.

1217   "Basie Bands." Jazz Journal 8:5, May 1955. Recording reviews.

1218   "Basie Soloists." Jazz Journal 8:5-6, May 1955.

1219   Gleason, R. J. "Perspectives." down beat 22:6, August 10, 1955.

1220   Dance, S. "The Man Who Kept the Blues Alive." Melody Maker
       31:7, October 22, 1955.

1221   Hammond, J. "Count Basie Marks 20th Anniversary." down beat
       22:11-12, November 2, 1955.

1222   Dahlgren, C. "Basie Bas pa Bygget." Orkester Journalen 24:10-11,
       January 1956.

1223   "Basie Beat." Jazz Journal 9:12, January 1956. Recording reviews.

1224   Korall, B. "Count Basie at Birdland." Metronome 72:8, January
       1956.

1225 Balliett, W. "A Buss for Basie ... Twenty Years of the 'One O'clock Jump.'" Saturday Review 39:28, January 14, 1956.

1226 "Band Reviews." Variety 201:46, January 25, 1956.

1227 Tracy, J. "The First Chorus." down beat 23:5, February 22, 1956.

1228 "Want to Buy a Band?" down beat 23:45, April 18, 1956.

1229 Willard, B. "Band Review." down beat 23:41, May 2, 1956.

1230 Freeman, D. "My Biggest Thrill? When Duke Roared Back: Basie." down beat 23:14, May 16, 1956.

1231 Dahlgren, C. "Basie Jazzhistoriker." Orkester Journalen 24:8-9, June 1956.

1232 "Basie Working on Jazz History Data, New Musical Revue." down beat 23:35, June 13, 1956.

1233 Wilson, J. S. "A Basie Treasure and Other Bounty from ARS' Jazz Club." High Fidelity 6:60, July 1956.

1234 "'Eased Out,' Says CBS; 'I Quit,' Counters Basie." down beat 23:9, July 25, 1956.

1235 "Dunes, Las Vegas." Variety 203:54, August 8, 1956.

1236 Östberg, L. "Basie Topp." Orkester Journalen 24:6-8, September 1956.

1237 Brand, P. "Basie--in Sweden." Melody Maker 31:11, September 8, 1956.

1238 "Basie Rhythm Makes Old Seem New." Jazz Today 1:24, October 1956.

1239 "Seven Dances with the Count; Basiemen Think and Live Just as They Play." Jazz Today 1:18-23, October 1956.

1240 "Since 1937 You Can Count on Basie." Jazz Today 1:26, October 1956.

1241 "'Too Much Jazz' Hurts Basie Draw in Berlin." Variety 204:56, October 10, 1956.

1242 "Basie Big, Treads Softly in Paris' Jazz Season Bow." Variety 204:54, October 17, 1956.

1243 "The Bands Swing Back." Metronome 72:19-20, November 1956.

1244 Lascelles, G. "Count Basie in Paris." Jazz Journal 9:1, November 1956.

1245 Anderson, L. "Reflexer." Orkester Journalen 24:18, December 1956.

1246 Horricks, Raymond. Count Basie and His Orchestra, Its Music and Its Musicians. With discography by Alun Morgan. Westport, Conn.:

Negro Universities Press, 1971.   Reprint of the 1957 edition published by Gollancz in London.

1247   Dahlgren, C.   "Sarah och Ella med Basie."   Orkester Journalen
       25:6-7, January 1957.

1248   "Reviewer Has No Times for Basie."   down beat 24:11, January 9,
       1957.

1249   "Count Basie to Open at Festival Hall."   Melody Maker 32:1, Jan-
       uary 26, 1957.

1250   "The 'Count.'"   International Musician 55:14, February 1957.

1251   "All About Basie."   Melody Maker 32:2-3, March 30, 1957.

1252   Bruynoghe, Y.   "Basie--the Soloists and the Repertoire."   Jazz Jour-
       nal 10:1, April 1957.

1253   Gehman, D.   "The Count Basie Band."   Jazz Journal 10:7-9, April
       1957.

1254   Jepsen, J. G.   "1950-1957; A Discography of the Count Basie Or-
       chestra."   Jazz Journal 10:10-11, April 1957.

1255   Panassie, H.   "Reminiscing About the Count."   Jazz Journal 10:15,
       April 1957.

1256   Jones, M.   "Out for the Count."   Melody Maker 32:8-9, April 6,
       1957.

1257   "Basie Boffo in London; SRO Debut Brings Out Specs at Quintuple
       Tabs."   Variety 206:69, April 10, 1957.

1258   Jones, M.   "You're Great, Basie Tells British Audiences."   Melody
       Maker 32:8, April 13, 1957.

1259   "Want to Buy a Band?"   down beat 24:41, April 18, 1957.

1260   "Bill Basie."   Jazz Journal 10:1, May 1957.

1261   Nicholls, B.   "Harold Fielding Presents Count Basie."   Jazz Journal
       10:26-27, May 1957.

1262   Korall, B.   "New Look at Basie Band."   Metronome 74:19, June
       1957.

1263   "Waldorf-Astoria, N.Y."   Variety 207:57, June 5, 1957.

1264   "Wows at the Waldorf."   Newsweek 50:66, July 1, 1957.

1265   "Swing Is Here to Stay; Interviews with the Basie Band."   Jazz Today
       2:17-19, August 1957.

1266   "Basie Voted World's Top Jazzman."   Melody Maker 32:1-2, October
       12, 1957.

1267   Jones, M., and S. Traill.   "Basie's Back in Town."   Melody Maker
       32:5, October 26, 1957.

1268 Jones, M. "Basie's Back in Town." Melody Maker 32:5, October 26, 1957.

1269 Gleason, R. J. "Perspectives." down beat 24:35-36, November 28, 1957.

1270 Dance, S. "The Conquering Count." Jazz Journal 10:7-8, December 1957.

1271 "Rock-'n'-Roll a Blessing--Basie." Melody Maker 33:7, January 4, 1958.

1272 Lyttelton, H. "He Originated the Basie Sound." Melody Maker 33:5, January 11, 1958.

1273 "Want to Buy a Band?" down beat 25:43, April 17, 1958.

1274 "Jazz in the Year 2,000." Sepia 6:28-33, May 1958.

1275 "Crescendo, Hollywood." Variety 211:71, June 25, 1958.

1276 "Basie Band Just Great at Birdland." Billboard 70:3, September 8, 1958.

1277 "Heard in Person." down beat 25:47, September 18, 1958.

1278 "Relaxin' with the Count." down beat 25:14-15, September 18, 1958.

1279 Driggs, F. "About My Life in Music; Interview with Walter Page." Jazz Review 1:12-15, November 1958.

1280 Race, S. "Here Is a Superb Jazz Experience; Count Basie's 'Li'l Darlin.'" Melody Maker 33:5, November 8, 1958.

1281 Hodeir, A. "Du Cote de Chez Basie; An Appraisal of the Count Basie Orchestra." Jazz Review 1:6-8, December 1958.

1282 "Count Basie." down beat 25:15, December 25, 1958.

1283 Gehman, R. "A Triumph of Enthusiasm." Esquire 51:79-80, January 1959.

1284 "Lewis, Basie and Satch." Jazz Journal 12:1, February 1959.

1285 Dawbarn, B., and T. Brown. "Two Views of the Basie Concerts." Melody Maker 34:3, February 14, 1959.

1286 "B. O. Count Strictly SRO for Basie's British Tour; 3d Swing Looks No. 1." Variety 213:50, February 25, 1959.

1287 "Basie Perfekt." Orkester Journalen 27:6-7, March 1959.

1288 "Danes Hail the Count." Billboard 71:10, March 9, 1959.

1289 Masson, J. R. "Sous le Signe de l'Energie l'Atomique Monsieur Basie." Jazz Magazine 5:16-19, April 1959.

1290 Wilson, J. S. "The Jazz Panorama." High Fidelity Review 2:77-78, April 1959.

1291 "Dance Band Directory." down beat 26:41, April 16, 1959.

1292 Lambert, G. E. "Count Basie Concert Report." Jazz Monthly 5:25,
      May 1959.

1293 Hentoff, N. "Basic Basie." High Fidelity Review 3:68-73, Decem-
      ber 1959.

1294 Ioakimidis, D. "L'Orchestre Basie Enregistre." Jazz Hot 25:28,
      February 1960.

1295 Morgenstern, D. "New York Scene." Jazz Journal 13:23, March
      1960.

1296 Jones, M. "Basie: Better than Ever." Melody Maker 35:4, April
      16, 1960.

1297 Gardner, B. J. "Count Basie! Portrait of a Band." down beat
      27:30-32, April 28, 1960.

1298 "Editorial." Jazz Journal 13:1, May 1960.

1299 Cooke, J. "Basie 1960: A Reflection of Ozymandias." Jazz Month-
      ly 6:27, June 1960.

1300 Ioakimidis, D. "Les Debuts de l'Orchestre Basie." Jazz Hot 26:16-
      19, July-August 1960.

1301 "Basie, Count." Metronome 77:42, August 1960.

1302 Dance, S. "No German Fourteenths." Jazz Journal 13:4-6, August 1960.

1303 Balliett, W. "Jazz Records." New Yorker 35:164, September 12,
      1959.

1304 Basie, Count. "The Story of Jazz." Music Journal 18:16, Novem-
      ber-December 1960.

1305 "Basie's 25th Anniversary." Metronome 77:14-15, November 1960.

1306 Feather, L. "Count Basie's Silver Jubilee." International Musician
      59:18-19, November 1960.

1307 "Guest Editor: Ruby Braff." Metronome 77:13, November 1960.

1308 Korall, B. "Background Music." Metronome 77:52, November 1960.

1309 "Les Noces d'Argent du Count." Jazz Magazine 6:18, November
      1960.

1310 Schiozzi, Bruno. Count Basie. Milano: Ricordi, 1961.

1311 Hentoff, N. "One More Time: Travels of Count Basie; Excerpt from
      Jazz Life." Jazz Review 4:4-8, January 1961.

1312 Gaspard, J. "Count Basie à Travers Ses Disques." Musica no.
      87:54-56, June 1961.

1313   Vartan, E. "Un Homme, un Esprit, une Histoire--l'Epopee Basie."
       Jazz Magazine 7:20-24, July 1961.

1314   "Count et Duke Dos à Dos." Jazz Magazine 7:16, September 1961.

1315   Morgenstern, D. "Heard & Seen." Metronome 78:7, September 1961.

1316   _____. "The Truth." Metronome 78:6, December 1961.

1317   Gazzaway, D. "Before Bird--Buster." Jazz Monthly 7:6-7, January
       1962.

1318   Dunbar, A. "Basie, Count: Twenty-Five Years of Deep Driving
       Rhythm." Sepia 11:63-65, February 1962.

1319   "Basie Counts in His New Men." Melody Maker 37:5, March 3,
       1962.

1320   Maher, J. "New York Is a Basie Festival." Billboard Music Week
       74:34, March 24, 1962.

1321   Williams, M. "When the Big Bands Played Swing." High Fidelity
       12:49-51, April 1962.

1322   Dawbarn, B. "Brilliant Basie!" Melody Maker 37:8-9, April 7,
       1962.

1323   Jones, M. "When I'm in Britain I'm Home; Interview with Count
       Basie." Melody Maker 37:8-9, April 7, 1962.

1324   "Les Adieux d'un Orchestre." Jazz Magazine 8:26-7, June 1962.

1325   "Basie in Concert." Jazz Hot no. 177:6-7, June 1962.

1326   "The British Audiences Are Swell; Interview with Count Basie." Mel-
       ody Maker 37:16-17, September 15, 1962.

1327   Schiozzi, B. "La Storia di Count Basie." Musica Jazz 18:12-16,
       November 1962; 18:36-39, 1962.

1328   Robertson, S. "Jazz World." Sepia 12:35, May 1963.

1329   Gelly, D. "The Count Basie Octet." Jazz Monthly 9:9-11, July 1963.

1330   "Three in the Afternoon." down beat 30:18-22, July 4, 1963.

1331   Lambert, G. E. "Count Basie: The Middle Years." Jazz Monthly
       9:4-8, September 1963.

1332   Dawbarn, B. "Basie's Back--Sarah too!" Melody Maker 38:8-9,
       September 7, 1963.

1333   "Count Basie in Japan; Benny Powell's Tour Diary." down beat
       30:13-15, September 12, 1963.

1334   Lefebvre, J. "Count Basie à Ostende." Jazz Magazine 9:14, Oc-
       tober 1963.

1335   Manglunki, A., and J. Manglunki. "Basie 63-64." Jazz Hot no.
       191:7-8, October 1963.

1336   Voce, S. "Basie--1963." Jazz Journal 16:1-3, October 1963.

1337   "Annuaire Biographique du Piano." Jazz Magazine 9:24-25, Novem-
       ber 1963.

1338   "Concert." Jazz Magazine 9:50-51, November 1963.

1339   "Count Basie and Sarah Vaughan." Jazz Monthly 9:6-9, November
       1963.

1340   Koechlin, P. "Concerts." Jazz Hot no. 192:5, November 1963.
       Basie gave a series of concerts in Paris.

1341   Traill, S. "Editorial." Jazz Journal 16:1, November 1963.

1342   "Homage to the Count." Time 83:55, January 10, 1964.

1343   Koechlin, P. "Count Basie et Ses Fonctionnaires du Swing." Mu-
       sica no. 120:25-27, March 1964.

1344   Hentoff, N. "Early Basie's Best." High Fidelity Review 12:58,
       June 1964.

1345   "Bill Evans, Herman, Basie, Ray Brown, Win Grammys." down
       beat 31:9-10, June 18, 1964.

1346   Balliett, W. "Jazz Records." New Yorker 40:194-198, October 3,
       1964.

1347   "Brubeck-Basie Bash at Philharmonic Hall, N.Y." Variety 236:59,
       October 21, 1964.

1348   Korall, B. "Caught in the Act." down beat 31:13, November 5,
       1964.

1349   Balliett, W. "Jazz." New Yorker 40:145-147, November 7, 1964.

1350   Shih, Hsio Wen. "Portrait of the Count." down beat 32:23-24, April
       22, 1965.

1351   Dance, S. "Academic Action." Jazz Journal 18:6-8, May 1965.
       Basie participates in a jazz festival at the Academy of Music in
       Philadelphia.

1352   "Why Count Basie Keeps Swinging." Sepia 14:36-40, May 1965.

1353   De Toledano, R. "Henderson, Basie, and Big-Band Jazz." National
       Review 17:385-387, May 4, 1965.

1354   Malson, L., and C. Bellest. "Gravures Celebres: 'One O'clock
       Jump.'" Jazz Magazine no. 121:30-34, August 1965.

1355   Traill, S. "Editorial." Jazz Journal 18:3, September 1965.

1356   Houston, B. "Basie Drives Away Those Blues." Melody Maker
       40:6, September 25, 1965.

1357 "Count Basie at Hammersmith." Jazz Monthly 11:24-25, October
      1965.

1358 "Basie: How to Keep It Swinging All the Time." Melody Maker
      40:6, October 2, 1965.

1359 Cullaz, M. "Basie en Jam." Jazz Hot no. 214:5-6, November 1965.

1360 Tenot, F. "Histoire de Comte." Jazz Magazine no. 124:16-17, No-
      vember 1965.

1361 "Riverboat, N.Y." Variety 241:58, December 22, 1965.

1362 Marne, G. "Count Basie Thirty Years a Leader." International
      Musician 64:4, January 1966.

1363 Feather, L. "Suddenly, Las Vegas Millionaires, Gamblers and
      Squares Are Digging the Band." Melody Maker 41:6, January 29,
      1966.

1364 Carles, P. "Bye Bye Basie." Jazz Magazine no. 127:14, February
      1966.

1365 Feather, L. "Caught in the Act." down beat 33:36-37, February
      24, 1966.

1366 _____. "Basie et Sinatra à Las Vegas." Jazz Magazine no.
      128:15, March 1966.

1367 Stewart, R. "Caught in the Act." down beat 33:39-40, June 16,
      1966.

1368 "Bellson Joins Basie." down beat 33:14, September 8, 1966.

1369 "Riverboat, N.Y." Variety 245:53, December 28, 1966.

1370 "Clean Sweep." ASCAP Today 1:5, no. 2, 1967.

1371 Lees, G. "From Spirituals to Swing, 1967." High Fidelity/Musical
      America 17MA7, April 1967.

1372 Hutton, J. "A Swing Cleaning for the Basie Band." Melody Maker
      42:7, May 20, 1967.

1373 Jones, M. "Harry Edison, Back with the Basie Band After 17
      Years." Melody Maker 42:6, May 27, 1967.

1374 Binchet, J. P. "Le Survivant des Temps Lointains." Jazz Maga-
      zine no. 143:5, June 1967.

1375 Le Moel, R. "Le Count Encore." Jazz Hot no. 232:6-7, June 1967.

1376 Welch, C. "Welcome to My Dreams...." Melody Maker 42:9, June
      3, 1967.

1377 "Basie, Fame Give a Royal, Rocking Concert in U.K." Billboard
      79:22, June 10, 1967.

1378 Dawson, J. "Basie." Melody Maker 42:6, June 17, 1967.

1379   Ginibre, J. L.   "Tony et le Comte."   Jazz Magazine no. 144:11,
       July 1967.

1380   Morgan, A.   "Count Basie in Chatham."   Jazz Monthly 13:15-16,
       July 1967.

1381   "Basie in Paris."   Variety 247:44, July 5, 1967.

1382   "Le Bistro, A. C."   Variety 247:52, July 19, 1967.

1383   "Sahara Tahoe, L. Tahoe."   Variety 248:67, September 13, 1967.

1384   Feather, L.   "The Rise and Fall of the Basie Band."   Melody Maker
       43:6, January 20: 1968.

1385   Dance, S.   "Count Basie: An American Institution."   down beat
       35:18-20, April 18, 1968.

1386   Houston, B.   "Fame/Basie."   Melody Maker 43:10, April 27, 1968.

1387   Hutton, J.   "Caught in the Act."   Melody Maker 43:6, May 4, 1968.

1388   Jones, M.   "Mitchell: Basie's 'New' Section Leader."   Melody Mak-
       er 43:8, May 4, 1968.

1389   "Basie with Fame."   Jazz Journal 21:3, June 1968.

1390   Holroyd, S.   "Four Decades of Basie, Aristocrat of Big Band Jazz."
       Melody Maker 43:10, August 17, 1968.

1391   "Tropicana, Las Vegas."   Variety 252:55, August 21, 1968.

1392   Holroyd, S.   "The Miraculous Basie--Keeping the Big Band Togeth-
       er."   Melody Maker 43:8, August 24, 1968.

1393   Östberg, L.   "Count Basie."   Orkester Journalen 36:15, September
       1968.

1394   Feather, L.   "Rediscovering Basie."   Melody Maker 43:8, September
       14, 1968.

1395   Jepsen, Jorgen Grunnet.   A Discography of Count Basie, 1951-1968.
       Copenhagen NV: Karl Emil Knudsen, 1969.

1396   Dance, S.   "Noblesse Oblige: Jazz Nobility on Tour."   Interna-
       tional Musician 67:24, January 1969.

1397   _____.   "Caught in the Act."   down beat 36:30-31, February 20,
       1969.

1398   "Caught in the Act."   Melody Maker 44:10, April 26, 1969.

1399   Burns, J.   "Lesser Known Bands of the Forties."   Jazz Monthly no.
       171[sic, i.e. 172]:8-10, June 1969.

1400   Lambert, E.   "Count Basie at Wakefield."   Jazz Monthly no. 171[sic.
       i.e. 172]:31, June 1969.

1401   Traill, S.   "Editorial."   Jazz Journal 22:1, June 1969.

1402 "Harrah's, Reno." Variety 255:60, June 25, 1969.

1403 McRae, B. "A B Basics; A Column for the Newcomer to Jazz."
      Jazz Journal 22:17, July 1969.

1404 Dance, S. "New Orleans, Jazz Capital?" Saturday Review 52:45,
      July 12, 1969.

1405 Vacher, A. "Montreal, le Duc et le Comte." Jazz Magazine no.
      169-170:11, September 1969.

1406 Albertson, C. "Jimmy Rushing: A Sturdy Branch of the Learning
      Tree." down beat 36:17, November 13, 1969.

1407 Korall, B. "Basie." Saturday Review 52:82-83, November 29, 1969.

1408 Feather, L. "Rocking on Board with Basie's Band." Melody Maker
      45:8, January 24, 1970.

1409 "Disques du Mois." Jazz Magazine no. 175:38, February 1970.

1410 "Caught in the Act." down beat 38:31-32, February 18, 1971.

1411 "Tropicana, Las Vegas." Variety 258:67, March 11, 1970.

1412 "Big Band Special." Melody Maker 45:18, March 21, 1970.

1413 Feather, L. "Count Meets Queen: A Diary of an Uncommon Cruise."
      down beat 37:14-15, April 2, 1970.

1414 Tiegel, E. "Talent in Action." Billboard 82:22, April 4, 1970.

1415 Feather, L. "Count Meets Queen: A Diary of an Uncommon Cruise."
      down beat 37:18-19, April 16, 1970.

1416 Callagham, P. "Basie à Paris." Jazz Hot no. 261:6, May 1970.

1417 Gerber, A. "La Dame et le Comte." Jazz Magazine no. 178:15,
      May 1970.

1418 "Ella, Basie Whip Up Lots of B. O. Noise in Tour of W. Germany."
      Variety 258:85, May 6, 1970.

1419 Yates, C. "Caught in the Act." Melody Maker 45:17, May 16, 1970.

1420 Dawson, J. "In Praise of the Kids--Basie." Melody Maker 45:8,
      May 23, 1970.

1421 "Basie Lever Paa Sina Saangare." Orkester Journalen 38:8-9, June
      1970.

1422 Dahlgren, R. "Stjaernmoete Paa Hoegsta Nivaa." Orkester Journalen
      38:12, June 1970.

1423 "Reeditions: Count Basie, Volume 2: 1946-1949." Jazz Magazine
      no. 179:48, June 1970.

1424 "Reeditions: The Best of Count Basie and His Orchestra, Volume
      1." Jazz Magazine no. 180:45, July-August 1970.

1425   "Count Basie." Muzsika 13:22-23, July 1970.

1426   Cullaz, M. "La Chronique des Disques." Jazz Hot no. 264:37, September 1970.

1427   Szantor, J. "Record Reviews: Basie on the Beatles." down beat 37:22, September 3, 1970.

1428   "Record Reviews: Basic Basie." Jazz Journal 23:30, November 1970; Jazz Monthly no. 190:18, December 1970.

1429   Tercinet, A., and B. Niquet. "La Chronique des Disques: The Best of Count Basie Vol. 2; Basic Basie." Jazz Hot no. 268:33, January 1971.

1430   Dance, S. "Lightly & Politely." Jazz Journal 24:8-9, February 1971.

1431   Gerber, A. "Disques du Mois: Basic Basie." Jazz Magazine no. 187:34, March 1971.

1432   Morgenstern, D. "Breakfast with Champions." down beat 38:14-15, April 15, 1971. Basic attends a victory party for Joe Frazier.

1433   "Concert Review." Variety 262:45, April 21, 1971.

1434   Laverdure, M. "Les Bases du Style Basie." Jazz Magazine no. 189:21-24, May 1971.

1435   "Caught in the Act." Melody Maker 46:30, May 15, 1971.

1436   Jones, M. "Jazz Records: On the Sunny Side of the Street." Melody Maker 46:38, May 22, 1971.

1437   Gerber, A. "Paris." Jazz Magazine no. 190:7-8, June-July 1971.

1438   "Basie i Skaane." Orkester Journalen 39:14, June 1971.

1439   Carter, J. "One More Time!: Basie and Ella '71." Crescendo International 9:20-22, June 1971.

1440   Cressant, P. "Basie + Ella." Jazz Hot no. 273:26, June 1971.

1441   Gamble, P. "Jazz in Britain." Jazz Journal 24:10, July 1971.

1442   Traill, S. "Record Reviews: Basie on the Air." Jazz Journal 24:30, August 1971.

1443   Szantor, J. "Record Reviews: Afrique." down beat 38:18, October 28, 1971.

1444   "Record Reviews: Afrique; High Voltage." Coda 10:28-29, no. 6, 1972.

1445   "Record Reviews: Basie on the Beatles." Coda 10:19-20, no. 5, 1972.

1446   "Basie Band at Cancer Benefit." Billboard 84:3, January 15, 1972.

1447   "Hotel St. Regis, N.Y." Variety 265:55, January 26, 1972.

1448   Dove, I. "Talent in Action." Billboard 84:20, February 5, 1972.

1449   "Jazz Records: At the Savoy Ballroom." Melody Maker 47:28, Feb-
       ruary 12, 1972.

1450   "Chronique des Disques: Volume 1." Jazz Hot no. 281:26, March
       1972.   Volume 1 consists of music by Basie from 1947.

1451   "Disques du Mois: Volume 1." Jazz Magazine no. 198:26, March
       1972.

1452   Tricot, J. "Handful of Records: Count Basie Vol. 1." Points du
       Jazz no. 6:125-127, March 1972.

1453   Morgenstern, D. "The Count in N.Y.: A Swinging Affair." down
       beat 39:9, March 2, 1972.

1454   Szantor, J. "Windy City Wails with Getz, Carmen, et al." down
       beat 39:12, March 30, 1972.

1455   "Disques du Mois: Jazz Spectrum Vol. 4; Afrique." Jazz Magazine
       no. 199:32-33, April 1972.

1456   "Record Reviews: At the Savoy Ballroom 1937." Jazz & Blues
       2:24-25, April 1972.

1457   "Jazz Records: Have a Nice Day." Melody Maker 47:28, April 1,
       1972.

1458   "Record Reviews: Have a Nice Day." down beat 39:22, April 13,
       1972.

1459   Feather, L. "Basie Afloat: High C's on the High Seas." Billboard
       84:16, April 29: 1972.

1460   _____. "Basie at Sea." Melody Maker 47:24, April 29, 1972.

1461   Balagri, D. "Paris." Jazz Magazine no. 200:60-61, May 1972.

1462   Dance, S. "Jazz." Music Journal 30:14, May 1972.

1463   "Schallplattenbesprechungen: Have a Nice Day." Jazz Podium 21:166,
       May 1972.

1464   "Caught in the Act." Melody Maker 47:22, May 13, 1972; 47:44, May
       20, 1972.

1465   "Jazz Records: The Kid from Red Bank, Vol. 1." Melody Maker
       47:32, May 20, 1972.

1466   Carriere, C. "Count Basie à Pleyel." Jazz Hot no. 284:28, June
       1972.

1467   Carter, J. "Concert Reviews." Crescendo International 10:40, June
       1972.

1468 Östberg, L., and C. Nilsson. "Tillbakablickande Basie." Orkester
      Journalen 40:11, June 1972.

1469 Tiegel, E. "Granz Bows Twin Bill: Disks and Jam Session." Bill-
      board 84:17, June 17, 1972.

1470 Lambert, E. "In Person." Jazz & Blues 2:9, July 1972.

1471 "Record Reviews: Summit Meeting." Jazz & Blues 2:28-29, July
      1972.

1472 "Record Reviews: The Kid from Red Bank, Vol. 1." Jazz & Blues
      2:28, July 1972.

1473 Tomkins, L. "You Could Listen to Twelve Bands a Night." Cre-
      scendo International 10:6-7, July 1972.

1474 "Records: Count Basie: Super Chief." Rolling Stone no. 112:60,
      July 6, 1972.

1475 "St. Regis Roof, N.Y." Variety 267:57, July 12, 1972.

1476 "Jazz Records: Afrique; Swinging at the Daisy Chain; You Can De-
      pend on Basie." Melody Maker 47:36, July 15, 1972.

1477 "The Four Sides of Superchief." Melody Maker 47:48, September
      23, 1972.

1478 "Hilton Int'l, L. V." Variety 268:53, September 27, 1972.

1479 "Count Basie in Europe." Jazz Forum no. 19:48-51, October 1972.

1480 "Disques du Mois: Featuring Al Hibbler & Joe Williams." Jazz
      Magazine no. 204:40, October 1972.

1481 "Disques du Mois: The Best of Basie." Jazz Magazine no. 106:36,
      December 1972. Recording from the 1938-1939 period.

1482 "Record Reviews: Bing 'n' Basie." down beat 39:19, December 7,
      1972.

1483 "On Record: From Broadway to Paris." Jazz & Blues 2:12-13, Jan-
      uary 1973.

1484 "Record Reviews: The Best of Basie." Jazz & Blues 2:24, January
      1973.

1485 Wyatt, F. "Ella, Basie Join Hands in California Stand." down beat
      40:11, February 1, 1973.

1486 "On Record: Swinging at the Daisy Chain." Jazz & Blues 2:20,
      March 1973.

1487 Voce, S. "In for the Count." Jazz Journal 26:13-14, March 1973.

1488 "Record Reviews: Super Chief." down beat 40:21, March 1, 1973.

1489 "Reviews on Record: You Can Depend on Basie." Jazz & Blues
      3:16, April 1973.

1490   "On Record: At the Savoy Ballroom; Super Chief." Jazz & Blues
       3:23-24, May 1973.

1491   "On Record: The Kid from Red Bank, Vol. II." Jazz & Blues
       3:18-19, June 1973.

1492   "Born to Swing." Jazz Journal 26:2-3, July 1973.

1493   "Caught in the Act." Melody Maker 48:27, September 29, 1973.

1494   Carriere, C. "Les Geants au Paris." Jazz Hot no. 299:23-24,
       November 1973.

1495   Kuehn, G. "Norman Granz Presents: Leise Spannung, Powerhouse
       und Marionetten-Show." Jazz Podium 22:29, November 1973.

1496   "Jazz en Direct." Jazz Magazine no. 217:15, December 1973.

1497   "Jazzens Giganter: Basie och Ellington." Musikern no. 12:12-13,
       December 1973.

1498   Giddins, G. "Weather Bird." down beat 40:29, December 8, 1973.
       Discussion of Basie's orchestra in the 1930's.

1499   Dugan, J., and J. Hammond. "An Early Black-Music Concert, From
       Spirituals to Swing." Black Perspectives in Music 2:196-198, no.
       2, 1974.

1500   "Concert Reviews." Variety 273:76, January 16, 1974.

1501   "Caught." down beat 41:25-26, February 28, 1974.

1502   "Concert Reviews." Variety 274:54, March 6, 1974.

1503   "Talent in Action." Billboard 86:20, March 9, 1974.

1504   Balliett, W. "Simplicity." New Yorker 50:117-118, March 25, 1974.

1505   "Caught in the Act." Melody Maker 49:58, June 8, 1974.

1506   "Count Basie Feted at Waldorf Soiree." Variety 276:47, September
       25, 1974.

1507   "Caught in the Act." Melody Maker 49:34, October 5, 1974.

1508   Brown, George F. "Count Basie Celebrates 70th Birthday." Jet
       47:14-16, October 10, 1974.

1509   "The Musical Whirl." High Fidelity/Musical America 24:MA16-17,
       November 1974.

1510   Carriere, C. "Ernie Wilkins." Jazz Hot no. 311:24-27, December
       1974.

1511   "Count Basie Siebzig Jahre Alt." Hifi-Stereophonie 13:1490, Decem-
       ber 1974.

1512   Douglas, C. C. "Count Basie 70th Birthday Party Is Kick-Off for
       Bandleader's Tour of Europe." Ebony 30:54-56, December 1974.

1513 Nass, K. H. "Hoechst Bemerkenswert; Peterson, NHOP, Basie und
      Turner in der Jahrhunderthalle." Jazz Podium 23:28-29, Decem-
      ber 1974.

1514 West, H. "Basie at 70." Radio Free Jazz 14:7, December 1974.
      Reprinted from the Washington Post.

1515 Count Basie and His Bands. Edited by Dan Morgenstern and Jack
      Bradley. New York: New York Jazz Museum, 1975.

1516 "Jazz Records: Rock-a-Bye Basie." Melody Maker 50:34, January
      11, 1975.

1517 "Concert Reviews." Variety 277:72, January 22, 1975; 277:80, Feb-
      ruary 5, 1975.

1518 Balliett, W. "Jazz: New York Notes." New Yorker 51:74, April
      7, 1975.

1519 Tomkins, L. "The Inimitable Basie Recalled by Bennie Morton."
      Crescendo International 13:10-11, July 1975.

1520 "See Record 2-Wk Gross for Sinatra, Ella, Basie at Uris, N.Y."
      Variety 280:74, September 10, 1975.

1521 McDonough, J. "Count Basie: A Hard Look at an Old Softie."
      down beat 42:17-18, September 11, 1975.

1522 "Basie à Mi-Voix." Jazz Magazine no. 237:16, October 1975.

1523 Dance, S. "Lightly and Politely: At Misquamicut." Jazz Journal
      28:11-12, October 1975.

1524 Byers, B., and W. L. Fowler. "How to Design Your Basie-Type
      Chart." down beat 42:44-45, October 23, 1975.

1525 Carter, J. "Count Basie Orchestra and Ella Fitzgerald at Royal
      Festival Hall." Crescendo International 14:9, November 1975.

1526 "Count Basie--Ella Fitzgerald." Jazz Hot no. 321:21, November
      1975.

1527 "Jazz in Britain." Jazz Journal 28:20, November 1975.

1528 "Caught in the Act." Melody Maker 50:28, November 15, 1975.

1529 "Concert Reviews." Variety 281:52, November 19, 1975.

1530 "Caught in the Act." Melody Maker 50:26, November 22, 1975.

1531 Jones, M. "Basie: Still Making History." Melody Maker 50:42,
      November 22, 1975.

1532 Tomkins, L., and J. Carter. "Sinatra at the Palladium." Crescendo
      International 14:25, December 1975.

1533 "Record Reviews: The Count at the Chatterbox." Coda no. 144:21,
      January-February 1976.

1534 "Jazz Records: Count Basie Jam Session at Montreux Festival 1975."
      Melody Maker 51:26, January 3, 1976.

1535 "Deauville, M. Beach." Variety 282:119, February 18, 1976.

1536 "Heard and Seen." Coda no. 148:31-32, June 1976.

1537 "Sahara, Las Vegas." Variety 283:63, June 2, 1976.

1538 "Talent in Action." Billboard 88:45, June 26, 1976.

1539 "Record Reviews: Basie & Zoot." Jazz Journal 29:28, July 1976.

1540 "Jazz Albums: Sixteen Big Band Greats." Melody Maker 51:24,
      July 3, 1976.

1541 "Jazz Albums: Swingin' with the Count." Melody Maker 51:26, July
      24, 1976.

1542 "Jazz Albums: Basie and Zoot." Melody Maker 51:23, August 28,
      1976.

1543 "Record Reviews: Blues by Basie." Jazz Journal 29:28, September
      1976.

1544 "It's a Ripley: Basie Jammed with Lombardo." Variety 284:72,
      September 8, 1976.

1545 "Concert Reviews." Variety 284:76, September 15, 1976.

1546 "Record Reviews: Basie and Zoot." down beat 43:32-33, October
      21, 1976.

1547 Francis, H. "As I Heard It--Jazz Development in Britain 1924-
      1974." Crescendo International 15:8, December 1976.

1548 "Record Reviews: Basie & Zoot; For the First Time; Jam Session
      at the Montreux." Coda no. 152:22, December 1976.

1549 "Record Reviews: 'Satch' and 'Josh.'" Coda no. 152:22-23, Decem-
      ber 1976.

1550 "Record Reviews: Chairman of the Board; The Atomic Mister Basie."
      Jazz Journal 29:30, January 1976.

1551 "Count Does Bottom Line." down beat 43:12, April 22, 1976.

1552 "Jazz Albums: Basie Big Band; The Atomic Mr. Basie; Chairman
      of the Board." Melody Maker 51:28, May 8, 1976.

1553 "Talent in Action." Billboard 88:42, May 22, 1976.

1554 Scherman, B. "Stor Basie-Kvaell Paa Groenan." Orkester Journalen
      44:8, September 1976.

1555 "Jazz Albums: Blues by Basie." Melody Maker 51:20, December
      18, 1976.

1556   Korall, B. "Basie After 40 Years: The Band." Jazz Magazine
       (U.S.) 1:64-65, no. 4, 1977.

1557   McElfresh, P. "Basie: Back on Road with New Lifestyle." Jazz
       Magazine (U.S.) 1:15, no. 3, 1977.

1558   Stites, T. "Basie After Forty Years: The Soloist." Jazz Magazine
       (U.S.) 1:65, no. 4, 1977. Examines Basie's recordings which
       have been reissued.

1559   Villani, G. "Butch Miles: Drivin' the Basie Rhythm Machine."
       Modern Drum 1:12-13, no. 3, 1977.

1560   Lambert, E. "Count Basie--the V-Discs." Jazz Journal 30:6-8,
       January 1977.

1561   Laverdure, M. "Les Tapeurs de la Bande." Jazz Magazine no.
       251:34-35, January 1977.

1562   Reda, J. "Les Anches Passent." Jazz Magazine no. 251:36-37,
       January 1977.

1563   "Record Reviews: I Told You So." down beat 44:24, January 27,
       1977; Jazz Journal 30:28, February 1977.

1564   Hentoff, N. "Indigenous Music: Basie Jam #2." Nation 224:222,
       February 19, 1977.

1565   "Jazz Albums: I Told You So." Melody Maker 52:29, February 19,
       1977.

1566   "Concert Reviews." Variety 286:63, February 23, 1977.

1567   "Record Reviews: Basie Jam No. 2." down beat 44:26, April 7,
       1977.

1568   "Talent in Action." Billboard 89:46, April 23, 1977.

1569   "Caught in the Act." Melody Maker 52:20, April 30, 1977.

1570   Tomkins, L. "Ella & Basie at the Palladium." Crescendo Interna-
       tional 15:36, May 1977.

1571   Carriere, C., and D. Nevers. "Count Basie." Jazz Hot no. 339-
       340:34-35, July-August 1977.

1572   Aikin, J. "Count Basie." Contemporary Keyboard 3:10-12, July
       1977.

1573   "Count Basie & Ella Fitzgerald at the London Palladium." Jazz Jour-
       nal International 30:32, July 1977.

1574   Lambert, E. "Basie's Top Ten." Jazz Journal International 30:26-
       27, July 1977.

1575   Balliett, W. "Jazz: New York Notes." New Yorker 53:85, July 18,
       1977.

1576   "Jazz Albums: Basie Jam 2." Melody Maker 52:24, August 27, 1977.

1577 "Reissues: The V-Discs Volume 2." Coda no. 157:23, September-
      October 1977.

1578 "En Direct." Jazz Magazine no. 258:9, October 1977.

1579 Endress, G. "Nur Nicht Solo!" Jazz Podium 26:9-12, October 1977.

1580 "Record Review: Prime Time; The ABC Collection." Radio Free
      Jazz 18:17-18, October 1977.

1581 "Concert Reviews." Variety 288:80, October 5, 1977.

1582 "Waxing On: Good Morning Blues." down beat 44:34, October 6,
      1977.

1583 "Jazz Albums: Prime Time." Melody Maker 52:36, October 8, 1977.

1584 Kisner, R. E. "Count Basie Gets Sickle Cell Award and Kisses
      from Friends." Jet 53:62-63, October 13, 1977.

1585 "Count Basie Tribute in K.C. Raises 20G for Jazz Hall of Fame."
      Variety 288:217, October 19, 1977.

1586 "Record Reviews: Prime Time." down beat 44:23, November 17,
      1977.

1587 "Record Reviews: Count Basie Jam." Jazz Journal International
      30:39, December 1977.

1588 "Caught." down beat 44:36-37, December 1, 1977.

1589 "Waxing On: Sessions, Live." down beat 44:38, December 15, 1977.
      Music recorded from "Stars of Jazz" shown on TV.

1590 "Jazz Albums: Count Basie Big Band Montreux '77." Melody Maker
      52:16, December 31, 1977.

1591 Jordon, G., and S. Paul. "Notes: Tribute to Basie." Jazz Maga-
      zine (U.S.) 2:14-15, no. 2, 1978.

1592 Skipper, J. K. "Count Basie 1977: Performance and Interview."
      Popular Music and Sociology 6:64-67, no. 1, 1978.

1593 "Count Basie Is Honored." International Musician 76:8, January
      1978.

1594 "Record Reviews: Lester Young Story Vol. 3: Enter the Count."
      down beat 45:20, January 26, 1978.

1595 "Jazz Albums: Golden Hour Presents." Melody Maker 53:23, Feb-
      ruary 4, 1978.

1596 "Jazz Albums: Sixteen Men Swinging." Melody Maker 53:24, Feb-
      ruary 4, 1978.

1597 Giddins, G. "Weatherbird: Jazz Holds Its Own in Granziland."
      Village Voice 23:56, February 6, 1978.

1598 "Jazz Albums: 8 & 16." Melody Maker 53:32, February 25, 1978.

1599   Feather, L. "Piano Giants of Jazz: Count Basie." Contemporary
       Keyboard 4:55, March 1978.

1600   "Talent in Action." Billboard 90:39, March 4, 1978.

1601   "Record Reviews: Count Basie Jam." down beat 45:21-22, March
       9, 1978.

1602   "Yankee Riverboat, N.Y." Variety 290:81, March 29, 1978.

1603   "Record Reviews: Sixteen Men Swinging." Jazz Journal International
       31:36, April 1978.

1604   "Count Basie on America's New Musical Era." U.S. News & World
       Report 84:77, April 3, 1978.

1605   "Basie and Zoot." Radio Free Jazz 17:13-14, May 1978.

1606   "Jazz; Disc: Count Basie Jam." Music Journal 36:32-33, May 1978.

1607   "Record Reviews: Switch and Josh Again; The Atomic Period." Jazz
       Journal International 31:37, June 1978.

1608   Kuehn, G. "Jazz Portraet: Count Basie, Cecil Taylor." Hifi-Ster-
       eophonie 17:832-839, July 1978.

1609   Von Konow, A. "Basie Har Varit Haer Igen." Orkester Journalen
       46:19, September 1978.

1610   "Jazz Albums: Jumpin' at the Woodside; Satch and Josh Again; That
       Atomic Period." Melody Maker 53:22, September 2, 1978.

1611   "Record Reviews: Satch and Josh Again." down beat 45:38, Septem-
       ber 7, 1978.

1612   "Record Reviews: Jumping at the Woodside." Jazz Journal Interna-
       tional 31:57, October 1978.

1613   "Waxing On: A Legend, Rock a Bye Basie." down beat 45:27, Oc-
       tober 19, 1978.

1614   "Record Reviews: Count Basie at the Famous Door, 1938-39; Lester
       Young & Charlie Christian, 1939-1940." down beat 45:38, Novem-
       ber 2, 1978.

1615   "Jazz Albums: The Big Band, Vol. 1 and 2." Melody Maker 53:26,
       November 4, 1978.

BEATTY, JOSEPHINE see HUNTER, ALBERTA

BECHET, SIDNEY, 1891-1959.

1616   "That Old Feeling." Time 49:52, March 31, 1947.

1617   "Bechet on Columbia." Melody Maker 25:6, May 21, 1949.

1618 "Bechet Triumphs." Playback 2:14, June 1949.

1619 Thompson, K. C. "An Interview with Sidney Bechet." Record
      Changer 8:9-10, July 1949.

1620 Anderson, J. L. "Evolution of Jazz." down beat 16:7, July 1, 1949.

1621 Preston, S. D. "Backstage with Bechet and Bop." Melody Maker
      25:3, August 27, 1949.

1622 Aurthur, B. "Sidney Bechet; A Profile." Playback 2:3-5, Septem-
      ber 1949.

1623 McGarvey, R. "Bechet's Records." Playback 2:5-15, September
      1949.

1624 Jones, M. "Scintillating Sides from Bechet." Melody Maker 25:3,
      October 22, 1949.

1625 Tanner, P. "Sidney Bechet's French Appearances." Melody Maker
      25:2, November 12, 1949.

1626 "Bechet at London Airport." Melody Maker 25:6, November 19, 1949.

1627 "Bechet Plays in London!" Melody Maker 25:1, November 19, 1949.

1628 McGarvey, R. "Techet's Records." Playback 2:18, December 1949.

1629 Dance, S. F. "Jazz at the Winter Gardens." Jazz Journal 3:2, Jan-
      uary 1950.

1630 "The Old-Time Stars Are Trying to Forget It!" Melody Maker 26:4,
      February 18, 1950.

1631 "Bechet Returning to Paris--for Good?" Melody Maker 26:6, May
      20, 1950.

1632 "Lightly and Politely." Jazz Journal 3:9, June 1950.

1633 Thompson, K. C. "Sidney Bechet in the Days of 'Nicks.'" Jazz
      Journal 3:1-2, June 1950.

1634 "Wilcox, Curtis, Hughes at Bow Street." Melody Maker 26:1-2,
      June 10, 1950.

1635 "Immigration Officers Tell of Hawkins, Bechet Interviews." Melody
      Maker 26:2, June 17, 1950.

1636 "'Jazz Illustrated' Quoted in Court; Hughes Pleads Guilty." Melody
      Maker 26:2-3, June 24, 1950.

1637 Jones, M. "Bechet Abounds: Fourteen Titles for the Library."
      Melody Maker 26:9, June 24, 1950.

1638 "What Happened at Heath Row? Jack Marshall Gives Evidence."
      Melody Maker 26:2, July 8, 1950.

1639 Traill, S. "Not the Best of Mr. Bechet." Melody Maker 26:9, De-
      cember 2, 1950.

1640 "Bechet Jazz Wins Paris." Billboard 62:2, December 16, 1950.

1641 Zwonicek, E. "Sidney Bechet's Recent Trip to Geneva." Melody
      Maker 27:9, January 13, 1951.

1642 "Mezzrow-Bechet on King Jazz--a Provisional Listing." Melody Mak-
      er 27:9, January 27, 1951.

1643 Anderson, J. L. "Evolution of Jazz." down beat 18:11, March 9,
      1951; 18:11, March 23, 1951.

1644 "Stan Getz, Sidney Bechet; En Kontrasternas Jazzkonsert." Orkester
      Journalen 19:10-11, April 1951.

1645 Kahn, H., and S. Bechet. "Jazz May be Dying in America ... but
      It's Brought New Life to the French." Melody Maker 27:3, April
      14, 1951.

1646 "Getz, Bechet Do Concerts in Stockholm." down beat 18:5, April 20,
      1951.

1647 "Bechet Injured in Car Smash on Way to Clamart Jazz Festival."
      Melody Maker 27:7, June 23, 1951.

1648 "Sidney Bechet Weds on Riviera as 200 Jazzmen Play." Melody Mak-
      er 27:1, August 11, 1951.

1649 "The Sidney Bechet Wedding." Melody Maker 27:6-7, August 25,
      1951.

1650 "Patriarch's Wedding." Time 58:82, August 27, 1951.

1651 Dobell, D. "Bechet at the Vieux Colombier." Melody Maker 27:9,
      September 8, 1951.

1652 Kahn, H. "A Jazz Throne Changes Hands!" Melody Maker 27:9,
      September 22, 1951.

1653 "Band Reviews." Variety 184:44, October 31, 1951.

1654 "Marriage on the Riviera." Our World 6:41-44, December 1951.

1655 "Bechet Discography." down beat 18:18, December 14, 1951.

1656 Hoefer, G. "Sid Bechet Has Led Long, Colorful Life as Jazzman."
      down beat 18:2, December 14, 1951.

1657 "Bechet Returns to Paris for Operation." Melody Maker 28:6, Jan-
      uary 12, 1952.

1658 Jones, M. "There Was Joyous Jazz on Sidney's Wedding Day!" Mel-
      ody Maker 28:9, January 12, 1952.

1659 _____, and S. Traill. "Collectors' Corner." Melody Maker
      28:9, January 19, 1952.

1660 Hentoff, N. "Sidney Bechet Faces Surgery." down beat 19:1, Jan-
      uary 25, 1952.

1661 Hobson, W. "Monuments of the Great." Saturday Review 35:44-45,
      January 26, 1952.

1662 Mylne, D. "A Latter-Day Discography of Sidney Bechet." Melody
      Maker 28:9, January 26, 1952.

1663 Kahn, H. "They Don't Appreciate Real Blues in France." Melody
      Maker 28:9, February 2, 1952.

1664 Mylne, D. "Bechet Discography." Melody Maker 28:9 February 9,
      1952; 28:9, February 16, 1952; 28:9, February 23, 1952; 28:9,
      March 8, 1952; 28:9, March 15, 1952.

1665 "Bechet's Ballet Score in Pas-de-Deux Groove." Variety 190:53,
      April 15, 1953.

1666 Wiedemann, E. "Corrections and Additions to the Sidney Bechet
      Discography." Melody Maker 28:9, April 19, 1952.

1667 "Sidney Bechet Quits Colombier and Luter Band." Melody Maker
      29:12, June 6, 1953.

1668 "Sidney Bechet Heads Coast Jazz Jubilee." Variety 192:49, Septem-
      ber 9, 1953.

1669 "Sidney Bechet Ballet to be Staged on Television." Melody Maker
      30:16, June 12, 1954. Bechet's ballet is entitled "La Nuit est une
      Sorciere."

1670 "'Recording Artists' Roster." down beat 21:89, June 30, 1954.

1671 "Along the Rue Bechet." Time 64:83-84, September 20, 1954.

1672 Lucas, J. "Satchmo or Pops." Jazz Journal 7:7-9, December 1954.

1673 "Bechet to Baton Bow of Ballet to His Music; Sombert in New Troupe."
      Variety 197:75, February 2, 1955.

1674 Kahn, H. "Bechet Ballet May be Staged in London." Melody Maker
      31:15, February 26, 1955.

1675 _____. "The Bechet-Roy Reunion." Melody Maker 31:7, Febru-
      ary 26, 1955.

1676 Hoefer, G. "The Hot Box." down beat 22:22, May 18, 1955.

1677 Jepsen, J. G. "Jazzens Instrumentalister: Sopransaxofonen." Or-
      kester Journalen 23:15, July 1955.

1678 "Bechet's Ballet Is Cheered." Melody Maker 31:16, September 17,
      1955. The premiere of Bechet's ballet "The Night Is a Witch" re-
      ceives much acclaim.

1679 Kahn, H. "The 'Murder' of Sidney Bechet." Melody Maker 31:13,
      October 15, 1955.

1680 "Ten Fans Hurt in Riot at Bechet Concert." Melody Maker 31:1,
      October 22, 1955.

1681   "Paris Gendarmerie Called in to Cool Off Rioting Bechet Fans."
       Variety 200:41, October 26, 1955.

1682   "Bechet Blew." Melody Maker 31:8, October 29, 1955.

1683   Borneman, E. "Bechet." Melody Maker 31:15, November 19, 1955.

1684   Wilson, J. S. "New Orleans Jazz." High Fidelity 6:77, June 1956.
       Recordings are discussed.

1685   "Jazz Photos." down beat 23:42, June 27, 1956.

1686   "Bechet Is Coming to Britain!" Melody Maker 31:1, June 30, 1956.

1687   "Belfast Fans to See Sidney Bechet." Melody Maker 31:2, August 4,
       1956.

1688   Kahn, H. "Bechet." Melody Maker 31:3, August 4, 1956.

1689   Hoefer, G. "The Hot Box." down beat 23:37, August 8, 1956.

1690   "Extra London Concert for Sidney Bechet." Melody Maker 31:16,
       August 18, 1956.

1691   Hutton, J. "Bechet--at the Albert Hall." Melody Maker 31:10,
       September 8, 1956.

1692   "Bechet, 70, Still Boff, Plays Pre-Midnight in Frankfurt with Gold
       Sax." Variety 204:43, November 28, 1956.

1693   Kahn, H. "Bechet's Ballet Fails to Impress." Melody Maker 33:11,
       January 4, 1958.

1694   Wood, B. "The Duke and Sidney Bechet." Jazz Journal 11:25-26,
       July 1958.

1695   Bass, M. R. "The Squares of Paris." High Fidelity/Musical Amer-
       ica 8:37, August 1958.

1696   Balliett, W. "Jazz Records." New Yorker 34:103-104, September
       27, 1958.

1697   Jones, M. "Bechet Getting Better After Serious Illness." Melody
       Maker 33:11, November 22, 1958.

1698   Kunst, Peter. Sidney Bechet, ein Porträt. Wetzlar: Pegasus, 1959.

1699   Mouly, Raymond. Sidney Bechet, Notre Ami. Paris: La Table
       Ronde, 1959.

1700   Lyttelton, H. "Bechet--No Stranger to the Hit Parade." Melody
       Maker 34:11, February 7, 1959.

1701   Gushee, L. "Sidney Bechet: The Fabulous Sidney Bechet." Jazz
       Review 2:22, April 1959.

1702   "Sidney Bechet Dies in Paris." Second Line 10:3, May-June 1959.

1703   "Bonnes Nouvelles de Sidney Bechet." Jazz Magazine 5:11, May 1959.

1704 Levi, G. "Bechet Is Fighting for His Life." Melody Maker 34:1,
      May 16, 1959.

1705 ["Obituary."] Variety 214:79, May 20, 1959.

1706 Levi, G. "3,000 Fans Say Adieu." Melody Maker 34:1, May 23,
      1959.

1707 Lyttelton, H. and H. Kahn. "This Was Sidney Bechet." Melody
      Maker 34:2-3, May 23, 1959.

1708 Lyttelton, H. "Sidney Bechet--a Postscript." Melody Maker 34:4,
      May 30, 1959.

1709 Anderson, L. "Bechet." Orkester Journalen 27:16, June 1959.

1710 "Bechet Dies." Music U.S.A. 76:6, June 1959.

1711 ["Obituary."] International Musician 57:16, June 1959; Musical Amer-
      ica 79:33, June 1959.

1712 "Sidney Bechet Est Mort." Jazz Magazine 5:11, June 1959.

1713 Stenbeck, L. "Sidney Bechet; In Memoriam." Orkester Journalen
      27:8-9, June 1959.

1714 "Sidney Bechet Dead." down beat 26:9, June 11, 1959.

1715 Hadlock, R. "Bechet Remembered: A Tribute." down beat 26:46-
      47, June 25, 1959.

1716 "In Memoriam." down beat 26:14, June 25, 1959.

1717 Lucas, J. "Sidney Bechet--Jazz King." Jazz Journal 12:5, July
      1959.

1718 "La Mort de Bechet Vue par la Grande Presse." Jazz Magazine
      5:11, July 1959.

1719 Gaspard, J. J. "Sidney Bechet." Musica no. 66:21, September
      1959.

1720 Morgenstern, D. "New York Scene." Jazz Journal 12:3-5, October
      1959.

1721 Bechet, Sidney. Treat It Gentle: An Autobiography. New York:
      Da Capo Press, 1978. Reprint of the first edition, published in
      1960 by Cassell, London.

1722 Kennedy, S. "Bronze Bust of Sidney Bechet Brightens Up French
      Riviera." Second Line 11:3, no. 11-12, 1960.

1723 O'Brien, Ralph. Armstrong. Mit Texten von Louis Armstrong, Sid-
      ney Bechet, Mezz Merrow, Bunk Johnson. Zürich: Sanssouci,
      1960.

1724 Manskleid, F. "Monsieur Bechet." Metronome 77:6-7, July 1960.

1725 Bureau, J. "Sidney Bechet." Musica no. 77:7-11, August 1960.

1726 "A Monument for Bechet." down beat 27:14, August 18, 1960.

1727 "L'Hommage de Juan-les-Pins au Grand Absent du Festival: Sidney
       Bechet." Jazz Magazine 6:18-19, September 1960.

1728 Bedrick, P. "A Summer Play in Three Scenes." Metronome 77:28-
       29, October 1960.

1729 "Way the Music Was; Excerpt from Treat It Gentle." Mademoiselle
       52:74, November 1960.

1730 "Inner Jazzman." Newsweek 56:76, November 21, 1960.

1731 Lyttelton, H. "Titanic Bechet." Melody Maker 36:5, March 11,
       1961.

1732 Flakser, H. "Bechet, 1928-1931." Jazz Magazine 7:31-33, Septem-
       ber 1961.

1733 Englin, M. "More About Sidney Bechet." Second Line 13:3, no.
       11-12, 1962.

1734 Jepsen, Jorgen Grunnet. Sidney Bechet Discography. Lübbecke:
       Uhle & Kleimann, 1962.

1735 Hodes, A. "Sittin' In." down beat 29:34, February 1, 1962; 29:42,
       April 12, 1962.

1736 Feather, L. "Inside Soviet Jazz." down beat 29:14, August 16,
       1962.

1737 Lucas, J. "Bechet v. Hodges; A Pair to Compare." Jazz Journal
       16:4-6, October 1963.

1738 Fayenz, F. "Un Vero Jazzman e una Leggenda--Sidney Bechet."
       Musica Jazz 20:7-13, February 1964.

1739 Balliett, W. "Jazz Records." New Yorker 41:175-179, May 15,
       1965.

1740 Ellington, D. "The Most Essential Instrument." Jazz Journal 18:14-
       15, December 1965.

1741 Lambert, E. "Quality Jazz." Jazz Journal 19:28, September 1966.

1742 Williams, M. "Bechet the Prophet." Saturday Review 50:64-65,
       February 11, 1967.

1743 McRae, B. "A B Basics; A Column for the Newcomer to Jazz."
       Jazz Journal 20:28, June 1967.

1744 Niquet, B. "Le Herault de la Nouvelle-Orleans." Jazz Hot no.
       240:11-13, April 1968.

1745 Williams, M. "Bechet the Prophet." Jazz Journal 21:4, April 1968.

1746 Sissle, Noble. "Anniversaire: Bechet Il y a Vingt Ans." Jazz Hot
       no. 241:30-31, May-July 1968.

1747 Mauerer, Hans J. A Discography of Sidney Bechet. Copenhagen: Karl Emil Knudsen, 1969.

1748 Averty, J. C. "Sidney Bechet, 1919-1922." Jazz Hot no. 250:22-23, May 1969.

1749 Arlt, II. "The Third Line." Second Line 21:191-192, July-August 1969.

1750 Voce, S. "It Don't Mean a Thing." Jazz Journal 22:9, July 1969.

1751 Englund, B. "Besoekte Bechet Sverige 1926?" Orkester Journalen 38:13, January 1970.

1752 Postif, F., and G. Conte. "La Chronique des Disques: Sidney Bechet, Volumes 2 and 3." Jazz Hot no. 265:37-38, October 1970.

1753 Barrell, A. "Sidney Bechet." Footnote 2:2-7, no. 5, 1971.

1754 Blesh, Rudi. Combo: USA; Eight Lives in Jazz. Philadelphia: Chilton Book Co., 1971. Includes Louis Armstrong, Eubie Blake, Charlie Christian, Billie Holiday, Gene Krupa, Jack Teagarden, Lester Young, and Sidney Bechet.

1755 Jones, M. "Jazz Records: Archive of Jazz, Vol. 14: Sidney Bechet." Melody Maker 46:26, January 16, 1971.

1756 Traill, S. "Record Reviews: Sidney Bechet." Jazz Journal 24:28, October 1971.

1757 "Record Reviews: Immortal Sessions--Sidney Bechet Album." Jazz & Blues 1:21, January 1972.

1758 "Chronique des Disques: The Fabulous Sidney Bechet." Jazz Hot no. 280:28, February 1972.

1759 "Disques du Mois: King Jazz Masters." Jazz Magazine no. 197:37-38, February 1972.

1760 Reid, J. D. "Bechet and Bunk in Boston." Second Line 24:12-14, Summer 1972.

1761 Cordle, O. "The Soprano Saxophone: From Bechet to Coltrane to Shorter." down beat 39:14-15, July 20, 1972.

1762 Lambert, E. "King Jazz." Jazz & Blues 2:12-15, August 1972. Recordings on the King Jazz label, 1945-47.

1763 "Handful of Records: Sidney Bechet & Friends." Points du Jazz no. 5:121-122, September 1971.

1764 Lambert, E. "King Jazz." Jazz & Blues 2:20-22, September, 1972; 2:28-30, October, 1972; 2:14-15, November 1972.

1765 Ahlstroem, T. "Jazzdiskoteket--New Orleans-Profiler: Sidney Bechet." Musikrevy 28:240-241, no. 4, 1973.

1766 Berendt, J. E. "The Soprano Saxophone." Jazz Forum 7:40-43, no.

26, 1973. Extracts taken from Berendt's book The Jazz Book--
From Rag to Rock.

1767   "Record Reviews: The Genius of Jazzology." Coda 11:17, no. 1,
       1973.

1768   "On Record: The Prodigious Sidney Bechet." Jazz & Blues 2:21,
       March 1973.

1769   Gerber, A. "Huit Faces de Coltrane." Jazz Magazine no. 213:22-
       24, July 1973.

1770   "Jazz Records: Sidney Bechet 1949." Melody Maker 48:50, July 14,
       1973.

1771   "On Record: Sidney Bechet 1949." Jazz & Blues 3:13, December
       1973.

1772   Reid, J. D. "Bechet at Camp Unity." Second Line 26:21-22, Spring
       1974.

1773   "Jazz Records: Jazz Classics Vol. Two." Melody Maker 49:64,
       March 2, 1974.

1774   Gleason, R. J. "Perspectives: Big Les & Little Sid." Rolling
       Stone no. 180:52, February 13, 1975.

1775   Lyttelton, H. "Spielen, Was Gefaellt." Jazz Podium 24:3-6, May
       1975.

1776   Endress, G. "Sammy Price--über die Musik mit den Menschen in
       Kontakt Kommen." Jazz Podium 24:7-9, September 1975.

1777   "Record Reviews: The Panassie Sessions." Jazz Journal 28:34,
       October 1975.

1778   Dance, S. "Jazz." Music Journal 34:22, March 1976.

1779   "Records: Master Musician." Creem 7:59, May 1976.

1780   Francis, H. "Jazz Development in Britain 1924-1974." Crescendo
       International 15:14, September 1976.

1781   Kolodin, I. "High Notes in the Honeysuckle: Clarinet à la Creole."
       Saturday Review 3:30-32, September 4, 1976.

1782   Berry, J. "Jazz Literature: Through a Rhythm, Joyously." Village
       Voice 23:61, May 8, 1978.

BELAFONTE, HARRY (Harold George), 1927- .

1783   "Unknown, Belafonte Just Sang Self into Roost Job." down beat 16:12,
       March 11, 1949.

1784   "Harry Learns." down beat 16:4, June 3, 1949.

1785   "New Acts." Variety 178:53, May 3, 1950.

1786 "Voices and Modern Jazz." Metronome 66:29, June 1950.

1787 "Belafonte's Fans." Our World 5:61, November 1950.

1788 "New Acts." Variety 184:51, October 31, 1951.

1789 "In Person." Metronome 68:17, January 1952.

1790 "New Belafonte; Harry Belafonte's Folk Songs a Hit." Our World
      7:59-61, May 1952.

1791 "Village Vanguard, N.Y." Variety 187:49, June 11, 1952.

1792 "The Boulevard, Long Island." Billboard 64:14, November 22, 1952.

1793 "After 4 Tries, Slipper Finally Fit the Cinderella Gentleman." down
      beat 20:2, February 11, 1953.

1794 "Cocoanut Grove, Ambassador Hotel, Los Angeles." Billboard 65:27,
      February 21, 1953.

1795 "Timber's Gotta Roll." Time 61:55, March 9, 1953.

1796 Freeman, D. "Sharp or Square, They All Like Harry Belafonte's
      Art in Song." down beat 20:2, May 6, 1953.

1797 "Reunion in Hollywood; Schoolmates Harry Belafonte and Tony Curtis
      Meet Again After Both Become Successful." Ebony 8:26-30, July
      1953.

1798 Coss, B. "Just Plain Folk." Metronome 69:15, October 1953.

1799 "Belafonte Strikes It Rich." Our World 8:8-11, November 1953.

1800 "Caught in the Act." down beat 20:2, November 4, 1953.

1801 "Box-Office Hits of 1953." Billboard 65:19, December 19, 1953.

1802 Whitcomb, J. "Backstage at the Birth of a Hit." Cosmopolitan
      136:59, March 1954.

1803 "La Vie en Rose, N.Y." Variety 194:53, March 17, 1954.

1804 "Splash with a Song." Newsweek 43:84-85, March 29, 1954.

1805 "Broadway's Newest Golden Boy; The Whole Town's Talking About
      the Belafonte Boy's Brilliant Success in His First Broadway Show."
      Our World 9:43-47, May 1954.

1806 "Harry." Metronome 70:20, June 1954.

1807 "'Recording Artists' Roster." down beat 21:89, June 30, 1954.

1808 "Call Me Actor." Theatre Arts 38:14, July 1954.

1809 "Belafonte Will Tour Negro Folk Musical." Variety 195:57, July 7,
      1954.

1810 "Cocoanut Grove, L.A." Variety 195:78, September 1, 1954.

1811   Friedman, J. "Belafonte's Showmanship High Spot in Grove Date."
        Billboard 66:34, September 4, 1954.

1812   "People Are Talking About...." Vogue 124:125, December 1954.

1813   "Belafonte Discusses Plans for 'Negro Anthology' Tour." down beat
        21:2, December 29, 1954.

1814   "Copacabana, N.Y." Variety 197:64, February 9, 1955.

1815   "Caught in the Act." down beat 22:4, March 23, 1955.

1816   "Fairmont, San Francisco." Variety 199:53, August 31, 1955.

1817   "Palmer House, Chi." Variety 200:64, November 16, 1955.

1818   "Chronicle and Comment." Catholic Choirmaster 41:181-182, Winter
        1955.

1819   "Belafonte's Best Year; Singer's Popularity, Income Soar." Ebony
        11:56-60, March 1956.

1820   "Eden Roc, Miami Beach." Variety 202:54, March 7, 1956.

1821   "Riviera, Las Vegas." Variety 203:116, July 25, 1956.

1822   "Palmer House, Chi." Variety 203:54, August 22, 1956.

1823   "Waldorf-Astoria, N.Y." Variety 204:54, September 26, 1956.

1824   "Ambassador, L.A." Variety 205:61, February 6, 1957.

1825   "Riviera, Las Vegas." Variety 205:54, February 27, 1957.

1826   Cerulli, D. "Belafonte; The Responsibility of an Artist." down beat
        24:17-18, March 6, 1957.

1827   _____. "Belafonte--'Just for the Record.'" down beat 24:14,
        March 21, 1957.

1828   _____. "Belafonte." down beat 24:17-18, April 4, 1957.

1829   Van Holmes, J. "Belafonte Gives It All He's Got." Saturday Eve-
        ning Post 229:28-29, April 29, 1957.

1830   "Guess Again!" Good Housekeeping 144:70, May 1957.

1831   Ross, I. "Story of a Restless Troubadour." Coronet 42:84-89, May
        1957.

1832   "I Wonder Why Nobody Don't Like Me." Life 42:85-86, May 27,
        1957.

1833   "Heard in Person." down beat 24:31, May 30, 1957.

1834   "Storm over Belafonte." Look 21:138-142, June 25, 1957.

1835   Belafonte, Harry. "Why I Married Julie." Ebony 12:90-95, July
        1957.

1836 "Wild About Harry." Time 70:66, July 1, 1957.

1837 "Harry Belafonte a Tough Critic." Variety 207:1, July 10, 1957.

1838 Kaufman, D. "Belafonte Riding Wax & P.A.s into $1,000,000 Cir-
      cle." Variety 207:55, July 24, 1957.

1839 "Alabama Rep. Summerlin Sees Belafonte's 'Sun' Pic as Commie
      'Propaganda.'" Variety 207:1, August 7, 1957.

1840 Sherman, R. "Guide to Record Collecting: Harry Belafonte Sug-
      gests a Basic Library of American Folk Music." High Fidelity/
      Musical America 4:40, January-February 1958.

1841 Grevatt, R. "The U.S. Pop Scene Is 'Miserable'; Interview with
      Harry Belafonte." Melody Maker 33:9, January 4, 1958.

1842 "Belafonte Becomes 'Big Business.'" Ebony 13:17-20, June 1958.

1843 "Belafonte Bombshell; U.S. Musicians Banned." Melody Maker 33:1,
      August 2, 1958.

1844 Brown, T. "I'm Not Just a Calypso Singer." Melody Maker 33:3,
      August 9, 1958.

1845 "Belafonte Scores in Four-Day Paris Stand; High-Priced Seats SRO."
      Variety 212:11, September 24, 1958.

1846 Ramsey, F. "Popular Folk." Saturday Review 41:61, October 25,
      1958.

1847 Noonan, T. "Belafonte Better Than Ever at Waldorf." Billboard
      70:5, November 24, 1958.

1848 Belafonte, Harry. "My Repertory Must Have Roots." HiFi/Stereo
      Review 2:42-43, January 1959.

1849 "Harry Belafonte and the World of Folk Music." World of Music no.
      6:8, January 1959.

1850 "Lead Man Holler." Time 73:40-42, March 2, 1959.

1851 "Belafonte Seeks Negro Films sans a Race Conflict." Variety 214:1,
      March 11, 1959.

1852 Belafonte, Harry. "Passing Trends in Popular Music." Music Jour-
      nal 17:16, April-May 1959.

1853 Young, A. S. "Harry Belafonte's Debut as a Hollywood Producer."
      Sepia 7:34-39, July 1959.

1854 "Tonight with Belafonte." Variety 215:53, June 17, 1959.

1855 "Movie Maker Belafonte." Ebony 14:94-96, July 1959.

1856 Hentoff, N. "Faces of Harry Belafonte." Reporter 21:38-39, August
      20, 1959.

1857   Morriwon, C. "Harry Belafonte: Transatlantic Troubador." Look
       23:90-94, December 8, 1959.

1858   Shaw, Arnold. Belafonte, an Unauthorized Biography. Philadelphia:
       Chilton Co., 1960.

1859   Chase, S. "Thoughts on Belafonte Palace Stint." Billboard 72:14,
       January 4, 1960.

1860   "Belafonte's Protégée." Ebony 15:109-110, February 1960.

1861   "Cole-Belafonte Start Production Firm." down beat 27:13, February
       4, 1960.

1862   "Harry Belafonte's 'Tonight with Belafonte' TV Program Named the
       Best Among Light Musical Programs of 1959 by Sylvania TV
       Awards." Jet p. 61, February 4, 1960.

1863   "Harry Belafonte and Sidney Poitier Make Show Business Pact: Will
       Appear in Films Each Will Produce in Their Independent Movie
       Companies." Jet p. 60-61, February 18, 1960.

1864   "Reads Jamaican Folk Tales to Youngsters on Reading Out Loud Pro-
       gram." Jet p. 17, March 3, 1960.

1865   "Organizes Cole-Belafonte Enterprises, Inc.; Company Will Produce
       Movies and TV Shows." Jet p. 59, March 10, 1960.

1866   "Actor-Singer, Signs with Revlon to Do 4 One Hour Shows in 1960
       and 1961; His 1st Spectacular, 'An Evening with Belafonte.' Done
       for Revlon in 1959 was Big Success." Jet p. 60, April 7, 1960.

1867   "An Evening with Belafonte Folk Singers." Jet p. 60, May 19, 1960.

1868   "Gets British West Indian Airways Vicki Doll for His Contribution to
       the Understanding of West Indian Culture; Nominated 2 Times for
       'Emmy' Awards in 2 TV Categories." Jet p. 60-61, June 9, 1960.

1869   "Wins a TV Academy Emmy for His Show 'Tonight with Belafonte.'"
       Jet p. 61, July 7, 1960.

1870   "Belafonte Enterprises, Inc., Expands into New Concepts in Music
       for All Media." Jet p. 62, July 14, 1960.

1871   "Belafonte Hits 'Escapist' Show Bizites; Asks More Political Action,
       Less Pools." Variety 219:48, August 10, 1960.

1872   "Belafonte's Melbourne Preem Delayed by Flu, His Pay an Aussie
       High." Variety 219:46, August 17, 1960.

1873   "Signs for 2 Hour Long CBS-TV Specials; One in Nov. 1960; the
       Other in Spring of 1961." Jet 18:58, September 8, 1960.

1874   Falk, R. "Belafonte in Japan." Sepia 8:36-39, October 1960.

1875   "Belafonte in the Holyland." Ebony 16:161-164, December 1960.

1876   "Harry Belafonte a Smash Hit in 2nd TV Spectacular 'New York 19'
       on CBS-TV." Jet 19:56, December 8, 1960.

1877   "Harry Sings Good, Clowns Bad." Billboard 72:35, December 12, 1960.

1878   "Belafonte." Variety 221:49, December 21, 1960.

1879   "Eden Roc, Miami B'ch." Variety 221:68, February 22, 1961.

1880   "Belafonte Forms Disk Operation; RCA to Distrib." Variety 222:43,
       May 24, 1961.

1881   Cartier, J. "Harry Belafonte, le Roi du Calypso." Musica no.
       87:4-8, June 1961.

1882   "One-Man Show." Variety 223:53, July 19, 1961.

1883   Hepburn, D. "Harry Belafonte, the Businessman." Sepia 10:8-11,
       August 1961.

1884   "Harrah's, Lake Tahoe." Variety 223:51, August 16, 1961.

1885   "Belafonte's 'Carnegie Hall' LP Racks Up $5-Mil. Sales Since '59
       Release." Variety 224:44, November 22, 1961.

1886   "Riviera, Las Vegas." Variety 225:46, December 27, 1961.

1887   "Today's Top Record Talent." Billboard Music Week 74:48, April
       7, 1962.

1888   "Harry Belafonte Talks to Teens." Seventeen 21:112, June 1962.

1889   Mendlowitz, L. "Belafonte Breaks Pitt Records." Billboard Music
       Week 74:10, September 8, 1962.

1890   "Americana Hotel, N.Y." Variety 228:58, October 10, 1962.

1891   Grevatt, R. "Belafonte Si, Americana No." Billboard Music Week
       74:6, October 20, 1962.

1892   "Harrah's, Lake Tahoe." Variety 228:42, November 21, 1962.

1893   "Redbook Dialogue." Redbook 120:54-55, March 1963.

1894   "Harrah's, Lake Tahoe." Variety 232:53, November 6, 1963.

1895   "Belafonte in Rights Fight as Duty, Not Fun." Variety 239:1, June
       9, 1965.

1896   "O'Keefe Centre, Toronto." Variety 239:56, June 9, 1965.

1897   "Unit Review." Variety 239:52, August 18, 1965.

1898   Tiegel, E. "Belafonte and Troupe Toast of the W. Coast." Bill-
       board 77:16, August 21, 1965.

1899   "Big-Star Stomp Through Oldtime Harlem; With Report by K. Gould-
       thorpe." Life 60:70-74, February 4, 1966.

1900   "Belafonte Buys Estate." Variety 247:2, July 19, 1967.

1901   "Caesar's Palace, L. V." Variety 248:58, September 20, 1967.

1902   "Cleve.   Benefit a Lotta Discord for Belafonte, His Sponsors, Aretha's
       Fans."   Variety 248:47, October 25, 1967.

1903   "Largest Miami Beach Hotel Nitery Preems with Belafonte, $100,000
       Star."   Variety 249:53, December 20, 1967.

1904   "Caesar's Palace, L. V."   Variety 252:95, September 11, 1968.

1905   Kotlowitz, R.   "Making of 'The Angel Levine.'"   Harper's Magazine
       239:98-100, July 1969.

1906   "Unit Review."   Variety 255:60, July 2, 1969.

1907   "Caesar's Palace, L. V."   Variety 256:112, September 10, 1969.

1908   "Belafonte and Lena Horne Team Up for Superb Show in Las Vegas,
       Nev. at Caesar's Palace."   Jet 36:60-61, September 18, 1969.

1909   "Belafonte Plays Angel on and off the Screen."   Ebony 24:76-78, Oc-
       tober 1967.

1910   "Harry and Lena Off the Cuff!"   Ebony 25:128-129, March 1970.

1911   "Caesar's Palace, L. V."   Variety 260:53, November 4, 1970.

1912   "The Collector's Harry Belafonte--a New Two-Disc Retrospective
       from RCA Displays a Formidable Talent in a Variety of Idioms."
       Stereo Review 25:81-82, December 1970.

1913   Joe, R.   "Talent in Action."   Billboard 82:28, December 5, 1970.

1914   "Belafonte, Others Support Hatcher in Gary."   Jet 4:54-55, April 29,
       1971.

1915   "Concert Reviews."   Variety 263:46, June 16, 1971.

1916   Tiegel, E.   "Talent in Action."   Billboard 83:14, October 30, 1971.

1917   "Caesar's Palace, L. V."   Variety 265:82, November 17, 1971.

1918   "Martin Luther King and W. E. B. Du Bois: A Personal Tribute."
       Freedomways 12, no. 1, 17-21, 1972.

1919   Thompson, M. C.   "Belafonte Bounces Back Big and Black."   Jet
       42:56-62, July 6, 1972.

1920   Gest, D., and J. Spiegelman.   "Harry Belafonte."   Soul 7:8, July
       31, 1972.

1921   "Caesar's Palace, L. V."   Variety 267:95, July 19, 1972; 268:61,
       October 25, 1972.

1922   Deni, L.   "Talent in Action."   Billboard 84:40, November 4, 1972.

1923   "Soul Review."   Soul 8:6, October 1, 1973.

1924   "Caesar's Palace, L. V."   Variety 272:55, October 24, 1973.

1925 "Harry Belafonte, Staples a Top Vegas Opener." Soul 8:8, Novem-
      ber 26, 1973.

1926 Belafonte, Harry. "Concerns and Outlooks; A Performing Artist
      Views the Contours of Contemporary American Culture." Arts in
      Society 11:452, no. 3, 1974.

1927 Robinson, L. "Calypso by Sparrow Is Tasty Dish." Billboard 86:48,
      January 29, 1974.

1928 Kirk, C. "The Screen Goes to Black as TV Opens Its Eyes." Soul
      9:22, April 29, 1974.

1929 "Belafonte Will Leave U. S. to Explore Other Worlds." Billboard
      88:19, July 13, 1974.

1930 "Concert Reviews." Variety 275:93, July 17, 1974.

1931 "Talent in Action." Billboard 86:16, July 20, 1974.

1932 "Caesar's Palace, L. V." Variety 275:55, July 31, 1974.

1933 "Concert Reviews." Variety 283:72, May 26, 1976; 284:54 August
      25, 1976.

1934 Williams, J. "Belafonte Show Masterful for Sickle Cell Audience."
      Billboard 88:28, September 18, 1976.

1935 "Belafonte Plans Turner Production for B'way; May Direct, Not
      Star." Variety 284:76, October 6, 1976.

1936 "Belafonte SRO in Tour of W. Germany." Variety 285:57, November
      10, 1976.

1937 "London, Palladium." Variety 285:118, November 24, 1976.

1938 "Belafonte Wraps Europe Tour with a $1-Mil. Take." Variety 285:67,
      December 1, 1976.

1939 "Belafonte Scores Well in 2d Zurich Booking Despite Steep Prices."
      Variety 288:85, October 12, 1977.

1940 "Concert Reviews." Variety 289:61, November 30, 1977.

1941 "Belafonte Benefits Orchestras." Performing Arts in Canada 15:19,
      no. 1, 1978.

1942 Henricksson, S. A. "Harry Belafonte--Succe Igen!" Musikrevy
      33:18-19, no. 1, 1978.

BENSON, GEORGE, 1943- .

1943 "Tvaa mya Förmaagor." Orkester Journalen 35:5, October 1967.

1944 Morgenstern, D. "Mellow McDuff." down beat 36:19, May 1, 1969.

1945   Albertson, C., et al. "Record Reviews" down beat 36:23, May 29,
       1969; 36:20, June 26, 1969.

1946   Feather, L., and M. Horne. "Newport 69." Jazz Magazine no.
       169-170:36, September 1969.

1947   Morgenstern, D. "Record Reviews: The Other Side of Abbey Road."
       down beat 37:20, June 11, 1970.

1948   "Record Reviews: Beyong the Blue Horizon." down beat 39:22,
       April 13, 1972.

1949   "Chateauvallon de A à Z." Jazz Magazine no. 203:8, August-Septem-
       ber 1972.

1950   Endress, G. "CTI Olympic Jazz." Jazz Podium 21:24-28, August
       1972.

1951   "Record Reviews: White Rabbit." down beat 39:16, October 26,
       1972.

1952   Nolan, H. "The Essence of George Benson." down beat 40:13-14,
       June 7, 1973.

1953   Yellin, R. "George Benson, 'Playing White Man's Music, but Play-
       ing It Black.'" Guitar Player 8:22-25, no. 1, 1974.

1954   "Caught in the Act." Melody Maker 49:24, March 9, 1974.

1955   Henshaw, L. "George Benson: Guitar Giant." Melody Maker 49:16,
       March 16, 1974.

1956   Tomkins, L. "Guitarist George Benson Speaks His Mind." Cre-
       scendo International 12:26-27, April 1974.

1957   "New Acts." Variety 275:68, June 26, 1974.

1958   "Talent in Action." Billboard 86:14, September 28, 1974.

1959   "Concert Reviews." Variety 278:61, April 9, 1975; 278:74, April
       16, 1975.

1960   "Talent in Action." Billboard 87:52, April 26, 1975.

1961   "Concert Reviews." Variety 278:54, April 30, 1975.

1962   "Caught in the Act America." Melody Maker 50:42, July 12, 1975.

1963   "Benson Hedges His Bets." Melody Maker 50:9, September 6, 1975.

1964   "Television Tribute to John Hammond." Coda no. 143:32-34, Novem-
       ber 1975.

1965   "Notes." Jazz Magazine (U.S.) 1:8, no. 2, 1976.

1966   "Concert Reviews." Variety 282:64, February 25, 1976; 282:74,
       March 3, 1976.

1967   "Talent in Action." Billboard 88:36, March 13, 1976.

1968 Williams, J. "Benson Tops R&B, Jazz Sales Charts." Billboard
     88:42, May 29, 1976.

1969 "Concert Reviews." Variety 283:62, June 9, 1976.

1970 "Record Reviews: Breezin'." down beat 43:20, June 17, 1976.

1971 "Talent in Action." Billboard 88:45, June 19, 1976.

1972 Silvert, C. "He's Not a Millionaire Yet, but George Benson, the
     Jazz Guitarist Gone Pop, Is Breezin' All the Way to the Bank."
     Rolling Stone no. 219:20, August 12, 1976.

1973 Mitchell, C. "George Benson: Breezin' Along with a Bullet." down
     beat 43:16-17, September 9, 1976.

1974 "Concert Reviews." Variety 284:74, September 15, 1976.

1975 Feather, L. "Benson--Breezing Through the Chart." Melody Maker
     51:34, September 25, 1976.

1976 "Talent in Action." Billboard 88:47, September 25, 1976.

1977 Feather, L. "Blindfold Test." down beat 43:37, October 21, 1976.

1978 "Records: Breezin'." Rolling Stone no. 225:75, November 4, 1976.

1979 Weathers, D. Benson. "Managing the Muses; The Business Side of
     Black Music." Black Enterprise 7:30, December 1976.

1980 Sippel, J. "Closeup." Billboard 88:66, December 25, 1976. Dis-
     cussion of Benson's recording "Benson Burner."

1981 Cassese, S. "Gold Again." Jazz Magazine (U.S.) 1:16, no. 4, 1977.
     Benson earns another gold record.

1982 Gitler, I. "People: New York." Jazz Magazine (U.S.) 1:10-11, no.
     4, 1977.

1983 Feather, L. "Benson: Man of the Year; The Ups and Downs of
     US Jazz in 1976." Melody Maker 52:24, January 1, 1977.

1984 Kozak, R. "'I Play for Money' George Benson Says." Billboard
     89:40, January 29, 1977.

1985 "Capsule Reviews: Blue Benson." Crawdaddy no. 69:78, February
     1977.

1986 Feather, L. "Fem Fulltraeffar foer George Benson." Orkester
     Journalen 45:5, February 1977.

1987 Heckman, D. "George Benson & Tommy LiPuma: The In Flight
     Sessions." High Fidelity/Musical America 27:134-136, February
     1977.

1988 "Record Reviews: Benson Burner; Blue Benson." Radio Free Jazz
     18:17, February 1977.

1989   Charlesworth, C. "Breezin' with Benson." Melody Maker 52:33,
       February 5, 1977.

1990   "Albums: In Flight." Melody Maker 52:29, February 26, 1977.

1991   Pareles, J. "Fretful Benson: Bop Is No Breeze." Crawdaddy no.
       70:20-21, March 1977.

1992   Ribowsky, M. "How George Benson Made His Million." Sepia 26:71-
       76, March 1977.

1993   "Concert Reviews." Variety 286:74, March 23, 1977.

1994   "Record Reviews: Benson Burner." down beat 44:24, March 24,
       1977.

1995   "Talent in Action." Billboard 89:36, March 26, 1977.

1996   "Records: In Flight." High Fidelity/Musical America 27:138, April
       1977.

1997   Adderton, D. "George Benson Breezes to Top on Twin Talents."
       Jet 52:20-23, April 28, 1977.

1998   Rosovsky, P. "A Man for All Tempos." Variety 287:114, May 18,
       1977.

1999   "Records: In Concert--Carnegie Hall; In Flight." Rolling Stone no.
       239:80, May 19, 1977.

2000   Mieses, S. "High-Flying Benson." Melody Maker 52:41, May 21,
       1977.

2001   "Talent in Action." Billboard 89:40, May 21, 1977.

2002   "Caught in the Act." Melody Maker 52:46, June 4, 1977.

2003   "The Breakout Trio: James, Mann, Benson." Billboard 89:58, July
       9, 1977.

2004   "Caught." down beat 44:50-51, September 8, 1977.

2005   "Records: The Greatest." Crawdaddy no. 77:73, October 1977.

2006   Johnson, H. "George Benson: Still Breezin'." Ebony 33:114-116,
       November 1977.

2007   "Albums: Weekend in L.A." Melody Maker 53:26, January 28, 1978.

2008   Feather, L. "The Good Life." Melody Maker 53:17, February 11,
       1978.

2009   Harrison, E. "Closeup." Billboard 90:74, February 18, 1978.

2010   Feather, L. "Blindfold Test." down beat 45:31, March 23, 1978.

2011   "Records: Weekend in L.A." Rolling Stone no. 261:68, March 23,
       1978; High Fidelity/Musical America 28:142, April 1978.

2012 Feather, L. "George Benson: Superstar Update." down beat 45:13, April 6, 1978.

2013 "Concert Reviews." Variety 290:124, April 19, 1978.

2014 "Record Reviews: Weekend in L.A." down beat 45:22, May 4, 1978.

2015 Stern, C. "Riffs: George Benson's Broadway Masquerade." Village Voice 23:65, May 15, 1978.

2016 "Talent in Action." Billboard 90:67, May 20, 1978.

2017 "Caught in the Act." Melody Maker 53:47, June 3, 1978.

2018 Palmer, R. "George Benson's Sweet Ride." Rolling Stone no. 268:7, June 29, 1978.

2019 "Album Reviews: George Benson/Jack McDuff." Crescendo International 16:26-27, July 1978.

2020 Tomkins, L. "The Jazz Success Story of George Benson." Crescendo International 16:20-22, July 1978.

2021 Adderton, D. "Benson Shares His Fame with Family." Jet 54:22-25, July 6, 1978.

2022 Roth, R. "Court Restrains 'Erotic Moods'; N.Y. Judge Prohibits Sale of Disputed Benson LP." Billboard 90:6, July 8, 1978.

2023 "Benson on Broadway." down beat 45:11, July 13, 1978.

2024 "George Benson--Brilliant or Bland?" Jazz Journal International 31:20, August 1978.

2025 Tomkins, L. "How to Make the Most of Yourself--George Benson." Crescendo International 17:6-7, August 1978.

BENTON, BROOK (Benjamin Franklin Peay).

2026 "'Matter of Time' Written by Benton." Billboard 71:6, February 23, 1959.

2027 "To Star on NBC 'Saturday Prom.'" Jet p. 66, November 1960.

2028 Hepburn, D. "Brook Benton the Hit-Maker." Sepia 9:22-23, March 1961.

2029 "Freddie's, Mpls." Variety 226:58, February 28, 1962.

2030 "Brook Benton." Ebony 18:44-50, May 1963.

2031 "Basin St. East, N.Y." Variety 230:213, May 8, 1963.

2032 "New Brook Benton." Sepia 12:25-30, September 1963.

2033 Coleman, R. "Welcome Benton!--Mystery Man of Pop Music." Melody Maker 38:7, October 12, 1963.

2034 "Copacabana, N.Y." <u>Variety</u> 243:46, June 29, 1966.

2035 "Hotel Roosevelt, N.O." <u>Variety</u> 243:53, August 17, 1966.

2036 "Harolds, Reno." <u>Variety</u> 244:62, September 14, 1966.

2037 "Piccadilly, Glasgow." <u>Variety</u> 249:59, January 10, 1968.

2038 "Huki Lau, New Orleans." <u>Variety</u> 278:343, May 7, 1975.

2039 Jones, M. "Golden Brook." <u>Melody Maker</u> 50:30, July 19, 1975.

2040 "Rainbow Grill, N.Y." <u>Variety</u> 280:79, September 24, 1975.

2041 Brown, G. "Solid Gold Benton." <u>Melody Maker</u> 51:46, April 10, 1976.

2042 Smallwood, D. "Rainy Years in America Sent Benton to Europe." <u>Jet</u> 53:60-61, January 5, 1978.

2043 "Brook Benton; On the Come-Back Trail." <u>Ebony</u> 33:164-166, May 1978.

BERRY, CHUCK (Charles Edward Anderson), 1926- .

2044 "New Acts." <u>Variety</u> 205:62, February 6, 1957.

2045 Roberts, C. "The Great Provider of the Big Beat Boom, That's Chuck Berry." <u>Melody Maker</u> 38:7, July 20, 1963.

2046 _____. "Berry's Back!" <u>Melody Maker</u> 38:8-9, November 16, 1963.

2047 Grevatt, R. "Chuck Berry Bounces Back." <u>Melody Maker</u> 39:9, April 25, 1964.

2048 Roberts, C. "Great, Chuck, Just Great!" <u>Melody Maker</u> 39:3, May 16, 1964.

2049 "Blind Date with Chuck Berry." <u>Melody Maker</u> 39:3, May 30, 1964.

2050 "Am I Coming Back? Yes! Definitely!" <u>Melody Maker</u> 39:7, June 6, 1964.

2051 Fox, C. "Chuck Berry, John Lee Hooker and Jimmy Witherspoon." <u>Jazz Monthly</u> 10:5, July 1964.

2052 "Industry Finds Gold Mine in Chuck Berry Material." <u>Cash Box</u> 25:6, August 29, 1964.

2053 "Berry Bounces Back." <u>Melody Maker</u> 39:1, October 3, 1964.

2054 Jones, M. "Berry's Formula--Old Songs with a New Sound." <u>Melody Maker</u> 39:13, November 14, 1964.

2055 "Chuck--Second Time Around." <u>Melody Maker</u> 40:8, January 9, 1965.

2056   Welch, C. "Backstage with Chuck." Melody Maker 40:16, January
       16, 1965.

2057   "Chuck by Chick." Melody Maker 40:7, February 20, 1965.

2058   "Berry Triomphe à l'Olympia." Jazz Magazine no. 116:14, March
       1965.

2059   "Father Figure Chuck." Melody Maker 42:7, February 25, 1967.

2060   Welch, C. "Caught in the Act." Melody Maker 42:14, March 1967.

2061   Pekar, H. "From Rock to ???" down beat 35:20, May 2, 1968.

2062   "A Gallery of the Greats." BMI p. 28, Summer 1969.

2063   Ochs, E. "Berry the Berries at Fillmore." Billboard 81:36, June
       21, 1969.

2064   Henshaw, L. "Enter the Cool Chuck Berry." Melody Maker 44:5,
       July 12, 1969.

2065   Dove, I. "Berrys, Bishop--Musical Brothers." Billboard 81:27,
       October 18, 1969.

2066   Lydon, M. "Chuck Berry." Ramparts 8:47-56, December 1969.

2067   "Record Reviews: Concerto in B. Goode." down beat 37:18-19,
       January 8, 1970.

2068   "Caught in the Act." down beat 37:29, January 22, 1970.

2069   "Caught in the Act." Melody Maker 45:18, June 27, 1970.

2070   Goodwin, N. "Records: Back Home." Rolling Stone no. 66:46,
       September 17, 1970.

2071   "What Have They Done to My Roots, Ma?" Melody Maker 46:25,
       October 30, 1971.

2072   Welding, P. "Records: San Francisco Dues." Rolling Stone no.
       95:60, November 11, 1971.

2073   Atlas, J. "Stones Roll Up for Chuck." Melody Maker 47:6, Feb-
       ruary 5, 1972.

2074   Hollingworth, R. "Reelin' and Rockin'." Melody Maker 47:24-25,
       February 12, 1972.

2075   Detheridge, D. "Paying Homage to Chuck." Melody Maker 47:14,
       ' April 1, 1972.

2076   Knobler, P. "Chuck Berry: 'Sweet Little 16' Is 32." Crawdaddy
       no. 9:25-27, April 16, 1972.

2077   "Albums: Chuck Berry's Golden Decade." Melody Maker 47:18,
       June 3, 1972.

2078   "Rock 'n' Roll Lives!" Melody Maker 47:24-25, August 5, 1972.

2079   "RecWords: The London Chuck Berry Sessions." Crawdaddy no.
       16:19, September 1972.

2080   Salvo, P. W. "A Conversation with Chuck Berry." Rolling Stone
       no. 122:34-36, November 23, 1972.

2081   Kerrigan, M. "Berry: Going Round and Round." Melody Maker
       47:60, December 9, 1972.

2082   Salvo, P. W. "Chuck Berry Speaks!" Melody Maker 47:32-34,
       December 16, 1972.

2083   "Living Legend Chuck Berry Still Being Discovered." Soul 7:9, De-
       cember 18, 1972.

2084   "A Gallery of the Greats." BMI no. 1:4-13, 1973.

2085   Sandner, W. "Frankfurt A. M: Chuck Berrys Erste Deutschland-
       Tournee." Neue Zeitschrift für Musik 134:235, no. 4, 1973.

2086   Gelormine, P. "Talent in Action." Billboard 85:18, January 20,
       1973.

2087   Plummer, M. "Chuck's Teenage Dream." Melody Maker 48:39,
       January 20, 1973.

2088   "Chuck Storms Out." Melody Maker 48:1, January 27, 1973.

2089   "Paris." Jazz Magazine no. 209:48, March 1973.

2090   Arrondelle, G. "Chuck Berry in Birmingham." Blues no. 100:50,
       April 1973.

2091   Horne, M. "A Student Speaks: Chuck Berry Is Funky--Plus."
       Music Journal 31:21, May 1973.

2092   "On Record: Chuck Berry's Golden Decade Vol. 2." Jazz & Blues
       3:24, May 1973.

2093   Salvo, P. "Man Who Invented Rock 'n' Roll." Sepia 22:44-46, July
       1973.

2094   "Caught in the Act." Melody Maker 48:36, September 15, 1973.

2095   Brown, G. "Chuck Berry: Daddy of Them All." Melody Maker
       48:35-36, October 6, 1973.

2096   "Records: Bio." Rolling Stone no. 148:79, November 22, 1973.

2097   Benjamin, S. "Chuck Berry's No-Show at Scranton Rock Date Stirs
       $6,435 Refund Snag." Variety 269:41, December 27, 1972.

2098   "Court Closes Berry's Mo. Park Six Months After Rock Concert
       'Disorders.'" Variety 276:78, September 18, 1974.

2099   Harrigan, B. "Reelin' and a-Rockin'." Melody Maker 50:31, March
       1, 1975.

2100 "Chuck Berry: 'Maybellene' the Beginning of Rock 'n' Roll." Soul
      9:11, April 14, 1975.

2101 Hilburn, R. "Chuck Berry." BMI p. 32-33, Fall 1975.

2102 "Spedding's Guitar Heroes." Melody Maker 51:31, April 17, 1976.

2103 Harrigan, B. "Scampi, Chips, and Chuck." Melody Maker 51:8,
      May 22, 1976.

2104 "Jazz en Direct." Jazz Magazine no. 245:4, June-July 1976.

2105 "Talent in Action." Billboard 89:37, February 12, 1977.

2106 "Caught in the Act." Melody Maker 52:67, May 14, 1977.

2107 "Concert Reviews." Variety 289:84, January 18, 1978.

2108 Stewart, J. "Guitar Notebook: Chuck Berry." Guitar Player 12:135,
      August 1978.

2109 "Chuck Berry Didn't Show His Best Side While Down Under." Variety
      292:49, August 9, 1978.

BIRD see PARKER, CHARLES CHRISTOPHER.

BLAKE, EUBIE (James Hubert), 1883- .

2110 "Sissle and Blake; Oldest Vaudeville Team Celebrates 40th Anniver-
      sary in Show Business." Ebony 10:113-114, March 1955.

2111 Montgomery, M. "Eubie Blake Rollography." Record Research no.
      27:19, March-April 1960.

2112 _____. "Revised Eubie Blake Rollography." Record Research
      no. 33:16, March 1961.

2113 Williams, M. "With Blake and Lee in Europe." down beat 31:14-
      17, May 7, 1964.

2114 "Eubie Blake Celebrates His 82nd Birthday." Second Line 16:23,
      January-February 1965.

2115 Davies, J. R. "Eubie Blake, His Life and Times." Storyville no.
      6:19-20, August 1966; no. 7:12-13, October 1966.

2116 Schwimmer, M. "4th Annual Ragtime Festival." Jazz Report 6:29-
      30, no. 3, 1968.

2117 Norris, J. "They Still Play Ragtime." down beat 35:14, October
      17, 1968.

2118 Ackerman, P. "Blues Pianist Blake Takes Session at Studio in
      Stride." Billboard 81:6, February 22, 1969.

2119   Bellantonio, D. D. "Eubie Blake." Jazz & Pop 8:24-26, March
       1969.

2120   Feather, L. "Ragtimer's Heros of Yore." Ragtimer p. 6-7, No-
       vember-December 1969.

2121   Albertson, C., et al. "Record Reviews." down beat 36:26, Decem-
       ber 25, 1969.

2122   Affeldt, P. E. "Jazz Miscellany." Jazz Report 7:4, no. 3, 1970.

2123   Stanleigh, B. "Jazz." Audio 54:76, February 1970.

2124   Wyndham, T. "Record Review." Ragtimer p. 4-6, March-April,
       1970.

2125   Winner, L. "Records: The Eighty-Six Years of Eubie Blake." Roll-
       ing Stone 54:50, March 19, 1970.

2126   "Yale University Band Recruits Ted Lewis, Sissle and Blake as Hon-
       orary Members." Variety 258:216, April 2, 1970.

2127   "Eubie Blake Honored." Variety 259:47, June 17, 1970.

2128   Wilson, J. S. "He's the Dean of Jazz Piano." Ragtimer p. 12,
       July-August 1970.

2129   "Eubie Blake Honored." International Musician 69:13, August 1970.
       Blake receives the first James P. Johnson Award.

2130   Harris, S. "3rd Discographical Conference." Jazz and Pop 9:51,
       September 1970.

2131   Blesh, Rudi. Combo: USA; Eight Lives in Jazz. Philadelphia:
       Chilton Book Co., 1971. Musicians discussed are Louis Arm-
       strong, Sidney Bechet, Charlie Christian, Billie Holiday, Gene
       Krupa, Jack Teagarden, Lester Young, and Blake.

2132   Mitchell, B. "Where It Was; A Ragtime Happening 1971." Jazz Re-
       port 7:3-4, no. 5, 1971.

2133   Saal, H. "Mr. Ragtime." Newsweek 72:99, February 22, 1971.

2134   Mohr, S. "Eubie Blake Evoque Ses Souvenirs." Jazz Hot no. 278:16-
       17, December 1971.

2135   Bingham, T. "Great American Dream Machine." Jazz Report 8:8,
       no. 2, 1972.

2136   "Record Reviews: The Eighty-Six Years of Eubie Blake." Coda
       10:20, no. 5, 1972.

2137   Fried, A. G. "New York Premiers of Two Works on Albright Pro-
       gram." Music 6:30-31, March 1972.

2138   "Concert Reviews." Variety 266:58, March 8, 1972.

2139   "Eubie Blake, 89, Is Life of His Party." down beat 39:13, March
       30, 1972.

2140 Dance, S. "Jazz." Music Journal 30:22, June 1972.

2141 "Recording of Special Merit: Eubie Blake." Stereo Review 28:105,
      June 1972.

2142 Citron, P. "Joe Jordan and Eubie Blake Combine Their Talents at
      Omaha." Ragtimer p. 8-10, July-August 1971. Reprinted from
      the Omaha World-Herald.

2143 Wilson, J. S. "Eubie Blake." International Musician 71:6, July
      1972.

2144 "Piano Professors Played Rag from Back Alleys to Concert Halls."
      Life 73:49, July 21, 1972.

2145 "Rebirth of Ragtime." Life 73:46-47, July 21, 1972.

2146 Hyder, W. "The Roaring Ragtime Odyssey of Eubie Blake." Rag-
      timer p. 4-10, January-February 1973. Reprinted from the Sun
      Magazine, Baltimore, October 15, 1972.

2147 Rusch, R. D. "Blake." Jazz Journal 25:5, September 1972.

2148 Bolcom, W. and R. Kimball. "The Words and Music of Noble Sis-
      sle & Eubie Blake." Stereo Review 29:56-64, November 1972.

2149 "Songsmith Eubie Blake Concertizing at Age 89." Variety 268:1,
      November 8, 1972.

2150 Gilmore, M. S. "King of Ragtime." Sepia 21:7-74, December 1972.

2151 "Baltimore in Tribute to Native Son Blake." down beat 39:9, Decem-
      ber 7, 1972.

2152 "Still Shuffling." Time 100:97, December 18, 1972.

2153 Affeldt, P. E. "Editorial." Jazz Report 8:4, no. 3, 1973.

2154 Earwaker, B. "Eubie Blake." Footnote 5:18-22, no. 1, 1973.

2155 Kimball, Robert, and William Bolcom. Reminiscing with Sissle and
      Blake. New York: Viking Press, 1973.

2156 King, Bobbi. "Eubie Blake, a Legend in His Own Lifetime." Black
      Perspectives in Music 1:151-156, no. 2, 1973.

2157 "Record Reviews: Eubie Blake, Volume 1." Coda 11:17-18, no. 1,
      1973.

2158 Southern, E. "A Legend in His Own Lifetime; Conversation with
      Eubie Blake." Black Perspectives in Music 1:50-59, no. 1, 1973.

2159 "Concert Reviews." Variety 269:57, January 17, 1973.

2160 "For Eubie Blake, Life Begins at Ninety." down beat 40:11-12,
      March 29, 1973.

2161 Feather, L. "Blindfold Test." down beat 40:27, May 24, 1973.

2162   Balliett, W. "Musical Events." New Yorker 49:96, June 16, 1973.

2163   MacInnes, I. "Dr. James Hubert Blake." Ragtimer p. 5, July-
       August 1973.

2164   Bailey, P. "A Love Song to Eubie." Ebony 28:94-99, July 1973.

2165   "On Record: His Earliest Piano Rolls." Jazz & Blues 3:17, Oc-
       tober 1973.

2166   Thacker, E. "Ragtime Roots: African and American Minstrels."
       Jazz & Blues 3:406, December 1973.

2167   ["Eubie Blake's 90th Birthday Celebration."] ASCAP Today 6:12,
       no. 2, 1974.

2168   "Happy Birthday Greetings to Eubie Blake on His 91st Birthday Feb.
       7, 1974." Ragtimer p. 5-9, January-February 1974.

2169   Lundberg, P. "Letters." Ragtimer p. 17-18, March-April 1974.

2170   Daubresse, J. P. "91 Years Young: Eubie Blake." Jazz Hot no.
       307:22, July-August 1974.

2171   Robinson, L. "Eubie Blake Remembers Rag Times." Billboard
       86:32, October 26, 1974.

2172   "Record Reviews: Eubie Blake Introducing Jim Hession." Coda
       12:13, no. 6, 1975.

2173   Choice, H. "Eubie: Ragtime to Broadway and Back Again." Rag-
       timer p. 4-8, January-February 1975.

2174   "Eubie Blake Goes to Harvard." Ragtimer p. 16-17, March-April
       1975. Reprinted from the Christian Science Monitor February 10,
       1975.

2175   MacInnes, I. "Eubie Blake." Ragtimer p. 4-5, May-June 1975.

2176   Nevers, D., et al. "Nice: Ragtime to Bop." Jazz Hot no. 319:22-
       26, September 1975.

2177   Cuff, J. "The Ragtime Society Annual Bash '1975.'" Ragtimer p.
       4-16, November-December 1975.

2178   "Talent in Action." Billboard 87:38, November 1, 1975.

2179   "Ivory Action in Triplicate." down beat 42:11, December 18, 1975.

2180   Newberger, E. H. "The Transition from Ragtime to Improvised
       Piano Style." Journal of Jazz Studies 3:10-11, no. 2, 1976.

2181   "To Our Active 93 Year Old Fellow Ragtimer Eubie Blake." Rag-
       timer p. 9, January-February 1976.

2182   "A Special Birthday Party for Eubie Blake." Ragtimer p. 12-14,
       March-April 1976. Reprinted from the New Yorker March 8, 1976.

2183   "Birthday Party." New Yorker 52:30-32, March 8, 1976.

2184 "Talent in Action." Billboard 88:29-30, April 24, 1976.

2185 "Eubie Blake--Is the Oldest Living Member of A.S.C.A.P." Rag-
      timer p. 18, July-August 1976.

2186 "Truman Library Gets Sissle & Blake's 'I'm Just Wild About Harry.'"
      Variety 248:1, September 27, 1976.

2187 Morath, M. "93 Years of Eubie Blake." American Heritage 27:56-
      65, October 1976.

2188 Newberger, E. H. "The Development of New Orleans and Stride
      Piano Styles." Journal of Jazz Studies 4:56, no. 2, 1977.

2189 "Around the World." Coda no. 155:31-32, May-June 1977.

2190 Isacoff, S. "Eubie Blake: Playing and Writing Great Ragtime for
      Eighty Years." Contemporary Keyboard 3:8-9, August 1977.

2191 "Broadway Jazz." Swinging Newsletter 8:5, no. 36, 1978.

2192 "Broadway Jazz." Swinging Newsletter 8:5, no. 36, 1978. A re-
      view of Blake's "Shuffle Along."

2193 Dobie, W. "'Eubie' Heading for Broadway." Swinging Newsletter
      8:7, no. 38, 1978.

2194 Kimball, R. "Eubie Blake at 95." ASCAP Today 9:20, no. 1, 1978.

2195 Vogel, F. G. "Eubie!!" Jazz Magazine (U.S.) 2:32-35, no. 4,
      1978.

2196 "The Dean of Ragtime." Ragtimer p. 8-9, January-February 1978.
      A celebration is held in honor of Blake's 95th birthday.

2197 Giddins, G. "Theatre: Wild About Eubie." Village Voice 23:71-72,
      February 13, 1978. Blake's "Shuffle Along" is examined.

2198 "Composer Eubie Blake Celebrates 95th Birthday." Music Trades
      126:75, March 1978.

2199 "Show Out of Town." Variety 291:86, June 21, 1978. A review of
      "Eubie" performed at the Walnut Street Theatre in Philadelphia.

2200 "You Will Be Just Wild About 'Eubie!'" Ragtimer p. 5-8, July-
      August 1978.

2201 Jones, M. "Eubie: Blooming Youth." Melody Maker 53:23, August
      5, 1978.

2202 "Pro-file: Eubie Blake--Ragtime Giant." International Musician
      77:8, September 1978.

2203 Ripp, A. "There's Also Eubie!" Horizon 21:92-93, September 1978.

2204 Fox, T. C. "Theatre: Shuffled Aback." Village Voice 23:136, Oc-
      tober 2, 1978.

2205 Joe, R. "Eubie Blake Songs Basis for 'Extraordinary' Show." Bill-
      board 90:14, October 21, 1978.

2206 Gottfried, M. "Theater: Openings in the Non-News Vacuum." Sat-
      urday Review 5:54, November 25, 1978.

2207 Montgomery, M. "Eubie Blake Piano Rollography." Record Re-
      search no. 159-160:4-5, December 1978.

2208 "Good-Looking." New Yorker 54:25-26, December 25, 1978.

2209 Carter, Lawrence T. Eubie Blake: Keys of Memory. Detroit: Ba-
      lamp Pub., 1979.

2210 Rose, Al. Eubie Blake. New York: Schirmer Books, 1979. In-
      cludes discography, piano rollography, and filmography.

BRAXTON, ANTHONY.

2211 Litweiler, J. "Caught in the Act." down beat 34:25-26, May 18,
      1967.

2212 Gifford, B. "Chigago: The 'New' Music." Jazz and Pop 8:40-41,
      January 1969.

2213 Alessandrini, P. "Jazz on the Grass." Jazz Magazine no. 169-
      170:9, September 1969.

2214 "Les Nouvelles Tetes de la Nouvelle Musique." Jazz Magazine no.
      171:23, October 1969.

2215 Caux, D. "A Propos du Groupe d'Anthony Braxton." Jazz Hot no.
      255:8-9, November 1969.

2216 Litweiler, J. "Three to Europe." Jazz Monthly no. 177:20-22, No-
      vember 1969.

2217 "Disques du Mois." Jazz Magazine no. 176:38, March 1970.

2218 Smith, W. "Chicago: Winds of Change." Jazz and Pop 9:18-20,
      April 1970.

2219 Cooke, J. "Record Review: Three Compositions of New Jazz."
      Jazz Monthly no. 183:18, May 1970.

2220 Smith, W. "Record Reviews: Anthony Braxton." Jazz and Pop
      9:54-55, September 1970.

2221 Levin, R. "Anthony Braxton and the Third Generation." Jazz and
      Pop 9:12-14, October 1970.

2222 Braxton, Anthony. "KN-(J-6) 1 R10." Source 5:40-45, no. 2, 1971.

2223 Constant, D. "La Quadrature du Cercle." Jazz Magazine no. 187:7,
      March 1971.

2224 Klee, J. H. "Record Reviews: For Alto." down beat 38:18, June 24, 1971.

2225 Charles, P. "Disques du Mois: This Time." Jazz Magazine no. 194:32-33, November 1971.

2226 Loupias, B. "Chronique des Disques: Recital Paris 71." Jazz Hot no. 278:33-34, December 1971.

2227 Millroth, T. "Great Black Music." Nutida Musik 16:43-50, no. 2, 1972-1973.

2228 Goddet, L. "Braxton au Centre Americain." Jazz Hot no. 279:25, January 1972.

2229 _____. "Den Nya Generationen." Orkester Journalen 40:10-11, January 1972.

2230 "Paris." Jazz Magazine no. 196:34-35, January 1972.

2231 "Disques du Mois: Recital Paris 71." Jazz Magazine no. 197:31, February 1972.

2232 "Paris." Jazz Magazine no. 197:41, February 1972.

2233 Goddet, L. "Braxton au Palace." Jazz Hot no. 281:22, March 1972.

2234 Loupias, B. "Braxton au Musee." Jazz Hot no. 281:22, March 1972.

2235 "Record Reviews: This Time." Jazz & Blues 1:25, March 1972.

2236 Echenoz, J., and B. Loupias. "Anthony Braxton." Jazz Hot no. 282:4-5, April 1972.

2237 "Caught in the Act." Melody Maker 47:58, June 24, 1972.

2238 "Disques du Mois: Saxophone Improvisations Series F; Donna Lee." Jazz Magazine no. 202:25, July 1972.

2239 "Chronique des Disques: Saxophone Improvisations Serie F." Jazz Hot no. 286:26, September 1972.

2240 Delmas, J. "Autour d'un Disque: Donna Lee, ou On Est Toujours Trop Bon avec les Femmes." Jazz Hot no. 286:23, September 1972.

2241 "Caught in the Act." down beat 39:36, September 14, 1972.

2242 Carles, P. "Braxton: Le Jazz Est une Musique Dangereuse." Jazz Magazine no. 205:12-17, November 1972.

2243 "American Center." Jazz Magazine no. 206:47, December 1972.

2244 Carles, P. "Braxton: Le Jazz Est une Musique Dangereuse." Jazz Magazine no. 206:18-21, December 1972.

2245 McRae, B. "Avant Courier." Jazz Journal 25:20-21, December 1972.

2246   Tepperman, B. "Heard and Seen." Coda 11:43-44, no. 3, 1973.

2247   Dutilh, A. "Anthony Braxton à l'American Center." Jazz Hot no.
       290:24, January 1973.

2248   Delmas, J. "Les Braxtons n'En Font qu'Un." Jazz Hot no. 293:18-
       19, April 1973.

2249   Cardat, P. "Braxton-Bailey aux Gemeaux." Jazz Hot no. 294:21,
       May 1973.

2250   "Jazz en Direct." Jazz Magazine no. 212:32, June 1973.

2251   "Pas d'Entrechats pour Braxton." Jazz Hot no. 295:22, June 1973.

2252   "Annan Bild av Braxton." Orkester Journalen 41:9, September 1973.

2253   Dutilh, A. "Chateauvallon." Jazz Hot no. 298:27-29, October 1973.

2254   Kumpf, H. "Chateauvallon Jazz Festival 1973." Jazz Podium 22:24-
       25, October 1973.

2255   "The Anthony Braxton Discography." Coda 11:10-11, no. 8, 1974.

2256   "Heard and Seen." Coda 12:37-38, no. 1, 1974. Review of Brax-
       ton's "ADGMB" and "HM--421."

2257   "Record Reviews: America 30; The Complete Braxton; Freedom;
       Saxophone Improvisations Series F; Town Hall 1972; Trio." Coda
       11:15-16, no. 8, 1974.

2258   Smith, B. "The Anthony Braxton Interview." Coda 11:2-8, no. 8,
       1974.

2259   Townley, R. "Anthony Braxton." down beat 41:12-13, February 14,
       1974.

2260   "Caught in the Act." Melody Maker 49:33, July 6, 1974.

2261   "Jazz Records: The Complete Braxton." Melody Maker 49:49, July
       27, 1974.

2262   McRae, B. "Avant Courier: Lookout Form." Jazz Journal 27:19,
       August 1974.

2263   Dutilh, A. "Anthony Braxton en Avignon." Jazz Hot no. 308:24,
       September 1974.

2264   Kumpf, H. "Solo Musik--ein Weg zur Emanzipation; Anthony Brax-
       ton." Jazz Podium 23:12-14, September 1974.

2265   Delmas, J. "Comment Anthony Ortega Fait Sa Musique avec un
       Jugement Circonstancie sur la Relation Konitz/Ortega/Braxton."
       Jazz Hot no. 311:14-17, December 1974.

2266   "Heard and Seen." Coda 12:35-37, no. 3, 1975; 12:37-38, no. 6,
       1975.

2267 "Record Reviews: New York, Fall 1974." Coda 12:24-25, no. 7,
      1975.

2268 "Record Reviews: Duo; In the Tradition; New York, Fall 1974."
      down beat 42:18, June 5, 1975.

2269 "Records: New York, Fall 1974." Rolling Stone no. 189:66, June
      19, 1975.

2270 Dutilh, A. "Anthony Braxton Solitaire et Sublime." Jazz Hot no.
      318:26, July-August 1975.

2271 Goddet, L. "Braxton's Back." Jazz Hot no. 318:21, July-August
      1975.

2272 "Anthony Braxton." Jazz Magazine no. 234:32-33, July 1975.

2273 "Reviews: Anthony Braxton New York, Fall 1974." Radio Free Jazz
      15:13-14, July 1975.

2274 Albertson, C. "Avant-garde Jazz Finds an Unexpected Outlet on the
      Arista Label." Stereo Review 35:90-91, August 1975.

2275 Lake, S. "I Made More Money at Chess Than at Music." Melody
      Maker 50:48, October 11, 1975.

2276 "Talent in Action." Billboard 87:38, November 1, 1975.

2277 "Heard and Seen." Coda no. 144:45, January-February 1976.

2278 "Record Reviews: Duo." Coda no. 144:23-24, January-February
      1976.

2279 "A Space Concert Series." Coda no. 144:32-33, January-February 1976.

2280 "Record Reviews: Five Pieces 1975." down beat 43:20, January 15,
      1976.

2281 Albertson, C. "Anthony Braxton: Improvisations as Liberated and
      Fresh as Louis Armstrong's." Stereo Review 36:76, February
      1976.

2282 "Caught." down beat 43:41, March 25, 1976.

2283 "Records: Five Pieces 1975." Crawdaddy no. 59:73-74, April 1976.

2284 "Around the World: Los Angeles." Coda no. 147:27, May 1976. A
      concert review.

2285 "Jazz Albums: Five Pieces 1975." Melody Maker 51:30, May 29,
      1976.

2286 "Record Reviews: In the Tradition--Vol. 2." Jazz Journal 29:30-31,
      June 1976.

2287 Dutilh, A. "Discographie d'Anthony Braxton." Jazz Hot no. 329:46-
      49, July-August 1976.

2288   Occhiogrosso, P.   "Anthony Braxton Explains Himself."   down beat
       43:15-16, August 12, 1976.

2289   "Records: Creative Orchestra Music 1976."   Rolling Stone no. 219:59-
       60, August 12, 1976.

2290   "Caught in the Act Extra."   Melody Maker 51:37, August 28, 1976.

2291   "Record Reviews: Creative Orchestra Music 1976; In the Tradition,
       Volume 2."   down beat 43:20, October 7, 1976.

2292   "Record Reviews: Saxophone Improvisations/Series F."   Jazz Journal
       29:24-25, November 1976.

2293   Berendt, J. E.   "Berlin Jazz Days 76."   Jazz Hot no. 333:19-21,
       December 1976.

2294   DeMuth, J.   "Anthony Braxton--George Lewis."   Cadence 2:3-4, De-
       cember 1976.

2295   _____.   "People: Chicago."   Jazz Magazine (U. S.) 1:19-20, no.
       3, 1977.

2296   "Record Reviews: Saxophone Improvisations/Series F."   Jazz Forum
       no. 45:64, 1977.

2297   Tepperman, B.   "Perspectives on Anthony Braxton."   Jazz Forum
       no. 45:34-37, 1977.

2298   "Record Reviews: Creative Orchestra Music 1976; Five Pieces."
       Coda no. 153:12-13, January-February 1977.

2299   "Record Reviews: Saxophone Improvisations/Series F."   down beat
       44:26, January 27, 1977.

2300   Buhles, G.   "Bebop und die Folgen: Avant Gardisten von Heute vor
       dem Hintergrund der Modernen Jazztradition."   Jazz Podium 26:14-
       16, February 1977.

2301   "Duets 1976."   Radio Free Jazz 18:12-13, February 1977.

2302   "Record Reviews: Duets 1976, with Muhal Richard Abrams."   down
       beat 44:20, February 10, 1977.

2303   "Around the World."   Coda no. 154:31, March-April 1977.

2304   "Records: Duets 1976."   High Fidelity/Musical America 27:138-139,
       April 1977.

2305   Balliett, W.   "Jazz: New York Notes."   New Yorker 53:84-90, April
       4, 1977.

2306   "Around the World: America."   Coda no. 155:26-28, May-June 1977.
       Review of concerts in Michigan.

2307   "En Direct."   Jazz Magazine no. 255:7, June 1977.

2308   Moussaron, J. P.   "L'Aube de Braxton."   Jazz Magazine no. 255:28-
       29, June 1977.

2309 Blumenthal, B. "Reedman Anthony Braxton Plays by His Own Rules." Rolling Stone no. 240:30-31, June 2, 1977.

2310 _____. "Anthony Braxton Topp i Goeteborg." Orkester Journalen 45:16, July-August 1977.

2311 Millroth, T. "Braxton Taende Publiken." Orkester Journalen 45:9, July-August 1977.

2312 Regnier, B. "Anthony Braxton Envahit l'Espace." Jazz Hot no. 339-340:60, July-August 1977.

2313 Wachtmeister, H. "Anthony Braxton--Skapare av Musiki Maanga Medier." Orkester Journalen 45:8-9, July-August 1977.

2314 Bachmann, K. R. "Anthony Braxton Quintett." Jazz Podium 26:19, July 1977.

2315 McRae, B. "Arena: Braxton, Bailey & Company--the Art of Ad Hoc Ad Lib." Jazz Journal International 30:22-23, July 1977.

2316 "Jazz Albums: Company 2." Melody Maker 52:30, July 16, 1977.

2317 Caroli, D. "Braxton Scores at Milan Festival." Jazz Journal International 30:16, August 1977.

2318 "Records: The Montreux/Berlin Concerts." Crawdaddy no. 75:70, August 1977.

2319 "Jazz Albums: The Montreux/Berlin Concerts." Melody Maker 52:18, August 6, 1977.

2320 Saal, H. "Two Free Spirits." Newsweek 90:52-53, August 8, 1977. Braxton and Keith Jarrett are discussed.

2321 "Caught." down beat 44:41, August 11, 1977.

2322 McRae, B. "Arena: Vive la Difference." Jazz Journal International 30:32-33, September 1977.

2323 "Record Reviews: The Complette Braxton." Jazz Journal International 30:35, September 1977.

2324 Wachtmeister, H. "Anthony Braxton." Orkester Journalen 45:15, September 1977.

2325 Kumpf, H. H. "Jazz und Avantgarde." Musik und Bildung 9:523-525, October 1977.

2326 Watchtmeister, H. "Anthony Braxton." Orkester Journalen 45:17, October 1977.

2327 "Record Reviews: The Montreux/Berlin Concerts; Time Zones." down beat 44:29, October 20, 1977.

2328 "Jazz Albums: Together Alone." Melody Maker 52:33, November 19, 1977.

2329 "Record Reviews: Duets 1976 with Richard Abrams; Solo Live at

Moers Festival; Trio and Duet." Coda no. 159:18-19, February 1, 1978.

2330 "Records: The Complete Braxton 1971." Rolling Stone no. 262:61, April 6, 1978.

2331 "Record Reviews: The Complete Braxton 1971." down beat 45:20, April 20, 1978.

2332 Albertson, C. "Loft Jazz." Stereo Review 40:80-83, May 1978.

2333 Dutilh, A., and L. Goddet. "Anthony Braxton ou l'Art de la Surprise." Jazz Hot no. 349:14, May 1978.

2334 Goddet, L. "Anthony Braxton ou l'Art de la Surprise." Jazz Hot no. 350:14-17, June 1978.

2335 "Record Reviews: The Montreux/Berlin Concerts." Coda no. 161:18, June 1, 1978.

2336 "Jazz en Direct." Jazz Magazine no. 266-267:12, July-August 1978.

2337 "Record Reviews: For Trio." Jazz Journal International 31:35, September 1978.

2338 "Jazz Albums: For Trio." Melody Maker 53:22, September 2, 1978.

2339 Cohen, E. "Anthony Braxton." Coda no. 163:32, October 1, 1978.

BROONZY, BIG BILL (William Lee Conley) (real name: Sammy Sampson), 1893-1958.

2340 "Do You Remember ... Big Bill Broonzy?" Negro Digest 9:25-26, August 1951.

2341 "Meet Bill Broonzy." Melody Maker 27:9, August 11, 1951.

2342 Panassie, H. "Big Bill Doesn't Sell His Music--He Gives it Away." Melody Maker 27:9, September 15, 1951.

2343 Stewart-Baxter, D. "A Date with the Blues." Melody Maker 27:9, September 15, 1951.

2344 "Bill Broonzy Sings Farewell to London." Melody Maker 27:6, September 29, 1951.

2345 Borneman, E. "Big Bill Talkin'." Melody Maker 27:2, September 29, 1951.

2346 Stewart-Baxter, D. "Preachin' the Blues." Jazz Journal 4:3, October 1951.

2347 "Lightly and Politely: About Big Bill Broonzy." Jazz Journal 4:2, November 1951.

2348 Stewart-Baxter, D. "Preachin' the Blues." Jazz Journal 4:13-14, November 1951; 5:8-9, February 1952.

2349   Kahn, H. "They Don't Appreciate Real Blues in France." Melody
       Maker 28:9, February 2, 1952.

2350   "Broonzy." Jazz Journal 5:8-9, March 1952.

2351   Phythian, L. "Broonzy in Liverpool." Jazz Journal 5:7, April 1952.

2352   Race, S. "The Other Side of the Picture." Jazz Journal 5:2, April
       1952.

2353   "Hughes Panassie on Blues Singers." Melody Maker 28:9, May 10,
       1952.

2354   Jackson, A. "Broonzy at the Cambridge Theatre." Jazz Journal
       5:3, December 1952.

2355   Stewart-Baxter, D. "Preachin' the Blues." Jazz Journal 6:4-5, Feb-
       ruary 1953.

2356   Broonzy, William. Big Bill Blues, William Broonzy's Story as Told
       to Yannick Bruynoghe. New York: Oak Publications, 1964, c1955.

2357   "Never Out of Style." Jazz Journal 8:6, April 1955.

2358   Broonzy, Big Bill. "It Was Born in Us to Sing the Blues." Melody
       Maker 31:3, August 27, 1955.

2359   _____. "A 19th Century Blues Session." Melody Maker 31:5,
       September 3, 1955.

2360   _____. "'No Drinking Here!'--Said the Club Boss." Melody
       Maker 31:7, September 17, 1955.

2361   _____. "Work-Songs on the Yellow Dog." Melody Maker 31:5,
       September 24, 1955.

2362   Hutton, J. "Big Bill Took a Back Seat." Melody Maker 31:3, No-
       vember 12, 1955.

2363   Balliett, W. "Billie, Big Bill, and Jelly Roll." Saturday Review
       39:32-33, July 14, 1956.

2364   "Caught in the Act." down beat 23:8, August 22, 1956.

2365   Nicholls, B. "Jazzman's Diary." Jazz Journal 10:3, April 1957.

2366   Olausson, R. "Big Bill Blues." Orkester Journalen 26:13, January
       1958.

2367   "Big Bill Broonzy Benefit Concert." down beat 25:37-38, January
       9, 1958.

2368   "Editorial." Jazz Journal 11:1, February 1958.

2369   "Charity Concert in March." Melody Maker 33:2, February 1, 1958.

2370   Gold, D. "Big Bill Broonzy." down beat 25:15-16, February 6, 1958.

2371   Asbell, B. "The Whisper of Big Bill Broonzy." Melody Maker
       33:13, February 8, 1958.

2372   Komer, A. "Big Bill Broonzy; Some Personal Memories." Jazz
       Journal 11:1, March 1958.

2373   "Maybe I'll Sing Again, Says Big Bill." Melody Maker 33:1, March
       15, 1958.

2374   "Big Bill Broonzy Interviewed by Studs Terkel." Jazz Journal 11:33-
       36, May 1958.

2375   ["Obituary."] Variety 211:79, August 29, 1958.

2376   "500 Pounds 'Blues' for Broonzy." Melody Maker 33:1, August 23,
       1958.

2377   Jones, M. "The Last of a Line." Melody Maker 33:12, August 23,
       1958.

2378   "Big Bill Broonzy Död." Orkester Journalen 26:4, September 1958.

2379   "Best of the Blues." Time 72:39, September 1, 1958.

2380   Lyttelton, H. "There's No Argument--the Money Is Big Bill's."
       Melody Maker 33:11, September 6, 1958. The reference is to
       money earned at charity concerts.

2381   ["Obituary."] down beat 25:11, September 18, 1958.

2382   Terkel, S. "Big Bill's Last Session." Jazz Journal no. 1:9-18, Oc-
       tober 1958.

2383   Gold, D. "Tangents." down beat 25:42, October 2, 1958.

2384   Balliett, W. "Jazz Records." New Yorker 34:94, October 25, 1958.

2385   "Weep No More; Photo-Editorial." Ebony 14:154-155, November 1958.

2386   Terkel, S. "On Big Bill Broonzy and the Blues." Jazz Review 1:28-
       29, December 1958.

2387   Bruynoghe, Y. "Mes Blues, Ma Guitare et Moi; Les Souvenirs de
       Big Bill Broonzy." Jazz Magazine 5:37-39, January 1959; 5:32-34,
       February 1959; 5:22-25, March 1959.

2388   Stewart-Baxter, D. "Blues in the Country." Jazz Journal 12:3-4,
       April 1959.

2389   Bruynoghe, Y. "Mes Blues, Ma Guitare et Moi; Les Souvenirs de
       Big Bill Broonzy." Jazz Magazine 5:27, May 1959.

2390   Vreede, M. E. "A Discography of Georgia Tom and His Associates."
       Matrix no. 31:3-22, October 1960. Broonzy was an associate of
       Thomas A. Dorsey.

2391   Hentoff, N. "Wild Bill's Last Date; Bill Broonzy Story." Reporter
       24:43-44, April 13, 1961.

2392 Hodes, A. "Sittin' in." down beat 28:44, April 13, 1961.

2393 "'Bill Broonzy Story' Set a Standout Contribution to History of the
     Blues." Variety 223:51, June 21, 1961.

2394 Hentoff, N. "A Life in the Blues." HiFi/Stereo Review 7:73, Au-
     gust 1961. Recording of "The Bill Broonzy Story."

2395 Yurchenco, H. "Three Giants of Folk Music." Sing Out 12:57, no.
     3, 1962.

2396 Voce, S. "Big Bill in Concert." Jazz Journal 15:8-10, March 1962.

2397 Huyton, T. "Big Bill's Blues." Matrix no. 57:18-19, February
     1965.

2398 Testoni, G. C. "Il Mondo del Blues." Musica Jazz 21:24-26, June
     1965; 21:14-16, November 1965.

2399 Jones, M. "Magnificent Seven." Melody Maker 43:8, January 13,
     1968.

2400 Korner, A. "A Guide to Blues Guitar." Melody Maker 43:17, Feb-
     ruary 17, 1968.

2401 Williams, M. "Epic II and Others." Saturday Review 52:56, Jan-
     uary 25, 1969.

2402 "A Gallery of the Greats." BMI p. 25, Summer 1969. Focus on
     top musicians in rhythm and blues.

2403 Oliver, P. "The Young Big Bill Broonzy 1928-1935." Jazz Monthly
     no. 173:20-21, July 1969. Discussion of some of Broonzy's earlier
     recordings.

2404 Astbury, R. "Big Bill Broonzy on Archive of Folk Music." Matrix
     no. 86:11, December 1969.

2405 Welding, P. "Big Bill Reconsidered." Saturday Review 53:62-63,
     February 14, 1970. Included in this examination of Broonzy is a
     partial list of his works.

2406 _____. "Blues 'n' Folk: The Young Big Bill Broonzy; Big Bill's
     Blues." down beat 37:22, February 19, 1970.

2407 "Chronique des Disques: Portrait in Blues." Jazz Hot no. 282:24,
     April 1972.

2408 "A Gallery of the Greats." BMI no. 1:4-13, 1973. An examination
     of great musicians in rhythm and blues during the past sixty years.

2409 Gleason, R. J. "Perspectives: The Presence of Legends in a Funky
     Hall." Rolling Stone no. 140:7, August 2, 1973.

2410 Jones, M. "Memories of Broonzy." Melody Maker 50:38, December
     6, 1975.

BROWN, OSCAR CICERO, JR., 1929- .

2411   "Ex-Radio Newscaster in Chicago Becomes a Hit Jazz Singer and
        Song Writer." Jet 19:62, December 22, 1960.

2412   Maher, J. "Promising Bow by Oscar Brown." Billboard Music
        Week 73:10, February 13, 1961.

2413   "New Acts." Variety 221:69, February 15, 1961.

2414   "New Show's Air Appeal for Finances." Life 50:102, April 7, 1961.

2415   "Oscar All the Way." Newsweek 57:90, April 10, 1961.

2416   "Unusual Appeals Bring Broadway Cash." Ebony 16:73-74, June 1961.

2417   "'Freedom Now Suite' May Go on Tour." down beat 28:13, October
        12, 1961.

2418   "People on the Way Up." Saturday Evening Post 234:34-35, Novem-
        ber 18, 1961.

2419   "Blue Angel Lounge, N.Y." Variety 226:60, March 21, 1962.

2420   "Mr. Kicks." Time 79:74, March 30, 1962.

2421   "Caught in the Act." down beat 29:31, August 2, 1962.

2422   Lucraft, H. "I'm Not a Jazz Songer; Interview with Oscar Brown."
        Melody Maker 37:9, August 25, 1962.

2423   "Many Faces of Oscar Brown, Jr." Sepia 11:72-74, September 1962.

2424   "Singer with a Soul." Negro Digest 11:41-43, September 1962.

2425   Feather, L. "Blindfold Test." down beat 29:43, October 11, 1962.

2426   "Crescendo, L.A." Variety 228:76, October 24, 1962.

2427   Gardner, B. "Oscar Brown: Rebel with a Cause." down beat 29:17-
        19, December 6, 1962.

2428   "Troubadour, L.A." Variety 230:59, April 19, 1963.

2429   "Oscar Brown, Jr.: The Flop That Flipped." Sepia 12:18-22, May
        1963.

2430   Dawbarn, B. "Oscar Brown Arrives." Melody Maker 38:9, August
        31, 1963.

2431   Barrett, L. "Oscar Brown, Junior." Jazz Monthly 9:12-14, October
        1963.

2432   Fox, C. "In Person." Jazz Monthly 9:4, November 1963.

2433   "Waldorf-Astoria, N.Y." Variety 233:58, January 15, 1964.

2434 Nahman, P. "Oscar Brown, Chanteur Engage." Jazz Hot no. 195:16-17, February 1964.

2435 Roth, M. "'Black Bottom' Negro Hitting America's Cultural Top, Asserts Oscar Brown Jr." Variety 234:2, April 8, 1964.

2436 "Derns Rest., Stockholm." Variety 234:180, April 29, 1964.

2437 "Cafe Au Go Go, N.Y." Variety 237:59, December 16, 1964.

2438 "Worlds of Oscar Brown, Jr." BMI p. 14, April 1965.

2439 "Cool Elephant, London." Variety 239:56, June 2, 1965.

2440 "In the Press." BMI p. 8-9, July 1967.

2441 "PJ's, L.A." Variety 250:62, May 1, 1968.

2442 "In the Press." BMI p. 10, January 1969.

2443 "Big Time Buck White." Variety 254:74, February 26, 1969.

2444 "'Big Time Buck White' Is Playing in S.F. as Musical." Billboard 81:12, March 15, 1969.

2445 Link, G. "Oscar Brown's Revise Swings at Neat Clip." Billboard 81:36, August 9, 1969.

2446 "Shows on Broadway." Variety 257:54, December 3, 1969. Review of "Big Time Buck White."

2447 "'Buck White' Jabs, Doesn't Jolt." Billboard 81:22, December 13, 1969.

2448 "Ford Foundation's 375 G Grant to Spur Serious Disks Recalls Gary Test." Variety 257:1, January 14, 1970.

2449 "On the Boards." BMI p. 18, February 1970.

2450 Kirby, F. "'Joy' a Joyful Revue as Music, Stars Click." Billboard 82:21, February 7, 1970.

2451 "Happy Medium, Chi." Variety 260:64, September 2, 1970.

2452 "Club Baron, N.Y." Variety 264:47, November 3, 1971.

2453 "Slave Song." BMI no. 5:38-39, 1972.

2454 "Oscar Brown's Showcase for Puerto Rican and Black Youthful Talent." Variety 266:1, March 1, 1972.

2455 "Mister Kelly's, Chi." Variety 270:83, February 14, 1973.

2456 Dove, I. "Talent in Action." Billboard 85:20, April 14, 1973.

2457 "New on the Charts." Billboard 86:21, May 25, 1974.

2458 "Brown Misses; Pointers Right On." Soul 9:14, July 8, 1974.

2459   "Ratso's, Chi." Variety 277:83, January 22, 1975.

2460   "New Acts." Variety 282:81, February 11, 1976.

2461   Carter, J. "Oscar Brown, Jr.: Reaching for the Plenty Cup." En-
       core 5:22-25, March 8, 1976.

2462   "Shows Out of Town." Variety 290:80, February 15, 1978. Brown's
       "In de Beginnin'" performed at the New Locust Theatre, Philadel-
       phia."

2463   "Oscar Brown Files Race Bias Charge vs. Moe Septee in Philly."
       Variety 290:103, March 8, 1978.

2464   "Correction." Variety 290:105, March 15, 1978. A correction to
       the preceding article about the race bias charge.

BULLOCK, AILLENE see TURNER, TINA

BUMBRY, GRACE (Mrs. Andreas Jaeckel).

2465   "Grace Bumbry." Music of the West 13:19, March 1958.

2466   Campbell, A. "San Francisco." Musical Courier 157:38, April
       1958.

2467   "Winning Personalities." Opera News 22:26, April 21, 1958.

2468   Tassie, P. "San Francisco Music Events." Music of the West
       13:16, May 1958.

2469   "Best in Opera." Music and Musicians 8:19, March 1960.

2470   Emery, J. "Bournemouth Symphony Orchestra." Musical Times
       101:173, March 1960.

2471   Senechaud, M. "Bayreuth." Revue Musicale de Suisse Romande
       14:130-131, no. 7, 1961.

2472   Müller, L. "Progressive Brussels." Opera News 25:32, April 8,
       1961.

2473   "Yankee Parsifal." Time 78:47, August 4, 1961.

2474   "Black Venus." Newsweek 58:36, August 7, 1961.

2475   "Negro Singer Stars as 'Venus' in Wagner Festival's Production of
       Opera 'Tannhäuser' at Bayreuth, Germany; Is first Negro to Ap-
       pear at Bayreuth Festival." Jet 20:60, August 19, 1961.

2476   Bernheimer, M. "Bayreuth 1961: The Troubles of Tannhäuser."
       Saturday Review 44:42-43, August 26, 1961.

2477   _____ . "A European Journal." Musical Courier 163:21, Septem-
       ber 1961.

2478   Brunner, G. "Bayreuth." Musical Courier 163:36, September 1961.

2479 Rabsch, E. "Kieler Woche." Musica 15:495, September 1961.

2480 Ruppel, K. H. "Wagner-Festspiele 1961." Neue Zeitschrift für Musik 122:360, September 1961.

2481 Thomas, E. "Danger Signs." Musical America 81:57, September 1961.

2482 Bernheimer, M. "Die Schwarze Venus." Opera News 26:21, October 28, 1961.

2483 Reid, C. "Notes from Abroad." High Fidelity 11:28, November 1961.

2484 Tircuit, H. "Tokyo." Music Magazine 163:58-59, November 1961.

2485 "Black Venus Triumph at Bayreuth." Music and Dance 52:13, December 1961.

2486 "Mademoiselle's Annual Merit Awards." Mademoiselle 54:52, January 1962.

2487 "American Negro Diva's 'Delilah,' a Swiss Click." Variety 255:1, January 3, 1962.

2488 Martin, B. E. "Oriental Variety." Opera News 26:33, February 10, 1962.

2489 "Command Performance." Time 79:46, March 2, 1962.

2490 Eland, C. E. "European Visitors." Opera 13:263, April 1962.

2491 "Dream Come True." Ebony 17:91-95, May 1962.

2492 "Government and the Arts." Music Magazine 164:8-9, May 1962.

2493 "New Mezzo." Time 80:70, November 16, 1962.

2494 "Test by Lieder." Newsweek 60:73, November 19, 1962.

2495 Kolodin, I. "Music to My Ears; Debut at Carnegie Hall." Saturday Review 45:43, November 24, 1962.

2496 Ardoin, J. "Ladies of the Lied." Musical America 82:53-54, December 1962.

2497 Sargeant, W. "Musical Events; Second New York Recital in Carnegie Hall." New Yorker 38:73, December 29, 1962.

2498 Freyse, R. "Schallplatten." Neue Zeitschrift für Musik 124:39-40, no. 1, 1963.

2499 "Grace Bumbry at the Garden." About the House 1:30, no. 3, 1963.

2500 Sigmon, C. "Recitals in New York." Musical America 83:110-111, January 1963.

2501 Cecil, W. "Singers Six." Saturday Review 46:58-59, January 26, 1963.

2502 Salzman, E. "Recitals in New York." Musical America 83:31, Feb-
      ruary 1963.

2503 Kelly, V. "Grace Bumbry: A Singer Comes Home." Look 27:66,
      February 26, 1963.

2504 "America Applauds Grace Bumbry After European Success." Sepia
      12:28-31, May 1963.

2505 Barker, F. G. "Glittering Revival." Music and Musicians 11:37,
      May 1963.

2506 "Covent Garden Opera." Musical Opinion 86:458, May 1963.

2507 "'Don Carlos;' Covent Garden." Opera 14:349-350, May 1963.

2508 Tracey, E. "'Cosi' and 'Don Carlos.'" Musical Times 104:346,
      May 1963.

2509 Knessl, L. "Salzburg: Festspielsommer im Strauss-Gedenkjahr."
      Neue Zeitschrift für Musik 125:443-444, no. 10, 1964.

2510 "Salzburg." Music Review 25:347, no. 4, 1964.

2511 Kolodin, I. "Music to My Ears." Saturday Review 47:28, January
      18, 1964.

2512 ["Recital, New York."] Musical America 84:32, February 1964.

2513 "New York." Musical Leader 96:23, February 1964.

2514 Mackinnon, D. A. "Salzburg Success." Opera News 29:27, Novem-
      ber 14, 1964.

2515 "With Our Honorary Artists." Pan Pipes 57:23, no. 4, 1965.

2516 Kolodin, I. "Music to My Ears." Saturday Review 48:54, October
      23, 1965.

2517 ["Recital, N.Y."] Variety 241:64, November 24, 1965; High Fidelity/
      Musical America 16:137, February 1966.

2518 Osborne, C. L. "Verdi's 'Don Carlo.'" High Fidelity/Musical Amer-
      ica 16:83-85, April 1966. Bumbry's recordings (London) are re-
      viewed.

2519 Seelmann-Eggebert, U. "Mailand: Natur und Schwärmerei." Neue
      Zeitschrift für Musik 127:295-297, July-August 1966.

2520 Boucher, A. "San Francisco." Opera News 31:30, December 24,
      1966.

2521 Price, G. "Barcelona." Opera 18:244, March 1967.

2522 Boucher, A. "San Francisco." Opera News 32:23, October 14, 1967.

2523 Bloomfield, A. "San Francisco." Opera 18:1003, December 1967.

2524 Salzman, E. "In the Cards." Opera News 32:26-27, December 16, 1967.

2525 Kolodin, I. "Music to My Ears." Saturday Review 50:38-39, December 30, 1967.

2526 Frankenstein, A. "San Francisco Report." High Fidelity/Musical America 18:MA19, January 1968.

2527 "People Are Talking About...." Vogue 151:162-163, February 1, 1968.

2528 Blyth, A. "All Is Not Gold...." Music and Musicians 16:33, March 1963.

2529 Chapman, E. "New 'Aida.'" Musical Events 23:26-27, March 1968.

2530 Koegler, H., and A. Jacobs. "'Aida;' Covent Garden." Opera 19:249-250, March 1968.

2531 McVeagh, D. "Aida." Musical Times 109:251, March 1968.

2532 Movshon, G. "Carmen." High Fidelity/Musical America 18:MA7-8, March 1968.

2533 Natan, A. "Gestoertes Gleichgewicht Swischen Szene und Musik." Opernwelt no. 3:20, March 1968.

2534 Smith, P. J. "And We Quote...." High Fidelity/Musical America 18:MA16, March 1968.

2535 Weinstock, H. "New York." Opera 19:210, March 1968.

2536 "Names, Dates and Places." Opera 32:4-5, March 2, 1968.

2537 Barker, F. G. "London." Opera News 32:30, March 9, 1968.

2538 Lang, P. H. "Two Properly Dutiful 'Orfeos' Need a Touch of Irreverence." High Fidelity/Musical America 18:66-67, May 1968.

2539 Tellini, E. "Naples." Opera News 32:27, May 18, 1968.

2540 Gualerzi, G. "Bologna." Opera 19:490, June 1968.

2541 Tellini, E. "Naples." Opera 19:493, June 1968.

2542 Weinstock, H. "Letters." Opera News 32:27, June 15, 1968.

2543 Blyth, A. "Music in London." Musical Times 109:1136, December 1968.

2544 "New York, N.Y." Music and Artists 2:30, no. 2, 1969.

2545 Strongin, T. "M & A Reviews: The Press." Music and Artists 2:45, no. 1, 1969.

2546 Wright, K. A. "From Flop to Pop--Some Thoughts on Bizet's 'Carmen.'" Music 3:6-8, no. 1, 1969.

2547   Spingel, H. O. "Journal des Monats." Opernwelt no. 4:14, April
       1969.

2548   "Names, Dates and Places." Opera News 33:5, April 12, 1969.

2549   Harewood, Lord. "A Week in New York." Opera 20:398, May 1969.

2550   Mayer, M. "The Metropolitan Opera." High Fidelity/Musical Amer-
       ica 19:MA12-13, May 1969.

2551   Oppens, K. "Verdi und Seine Interpreten." Opernwelt no. 6:24,
       June 1969.

2552   Barker, F. G. Women in Conflict." Music and Musicians 17:58,
       July 1969.

2553   "Opera and Ballet in London." Musical Opinion 92:514, July 1969.

2554   "London Opera Diary." Opera 20:726-728, August 1969.

2555   Dettmer, R. "Chicago." Opera 20:1037, December 1969.

2556   McMullen, R. "EMI's New Spoken/Sung 'Carmen.'" High Fidelity/
       Musical America 20:20, January 1970, section 1.

2557   Kolodin, I. "Music to My Ears." Saturday Review 53:21, January
       24, 1970.

2558   "Names, Dates and Places." Opera News 34:5, April 18, 1970.

2559   "Neapel." Oper und Konzert 8:24, May 1970.

2560   Blyth, A. "Grace Bumbry." Opera (Eng) 21:506-510, June 1970.

2561   Weaver, W. "Rome." Opera (Eng) 21:555-556, June 1970.

2562   "London." Oper und Konzert 8:25, July 1970.

2563   Chapman, E. "New 'Salome' Production." Musical Events 25:10-11,
       August 1970.

2564   Goodwin, N. "Innocence and Desire." Music and Musicians 18:28-
       29, August 1970.

2565   Natan, A. "Das Schoene Wilde Tier." Opernwelt no. 8:34-35, Au-
       gust 1970.

2566   Rosenthal, H. "London Opera Diary." Opera (Eng) 21:787-790, Au-
       gust 1970.

2567   "London." Opera News 35:26, September 5, 1970.

2568   Davis, P. G. "Opera on Film: Pitfalls Aplenty." High Fidelity/
       Musical America 20:MA12, October 1970.

2569   Kolodin, I. "Music to My Ears." Saturday Review 53:41, October
       10, 1970.

2570 Oppens, K. "Gemischte Freuden bei Gluck und Verdi." Opernwelt
no. 12:29, December 1970.

2571 Silver, E. "People, Portrait." Essence 1:48-49, January 1971.

2572 "Muenchner Konzerte." Oper und Konzert 9:32, February 1971.

2573 Chapin, L. "Orfeo Races the Furies!" Music Journal 29:26-27,
March 1971.

2574 "Names, Dates and Places." Opera News 35:4-5, April 3, 1971.

2575 "Opera and Ballet in London." Musical Opinion 94:333, April 1971.

2576 Thomas, S. "Grace Bumbry's 'Salome.'" Musical Events 26:30-31,
April 1971.

2577 Greenhalgh, J. "Salome." Music and Musicians 19:53-54, May 1971.

2578 Osborne, C. "London Opera Diary." Opera (Eng) 22:453-454, May
1971.

2579 Kertesz, I. "Vendeguenk: Grace Bumbry." Muzsika 14:30-31, July
1971.

2580 Kolodin, I. "Bach by Rostropovich; Tucker as Samson." Saturday
Review 54:60, December 25, 1971.

2581 Fitzgerald, G. "A New Grace." Opera News 36:14-16, January 8,
1972.

2582 _____. "New York." Opera News 36:30, January 29, 1972. A
review of "Samson et Dalila."

2583 Movshon, G. "America: New Look Forecast." Opera (Eng) 23:127-
128, February 1972.

2584 Schaumkell, C. D. "Saengerstars." Opernwelt no. 7:17, July 1972.

2585 Gualerzi, G. "Florence." Opera (Eng) 23:933, October 1972.

2586 Jacobson, R. "Sacred and Profane." Opera News 38:29, December
29, 1973-January 5, 1974.

2587 "London." Oper und Konzert 11:32-33, no. 6, 1973.

2588 "Muenchen." Oper und Konzert 11:22, no. 4, 1973.

2589 "Names, Dates and Places." Opera News 37:6-7, March 31, 1973.

2590 Stevenson, F. "Dame Judith Speaks of Shakespeare, Verdi and the
Theater." Opera News 37:22-23, May 1973.

2591 Milnes, R. "'Tosca;' Royal Opera." Opera (Eng) 24:553-554, June
1973.

2592 Morris, G. "'Maria Padilla,' 'Lucia' and 'Tosca.'" Music and
Musicians 21:58-60, July 1973.

2593   "Opera and Ballet in London." Musical Opinion 96:508-509, July
        1973.

2594   Movshon, G. "New York." Opera (Eng) 24:797-800, September 1973.

2595   _____, and R. Lawrence. "Summer Singers at the Met; Some
        First Time Roles Highlight June Festival Weeks." High Fidelity/
        Musical America 23:MA12-13, September 1973.

2596   Bailey, P. A. "Grace Bumbry: Singing Is Terrific--But Living Is
        an Art." Ebony 29:66-68, December 1973.

2597   Movshon, G. "Lincoln Center's Opera Houses: The Sound of Mon-
        ey." High Fidelity/Musical America 23:MA15, December 1973.

2598   "Names, Dates and Places." Opera News 38:10-11, December 8,
        1973.

2599   "Muenchen." Oper und Konzert 12:22, no. 6, 1974.

2600   Jenkins, S. "Grace Melzia Bumbry." Stereo Review 32:70-71, Jan-
        uary 1974.

2601   Movshon, G. "New York." Opera (Eng) 25:31-35, January 1974.

2602   Jacobson, R. "Newark." Opera News 38:22, March 30, 1974.

2603   Haynes, H. "Grace Bumbry: International Opera's Super Star."
        Sepia 23:46-48, June 1974.

2604   Galalopoulos, S. "Tosca." Music and Musicians 22:44-45, July
        1974.

2605   "Toronto." Opera Canada 16:36-37, no. 5, 1975. Productions of
        "Salome" and "Louis Riel" in which Bumbry sang major roles.

2606   Davidson, E. "Siciliani." Opera News 39:15, January 18, 1975.

2607   Gould, S. "Milan." Opera (Eng) 26:357-358, April 1975.

2608   "Names, Dates and Places." Opera News 39:7, April 19, 1975.

2609   Bramble, R. "Verona's Subtle 'Turandot.'" Opera (Eng) 26:111,
        Autumn 1975.

2610   Harris, D. "Paris Opera Reaches New Heights; Dukas' 'Ariane'
        Reaffirms French Tradition." High Fidelity/Musical America
        25:MA34-35, December 1975.

2611   Sachs, H., and R. Covello. "Italy--La Scala, Milan." Opera Can-
        ada 17:43-44, no. 2, 1976.

2612   "Names, Dates and Places." Opera News 40:6-7, March 20, 1976.

2613   Lanier, T. P. "New York." Opera News 40:39, April 17, 1976.

2614   "Bumbry to Bolshoi." Variety 284:58, August 11, 1976.

2615   "Grace Bumbry Writes." Opera (Eng) 27:1013, November 1976.

2616   Barker, F. G. "Covent Garden: 'Macbeth.'" Music and Musicians
       25:46, December 1976.

2617   Rosenthal, H. "'Macbeth;' Royal Opera, Covent Garden." Opera
       (Eng) 27:1156-1158, December 1976.

2618   Davis, B. R. "Houston Grand Opera." Opera Canada 18:38, no. 3,
       1977.

2619   Gualerzi, G. "Da Martina Franca: II, III Festival Della Valle
       d'Itria." Revista Italiana di Musicologia 11:406-408, no. 3, 1977.

2620   Pedemonte, V. "Busseto e Martina Franca." Rassegna Musicale
       Curci 30:62-66, no. 2, 1977.

2621   Fischer-Williams, B. "Roman Forum." Opera News 41:31, January
       1, 1977.

2622   Gusev, A. "Greys Meltsiya Bambri." Sovetskaya Muzyka 41:123-
       125, February 1977.

2623   Weber, H. "Frankfurt: Transitional Season." Opera (Eng) 28:280,
       March 1977.

2624   Tellini, E. "Naples: Unrest in Naples." Opera (Eng) 28:889-891,
       September 1977.

2625   "Names, Dates and Places." Opera News 42:8-9, October 1977.

2626   Barker, F. G. "Grace Bumbry." Music and Musicians 26:20-22,
       November 1977.

2627   Hoelterhoff, M. "Interview with Grace Bumbry." Music Journal
       35:4-6, November 1977.

2628   Morsell, F. A. "Grace Bumbry." Crisis 84:446-450, November
       1977.

2629   Blyth, A. "'Don Carlos;' Royal Opera, Covent Garden 7." Opera
       (Eng) 28:1190-1192, December 1977.

2630   Gualerzi, G. "Itria Valley." Opera (Eng) 28:1146, December 1977.

2631   Belotti, G. "'Norma' Nareszcie Wiernie Zrealizowana." Ruch Mu-
       zyczny 22:10-11, no. 9, 1978.

2632   "London: Royal Opera." Opera Canada 19:30-31, no. 4, 1978. Re-
       view of Bumbry's performance in "Norma."

2633   Lingg, A. M. "In the Contest." Opera News 42:23, January 21,
       1978.

2634   "Concert Reviews." Variety 289:91, February 1, 1978.

2635   Movshon, G. "The Metropolitan Opera." High Fidelity/Musical
       America 28:MA28, April 1978.

2636   Barker, F. G. and J. Greenhalgh. "Covent Garden: 'Norma.'"
       Music and Musicians 27:31-32, September 1978.

2637   Jacobs, A. "'Norma;' Royal Opera, Covent Garden." Opera (Eng)
       29:916-919, September 1978.

BURT, GLORIA.

2638   "Little Girl, Big Harp; Playing Since She Was Five, Gloria Burt
       Hopes to Perform with Symphony Orchestra." Ebony 11:31-33,
       August 1956.

2639   Roy, J. H. "Angel and Her Harp." Negro History Bulletin 20:67,
       December 1956.

BUTLER, JERRY (Iceman), 1940- .

2640   "Butler's 'Break Your Heart' Big on Hot 100." Billboard 72:23, De-
       cember 12, 1960.

2641   "R 'n' R May Be on the Way Out but Kids Will Stay with It: Jerry
       Butler." Variety 225:48, February 14, 1962.

2642   "Today's Top Record Talent." Billboard 74:49, April 7, 1962.

2643   "'Moon River'--the Men Who Made the Hit." Billboard 74:19, April
       21, 1962.

2644   "Jerry Butler: History's Hottest Iceman." Ebony 25:64-66, Decem-
       ber 1969.

2645   Eldridge, R. "Jerry Butler, the Ice Man, Cometh." Melody Maker
       45:15, April 11, 1970.

2646   Aletti, V. "Jerry Butler." Rolling Stone no. 57:34-37, April 30,
       1970.

2647   "Apollo, N.Y." Variety 259:56, May 27, 1970.

2648   "Jerry Butler; Some Cool Words About the 'Ice Man.'" Sepia 19:48,
       July 1970.

2649   Butler, Jerry. "Black Music Is Getting Intellectually Involved."
       Billboard 82:18, August 22, 1970.

2650   "Chicago--to Build a Creative Soul Center." Billboard 82:20, August
       22, 1970.

2651   Aletti, V. "Records: Jerry Butler Sings." Rolling Stone no. 76:49,
       February 18, 1971.

2652   "Records: The Sagittarius Movement." Rolling Stone no. 108:58,
       May 11, 1972.

2653   Bartley, G. F. "Jerry Butler--the Survivor." Soul 7:4, August 14,
       1972.

2654   "Jerry Butler Scores Film." Soul 7:11, September 11, 1972.

2655   "Records: Spice of Life." Rolling Stone no. 118:52, September 28,
       1972.

2656   "Copacabana, N.Y." Variety 269:61, January 10, 1973.

2657   Werbin, S. "Jerry Butler, Mr. Contemporary." Rolling Stone no.
       128:18, February 15, 1973.

2658   Gibbs, V. "Soul, Man." Crawdaddy no. 23:16, April 1973.

2659   Grant, C. D. "In Both Ears: Jerry Butler." Essence 4:70, April
       1974.

2660   "Records: It All Comes Out in My Song." Rolling Stone no. 258:99,
       February 9, 1978.

2661   "Albums: It All Comes Out in My Song." Melody Maker 53:24, Feb-
       ruary 11, 1978.

2662   "Albums: Two to One." Melody Maker 53:20, September 23, 1978.

CALLOWAY, CAB (Cabell), 1908- .

2663   Calloway, Cab. The New Cab Calloway's Hepsters Dictionary; Lang-
       uage of Jive. New York: C. Calloway, Inc., 1944.

2664   Crow, J. "Cab Calloway at Clover Club is 4th to Crack Miami."
       Billboard 61:45, February 5, 1949.

2665   Calloway, Cab. "Is Dope Killing Our Musicians?" Ebony 6:22-24,
       February 1951. Calloway feels that narcotics are ruining many
       musicians.

2666   Whiston, H. "Senor Calloway Is Going South!" Melody Maker 27:2,
       February 17, 1951.

2667   "Cab Re-forms Big Ork for Trip to Uruguay." down beat 18:1, Feb-
       ruary 24, 1951.

2668   "Three U.S. Orks Hits in Montevideo Appearances." down beat 18:1,
       April 6, 1951.

2669   Whiston, H. "Back Comes the King of Hi-de-ho!" Melody Maker
       27:3, August 11, 1951.

2670   _____. "Cab's Big Band Sounds Great in Canadian Date." down
       beat 18:13, August 24, 1951.

2671   "Video Means the Rebirth of Band Biz, Says Calloway." down beat
       18:3, November 16, 1951.

2672   "Birdland, N.Y." Variety 184:60, December 5, 1951.

2673   "Calloway Debunks Story of Dope Arrest in S. America." Melody
       Maker 28:6, April 19, 1952.

2674   "How Dead Is Cab?" Our World 7:28, August 1952.

2675   "Cab Calloway Arrives in London as MU Considers Axing 'Porgy'
       MD." Melody Maker 28:1, October 4, 1952.

2676   Jones, M. "The Man with the Double Profile." Melody Maker 28:5,
       October 11, 1952.

2677   "MU Man Watches as Calloway Crashes British Jazz Package." Mel-
       ody Maker 28:6, October 11, 1952.

2678   "Calloway Shaken by Porgy Closure." Melody Maker 29:7, February
       14, 1953.

2679   "Bandbox, N.Y." Variety 192:69, October 7, 1953.

2680   "Cab Calloway Plans Own Series for New Negro Radio Network."
       Variety 193:2, February 3, 1954.

2681   "Cab Won't Return to Band Biz, Will Do Single." Variety 194:49,
       June 2, 1954.

2682   "Amato's, Portland, Ore." Variety 195:53, June 16, 1954.

2683   "'Recording Artists' Roster." down beat 21:91, June 30, 1954.

2684   "Cab's Coast Music Dates After 2 Years in 'Porgy.'" Variety 195:54,
       August 18, 1954.

2685   "Cab Forming Small Combo." down beat 21:1, September 8, 1954.

2686   "Calloway Gets Carver Award." down beat 21:16, December 1, 1954.

2687   "Cab Calloway Voted 'an Inspiration.'" Melody Maker 30:12, Decem-
       ber 25, 1954.

2688   "Latin Quarter, N.Y." Variety 197:52, January 26, 1955.

2689   Nevard, M. "The Old Man & the King of Hi-de-ho." Melody Maker
       31:7, August 27, 1955.

2690   Francis, B. "Cab Calloway's One for the Books." Billboard 67:15,
       November 5, 1955.

2691   "Calloway Alumni Form New Band." down beat 23:6, April 4, 1956.

2692   "Cab Calloway Comes Back." Ebony 12:33-34, May 1957.

2693   "Town Casino, Buffalo." Variety 208:63, September 25, 1957.

2694   Voce, S. "The Marquis of Harlem." Jazz Journal 11:9-11, June
       1958.

2695   Burley, D. "What Became of....: Prince Hi-de-ho, Cab Callo-
       way?" Sepia 7:53, May 1959.

2696   "Cab Calloway's Secret of Youth." Ebony 14:89-90, June 1959.

2697   McCarthy, A. J. "The Big Band Era." Jazz Monthly 5:7-9, Feb-
       ruary 1960.

2698 Flückiger, O. "Cab Calloway: Discography and Solography." Jazz
      Journal 14:1-4, May 1961; 14:13-14, June 1961; 14:11-12, July
      1961.

2699 Burke, D. "They Don't Make Days Like They Used To." Second
      Line 14:3-4, no. 7-8, 1963.

2700 Matteson, L. "Liten Intervju med Cab Calloway." Orkester Jour-
      nalen 33:14, December 1965.

2701 "Riverboat, N.Y." Variety 243:61, May 25, 1966.

2702 "Eden Roc, M.B." Variety 243:61, July 20, 1966.

2703 McDonough, J. "Talent in Action." Billboard 82:26, October 24,
      1970.

2704 "Rainbow Grill, N.Y." Variety 270:83, February 14, 1973.

2705 "Focus on Cab Calloway." Harper's Bazaar 107:49, January 1974.

2706 "Newport, M.B." Variety 274:61, March 6, 1974.

2707 Calloway, Cab and Bryant Rollins. Of Minnie the Moocher and Me.
      New York: Crowell, 1976.

2708 Baker, J. F. "PW Interviews." Publishers Weekly 209:6-7, May
      17, 1976.

2709 Hippenmeyer, J. R. "Cab Calloway; ou, les Nouvelles Aventures
      d'un Maitre Chanteur." Revue Musicale de Suisse Romande 30:128-
      129, no. 4, 1977.

2710 Daubresse, J. P. "Cab Calloway." Jazz Hot no. 339-340:30-33,
      July-August 1977.

2711 Nevers, D. "Les Jours d'Avant Cab." Jazz Hot no. 339-340:28-30,
      July-August 1977.

2712 Hoberman, J. "If Youse a Viper: Pot Luck Behind the Bandstand."
      Crawdaddy no. 79:18, December 1977.

2713 "'Immer First Class' Cab Calloway im Gespraech." Jazz Podium
      26:8-10, December 1977.

2714 Joe, R. "It's Calloway & 'Minnie' Again." Billboard 90:44, Septem-
      ber 16, 1978.

CARRINGTON, TERRI LYNE.

2715 London, J. "Terri Lyne Carrington: She's Only Just Begun." Mod-
      ern Drum 1:10, no. 4, 1977.

2716 "Oooowe, Man, That Little Girl Can Play!" Ebony 32:130-132, April
      1977.

CARROLL, DIAHANN (real name: Carol Diahann Johnson), (Mrs. Robert
A. De Leon), 1930- .

2717   "Change of a Lifetime: Diahann Carroll Wins Fame, Fortune and a
       Celebrity's Headaches on TV Talent Show." Our World 9:12-17,
       May 1954.

2718   "New Acts." Variety 199:51, August 3, 1955.

2719   "Caught in the Act." down beat 22:8-9, October 5, 1955.

2720   "El Morocco, Mont'l." Variety 202:80, April 18, 1956.

2721   "Fontainebleau, M. B'ch." Variety 202:69, April 25, 1956.

2722   "Unlikely Corners." American Record Guide 23:179, August 1957.
       Review of Carroll's recording of Arlen songs.

2723   "Tables for Two." New Yorker 33:75, August 10, 1957.

2724   "Riverside, Ren." Variety 211:70, August 20, 1958.

2725   "Hotel Plaza, N.Y." Variety 214:73, March 11, 1959.

2726   Cook, H. "Diahann Carroll Scores at Plaza." Billboard 71:23,
       March 23, 1959.

2727   "Cloister, L.A." Variety 216:72, September 23, 1959.

2728   Carroll, Diahann. "My Musical Me." Music Journal 17:18, October
       1959.

2729   "Hotel Plaza, N.Y." Variety 216:67, November 25, 1959.

2730   "Bottom of the Top." Time 74:48, December 7, 1959.

2731   "Hands at the Heart of a Song." Life 47:57-58, December 7, 1959.

2732   "Fairmont, San Francisco." Variety 218:66, March 30, 1960.

2733   Tynan, J. "Caught in the Act." down beat 27:42-43, May 26, 1960.

2734   "Paris Bound with Diahann." Life 51:67-68, November 3, 1961.

2735   Rolontz, B. "Drama Makes Diahann Dynamite." Billboard 73:28,
       November 20, 1961.

2736   "Persian Room, N.Y." Variety 224:52, November 22, 1961.

2737   "Carroll, Diahann: Talented Bombshell." Sepia 11:57-59, March
       1962.

2738   "Talk with the Star." Newsweek 59:85, March 26, 1962.

2739   "Fancy Wrappings and Sweet Music for Diahann." Life 52:111-112,
       April 27, 1962. Carroll has received good reviews for her sing-
       ing and wardrobe in the Broadway musical "No Strings."

2740 Kelly, V. "Diahann Carroll: Show Stopper." Look 26:110-112, May 22, 1962.

2741 "Broadway's Newest Star." Ebony 17:40-42, July 1962.

2742 "Diahann Carroll Hits SRO 14 G in Concert Bow at Philharmonic Hall, N.Y." Variety 229:43, December 5, 1962.

2743 Barrow, W. "Five Fabulous Females." Negro Digest 12:78-83, July 1963.

2744 "New Acts." Variety 232:69, October 2, 1963.

2745 "Royal Box, N.Y." Variety 232:53, November 6, 1963.

2746 "Eden Roc, Miami Beach." Variety 233:52, February 19, 1964.

2747 "Cocoanut Grove, L.A." Variety 238:60, March 31, 1965.

2748 Tiegel, E. "Miss Carroll's L.A. Debut is 'Diahannimite.'" Billboard 77:12, April 3, 1965.

2749 "Sidney Poitier-Diahann Carroll: What Will It Be?" Sepia 14:8-12, June 1965.

2750 "Harold's, Reno." Variety 239:59, June 9, 1965; 241:52, February 9, 1966.

2751 "Hotel Plaza, N.Y." Variety 242:66, March 16, 1966.

2752 "Harrah's, Reno." Variety 245:61, November 23, 1966.

2753 "Plaza Hotel, N.Y." Variety 245:53, February 15, 1967.

2754 Sternfield, A. "Diahann Carroll Gives Out with Hot Act Despite Cold." Billboard 79:12, February 18, 1967.

2755 "Gallic-American Spectacular." Ebony 22:36, April 1967.

2756 Shayon, R. L. "Julia: A Political Relevance?" Saturday Review 51:37, July 20, 1968.

2757 Wolff, A. "Diahann Carroll: A New Kind of Glamour on TV." Look 32:66-69, October 29, 1968.

2758 "Entertaining Diahann Carroll." Harper's Bazaar 102:236-237, November 1968.

2759 "Julia." Ebony 24:56-58, November 1968.

2760 "Diahann's Dash Is Designers' Dish." Life 65:88-90, November 8, 1968.

2761 "Sands, Las Vegas." Variety 255:66, May 28, 1969.

2762 Shayon, R. L. "Changes." Saturday Review 53:46, April 18, 1970.

2763 Evers, Mrs. M. W. "Tale of Two Julias." Ladies Home Journal 87:60, May 1970.

2764   "Ambassador, L.A." Variety 258:59, May 13, 1970.

2765   Tepper, R. "Talent in Action." Billboard 82:18, May 16, 1970.

2766   "Did Diahann Carroll 'Sell Out' to T.V.?" Sepia 19:56-57, August
       1970.

2767   "Julia Models a Look for the Beach." Ebony 26:106-109, January
       1971.

2768   "Name Three Blacks on Global Best Dressed List." Jet 39:58, Jan-
       uary 28, 1971.

2769   Green, T. "New Honors for TV's Diahann Carroll." Jet 39:4-42,
       March 18, 1971.

2770   "Sands, Las Vegas." Variety 263:52, June 1971.

2771   King, R. "Stargazing." Essence 2:24-39, December 1971.

2772   Pierce, P. "To Begin with, I Am an Individual." McCalls 99:92-
       93, February 1972.

2773   "Diahann Carroll Among 10 Best Dressed." Jet 41:61, February 3,
       1972.

2774   "Hilton Intl., Las Vegas." Variety 266:63, March 8, 1972.

2775   "Hilton, Las Vegas." Variety 267:63, June 21, 1972.

2776   "David and Diahann: Prime Time to Get Married." Life 73:97, No-
       vember 17, 1972.

2777   "Kings Castle, Reno." Variety 271:71, June 27, 1973.

2778   Burrell, W. "The Image Is Charged: Flawless Julia Becomes Sim-
       ple Claudine." Soul 8:13, March 18, 1974.

2779   Ebert, A. "Diahann Carroll." Essence 5:44-45, July 1974.

2780   Morgan, A. J. "Will the Real Diahann Carroll Please Stand Up?"
       Soul 9:14-15, October 28, 1974.

2781   De Leon, Robert A. "Diahann Carroll: 'I've Been Black All the
       Time.'" Jet 48:58-63, April 3, 1975.

2782   "Palmer House, Chi." Variety 278:69, April 9, 1975.

2783   De Leon, Robert A. "Diahann Carroll's 'Oscar' Diary." Jet 48:12-
       15, April 24, 1975.

2784   Mitchell, G. "Jet Managing Editor Robert A. De Leon Weds Diahann
       Carroll." Jet 48:12-16, June 12, 1975.

2785   Neimark, P. "Diahann Carroll's Battle to Be Black." Sepai 24:36-
       43, July 1975.

2786   "Diahann Carroll Weds." Soul 10:1, July 7, 1975.

2787   "Dunes, Las Vegas." Variety 281:55, December 3, 1975.

2788   "TV Season Previews New Diahann Carroll." Jet 50:60-63, August
          19, 1976.

2789   Sanders, C. L. "We're Still Very Much in Love." Ebony 31:152-
          154, September 1976.

2790   Lucas, B. "How Famous Widows Get Along Now Without Mates."
          Jet 52:14-17, June 16, 1977.

2791   "Records: A Tribute to Ethel Waters." High Fidelity/Musical Amer-
          ica 28:170-171, October 1978.

2792   Kresh P. "Diahann Carroll Sings for Ethel Waters." Stereo Review
          41:107, December 1978.

CHARLES, RAY (real name: Ray Charles Robinson), 1930- .

2793   Cage, R. "Rhythm & Blues." down beat 22:13, December 14, 1955.

2794   Mulford, E. "Philadelphia Again." Metronome 72:28-29, January 1956.

2795   Cerulli, D. "Ray Charles." down beat 23:54, November 28, 1956.

2796   "Atlantic Record Artists." Billboard 70:25, January 13, 1958.

2797   Jones, M. "This World of Jazz." Melody Maker 33:13, May 24, 1958.

2798   Stewart-Baxter, D. "A Portrait of Ray Charles." Jazz Journal
          11:33, December 1958.

2799   Clar, M., and J. Goldberg. "Ray Charles." Jazz Review 2:32-33,
          January 1959.

2800   Grevatt, R. "Ray Loves Gospel." Melody Maker 34:v, Supplement,
          February 14, 1959.

2801   "Charles Hits Again with 'What'd I Say.'" Billboard 71:16, July 13, 1959.

2802   Gardner, B. "The Bright Night World of Ray Charles." down beat
          27:20-22, July 7, 1960.

2803   "Cloister, H'wood." Variety 219:55, August 3, 1960.

2804   "The Soul of Ray Charles." Ebony 15:99-107, September 1960.

2805   Postif, F. "New York in Jazz Time." Jazz Hot 26:17-18, Nov. 1960.

2806   Newton, F. "That Night with Ray Charles." Melody Maker 35:12-
          13, November 19, 1960.

2807   Morrison, A. "Ray Charles." Jazz Journal 13:3-6, December 1960.

2808   Tenot, F. "Lumieres sur Ray Charles." Jazz Magazine 6:36-40,
          December 1960.

2809   "Ray Charles' Late Showing Sparks Riot; Promoter Robbed During
       Melee." Variety 221:59, February 1, 1961.

2810   "Ray Charles Orchestra." down beat 28:36-37, March 16, 1961.

2811   "Ray Charles' Carnegie Hall Date Pulls Concert Tour B.O. Over
       220 G." Variety 222:67, May 3, 1961.

2812   Tronchot, J. "Ray Charles." Jazz Hot no. 167:16-20, July-August
       1961.

2813   Brand, P. "Ray Charles Is the Star, but Ball Wins on Applause."
       Melody Maker 36:7, July 22, 1961.

2814   "Ray Charles Makes History in Memphis; 1st Integrated Show a Social
       & B.O. Click." Variety 223:1, August 23, 1961.

2815   "Ray Charles, Ray Charles." Billboard 73:3, September 18, 1961.

2816   "Palace, N.Y." Variety 224:61, September 27, 1961.

2817   "Un Beau Remue-Menage." Jazz Magazine 7:15-16, October 1961.

2818   "Le Retour de Ray." Jazz Magazine 7:15, October 1961.

2819   Kahn, H. "I Live to Sing, Says Ray Charles." Melody Maker 36:12-
       13, October 28, 1961.

2820   Postif, F. "Marjorie Hendricks, David Newman et John Hunt Nous
       Aident à Mieux Connaitre les Veritables Debuts de Ray Charles."
       Jazz Hot no. 170:14-17, November 1961.

2821   "Ray Charles Wows Crix, Audiences in 4 Capacity Concerts at Paris
       Arena." Variety 224:69, November 1, 1961.

2822   "One of the Immortals." Newsweek 58:96, November 13, 1961.

2823   "Ray Charles Dope Rap Hypoes Take in Nashville Gig." Variety
       224:48, November 22, 1961.

2824   "SMU Cancels Ray Charles Because of Dope Arrest." Variety 225:1,
       November 29, 1961.

2825   Bremond, G. "Ray Charles, le Plus Humain des Chanteurs." Jazz
       Hot no. 171:30-31, December 1961.

2826   Lattes, P. and P. Nahman. "Un Roi à Paris." Jazz Magazine
       7:39-41, December 1961.

2827   Polillo, A. "Il Caso Charles." Musica Jazz 17:25, December 1961.

2828   "Ray Charles à Regne Cinq Jours sur Paris." Jazz Magazine 7:26-
       35, December 1961.

2829   Tenot, F. "Un Mouton à Cinq Pattes." Jazz Magazine 7:25, De-
       cember 1961.

2830   Tronchot, J. "Avec l'Orgue, un Cote 'Preacher' Tres Attrayant."
       Jazz Hot no. 171:31-32, December 1961.

2831 "The Genius & the Kids." down beat 28:15, December 7, 1961.

2832 "Balliamo Il 'Twist' con Ray Charles." Musica e Dischi 18:49, January 1962.

2833 Tenot, F. "L'Homme à la Voix d'Or." Jazz Magazine 8:17, January 1962.

2834 "The Ray Charles Case." down beat 29:12, January 4, 1962.

2835 "Charles, Ray, Speaks Facts and Insights." Sepia 11:23, February 1962.

2836 Perlberg, R. "Blind World of Ray Charles." Sepia 11:24-26, February 1962.

2837 Cartier, J. "Ray Charles, 'the Genius,' Aveugle Comme la Fortune." Musica no. 96:12-16, March 1962.

2838 "Ray Charles Forms Label; Inks New Pact with ABC-Paramount." Cash Box 23:7, March 10, 1962.

2839 "Ray Charles Freed on Narcotics Charge." down beat 29:15, March 15, 1962.

2840 "Ray Charles Forming Own Tangerine Label." Billboard 74:8, March 17, 1962.

2841 "Today's Top Record Talent." Billboard 74:52, April 7, 1962.

2842 Mohr, K., and M. Chauvard. "Discographie de Ray Charles." Jazz Hot no. 176:8-9, May 1962.

2843 "Ray Charles and Band Pull O.K. $36,000 in Four N.Y. Area Gigs." Variety 226:54, May 16, 1962.

2844 Thompson, R. F. "Music in the Market Place." Saturday Review 45:43, May 26, 1962.

2845 Mohr, K., and M. Chauvard. "Discographie de Ray Charles." Jazz Hot no. 177:37, June 1962.

2846 "Ray Charles: La Revolte." Jazz Hot no. 177:6, June 1962.

2847 Roberts, C. "Ray Charles--the Singer Who Sells Soul." Melody Maker 37:8-9, June 30, 1962.

2848 "Dix Jours avec Ray Charles; Sa Tournee en France." Jazz Hot no. 178:24-27, July-August 1962.

2849 Mohr, K., and M. Chauvard. "Discographie de Ray Charles." Jazz Hot no. 178:44, July-August 1962.

2850 Mouly, R. "Moi, J'Aime Ray Charles." Jazz Magazine 8:31-33, July 1962.

2851 King, G. "Being Black and Blind Helped Me! Interview with Ray Charles." Melody Maker 37:8, July 28, 1962.

2852   "Dix Jours avec Ray Charles; Sa Tournee en France." Jazz Hot no.
       179:28, September 1962.

2853   "Les Plaideurs." Jazz Magazine 8:11, September 1962.

2854   "Why Ray Charles Sings Country Music." Sepia 11:49-52, September
       1962.

2855   Morgenstern, D. "The Impact of Ray Charles." Jazz 1:4-5, Oc-
       tober 1962.

2856   Panassie, H. "Ray Charles in France." Jazz 1:6, October 1962.

2857   Maher, J. "Ray Charles Carried the Ball--Then Everybody Else
       Began Scoring Big." Billboard 74:34, November 10, 1962.

2858   "Little Casino, N.J." Variety 229:53, December 5, 1962.

2859   "Charles, Ray, Speaks Facts and Insights." Sepia 11:23, February
       1962.

2860   Feather, L. "I Don't Like Being Copied; Interview with Ray Charles."
       Melody Maker 38:11, March 30, 1963.

2861   Robinson, L. "Blues Becomes Big Business; Ray Charles Enterpris-
       es." Ebony 18:34-36, April 1963.

2862   "Ray Charles Hits Capacity 24 G in Two Carnegie Hall Perfs., but
       Show's Uneven." Variety 230:67, May 1, 1963.

2863   "That's All Right." Time 81:43, May 10, 1963.

2864   "Fantastic! That's Charles in Person." Melody Maker 38:7, May
       11, 1963.

2865   Doncaster, P., and C. Roberts. "X-Ray on Charles." Melody
       Maker 38:4-5, May 18, 1963.

2866   Jones, M. "Success Didn't Come Suddenly." Melody Maker 38:8-9,
       May 25, 1963.

2867   "Early Charles." Jazz Journal 16:4-5, June 1963. Early recordings
       made by Charles are examined.

2868   Masson, J. R. "Le Retour de Ray Charles." Jazz Magazine 9:20-
       27, June 1963.

2869   "Ray Charles; Du Blues au Music-Hall." Jazz Hot no. 188:6, June
       1963.

2870   Traill, S. "The Visitors." Jazz Journal 16:1-2, June 1963.

2871   "Premiere Tribute to Ray Charles and Nancy Wilson." Sepia 12:78-
       81, July 1963.

2872   Cooke, J. "Ray Charles: In Person." Jazz Monthly 9:6-8, July
       1963.

2873   "Premier Tribute to Ray Charles and Nancy Wilson." Sepia 12:78-81, July 1961.

2874   Tenot, F. "La Semaine Eblouissante." Jazz Magazine 9:30-32, July 1963.

2875   Aronowitz, A. G. "What's So Great About Ray Charles?" Saturday Evening Post 236:74-76, August 24, 1963.

2876   Feather, L. "Free Flow; A Conversation with Ray Charles." down beat 30:18-19, September 12, 1963.

2877   "Ray Charles' New Girl Singer." Sepia 12:57-60, October 1963.

2878   "Annuaire Biographique du Piano." Jazz Magazine 9:25, November 1963.

2879   "Ray Charles--Sandra Betts Affair." Sepia 12:70-72, November 1963; 12:6-9, December 1963.

2880   "His Business Is Show Business." Sepia 13:28-33, February 1964.

2881   Roberts, C. "The Genius Slows Down." Melody Maker 39:7, June 13, 1964.

2882   Houston, B. "The Trouble with the Ray Charles Band." Melody Maker 39:9, July 18, 1964.

2883   Priestley, B. "Ray Charles in Manchester." Jazz Monthly 10:4-5, September 1964.

2884   "Ray Charles' Reefer Blues After Arrest in Hub on Dope Charges." Variety 236:55, November 4, 1964.

2885   "Ray Charles Riot." Sepia 13:68-72, December 1964.

2886   "Man Who Outsings Ray Charles." Sepia 14:26-31, February 1965.

2887   "Order Ray Charles to Pay N.C. Promoter $6,300 for No-Show in '62 Booking." Variety 238:53, April 7, 1965.

2888   Hentoff, N. "The Night Ray Charles Came to Town." HiFi/Stereo Review 14:62, June 1965.

2889   "Charles Hospital Mystery." Melody Maker 40:5, August 28, 1965.

2890   "Ray Charles en Tournee." Jazz Magazine no. 130:14, May 1966.

2891   "New Band for Charles." down beat 33:13, May 5, 1966.

2892   Thompson, T. "Music Soaring in a Darkened World." Life 61:54-56, July 29, 1966.

2893   "Ray Charles Troupe, in Forest Hills Fest Finale, Draws Near-Capacity Biz." Variety 244:44, August 31, 1966.

2894   "In the Press." BMI p. 21, October 1966.

2895   "A Touch of Genius; The Ray Charles Story." Billboard 78:RC1-15,
       October 15, 1966.

2896   "Suspend Sentence in Ray Charles' Dope Rap." Variety 245:45, No-
       vember 30, 1966.

2897   Bird, C. "Ray Charles Bridges Gap." Melody Maker 42:3, April
       29, 1967.

2898   "Shipping Out with Ray Charles." down beat 34:11, May 4, 1967.

2899   Hofstein, F. "Le Retour de Ray." Jazz Magazine no. 143:5-7,
       June 1967.

2900   Illingworth, D. "Jazz in Britain." Jazz Journal 20:15, June 1967.

2901   Niquet, B. "Le Retour du Genius." Jazz Hot no. 232:6, June 1967.

2902   Sundin, B. "Avspänd Ray Charles." Orkester Journalen 35:11, June
       1967.

2903   "The Year of Ray Charles." Sepia 16:8-14, June 1967.

2904   Teigel, E. "Jazz Beat." Billboard 79:12, June 24, 1967.

2905   "Harrah's, Reno." Variety 248:55, October 4, 1967.

2906   "Copacabana, N.Y." Variety 249:45, November 29, 1967.

2907   Siders, H. "Subject: Ray Charles--an Open Letter to Future Inter-
       viewers." down beat 34:16-17, November 30, 1967.

2908   Sternfield, A. "Charles a Thanksgiving Treat with All Musical Trim-
       mings." Billboard 79:6, December 2, 1967.

2909   "Writer Report." BMI p. 7, January 1968.

2910   "Jet Magazine Sued for Libel by Ray Charles." down beat 35:12,
       January 25, 1968.

2911   Gleason, R. "Like a Rolling Stone." Jazz and Pop 7:20, February
       1968.

2912   Pekar, H. "From Rock to ???" down beat 35:21, May 2, 1968.

2913   Balliett, W. "Jazz Concerts; Performance at Carnegie Hall." New
       Yorker 44:136, May 25, 1968.

2914   "Cocoanut Grove, L.A." Variety 251:53, July 24, 1968.

2915   Tiegel, E. "Ray Charles Funky Jazz Format Wins at Grove." Bill-
       board 80:12, July 27, 1968.

2916   "Mr. D's, San Francisco." Variety 251:63, August 14, 1968.

2917   "Raelettes Leave Ray." Rolling Stone no. 17:8, September 14, 1968.

2918   "Raelets Walk Out on Ray Charles in L.A." down beat 35:13, Sep-
       tember 19, 1968.

2919   Jones, M. "Backstage with Ray, 'the Genius.'" Melody Maker
       43:10, September 28, 1968.

2920   _____. "Healthy Noise Behind the Genius." Melody Maker 43:23,
       October 5, 1968.

2921   _____. "Ray Charles in London." Rolling Stone 20:10, October
       26, 1968.

2922   Wilmer, V. "Second Opinion." Melody Maker 43:12, November 16,
       1968.

2923   "Copacabana, N.Y." Variety 253:58, December 11, 1968.

2924   "Fla. to Fete Ray Charles for Aiding Deaf & Blind." Variety 253:46,
       January 22, 1969.

2925   "A Gallery of the Greats." BMI p. 29, Summer 1969.

2926   Atkins, R. "Ray Charles at Newport." Jazz Monthly no. 173:22-23,
       July 1969.

2927   McRae, B. "A B Basics; A Column for the Newcomer to Jazz."
       Jazz Journal 22:17, August 1969.

2928   "Cocoanut Grove, L.A." Variety 256:61, August 20, 1969.

2929   Feather, L. "A Fighter Who Has Won the Toughest Battles." Mel-
       ody Maker 44:5, September 13, 1969.

2930   Welch, C. "Caught in the Act." Melody Maker 44:6, October 4,
       1969.

2931   Cullaz, M. "Ray Charles." Jazz Hot no. 255:6-7, November 1969.

2932   Gerber, A. "Ray Charles: La Verite." Jazz Magazine no. 172:13,
       November 1969.

2933   Tenot, F. "Les Triomphes de Ray." Jazz Magazine no. 160:13,
       November 1968.

2934   Westin, K. O. "Ray Charles Populaer." Orkester Journalen 37:19,
       December 1969.

2935   "Ray Charles Ends 11-Yr. Tie with ABC Records; He'll Do More
       Writing." Variety 257:43, December 3, 1969.

2936   "Charles and ABC Call It Quits; Singer Cites Personal Reasons."
       Billboard 81:3, December 6, 1969.

2937   Charles, Ray. "I Don't Need to See." Music Journal 28:30-31, Jan-
       uary 1970.

2938   "Random Notes." Rolling Stone no. 51:4, February 7, 1970.

2939   "La Chronique des Disques." Jazz Hot no. 259:31-32, March 1970.

2940   Balliett, W. "Profiles: R. Charles." New Yorker 46:44-46, March
       28, 1970.

2941   "Concert Reviews." Variety 258:56, April 22, 1970.

2942   Glassenberg, B. "Talent in Action." Billboard 82:24, May 2, 1970.

2943   "Charles' Label Stepping Up Disk Action; Have 16 Acts." Billboard
       82:8, July 4, 1970.

2944   "Caught in the Act." down beat 37:29-30, August 6, 1970.

2945   Feather, L. "Charles Grooves at the Grove." Melody Maker 45:25,
       August 29, 1970.

2946   _____. "Sassy, le Genius et Compagnie." Jazz Magazine no.
       182:11, October 1970.

2947   "Ray Charles Bows Top Pop Recitals at Rome Theatre." Variety
       260:41, October 7, 1970.

2948   "Caught in the Act." Melody Maker 45:39, October 31, 1970.

2949   Jones, M. "Ray Doing His Thing Despite the Critics." Melody
       Maker 45:21, October 31, 1970.

2950   Brown, R. "Record Reviews: My Kind of Jazz." Jazz Journal
       23:31, November 1970.

2951   Niquet, B. "Ray Charles à Pleyel." Jazz Hot no. 266:28-29, No-
       vember 1970.

2952   Olsson, J. "Ray Charles Som Vanligt." Orkester Journalen 38:13,
       November 1970.

2953   Tenot, F. "Ray l'Incomparable." Jazz Magazine no. 183:10, No-
       vember 1970.

2954   Atkins, R. "Jazz Expo '70: A Step Backward?" down beat 38:14,
       January 7, 1971.

2955   "L'Actualite Discographique: My Kind of Jazz." Points du Jazz no.
       4:108, March 1971.

2956   Flippo, C. "A Volcano in Ray Charles' Soul." Rolling Stone no.
       79:16, April 1, 1971.

2957   Klee, J. H. "Record Reviews: Volcanic Action of My Soul." down
       beat 38:24, September 16, 1971.

2958   Southall, B. "Caught in the Act." Melody Maker 46:22, October
       2, 1971.

2959   Charles, P. "Paris." Jazz Magazine no. 194:43, November 1971.

2960   Charles, Ray. "I'd Love to Work with a Small Combo Again."
       Crescendo International 10:14-15, November 1971.

2961   Cullaz, M. "Ray Charles à Pleyel." Jazz Hot no. 277:29, Novem-
       ber 1971.

2962   Gonda, J. "Ray Charles." Muzsika 14:43-44, December 1971.

2963 "Albums: His All-Time Great Performances." Melody Maker 47:21,
      January 22, 1972.

2964 "Disques du Mois: Vingt-Cinq Ans de Ray Charles, Ses Plus Grands
      Succes." Jazz Magazine no. 197:32, February 1972.

2965 "Concert Reviews." Variety 267:50, May 31, 1972.

2966 Feather, L. "Caught in the Act." Melody Maker 47:26, June 10,
      1972.

2967 "Ray Charles." Soul 7:14, June 19, 1972.

2968 "Records: A Message from the People." Rolling Stone no. 111:54-
      55, June 22, 1972.

2969 Feather, L. "A Message from Ray." Melody Maker 47:49, July
      15, 1972.

2970 Truck, B. "Second Line Jump; Reelin' and Rockin' Down in New Or-
      leans." Jazz & Blues 2:8-14, October 1972.

2971 "Record Reviews: A Message from the People." down beat 39:19,
      October 12, 1972.

2972 Blomberg, L. "Ray Charles i Goeteborg." Orkester Journalen
      40:13, November 1972.

2973 Cullaz, M. "Ray Charles à Pleyel." Jazz Hot no. 288:23, Novem-
      ber 1972.

2974 Brown, R. "Jazz in Britain." Jazz Journal 25:26, December 1972.

2975 "Disques du mois: A Message from the People." Jazz Magazine
      no. 206:38-39, December 1972.

2976 "Film Ray Charles in Holy Land for TV Sale." Variety 269:1, De-
      cember 20, 1972.

2977 Feather, L. "Caught in the Act." Melody Maker 47:39, December
      23, 1972.

2978 "A Gallery of the Greats." BMI no. 1:4-13, 1973. A survey of 60
      years of rhythm and blues musicians.

2979 Mathis, Sharon Bell. Ray Charles. New York: Crowell, 1973. A
      book for children.

2980 Fong-Torres, B. "Ray Charles." Rolling Stone no. 126:28-36, Jan-
      uary 18, 1973.

2981 "Records: All-Time Great Country & Western Hits." Rolling Stone
      no. 131:58, March 29, 1973.

2982 "Ray Charles: 'Who's Still on Chart After 26 Years?'" Billboard
      85:22, May 26, 1973.

2983 Howard, N. "New York pour Vous." Jazz Hot no. 295:16-17, June
      1973.

2984   Carriere, C. "Les Geants au Palais." Jazz Hot no. 299:23-24, November 1973.

2985   Kuehn, G. "Norman Granz Presents: Leise Spannung, Powerhouse und Marionetten-Show." Jazz Podium 22:29, November 1973.

2986   Von Konow, A. "Ray Charles Fast i Maner." Orkester Journalen 41:10, November 1973.

2987   "Two U.S. Army MPs at Ray Charles' Frankfurt Concert Stir Up Critics." Variety 273:71, November 21, 1973.

2988   "Jazz en Direct." Jazz Magazine no. 217:15, December 1973.

2989   "Waldorf-Astoria, N.Y." Variety 274:279, May 8, 1974.

2990   "Talent in Action." Billboard 86:18, May 11, 1974.

2991   "Bomb Scare Aborts SRO Ray Charles Concert at New York's Central Park." Variety 276:44, August 28, 1974.

2992   "Concert Reviews." Variety 276:57, September 4, 1974.

2993   Robinson, L. "Enduring Genius of Ray Charles: From Folk to Rock, Most Artists Owe a Debt to Multi-talented Musician." Ebony 29:125-128, October 1974.

2994   "Concert Reviews." Variety 278:74, April 16, 1975.

2995   "Caught in the Act." Melody Maker 50:29, April 26, 1975.

2996   "Talent in Action." Billboard 87:30, April 26, 1975.

2997   "Jazz en Direct." Jazz Magazine no. 233:16, May-June 1975.

2998   "Honor Ray Charles." Variety 279:149, May 14, 1975. The National Association of Sickle Cell Disease honored Charles.

2999   "Le Genius à Paris." Jazz Hot no. 317:27-28, June 1975.

3000   "Honor Ray Charles." Billboard 87:29, June 7, 1975.

3001   "Blue Room, New Orleans." Variety 279:67, June 18, 1975.

3002   Mayer, B. "Show Biz Salutes Ray Charles at Sickle Cell Anemia Benefit." Variety 279:64, June 18, 1975.

3003   "Jazz en Direct." Jazz Magazine no. 234:6, July 1975.

3004   Salvo, P., and B. Salvo. "Ray Charles on Soul, Dope and Blindness." Sepia 24:44-50, July 1975.

3005   "N. Z. Finally Forgets Charles' Old Drug Rap." Variety 280:63, October 8, 1975.

3006   "Ray Charles' Troupe in a Hairy Situation for Singapore Stand." Variety 281:1, November 19, 1975.

3007   Williams, J. "Ray Charles & His Special Concerts; Noted Perform-

er Does 2 Shows for Female Inmates at L.A. Prison." Billboard
88:31, April 24, 1976.

3008 Gourgues, M., and P. Carles. "Ray Charles: Je Ne Suis Pas un
Pur Chanteur." Jazz Magazine 245:26-27, June-July 1976.

3009 Ray Charles Pas à Pas." Jazz Hot no. 329:8-12, July-August 1976.

3010 Balliett, W. "Jazz: New York Notes." New Yorker 52:64-68, July
5, 1976.

3011 "Concert Reviews." Variety 284:74, September 29: 1976.

3012 Collier, J. L. "Remarkable Saga of Ray Charles." Reader's Digest
109:229-230, October 1976.

3013 Rusch, B. "Rapping with Ray Charles." Cadence 1:3-4, October
1976.

3014 "Talent in Action." Billboard 88:32, October 9, 1976.

3015 Wilmer, V. "Charles: Still Got the Blues." Melody Maker 51:49,
October 23, 1976.

3016 "En Direct." Jazz Magazine no. 250:12, December 1976.

3017 Reilly, P. "'Porgy and Bess': Ray and Cleo." Stereo Review
37:130, December 1976.

3018 Wilson, J. S. "Louis and Ella and Ray and Cleo." High Fidelity/
Musical America 26:95, December 1976. Review of the "Porgy
and Bess" recordings.

3019 Balliett, W. "Jazz: New York Notes." New Yorker 52:136, December 6, 1976. Review of the album "Porgy and Bess."

3020 "Reviews: "Porgy and Bess." Jazz Magazine (U.S.) 1:55, no. 3,
1977.

3021 "Records: Porgy & Bess." Creem 8:60, January 1977.

3022 "Record Reviews: Porgy and Bess." Jazz Journal 30:29, February
1977.

3023 "Albums: Porgy and Bess." Melody Maker 52:24, February 26,
1977.

3024 "Record Reviews: Porgy & Bess." down beat 44:18, March 24,
1977.

3025 Welding, P. "Ray Charles: Senior Diplomat of Soul." down beat
44:12-15, May 5, 1977.

3026 "Talent in Action." Billboard 89:38, September 17, 1977; 89:60,
October 8, 1977.

3027 "Concert Reviews." Variety 289:49, December 28, 1977.

3028   Charles, Ray and David Ritz. Brother Ray; Ray Charles' Own Story. New York: Dial Press, 1978.

3029   "Records: True to Life." High Fidelity/Musical America 28:129-130, January 1978.

3030   Jones, M. "A Ray of Sunshine." Melody Maker 53:13, January 14, 1978.

3031   Vance, J. "Remarkable Authority and Rekindling Vigor in Ray Charles' New True to Life." Stereo Review 40:112, February 1978.

3032   Palmer, R. "Soul Survivor Ray Charles." Rolling Stone no. 258:11-14, February 9, 1978.

3033   "Record Reviews: True to Life." down beat 45:22, February 9, 1978.

3034   "Waxing On: 14 Hits." down beat 45:36-37, February 23, 1978.

3035   "Albums: True to Life." Melody Maker 53:28, April 15, 1978.

3036   "Concert Reviews." Variety 292:77, August 30, 1978.

3037   "Talent in Action." Billboard 90:46, December 16, 1978.

COBB, ARNETT CLEOPHUS.

3038   "Caught in the Act." down beat 19:6, August 27, 1952.

3039   "'Recording Artists' Roster." down beat 21:93, June 30, 1954.

3040   Demeusy, Bertrand and Otto Flückiger. Arnett Cobb; The Wild Man of the Tenor Sax. Basel: Jazz Publications, 1962.

3041   Ioakimidis, D. "Revenants." Jazz Hot no. 185:24-26, March 1963.

3042   Cressant, P. "Cobb au 104." Jazz Hot no. 306:35, June 1974.

3043   "Jazz Records in Other Countries: Jumpin' the Blues." Jazz Digest 3:17, January 1974.

3044   "Whatever Happened to: Arnett Cobb?" Ebony 30:76, March 1975.

3045   Heribel, S., and G. Rouy. "Arnett Cobb: 'On M'Appelait the Wild Man.'" Jazz Magazine no. 257:24-25, September 1977.

3046   "Record Reviews: Arnett Cobb and His Mob." Jazz Journal International 30:40, October 1977.

COLE, NAT KING (real name: Nathaniel Adams Coles), 1919-1965.

3047   "Fiddlers Three." Newsweek 28:97, August 12, 1946.

3048   "King Cole Trio." Opportunity 25:28, January 1947.

3049   "Nat Cole." Metronome 65:20, January 1949.

3050   "Cole Trio Added to Herman Tour." Billboard 61:21, February 5,
       1949.

3051   "Nat Nominates Himself Advance Man for Bop." down beat 16:1,
       April 22, 1949.

3052   "Cole's Costanzo." Metronome 65:18, May 1949.

3053   "Cole Gets 55 G Guarantee for Southern Tour." Billboard 61:20,
       May 14, 1949.

3054   "Nat Cole." Metronome 65:27, July 1949.

3055   Emge, C. "Cole-Woody Concerts to Revitalize Coast Music?" down
       beat 16:2, September 9, 1949.

3056   "King Cole Baby; Bringing First Born Home from Hospital Is Big
       Moment for Popular Trio Leader and Singer-Wife." Ebony 5:31-
       34, June 1950.

3057   "Concerts, Variety for 'King' Cole and Trio." Melody Maker 26:4,
       September 16, 1950.

3058   Cole, Nat. "Why I Made the Trio a Quartet." Melody Maker 26:3,
       September 23, 1950.

3059   "I Want to Make Money, Not Play Jazz: Nat Cole." down beat 17:1,
       October 6, 1950.

3060   Boulton, D. "Horne Scores, Not Nat, at London Palladium Shows."
       down beat 17:15, October 20, 1950.

3061   Lindgren, C. E. "King Cole--Kung pa Underhallning." Orkester
       Journalen 18:8-9, November 1950.

3062   "Television." Metronome 67:32, January 1951.

3063   "How to Make and Lose Money." down beat 18:10, April 20, 1951.

3064   "Nat 'Always Comes Through Bigger Than Ever.'" down beat 18:2,
       July 13, 1951.

3065   "Pianists Salute Cole's Ability." down beat 18:19, July 13, 1951.

3066   "Remember the Public." Time 58:63-64, July 30, 1951.

3067   "Cole Breaks Up Trio for Sole Billing." Billboard 63:18, September
       1, 1951.

3068   "Ellington-Vaughan-Cole in Sock $4.80-Top Show at N.Y.'s Carnegie
       Hall." Variety 184:52, October 3, 1951.

3069   Freeman, D. "Critics to Blame for Confusion in Music: Cole."
       down beat 18:3, October 5, 1951.

3070   "Nat to Be Billed as Soloist from Now On."   down beat 18:1, Oc-
       tober 15, 1951.

3071   "King Cole Trio Isn't Dead, Beams Feather."   down beat 19:2, Feb-
       ruary 22, 1952.

3072   Whiston, H. F.   "You Can Go a Little Commercial--and Still Play
       Good Jazz; Interview with Nat Cole."   Melody Maker 28:3, Febru-
       ary 23, 1952.

3073   "Nat 'King' Cole; No. 1 Hitmaker."   Our World 7:28-31, April 1952.

3074   "No More Gimmicks to Invent--So Let's Play Music Again."   Melody
       Maker 28:3, July 26, 1952.

3075   Feather, L.   "'My Heart Is Still with Jazz'--Nat."   down beat 19:12,
       July 30, 1952.

3076   "The Hits and the Artists Who Made Them."   Billboard 64:68, August
       2, 1952.

3077   "Nat Cole."   Metronome 68:13, October 1952.

3078   "La Vie en Rose, N.Y."   Variety 189:59, December 10, 1952.

3079   Freeman, D.   "The Real Reason Nat Cole Cut His Piano-Only Al-
       bum."   down beat 20:3, January 28, 1953.

3080   Cole, Nat.   "Are Second Marriages Best."   Ebony 8:82-84, March
       1953.

3081   "King Cole Turns Actor."   Our World 8:45-47, April 1953.

3082   "Nate Cole Is Hospitalized Just as Tour Takes Off."   down beat 20:1,
       May 6, 1953.

3083   "King Cole Gravely Ill: Wife and Manager at Bedside."   Melody
       Maker 29:1, June 6, 1953.

3084   "Hotel Del Mar, Cal."   Variety 191:54, July 22, 1953.

3085   "$50,000 a Day; Nat Cole May Gross Amount from Singing Just One
       Song."   Ebony 8:85-88, October 1953.

3086   "Nat Cole Hits 10-Year Mark."   Billboard 65:1, December 26, 1953.

3087   "Caught in the Act."   down beat 20:4, December 30, 1953.

3088   "Cole Wary of Disk Juve 'Exclusivity;' Need Adult Fans."   Variety
       193:43, December 30, 1953.

3089   "El Rancho, Las Vegas."   Variety 193:64, January 13, 1954.

3090   "Can't Sing Any Way but Soft, Explains Nat Cole."   down beat 21:2,
       January 27, 1954.

3091   "The Singer Who Beat the Evil Eye."   Melody Maker 30:3, March
       20, 1954.

3092 Brown, T. "Ace-High 'King.'" Melody Maker 30:3, March 27, 1954.

3093 Lindgren, C. E. "Polerad Cole Inte Sa Kul." Orkester Journalen
      22:9, May 1954.

3094 "Chez Paree, Chi." Variety 194:52, June 2, 1954.

3095 "'Recording Artists' Roster." down beat 21:93, June 30, 1954.

3096 Race, S. "A Toast to Mr. Charm." Melody Maker 30:2, July 3,
      1954.

3097 Cole, M. "King and I." Our World 9:22-27, July 1954.

3098 "Caught in the Act." down beat 21:24, July 14, 1954.

3099 Hubler, R. G. "$12,000-a-Week Preacher's Boy." Saturday Evening
      Post 227:30, July 17, 1954.

3100 "Nat 'King' Cole's Second Honeymoon." Ebony 9:17-22, August 1954.

3101 Gleason, R. J. "Perspectives." down beat 21:4, August 11, 1954.

3102 "Ciro's, Hollywood." Variety 195:78, September 1, 1954.

3103 Hutton, J. "Nat 'King' Cole--His Voice Was an Accident." Melody
      Maker 30:15, September 4, 1954.

3104 "Billy Eckstine Reaches the Finale." Melody Maker 30:9, September
      11, 1954.

3105 Francis, B. "Nat Cole's Indeed King of Song at the Copa." Bill-
      board 66:19, November 6, 1954.

3106 "Melancholy Monarch." Look 19:119-121, April 19, 1955.

3107 "Nat 'King' Cole Learns to Dance." Ebony 10:24, May 1955.

3108 Lewis, V. "Ray, Laine, Cole--the Men as They Really Are." Mel-
      ody Maker 31:11, June 25, 1955. Discussion of musicians Johnnie
      Ray, Frankie Laine, and Cole.

3109 "Copacabana, N. Y." Variety 200:51, October 26, 1955.

3110 Francis, B. "Cole Restored to Copa's Throne." Billboard 67:11,
      October 29, 1955.

3111 Freeman, D. "Nat Cole Cuts Piano Set: 'It's One I'm Happy About.'"
      down beat 22:16, November 2, 1955.

3112 "King Cole's Wife Goes Back to Work." Ebony 11:132-138, Decem-
      ber 1955.

3113 "Jazz Photos." down beat 23:42, March 21, 1956.

3114 "Nat Cole-Ted Heath Package Draws Solid $83,000 in Tour's First
      Week." Variety 202:45, April 11, 1956.

3115 "Hooligan Attack on Nat Cole Ricochets Vs. Racists; Even Dixie
      Press Irate." Variety 202:1, April 18, 1956.

3116 "Hoodlums Vs. Decency." Billboard 68:29, April 21, 1956.

3117 "Promoters Holding to Southern Bookings, Despite Cole Incident."
      Billboard 68:29, April 21, 1956.

3118 "Unscheduled Appearance." Time 67:31, April 23, 1956. Nat King
      Cole was attacked in Birmingham, Alabama.

3119 "Who the Hoodlums Are." Newsweek 47:31-32, April 23, 1956.

3120 "Swift Justice." Time 67:23, April 30, 1956.

3121 Cole, Nat. "Chords and Discords." down beat 23:4, May 30, 1956.
      Cole expresses his opinions about discrimination problems.

3122 Feather, L. "Feather's Nest." down beat 23:33, May 30, 1956.

3123 "The Nat King Cole Nobody Knows." Ebony 11:42-48, October 1956.

3124 "New King Cole." Jazz Today 1:46, December 1956.

3125 "Eden Roc, Miami Beach." Variety 205:55, February 20, 1957.

3126 Kelley, F. "This King Cole Is a Wise Old Soul." Metronome 74:6,
      April 1957.

3127 Tynan, J. "Nat Cole." down beat 24:13, May 2, 1957; 24:15, May
      16, 1957.

3128 "Chez Paree, Chi." Variety 206:64, May 29, 1957.

3129 "Crooner Nat King Cole Turns Actor." Ebony 12:74, June 1957.

3130 "King's Own Show." Newsweek 50:90, July 15, 1957.

3131 "Pioneer." Time 70:66, July 15, 1957.

3132 "Ambassador Hotel, L.A." Variety 207:68, July 24, 1957.

3133 "King Cole Versus Jim Crow." Melody Maker 32:6, August 17, 1957.

3134 "500 Club, A.C." Variety 207:55, August 21, 1957.

3135 Kaufman, D. "Nat Cole Hits Madison Ave. Resistance to Negroes
      on TV." Variety 208:2, September 11, 1957.

3136 "Host with the Most." Time 70:56, September 23, 1957.

3137 "Some Background." down beat 25:13, January 9, 1958. Cole de-
      cides to discontinue his association with NBC television.

3138 "Copacabana, N.Y." Variety 209:66, January 15, 1958.

3139 Cole, Nat, and L. Bennett. "Why I Quit My TV Show." Ebony
      13:29-34, February 1958.

3140   Feather, L. "Colour-Bar Ruined Me on TV; Nat 'King' Cole Tells
        How He Lost His TV Show Because of Colour-Conscious Sponsors."
        Melody Maker 33:2-3, February 22, 1958.

3141   Grevatt, R. "'King' Again Sells Charm & Good Taste." Billboard
        70:9, March 3, 1958.

3142   "Sands, Las Vegas." Variety 210:86, March 19, 1958.

3143   "Ambassador, L.A." Variety 210:83, April 30, 1958.

3144   Cole, Nat. "I'm Proud of This Picture." Melody Maker 33:3, May
        24, 1958.

3145   "Chez Paree, Chi." Variety 212:61, October 1, 1958.

3146   "Copacabana, N.Y." Variety 212:55, October 29, 1958.

3147   Malson, L. "Jazz d'Aujourd'hui." Jazz Magazine 5:33, January
        1959.

3148   Young, A. S. "Nat 'King' Cole's Hottest Rival." Sepia 7:29-35,
        January 1959.

3149   "Sands, Las Vegas." Variety 214:55, March 4, 1959.

3150   Cole, Nat. "Why I Decided to Learn Spanish." Melody Maker 34:7,
        April 18, 1959.

3151   "Cole Blasts Music Graft." down beat 26:9, May 28, 1959.

3152   "Copacabana, N.Y." Variety 216:61, October 28, 1959.

3153   "I Found the Answer." Sepia 7:31-36, December 1959.

3154   "New Arena, Pittsburgh." Variety 217:55, December 16, 1959.

3155   "Cole-Belafonte Start Production Firm." down beat 27:13, February
        4, 1960.

3156   Steif, B. "Frisco Masonic Temple's Cryptic Nix of Cole, Who Shifts
        to Civic Aud." Variety 217:49-50, February 17, 1960.

3157   "Nat Cole Gives Frisco the Brushoff; Masons Claim Nix Not Race-
        Based." Variety 217:2, February 24, 1960.

3158   "Organizes Cole-Belafonte Enterprises, Inc.; Company Will Produce
        Movies and TV Shows." Jet p. 59, March 10, 1960.

3159   "Why We Adopted Kelly." Ebony 15:35-38, April 1960.

3160   Masson, J. R. "Nat King Cole: Le Roi du Double Jeu." Jazz Mag-
        azine 6:20-21, April 1960.

3161   "Nat Cole Knocks No-Talent Singers in U.S. Disk Biz." Variety
        218:1, May 4, 1960.

3162   "To Try a Broadway Show in Fall of 1960." Jet p. 58, May 19, 1960.

3163   "Scintillating Nat Cole Is Still the King." Melody Maker 35:12, May
       21, 1960.

3164   Guild, H. "Nat King Cole Hits Diskeries' Yet for Rock 'n' Roll, but
       Sez TV Will Kill It." Variety 218:57, May 25, 1960.

3165   Balli, E. "Quincy Jones e King Cole a Milano." Musica Jazz 16:24-
       25, June 1960.

3166   "Norman Granz Rebuts Nat Cole on State of Jazz Here and Abroad."
       Variety 219:51-52, June 8, 1960.

3167   "Forms Kell-Cole Productions in New York City for Production of
       Theatrical Feature Films, TV Properties and Stage Ventures."
       Jet p. 44, July 7, 1960.

3168   McAndrew, J. "Star Studded Shellac." Record Research no. 29:24,
       August 1960.

3169   "Fairmont, San Francisco." Variety 220:53, September 7, 1960.

3170   Cole, Nat. "Musical Good Neighbors." Music Journal 19:12, Feb-
       ruary 1961.

3171   "Nat Cole Stands on Artist's Right to Plug New Disk in Sullivan Row."
       Variety 221:57, February 1, 1961.

3172   "Eden Roc, Miami Beach." Variety 221:66, February 15, 1961.

3173   Ioakimidis, D. "Coup d'Oeil retrospectif sur King Cole et Son Trio."
       Jazz Hot no. 163:26-27, March 1961.

3174   Ackerman, P. "Cole Sheer Class at Copa." Billboard 73:11, March
       20, 1961.

3175   "Cole Raps Fast-Buck Diskers, Agencies for Disintegrating Show Biz
       Standards." Variety 223:47, May 31, 1961.

3176   "Nat Cole's New 10-Yr. Deal with Cap but Leaves Door Open for
       Own Prod. Set." Variety 223:43, June 14, 1961.

3177   "Caught in the Act." down beat 28:38, October 12, 1961.

3178   "Nat Cole Forms Pop Label; Artist to Stay with Capitol." Billboard
       73:1, October 16, 1961.

3179   "Nat King Cole Answers Teen Questions." Sepia 10:71, November
       1961.

3180   Arneel, G. "Negro Pix on Do-It-Yourself." Variety 224:5, Novem-
       ber 1, 1961.

3181   "Copacabana, N.Y." Variety 224:65, November 1, 1961.

3182   "Cocoanut Grove, L.A." Variety 225:63, November 29, 1961.

3183   "Cole, Nat King, Answers Teen Questions." Sepia 11:71, January
       1962.

3184   "Sands, Las Vegas." Variety 225:66, January 17, 1962.

3185   "Fairmont, San Francisco." Variety 225:55, February 14, 1962.

3186   "Eden Roc, Miami Beach." Variety 226:57, February 28, 1962.

3187   "Palmer House, Chi." Variety 226:77, April 4, 1962.

3188   "Cole, Nat King, Answers Teen Questions." Sepia 11:70, July 1962.

3189   Pryor, T. M. "Show Biz, Civic Notables' Salute to Nat King Cole."
       Variety 227:2, August 8, 1962.

3190   "Fete Nat Cole for 25 Years' Entertaining." Billboard 74:5, August
       18, 1962.

3191   "Unit Reviews." Variety 228:45, August 29, 1962.

3192   "Bios." Cash Box 24:44, September 22, 1962.

3193   Dewar, C. "Nat Cole's Royal Gifts." Billboard 74:10, September
       22, 1962.

3194   "Un Diner au Sirop." Jazz Magazine 8:18, October 1962.

3195   "Hollywood Honors Nat King Cole." Sepia 11:17-18, October 1962.

3196   "Copacabana, N.Y." Variety 228:70, October 24, 1962.

3197   Grevatt, R. "Nat Keeps Topping That Cole." Billboard 74:10, Oc-
       tober 27, 1962.

3198   "Harrah's, Lake Tahoe." Variety 229:59, January 30, 1963.

3199   "Nat Cole SRO in 2d Japan Tour." Variety 230:64, March 13, 1963.

3200   "Cocoanut Grove, L.A." Variety 230:213, May 8, 1963.

3201   "Cole on Colour Crisis." Melody Maker 38:5, June 22, 1963.

3202   Coleman, R. "Nat Cole Blasts Jazz Fans!" Melody Maker 38:7-9,
       July 1963.

3203   "Cole Disclaims Entertainers' Role in Integration Fight." down beat
       30:11-12, July 4, 1963.

3204   Feather, L. "Nat Cole--the Man Behind the Image." Melody Maker
       38:8-9, July 6, 1963.

3205   "Nat King Cole Fans Jam Astoria, London, as Singer Opens Brit.
       Concert Tour." Variety 231:53, July 24, 1963.

3206   "Nat King Cole, on Scot-Nighter Tour, Would Ride That 'Freedom
       Bus.'" Variety 231:95, July 31, 1963.

3207   "Nat King Cole Twins." Ebony 18:106-112, August 1963.

3208   "End of a Long Business Association." down beat 30:13, August 1,
       1963.

3209   "Singers Pledge Money for Civil-Rights Struggle." down beat 30:11,
       August 15, 1963.

3210   Cole, Nat. "Fads, Fans and Foreign Ambassadors." Music Journal
       21:37, September 1963.

3211   "Annuaire Biographique du Piano." Jazz Magazine 9:26, November
       1963.

3212   "Nat Cole's Salute to Freedom." Sepia 12:28-34, November 1963.

3213   "Friars' Luncheon for Nat King Cole a Not Too Ribald Ribfest."
       Variety 233:62, January 29, 1964.

3214   "Copacabana, N.Y." Variety 233:52, February 5, 1964.

3215   "Harrah's, Lake Tahoe." Variety 234:53, May 20, 1964; 236:69, Oc-
       tober 21, 1964.

3216   "Nat Cole, Hit by Lung Tumor, Cancels His Bookings Thru March."
       Variety 237:39, December 23, 1964.

3217   "King Cole Hospitalise." Jazz Magazine no. 114:16, January 1965.

3218   "Illness Strikes Nat King Cole." Melody Maker 40:11, January 2,
       1965.

3219   Coleman, R. "Nat Cole Fights for His Life." Melody Maker 40:11,
       January 23, 1965.

3220   "Nat Cole's Illness Cancels All Appearances." down beat 32:10, Jan-
       uary 28, 1965.

3221   Dawbarn, B. "He Could Have Been a Jazz Great." Melody Maker
       40:3, February 20, 1965.

3222   "Stars Pay Tribute to Nat Cole." Melody Maker 40:3, February 20,
       1965.

3223   "Form Cole Cancer Fund for Research." Variety 238:58, February
       24, 1965.

3224   "400 Attend L.A. Rites for Nat Cole." Variety 238:58, February 24,
       1965.

3225   "Two Colleges Planned Degree for Cole; L.A. to Build a Memorial."
       Variety 238:58, February 24, 1965.

3226   Feather, L. "Now Come the Tributes to Nat King Cole." Melody
       Maker 41:9, February 26, 1966.

3227   "King." Time 86:60, February 26, 1965. Cole is remembered for
       his music after his death.

3228   Thompson, T. "King of Song Dies, and a Friend Remembers Him."
       Life 58:36, February 26, 1965.

3229   "400 at Funeral Services for Cole." Billboard 77:1, February 27,
       1965.

3230 "Long Live the King." Billboard 77:4, February 27, 1965.

3231 Lucraft, H. "Stars Flock to Nat Cole Funeral." Melody Maker 40:19, February 27, 1965.

3232 "'Unforgettable' Nat Cole Truly a King to the Last." Billboard 77:4, February 27, 1965.

3233 "Cancer Strikes Nat Cole." Sepia 14:9-13, March 1965.

3234 Dahlgren, R. "Nat King Cole." Orkester Journalen 33: 18-19, March 1965.

3235 Feather, L. "Nytt Fraan USA." Orkester Journalen 33:9, March 1965.

3236 "Mort de Nat 'King' Cole." Jazz Hot no. 207:5, March 1965.

3237 "Nat King Cole." International Musician 63:41, March 1965.

3238 "Ora Anche King Cole." Musica Jazz 21:12, March 1965.

3239 "Le Roi Est Mort." Jazz Magazine no. 116:13-14, March 1965.

3240 "Soft Answers." Newsweek 65:81, March 1, 1965. A eulogy for Cole.

3241 "Bulk of Cole Estate Bequeathed to Widow." Variety 238:55, March 3, 1965.

3242 "Music City Stores Aid Cole Fund." Billboard 77:3, March 20, 1965.

3243 "Form Nat Cole Cancer Foundation as a 'Living Memorial' to Late Singer." Variety 238:72, March 24, 1965.

3244 "Nat 'King' Cole, 1917-1965." down beat 32:14, March 25, 1965.

3245 "Jazz Notes." International Musician 63:17, April 1965.

3246 Koechlin, P. "Nat King Cole, du Jazz à la Chanson." Musica no. 133:54-55, April 1965.

3247 "Last Days of Nat 'King' Cole." Sepia 14:8-14, April 1965.

3248 "Les Obseques du Roi." Jazz Magazine no. 117:9, April 1965.

3249 Pye, B. "Funeralized in Simple Dignity." Sepia 14:15-17, April 1965.

3250 Robertson, S. "Gentle Giant." Sepia 14:18-21, April 1965.

3251 Robinson, L. "Life and Death of Nat King Cole." Ebony 20:123-134, April 1965.

3252 Young, A. S. "Nat King Cole." Sepia 14:22-26, April 1965.

3253 Zaccagnino, M. "Nat Is Gone." Record Research no. 67-12, April 1965.

3254 "Nat Cole's Will Probated; Cancer Fund Begun in His Name." down
      beat 32:12, April 8, 1965.

3255 Feather, L. "Feather's Nest." down beat 32:39, May 6, 1965.

3256 "Eddie Albert Will Head Nat Cole Foundation." Billboard 77:4, June
      26, 1965.

3257 Tanner, P. "Oh Didn't They Ramble." Jazz Journal 19:4, July 1966.

3258 "Nat Cole Foundation Hits Heavy Returns at $100 Top in L.A. Bene-
      fit." Variety 241:62, December 15, 1965.

3259 "Launch Cole Cancer Drive." Billboard 77:3, December 25, 1965.

3260 "Cole Estate & Cap Sue Over 'Poor' LP." Variety 242:55, March
      16, 1966.

3261 "Cole Memorial Ball May Raise 100G." Billboard 79:3, March 18,
      1967.

3262 "King Cole Still Reigns as a Top Seller at Cap." Billboard 79:8,
      November 11, 1967.

3263 "Nat King Cole Still Rules Record Roost." down beat 35:13, Jan-
      uary 11, 1968.

3264 Cole, Maria, and Louie Robinson. Nat King Cole; An Intimate Biog-
      raphy. New York: W. Morrow, 1971. A biography by Cole's
      wife.

3265 Gardner, M. "Record Reviews: Anatomy of a Jam Session." Jazz
      Journal 24:34, June 1971.

3266 Jones, M. "Jazz Records: Anatomy of a Jam Session." Melody
      Maker 46:47, June 19, 1971.

3267 "Record Reviews: Capitol Jazz Classics, Vols. 1-10." Coda 10:15-
      16, no. 10, 1972.

3268 "Chronique des Disques: Trio Days." Jazz Hot no. 282:25, April
      1972.

3269 "Disques du Mois: Trio Days." Jazz Magazine no. 200:44-45, May
      1972.

3270 "Jazz Records: Trio Days." Melody Maker 48:38, August 25, 1973.

3271 Tiegel, E. "Leonard Feathers MCA's Nest with Nat, Duke, Tatum
      Vintages." Billboard 85:15, October 20, 1973.

3272 "On Record: Trio Days." Jazz & Blues 3:23, November 1973.

3273 "Jazz Records: Nat Cole Meets the Master Saxes." Melody Maker
      49:48, July 13, 1974.

3274 "Hearings Held on Cap. Vs. Cole Estate Dispute." Billboard 86:3,
      July 27, 1974.

3275   "Schallplatten-Besprechungen: From the Very Beginning." Jazz Po-
       dium 23:35, December 1974.

3276   Laverdure, M. "Il Ya Dix Ans, King Cole." Jazz Magazine no.
       230:24-26, February 1975.

3277   Tiegel, E. "Brothers & Daughter Keep Nat Cole Tradition Alive."
       Billboard 87:37, July 26, 1975. Freddie, Ike, and Natalie are
       Cole's children who are also singers.

3278   Brown, G. F. "Nat Cole's Daughter Follows in His Footsteps."
       Jet 48:58-61, September 4, 1975.

3279   "Record Reviews: Inseparable." down beat 43:28-29, January 15,
       1976.

3280   "Jazz Albums: Jazz at the Philharmonic 1944-46." Melody Maker
       51:24, July 10, 1976.

3281   Murphy, F. D. "Natalie Gives Nat the Cole Shoulder." Encore
       5:24-26, October 4, 1976.

3282   Dexter, D. "Rare Cole Trio Transcriptions Issued." Billboard
       88:46, December 11, 1976.

3283   "Caught in the Act Extra." Melody Maker 51:30, December 25, 1976.

3284   Feather, L. "Nat King Cole." Contemporary Keyboard 4:57, April
       1978.

COLE, NATALIE (Mrs. Marvin Yancy), 1950- .

3285   "New Acts." Variety 269:64, January 31, 1973.

3286   "Copacabana, N.Y." Variety 271:117, May 16, 1973.

3287   "Talent in Action." Billboard 85:16, June 9, 1973.

3288   "Nat King Cole's Daughter of Soul." Ebony 28:54-56, September 1973.

3289   "Shepheard's, N.Y." Variety 272:49, September 26, 1973.

3290   "'Nat's Little Girl' Is Her Own Lady." Soul 9:10, June 10, 1974.

3291   "New Acts." Variety 275:56, July 3, 1974.

3292   Tiegel, E. "Brothers & Daughter Keep Nat Cole Tradition Alive."
       Billboard 87:37, July 26, 1975. Freddie, Ike and Natalie have al-
       so become singers.

3293   "Talent in Action." Billboard 87:47, August 23, 1975.

3294   Jefferson, M., and A. Kuflik. "Princess Cole." Newsweek 86:75,
       August 25, 1975.

3295   Brown, G. F. "Nat Cole's Daughter Follows in His Footsteps."
       Jet 48:58-61, September 4, 1975.

3296 Nassour, E. "Natalie Cole Finds Her Own Style." Encore 4:32, October 20, 1975.

3297 Brown, G. "Young Queen Cole." Melody Maker 50:3, October 25, 1975.

3298 "Caught in the Act America." Melody Maker 50:42, October 25, 1975.

3299 Smith, N. "Inseparable." Black Collegian 6:61, November-December 1975.

3300 "Records: Inseparable." Rolling Stone no. 199:66, November 6, 1975.

3301 Johnson, H. "Natalie Cole: Nat King Cole's Daughter Zooms Toward Stardom." Ebony 31:35-37, December 1975.

3302 McGee, D. "Singles: Natalie Cole's Merry Old Gospel Soul." Rolling Stone no. 201:12, December 4, 1975.

3303 "Concert Reviews." Variety 281:52, February 4, 1976.

3304 "Caught in the Act." Melody Maker 51:27, February 14, 1976.

3305 "Performance." Rolling Stone no. 209:78, March 25, 1976.

3306 "Hilton, Las Vegas." Variety 282:69, April 28, 1976.

3307 "Talent in Action." Billboard 88:55, May 8, 1976.

3308 "New Albums: Natalie." Melody Maker 51:24, June 12, 1976.

3309 Snyder, P. "Natalie Cole: Soul Survivor." Rolling Stone no. 215:18, June 17, 1976.

3310 Williams, J. "Natalie Cole: Singer Looks for Longevity; Writing Songs, Will Produce." Billboard 88:45, September 4, 1976.

3311 No entry.

3312 Reilly, P. "The Arrival of Singer Natalie Cole: In Every Way, Her Illustrious Father's Daughter." Stereo Review 37:85-86, October 1976.

3313 Murphy, F. D. "Natalie Gives Nat the Cole Shoulder." Encore 5:24-26, October 4, 1976.

3314 "Caught in the Act Extra." Melody Maker 51:67, October 9, 1976.

3315 "Making Waves." Melody Maker 51:34, October 16, 1976.

3316 Grossman, J. "Natalie Cole's Sophisticated Soul: Always Smilin', Always Sweet, and Don't Say It's R&B." Crawdaddy no. 67:28, December 1976.

3317 "Concert Reviews." Variety 285:58, December 1, 1976.

3318   Jacobs, Linda. Natalie Cole: Star Child. St. Paul, Minn.: EMC
       Corp., 1977.

3319   Roberts, J. S. "Natalie Cole: Producers' Puppet, Father's Daugh-
       ter, or the New Queen of R&B?" High Fidelity/Musical America
       27:125, February 1977.

3320   "Talent in Action." Billboard 89:37, February 19, 1977.

3321   Rankin, E. L. "Natalie Cole Is Wed to Songwriter: Will Keep Sep-
       arate Careers." Jet 51:16-17, February 24, 1977.

3322   Cole, Natalie, and L. Gite. "Natalie Cole." Black Collegian 7:48-
       49, March-April 1977.

3323   Kisner, R. E. "Natalie and Her Mr. Melody Talk About Their Fu-
       ture." Jet 51:22-26, March 17, 1977.

3324   "Records: Unpredictable." High Fidelity/Musical America 27:114-
       115, May 1977.

3325   "Records: Unpredictable." Rolling Stone no. 239:86, May 19, 1977.

3326   Rankin, E. L. "Natalie and Marvin: Their Long-Distance Marriage
       Tests Love." Jet 52:20-23, June 23, 1977.

3327   Miller, E. "Daddy's Girl Makes Good." Seventeen 36:98-99, July
       1977.

3328   Salvo, P. "King's Daughter Inherits a New Realm of Music." Sepia
       26:34-36, July 1977.

3329   "Concert Reviews." Variety 288:60, August 31, 1977.

3330   "Talent in Action." Billboard 89:38, September 3, 1977.

3331   Kisner, R. E. "Is There Room at the Top for Big Three of Songs."
       Jet 52:58-60, September 15, 1977.

3332   "Records: Thankful." Rolling Stone no. 257:52, January 26, 1978.

3333   "Concert Reviews." Variety 290:116, April 19, 1978.

3334   "Talent in Action." Billboard 90:50, April 29, 1978.

3335   Robinson, L. "Revealing Talk with Natalie Cole." Ebony 33:32-34,
       May 1978.

3336   "Television Reviews." Variety 290:64, May 3, 1978.

3337   Wansley, J. "Couples." People 9:74-76, May 8, 1978.

3338   Antoine, R. "Natalie Cole Does It Her Way." Sepia 27:39-40, July
       1978.

3339   "Albums: Natalie--Live." Melody Maker 53:18, July 29, 1978.

3340   "Resorts Int'l, A.C." Variety 291:77, July 26, 1978.

3341 "Talent in Action." Billboard 90:86, August 26, 1978.

3342 "Concert Reviews." Variety 292:66, November 1, 1978.

COLEMAN, ORNETTE, 1930- .

3343 Jones, Q. "Ornette Coleman." Jazz Review 2:29, May 1959.

3344 Farmer, A. "Something Else!!!" Jazz Review 2:18, July 1959.

3345 Maher, J. "The School of Jazz." Music U.S.A. 76:15, October
      1959.

3346 Dahlgren, C. "Amerikanska Nyheter." Orkester Journalen 27:10-11,
      December 1959.

3347 Morgenstern, D. "New York Scene." Jazz Journal 13:22-23, Jan-
      uary 1960.

3348 Williams, M. "Ornette Coleman." Jazz Magazine 6:26-29, January
      1960.

3349 Feather, L. "The Blindfold Test." down beat 27:39-40, January 7,
      1960.

3350 Hoefer, G. "Caught in the Act." down beat 27:40-41, January 7,
      1960.

3351 Gleason, R. J. "Perspectives." down beat 27:44, January 21, 1960.

3352 Hoefer, G. "The Hot Box." down beat 27:42, January 21, 1960.

3353 Dance, S. "First Time in New York." Jazz Journal 13:23, Febru-
      ary 1960.

3354 Balliett, W. "Jazz Concerts." New Yorker 35:116-118, February
      6, 1960.

3355 Craddock, J. "Ornette Coleman at the Five Spot." Jazz Journal
      13:25, April 1960.

3356 Balliett, W. "Jazz Concerts." New Yorker 36:169-171, April 16,
      1960.

3357 Batten, J. H. "The Morning Line on Ornette Coleman: Some Criti-
      cal Motives." Jazz Monthly 6:12, May 1960.

3358 Adderley, J. "Cannon Ball Looks at Ornette Coleman." down beat
      27:20-21, May 26, 1960.

3359 Mingus, C. "Another View of Coleman." down beat 27:21, May 26,
      1960.

3360 Arrigoni, A. Qualcosa Sta Cambiando." Musica Jazz 16:17-21, June
      1960.

3361 Mortara, A. "Giuffre, Coleman e la Rivoluzione." Musica Jazz 16:14-16, June 1960.

3362 Russell, G., and M. Williams. "Ornette Coleman and Tonality." Jazz Review 3:6-10, June 1960.

3363 White, T. E. "Ornette Coleman; Too Much Too Soon?" Metronome 77:41, June 1960.

3364 "The True Essence." New Yorker 36:33-34, June 4, 1960.

3365 "Beyond the Cool." Time 75:56, June 27, 1960.

3366 Morgenstern, D. "Dionysius in New York." Jazz Journal 13:17-19, July 1960.

3367 Polillo, A. "Tiro al Piccione." Musica Jazz 16:20-22, July 1960.

3368 Tynan, J. "Ornette: The First Beginning." down beat 27:32-33, July 21, 1960.

3369 Mortara, A. "Ancora Su Coleman e Giuffre." Musica Jazz 16:17-18, August-September 1960.

3370 Abel, B. "The Man with the White Plastic Sax." HiFi/Stereo Review 5:40-44, August 1960.

3371 Morgenstern, D. "Jazz by Schuller." Metronome 77:43-45, August 1960.

3372 "Two Views of Ornette Coleman." American Record Guide 26:1017, August 1960.

3373 Korall, B. "Coleman Finally Wins Through." Melody Maker 35:13, August 6, 1960.

3374 "Triple Play." Metronome 77:38-40, September 1960. Coleman reviews three of his records.

3375 White, T. "Ornette and Jimmy." Metronome 77:44, September 1960.

3376 Kofsky, F. "It Happened in Monterey." Jazz Journal 13:1-4, November 1960.

3377 Masson, J. R. "Alors Faut-Il le Mettre au Poteau ou sur un Piedestal ce Fameux Ornette Coleman?" Jazz Magazine 6:26-29, November 1960.

3378 Arrigoni, A. "Il Nuovo Jazz di Ornette Coleman." Musica Jazz 17:14-17, January 1961.

3379 Close, A. "Ornette Coleman and Feeling." Jazz Monthly 6:9, January 1961.

3380 Coss, B., and D. Solomon. "A Visit to the King in Queens: An Interview with Dizzy Gillespie." Metronome 78:15-18, February 1961.

3381 Postgate, J. "Between You and Me." Jazz Monthly 6:16, February 1961.

3382 Hentoff, N. "Ornette Coleman: Biggest Noise in Jazz." Esquire
      55:82-87, March 1961.

3383 Morgenstern, D. "Ornette Meets Dizzy." Metronome 78:24-25,
      March 1961.

3384 "Combo Reviews." Variety 223:55, July 26, 1961.

3385 Morgenstern, D. "Heard & Seen." Metronome 78:7, October 1961.

3386 Balliett, W. "Jazz Records." New Yorker 37:164-168, October 28,
      1961.

3387 Williams, M. "Rehearsing with Ornette." Metronome 78:19, De-
      cember 1961.

3388 Feather, L. "Jazz: Going Nowhere." Show 2:12-14, January 1962.

3389 Williams, M. "Ornette Coleman." International Musician 60:20,
      January 1962.

3390 "Free Jazz Hits Cincinnati Snag." down beat 29:16-17, January 18,
      1962.

3391 Williams, M. "The Bystander." down beat 29:39, May 10, 1962.

3392 Voce, S. "No, No Ornette." Jazz Journal 15:15, August 1962.

3393 Korall, B. "I've Talked Enough; Interviews with Sonny Rollins, John
      Coltrane and Ornette Coleman." Melody Maker 37:8-9, September
      15, 1962.

3394 Quersin, B. "L'Homme au Plastique Entre les Dents." Jazz Mag-
      azine 8:48-49, December 1962.

3395 "Ornette to Premiere String Quartet, R&B Trio." down beat 30:11-
      12, January 3, 1963.

3396 Balliett, W. "Jazz Concerts; O. Coleman at Town Hall." New York-
      er 38:80-82, January 5, 1963.

3397 Heckman, D. "Ornette Coleman and the Quiet Revolution." Saturday
      Review 46:78-79, January 12, 1963.

3398 Tynan, J. "Jimmy Woods, Fire in the West." down beat 30:22,
      January 17, 1963.

3399 Coss, B. "Caught in the Act." down beat 30:32, January 31, 1963.

3400 Dahlgren, C. "Ornette Coleman, Man Med Problem." Orkester
      Journalen 31:10-11, February 1963.

3401 Dance, S. "Ornette Ennobled." Jazz Journal 16:22-24, February
      1963.

3402 Gaskell, P. "Can You Follow Ornette?" Jazz Monthly 8:6-7, Feb-
      ruary 1963.

3403 "Ornette's Concert." Jazz 2:14-15, February 1963.

3404   Jezer, M. "Ornette Coleman on the Frontiers of Jazz." Music
       Journal 21:77-80, March 1963.

3405   Feather, L. "Naked--That's Ornette Coleman." Melody Maker 38:7,
       September 14, 1963.

3406   Williams, M. "Ornette Coleman." Jazz 2:24-25, November-Decem-
       ber 1963.

3407   _____. "Ornette, le Coupable No. 1?" Jazz Hot no. 193:39-41,
       December 1963.

3408   Martin, T. E. "The Plastic Muse." Jazz Monthly 10:13-15, May
       1964; 10:14-18, June 1964.

3409   Heckman, D. "Ornette and the Sixties." down beat 31:58-62, July
       2, 1964.

3410   Martin, T. E. "The Plastic Muse." Jazz Monthly 10:20-21, August
       1964; 10:5-6, September 1964.

3411   Vikharieff, Y. "The 'New Thing' in Russia." down beat 31:16-18,
       September 10, 1964.

3412   Heckman, D. "Ornette '65." Jazz 4:24, no. 3, 1965.

3413   Kofsky, F. "Revolution, Coltrane and the Avant-Garde." Jazz 4:13-
       16, no. 7, 1965.

3414   Paudras, F. "Nouvelle Dimension: Ornette." Jazz Hot no. 205:16-
       23, January 1965.

3415   Balliett, W. "Jazz; O. Coleman's Music." New Yorker 40:117-118,
       January 16, 1965.

3416   "Back from Exile." Time 85:43, January 22, 1965.

3417   "Play Sincere." Newsweek 65:84, January 25, 1965.

3418   Morgenstern, D. "Caught in the Act." down beat 32:15, February
       25, 1965.

3419   Balliett, W. "Jazz Concerts; Composer of the New Thing." New
       Yorker 41:122-124, February 27, 1965.

3420   "Il Ritorno di Coleman." Musica Jazz 21:13, March 1965.

3421   Morgenstern, D. "Ornette Coleman from the Heart." down beat
       32:16-18, April 8, 1965.

3422   Martin, T. "Ornette Coleman on Atlantic." Jazz Monthly 11:21-22,
       May 1965.

3423   Binchet, J. P. "Honnete Ornette." Jazz Magazine no. 119:20-23,
       June 1965.

3424   Dawbarn, B. "Coleman: It's All Over the Ridge." Melody Maker
       40:6, August 14, 1965.

3425   Whitworth, B. "Ornette Coleman: Innovator or Incompetent?" Hol-
       iday 38:81-82, September 1965.

3426   "Ornette: Justification for the Faithful." Melody Maker 40:6, Sep-
       tember 4, 1965.

3427   Heckman, D. "Inside Ornette Coleman." down beat 32:13-15, Sep-
       tember 9, 1965.

3428   "U. S. Jazzman's Permit Irks British Musicians Because of 'Concert'
       Tag." Variety 240:65, September 15, 1965

3429   "Ornette in London, Plans Extended Stay Out of U. S." down beat
       32:17, September 23, 1965.

3430   Cooke, J. "Ornette Coleman at Crydon." Jazz Monthly 11:22-24,
       October 1965.

3431   Harrison, M. "David Mack & Serial Jazz." Jazz Monthly 11:14-15,
       October 1965.

3432   McRae, B. "Ornette Coleman Live." Jazz Journal 18:8-9, October
       1965.

3433   Nahman, P. "En Angleterre, Premier Triomphe Europeen pour Or-
       nette Coleman." Jazz Hot no. 213:7-8, October 1965.

3434   "Givande Jazzhöst." Orkester Journalen 33:10-11, December 1965.

3435   Van Peebles, M. "Tete à Tete avec Ornette." Jazz Magazine no.
       125:26-31, December 1965.

3436   Heckman, D. "Inside Ornette." down beat 32:20-21, December 16,
       1965.

3437   Hennessey, M. "Ornette: There Is No Bad Music, Only Bad Mu-
       sicians." Melody Maker 40:8, December 18, 1965.

3438   Andre, J. "Jazz-Brief: Wird Ornette Coleman Doch Siegen? Die
       Junge Avantgarde auf dem 10. Deutschen Jazz-Festival in Frank-
       furt." Gottesdienst und Kirchenmusik no. 4-5:174-175, 1966.

3439   Smith, F. "Music and Internal Activities; Contacting Greatness in
       Art and the Music of Ornette Coleman." Jazz 5:13-15, no. 4,
       1966; 5:22-23, no. 5, 1966; 5:18-20, no. 6, 1966.

3440   Spellman, A. B. Black Music, Four Lives. New York: Schocken
       Books, 1970, c1966. The first edition in 1966 had the title: Four
       Lives in the Bebop Business. The four musicians examined are
       Cecil Taylor, Herbie Nichols, Jackie McLean, and Coleman.

3441   "Ornette Coleman in Paris." Melody Maker 41:23, February 26,
       1966.

3442   Reda, J. "Du Free Jazz Prisonnier." Jazz Magazine no. 128:9,
       March 1966.

3443   Delorme, M., et al. "Consecration d'Ornette." Jazz Hot no. 219:5-
       6, April 1966.

3444 "Ornette à la Mutualite." Jazz Magazine no. 129:13-14, April 1966.

3445 Houston, B. "Ornette; The New Wave, Resident in London." Mel-
      ody Maker 41:6, April 16, 1966.

3446 Walker, M. "Ornette Coleman." Jazz Monthly 12:24-25, May 1966.

3447 Wilmer, V. "Ornette Coleman." Jazz Monthly 12:13-14, May 1966.

3448 "Ornette, Noise or Music--the Controversy Continues." Melody Mak-
      er 41:6, May 7, 1966.

3449 "Seven Steps to Jazz." Melody Maker 41:8, May 7, 1966.

3450 Harrison, M. "Coleman and the Consequences." Jazz Monthly 12:10-
      15, June 1966.

3451 McRae, B. "The Ornette Coleman Trio at Ronnie Scott's Club."
      Jazz Journal 19:9, June 1966.

3452 Williams, M. "Ornette Coleman in Stockholm." Saturday Review
      49:83, June 11, 1966.

3453 _____. "No Work in U.S. for Ornette?" down beat 33:12, June
      30, 1966.

3454 Cooke, J. "Ornette Coleman Revisited." Jazz Monthly 12:9-11,
      July 1966.

3455 Schonfield, V. "Caught in the Act." down beat 33:31, July 14, 1966.

3456 Heckman, D. "The Month's Jazz." American Record Guide 32:1166-
      1167, August 1966.

3457 Delorme, M. "Ornette Prophete en Son Pays?" Jazz Hot no. 224:3,
      October 1966.

3458 Williams, M. "Coltrane, Coleman Up to Date." Jazz Journal 19:4-
      5, November 1966.

3459 "Dictionnaire de l'Alto." Jazz Magazine no. 137:41, December 1966.

3460 "New Jazz." Newsweek 68:101-104, December 12, 1966.

3461 Baronijan, V. "Atonalnost u Dzezu." Zvuk no. 75-76: 18-19, 1967.

3462 "Honors for Members." ASCAP Today 1:18, no. 2, 1967.

3463 Zwerin, M. "A State of Mind; The Excellence of Ornette." down
      beat 34:16, March 9, 1967.

3464 Balliett, W. "Jazz Concerts; Quartet and the Philadelphia Woodwind
      Quintet at the Village Theatre." New Yorker 43:125-126, March
      25, 1967.

3465 Morgenstern, D. "Caught in the Act." down beat 34:24, May 18,
      1967.

3466 "Ornette Gets Grant." down beat 34:13, May 18, 1967.

3467 Coleman, Ornette. "To Whom It May Concern." down beat 34:19, June 1, 1967.

3468 Cooke, J. "Ornette and Son." Jazz Monthly 13:13-15, July 1967.

3469 Williams, M. "Ornette Coleman: Father and Son." Saturday Review 50:45, July 29, 1967.

3470 "Ayler, Coleman Quartets Play for Trane Funeral." Melody Maker 42:3, August 5, 1967.

3471 Berendt, J. E. "Free Jazz--der Neue Jazz der Sechziger Jahre." Melos 34:344-345, October 1967.

3472 "Put Down That Saxophone." Jazz Journal 20:13, October 1967.

3473 Coleman, Ornette, et al. "'Round 'The Empty Foxhole.'" down beat 34:16-17, November 2, 1967.

3474 Dawbarn, B. "Ornette Stirs It Up Again." Melody Maker 43:10, March 2, 1968.

3475 _____. "The Controversy, Jazz or Concert Artist?" Melody Maker 43:10, March 9, 1968.

3476 McRae, B. "Emotion Modulation; Ornette Coleman in Concert." Jazz Journal 21:5, April 1968.

3477 Priestley, B. "In Person." Jazz Monthly 14:28-29, April 1968.

3478 "Caught in the Act." down beat 35:32-33, May 2, 1968.

3479 Heckman, D., and A. Cohn. "Jazzman as Serious Composer: Two Views of Ornette Coleman." American Record Guide 35:24-25, September 1968.

3480 "Caught in the Act." down beat 35:30, September 5, 1968.

3481 Hunt, D. C. "Coleman, Coltrane and Shepp: The Need for an Educated Audience." Jazz and Pop 7:18-21, October 1968.

3482 Raben, Erik. A Discography of Free Jazz. Copenhagen: Karl Emil Knudsen, 1969. Discographies of Coleman, Albert Ayler, Don Cherry, Pharoah Sanders, Archie Shepp, and Cecil Taylor.

3483 Williams, M. "Ornette Coleman." ASCAP Today 3:14-15, no. 2, 1969.

3484 "Record Reviews." down beat 36:21-22, January 23, 1969.

3485 Harrison, M. "Two from Coleman." Jazz Monthly no. 168:17, February 1969.

3486 "Good News: Coleman, Don Cherry Reunite." down beat 36:14, March 20, 1969.

3487 Williams, M. "Caught in the Act." down beat 36:30, May 15, 1969.

3488 "Record Reviews." down beat 36:21, June 12, 1969.

3489 Dawbarn, B. "Saxists Always the Innovators." Melody Maker 44:16, June 14, 1969.

3490 Wilmer, V. "Second Opinion." Melody Maker 44:14, September 27, 1969.

3491 Carles, P. "O. C. et la Centrifugeuse." Jazz Magazine no. 171:15, October 1969.

3492 Cressant, P. "Ornette Coleman." Jazz Hot no. 254:6-7, October 1969.

3493 Lecomte, H. "Ornette à Bilzen." Jazz Magazine no. 171:12-13, October 1969.

3494 "Record Reviews." Jazz Journal 22:29, November 1969.

3495 Williams, M. "Ornette Coleman: Ten Years After." down beat 36:24-25, December 25, 1969.

3496 Jost, E. "Zur Musik Ornette Colemans." Jazz Research 2:105-124, 1970.

3497 Williams, M. "Thriving on Challenge and Change." American Musical Digest 1:39-40, no. 4, 1970.

3498 West, H. I. "How Jazz Was Orphaned." American Musical Digest 1:34-35, no. 4, 1970. Reprinted from the Washington Post January 4, 1970.

3499 Williams, M. "Ornette Coleman Ten Years After." down beat 37:11, January 8, 1970.

3500 Malson, L., et al. "Sur Quelques Oeuvres Contemporaines." Jazz Magazine no. 176:xxii-xxiii, March 1970.

3501 Glassenberg, B. "Talent in Action." Billboard 82:44, August 22, 1970.

3502 Strongin, D. "Record Reviews: Friends and Neighbors, Live at Prince Street." Jazz and Pop 9:55-56, September 1970.

3503 Kofsky, F. "Ornette Coleman: 'Jazz' Musician." Jazz and Pop 9:34-35, November 1970.

3504 Noel, G. "La Chronique des Disques: The Best of Ornette Coleman." Jazz Hot no. 266:40, November 1970.

3505 Brauer, C. "Records: Friends and Neighbors, Ornette Live at Prince Street." Rolling Stone no. 72:56, December 2, 1970.

3506 Mitchell, S. "Caught in the Act: Ornette Coleman." down beat 37:34, November 12, 1970.

3507 Brown, D. "Record Reviews: The Art of the Improvisers; Friends and Neighbors--Ornette Live at Prince Street." Coda 10:16, no. 2, 1971.

3508 Norris, J. "Heard and Seen: Ornette Coleman, Town Tavern, Tor-
      onto." Coda 9:41-42, no. 11, 1971.

3509 "Record Reviews: The Art of the Improvisers." Hip 9:19, no. 4,
      1971.

3510 Santucci, U. "Da Milano." Rivista Italiana di Musicologia 5:1055-
      1056, no. 6, 1971.

3511 Goldman, A. "Jazz Meets Rock." Atlantic Monthly 227:100-101,
      February 1971.

3512 Cole, B. "Caught in the Act." down beat 38:31, February 18, 1971.

3513 "Jazz Records: Love Call; The Art of the Improvisers." Melody
      Maker 46:27, March 27, 1971.

3514 Williams, R. "Memories of Ornette." Melody Maker 46:28, July
      17, 1971.

3515 Wilmer, V. "The Art of Insecurity." Melody Maker 46:18, October
      30, 1971.

3516 Gilmore, M. S. "Newport '71--Festival Misfortune." Jazz Journal
      24:6-7, November 1971.

3517 Wilmer, V. "The Art of Insecurity." Melody Maker 46:12, Novem-
      ber 6, 1971.

3518 Welch, C. "Weekend of Jazz Giants." Melody Maker 46:25, Novem-
      ber 20, 1971.

3519 Delaunay, C., et al. "Les Festivals d'Automne." Jazz Hot no.
      278:8, December 1971.

3520 McRae, B. "A B Basics; A Column for the Newcomer to Jazz."
      Jazz Journal 24:7, December 1971.

3521 Marmande, F. "Ornette Coleman." Jazz Magazine no. 195:28-29,
      December 1971.

3522 "News & Honors." ASCAP Today 5:30, no. 3, 1972. Performance
      of Coleman's "Quintet for Trumpet and String Quartet."

3523 Norris, J. "Newport, N.Y., N.Y." Coda 10:10-11, no. 8, 1972.

3524 "Record Reviews: Love Call." Coda 10:22-23, no. 5, 1972.

3525 Stanilewicz, M. "'Jazz Jamboree' 71." Ruch Muzycany 16:15, no.
      1, 1972.

3526 "Record Reviews: The Art of the Improvisers." Jazz and Pop 10:50-
      51, January 1971; down beat 38:21, February 18, 1971.

3527 "Ornette Coleman." Jazz Hot no. 281:12-15, March 1972.

3528 "Jazz Records: In Europe, Vol. 1." Melody Maker 47:32, March
      11, 1972.

3529 "Records: Science Fiction." Rolling Stone no. 104:60, March 16, 1972.

3530 "Disques du Mois: Friends and Neighbors; Ornette Live at Prince Street." Jazz Magazine no. 199:37, April 1972.

3531 "Record Reviews: Love Call." Jazz Journal 24:38, April 1971.

3532 "RecWords: Science Fiction." Crawdaddy no. 8:19, April 2, 1972.

3533 Williams, R. "Ornette in the Studio." Melody Maker 47:21, April 22, 1972.

3534 "Record Reviews: Science Fiction." down beat 39:17-18, April 27, 1972.

3535 "Record Reviews: Ornette Coleman in Europe, Vol. 1, 2." Jazz & Blues 2:21, May 1972.

3536 "Record Reviews: The Art of the Improvisers." Jazz Journal 24:35, May 1971.

3537 "Record Reviews: Twins." down beat 39:18, May 25, 1972.

3538 "Record Reviews: Love Call." Jazz and Pop 10:43-44, June 1971; down beat 36:16, June 10, 1971.

3539 "Jazz Records: Twins; Crisis; Science Fiction; Skies of America." Melody Maker 47:44, July 22, 1972.

3540 "Impressive Preview of Coleman's Magnum Opus." down beat 39:10-11, August 17, 1972.

3541 "Records: Skies of America." Rolling Stone no. 115:52, August 17, 1972.

3542 "Record Reviews: Twins." Jazz & Blues 2:26, October 1972.

3543 Palmer, R. "Ornette Coleman and the Circle with a Hole in the Middle." Atlantic 230:91-93, December 1972.

3544 Bachmann, C. H. "Viktring: Die Schule der Improvisation." Neue Zeitschrift für Musik 134:590-592, no. 9, 1973.

3545 James, M. "Some Interesting Contemporaries." Jazz & Blues 2:8-14, January 1973.

3546 Marmande, F. "Retour sur Ornette." Jazz Magazine no. 207:14-17, January 1973.

3547 McRae, B. "Avant Courier: Kaleidoscope." Jazz Journal 26:10, February 1973.

3548 Klee, J. "Caught in the Act." down beat 40:30, February 1, 1973.

3549 "Record Reviews: Crisis." down beat 40:20, February 15, 1973.

3550 Williams, R. "Ornette and the Pipes of Joujouka." Melody Maker 48:22-23, March 17, 1973.

3551 "Reviews on Record: Ornette on Tenor." Jazz & Blues 3:17, April
      1973.

3552 Carles, P. "Ornette: Musique Non Temperee." Jazz Magazine no.
      212:16-17, June 1973.

3553 "On Record: This Is Our Music." Jazz & Blues 3:20, June 1973.

3554 Friedli, H. "5. Internationales Musik-Forum." Jazz Podium 22:26-
      27, September 1973.

3555 "Chronique des Disques: Ornette Coleman in Europe, Vols. 1 et 2."
      Jazz Hot no. 287:25, October 1972.

3556 "Chronique des Disques: Crisis." Jazz Hot no. 288:29, November
      1972.

3557 Bourne, M. "Ornette's Interview." down beat 40:16-17, November
      22, 1973.

3558 Palmer, R. "Ornette Coleman and the Circle with a Hole in the
      Middle." Atlantic 230:91-93, December 1972.

3559 "Record Reviews: Skies of America." down beat 40:20, January
      18, 1973; Jazz Journal 26:26-27, February 1973.

3560 Williams, R. "Ornette and the Pipes of Joujouka." Melody Maker
      48:22-23, March 17, 1973.

3561 Berendt, J. E. "Kleine Combo-Geschichte des Neuen Jazz." Jazz
      Podium 22:12-15, November 1973. Reprinted from Berendt's book
      Jazzbuch--von Rag bis Rock.

3562 Bourne, M. "Ornette's Interview." down beat 40:16-17, November
      22, 1973.

3563 "Heard and Seen." Coda 12:36, no. 2, 1974.

3564 Pailhe, J. "1965: The Ornette Coleman Trio." Jazz Hot no. 302:20-
      23, February 1974.

3565 "Readers' Profiles." Jazz Forum no. 27:5, February 1974.

3566 "Caught in the Act." Melody Maker 49:58, May 18, 1974.

3567 Anders, J. "Ornette Coleman in der Schweiz." Jazz Podium 23:13-
      14, July 1974.

3568 Lake, S. "Stirring Up Ornette's Nest." Melody Maker 49:24, Au-
      gust 17, 1974.

3569 Kumpf, H. "Skies of America: Ornette Coleman." Jazz Podium
      23:18-19, November 1974.

3570 McRae, B. "Avant Courier: The Ornette Coleman Atlantics." Jazz
      Journal 28:14-16, April 1975.

3571 Goddet, L. "La Deuxieme Voix." Jazz Hot no. 323:6-7, January
      1976.

3572 "Jazz en Direct." Jazz Magazine no. 240:10, January 1976.

3573 Hardy, A. R. "Deux Avant-Gardes." Jazz Magazine no. 241:20-21, February 1976.

3574 McRae, B. "Avant Courier: Practising in Public." Jazz Journal 29:14-16, March 1976.

3575 "Les Faces d'Ornette." Jazz Magazine no. 250:20-22, December 1976.

3576 Blumenthal, B. "Ornette: An Experimental Music that Has Aged Gracefully." Jazz Magazine (U.S.) 1:39-42, no. 3, 1977.

3577 "Reviews: Dancing in Your Head." Jazz Magazine (U.S.) 2:56-57, no. 1, 1977.

3578 "Closeness." Radio Free Jazz 18:12-13, February 1977.

3579 Ruppli, M. "Discographie d'Ornette Coleman." Jazz Hot no. 334:24-25, February 1977.

3580 Balliett, W. "Jazz: New York Notes." New Yorker 53:84-85, July 18, 1977.

3581 Occhiogrosso, P. "Ornette--Miles of the Eighties." Melody Maker 52:32-33, July 30, 1977.

3582 Morgenstern, D. "Report from Newport--Sarah and Ornette Take the Honors." Jazz Journal International 30:26-27, August 1977.

3583 "Jazz Albums: Dancing in Your Head." Melody Maker 52:22, August 13, 1977.

3584 Palmer, R. "Ornette Coleman Makes New Waves." Rolling Stone no. 246:17, August 25, 1977.

3585 Weber, M. "Bobby Bradford." Coda no. 157:2-5, September-October 1977.

3586 "Capsule Reviews: Dancing in Your Head." Crawdaddy no. 76:81, September 1977.

3587 "Records: Dancing in Your Head." Rolling Stone no. 248:72, September 22, 1977; Creem 96:60, October 1977.

3588 "Record Reviews: Dancing in Your Head." down beat 44:24, October 6, 1977.

3589 "Jazz Albums: Paris Concert; To Whom Keeps a Record." Melody Maker 52:24, December 17, 1977.

3590 Berendt, J. E. "Jazz Highlights of 1977, in Retrospect." Jazz Forum no. 51:31-32, 1978.

3591 "Record Reviews: Paris Concert." Jazz Forum no. 52:48, 1978.

3592 Mandel, H. "Predatory Prawns; With Biographical Sketch." Sea Frontiers 24:89-90, March 1978.

3593 "Jazz Records: Coleman Classics Vol. 1." Melody Maker 53:17,
      May 6, 1978.

3594 "Record Reviews: Coleman Classics 1." Coda no. 161:19-20, June
      1, 1978.

3595 "Record Reviews: Coleman Classics Vol. 1." down beat 45:24, June
      1, 1978; Radio Free Jazz 19:22, July 1978.

3596 Dallas, K. "Ornette Makes It All Worthwhile." Melody Maker 53:44-
      45, July 15, 1978.

3597 Jaenichen, L. "Ornette Coleman." Jazz Podium 27:15, August 1978.

3598 "Ornette Coleman." Jazz Podium 27:10-15, September 1978.

3599 "Record Reviews: Coleman Classics Vol. 1." Jazz Journal Interna-
      tional 31:35-36, September 1978.

3600 "Jazz Albums: The Unprecedented Music of Ornette Coleman." Mel-
      ody Maker 53:28, September 30, 1978.

3601 Mandel, H. "Ornette Coleman: The Creator as Harmolodic Magi-
      cian." down beat 45:17-19, October 5, 1978.

COLERIDGE-TAYLOR, SAMUEL, 1875-1912.

3602 "Higher Music of Negroes." Literary Digest 45:565, October 5,
      1912.

3603 Kramer, A. W. "Impressions of Coleridge-Taylor's New Violin Con-
      certo." Musician 19:201, March 1914.

3604 Sayers, William Charles Berwick. Samuel Coleridge-Taylor, Mu-
      sician; His Life and Letters. Chicago: Afro-Am Press, 1969.
      Original edition published by Cassell in London, 1915.

3605 "The Composer and the Organ Grinder." Music Box 22:240, no. 3,
      1976. Reprinted from Etude April 1916.

3606 Gaul, H. B. "Afro-British Composer." Musician 22:577, August
      1917.

3607 Antcliffe, H. "Some Notes on Coleridge-Taylor." Musical Quarter-
      ly 8:180-192, April 1922.

3608 Dashwood, G. C. "Samuel Coleridge-Taylor." Crisis 29:158-161,
      February 1925.

3609 "Samuel Coleridge-Taylor." Canon 10:399, July 1957.

3610 "Samuel Coleridge-Taylor in Washington." Phylon 28:185-196, 2d
      quarter, Summer 1967.

3611 Simms, L. M. "Samuel Coleridge-Taylor, Black Composer." Crisis
      78:291-292, November 1971.

3612 Arvey, V. "Symphonies in Black." Music Journal 32:28-29, April
      1974.

3613 "Here and There." Gramophone 53:307, August 1975.

3614 "Samuel Coleridge-Taylor." Music and Musicians 23:6-7, August
      1975.

3615 Tortolano, W. "Samuel/Colerige[sic]-Taylor, 1875-1912." Music
      9:25-27, August 1975.

3616 Young, P. M. "Samuel Coleridge-Taylor, 1875-1912." Music Teach-
      er 116:703-705, August 1975.

3617 Tortolano, William. Samuel Coleridge-Taylor: Anglo-Black Com-
      poser, 1875-1912. Metuchen, N.J.: Scarecrow Press, 1977. In-
      cludes "Catalog of Music by Coleridge-Taylor," discography, and
      bibliography.

COLES, NATHANIEL ADAMS see COLE, NAT KING

COLLINS, MRS. WALTER see ANDERSON, IVIE MARY

COLTRANE, JOHN WILLIAM, 1926-1967.

3618 Fremer, B. "John Coltrane." Orkester Journalen 26:12-13, March
      1958.

3619 Jepsen, J. G. "John Coltrane Diskografi." Orkester Journalen
      26:42, March 1958; 26:46, April 1958.

3620 Gitler, I. "'Trane on the Track." down beat 25:16-17, October 16,
      1958.

3621 Blume, A. "An Interview with John Coltrane." Jazz Review 2:25,
      January 1959.

3622 Taylor, C. "John Coltrane." Jazz Review 2:34, January 1959.

3623 Feather, L. "Honest John." down beat 26:39, February 19, 1959.

3624 Clar, M. "John Coltrane: Soultrane." Jazz Review 2:24, April
      1959.

3625 Morgenstern, D. "Modern Reeds--and How They Grew." down beat
      26:17, May 14, 1959.

3626 Carno, Z. "The Style of John Coltrane." Jazz Review 2:27-21, Oc-
      tober 1959; 2:13-17, November 1959.

3627 "Controverse Autour de Coltrane." Jazz Hot 26:28-29, May 1960.

3728 "Le Dossier Coltrane." Jazz Magazine 6:22-27, May 1960.

3729 "Jazz Gallery, N.Y." Variety 218:66, May 25, 1960.

3730   Arrigoni, A. "Qualcosa sat Cambiando." Musica Jazz 16:17-21,
       June 1960.

3731   Gibson, M. "John Coltrane: The Formative Years." Jazz Journal
       13:9-10, June 1960.

3732   "Lettere al Direttore: Pro e Contro Coltrane." Musica Jazz 16:10-
       12, July 1960.

3733   Coltrane, John. "Coltrane on Coltrane." down beat 39:30-31, July
       20, 1972. Reprinted from down beat 27:26-27, September 19, 1960.

3734   Newton, F. "Me Dig Coltrane? That Old Traddy!" Melody Maker
       35:8, October 29, 1960.

3735   Guastone, G. "Quattro Chiacchiere con Gianni Basso su Cinque Sas-
       sofonisti." Musica Jazz 16:29, November 1960.

3736   Postif, F. "New York in Jazz Time." Jazz Hot 26:25, December
       1960.

3737   "John Coltrane et Cannonball Adderley, Premiers au Referendum de
       la Revue down beat." Jazz Magazine 7:26, January 1961.

3738   Mortara, A. "Coltrane (e Altri); la Crisi del Parkerismo." Musica
       Jazz 17:18-22, March 1961.

3739   Hobson, W. "The Amen Corner." Saturday Review 44:51, April 29,
       1961.

3740   Mortara, A. "John Coltrane; La Maturazione di Uno Stile." Musica
       Jazz 17:10-14, May 1961.

3741   "Finally Made." Newsweek 58:64, July 24, 1961.

3742   "Combo Reviews." Variety 223:55, July 26, 1961.

3743   Grigson, L. "Directions in Modern Jazz." Jazz Monthly 7:17, Sep-
       tember 1971.

3744   Lees, G. "L'Homme Coltrane." Jazz Magazine 7:34-35, November
       1961.

3745   Spellman, A. B. "Heard & Seen." Metronome 78:8, November 1961.

3746   Dawbarn, B. "What Happened?" Melody Maker 36:15, November
       18, 1961.

3747   Tynan, J. "Take 5." down beat 28:40, November 23, 1961.

3748   Dawbarn, B. "I'd Like to Play Your Clubs; Interview with John
       Coltrane." Melody Maker 36:8, November 25, 1961.

3749   Jones, L. "A Coltrane Triology." Metronome 78:34-36, December
       1961.

3750   "Cinq Personnages en Quete de 'Trane.'" Jazz Hot no. 172:16-21,
       January 1962.

3751   Feather, L. "Jazz: Going Nowhere." Show 2:12-14, January 1962.

3752   Postif, F. "John Coltrane: Une Interview." Jazz Hot no. 172:12-14, January 1962.

3753   Tenot, F., M. Poulain, and J. C. Dargenpierre. "John Coltrane." Jazz Magazine 8:18-19, January 1962.

3754   Wilmer, V. "Conversation with Coltrane." Jazz Journal 15:1-2, January 1962.

3755   Atkins, R. "John Coltrane and Dizzy Gillespie in Britain." Jazz Monthly 7:11-12, February 1962.

3756   Hentoff, N. "John Coltrane; Challenges Without End." International Musician 60:12-13, March 1962.

3757   "Grand Prix pour Coltrane." Jazz Magazine 8:16, April 1962.

3758   DeMicheal, D. "John Coltrane and Eric Dolphy Answer the Jazz Critics." down beat 29:20-23, April 12, 1962.

3759   Williams, M. "The Bystander." down beat 29:39, May 10, 1962.

3760   Green, B. "A Matter of Form." Jazz Journal 15:11-12, June 1962.

3761   Ioakimidis, D. "Sonny Rollins et John Coltrane en Parallele." Jazz Hot no. 179:24-27, September 1962.

3762   Korall, B. "I've Talked Enough; Interviews with Sonny Rollins, John Coltrane and Ornette Coleman." Melody Maker 37:8-9, September 15, 1962.

3763   Bolognani, M. "John Coltrane; Sensibilita o Transformismo?" Musica Jazz 18:37-38, November 1962.

3764   Gilson, J., and C. Lenissois. "Les Concerts Coltrane." Jazz Hot no. 182:17-19, December 1962.

3765   Ioakimidis, D. "Sonny Rollins et John Coltrane." Jazz Hot no. 182:30-34, December 1962.

3766   Sundin, B. "Coltranes Musik Angelägen och Krävande." Orkester Journalen 30:10-11, December 1962.

3767   Williams, M. "New Coltrane, the Old Parker." Saturday Review 45:38, December 15, 1962.

3768   Cooke, J. "Better Times Ahead." Jazz Monthly 8:4-5, January 1963.

3769   Masson, J. R. "La Nuit des Magiciens." Jazz Magazine 9:22-29, January 1963.

3770   Quersin, B. "La Passe Dangereuse." Jazz Magazine 9:39-40, January 1963.

3771   "Sentiamo ora le Opinioni di Alcuni Noti Musicisti." Musica Jazz 19:15-16, January 1963.

3772 Testoni, G. C., and A. Polillo. "Impressioni su Coltrane." Mu-
      sica Jazz 19:10-14, January 1963.

3773 Lees, G. "Consider Coltrane." Jazz 2:7, February 1963.

3774 Santucci, U. "Jazz + Microstruttura + John = Coltrane." Musica
      Jazz 19:12-17, July-August 1963.

3775 "Coltrane--Anti-Jazz or the Wave of the Future?" Melody Maker
      38:11, September 28, 1963.

3776 Delorme, M. "Coltrane 1963: Vers la Composition." Jazz Hot no.
      193:10-11, December 1963.

3777 James, M. "The John Coltrane Quartet in Amsterdam." Jazz Month-
      ly 9:16-17, December 1963.

3778 Lenissois, C., and J. Gilson. "Les Fabuleux Demons Coltraniens
      Sont Revenus le 1er Novembre." Jazz Hot no. 193:9-10, Decem-
      ber 1963.

3779 "E Tornato John Coltrane." Musica Jazz 19:16-17, December 1963.

3780 Koechlin, P. "L'Ombre de Coltrane sous le Soleil de Parker." Jazz
      Hot no. 194:10, January 1964.

3781 Fresia, E. "Discografia." Musica Jazz 20:42-43, February 1964.
      Lists recordings of John Coltrane and Oscar Peterson from 1961-
      1963.

3782 "Caught in the Act." down beat 31:34, February 27, 1964.

3783 Coleman, R. "Coltrane." Melody Maker 39:6, July 11, 1964.

3784 Feather, L. "For Coltrane the Time Is Now." Melody Maker 39:10,
      December 19, 1964.

3785 Coltrane, John. "A Love Supreme." Jazz 4:16-17, no. 3, 1965. A
      poem by Coltrane.

3786 Kofsky, F. "Revolution, Coltrane and the Avant-garde." Jazz 4:13-
      16, no. 7, 1965; 4:18-22, no. 8, 1965.

3787 Williams, M. "Coltrane Triumphant." Saturday Review 48:73-74,
      January 16, 1965.

3788 Lemery, D. "Comme un Seul Homme." Jazz Magazine no. 115:30-
      34, February 1965.

3789 Stenbeck, L. "Coltrane och Guds Kärlek." Orkester Journalen 33:7,
      July-August 1965.

3790 Hennessey, M. "Forty-Seven Minutes of Magnificent Coltrane."
      Melody Maker 40:8, July 31, 1965.

3791 _____. Coltrane: Dropping the Ball and Chain from Jazz." Mel-
      ody Maker 40:6, August 14, 1965.

3792 Delorme, M., and C. Lenissois. "Coltrane, Vedettre d'Antibes." Jazz Hot no. 212:5-6, September 1965.

3793 Koechlin, P. "Coltrane à Paris." Jazz Hot no. 212:10, September 1965.

3794 "Trane et Woody à Paris." Jazz Magazine no. 122:7-8, September 1965.

3795 Noames, J. L. "Jazz à New York." Jazz Magazine no. 123:21, October 1965.

3796 Spellman, A. B. "Trane + 7 = a Wild Night at the Gate." down beat 32:15, December 30, 1965.

3797 "About John Coltrane." Jazz 5:22, no. 8, 1966. Bob Thiele's views of Coltrane.

3798 Kofsky, F. "John Coltrane and the Jazz Revolution; The Case of Albert Ayler." Jazz 5:24-25, no. 9, 1966, no. 10, 1966.

3799 "Who's on First?" down beat 33:8, March 10, 1966.

3800 "Plugged Nickel, Chi." Variety 242:65, March 16, 1966.

3801 Feather, L. "Coltrane; Does It Now Mean a Thing, If It Ain't Got That Swing?" Melody Maker 41:6, April 16, 1966.

3802 Williams, M. "Coltrane Up to Date." Saturday Review 49:67, April 30, 1966.

3803 Mathieu, B. A Review of Ascension by John Coltrane." down beat 33:25, May 5, 1966.

3804 Walker, M., and E. Raben. "John Coltrane." Jazz Monthly 12:11-13, August 1966; 12:30-31, September 1966; 12:23-24, October 1966.

3805 Dawbarn, B. "Coltrane." Melody Maker 41:8, October 15, 1966.

3806 Walker, M., and E. Raben. "John Coltrane." Jazz Monthly 12:29-31, November 1966.

3807 Williams, M. "Coltrane, Coleman Up to Date." Jazz Journal 19:4-5, November 1966.

3808 "New Jazz." Newsweek 68:103-104, December 12, 1966.

3809 ["Obituary."] Musikalische Jugend 16:14, no. 4, 1967.

3810 Kofsky, F. "A Note on Jazz Rhythm." Jazz 6:16-17, January 1967.

3811 Heckman, D. "After Coltrane." down beat 34:18-19, March 9, 1967.

3812 Buin, Y. "Coltrane ou la Mise à Mort." Jazz Hot no. 231:14-17, May 1967.

3813 ["Obituary."] Variety 247:63, July 19, 1967.

3814   "Coltrane Dies in New York." Melody Maker 42:1, July 22, 1967.

3815   "Coltrane Dead of a Liver Ailment." Billboard 79:12, July 29, 1967.

3816   Houston, B. "Always Expect the Unexpected." Melody Maker 42:6,
       July 29, 1967.

3817   Zimmerman, P. D. "Death of a Jazzman." Newsweek 70:78-79,
       July 31, 1967.

3818   Berger, D. "John Coltrane." Jazz Hot no. 234:5, August 1967.

3819   Delorme, M. "John Coltrane Est Mort." Jazz Hot no. 234:15-16,
       August 1967.

3820   "John Coltrane 1926-1967." Jazz Magazine no. 145:16-23, August
       1967.

3821   ["Obituary."] International Musician 66:17, August 1967.

3822   Voce, S. "Basic Trane-ing." Jazz Journal 20:10, August 1967.

3823   "Ayler, Coleman Quartets Play for Trane Funeral." Melody Maker
       42:3, August 5, 1967.

3824   Spellman, A. B. "John Coltrane: 1926-1967." Nation 205:119-120,
       August 14, 1967.

3825   Wilmer, V. "When You Lose an 'Elder Brother.'" Melody Maker
       42:8, August 19, 1967. An interview with McCoy Tyner.

3826   "John Coltrane Dies." down beat 34:12-13, August 24, 1967.

3827   "In Memoriam." Freedomways 7:387, Fall 1967.

3828   Cooke, J. "In Memoriam." Jazz Monthly 13:2, September 1967.

3829   Dance, S. "Jazz." Music Journal 25:92, September 1967.

3830   "Editorial." Jazz and Pop 6:7, September 1967.

3831   "Hommage à John Coltrane." Jazz Magazine no. 146:12-15, Septem-
       ber 1967.

3832   Idestam-Almquist, D. "In Memoriam." Orkester Journalen 35:6-7,
       September 1967.

3833   Kofsky, F. "John Coltrane." Jazz and Pop 6:23-31, September
       1967.

3834   McRae, B. "A B Basics: A Column for the Newcomer to Jazz."
       Jazz Journal 20:8, September 1967.

3835   "John William Coltrane, 1926-1967: Tributes." down beat 34:15-17,
       September 7, 1967.

3836   Williams, M. "Legacy of John Coltrane." Saturday Review 50:69,
       September 16, 1967.

3837 Toomajian, S. "Caught in the Act." down beat 34:26, September
      21, 1967.

3838 Berendt, J. E. "Free Jazz--der Neue Jazz der Sechziger Jahre."
      Melos 34:349-351, October 1967.

3839 Hunt, D. C. "Coleman, Coltrane and Shepp: The Need for an Ed-
      ucated Audience." Jazz and Pop 7:18-21, October 1968.

3840 "In Memoriam." BMI p. 26-27, October 1967.

3841 ["Obituary."] High Fidelity/Musical America 17:MA13, October 1967.

3842 Litweiler, J. "Caught in the Act." down beat 34:44, October 19,
      1967. A tribute to Coltrane performed at the Meadows Club, Chi-
      cago.

3843 "L'Enterrement de Coltrane." Jazz Hot no. 236:7, November 1967.
      Freddy Santamaria is interviewed.

3844 Garland, P. "Requiem for 'Trane." Ebony 23:66-68, November
      1967.

3845 Heckman, D. "The Month's Jazz." American Record Guide 34:339,
      December 1967.

3846 Williams, M. "John Coltrane: Man in the Middle." down beat 34:15-
      17, December 14, 1967.

3847 Jones, M. "It's True--We'll Never Hear Their Like Again." Melody
      Maker 42:6, December 30, 1967.

3848 Berendt, J. E. "Jazz Meets the World." World of Music 10:9, no.
      3, 1968.

3849 Lindgren, G. "Coltranes Konturer." Orkester Journalen 36:8-9,
      January 1968.

3850 Goodman, J. "Looking for the Black Message." New Leader 51:26-
      28, January 1, 1968.

3851 Lindgren, G. "Coltranes Konturer." Orkester Journalen 36:10-11,
      March 1968; 36:10, April 1968.

3852 Balliett, W. "Jazz Concerts; Memorial at Carnegie Hall." New
      Yorker 44:158, April 27, 1968.

3853 Lindgren, G. "Coltranes Konturer." Orkester Journalen 36:8-9,
      May 1968.

3854 Spellman, A. B. "Small Band Jazz; J. Coltrane's Om and M. Dav-
      is' Nefertiti." New Republic 159:40-41, August 17, 1968.

3855 Rivelli, P. "Alice Coltrane." Jazz and Pop 7:26-30, September
      1968. An interview with the wife of John Coltrane.

3856 "Impulse, Mrs. Coltrane in Legacy Agreement." down beat 35:13,
      September 5, 1968.

3857   Hunt, D. C. "Coleman, Coltrane and Shepp: The Need for an Educated Audience." Jazz and Pop 7:18-21, October 1968.

3858   Jepsen, Jorgen Grunnet. A Discography of John Coltrane. Copenhagen NV: Karl Emil Knudsen, 1969.

3859   Jones, M. "Putting the Greats on Record." Melody Maker 44:8, January 25, 1969.

3860   Wiskirchen, G. "Jazz on Campus." down beat 36:45-46, May 1, 1969.

3861   Locke, D. "Cosmic Music." Jazz Monthly no. 173:23, July 1969.

3862   "Record Reviews." Jazz Journal 22:29-30, October 1969; Jazz Monthly no. 177:5, November 1969.

3863   West, H. I. "How Jazz Was Orphaned." American Musical Digest 1:34-35, no. 4, 1970. Reprinted from the Washington Post January 4, 1970.

3864   Cooke, J. "Late Trane." Jazz Monthly no. 179:2-6, January 1970.

3865   "Record Reviews: Selflessness." Jazz and Pop 9:52, March 1970.

3866   "Disques du Mois: Selflessness." Jazz Magazine no. 177:36, April 1970.

3867   "Disques du Mois: Ascension." Jazz Magazine no. 178:48, May 1970.

3868   "Record Reviews: Selflessness." Jazz Monthly no. 184:12, June 1970.

3869   "Shepp Big Band Stars in Coltrane Tribute." down beat 37:12, August 20, 1970.

3870   Tercinet, A., et al. "Special Coltrane." Jazz Hot no. 265:6-25, October 1970.

3871   "Record Reviews: Africa/Brass." Jazz 23:31, November 1970.

3872   "Disques du Mois: The Coltrane Legacy." Jazz Magazine no. 184:52-53, December 1970.

3873   Postgate, J. "The Black and White Show 1970-80: A Speculation on the Future of Jazz." Jazz Monthly no. 190:2-6, December 1970.

3874   "Record Reviews: Africa/Brass." Jazz Monthly no. 190:19-20, December 1970.

3875   Litweiler, J. "Record Reviews: Transition." down beat 37:22, December 24, 1970.

3876   "Record Reviews: The Coltrane Legacy." Coda 10:16, no. 2, 1971.

3877   Tepperman, B. "Record Reviews: Trane's Reign." Coda 9:19, no. 12, 1971.

3878   Goddet, L.   "La Chronique des Disques: Transition."   Jazz Hot no.
       268:34, January 1971.

3879   Williams, R.   "Jazz Records: New Wave in Jazz."   Melody Maker
       46:24, April 3, 1971.

3880   "Record Reviews: The Coltrane Legacy."   down beat 38:22, May 13,
       1971.

3881   McRae, B.   "John Coltrane--the Impulse Years."   Jazz Journal 24:2-
       6, July 1971.   Discussion of Coltrane's recordings under the Im-
       pulse label.

3882   Kopulos, G.   "John Coltrane: Retrospective Perspective."   down
       beat 38:14-15, July 22, 1971.

3883   Seidel, R.   "Caught in the Act."   down beat 38:24-26, November 11,
       1971.   Review of a memorial concert in John Coltrane's honor.

3884   Dews, A.   "Alice Coltrane."   Essence 2:42-43, December 1971.
       Mrs. Coltrane reminisces about her husband.

3885   Gerber, A.   "Disques du Mois: Sun Ship."   Jazz Magazine no.
       195:37-38, December 1971.

3886   "Record Reviews: Live in Seattle."   Coda 10:24, no. 5, 1972.

3887   "Disques du Mois: Live in Seattle."   Jazz Magazine no. 196:27,
       January 1972.

3888   "Le 17 Juillet 1967--Disparaissait John Coltrane."   Jazz Hot no.
       280:16-17, February 1972.

3889   "Schallplattenbesprechungen: Transition."   Jazz Podium 21:82, March
       1972.

3890   "Disques du Mois: Cannonball & Coltrane."   Jazz Magazine no.
       199:30, April 1972.

3891   Roach, M.   "What 'Jazz' Means to Me."   Black Scholar 3:2-6, Sum-
       mer 1972.

3892   Gerber, A.   "Huit Faces de Coltrane."   Jazz Magazine no. 201:25-
       31, June 1972.

3893   "Chronique des Disques: John Coltrane."   Jazz Hot no. 285:29, July-
       August 1972.

3894   Gerber, A.   "Huit Faces de Coltrane."   Jazz Magazine no. 202:14-
       17, July 1972.

3895   Cordle, O.   "The Soprano Saxophone: From Bechet to Coltrane to
       Shorter."   down beat 39:14-15, July 20, 1972.

3896   "Chronique des Disques: Giant Steps."   Jazz Hot no. 286:27, Sep-
       tember 1972.

3897   "Disques du Mois: John Coltrane."   Jazz Magazine no. 204:45, Oc-
       tober 1972.

3898 Cailhe, J. "My Favorite Things." Jazz Hot no. 289:14-16, December 1972.

3899 "Record Reviews: The Master." Coda 10:21, no. 11, 1973.

3900 Taylor, J. R. "The Prestige 24000 Series." Journal of Jazz Studies 1:90-110, no. 1, 1973.

3901 Tomkins, L. "There Is a Future for the Jazz Player; Elvin Jones Speaks His Mind." Crescendo International 11:26-27, January 1973.

3902 "Record Reviews: Infinity." Coda 11:25-26, no. 3, 1973; down beat 40:20, February 15, 1973.

3903 "On Record: Giant Steps." Jazz & Blues 3:21-22, July 1973.

3904 Albertson, C. "John Coltrane: Icing on the Cake--Prestige Restores to the Catalog Two Eloquent Sessions with the Red Garland Quintet." Stereo Review 31:78, August 1973.

3905 "On Record: More Lasting than Bronze." Jazz & Blues 3:15, September 1973.

3906 "On Record: Coltrane Plays the Blues." Jazz & Blues 3:19-20, October 1973.

3907 "On Record: Expression." Jazz & Blues 3:23-24, November 1973.

3908 Berendt, J. E. "The Soprano Saxophone." Jazz Forum no. 26:40-43, December 1973. Portions from Berendt's book: The Jazz Book--from Rag to Rock.

3909 Gerber, A. "Huit Faces de Coltrane." Jazz Magazine no. 217:32-35, December 1973.

3910 "On Record: Coltrane Time." Jazz & Blues 3:15, December 1973.

3911 Chapman, A. "An Interview with Michael S. Harper." Arts in Society 11:462-471, no. 3, 1974.

3912 "Autour de Coltrane." Jazz Magazine no. 218:13-19, January 1974.

3913 Gourgues, M. "Guide pour 'Ascension': Pour Ecouter un des Chefs-d'Oeuvre du Free-Jazz." Jazz Magazine no. 219:14-15, February 1974.

3914 Ramsey, D. "With Respect to 'Respect.'" down beat 41:38, March 14, 1974.

3915 Goddet, L., and A. Dutilh. "McCoy Tyner." Jazz Hot no. 311:8-9, December 1974.

3916 Logan, W. "The Case of Mr. John Coltrane: A Compositional Review." Numus-West 2:40-45, no. 2, 1975.

3917 "Record Reviews: The Africa Brass Sessions, Vol. 2." Coda 12:13-14, no. 5, 1975.

3918 "Record Reviews: Jazz at the Plaza." Coda 12:17, no. 4, 1975.

3919 Simpkins, Cuthbert Ormond. Coltrane: A Biography. New York:
      Herdon House Publishers, 1975.

3920 Thomas, J. Chasin' the Trane: The Music and Mystique of John
      Coltrane. Garden City, N.Y.: Doubleday, 1975.

3921 Turner, R. "John Coltrane: A Biographical Sketch." Black Per-
      spectives in Music 3:3-16, no. 1, 1975.

3922 "Records: Interstellar Space." Crawdaddy no. 46:68-69, March
      1975.

3923 Dutilh, A. "McCoy Tyner Sorti de l'Ombre; Un Eblouissement."
      Jazz Hot no. 318:6-9, July-August 1975.

3924 "McCoy Tyner." Jazz Magazine no. 234:19-22, July 1975.

3925 "Records: Interstellar Space." Rolling Stone no. 190:61, July 3,
      1975.

3926 Dutilh, A. "La Transition." Jazz Hot no. 322:36-37, December
      1975.

3927 Cole, Bill. John Coltrane. New York: Schirmer Books, 1976.

3928 Kofsky, F. "Elvin Jones--Part 1: Rhythmic Innovator." Journal
      of Jazz Studies 4:3-24, no. 1, 1976.

3929 "Record Reviews: Cannonball and Coltrane." Coda no. 144:18, Jan-
      uary-February 1976.

3930 McRae, B. "Avant Courier: Practising in Public." Jazz Journal
      29:14-16, March 1976.

3931 _____. "Arena." Jazz Journal 29:10, August 1976.

3932 "Jazz Albums: Giant Steps." Melody Maker 51:20, August 21, 1976.

3933 "Record Reviews: In Europe Vol. 3." Jazz Journal 29:31, October
      1976.

3934 "Waxing On: Kenny Burrell-John Coltrane." down beat 43:34, Oc-
      tober 21, 1976.

3935 "Record Reviews: Countdown." Jazz Journal 29:26, December 1976.

3936 "Coltrane Works." Jazz Forum no. 50:14-15, 1977.

3937 Kofsky, F. "Elvin Jones: Rhythmic Displacement in the Art of El-
      vin Jones." Journal of Jazz Studies 4:11-32, no. 2, 1977.

3938 "Record Reviews: Interstellar Space." Coda no. 153:17-18, January-
      February 1977.

3939 Williams, R. "Richard Williams." Melody Maker 52:32, March 12,
      1977.

3940 _____. "In My Lifetime, No Artist Has Been So Intent on Devel-

opment as Coltrane." Melody Maker 52:45, April 9, 1977. Review of the recording "The Other Village Vanguard Tapes."

3941 "Records: The Other Village Vanguard Tapes." Rolling Stone no.
      239:89, May 19, 1977.

3942 "Jazz Albums: Creation." Melody Maker 52:28, May 21, 1977.

3943 "Records: The Other Village Vanguard Tapes." Crawdaddy no. 73:72-
      73, June 1977.

3944 Dutilh, A. "Trane Vu par Jeanneau." Jazz Hot no. 339-340:44-50,
      July-August 1977.

3945 Pailhe, J. "Coltrane 1967/1977." Jazz Hot no. 339-340:52-56, July-
      August 1977.

3946 Tercinet, A. "Discographie de John Coltrane." Jazz Hot no. 339-
      340:36-42, July-August 1977.

3947 Wilmer, V. "Coltrane: The Spirit Lives On." Melody Maker 52:46,
      July 16, 1977. Review of recent books about Coltrane by Thomas,
      Simpkins, and Cole.

3948 Heckman, D. "John Coltrane & Eric Dolphy: The Vanguard Years."
      High Fidelity/Musical America 27:116-117, August 1977. Record-
      ings discussed are "The Other Village Vanguard Tapes" and "Wheel-
      in'."

3949 "Record Reviews: The Other Village Vanguard Tapes." down beat
      44:30, September 8, 1977.

3950 "Record Reviews: Dial Africa." Jazz Journal International 30:41,
      October 1977.

3951 "Jazz Albums: Afro-Blue Impressions." Melody Maker 52:28, Oc-
      tober 22, 1977.

3952 "Reissues: Dial Africa; Turning Point." Coda no. 158:22, Novem-
      ber-December 1977.

3953 "Record Reviews: Afro Blue Impressions." down beat 44:28, De-
      cember 15, 1977.

3954 "Coltrane's Transcription." Swinging Newsletter 7:4, no. 34, 1978.

3955 "Waxing On: Dial Africa." down beat 45:34, January 12, 1978.

3956 "Jazz Albums: First Meditations." Melody Maker 53:26, January
      21, 1978.

3957 "Record Reviews: Afro Blue Impressions." Coda no. 159:21, Feb-
      ruary 1, 1978.

3958 Loftus, A. "Thoughts of 'Trane." Jazz Journal International 31:14-
      15, March 1978.

3959 "Record Reviews: First Meditations." down beat 45:24, May 18, 1978.

3960   "Record Reviews: Gold Coast." Radio Free Jazz 19:15, November
           1978.

3961   "Jazz Albums: Coltranology, Vol. 1." Melody Maker 53:47, De-
           cember 9, 1978.

3962   Primack, B. "Archie Shepp: Back to Schooldays." down beat 45:27-
           28, December 21, 1978.

3963   Wild, David Anthony. The Recordings of John Coltrane: A Discog-
           raphy. 2d ed. Ann Arbor, Mich.: Wildmusic, 1979.

CUNNINGHAM, MRS. KENNY see FRANKLIN, ARETHA LOUISE

DALE, CLAMMA.

3964   "More Contest Winners." Clavier 14:40, no. 9, 1975.

3965   "Pianist and Two Sopranos Win Naumburg Competition." School Mu-
           sician 47:27, January 1976.

3966   "Clamma Dale, Soprano; Concert at Alice Tully Hall." High Fidelity/
           Musical America 26:MA25-26, August 1976. Also lists her achieve-
           ments in addition to her concert review.

3967   "Brash Bess Is on Her Way." Newsweek 88:119, October 11, 1976.

3968   Kolodin, I. "Young Old 'Porgy,' New Young Pianist." Saturday Re-
           view 4:48-49, November 13, 1976.

3969   "Porgy & Clamma--Bess." Vogue 166:196-197, December 1976.

3970   Van Cleave, Kit. "Essence Women: Clamma Dale." Essence 4:6,
           December 1976.

3971   "Creative Woman: Success Requires Talent and Drive." Ebony
           32:135-138, August 1977.

3972   Kresh, P. "The Inexhaustible 'Porgy and Bess.'" Stereo Review
           39:130, September 1977.

3973   Hiemenz, J. "Musician of the Month: Clamma Dale." High Fidel-
           ity/Musical America 27:MA4-5, December 1977.

3974   Belsom, J. "Santa Fe: An Ideal 'Onegin.'" Opera 29:113, Autumn
           1978.

3975   Eaton, Q. "Wolf Trap--Santa Fe: A Critical Look." Music Journal
           36:7, November 1978. Review of Dale's performances of "Tosca."

3976   Von Buchau, S. "Santa Fe." Opera News 43:73, November 1978.

DASH, SARAH see LABELLE

DAVIS, MILES DEWEY, JR., 1926- .

3977   Russell, R.   "Brass Instrumentation in Be-bop."   Record Changer
       8:9-10, January 1949.

3978   Harris, P.   "Nothing But Bop?   'Stupid,' Says Miles."   down beat
       17:18-19, January 27, 1950.

3979   "Miles Davis Arrested on Narcotics Charge."   Melody Maker 26:1,
       September 30, 1950.

3980   Ohman, A. R.   "Miles Davis Elegant Stilbildare."   Orkester Journal-
       en 18:12-13, October 1950.

3981   "Miles Davis Acquitted of Dope Charge."   Melody Maker 27:6, January
       27, 1951.

3982   "All Stars."   Metronome 67:15, February 1951.

3983   Russo, B., and L. Lifton.   "Jazz Off the Record."   down beat 18:12,
       March 9, 1951.

3984   Davis, Miles.   "My Best on Wax."   down beat 18:7, March 23, 1951.

3985   "U.S.A.--Intervju i Kickformat: Miles Davis."   Orkester Journalen
       19:8, May 1951.

3986   Russo, B., and L. Lifton.   "Jazz Off the Record."   down beat 18:12,
       September 21, 1951.

3987   Lindgren, C. E.   "Mina Sex Stora Jazzminnen."   Orkester Journalen
       19:26, December 1951.

3988   Feather, L.   "Poll-Topper Miles Has Been at a Standstill Since Back
       in 1950."   Melody Maker 28:4, February 23, 1952.

3989   Morgan, A.   "Retrospection."   Jazz Journal 5:10, June 1952.

3990   _____.   "Music by Miles Davis and Lars Gullin; Two New Long
       Playing Records."   Jazz Journal 6:21, November 1953.

3991   "'Recording Artists' Roster."   down beat 21:94, June 30, 1954.

3992   Eckstine, B.   "Dizzy, Bird and the Birth of Bop."   Melody Maker
       30:5, September 4, 1954.

3993   Dahlgren, C.   "Glimtar om Glimtar."   Orkester Journalen 22:22-23,
       December 1954.

3994   Horricks, R.   "A Milestone from Capitol."   Jazz Journal 7:34, De-
       cember 1954.

3995   Jepsen, J. G.   "Jazzens Instrumentalister: Trumpeten."   Orkester
       Journalen 23:11, February 1955.

3996   Dahlgren, C.   "Dizzy, Miles och Chet i Birdland-Duell."   Orkester
       Journalen 23:8-9, July 1955.

3997   Feather, L. "Miles and Miles of Trumpet Players." down beat
       22:33, September 21, 1955.

3998   Hentoff, N. "Miles." down beat 22:13-14, November 2, 1955. Com-
       ments on the jazz styles which are currently in favor.

3999   Mingus, C. "An Open Letter to Miles Davis." down beat 22:12-13,
       November 30, 1955.

4000   Wood, B. "Miles Davis." Jazz Journal 9:25, May 1956.

4001   Ferrara, D. "The Trumpet." Metronome 72:22, July 1956.

4002   "Davis-Charles at the Bohemia." Metronome 72:8, August 1956.

4003   O'Brien, N. C. "Miles Davis." Jazz Journal 9:9, August 1956.

4004   Stewart-Baxter, D. "Miles Davis." Jazz Journal 9:7, November
       1956.

4005   Frost, H. "Miles Davis." Metronome 74:27-28, May 1957.

4006   "Miles Davis Quintet." down beat 24:31, August 8, 1957.

4007   "Post-Bopper." Time 71:63, January 20, 1958.

4008   Feather, L. "The Trumpet in Jazz." down beat 25:16, January
       23, 1958.

4009   Davis, Miles. "You Don't Learn the Blues." Melody Maker 33:12,
       February 22, 1958.

4010   "Self-Portrait: Miles Davis." down beat 25:17, March 6, 1958.

4011   Larrabee, E. "Jazz Notes." Harper's Magazine 216:96, May 1958.

4012   Balliett, W. "Chameleon." New Yorker 34:121-125, May 17, 1958.

4013   Rolontz, B. "Miles Davis Group Is Strong as Ethel Ennis Debuts
       Well." Billboard 70:5, July 28, 1958.

4014   Feather, L. "More Miles." down beat 25:29, August 7, 1958.

4015   Anderson, J. L. "Musings of Miles." Saturday Review 41:58-59,
       October 11, 1958.

4016   Race, S. "Birth of an Era." Melody Maker 33:7, October 18, 1958.
       Discussion of the "Boplicity" recording.

4017   Jepsen, J. G. "Miles Davis Diskografi." Orkester Journalen 26:58,
       November 1958.

4018   Hentoff, N. "An Afternoon with Miles Davis." Jazz Review 1:9-12,
       December 1958.

4019   James, M. "Miles Davis." Orkester Journalen 26:10-13, December
       1958.

4020   Jepsen, J. G. "Miles Davis Diskografi." Orkester Journalen 26:64-
        65, December 1958.

4021   Williams, M. "Extended Improvisation and Form: Some Solutions."
        Jazz Review 1:13-15, December 1958.

4022   "Apollo, N.Y." Variety 214:87, March 18, 1959.

4023   Gibson, M. "Miles Davis--an Appreciation." Jazz Journal 12:7-8,
        June 1959.

4024   Feather, L. "That Birdland Beating." Melody Maker 34:5, Septem-
        ber 5, 1959.

4025   Grevatt, R., and B. Korall. "Probe into Birdland Beating-Up."
        Melody Maker 34:1, September 5, 1959.

4026   Kolodin, I. "'Miles Ahead' or Miles' Head?" Saturday Review
        42:60-61, September 12, 1959.

4027   Korall, B. "Miles Davis's Band Is a Laboratory." Melody Maker
        34:12, September 12, 1959.

4028   "This Is What They Did to Miles Davis." Melody Maker 34:1, Sep-
        tember 12, 1959.

4029   "Miles Davis to Sue N.Y. City." Melody Maker 34:1, September 19,
        1959.

4030   Gaspard, J. J. "Miles Davis." Musica no. 67:29, October 1959.

4031   "Sauvage Agression Contre Miles Davis." Jazz Magazine 5:13, Oc-
        tober 1959.

4032   "The Slugging of Miles." down beat 26:11-12, October 1, 1959.

4033   "Judge Finds Miles Not Guilty." Melody Maker 34:1, October 24,
        1959.

4034   "Aftermath for Miles." down beat 26:11, October 29, 1959.

4035   "Charge Dismissed." down beat 26:11, November 12, 1959.

4036   Thorne, F. "Microsolco al Microscopio." Jazz di Ieri e di Oggi
        11:48-53, January-February 1960.

4037   Crawford, M. "Miles Davis: Evil Genius of Jazz." Ebony 16:69-
        72, January 1960.

4038   Stenbeck, L. "Qua Vadis, Miles?" Orkester Journalen 28:8-9, Jan-
        uary 1960.

4039   Gardner, B. J. "The Enigma of Miles Davis." down beat 27:20-23,
        January 7, 1960.

4040   Harrison, M. "Gil Evans and Miles Davis." Jazz Monthly 5:10-12,
        February 1960.

4041 Hentoff, N. "Miles Davis Now Recording." HiFi/Stereo Review 4:52-56, February 1960.

4042 "Miles Exonerated." down beat 27:12, February 18, 1960.

4043 Vartan, E. "Miles Davis, le Solitaire." Jazz Magazine 6:20-25, March 1960.

4044 "Miles Files." down beat 27:13, March 31, 1960.

4045 Vitet, B. "Miles Davis." Jazz Hot 26:10-13, April 1960.

4046 Tynan, J. "Caught in the Act." down beat 27:42, April 14, 1960.

4047 Vitet, B. "Miles Davis." Jazz Hot 26:12-13, May 1960.

4048 Mathieu, B. "The Inner Ear." down beat 27:47, May 26, 1960.

4049 Arrigoni, A. "Qualcosa Sta Cambiando." Musica Jazz 16:17-21, June 1960.

4050 "Davis, Miles." Metronome 77:43, June 1960.

4051 Vitet, B. "Miles Davis." Jazz Hot 26:12-13, June 1960.

4052 "Miles Davis, Jazz Trumpeter, to Appear on Robert Herridge Theater, July 21 on CBS-TV with His Quintet and with a 19 Piece Orchestra." Jet p. 66, July 21, 1960.

4053 "Miles Davis and Dizzy Gillespie Tie in downbeat International Critics Poll for Top Trumpet." Jet p. 59, July 28, 1960.

4054 "Quattro Chiacchiere con Oscar Valdambrini su Cinque Trombettisti." Musica Jazz 16:28, August-September 1960.

4055 "The Sound of Miles." down beat 27:13, August 18, 1960.

4056 "Bodyguard for Miles Davis." Melody Maker 35:1, August 27, 1960.

4057 "Miles Davis Says 'Yes' to the Press." Melody Maker 35:1, September 10, 1960.

4058 Feather, L. "The Real Miles Davis." Melody Maker 35:2-3, September 17, 1960.

4059 Lyttelton, H. "Miles Has Rights, Too." Melody Maker 35:10, September 17, 1960.

4060 Green, B. "Famous Last Words." Jazz Journal 13:1, October 1960.

4061 "Pourquoi si Mechant? Miles." Jazz Magazine 6:24-27, October 1960.

4062 Dawbarn, B. "Miles Davis Is a Genius." Melody Maker 35:2-3, October 1, 1960.

4063 Lyttelton, H. "Here's My Theory." Melody Maker 35:3, October 1, 1960.

4064 Jones, M. "Miles Is Taking a Chance." Melody Maker 35:8-9, October 8, 1960.

4065 Hoefer, G. "The Hot Box." down beat 27:57, October 27, 1960.

4066 "Pourquoi si Gentil Miles?" Jazz Magazine 6:17-18, November 1960.

4067 Renaud, H. "Propos sur le Premier Concert Miles Davis à l'Olympia." Jazz Hot 26:22-23, November 1960.

4068 Shaw, R. B. "Miles Above." Jazz Journal 13:15-16, November 1960.

4069 "Miles Davis, Cry 'Genius' Trumpeter, Scowls in England." Jet p. 58-59, November 3, 1960.

4070 "Miles Davis Wows 'em at Vanguard." Billboard 72:17, November 21, 1960.

4071 "Village Vanguard, N.Y." Variety 220:60, November 23, 1960.

4072 Harrison, M. "Miles Davis Concert Review." Jazz Monthly 6:14-15, December 1960.

4073 Lyttelton, H. "Miles Davis in England: Boor or Businessman?" Metronome 77:53, December 1960.

4074 "Merci, Miles!" Jazz Magazine 6:22, December 1960.

4075 James, Michael. Miles Davis. New York: Barnes, 1961.

4076 Crawford, M. "Miles Davis: Evil Genius of Jazz." Ebony 16:69-72, January 1961.

4077 Hentoff, N. "Miles Davis." International Musician 59:20-21, February 1961.

4078 Crawford, M. "Miles and Gil--Portrait of a Friendship." down beat 28:18-19, February 16, 1961.

4079 Mortara, A. "Coltrane (e Al tri); La Crisi del Parkerismo." Musica Jazz 17:18-22, March 1961.

4080 "Village Vanguard, N.Y." Variety 222:67, March 8, 1961.

4081 Jones, M. "U.S. Jazzmen Quiz Critics--a 'Bristling Evening!'" Melody Maker 36:10, March 18, 1961. Jazz musicians talk with jazz writers at Davis's home.

4082 Millstein, G. "On Stage: Miles Davis." Horizon 3:100-101, May 1961.

4083 Morgenstern, D. "Sippin' at Miles', or a Press Conference in Reverse." Metronome 78:8, May 1961.

4084 "Black Hawk, S.F." Variety 222:77, May 3, 1961.

4085 "Frisco's Masonic Temple Turns Down Miles Davis Benefit Show for NAACP." Variety 222:1, May 3, 1961.

4086   "Miles Davis--Gil Evans Carnegie Hall Concert Spiked with Politics."
       Variety 222:15, May 24, 1961.

4087   Balliett, W.   "Musical Events."   New Yorker 37:79-80, May 27, 1961.

4088   "Frisco's Masonic Temple Drops Miles Davis' Ban; Feared 'Wrong'
       Audience."   Variety 223:1, June 14, 1961.

4089   "Miles au Pilon."   Jazz Magazine 7:15, July 1961.

4090   "Combo Reviews."   Variety 223:44, July 5, 1961.

4091   "Caught in the Act."   down beat 28:42, July 6, 1961.

4092   "Miles Davis to Retire?"   down beat 28:13, July 6, 1961.

4093   "Miles Davis 'Approved' for Bay Concert."   down beat 28:13-14, July
       20, 1961.

4094   Feather, L.   "Feather's Nest."   down beat 28:43-44, August 17, 1961.

4095   Haley, A.   "Two Faces of Miles Davis."   Negro Digest 10:81-88,
       August 1961.   Reprinted from Climax.

4096   Grigson, L.   "Directions in Modern Jazz."   Jazz Monthly 7:16-17,
       September 1961.

4097   Morgenstern, D.   "Heard & Seen."   Metronome 78:7, September
       1961.

4098   Feather, L.   "Voyages en Quarantaine."   Jazz Magazine 7:31, Oc-
       tober 1961.

4099   _____.   "Jazz Records."   Show 2:102-103, February 1962.

4100   James, M.   "Some Notes on 'Lift to the Scaffold.'"   Jazz Monthly
       7:4-5, February 1962.

4101   "Miles Davis."   Esquire 57:59, March 1962.

4102   James, M.   "Out of the Bay."   Jazz Monthly 8:16-17, July 1962.

4103   "Caught in the Act."   down beat 29:31, August 2, 1962.

4104   Heckman, D.   "Miles Davis Times Three; The Evolution of a Jazz
       Artist."   down beat 29:16-19, August 30, 1962.

4105   Williams, M.   "Miles Davis; A Man Walking."   Saturday Review
       45:54-55, November 10, 1962.

4106   "L. P. Recordings of Miles Davis."   Holiday 33:109, February 1963.

4107   Tynan, K.   "Antic Arts; M. Davis, Moody Potentate of Jazz."   Holi-
       day 33:101-103, February 1963.

4108   Wagner, J.   "Voici Miles, l'Iconoclaste."   Jazz Magazine 9:26-31,
       April 1963.

4109   "The New Miles Davis Sextet."   down beat 30:17, April 25, 1963.

4110 "Sextette New-Look." Jazz Magazine 9:13, May 1963.

4111 Turley, P. "Miles." Jazz 2:11, June 1963. Review of the record-
        ing entitled "Miles."

4112 Jalard, M. C. "Notes pour Miles." Jazz Magazine 9:22-25, July
        1963.

4113 "Village Vanguard, N.Y." Variety 231:74, July 17, 1963.

4114 Bianco, F. "Trionfo di Davis ad Antibes." Musica Jazz 19:17-19,
        September 1963.

4115 Jalard, M. C. "Miles Aujourd'hui." Jazz Magazine 9:37-39, Oc-
        tober 1963.

4116 "One Pays--Another Gets It." down beat 30:11, November 7, 1963.

4117 Idestam-Almquist, D. "Miles Davis." Orkester Journalen 32:12-13,
        January 1964.

4118 Houston, B. "Miles Davis Talks about Birdland, Europe, Britain."
        Melody Maker 39:16, February 1, 1964.

4119 "Concert Review." Variety 233:61, February 19, 1964.

4120 "Le Palais Merveilleux." Jazz Magazine no. 104:30-33, March 1964.

4121 Balliett, W. "Jazz Records." New Yorker 40:194-197, April 25,
        1964.

4122 Feather, L. "Musing with Miles." Melody Maker 39:12, June 6,
        1964.

4123 _____. "Blindfold Test." down beat 31:31, June 18, 1964.

4124 _____. "Miles and the Fifties." down beat 31:44-48, July 2,
        1964.

4125 _____. "Now It's Miles the Mikado." Melody Maker 39:6, August
        8, 1964.

4126 Koechlin, P. "Miles Davis." Musica no. 126:60-61, September
        1964.

4127 Feather, L. "Tokyo Blues; Japan's Recent World Jazz Festival."
        down beat 31:20-23, September 10, 1964.

4128 Williams, M. "The Public Miles Davis." Saturday Review 47:72-
        73, September 26, 1964.

4129 "Miles Hospitalise." Jazz Magazine no. 118:15, May 1965.

4130 Santucci, C. "Il Mestiere di Miles." Musica Jazz 21:10-19, August-
        September 1965.

4131 Williams, M. "Miles Davis: Conception in Search of a Sound."
        Jazz 4:8-11, October 1965.

4132   Hentoff, N.   "The Singular Trumpet of Miles Davis."   HiFi/Stereo
       Review 15:86, December 1965.

4133   "Miles Back in Action."   down beat 32:14, December 30, 1965.

4134   "Plugged Nickel, Chi."   Variety 241:70, January 12, 1966.

4135   "Jazz."   BMI p. 20, March 1966.

4136   Zwerin, M.   "Miles Davis; A Most Curious Friendship."   down beat
       33:18-19, March 10, 1966.

4137   Dawbarn, B.   "Great Jazz Solos."   Melody Maker 41:8, December
       3, 1966.

4138   Houston, B.   "Great Jazz Solos."   Melody Maker 42:6, March 11,
       1967.

4139   Atterton, J.   "Miles; Henderson Joins the Sextet."   Melody Maker
       42:6, March 25, 1967.

4140   Hoefer, G.   "Early Miles."   down beat 34:16-19, April 6, 1967.

4141   Hentoff, N.   "Miles Davis: Best Rhythm Team Yet."   HiFi/Stereo
       Review 18:62, June 1967.   Review of the "Miles Smiles" recording.

4142   Cotterrell, R.   "Interlude; Miles Davis with Hank Mobley."   Jazz
       Monthly 13:3-4, October 1967.

4143   Gleason, R.   "Miles Davis."   Melody Maker 42:21, October 14, 1967.

4144   Cooke, J.   "Miles Davis and Archie Shepp."   Jazz Monthly 13:16,
       December 1967.

4145   McRae, B.   "Davis/Shepp."   Jazz Journal 20:12, December 1967.

4146   Mallofre, A.   "Scandale à Barcelone."   Jazz Magazine no. 150:17-
       18, January 1968.

4147   Korall, B.   "The Davis Phenomenon."   Saturday Review 51:50-51,
       February 10, 1966.

4148   Postgate, J.   "The St. Louis Sound."   Jazz Monthly 14:2-6, April
       1968.

4149   Feather, L.   "Miles: A View from the Top."   Melody Maker 43:11,
       April 20, 1968.

4150   _____.   "Miles au 'Manne.'"   Jazz Magazine no. 154:15, May
       1968.

4151   _____.   "Blindfold Test."   down beat 35:34, June 13, 1968.

4152   "Village Gate, N.Y."   Variety 251:52, July 24, 1968.

4153   Gleason, R.   "Mailer, Miles and Johnny Cash."   Jazz and Pop 7:12,
       August 1968.

4154   Spellman, A. B.   "Small Band Jazz; J. Coltrane's Om and M. Dav-
       is' Nefertiti."   New Republic 159:40-41, August 17, 1968.

4155   Atterton, J.   "Dave Holland at Home in Harlem."   Melody Maker
       43:8, September 7, 1968.

4156   Gleason, R. J.   "Davis Quintet in Its Totality."   Jazz and Pop 7:12,
       October 1968.

4157   "Shelly's Manne-Hole."   Variety 252:69, October 30, 1968.

4158   "Miles Davis Takes New Bride of Many Talents."   down beat 35:10-
       11, November 14, 1968.

4159   Carr, I.   "Second Opinion."   Melody Maker 43:8, December 28,
       1968.

4160   Jepsen, Jorgen Grunnet.   A Discography of Miles Davis.   Copenhagen
       NV: Karl Emil Knudsen, 1969.

4161   Russell, R.   "Jazz Record Reviews."   Jazz and Pop 8:48-49, Jan-
       uary 1969.

4162   Williams, M.   "Recording Miles Davis."   Stereo Review 22:68-70,
       February 1969.

4163   "Japanese Wreck Tour by Miles Davis Group."   down beat 36:10,
       February 20, 1969.

4164   Snell, P.   "Miles Davis: 1955."   Jazz Journal 22:19, March 1969.

4165   Williams, M.   "Miles Davis."   BMI p. 14, May 1969.

4166   Albertson, C., et al.   "Record Reviews."   down beat 36:21, May
       29, 1969.

4167   Ginguet, F.   "Miles Davis."   Jazz Hot no. 252:14-17, July-August
       1969.

4168   "Miles Davis' 'Filles de Kilimanjaro.'"   Stereo Review 23:77, July
       1969.

4169   Walsh, A., and J. Hutton.   "Miles, Peterson and Nina on Form."
       Melody Maker 44:6, August 2, 1969.

4170   "Caught in the Act."   down beat 36:28, August 7, 1969.

4171   Delorme, M.   "Deux Nuits à Antibes."   Jazz Hot no. 253:20-21,
       September 1969.

4172   Gerber, A.   "Antibes an 10."   Jazz Magazine no. 169-170:51, Sep-
       tember 1969.

4173   Hopkins, B.   "Scandale à Newport."   Jazz Hot no. 253:8-9, Septem-
       ber 1969.

4174   Peterson, O.   "Tales of Manhattan."   Jazz Monthly no. 175:9, Sep-
       tember 1969.

4175 "Shelly's Manne-Hole, Los Angeles." Variety 256:53, September 17, 1969.

4176 "Caught in the Act." down beat 36:25, October 2, 1969.

4177 "Miles Davis, Wounded by N.Y. Gunman, Posts 4 G Reward for His Arrest." Variety 256:53, October 15, 1969.

4178 Williams, M. "Miles Davis." Saturday Review 52:75, October 25, 1969.

4179 Albertson, C., et al. "Record Reviews." down beat 36:20-21, October 30, 1969.

4180 "Flashes." Jazz Magazine no. 172:14, November 1969.

4181 "The Duke in Berlin." American Musical Digest 1:40, no. 4, 1970. Originally published in the Frankfurter Neue Press November 11, 1969.

4182 "Miles Davis Shot in N.Y. Extortion Plot." down beat 36:11, November 13, 1969.

4183 Bangs, L. "Records: In a Silent Way." Rolling Stone no. 46:33, November 15, 1969.

4184 Burde, W. "Jazz-Tage 1969." Neue Zeitschrift für Musik 130:559, December 1969.

4185 Selbert, T. "Record Reviews." Jazz and Pop 8:49, December 1969.

4186 "Caught in the Act." down beat 36:31, December 11, 1969.

4187 DeMicheal, D. "And in This Corner, the Sidewalk Kid...." down beat 36:12, December 11, 1969.

4188 _____. "Miles Davis." Rolling Stone no. 48:23-26, December 13, 1969.

4189 Gleason, R. "Miles Davis." Rolling Stone no. 48:22, December 13, 1969.

4190 Heckman, D. "Jazz: Optimism." American Musical Digest 1:16-17, no. 6, 1970. Excerpt from an article in the Village Voice March 12, 1970.

4191 Miller, M. "'Bitches Brew' und das Neue Afrika." Neue Musikzeitung 19:9, no. 4, 1970.

4192 Alessandrini, P., et al. "Disques du Mois." Jazz Magazine no. 174:47, January 1970.

4193 Burns, J. "Miles Davis: The Early Years." Jazz Journal 23:2-4, January 1970.

4194 Wilmer, V. "Caught in the Act: Berlin Jazz Days." down beat 37:26, January 22, 1970.

4195 "Talent in Action." Billboard 82:26, March 21, 1970.

4196   Saal, H. "Miles of Music; M. Davis at the Fillmore East." News-
        week 75:99-100, March 23, 1970.

4197   "Disques du Mois: Miles at Newport." Jazz Magazine no. 177:44-
        45, April 1970.

4198   Aletti, V. "Red Roses from Laura for Miles." Rolling Stone no.
        56:20, April 16, 1970.

4199   "Days in the Lives of Our Jazz Superstars." down beat 37:11, April
        16, 1970.

4200   Cooke, J. "Record Review: In a Silent Way." Jazz Monthly no.
        183:19, May 1970.

4201   Gardner, A. J., and B. Priestley. "Readers' Letters: Miles Dav-
        is." Jazz Monthly no. 183:31, May 1970.

4202   Stratton, B. "Miles Ahead in Rock Country." down beat 37:19, May
        14, 1970.

4203   "Record Reviews: Bitches Brew." Rolling Stone no. 59:50, May 28,
        1970.

4204   Goddet, L. "La Chronique des Disques: Bitches Brew." Jazz Hot
        no. 263:42, Summer 1970.

4205   Russell, R. "Miles Davis en Direct au Shelly's." Jazz Hot no.
        262:7, June 1970.

4206   "Clapton and Bruce to Join Miles!" Melody Maker 45:1, June 6,
        1970.

4207   "Record Reviews: Bitches Brew." down beat 37:20-21, June 11,
        1970.

4208   Williams, R. "What Made Miles Davis Go Pop?" Melody Maker
        45:20-21, June 13, 1970.

4209   "Eric Joins Miles' New Rock Group." Rolling Stone no. 61:10, June
        25, 1970.

4210   "Disques du Mois: Bitches Brew." Jazz Magazine no. 180:40, July-
        August 1970.

4211   "Talent in Action." Billboard 82:42, July 4, 1970.

4212   Burks, J. "Miles & a Lot of Different Bitches." Rolling Stone no.
        62:15, July 9, 1970.

4213   "Caught in the Act." down beat 37:28, July 23, 1970.

4214   Lucraft, H. "Miles and the Band at the Bowl." Melody Maker
        45:14, July 25, 1970.

4215   "Talent in Action." Billboard 82:21, August 8, 1970.

4216   "Record Reviews: Bitches Brew." Jazz Monthly no. 187:16, Sep-
        tember 1970.

4217 Morgenstern, D. "Miles in Motion." down beat 37:16-17, September 3, 1970.

4218 Williams, R., et al. "Five Days that Rocked Britain." Melody Maker 45:24-26, September 5, 1970.

4219 Feather, L. ".Jazz at the Crossroads." Melody Maker 45:35, September 12, 1970.

4220 Albertson, C. "Blood, Sweat & Tears: With Miles Davis." down beat 37:12, September 17, 1970.

4221 Gros-Claude, P. "Miles Davis à Wight." Jazz Magazine no. 182:12-13, October 1970.

4222 Feather, L. "The Name of the Game." down beat 37:11, October 15, 1970.

4223 Aronowitz, A. "Rock Is a White Man's Word, Says Miles." Melody Maker 45:25, October 17, 1970.

4224 Feather, L. "Miles Hits the Mood of Today." Melody Maker 45:39, October 24, 1970.

4225 "Caught in the Act." down beat 37:34, December 24, 1970.

4226 Palmer, B. "Records: Miles Davis at Fillmore." Rolling Stone no. 73:54, December 24, 1970.

4227 Kerschbaumer, F. "Zum Personalstil von Miles Davis." Jazz Research 3-4:225-232, 1971-1972.

4228 Norris, J. "Heard and Seen: Miles Davis, Massey Hall, Toronto." Coda 9:42, no. 11, 1971.

4229 "Record Reviews: Oleo." Hip 10:5, no. 2, 1971.

4230 Peterson, O. "West Coast Highlights." Jazz Journal 24:12-15, January 1971.

4231 "Miles Davis Rips Record Firm for Bias." Jet 39:59, January 7, 1971.

4232 Eniss, J. "Miles Smiles." Melody Maker 46:16-17, January 9, 1971.

4233 Williams, R. "Jazz Records: Miles at Fillmore." Melody Maker 46:26, January 16, 1971.

4234 "Dave Holland Forms Circle." Jazz and Pop 10:25-26, February 1971.

4235 Goldman, A. "Jazz Meets Rock." Atlantic Monthly 227:98, February 1971.

4236 Tercinet, A. "Chronique des Disques: At Fillmore." Jazz Hot no. 269:34, February 1971.

4237 Hess, J. B., et al. "Miles Davis: La Volonte de Puissance." Jazz Magazine no. 187:28-33, March 1971.

4238   McRae, B. "Record Reviews: At Fillmore." Jazz Journal 24:35-
       36, March 1971.

4239   "Polls and Awards." BMI p. 11-13, March 1971.

4240   "Disques du Mois: Miles Davis at Fillmore." Jazz Magazine no.
       188:38-39, April 1971.

4241   "Caught in the Act." down beat 38:28, April 15, 1971.

4242   Aronowitz, A. "James Has the Vision of a Blind Man." Melody
       Maker 46:26, April 24, 1971.

4243   "Talent in Action." Billboard 83:52, April 24, 1971.

4244   Feather, L. "Los Angeles." Jazz Magazine no. 189:11, May 1971.

4245   Napoleon, A. "Record Reviews: The Essential Miles Davis." Jazz
       Journal 24:29-30, May 1971.

4246   "Caught in the Act." Melody Maker 46:32, May 8, 1971.

4247   "Record Reviews." Melody Maker 46:26, May 29, 1971.

4248   Aronowitz, A. "The 11,000 Dollar Bash." Melody Maker 46:24,
       June 5, 1971.

4249   Goddet, L. "La Chronique des Disques: Jack Johnson." Jazz Hot
       no. 274:29, July 1971.

4250   "Miles Davis' Movie Music." Stereo Review 27:78, July 1971.

4251   "Record Reviews." Jazz and Pop 10:45, July 1971; Rolling Stone no.
       86:44, July 8, 1971.

4252   "Is Miles Quitting?" Melody Maker 46:4, July 31, 1971.

4253   "Les Malheurs de Miles: Le Trompettiste à Annonce Son Intention
       de Renoncer à Toute Activite Professionnelle." Jazz Magazine no.
       191:8, August 1971.

4254   "Record Reviews." Jazz Journal 24:30-31, August 1971.

4255   "Concert Reviews." Variety 263:43, August 4, 1971.

4256   "Divergences: Miles Davis at Fillmore." Points du Jazz no. 5:35-
       39, September 1971.

4257   Ramsey, D. "Record Reviews: Jack Johnson." down beat 38:29-30,
       September 16, 1971.

4258   Tirfoin, G. "New York." Jazz Magazine no. 193:51, October 1971.

4259   Welch, C. "Miles and the MM." Melody Maker 46:15, October 30,
       1971.

4260   Gerber, A. "Disques du Mois: Jack Johnson." Jazz Magazine no.
       194:33, November 1971.

4261 Watts, M. "Weekend of Jazz Giants." Melody Maker 46:25, November 20, 1971.

4262 Albertson, C. "The Unmasking of Miles Davis." Saturday Review 54:67, November 27, 1971.

4263 Carles, P. "Miles Davis." Jazz Magazine no. 195:24-25, December 1971.

4264 Delaunay, C., et al. "Les Festivals d'Automne." Jazz Hot no. 278:7-8, December 1971.

4265 "Skiftande Stjaernspel i Uppsala." Orkester Journalen 39:8, December 1971.

4266 "Concert Reviews." Variety 265:46, December 1, 1971.

4267 "Talent in Action." Billboard 83:22, December 11, 1971.

4268 "Live/Evil." Soul Illustrated 3:22, no. 5, 1972.

4269 "Record Reviews: Capitol Jazz Classics, Vols. 1-10." Coda 10:15-16, no. 10, 1972.

4270 "Record Reviews: Jack Johnson; Oleo." Coda 10:25, no. 5, 1972.

4271 "Record Reviews: Live/Evil." Coda 10:22, no. 8, 1972.

4272 Burde, W. "Berlin: Jazz, Gulda, Schostakowitsch, Humperdinck." Neue Zeitschrift für Musik 133:27, January 1972.

4273 Burns, J. "The Charlie Parker 'Ko Ko' Date." Jazz & Blues 1:10, January 1972.

4274 "Record Reviews: Live-Evil." Rolling Stone no. 100:50, January 20, 1972.

4275 "Live/Evil." Melody Maker 47:26, February 29, 1972.

4276 "Chronique des Disques: Miles Davis." Jazz Hot no. 281:27, March 1972.

4277 Gilmore, M. S. "Jazz & Blues: Tribute to Jack Johnson." Audio 56:82-83, March 1972.

4278 "Blacks Win 17 Grammy Awards, but Miles Davis, Motown, etc. Walk Out." Jet 42:58, March 3, 1972.

4279 "Chronique des Disques: Live-Evil." Jazz Hot no. 282:26-27, April 1972.

4280 "Schallplattenbesprechungen: Live-Evil." Jazz Podium 21:130, April 1972.

4281 "Record Reviews: Live-Evil." down beat 39:22, April 13, 1972.

4282 "Disques du Mois: Miles Davis Live." Jazz Magazine no. 200:45, May 1972.

4283   Scott, R. E. "Miles Davis: Live/Evil." Black Scholar 3:57-58,
       Summer 1972.

4284   "Classics on Capitol: Capitol Jazz Classics Vol. 1." Jazz & Blues
       2:7, June 1972.

4285   Lee, R. M. "Live Performance: Miles Davis at the Royal Festival
       Hall, London." Jazz Forum no. 17:78-79, June 1972.

4286   Gibbs, V. "John McLaughlin as the Mahavishnu: I Work for the
       Divine Now." Crawdaddy no. 14:30-32, July 1972.

4287   McRae, B. "Avant Courier." Jazz Journal 25:24, July 1972.

4288   Scott, R. E. "Live/Evil." Black World 21:19, September 1972.

4289   "Disques du Mois: Miles Davis." Jazz Magazine no. 204:45, Oc-
       tober 1972.

4290   "Concert Reviews." Variety 268:49, October 4, 1972.

4291   "Miles Davis Recovering After N.Y. Auto Mishap." Variety 268:57,
       October 25, 1972.

4292   "Davis into New Thing; LP Is Free Form & Open." Billboard 84:16,
       October 28, 1972.

4293   "Record Reviews: Miles Davis." Jazz & Blues 2:24, November
       1972.

4294   "Records: In a Silent Way." Crawdaddy no. 18:86, November 1972.

4295   "Miles Davis Almost Waved." Rolling Stone no. 121:18, November
       9, 1972.

4296   "Jazz Records: On the Corner." Melody Maker 47:46, November
       18, 1972.

4297   "Miles Breaks Both Legs in Car Crash." down beat 39:9, December
       7, 1972.

4298   "Records: On the Corner." Rolling Stone no. 123:62, December 7,
       1972.

4299   Chadbourne, E. "Heard and Seen." Coda 11:45-46, no. 1, 1973.

4300   "Record Reviews: Miles Ahead!" Coda 10:24, No. 11, 1973.

4301   Taylor, J. R. "The Prestige 24000 Series." Journal of Jazz Studies
       1:90-110, no. 1, 1973.

4302   Lohmann, J., and N. Winther. "Discographie des Enregistrements
       Inedits de Miles Davis." Jazz Hot no. 290:20-21, January 1973.

4303   Watts, M. "Miles." Melody Maker 48:28-29, January 20, 1973.

4304   "Concert Reviews." Variety 269:50, January 24, 1973.

4305 Sutherland, S. "Talent in Action." Billboard 85:28, January 27, 1973.

4306 "Arrest Miles Davis on Drug, Gun Raps." Variety 270:57, February 28, 1973.

4307 Cooke, J. "Miles Davis, March 6th 1954." Jazz & Blues 2:15, March 1973.

4308 "Records: On the Corner." Crawdaddy no. 22:76, March 1973.

4309 "Miles Back in Action; Liebman Joins Group." down beat 40:10, March 1, 1973.

4310 "New York--Miles Davis." Melody Maker 48:5, March 10, 1973.

4311 "Record Reviews: On the Corner." down beat 40:22-23, March 29, 1973.

4312 "At Last: Correct on the Corner Personnel." down beat 40:9, April 26, 1973.

4313 "On Record: Tallest Trees." Jazz & Blues 3:24, May 1973.

4314 "Miles Casts a Spell." Soul 8:12, June 11, 1973.

4315 "Miles Tours Japan." down beat 40:11, June 21, 1973.

4316 "Records: Miles Davis in Concert." Rolling Stone no. 137:66, June 21, 1973.

4317 Goddet, L. "Miles Ahead." Jazz Hot no. 296:4-5, July-August 1973.

4318 Lohmann, J., and N. Winther. "Discographie des Enregistrements Inedits de Miles Davis." Jazz Hot no. 296:6-7, July-August 1973.

4319 Feather, L. "Blindfold Test." down beat 40:30, July 19, 1973.

4320 "Caught in the Act." Melody Maker 48:48, July 21, 1973.

4321 "Jazz en Direct." Jazz Magazine no. 214:32-33, August 1973.

4322 "Jazz in Britain." Jazz Journal 26:18-19, September 1973.

4323 Lequime, M. "Miles Davis à l'Olympia." Jazz Hot no. 297:28, September 1973.

4324 Tercinet, A., and M. Cullaz. "Antibes." Jazz Hot no. 297:26, September 1973.

4325 Goddet, L. "Les Hommes de Miles." Jazz Hot no. 299:6-8, November 1973.

4326 "On Record: In Concert." Jazz & Blues 3:24, November 1973.

4327 Toner, J. "Electric and Eclectic." Jazz & Blues 3:18-19, November 1973.

4328   "Caught in the Act." Melody Maker 48:26, November 24, 1973.

4329   "Davis Grupp Fungerade." Orkester Journalen 41:25, December 1973.

4330   De Radzitzky, C. "Jazziana: D'un Davis à l'Autre." Points du
       Jazz no. 9:30-32, December 1973.

4331   Dutilh, A. "Concerts." Jazz Hot no. 300:23, December 1973.

4332   "On Record: The Essential Miles Davis, Vol. 1." Jazz & Blues
       3:15-16, December 1973.

4333   "Concert Reviews." Variety 273:50, December 5, 1973.

4334   Burde, W. "Berlin: Jazztage '73." Neue Zeitschrift für Musik
       135:34-36, no. 1, 1974.

4335   Cole, Bill. Miles Davis: A Musical Biography. New York: W.
       Morrow, 1974. A revision of the author's thesis (M.A.), Univer-
       sity of Pittsburgh.

4336   "Record Reviews: In Concert." Coda 11:17, no. 7, 1974; 11:18, no.
       10, 1974.

4337   Balagri, D., et al. "Trois Jours san Surprises." Jazz Magazine
       no. 218:20-21, January 1974.

4338   Berendt, J. E. "Kleine Combo--Geschichte des Neuen Jazz." Jazz
       Podium 23:13-16, January 1974. Reprinted from Berendt's book
       Jazzbuch--von Rag bis Rock.

4339   "Caught in the Act." Melody Maker 49:29, February 9, 1974.

4340   "Concert Reviews." Variety 274:58-59, April 3, 1974.

4341   "Performance." Rolling Stone no. 160:78, May 9, 1974.

4342   Gleason, R. J. "Perspectives: Miles Davis Still Accepts the Chal-
       lenge." Rolling Stone no. 161:13, May 23, 1974.

4343   Hall, G. "Miles: Today's Most Influential Contemporary Musician."
       down beat 41:16-20, July 18, 1974.

4344   _____. "Teo--the Man Behind the Scene." down beat 41:13-15,
       July 18, 1974.

4345   "Selected Miles Discography: Recorded Miles as a Leader, with
       Special Emphasis on the Years 1959-1974." down beat 41:20, July
       18, 1974.

4346   "Records: Big Fun." Crawdaddy no. 39:71-72, August 1974; Creem
       6:71, August 1974.

4347   Palmer, B. "Jazz/Rock '74: The Plain Funky Truth." Rolling
       Stone no. 166:16-17, August 1, 1974.

4348   Runcie, J. "Miles: Big Fun!" Melody Maker 49:22, September
       7, 1974.

4349   "Talent in Action." Billboard 86:14, September 28, 1974.

4350   Heckman, D. "Jazz-Rock." Stereo Review 33:74-48, November 1974.

4351   Gleason, Ralph J. Celebrating the Duke, and Louis, Bessie, Billie,
        Bird, Carmen, Miles, Dizzy, and Other Heroes. Boston: Little,
        Brown, 1975.

4352   "Record Reviews: Big Fun." Coda 12:16, no. 6, 1975.

4353   "Record Reviews: Jazz at the Plaza." Coda 12:17, no. 4, 1975.

4354   "Record Reviews: Pre-Birth of Cool." Jazz Journal 28:35, January
        1975.

4355   "Caught in the Act." Melody Maker 50:21, February 1, 1975.

4356   "Jazz Records: Get Up with It." Melody Maker 50:42, February 1,
        1975.

4357   Underwood, L. "Miles Did Not 'Get Up with It.'" Soul 9:15, March
        3, 1975.

4358   "Caught." down beat 42:36, March 13, 1975.

4359   "Miles Bien Entendu." Jazz Magazine no. 232:13-15, April 1975.

4360   "Records: Get Up with It." Creem 6:62, April 1975; Rolling Stone
        no. 184:70, April 10, 1975.

4361   Fleming, R. "Miles Davis." Black Collegian 5:26-27, May-June
        1975.

4362   "Miles ou le Defi." Jazz Magazine no. 233:38-39, May-June 1975.

4363   "Record Reviews: Get Up with It." Jazz Journal 28:35-36, May
        1975.

4364   McRae, B. "Miles Davis: Since Philharmonic Hall, Berlin--1964."
        Jazz Journal 28:10-12, June 1975.

4365   Lake, S. "Miles Saves the Day!" Melody Maker 50:37, July 12,
        1975. A report on the Newport Jazz Festival.

4366   Murphy, F. D. "Miles Davis: The Monster of Modern Music."
        Encore 4:36-39, July 21, 1975.

4367   Balliett, W. "Jazz: New York Notes." New Yorker 51:54, July 28,
        1975.

4368   Gourgues, M. "Miles en Morceaux." Jazz Magazine no. 235:24-25,
        August 1975.

4369   Buhles, G. "Jazz Portraet: Miles Davis." Hifi-Stereophonie 14:932,
        September 1975.

4370   Hurwitz, R. "Jazz-Rock: Musical Artistry or Lucrative Copout?"
        High Fidelity/Musical America 25:54-55, September 1975.

4371   "Record Reviews: Miles Davis & His Tuba Band: Prebirth of the
       Cool." down beat 42:34, September 11, 1975.

4372   Goddert, L. "Jazz 1975." Jazz Hot no. 322:42-43, December 1975.

4373   "Schallplatten-Besprechungen: Miles Davis Classics." Jazz Podium
       24:35, December 1975.

4374   Lowe, E., and S. Johnson. "Miles." Jazz Magazine (U.S.) 1:20-
       27, no. 2, 1976.

4375   "Record Reviews: Agharta." Jazz Forum no. 44:74, 1975.

4376   Scott, R. "Miles Davis at the Troubadour." Black Scholar 7:41-42,
       January-February 1976.

4377   Paihle, J. "Piano Miles." Jazz Hot no. 323:9-15, January 1976.

4378   Silvert, C. "Miles Davis Brews Up a Recovery." Rolling Stone no.
       208:18, March 11, 1976.

4379   Pekar, H. "Miles Davis: 1964-69 Recordings." Coda no. 147:8-
       14, May 1976.

4380   "Record Reviews: Agharta." down beat 43:22, May 6, 1976.

4381   Lake, S. "Miles at 50." Melody Maker 51:13, May 29, 1976.

4382   Quinke, R. "Miles Davis und der Jazz der Siebziger Jahre." Musik
       und Bildung 8:419-421, July-August 1976.

4383   Endress, G. "Ian Carr--auf den Spuren von Miles Davis." Jazz
       Podium 25:16-17, August 1976.

4384   "Record Reviews: At Birdland 1951." Jazz Journal 29:29, Septem-
       ber 1976.

4385   "Record Reviews: Charlie Parker/Miles Davis/Dizzy Gillespie."
       Jazz Journal 29:35-36, December 1976.

4386   "Waxing On: Green Haze." down beat 43:36-39, December 16, 1976.

4387   Williams, R. "Miles Davis and Weather Report Are Denying Their
       Musical History." Melody Maker 51:12, December 25, 1976.

4388   "Gallery." Jazz Magazine (U.S.) 1:41, no. 4, 1977.

4389   Jost, E. "Zur Oekonomie und Ideologie der Sogenannten Fusion Mu-
       sic." Jazz Research 9:9-24, 1977. A summary in English is in-
       cluded.

4390   Lowe, E. "Miles Emerges, Almost...." Jazz Magazine (U.S.)
       2:16, no. 1, 1977.

4391   "Reviews: Water Babies." Jazz Magazine (U.S.) 1:50, no. 4, 1977.

4392   Roszczuk, A. "Teo Macero: 'A Producer Must Encourage the Artist
       to Do New Things.'" Jazz Forum no. 50:38-40, 1977.

4393 Savicky, R. "Miles and Gil Again." Jazz Magazine (U.S.) 1:12, no.
      4, 1977.

4394 "Record Reviews: Green Haze." Jazz Journal 30:27, January 1977.

4395 "Records: Water Babies." Crawdaddy no. 71:96-97, April 1977;
      Rolling Stone no. 237:87, April 21, 1977.

4396 "Record Reviews: Water Babies." down beat 44:20, May 5, 1977.

4397 Clark, D. "Miles into Jazz-Rock Territory." Jazz Journal Interna-
      tional 30:12-14, June 1977. Review and discussion of the album
      "Water Babies."

4398 "Records: Water Babies." High Fidelity/Musical America 27:119,
      June 1977.

4399 "Jazz Albums: Water Babies." Melody Maker 52:32, June 4, 1977.

4400 Albertson, C. "New (Old) Miles: An Album That Will Be Relevant
      Long After All the Electronic Groups Short-Circuit." Stereo Re-
      view 39:87-88, July 1977.

4401 "Records: Water Babies." Creem 9:72, July 1977.

4402 "Spotlight Review: Water Babies." Radio Free Jazz 18:14, July 1977.

4403 "Gil & Miles Fusion?" down beat 44:11, July 14, 1977.

4404 Occhiogrosso, P. "Ornette--Miles of the Eighties." Melody Maker
      52:32-33, July 30, 1977. Discussion of new innovations at the
      Newport Jazz Festival.

4405 Morgenstern, D. "Dogg' Around: One More Time--Miles and Gil."
      Jazz Journal International 30:14, August 1977.

4406 "Record Reviews: A New Approach to Jazz Improvisation, Volumes
      VII-X." down beat 44:25, December 1, 1977.

4407 "Miles in the Studio." Jazz Magazine (U.S.) 2:11, no. 3, 1978.

4408 "Reviews: Contemporary Masters on Columbia." Jazz Magazine
      (U.S.) 2:71, no. 3, 1978.

4409 "Jazz Albums: Dark Magus." Melody Maker 53:28, January 28,
      1978.

4410 Ganke, W. "Jazz-Rock und Mehr: Weather Report." Hifi-Stereo-
      phonie 17:154, February 1978.

4411 "Records: The Miles Davis/Tadd Dameron Quintet in Paris Festival
      International de Jazz-May, 1949." High Fidelity/Musical America
      28:119, February 1978.

4412 Wilson, J. S. "Contemporary Masters Series: Davis, Mulligan,
      Parker, Young." High Fidelity/Musical America 28:118-119, Feb-
      ruary 1978.

4413   "Jazz Albums: Paris Festival 1949." Melody Maker 53:24, February 4, 1978.

4414   Albertson, C. "A Little Early Miles." Stereo Review 40:134, March 1978.

4415   "Album Reviews: Paris Festival International, May 1949." Crescendo International 16:30, March 1978.

4416   "Miles Davis/Tadd Dameron Quintet in Paris, Festival International de Jazz, May 1949." Stereo Review 40:134, March 1978.

4417   "Record Reviews: Paris Festival 1949." Jazz Journal International 31:36, April 1978.

4418   "Record Reviews: The Paris Festival International." down beat 45:23-24, May 4, 1978.

4419   "Waxing On: Tune Up." down beat 45:27, May 4, 1978.

4420   Primack, B. "Dave Holland: Diverse and Dedicated." down beat 45:18-20, May 18, 1978.

4421   "Record Reviews: In Paris." Coda no. 161:21-22, June 1, 1978.

4422   "Record Reviews--Reissues: Tune Up." Coda no. 161:25, June 1, 1978.

4423   "The CBS Jazz Roster." Radio Free Jazz 19:H, July 1978.

4424   "Record Reviews: Tune Up." Radio Free Jazz 19:20-21, July 1978.

4425   "Prez Awards." Jazz Journal International 31:36, August 1978.

DE LEON, MRS. ROBERT A. see CARROLL, DIAHANN

DUNCAN, TODD, 1903-   .

4426   "Porgy to Pagliacci." Time 46:59, October 8, 1945.

4427   Greene, M. "It Is That Perfection Which I Seek." Opportunity 25:24-25, January 1947.

4428   Craig, M. "Todd Duncan Speaks for the Recitalist." Musical Courier 140:14, July 1949.

4429   "Mr. Duncan Returns to B'way." Our World 5:32-34, March 1950.

4430   Duncan, Todd. "South African Songs and Negro Spirituals." Music Journal 8:19, May-June 1950.

4431   Craig, M. "New Doctor of Letters, Todd Duncan, Versatile." Musical Courier 142:16, July 1950.

4432   Duncan, Todd. "To Sing ... but Where?" Opera 15:8-10, August 1950.

4433 "Todd Duncan." Musical Courier 144:31, December 1, 1951; Chicago Symphony Orchestra Program Notes p. 45, December 6, 1951.

4434 "Chicago Concerts." Music News 44:14-15, January 1952.

4435 "Unchained." Our World 9:24-27, November 1954.

4436 "Unchained; Todd Duncan Makes Return to Screen in Hollywood Film on Honor Prison." Ebony 10:107-110, November 1954.

4437 Lyons, J. "Baritone Saga." Musical America 75:10, February 1, 1955.

4438 "Whatever Happened to Todd Duncan?" Ebony 31:182, December 1975.

4439 Black, D. "Yesterday's Hit Makers: Todd Duncan." Sepai 25:80, January 1976.

ELLINGTON, DUKE (Edward Kennedy), 1899-1974.

4440 Antrim, Doron Kemp. Paul Whiteman, Jimmy Dorsey, Rudy Vallee, Freddie Rich, Glen Gray, Frank Skinner, Enric Madriguers, Jimmy Dale, Merle Johnston, Guy Lombardo, Uriel Davis and Duke Ellington Give Their Secrets of Dance Band Success. New York: Famous Stars Publishing Co., 1936.

4441 "Duke Marks His Band's 20 Fabulous Years with Ellington Week and Carnegie Concert." Newsweek 21:50, February 1, 1943.

4442 "Duke of Jazz." Time 41:66, February 1, 1943.

4443 Zolotow, M. "Duke of Hot." Saturday Evening Post 216:24-25, August 7, 1943.

4444 Mize, J. T. H. "Good Lick for Black, Brown and Beige, a Creation of D. Ellington and His Orchestra of Swing Virtuosi." Musician 48:159, December 1943.

4445 "Defense of Jazz." American Mercury 58:124, January 1944.

4446 Boyer, R. O. "Hot Bach." New Yorker 20:30-34, June 24, 1944; 20:32, July 1, 1944; 20:26-31, July 8, 1944.

4447 "Highbrow Blues." Time 47:63, January 14, 1946.

4448 Ulanov, Barry. Duke Ellington. New York: Da Capo Press, 1975. Reprint of the 1946 edition published by Musicians Press, London.

4449 "Double Duke." Newsweek 27:90, January 21, 1946.

4450 Asklund, G. "Interpretations in Jazz." Etude 65:134, March 1947.

4451 "Duke." Time 49:47-48, May 19, 1947.

4452 "New Ventures." Time 51:69, January 12, 1948.

4453   Wilder, A. "Look at the Duke." Saturday Review of Literature
       31:43-44, August 28, 1948.

4454   "Four of Duke's Winning Men Give Bop Views." down beat 16:2,
       January 28, 1949.

4455   "Duke's Sock 16 G in Five Nights Is New Coast Mark." Billboard
       61:17, February 12, 1949.

4456   Mohr, K. "Miley, Metcalf, Whetsol, Jenkins; The Four Trumpet
       Soloists on the Early Ellingtons." Playback 2:17, March 1949.

4457   "Duke Shows He's Got Band with More Class Than Any." down beat
       16:2, March 11, 1949.

4458   Jackson, E. "Artistry in Modern Jazz by Duke and Kenton." Mel-
       ody Maker 25:3, March 19, 1949.

4459   _____. "These Ellingtons Have Plenty of Drive." Melody Maker
       25:2, April 30, 1949.

4460   Lewerke, J. "George Davis Collects the Recordings of Duke Elling-
       ton." Record Changer 8:6, June 1949.

4461   "Rare Ellington on American Parlophone." Playback 2:30-32, June
       1949.

4462   Ulanov, B. "The Duke at 50." Metronome 65:11-12, June 1949.

4463   "Doctorate for Duke." Variety 175:39, June 15, 1949.

4464   Levin, M. "Reputation Shredded, Duke Should Disband, Mix Claims."
       down beat 16:1, June 17, 1949.

4465   Barnet, C. "Storm Rages over Duke Story." down beat 16:1, July
       15, 1949.

4466   Wilson, J. S. "NYC Radio Forum Calls Mix Insincere, Irrelevant."
       down beat 16:1, July 15, 1949.

4467   Jackson, E. "A 'New Indigo,' a Modern 'Miss Muffitt' from the Two
       Ellingtons." Melody Maker 25:5, August 6, 1949.

4468   Harris, P. "I Like Way Band Sounds--Duke." down beat 16:1, Au-
       gust 12, 1949.

4469   "The Grand Duke of Jazz." International Musician 48:14, December
       1949.

4470   "Heath, Geraldo, Ellington, Ros Voted Top Bands." Melody Maker
       25:1, December 17, 1949.

4471   Arnaud, Noël. Duke Ellington. Paris: Messager Boiteux, 1950.

4472   Otto, A. S. "The Duke--at the Half Century Mark." Jazz Journal
       3:12, February 1950.

4473   Hoefer, G. "Ellington's Annual Chicago Concert 'a Gala Evening.'"
       down beat 17:7, March 10, 1950.

4474 "Ellington's Ork to Tour Europe." Billboard 62:46, March 25, 1950.

4475 "Honor Roll of Popular Songwriters. No. 53-54--Duke Ellington." Billboard 62:42, March 25, 1950.

4476 "Duke and Orchestra Sailing for Europe." Melody Maker 26:1, April 1, 1950.

4477 Feather, L. "Ellington: Jazz Pioneer for 25 Years." Melody Maker 26:3, April 1, 1950.

4478 "Honor Roll of Popular Songwriters. No. 53-54--Duke Ellington." Billboard 62:46, April 1, 1950.

4479 Jones, M. "Duke Is Still Tops with a Stage Show Plus." Melody Maker 26:3, April 15, 1950.

4480 Dawson, J. "French Fans Refuse to Bury Their Dead." Melody Maker 26:2, April 22, 1950.

4481 "Duke's Concerts." Melody Maker 26:9, April 22, 1950.

4482 Grut, H. "Portrait of the Duke." Orkester Journalen 18:10-11, June 1950.

4483 Kahn, H. "Ellington Plays His Farewell Paris Concert." Melody Maker 26:3, June 24, 1950.

4484 Goepfert, A. "Ellington and Goodman Visit Switzerland." Jazz Journal 3:12-13, July 1950.

4485 Kahn, H. "Ellington's Music for Orson's 'Faust.'" Melody Maker 26:3, July 8, 1950.

4486 Hoefer, G. "Chicagoan Unearths Rare Duke Nickelodeon Roll." down beat 17:11, July 28, 1950.

4487 "My Nights in 'Frisco." Our World 5:54-55, August 1950.

4488 "Ellington to Sue on Use of Name in 'Peace' Appeal; Claims He Never Signed." Variety 180:41, October 4, 1950.

4489 "Ducal Movements." Metronome 66:6, December 1950.

4490 Feather, L. "Mighty Man of Music." Negro Digest 9:9-13, December 1950.

4491 "Wows 'em on Seine; Duke, Mezz Popular." Billboard 62:2, December 23, 1950.

4492 "Duke Ellington Rocks Met Opera in Recital Under NAACP Auspices." Variety 181:37, January 24, 1951.

4493 Feather, L. "Duke Readies New Works for Met Opera House Bow." down beat 18:1, January 26, 1951.

4494 "Armstrong Still King." International Musician 49:14, February 1951.

4495 "Duke Ellington at the Met." International Musician 49:12, February 1951.

4496   Goffin, R.   "Horn of Plenty."   Jazz Journal 4:4, February 1951.

4497   Feather, L.   "Duke's Programme Was Spectacular!"   Melody Maker
       27:3, February 17, 1951.

4498   Levin, M.   "Duke's Concert 'Best in Years.'"   down beat 18:1, Feb-
       ruary 24, 1951.

4499   "Duke Ellington Selects the Best in Jazz."   Coronet 29:121-124, March
       1951.

4500   "Duke Flays NAACP for Halting Richmond Concert."   down beat 18:1,
       March 9, 1951.

4501   "The Famous Turned Out to Greet Duke, Aid NAACP at the Met."
       down beat 18:3, March 9, 1951.

4502   Gleason, R. J.   "AFM Cancels Ellington Frisco Concert Onstage."
       down beat 18:1, March 23, 1951.

4503   "Concert of the Year."   Metronome 67:14, April 1951.

4504   "Duke at the 'Met.'"   Our World 6:30-33, April 1951.

4505   "New Musicians Mean a New Sound in My Band: Ellington."   down
       beat 18:13, April 6, 1951.

4506   "Duke Hires Tizol, Lou Bellson, Smith."   down beat 18:1, April 20,
       1951.

4507   "I Was Jealous of My Father."   Negro Digest 9:52-59, May 1951.
       Mercer K. Ellington, also a musician, talks about his father, Duke
       Ellington.

4508   "Louis Wins Again; All-Time All Star No. 1."   Record Changer 10:3,
       May 1951.

4509   "When Johnny Left the Duke."   Metronome 67:5, May 1951.

4510   "N.Y. Swing Revival Is Like Old Times."   Billboard 63:10, May 12,
       1951.

4511   Tracy, J.   "Ellington Crew 'Powerful, Thrilling.'"   down beat 18:1,
       May 18, 1951.

4512   Feather, L.   "Drummer Bellson Makes the New Ellington Band Rock."
       Melody Maker 27:8, May 26, 1951.

4513   Grauer, W.   "Letter to Louis."   Record Changer 10:5, June 1951.

4514   Freeman, D.   "Have to Learn Your Horn, Says Armstrong."   down
       beat 18:18, June 1, 1951.

4515   "Ellingtonia."   Record Changer 10:38-39, July-August 1951.

4516   "Ellington Conducts Orchestra at Stadium."   Musical America 71:18,
       July 1951.

4517   "Band Review."   Variety 183:100, July 11, 1951.

4518 Hodgkins, B. "New Men Continue to Inspire Ellington Band." down beat 18:3, July 27, 1951.

4519 "Louis: 1925-1947." Metronome 67:18-19, August 1951.

4520 Simon, G. T., and M. Ellington. "Duke 1951." Metronome 67:11-13, August 1951.

4521 Pease, S. A. "Duke Piano Style Shows Same Sound Tenets His Writing Do." down beat 18:18, August 10, 1951.

4522 "Duke Ellington." Metronome 67:19-20, September 1951.

4523 "The Top Active Songwriters and Records of Their Greatest Songs." Billboard 63:100-101, September 15, 1951.

4524 "Ellington-Vaughan-Cole in Sock $4.80-Top Show at N.Y.'s Carnegie Hall." Variety 184:52, October 3, 1951.

4525 Nilsson, O. G. "The Duke of Sugar Hill." Orkester Journalen 19:8, November 1951.

4526 Armstrong, L. "Jazz on a High Note." Esquire 36:85-86, December 1951.

4527 Lindgren, C. E. "Mina Sex Stora Jazzminnen." Orkester Journalen 19:26, December 1951.

4528 Traill, S. "Requiem for the All Stars." Jazz Journal 4:1-2, December 1951.

4529 "Most Exciting Women I've Known." Ebony 7:23-24, April 1952.

4530 Gleason, R. J. "Duke's Band 'Magnificent' in San Francisco Concert." down beat 18:7, April 4, 1952.

4531 "Perennial Ellington." Jazz Journal 5:20-21, May 1952. Review of the Columbia recording "Masterpieces by Ellington."

4532 Hallock, T. "Things Ain't What They Ought to Be with Ellington's Band." down beat 19:2, May 21, 1952.

4533 "Ellington Fans Pursue Hallock's Scalp; 'Better Just to Forget It,' Says Duke." down beat 19:6, June 18, 1952.

4534 "Rocking Chair Not for Duke Despite 25 Restless Years." down beat 19:6, August 13, 1952.

4535 Simon, G. "The New Duke Ellington." Metronome 68:11, September 1952.

4536 "Music World to Salute Ellington on Silver Jubilee." down beat 19:1, September 24, 1952.

4537 "Mills Plans Big Jubilee Promotion on the Duke." Billboard 64:23, October 4, 1952.

4538 Feather, L. "They No Longer Care What Musicians I Use ... Interview with Duke Ellington." Melody Maker 28:3, October 25, 1952.

4539   "Ellington Silver Jubilee." Jazz Journal 5:3, November 1952.

4540   "2-Week Fete for Ellington Is Underway." Billboard 64:18, November 1, 1952.

4541   "Duke's Anniversary." Time 60:85, November 3, 1952.

4542   Hughes, S. "My 13 Years as 'Mike.'" Melody Maker 28:iv, November 15, 1952 Supplement.

4543   "Ellington, Eckstine Almost Trip Each Other Up at Carnegie, but Not at B.O." Variety 188:45, November 19, 1952.

4544   Mallows, L. "The Ellington Gap of 1937-1939." Jazz Journal 5:16-17, December 1952.

4545   "Duke Ellington--First Gentleman of Jazz." Melody Maker 28:3, December 6, 1952.

4546   Preston, D. "Petit Maitre or Thwarted Genius?" Melody Maker 28:5, December 6, 1952.

4547   "In Person." Metronome 69:19, January 1953.

4548   Mallows, L. "The Ellington Gap of 1937-39." Jazz Journal 6:15, January 1953.

4549   Borneman, E. "A Real Composer." Melody Maker 29:4, January 10, 1953.

4550   Watt, D. "The Enormous Room." New Yorker 28:54-56, February 7, 1953.

4551   Coss, B. "Duke Ellington at the Bandbox." Metronome 69:18, April 1953.

4552   "Erroll and Dizzy Are Heady Fare." Billboard 65:18, April 4, 1953.

4553   Wilford, C. "A Festival for Duke." Melody Maker 29:3, April 18, 1953.

4554   Morgan, A. "Retrospection." Jazz Journal 6:5, June 1953.

4555   Freeman, D. "'Only One Bellson,' Sighs Wistful Duke." down beat 20:20, June 17, 1953.

4556   Gleason, R. J. "'It's Tough to Compete with Yourself': Duke." down beat 20:15-S, July 15, 1953.

4557   Tracy, J. "Ellington, Brubeck Winners in Critics' Jazz Poll." down beat 20:1, August 26, 1953.

4558   Simon, G. T. "Duke Ellington." Metronome 69:19, September 1953.

4559   "Ellington '55--and Younger." Metronome 70:23, October 1953.

4560   Feather, L. "Kenton Calls off Joint Tour with Ellington Band." down beat 20:1, October 7, 1953.

4561 "The Greatest." Jazz Journal 6:17, November 1953.

4562 "Best Years of My Life." Our World 8:32-37, December 1953.

4563 Morgan, A. "The Duke Up to Date." Jazz Journal 6:21-22, Decem-
        ber 1953.

4564 Aasland, Benny H. The "Wax Works" of Duke Ellington. Danderyd,
        Sweden: Aasland, 1954. A limited edition published for the Duke
        Ellington Jazz Society.

4565 Horricks, R. "Duke Ellington Plays." Jazz Journal 7:1-2, January
        1954.

4566 Feather, L. "Noblesse Oblige; Duke Lauds His Interpreters." down
        beat 21:23, January 13, 1954.

4567 "Duke, Stan Merge." down beat 21:8, March 24, 1954.

4568 "Sex Is No Sin." Ebony 9:100-102, May 1954.

4569 "Flight Fear May Cancel Ellington's Europe Trip." Billboard 66:20,
        May 1, 1954.

4570 "Caught in the Act." down beat 21:4, May 19, 1954.

4571 "Birdland, N.Y." Variety 195:53, June 16, 1954.

4572 "'Recording Artists' Roster." down beat 21:97, June 30, 1954.

4573 "Duke Ellington Writing Musical History of Negro." down beat 21:1,
        July 28, 1954.

4574 "Lightly and Politely." Jazz Journal 7:7, August 1954.

4575 "Downbeat Club, Frisco." Variety 195:53, August 4, 1954.

4576 "Ellington '55--and Younger." Metronome 70:23, October 1954. Re-
        cordings of Ellington are reviewed.

4577 "Duke-Getz-Mulligan-Brubeck Package Heard at Carnegie." down beat
        21:4, December 1, 1954.

4578 "Basin Street, N.Y." Variety 197:52, December 8, 1954.

4579 Rolontz, B. "Alec, Duke Combine to Pace Basin St. Show." Bill-
        board 66:12, December 11, 1954.

4580 "Duke Finally Set on Europe Tour." Billboard 66:22, December 25,
        1954.

4581 "Twenty-Three Years at the Top." Jazz Journal 8:5-6, January 1955.

4582 Feather, L. "Ellington Fifty-Five." Melody Maker 31:2-3, January
        1, 1955.

4583 Hulsizer, K. "The Early Ellington Orchestra." Jazz Journal 8:2-4,
        February 1955.

4584   Mulligan, G. "The Greatness of Duke Ellington." <u>Melody Maker</u>
       31:5, March 19, 1955.

4585   "Ellington Jumps at Carnegie Hall but B. O. Doesn't Swing." <u>Var-
       iety</u> 198:43, March 23, 1955.

4586   "Symphony of Air to Play New Ellington Work; Duke Leader." <u>down
       beat</u> 22:19, March 23, 1955.

4587   "Duke Ellington Conducts Symphony of the Air." <u>Musical America</u>
       75:21-22, April 1955.

4588   Simon, G. T. "An Ellington Revelation." <u>Metronome</u> 71:22, April
       1955.

4589   Feather, L. "The 'Night Creature' at Carnegie." <u>Melody Maker</u>
       31:3, April 2, 1955.

4590   "Newport Festival Signs Ellington." <u>down beat</u> 22:1, April 6, 1955.

4591   "Want to Buy a Band?" <u>down beat</u> 22:47, April 20, 1955.

4592   "Duke Ellington." <u>Metronome</u> 71:41-42, May 1955.

4593   "Symphony of the Air." <u>Musical Courier</u> 151:14, May 1955.

4594   "Duke." <u>Jazz Journal</u> 8:27-28, June 1955.

4595   "Ellington Ork Revamped." <u>down beat</u> 22:7, July 27, 1955.

4596   Gleason, J. "Tops in Tunesmiths." <u>Coronet</u> 38:78-79, August 1955.

4597   Feather, L. "Jazz Achieves Social Prestige." <u>down beat</u> 22:11,
       September 21, 1955.

4598   "Duke Ellington." <u>Melody Maker</u> 31:3, October 1, 1955.

4599   "Music Biz Needs Tunes That Last Years: Duke." <u>down beat</u> 22:15,
       October 5, 1955.

4600   Feather, L. "Duke Unloads the Deadwood." <u>Melody Maker</u> 31:6,
       October 22, 1955.

4601   "The Duke Rides Again." <u>Time</u> 67:53, January 23, 1956.

4602   "Band Review." <u>down beat</u> 23:6, March 7, 1956.

4603   "Basin Street, N.Y." <u>Variety</u> 202:80, April 18, 1956.

4604   "Want to Buy a Band?" <u>down beat</u> 23:48, April 18, 1956.

4605   Balliett, W. "Celebration for the Duke." <u>Saturday Review</u> 39:30-31,
       May 12, 1956.

4606   "Duke, Fiedler Discuss a Project." <u>down beat</u> 23:17, May 16, 1956.

4607   Freeman, D. "My Biggest Thrill? When Duke Roared Back: Bas-
       ie." <u>down beat</u> 23:14, May 16, 1956.

4608 "Music Fraternity Honors Ellington." down beat 23:27, May 16, 1956.

4609 "Swee'pea Is Still Amazed at Freedom Allowed in Writing for Elling-
      ton Orchestra." down beat 23:15, May 30, 1956.

4610 "Duke Har Sagt...." Orkester Journalen 24:6-7, June 1956.

4611 Jepsen, J. G. "Jazzens Instrumentalister: Arrangören." Orkester
      Journalen 24:12-13, June 1956.

4612 Mulford, E. "Duke Ellington, Doylestown, Pa." Metronome 72:12,
      June 1956.

4613 "Caught in the Act." down beat 23:8, June 13, 1956.

4614 Aaslund, B. H. "Duke--Och i Sa Fall Varför?" Orkester Journalen
      24:7, July 1956.

4615 Kay, G. W. "Wilbur De Paris and His New New Orleans Jazz."
      Jazz Journal 9:3, July 1956.

4616 Gleason, R. J. "Perspectives." down beat 23:19, July 25, 1956.

4617 "Mood Indigo & Beyond." Time 68:54-56, August 20, 1956.

4618 "Band Reviews." Variety 203:48, August 29, 1956.

4619 Hentoff, N. "Music Mediocre, Presentation Poor at Connecticut Fes-
      tival." down beat 23:17-18, September 5, 1956.

4620 Sharpe, D. "An Appreciation of Duke Ellington." Jazz Journal 9:13-
      14, October 1956.

4621 Bellerby, V. "Ellington '56." Melody Maker 31:6, October 13, 1956.

4622 "The Bands Swing Back." Metronome 72:20-21, November 1956.

4623 "Band Reviews." down beat 23:19, November 28, 1956.

4624 Aaslund, B. H.   "Duke och Piratema; Rövarpressade Godbitar för
      Discofilen." Orkester Journalen 24:24-25, December 1956.

4625 Anderson, L. "Reflexer." Orkester Journalen 24:18, December
      1956.

4626 "In Person." Metronome 72:8, December 1956.

4627 Feather, L. "Feather's Nest." down beat 23:47-48, December 12,
      1956.

4628 Hentoff, N. "The Duke." down beat 23:12, December 26, 1956.

4629 "Duke Ellington in Washington." Metronome 74:30, January 1957.

4630 Hentoff, N. "The Duke." down beat 24:20, January 9, 1957.

4631 Feather, L. "Feather's Nest." down beat 24:18, February 20, 1957.

4632   Watt, D. "Musical Events; Popular Records." New Yorker 33:123-
        126, March 9, 1957.

4633   Kolodin, I. "Rodgers and Hart, Ella and Ellington." Saturday Re-
        view 40:43, March 16, 1957.

4634   "Duke Ellington Again the Composer." Jazz Today 2:17, April 1957.
        Discussion of Ellington's work "A Drum Is a Woman."

4635   "From My Point of View." Jazz Today 2:50, April 1957.

4636   "Want to Buy a Band?" down beat 24:45, April 18, 1957.

4637   Dahlgren, C. "Duke i Ramplijuset." Orkester Journalen 25:6, May
        1957.

4638   Grut, H. "Ellingtons Musiker." Orkester Journalen 25:10-11, May
        1957.

4639   "Music for Moderns Begins Series." Musical America 77:25, May
        1957. First performance of Ellington's "Such Sweet Thunder."

4640   Langman, A. W. "Television." Nation 184:400, May 4, 1957.

4641   "Crazy Little Story." Newsweek 49:66, May 6, 1957.

4642   Balliett, W. "Duke at Play." New Yorker 33:150-152, May 18,
        1957.

4643   Feather, L. "The Duke Orchestrated the Bard." Melody Maker
        32:9, May 18, 1957. Review of "Such Sweet Thunder" in its first
        performance.

4644   "A Drum Is a Woman." Orkester Journalen 25:13, June 1957.

4645   "Duke Ellington the Composer." Metronome 74:13-14, June 1957.

4646   Grut, H. "Ellingtons Musiker." Orkester Journalen 25:12-13, June
        1957.

4647   "Music for Moderns." Musical Courier 155:35-36, June 1957.

4648   Wilson, J. S. "The Sidemen Are Moving Way Out Yonder." High
        Fidelity/Musical America 7:77, June 1957.

4649   Feather, L., and B. Ulanov. "Two Thumps on 'a Drum.'" down
        beat 24:18, June 27, 1957.

4650   Grut, H. "Ellingtons Musiker." Orkester Journalen 25:18-19, July-
        August, 1957.

4651   Flakser, H. "Duke Ellington and the Talking Record." Record Re-
        search 3:9, August-September 1957.

4652   Katz, R. "Music Festival at Brandeis University." Jazz Today
        2:30, August 1957. Discussion of Ellington's "Reminiscing in
        Tempo."

4653   "Ravinia Festival." down beat 24:31-32, August 8, 1957.

4654   "Duke Ellington: A Living Legend Swings On." Look 21:82-86, August 20, 1957.

4655   Grut, H. "Ellingtons Musiker." Orkester Journalen 25:14-15, September 1957.

4656   Dance, S. "A Drum Is a Woman." Melody Maker 32:17, September 7, 1957.

4657   Grut, H. "Ellingtons Musiker." Orkester Journalen 25:14-15, October 1957.

4658   Townley, E. "The Duke and His Sidemen." Jazz Journal 10:9-10, October 1957.

4659   Wilson, J. S. "Ellington's Sweet Thunder Spoofs the Bard." High Fidelity/Musical America 7:96, November 1957.

4660   Feather, L. "Duke Tops Them All." Melody Maker 32:7, December 14, 1957.

4661   Gammond, Peter, ed. Duke Ellington: His Life and Music. Contributions by Jeff Aldam, et al. New York: Da Capo Press, 1977. Reprint of the 1958 edition published by Phoenix House, London.

4662   "Duke's 'Heart' Disk a Career Milestone." Billboard 70:30, January 20, 1958.

4663   Dance, S. "Such Sweet Thunder." Jazz Journal 11:26-27, March 1958.

4664   "'58 Is 33 for Duke." down beat 25:11-12, March 6, 1958. 1958 marks Duke's thirty-third year of recording his music.

4665   Kolodin, I. "Duke Ellington and Queen Ella." Saturday Review 41:50, April 12, 1958.

4666   "Want to Buy a Band?" down beat 25:48, April 17, 1958.

4667   Wilson, J. S. "Ella and the Duke Assemble a Somewhat Mixed-Up Songbook." High Fidelity/Musical America 8:79, May 1958.

4668   Wood, B. "The Duke and Sidney Bechet." Jazz Journal 11:25-26, July 1958.

4669   "Duke's Back." Jazz Journal 11:1, October 1958.

4670   Gammond, P. "Duke Ellington, Pianist." Jazz Journal 11:7-8, October 1958.

4671   Hentoff, N. "Duke Ellington, Composer." Jazz Journal 11:5-6, October 1958.

4672   Voce, S. "And All the Duke's Men." Jazz Journal 11:2-4, October 1958.

4673   Feather, L. "Ellington--Meet the Band." Melody Maker 33:2, October 4, 1958.

4674 "Ellington's 1st Date in Brit. in 25 Years." Variety 212:64, October 8, 1958.

4675 Jones, M. "A Knockout of Course, but...." Melody Maker 33:3, October 11, 1958.

4676 "The Duke Comes Back to Brit." Variety 212:58, October 15, 1958.

4677 "Ducal Details." down beat 25:11-12, October 16, 1958.

4678 Houlden, D., and F. Dutton. "The Duke Steps Out--Once More." Jazz Journal 11:3-7, November 1958. Lists the personnel in Ellington's band during various periods.

4679 "Leeds: Music and Musicians." Jazz Journal 11:1, November 1958.

4680 "Stor Succe för Ellington." Orkester Journalen 26:14-15, November 1958.

4681 "This World of Jazz." Melody Maker 33:11, November 1, 1958. Three critics comment on Ellington's European tour.

4682 "Ellington Concert 20% Empty in Berlin Even with Lotsa Longhairs." Variety 212:62, November 19, 1958.

4683 Guild, H. "Ellington's Riot-Less German Tour; Old Fogies Dig Duke Quiet-Like." Variety 212:60, November 26, 1958.

4684 "One of the First Gentlemen of Jazz." Sepia 6:78, December 1958.

4685 Dance, S. "48 in Boston." Jazz Journal 13:25, January 1960.

4686 Schuller, G. "Early Duke." Jazz Review 3:18-22, January 1960.

4687 "Large Ellington Shuffle." down beat 27:12, January 21, 1960.

4688 "'Most Honored' Musician of 1959; He Received 8 Awards." Jet p. 59, January 21, 1960.

4689 Schuller, G. "Early Duke." Jazz Review 3:18-25, February 1960.

4690 "Named 'Musician of the Year' in International Jazz Poll of British Weekly 'Melody Maker.'" Jet p. 58, February 18, 1960.

4691 "Ellington and Other Masters." down beat 27:13, March 17, 1960.

4692 Feather, L. "The Duke Ellington Story, as Hollywood Might Do It." down beat 27:20-23, March 17, 1960.

4693 Ioakimidis, D. "1er Avril 1960; Pres de 35 Ans de Fidelite à Duke Ellington le Jour de Son 50e Anniversaire." Jazz Hot 26:22-23, April 1960.

4694 Jacobs, I. L. "Duke Ellington on Transcriptions." Jazz Review 3:41-42, June 1960.

4695 Dance, S. "In the Arena." Jazz Journal 13:11-12, October 1960.

4696 "Sweetness & Fruit." Time 76:59, October 10, 1960.

4697   "Caught in the Act." down beat 27:10, October 13, 1960.

4698   "His Version of 'Nutcracker Suite' Praised by N.Y. Herald Tribune
        Music Critic." Jet p. 62, November 3, 1960. Ellington's version
        of Tchaikovsky's "Nutcracker Suite" was adapted by Billy Strayhorn.

4699   Dance, S. "Johnny Hodges on Hodges & the Duke." Metronome
        77:22-23, December 1960.

4700   Hadlock, D. "Special Report: Monterey Jazz Festival." Metronome
        77:8, December 1960. Ellington's "Suite Thursday" was performed.

4701   Jalard, M. C. "Trois Apotres du Discontinu." Jazz Magazine 6:42-
        47, December 1960.

4702   Testoni, G. "Lo Spettacolo Negro e Il Jazz." Musica Jazz 16:20-
        22, December 1960.

4703   White, T. "Duke Ellington: The Slumbering Giant." Metronome
        77:42-43, December 1960.

4704   "Commissioned by the 3rd Annual Monterey Jazz Festival to Write a
        Special Work Titled 'Suite Thursday' Based on the Characters in
        Certain John Steinbeck Novels." Jet 18:60, December 8, 1960.

4705   "He and Billy Strayhorn Writing Musical Score for Movie 'Paris
        Blues' in Paris." Jet 19:61, December 15, 1960.

4706   Pilon, G. "Edward Kennedy 'Duke' Ellington." Sveta Cecilija 10:38-
        46, no. 4, 1961.

4707   Lambert, G. E. "Trumpets No End." Jazz Journal 14:8-10, Jan-
        uary 1961.

4708   "Writes Music Score for ABC-TV Dramatic Series." Jet 19:55, January
        12, 1961. A series, "The Asphalt Jungle," will use Ellington's com-
        positions.

4709   Jones, M. "'It Was a Challenge' Says Duke." Melody Maker 36:5, Jan-
        uary 14, 1961. Ellington on his recording of the "Nutcracker Suite."

4710   Berini, A., and G. Volontè. "La 'Controversial Suite.'" Musica
        Jazz 17:22-24, February 1961.

4711   "Ellington au T. N. P." Jazz Magazine 7:15, February 1961.

4712   "Duke's Mad, Mad Paris Visit." down beat 28:12, February 16, 1961.

4713   Ioakimidis, D. "Un Pianiste Nomme Ellington." Jazz Hot no. 163:12-
        15, March 1861.

4714   Traill, S. "With Duke and Louis in Paris." Jazz Journal 14:1,
        March 1961.

4715   "Four Ellingtonians Arrested in Vegas." down beat 28:11, March
        16, 1961.

4716   Feather, L. "Duke Ellington." International Musician 59:18-19,
        April 1961.

4717   Ioakimidis, D. "Un Pianiste Nomme Ellington." Jazz Hot no. 164:18-
       19, April 1961.

4718   Traill, S. "Paris Blues." Metronome 78:16-17, April 1961.

4719   Lyttelton, H. "Duke--the Greatest Poet in Jazz." Melody Maker
       36:5, April 8, 1961.

4720   "Writes Musical Score for ABC-TV's New Asphalt Jungle Series
       Titled 'The Lady and Lawyer.'" Jet 20:60, April 27, 1961.

4721   "The Beautiful Americans." Jazz Journal 14:19, May 1961.

4722   Fresia, E. "Discografia." Musica Jazz 17:41-42, May 1961. Cov-
       ers Ellington discography March 1959-October 1960.

4723   Ioakimidis, D. "Un Pianiste Nomme Ellington." Jazz Hot no. 165:22-
       25, May 1961.

4724   "Quincy Hamp Duke." Jazz Magazine 7:26-29, May 1961.

4725   Ioakimidis, D. "Un Pianiste Nomme Ellington." Jazz Hot no. 166:20-
       25, June 1961.

4726   "Satchmo et Duke Face à Face." Jazz Magazine 7:15, June 1961.

4727   Feather, L. "Duke Ellington; Et Geni paa 60 Aar." Norsk Musik-
       erblad 50:5-7, July-August 1961.

4728   Dance, S. "Festival: Preparation and Aftermath." Metronome
       78:22-23, July 1961.

4729   "More 'Paris Blues.'" Jazz Journal 14:18-19, July 1961.

4730   "Count et Duke Dos à Dos." Jazz Magazine 7:16, September 1961.

4731   Saran, S. "Ellington a Ravinia Hit." Musical Courier 163:29, Sep-
       tember 1961.

4732   "Composed Music for ABC-TV Show 'Asphalt Jungle.'" Jet 20:61,
       September 7, 1961. Ellington's theme song used on the TV series
       has been released as a single and is selling well. In addition his
       "Nutcracker Suite" has reached the top of London's "Jazz Top Ten."

4733   "Duke Objects to Jazz as a Term." down beat 28:13, October 26,
       1961.

4734   "'Jazz Fakers' Can't Make It Now." Negro Digest 11:76-79, Novem-
       ber 1961.

4735   Tynan, J. "Paris Blues." down beat 28:16, November 23, 1961.

4736   "Duke Ellington Racks Up Mild $3,090 in Polished Town Hall, N.Y.
       Concert." Variety 225:54, November 29, 1961.

4737   Jepsen, Jorgen Grunnet. Discography of Duke Ellington. 2d ed.
       Brande, Denmark: Debut Records, 1959- . Contents: vi. 1.
       1925-37.--v. 2. 1937-47.--v. 3. 1948-60.

4738 Lambert, George Edmund. Duke Ellington. New York: Barnes, 1959.

4739 "Ellington sur Scene." Jazz Magazine 5:12, January 1959.

4740 Mouly, R. "Ella et Duke et Duke et Mahalia." Jazz Magazine 5:16-17, January 1959.

4741 Race, S. "Ellington's Best." Melody Maker 34:5, January 10, 1959.

4742 Schmidt-Garre, H. "Zum Letztenmal Duke Ellington?" Neue Zeitschrift für Musik 120:26, January 1959.

4743 Crowley, R. "'Black, Brown and Beige' After 16 Years." Jazz no. 2:98-104, Spring 1959.

4744 Ellington, Duke. "A Royal View of Jazz." Jazz no. 2:83-87, Spring 1959.

4745 Hodeir, A. "A Renaissance of Ellingtonism; A Tribute to Gil Evans." Jazz no. 2:95-97, Spring 1959.

4746 Postgate, J. "Between You and Me." Jazz Monthly 5:31-32, March 1959.

4747 Crawford, M. "Visit with Mrs. Duke Ellington." Ebony 14:132-136, March 1959.

4748 Voce, S. "Quoth the Duke." Jazz Journal 12:2-4, March 1959. Treats interviews with Ellington by B.B.C. announcers.

4749 Anderson, L. "Ellington 60 Ar." Orkester Journalen 27:15, April 1959.

4750 Clar, M. "The Style of Duke Ellington." Jazz Review 2:6-10, April 1959.

4751 Wilson, J. S. "The Jazz Panorama." HiFi/Stereo Review 2:75, April 1959.

4752 "Dance Band Directory." down beat 26:44, April 16, 1959.

4753 "Duke to Write Movie Score." down beat 26:13, April 16, 1959. Ellington will compose the music for "Anatomy of a Murder."

4754 Jones, Q. "Duke Ellington, Newport 1958." Jazz Review 2:30, May 1959.

4755 "Another Film for Duke." down beat 26:13, May 14, 1959.

4756 McKinney, J. "Duke in New Jersey." Music U.S.A. 76:7-8, July 1959.

4757 Wilson, J. S. "Three Decades of Ellington Documented on Three Discs." High Fidelity/Musical America 9:75, July 1959.

4758 "Duke Swings." Variety 215:47, July 1, 1959.

4759   Mulford, E. "Duke's Film Score." Music U.S.A. 76:33-34, August
       1959.

4760   Dance, S. "Dukesville." Jazz Journal 12:10-12, September 1959.

4761   Gaspard, J. J. "Duke Ellington." Musica no. 66:23, September
       1959.

4762   Hentoff, N. "The Well-Constructed 'Anatomy.'" HiFi/Stereo Re-
       view 3:55, September 1959.

4763   "High Honor to Ellington." Billboard 71:4, September 21, 1959.

4764   Anderson, L. "Ellingtonia '59." Orkester Journalen 27:8-9, Oc-
       tober 1959.

4765   "Jazz B. O. In Sweden Goes from Hot to Cool to Cold; Dizzy, Duke
       Concerts NSG." Variety 216:48, October 14, 1959.

4766   "A Medal for Duke." down beat 26:9, October 15, 1959.

4767   Dance, S. "In the Round." Jazz Journal 12:4, November 1959.

4768   Harrison, M. "Anatomy of a Murder." Jazz Review 2:35-36, No-
       vember 1959.

4769   Lambert, G. E. "Ella Fitzgerald Sings Duke Ellington." Jazz
       Monthly 5:22-24, November 1959.

4770   Traill, S. "Duke in Paris." Jazz Journal 12:10-11, November
       1959.

4771   Anderson, L. "Reflexer." Orkester Journalen 27:24-25, December
       1959.

4772   Candini, P. "Anatomia di un Omicidio." Musica Jazz 15:28, De-
       cember 1959.

4773   Schuller, G. "Early Duke." Jazz Review 2:6-14, December 1959.

4774   Hoefer, G. "The Hot Box." down beat 26:63, December 10, 1959.

4775   "Pace-Setters in the World of Jazz." International Musician 60:10,
       January 1962.

4776   Balliett, W. "Jazz Concerts." New Yorker 37:101-102, January 13,
       1962.

4777   "Ellington Premiere." Jazz Journal 15:8-9, February 1962. Re-
       view of Ellington's first public piano recital.

4778   Williams, M. "Jazz Composition; What Is It?" down beat 29:20-23,
       February 15, 1962.

4779   Ellington, Duke. "Where Is Jazz Going?" Music Journal 20:31,
       March 1962.

4780   Williams, M. "When the Big Bands Played Swing." High Fidelity
       12:49-51, April 1962.

4781 "Credit Where Due on 'Paris Blues.'" down beat 29:13, May 24, 1962.

4782 Tollara, G., and L. Massagli. "Discografia." Musica Jazz 13:42-44, June 1962. Covers recordings made by Ellington and his orchestra 1939-1943.

4783 Dance, S. "The Art Is in the Cooking." down beat 29:13-15, June 7, 1962.

4784 DeMicheal, D. "Double Play." down beat 29:20-21, June 7, 1962.

4785 "Ellington & Strayhorn, Inc." down beat 29:22-23, June 7, 1962.

4786 Feather, L. "The Duke's Progress." down beat 29:16-19, June 7, 1962.

4787 McCuen, B. "A Rose by Any Other Name." down beat 29:26, June 7, 1962.

4788 Welding, P. "Long Day's Journey; On the Road with the Duke Ellington Orchestra." down beat 29:24-25, June 7, 1962.

4789 Morgenstern, D. "Jazz Goes to Washington." Musical America 82:18-19, July 1962.

4790 "Hub Producer Files 100 G Counterclaim Vs. Ellington over May 26 Gig Dispute." Variety 227:41, July 18, 1962.

4791 "Ellington Sues and Is Sued in Return." down beat 29:12, September 13, 1962.

4792 "Up to My Ears in All of It." Melody Maker 37:20-21, September 15, 1962.

4793 Dance, S. "It's Really a Twisting World." Jazz 1:8-9, October 1962.

4794 Balliett, W. "Jazz Records." New Yorker 39:179-83, October 26, 1962.

4795 "Duke Ellington Orch Wins Honors Before 1,800 Fans at Washington College Gig." Variety 228:39, November 21, 1962.

4796 "Free-Loaders Mill as Frank Signs Ellington." Billboard 74:4, December 8, 1962.

4797 "Duke's Back Again." Jazz Journal 16:1-2, January 1963.

4798 Ellington, Duke. "Thoughts on Composing." Jazz Journal 16:3, January 1963.

4799 Heughan, G. W. "Historical Calendar of Duke Ellington's Career." Jazz Journal 16:10-13, January 1963.

4800 Ioakimidis, D. "Ellington's Drummers." Jazz Journal 16:4-5, January 1963.

4801   Pekar, H. "The Duke Ellington Small Bands." Jazz Journal 16:6-7,
       January 1963.

4802   "Duke Signs with Reprise, Will Also Supervise Sessions." down beat
       30:11, January 3, 1963.

4803   "New Blood from Some Old Hands." down beat 30:13, January 3,
       1963.

4804   Henshaw, L. "Ellingtonia '63." Melody Maker 38:10-11, January
       19, 1963.

4805   _____. "Rehearsing with Duke." Melody Maker 38:i, January
       26, 1963.

4806   Anderson, L., and L. Östberg. "Duke Ellington: 'We Do Love
       You Madly.'" Orkester Journalen 31:12-13, February 1963.

4807   "Duke Ellington and His Famous Orchestra." Jazz Monthly 8:2-5,
       February 1963.

4808   Traill, S. "Editorial." Jazz Journal 16:1, February 1963.

4809   Wagner, J. "L'Aristocrate aux Prises avec la Foule." Jazz Mag-
       azine 9:23-26, February 1963.

4810   Lyttelton, H. "Tin Pan Alley Can Do Its Worst!" Melody Maker
       38:11, February 2, 1963.

4811   Dance, S. "Duke at Reprise." Jazz 2:14-18, March 1963.

4812   "Le Duke et Sa Suite; Ou, la Bataille de Wagram." Jazz Magazine
       9:20-27, March 1963.

4813   Hoefer, G. "Ellington Memories." Jazz 2:11, March 1963.

4814   Lambert, E. "Duke Ellington--1963." Jazz Journal 16:1-3, March
       1963.

4815   Postif, F. "Le Duke Parle." Jazz Hot no. 185:14-18, March 1963.

4816   Reda, J. "Veni, Vidi, Vici." Jazz Magazine 9:28-29, March 1963.

4817   Testoni, G. C., and P. Candini. "Ellington non Invecchia; Il Trion-
       fo del 'Duca' al Conservatorio di Milano." Musica Jazz 19:12-16,
       March 1963.

4818   "Vive le Duke!" Jazz Hot no. 185:6-7, March 1963.

4819   Williams, M. "Mid-Month Recordings; The Enduring Ellington."
       Saturday Review 46:96, March 16, 1963.

4820   "La 'Creole Rhapsody.'" Musica Jazz 19:20-22, April 1963.

4821   Robertson, S. "Jazz World." Sepia 12:16, April 1963.

4822   Wilson, J. S. "Ellington, After Four Decades, a New Luster."
       High Fidelity/Musical America 13:106, April 1963. Ellington cel-
       ebrates his sixty-fourth birthday.

4823 "Caught in the Act." down beat 30:35-36, May 9, 1963.

4824 "All Week Long." Jazz Journal 16:6, June 1963.

4825 Anderson, L. "Dans till Duke." Orkester Journalen 31:13, June 1963.

4826 "Wa-Wa-Wa." New Yorker 39:25-27, June 1, 1963.

4827 O'Connor, N. J. "Inspiration Is Like Mingling of Colors." Jazz 2:15, July-August 1963.

4828 Lees, G. "The Jazz Composer; A Study in Symbiosis." High Fidelity/Musical America 13:55-57, August 1963.

4829 "Basin St. East, N.Y." Variety 231:60, August 7, 1963.

4830 "Duke Ellington Jazz Society." down beat 30:32, August 15, 1963.

4831 "Ellington Puts Together Show for Emancipation Celebration." down beat 30:11, August 15, 1963.

4832 "Duke at Sixty-Four." Newsweek 62:71, August 26, 1963.

4833 "Major Ellington Opuses Slated for LP Release." down beat 30:9, August 29, 1963.

4834 "My People." down beat 30:41, September 26, 1963.

4835 Dance, S. "Ellington's 'My People.'" Saturday Review 46:73, September 28, 1963.

4836 _____. "Jazz." Music Journal 21:84-85, October 1963.

4837 Fresia, E. "Discografia." Musica Jazz 19:50-51, October 1963.

4838 Balliett, W. "Jazz Records." New Yorker 39:179-183, October 26, 1963.

4839 "The Ellington Tempo." Jazz 2:27, November-December 1963. Refers to the jazz and cultural exchange program in which Ellington's group toured the Middle East.

4840 "Annuaire Biographique du Piano." Jazz Magazine 9:26, November 1963.

4841 Bishop, A. J. "Duke's 'Creole Rhapsody.'" Jazz Monthly 9:12-13, November 1963.

4842 Williams, M. "The Ellington Era." Saturday Review 46:59-60, November 16, 1963.

4843 Morgenstern, D. "The Ellington Era." Listen 1:15-16, December 1963.

4844 "Repertoire." Jazz Journal 16:14-15, December 1963.

4845 "Ellington, on Asian Tour, 'Tears Down the Clouds.'" down beat 30:15, December 19, 1963.

4846   "Duke Ellington's 'My People.'"   Jazz 3:21-23, January-February
       1964.

4847   "The Ellington Era, 1927-1940, Vol. I."   Jazz 3:13-15, January-
       February 1964.

4848   Craik, R.   "Duke in Dacca."   Jazz Journal 17:12-13, January 1964.

4849   Dance, S.   "In the Hands of Artists."   Jazz Journal 17:18-19, Jan-
       uary 1964.   Description of the cultural exchange program tour to
       the Middle East by Ellington's band.

4850   Harrison, M.   "Duke Ellington; Reflections on Some of the Larger
       Works."   Jazz Monthly 9:12-15, January 1964.

4851   Lambert, E.   "The Ellington Era, Volume One."   Jazz Journal 17:36-
       37, January 1964.

4852   Dance, S.   "Duke in India."   Saturday Review 47:66-67, January 11,
       1964.

4853   "Basin St. East, N.Y."   Variety 233:59, January 15, 1964.

4854   Balliett, W.   "Jazz Records."   New Yorker 39:97-101, January 25,
       1964.

4855   Bishop, A.   "Reminiscing in Tempo."   Jazz Journal 17:5-6, Febru-
       ary 1964.

4856   Dance, S.   "My People."   Jazz Journal 17:19, February 1964.

4857   "Duke Ellington's 'My People.'"   Jazz 3:21-23, February 1964.

4858   Lambert, G. E.   "The Duke Steps Out."   Jazz Journal 17:2-4, Feb-
       ruary 1964.

4859   Malson, L., and C. Bellest.   "Gravures Celebres."   Jazz Magazine
       no. 103:30-32, February 1964.

4860   Traill, S.   "Editorial."   Jazz Journal 17:1, February 1964.

4861   Jones, M.   "I'll Have to Start Practising."   Melody Maker 39:6, Feb-
       ruary 1, 1964.

4862   _____, and B. Houston.   "Two Views of Ellington."   Melody Mak-
       er 39:5, February 22, 1964.

4863   Bate, B.   "With Duke on Tour."   down beat 31:14-15, February 27,
       1964.

4864   Bellerby, V.   "Phase Three of Ellington."   Melody Maker 39:6, Feb-
       ruary 29, 1964.

4865   Jones, M.   "I'm Right at Home with Duke Says Rolf."   Melody Maker
       39:6, February 29, 1964.

4866   Ellington, Duke.   "Orientations: Adventures in the Mid-East."   Mu-
       sic Journal 22:34-36, March 1964.

4867 Traill, S. "Editorial." Jazz Journal 17:1, March 1964.

4868 Dommett, K. "Birmingham." Music Teacher 105:281, April 1964.

4869 "Duke Ellington in England." Jazz Monthly 10:4-5, April 1964.

4870 Lambert, G. E. "Ellingtonia '64." Jazz Journal 17:2-4, April 1964.

4871 _____. "The Ellingtonians." Jazz Monthly 10:16-17, April 1964.

4872 Östberg, L. "Ellington Med Nytt Material." Orkester Journalen 32:8-9, April 1964.

4873 Stearns, M. W. "Our Man in Music." Musical America 84:63, April 1964.

4874 Testoni, G. "Ellington a Milano." Musica Jazz 20:22-23, April 1964.

4875 Wilson, J. S. "Major Phases of the Latest Ellington." High Fidelity/Musical America 14:114, April 1964.

4876 "Ellington Rocks Carnegie Hall in New York Return." Variety 234:67, April 1, 1964.

4877 Balliett, W. "Jazz Concerts." New Yorker 40:100-102, April 11, 1964.

4878 Coss, B. "Duke's Concert Shows New Areas Conquered." Billboard 76:10, April 11, 1964.

4879 "Duke's Ball." Newsweek 63:84, April 13, 1964.

4880 Dance, S. "Jazz." Music Journal 22:70, May 1964.

4881 Destombes, A. "La Caravane Eternelle." Jazz Magazine no. 106:35, May 1964.

4882 Lattes, P. "Ellington 64." Jazz Hot no. 198:18-21, May 1964.

4883 Hentoff, N. "Durable Duke." Reporter 30:45-48, May 7, 1964.

4884 Williams, M. "Bigger Monk and Bigger Duke." Saturday Review 47:63-64, May 16, 1964.

4885 DeMicheal, D. "Caught in the Act." down beat 31:30, May 21, 1964.

4886 Koechlin, P. "Duke Ellington, l'Aristocrate du Jazz." Musica no. 123:42-43, June 1964.

4887 Postgate, J. "Between You and Me." Jazz Monthly 10:2, June 1964.

4888 "Robert Herridge Films and Hour of Ellington for TV." down beat 31:9, June 4, 1964.

4889 "Duke's Day." Time 83:60, June 5, 1964.

4890 Hentoff, N. "The Incompleat Duke Ellington." Show 4:70-72, July-August 1964.

4891   Ellington, Duke. "Reminiscing in Tempo." down beat 31:8-9, July
       2, 1964.

4892   DeMicheal, D. "Caught in the Act." down beat 31:42-43, July 16,
       1964.

4893   De Toledano, R. "Duke." National Review 16:658-659, July 28,
       1964.

4894   Jampel, D. "Duke Ellington's Beat Wows Japan Auds but Promoter
       Drops $40,000." Variety 235:47, August 1964.

4895   Williams, M. "Videotaping with Duke." down beat 31:20-23, August
       27, 1964.

4896   Lambert, G. E. "The Essential Ellington on French R.C.A." Jazz
       Monthly 10:15-17, October 1964.

4897   "New York." Music Journal 22:65, October 1964.

4898   Reda, J. "Le Duc Joue Ellington." Jazz Magazine no. 113:82-84,
       December 1964.

4899   "Swimming Pool Named for Duke Ellington in California." down beat
       31:10, December 17, 1964.

4900   "Basin St. Easty, N.Y." Variety 237:47, December 23, 1964. .

4901   Berendt, J. E. "Mingus and the Shadow of Duke Ellington." Jazz
       4:17-19, no. 4, 1965.

4902   Conniff, F. "Editorial." Jazz 4:3, no. 6, 1965. An expected Pul-
       itzer prize is not awarded to Ellington.

4903   Hoefer, G. "History of the Drum in Jazz." Jazz 4:12, no. 10,
       1965.

4904   "Ellington Jr. Joins Duke Trumpets." Melody Maker 40:5, January
       9, 1965.

4905   "College Gives Ellington Honorary Doctor's Degree." down beat
       32:9-10, January 14, 1965.

4906   Feather, L. "Feather's Nest." down beat 32:34, January 28, 1965.

4907   Anderson, L., and B. Sundin. "Ellington '65." Orkester Journalen
       33:10-11, February 1965.

4908   Lambert, E. "Duke Ellington and the Modernists." Jazz Journal
       18:24-26, February 1965.

4909   _____. "Quality Jazz." Jazz Journal 18:17, February 1965.

4910   Reda, J. "Le Duc Joue Ellington." Jazz Magazine no. 115:36-39,
       February 1965.

4911   Williams, M. "The Genesis of Duke." Jazz Journal 18:6-9, Feb-
       ruary 1965.

4912 "Duke--in Danger of Becoming a Jazz Museum?" Melody Maker
      40:10-11, February 6, 1965.

4913 Jones, M. "The Son of Duke!" Melody Maker 40:6, February 13,
      1965.

4914 "Out Go the Drum Solo, Medley, and on Comes Jazz." Melody Mak-
      er 40:6, February 20, 1965.

4915 Ramonet, M. C. "Duke!" Jazz Hot no. 207:10, March 1965.

4916 Tenot, F. "Une Societe en Plein Essor." Jazz Magazine no. 116:49-
      50, March 1965.

4917 Priestley, B. "Duke Ellington in Bournemouth." Jazz Monthly 11:22-
      24, April 1965.

4918 Traill, S. "Editorial." Jazz Journal 18:3, April 1965. Discussion
      of the jazz musicians Earl "Fatha" Hines and Ellington.

4919 Stewart, R. "The Days with Duke." down beat 32:20-22, April 22,
      1965.

4920 Dance, S. "Academic Action." Jazz Magazine 18:6-8, May 1965.
      Ellington participated in Philadelphia's Academy of Music Jazz
      Festival.

4921 "Pulitzer's Bum Duke to Ellington." Variety 238:187, May 12, 1965.

4922 "Notes and Comment; Decision Not to Award Pulitzer Prize for Mu-
      sic." New Yorker 41:43, May 15, 1965.

4923 "Repercussions on Pulitzer Nix to Duke Ellington." Variety 238:17,
      May 19, 1965.

4924 Kolodin, I. "Music to My Ears; No Duke for the Duke." Saturday
      Review 48:22, May 29, 1965.

4925 Shields, D. "The Jazz Beat." Billboard 77:10, May 29, 1965.

4926 Lambert, G. E. "Al Sears." Jazz Monthly 11:19-20, June 1965.

4927 "Duke and the Pulitzer Prize." down beat 32:12, June 17, 1965.

4928 Dance, S. "Lightly & Politely." Jazz Journal 18:24-26, July 1965.

4929 "Ellington and 'the Prize.'" International Musician 64:18, July 1965.

4930 "Mingus et l'Ombre de Duke." Jazz Magazine no. 120:28-34, July
      1965.

4931 Darke, P. "Gala and All That Jazz." Matrix no. 60:10-11, August
      1965.

4932 Flakser, H. "The 1933 Duke Ellington European Sojourn." Record
      Research no. 70:4, August 1965.

4933 "Bronze Medal." New Yorker 41:19-20, August 14, 1965.

4934 "Ellington Goes Down a Bomb on Symphony Dates." Melody Maker
      40:27, August 21, 1965.

4935 Harman, C. "Duke Clicks in Squaresville, at the Philharmonic."
      Life 59:15, August 27, 1965.

4936 Dance, S. "Jazz." Music Journal 23:92-93, September 1965.

4937 "Ellington Honored." International Musician 64:8, September 1965.
      The Medallion of Honor is presented to Ellington by New York City.

4938 "New Works." Music Journal 23:88, September 1965. Review of
      Ellington's "The Golden Broom and the Green Apple."

4939 "Duke Ellington Honored by City of New York." down beat 32:11,
      September 9, 1965.

4940 Morgenstern, D. "Caught in the Act." down beat 32:38, September
      9, 1965.

4941 Williams, M. "Last Trip up the River." Jazz Journal 18:7, Oc-
      tober 1965.

4942 Feather, L. "Back to Duke." down beat 32:15-17, October 7, 1965.

4943 "S. F.'s Grace Cathedral Site of Unique Ellington Concert." down
      beat 32:13, October 7, 1965.

4944 "Isy's, Vancouver." Variety 240:72, October 13, 1965.

4945 Dance, S. "Ecumenical Ellington; Concert in San Francisco's Grace
      Cathedral." Saturday Review 48:70-71, 1965.

4946 Berini, A., and G. Volontè. "Un Capolavoro di Ellington, 'The
      Mooche.'" Musica Jazz 21:9-13, November 1965.

4947 DeMicheal, D. "Duke Scores with Sacred Music in Grace Cathedral."
      down beat 32:13, November 4, 1965.

4948 "Documentary to Symphony--Duke's World of Challenge." down beat
      32:9-10, November 4, 1965.

4949 Ellington, Duke. "The Most Essential Instrument." Jazz Journal
      18:14-15, December 1965.

4950 "Ellington and More Ellington." International Musician 64:5, Decem-
      ber 1965.

4951 "A New Umbrella for Duke and Ella." down beat 32:10-11, Decem-
      ber 2, 1965.

4952 Kolodin, I. "Music to My Ears; Philharmonic Hall Concert." Sat-
      urday Review 48:60, December 25, 1965.

4953 "Ellington SRO in N.Y. Church Bash." Variety 241:40, December
      29, 1965.

4954 Granz, N. "Ella at 'Duke's Place.'" Jazz 5:8-9, no. 1, 1966.

4955 Sanfilippo, Luigi. General Catalogue of Duke Ellington's Recorded
      Music. 2d ed. Palermo: Centro Studi di Musica Contemporanea,
      1966.

4956 Solin, V. "Festival s Ellingtonem." Hudebni Rozhledy 19:543, no.
      17, 1966.

4957 Willard, P. "The King Scores." Jazz 5:10-12, no. 4, 1966.

4958 "Rex Stewart Attends a Duke Ellington Recording Session." Jazz
      Journal 19:15, January 1966.

4959 Morgenstern, D. "Caught in the Act." down beat 33:36-37, January
      27, 1966.

4960 "Ellington." International Musician 64:7, February 1966.

4961 "I. T. M. A." Jazz Journal 19:27, February 1966. Discussion of re-
      cordings by Ellington which have not been issued.

4962 "The Maestro." Jazz Journal 19:24-25, February 1966.

4963 "Pousse-Cafe." Variety 241:58, February 2, 1966.

4964 Dawson, J. "Ella: Having a Ball with Duke." Melody Maker 41:20,
      February 26, 1966.

4965 "Duke Swings in the Aisles." Melody Maker 41:23, February 26,
      1966. Review of Ellington's concert in Coventry Cathedral.

4966 "Gonsalves: Bands Are Forever." Melody Maker 41:20, February
      26, 1966.

4967 "Duke Ellington: Musical Genius." Sepia 15:8-10, March 1966.

4968 "I. T. B. G. in the Cathedral." Jazz Monthly 12:18-19, March 1966.

4969 "La Lady & Son Duc." Jazz Magazine no. 128:24-27, March 1966.

4970 Lattes, P. "Ella + Duke à Paris." Jazz Hot no. 218:9, March
      1966.

4971 "Stor Succe för Ella och Duke." Orkester Journalen 34:6-7, March
      1966.

4972 McNamara, H. "Caught in the Act." down beat 33:34, March 19,
      1966.

4973 Bellerby, V. "Duke Ellington, Coventry Cathedral." Jazz Journal
      19:4-5, April 1966.

4974 Dommett, K. "Cathedral Jazz." Music and Musicians 14:53, April
      1966.

4975 "Jazz Goes to Church." Ebony 21:76-80, April 1966.

4976 Lambert, E. "Duke at the University." Jazz Journal 19:4-5, April
      1966. Ellington performed at Liverpool University.

4977   "One Doesn't Snap One's Finger's [sic] on the Beat."   Jazz Journal
       19:12-13, April 1966.

4978   Traill, S.   "Editorial."   Jazz Journal 19:3, April 1966.

4979   Feather, L.   "Ellington; Hollywood, Africa, Japan--the World Shrinks
       for the Duke."   Melody Maker 41:8, May 28, 1966.

4980   Dance, S.   "Jazz."   Music Journal 24:62, June 1966.

4981   "April in Cincinnati."   Jazz Journal 19:16-17, June 1966.

4982   Quersin, B.   "Le Festival des Arts Negres."   Jazz Magazine no.
       131:13, June 1966.

4983   Williams, M.   "More of the Ellington Era."   Saturday Review 49:53,
       July 30, 1966.

4984   "Le Duke Parle d'Ellington."   Jazz Magazine no. 133:12-17, August
       1966.

4985   Hennessey, M.   "Ella, Duke Make Antibes Swing."   Billboard 78:16,
       August 13, 1966.

4986   "Ellington & Waring's 50th Annis."   Variety 243:43, August 17, 1966.

4987   "Granz Grooves 3 LPs, Gets Pie Too from Ella & Duke's Jazz on
       Riviera."   Variety 244:51, September 28, 1966.

4988   "Ellington Denies He Owes 125 G in Back U.S. Taxes."   Variety
       244:60, October 12, 1966.

4989   Bowes, M.   "Jazz in the Chapel."   Music Journal 24:45, November
       1966.

4990   Valburn, J.   "The Recordings of Duke Ellington for the Pathe/Cameo
       Groups 1928-29."   Record Research no. 80:6, November 1966.

4991   "Riverboat, N.Y."   Variety 245:53, November 30, 1966.

4992   Frazier, G.   "Sophistication of Duke Ellington."   Esquire 66:244-245,
       December 1966.

4993   "Clean Sweep."   ASCAP Today 1:5, no. 2, 1967.   Lists Ellington's
       "Here's to Morgan State," as well as his honorary doctorate of
       music awarded by Yale University.

4994   "Honors for Members."   ASCAP Today 1:20, no. 2, 1967.   "Here's
       to Morgan State," as well as his honorary doctorate of music award-
       ed by Yale University.

4995   Massagli, Luciano, Liborio Pusateri, and Giovanni M. Volontè.   Duke
       Ellington's Story on Records, 1923-?   Milan: Musica Jazz, 1967-?
       At least four volumes published: v. 1: 1923-1931; v. 2: 1932-
       1938; v. 3: 1939-1942; vo. 4: 1943-1944.

4996   "Ellington-Fitzgerald Nästa."   Orkester Journalen 35:4, January
       1967.

4997   "Duke's Sacred Music Blasted by Baptists."   down beat 34:11, Jan-
       uary 12, 1967.

4998 Feather, L. "Duke: Well, What Is Jazz?" Melody Maker 42:6,
January 14, 1967.

4999 "Caught in the Act." Melody Maker 42:7, February 4, 1967.

5000 "Duke Always Has a Trick up His Sleeve." Melody Maker 42:15,
February 11, 1967.

5001 "Ella and Duke Having a Ball." Melody Maker 42:11, February 18,
1967.

5002 Jones, M. "Duke Suites in a Hotel Suite." Melody Maker 42:8,
February 18, 1967.

5003 Bellerby, V. "Duke Plus the LPO." Melody Maker 42:9, February
25, 1967.

5004 _____. "Jazz in Britain." Jazz Journal 20:26, March 1967.

5005 Binchet, J. P. "La Tournee de Grand Duke." Jazz Magazine no.
140:18-25, March 1967.

5006 Carles, P. "Des Hommes et une Femme." Jazz Magazine no. 140:11,
March 1967.

5007 Nilsson, C. "Babs med Duke i Malmö." Orkester Journalen 35:13,
March 1967.

5008 Östberg, L. "Ellington med Nytt Material." Orkester Journalen
35:7, March 1967.

5009 Rado, A. "Duke Toujours Mieux." Jazz Hot no. 229:20-24, March
1967.

5010 Jones, M. "Jimmy Jones; Composing and Playing with Ella and the
Duke." Melody Maker 42:8, March 4, 1967.

5011 "Duke, One More Time." Jazz Magazine no. 141:12-13, April 1967.

5012 "Ellington & the L. P. O." Musical Events 22:30, April 1967.

5013 Feather, L. "Duke Ellington." International Musician 65:8, April
1967.

5014 Traill, S. "Editorial." Jazz Journal 20:3, April 1967.

5015 "Caught in the Act." down beat 34:28-29, April 6, 1967. Review of
concerts at Great St. Mary's Church and Royal Albert Hall in England.

5016 "Keeping up with the Duke." Time 89:73, April 14, 1967.

5017 "The Duke Ellington Stamp." Jazz 6:11, May 1967.

5018 "Duke's Honorary Degree." Variety 246:57, May 3, 1967.

5019 "Ellington Named Doctor of Music." down beat 34:13, June 15, 1967.

5020 "Inside Stuff--Music." Variety 247:54, June 21, 1967.

5021 "Ellington Honored by Yale University." down beat 34:11, July 27,
      1967. Ellington received the honorary doctor of music degree.

5022 Ackerman, P. "Duke Has No Peers; Is Still a Great U.S. Musical
      Force." Billboard 79:21, August 12, 1967.

5023 Balliett, W. "Jazz." New Yorker 43:86, August 19, 1967.

5024 Dance, S. "CAPAC & CAB." Jazz Journal 20:16-18, September
      1967.

5025 _____. "Jazz." Music Journal 25:92, September 1967.

5026 "Canadian Composers Get Ellington Touch." down beat 34:13, Sep-
      tember 7, 1967.

5027 Korall, B. "Strayhorn and the Duke." Saturday Review 50:71-72,
      September 16, 1967.

5028 Norris, J. "Duke Ellington, Pianist." down beat 34:15, October
      19, 1967.

5029 Lambert, G. E. "Microgroove Re-issues of Rare Early Ellington
      Recordings." Jazz Monthly 13:29-30, November 1967.

5030 Vacher, A. "Duke et Sarah à Montreal." Jazz Magazine no. 148:12,
      November 1967.

5031 Gitler, I. "Caught in the Act." down beat 34:28, November 16,
      1967.

5032 Atterton, J. "Ellington: Doesn't God Accept Singers Any More Now?"
      Melody Maker 41:8, December 17, 1966.

5033 Dance, S. "The Peerless Ellington." ASCAP Today 2:5-8, no. 2,
      1968.

5034 Ellington, Duke. "Wir Haben Einige Wichtige Dinge zu Sagen."
      Melos, Neue Zeitschrift für Musik 36:296-297, July-August 1969.
      Translated from the Christian Science Monitor 1968.

5035 McHugh, J. "Duke's Big Night." ASCAP Today 2:5, no. 2, 1968.

5036 Bennett, M. "Ellington's 'Sacred Concert' Fills N.Y. Church with
      5,000 Faithful at $15 Top." Variety 249:51, January 24, 1968.

5037 "Ellington a Hit with Seattle School Kids." down beat 35:13, Jan-
      uary 25, 1968.

5038 Des Malades Chez le Duke." Jazz Magazine no. 151:20, February
      1968.

5039 Jacobs, I. "Hail to the Duke." Matrix no. 75:5, February 1968.

5040 "Stor Succe för Babs och Duke." Orkester Journalen 36:11, Febru-
      ary 1968.

5041 Balliett, W. "Jazz Concerts." New Yorker 43:97, February 3,

1968. Review of the sacred concert Ellington gave at the Cathedral of St. John the Divine.

5042 Dance, S. "Ellington at St. John's." Saturday Review 51:53-54, February 10, 1968.

5043 _____. "Jazz." Music Journal 26:100, March 1968.

5044 _____. "Something about Believing." Jazz Journal 21:8-10, March 1968.

5045 Ellington, Duke. "Meningen med Min Kyrkomusik." Orkester Journalen 36:7, March 1968.

5046 _____. "La Signification de Mes Concerts de Musique Sacree." Jazz Magazine no. 152:11, March 1968.

5047 Feather, L. "Le Duke à l'Eglise." Jazz Magazine no. 152:10-11, March 1968. Ellington's sacred music concert at St. John the Divine is noted.

5048 _____. "Dukes Kyrkokonsert Inspelad." Orkester Journalen 36:6-7, March 1968. Duke Ellington's concert of religious works at the Cathedral of St. John the Divine is reviewed.

5049 "Bennett-Ellington-Leonard Package Packs Philharmonic for 53 G Gross." Variety 250:62, March 6, 1968.

5050 "Flamingo, Las Vegas." Variety 250:67, March 20, 1968.

5051 Dance, S. "Ellington Marches On." down beat 35:18, March 21, 1968.

5052 Wilson, J. S. "Duke Ellington's 'Sacred Concert.'" High Fidelity/ Musical America 18:MA20, April 1968.

5053 Dance, H. "God Has Those Angels." Saturday Review 51:60-61, April 13, 1968. Reprinted in Jazz Journal 21:2-3, August 1968. A review of Ellington's recording of religious music.

5054 Reilly, P. "Meeting on Parnassus: Sinatra and Ellington." HiFi/ Stereo Review 20:71, May 1968.

5055 "Rainbow Grill, N.Y." Variety 251:51, May 29, 1968.

5056 "Lincoln Center to House Duke Ellington Collection." Variety 251:45, June 12, 1968.

5057 Balliett, W. "Jazz." New Yorker 44:97-98, June 15, 1968.

5058 McDonough, J. "Inside Ellington." down beat 35:20-21, July 25, 1968.

5059 Malings, R. "Duke Ellington Forum." Matrix no. 78:11-12, August 1968.

5060 Mitchell, S. "Caught in the Act." down beat 35:32-33, August 8, 1968. Review of Ellington's concert in San Francisco's Grace Cathedral.

5061 "Wynn Humanitarian Award to Ellington." Variety 251:53, August
      14, 1968.

5062 Heckman, D. "Duke Ellington Plays Billy Strayhorn." HiFi/Stereo
      Review 21:74, September 1968.

5063 Dutton, F. "Alice Babs--Duke Ellington." Matrix no. 79:12-13,
      October 1968.

5064 Dance, S. "Interlude: Latin American Sunshine." Jazz Journal
      21:22-24, November 1968.

5065 _____. "Jazz." Music Journal 26:96, December 1968.

5066 Lindholm, O. "Bland Ellington-Vaenner i N.Y." Orkester Journalen
      36:14-15, December 1968.

5067 Malings, R. "Duke Ellington Forum." Matrix no. 80:16, December
      1968.

5068 Dance, S. "'Otra, Otra' Ellington Conquers Latin America." down
      beat 35:16, December 12, 1968.

5069 "Duke Ellington: Chceme Rici Neco Duleziteho." Hudebni Rozhledy
      22:509-510, no. 20, 1969.

5070 "Ellington Birthday Honored at White House on April 29th." ASCAP
      Today 3:13, no. 1, 1969.

5071 "Notes for Notes." Notes 25:470-471, no. 3, 1969.

5072 Polednak, I. "Jazzfestival '69." Hudebni Rozhledy 22:686-688, no.
      22, 1969.

5073 Dance, S. "Noblesse Oblige; Jazz Nobility on Tour." International
      Musician 67:5, January 1969.

5074 "LBJ Appoints Duke to Art Council." down beat 36:12, January 23,
      1969.

5075 Bolling, C. "Le Compositeur et l'Orchestrateur." Jazz Hot no.
      247:16-17, February 1969.

5076 _____, and G. Arvanitas. "Le Pianiste." Jazz Hot no. 247:16-
      17, February 1969.

5077 Dance, S. "L'Incomparable Ellington." Jazz Hot no. 247:14-15,
      February 1969. Reprinted from ASCAP Today.

5078 "Ellington 69." Jazz Magazine no. 163:19, February 1969.

5079 Priestly, B. "Duke Ellington's Greatest Hits and the Far East
      Suite." Jazz Monthly no. 169:17-19, March 1969.

5080 "Sahara, Las Vegas." Variety 254:100, March 19, 1969.

5081 Jones, M. "President Nixon's Dinner Tribute to Ellington." Melody
      Maker 44:4, March 22, 1969.

5082 Anderson, L. "Duke Ellington 70 Aar." Orkester Journalen 37:9, April 1969.

5083 Malings, R. "Duke Ellington Forum." Matrix no. 82:9-10, April 1969.

5084 "Ellington Now 100 Percent Owner of Tempo Pub." Variety 254:58, April 16, 1969.

5085 Feather, L. "King of the Big Band Road." down beat 36:18, April 17, 1969.

5086 McDonough, J. "Reminiscing in Tempo--Guitarist Freddy Guy's Ellington Memories." down beat 36:16-17, April 17, 1969.

5087 Bellerby, V. "Second Opinion on the Duke." Melody Maker 44:19, April 26, 1969.

5088 Chilton, J. "What Brassmen Owe to Ellington." Melody Maker 44:20, April 26, 1969.

5089 "70 Years of Ellington!" Melody Maker 44:18-23, April 26, 1969.

5090 Lambert, E. "Duke Ellington on Reprise." Jazz Journal 22:2-4, May 1969.

5091 Traill, S. "Editorial." Jazz Journal 22:1, May 1969.

5092 "Buys Billy Strayhorn's Stock in the Tempo Music Publishing Co., N.Y.C. for $100,000." Jet 36:60, May 8, 1969.

5093 "Medal for Duke and a Kiss for the Chief." Life 66:97-98, May 9, 1969.

5094 "Duke's Party." New Yorker 45:31-33, May 10, 1969.

5095 Saal, H. "Duke at Seventy." Newsweek 73:117, May 12, 1969.

5096 "Jazz Night at the White House Honoring the Duke." U.S. News & World Report 66:10-11, May 12, 1969.

5097 "Taking the A Train." Newsweek 73:34-35, May 12, 1969.

5098 "Pres. Nixon Gives Ellington a History-Making 70th Birthday Party at the White House." Jet 36:22-53, May 15, 1969.

5099 "Concert Reviews." Variety 255:62, May 28, 1969.

5100 Dance, S. "Ellington at the White House." Saturday Review 52:48-49, May 31, 1969.

5101 Berendt, J. E. "Jazz & Pop Mailbox: Happy Birthday, Duke!" Jazz and Pop 8:8-9, June 1969.

5102 Dance, S. "Lightly & Politely." Jazz Journal 22:12-13, June 1969.

5103 Feather, L. "Le Duc et le President." Jazz Magazine no. 167:16-17, June 1969.

5104 _____. "Fin Foedelsedagsfest foer Duke." Orkester Journalen
      37:7, June 1969.

5105 Gingrich, A. "Homage to Ellington in the Nixon Style." Esquire
      71:10, June 1969.

5106 Malings, R. "Duke Ellington Forum." Matrix no. 83:8, June 1969.

5107 Morgenstern, D. "Swinging at the White House." down beat 36:14,
      June 12, 1969.

5108 Henshaw, L. "McHugh--the Man Who Found Duke Ellington." Mel-
      ody Maker 44:9, June 14, 1969.

5109 Garland, P. "Duke Ellington." Ebony 24:29-32, July 1969.

5110 "Ellington's Medallion." Variety 255:54, July 2, 1969.

5111 "Composes a Song, 'Moon Maiden,' for the Moon-Bound Astronauts."
      Jet 36:60-61, July 31, 1969.

5112 "Rainbow Grill, N.Y." Variety 255:46, August 6, 1969.

5113 Dove, I. "Quality, Taste & Warmth Mark Duke's Performance."
      Billboard 81:32, August 9, 1969.

5114 "Notes and Comment." New Yorker 45:23, August 9, 1969.

5115 "Wins Four Awards in the Annual down beat Critics Poll: For Best
      Band, Best Composer, Best Arranger and Best Record of the Year."
      Jet 36:59, August 14, 1969.

5116 Finola, G. "'Guy Throws a Good Paint Brush' ... Duke." Second
      Line 22:225-226, September-October 1969.

5117 Vacher, A. "Montreal, le Duc et le Comte." Jazz Magazine no.
      169-170:11, September 1969.

5118 "Gets Elijah Lovejoy Award from the Elks at Their 70th Convention
      in Washington, D.C. Photo." Jet 36:8, September 11, 1969.

5119 Lambert, E. "In Harlem." Jazz Monthly no. 176:17-18, October
      1969.

5120 Malings, R. "Duke Ellington Forum." Matrix no. 85:8-9, October
      1969.

5121 "Plays a Selection from His Sacred Music Concert at the Mass for
      Dr. James A. Pike in N.Y. City's St. Clement's Episcopal Church."
      Jet 36:51, October 2, 1969.

5122 "Berkeley Fetes Duke; Musicians Pay Tribute." down beat 36:12, Oc-
      tober 16, 1969.

5123 Gitler, I. "Chasin' the 'Apple.'" down beat 36:13, October 30,
      1969.

5124 James, B. "What Jazz Influence?" American Musical Digest 1:38-
      39, no. 4, 1970. Abridged from Audio Record Review November 1969.

5125   Lambert, E. "Quality Jazz." Jazz Journal 22:11, November 1969.
       Discussion of Ellington's "Nutcracker Suite" recording.

5126   Lucas, J. "The Duchy of Ellington." Jazz Journal 22:22-24, No-
       vember 1969.

5127   McCarthy, A. "Record Reviews." Jazz Monthly no. 177:12-13, No-
       vember 1969. Covers the recording made 1927-1940.

5128   Rado, A. "Duke Ellington." Jazz Hot no. 255:12-15, November
       1969.

5129   Reddy, J. "Man Who Put the Top Hat on Jazz." Reader's Digest
       95:108-112, November 1969.

5130   "Chevalier to Emcee Duke's Paris Salute." Variety 256:1, November
       5, 1969.

5131   "The Duke in Berlin." American Musical Digest 1:40, no. 4, 1970.
       Translated from the Frankfurter Neue Press November 11, 1969.

5132   "Even Duke Ellington Can't Make It on Czech TV as Red Grip Tight-
       ens." Variety 257:53, November 26, 1969.

5133   Hadlock, D. "The Ultimate Ellington Tribute." down beat 36:12,
       November 27, 1969.

5134   Burde, W. "Jazz-Tage 1969." Neue Zeitschrift für Musik 130:556-
       559, December 1969.

5135   Dance, S. "Duke Ellington." Stereo Review 23:69-80, December
       1969.

5136   "Ellington on Records: A Selective Discography." Stereo Review
       23:78, December 1969.

5137   Gilson, J. "Duke Ellington à Saint-Sulpice." Jazz Hot no. 256:14,
       December 1969.

5138   Levin, J. "Sacre Duke." Jazz Magazine no. 173:15, December
       1969.

5139   Miller, S. "Jazzfestivalen i Prag." Musikern no. 12:6, December
       1969.

5140   "There Will Always Be an Ellington." Melody Maker 44:8, December
       6, 1969.

5141   Dance, Stanley. The World of Duke Ellington. New York: C. Scrib-
       ner's Sons, 1970. A heavily illustrated biography utilizing inter-
       views with Ellington as well as musicians who knew him.

5142   Levin, F. "The Duke Ellington 'Sacred Music Concert,' New Orleans
       1970." Jazz Report 7:27-28, no. 3, 1970.

5143   Yuhasz, Sister M. J. "Black Composers and Their Piano Music."
       American Music Teacher 19:28-29, no. 5, 1970.

5144   Alessandrini, P., et al. "Disques du Mois." Jazz Magazine no.
       174:46-47, January 1970.

5145   Bruer, J. "Samtal Med Carney." Orkester Journalen 38:10-11,
       January 1970.

5146   Goddet, L. "Svenskar Med Duke i Paris." Orkester Journalen 38:9,
       January 1970.

5147   Traill, S. "Editorial." Jazz Journal 23:1, January 1970. Discus-
       sion of Ellington's recording session in London.

5148   _____. "Jazz in Britain." Jazz Journal 23:6, January 1970.

5149   Voce, S. "It Don't Mean a Thing." Jazz Journal 23:18-19, Jan-
       uary 1970.

5150   Dance, S. "New Crop of Honors Reaped by Ellington." down beat
       37:8-9, January 22, 1970.

5151   Wilmer, V. "Caught in the Act: Berlin Jazz Days." down beat
       37:27, January 22, 1970.

5152   Dance, S. "Lightly & Politely." Jazz Journal 23:8-9, February 1970.

5153   Marr, W., et al. "NAACP Benefit and Tribute to Duke Ellington."
       Crisis 77:97-101, March 1970.

5154   Locke, D. "Random Reflections." Jazz Monthly no. 181:11-12,
       March 1970. Discusses Ellington's "And His Mother Called Him
       Bill" on the album done as a tribute to Strayhorn.

5155   "La Plume d'Or." Jazz Hot no. 259:9, March 1970.

5156   Dove, I. "Tribute Packed with Elegant Ellingtonia." Billboard 82:26,
       March 7, 1970.

5157   Goodman, J. "Unsold Soul." New Leader 53:32-33, March 16, 1970.

5158   "Big Band Special." Melody Maker 45:18, March 21, 1970.

5159   Feather, L. "Caught in the Act." Melody Maker 45:12, March 21,
       1970.

5160   Horne, M. "Ellingtonia 70." Jazz Magazine no. 177:9-10, April 1970.

5161   Tortolano, W. "Music in Today's Churches." Musical Opinion 93:375,
       April 1970.

5162   Dance, S. "New Conquests for Duke." down beat 37:12, April 16, 1970.

5163   Hughes, D. "Caught in the Act: Duke Ellington." down beat 37:26-
       28, April 16, 1970.

5164   Bolton, C. "The Eternal Ellington." Second Line 23:335-336, May-
       June 1970.

5165   Levin, F. "The Duke Ellington Sacred Music Concert, New Orleans
       1970." Second Line 23:322-323, May-June 1970.

5166 "Two Ellington Concerts." Second Line 23:321, May-June 1970.

5167 Dance, S. "Continued, or Limeside Defied." Jazz Journal 236:237, May 1970.

5168 Krajewski, F. "The Ellington Legend." Music Journal 28:32, May 1970.

5169 Niquet, B. "La Chronique des Disques: 70th Birthday Concert." Jazz Hot no. 263:43, Summer 1970.

5170 "Honour." Storyville no. 29:193, June-July 1970. Ellington is honored by election to the National Institute of Arts and Letters.

5171 Lambert, E. "Record Reviews: Flaming Youth; Cottontail." Jazz Monthly no. 184:13-14, June 1970.

5172 "Reeditions: The Great Reunion." Jazz Magazine no. 179:49, June 1970.

5173 "Duke Ellington Plays a Near Secret Date at Richmond Country Club." Variety 259:46, June 24, 1970.

5174 Balliett, W. "Our Local Correspondents; A Day with the Duke." New Yorker 46:52-55, June 27, 1970.

5175 "Disques du Mois: 70th Birthday Concert." Jazz Magazine no. 180:41, July-August 1970.

5176 "Reeditions: At His Very Best." Jazz Magazine no. 180:45-46, July-August 1970.

5177 "Reeditions: Masterpieces." Jazz Magazine no. 180:47-48, July-August 1970.

5178 Saal, H. "Dance Me a River." Newsweek 76:86, July 6, 1970.

5179 Ellington, Duke, et al. "Roses for Satchmo." down beat 37:14-19, July 9, 1970.

5180 Lockhart, G. "Chords & Discords: It Don't Mean a Thing." down beat 37:10, July 23, 1970.

5181 Dance, S. "Ellington Notes--May-June." Jazz Journal 23:6-7, August 1970.

5182 Levin, F. "The Duke in New Orleans." Jazz Journal 23:35, August 1970.

5183 "Rainbow Grill, N.Y." Variety 259:53, August 5, 1970.

5184 Roberts, A. "Caught in the Act Extra." Melody Maker 45:37, August 8, 1970.

5185 "Talent in Action." Billboard 82:30, August 15, 1970.

5186 Vinding, T. "The Duke in Music City, U.S.A." Second Line 23:379, September-October 1970.

5187   Dance, S.   "Jazz."   Music Journal 28:38, September 1970.

5188   Delorme, M.   "Duke à Menton."   Jazz Hot no. 264:12, September
       1970.

5189   Polillo, A.   "Italie: Festival par Cinq."   Jazz Magazine no. 181:45-
       46, September 1970.

5190   Rado, A.   "Duke en Tournee."   Jazz Magazine no. 181:8-9, Septem-
       ber 1970.

5191   Tenot, F.   "Ellington à Provins."   Jazz Magazine no. 181:7-8, Sep-
       tember 1970.

5192   Jones, M.   "Jazz Records: 70th Birthday Concert."   Melody Maker
       45:34, September 26, 1970.

5193   Bruer, J.   "Svensk Saangerska Med Duke Ellington."   Orkester Jour-
       nalen 38:7, October 1970.

5194   Dance, S.   "Lightly & Politely."   Jazz Journal 23:8-9, October 1970.
       Review of Ellington's Rainbow Grill performances.

5195   Maskey, J.   "The Dance."   High Fidelity/Musical America 20:MA10,
       October 1970.

5196   "Record Reviews: 70th Birthday Concert."   Jazz Journal 23:27, Oc-
       tober 1970.

5197   Allan, J. W.   "Chords & Discords: Prescription."   down beat 37:7,
       October 29, 1970.   Review of Ellington's concert in Melbourne,
       Australia.

5198   Carriere, C.   "La Chronique des Disques: Masterpieces."   Jazz Hot
       no. 266:40, November 1970.

5199   Niquet, B.   "La Chronique des Disques: The Great Reunion."   Jazz
       Hot no. 266:39, November 1970.

5200   "Record Reviews: 70th Birthday Concert."   Jazz Monthly no. 189:16-
       17, November 1970.

5201   Siders, H.   "Monterey Diary."   down beat 37:17, November 12, 1970.

5202   "Now Grove, L.A."   Variety 261:74, November 18, 1970.

5203   Feather, L.   "Ella and Duke--Together."   Melody Maker 45:39, No-
       vember 21, 1970.

5204   "Talent in Action."   Billboard 82:25, November 21, 1970.

5205   Feather, L.   "Caught in the Act."   Melody Maker 45:16, November
       28, 1970.

5206   Kumm, B.   "Record Reviews: 70th Birthday Concert."   Storyville
       no. 32:79, December 1970-January 1971.

5207   Feather, L.   "Monterey 70."   Jazz Magazine no. 184:45-46, Decem-
       ber 1970.

5208   James, B. "Johnny Hodges on Record." Jazz Journal 23:18-19,
       December 1970.

5209   Tercinet, A. "La Chronique des Disques: My People; The Great
       Duke Ellington." Jazz Hot no. 267:45, December 1970.

5210   "Ellington Wows Muscovites." Music and Artists 4:5, no. 5, 1971-
       1972.

5211   Barrell, A. "The Ellington Orchestra 1926-1930." Footnote 2:2-6,
       no. 3, 1971.

5212   "Ellington Concert." Footnote 3:14-15, no. 2, 1971.

5213   Norris, J. W. "Record Reviews: Ellington Encore." Coda 10:18-
       19, no. 2, 1971.

5214   Fabio, S. W. "Tribute to Duke." Black World 2:42-45, January
       1971. A poem in Ellington's honor.

5215   "Record Reviews: My People." Coda 9:22, no. 11, 1971; Jazz Jour-
       nal 24:31, January 1971.

5216   "Reeditions: Duke Ellington's My People; The Great Duke Elling-
       ton." Jazz Magazine no. 185:45-46, January 1971.

5217   Tercinet, A. "La Chronique des Disques: The Beginning." Jazz
       Hot no. 268:34, January 1971.

5218   "Caught in the Act." down beat 38:30-31, January 7, 1971.

5219   Kolodin, I. "Hodeir on 'Finnegans Wake.'" Saturday Review 54:53,
       January 30, 1971.

5220   "Three Decades of Ellington: A Fascinating Decca Release." Amer-
       ican Record Guide 37:370-371, February 1971. Discusses Elling-
       ton's "Harlem," "New World a 'Coming," and "The Golden Broom
       and the Green Apple."

5221   Traill, S. "Record Reviews: Ellington 55." Jazz Journal 24:33,
       February 1971.

5222   McDonough, J. "Old Wine--New Bottles." down beat 38:28-29, Feb-
       ruary 18, 1971.

5223   "Royal Swedish Academy Taps Duke Ellington." down beat 38:12,
       April 15, 1971.

5224   "Concert Reviews." Variety 262:59, April 28, 1971.

5225   Lewis, J. S., and D. Metcalf. "I've Heard That Song Before."
       Record Research no. 110:8, May 1971.

5226   Boatfield, G. "Record Reviews: At the Southland and the Cotton
       Club." Jazz Journal 24:35, June 1971.

5227   Dance, S. "Jazz." Music Journal 29:38, June 1971.

5228   _____. "Lightly & Politely." Jazz Journal 24:25, June 1971.

5229   "Record Reviews: Second Sacred Concert." Jazz and Pop 10:44-45,
       June 1971; down beat 38:19, June 10, 1971.

5230   "Concert Reviews." Variety 263:51, June 30, 1971.

5231   Tercinet, A. "La Chronique des Disques: The Works of Duke, Vol.
       1." Jazz Hot no. 272:29, July 1971.

5232   "The River." Jet 4:56, July 22, 1971.

5233   "Doctor Jazz." Jazz Magazine no. 191:5, August 1971.

5234   Reda, J. "Reeditions: The Works of Duke; Integrale, Vol. 1."
       Jazz Magazine no. 191:51, August 1971.

5235   Jones, M. "Jazz Records: New Orleans Suite." Melody Maker
       46:26, August 14, 1971.

5236   "Caught in the Act." Melody Maker 46:26, August 21, 1971.

5237   "Autour d'un Disque: Suite Autour d'une Chaise Vide." Jazz Hot no.
       275:34, September 1971. Review of Ellington's "New Orleans
       Suite."

5238   Debroe, G. "Ellingtonia." Points du Jazz no. 5:97-104, September
       1971.

5239   Atterton, J., and L. Feather. "Ellington's Free Concert." Melody
       Maker 46:6, September 11, 1971.

5240   Morgenstern, D. "Record Reviews: New Orleans Suite." down beat
       38:30, September 16, 1971.

5241   Thompson, C. S. "Duke Ellington's New Musical Discovery." Jet
       4:6-63, September 16, 1971.

5242   Bishop, A. J. "The Protean Imagination of Duke Ellington--the Ear-
       ly Years." Jazz Journal 24:2-4, October 1971.

5243   "Dusques du Mois: Second Sacred Concert." Jazz Magazine no.
       193:44-45, October 1971.

5244   McRae, B. "A B Basics." Jazz Journal 24:22, October 1971.

5245   Traill, S. "Editorial." Jazz Journal 24:1, October 1971.

5246   _____. "Record Reviews: Back to Back and Side by Side." Jazz
       Journal 24:29, October 1971.

5247   "Duke's Old 'A Train' on Time in USSR." Billboard 83:20, October
       2, 1971.

5248   "Ellington in Russia; They Love Him Madly." down beat 38:9, Oc-
       tober 28, 1971.

5249   Jones, M. "The Duke Steps Out, 71 Style." Melody Maker 46:34-
       35, October 30, 1971.

5250 "Black Academy of Arts and Letters." Black World 21:68-71, November 1971.

5251 Carriere, C. "La Chronique des Disques: Anatomy of a Murder." Jazz Hot no. 277:35, November 1971.

5252 _____. "La Chronique des Disques: Second Sacred Concert." Jazz Hot no. 277:34-35, November 1971.

5253 Levin, J. "Disques du Mois: Anatomy of a Murder." Jazz Magazine no. 149:33-34, November 1971.

5254 Oberg, C. "Disques du Mois: New Orleans Suite." Jazz Magazine no. 194:34, November 1971.

5255 "Russia Was Great But." Melody Maker 46:24, November 6, 1971.

5256 Bishop, A. J. "The Protean Imagination of Duke Ellington--the Early Years." Jazz Journal 24:12-14, December 1971.

5257 Delaunay, C., et al. "Les Festivals d'Automne." Jazz Hot no. 278:10, December 1971.

5258 "Duke en U.R.S.S." Jazz Magazine no. 195:8, December 1971.

5259 "Ellingtonians Talking." Crescendo International 10:20, December 1971.

5260 Nilsson, C. "Ellington i Malmoe." Orkester Journalen 39:11, December 1971.

5261 "Record Reviews: 'Second Sacred Concert.'" Jazz Journal 24:36, December 1971.

5262 Reda, J. "Duke Ellington." Jazz Magazine no. 195:30-31, December 1971.

5263 "Skiftande Stjaernspel i Uppsala." Orkester Journalen 39:8, December 1971.

5264 Staples, J. "Duke Still Comes up with Some Surprises." Crescendo International 10:22, December 1971.

5265 _____. "Instrumental Reflections." Crescendo International 10:10, December 1971.

5266 Tercinet, A. "La Chronique des Disques: The Works of Duke." Jazz Hot no. 278:34, December 1971.

5267 Traill, S. "Editorial." Jazz Journal 24:1, December 1971.

5268 "Rainbow Grill, N.Y." Variety 265:57, December 22, 1971.

5269 "Caught in the Act." down beat 38:36, December 23, 1971.

5270 Montgomery, Elizabeth Rider. Duke Ellington: King of Jazz. Champaign, Ill.: Garrard Pub. Co., 1972. Juvenile literature.

5271 "Record Reviews: Big Bands--1933." Coda 10:26-27, no. 8, 1972.

5272 "Record Reviews: Integrale, Vols. 1 and 3." Coda 10:25-26, no.
      7, 1972.

5273 Syman, O. "Atlantic City; Potsdam University." Coda 10:40-42, no.
      10, 1972.

5274 Dance, S. "Jazz." Music Journal 30:66, January 1972.

5275 Lambert, E. "In Person: Duke Ellington and His Orchestra." Jazz
      & Blues 1:12-13, January 1972.

5276 "Schallplattenbesprechungen: The Popular Duke Ellington." Jazz Po-
      dium 21:24, January 1972.

5277 "Disques du Mois: The Works of Duke, Vol. 2." Jazz Magazine no.
      197:33, February 1972.

5278 "Record Reviews: Duke Ellington and His Orchestra--in a Mellotone."
      Jazz & Blues 1:27-28, February 1972.

5279 "Record Reviews: Masterpieces." Jazz & Blues 1:27-28, February
      1972.

5280 "Record Reviews: Second Sacred Concert." Jazz & Blues 1:27-28,
      February 1972.

5281 Dance, S. "Duke's Grand Tour: The Inside Story." down beat
      39:17, February 3, 1972.

5282 "Jazz Records: His Most Important Second War Concert." Melody
      Maker 47:32, February 26, 1972.

5283 "Chronique des Disques: Integrale Volume 3." Jazz Hot no. 281:27,
      March 1972.

5284 Debroe, G. "Ellington en Microsillons." Points du Jazz no. 6:101-
      102, March 1972.

5285 _____ . "Ellingtonia: Ellington en Question." Points du Jazz no.
      6:99-100, March 1972.

5286 Gordeyeva, M. "Duke Ellington: 'Very Sensitive Audience.'" Soviet
      Life no. 3(186):60-62, March 1962.

5287 Mellers, W. "The Duke at 70." Music and Musicians 20:34-35,
      March 1972.

5288 Niquet, B. "Handful of Records: Second Sacred Concert." Points
      du Jazz no. 6:128-130, March 1972.

5289 "Chronique des Disques: Piano Reflections." Jazz Hot no. 282:27,
      April 1972.

5290 "Record Reviews: His Most Important Second War Concert." Jazz
      & Blues 2:25, April 1972.

5291 "Concert Reviews." Variety 266:88, April 12, 1972.

5292   "The Long Road Home; Mercer Ellington Talks to Stanley Dance."
       down beat 39:14-15, April 13, 1972.

5293   "Bill Evans, Ellington Cop Grammy Awards." down beat 39:9, April
       27, 1972.

5294   Kolodin, I. "Music to My Ears." Saturday Review 55:7, April 29,
       1972. Ellington performed at New York City's Whitney Museum in
       the Composer's Showcase.

5295   Roach, M. "What 'Jazz' Means to Me." Black Scholar 3:2-6, Sum-
       mer 1972.

5296   Dance, S. "Jazz." Music Journal 30:22, June 1972.

5297   "Chronique des Disques: The Cosmic Scene." Jazz Hot no. 285:30,
       July-August 1972.

5298   Dance, S. "Celebration." Jazz Journal 25:4, July 1972.

5299   "18th Annual Mr. Travel Award." Travel 138:56-57, July 1972.

5300   "Record Reviews: The Beautiful Americans." Jazz & Blues 2:28,
       July 1972.

5301   Traill, S. "Editorial." Jazz Journal 25:3, July 1972. Ellington
       has reached his 73rd birthday.

5302   "Ellington Refutes Cry that Swing Started Sex Crimes!" down beat
       39:24, July 20, 1972.

5303   Stickney, D. B. "Happenings Then and Now--from David to the
       Duke." Music Ministry 4:34-35, August 1972.

5304   "Rainbow Grill, N.Y." Variety 267:53, August 9, 1972.

5305   "Carnegie Hall." Music Journal 30:65, September 1972.

5306   "Chronique des Disques: The Works of Duke, Vol. 4." Jazz Hot no.
       286:28, September 1972.

5307   "$1 Million Ellington Chair to be Established at Yale U." Jet 42:6,
       September 21, 1972.

5308   "Yale Rolls $1-Mil. Ellington Program." Variety 268:1, September 27,
       1972.

5309   Dance, S. "Jazz." Music Journal 30:66-67, October 1972.

5310   _____. "Uwis." Jazz Journal 25:22-23, October 1972.

5311   Debroe, G. "Ellingtonia." Points du Jazz no. 7:157-158, October 1972.

5312   "Disques du Mois: Hot in Harlem; The Beginning." Jazz Magazine
       no. 204:45-46, October 1972. Covers recordings from 1928-1929
       and 1926-1928, respectively.

5313   "Ellington Fellowship to Honor 36 Black Greats of Music at Yale Uni-
       versity." Music Trades 120:34, October 1972.

5314   "30 Black Musicians Get Ellington Medal in Yale's New Program."
       Variety 268:55, October 11, 1972.

5315   "Ellington Fellowship Program Set for Yale." down beat 39:10, Oc-
       tober 12, 1972.

5316   Willard, P. "Love and Learn: The Ellingtonians at UW." down
       beat 39:12-14, October 12, 1972.

5317   Atterton, J. "Jazz." Melody Maker 47:6, October 21, 1972. Notes
       on the Duke Ellington Fellowship Program at Yale University's
       Conservatory Without Walls.

5318   "Musicians Celebrate Black Heritage." Jet 43:56-58, October 26,
       1972.

5319   Dance, S. "Conservatory Without Walls." Jazz Journal 25:10-11,
       November 1972.

5320   Duckett, A. "Duke Ellington: Greatest Living Popular Musician."
       Sepia 21:38-44, November 1972.

5321   "Hilton, Las Vegas." Variety 269:61, November 29, 1972.

5322   Dance, S. "Jazz: Conservatory Without Walls." Music Journal
       30:12, December 1972.

5323   "Disques du Mois: The Works of Duke, Integrale Vols. 3, 4, 5."
       Jazz Magazine no 206:40, December 1972.

5324   "Yale's Ellington Fellowship Program to Preserve Black Musical
       Legacy." School Musician 44:61, December 1972.

5325   Morgenstern, D. "Yale's Conservatory Without Walls." down beat
       39:11, December 7, 1972.

5326   "Record Reviews: Earl Hines Plays Duke Ellington." down beat
       39:22, December 7, 1972.

5327   "Duke Ellington Repeatedly Honored." Jazz Forum 7:13, no. 25,
       1973.

5328   Ellington, Duke. Music Is My Mistress. New York: Da Capo Press,
       1976. Reprint of the 1973 edition published by Doubleday, Garden
       City, N.Y.

5329   Hippenmeyer, J. R. "Un Duc à la Tete d'un Royaume--'Duke' El-
       lington. L'Ascension: 1926-1942." Revue Musicale de Suisse
       Romande 26:17, no. 4, 1973.

5330   "Premieres." Symphony News 24:21, no. 1, 1973.

5331   "Record Reviews: Latin American Suite; Togo Brava Suite." Popular
       Music and Society 2:172-174, no. 2, 1973.

5332   "Record Reviews: Rockin' in Rhythm." Coda 10:24, no. 11, 1973.

5333   Wayne, Bennett. 3 Jazz Greats. Champaign, Ill.: Garrard Pub.

Co., 1973. William Christopher Handy, Louis Armstrong, and Ellington are discussed in this book designed for children.

5334 "Record Reviews: Complete Edition, Vol. Five; Far East Suite; The Popular Duke Ellington." Jazz & Blues 2:26-28, January 1973.

5335 Sobel, R. "Talent in Action." Billboard 85:19, January 13, 1973.

5336 Ioakimidis, D. "Ellington: A Time of Transition." Jazz & Blues 2:5-7, February 1973.

5337 "On Record: 'Anatomy of a Murder.'" Jazz & Blues 2:12-13, February 1973.

5338 Traill, S. "Editorial." Jazz Journal 26:1, February 1973.

5339 Wasserman, J. L. "Love Song to the Duke, from Just About Everybody." Saturday Review of the Arts 1:7-8, February 1973.

5340 Feather, L. "The 10 Worlds of Edward Kennedy Ellington." Billboard 85:14-15, February 10, 1973.

5341 "From Jazzman to Pop Composer, That's the Way Things Developed." Billboard 85:25, February 10, 1973.

5342 "One a Year, That's Been the Way Duke's Been Writing Extended Works Since 1943." Billboard 85:22, February 10, 1973.

5343 "Recordings Reflect the Evolution of the Ellington Sound." Billboard 85:16, February 10, 1973.

5344 Tiegel, E. "Duke and Irving Mills: They Helped Each Other Grow in the Early Years." Billboard 85:18, February 10, 1973.

5345 Nickerson, R. "Shaking the 'Losing Human Syndrome': A Lesson in Living from Duke Ellington." Soul 7:2-3, February 12, 1973.

5346 Dance, S. "Ain't But the One." Jazz Journal 26:9, March 1973.

5347 Siders, H. "The Ellington Special: A Labor of Love." down beat 40:18-19, March 1, 1973.

5348 "Caught in the Act." Melody Maker 48:45, March 3, 1973.

5349 "Jazz Records: Ellington on the Air." Melody Maker 48:48, March 3, 1973.

5350 Giddins, G. "Duke Back in Action: After Brief Layoff." down beat 40:12, March 15, 1973.

5351 "Reviews on Record: Great Times!" Jazz & Blues 3:18, April 1973.

5352 "Duke, Hubbard, Burton Cop Grammy Awards." down beat 40:9, April 26, 1973.

5353 Keating, L. "On Screen: BBC TV." Jazz & Blues 3:34, May 1973.

5354 "On Record: His Most Important Second War Concert." Jazz & Blues 3:26, May 1973.

5355 "Record Reviews: Latin American Suite." down beat 40:20, May 24, 1973.

5356 "Columbia Honors Duke with Honorary Degree." Jet 44:61, May 31, 1973.

5357 Cholinski, H. "Collectors Corner: Duke Ellington on LPs." Jazz Forum no. 23:58-62, June 1973.

5358 Dance, S. "Lightly & Politely." Jazz Journal 26:12-14, June 1973.

5359 "Duke Ellington, Sine Qua Non." Esquire 79:130-133, June 1973. An excerpt from Ellington's book Music Is My Mistress.

5360 "On Record: The Duke Plays Ellington." Jazz & Blues 3:20, June 1973.

5361 Cholinski, H. "Collectors Corner: Duke Ellington on LPs." Jazz Forum no. 24:51-55, August 1973.

5362 "Duke Ellington Gets France's Top Honor." Jet 44:60, August 2, 1973.

5363 "Rainbow Grill, N.Y." Variety 272:39, August 15, 1973.

5364 McDonough, J. "Four Big Bands." down beat 40:19, August 16, 1973.

5365 Borall, B. "Monsieur le Duc." International Musician 72:11, September 1973. Ellington received the Legion of Honor award.

5366 Dance, S. "Lightly & Politely." Jazz Journal 26:16-17, September 1973.

5367 Carriere, C., and J. Delmas. "Elements pour l'Extraordinaire, Incroyable & Fabuleuse Histoire de Duke Ellington and His Famous Orchestra." Jazz Hot no. 298:13-19, October 1973.

5368 Carriere, C. "Stomp, Look & Listen: Discographie Selective des Microsillons du Duke." Jazz Hot no. 298:22-23, October 1973.

5369 Cholinski, H. "Collectors Corner: Duke Ellington on LPs." Jazz Forum no. 25:53-58, October 1973.

5370 _____. "Duke Ellington on LPs." Jazz Forum no. 25:13, October 1973.

5371 "Irving Mills Reminisces About His Friend and Colleague Duke Ellington." Crescendo International 12:14-16, October 1973.

5372 Mialy, L. V. "Kinda Dukish." Jazz Hot no. 298:4-5, October 1973.

5373 Tercinet, A. "Hollywood Hanover: Filmographie de Duke Ellington." Jazz Hot no. 298:24-26, October 1973.

5374 Whiston, H. "Reminiscing in Tempo." Jazz Hot no. 298:6-12, October 1973. Reprinted from Coda.

5375 Wong, H. "Happy Reunion." Jazz Hot no. 298:20-21, October 1973.

5376 "Mister Kelly's, Chi." Variety 272:41, October 17, 1973.

5377 Tiegel, E. "Leonard Feathers MCA's Nest with Nat, Duke, Tatum Vintages." Billboard 85:15, October 20, 1973.

5378 Jewell, D. "Iron Duke." Melody Maker 48:49, October 27, 1973.

5379 Palmer, C. "A Tribute to Constant Lambert." Crescendo International 12:16, November 1973.

5380 "What Did Duke Ellington Know, and When Did He Know It?" Esquire 80:158-162, November 1973.

5381 Jones, M. "Duke at the Abbey." Melody Maker 48:14, November 3, 1973.

5382 "Jazz Records: Latin American Suite." Melody Maker 48:61, November 17, 1973.

5383 Carriere, C. "Concerts." Jazz Hot no. 300:22, December 1973.

5384 Debroe, G. "Ellingtonia." Points du Jazz no. 9:124-126, December 1973.

5385 "Fiasko i Berlin foer Duke Ellington." Orkester Journalen 41:7, December 1973.

5386 "Jazzens Giganter: Basie och Ellington." Musikern no. 12:12-13, December 1973.

5387 "Mot Slutet av en Epok." Orkester Journalen 41:24-25, December 1973.

5388 Olsson, J., and C. Nilsson. "Maerklig Ellingtonkonsert i Malmoe." Orkester Journalen 41:27, December 1973.

5389 "On Record: Earl Hines Plays Duke Ellington." Jazz & Blues 3:20, December 1973.

5390 Tomkins, L. "Duke Ellington at the Abbey." Crescendo International 12:22, December 1973.

5391 Traill, S. "Ellington at the Abbey." Jazz Journal 26:8, December 1973.

5392 Voce, S. "It Don't Mean a Thing." Jazz Journal 26:6-7, December 1973.

5393 "Jazz Records: Black, Brown and Beige." Melody Maker 48:60, December 1, 1973.

5394 "Caught in the Act." Melody Maker 48:19, December 8, 1973.

5395 Jones, M. "Loch Here!" Melody Maker 48:60, December 8, 1973.

5396 "Rainbow Grill, N.Y." Variety 273:39, December 19, 1973.

5397 Bakker, Dick M. Duke Ellington on Microgroove, 1923-1942. Alphen aan de Rijn, Holland: Micrography, 1974. Augmented version of a 1972 booklet, Duke Ellington on Microgroove 1923-February

1940, based on Duke Ellington's Story on Records by L. Massagli, L. Pusateri, and G. M. Volontè.

5398 Barclay, Pamela. Duke Ellington; Ambassador of Music. Mankato, Minn: Creative Education; distributed by Childrens Press, Chicago, 1974. Juvenile literature.

5399 Burde, W. "Berlin: Jazzrage '73." Neue Zeitschrift für Musik 135:34-36, no. 1, 1974.

5400 Current, G. B. "Duke Ellington." Black Perspectives in Music 2:172-178, no. 2, 1974.

5401 "Duke Ellington Ist Tot." Neue Musikzeitung 23:11, no. 3, 1974.

5402 "Heard and Seen: Ravinia Festival, Highland Park, Illinois, U.S.A." Coda 11:33-34, no. 12, 1974.

5403 Hosiasson, J. "Duke Ellington." Revista Musical Chilena 28:151-152, no. 126-127, 1974.

5404 Norris, J., and E. Taylor. "Duke Ellington." Coda 11:8-9, no. 11, 1974.

5405 ["Obituary."] Black Perspectives in Music 2:225, no. 2, 1974; Musikhandel 25:217, no. 5, 1974; Nuova Rivista Musicale Italiana 8:343, no. 2, 1974.

5406 "Record Reviews: The Great Paris Concert; The London Concert." Coda 11:18-19, no. 10, 1974.

5407 Schuller, G. "A Eulogy to Edward Kennedy 'Duke' Ellington." Jazz Report 8:4, no. 5, 1974.

5408 Balagri, D., et al. "Trois Jours sans Surprises." Jazz Magazine no. 218:20-21, January 1974.

5409 "Duke Ellington Talks to Les Tomkins on the Subject of His Sacred Music." Crescendo International 12:6-7, January 1974.

5410 Ellington, Duke. "Music Is My Mistress." Ebony 29:60-61, January 1974. An excerpt from Ellington's book with the same name.

5411 "Jazz in Britain." Jazz Journal 27:18-20, January 1974.

5412 Palmer, C. "The Duke and the Voice; An Assessment of This Aspect of Ellington." Crescendo International 12:8-9, January 1974.

5413 "Talent in Action." Billboard 86:16, January 12, 1974.

5414 Voce, S. "It Don't Mean a Thing." Jazz Journal 27:20-21, February 1974.

5415 Priestley, B., and A. Cohen. "Black, Brown & Beige." Composer (London) no. 51:33-37, Spring 1974.

5416 "Record Reviews: The English Concert." Jazz Journal 27:31, March 1974.

5417   Valburn, J. "Fargo Dance Date, November 7th, 1940." Jazz Digest
       3:1-4, March 1974.

5418   "Jazz Records: The English Concert." Melody Maker 49:50, March
       9, 1974.

5419   "Duke Ellington to Celebrate 75th Birthday." School Musician 45:51,
       April 1974.

5420   "Ellington Is Ill, Cancels Dates." Billboard 86:4, April 20, 1974.

5421   "Happy Birthday, Duke." down beat 41:16-19, April 25, 1974.

5422   Suber, C. "The First Chorus." down beat 41:6, April 25, 1974.

5423   Willard, P. "Diamonds for Duke." down beat 41:11, April 25, 1974.

5424   _____. "Love You Madly." down beat 41:14-15, April 25, 1974.
       Musicians who have known Ellington remember him.

5425   "Duke's 75th Birthday Gets Royal Salute." Billboard 86:3, April 27,
       1974.

5426   Cuff, J. "Duke Ellington 1899-1974." Ragtimer p. 10-11, May-June
       1974.

5427   "Jazz Records: Duke's Big Four." Melody Maker 49:42, May 4,
       1974.

5428   Robinson, L. "Black Pride Takes Note of Ellington." Billboard
       86:32, May 11, 1974.

5429   "Duke Ellington, Major Influence in 20th Cent. Music, Dies at 75."
       Variety 275:43, May 29, 1974.

5430   "The Duke Steps Out." Second Line 26:18-19, Summer 1974.

5431   ["Obituary."] Central Opera Service Bulletin 16:20, Summer 1974.

5432   Priestley, B., and A. Cohen. "Black, Brown & Beige." Composer
       (London) no. 52:29-32, Summer 1974.

5433   Dance, S. "Lightly & Politely: Seventy-Fifth." Jazz Journal 27:16-
       18, June 1974.

5434   Davis, H. "The Duke." International Musician 72:3, June 1974.

5435   "Duke Ellington." Jazz Digest 3:1, June 1974.

5436   "Farewell to a Musical Giant." International Musician 72:10, June
       1974.

5437   "Fred Stone Recalls: Balling with the Duke." Jazz Forum no. 29:42-
       45, June 1974.

5438   "Informations." Jazz Hot no. 306:36, June 1974.

5439   Parks, Carole A. "Duke Ellington--Communicator." Black World
       23:49-50, June 1974.

5440   Bellerby, V. "Ellington's Legacy on Record." Melody Maker 49:37,
       June 1, 1974.

5441   Chilton, J. "Ducal Datelines." Melody Maker 49:38, June 1, 1974.

5442   "Ellington Dies of Pneumonia." Billboard 86:6, June 1, 1974.

5443   Feather, L. "Duke of Jazz." Melody Maker 49:36-37, June 1, 1974.

5444   Jones, M. "Jazz's First Great Virtuoso." Melody Maker 49:38,
       June 1, 1974.

5445   "Musicians Pay Tribute to Duke Ellington." Melody Maker 49:1,
       June 1, 1974.

5446   "Duke, Jelly Roll Due for Revivals in Ragtime Wake." Variety
       275:1, June 5, 1974.

5447   Robinson, L. "Ellington's Soul Lives in His Music." Billboard
       86:28, June 8, 1974.

5448   "Thank You, Duke." Billboard 86:3, June 8, 1974.

5449   "Thousands Mourn Duke." Melody Maker 49:22, June 8, 1974.

5450   Ellington, Duke. "Duke Introduces Sacred Music Concerts." Jet
       46:54-56, June 13, 1974.

5451   "Duke Is Remembered." Jet 46:14-16, June 13, 1974.

5452   "Ellington, Edward Kennedy (1899-1974)." Jet 46:12-13, June 13,
       1974.

5453   "Ellington Joins Distinguished Musicians and Sidemen in Death."
       Jet 18-19, June 13, 1974.

5454   "Ellington Sought Privacy When Not Playing Onstage." Jet 46:53,
       June 13, 1974.

5455   Thompson, M. C. "Thousands Bid Farewell to Duke." Jet 46:20-24,
       June 13, 1974.

5456   Atterton, J. "Mercer Takes Over." Melody Maker 49:20, June 15,
       1974. Ellington's son Mercer takes charge of the orchestra after
       his father's death.

5457   "Honor Duke in London." Variety 275:46, June 19, 1974.

5458   "'Jeremiah' Oratorio, Dedicated to Duke, Impresses on Coast."
       Variety 275:44, June 19, 1974.

5459   "Industry Members Probe Ellington Cancer Center." Billboard 86:6,
       June 22, 1974.

5460   Jones, M. "Homage to the Duke." Melody Maker 49:24, June 22,
       1974. A memorial service is held at St. Martin-in-the-Fields,
       Trafalgar Square.

5461   Dance, S. "Duke Ellington's Musical Legacy: A Gift for Everyone."
       Billboard 86:32, June 29, 1974.

5462   Aaslund, B. "Glimtar av en Unik Hertig." Orkester Journalen
       42:8, July-August 1974.

5463   Anderson, L. "Saddest Tale en Hyllning till Duke Ellington." Or-
       kester Journalen 42:6-7, July-August 1974.

5464   Astrup, O. J. "Ur Dukes Repertoar." Orkester Journalen 42:9,
       July-August 1974.

5465   Domnerus, L. "Duke Ellington, en Maestare Som Lever Kvar."
       Musikern no. 7-8, July-August 1974.

5466   Feather, L. "Dukes Band Lever Vidare." Orkester Journalen 42:7,
       July-August 1974.

5467   [Chilton, J.] "Saluting Duke Ellington." Record Research [entire is-
       sue] no. 128, July 1974.

5468   Dance, S. "The Funeral Address." Jazz Journal 27:14-15, July
       1974. Address given at the Cathedral Church of St. John the Di-
       vine, New York, at Ellington's funeral May 27, 1974.

5469   Edwards, C. "Duke Is Gone." Sepia 23:79-82, July 1974.

5470   Francis, H. "Duke Ellington." Crescendo International 12:6, July
       1974.

5471   "Joyful Tribute to the Duke." Crescendo International 12:1, July
       1974.

5472   "Music Industry to Establish Duke Ellington Cancer Center." Music
       Trades 122:123-124, July 1974.

5473   ["Obituary."] Jazz Podium 23:3, July 1974.

5474   Schuller, G. "Ellington Tribute." Music Journal 32:79, July 1974.

5475   Gleason, R. J. "Farewell to the Duke." Rolling Stone no. 164:34-
       37, July 4, 1974.

5476   Cook, B. "Jazz." New Republic 171:27-28, July 6, 1974.

5477   "World Mourns Duke's Death." Soul 9:13, July 8, 1974.

5478   Dance, S. "Citizen of the World." Saturday Review/World 1:42-43,
       July 13, 1974.

5479   Kolodin, I. "The Ecumenical Ellington." Saturday Review /World
       1:42, 1:42, July 13, 1974.

5480   "Talent in Action." Billboard 86:14, July 13, 1974.

5481   ["Obituary."] down beat 41:9, July 18, 1974.

5482   "Wein Launches Duke's Cancer Fund Campaign." Billboard 86:27, July
       27, 1974.

5483 Berendt, J. E. "In Memoriam: Duke Ellington." Jazz Forum no.
      30:28-33, August 1974.

5484 "Duke Ellington: Ausdruck Schoepferischer Kraft--ein Gebet." Jazz
      Podium 23:10-12, August 1974.

5485 Nalle, B. "Letters: Duke Ellington." Music 8:4, August 1974.

5486 ["Obituary."] Gramophone 52:351, August 1974; Jazz Forum no.
      30:24, August 1974; Music Teacher 115:685, August 1974.

5487 "Duke Cancer Center." down beat 41:9, August 15, 1974.

5488 Current, G. "Duke Ellington." Black Perspectives in Music 2:173-
      178, Fall 1974.

5489 Ebert, A. "Duke: Loving You Madly: As Told to Alan Ebert."
      Essence 5:50-51, September 1974.

5490 "Ellington Items." International Musician 73:11, September 1974.
      A Cancer Care Center has been established in Duke Ellington's
      name.

5491 Grant, C. D. "Best of Ellington." Essence 5:40, September 1974.

5492 "Tribute to Duke Ellington." Ebony 29:43-45, September 1974.

5493 Voce, S. "It Don't Mean a Thing." Jazz Journal 27:28-30, Septem-
      ber 1974.

5494 Thompson, M. C. "Son Keeps Duke Ellington and His Great Music
      Alive." Jet 46:52-58, September 5, 1974.

5495 Dance, S. "Lightly & Politely: Tone." Jazz Journal 27:14, Oc-
      tober 1974.

5496 Debroe, G. "Ellingtonia: Ellington en Microsillons." Points du
      Jazz no. 10:93-96, October 1974.

5497 ["Obituary."] Musik und Bildung 6:580, October 1974.

5498 "Record Reviews: Duke's Big 4." Radio Free Jazz 14:8, October
      1974.

5499 West, H. "Mercer Ellington: Perpetuating Dad's Legacy." Radio
      Free Jazz 14:6, October 1974.

5500 "Duke's Noble Legacy." down beat 41:34, October 10, 1974.

5501 "Ellington Film." Melody Maker 49:72, October 19, 1974.

5502 Feather, L. "Mercer Carries Duke's Torch." Melody Maker 49:60,
      October 26, 1974.

5503 "Duke on Discs; A Key to All Currently Available Recordings." High
      Fidelity/Musical America 24:79-80, November 1974.

5504 "An Ellington Garland; Edward Kennedy Ellington." Stereo Review
      33:70-71, November 1974.

5505 Elliott, M. "Duke and the Blues." Jazz Journal 27:18-19, November 1974.

5506 Hodara, M. "The Duke on Discs--a Key to All Currently Available Recordings." High Fidelity/Musical America 24:79-80, November 1974.

5507 "Im Schatten des Duke: Mercer Ellington." Jazz Podium 23:20-22, November 1974.

5508 Lees, G. "Ellington Remembered, a Minority Report." High Fidelity/Musical America 24:28, November 1974.

5509 Schuller, G. "Are the Recordings Enough?" High Fidelity/Musical America 24:87-88, November 1974.

5510 _____. "Ellington in the Pantheon." High Fidelity/Musical America 24:63-64, November 1974.

5511 Wilson, J. S. "The Duke in the Recording Studio." High Fidelity/Musical America 24:65-68, November 1974.

5512 "Jazz Records: Edward Kennedy Ellington." Melody Maker 49:68, November 2, 1974.

5513 Priestley, B., and A. Cohen. "Black, Brown & Beige." Composer (London) no. 53:29-32, Winter 1974-1975.

5514 Dance, S. "Lightly & Politely." Jazz Journal 27:12-13, December 1974.

5515 Pereverzev, L. "Dyuka Ellingtona." Soviet Muzyka 38:140-141, December 1974.

5516 "London House, Chi." Variety 277:57, December 4, 1974.

5517 Feather, L. "More Ellington Changes." down beat 41:10, December 5, 1974.

5518 Gleason, Ralph J. Celebrating the Duke, and Louis, Bessie, Billie, Bird, Carmen, Miles, Dizzy, and Other Heroes. Boston: Little, Brown, 1975.

5519 "Record Reviews: The Golden Duke." Coda 12:17-18, no. 4, 1975.

5520 Schaaf, Martha E. Duke Ellington: Young Music Master. Indianapolis: Bobbs-Merrill, 1975. Juvenile material concentrating on Ellington's childhood.

5521 Dance, S. "Jazz." Music Journal 33:22-23, January 1975.

5522 ["Obituary."] Crescendo International 13:39, January 1975.

5523 "Record Reviews: Date with the Duke, 2V." Jazz Journal 28:36, January 1975.

5524 Williams, M. "And What Might a Jazz Composer Do?" Music Educators Journal 61:24-31, January 1975.

5525   Dahlgren, R.   "Duke Hyllad i Storkyrkan."   Orkester Journalen 43:7,
       March 1975.

5526   Tomkins, L.   "Mercer Ellington Talking."   Crescendo International
       13:6-7, March 1975.

5527   "Caught in the Act."   Melody Maker 50:56, March 1, 1975.

5528   Jones, M.   "Steward to the Duke."   Melody Maker 50:46, March 1,
       1975.

5529   "Jazz Records: Third Sacred Concert--the Majesty of God."   Mel-
       ody Maker 50:50, March 22, 1975.

5530   Carriere, C.   "Ellington Sans Duke."   Jazz Hot no. 315:26, April
       1975.

5531   Domnerus, L.   "Git Paa Atlantic Bokar Duke Ellingtons Orkester."
       Musikern no. 4:16-17, April 1975.

5532   "Jazz en Direct."   Jazz Magazine no. 232:8, April 1975.

5533   "Jazz in Britain."   Jazz Journal 28:22-23, April 1975.

5534   Korall, B.   "Mercer Ellington--and the Beat Goes On."   International
       Musician 73:4, April 1975.

5535   "Record Reviews: Third Sacred Concert."   Jazz Journal 28:35, April
       1975.

5536   Tomkins, L.   "Mercer Ellington."   Crescendo International 13:14-15,
       April 1975.

5537   Traill, S.   "Editorial."   Jazz Journal 28:3, April 1975.   Ellington's
       son Mercer continues the family tradition by leading the Ellington
       Orchestra.

5538   "Town Hall 'Concept' Shows in Solid Bow with 'Cotton Club.'"   Variety
       278:80, April 2, 1975.

5539   Carriere, C.   "Pitter Panther Patter: Les Bassistes de Duke El-
       lington."   Jazz Hot no. 316:10-15, May 1975.

5540   Dance, S.   "Lightly & Politely."   Jazz Journal 28:12-13, May 1975.
       Examines Ellington's "Third Sacred Concert" album.

5541   "Premieres."   Music Journal 33:29, May 1975.   Review of Elling-
       ton's work "Theme and Variations for the Flatted Fifth."

5542   "Schallplatten-besprechungen: The Works of Duke."   Jazz Podium
       24:35, May 1975.

5543   Townsend, I.   "Ellington in Private."   Atlantic Monthly 235:78-83,
       May 1975.

5544   "Concert Reviews."   Variety 279:152, May 14, 1975.

5545   Atterton, J.   "24-Hour Tribute to the Duke."   Melody Maker 50:20,

   May 17, 1975.   New York City's Central Church on Park Avenue
   presents music of Ellington.

5546   Debroe, G.   "Ellington en Microsillons."   Points du Jazz no. 11:87-
       88, June 1975.

5547   Korall, B.   "The Pop and Jazz Scene."   International Musician 73:10,
       June 1975.   Discusses the 24-hour tribute at Central Church in
       New York.

5548   "Reviews: Duke Ellington's Third Sacred Concert: The Majesty of
       God."   Radio Free Jazz 15:11, June 1975.

5549   Terry, W.   "A Huge 'Ivan'; a Rousing 'Mooche.'"   Saturday Review
       2:47-48, June 14, 1975.

5550   Dance, S.   "Lightly & Politely."   Jazz Journal 28:14-16, July 1975.
       The Duke Ellington Orchestra and the Duke Ellington Society pre-
       sent an annual concert.

5551   Martin, H.   "Exempli Gratia: As You Like It."   In Theory Only
       1:37, October 1975.   Ellington's "Satin Doll" is examined for chord
       substitutions.

5552   Carriere, C.   "Les Grands Orchestres."   Jazz Hot no. 322:26-27,
       December 1975.

5553   Parks, G.   "Jazz."   Esquire 84:138-145, December 1975.

5554   Blumenthal, B.   "After the Duke."   Jazz Magazine (U.S.) 1:20-23,
       no. 1, 1976.

5555   Hentoff, N.   "The Political Economy of Jazz."   Social Policy 6:53-
       56, no. 5, 1976.

5556   "Swinging News: USA."   Jazz Forum no. 42:18-19, 1976.

5557   "Record Reviews."   down beat 43:24-27, January 29, 1976.   Reviews
       include: A Date with the Duke, Vols. 1 through 6; Duke Ellington;
       Duke Ellington: Blue Skies; Duke Ellington: Eastbourne Perform-
       ance; Duke Ellington in Hollywood/on the Air; Duke Ellington: Love
       You Madly; Duke Ellington: October 20, 1945; Duke Ellington: on
       the Air, 38/39; Duke Ellington: on the Air, 1940; Duke Ellington:
       Suddenly It Jumped; Duke Ellington: the Jimmy Blanton Years;
       Duke Ellington, Volume One; Duke Ellington: Vol. 1, Fickle Fling;
       Duke Ellington: Vol. 2, Unbooted Character; Duke Ellington with
       Django Reinnardt: Chicago Opera House; Duke Ellington's Third
       Sacred Concert; the Duke Is on the Air at the Blue Note; Duke's
       Big Four; One Night Stand with Duke Ellington; Recollections of the
       Big Band Era; This One's for Blanton.

5558   Carriere, C., and C. Guyot.   "The Duke Plays Ellington."   Jazz Hot
       no. 324:16-19, February 1976.

5559   Lambert, E.   "Duke Ellington on Tax."   Jazz Journal 29:6-8, Feb-
       ruary 1976.

5560   "Record Reviews: The Works of Duke Ellington Vols. 14 & 15."
       Jazz Journal 29:28, February 1976.

5561 "Jazz Albums: Continuum." Melody Maker 51:26, February 7, 1976.

5562 "$25,000 Grant to Ensure Duke's Music at Newport." Billboard 88:66,
      February 14, 1976.

5563 "Ailey Lauds Duke." down beat 43:9, February 26, 1976.

5564 "Duke Ellington Cancer Center for Musicians." Instrumentalist 30:21,
      March 1976.

5565 Shaw, A. J. "Ellingtoniana." Dance Magazine 50:21-22, March
      1976.

5566 Lambert, E. "Duke Ellington on Tax." Jazz Journal 29:8-10, April
      1976. Discussion of recordings by individual Ellington band mem-
      bers.

5567 "Record Reviews: At Carnegie Hall." Jazz Journal 29:28, May
      1976. Reviews the 1946 performance of Ellington.

5568 "Caught in the Act, USA." Melody Maker 51:14, May 22, 1976. The
      Duke Ellington Orchestra performs a 77th birthday concert tribute
      in New York City.

5569 Lucas, J. "Bicentennial Canticles." Second Line 28:9, Summer
      1976.

5570 Dance, S. "Lightly & Politely: Ellington Is Forever." Jazz Journal
      29:14, June 1976.

5571 "Record Reviews: Duke's Big 4; The Duke Is on the Air--from the
      Blue Note." Coda no. 148:18-19, June 1976.

5572 "Jazz Albums: All That Jazz." Melody Maker 51:22, June 5, 1976.

5573 "Four Ellington Concerts Booked at Carnegie Hall." Billboard 88:6,
      June 12, 1976.

5574 Kolodin, I. "'Ellington Is Forever,' Likewise Mozart." Saturday
      Review 3:51-52, June 12, 1976.

5575 "Ellington Forever." down beat 43:10, June 17, 1976.

5576 Hansen, J. "Ellingtons Stoerre Verk." Orkester Journalen 44:10-11,
      July-August 1976.

5577 "Heard and Seen." Coda no. 149:30-31, July 1976.

5578 "Jazz Albums: The Works of Duke--Complete Edition, Volume 1."
      Melody Maker 51:24, July 3, 1976.

5579 Balliett, W. "Jazz: New York Notes." New Yorker 52:82-85, July
      19, 1976. Critique of Ellington's "Black, Brown and Beige" at
      the Newport Jazz Festival.

5580 "Jazz Albums: At Carnegie Hall, 1964." Melody Maker 51:26, July
      24, 1976.

5581   Keating, L. "Jazz on the Screen." Jazz Journal 29:20-21, August
       1976.

5582   "Record Reviews: The Complete Duke Ellington." Jazz Journal
       29:30-31, August 1976.

5583   "Record Reviews: Afro-Eurasian Eclipse; The Bethlehem Years,
       Vol. 9; The Ellington Suites." down beat 43:26, August 12, 1976.

5584   Croce, A. "Dancing." New Yorker 52:75-77, August 30, 1976.
       The Ellington series is lauded by Ailey.

5585   Hansen, J. "Ellingtons Stoerre Verk." Orkester Journalen 44:9,
       September 1976.

5586   "Jazz Albums: The Duke Is on the Air--from the Blue Note." Mel-
       ody Maker 51:25, September 18, 1976.

5587   Hansen, J. "Ellingtons Stoerre Verk." Orkester Journalen 44:13,
       October 1976.

5588   Townsend, I. "Ellington in Private." Jazz Journal 29:4-8, October
       1976.

5589   Dance, S. "Alvin Ailey Celebrates Ellington." Music Journal 34:42,
       November 1976.

5590   Parker, A. "The Day Duke Ellington Played to Only 150 People."
       Crescendo International 15:8, November 1976.

5591   "Record Reviews: Duke Ellington and the Ellingtonians." Jazz Jour-
       nal 29:26, November 1976.

5592   "Jazz Albums: Concert at Carnegie Hall." Melody Maker 51:31,
       November 13, 1976.

5593   Hansen, J. "Ellingtons Stoerre Verk." Orkester Journalen 44:21,
       December 1976.

5594   Hentoff, N. "Indigenous Music; Smithsonian Institution Recordings of
       D. Ellington." Nation 223:606, December 4, 1976.

5595   Conover, W. "May Recessional." Jazz Forum no. 48:3, 1977.

5596   "Duke Ellington." Jazz Magazine (U.S.) 2:21, no. 1, 1977.

5597   Gutman, Bill. Duke: The Musical Life of Duke Ellington. New
       York: Random House, 1977. Juvenile literature.

5598   Jewell, Derek. Duke: A Portrait of Duke Ellington. London: Elm
       Tree Books, 1977.

5599   _____. "Duke: A Portrait of Duke Ellington." Educator 9:4-5,
       no. 4, 1977. Chapter 11 covering the period 1899-1928 reprinted
       from Jewell's book with the same title.

5600   "Record Reviews: Duke Ellington's Jazz Violin Session." Popular
       Music and Society 5:110-111, no. 5, 1977.

5601 Hansen, J. "Ellington Stoerre Verk." Orkester Journalen 45:17, January 1977.

5602 "Record Reviews: Duke Ellington's Jazz Violin Session." down beat 44:27-28, January 13, 1977.

5603 "Caught." down beat 44:35-36, January 27, 1977.

5604 "Records: Duke Ellington 1938." High Fidelity/Musical America 27:142-143, February 1977.

5605 "Schallplatten-Besprechungen: The Complete Duke Ellington, Vol. 2-4." Jazz Podium 26:31, February 1977.

5606 "Record Reviews: The Afro-Eurasian Eclipse." Coda no. 154:14, March-April 1977.

5607 "Record Reviews: The Intimate Ellington." Jazz Journal 30:31, March 1977.

5608 Hentoff, N. "Indigenous Music: Intimate Ellington." Nation 224:314-315, March 12, 1977.

5609 Jewell, D. "Duke: Early Years at the Cotton Club." Melody Maker 52:32, March 26, 1977. An excerpt from Jewell's biography: Duke: A Portrait of Duke Ellington.

5610 _____. "Duke on Tour in Russia." Melody Maker 52:43, April 2, 1977. An excerpt from Jewell's biography of Ellington.

5611 "Waxing On: 1938; The World of Duke Ellington." down beat 44:31-33, April 7, 1977.

5612 Berendt, J. E. "Der Jazz als Amerikas Klassische Musik." Jazz Podium 26:7-9, May 1977.

5613 "Spotlight Review: Duke Ellington 1938." Radio Free Jazz 18:11, May 1977.

5614 "Schallplatten-Besprechungen: The Complete Duke Ellington Vol. 10, 1937-38." Jazz Podium 26:34, June 1977.

5615 "Records in Brief--Reissues: The World of Duke Ellington: Volume 3." Coda no. 156:22, July-August 1977.

5616 "Jazz Albums: The Complete Duke Ellington, Vol. 5: 1932-1933." Melody Maker 52:30, July 16, 1977.

5617 "Reviews: The Duke 1940." Coda no. 157:23-24, September-October 1977.

5618 Lees, G. "The Lees Side--Mu$ic U.$.A.: The Big Bands." High Fidelity/Musical America 27:24-26, September 1977.

5619 "Record Reviews: The Bethlehem Years, Vol. 1." Jazz Journal International 30:36, September 1977.

5620 "Record Reviews: Volume 18: Complete Edition." Jazz Journal International 30:35-36, September 1977.

5621 Albertson, C. "Ellington, Summer of '45: Eight Discs Off the Air."
      Stereo Review 39:132-133, October 1977.

5622 Buhles, G. "Jazz Portrat: Duke Ellington." Hifi-Stereophonie
      16:1278-1280, October 1977.

5623 Cooper, P. "On Education: A Statement to Congress." High Fidel-
      ity/Musical America 27:MA16-18, October 1977.

5624 "Mercer Ork for Britain." Melody Maker 52:6, October 1, 1977.

5625 "Record Reviews: Collectors Item." Jazz Journal International 30:41,
      November 1977.

5626 "Jazz Albums: The Hollywood Bowl Concert." Melody Maker 52:32,
      November 5, 1977.

5627 "Caught in the Act." Melody Maker 52:68, November 19, 1977.

5628 "Duke Ellington Opus Set for Atlanta Bow." Variety 289:119, Novem-
      ber 23, 1977. Ellington's "Saturday Laughter" is to be presented.

5629 Jewell, D. "Write on! Duke." Jazz Journal International 30:16,
      December 1977. Jewell justifies his book Duke: A Portrait of
      Duke Ellington in view of a review by S. Dance.

5630 Otto, A. S. "Reminiscing in Tempo." Educator 10:11-12, no. 2,
      1978-1979. Includes personnel in the band of Ellington.

5631 Ellington, Mercer and Stanley Dance. Duke Ellington in Person: An
      Intimate Memoir. Boston: Houghton Mifflin, 1978.

5632 "Ellington's 79th Birthday Hailed." Swinging Newsletter 8:5, no. 37,
      1978.

5633 Gitler, I. "Notes: New York." Jazz Magazine (U.S.) 2:13-14, no.
      3, 1978.

5634 Moss, B. "Notes: Center for Duke." Jazz Magazine (U.S.) 2:16,
      no. 2, 1978.

5635 "Notes from All Over." Jazz Magazine (U.S.) 2:20, no. 3, 1978.

5636 Holmberg, G. "Tunt Ellingtonband." Orkester Journalen 46:7, Jan-
      uary 1978.

5637 Hentoff, N. "Indigenous Music: Record Reviews: Duke Ellington/
      1939." Nation 226:59-60, January 21, 1978.

5638 "Jazz Albums: A Duke Ellington Collector's Item." Melody Maker
      53:26, January 21, 1978.

5639 "Concert Reviews." Variety 289:72, January 25, 1978.

5640 "Album Reviews: New Orleans Suite." Crescendo International
      16:30, February 1978.

5641 Dance, S. "Jazz." Music Journal 36:23-24, February 1978.

5642   Jacobs, I. L.   "Meanwhile, in the Vaults of MGM."   Radio Free
       Jazz 19:3, February 1978.

5643   Jewell, D.   "Letters to the Editor: On Duke."   Radio Free Jazz
       19:3, February 1978.

5644   "Records: The Duke Ellington Carnegie Hall Concerts, Number 1:
       January 23rd, 1943; Number 2:   December 19th, 1944; Number 3:
       January 4th, 1946; Number 4:   December 27th, 1947."   Rolling
       Stone no. 258:91, February 9, 1978.

5645   "Ellington Blvd. Opens."   down beat 45:9, March 9, 1978.

5646   Ellington, Mercer.   "Things Ain't What They Used to Be."   Jazz
       Podium 27:4-7, April 1978.

5647   "Letters to the Editor."   Radio Free Jazz 19:3, April 1978.

5648   "Record Reviews: A Tribute to Duke; New Orleans Suite."   Jazz
       Journal International 31:36-37, April 1978.

5649   Reilly, P.   "Ellington by Crosby, Clooney, Bennett, and Herman:
       A Great Tribute to a Great Composer."   Stereo Review 40:87,
       April 1978.

5650   "Spotlight Review: Duke Ellington 1939."   Radio Free Jazz 19:19,
       April 1978.

5651   Traill, S.   "Editorial: Dancing and Duelling over Duke."   Jazz Jour-
       nal International 31:4, April 1978.

5652   "Record Reviews: The Duke Ellington Carnegie Hall Concerts: Jan-
       uary 1943; December 1944; January 1946; December 1947."   down
       beat 45:20-22, April 6, 1978.

5653   Tercinet, A.   "Duke à Carnegie Hall."   Jazz Hot no. 349:26-28,
       May 1978.

5654   "Party Spots Duke's Music."   Billboard 90:6, May 13, 1978.

5655   Balliett, W.   "Jazz."   New Yorker 54:145-148, May 15, 1978.

5656   "Son's Revealing Book Says Duke Ellington ..."   Jet 54:12-18, May
       25, 1978.   Mercer Ellington's book is Duke Ellington in Person:
       An Intimate Memoir.

5657   "Record Reviews: The English Concert."   Jazz Journal International
       31:40-41, June 1978.

5658   Hentoff, N.   "Indigenous Music: Duke Ellington Carnegie Hall Con-
       certs."   Nation 226:710, June 10, 1978.

5659   Feather, L.   "Duke Ellington."   Contemporary Keyboard 4:55, July
       1978.

5660   Cook, B.   "Ellington Playing the Band."   New Leader 61:25-26, July
       17, 1978.

5661   Dance, S.   "Letter to the Editor."   Radio Free Jazz 18:2, August

1977. Dance comments on an earlier review of Jewell's Duke: A Portrait of Duke Ellington by Leonard Feather.

5662 Weiss, P. "Songwriters' Hall of Fame." Stereo Review 41:60, August 1978.

5663 "Record Reviews: Earl Hines Plays Duke Ellington, Vol. 4." Coda no. 162:21, August 1, 1978.

5664 Jacobs, I. "Symposium with Duke Ellington." Cadence 4:6-14, September 1978.

5665 "Record Reviews: The Carnegie Hall Concerts, Dec. 1944." Radio Free Jazz 19:15, September 1978.

5666 "Records--Jazz: Duke Ellington's Band Shorts." High Fidelity/Musical America 28:142, September 1978.

5667 "Editorial: How Mule Took the King and the Duke to the Union and Survived!" Jazz Journal International 31:4, October 1978.

5668 "Record Reviews: Duke Ellington, Vol. 1." Jazz Journal International 31:58, October 1978.

5669 "Records: A Tribute to Ethel Waters." High Fidelity/Musical America 28:170-171, October 1978. The Duke Ellington Orchestra records a tribute to Waters.

5670 "Vibe Trio Renders Duke." down beat 45:12, October 5, 1978.

5671 "Waxing On: 1939; 1940 Fargo Concert." down beat 45:30, October 19, 1978.

5672 Crockett, J. "From the Publisher." Contemporary Keyboard 4:3, November 1978.

5673 Doerschuk, B. "Ellington Protege--Brooks Kerr." Contemporary Keyboard 4:41, November 1978.

5674 "Duke Ellington: Images in Retrospect." Contemporary Keyboard 4:34-35, November 1978.

5675 "Duke Ellington Symposium." Cadence 4:14-20, November 1978.

5676 "An Ellington Solo." Contemporary Keyboard 4:38-40, November 1978.

5677 "Ellington Tributes and Recollections." Contemporary Keyboard 4:37, November 1978.

5678 Feather, L. "Duke Ellington." Contemporary Keyboard 4:32-33, November 1978.

5679 _____. "Duke Ellington: A Selected and Annotated Discography." Contemporary Keyboard 4:76, November 1978.

5680 Jeske, L. "Sonny Greer, 83, Recalls the Time When the Aristocrats of Harlem Took London by Storm." Jazz Journal International 31:22-23, November 1978.

5681 "Record Reviews: The Fabulous Forties; The Transcription Years, Vol. 1." Jazz Journal International 31:38, November 1978.

5682 Balliett, W. "Jazz: Duke Ellington at Fargo, 1940, Live." New Yorker 54:117-180, November 27, 1978.

FAGAN, ELEANORA see HOLIDAY, BILLIE

FATHA see HINES, EARL KENNETH

FIFTH DIMENSION.

5683 "Ciro's, L.A." Variety 246:63, March 15, 1967.

5684 "Marco Polo, V'ncouver." Variety 248:58, August 30, 1967.

5685 "Fifth Dimension." Ebony 22:152-154, October 1967.

5686 "P. J.'s, L.A." Variety 250:54, April 17, 1968.

5687 "New Acts." Variety 251:59, May 22, 1968.

5688 Fox, H. "5th Dimension Gives Superb Performance." Billboard 80:17, May 25, 1968.

5689 Dawbarn, B. "Fifth Dimension Hope to Be Up, Up and Away Here Too." Melody Maker 43:31, September 21, 1968.

5690 "Deauville, M. B." Variety 253:47, December 25, 1968.

5691 "5th Dimension Stirs MIDEM." Billboard 81:11, February 1, 1969.

5692 Hall, C. "Fifth Dimension Behind Spot Wheel of Chevrolet." Billboard 81:32, February 15, 1969.

5693 "Success and the 5th Dimension." Sepia 18:22-25, March 1969.

5694 "Satin, Silky, Sexy; 5th Dimension." Time 93:72-73, April 18, 1969.

5695 "Americana, N.Y." Variety 255:63, May 21, 1969.

5696 Dove, I. "Fifth Dimension Soar Up, Up and Away as Cabaret Artists." Billboard 81:8, May 24, 1969.

5697 Reilly, P. "The 5th Dimension's 'Age of Aquarius.'" Stereo Review 23:73-74, August 1969.

5698 Taras, J. "5th Dimension Gives 'Up Away' Act; Oliver Pleases." Billboard 81:20, August 30, 1969.

5699 "Latin Casino, N.J." Variety 256:61, September 24, 1969.

5700 Feather, L. "Fifth Dimension, a Group Designed to Entertain." Melody Maker 44:7, October 4, 1969.

5701 "Concert Reviews." Variety 258:60, February 18, 1970.

5702 "Talent in Action." Billboard 82:20, February 28, 1970.

5703 "Caesars Palace, L.V." Variety 259:54, May 20, 1970.

5704 "Talent in Action." Billboard 82:22, August 1, 1970.

5705 "Concert Reviews." Variety 260:58, October 28, 1970.

5706 "Caesars Palace, L.V." Variety 261:52, February 10, 1971.

5707 "What's Going on with the Fifth Dimension." Jet 4:54-57, June 1, 1971.

5708 Feather, L. "Caught in the Act Stateside." Melody Maker 46:6, August 21, 1971.

5709 Tiegel, E. "Talent in Action." Billboard 83:36, September 4, 1971.

5710 "Gordon Changes Disk's Name; Slates 'Fifth' Europe Trek." Billboard 3:14, December 11, 1971.

5711 "Riviera, Las Vegas." Variety 265:32, December 29, 1971.

5712 Brown, G. "Fifths: Tale of Two Styles." Melody Maker 47:22, February 5, 1972.

5713 Charlesworth, C. "Soul Picnic." Melody Maker 47:31, June 29, 1972.

5714 "Talent in Action." Billboard 84:10, August 26, 1972.

5715 Gest, D. "5th Dimension & Bill Withers in Summer Spectacular." Soul 7:8, September 11, 1972.

5716 "Riviera, Las Vegas." Variety 268:87, September 13, 1972.

5717 "Concert Reviews." Variety 269:66, November 22, 1972.

5718 "Talent in Action." Billboard 84:16, December 2, 1972.

5719 Gest, D. "An Institution? Not All in 5th Dimension Think They Are." Soul 7:6-7, February 12, 1973.

5720 "5th Dimension to Tour for State Department." down beat 40:11, March 29, 1973.

5721 "Riviera, Las Vegas." Variety 271:69, May 23, 1973.

5722 Trubo, R. "Up, Up to Stardom for 5th Dimension." Sepia 22:34-36, July 1973.

5723 "Sahara, Tahoe." Variety 271:54, July 4, 1973.

5724 "Novi Singers Meet the Fifth Dimension." Jazz Forum no. 24:23-24, August 1973.

5725 "Caught in the Act." Melody Maker 48:40, September 15, 1973.

5726 "Soul Reviews." Soul 8:12, November 12, 1973.

5727   "Riviera, Las Vegas." Variety 273:40, January 2, 1974; 273:40,
        June 26, 1974.

5728   "Concert Reviews." Variety 276:44, August 28, 1974.

5729   "Riviera, Las Vegas." Variety 277:55, November 20, 1974.

5730   "Talent in Action." Billboard 86:30, December 7, 1974.

5731   "Riviera, Las Vegas." Variety 277:84, January 15, 1975.

5732   Deni, L. "Fifth Dimension Looking to a Reunion with Jim Webb."
        Billboard 87:24, January 25, 1975.

5733   "Fontainebleau, M. B." Variety 278:54, February 19, 1975.

5734   "Riviera, Las Vegas." Variety 279:71, May 21, 1975; 280:67, Oc-
        tober 29, 1975.

5735   Reilly, P. "An Ideal Combination: Songs by Jimmy Webb, Per-
        formances by the 5th Dimension." Stereo Review 35:83-84, De-
        cember 1975.

5736   "Hilton, Las Vegas." Variety 281:61, February 4, 1976.

5737   "Talent in Action." Billboard 88:30, February 28, 1976.

5738   "Waldorf-Astoria, N.Y." Variety 283:69, June 9, 1976.

5739   "Talent in Action." Billboard 88:41, June 12, 1976.

5740   "To the New Fifth." Billboard 88:50, June 26, 1976.

5741   "Record Contract Provided Cushion as McCoo-Davis Left Dimension."
        Variety 284:78, October 13, 1976.

5742   "Talent in Action." Billboard 89:34, January 8, 1977.

5743   "Concert Reviews." Variety 286:64, March 9, 1977.

5744   "Music Hall, N.Y." Variety 292:285, October 18, 1978.

FISHER, MRS. MARSHALL see VAUGHAN, SARAH LOIS

FLAKE, RUBINA see FLACK, ROBERTA

FITZGERALD, ELLA, 1918- .

5745   "Ella Fitzgerald." Ebony 4:45-46, May 1949.

5746   Hoefer, G. "Singer 'Evelyn Fields' on Trans Really Fitzgerald."
        down beat 17:15, February 24, 1950.

5747   "Capsule Comments." down beat 17:12, March 10, 1950.

5748   "Ella Fitzgerald."   Metronome 66:13-14, April 1950.

5749   "Apollo's Girl."   Time 55:70-71, April 3, 1950.

5750   "Ella Fitzgerald."   Metronome 66:15, May 1950.

5751   "Ella, Oscar Peterson Star as 'JATP' Tour Begins."   down beat
       18:1, October 19, 1951.

5752   "Ella Steals the Show at JATP Debut."   Melody Maker 28:1, April
       5, 1952.   Review of Fitzgerald's performance at Jazz at the Phil-
       harmonic.

5753   "Caught in the Act."   down beat 20:4, July 1, 1953.

5754   "Ella!"   Metronome 69:13, October 1953.

5755   "Ella Fitzgerald Divorces Brown."   down beat 20:3, October 7, 1953.

5756   Dahlgren, C.   "Fitzgerald Festlight Firad."   Orkester Journalen
       22:6-7, June 1954.

5757   "Any Style Will Do."   Newsweek 43:82, June 7, 1954.

5758   Feather, L.   "When They All Went Wild About Ella!"   Melody Maker
       30:4, June 12, 1954.

5759   "'Recording Artists' Roster."   down beat 21:98, June 30, 1954.

5760   "In Person."   Metronome 70:8-9, August 1954.

5761   "Tiffany, Los Angeles."   Variety 196:61, November 10, 1954.

5762   Race, S.   "Oscar and Ella."   Melody Maker 31:3, January 15, 1955.

5763   "Ella, Granz Sue Pan Am Airline."   down beat 22:12, February 9,
       1955.

5764   "Ella, Peterson Due in England."   down beat 22:6, February 23,
       1955.

5765   Hentoff, N.   "Ella Tells of Trouble in Mind Concerning Discs, Tele-
       vision."   down beat 22:2, February 23, 1955.

5766   "London Cheers Oscar and Ella--But Tour Cut."   Melody Maker 31:1,
       February 26, 1955.

5767   "A Night of Jazz."   Melody Maker 31:3, February 26, 1955.

5768   Traill, S.   "Ella and Oscar at the Albert."   Jazz Journal 8:1, March
       1955.

5769   "Oscar and Ella in Your Town."   Melody Maker 31:8, March 5, 1955.

5770   "Mocambo, Hollywood."   Variety 198:53, March 23, 1955.

5771   "Fairmont, San Francisco."   Variety 198:69, April 13, 1955.

5772   "New Work for Ella Fitzgerald."   down beat 22:27, May 4, 1955.

5773   "Pete Kelly's Blues; Ella Fitzgerald Draws a Hot Jazz Assignment
       for Her First Major Role in Movies." Ebony 10:115-117, October
       1955.

5774   Feather, L. "Ella Gives Carmen, Peggy, Hackett 5." down beat
       22:51, October 5, 1955.

5775   "Flamingo, Las Vegas." Variety 200:48, November 9, 1955.

5776   "Caught in the Act." down beat 22:8, December 14, 1955.

5777   "Tribute Paid to Fitzgerald." down beat 22:31, December 28, 1955.

5778   Jepsen, J. G. "Kvinnliga Vokalister." Orkester Journalen 24:15,
       February 1956.

5779   Wilkinson, G. "Oscar, Ella and Louis." Jazz Journal 9:1, June
       1956.

5780   Race, S. "Ella." Melody Maker 31:4, September 22, 1956.

5781   "New Frontier, Las Vegas." Variety 204:67, November 14, 1956.

5782   Tynan, J. "Ella." down beat 23:13, November 28, 1956.

5783   Dahlgren, C. "Sarah och Ella med Basie." Orkester Journalen
       25:6-7, January 1957.

5784   "Ella Fitzgerald, Others Win $7,500 Settlement from PanAm on
       Bias Rap." Variety 205:41, January 23, 1957.

5785   "Ella, Granz, Lewis Party Win $7,500 in Pan American Suit." down
       beat 24:15, March 6, 1957.

5786   "Ella Resting After Surgery." down beat 24:13, March 6, 1957.

5787   Kolodin, I. "Rodgers and Hart, Ella and Ellington." Saturday Re-
       view 40:43, March 16, 1957.

5788   "Ella Fitzgerald." Jazz Today 2:11, May 1957.

5789   "Copacabana, N.Y." Variety 207:67, June 19, 1957.

5790   "Ella Fitzgerald Attacked by Man with Same Name on A.C. Stage."
       Variety 207:50, July 17, 1957.

5791   "Heard in Person." down beat 24:43, July 25, 1957.

5792   "Mocambo, Hollywood." Variety 208:69, November 6, 1957.

5793   "Fairmont, San Francisco." Variety 209:71, December 11, 1957.

5794   "Chez Paree, Chi." Variety 209:67-68, January 15, 1958.

5795   Barrett, M. E., and M. Barrett. "Music: Gingham and Ginger
       Ale." Good Housekeeping 146:40, February 1958.

5796   "Moulin Rouge, L.A." Variety 212:71, March 5, 1958.

5797 Balliett, W. "Close, but No Cigar." New Yorker 34:117-120, April 5, 1958.

5798 Kolodin, I. "Duke Ellington and Queen Ella." Saturday Review 41:50, April 12, 1958.

5799 Wilson, J. S. "Ella and the Duke Assemble a Somewhat Mixed-Up Songbook." High Fidelity 8:79, May 1958.

5800 Burman, M. "Ella." Melody Maker 33:5, May 10, 1958.

5801 Race, S. "It Was Ella's Night! Opening Night of JATP." Melody Maker 33:10-11, May 10, 1958.

5802 "Brit. & All That Jazz; 'JATP' All-Time Click with Ella, Oscar & Co." Variety 210:42, May 14, 1958.

5803 "Copacabana, N.Y." Variety 211:55, June 11, 1958.

5804 Sinclair, C. "Ella Mellow and Magnetic with Standards at Copa." Billboard 70:7, June 16, 1958.

5805 "What Ella Does Best." Newsweek 51:67, June 23, 1958.

5806 "Ella Fitzgerald Pulls 'em, Peterson Trio Chases 'em in New Granz Jazz Show." Variety 212:68, September 17, 1958.

5807 "Pop Records." Time 72:45, October 6, 1958.

5808 "Fairmont, San Francisco." Variety 212:68, November 5, 1958.

5809 "Shy Ella Fitzgerald Bridges Two Generations of Jazz Singing." Sepia 6:20-24, December 1958.

5810 Mouly, R. "Ella et Duke et Duke et Mahalia." Jazz Magazine 5:16-17, January 1959.

5811 "Waldorf-Astoria, N.Y." Variety 215:53, January 3, 1959.

5812 Vincent, L. "Ella och Getz pa Busigt Bohemia." Orkester Journalen 27:16, May 1959.

5813 Dawbarn, B. "Once Again--It's Ella All the Way." Melody Maker 34:3, May 9, 1959.

5814 "Ella Fitzgerald." Variety 215:54, July 1, 1959.

5815 "Ella Fitzgerald Show." Variety 216:75, October 7, 1959.

5816 Lambert, G. E. "Ella Fitzgerald Sings Duke Ellington." Jazz Monthly 5:22-24, November 1959.

5817 Jungermann, Jimmy. Ella Fitzgerald; Ein Porträt. Wetzlar: Pegasus Verlag, 1960.

5818 Wilson, J. S. "Ella Meets the Gershwins." High Fidelity 10:63-64, January 1960.

5819 "Fairmont Hotel, S.F." Variety 217:53, January 27, 1960.

5820   Shaw, R. B. "'Little Jazz' at the Philharmonic." Jazz Journal
        13:2, April 1960.

5821   "Ella Fitzgerald, Guest on 'Person to Person.'" Jet p. 66, June 9,
        1960.

5822   McAndres, J. "Star Studded Shellac." Record Research no. 29:24,
        August 1960.

5823   "Fairmont, San Francisco." Variety 220:55, October 19, 1960.

5824   Babic, K. "Beograd." Zvuk no. 47-48:397, 1961.

5825   "Ella Schedules Biggest Overseas Tour to Date." down beat 28:13,
        January 19, 1961.

5826   "Wins Jet Magazine's Best Female Singer Award." Jet 19:62, Jan-
        uary 26, 1961.

5827   Littler, F. "Oral Solos." Jazz Monthly 6:11, February 1961.

5828   "Eden Roc, Miami Beach." Variety 221:69, February 1, 1961.

5829   "Fraught v Unfraught." Jazz Journal 14:18, March 1961.

5830   Hutton, J. "Incredible Ella Does It Again!" Melody Maker 36:9,
        March 11, 1961.

5831   De Toledano, R. "Perennial Ella." National Review 10:194, March
        25, 1961.

5832   Destombes, A. "A Good Evening for We." Jazz Hot no. 164:29,
        April 1961. Review of a performance by Fitzgerald and Oscar
        Peterson.

5833   "Le Double Concert Ella Fitzgerald." Jazz Magazine 7:17, April
        1961.

5834   "Trionfo per Ella e Oscar." Musica Jazz 17:19-20, April 1961.

5835   Jones, M. "Ella Crashes the Barrier." Melody Maker 36:10, April
        1, 1961.

5836   Lapid, J. "Ella-Peterson Click in Tel Aviv Due to Disks; 'Philhar-
        monic' Tag Beef." Variety 222:45, April 12, 1961.

5837   "Basin Street East, N.Y." Variety 222:68, April 19, 1961.

5838   Rolontz, B. "Basin St. in Flurry Over Ella." Billboard 73:5, April
        24, 1961.

5839   "Un Grand Orchestre, S.V.P.!" Jazz Magazine 7:19, May 1961.

5840   "Crescendo, L.A." Variety 222:67, May 17, 1961.

5841   "Ella Sings Her Heart Out--and Everything's Absolutely Right."
        High Fidelity 11:109-110, September 1961.

5842 Watt, D. "Popular Records: Miss Ella." Show 1:122-123, October
      1961.

5843 Robinson, L. "First Lady of Jazz." Ebony 17:131-132, November
      1961.

5844 "Tahoe Harrah's." Variety 224:76, November 1, 1961.

5845 "Fairmont, S. F." Variety 225:63, November 29, 1961.

5846 "Basin Street East, N.Y." Variety 225:67, January 17, 1962.

5847 "Eden Roc, Miami Beach." Variety 225:55, February 14, 1962.

5848 "Eartha and Ella." Melody Maker 37:9, February 24, 1962.

5849 "Whatever She Is, Ella Hits with French Jazz Buffs on 10th O'seas
      Tour." Variety 226:43, March 28, 1962.

5850 Keating, L. "In Person." Jazz Monthly 8:25, April 1962.

5851 "Today's Top Record Talent." Billboard 74:56, April 7, 1962.

5852 Poulain, M. "Ella, Toujours." Jazz Magazine 8:21-23, May 1962.

5853 Zylberstein, J. C. "Les Girls." Jazz Magazine 8:32-33, May 1962.

5854 Levy, L. "Ella and Peggy." Melody Maker 37:8-9, June 16, 1962.

5855 "Crescendo, L.A." Variety 227:59, June 20, 1962.

5856 "Inside Stuff--Music." Variety 227:40, August 1, 1962.

5857 Hentoff, N., and L. Feather. "Is Ella a Great Jazz Singer?" Ne-
      gro Digest 11:23-28, September 1962. Reprinted from HiFi/Stereo
      Review.

5858 "Sahara Inn, Chi." Variety 228:45, October 31, 1962.

5859 "Latin Casino, N.J." Variety 228:42, November 21, 1962.

5860 "False Alarm Brings a Few Lyons' Roars." down beat 29:15-16,
      November 22, 1962. Review of Fitzgerald's recital at Lincoln Cen-
      ter, New York.

5861 "Basin Street East, N.Y." Variety 229:54, January 30, 1963.

5862 Jones, M. "Ella's New Fellas." Melody Maker 38:10-11, February
      23, 1963.

5863 "Ella and Millie." Melody Maker 38:8-9, March 2, 1963.

5864 Clayton, P. "Dome of Discovery." Jazz Journal 16:1-2, April 1963.
      Review of a concert in Brighton, England by Oscar Peterson and
      Fitzgerald.

5865 "Revamped Royal Box, N.Y., Now Looms a 'Hit' Room; Ella Fitz-
      gerald's Big Biz." Variety 230:61, April 17, 1963.

5866 Grevatt, R. "Ella & the Room Both Good Show." Billboard 75:12,
       April 27, 1963.

5867 "Oscar et Ella." Jazz Hot no. 187:8-9, May 1963.

5868 "Crescendo, L. A." Variety 231:63, June 26, 1963.

5869 Koechlin, P. "Ella Fitzgerald, Premiere Dame du Jazz." Musica
       no. 115:26-30, October 1963.

5870 "Americana, N. Y." Variety 233:52, February 5, 1964.

5871 Myatt, C. "Ella Wins Hong Kong." Billboard 76:10, February 15,
       1964.

5872 Hutton, J., and M. Jones. "I'd Like to Do an Album with Strings--
       No Jazz!" Melody Maker 39:7, March 28, 1964.

5873 Dahlgren, R. "Ella Bättre än Naagonsin." Orkester Journalen 32:11,
       May 1964.

5874 Priestly, B. "Ella Fitzgerald and Oscar Peterson." Jazz Monthly
       10:10-12, May 1964.

5875 "Basin St. East, N. Y." Variety 234:53, May 20, 1964.

5876 "La Joie des Retrouvailles." Jazz Magazine no. 107:45-46, June
       1964.

5877 "Nugget, Sparks." Variety 236:54, September 30, 1964.

5878 "She Who Is Ella." Time 84:86, November 27, 1964.

5879 Williams, M. "Ella and Others." Saturday Review 47:51, Novem-
       ber 28, 1964.

5880 Zylber, J. "Trio Petersona i Ella Fitzgerald." Ruch Muzyczny
       9:18, no. 10, 1975.

5881 "No Financial Interest, but the Touch Is There." down beat 32:11,
       March 11, 1965.

5882 Tynan, J. A. "Caught in the Act." down beat 32:34, March 11,
       1965.

5883 Dahlgren, R. "Perfekt Show av Ella och Oscar." Orkester Jour-
       nalen 33:4, April 1965.

5884 "More Ella Please, and a Little Less Oscar." Melody Maker 40:8,
       April 17, 1965.

5885 "Basin St. East, N. Y." Variety 238:197, May 12, 1965.

5886 Sternfield, A. "Ageless Ella Brings Back Some of the Old Favor-
       ites." Billboard 77:18, May 22, 1965.

5887 "Strictly Ad Lib." down beat 32:16, June 17, 1965.

5888   Siders, H. "Caught in the Act." <u>down beat</u> 32:37-38, September
       9, 1965.

5889   Feather, L. "Ella Today and Yesterday Too." <u>down beat</u> 32:20-23,
       November 18, 1965.

5890   "A New Umbrella for Duke and Ella." <u>down beat</u> 32:10-11, Decem-
       ber 2, 1965.

5891   "Ella: Only Room for One at the Top." <u>Melody Maker</u> 40:6, Decem-
       ber 25, 1965.

5892   Granz, N. "Ella at 'Duke's Place.'" <u>Jazz</u> 5:8-9, no. 1, 1966.

5893   Dawson, J. "Ella: Having a Ball with Duke." <u>Melody Maker</u> 41:20,
       February 26, 1966.

5894   "La Lady & Son Duc." <u>Jazz Magazine</u> no. 128:24-27, March 1966.

5895   Latters, P. "Ella + Duke à Paris." <u>Jazz Hot</u> no. 218:9, March
       1966.

5896   "Stor Succe for Ella och Duke." <u>Orkester Journalen</u> 34:6-7, March
       1966.

5897   "Americana, N.Y." <u>Variety</u> 242:65, March 16, 1966.

5898   "Ella Fitzgerald Exits Verve; Will Trim Disk Output & Live Book-
       ings." <u>Variety</u> 243:38, July 6, 1966.

5899   Hennessey, M. "Ella, Duke Make Antibes Swing." <u>Billboard</u> 78:16,
       August 13, 1966.

5900   "Granz Grooves 3 LPs, Gets Pic Too from Ella & Duke's Jazz on
       Riviera." <u>Variety</u> 244:51, September 28, 1966.

5901   "Riverboat, N.Y." <u>Variety</u> 244:59, November 16, 1966.

5902   "Clean Sweep." <u>ASCAP Today</u> 1:5, no. 2, 1967. Fitzgerald receives
       acclaim at the <u>Playboy Jazz</u> Hall of Fame.

5903   "Ellington-Fitzgerald Nasta." <u>Orkester Journalen</u> 35:4, January 1967.

5904   Morgenstern, D. "Caught in the Act." <u>down beat</u> 34:23, January
       12, 1967.

5905   "Ella and Duke Having a Ball." <u>Melody Maker</u> 42:11, February 18,
       1967.

5906   Carles, P. "Des Hommes et une Femme." <u>Jazz Magazine</u> no.
       140:11, March 1967.

5907   Rado, A. "Duke Toujours Mieux." <u>Jazz Hot</u> no. 229:20-24, March
       1967.

5908   Jones, M. "Jimmy Jones; Composing and Playing with Ella and the
       Duke." <u>Melody Maker</u> 42:8, March 4, 1967.

5909   Locke, D. "The Jazz Vocal." Jazz Monthly 13:10-11, September
       1967.

5910   "Americana, N.Y." Variety 248:52, October 25, 1967.

5911   Sternfield, A. "Elegant Ella Does It Again--Rocks Philharmonic
       Hall." Billboard 79:37, December 9, 1967.

5912   "Cocoanut Grove, L.A." Variety 249:58, January 10, 1968.

5913   "Ella Cuts Iron Curtain with a Budapest Concert." Variety 249:2,
       January 31, 1968.

5914   "Ella's Fullscale Iron Curtain Tour." Variety 250:2, April 17, 1968.

5915   Gonda, J. "Ella Fitzgerald Budapesten." Muzsika 11:1-7, May 1968.

5916   Hegedüs, L. "Csütörtok, Ella." Muzsika 11:7-8, May 1968.

5917   "Rainbow Grill, N.Y." Variety 250:62, May 1, 1968.

5918   Sternfield, A. "Ella Fitzgerald: Strong as Ever." Billboard 80:12,
       May 11, 1968.

5919   "Ella Accepts Honorary Chair with King F'dation." Variety 251:50,
       May 22, 1968.

5920   "Flamingo, Las Vegas." Variety 251:53, June 12, 1968.

5921   "Sherman House, Chi." Variety 251:53, July 31, 1968.

5922   "Ella Is King Foundation Chairman." Jazz and Pop 7:10, August
       1968.

5923   "Americana, N.Y." Variety 253:56, December 4, 1968.

5924   Skala, P. "Ella Byla v Praze." Hudebni Rozhledy 22:739, no. 14,
       1969.

5925   "Flamingo, Las Vegas." Variety 253:82, January 15, 1969.

5926   Feather, L. "TV Soundings." down beat 36:14, February 6, 1969.

5927   "Sherman House, Chi." Variety 254:64, April 16, 1969.

5928   "Ella paa Berns." Orkester Journalen 37:4, June 1969.

5929   Welch, C. "Ella's Very Own Brand of Sunshine." Melody Maker
       44:19, June 28, 1969.

5930   Hennessey, M. "13-Nation Band's Spark & Ella's Fire Ignite Mon-
       treux Jazz Fest." Billboard 81:22, July 12, 1969.

5931   Hutton, J. "Caught in the Act." Melody Maker 44:6, August 9,
       1969.

5932   Cressant, P. "Ella Fitzgerald." Jazz Hot no. 253:38-39, Septem-
       ber 1969.

5933   Gerber, A.   "Antibes an 10."   Jazz Magazine no. 169-170:62, September 1969.

5934   "Hotel Roosevelt, N.O."   Variety 256:65, October 1, 1969.

5935   "Concert Reviews."   Variety 257:56, November 26, 1969.

5936   Dove, I.   "Ella Turns 'Contemporary' with Old-Fashioned Grace."   Billboard 81:35, December 6, 1969.

5937   Albertson, C., et al.   "Record Reviews."   down beat 36:28, December 25, 1969.

5938   Unias, A. Q.   "Records: Ella."   Rolling Stone no. 51:38, February 7, 1970.

5939   "Flamingo, Las Vegas."   Variety 258:54, March 4, 1970.

5940   "Waldorf-Astoria, N.Y."   Variety 258:115, April 8, 1970.

5941   "Talent in Action."   Billboard 82:20, April 11, 1970.

5942   Callagham, P.   "Basie à Paris."   Jazz Hot no. 261:6-7, May 1970.

5943   Gerber, A.   "La Dame et le Comte."   Jazz Magazine no. 178:15, May 1970.

5944   Reed, R.   "Just Plain 'Ella.'"   Stereo Review 24:81-82, May 1970.

5945   "Ella, Basie Whip Up Lots of B. O. Noise in Tour of W. Germany."   Variety 258:85, May 6, 1970.

5946   Henshaw, L.   "Caught in the Act."   Melody Maker 45:17, May 16, 1970.

5947   Dahlgren, R.   "Stjaermoete paa Hoegsta Nivaa."   Orkester Journalen 38:12, June 1970.

5948   Tercinet, A.   "La Chronique des Disques, Vol. 1."   Jazz Hot no. 262:35, June 1970.

5949   "Tivoli, Copenhagen."   Variety 259:62, June 10, 1970.

5950   Pernye, A.   "Ella."   Muzsika 13:24-25, July 1970.

5951   Feather, L.   "Newport sans Grise."   Jazz Magazine no. 181:62-63, September 1970.

5952   "Royal York, Toronto."   Variety 260:71, September 23, 1970.

5953   "Now Grove, L.A."   Variety 261:74, November 18, 1970.

5954   Feather, L.   "Ella and Duke--Together."   Melody Maker 45:39, November 21, 1970.

5955   "Granz Produces Ella LP After Ten Year Layoff."   Billboard 82:4, November 21, 1970.

5956   "Talent in Action."   Billboard 82:25, November 21, 1970.

5957 Constant, D. "Ella et Oscar: Une Habitude." Jazz Magazine no. 185:14-15, January 1971.

5958 "Caught in the Act." down beat 38:30-31, January 7, 1971.

5959 "Flamingo, Las Vegas." Variety 261:65, January 13, 1971.

5960 Traill, S. "Record Reviews: In Concert." Jazz Journal 24:33-34, February 1971.

5961 "Elmwood, Windsor." Variety 262:66, February 17, 1971.

5962 "Concert Review." Variety 262:45, April 21, 1971.

5963 Jones, M. "A Jazz Panorama with Ella in Top Form." Melody Maker 46:36, May 8, 1971.

5964 "Caught in the Act." Melody Maker 46:30, May 15, 1971.

5965 Jones, M. "It's Ella Week." Melody Maker 46:40, May 15, 1971.

5966 _____. "Jazz Records: On the Sunny Side of the Street." Melody Maker 46:38, May 22, 1971.

5967 Gerber, A. "Paris." Jazz Magazine no. 190:7-8, June-July 1971.

5968 Carter, J. "One More Time!; Basie and Ella '71." Crescendo International 9:20-22, June 1971.

5969 Cressant, P. "Basie + Ella." Jazz Hot no. 273:26, June 1971.

5970 Gonda, J. "Hampton, Gojkovic, Fitzgerald." Muzsika 14:35-38, June 1971.

5971 Jones, M. "Any Song for Ella--as Long as It Leaves Her Happy." Melody Maker 46:14, June 5, 1971.

5972 Boatfield, G. "Record Reviews: Sweet and Hot." Jazz Journal 24:31, July 1971.

5973 Gamble, P. "Jazz in Britain." Jazz Journal 24:10, July 1971.

5974 "Ella Fitzgerald Hit by Eye Trouble O'seas." Variety 263:35, July 28, 1971.

5975 "Handful of Records: Chick Webb and His Orchestra Featuring Ella Fitzgerald (1936-1939)." Points du Jazz no. 5:133-134, September 1971.

5976 Levin, J. "Disques du Mois: Things Ain't What They Used to Be." Jazz Magazine no. 193:45-46, October 1971.

5977 "Flamingo, Las Vegas." Variety 264:47, November 10, 1971.

5978 Deni, L. "Talent in Action." Billboard 83:22, November 20, 1971.

5979 Feather, L. "Welcome Back, Ella." Melody Maker 46:60, November 20, 1971.

5980 Jones, M. "Jazz Records: Ella Sings Gershwin." Melody Maker 46:48, November 27, 1971.

5981 "Disques du Mois: Jazz Spectrum Vol. 1." Jazz Magazine no. 196:27, January 1972.

5982 Bennett, R. R. "Technique of the Jazz Singer." Music and Musicians 20:30-32, February 1972.

5983 "Record Reviews: Ella Sings Gershwin, Vol. 2." Jazz & Blues 2:26, April 1972.

5984 "Jazz Records: Ella Sings Gershwin, Vol. 2." Melody Maker 47:36, April 15, 1972.

5985 "Concert Reviews." Variety 267:60, May 17, 1972.

5986 Tiegel, E. "Granz Bows Twin Bill: Disks and Jam Session." Billboard 84:17, June 17, 1972.

5987 "Elmwood, Windsor, Ont." Variety 267:63, June 21, 1972.

5988 "Ella's Eye Tragedy." Melody Maker 47:1, August 5, 1972.

5989 "Nice." Jazz Hot no. 286:15-16, September 1972.

5990 "Disques du Mois: Ella à Nice." Jazz Magazine no. 204:46, October 1972.

5991 "Jazz Records: Ella Swings with Nelson." Melody Maker 47:64, December 2, 1972.

5992 Wyatt, F. "Caught in the Act." Melody Maker 47:32, December 23, 1972.

5993 Bennett, R. R. "Technique of the Jazz Singer." Educator 5:2-4, no. 3, 1973. Reprinted from Music and Musicians.

5994 "Concert Reviews." Variety 269:50, January 25, 1973.

5995 Wyatt, F. "Ella, Basie Join Hands in California Stand." down beat 40:11, February 1, 1973.

5996 "Elmwood, Windsor, Ont." Variety 270:53, February 21, 1973.

5997 "Reviews on Record: Ella Loves Cole." Jazz & Blues 3:19, April 1973.

5998 "On Record: Ella Swings with Nelson." Jazz & Blues 3:26, May 1973.

5999 Pleasants, H. "Bel Canto in Jazz and Pop Singing." Music Educators Journal 59:54059, May 1973.

6000 "Caesars Palace, L. V." Variety 270:63, May 2, 1973.

6001 "Disques du Mois: Ella à Nice." Jazz Magazine no. 204:46, October 1972.

6002 "Jazz Records: Ella Swings with Nelson." Melody Maker 47:64, December 2, 1972.

6003 Wyatt, F. "Caught in the Act." Melody Maker 47:32, December 23, 1972.

6004 "Concert Reviews." Variety 273:46, January 23, 1974.

6005 Dahlgren, R. "Ella--Alltid Samma Succe." Orkester Journalen 42:13, April 1974.

6006 "The 'First Lady.'" Jazz Podium 23:16, April 1974.

6007 "Caught in the Act." Melody Maker 49:31, April 6, 1974; 49:51, April 13, 1974.

6008 Jones, M. "Smoke Gets in Your Eyes." Melody Maker 49:8, April 13, 1974.

6009 Kresh, P. "Ella Fitzgerald at Carnegie Hall." Stereo Review 32:90, May 1974.

6010 Tomkins, L. "Ella at Ronnie's." Crescendo International 12:4, May 1974.

6011 "Ella in Austria." Jazz Forum no. 29:16-17, June 1974.

6012 Lindenberger, H. "Jazz-Konzerte." HiFi-Stereophonie 13:640, June 1974.

6013 Tiegel, E. "Frank, Ella, Basie." Billboard 86:4, June 22, 1974.

6014 "Caught in the Act." Melody Maker 49:23, November 2, 1974.

6015 "Dedicate Ella Fitzgerald Center for Perf. Arts at U. of Md., Eastern Shore." Variety 276:56, November 6, 1974.

6016 "Concert Reviews." Variety 277:54, December 4, 1974.

6017 "Performance." Rolling Stone no. 175:94, December 5, 1974.

6018 Renninger, C. "The Ella Fitzgerald Center for the Performing Arts." Radio Free Jazz 15:4, January 1975.

6019 "Records: With Everything I Feel in Me." Rolling Stone no. 179:50, January 30, 1975.

6020 "Caught in the Act." Melody Maker 50:59, March 29, 1975; 50:16, April 5, 1975.

6021 "Circus Tavern, Purflect." Variety 278:51, April 23, 1975.

6022 "Caught in the Act." Melody Maker 50:29, April 26, 1975.

6023 Jones, M. "Queen of Song." Melody Maker 50:33, May 3, 1975.

6024 "See Record 2-Wk Gross for Sinatra, Ella, Basie at Uris, N.Y." Variety 280:74, September 10, 1975.

6025 "Caught in the Act." Melody Maker 50:14, October 11, 1975.

6026 Carter, J. "Count Basie Orchestra and Ella Fitzgerald at Royal Festival Hall." Crescendo International 14:9, November 1975.

6027 "Count Basie-Ella Fitzgerald." Jazz Hot no. 321:21, November 1975.

6028 "Jazz in Britain." Jazz Journal 28:20, November 1975.

6029 Cressant, P. "Les Petites Formations." Jazz Hot no. 322:28-29, December 1975.

6030 "Concert Reviews." Variety 282:66, March 24, 1976.

6031 "Caught in the Act." Melody Maker 51:26, April 3, 1976.

6032 "Talent in Action." Billboard 88:26-27, April 10, 1976; 88:42, May 22, 1976.

6033 Endress, G. "Feelings." Jazz Podium 25:4-6, June 1976.

6034 "Record Reviews: Ella Swings Lightly." Jazz Journal 29:31, June 1976.

6035 "Ella Repays Retina Foundation in Hub." Variety 283:60, June 9, 1976.

6036 Daubresse, J. P. "Ella Fitzgerald au Palais des Congres--le 20 Mai 1976." Jazz Hot no. 329:54, July-August 1976.

6037 "Jazz Albums: Ella and Oscar." Melody Maker 51:20, August 7, 1976.

6038 "Ella Honored by AMC." School Musician 48:41, October 1976.

6039 "Tribute to Fitzgerald." Billboard 88:57, October 30, 1976.

6040 "Jazz Albums: Fitzgerald and Pass ... Again." Melody Maker 51:25, November 6, 1976.

6041 "Waxing On: Porgy and Bess." down beat 43:30-32, November 18, 1976.

6042 "Concert Reviews." Variety 285:112, November 24, 1976.

6043 Mitz, R. "Sibling Rock." Stereo Review 37:88-91, December 1976.

6044 "Record Reviews: Sings the Jerome Kern/Johnny Mercer Songbooks." Jazz Journal 29:27-28, December 1976.

6045 Wilson, J. S. "Louis and Ella and Ray and Cleo." High Fidelity/ Musical America 26:95, December 1976. Review of the recordings made of "Porgy and Bess."

6046 "Reviews--MCA Reissues: Billie Holiday and Ella Fitzgerald." Jazz Magazine (U.S.) 1:56, no. 3, 1977.

6047 "Jazz Albums: Ella." Melody Maker 52:32, March 5, 1977.

6048   "Caught in the Act." Melody Maker 52:20, April 30, 1977.

6049   Tomkins, L. "Ella & Basie at the Palladium." Crescendo International 15:36, May 1977.

6050   "Concert Reviews." Crescendo International 15:8, June 1977.

6051   "Ella à la Nouvelle Orleans." Jazz Hot no. 338:30-31, June 1977.

6052   Everett, T. "Ella Fitzgerald Interview." Cadence 2:7-8, June 1977.

6053   Robbins, R. J. "Ella and Roy in Philadelphia." Crescendo International 15:38, June 1977.

6054   "Count Basie & Ella Fitzgerald at the London Palladium." Jazz Journal International 30:32, July 1977.

6055   "Waxing On: The Cole Porter Songbook." down beat 44:45, July 14, 1977.

6056   "Reviews: Montreaux '77." Jazz Magazine (U.S.) 2:64, no. 3, 1978.

6057   "Waxing On: The Rodgers and Hart Songbook." down beat 45:36, January 12, 1978.

6058   "Talent in Action." Billboard 90:39, March 4, 1978.

6059   "Concert Reviews." Variety 290:84, March 15, 1978; 291:62, June 14, 1978.

6060   "Ella Wraps It All Up." Melody Maker 53:20, July 29, 1978. Review of her performance at the Cleveland, England International Jazz Festival.

6061   "Record Reviews: Ella Fitzgerald & Cole Porter." Jazz Journal International 31:37, December 1978.

6062   "Record Reviews: Lady Time." down beat 45:26, December 7, 1978.

FLACK, ROBERTA (Rubina Flake; Mrs. Stephen Novosel), 1940- .

6063   Berton, R. "Caught in the Act." down beat 36:26, October 2, 1969. Review of Flack's performance at the Rutgers Jazz Festival.

6064   Dilts, J. D. "Caught in the Act." down beat 36:27, October 16, 1969. Concert review of Flack's singing at the Third Annual Laurel Jazz Festival.

6065   "New Acts." Variety 258:86, April 22, 1970.

6066   "Shelly's Manne Hole." Variety 259:53, July 29, 1970.

6067   Feather, L. "Caught in the Act." Melody Maker 45:24, August 8, 1970.

6068   Tiegel, E. "Talent in Action." Billboard 82:22, August 8, 1970.

6069   Feather, L. "Newport sans Grise." Jazz Magazine no. 181:12,
       September 1970.

6070   Lester, J. "Records: Chapter Two; First Take." Rolling Stone
       no. 69:42, October 29, 1970.

6071   "Recording of Special Merit: Chapter Two." Stereo Review 25:120,
       November 1970.

6072   Feather, L. "Blindfold Test." down beat 37:32, November 12, 1970.

6073   Morgenstern, D. "Roberta Flack: Sure Bet for Stardom." down
       beat 37:14, November 12, 1970.

6074   "Concert Reviews." Variety 261:34, December 30, 1970.

6075   Brown, D. "Record Reviews: Roberta Flack, Chapter Two." Coda
       10:29, no. 3, 1971.

6076   Lee, B. "Who Is Roberta Flack?" Soul Illustrated 3:18-21, no. 1,
       1971.

6077   Cuscuna, M. "Roberta Flack." Jazz and Pop 10:14-18, January
       1971.

6078   Friend, R., and L. V. Mialy. "Roberta Flack." Jazz Hot no.
       268:10-12, January 1971.

6079   Garland, P. "Roberta Flack: New Musical Messenger." Ebony
       26:54-56, January 1971.

6080   "Roberta Flack, Her Own Drumbeat." Sepia 2:52-55, January 1971.

6081   "Caught in the Act." down beat 38:31, January 7, 1971.

6082   "Talent in Action." Billboard 83:18, January 9, 1971.

6083   Oberbeck, S. K. "Roberta." Newsweek 77:91, January 11, 1971.

6084   Wickham, V. "Young, Gifted and Flack." Melody Maker 46:6, Jan-
       uary 16, 1971.

6085   "Concert Reviews." Variety 262:60, February 17, 1971.

6086   "Disques du Mois: Chapter Two." Jazz Magazine no. 188:41, April
       1971.

6087   "Caught in the Act." down beat 38:28, May 13, 1971.

6088   "Talent in Action." Billboard 83:22, May 22, 1971.

6089   Wickham, V. "America." Melody Maker 46:8, May 22, 1971.

6090   Hennessey, M. "Burton, Santamaria & Flack Give Montreux Solid
       Wind-Up." Billboard 83:38, July 3, 1971.

6091   Williams, R. "Flack Magic." Melody Maker 46:13, July 31, 1971.

6092   "Jazzfesztival--Montreux." Muzsika 14:32-33, September 1971.

6093   "Talent in Action."   Billboard 83:22, September 11, 1971.

6094   King, R. "Stargazing."   Essence 2:24-39, December 1971.

6095   Let's Save the Children, Inc. Roberta Flack. Staff: Helen King,
       et al. Chicago: Let's Save the Children, Inc., 1972. A 22-page
       biography for children.

6096   Phillips, G. "Roberta's Quiet Fire Lights Campus Night."   Soul
       6:15, January 4, 1972.

6097   Aletti, V. "Records: Quiet Fire."   Rolling Stone no. 99:66, Jan-
       uary 6, 1972.

6098   Fong-Torres, B. "Roberta Flack & Her Quiet Fire."   Rolling Stone
       no. 103:24, March 2, 1972.

6099   Feather, L. "Blindfold Test."   down beat 39:27, March 30, 1972.

6100   "Disques du Mois: Quiet Fire."   Jazz Magazine no. 200:51, May
       1972.

6101   "Schallplattenbesprechungen: Chapter Two; Quiet Fire."   Jazz Podi-
       um 21:167-168, May 1972.

6102   Griffith, P. "Quiet Fire."   Melody Maker 47:21, June 3, 1972.

6103   "Lady with a Low Flame."   Time 99:73-74, June 5, 1972.

6104   Moore, E. "Unraveling Roberta."   Saturday Review 55:56-60, June
       17, 1972.

6105   Comas, B. "Roberta & Donny Tear Up L.A."   Soul 7:12, June 19,
       1972.

6106   Lewis, A. "Roberta: Black Pride, White Songs."   Melody Maker
       47:29, August 5, 1972.

6107   "Records: Roberta Flack and Donny Hathaway."   Rolling Stone no.
       115:49, August 17, 1972.

6108   Tiegel, E. "Monterey: Roberta, Quincy Sensational at 15th Anny."
       Billboard 84:21-22, September 30, 1972.

6109   Hoffmann, R. "Roberta Flack: Zwischen Soul und Seele."   Neue
       Musikzeitung 21:10, October-November 1972.

6110   Kerrigan, M. "Caught in the Act."   Melody Maker 47:57, October
       28, 1972.

6111   Goddard, R. "Quincy--Roberta So-So at Center."   Soul 7:12, Decem-
       ber 4, 1972.

6112   Williams, R. "Caught in the Act."   Melody Maker 48:39, January
       27, 1973.

6113   Cullaz, M. "Merveilleuse Roberta Flack."   Jazz Hot no. 292:22,
       March 1973.

6114 Kuehn, G., et al. "This Here Dat Dere." Jazz Podium 22:21-23,
      March 1973.

6115 Choice, H. "Roberta Flack: No. 1 Singing Superstar of 70's."
      Sepia 22:56-60, April 1973.

6116 Gelormine, P. "Talent in Action." Billboard 85:20, April 14, 1973.

6117 "American Woman in Song." Vogue 161:106-107, June 1973.

6118 "Roberta Warms Up a Chilled Crowd." Soul 8:12, September 3, 1973.

6119 "Records: Killing Me Softly." Rolling Stone no. 144:95, September
      27, 1973.

6120 "Roberta Flack Takes Career Success in Stride." Jet 45:86-92, De-
      cember 6, 1973.

6121 Morse, Charles, and Ann Morse. Roberta Flack. Mankato, Minn.:
      Creative Education, Distributed by Childrens Press, Chicago, 1974,
      c1975. Biography for children.

6122 "Roberta Flack Vs. Film Co. for Huckleberry Finn Cut." Billboard
      86:54, June 22, 1974.

6123 Haynes, H. "Roberta Flack: Her Secret Ingredient Is Humanity."
      Sepia 23:73-74, July 1974.

6124 Eguchi, H. "Flack Cancels; Big Losses Shake Japanese Promoters."
      Billboard 86:18, July 27, 1974.

6125 Ebert, A. "Song Named Roberta." Essence 5:46-47, November 1974.

6126 Jacobs, Linda. Roberta Flack, Sound of Velvet Melting. St. Paul:
      EMC Corp., 1975. Juvenile literature.

6127 "Record Reviews: Feel Like Makin' Love." Popular Music and So-
      ciety 4:118-120, no. 2, 1975.

6128 "Records: Feel Like Makin' Love." Rolling Stone no. 185:58, April
      24, 1975.

6129 "What Ever Happened to Rubina Flake?" Time 105:62-63, May 12,
      1975.

6130 "Talent in Action." Billboard 87:41, July 26, 1975.

6131 "Concert Reviews." Variety 280:62, October 8, 1975.

6132 "Talent in Action." Billboard 87:28, October 18, 1975.

6133 "Concert Reviews." Variety 283:450, May 12, 1976; 286:58, March
      30, 1977.

6134 "Aladdin, Las Vegas." Variety 289:117, November 23, 1977.

6135 "Talent in Action." Billboard 89:61, December 17, 1977.

6136   "Soul/Reggae Albums; Blue Lights in the Basement." Melody Maker
       53:23, January 14, 1978.

6137   "Records: Blue Lights in the Basement." High Fidelity/Musical
       America 28:126, March 1978; Rolling Stone no. 261:67-68, March
       23, 1978.

6138   "Talent in Action." Billboard 90:60, April 15, 1978.

6139   Garland, P. "Flack's Back." Stereo Review 40:132, May 1978. Re-
       view of Flack's "Blue Lights in the Basement."

6140   Snow, L. "Inevitably, Roberta Flack." High Fidelity/Musical Amer-
       ica 28:121-124, May 1978.

6141   White, A. "'Closer' Tie Tees Flack-Hathaway." Billboard 90:44-45,
       May 27, 1978.

6142   Wansley, J. "On the Move." People 10:124, October 9, 1978.

6143   "Albums: Roberta Flack." Melody Maker 53:22, November 4, 1978.

FLAKE, RUBINA see FLACK, ROBERTA

FRANKLIN, ARETHA LOUISE (Mrs. Kenny Cunningham; Mrs. Glynn Turman), 1942- .

6144   "Combo Reviews." Variety 223:55, July 26, 1961.

6145   "International Jazz Critic's Poll: The Winners." down beat 28:17,
       August 3, 1961.

6146   Welding, P. "Aretha Franklin." down beat 28:18, September 28,
       1961.

6147   "Aretha Franklin." Sepia 10:69, December 1961.

6148   Grevatt, R. "The Girls Are Moving In." Melody Maker 36:9, De-
       cember 16, 1961.

6149   "Today's Top Recording Talent." Billboard 74:57, April 7, 1962.

6150   "Aretha Franklin: Soul Singer." Sepia 12:56-58, February 1963.

6151   "Swingin' Aretha." Ebony 19:85, March 1964.

6152   Payne, J. "Aretha Franklin--I Never Loved a Man." Crawdaddy no.
       10:33, July-August 1967.

6153   "Concert Reviews." Variety 251:54, May 22, 1968.

6154   Jones, M. "What Do You Want to Tell Me About That?" Melody
       Maker 43:7, May 25, 1968.

6155   Feather, L. "Blindfold Test." down beat 35:33, May 30, 1968.

6156 Hofstein, F. "Aretha, C'est Ca." Jazz Magazine no. 155:9, June 1968.

6157 Illingworth, D. "Jazz in Britain." Jazz Journal 21:16-17, June 1968.

6158 "Lady Soul paa Berns." Orkester Journalcn 36:11, June 1968.

6159 "Aretha's 96 G Guarantee for West German Tour." Variety 251:49, June 12, 1968.

6160 "Lady Soul: Singing It Like It Is." Time 91:62-66, June 28, 1968.

6161 Landau, J. "Aretha." Rolling Stone no. 13:11, July 6, 1968.

6162 Wilmer, V. "Caught in the Act." down beat 35:34-35, July 11, 1968.

6163 Ochs, E. "Aretha Franklin: From Sermons on Sunday to All-Week Success." Billboard 80:12, July 13, 1968.

6164 "Aretha Femme Goldisk Champ, Corrals Her 6th." Variety 251:44, July 31, 1968.

6165 Hackenbush, J. F. "Lady Soul: Aretha Franklin." Jazz Hot no. 242:36-38, August-September 1968.

6166 Dance, H. "Aretha Lady Soul." down beat 35:17-18, August 8, 1968.

6167 Wilmer, V. "Aretha Lady Soul." down beat 35:16, August 8, 1968.

6168 "'Half-Paid' Aretha Balks at Denver Date & Fans Break up Amphitheatre." Variety 251:62, August 14, 1968.

6169 "NATRA Gives Mrs. Martin Luther King and Bill Cosby Top Honors in Miami." Variety 252:45-46, August 21, 1968.

6170 Henshaw, L. "Aretha, the Girl Draws Pictures When She Sings." Melody Maker 43:7, September 7, 1968.

6171 Ochs, E. "Aretha Wailer, Wooer, Winner." Billboard 80:12, October 26, 1968.

6172 "Aretha, in Wheelchair, Pulls 53 G in Hawaii; Delay Concerts 1 Day." Variety 253:80, November 20, 1968.

6173 Willis, Ellen. "Records: Rock Etc." New Yorker 44:134-136, November 23, 1968.

6174 "Random Notes." Rolling Stone no. 24:8, December 21, 1968.

6175 "Aretha Gets R & B Award." Billboard 81:70, April 19, 1969.

6176 "Soul Night." Time 93:25, May 9, 1969.

6177 "A Gallery of the Greats." BMI p. 31, Summer 1969.

6178 "Aretha Unanimous Winner." BMI p. 5, June 1969.

6179 Tiegel, E. "Aretha Conquers Caesars Palace." Billboard 81:22,
      June 28, 1969.

6180 "135 G Refunds Due as Fla. Soul Show Promoter Concedes Aretha
      Cancelled." Variety 255:52, July 9, 1969.

6181 Eldridge, R. "Magnificent Seven of Soul." Melody Maker 44:10,
      July 26, 1969.

6182 Shaw, A. "The Rhythm & Blues Revival--No White Gloved, Black
      Hits." Billboard 81:S3, August 16, 1969.

6183 "Aretha: Troubles in Motor City." Rolling Stone no. 40:8, August
      23, 1969.

6184 "J. Brown, Aretha, Sly, Supremes Win 'Mikes.'" Billboard 81:34,
      August 30, 1969.

6185 "Aretha Shouts the Blues Briefly." Billboard 81:SC5, October 4,
      1969.

6186 "Random Notes." Rolling Stone no. 43:4, October 4, 1969.

6187 "Aretha's Old Man Comes Up Shooting." Rolling Stone no. 51:16,
      February 7, 1970.

6188 "Aretha Cooks Up Some Pigs' Feet." Rolling Stone no. 55:14, April
      2, 1970.

6189 "Aretha Franklin Back on the Concert Trail." Variety 259:47, May
      20, 1970.

6190 "International, Las Vegas." Variety 259:58, June 10, 1970.

6191 Atlas, J. "Aretha's Great Re-birth." Melody Maker 45:6, June 20,
      1970.

6192 "Talent in Action." Billboard 82:24, June 27, 1970.

6193 "Aretha Cancels London Concert Due to Illness." Variety 259:40,
      July 15, 1970.

6194 "Aretha Show a Sell-Out." Melody Maker 45:5, July 18, 1970.

6195 Coleman, R. "Aretha in Antibes." Melody Maker 45:20, August 1,
      1970.

6196 Jones, M. "The Gospel Truth from Aretha." Melody Maker 45:20-
      21, August 1, 1970.

6197 Lewis, A. "Aretha's Still the Queen But ..." Melody Maker 45:24,
      August 8, 1970.

6198 Cullaz, M. "Aretha Franklin Parle ..." Jazz Hot no. 264:11, Sep-
      tember 1970.

6199 _____. "La Chronique des Disques: Aretha's Gold; This Girl's
      in Love with You." Jazz Hot no. 264:39, September 1970.

6200 Gerber, A. "Les Hauts et les Bas d'Antibes." Jazz Magazine no. 181:57-58, September 1970.

6201 Feather, L. "Caught in the Act." Melody Maker 45:16, September 26, 1970.

6202 "Concert Reviews." Variety 260:58, October 28, 1970.

6203 "Santana, Aretha Wrap Up More Gold Disks." Variety 260:49, November 4, 1970.

6204 "Talent in Action." Billboard 82:23, November 7, 1970.

6205 Amatneedk, B. "Records: Spirit in the Dark." Rolling Stone no. 70:36, November 12, 1970.

6206 "Record Reviews: Spirit in the Dark." down beat 37:22, November 12, 1970.

6207 Cullaz, M. "La Chronique des Disques: Spirit in the Dark." Jazz Hot no. 267:47, December 1970.

6208 "Record Reviews: Spirit in the Dark." Jazz and Pop 9:59, December 1970.

6209 Aletti, V. "Aretha Franklin Returns to Life." Rolling Stone no. 72:10, December 2, 1970.

6210 "NATRA Prexy Praises Aretha Support of Angela." Jet 39:62, March 18, 1971.

6211 "San Francisco." Rolling Stone no. 80:23, April 15, 1971.

6212 "Aretha." Jazz and Pop 10:14-17, June 1971.

6213 "Pop Albums: Live at the Fillmore West." Melody Maker 46:34, June 12, 1971.

6214 "Talent in Action." Billboard 83:27, June 12, 1971.

6215 Wickham, V. "Lady Soul Back at the Apollo." Melody Maker 46:6, June 19, 1971.

6216 Hennessey, M. "Aretha and Curtis Give Montreux Power Packed Soulful Opening." Billboard 83:24, June 26, 1971.

6217 "Big Disc(h)ord in Rome for Aretha." Variety 263:1, July 7, 1971.

6218 Aletti, V. "Records: Live at Fillmore West." Rolling Stone no. 87:36, July 22, 1971.

6219 "Life Is Change, Says Aretha." Rolling Stone no. 88:12, August 5, 1971.

6220 "Aretha, Marvin Gaye Win Top NATRA 1971 Awards." Billboard 83:8, August 28, 1971.

6221 Cullaz, M. "La Chronique des Disques: Live at Fillmore West." Jazz Hot no. 275:36, September 1971.

6222 Lydon, M. "Soul Kaleidoscope: Aretha at the Fillmore." Ramparts Magazine 10:30-39, October 1971.

6223 "Concert Reviews." Variety 264:43, November 3, 1971.

6224 "Talent in Action." Billboard 83:14, November 6, 1971.

6225 Feather, L. "Caught in the Act." Melody Maker 46:58, November 27, 1971.

6226 "Pop Albums: Aretha's Greatest Hits." Melody Maker 46:10, November 27, 1971.

6227 King, R. "Stargazing." Essence 2:24-39, December 1971.

6228 Sanders, C. L. "Aretha; A Close-Up Look at Sister Superstar." Ebony 27:124-135, December 1971.

6229 Gersten, R. "Records: Aretha's Greatest Hits." Rolling Stone no. 97:56, December 9, 1971.

6230 "Aretha's 12th Goldisk." Variety 265:53, December 22, 1971.

6231 Korall, B. "Aretha's Greatest Hits." Saturday Review 54:59, December 25, 1971.

6232 "Lady Soul." BMI no. 6:38-39, 1972.

6233 Spiegelman, J. "After Ten Years Aretha Brings It All Back Home." Soul 6:1-5, February 28, 1972.

6234 "Chronique des Disques: Young, Gifted and Black." Jazz Hot no. 281:27-28, March 1972.

6235 Thompson, M. C. "Aretha Is Rocking Steady Now." Jet 41:58-63, March 9, 1972.

6236 "Records: Young, Gifted and Black." Rolling Stone no. 104:58, March 16, 1972.

6237 Feather, L. "Aretha in Angela Davis Benefit." Melody Maker 47:6, March 18, 1972.

6238 "Disques du Mois: Young, Gifted and Black." Jazz Magazine no. 199:38, April 1972.

6239 "Aretha Franklin Awarded $5,000 and Dorie Miller Medal of Honor for 1972." Jet 42:62, April 2, 1972.

6240 Chorush, B. "Aretha Sings in a Church in Watts." Rolling Stone no. 106:22, April 13, 1972.

6241 "RecWords: Young, Gifted and Black." Crawdaddy no. 9:14, April 16, 1972.

6242 Spiegelman, J. "Female Vocalist of 1971." Soul 7:4, May 1, 1972.

6243 "Aretha Package a Triumph." Billboard 84:4, June 10, 1972.

6244 "Recording of Special Merit: Young, Gifted and Black." Stereo Review 29:92, July 1972.

6245 "Records: Amazing Grace." Rolling Stone no. 114:36, August 3, 1972.

6246 "Chronique des Disques: Amazing Grace." Jazz Hot no. 286:28, September 1972.

6247 "Records: Amazing Grace; Aretha Franklin--in the Beginning 1960-1967; The Gospel Soul of Aretha Franklin." Crawdaddy no. 17:74-76, October 1972.

6248 "Records: In the Beginning: The World of Aretha Franklin, 1960-1967." Rolling Stone no. 120:60, October 26, 1972.

6249 Coombs, O. "Aretha." Essence 3:42-43, December 1972.

6250 "A Gallery of the Greats." BMI no. 1:4-13, 1973. Lists great rhythm and blues musicians from the past sixty years.

6251 "Random Notes." Rolling Stone no. 125:5, January 4, 1973.

6252 Black, D. "How Black Churches Became a School for Singing Stars." Sepia 22:70-74, February 1973.

6253 "Record Reviews: Amazing Grace." Jazz & Blues 2:25, March 1973.

6254 "Aretha Franklin's 'Mini Meals' Diet Helps Shed Pounds." Jet 44:50-51, March 29, 1973.

6255 "Aretha Buries Rumors About 'Going Crazy.'" Jet 44:12, April 12, 1973.

6256 Hamilton, E. "Aretha Franklin--Female Vocalist 1972." Soul 7:2, April 23, 1973.

6257 Alterman, L. "In the Studio with Lady Soul." Melody Maker 48:15, April 28, 1973.

6258 "Talent in Action." Billboard 85:16, June 9, 1973.

6259 "Review: Aretha Turned On." Soul 8:14, July 23, 1973.

6260 "Records: Hey Now Hey, the Other Side of the Sky." Rolling Stone no. 140:47-48, August 2, 1973.

6261 Ebert, A. "Aretha." Essence 4:38-39, December 1973.

6262 Jones, Hettie. Big Star Fallin' Mama; Five Women in Black Music. New York: Viking Press, 1974. The five women are Ma Rainey, Bessie Smith, Mahalia Jackson, Billie Holiday, and Franklin. Juvenile literature.

6263 Olsen, James T. Aretha Franklin. Mankato, Minn.: Creative Education; Distributed by Childrens Press, Chicago, 1974 c1975. Juvenile literature.

6264 "The Soul Report." Melody Maker 49:28-29, January 12, 1974.

6265   "Two Gatherings." New Yorker 50:31-32, March 25, 1974.

6266   "Records: Let Me in Your Life." Rolling Stone no. 158:61-62, April 11, 1974.

6267   "Records: Let Me into Your Life." Crawdaddy no. 36:73-74, May 1974.

6268   Thompson, M. C. "Visit with Aretha Franklin." Jet 46:58-62, May 2, 1974.

6269   Hodenfield, C. "Reassessing Aretha." Rolling Stone no. 161:62-64, May 23, 1974.

6270   "Concert Reviews." Variety 276:42, August 14, 1974.

6271   "New Aretha: Her Simple Diet Helps Singer Shed 40 Pounds." Ebony 29:178-180, October 1974.

6272   "Concert Reviews." Variety 276:78, October 30, 1974.

6273   Brown, G. F. "Aretha Franklin's Back-up Singers Get Big Break." Jet 48:58-61, May 15, 1975.

6274   "Tampa Promoter Wins a $47,500 Award over Franklin's '69 No-Show." Variety 279:73, May 28, 1975.

6275   "Talent in Action." Billboard 87:27-28, June 14, 1975.

6276   Cullaz, M. "La Voix dans la Musique Negro-Americaine." Jazz Hot no. 322:16-19, December 1975.

6277   "Concert Reviews." Variety 281:52, December 17, 1975.

6278   "Soul Food: You." Melody Maker 51:39, January 17, 1976.

6279   "Talent in Action." Billboard 88:28, January 31, 1976.

6280   Lucas, B. "Looking Ahead with Aretha Franklin." Jet 49:60-63, February 26, 1976.

6281   Burgess, A. "Aretha Franklin's Hidden Asset: Her Brother Cecil." Jet 50:58-61, July 15, 1976.

6282   "Records: Sparkle." Rolling Stone no. 219:56, August 12, 1976.

6283   "Soul Albums: Sparkle." Melody Maker 51:26, October 16, 1976.

6284   "Women in Music." BMI no. 4:18, 1977.

6285   "Albums: Sweet Passion." Melody Maker 52:21, July 2, 1977.

6286   "Concert Reviews." Variety 288:61, August 31, 1977.

6287   "Records: Sweet Passion." High Fidelity/Musical America 27:138, September 1977.

6288   "Talent in Action." Billboard 89:38, September 3, 1977.

6289   Kisner, R. E. "Is There Room at the Top for Big Three of Songs?"
       Jet 52:58-60, September 15, 1977.

6290   "Aretha Faces Ban." Melody Maker 52:4, November 19, 1977.
       Franklin might be banned from giving performances in Great Brit-
       ain.

6291   Lucas, B. "Aretha, Stevie Chosen SBT 20 Queen, King." Jet 53:78-
       80, November 24, 1977.

6292   Cullaz, M. "Aretha Boycottee." Jazz Hot no. 346:63, February
       1978.

6293   Lucas, B. "Aretha's New Life and New Husband." Jet 54:12-17,
       April 27, 1978.

6294   "Concert Reviews." Variety 291:78, May 31, 1978.

6295   Trebay, G. "Riffs: Aretha's Slow Burn." Village Voice 23:50,
       June 12, 1978.

6296   Davis, C. "Aretha's Lament." Encore 7:34, June 19, 1978.

6297   "Records: Almighty Fire." Rolling Stone no. 268:56, June 29, 1978.

6298   "Capsule Reviews: Almight Five." Crawdaddy no. 86:76, July 1978.

6299   Sanders, C. L. "Aretha and Glynn." Ebony 33:104-106, July 1978.

6300   "Talent in Action." Billboard 90:40, July 8, 1978.

6301   Williams, J. "Soul Sauce: Los Angeles Aretha Fete a Puzzler."
       Billboard 90:78-79, July 22, 1978.

6302   Garland, P. "Aretha: She May Be Just Your Speed." Stereo Re-
       view 41:104, August 1978.

6303   Armstrong, L. "Couples." People 10:79-80, November 6, 1978.

GAHOWAY, MRS. SIGMUND see JACKSON, MAHALIA

GAINES, DONNA see SUMMER, DONNA

GAYE, MARVIN PENZE, 1939- .

6304   "Bios." Cash Box 24:32, June 1, 1963.

6305   "Blind Date." Melody Maker 39:12, November 28, 1964.

6306   "Marvin Gaye; A Performer's Performer." Sepia 14:46-50, January
       1965.

6307   Noonan, T. "'Hitsville, USA' Act in Detroit a Hitsville." Billboard
       77:12, March 13, 1965.

6308   "The 'In' Crowd."   Melody Maker 40:8, May 1, 1965.

6309   "Copacabana, N.Y."   Variety 243:56, August 10, 1966.

6310   Ovens, D.   "Gaye Makes It Big in Major Bistro Debut."   Billboard
        78:14, August 20, 1966.

6311   Landau, J.   "A Whiter Shade of Black."   Crawdaddy no. 11:35-40,
        September-October 1967.

6312   "Marvin Joins the Tamla Take-Over."   Melody Maker 44:21, March
        22, 1969.

6313   Eldridge, R.   "With the Solo Success Comes a Little Sadness."
        Melody Maker 44:5, April 5, 1969.

6314   Egan, J.   "Records."   Rolling Stone no. 40:37, August 23, 1969.

6315   Brodsky, A.   "Records: That's the Way Love Is."   Rolling Stone no.
        59:52, May 28, 1970.

6316   Aletti, V.   "Records: What's Going On."   Rolling Stone no. 88:43-
        44, August 5, 1971.

6317   "Aretha, Marvin Gaye Win Top NATRA 1971 Awards."   Billboard
        83:8, August 28, 1971.

6318   "Motown Beatitudes."   Time 98:69, October 11, 1971.

6319   "Pop Albums: What's Going On."   Melody Maker 46:54, October 16,
        1971.

6320   Let's Save the Children, Inc.   Marvin Gaye.   Staff: Helen King, et
        al.   Chicago: Let's Save the Children, Inc., 1972.   Juvenile liter-
        ature.

6321   Coleman, B.   "Marvin Gaye, Bill Withers--Enjoy Soulfulizing for
        Everybody."   Billboard 84:36, January 29, 1972.

6322   "Albums of the Year."   Rolling Stone no. 101:39, February 3, 1972.

6323   "Marvin Gaye Returns to Stage, Collects Multiple Honors."   Soul
        6:1, February 14, 1972.

6324   "Albums: The Hits of Marvin Gaye."   Melody Maker 47:31, Febru-
        ary 19, 1972.

6325   "Blacks Win 17 Grammy Awards, but Miles Davis, Motown Exec.
        Walk Out."   Jet 42:58, March 3, 1972.

6326   Fong-Torres, B.   "A Visit with Marvin Gaye."   Rolling Stone no.
        107:32-34, April 27, 1972.

6327   Siler, C.   "Male Vocalist."   Soul 7:10, May 1, 1972.

6328   Spiegelman, J.   "'What's Going On'; Record of 1971."   Soul 7:2-3,
        May 1, 1972.

6329   "Marvin Gaye Goes Home for First Concert in 4 Years." Soul 7:14,
       July 3, 1972.

6330   "Record Reviews: Trouble Man." down beat 40:22-23, January 7,
       1973.

6331   Berry, W. E. "Marvin Gaye: Inner City Musical Poet." Jet 43:58-
       62, February 1, 1973.

6332   "Records: Trouble Man." Rolling Stone no. 129:63, March 1, 1973.

6333   Peters, A. "Secret Terror of Marvin Gaye." Sepia 22:44-46, June
       1973.

6334   Bernstein, P., and B. Eisner. "Marvin Gaye: Paradox Makes Per-
       fect." Crawdaddy no. 26:50-55, July 1973.

6335   "Records: Let's Get It On." Crawdaddy no. 31:71-72, December
       1973.

6336   "Albums: Diana and Marvin." Melody Maker 48:37, December 15,
       1973.

6337   "The Soul Report." Melody Maker 49:28-29, January 12, 1974.

6338   "Marvin Gaye Gets It On: First Show in Four Years." Jet 45:56-
       57, January 24, 1974.

6339   "Recording of Special Merit: Let's Get It On." Stereo Review 32:90,
       February 1974.

6340   "Gaye Back to Concert." Billboard 86:24, February 2, 1974.

6341   "Marvin Gets It on for 13,000 Fans." Soul 8:14, March 4, 1974.

6342   Cahill, T. "The Spirit, the Flesh and Marvin Gaye." Rolling Stone
       no. 158:40-44, April 11, 1974.

6343   Burrell, W. "A Rare, Frank Talk with the Rare Marvin Gaye."
       Soul 8:2-3, April 15, 1974.

6344   Ruffin, W. D. "Marvin's Back--a Mighty Magnet." Soul 9:12, July
       8, 1974.

6345   Salvo, P., and B. Salvo. "America's Biggest Black Business: The
       Motown Empire." Sepia 23:34-36, September 1974.

6346   "Talent in Action." Billboard 86:18, September 7, 1974.

6347   "Performance." Rolling Stone no. 170:110, September 26, 1974.

6348   "Concert Reviews." Variety 276:58, October 2, 1974.

6349   Douglas, C. C. "Marvin Gaye." Ebony 30:50-52, November 1974.

6350   "Talent in Action." Billboard 87:54, July 19, 1975.

6351   "Concert Reviews." Variety 280:60, October 15, 1975.

6352   "Talent in Action." Billboard 87:33, October 25, 1975.

6353   "New Albums: I Want You." Melody Maker 51:29, May 1, 1976.

6354   "Records: I Want You." Rolling Stone no. 214:69, June 3, 1976;
       down beat 43:26, July 15, 1976.

6355   "Marvin Gaye Faces Jail for Contempt in Alimony Dispute." Variety
       284:56, August 18, 1976.

3656   "No Money, No Concert, So Gaye Does Freebie While Rain Pelts
       Fans." Variety 284:52, August 25, 1976.

6357   "Caught in the Act." Melody Maker 51:33, October 2, 1976.

6358   Brown, G. "What's Going On?" Melody Maker 51:8-10, October 9,
       1976.

6359   "New Albums: The Best of Marvin Gaye." Melody Maker 51:27, Oc-
       tober 23, 1976.

6360   "Talent in Action." Billboard 88:54-55, October 23, 1976.

6361   Goddet, L. "Marvin Gaye à Paris." Jazz Hot no. 332:12-17, No-
       vember 1976.

6362   "Jazz en Direct." Jazz Magazine no. 249:6, November 1976.

6363   Brown, G. "Gaye, Knight Beat the Disco Machine: The Year of
       Soul." Melody Maker 51:8, December 25, 1976.

6364   "Soul Albums: Live at the London Palladium." Melody Maker 52:29,
       May 28, 1977.

6365   "Records: Live at the London Palladium." Rolling Stone no. 240:76,
       January 2, 1977.

6366   "Concert Reviews." Variety 288:86, September 21, 1977.

6367   "Talent in Action." Billboard 89:58, October 1, 1977.

6368   "Order Marvin Gaye to Pay Four Tooters 197 G in Back Salary."
       Variety 289:73, December 14, 1977.

6369   Salvo, P. W. "What's Really Going on with Marvin Gaye." Sepia
       27:14, April 1978.

6370   Hunter, J., and P. W. Salvo. "Interview with Janis Hunter." Sepia
       27:47-50, June 1978.

6371   Sippel, J. "Gaye Files 2 Bankruptcy Pleas." Billboard 90:20, Oc-
       tober 7, 1978.

6372   Gilmore, M. "Marvin Gaye Declares Bankruptcy." Rolling Stone
       no. 279:14, November 30, 1978.

GILLESPIE, DIZZY (John Birks), 1917- .

6373 "How Deaf Can You Get? Bebop." Time 51:74, May 17, 1948.

6374 Boyer, R. O. "Bop; Bebop." New Yorker 24:28-32, July 3, 1948.

6375 "Dizzy Gillespie." Metronome 65:29, January 1949.

6376 Russell, R. "Brass Instrumentation in Be-bop." Record Changer
      8:9-10, January 1949.

6377 Ulanov, B. "He's In and He's Out!" Stan Kenton Wins Poll, Dis-
      bands to Fight for Decent Working Conditions for His Music."
      Metronome 65:15-16, January 1949.

6378 "DJs, Diz' Humor (?), Plus Other Mess Mar Concert." down beat
      16:3, January 14, 1949.

6379 Allen, S. "What Is Bop? It's Just the Way I Think and Feel Jazz,
      Says Dizzy Gillespie." Melody Maker 25:3, February 12, 1949.

6380 "Diz Cracks S. F. Mark; Back in Spring." down beat 16:2, February
      25, 1949.

6381 Gleason, R. J. "Dizzy Proves He's Tops in Showmanship Ability."
      down beat 16:13, April 8, 1949.

6382 "Dizzy's Now a Real Gone Maracas Man." down beat 16:5, April 22,
      1949.

6383 Jackson, E. "Dizzy with No Punches Pulled." Melody Maker 25:2,
      May 7, 1949.

6384 "Shaw Summons Dizzy Gillespie." Billboard 61:17, June 11, 1949.

6385 Weinstock, B. "Dizzy Gillespie; A Complete Discography." Record
      Changer 8:8, July 1949.

6386 "Dizzy's New Idea Would Help Interpret Arrangers." down beat 16:13,
      July 1, 1949.

6387 "Dizzy Gillespie Orch." Variety 175:47, July 13, 1949.

6388 "Bird Wrong; Bop Must Get a Beat: Diz." down beat 16:1, October
      7, 1949.

6389 Wilson, J. S. "Shearing Makes Concert Bow." down beat 16:1, No-
      vember 18, 1949.

6390 "Dizzy Gillespie." Metronome 66:18, January 1950.

6391 Harris, P. "Dix Sacrifices Spark to Get His 'Bop with Beat.'"
      down beat 17:8, January 13, 1950.

6392 Burman, M. "Bop." Jazz Journal 3:10-11, April 1950.

6393 "Dizzy Gillespie." Metronome 66:20, April 1950.

6394 Tracy, J. "Gillespie's Crew Great Again, but May Break Up."
      down beat 17:1, June 16, 1950.

6395 "Decline of the Big Band--Gillespie Division." Metronome 66:6,
      July 1950.

6396 "Good-by, Bop." Newsweek 36:76, September 4, 1950.

6397 Wilson, J. S. "Bop at End of Road, Says Dizzy." down beat 17:1,
      September 8, 1950.

6398 "Also in Person." Metronome 66:21, October 1950.

6399 Gleason, R. J. "Dizzy Getting a Bad Deal from Music Biz." down
      beat 17:14, November 17, 1950.

6400 Gillespie, Dizzy. "Leading a Big Band Was Too Much of a Head-
      ache!" Melody Maker 27:2, April 21, 1951.

6401 "They're Making Music News." International Musician 49:20, May
      1951.

6402 Hoefer, G. "Diz Starts Own Disc Firm to Wax What He Pleases."
      down beat 18:9, June 1, 1951.

6403 Jackson, E. "Dizzy Gillespie Plays--Johnny Richards Conducts."
      Melody Maker 27:5, June 23, 1951.

6404 "Art of Banana-Eating; Bebop King Demonstrates His Talent as a
      Comic." Ebony 6:32, October 1951.

6405 "In Person." Metronome 67:20-22, October 1951.

6406 Ulanov, B. "History of Jazz." Metronome 67:16, October 1951;
      67:18-20, November 1951.

6407 "Diz Strikes Happy Compromise Between Jazz, Commercialism."
      down beat 19:18, February 8, 1952.

6408 "Dizzy Drops Everything to Play at Paris Jazz Fair." Melody Maker
      28:1, March 8, 1952.

6409 Kahn, H. "Dizzy Arrives with a Truckful of Tinned Apple Juice!"
      Melody Maker 28:3, March 22, 1952.

6410 "Dizzy Could Do No Wrong." Melody Maker 28:1, April 5, 1952.

6411 Callender, R. "Bop Is Just Everybody Playing Like Diz or Bird."
      Melody Maker 28:4, May 10, 1952.

6412 Hentoff, N. "Crazy Like a Fox." down beat 19:15, June 18, 1952.

6413 "They Talk About Louis and Dizzy in the Same Breath." Melody
      Maker 28:9, August 9, 1952.

6414 Feather, L. "When Dizzy's Bop Clique Played 'Muskrat Ramble.'"
      Melody Maker 29:5, January 3, 1953.

6415 "Ett Galajam." Orkester Journalen 21:8, February 1953.

6416 Linde, U. "Rytm och Tempo." Orkester Journalen 21:7, February
      1953.

6417 "Our Jazz Had Entered a Dangerous Phase." Melody Maker 29:1,
      February 7, 1953.

6418 Condon, B. "Gillespie Bebops Svenska Cats Dizzy." Variety 189:2,
      February 11, 1953.

6419 "The Dizzy Boys." Melody Maker 29:3, February 14, 1953.

6420 Fremer, B. "Varför Inte en Pungratta Ocksa?" Orkester Journalen
      21:15, March 1953.

6421 "Gillespie Flops in Germany." Melody Maker 29:6, March 21, 1953.

6422 "Dizzy, Django, Doc, et al." Saturday Review 36:76, November 28,
      1953.

6423 "Operations on Gillespie and Oscar Peterson." Melody Maker 29:1,
      December 12, 1953.

6424 "Perspectives." down beat 21:8, April 7, 1954.

6425 "'Recording Artists' Roster." down beat 21:99, June 30, 1954.

6426 "Dizzy Designs New Trumpet, Claims Improvement in Tone." down
      beat 21:29, July 14, 1954.

6427 "Granz Will Back Diz in Big Band." down beat 21:6, July 28, 1954.

6428 Eckstine, B. "Dizzy, Bird, and the Birth of Bop." Melody Maker
      30:5, September 4, 1954.

6429 Peterson, O. "The Jazz Scene Today." down beat 21:22, September
      8, 1954.

6430 Morgan, A. "Gillespie in Concert." Jazz Journal 8:3, November
      1954.

6431 Jepsen, J. G. "Jazzens Instrumentalister: Trumpeten." Orkester
      Journalen 23:11, February 1955.

6432 Coss, B. "Bop 1955, a Summing Up." Metronome 71:20-21, April
      1955.

6433 Dahlgren, C. "Dizzy, Miles och Chet i Birdland-Duell." Orkester
      Journalen 23:8-9, July 1955.

6434 "Dizzy Names Touring Band." down beat 23:7, March 7, 1956.

6435 "Tentative Gillespie Itinerary Disclosed." down beat 23:7, March 21,
      1956.

6436 "Dizzy Gillespie a Hit with Middle East Cats on U.S. Goodwill Tour."
      Variety 202:61, April 25, 1956.

6437 "History of Jazz Big Feature of Gillespie Overseas Tour." down
      beat 23:9, May 2, 1956.

6438   "Dizzy Flies in as Louis Leaves Britain." Melody Maker 31:1, May
       26, 1956.

6439   "Near East Click Cues Woo of Dizzy in Latin Lands; Satchmo's
       O'seas Coin." Variety 202:43, May 30, 1956.

6440   Ferrara, D.   "The Trumpet." Metronome 72:22, June 1956.

6441   Feather, L.   "Ambassador Diz Has Made Jazz History." Melody
       Maker 31:2, June 2, 1956.

6442   "Good Will with Horns." Newsweek 47:50, June 4, 1956.

6443   "Birdland, N.Y." Variety 203:53, June 6, 1956.

6444   "Dizzy's Troupe Casts Spell Over Mideast Audiences." down beat
       23:17, June 13, 1956.

6445   "Turkey Resounds, Reacts to Dizzy Gillespie Band." down beat 23:16,
       June 27, 1956.

6446   Mimaroglu, I.   "Gillespie in Ankara." Metronome 72:15-16, July
       1956.

6447   Stearns, M. W.   "Is Jazz Good Propaganda?" Saturday Review 39:28-
       31, July 14, 1956.

6448   Feather, L.   "Gillespie Really Digs Brownie, Thad." down beat
       23:39, July 25, 1956.

6449   "Capsule Reviews." Metronome 72:9, August 1956.

6450   Feather, L.   "Feather's Nest." down beat 23:32, August 8, 1956.

6451   "Despite Some Sour Notes, Dizzy Gillespie Troupe Makes Goodwill
       in Arg." Variety 203:45, August 22, 1956.

6452   "Gillespie Band Swinging Through Latin America." down beat 23:11,
       September 5, 1956.

6453   "The Bands Swing Back." Metronome 72:22, November 1956.

6454   "Gillespie Band Members Listed." down beat 23:11, December 12,
       1956.

6455   "No More Tizzy Re Dizzy on Coast; Berkeley Gets Gillespie, Trumpet
       & All." Variety 205:48, January 23, 1957.

6456   Steif, B.   "Gillespie's Glory in Greece." Variety 205:43, January
       30, 1957.

6457   Gleason, R. J.   "Frisco in Stew Over Banning of Dizzy Band." down
       beat 24:9, February 20, 1957.

6458   Segal, J.   "Gillespie Wails in Windy City." Metronome 74:9-11,
       March 1957.

6459   Gleason, R. J.   "Perspectives." down beat 24:8, March 6, 1957.

6460 "Gillespie's Higher-than-Ike 'Gov't' Fee Defended, USIA Film Rapped
      in Hub." Variety 206:45, April 17, 1957.

6461 Simon, B. "Dizzy Attacks Louis." Melody Maker 32:5, May 18,
      1957. Gillespie criticizes Armstrong in "Jazz Is Too Good for
      Americans" published in Esquire.

6462 "Dizzy Gillespie." Metronome 74:19, June 1957.

6463 Hague, D. "Town Hall Concert." Jazz Journal 10:9-10, June 1957.

6464 "Nothing New Since Dizzy." Melody Maker 32:6, June 8, 1957.

6465 Tracy, J. "The First Chorus." down beat 24:5, June 13, 1957.

6466 Korall, B., and R. Grevatt. "Bop King Gillespie Carries the Day."
      Melody Maker 32:4, July 20, 1957.

6467 "Barry Ulanov." down beat 24:6, August 8, 1957.

6468 Gold, D. "Dizzy Gillespie." down beat 24:12, September 19, 1957.

6469 "Dizzy Gillespie." down beat 25:11-12, January 23, 1958.

6470 Feather, L. "The Trumpet in Jazz." down beat 25:16, January 23,
      1958.

6471 James, Michael. Dizzy Gillespie. New York: A. S. Barnes, 1959.

6472 Feather, L. "Dizzy Gillespie." down beat 26:33, May 14, 1959.

6473 "Dizzy's Day; Jazz Star Is Honored by South Carolina Hometown."
      Ebony 14:67-68, June 1959.

6474 "Ears Catch Up." Newsweek 54:106, September 14, 1959.

6475 Gaspard, J. J. "Dizzy Gillespie." Musica no. 67:26, October 1959.

6476 "Gillespie Storms as Fans Walk Out." Melody Maker 34:11, October
      10, 1959.

6477 "Jazz B. O. in Sweden Goes from Hot to Cool to Cold; Dizzy, Duke
      Concerts NSG." Variety 216:48, October 14, 1959.

6478 Boatfield, G. "Full Packages." Jazz Journal 12:3, November 1959.

6479 Harrison, M. "Record Reviews." Jazz Review 2:28-31, November
      1959.

6480 Balliett, W. "Jazz Records." New Yorker 35:154-160, November 7,
      1959.

6481 Fayenz, F. "Buck e Dizzy in Italia." Musica Jazz 15:11-12, De-
      cember 1959.

6482 The Dizzy Gillespie Big Bands. [n. p., 196-?]. A 12-page biography
      and discography of Gillespie.

6483 Götze, Werner. Dizzy Gillespie; Ein Porträt. Wetzlar: Pegasus, 1960. Biography of Gillespie including bibliography and discography.

6484 Hoefer, G. "Caught in the Act." down beat 27:41, February 18, 1960.

6485 Gillespie, Dizzy. "Charlie Parker Tel que Je l'Ai." Jazz Hot 26:38-39, March 1960.

6486 Lees, G. "Dizzy Gillespie: Problems of Life on a Pedestal." down beat 27:16-19, June 23, 1960.

6487 "Gillespie, Dizzy." Metronome 77:42, July 1960.

6488 "Miles Davis and Dizzy Gillespie Tie in down beat International Critics Poll for Top Trumpet." Jet July 28, 1960.

6489 White, T. "Dizzy Gillespie, the Man Who Walks Alone." Metronome 77:42-43, October 1960.

6490 Manskleid, N. "Diz on Bird." Jazz Review 4:11-13, January 1961.

6491 Coss, B., and D. Solomon. "A Visit to the King in Queens: An Interview with Dizzy Gillespie." Metronome 78:15-18, February 1961.

6492 Morgenstern, D. "Ornette Meets Dizzy." Metronome 78:24-25, March 1961.

6493 Maher, J. "Brass, Acoustics Hamper Dizzy." Billboard 73:7, March 13, 1961.

6494 Diether, J. "Dizzy Gillespie Quintet." Musical America 81:65-66, April 1961.

6495 Dance, S. "Three Score; A Quiz for Jazz Musicians." Metronome 78:48, May 1961.

6496 Lees, G. "The Years with 'Yard': Interview with Dizzy Gillespie." down beat 28:22, May 25, 1961.

6497 Welding, P. "Caught in the Act." down beat 28:58, July 20, 1961.

6498 Cerulli, D. "Dizzy Gillespie." International Musician 60:20-21, August 1961.

6499 Lees, G. "Bird et Diz." Jazz Magazine 7:29-31, August 1961.

6500 Hoefer, G. "The Hot Box." down beat 28:48, August 17, 1961.

6501 Gleason, R. J. "Perspectives." down beat 28:38-39, September 14, 1961.

6502 Hoefer, G. "The Hot Box." down beat 28:37-38, September 14, 1961. Discussion of Gillespie and Cab Calloway with a discography.

6503 "Gillespie Brime." Jazz Magazine 8:13, January 1962.

6504 Feather, L. "Blindfold Test." down beat 29:37, January 18, 1962.

6505 Baker, K. "Dizzy Gillespie--He's a Law unto Himself." Melody
      Maker 37:i, January 27, 1962.

6506 Atkins, R. "John Coltrane and Dizzy Gillespie in Britain." Jazz
      Monthly 7:11-12, February 1962.

6507 Feather, L. "Jazz Records." Show 2:103, February 1962.

6508 "Bad Atmosphere for Dizzy in Chicago." down beat 29:15, February
      15, 1962.

6509 Lees, G. "Lalo = Brilliance." down beat 29:18-19, April 12, 1962.

6510 Destombes, A. "Dizzy Gillespie + Grand Orchestre = ?" Jazz Hot
      no. 178:23, July-August 1962.

6511 Williams, M. "Gillespie in Concert." Saturday Review 45:41, August
      25, 1962.

6512 "Jazz Belongs in the Dance Hall, Says Dizzy Gillespie." Melody
      Maker 37:3, September 15, 1962.

6513 "Dizzy Arrangements While You Wait." down beat 29:14, September
      27, 1962.

6514 Butterfield, D. "Dizzy's Brass Band." down beat 29:17, October
      25, 1962.

6515 "Lalo Apres Leo." Jazz Magazine 8:17, December 1962.

6516 Cooke, J. "Better Times Ahead." Jazz Monthly 8:2-5, January
      1963.

6517 Hoefer, G. "Earl Hines in the 1940s." down beat 30:25, April 25,
      1963.

6518 Gillespie, Dizzy. "James Moody's My Man Now." Melody Maker
      38:8, June 15, 1963.

6519 Hoefer, G. "The First Bop Combo." down beat 30:19, June 20,
      1963.

6520 Dance, S. "Dizzy Gillespie: Past, Present and Future." Jazz
      2:8-10, July-August 1963.

6521 "Basin Street West, L.A." Variety 232:52, October 23, 1963.

6522 "Gillespie Presidential Campaign Gathers California Momentum."
      down beat 30:11-12, November 7, 1963.

6523 "Candidate Gillespie Lectures at College." down beat 30:12, Novem-
      ber 21, 1963.

6524 Morrison, A. "Man Behind the Horn." Ebony 19:143-144, June 1964.

6525 Gitler, I. "Bird and the Forties." down beat 31:32-36, July 2, 1964.

6526   Grevatt, R.   "Here's Jazz at Its Frantic Best."   Melody Maker 39:5,
       August 8, 1964.

6527   "Manne-Hole, L.A."   Variety 236:48, September 2, 1964.

6528   Woodfin, H.   "The Dizzy Gillespie Band: 1946-1950."   Jazz Monthly
       10:12-14, October 1964.

6529   "The Candidate Meets the Press."   down beat 31:10-12, November 5,
       1964.

6530   Morgenstern, D.   "Framework for Blowing: The Dizzy Gillespie
       Quintet."   down beat 32:22-23, June 17, 1965.

6531   "Gillespie Keeps Dizzy Pace with Activities."   down beat 32:12, March
       25, 1965.

6532   Siders, H.   "Caught in the Act."   down beat 32:29-30, March 25,
       1965.

6533   "Playboy Club, Chi."   Variety 240:74, September 15, 1965.

6534   "Dizzy and Bop Subjects of National Educational TV Show."   down
       beat 32:13, October 7, 1965.

6535   "Dizzy paa Sparlaaga."   Orkester Journalen 33:11, December 1965.

6536   Lattes, P.   "Ponty, Gillespie et le Monstre."   Jazz Hot no. 216:5-
       6, January 1966.

6537   Stark, J. A.   "Gillespie Plays 'Bopthoven' with the Cincy Symphony."
       Billboard 78:56, January 15, 1966.

6538   Hentoff, N.   "A Challenging Big-Band Jazz Summation."   High Fidel-
       ity/Musical America 16:80, February 1966.

6539   "Two-Timing in Cincy."   down beat 33:14, February 24, 1966.

6540   "Isy's, Vancouver."   Variety 242:66, April 13, 1966.

6541   Hoefer, G.   "The Glorious Dizzy Gillespie Orchestra."   down beat
       33:27-30, April 21, 1966.

6542   Goldberg, J.   "Early and Essential Dizzy Gillespie; Vintage Record-
       ings from the Thirties and Forties Are Both Pleasant and Instruc-
       tive."   HiFi/Stereo Review 17:106-107, October 1966.

6543   "Basin Street, W., Frisco."   Variety 245:59, January 25, 1967.

6544   Feather, L.   "Dizzy Gillespie."   Melody Maker 42:6, January 28,
       1967.

6545   McCoy, F.   "Dizzy à Frisco."   Jazz Magazine no. 140:12, March
       1967.

6546   Feather, L.   "Blindfold Test."   down beat 34:40-41, March 23, 1967.

6547   "Village Gate, N.Y."   Variety 251:52, July 24, 1968.

6548   Vacher, A. "Un Ete Canadien." Jazz Magazine no. 158:8, September 1968.

6549   Clarke, K., and G. Arvanitas. "Temoignages." Jazz Hot no. 244:33, November 1968.

6550   Guerin, R. "Dizzy Gillespie Toujours Actuel?" Jazz Hot no. 244:30-33, November 1968.

6551   "5e Paris Jazz Festival." Jazz Hot no. 245:17, December 1968.

6552   Dahlgren, R. "Stor Jazzkvaell med Storband." Orkester Journalen 36:7, December 1968.

6553   Gardner, M. "Jazz in Britain." Jazz Journal 21:19, December 1968.

6554   Jepsen, Jorgen Grunnet. A Discography of Dizzy Gillespie. Copenhagen NV: Karl Emil Knudsen, 1969. A two-volume set covering the years 1937-1968.

6555   Burns, J. "Dizzy Gillespie: The Early 1950s." Jazz Journal 22:2, January 1969.

6556   Feather, L. "Second Opinion: Dizzy Gillespie." Melody Maker 44:8, January 11, 1969.

6557   Hentoff, N. "Dizzy Gillespie." International Musician 67:8, February 1969.

6558   Albertson, C., et al. "Record Reviews." down beat 36:24, February 6, 1969.

6559   Burns, J. "Lesser Known Bands of the Forties." Jazz Monthly no. 169:10-12, March 1969.

6560   "Cool Hand in Hollywood." Time 93:74-75, June 13, 1969.

6561   McRae, B. "A B Basics: A Column for the Newcomer to Jazz." Jazz Journal 22:4, September 1969.

6562   Albertson, C., et al. "Record Reviews." down beat 36:17-18, October 2, 1969.

6563   Berton, R. "Caught in the Act." down beat 36:24, October 2, 1969. Review of Gillespie's performance at the Rutgers Jazz Festival.

6564   Nedzella, M. "San Francisco by Night." Jazz Magazine no. 173:21, December 1969.

6565   "Disques du Mois." Jazz Magazine no. 175:40, February 1970.

6566   Feather, L. "Dizzy Gillespie Blindfold Test." down beat 37:24, February 5, 1970.

6567   "Caught in the Act." down beat 37:28-29, February 19, 1970.

6568   Feather, L. "Dizzy Gillespie Blindfold Test." down beat 37:26, February 19, 1970.

6569   Peterson, O. "The Massey Hall Concert." Jazz Journal 23:8-10,
       March 1970.

6570   "Big Band Special." Melody Maker 45:18, March 21, 1970.

6571   Gerber, A. "Un Triomphe pour Diz." Jazz Magazine no. 177:9,
       April 1970.

6572   Savy, M. "Dizzy Gillespie à l'ORTF." Jazz Hot no. 260:6, April
       1970.

6573   "Caught in the Act." Melody Maker 45:10, April 11, 1970.

6574   "Concert Reviews." Variety 258:56, April 22, 1970.

6575   Jones, M. "Yesterday, Today and Tomorrow." Melody Maker 45:8,
       April 25, 1970.

6576   O'Gilvie, B. "Dizzy Gillespie Quintet." Jazz Magazine no. 178:14,
       May 1970.

6577   Glassenberg, B. "Talent in Action." Billboard 82:24, May 2, 1970.

6578   Nibzen, A. "La Chronique des Disques: The Dizzy Gillespie Re-
       union Big Band 20th and 30th Anniversary." Jazz Hot no. 262:35-
       36, June 1970.

6579   "Caught in the Act." down beat 37:29-30, August 6, 1970.

6580   Cressant, P. "La Chronique des Disques: Vintage Series No. 16."
       Jazz Hot no. 264:39, September 1970.

6581   Woods, P., and J. L. Ginibre. "D'Hier et d'Aujourd'hui: Dizzy."
       Jazz Magazine no. 183:18-23, November 1970.

6582   Williams, R. "Sun Shines and Dizzy Dazzles." Melody Maker 45:24-
       25, November 14, 1970.

6583   Gerber, A. "Newport à Paris." Jazz Magazine no. 184:61, Decem-
       ber 1970.

6584   "Caught in the Act." down beat 37:31, December 10, 1970.

6585   "Record Reviews: At Salle Pleyel '48." Coda 10:16, no. 4, 1971.

6586   Storb, I. "Berliner Jazztage 1970." Musik und Bildung 3:41-42,
       January 1971.

6587   Morgenstern, D. "Record Reviews: The Real Thing." down beat
       38:22, February 4, 1971.

6588   Burns, J. "Early Birks." Jazz Journal 24:18-19, March 1971.

6589   Niquet, B. "Chronique des Disques: Live at the Village Vanguard."
       Jazz Hot no. 270:32, March 1971.

6590   "Gillespie and Hackett Meet in Super Summit." down beat 38:12-13,
       March 18, 1971.

6591 "Record Reviews: Reunion Big Band." down beat 38:20, April 15, 1971.

6592 Ramsey, D. "Record Reviews: The Dizzy Gillespie Orchestra at Salle Pleyel; Paris, France." down beat 38:20, April 29, 1971.

6593 "Concert Reviews." Variety 263:40, June 2, 1971.

6594 "Record Reviews: Reunion Big Band." Jazz and Pop 10:45-46, July 1971.

6595 Lentz, P. "Festival Focus; New Orleans '71." down beat 38:16-19, July 22, 1971.

6596 "Caught in the Act." down beat 38:37-38, September 16, 1971.

6597 Fiofori, T. "Getting Dizzy." Melody Maker 46:12, September 25, 1971.

6598 Feather, L. "Dizzy: Un Nouveau Gag? Pourquoi le Trompettiste à Retire Sa Candidature à la Presidence des Etats-Unis." Jazz Magazine no. 193:6, October 1971.

6599 "Disques du Mois: The Great Dizzy Gillespie." Jazz Magazine no. 194:34-35, November 1971.

6600 Gardner, M. "Record Reviews: The Ebullient Mr. Gillespie." Jazz Journal 24:28-29, November 1971.

6601 Williams, R. "The Giants of Jazz." Melody Maker 46:12, November 13, 1971.

6602 Morgenstern, D. "Record Reviews: Giants." down beat 38:18, November 25, 1971.

6603 Delaunay, C., et al. "Les Festivals d'Automne." Jazz Hot no. 278:7, December 1971.

6604 Gerber, A. "Giants of Jazz." Jazz Magazine no. 195:22-24, December 1971.

6605 "Caught in the Act." down beat 38:27-28, December 9, 1971.

6606 Burns, J. "The Charlie Parker 'Ko Ko' Date." Jazz & Blues 1:10, January 1972.

6607 Callahan, C. "Dizzy Gillespie--Artist-in-Residence." Instrumentalist 26:48-49, January 1972.

6608 "La Chronique des Disques: And His Orchestra, Vol. 2." Jazz Hot no. 279:31, January 1972.

6609 "Record Reviews: Dizzy Gillespie and the Mitchell-Ruff Duo; A Portrait of Jenny." down beat 39:22, January 20, 1972.

6610 "Chronique des Disques: Jazz Spectrum, Vol. 11." Jazz Hot no. 281:28, March 1972.

6611 Fiofori, T. "'Jaq Gillar Ordet Jazz'; Dizzy Gillespie." Orkester
      Journalen 40:8-9, March 1972.

6612 "Dizzy and Buddy Down but Far from Out." down beat 39:9, March
      2, 1972.

6613 Gilmore, M. S. "Caught in the Act." Melody Maker 47:22, March
      11, 1972.

6614 Bourne, M. "Fat Cats at Lunch: An Interview with Dizzy Gillespie."
      down beat 39:16-17, May 11, 1972.

6615 "Jazz Records: The Original Dizzy Gillespie Big Band in Concert."
      Melody Maker 47:36, May 27, 1972.

6616 "Disques du Mois: Dizzy Gillespie." Jazz Magazine no. 202:26,
      July 1972.

6617 "Dizzy Gets New York's Highest Cultural Award." Jet 42:59, July
      27, 1972.

6618 "Record Reviews: The Original Dizzy Gillespie Big Band in Concert."
      Jazz & Blues 2:27, October 1972.

6619 Bourne, M. "Dizzy Bows Out of Presidential Race." down beat
      39:10-11, November 9, 1972.

6620 "Disques du Mois: Portrait of Jenny." Jazz Magazine no. 206:41,
      December 1972.

6621 Morgenstern, Dan, Ira Gitler, and Jack Bradley. Bird & Diz: A
      Bibliography. New York: New York Jazz Museum, 1973.

6622 Want, R. "Jazz Circa 1945: A Confluence of Styles." Musical
      Quarterly 59:532, no. 4, 1973.

6623 Burns, J. "Boppin' in Paris." Jazz Journal 26:14-17, January 1973.

6624 "Caught in the Act." down beat 40:36, January 18, 1973.

6625 "Concert Reviews." Variety 269:50, January 24, 1973.

6626 "Half Note, N.Y." Variety 269:63, January 31, 1973.

6627 Russell, R. "West Coast Bop." Jazz & Blues 3:8-11, May 1973.

6628 Albertson, C. "Gillespie and Parker: An Important Reissue--'the
      Greatest Jazz Concert Ever.'" Stereo Review 30:84-85, June 1973.

6629 "Jazz Records: Trumpet Kings." Melody Maker 48:40, June 2, 1973.

6630 "On Record: The Dizzy Gillespie Story." Jazz & Blues 3:24, July
      1973.

6631 "Caught in the Act." Melody Maker 48:51, July 28, 1973.

6632 "Jazz Records: The Greatest Jazz Concert Ever." Melody Maker
      48:51, August 4, 1973.

6633 Welch, C. "Dizzy Has London in a Spin." Melody Maker 48:20,
      August 4, 1973.

6634 "Caught in the Act." Melody Maker 48:36-37, August 11, 1973.

6635 Nolan, H. "Dizzy: 'A Primary Force!'" down beat 40:20, August
      16, 1973.

6636 "Jazz in Britain." Jazz Journal 26:18-19, September 1973.

6637 Tomkins, L. "Dizzy Gillespie Tells His Story." Crescendo Interna-
      tional 20:20-22, September 6-7, 1973.

6638 East, L. "Summer Music." Music and Musicians 22:74, October
      1973.

6639 Olsson, J. "Dizzy Gladde Kristianstad." Orkester Journalen 41:24,
      October 1973.

6640 "On Record: The Small Groups." Jazz & Blues 3:20-21, October
      1973.

6641 "On Stage." Jazz & Blues 3:15-16, October 1973.

6642 Tomkins, L. "Dizzy Gillespie Tells His Story." Crescendo Interna-
      tional 20:6-7, October 1973.

6643 Woolley, S. J. "With Strings Attached." Jazz & Blues 3:10-11,
      October 1973.

6644 "On Record: Trumpet Kings." Jazz & Blues 3:24-25, November
      1973.

6645 "Record Reviews: The Small Groups." Coda 11:13-14, no. 11, 1974.

6646 Feather, L. "Dizzy--Soul to Soul." Melody Maker 49:53, February
      2, 1974.

6647 "Caught in the Act." Melody Maker 49:22, September 28, 1974.

6648 Feather, L. "Blindfold Test." down beat 41:25, December 5, 1974.

6649 "New Acts." Variety 277:52, December 11, 1974.

6650 Gleason, Ralph J. Celebrating the Duke, and Louis, Bessie, Billie,
      Bird, Carmen, Miles, Dizzy, and Other Heroes. Boston: Little,
      Brown, 1975.

6651 "Heard and Seen." Coda 12:36-37, no. 7, 1975.

6652 "Jazz in Britain." Jazz Journal 28:19, January 1975.

6653 Nilsson, C. "Dizzy med Storband." Orkester Journalen 43:10, Feb-
      ruary 1975.

6654 Blomberg, L. "Diger Jazzmaanad i Goeteborg." Orkester Journalen
      43:18, March 1975.

6655   Brodowski, P., et al. "Sweet Success!" Jazz Forum no. 34:34,
       April 1975.

6656   "Town Hall 'Concept' Shows in Solid Bow with 'Cotton Club.'" Vari-
       ety 278:80, April 2, 1975.

6657   "Record Reviews: Dizzy Gillespie's Big Four." Jazz Journal 28:28,
       June 1975.

6658   "Buddy's Place, N.Y." Variety 279:67, July 2, 1975.

6659   "Heard and Seen." Coda no. 141:36-37, September 1975.

6660   "Record Reviews: The Giant." down beat 42:30, September 11,
       1975.

6661   "Talent in Action." Billboard 87:44, October 11, 1975.

6662   Smith, A. J. "Dizzy Gillespie: The Man Who Invented Bebop."
       Encore 4:30-31, October 20, 1975.

6663   "Caught." down beat 42:37-38, October 23, 1975.

6664   "Diz Toasts Self." down beat 42:9, November 20, 1975.

6665   Goddet, L. "Le Be-bop." Jazz Hot no. 322:30-31, December 1975.

6666   "Record Reviews: Oscar Peterson & Dizzy Gillespie." down beat
       42:26-28, December 4, 1975.

6667   Sokolow, G. "Bopper Steve Was a Smash." IAJRC Journal 9:9-11,
       no. 1, 1976.

6668   Lees, G. "Dizzy Gillespie--More Credit, Please." High Fidelity/
       Musical America 26:16, January 1976.

6669   Fisher, M. "A Dizzy Idea; Gillespie Hopes to Explain Jazz Through
       Videocassettes." Billboard 88:40, March 13, 1976.

6670   Olsson, J. "Big Band Battle in Malmoe." Orkester Journalen 44:8,
       April 1976.

6671   "Jazz Albums: Oscar Peterson & Dizzy Gillespie." Melody Maker
       51:28, May 8, 1976.

6672   Goddet, L. "Dizzy Gillespie--Dizzy Atmosphere." Jazz Hot no.
       328:8-12, June 1976.

6673   "Record Reviews: The Giant." Coda no. 148:21, June 1976.

6674   Woolley, S. "Dizzy Gillespie: Reflections on Bebop." Jazz Journal
       29:18-19, June 1976.

6675   "Record Reviews: Bahiana." down beat 43:20, June 3, 1976; Jazz
       Journal 29:30, July 1976.

6676   "Caught in the Act." Melody Maker 51:20, July 31, 1976.

6677 "Record Reviews: Big 4; Something Old, Something New." Coda
      no. 150:12, August-September 1976.

6678 "Jazz Albums: Bahiana." Melody Maker 51:20, August 7, 1976.

6679 Feather, L. "Dizzy: Helping Out Old and New." Melody Maker
      51:36, October 23, 1976.

6680 "Jazz en Direct." Jazz Magazine no. 249:7, November 1976.

6681 "Trumpet Tribute." down beat 43:9, November 4, 1976. The Grand
      Master's Award is presented to Gillespie by the Jazzmobile.

6682 "Jazz Albums: Jazz at the Philharmonic 1946 Vol. 2." Melody Mak-
      er 51:30, November 20, 1976.

6683 "Record Reviews: Charlie Parker/Miles Davis/Dizzy Gillespie."
      Jazz Journal 29:35-36, December 1976.

6684 "From the Smithsonian: The Development of an American Artist,
      1940-1946." Jazz Magazine (U.S.) 1:52-53, no. 4, 1977.

6685 "Record Reviews: Live at the Spotlite." Jazz Forum no. 49:46,
      1977.

6686 "Jazz Albums: Dee Gee Days." Melody Maker 52:17, January 1,
      1977.

6687 Roberts, J. S. "Latin Jazz: Dizzy & Machito." Stereo Review
      38:110-111, January 1977.

6688 "Record Reviews: Dee Gee Days--the Savoy Sessions." Jazz Journal
      30:31, February 1977.

6689 "Concert Reviews." Variety 285:78, February 2, 1977.

6690 "Record Reviews: Afro-Cuban Jazz Moods." down beat 44:22, Feb-
      ruary 24, 1977; Coda no. 154:16, March-April 1977.

6691 Gladwell, B. "A Year of Radio 3 Jazz Interviews." Crescendo Inter-
      national 15:16-17, March 1977.

6692 Hentoff, N. "Indigenous Music: Dizzy Gillespie: The Development of
      an American Artist, 1940-46." Nation 224:350, March 19, 1977.

6693 "Record Reviews: Carter, Gillespie, Inc." down beat 44:30, April
      7, 1977.

6694 Welch, C. "Dizzy Heights." Melody Maker 52:34, April 16, 1977.

6695 "Record Reviews: Carter, Gillespie, Inc." Jazz Journal International
      30:44, May 1977.

6696 Voce, S. "It Don't Mean a Thing." Jazz Journal International 30:16-
      18, May 1977.

6697 Coleman, R. "Beaulieu: Great Music--but Where Was the Audience?"
      Melody Maker 52:44-45, July 16, 1977.

6698   "Caught in the Act." Melody Maker 52:39, July 30, 1977.

6699   "Record Reviews: Good Bait." Jazz Journal International 30:30-31,
       August 1977.

6700   Smith, A. J. "Voyage of the Jammed." down beat 44:17-18, August
       11, 1977.

6701   "Arena: Dizzy Moods." Jazz Journal International 30:33, September
       1977.

6702   Holmberg, G. "Jaettekoeer foer Dizzy i Koepenhamn." Orkester
       Journalen 45:16, September 1977.

6703   Kuehn, G. "Jazz Portraet: Dizzy Gillespie." HiFi Stereophonie
       16:1048-1050, September 1977.

6704   "Record Reviews: Diz and Gertz." Jazz Journal International 30:37,
       September 1977.

6705   "Capsule Reviews: Afro-Cuban Jazz." Crawdaddy no. 78:109-110,
       November 1977.

6706   Cressant, P. "Dizzy au Palais des Glaces." Jazz Hot no. 343:41,
       November 1977.

6707   "Dizzy Atmosphere." Jazz Magazine no. 259:34-35, November 1977.

6708   "Dizzy Disco." Jazz Magazine no. 259:36-37, November 1977.

6709   Feda, J. "Les Fetes de Dizzy." Jazz Magazine no. 259:33-35, No-
       vember 1977.

6710   "En Direct." Jazz Magazine no. 260:11, December 1977.

6711   "Record Reviews: Modern Trumpet Leaders." Jazz Journal Interna-
       tional 30:42, December 1977.

6712   "Reviews: Jazz Maturity--Where It's Coming From!" Jazz Magazine
       (U. S.) 3:61-62, no. 1, 1978.

6713   "Record Reviews: Dizzy Gillespie." Jazz Journal International 31:40,
       January-February 1978.

6714   "Waxing On: Afro-Cuban Jazz; Diz and Getz." down beat 45:34, Jan-
       uary 12, 1978.

6715   "Concert Reviews." Variety 289:72, January 25, 1978.

6716   Woolley, S. "Milt Hinton." Coda no. 159:10-11, February 1, 1978.

6717   "Caught!" down beat 45:42, February 23, 1978.

6718   Terry, C., and L. Underwood. "Dizzy Gillespie: Blowin' with Diz,
       via Mumbles." down beat 45:12-14, April 20, 1978.

6719   "Diz Joins Magnate Musicians." down beat 45:14, July 13, 1978.

6720   "Prez Awards." Jazz Journal International 31:36, August 1978.

6721 "Record Reviews: At the Downbeat Club Summer 1947." Coda no.
      162:19-20, August 1, 1978.

6722 "Jazz Albums: Dee Gee Days." Melody Maker 53:24, October 14,
      1978.

6723 "Record Reviews: Jazz Maturity--Where It's Coming From." down
      beat 45:32, November 16, 1978.

6724 Gillespie, Dizzy. To Be, or Not ... to Bop: Memoirs. Garden
      City, N.Y.: Doubleday, 1979.

HANCOCK, HERBIE (Herbert Jeffrey; Mwandishi), 1940- .

6725 Borneman, E. "Handy in Cuba." Melody Maker 28:5, August 23,
      1952.

6726 "Back Home." down beat 24:32, January 9, 1957.

6727 "Paul et Wynton; Tabliers Rendus." Jazz Magazine 9:18, April 1963.

6728 "Annuaire Biographique du Piano." Jazz Magazine 9:27, November
      1963.

6729 "Discussion; Herbie Hancock Talks to John Mehegan." Jazz 3:23-25,
      September 1964.

6730 Heckman, D. "Herbie Hancock." down beat 32:12-13, October 21,
      1965; BMI p. 22, March 1967.

6731 Wilmer, V. "Herbie--One of New York's Inner Circle." Melody
      Maker 42:8, September 23, 1967.

6732 Korall, B. "Herbie Hancock." Orkester Journalen 36:8-9, March
      1968.

6733 _____. "Herbie Hancock Continued Growth." International Mu-
      sician 66:11, April 1968.

6734 Gerber, A. "Hancock en Tete." Jazz Magazine no. 160:32-37, No-
      vember 1968.

6735 Williams, M. "Recording Miles Davis." Stereo Review 22:68-70,
      February 1969.

6736 Cuscuna, M. "Herbie Hancock's Declaration of Independence." down
      beat 36:18, May 1, 1969.

6737 Ginguet, F. "Miles Davis." Jazz Hot no. 252:14-17, July-August
      1969.

6738 Gallagher, J. "Caught in the Act." down beat 36:27-28, July 24,
      1969.

6739 Feather, L. "Herbie's Set to Clear the Last Hurdle." Melody Mak-
      er 44:8, August 16, 1969.

6740 _____, and M. Horne. "Newport 69." Jazz Magazine no. 169-170:66, September 1969.

6741 Feather, L. "Blindfold Test." down beat 36:28, September 18, 1969.

6742 Heckman, D. "Jazz: Optimism." American Musical Digest 1:16-17, no. 6, 1970.

6743 Feather, L. "Anciens et Modernes." Jazz Magazine no. 176:12, March 1970.

6744 "Concert Reviews." Variety 258:58, March 11, 1970.

6745 Dove, I. "Talent in Action." Billboard 82:28, May 2, 1970.

6746 Savy, M. "La Chronique des Disques: The Prisoner." Jazz Hot no. 262:36, June 1970.

6747 "Record Reviews: The Prisoner." down beat 37:21, June 11, 1970; Jazz Monthly no. 185:17, July 1970.

6748 Williams, R. "Herbie: Jazz, Jingles and Rock." Melody Maker 45:24, August 29, 1970.

6749 Strongin, D. "Record Reviews: Fat Albert Rotunda." Jazz and Pop 9:55, September 1970.

6750 _____. "Herbie Hancock." Jazz and Pop 9:30-32, October 1970.

6751 Mitchell, S. "Caught in the Act." down beat 37:36, December 24, 1970.

6752 "'I Am a Vehicle for the Flow of Music that Already Exists'--Herbie Hancock, in Conversation with the Editor." Hip 10:2-4, no. 4, 1971; 10:6-8, no. 5, 1971; 10:1-4, no. 6, 1971.

6753 "Caught in the Act." down beat 38:32, January 7, 1971.

6754 Johnson, B. "Herbie Hancock: Into His Own Thing." down beat 38:14-15, January 21, 1971.

6755 Feather, L. "Caught in the Act Stateside." Melody Maker 46:6, March 13, 1971.

6756 "Talent in Action." Billboard 83:52, April 24, 1971.

6757 Comas, B. "The Jazz Rap of Herbie Hancock." Soul 6:30, May 10, 1971.

6758 "Record Reviews: Mwandishi." Jazz and Pop 10:46, June 1971; Jazz Journal 24:36-37, June 1971.

6759 "Study; Interview." New Yorker 47:29, June 12, 1971.

6760 "Talent in Action." Billboard 83:28, June 12, 1971.

6761 "Caught in the Act." Melody Maker 46:16, June 31, 1971; 46:16, August 7, 1971.

6762   Williams, R. "Hancock's Heritage." Melody Maker 46:18, August
       7, 1971.

6763   _____. "Jazz Records: Mwandishi." Melody Maker 46:26, Au-
       gust 14, 1971.

6764   Gerber, A. "Disques du Mois: The Best of Herbie Hancock." Jazz
       Magazine no. 192:41, September 1971.

6765   Bangs, L. "Records: Mwandishi; The Best of Herbie Hancock."
       Rolling Stone no. 90:44, September 2, 1971.

6766   "Caught in the Act." down beat 38:32, October 28, 1971.

6767   "Concert Reviews." Variety 265:80, November 17, 1971.

6768   "Hancock Looks at Jazz." BMI p. 5, December 1971.

6769   "Esquire Show Bar, Montreal." Coda 10:41, no. 6, 1972.

6770   Gibbs, V. "Inventions and Dimensions." Crawdaddy no. 4:45-47,
       January 30, 1972.

6771   Meadow, E. "Harlem Music Center: More than a Dream." down
       beat 39:10, February 17, 1972.

6772   Martin, E. "Live Performance: Hancock at Scott's." Jazz Forum
       no. 16:80-81, March-April 1972.

6773   Feather, L. "Jazz Scene." Melody Maker 47:28, March 11, 1972.

6774   Blomberg, L. "Hancock Intressant Men Omogen." Orkester Jour-
       nalen 40:14, May 1972.

6775   Delmas, J. "Herbie Hancock ou la Musique en Creux." Jazz Hot
       no. 283:82, May 1972.

6776   Savy, M. "Paris." Jazz Magazine no. 200:61, May 1972.

6777   "Records: Crossing." Rolling Stone no. 112:55, July 6, 1972.

6778   Grant, C. D. "Beginnings: The Harlem Music Center." Essence
       3:36-37, October 1972.

6779   Levinson, J. C. "Hancock Leader, ou les Ambiguites de la Pudeur."
       Jazz Hot no. 290:5-9, January 1973.

6780   "Caught in the Act." down beat 40:32-33, May 10, 1973.

6781   Jagajivan. "Musing with Mwandishi." down beat 40:14-15, May 24,
       1973.

6782   "Caught in the Act." Melody Maker 48:65, June 9, 1973.

6783   "Talent in Action." Billboard 85:20, June 16, 1973.

6784   "Records: Sextant." Crawdaddy no. 27:70, August 1973.

6785   Gaer, E. "Herbie Hancock Fires His Band." down beat 40:12, Au-
       gust 16, 1973.

6786   "Caught in the Act." Melody Maker 48:46-47, August 18, 1973.

6787   "Herbie 'Singing' a New Tune." Soul 8:11, September 17, 1973.

6788   Toner, J. "Electric and Eclectic." Jazz & Blues 3:18-19, Novem-
       ber 1973.

6789   "Caught in the Act." down beat 40:36, November 8, 1973.

6790   "Heard and Seen." Coda 12:35, no. 2, 1974.

6791   "Record Reviews: Sextant." Coda 11:21, no. 7, 1974; 11:22, no.
       10, 1974.

6792   "Talent in Action." Billboard 86:29, January 19, 1974.

6793   Ivy, A. "Hancock Rocks Roxy with a New Funk." Soul 8:6, Febru-
       ary 18, 1974.

6794   "Herbie Hancock: Hunting Heads." Melody Maker 49:25, April 6,
       1974.

6795   "Concert Reviews." Variety 274:76, April 17, 1974.

6796   Gibbs, V. "Head Hunting with Herbie Hancock." Crawdaddy no.
       37:24-25, June 1974.

6797   Freedland, N. "Herbie Hancock; A Crossover Artist Who Feels None
       the Worse for the Trip." Billboard 86:40, June 29, 1974.

6798   "Improvising on the Beat." Time 104:37-38, July 8, 1974.

6799   Palmer, B. "Jazz/Rock '74: The Plain Funky Truth." Rolling
       Stone no. 166:16-17, August 1, 1974.

6800   Lake, S. "Herbie Rides Again." Melody Maker 49:31, August 10,
       1974.

6801   "Coarse Hancock." Melody Maker 49:15, October 12, 1974.

6802   Townley, R. "Hancock Plugs In." down beat 41:13-15, October 24,
       1974.

6803   "Caught in the Act." Melody Maker 49:34, November 2, 1974.

6804   "Talent in Action." Billboard 86:17-18, November 2, 1974.

6805   Goddet, L. "Herbie Hancock." Jazz Hot no. 311:5, December 1974.

6806   "Caught." down beat 42:36, January 16, 1975.

6807   Tiegel, E. "The Synthesizer; Improvising Requires Special Care
       Claims Herbie Hancock." Billboard 87:30, February 8, 1975.

6808   "Records: Thrust." Rolling Stone no. 180:80, February 13, 1975.

6809 Berendt, J. E. "I Wanna Make It: The Problems of Success in Jazz." Jazz Forum no. 34:39-41, April 1975.

6810 Solothurnmann, J. "An Open Talk with Herbie Hancock." Jazz Forum no. 34:42-48, April 1975.

6811 "Concert Reviews." Variety 278:61, April 9, 1975.

6812 "Herbie Hancock pour le Plaisir." Jazz Magazine no. 233:18-19, May-June 1975.

6813 Constant, D. "Hancock, Corea: Qu'est-ce qui les Fait Courir?" Jazz Magazine no. 235:20-21, August 1975.

6814 Hurwitz, R. "Jazz-Rock: Musical Artistry or Lucrative Copout?" High Fidelity/Musical America 25:62-63, September 1975.

6815 "Record Reviews: Herbie Hancock." down beat 42:32-34, September 11, 1975.

6816 "Around the World: Los Angeles." Coda no. 143:30, November 1975.

6817 "Concert Reviews." Variety 281:52, November 12, 1975.

6818 "Caught." down beat 42:34, December 4, 1975.

6819 "Talent in Action." Billboard 87:47, December 13, 1975.

6820 Stites, T. "Herbie Hancock." Jazz Magazine (U.S.) 1:15, no. 1, 1976.

6821 Ferdinand, V. "Electric, Ritual-Rhythm Juice, Ju-Ju Man--Herbie Hancock." Black Collegian 6:29, January-February 1976.

6822 Paihle, J. "Piano Miles." Jazz Hot no. 323:9-15, January 1976.

6823 "Records: Man-Child." Rolling Stone no. 204:53, January 15, 1976.

6824 Silvert, C. "Herbie Hancock: Man-Child in the Promised Land." Rolling Stone no. 205:15, January 29, 1976.

6825 Naura, M. "Herbie Hancock: Ausdruck des Ober Flaechlichen Ichs?" Jazz Podium 25:9-12, February 1976.

6826 "Axes of the Aces." Rolling Stone no. 206:55, February 12, 1976.

6827 "Herbie Splits Headhunters." down beat 43:9, April 8, 1976.

6828 "Caught in the Act." Melody Maker 51:26, August 14, 1976.

6829 "Reviews." Crescendo International 15:2, September 1976.

6830 "Herbie Hancock in Offenbach." Jazz Podium 25:20-21, October 1976.

6831 "Records: Secrets." Crawdaddy no. 66:70, November 1976.

6832 "Record Reviews: Secrets." down beat 43:18, November 18, 1976.

6833   Keepnews, P. "Notes: Hancock." Jazz Magazine (U.S.) 2:24, no.
       1, 1977.

6834   Giddins, G. "Herbie Hancock and the Electric-Piano Possibility."
       Esquire 87:134-135, January 1977.

6835   Lyons, L. "Herbie Vs. the Brain: 'Doin' It' Till You're Synthe-
       sized." Crawdaddy no. 68:24, January 1977.

6836   Davis, C. "Hancock + Watson = Musical Synthesis." Encore 6:34-
       35, January 17, 1977.

6837   Feather, L., et al. " A Time for Silver." Radio Free Jazz 18:14,
       March 1977. A celebration of Hancock's 25th anniversary in music.

6838   Lyons, L. "Piano Panorama: Insights into the Ivories." down beat
       44:18-19, March 10. 1977.

6839   Hancock, M. "Music in the Community: 80,000 Take Part in An-
       nual Festivals." Musicanada no. 32:10, May 1977.

6840   "Record Reviews: Chick Corea, Herbie Hancock, Keith Jarrett, Mc-
       Coy Tyner." down beat 44:22, May 5, 1977.

6841   "Miles into Jazz-Rock Territory." Jazz Journal International 30:12-
       14, June 1977. Review of the album "Water Babies."

6842   "Jazz Albums: V.S.O.P." Melody Maker 52:24, July 9, 1977.

6843   "Records: Chick Corea/Herbie Hancock/Keith Jarrett/McCoy Tyner."
       Crawdaddy no. 75:65, August 1977.

6844   "Records: V.S.O.P." Contemporary Keyboard 3:48, August 1977.

6845   "Record Reviews: V.S.O.P." down beat 44:23, August 11, 1977.

6846   Lyons, L. "Herbie Hancock's Fifth Incarnation." High Fidelity/
       Musical America 27:121-123, September 1977.

6847   Silvert, C. "Herbie Hancock--Revamping the Past, Creating the Fu-
       ture." down beat 44:16-17, September 8, 1977.

6848   Palmer, R. "Hancock's All-Star Reunion." Rolling Stone no. 249:28-
       29, October 6, 1977.

6849   Aikin, J. "Herbie Hancock: Producer David Rubinson." Contempor-
       ary Keyboard 3:29, November 1977.

6850   Milano, D. "Herbie Hancock: New Keyboards, New Music, New
       Techniques." Contemporary Keyboard 3:26-27, November 1977.

6851   Coleman, R. "Jazz Funk: Herbie Hancock: What's in a Label?"
       Melody Maker 52:10, December 24, 1977.

6852   "Reviews: Sunlight." Jazz Magazine (U.S.) 2:67-68, no. 4, 1978.

6853   Savicky, R. "Acoustic Duo on Tour: Corea and Hancock." Jazz
       Magazine (U.S.) 2:22, no. 3, 1978.

6854 Albertson, C. "A Very Special Quintet." Stereo Review 40:136, February 1978.

6855 Giddins, G. "Riffs: Hancock and Corea Electrify Acoustically." Village Voice 23:53, February 13, 1978.

6856 "Concert Reviews." Variety 290:64, February 15, 1978.

6857 "Talent in Action." Billboard 90:39, February 18, 1978.

6858 "Caught in the Act." Melody Maker 53:18, February 25, 1978.

6859 "Herbie Hancock & Chick Corea." Jazz Hot no. 347:8-13, March 1978.

6860 Harrison, E. "Hancock-Corea Tour Melds Two Forces." Billboard 90:36, March 4, 1978.

6861 Blumenthal, B. "Corea and Hancock: Dueling Pianos." Rolling Stone no. 261:27-28, March 23, 1978.

6862 Swenson, J. "Corea and Hancock Go Full Circle." Rolling Stone no. 261:76, March 23, 1978.

6863 "Jazz Live!" Jazz Journal International 31:31, April 1978.

6864 Liefland, W. "Europaeischer Piano-Zenith." Jazz Podium 27:18, April 1978.

6865 "Jazz en Direct." Jazz Magazine no. 264:7, May 1978.

6866 Cozzetti, R. "Herbie Hancock/Chick Corea: Paramount Northwest." down beat 45:33-34, May 4, 1978.

6867 Robbins, R. J. "Live Reviews from the States." Crescendo International 16:8, June 1978.

6868 Tiegel, E. "Hancock Sings, More or Less; Uses Vocoder on 'Sunlight' LP." Billboard 90:94, June 24, 1978.

6869 "Records--Jazz: Sunlight." High Fidelity/Musical America 28:142, September 1978.

6870 Albertson, C. "Herbie Hancock." Stereo Review 41:106-108, November 1978.

6871 "Musicware." Crawdaddy p. 96, November 1978.

HANDY, WILLIAM CHRISTOPHER, 1873-1958.

6872 Scarborough, D. "The 'Blues' as Folksongs." Texas Folklore Society Publications no. 2:52-66, 1923.

6873 Handy, William Christopher. Negro Authors and Composers of the United States. New York: AMS Press, 1976. Reprint of the 1938? edition published by Handy Bros. Music Co., New York.

6874 Fellowes, M. H. "Heart of the Blues." Etude 58:152, March 1940.

6875   Handy, William Christopher. Father of the Blues; An Autobiogra-
       phy of W. C. Handy. Edited by Arna Bontemps. New York: Mac-
       millan, 1941.

6876   _____. "Father of the Blues; Autobiography." Scholastic 40:21-
       22, February 9, 1942. An excerpt from Handy's book of the same
       name.

6877   _____. Unsung Americans Sung. New York: n.p., 1944. "Prin-
       cipally biographical sketches of prominent Negroes, with music
       written about them." Includes music.

6878   "St. Louis Honors Handy for Famous Blues Tune." Variety 174:1,
       May 25, 1949.

6879   Burton, J. "Honor Roll of Popular Songwriters: No. 30--William
       C. Handy." Billboard 61:63, July 30, 1949 Supplement.

6880   "About W. C. Handy." Music Journal 8:32-33, November 1950.

6881   Borneman, E. "A Letter from the Days When Jazz Was King."
       Melody Maker 27:3, August 11, 1951.

6882   "Handy Back to Beale St. to Plug Football Game with Old Jazz Side-
       men." Variety 184:50, December 5, 1951.

6883   Souchon, E. "W. C. Handy: An Enigma." Record Changer 11:3-4,
       May 1952.

6884   "W. C. Handy Cuts LP for Archives." down beat 19:14, May 21,
       1952.

6885   Handy, William Christopher. "Wyer Was Wrong." down beat 19:8,
       May 21, 1952.

6886   Borneman, E. "Handy in Cuba." Melody Maker 28:5, August 23,
       1952.

6887   "Letter from William C. Handy." Negro History Bulletin 16:13, Oc-
       tober 1952.

6888   Roy, J. H. "Where There's a Will; Story." Negro History Bulletin
       16:66, December 1952.

6889   "Handy Likes Ike." Negro History Bulletin 16:117-118, February
       1953.

6890   Morrison, A. "W. C. Handy: Broadway's Grand Old Man of Music."
       Ebony 9:59-62, November 1953.

6891   Hentoff, N. "A Visit with W. C. Handy: At 80, a Link with the
       Past." down beat 20:3, December 30, 1953.

6892   Handy, William Christopher. "From Minstrel Songs to 'St. Louis
       Blues.'" Variety 196:51, October 20, 1954.

6893   "Just Like Old Times." Time 65:47, June 13, 1955.

6894   Allen, W. C. "St. Louis Blues." Jazz Journal 8:24, November
       1955.

6895   "Surgery for W. C. Handy." down beat 23:9, February 8, 1956.

6896   Handy, William Christopher. "An Explanation of the 'Blues.'" Mu-
       sic Journal 15:8-9, November-December 1957.

6897   "Honor 'Father of the Blues.'" Billboard 69:1, November 18, 1957.

6898   Green, A. "Show Biz Salutes W. C. Handy." Variety 208:2, No-
       vember 20, 1957.

6899   "How Handy Wrote the Blues." Ebony 13:69-70, December 1957.

6900   "Two for Number 84." down beat 24:7, December 26, 1957.

6901   "Father of the Blues." Record Research 3:3, March-April 1958.

6902   Platt, D. "Handy Archives '1956.'" Record Research 3:3, March-
       April 1958.

6903   ["Obituary."] Orkester Journalen 26:6, April 1958.

6904   "Father of Blues Just Misses His 'St. Louis' Biopic." Variety 210:1,
       April 2, 1958.

6905   ["Obituary."] Variety 210:68, April 2, 1958.

6906   Cerulli, D. "W. C. Handy's Story of the Blues." down beat 25:15-
       16, April 3, 1958.

6907   Tynan, J. "St. Louis Blues." down beat 25:13-14, April 3, 1958.

6908   "Father of the Blues." Melody Maker 33:3, April 5, 1958.

6909   Jones, M. "This World of Jazz." Melody Maker 33:10, April 5,
       1958.

6910   Sinclair, C. "'St. Louis Blues' Fine Handy Epitaph." Billboard
       70:7, April 7, 1958.

6911   Lyttelton, H. "The Father of the Blues." Melody Maker 33:4, April
       12, 1958.

6912   "End on a Blue Note; Jazzman W. C. Handy Is Given a Musical Fu-
       neral." Life 44:109-110, April 14, 1958.

6913   Lyttleton, H. "The Paradox of W. C. Handy." Melody Maker 33:4,
       April 19, 1958.

6914   ["Obituary."] International Musician 56:32, May 1958; down beat 25:11,
       May 1, 1958.

6915   Traill, S. "St. Louis Blues; The Story of W. C. Handy--Father of
       the Blues." Jazz Journal 11:9-10, May 1958.

6916   Cole, Nat King. "I'm Proud of This Picture." Melody Maker 33:3,
       May 24, 1958. Refers to the film about Handy: "St. Louis Blues."

6917 "Evening Sun Goes Down." Ebony 13:96-98, June 1958.

6918 Wellstood, D. "W. C. Handy Blues." Jazz Review 1:34-35, December 1958.

6919 "Ebony Hall of Fame." Ebony 14:61-63, February 1959.

6920 "Eight Foot Tall Statue of Handy to Be Placed in Memphis, Tenn.; Handy Park, May 1, 1960." Jet p. 58, May 5, 1960.

6921 "W. C. Handy Memorial, an 8 Foot Bronze Statue, Dedicated in Handy Park, Memphis, Tenn." Jet p. 60, May 19, 1960.

6922 Hardin, G. E. "Mr. Handy's Beale Street." Sepia 8:24-28, July 1960.

6923 Walsh, J. "50th Anni. of Handy's First Blues." Variety 220:62, October 5, 1960.

6924 Smith, N. "Der Vater des Blues." Musikhandel 12:66, no. 2, 1961.

6925 Blau, George. "W. C. Handy." Music Memories 3:16-18, no. 2, 1963.

6926 Testoni, G. "Il Mondo del Blues." Musica Jazz 20:11-12, January 1964; 20:21-23, March 1964.

6927 "Polls: Tales of Mr. Crump." Melody Maker 41:8, March 26, 1966.

6928 Godwin, H. E. "Where de Southern Cross de Yellow Dog." Second Line 17:112, September-October 1966.

6929 Hutton, J. "Now Handy Takes the Flower Road." Melody Maker 42:6, August 5, 1967.

6930 Montgomery, Elizabeth Rider. William C. Handy, Father of the Blues. Champaign, Ill.: Garrard Publishing Co., 1968. Juvenile literature.

6931 Leonard, A. G. "Handy Stamp." Jazz Journal 21:25, December 1968.

6932 "American Society of Composers, Authors and Publishers." National Music Council Bulletin 29:24-25, no. 3, 1969.

6933 "U.S. Honors W. C. Handy." ASCAP Today 3:9, no. 1, 1969. A postage stamp depicting Handy will commemorate his music.

6934 "W. C. Handy." ASCAP Today 3:4-8, no. 2, 1969.

6935 Wolf, J. Q. "Aunt Caroline Dye: The Gypsy in the 'St. Louis Blues.'" Southern Folklore Quarterly 33:339-346, no. 4, 1969.

6936 "Memphis Sets Memorial Concert for W. C. Handy; Proceeds to Aid Studies." Variety 254:57, February 19, 1969.

6937 "Davis Eulogizes Handy." Billboard 81:MS30, March 29, 1969.

6938 Williams, B. "Home of Blues and Soul." Billboard 81:MS3-4, March 29, 1969.

6939 "A 6-Cents Postage Stamp Depicting W. C. Handy." Journal of Negro History 54:212, April 1969.

6940 "His Widow Accepts W. C. Handy Commemorative Stamps in Memphis, Tenn." Jet 36:36, June 5, 1969.

6941 Williams, B. "Memphis, Handy Fests Coupled." Billboard 81:6, June 7, 1969.

6942 "W. C. Handy Fest Sings the Blues in Memphis; In the Red for $15,000." Variety 255:73, June 11, 1969.

6943 Levine, H. "Gershwin, Handy and the Blues." Clavier 9:10-20, no. 7, 1970.

6944 "Muscle Shoals Honors W. C. Handy." Billboard 82:46, December 5, 1970.

6945 "Handy Home Museum." ASCAP Today 5:21, no. 1, 1971.

6946 Kay, G. W. "William Christopher Handy, Father of the Blues--a History of Published Blues." Jazz Journal 24:10-12, March 1971.

6947 Traill, S. "Editorial." Jazz Journal 24:1, March 1971.

6948 Rossi, N. "Father of the Blues." Music Journal 29:24-26, May 1971.

6949 Neal, L. "The Ethos of the Blues." Black Scholar 3:42-48, Summer 1972.

6950 "Stamps of Musical Interest." Musical Opinion 95:521, July 1972.

6951 "99th Anni. of W. C. Handy at Riverdale Library." Variety 269:65, November 22, 1972.

6952 Wayne, Bennett. 3 Jazz Greats. Champaign, Ill.: Garrard Pub. Co., 1972. Juvenile literature concerning Duke Ellington, Louis Armstrong, and W. C. Handy.

6953 "Handy Portrait 1st Black to Hang in Tenn. Capitol." Jet 43:55, March 15, 1973.

6954 "W. C. Handy Centennial Honored with Concerts, Shows." Music Trades 121:18, December 1973.

6955 "W. C. Handy, Bessie Smith Honored." down beat 40:10, December 20, 1973.

6956 Starks, G. L. "Tribute to W. C. Handy and the Blues Tradition." Black World 23:49-50, April 1974.

6957 Lucas, J. "Bicentennial Canticles." Second Line 28:7-8, Summer 1976.

6958   "Concert Reviews." Variety 283:52, June 2, 1976. Review of a
       concert in the District of Columbia in honor of Handy.

6959   Dobie, W. "Not All Jazz Historians Remember W. C. Handy's 1928
       Carnegie Concert." Swinging Newsletter 8:5, no. 35, 1978.

6960   Lucas, J. "Music of the Mississippi." Second Line 30:28-29, Win-
       ter 1978.

HARDAWAY, STEVELAND JUDKINS   see   WONDER, STEVIE

HARDIN, LIL   see   ARMSTRONG, LIL HARDIN

HAYTON, MRS. LENNIE   see   HORNE, LENA

HENDRYX, NONA   see   LABELLE

HINES, EARL KENNETH (Fatha), 1905- .

6961   "Hines to Form Own Full Band." down beat 16:1, March 25, 1949.

6962   Jones, M., and S. Traill. "Corner Scoops World on 1930 Armstrong
       Disc." Melody Maker 25:9, November 19, 1959.

6963   Traill, S. "Fatha's Back for Xmas!" Melody Maker 25:6, December
       17, 1949.

6964   "Tidig Svart Swing." Orkester Journalen 18:14-15, September 1950.

6965   Pease, S. A. "Earl Hines the 'Dean of U.S. Dance Pianists.'"
       down beat 17:12, November 3, 1950.

6966   "Lightly and Politely." Jazz Journal 4:7-8, April 1951.

6967   Hobson, W. "Hits and Misses." Saturday Review of Literature 34:56,
       June 30, 1951.

6968   Whiston, H. F. "Soon I'll Be Leaving Louis to Record with My Own
       Band ... Says Earl Hines." Melody Maker 27:3, October 6, 1951.

6969   Traill, S. "Requiem for the All Stars." Jazz Journal 4:1-2, Decem-
       ber 1951.

6970   Gleason, R. J. "Though Already a Legend, Earl Hines Is Still a
       Provocative, Influential Pianist." down beat 19:2, February 8,
       1952.

6971   Freeman, D. "We'll Get Along Without Hines' Ego, Says Armstrong."
       down beat 19:3, February 22, 1952.

6972   "Never Had Any Hassels with Louis, Says Hines." down beat 19:3,
       March 21, 1952.

6973 "Hines Has 57 Varieties of Moods--from Dixie to Bop." down beat
      19:12, July 30, 1952.

6974 "Band Review." Variety 189:41, February 25, 1953.

6975 "Caught in the Act." down beat 20:4, April 8, 1953.

6976 "Public Sated by TV, Wants Bands: Hines." down beat 20:2, May
      20, 1953.

6977 Hines, Earl. "Chasing a Fast Dollar." Melody Maker 29:3, July 11,
      1953.

6978 _____. "The Jazz Scene Today." down beat 20:6, July 15, 1953.

6979 Feather, L. "Fatha Digs Tatum, Nixes Brubeck." down beat 20:19,
      September 23, 1953.

6980 Kenton, S. "Kenton Talking." Melody Maker 29:9, December 12,
      1953.

6981 "Fatha Plans to Start a 'New Sound' Ork." down beat 21:3, May 19,
      1954.

6982 "Crescendo, Hollywood." Variety 195:52, June 30, 1954.

6983 "'Recording Artists' Roster." down beat 21:105, June 30, 1954.

6984 "Hines Preems Newest Band." down beat 21:5, July 14, 1954.

6985 Eckstine, B. "Bird Blew in His Socks!" Melody Maker 30:3, August
      14, 1954.

6986 _____. "When Sarah Vaughan Began to Sing." Melody Maker 30:5,
      August 21, 1954.

6987 Dance, S. "Fatha's Back." Melody Maker 30:4, December 25, 1954.

6988 "The Father!" Metronome 71:21, January 1955.

6989 "Lightly and Politely." Jazz Journal 8:26, June 1955.

6990 Jepsen, J. G. "Jazzens Instrumentalister: Pianot." Orkester Jour-
      nalen 23:12, September 1955.

6991 Dance, S. "He Played Trumpet on the Piano." Melody Maker 31:5,
      December 17, 1955.

6992 Hines, Earl. "Piano Man." Jazz Journal 9:3-4, December 1956.

6993 Coss, B. "Jazz Pianists and the Jazz Piano." Jazz Today 2:18,
      March 1957.

6994 Wilson, J. S. "Jazz Pianists; A Discography." High Fidelity 7:66,
      August 1957.

6995 "This Is a Wonderful Chance." Melody Maker 32:2-3, September 28,
      1957.

6996 "Earl 'Fatha' Hines." Jazz Journal 10:1, October 1957.

6997 Dance, S. "The Season Opens." Jazz Journal 10:24-26, November
      1957. Hines' concert in London is reviewed.

6998 "Fatha Speaks." Jazz Journal 11:28-29, April 1958.

6999 Hadlock, R. "Fatha Knows Best." down beat 25:19, October 30,
      1958.

7000 Waterman, G. "Earl Hines-Cozy Cole: Earl's 'Backroom' and Cozy's
      'Caravan.'" Jazz Review 2:22, June 1959.

7001 "Combo Review." Variety 216:62, November 11, 1959.

7002 Morgenstern, D. "Three Giants." Jazz Journal 13:16, February
      1960.

7003 Dance, S. "Earl's Four." Jazz Journal 13:9-10, July 1960.

7004 _____. "Earl Hines: Aspects of a Jazz Genius." Metronome
      77:20-21, September 1960.

7005 Hadlock, D. "Earl Hines on Bird." Jazz Review 3:12-13, Novem-
      ber 1960.

7006 Erskine, G. M. "Caught in the Act." down beat 28:46, February
      2, 1961.

7007 "Earl Hines' Sentimental Journey." Ebony 16:96-98, July 1961.

7008 Coss, B. "Jazz Piano--Three Fountainheads." down beat 28:16-17,
      October 26, 1961.

7009 Hobson, W. "The Amen Corner." Saturday Review 45:54-55, Jan-
      uary 27, 1962.

7010 Harrison, M. "Backlog Eleven--Earl Hines." Jazz Monthly 8:9-10,
      July 1962.

7011 "57th Birthday Celebrated by Earl 'Fatha' Hines on December 28th,
      1962." Second Line 14:10, no. 1-2, 1963.

7012 Hoefer, G. "Earl Hines in the 1940's." down beat 30:25, April 25,
      1963.

7013 Wilson, R. "Bringing Up 'Fatha.'" down beat 30:18-19, June 6,
      1963.

7014 "Annuaire Biographique du Piano." Jazz Magazine 9:28, November
      1963.

7015 Balliett, W. "Jazz Concerts; Third of Jazz on Broadway Series at
      Little Theatre." New Yorker 40:159-162, March 14, 1964.

7016 Dance, S. "Lightly & Politely." Jazz Journal 17:16-18, April 1964.

7017 Williams, M. "Earl Hines in Renaissance." Listen 1:21, May-June
      1964.

7018 Dance, S. "Jazz." Music Journal 22:69-70, May 1964.

7019 "The Perennial Hines." Jazz 4:12, no. 4, 1965.

7020 Balliett, W. "Rhythm in My Mind." New Yorker 40:39-42, January 2, 1965.

7021 _____. "Jazz; Concerts at Village Vanguard Performed by E. Hines, C. Hawkins, and C. Mingus." New Yorker 41:174, March 27, 1965.

7022 Feather, L. "Earl Without Honour." Melody Maker 40:6, March 27, 1965.

7023 Balliet, W. "Earl 'Fatha' Hines." Jazz Journal 18:4-9, April 1965.

7024 Reda, J. "Hines Toujours." Jazz Magazine no. 117:9, April 1965.

7025 Traill, S. "Editorial." Jazz Journal 18:3, April 1965.

7026 Hines--the One-Man Band of the Piano." Melody Maker 40:11, April 10, 1965.

7027 "My First Love? Big Bands." Melody Maker 40:6, April 17, 1965.

7028 Chevalier, L. "Le 'Pere' à Pacra." Jazz Hot no. 209:3-4, May 1965.

7029 Dahlgren, R. "En Levande Jazzlegend." Orkester Journalen 33:7, May 1965.

7030 Stevens, A. "Earl Hines and the Alan Hare Big Band." Jazz Journal 18:22-23, May 1965.

7031 Morgenstern, D. "Monitoring Hawk and Hines." down beat 32:22, May 6, 1965.

7032 "Hines Honored; On Jazz Mission." Billboard 77:22, May 29, 1965.

7033 Dance, S. "Earl in a Whirl." Jazz Journal 18:12, June 1965.

7034 Ioakimidis, D. "Lu, Vu, Entendu." Jazz Hot no. 210:6, June 1965.

7035 Lambert, G. E. "Earl Hines in Manchester." Jazz Monthly 11:17-18, June 1965.

7036 Traill, S. "Editorial." Jazz Journal 18:3, June 1965. Discussion of Hines' England tour.

7037 Williams, M. "Rediscovery of Earl Hines." Saturday Review 48:59, June 26, 1965.

7038 "Village Vanguard, N.Y." Variety 239:63, June 30, 1965.

7039 Boujut, M. "Au Nom du Pere." Jazz Magazine no. 120:53-55, July 1965.

7040 "Hines Triumph." International Musician 64:23, July 1965.

7041 Reda, J. "Earl au Studio." Jazz Magazine no. 120:17-18, July
      1965.

7042 Hentoff, N. "'Fatha' Hines: Still the Master Improviser." HiFi/
      Stereo Review 15:64, August 1965. Review of Hines' album "Spon-
      taneous Explorations."

7043 Dance, S. "Caught in the Act." down beat 32:35, August 26, 1965.

7044 Morgenstern, D. "Today's Life with Fatha Hines." down beat 32:25-
      27, August 26, 1965.

7045 Niquet, B. "Earl Hines Encores!" Jazz Hot no. 213:8, October
      1965.

7046 Stewart-Baxter, D. "The Distinguished Visitors, Hines-Braff." Jazz
      Journal 18:22-23, October 1965.

7047 "Life with Fatha; Comeback Trial." Newsweek 66:108, October 18,
      1965.

7048 "Ambassadors to Russia." Jazz 5:13, no. 9, 1966.

7049 Jepsen, J. G. "Earl Hines 1965 aars Jazzmusiker." Orkester Jour-
      nalen 34:8-9, January 1966.

7050 "Earl Hines on Topps." Matrix no. 63:7, February 1966.

7051 "Fatha at the Gate." Jazz Journal 19:24, February 1966.

7052 Hines, Earl. "In My Opinion." Jazz Journal 19:7-8, March 1966.

7053 "Earl Hines: A New Career at Sixty for the Reluctant Soloist."
      Melody Maker 41:6, March 19, 1966.

7054 "Fatha Co-operates." Jazz Journal 19:16, May 1966.

7055 Lambert, G. E. "Earl Hines in Liverpool." Jazz Monthly 12:9,
      May 1966.

7056 "State Dept. Sets Hines for Russian Tour." down beat 33:12, May 5,
      1966.

7057 Cullaz, M. "Earl Hines à Paris." Jazz Hot no. 221:7, June 1966.

7058 "U.S. Visitors." Storyville no. 5:2, June 1966.

7059 "Fatha Knows Best." Time 88:72, August 5, 1966.

7060 Dance, S. "Caught in the Act." down beat 33:34-35, August 11,
      1966.

7061 "The Long, Hard Road." down beat 33:11, August 11, 1966. Hines
      on tour in Georgia, U.S.S.R.

7062 Dance, S. "Fatha in Russia." Jazz Journal 19:24, September 1966.

7063 "Earl Hines en Russie." Jazz Magazine no. 135:15, October 1966.

7064 "London House, Chi." Variety 244:67, October 12, 1966.

7065 Zwerin, M. "You're Not Going to Like This, but...." down beat 33:18-19, November 3, 1966.

7066 Feather, L. "Roubles et Troubles." Jazz Magazine no. 138:17-18, January 1967.

7067 Morgenstern, D. "Caught in the Act." down beat 34:23, January 12, 1967.

7068 "Shepheard's, N.Y." Variety 246:101, April 19, 1967.

7069 "Riverboat, N.Y." Variety 247:54, May 24, 1967.

7070 "Earl Hines Signs Lifetime Contract." down beat 34:13-14, June 29, 1967.

7071 "At the Riverboat Again." Jazz Journal 20:15-16, July 1967.

7072 "Al Hirt's Club, N.O." Variety 247:55, July 12, 1967.

7073 "Un Contrat pour Fatha." Jazz Magazine no. 145:14, August 1967.

7074 Larrabee, E. "Golden Autumn of Fatha Hines." Harper's Magazine 235:97-99, August 1967.

7075 Dance, S. "Jazz." Music Journal 25:92, September 1967.

7076 _____. "Fatha Hines, Meet Papa Haydn...." down beat 34:14, October 19, 1967.

7077 Bessom, M. E. "Earl Hines and His Trumpet-Style Piano." Jazz and Pop 7:30-32, January 1968.

7078 Williams, M. "The Grand Return of Earl Hines." International Musician 66:4, March 1968.

7079 Dance, S. "Shine on, Father Hines." Jazz Journal 21:9-10, April 1968.

7080 Lambert, E. "Quality Jazz." Jazz Journal 21:33, October 1968.

7081 Kington, M. "Second Opinion." Melody Maker 43:8, November 2, 1968.

7082 Traill, S. "Jazz in Britain." Jazz Journal 21:18, December 1968.

7083 Arvanitas, G., et al. "Panorama des Pianistes." Jazz Hot no. 246:28, January 1969.

7084 Dance, S. "Lightly & Politely." Jazz Journal 22:10, January 1969. Lists Hines' band members during 1934-1935.

7085 _____. "Noblesse Oblige; Jazz Nobility on Tour." International Musician 67:24, January 1969.

7086 Darlays, P. "Hines Toujours Vivant." Jazz Magazine no. 162:15, January 1969.

7087   Mattsson, L. "Traakigt naer Idoler Spricker." Orkester Journalen
       37:5, January 1969.

7088   Williams, M. "Further Notes of an LP Listener." down beat 36:15,
       May 1, 1969.

7089   Dance, S. "Ellington at the White House." Saturday Review 52:49,
       May 31, 1969.

7090   _____. "Musical Banquet." Jazz Journal 22:3, September 1969.

7091   _____. "Fatha's Day in Frisco." down beat 36:8, October 2,
       1969.

7092   Albertson, C., et al. "Record Reviews." down beat 36:21-22, Oc-
       tober 30, 1969.

7093   Dance, S. "Lightly & Politely." Jazz Journal 22:8-9, November
       1969.

7094   "Plaza 9, N.Y." Variety 257:56, December 17, 1969.

7095   Miller, M. "Geben Sie Bewegungsfreiheit, Sire! Subjektive Bemer-
       kungen zu Drei Jazz-Festivals." Neue Musikzeitung 19:9, no. 6,
       1970-1971.

7096   "Disques du Mois: Earl Hines Plays Fats Waller." Jazz Magazine
       no. 177:42, April 1970.

7097   Morh, S. H. "A Monday Date par Earl 'Fatha' Hines." Jazz Hot
       no. 263:12-15, Summer 1970.

7098   "Club Atlantis, Atlanta." Variety 259:49, July 1, 1970.

7099   "La Chronique des Disques: Earl Hines Plays Fats Waller." Jazz
       Hot no. 264:40, September 1970.

7100   Mitchell, S. "Concord Cornucopia." down beat 37:16, October 29,
       1970.

7101   Carriere, C. "Newport à Paris: Jazz au T.N.P." Jazz Hot no.
       267:7, December 1970.

7102   Gerber, A. "Newport à Paris." Jazz Magazine no. 184:57, Decem-
       ber 1970.

7103   "In Person." Jazz Monthly no. 190:8-10, December 1970.

7104   Jones, M. "Caught in the Act." Melody Maker 45:27, December
       5, 1970.

7105   _____. "Fatha Knows Best." Melody Maker 45:20, December 12,
       1970.

7106   "Earl Hines at Home." Jazz Report 7:18, no. 6, 1971.

7107   Kramer, E. "Record Reviews: Quintessential Recording Session."
       Coda 10:22, no. 2, 1971.

7108 Callagham, P. "La Chronique des Disques: At the Apex Club." Jazz Hot no. 268:36-37, January 1971.

7109 McRae, B. "A B Basics; A Column for the Newcomer to Jazz." Jazz Journal 24:15, January 1971.

7110 "Reeditions: Snappy Rhythm." Jazz Magazine no. 185:48-49, January 1971.

7111 Strassberg, P. "Talent in Action." Billboard 83:24, January 23, 1971.

7112 Stewart-Baxter, D. "Record Reviews: Swinging in Chicago." Jazz Journal 24:35, February 1971.

7113 Laverdure, M. "Reeditions: Earl Hines and His Orchestra." Jazz Magazine no. 187:41-42, March 1971.

7114 Morgenstern, D. "Record Reviews: A Monday Date; Quintessential Recording Session." down beat 38:24, March 4, 1971.

7115 "Jazz Records: Swinging in Chicago." Melody Maker 46:34, March 20, 1971.

7116 Gerber, A. "Disques du Mois: Earl Hines in Paris." Jazz Magazine no. 189:42-43, May 1971.

7117 Traill, S. "Earl Hines and Marva Josie." Jazz Journal 24:2-3, May 1971.

7118 Ramsey, D. "Record Reviews: Earl Hines at Home." down beat 38:22, May 13, 1971.

7119 "Landmark, K.C." Variety 263:71, May 19, 1971.

7120 Traill, S. "Record Reviews: Tea for Two." Jazz Journal 24:37, June 1971.

7121 Jones, M. "Jazz Records: Tea for Two." Melody Maker 46:28, June 5, 1971.

7122 Sportis, F. "Contribution à la Connaissance des Maitres du Jazz: Earl Hines." Points du Jazz no. 5:49-84, September 1971.

7123 Traill, S. "Record Reviews: Blues & Things." Jazz Journal 24:30, October 1971.

7124 Dance, S. "Hines Reunited with Old Chicago Sidemen." down beat 38:11, October 14, 1971.

7125 Traill, S. "Record Reviews: At Home." Jazz Journal 24:30, November 1971.

7126 "Record Reviews: Live at the Overseas Press Club." Coda 10:18-19, no. 9, 1972.

7127 "Record Reviews: My Tribute to Louis." Coda 10:16, no. 9, 1972.

7128   "La Chronique des Disques: The Indispensable Earl Hines, Vol. 1:
       1929-1939." <u>Jazz Hot</u> no. 279:32, January 1972.

7129   "Disques du Mois: The Indispensable Earl Hines/Volume 1." <u>Jazz
       Magazine</u> no. 198:27-28, March 1972.

7130   "Handful of Records: Fatha & His Flock on Tour." <u>Points du Jazz</u>
       no. 6:137-138, March 1972.

7131   Gilmore, M. S. "Caught in the Act." <u>down beat</u> 39:29, March 30,
       1972.

7132   "Chronique des Disques: Fatha and His Flock on Tour." <u>Jazz Hot</u>
       no. 282:29, April 1972.

7133   Balliett, W. "Jazz Records." <u>New Yorker</u> 48:123-126, May 6, 1972.

7134   Dance, S. "Jazz." <u>Music Journal</u> 30:22, June 1972.

7135   "Record Reviews: Hines '65; My Tribute to Louis." <u>down beat</u> 39:20-
       21, June 8, 1972.

7136   "Record Reviews: Earl Hines and Maxine Sullivan." <u>down beat</u> 39:22,
       December 7, 1972.

7137   Dance, S. "Lightly & Politely." <u>Jazz Journal</u> 26:14-16, May, 1973.

7138   "Caught in the Act." <u>down beat</u> 40:34, June 7, 1973.

7139   "Concerts by the Sea, L.A." <u>Variety</u> 271:55, June 13, 1973.

7140   "Michael's Pub, N.Y." <u>Variety</u> 272:39, August 15, 1973.

7141   "Record Reviews: Hines Does Hoagy." <u>down beat</u> 40:22, August 16,
       1973.

7142   Dance, S. "Lightly & Politely." <u>Jazz Journal</u> 26:16-17, September
       1973.

7143   "On Record: Earl Hines Plays Duke Ellington; Tour de Force."
       <u>Jazz & Blues</u> 3:19-20, December 1973.

7144   Elias, M. "Dr. John Newman: Lost in Obscurity--Ex-Pittsburgh
       Bandleader Gives His View on Hines--Deppe Gennetts." <u>IAJRC
       Journal</u> 7:14-17, no. 3, 1974.

7145   Dance, S. "Earl 'Fatha' Hines." <u>Stereo Review</u> 32:76-82, January
       1974.

7146   "Talent in Action." <u>Billboard</u> 86:9, January 5, 1974.

7147   "Michael's Pub, N.Y." <u>Variety</u> 274:71, March 20, 1974.

7148   "Quelques Grands Pianistes." <u>Jazz Hot</u> no. 305:11, May 1974.

7149   Nevers, D. "Earl Hines Portrait d'un Piano Bien Tempere." <u>Jazz
       Hot</u> no. 307:10-13, July-August 1974.

7150   "Caught in the Act." <u>Melody Maker</u> 49:26, December 7, 1974.

7151 "Hines: Stretching Out a Little." Melody Maker 49:56, December 7, 1974.

7152 "Caught." down beat 41:37, December 19, 1974.

7153 Feather, L. "Blindfold Test." down beat 42:33, January 16, 1975.

7154 Dance, S. "Lightly & Politely." Jazz Journal 28:10, April 1975.

7155 "Schallplattenbesprechungen: Young Earl Hines--1929 Complete Recordings." Jazz Podium 24:36, May 1975.

7156 "Tropicana, Las Vegas." Variety 279:85, May 28, 1975.

7157 "Earl Hines." Jazz Magazine no. 234:28-29, July 1975.

7158 "Rainbow Grill, N.Y." Variety 279:67, July 2, 1975.

7159 "Heard and Seen." Coda no. 141:35, September 1975.

7160 "Schallplatten Besprechungen: Tour de Force Encore." Jazz Podium 24:36, September 1975.

7161 "Talent in Action." Billboard 87:38, November 1, 1975.

7162 Horton, J. "Life with Fatha at 70." Sepia 24:70-76, December 1975.

7163 "Ivory Action in Triplicate." down beat 42:11, December 18, 1975.

7164 Lyles, T. "Jazz Great Earl Hines on Discipline." Jazz Forum no. 43:20-23, 1976.

7165 "Record Reviews: Duet!" Jazz Forum no. 41:62-63, 1976.

7166 "Jazz Records: West Side Story." Melody Maker 51:26, January 3, 1976.

7167 James, B. "Fatha on the Box." Jazz Journal 29:16, February 1976.

7168 "Lightly and Politely: Fatha's 70." Jazz Journal 29:13, February 1976.

7169 Renninger, C. "Earl Hines: Always Exploring." Radio Free Jazz 17:8, March 1976.

7170 Wilson, J. S. "From the Smithsonian: Perspective on King Oliver, Hines, and Satchmo." High Fidelity/Musical America 26:140, April 1976.

7171 "LP's: Blues & Things." Living Blues no. 27:38-39, May-June 1976.

7172 "Record Reviews: Armstrong and Hines, 1928." down beat 43:30-31, May 20, 1976.

7173 Dance, S. "Lightly & Politely; Fatha at the White House." Jazz Journal 29:24, July 1976.

7174 Miller, S., and B. Rusch. "Chattin' with the Fatha." Cadence 1:3-4, August 1976.

7175   Vance, J. "The 1938 Collaborations of Louis Armstrong and Earl
       Hines." Stereo Review 37:88, August 1976.

7176   "Records: Louis Armstrong and Earl Hines--1928." Creem 8:71,
       October 1976.

7177   "Record Reviews: Louis Armstrong and Earl Hines." Coda no.
       152:21-22, December 1976.

7178   Dance, Stanley. The World of Earl Hines. New York: Scribner,
       1977.

7179   "Record Reviews: Live at the Downtown Club, the Statler Hilton,
       Buffalo." Radio Free Jazz 18:15, January 1977.

7180   "Record Reviews: At the Village Vanguard." Coda no. 154:18,
       March-April 1977.

7181   "Record Reviews: Dinah." Jazz Journal 30:33, March 1977.

7182   Colombe, G. "Side by Side." Jazz Journal 30:26-27, April 1977.
       Hines and Art Tatum are compared.

7183   "Record Reviews: At Saralee's." Jazz Journal 30:30, April 1977.

7184   Smith, A. J. "Voyage of the Jammed." down beat 44:17-18, Au-
       gust 11, 1977.

7185   "Record Reviews: Jazz Is His Old Lady & My Old Man." Jazz Jour-
       nal International 30:39, September 1977.

7186   "Record Reviews: The Giants." Jazz Journal International 30:37,
       September 1977.

7187   Youngren, W. "National Public Radio." New Republic 177:23, Sep-
       tember 24, 1977.

7188   "Record Reviews: Swingin' Away." Jazz Journal International 30:45,
       October 1977.

7189   Dance, S. "Earl 'Fatha' Hines: More than Fifty Years of Great
       Jazz Piano." Contemporary Keyboard 3:14-15, November 1977.

7190   Feather, L. "Piano Giants of Jazz: Earl 'Fatha' Hines." Contem-
       porary Keyboard 3:55, November 1977.

7191   "Jazz Albums: Jazz Is His Old Lady." Melody Maker 52:34, Novem-
       ber 12, 1977.

7192   "Record Reviews: Earl Hines Plays George Gershwin." down beat
       44:28-29, December 1, 1977.

7193   DeMuth, J. "Notes: Chicago." Jazz Magazine (U.S.) 2:17, no. 2,
       1978.

7194   "Record Reviews: Solo Walk in Tokyo." down beat 45:28, January
       26, 1978.

7195   "Caught in the Act." Melody Maker 53:66, April 15, 1978.

7196 "Ronnie Scott's Ldn." Variety 290:85, May 3, 1978.

7197 "Jazz Live!" Jazz Journal International 31:36, June 1978.

7198 "Record Reviews: Earl Hines Plays Duke Ellington, Vol. 4." Coda
      no. 162:21, August 1, 1978.

7199 Vance, J. "Ry Cooder, Earl Hines, and Others Have Some Shame-
      less Fun with Feel-Good Jazz." Stereo Review 41:103, September
      1978.

HOLIDAY, BILLIE (Lady Day; Eleanor Gough McKay; Eleanora Fagan),
      1915-1959.

7200 "Billie, Manager Face 3 Assault Counts in Fight." down beat 16:1,
      January 28, 1949.

7201 "Billie Holiday Rap Hypoes Frisco B.O." Variety 173:43, February
      2, 1949.

7202 "Billie, Berg's Sued in Melee." down beat 16:8, February 25, 1949.

7203 "Billie, Levy Arrested on Opium Count." down beat 16:5, February
      25, 1949.

7204 Ulanov, B. "The Real Villains." Metronome 65:42, March 1949.

7205 "Acquit Billie Holiday on Opium Charge." Variety 174:51, June 8,
      1949.

7206 "Billie Holiday Put on Trial over Drugs." Billboard 61:4, June 11,
      1949.

7207 "I'm Cured for Good." Ebony 4:26-32, July 1949.

7208 "Broke, Alone, Billie Goes Back to Work." down beat 16:3, July 15,
      1949.

7209 Feather, L. "Lady Day Has Her Say." Metronome 66:16, February
      1950.

7210 "Billie Holiday." Metronome 66:27, May 1950.

7211 Torme, M. "Of Singing and Singers." Metronome 66:22, May 1950.

7212 "Billie in Hassel in Frisco Again." down beat 17:1, November 17,
      1950.

7213 Ulanov, B. "History of Jazz." Metronome 67:17, September 1951.

7214 Hentoff, N. "Billie Holiday, Now Remarried, Finds Happiness, a
      New Sense of Security." down beat 19:2, January 11, 1952.

7215 "How I Blew a Million Dollars." Our World 8:30-33, March 1953.

7216 Feather, L. "Billie Holiday Tells About the Dope Leeches." Melody
      Maker 29:3, October 31, 1953.

7217   "Billie Holiday Reaps Fair Europe Response." Billboard 66:14, February 6, 1954.

7218   Stewart-Baxter, D. "Billie Holiday Sings." Jazz Journal 8:11, October 1955.

7219   "Caught in the Act." down beat 22:6, November 30, 1955.

7220   Holiday, Billie and William Dufty. Lady Sings the Blues. Garden City, N.Y.: Doubleday, 1956. Autobiography.

7221   Jepsen, J. G. "Kvinnliga Vokalister." Orkester Journalen 24:14-15, February 1956.

7222   Dahlgren, C. "Mörkt för Lady Day; Amerikanska Nyheter." Orkester Journalen 24:8-9, March 1956.

7223   Stewart-Baxter, D. "Billie Holiday To-day." Jazz Journal 9:10, April 1956.

7224   "Billie Holiday Out on Bail." down beat 23:7, April 4, 1956.

7225   "Right to Sing the Blues." Time 68:80, July 9, 1956.

7226   Balliett, W. "Billie, Big Bill, and Jelly Roll." Saturday Review 39:32-33, July 14, 1956.

7227   "Dunes, Las Vegas." Variety 203:119, July 25, 1956.

7228   "Billie Holiday's Tragic Life." Ebony 11:47-51, September 1956.

7229   Holiday, Billie and William Dufty. "Lady Sings the Blues; Condensation." Coronet 41:68-86, November 1956.

7230   Schoenfeld, H. "Lady Sings the Blues; Billie Holiday a Sock Echo of BG '38 in N.Y." Variety 204:53, November 14, 1956.

7231   Dahlgren, C. "Billie Holiday Superb i Carnegie Hall." Orkester Journalen 24:10-11, December 1956.

7232   "Lady Day at Carnegie." Jazz Today 1:44-45, December 1956.

7233   "Caught in the Act." down beat 23:10, December 12, 1956.

7234   Conover, W. "Billie Holiday." Metronome 74:24-25, February 1957.

7235   "Mr. Kelly's, Chi." Variety 206:69, March 20, 1957.

7236   Kahn, H. "'They Call Me an Artist in Britain,' Says Billie Holiday." Melody Maker 33:3, November 22, 1958.

7237   "Billie à l'Olympia: Emouvante et Fatiguee." Jazz Magazine 5:15, January 1959.

7238   "Billie Holiday, the One Singer Who Always Sings Jazz." Music U.S.A. 76:5, February 1959.

7239   Race, S. "Lady Day." Melody Maker 34:5, February 21, 1959. Review of Holiday's recording of "Porgy and Bess."

7240 Jones, M. "I'm Settling in London, Says Billie Holiday." Melody Maker 34:5, February 28, 1959.

7241 Clar, M. "Billie Holiday." Jazz Review 2:33, May 1959.

7242 "Happy Birthday, Billie!" Jazz Magazine 5:14, June 1959.

7243 "'Lady Day' Arrested." Melody Maker 34:12, June 20, 1959.

7244 "Billie's Blues." down beat 26:10, July 9, 1959.

7245 Hoefer, G. "How Death Came Near for Lady Day." down beat 26:11, July 9, 1959.

7246 "Lady Day Is Gone; Singer Dies at 44." Billboard 71:3, July 20, 1959.

7247 "The Paradox of Billie Holiday." Variety 215:43, July 22, 1959.

7248 Maffei, P. "E Morta Billie Holiday." Musica Jazz 15:30, August-September 1959.

7249 "Billie Holiday: 1915-1959." Music U.S.A. 76:35, August 1959.

7250 James, B. "Billie Holiday and the Art of Communication." Jazz Monthly 5:9-11, August 1959.

7251 Jones, M. "She Was Original, Honest--Unique." Melody Maker 34:5, August 8, 1959.

7252 White, J. "A Fighter." Melody Maker 34:5, August 8, 1959.

7253 Gehman, R. "Lady (for a) Day." Saturday Review 42:39, August 29, 1959.

7254 "Billie Holiday." Music U.S.A. 76:9, September 1959.

7255 Sundin, B. "Lady Day Är Död." Orkester Journalen 27:10-12, September 1959.

7256 Dufty, W., and F. Postif. "Quand Lady Day Mous Enchantait." Jazz Magazine 5:34-35, October 1959.

7257 Morgenstern, D. "New York Scene." Jazz Journal 12:3, October 1959.

7258 Jepsen, Jorgen Grunnet. A Discography of Billie Holiday. Copenhagen NV: Karl Emil Knudsen, 196-?

7259 "The Billie Holiday Story, to Be Filmed." Jet p. 63, January 7, 1960.

7260 Bush, J. B. "I'll Remember Lady." Negro History Bulletin 23:110-111, February 1960.

7261 Balliett, W. "Jazz Records." New Yorker 36:84, March 26, 1960.

7262 Feather, L. "The Scandal of Billie's Grave." Melody Maker 35:20, April 30, 1960.

7263 "$2,500 Headstone to Mark Her Grave in Bronx, N.Y.C. Cemetery."
       Jet p. 57, May 12, 1960.

7264 "Billie Holiday Memorial Foundation Formed in New York." Jet p.
       59, June 16, 1960. The Holiday Foundation will aid drug addicts.

7265 "A Stone for Lady Day." down beat 27:14, June 23, 1960.

7266 Green, B. "Billie Holiday; A Reflection." Jazz Journal 13:4, July
       1960.

7267 "The Unmarked Grave." down beat 27:16, July 21, 1960.

7268 "Set Up Disk, Publishing Firms for Billie Holiday, Parker; Seek
       Royalties." Variety 221:55, February 22, 1961.

7269 "Two Estates Seek Royalties." down beat 28:15, April 13, 1961.

7270 Lyttelton, H. "Lady Is Still the Greatest." Melody Maker 36:5,
       April 15, 1961.

7271 Shera, M. G. "Billie Holiday & Lester Young 1937-1941; A Dis-
       cography." Jazz Journal 14:16, August 1961.

7272 "No AGVA Death Benefit Holiday Estate Charges." Variety 224:49,
       August 30, 1961.

7273 "How Many Dues Need to Be Paid?" down beat 28:14, October 12,
       1961.

7274 Hentoff, N. "The Soft Mythology of Jazz." Show 1:14, November
       1961.

7275 Green, Benny. The Reluctant Art: The Growth of Jazz. Plainview,
       N.Y.: Books for Libraries Press, 1975. Reprint of the 1962 edi-
       tion published by Horizon Press, New York which has one chapter
       devoted to Holiday.

7276 Welding, P. J. "The Art of Billie Holiday; A Performance Record-
       ing of a 1956 Concert." HiFi/Stereo Review 8:64-65, January 1962.

7277 Feather, L. "Billie Holiday, the Voice of Jazz." down beat 29:18-
       21, February 1, 1962.

7278 Rolontz, B. "'Golden Years' Is Golden Billie." Billboard 74:32,
       April 14, 1962.

7279 "MGM Lifted His Billie Holiday Tape, Promoter Charges in $1,750,000
       Suit." Variety 226:47, April 18, 1962.

7280 Zylberstein, J. C. "Les Girls." Jazz Magazine 8:32, May 1962.

7281 "Billie Holiday Benefit for Narcotics Centre Cool at Carnegie B.O."
       Variety 226:2, May 9, 1962.

7282 Schiozzi, B. "Ricordo di Billie Holiday." Musica Jazz 18:22-25,
       July-August 1962.

7283   "Billie Holiday Album Brings Lawsuit." down beat 29:11, July 5,
       1962.

7284   Griffiths, I. "The Columbia-Clef Recordings of Billie Holiday."
       Jazz Journal 15:17-18, August 1962.

7285   Jones, M. "Lady the Great." Melody Maker 37:7, September 29,
       1962.

7286   Dance, S., and H. Dance. "Lovelorn Lady." Saturday Review 46:82-
       83, January 12, 1963.

7287   "Verve's Billie Holiday LP Spins Up Legal Discords, Hamilton Sues
       for 150 G." Variety 231:45, May 29, 1963.

7288   "Chico Hamilton Sues Verve over Billie Holiday Album." down beat
       30:12, July 4, 1963.

7289   Balliett, W. "Jazz Records." New Yorker 39:86-89, August 24,
       1963.

7290   "A Lady Well Remembered." Jazz 2:27, October 1963.

7291   Feather, L. "Over My Jazz Shoulder." Melody Maker 39:5, Jan-
       uary 4, 1964.

7292   Williams, M. "Billie Holiday; Triumphant Decline." Saturday Re-
       view 47:68, October 31, 1964.

7293   Martell, M. "Billie--She Was Planning to Live in London." Melody
       Maker 40:6, May 1, 1965. Interview with Mal Waldron about Holi-
       day.

7294   Allan, L. "Chords & Discords: The Roots of 'Fruit.'" down beat
       32:8-9, September 9, 1965.

7295   Lambert, E. "Quality Jazz." Jazz Journal 19:18-19, February
       1966.

7296   Hentoff, N. "The Indispensable Billy Holiday; Columbia's Second
       Golden Years Album." HiFi/Stereo Review 17:57, July 1966.

7297   Lambert, G. E. "Billie Holiday on Decca." Jazz Monthly 12:11-12,
       July 1966.

7298   Sundin, B. "Mer än ett Nostalgiskt Skimmer." Orkester Journalen
       35:26-27, March 1967.

7299   "Fine and Mellow." Storyville no. 10:20-23, April-May 1967.

7300   Shaw, A. "Billie Holiday and the Blues." Billboard 79:12-13, June
       24, 1967 Supplement.

7301   Locke, D. "The Jazz Vocal." Jazz Monthly 13:6, September 1967.

7302   Morgan, A. "Collectors' Notes; Discography." Jazz Monthly 13:26,
       October 1967.

7303 Ellis, G. "Billie Holiday's Golden Years." Jazz Monthly 13:28-29,
      January 1968.

7304 Gerber, A. "Billie Neuf Ans Deja." Jazz Magazine no. 152:18-21,
      March 1968.

7305 Williams, M. "Billie Holiday--Actress Without an Act." Jazz Jour-
      nal 21:22-23, October 1968.

7306 "Rival Billie Holiday Versions; Public Domain and Heirs' Nights
      Pitted." Variety 252:7, October 9, 1968.

7307 O'Hara, F. "The Day Lady Died." down beat 36:18, April 3, 1969.
      A poem in Holiday's honor.

7308 "'God Bless the Child,' Billie Holiday Standard, Scores on Rock
      Scene." Variety 255:47, July 23, 1969.

7309 Jones, M. "Lady Day--the True Sound of Soul." Melody Maker
      44:8, August 2, 1969.

7310 Lambert, E. "The Voice of Jazz." Jazz Monthly no. 176:18-19,
      October 1969.

7311 McRae, B. "A B Basics; A Column for the Newcomer to Jazz."
      Jazz Journal 22:26, October 1969.

7312 Miller, J. "Billie Holiday at the Storyville Club in October 1951."
      Matrix no. 85:10, October 1969.

7313 Perrin, M. "La Chronique des Disques: Billie Holiday Story Vol.
      1." Jazz Hot no. 263:45, Summer 1970.

7314 Jones, M. "Jazz Records: Back to Back." Melody Maker 45:38,
      October 10, 1970.

7315 Blesh, Rudi. Combo: USA; Eight Lives in Jazz. Philadelphia:
      Chilton Book Co., 1971. The eight musicians are Armstrong,
      Bechet, Blake, Christian, Krupa, Teagarden, Young, and Holiday.

7316 "Reeditions: Billie Holiday Story--Volume I and II." Jazz Magazine
      no. 185:49, January 1971.

7317 Noel, G. "Chronique des Disques: Billie Holiday Story." Jazz Hot
      no. 269:35-36, February 1971.

7318 Traill, S. "Record Reviews: In Concert." Jazz Journal 24:33-34,
      February 1971.

7319 Niquet, B., and A. Fonteyne. "Aimer le Jazz: Billie Holiday."
      Points du Jazz no. 4:23-27, March 1971.

7320 "Diana Ross as Holiday for Motown." Variety 262:2, March 31, 1971.

7321 Brown, R. "Record Reviews: Back to Back." Jazz Journal 24:39,
      April 1971.

7322 Perrin, M. "Billie." Jazz Hot no. 272:5-8, May 1971.

7323 Feather, L. "Tvaa Billie Holiday-Filmer paa Gaang." Orkester Journalen 39:6, June 1971.

7324 Siders, H. "Diana Ross to Star in Billie Holiday Movie." down beat 38:10, June 10, 1971.

7325 "Conflicting Projects on Billie Holiday." Variety 263:1, July 7, 1971.

7326 McDonough, J. "Record Reviews: The Lady Lives." down beat 38:26-27, August 19, 1971.

7327 Knight, A. "Two Educations." Saturday Review 55:81, no. 46, 1972.

7328 "Vinyl Highlights: Billie Holiday--God Bless the Child." Jazz Report 8:17-18, no. 1, 1972.

7329 Bennett, R. R. "Technique of the Jazz Singer." Music and Musicians 20:30-32, February 1972.

7330 "Jazz Records: The Lady Lives." Melody Maker 47:36, March 25, 1972.

7331 Miller, J. "A Preliminary Listing of the Alternative Masters Featuring Vocal by Billie Holiday." Matrix no. 96:14-15, April 1972.

7332 Westin, K. Otto. "Filmen om Billie Holiday Klar." Orkester Journalen 40:7, July-August 1972.

7333 McKaie, A. "Billie Holiday; An Appreciation." Crawdaddy no. 14:46-47, July 1972.

7334 Miller, J. "An Analysis of the Alternative Masters Made by Billie Holiday." Matrix no. 97:12-14, September 1972.

7335 "Record Reviews: Billie Holiday, Vol. 1." Jazz & Blues 2:26, September 1972.

7336 "Lady Sings the Blues." Variety 268:18, October 18, 1972.

7337 Berry, W. E. "Diana Ross Brings Back Billie Holiday in New Movie." Jet 43:56-61, October 19, 1972.

7338 Miller, J. "An Analysis of the Alternative Masters Made by Billie Holiday." Matrix no. 98:9, November 1972.

7339 Robinson, L. "Lady Sings the Blues." Ebony 27:37-46, November 1972.

7340 Cocks, J. "Holiday on Ice." Time 100:86-87, November 6, 1972. Discussion of Ross playing the part of Holiday in the film "Lady Sings the Blues."

7341 Kroll, J. "Blues for Billie." Newsweek 81:133-134, November 6, 1972.

7342 Bates, J. "La Ross Piques Holiday Movie." Billboard 84:4, November 11, 1972.

7343   Knight, A. "Two Educations." Saturday Review 55:81, November 11,
       1972.

7344   Watts, M. "Diana Triumphs as Billie." Melody Maker 47:38, No-
       vember 11, 1972.

7345   Bailey, P. "Billy Holiday's Husband Objects to Play About Her."
       Jet 43:6, November 16, 1972.

7346   Nickerson, R. "The Lady Sings the Blues." Soul 7:1-3, November
       20, 1972.

7347   Gleason, R. J. "Perspectives: Diana Ross Is Billie Holiday." Roll-
       ing Stone no. 122:22, November 23, 1972.

7348   Morgenstern, D. "Diana Ross Almost Saves Billie 'Bio.'" down beat
       39:11, November 23, 1972.

7349   Feather, L. "Truth Takes a Holiday." Melody Maker 47:63, Decem-
       ber 2, 1972.

7350   Bennett, R. R. "Technique of the Jazz Singer." Educator 5:2-4, no.
       3, 1973.

7351   Billie Holiday Remembered. Compiled by Linda Kuehl and Ellie
       Schocket; assisted by Dan Morgenstern. New York: New York
       Jazz Museum, 1973. A 20-page booklet on Holiday's life.

7352   Lutsky, I., and J. Norris. "The Billie Holiday Story." Coda 11:12-
       14, no. 1, 1973. A critique of Holiday's recordings.

7353   Walling, W., and R. Shatzkin. "'It Ain't the Blues': Billie Holiday,
       Sidney J. Furie, and Kitsch." Journal of Jazz Studies 1:21-33, no.
       1, 1973.

7354   Sanders, C. L. "Lady Didn't Always Sing the Blues." Ebony 28:110-
       116, January 1973.

7355   Comas, B. "Black Films: Is Quality Coming?" Soul 7:3, January
       1, 1973.

7356   Feather, L. "Final Days of 'Lady Day.'" Variety 269:134, January
       3, 1973. A portion of Feather's book From Satchmo to Miles.

7357   Batten, J. "On Screen." Jazz & Blues 2:30, February 1973.

7358   "Swinging News: Lady Day on Screen and Stage: Double Failure?"
       Jazz Forum no. 21:22, February 1973.

7359   "Records." Rolling Stone no. 130:54-55, March 15, 1973.

7360   "Diana Sings Billie." Melody Maker 48:33, March 17, 1973.

7361   Jones, M. "The Legend of Lady Day." Melody Maker 48:33-34,
       March 17, 1973.

7362   Gabler, M. "A Lady Named Billie--and I." down beat 40:16-17,
       March 29, 1973.

7363 "Jazz Records: The Voice of Jazz." Melody Maker 48:42, March
      31, 1973.

7364 "Billie Holiday Boom." Jazz Podium 22:8, April 1973.

7365 "Jazz Records: Lady Sings the Blues." Melody Maker 48:50, April
      14, 1973.

7366 Jones, M. "Lady Ross." Melody Maker 48:3, April 14, 1973.

7367 Ivy, A. "'Lady Sings the Blues'--Film of 1972." Soul 7:26, April
      23, 1973.

7368 "Remembering Lady Day." Essence 4:31, May 1973.

7369 Cullaz, M. "Billie Holiday: Lady Sings the Blues." Jazz Hot no.
      295:4-7, June 1973. A portion of Holiday's autobiography Lady
      Sings the Blues.

7370 Noakes, K. W. "Lady in Satin; An Appreciation of Billie Holiday's
      Last Record." Jazz Journal 26:22-23, June 1973.

7371 Voce, S. "It Don't Mean a Thing." Jazz Journal 26:24-25, June
      1973.

7372 Gleason, R. J. "Perspectives: 'Cover' Versions and Their Origins."
      Rolling Stone no. 136:7, 1973.

7373 Tiegel, E. "Soft Sounds Spell Success for Today." Billboard 85:26,
      July 21, 1973.

7374 Cooke, J. "Billie Holiday: A Continuing Musical Conception." Jazz
      & Blues 3:4-6, September 1973.

7375 "On Record: Lady Sings the Blues." Jazz & Blues 3:21, September
      1973.

7376 Tenot, F. "Chronique d'un Vieus Con: 'Lady Sings the Blues' ou
      la Vie en Loss." Jazz Magazine no. 216:8, October-November
      1973.

7377 "On Record: Gallant Lady." Jazz & Blues 3:21, October 1973.

7378 "On Record: The Voice of Jazz Volume Two." Jazz & Blues 3:21-
      22, October 1973.

7379 "Ross Ingen Holiday." Orkester Journalen 41:10, October 1973.

7380 "On Record: The Lady Lives, Vol. 1." Jazz & Blues 3:20-21, De-
      cember 1973.

7381 Jones, Hettie. Big Star Fallin' Mama; Five Women in Black Music.
      New York: Viking Press, 1974. The five women are Ma Rainy,
      Bessie Smith, Mahalia Jackson, Aretha Franklin, and Holiday.
      Juvenile literature.

7382 Hawes, H., and D. Asher. "Remembering Billie and Bird; Excerpt
      from Raise Up Off Me." Harper's Magazine 248:44, June 1974.

7383 Miller, J. "Billie Holiday Further Alternative Masters." Matrix no. 105:7-8, November 1974.

7384 Bakker, Dick M. Billie & Teddy on Microgroove, 1932-1944. Alphen aan den Rijn, Holladn: Micrography, 1975? A 52-page discography of Teddy Wilson and Holiday.

7385 Chilton, John. Billie's Blues: Billie Holiday's Story 1933-1959. New York: Stein and Day, 1975.

7386 Gleason, Ralph J. Celebrating the Duke, and Louis, Bessie, Billie, Bird, Carmen, Miles, Dizzy, and Other Heroes. Boston: Little, Brown, 1975.

7387 Wilmer, V. "Blues for a Lady." Melody Maker 50:40, May 3, 1975.

7388 Simmen, J. "Lady Day." Points du Jazz no. 11:41, June 1975.

7389 Cullaz, M. "La Voix dans la Musique Negro-Americaine." Jazz Hot no. 322:16-19, December 1975.

7390 Miller, J. "A Billie Holiday Investigation." Matrix no. 107-108:7-8, December 1975. An examination of Holiday's recordings.

7391 "Record Reviews: A Day in the Life of Billie Holiday." down beat 42:36, December 18, 1975.

7392 Hentoff, N. "Indigenous Music; Billie Holiday/Songs & Conversations." Nation 222:764-765, June 19, 1976.

7393 Olsson, J. "Sagt om Billie Holliday." Orkester Journalen 44:8-9, July-August 1976.

7394 Hentoff, N. "Indigenous Music; Billie Holiday/Songs & Conversations." Nation 233:61, July 17, 1976.

7395 "Jazz Albums: Billie's Blues." Melody Maker 51:26, September 25, 1976.

7396 "Records: The First Verve Sessions." Creem 8:61, September 1976. Discussion of recordings made for Jazz at the Philharmonic.

7397 Jannotta, R. "'Glad Bless the Child': An Analysis of Unaccompanied Bass Clarinet Solo by Eric Dolphy." Jazz Research 9:37-48, 1977.

7398 Pleasants, H. "The Great American Popular Singers--Billie Holiday." Educator 10:4-5, no. 1, 1977. Taken from Pleasants' book The Great American Popular Singers.

7399 "Reviews--MCA Reissues: Billie Holiday and Ella Fitzgerald." Jazz Magazine (U.S.) 1:56, no. 3, 1977.

7400 "Women in Music." BMI no. 4:23-24, 1977.

7401 "Waxing On: Stormy Blues." down beat 44:45, July 14, 1977.

7402 "Record Reviews: For a Lady Named Billie." Jazz Journal International 30:32-33, August 1977.

7403 "Record Reviews: Stormy Blues." Radio Free Jazz 18:12-13, September 1977.

7404 "John Hammond." Jazz Magazine (U.S.) 2:33, no. 2, 1978. Discusses Bessie Smith and Holiday.

7405 "Record Reviews: Lester Young Story Vol. 2: A Musical Romance." down beat 45:20, January 26, 1978.

7406 "Prez Awards." Jazz Journal International 31:36, August 1978. Holiday, Art Tatum, and Sarah Vaughan are among those who received Prez awards.

HOLT, PATRICIA LOUISE (Patti Labelle) see LABELLE

HOPKINS, LINDA.

7407 Edwards, H. "A Musical About Muggins." Crawdaddy no. 7:13, March 19, 1972.

7408 Westin, K. O. "2 Saangerskar paa Vaeg Upp." Orkester Journalen 40:6, May 1972.

7409 "Linda Hopkins." Soul 7:10, September 25, 1972.

7410 "Spiritual Singer Overcomes Defeat." Soul 8:11, June 25, 1973.

7411 "Linda Hopkins: 'Why I Submerge My Act in Bessie Smith Saga.'" Variety 273:46, January 23, 1974.

7412 "Talent in Action." Billboard 86:20, March 23, 1974.

7413 Ainslie, P. "Novella & Linda: A Tale of Two Singers." Rolling Stone no. 165:26, July 18, 1974.

7414 "Grand Finale, N.Y." Variety 275:48, August 7, 1974.

7415 "Me and Bessie." Melody Maker 49:32, October 19, 1974.

7416 Lees, G. "Linda as Bessie." High Fidelity/Musical America 25:14-15, May 1975.

7417 Williams, J. "Linda Hopkins Feels Role of Bessie Smith in Play." Billboard 87:37, June 7, 1975.

7418 "Shows on Broadway: Me and Bessie." Variety 280:72, October 29, 1975.

7419 Joe, R. "Linda Hopkins Resembles Blues Queen Bessie Smith." Billboard 87:32, November 1, 1975.

7420 Downs, J. "Upbeat Blues." Time 106:66, November 3, 1975.

7421 Balliett, W. "Jazz." New Yorker 51:151-152, November 10, 1975.

7422 Davis, C. "Me and Bessie." Encore 4:34, December 8, 1975.

7423 "'Me and Bessie' Hits Broadway." down beat 42:10, December 18, 1975.

7424 Robles, R. "Linda Hopkins Outside of Bessie Smith." Encore 4:29, December 22, 1975.

7425 Dance, S. "Lightly and Politely." Jazz Journal 29:11-12, January 1976. Discussion of the Broadway play "Me and Bessie."

7426 Peterson, M. "Spotlight on Linda Hopkins." Essence 7:45, June 1976.

7427 "One Woman Show." Variety 289:54, December 28, 1977.

7428 "Studio One, L. A." Variety 290:116, March 22, 1978.

7429 "Scandals, L. A." Variety 293:121, November 22, 1978.

HORNE, LENA (Mrs. Lennie Hayton), 1917- .

7430 "Chocolate Cream Chanteuse." Time 41:62, January 4, 1943.

7431 "Song Seller." Newsweek 21:65, January 4, 1943.

7432 "Young Negro with Haunting Voice Charms New York with Old Songs." Life 14:20-21, January 4, 1943.

7433 Crichton, K. "Horne Solo." Collier's 111:12, June 26, 1943.

7434 "Lena in Paris." Time 50:67-68, December 8, 1947.

7435 "Lena Horne." Life 25:101-102, October 18, 1948.

7436 "Lena Horne Scenes Out of 'Words' in Memphis." Variety 173:3, January 5, 1949.

7437 "Memphis Censors Go Snip, Snip on Lena." down beat 16:3, January 28, 1949.

7438 "Clear the Decks--Sinatra Called Red." down beat 16:16, July 29, 1949.

7439 Horne, Lena. In Person; Lena Horne. As Told to Helen Arstein and Carlton Moss. New York: Greenberg, 1950.

7440 "Copacabana, N.Y." Variety 177:50, January 11, 1950.

7441 "Lena Horne: Our World's First Cover Girl." Our World 5:11-13, April 1950.

7442 "Lena All Set for Britain." Melody Maker 26:1, June 24, 1950.

7443 "Lena Conquers Formidable 'Opposition.'" Melody Maker 26:6, July 8, 1950.

7444 Scott, G. "Films? Cabaret?--Give Me Television, Says Lena Horne." Melody Maker 26:11, August 19, 1950.

7445 "Lena Horne's New Singing Style." Ebony 5:35-36, October 1950.

7446 Boulton, D. "Horne Scores, Not Nat, at London Palladium Shows."
      down beat 17:15, October 20, 1950.

7447 "Hotel Ambassador, L.A." Variety 182:52, May 16, 1951.

7448 "Can't Solve Problems by Running, Lena Tells Roy." down beat 18:1,
      June 15, 1951.

7449 "Comeback for Lena Horne; Singer Has Greatest Triumph in Big Hol-
      lywood Opening." Ebony 6:29-32, August 1951.

7450 "Riviera, Ft. Lee, N.J." Variety 184:52, September 12, 1951.

7451 "Hearst Press Off Again; This Time Vs. Lena Horne." down beat
      18:3, October 19, 1951.

7452 "El Rancho, Las Vegas." Variety 184:53, November 28, 1951.

7453 Feather, L. "Big Bands Hold Thrill for Lena." down beat 18:16,
      December 28, 1951.

7454 Rau, H. "Lena Horne's Miami Debut Draws SRO for Socko Clover
      Club Bill." Billboard 64:3, February 2, 1952.

7455 "Lena Horne Ups Lido 3 G Per Day in Paris." Variety 186:63, April
      2, 1952.

7456 Kahn, H. "A Singer Who Studies Her Songs." Melody Maker 28:2,
      April 5, 1952.

7457 "Max, Mike and Marie Drop in on Lena." Melody Maker 28:8, May
      31, 1952.

7458 Jones, M. "Fascinating Lena." Melody Maker 28:9, June 7, 1952.

7459 Race, S. "Searchlight." Melody Maker 28:2, June 21, 1952.

7460 Winquist, S. G. "The MM Reports Exclusively on the Parnell-Lena
      Horne Scandinavian Tour." Melody Maker 28:3, August 23, 1952.

7461 "Horne a Hit in Copenhagen." Billboard 64:23, August 30, 1952.

7462 "Lena Horne Raffinerad Men även Affekterad." Orkester Journalen
      20:8, September 1952.

7463 Ruark, R. "Lady in a High Key." Esquire 38:32-33, September
      1952.

7464 "Lena Horne Loses Dancing Partner." Ebony 8:29-30, November
      1952.

7465 "Caught in the Act." down beat 20:4, May 6, 1953.

7466 "The Private Life of Lena Horne." Ebony 8:65-70, September 1953.

7467 "This Is Show Business." Our World 8:32-36, September 1953.

7468 "Ambassador Hotel, L.A." Variety 192:64, November 25, 1953.

7469 "Caught in the Act." down beat 20:4, December 30, 1953.

7470 Jones, M. "The Singer They Went to See." Melody Maker 30:2, October 30, 1954.

7471 "Lena Horne Enjoys Her Longest Vacation." Ebony 10:64-68, 1954.

7472 "Sands, Las Vegas." Variety 197:47, December 29, 1954.

7473 "Chez Paree, Chi." Variety 197:52, January 26, 1955.

7474 "Caught in the Act." down beat 22:13, February 9, 1955.

7475 "Hint Negro Bias, Anti-Davis H. O. in Lena Horne's Copa City Scram." Variety 197:50, February 1955.

7476 Powers, C. "That Fabulous Lena." down beat 22:6, June 1, 1955.

7477 "Caught in the Act." down beat 22:52, October 5, 1955.

7478 "Savoy Hotel, London." Variety 200:51, October 26, 1955.

7479 "Is Lena Still the Queen?" Ebony 11:43-47, February 1956.

7480 "Sands, Las Vegas." Variety 204:53, November 7, 1956.

7481 "Waldorf-Astoria, N.Y." Variety 205:276, January 9, 1957.

7482 Watt, D. "Tables for Two." New Yorker 32:95, February 2, 1957.

7483 "Eden Roc, Miami Beach." Variety 206:68, March 20, 1957.

7484 "Cocoanut Grove, L.A." Variety 207:67, June 19, 1957.

7485 Coss, B. "The Articulate Lena Horne." Metronome 74:12, November 1957.

7486 Gibbs, W. "Music and Words." New Yorker 33:100, November 9, 1957.

7487 "Lena Lights Up Jamaica." Life 43:112, November 18, 1957.

7488 Jablonski, E. "Lena Horne, on Stage and on Records." High Fidelity/Musical America 4:36-37, January-February 1958.

7489 "Lena Horne Returns to Broadway." Ebony 13:74-76, January 1958.

7490 "Million Dollar Beauty, Lena Horne." Sepia 6:7-13, January 1958.

7491 Feather, L. "The Horne of Plenty." down beat 25:14-15, January 9, 1958.

7492 Horne, Lena. "I'm Proud to Be a Mother." Ebony 14:56-58, April 1959.

7493 "Sands, Las Vegas." Variety 215:115, June 24, 1959.

7494 "Cal-Neva, Lake Tahoe." Variety 215:69, August 12, 1959.

7495 "Savoy Hotel, London." Variety 216:53, September 30, 1959.

7496 Burman, M. "Lena." Melody Maker 34:6-7, October 10, 1959.

7497 "Lena Horne, Singer, Is Guest Star on Perry Como Show." Jet p. 66, January 21, 1960.

7498 "Cocoanut Grove, L.A." Variety 217:53, February 17, 1960.

7499 "She Won't Apologize After Hitting White Heckler in Beverly Hills Night Club." Jet p. 60-61, March 3, 1960.

7500 "Eden Roc, Miami Beach." Variety 218:53, March 23, 1960.

7501 Grevatt, R. "Lena Horne in Smart Florida Stint." Billboard 72:41, April 4, 1960.

7502 "Waldorf-Astoria, N.Y." Variety 218:78, April 6, 1960.

7503 "Fairmont, San Francisco." Variety 219:63, July 6, 1960.

7504 "Talk of Town, London." Variety 222:66, April 5, 1961.

7505 Hepburn, D. "Lena Horne: Her Quiet Fight for Equality." Sepia 10:41-45, November 1961.

7506 "Cocoanut Grove, L.A." Variety 225:55, February 14, 1962.

7507 "Chi Chi, Palm Springs." Variety 226:59, April 18, 1962.

7508 "Cave, Vancouver." Variety 227:59, June 20, 1962.

7509 "Waldorf-Astoria, N.Y." Variety 229:56, February 13, 1963.

7510 "Latin Casino, N.J." Variety 230:60, March 27, 1963.

7511 Feinstein, H. "Lena Horne Speaks Freely on Race, Marriage, Stage." Ebony 18:61-67, May 1963.

7512 Horne, Lena. "I Just Want to Be Myself." Show 3:62-65, September 1963.

7513 "2 Sinatra-Horne Carnegie Hall Benefits Garner 100 G for Civil Rights & Kids." Variety 232:47, October 9, 1963.

7514 "Cocoanut Grove, L.A." Variety 235:60, January 10, 1964.

7515 Jones, M. "Look Out--Here Comes Lena!" Melody Maker 39:8, September 19, 1964.

7516 "Talk of Town, London." Variety 236:93, September 23, 1964.

7517 Pitman, J. "Lena Horne Made It Non-ethic and Will Tell Her Tale." Variety 237:1, December 23, 1964.

7518 Horne, Lena and Richard Schickel. Lena. New York: Doubleday, 1965.

7519 "My Life with Lennie; Excerpt from Lena." Ebony 21:176-178, November 1965.

7520 "Successful Autographing Tours by Three Personalities." Publishers' Weekly 188:53-56, December 13, 1965.

7521 Noble, J. L. "Three-Horned Dilemma Facing Negro Women." Ebony 21:118-122, August 1966.

7522 "Sands, Las Vegas." Variety 244:58, September 28, 1966.

7523 "Nugget, Sparks, Nev." Variety 244:59, November 16, 1966.

7524 Pierce, P. "Lena at 51." Ebony 23:124-126, July 1968.

7525 "Caesars Palace, L. V." Variety 256:112, September 10, 1969.

7526 "Belafonte and Lena Horne Team up for Superb Show in Las Vegas." Jet 36:60-61, September 18, 1969.

7527 "Harry and Lena Off the Cuff!" Ebony 25:128-129, March 1970.

7528 "Szabo Produces LP with Lena Horne; Plays It Cool." Billboard 82:27, July 11, 1970.

7529 "Tribute to Paul Robeson." Freedomways 11:7-8, no. 1, 1971.

7530 Feather, L. "TV Soundings." down beat 38:12, March 4, 1971.

7531 Heckman, D. "The Imperishable Lena Horne." Stereo Review 27:71-72, September 1971.

7532 Dobrin, Arnold. Voices of Joy, Voices of Freedom: Ethel Waters, Sammy Davis, Jr., Marian Anderson, Paul Robeson, Lena Horne. New York: Coward, McCann & Geoghegan, 1972.

7533 "Caesars Palace, L. V." Variety 266:87, March 29, 1972.

7534 "Disques du Mois: The Fabulous Lena Horne." Jazz Magazine no. 199:40, April 1972.

7535 Gruen, J. "Lena Horne's New Love for Life." Vogue 159:92-95, June 1972.

7536 Duckett, A. "Triple Tragedy for Lena Horne." Sepia 21:16, August 1972.

7537 "Still Glamorous at 55, Lena Horne Has No Big Show-Business Plans." Jet 42:44-45, August 3, 1972.

7538 "Elmwood, Windsor." Variety 269:55, December 13, 1972.

7539 Ebert, A. "Sometimes Sunshine, Most Times Storm." Essence 4:46-49, May 1973.

7540 "Sands, Las Vegas." Variety 273:55, December 12, 1973; 275:101, May 15, 1974.

7541 "Concert Reviews." Variety 275:44, June 19, 1974.

7542 "Minskoff, N.Y." Variety 276:56, November 6, 1974.

7543 "Talent in Action." Billboard 86:22, November 23, 1974.

7544 Balliett, W. "Jazz--New York Notes." New Yorker 50:75, December 23, 1974.

7545 "Deauville, M. B." Variety 277:83, January 22, 1975.

7546 Connolly, R. "Cabaret!" Stereo Review 34:70-75, February 1975.

7547 "Concert Reviews." Variety 279:74, May 28, 1975.

7548 Reilly, P. "The Art of La Belle Lena: Far Too Special to Categorize." Stereo Review 35:73-74, October 1975.

7549 "Talent in Action." Billboard 87:39, November 29, 1975.

7550 "Caught in the Act." Melody Maker 51:23, May 8, 1976.

7551 "Concert Reviews." Variety 283:450, May 12, 1976.

7552 "Jazz Albums: Lena--a New Album." Melody Maker 52:28, January 29, 1977.

7553 "Concert Reviews." Variety 286:63, February 23, 1977.

7554 Davis, C. "Lena Horne's Everlasting Magic." Encore 6:42, April 4, 1977.

7555 "Fairmont Hotel, S.F." Variety 287:119, May 18, 1977.

7556 Norman, S. "Lena Horne at 60." Sepia 26:26-28, June 1977.

7557 Lucas, B. "How Famous Widows Get Along Now Without Mates." Jet 52:14-17, June 16, 1977.

7558 Coombs, O. "Lena Horne Is 60." Esquire 88:66-68, August 1977.

7559 Pyatt, R. I. "Great God A'mighty, Lena Horne Is 'Me at Last.'" Encore 6:32-35, August 15, 1977.

7560 Nilsson, C. "Lena Horne Fascinerande." Orkester Journalen 45:20, December 1977.

7561 "Readers Respond to Ebony Poll on Class and Style." Ebony 33:40-41, March 1978.

7562 Williams, J. "Lena Horne Dazzles in Black 'Pal Joey.'" Billboard 90:51, May 13, 1978.

7563 "Lena Horne's Stage Lover Is Clifton Davis." Jet 55:22-25, September 28, 1978.

7564 "Sands, Las Vegas." Variety 293:99, December 13, 1978.

7565 "50 Plus Beauty." 50 Plus 19:36-37, January 1979.

HUMES, HELEN, 1913- .

7566   Hobson, W. "To Miss Humes, in Spring." Saturday Review 43:54,
       April 30, 1960.

7567   Feather, L. "The Blindfold Test." down beat 28:35, May 11, 1961.

7568   _____. "Riscoperta di Helen Humes. Musica Jazz 17:39-40, June
       1961.

7569   _____. "Les Charmes de l'Existence." Jazz Magazine 164:32,
       June 1962.

7570   Dugan, J., and J. Hammond. "An Early Black-Music Concert: From
       Spirituals to Swing." Black Perspectives in Music 2:200, no. 2,
       1974. Discussion of the Carnegie Hall concert held December 23,
       1938.

7571   "Some Records: Helen Comes Back." Jazz Journal 27:7-8, March
       1974.

7572   Cullaz, M. "Festival du Son." Jazz Hot no. 304:23, April 1974.

7573   "Helen Humes." Jazz Hot no. 310:20-21, November 1974.

7574   Dance, S. "Lightly & Politely: Helen Humes & Roomful of Blues."
       Jazz Journal 27:16-17, December 1974.

7575   "Talent in Action." Billboard 87:36, February 22, 1975.

7576   Balliett, W. "Our Local Correspondents; Just a Singer." New York-
       er 51:98, February 24, 1975.

7577   Dance, S. "Lightly & Politely." Jazz Journal 28:10-11, April 1975.

7578   "Helen Humes: Vindicating the Critics." Stereo Review 35:76, July
       1975. Crituque of "It's All over Town."

7579   "Record Reviews: Helen Comes Back; Helen Humes: Talk of the
       Town." down beat 42:26-28, August 14, 1975.

7580   "Record Reviews: Helen Humes with Red Norvo and His Orchestra:
       RCA." down beat 42:26-28, August 14, 1975.

7581   "Rainbow Grill, N.Y." Variety 281:60, December 1975.

7582   "Talent in Action." Billboard 88:63, January 24, 1976.

7583   McDonough, J. "Helen Humes: Still the Talk of the Town." down
       beat 43:17-18, May 20, 1976.

7584   Soutif, D. "Les Voix de Basie." Jazz Magazine no. 251:30, January
       1977.

7585   Joyce, M. "Helen Humes: Interview." Cadence 3:6, January 1978.

7586   "Caught in the Act." Melody Maker 53:18, June 24, 1978.

7587   "Le Club, N.O." Variety 290:91, February 22, 1978.

7588 Gelly, D. "Helen Humes at Ronnie Scott's." Jazz Journal International 31:21, September 1978.

HUNTER, ALBERTA (Josephine Beatty), 1895- .

7589 Whiston, H. F. "Back Comes Alberta Hunter." Melody Maker 26:9, December 9, 1950.

7590 Hobson, W. "The Amen Corner." Saturday Review 45:54-55, January 27, 1962.

7591 Stewart-Baxter, D. "Blues & Views." Jazz Journal 28:18, February 1975. Review of the recording "Jack Jackson & His Orchestra."

7592 "Alberta Hunter Retires to Go Back to Work." Jazz Report 9:33, no. 4, 1977.

7593 Giddins, G. "Riffs: Alberta Hunter Goes Back to Work." Village Voice 22:87-88, October 24, 1977.

7594 Balliett, W. "Our Local Correspondents." New Yorker 53:100-101, October 31, 1977.

7595 Saal, H. "Rebirth of the Blues." Newsweek 90:101, October 31, 1977.

7596 "Cookery, N.Y." Variety 289:61, November 9, 1977.

7597 Traill, S. "From the Jazz Corners of the World: Home Is the Hunter." Jazz Journal International 30:21, December 1977.

7598 "Comeback at 82." Swinging Newsletter 8:5, no. 36, 1978.

7599 "Jazz en Direct." Jazz Magazine no. 265:10, June 1978.

7600 Jeske, L. "Home Is the Hunter--and Her Castle's Still Rockin'." Jazz Journal International 31:28, June 1978.

7601 Bourget, J. L. "Alberta Hunter: Remember My Name." Jazz Magazine no. 266-267:28-29, July-August 1978.

7602 Mitz, R. "Pop Rotogravure." Stereo Review 41:124, August 1978.

7603 "83 and Evermore." down beat 45:12, August 10, 1978.

7604 Palmer, R. "Jazz: Alberta Hunter: Young at 83." Rolling Stone no. 272:18, August 24, 1978.

7605 Darden, N. J. "No Tea for the Fever." Essence 9:82-83, October 1978.

7606 "On Stage." People 10:118-119, November 13, 1978.

7607 Weiss, P. "Two Ways to Stretch Your Ears." Stereo Review 42:61, January 1979.

ICEMAN   see   BUTLER, JERRY

JACKSON, MAHALIA (Mahala; Mrs. Sigmund Gahoway), 1911-1972.

7608   Jackson, Mahalia. "On the Interpretation of Negro Spirituals." Etude
       52:486, August 1934.

7609   Moon, B. "Mahalia Jackson, a Great Gospel Singer." Record Chang-
       er 8:15-16, April 1949.

7610   Schuler, V. "Mahalia Jackson--Queen of the Gospel Singers." Mel-
       ody Maker 26:9, April 15, 1950.

7611   Jones, M. "Magnificent Mahalia--the Greatest Gospel Voice." Mel-
       ody Maker 27:9, January 2, 1951.

7612   "Mahalia Jackson to Mark 25th Year in Music." down beat 18:16,
       November 2, 1951.

7613   Grut, H. "Mahalia Jackson; Kyrkosangerska med Swing." Orkester
       Journalen 19:24-25, December 1951.

7614   Whitton, D. "The Gospel Queen." Jazz Journal 5:1, November 1952.

7615   Jackson, Mahalia. "Singing the Gospel Makes Me Feel Good All
       Over." Melody Maker 28:3, November 1, 1952.

7616   Kahn, H. "Mahalia--Greatest of Gospellers." Melody Maker 28:3,
       November 1, 1952.

7617   "Mahalia--Cold, Tired, Hungry--Is Still Great!" Melody Maker 28:9,
       November 15, 1952.

7618   Hammond, J. "Gospel Singers' Progress--from Churches to Car-
       negie." down beat 19:7, November 19, 1952.

7619   Borneman, E. "Ageing Collectors, Baptist Ladies, Fans--I Tell
       You It Was Weird!" Melody Maker 28:8, November 22, 1952.

7620   Stewart-Baxter, D. "Preachin' the Blues." Jazz Journal 6:2-3, Jan-
       uary 1953.

7621   "Gospel Music Festival Stirs Carnegie Hall." Billboard 65:20, Oc-
       tober 17, 1953.

7622   Thompson, E. B. "When Mahalia Sings." Ebony 9:35-38, January
       1954.

7623   "Born to Sing." Newsweek 43:98, February 22, 1954.

7624   "Columbia to Sign Mahalia Jackson." down beat 21:11, September 22,
       1954.

7625   "Gospel with a Bounce." Time 64:46, October 4, 1954.

7626   Sargent, M. "Meet Mahalia Jackson--Classicist of the Spiritual."
       down beat 21:10, November 17, 1954.

7627 "Gospel Queen Mahalia." Life 37:63-66, November 29, 1954.

7628 Simon, G. "Mahalia Jackson; Veteran Gospel Singer Thinks Jazz Should Have a Soul." Metronome 70:16, December 1954.

7629 "Mahalia to Keep to Her Own Pattern on Discs." down beat 21:8, December 1, 1954.

7630 Harper, Mr. "Joyful Noise." Harper's Magazine 213:82, August 1956.

7631 Hentoff, N. "You Can Still Hear Her Voice When the Music Has Stopped." Reporter 16:34-36, June 27, 1957.

7632 "Music for Moderns." Musical Courier 156:11, July 1957.

7633 "A New Dignity." down beat 24:34, August 22, 1957. Review of her appearance in Newport, R.I. at Trinity Episcopal Church.

7634 Shipman, J. "The Newport Jazz Festival." Jazz Journal 10:8, October 1957.

7635 Stearns, M. W. "Make a Joyous Noise unto the Lord." Saturday Review 41:47, January 25, 1958.

7636 Hentoff, N. "Mahalia Jackson." Jazz Journal 11:16-17, May 1958. Reprinted from the Reporter.

7637 "Mahalia Jackson." down beat 25:34, June 26, 1958.

7638 Jones, M. "This World of Jazz." Melody Maker 33:11, July 19, 1958.

7639 Ellison, R. "As the Spirit Moves Mahalia." Saturday Review 41:41, September 27, 1958.

7640 Richards, M. "Best in Records." Cosmopolitan 145:6, December 1958.

7641 Terkel, S. "A Profile of Mahalia." down beat 25:13-15, December 11, 1958.

7642 Mouly, R. "Ella et Duke et Duke et Mahalia." Jazz Magazine 5:16-17, January 1959.

7643 Hadlock, D. "Heard in Person." down beat 26:42, February 5, 1959.

7644 Brown, F. L. "Mahalia the Great." Ebony 14:69-72, March 1959.

7645 Testoni, G. "Gli Autori dei Temi." Musica Jazz 15:38, November 1959.

7646 Sylie, E. M. "I Can't Stop Singing." Saturday Evening Post 232:19-21, December 5, 1959.

7647 "Mahalia Jackson's Constitution Hall." Variety 217:2, February 24, 1960.

7648 "Promise Kept." down beat 27:14, March 3, 1960.

7649   "Gospel in Washington." Newsweek 55:68, April 4, 1960.

7650   "Gospel Singer Is Guest on Ed Sullivan Show." Jet p. 66, April 21,
       1960.

7651   "Gospel Goes to Washington." Ebony 15:52-54, July 1960.

7652   "Mahalia Jackson, Singer to Star in Special Program of Spirituals on
       'Look Up and Live.'" Jet p. 66, August 4, 1960.

7653   "Mahalia Jackson, Gospel Singer on Ed Sullivan Show." Jet p. 66,
       November 10, 1960.

7654   Affeldt, P. "And an Angel Sang His Praises." Jazz Report 1:1-3,
       December 1960.

7655   "Mahalia Jackson, Gospel Singer, on Ed Sullivan Show." Jet 19:66,
       December 22, 1960.

7656   Tallmadge, W. H. "Dr. Watts and Mahalia Jackson--the Develop-
       ment, Decline, and Survival of a Folk Style in America." Ethno-
       musicology 5:95-99, no. 2, 1961.

7657   "Editorial." Jazz Journal 14:1, April 1961.

7658   Masson, J. R. "Mahalia, la Precheuse du XX Siecle." Jazz Maga-
       zine 7:24-27, April 1961.

7659   Jones, M. "I'm Glad I Didn't Miss Mahalia." Melody Maker 36:10,
       April 15, 1961.

7660   Mouly, R., and J. R. Masson. "Monk, Newport, Cannonball, Ma-
       halia." Jazz Magazine 7:22-27, June 1961.

7661   Tronchot, J. "Les Concerts." Jazz Hot no. 166:14-15, June 1961.

7662   "Balto Agency Countersues Mahalia Jackson for 86 G in Row over
       2½ G Payoff." Variety 223:45, June 14, 1961.

7663   Cartier, J. "Mahalia Jackson, la Premiere Chanteuse Biblique du
       Monde." Musica no. 88:51-56, July 1961.

7664   Terkel, S. "Mahalia: Songbird for God." Negro Digest 10:8-12,
       July 1961.

7665   Schweizer, G. "Gospelgesänge." Musica 15:501, September 1961.

7666   "To Europe and the Holy Land with Mahalia Jackson." Ebony 16:44-
       46, October 1961.

7667   Haley, A. "She Makes a Joyful Music." Reader's Digest 79:196-198,
       November 1961.

7668   Wylie, E. M. "I Walked in Jerusalem." Good Housekeeping 153:110-
       111, December 1961.

7669   "Slurs to Mahalia & India Dance Troupe Cue Fresh Racial Picketing
       in N.C." Variety 225:1, December 13, 1961.

7670 Kayser, Erhard. Mahalia Jackson. Wetzlar: Pegasus, 1962.

7671 Uyldert, Herman. Vorstin van de Gospel; Mahalia Jackson. Tielt:
      Lannoo, 1962.

7672 Palmer, M. "Jackson, Mahalia, at the Garden." Sepia 11:19-20,
      February 1962.

7673 "Joyful Noise in Israel." Time 80:70, September 21, 1962.

7674 "Mahalia Jackson's First Love." Sepia 11:12-16, December 1962.

7675 Jackson, Mahalia. "I Sing for the Lord." Music Journal 21:19, Jan-
      uary 1963.

7676 "Mahalia Jackson's Lenten Recipe." Ebony 18:120, March 1963.

7677 "Mahalia Jackson Enlists Show Biz to Raise Coin for Desegregation
      Fight." Variety 231:53-54, June 5, 1963.

7678 "Gospel's 'Blasphemous' Beat." Variety 231:53, June 19, 1963.

7679 Gold, D. "In God She Trusts." Ladies' Home Journal 80:66-67, No-
      vember 1963.

7680 "Mahalia Jackson: 'Gospel Isn't Pop.'" down beat 30:12, August 15,
      1963.

7681 Tiegel, E. "Pop Gospel Not of U.S.--Mahalia." Billboard 75:1,
      September 28, 1963.

7682 Feather, L. "Spitting in God's Face; Pop Gospel." Show 3:47, Oc-
      tober 1963.

7683 "Mahalia Swings Again." Sepia 13:42-45, March 1964.

7684 Jones, M. "How Cheap Can You Get--Mahalia Jackson Asks Max
      Jones." Melody Maker 39:6, May 23, 1964.

7685 "Will Mahalia Jackson's Second Marriage Last?" Sepia 13:78-81,
      September 1964.

7686 Thompson, E. B. "Love Comes to Mahalia." Ebony 20:50-52, No-
      vember 1964.

7687 Jackson, M. "Make a Joyful Noise!" Music Journal 23:60, January
      1965.

7688 Hayes, C. J. "Mahalia Jackson, a Discography." Matrix no. 60:3-8,
      August 1965; no. 61:3-8, October 1965.

7689 "Mahalia Jackson Back in Business." Billboard 77:82, October 23,
      1965 Supplement.

7690 Hayes, C. J. "Mahalia Jackson, a Discography." Matrix no. 62:3-
      5, December 1965.

7691 Jackson, Mahalia and Evan McLeod Wylie. Movin' on Up. New
      York: Hawthorn Books, 1966. Autobiography.

7692 "Mahalia Jackson Back on Concert Trail After Illness; Pulls 11 G
      in Tex." Variety 242:51, April 6, 1966.

7693 "Mahalia Is 'Satisfactory' After Illness." Billboard 78:15, May 14,
      1966.

7694 Atterton, J. "Mahalia Jackson Recuperating from a Heart Attack."
      Melody Maker 41:15, May 28, 1966.

7695 Balliett, W. "Jazz Concerts; Recital at Philharmonic Hall." New
      Yorker 43:164-165, April 8, 1967.

7696 "How God Rescued Mahalia from a Tragic Marriage." Sepia 16:6-10,
      July 1967.

6797 Toomajian, S. "Caught in the Act." down beat 34:37, October 5,
      1967.

7698 "Marital Bliss Vs. Single Blessedness." Ebony 23:89-90, April 1968.

7699 Hobson, C. "The Gospel Truth." down beat 35:19, May 30, 1968.

7700 "Mahalia Also Savors That Fried Chicken Biz." Variety 251:2, July
      3, 1968.

7701 Feather, L. "Carrot Juice and the Word of the Lord." Melody Mak-
      er 44:21, March 29, 1969.

7702 Jones, M. "Why Mahalia's Still in the Book." Melody Maker 44:8,
      May 31, 1969.

7703 Stenbeck, L. "Haerlig Mahalia paa Groenan." Orkester Journalen
      37:9, July-August 1969.

7704 Wilmer, V. "Caught in the Act." down beat 36:31, August 7, 1969.

7705 Thompson, E. B. "Love Comes to Mahalia." Ebony 25:50-61, No-
      vember 1969.

7706 Joe, R. "Mahalia Jackson Is Still Gospel Queen." Billboard 81:20,
      November 22, 1969.

7707 "Mahalia Jackson Goes Home." Second Line 23:320, May-June 1970.

7708 "Mahalia Jackson Says Rock & Jazz Have No Place in Church Rites."
      Variety 259:1, July 22, 1970.

7709 Feather, L. "Newport sans Grise." Jazz Magazine no. 181:59,
      September 1970.

7710 _____. "Mahalia Spreads the Good Word." Melody Maker 46:35,
      August 7, 1971.

7711 Demetre, J. "La Chronique des Disques: Silent Night." Jazz Hot
      no. 277:36, November 1971.

7712 "Mahalia Is OK." Rolling Stone no. 95:14, November 11, 1971.

7713 "Moving on Up." Newsweek 47:49, December 18, 1971.

7714 ["Obituary."] Coda 10:38, no. 6, 1972.

7715 Affeldt, P. E. ["Obituary."] Jazz Report 8:15-16, no. 1, 1972.

7716 "Mahalia Jackson's Concert Tour to India." Jazz Forum no. 15:34, 1972.

7717 ["Obituary."] Musikhandel 23:110, no. 3, 1972; Nuova Rivista Musicale Italiana 6:152, no. 1, 1972.

7718 Higgins, C. "Death Robs World of Greatest Gospel Singer; Mahalia Jackson Rites in Chicago." Jet 41:56-61, February 1, 1972.

7719 ["Obituary."] Variety 265:71, February 2, 1972.

7720 "Heart Attack Takes Mahalia." Billboard 84:3, February 5, 1972.

7721 Jones, M. "Mahalia, the Golden Voice of Gospel." Melody Maker 47:24, February 5, 1972.

7722 Leiser, W. "Cinq Journees avec Mahalia Jackson." Points du Jazz no. 7:127-132, October 1972. Reprinted from Feuille d'Avis de Lausanne February 5-6, 1972.

7723 "Moving on Up." Newsweek 79:49, February 7, 1972; Time 99:89, February 7, 1972.

7724 "Tribute to Mahalia." Melody Maker 47:3, February 12, 1972.

7725 Brown, W. "Sorrow, Pomp, Anger Mark Mahalia's Rites." Jet 41:18-22, February 17, 1972.

7726 Higgins, C. "Mahalia Jackson: A Millionairess' Legacy." Jet 41:22-34, February 17, 1972.

7727 ["Obituary."] Christianity Today 16:44, February 18, 1972.

7728 Goreau, L. "The Queen at Rest." Second Line 24:25-28, Spring 1972.

7729 "A Great Voice Is Stilled." Ebony 27:122-123, March 1972.

7730 Masson, J. R., and J. Reda. "La Place de Mahalia Jackson." Jazz Magazine no. 198:8-15, March 1972.

7731 ["Obituary."] Diapason 63:10-11, March; Ebony 27:122-123, March 1972; Jazz Hot no. 281:16, March 1972; Jazz Podium 21:79, March 1972; Musik und Bildung 4:155, March 1972; Neue Zeitschrift für Musik 133:155, March 1972.

7732 "Two Cities Pay Tribute to Mahalia Jackson." Ebony 27:122-123, March 1972. Chicago and New Orleans hold memorial services to commemorate her many years as a gospel singer.

7733 Von Konow, A. "In Memoriam." Orkester Journalen 40:5, March 1972.

7734 McDaniel, C. G. "Funeralizing Mahalia." Christian Century 89:253-254, March 1, 1972.

7735   Rogers, C. "Mahalia Jackson: Saturday Night Rhythms and Sunday
       Morning Lyrics." Christian Century 89:241-242, March 1, 1972.

7736   Goldberg, J. "When Mahalia Had Her Own TV Show." Rolling Stone
       no. 103:20, March 2, 1972.

7737   "Mahalia Jackson Dead at 60." Rolling Stone no. 103:18, March 2,
       1972.

7738   ["Obituary."] down beat 39:11, March 2, 1972.

7739   "Blacks Win 17 Grammy Awards, but Miles Davis, Motown Exec.
       Walk Out." Jet 42:58, March 3, 1972.

7740   Siler, C. "Mahalia." Soul 6:4, March 6, 1972.

7741   "Mahalia Jackson 1911-1972." down beat 39:10, March 16, 1972.

7742   Terkel, S. "Mahalia Remembered." down beat 39:11, March 16,
       1972. Reprinted from the Chicago Sun Times.

7743   Solomon, L. "Mahalia Jackson, Sanctified." Crawdaddy no. 7:10,
       March 19, 1972.

7744   Lentz, P. "Mahalia Comes Home." down beat 39:13, March 30,
       1972.

7745   Duckett, A. "I Remember Mahalia." Sepia 21:36, April 1972.

7746   Gonda, J. "Mahalia Jackson Halalara." Muzsika 15:30-31, April
       1972.

7747   "In Memory of Mahalia Jackson." Sepia 21:5, April 1972.

7748   Lindenberger, H. "Die Koenigin des Gospelsongs." HiFi-Stereo-
       phonie 11:311-312, April 1972.

7749   ["Obituary."] Music Educators Journal 58:96, April 1972.

7750   Roach, M. "What 'Jazz' Means to Me." Black Scholar 3:2-6, Sum-
       mer 1972.

7751   Grant, C. D. "Mahalia." Essence 3:62, June 1972.

7752   ["Obituary."] Jazz Forum no. 17:36-37, June 1972.

7753   Raney, C. "The Great Thanksgiving for Mahalia." Music 6:19, Sep-
       tember 1972.

7754   "Jazz im Film: In Memoriam Mahalia Jackson und Louis Armstrong."
       Jazz Podium 21:21-22, August 1972.

7755   ["Obituary."] Black Perspectives in Music 1:198, no. 2, 1973.

7756   Cornell, Jean Gay. Mahalia Jackson: Queen of Gospel Song. Cham-
       paign, Ill.: Garrard Pub. Co., 1974. Juvenile literature.

7757   Dunham, Montrew. Mahalia Jackson: Young Gospel Singer. Indian-
       apolis: Bobbs-Merrill, 1974. Juvenile literature.

7758   Jackson, Jesse. Make a Joyful Noise unto the Lord! The Life of
       Mahalia Jackson, Queen of Gospel Singers. New York: T. Y.
       Crowell, 1974. Juvenile literature.

7759   Jones, Hettie. Big Star Fallin' Mama; Five Women in Black Music.
       New York: Viking Press, 1974. Juvenile literature about Ma
       Rainey, Bessie Smith, Billie Holiday, Aretha Franklin, and Jack-
       son.

7760   Lehmann, Theo. Mahalia Jackson: Gospelmusik Ist Mein Leben.
       Berlin: Union-Verlag, 1974.

7761   Falls, M. "Unforgettable Mahalia Jackson." Reader's Digest 104:102-
       106, March 1974.

7762   Goreau, Laurraine R. Just Mahalia, Baby. Waco, Tex.: Word
       Books, 1975.

7763   McDearmon, Kay. Mahalia, Gospel Singer. New York: Dodd, Mead
       1976.

7764   Jones, M. "Mahalia and Gospel Roots." Melody Maker 52:38, Feb-
       ruary 1977.

7765   Mays, Benjamin E., et al. "Most Extraordinary Black Woman I
       Have Ever Known." Ebony 32:139-140, August 1977.

7766   Record Reviews: Gospel." Jazz Journal International 30:38-39, De-
       cember 1977.

7767   "Blues/Folk Albums: Gospel." Melody Maker 53:30, February 25,
       1978.

JACKSON FIVE (later, the Jacksons).

7768   Winner, L. "Records: Diana Ross Presents the Jackson Five."
       Rolling Stone no. 53:46, March 7, 1970.

7769   "Soul Brothers; The Jackson 5." Newsweek 75:98, April 20, 1970.

7770   "Talent in Action." Billboard 82:42, July 4, 1970.

7771   Dunbar, E. "Jackson Five." Look 34:18-21, August 25, 1970.

7772   Robinson, L. "The Jackson Five." Ebony 25:150-154, September
       1970.

7773   Brodsky, A. "Records: ABC." Rolling Stone no. 65:46, September
       3, 1970.

7774   Wickham, V. "Jackson Five Are on Top." Melody Maker 45:6, Sep-
       tember 19, 1970.

7775   "Concert Reviews." Variety 260:42, October 21, 1970.

7776   "Talent in Action." Billboard 82:24, October 31, 1970.

7777   Aletti, V. "Jackson Five: The Biggest Thing Since the Stones."
        Rolling Stone no. 71:12, November 26, 1970. Discussion of a con-
        cert at Madison Square Garden.

7777a   Goldman, A. "A Black Teen Breakthrough." Life 69:12, November 27,
        1970.

7778   "Series of Death Threats to Jackson 5's Youngest Cancels Show in
        Buffalo." Variety 261:41, December 2, 1970.

7779   Spiegelman, J. "The Jackson 5." Soul 3:34-38, no. 1, 1971.

7780   Taylor, J. "The Jackson 5 'Go Home.'" Sepia 2:21-26, April 1971.

7781   Fong-Torres, B. "The Jackson 5." Rolling Stone no. 81:24-27,
        April 29, 1971.

7782   Tyler, T. "Jackson Five at Home." Time 97:64, June 14, 1971.

7783   Aletti, V. "Records: Maybe Tomorrow." Rolling Stone no. 87:39,
        July 22, 1971.

7783a   "Talent in Action." Billboard 83:22, July 31, 1971; 83:20, September 11,
        1971.

7784   "Jackson Five's 35 G Fee at Ohio Fair, Not $25,000." Variety
        264:42, August 18, 1971.

7785   "New Heights for the Jackson Five." Ebony 26:126-131, September
        1971.

7786   "Jackson Five." Life 71:50-51, September 24, 1971.

7787   Lucas, B. "Jackson 5: Hottest Music Act in Show Business." Sepia
        20:35-45, October 1971.

7788   Let's Save the Children, Inc. The Jackson Five. Staff: Helen King,
        et al. Chicago: Let's Save the Children, Inc., 1972. Juvenile
        literature.

7789   Spiegelman, J. "What Does the Future Hold for the Jackson Five?"
        Soul 6:2-4, February 14, 1972.

7790   "Records: Jackson 5 Greatest Hits." Rolling Stone no. 102:49, Feb-
        ruary 17, 1972.

7791   Davis, L. "Will Jackie Leave Home?" Soul 6:1-2, March 6, 1972.

7792   Spiegelman, J. "Male Group of 1971." Soul 7:22-23, May 1, 1972.

7793   "Tito of Jackson Five Gets Married at 19." Jet 42:12-13, June 29,
        1972.

7794   "Concert Reviews." Variety 267:55, July 12, 1972.

7795   Berry, W. E. "Jermaine Jackson Becomes Idol of Teenagers." Jet
        42:58-61, August 31, 1972.

7796 "6,000 Fans Mob J-5 Member Jermaine." Jet 42:62-63, August 3, 1972.

7797 Bartley, G. F. "Jackson 5 in New York; A Night to Remember." Soul 7:14, August 28, 1972.

7798 Hetherington, B. "Caught in the Act Extra." Melody Maker 46:38, September 11, 1971.

7799 Gest, D. "Jackson 5 Electrify Forum." Soul 7:14, October 23, 1972.

7800 Alterman, L. "On the Eve of the British Tour." Melody Maker 47:53, October 28, 1972.

7801 "Albums: Lookin' Through the Windows." Melody Maker 47:30, November 4, 1972.

7802 Williams, R. "Who Said It Couldn't Happen Again?" Melody Maker 47:34-35, November 4, 1972.

7803 "Jacksons Set Extra Concert." Melody Maker 47:5, November 11, 1972.

7804 Charlesworth, C. "Battle of the Boppers!" Melody Maker 47:34, November 11, 1972.

7805 _____. "Jacksons' ABC of Soul." Melody Maker 47:41, November 18, 1972.

7806/8 "Jackson 5, Osmonds Plan Returns." Melody Maker 47:5, November 18, 1972.

7809 "Records: Looking Through the Windows." Rolling Stone no. 123:68, December 7, 1972.

7810 Sandner, W. "Frankfurt A.M." Soul-Gruppen 'Jackson-Five,' 'Ike & Tina Turner' und 'The Four Tops' in Deutschland." Neue Zeitschrift für Musik 134:37-38, no. 1, 1973.

7811 Nickerson, R. "Hair-Pulling, Choking and Knives: Europe Greets the Jackson Five." Soul 7:2, January 15, 1973.

7812 "Jacksonmania Hits Watts." Soul 7:13, January 29, 1973.

7813 Aubrey, D. "Jackson Five--Male Group 1972." Soul 7:6, April 23, 1973.

7814 "Records: Skywriter." Rolling Stone no. 136:58, June 7, 1973.

7815 Spiegelman, J. "Jackson Family Journeys to Japan." Soul 8:2-3, June 25, 1973.

7816 Rubine, N. "Papa Joe Reflects on His Talented Sons." Soul 8:2-3, July 9, 1973.

7817 "Concert Reviews." Variety 271:38, July 25, 1973.

7818   Trubo, R. "Very Private Life of Jackson 5." Sepia 22:42-49, October 1973.

7819   "Tito Jackson's First Wedding Anniversary Starts New Life." Jet 44:74-79, October 4, 1973.

7820   Crenshaw, J. "Jackson Five Stir Up Some Great Vibrations." Soul 8:6, October 15, 1973.

7821   Milton, D. "Confident Jacksons." Melody Maker 48:51, November 10, 1973.

7822   "Records: Get It Together." Rolling Stone no. 148:76, November 22, 1973.

7823   "Love Comes to a Jackson Five." Ebony 29:142-143, December 1973.

7824   Morse, Charles and Ann Morse. Jackson Five. Mankato, Minn.: Creative Education; Distributed by Childrens Press, Chicago, 1974, c1975. Juvenile literature.

7825   Mitchell, G. "Jackson Five Wins New Acclaim on Tour of Africa." Jet 45:54-61, March 7, 1974.

7826   "MGM Grand Hotel, L.V." Variety 274:84, April 17, 1974.

7827   "Everybody in the Act; Jackson Five 'Turn on' Las Vegas." Soul 9:12-13, May 27, 1974.

7828   Atlas, J. "Jacksons: All You Need for a Hit Is the Right Feeling." Melody Maker 49:11, June 12, 1974.

7829   "The Soul Report." Melody Maker 49:28-29, January 12, 1974.

7830   Brown, G. "How the Boppers Stopped the Jacksons." Melody Maker 49:8-9, June 15, 1974.

7831   Rubine, N. "What 3 Super, Super Fans Will Do to Meet the J-5!" Soul 9:14-15, June 24, 1974.

7832   "Concert Reviews." Variety 275:46, July 31, 1974.

7833   Brown, C. "Jackson Five Plus Three Equal a New Entertainment Act." Jet 46:54-57, August 1, 1974.

7834   "'I'm Trapped,' Jackie Yells After J5 Smash Show." Soul 9:2-3, August 5, 1974.

7835   "Talent in Action." Billboard 86:22, August 10, 1974.

7836   "Performance." Rolling Stone no. 167:62, August 15, 1974.

7837   "Caught in the Act." Melody Maker 49:44, August 31, 1974.

7838   "MGM Grand, Las Vegas." Variety 276:63, September 4, 1974; 277:79, November 27, 1974.

7839   Robinson, L. "Family Life of the Jackson Five." Ebony 30:33-36, December 1974.

7840 Ruffin, W. D. "No 'Hum-Drum' for Jackson Five." Soul 9:15, January 20, 1975. Review of performance at MGM Grand in Las Vegas.

7841 "Concert Reviews." Variety 278:72, February 12, 1975.

7842 "Talent in Action." Billboard 87:36, February 22, 1975.

7843 "MGM Grand, Las Vegas." Variety 278:85, April 16, 1975.

7844 Sims, J. "Singles: J5 Come of Age on 'I Am Love.'" Rolling Stone no. 186:24, May 8, 1975.

7845 "A. C. Turns Down Convention Hall for Jackson 5; Fear Unruly Crowd." Variety 279:65, July 2, 1975.

7846 "It's Now Jackson 4 in Diskery Switch: Motown to Epic." Variety 279:61, July 2, 1975.

7847 Brown, G. F. "Randy and Janet Add New Dimension to J-5." Jet 48:56-59, July 3, 1975.

7848 "Leaving Motown." New Yorker 51:26-27, July 14, 1975.

7849 "MGM Grand, Las Vegas." Variety 279:102, July 16, 1975.

7850 "Records: Moving Violation." Rolling Stone no. 192:56, July 31, 1975.

7851 "Joe Jackson on J-5 Motown Split: 'Never Gave Us an Opportunity.'" Soul 10:4, August 18, 1975.

7852 Kirk, C. "Why J5 Switched to Epic Revealed." Soul 10:1, August 18, 1975.

7853 Kirby, F. "Combo Members Going Solo; Artist of Faces, Jackson 5, Allman Bros., et al., Cut Solo LPs but Retain Group Ties." Variety 280:59, August 20, 1975.

7854 "Concert Reviews." Variety 280:84, September 3, 1975.

7855 "Talent in Action." Billboard 87:35, September 13, 1975.

7856 "Performance." Rolling Stone no. 196:118, September 25, 1975.

7857 "Can Randy & Janet Survive the Rigors of Show Business?" Soul 10:2-3, September 29, 1975.

7858 Lucas, B. "Tito Jackson: His Music and His Family Life." Jet 49:20-24, November 20, 1975.

7859 Lake, Harriet. On Stage, Jackson Five. Mankato, Minn.: Creative Education; Distributed by Childrens Press, Chicago, 1976. Juvenile literature.

7860 "Motown Sued by 4 of Jackson 5." Billboard 88:12, April 10, 1976.

7861 "Clear Jackson 5 for Epic Etchings." Variety 283:67, May 26, 1976.

7862   Lucas, B.   "Summer TV Debut: 'The Jacksons ... and Then Some.'"
       Jet 50:60-63, June 24, 1976.

7863   Norman, Shirley.   "New Show and a New Career for New Jackson
       5."   Sepia 25:34-36, July 1976.

7864   Lucas, B.   "Jermaine Jackson Goes It Alone."   Jet 50:58-61, Sep-
       tember 2, 1976.

7865   _____ .   "Jacksons: New TV Show to Give New Boost to Career."
       Jet 51:60-63, December 2, 1976.

7866   "$20 Million Suit: Motown & CBS."   Billboard 89:18, February 19,
       1977.

7867   Lemieux, M.   "Jacksons."   Black Collegian 7:80, March-April 1977.

7868   "Motown Sues CBS in Jackson Five Action."   Variety 286:65, March
       9, 1977.

7869   Lucas, B.   "Michael Jackson: A Young Bachelor Married to Music."
       Jet 52:60-63, March 31, 1977.

7870   "Albums: Goin' Places."   Melody Maker 52:23, December 3, 1977.

7871   "Records: Goin' Places."   Rolling Stone no. 255:25, December 29,
       1977.

7872   Norman, S.   "Jackson Girls: Like the Jackson 5, They're Making
       Their Marks."   Sepia 27:40-46, May 1978.

7873   Peterson, S.   "The Jacksons Tenth Anniversary Special."   Billboard
       90:J1, November 18, 1978.

7874   White, T.   "Blame It on the Boogie?"   Crawdaddy no. 91:48-51, De-
       cember 1978.

JAECKEL, MRS. ANDREAS   see   BUMBRY, GRACE

JARRETT, KEITH, 1945- .

7875   Hennessey, M.   "Keith Jarrett, Pianist Who Makes Sounds That Fit."
       Melody Maker 42:6, May 20, 1967.

7876   "Fin de Liaisons."   Jazz Magazine no. 158:13, September 1968.

7877   Albertson, C., et al.   "Record Reviews."   down beat 36:24, April
       17, 1969.

7878   Wilson, J. S.   "Caught in the Act."   down beat 36:40, May 1, 1969.

7879   Gerber, A.   "Prelude to a Keith."   Jazz Magazine no. 168:26-29,
       July-August 1969.

7880   Albertson, C., et al.   "Record Reviews."   down beat 36:23-24, Sep-
       tember 4, 1969.

7881 Williams, R. "Keith Finds the Going Much Tougher." Melody Maker 44:14, October 4, 1969.

7882 Carles, P. "Les Trois Nuits de Bologne." Jazz Magazine no. 172:18-21, November 1969.

7883 Gerber, A. "Une Demystification Corrosive." Jazz Magazine no. 173:17-18, December 1969.

7884 Postif, F. "Keith Jarrett." Jazz Hot no. 256:18-20, December 1969.

7885 "Pieges pour Keith." Jazz Magazine no. 176:32-33, March 1970.

7886 Gerber, A. "Une Minutieuse Luxuriance." Jazz Magazine no. 177:15, April 1970.

7887 "Jean-Luc Ponty, Keith Jarrett et Annie Ross à l'Apollo." Jazz Hot no. 262:26, June 1970.

7888 "Record Reviews: Gary Burton & Keith Jarrett." down beat 38:21, May 13, 1971; Jazz and Pop 10:42, May 1971; Jazz Journal 24:28-29, October 1971; Rolling Stone no. 90:48, September 2, 1971.

7889 "Record Reviews: The Mourning of a Star." Coda 10:17, no. 6, 1972.

7890 Wilmer, V. "Keith Jarrett." Jazz Forum no. 15:67-69, 1972.

7891 Klee, J. H. "Keith Jarrett: Spontaneous Composer." down beat 39:12, January 20, 1972.

7892 "Record Reviews: The Mourning of a Star." down beat 39:22, February 3, 1972.

7893 "Records: The Mourning of a Star." Rolling Stone no. 101:44, February 3, 1972.

7894 "Records: Gary Burton and Keith Jarrett." Jazz Forum no. 16:83-84, March-April 1972.

7895 "RecWords: The Mourning of a Star." Crawdaddy no. 6:17, March 5, 1972.

7896 "Chronique des Disques: Facing You." Jazz Hot no. 282:29, April 1972.

7897 "Chronique des Disques: Gary Burton & Keith Jarrett." Jazz Hot no. 282:25, April 1972.

7898 "Disques du Mois: Gary Burton and Keith Jarrett." Jazz Magazine no. 199:36, April 1972.

7899 "Schallplattenbesprechungen: Facing You." Jazz Podium 21:132, April 1972.

7900 "Jazz Records: Facing You." Melody Maker 47:40, May 6, 1972.

7901 "Five Guggenheims to Artists in Jazz Field." down beat 39:9, June 8, 1972.

7902   Goddet, L., and C. Flicker. "Keith Jarrett Trio à l'ORTF." <u>Jazz</u>
       <u>Hot</u> no. 285:24-25, July-August 1972.

7903   Gerber, A. "Paris." <u>Jazz Magazine</u> no. 202:29-30, July 1972.

7904   "Jazz Records: The Mourning of a Star." <u>Melody Maker</u> 47:16, July
       29, 1972.

7905   "Record Reviews: Facing You." <u>Jazz & Blues</u> 2:30, August 1972.

7906   Gonda, J. "Utohang a Videoton Jazzfesztivalrol." <u>Muzsika</u> 15:44,
       September 1972.

7907   "Record Reviews: The Mourning of a Star." <u>Jazz & Blues</u> 2:25,
       September 1972.

7908   "Records: Birth; Expectations; Facing You." <u>Rolling Stone</u> no.
       124:66, December 21, 1972.

7909   Offstein, A. "ECM." <u>Coda</u> 10:7-14, no. 12, 1973.

7910   "Record Reviews: Gary Burton and Keith Jarrett." <u>Coda</u> 10:19-20,
       no. 11, 1973.

7911   Mimaroglu, I. "Caught in the Act." <u>down beat</u> 40:36, January 18,
       1973.

7912   "Record Reviews: Expectations." <u>down beat</u> 40:21-22, March 29,
       1973.

7913   Rockwell, J. "New York." <u>Music and Musicians</u> 22:84, October
       1973.

7914   _____. "What's New?" <u>High Fidelity/Musical America</u> 23:MA10-
       11, October 1973.

7915   "Talent in Action." <u>Billboard</u> 85:22, November 10, 1973.

7916   "Jarrett Brand of Jazz Like Brandy." <u>Soul</u> 8:11, December 10, 1973.

7917   "Jazz Records: Solo Concerts." <u>Melody Maker</u> 48:36, December 29,
       1973.

7918   Burde, W. "Berlin: Jazztage '73." <u>Neue Zeitschrift für Musik</u>
       135:34-36, no. 1, 1974.

7919   "Heard and Seen." <u>Coda</u> 11:36-37, no. 5, 1974; 11:37, no. 11, 1974.

7920   Berendt, J. E. "Kleine Combo--Geschichte des Neuen Jazz." <u>Jazz</u>
       <u>Podium</u> 23:13-16, January 1974.

7921   Anders, J. "Keith Jarrett in Willisau." <u>Jazz Podium</u> 23:24, Febru-
       ary 1974.

7922   "Jazz Records: In the Light." <u>Melody Maker</u> 49:64, March 30, 1974.

7923   "Records: Fort Yawuh." <u>Crawdaddy</u> no. 34: 74, March 1974.

7924 Albertson, C. "On Importing Our Own Jazz." Stereo Review 32:91, May 1974.

7925 Berendt, J. E. "The Whole World in a Piano." Jazz Forum no. 29:35-37, June 1974.

7926 McRae, B. "Avant Courier: You Know, You Know." Jazz Journal 27:25, June 1974.

7927 Bompard, P. "Jarrett Calls 'Free Music' Idea of Leftists Mere 'Gate Crashing.'" Variety 275:2, August 7, 1974.

7928 "Records: In the Light; Solo Concerts; Treasure Island." Crawdaddy no. 41:72-73, October 1974.

7929 "Records: Solo Concerts." Cream 6:66, October 1974.

7930 Palmer, B. "The Inner Octaves of Keith Jarrett." down beat 41:16-17, October 24, 1974.

7931 Albertson, C. "Keith Jarrett's New Jazz Piano." Stereo Review 33:89-90, November 1974.

7932 "Heard and Seen." Coda 12:38, no. 6, 1975.

7933 "Keith Jarrett: Face à Vous." Jazz Magazine no. 230:13-15, February 1975.

7934 "Concerts: Jarrett aux Champs." Jazz Hot no. 314:42, March 1975.

7935 "Jazz en Direct." Jazz Magazine no. 231:9-10, March 1975.

7936 "Concert Reviews." Variety 278:60, March 5, 1975.

7937 "Caught in the Act." Melody Maker 50:26, March 15, 1975.

7938 "Talent in Action." Billboard 87:53, March 22, 1975.

7939 "Caught." down beat 42:30, April 10, 1975.

7940 Hurwitz, R. "Parallel Careers of Keith Jarrett." High Fidelity/ Musical America 25:63-65, May 1975.

7941 "Record Reviews: Belonging." down beat 42:22, June 19, 1975.

7942 Anders, J. "Grosser Deutscher Schallplattenpreis für Keith Jarrett und Eberhard Weber." Jazz Podium 24:29, August 1975.

7943 "Record Reviews: Becoming." Coda no. 142:15, October 1975.

7944 "Records: Luminessence; The Koeln Concert." Rolling Stone no. 200:68, November 20, 1975.

7945 Bachmann, K. R. "Brillant, aber Gegaengelt: Keith Jarrett und Jan Garbarek mit Streichern." Jazz Podium 24:21, December 1975.

7946 Commanday, R. "New Music at Cabrillo; Ballard and List Get a

Fair Hearing and a Mixed Sentence." High Fidelity/Musical America 25:MA32, December 1975.

7947 "Schallplatten-Besprechungen: The Koeln Concert." Jazz Podium 24:36, December 1975.

7948 "Record Reviews: Belonging; Luminessence; The Koeln Concert." Jazz Forum no. 41:60-61, 1976.

7949 Tesser, N. "Keith Jarrett." Jazz Forum no. 40:50, 1976.

7950 "Record Reviews: El Juicio." down beat 43:23-24, January 15, 1976.

7951 "Record Reviews: Luminessence." down beat 43:22, January 29, 1976.

7952 Chesnel, J. "La Vraie Nature de Keith Jarrett." Jazz Hot no. 324:6-10, February 1976.

7953 Goddet, L. "Keith Jarrett." Jazz Hot no. 324:11, February 1976.

7954 "Record Reviews: The Koeln Concert." down beat 43:22, February 12, 1976.

7955 "Caught in the Act." Melody Maker 51:27, March 20, 1976.

7956 "Records: Backhand; The Koeln Concert." Crawdaddy no. 59:73-74, April 1976.

7957 "Record Reviews: Back Hand-ABC." down beat 43:24, May 6, 1976.

7958 "In Concert--Complete Artistry." Melody Maker 51:29, May 22, 1976. Review of concert in Willisau, Switzerland.

7959 Lake, S. "Genius on a Razor's Edge." Melody Maker 51:29, May 22, 1976.

7960 "Jazz en Direct." Jazz Magazine no. 245:4, June-July 1976.

7961 "Jazz Albums: Arbour Zena." Melody Maker 51:26, June 26, 1976.

7962 Goddet, L. "Keith Jarret à Pleyel." Jazz Hot no. 329:50, July-August 1976.

7963 Ogan, B. "Jazzmarathon aus Ost und West." Jazz Podium 25:4-6, July 1976.

7964 "Record Reviews: Death and the Flower." Coda no. 149:16, July 1976.

7965 Balliett, W. "Jazz: New York Notes." New Yorker 52:83, July 19, 1976.

7966 "Record Reviews: Mysteries." Jazz Journal 29:35-36, August 1976; down beat 43:25-26, September 9, 1976.

7967 Lake, S. "Piano Giants." Melody Maker 51:44-45, October 2, 1976.

7968 "Record Reviews: Arbour Zena." down beat 43:20, October 21, 1976.

7969 "Jazz Albums: Hymns Spheres." Melody Maker 52:20, January 15, 1977.

7970 "Closeness." Radio Free Jazz 18:12-13, February 1977.

7971 "Records: Shades." High Fidelity/Musical America 27:143, February 1977.

7972 "Records: Shades." Cream 8:70, May 1977.

7973 "Record Reviews: Chick Corea, Herbie Hancock, Keith Jarrett, McCoy Tyner." down beat 44:22, May 5, 1977.

7974 "Jazz Albums: Staircase." Melody Maker 52:36, May 14, 1977.

7975 "Record Reviews: Shades." down beat 44:26, May 19, 1977.

7976 "Hymn/Spheres." down beat 44:20, June 2, 1977.

7977 "Records: Chick Corea/Herbie Hancock/Keith Jarrett/McCoy Tyner." Crawdaddy no. 75:65, August 1977.

7978 Saal, H. "Two Free Spirits." Newsweek 90:52-53, August 8, 1977. The music of Anthony Braxton and Jarrett is discussed.

7979 "Records: Staircase." High Fidelity/Musical America 27:139, September 1977.

7980 Youngren, W. "National Public Radio." New Republic 177:23, September 24, 1977.

7981 "Record Reviews: Tales of Another." Jazz Journal International 30:50, October 1977.

7982 Simmons, W. "Jarrett: Various Works." American Record Guide 40:34, October 1977.

7983 "Record Reviews: Staircase." down beat 44:27, October 6, 1977.

7984 "Caught in the Act." Melody Maker 52:17, October 29, 1977.

7985 "Records: Staircase." Rolling Stone no. 251:110, November 3, 1977.

7986 Carr, I. "Acoustic Music for the Mind and Bod." Melody Maker 52:10, November 5, 1977.

7987 "Jazz Albums: The Survivors' Suite." Melody Maker 52:32, November 5, 1977.

7988 "Concert Reviews." Variety 289:58, November 30, 1977.

7989 "En Direct." Jazz Magazine no. 260:12, December 1977.

7990 McRae, B., and D. Gelly. "Jazz Live!: Two Views on Jarrett." Jazz Journal International 30:27, December 1977.

7991 Giddins, G. "Weatherbird: Keith Jarrett: Virtuosity Is Not Enough."
      Village Voice 22:65, December 5, 1977.

7992 Coleman, R., et al. "MM Albums of the Year." Melody Maker
      52:31, December 17, 1977.

7993 "Talent in Action." Billboard 89:50, December 17, 1977.

7994 "Record Reviews: The Survivors' Suite." Jazz Forum no. 54:43-44,
      1978.

7995 "Reviews: Bop-Be; My Song; Keith Jarrett." Jazz Magazine (U.S.)
      2:68-69, no. 4, 1978.

7996 Solothurnmann, J. "Jan Garbarek: A Thinking Improviser." Jazz
      Forum no. 54:33-37, 1978.

7997 "Record Reviews: Byablue." down beat 45:24, January 12, 1978.

7998 "Record Reviews: The Survivors Suite." down beat 45:20, January
      26, 1978.

7999 Moussaron, J. P. "Du Lyrisme en Piano-Jazz." Jazz Magazine
      no. 262:36-39, February 1978.

8000 "Jazz Albums: Byablue." Melody Maker 53:24, February 4, 1978.

8001 "Record Reviews: The Survivors' Suite." Jazz Journal International
      31:39, April 1978.

8002 Ruppli, M. "Discographie: Keith Jarrett." Jazz Hot no. 348:22-25,
      April 1978.

8003 Henschen, R. "Keith Jarrett: Classical Sides of Jazz." Music Jour-
      nal 36:3-5, May 1978.

8004 "Jazz Albums: My Song." Melody Maker 53:32, May 20, 1978.

8005 "Records--Jazz: Bop-Be." High Fidelity/Musical America 28:124-
      125, August 1978.

8006 Ripp, A. "Keith Jarrett." Horizon 21:80-84, August 1978.

8007 "Jazz Albums: Bop-Be." Melody Maker 53:22, September 16, 1978.

8008 "Concert Reviews." Variety 292:66, October 25, 1978.

8009 "Talent in Action." Billboard 90:60, October 28, 1978.

8010 Albertson, C. "Jarrett: Out of Superlatives." Stereo Review 41:182,
      November 1978. Review of "My Song."

8011 "Jazz Albums: Sun Bear Concerts." Melody Maker 53:55, December
      2, 1978.

8012 "Record Reviews: My Song." down beat 45:18, December 7, 1978.

JELLY ROLL see MORTON, FERDINAND JOSEPH

JOHNSON, CAROL DIAHANN see CARROLL, DIAHANN

JONES, QUINCY DELIGHT, 1933- .

8013 Hentoff, N. "Counterpoint." down beat 21:36, April 21, 1954; 21:12,
      May 5, 1954.

8014 Cage, R. "Arranger Quincy Jones Says Quality of R&B Sides Bet-
      ter." down beat 22:42, September 21, 1955.

8015 Feather, L. "A Jones Boy." down beat 24:37, February 6, 1957.

8016 Östberg, L. "Quincy Jones." Orkester Journalen 26:10-11, May 1958.

8017 "Jones Forming Band." down beat 26:12, April 30, 1959.

8018 Jones, Quincy. "Starting a Big Band." Jazz Review 2:16-17, Sep-
      tember 1959.

8019 Feather, L. "The Blindfold Test." down beat 26:35, September 17,
      1959.

8020 "Quincy Scoring Show." down beat 26:12, October 15, 1959.

8021 "Clark Terry Rejoint Quincy Jones." Jazz Magazine 6:13, December
      1959.

8022 De Radzitzky, C. "Demarrage à Bruxelles du Grand Orchestre de
      Quincy Jones avec la Revue 'Free and Easy.'" Jazz Magazine
      6:11, January 1960.

8023 "Succe for Nya Negeroperan 'Free and Easy.'" Orkester Journalen
      28:13, January 1960.

8024 Kopel, G. "Biographie de Quincy Jones." Jazz Magazine 6:25, Feb-
      ruary 1960.

8025 Tenot, F. "Quincy Jones Face à Son Destin." Jazz Magazine 6:19-
      24, February 1960.

8026 "Tout l'Orchestre de Quincy Jones." Jazz Hot 25:24-25, February
      1960.

8027 Lees, G. "The Great Wide World of Quincy Jones." down beat
      27:19-20, February 4, 1960.

8028 Mathieu, B. "Nothing New in Quincy, but...." down beat 27:22,
      February 4, 1960.

8029 Destombes, A. "Un Ensemble Homogene et Hors Serie." Jazz Hot
      26:46, March 1960.

8030 "European Try-Out Cut Short." down beat 27:13-14, March 31, 1960.

8031 Helander, O. "Quincy Jones Orchestra in Concert in Stockholm."
      down beat 27:50, April 28, 1960.

8032   Balli, E. "Quincy Jones e King Cole a Milano." Musica Jazz 16:24-25, June 1960.

8033   Schiozzi, B. "Intervista con Quincy." Musica Jazz 16:18-19, July 1960.

8034   Parnell, C. "The Band Business in Europe Is a Headache: Interview with Quincy Jones." Melody Maker 35:8-9, September 24, 1960.

8035   Masson, J. R. "Quincy Jones à Quitte l'Europe." Jazz Magazine 6:16-17, October 1960.

8036   "Band Reviews." Variety 220:48, November 2, 1960.

8037   Feather, L. "The Blindfold Test." down beat 28:45, February 16, 1961.

8038   "Quincy Jones." Ebony 16:69-73, March 1961.

8039   Feather, L. "The Blindfold Test." down beat 28:43, March 2, 1961.

8040   Hennessey, M. "Who Says Europeans Can't Play Jazz?" Melody Maker 36:13, March 25, 1961.

8041   "La Renaissance d'un Orchestre." Jazz Magazine 7:18, April 1961.

8042   Renaud, H. "Le Groupement de Quincy Jones est un Orchestre Jeune, Enthousiaste, mais Discipline et Efficace." Jazz Hot no. 164:21, April 1961.

8043   "Le Retour de Quincy Jones." Jazz Hot no. 164:20, April 1961.

8044   Dance, H., and S. Dance. "Quincy Jones Discusses Aspects of the Contemporary Scene." Metronome 78:22-23, May 1961.

8045   Dance, S. "Three Score; A Quiz for Jazz Musicians." Metronome 78:48, May 1961.

8046   "Quincy Hamp Duke." Jazz Magazine 7:22-30, May 1961.

8047   "Du Galon pour Quincy." Jazz Magazine 7:14, September 1961.

8048   Hentoff, N. "Quincy Jones." International Musician 60:22-23, December 1961.

8049   Jones, M. "Quincy Jones in London for Flying Visit." Melody Maker 37:9, February 10, 1962.

8050   Feather, L. "How to Lose a Big Band Without Really Trying." down beat 29:22-23, April 26, 1962.

8051   Hentoff, N. "The Scope of Quincy Jones." Philips Music Herald p. 18-20, Spring 1963.

8052   Jones, Quincy. "Sarah Makes It All Worth While." Melody Maker 38:12, October 12, 1963.

8053   Traill, S. "Editorial." Jazz Journal 16:1, November 1963.

8054 _____. "In My Opinion." Jazz Journal 17:5-6, April 1964.

8055 "American Recording Director Has One Foot in Europe." Philips Music Herald p. 26-29, Winter 1964-1965.

8056 "Quincy Jones New Mercury Vice-President." Cash Box 26:7, December 19, 1964.

8057 Tiegel, E. "Quincy at the Movies." Billboard 77:26, December 18, 1965.

8058 "The Busy Mr. Jones." down beat 33:13, May 5, 1966.

8059 Raben, E. "Quincy Jones Diskografi." Orkester Journalen 34:32, November 1966.

8060 _____. "Quincy Jones Diskografi." Orkester Journalen 35:31, January 1967; 35:28, February 1967; 35:28, March 1967.

8061 Lees, G. "The New Sound on the Soundtracks." High Fidelity/Musical America 17:58-61, August 1967.

8062 Feather, L. "Quincy in Hollywood." Melody Maker 43:8, March 30, 1968.

8063 _____. "From Pen to Screen." International Musician 66:4, June 1968.

8064 "Bli Musikalisk Skrothandlare Sager Quincy Jones." Orkester Journalen 36:10-11, July-August 1968.

8065 Holroyd, S. "Soul Brother in Hollywood." Melody Maker 43:8, July 20, 1968.

8066 McPartland, M. "Quincy Jones." down beat 36:39, March 6, 1969.

8067 "Harold Robbins' Novel Entry into Disk Biz." Variety 256:57, October 29, 1969.

8068 Siders, H. "Keeping up with Quincy Jones." down beat 36:13, November 27, 1969.

8069 "Composer-Arrangers Appointed to Berklee Board of Trustees." Jazz and Pop 8:46, December 1969.

8070 Feather, L. "Blindfold Test." down beat 37:30, March 5, 1970.

8071 "Quincy Jones Plans Studio." Billboard 82:32, October 3, 1970.

8072 "Record Review: Gula Matari." Melody Maker 45:14, November 14, 1970.

8073 Siders, H. "Quincy's Got a Brand New (Old) Bag." down beat 37:13, November 26, 1970.

8074 Jones, Quincy. "The Institute of Black American Music." down beat 37:14, December 24, 1970.

8075 Traill, S. "Record Reviews: Gula Matari." Jazz Journal 24:37,
      March 1971.

8076 "Quincy Jones Cops Oscar Show M. C. Job." down beat 38:11,
      March 4, 1971.

8077 Traill, S. "Record Reviews: Walking in Space." Jazz Journal
      24:39, April 1971.

8078 Flippo, C. "A Volcano in Ray Charles' Soul." Rolling Stone no.
      79:16, April 1, 1971.

8079 Gerber, A. "Disques du Mois: Gula Matari." Jazz Magazine no.
      189:44, May 1971.

8080 Niquet, B. "Chronique des Disques: Gula Matari." Jazz Hot no.
      272:33, May 1971.

8081 "Other Premieres." BMI p. 12-13, May 1971. Discussion of "Black
      Requiem."

8082 Tiegel, E. "Talent in Action." Billboard 83:22, September 11, 1971.

8083 Henshaw, L. "The Album Every Guitarist Should Hear." Melody
      Maker 46:35, November 6, 1971. Critique of Jones' "Smackwater
      Jack."

8084 Szantor, J. "Record Reviews: Smackwater Jack." down beat 38:24,
      December 9, 1971.

8085 Tiegel, E. "Quincy Returns to Clef Disks." Billboard 83:1, Decem-
      ber 25, 1971.

8086 "Happenings." Symphony News 23:18, no. 2, 1972. Discussion of
      performance of Jones' "Music for Malcolm."

8087 Carter, J. "Quincy Jones--the Prolific Powerhouse." Crescendo In-
      ternational 10:26, January 1972.

8088 Jones, Quincy. "The Problems of A & R Work." Crescendo Inter-
      national 10:19, March 1972.

8089 Siders, H. "The Jazz Composers in Hollywood." down beat 39:12-
      15, March 2, 1972.

8090 Meyers, R. "Quincy Jones Sees the Whole Thread." Rolling Stone
      no. 104:22, March 16, 1972.

8091 Robinson, L. "Quincy Jones: Man Behind the Music." Ebony 27:92-
      94, June 1972.

8092 "Concert Reviews." Variety 267:55, July 12, 1972.

8093 Tiegel, E. "Monterey: Roberta, Quincy Sensational at 15th Anny."
      Billboard 84:21, September 30, 1972.

8094 Feather, L. "Quincy Jones." Melody Maker 47:22, October 28,
      1972.

8095 Goddard, R. "Quincy--Roberta So-So at Center." Soul 7:12, December 4, 1972.

8096 Nickerson, R. "Shaking the 'Losing Human Syndrome': A Lesson in Living from Duke Ellington." Soul 7:2-3, February 12, 1973.

8097 Carles, P. "Cinq de la Bande Son." Jazz Magazine no. 212:6-7, June 1973.

8098 Salvo, P. W. "Quincy Jones: A Musical Legend." Sepia 22:24-28, October 1973.

8099 "Three Music Names That Spell Greatness." Soul 8:10-11, October 1, 1973.

8100 Nolan, H. "Quincy Jones." down beat 40:12-13, November 22, 1973.

8101 Robinson, L. "Big Band Arranger Quincy Jones Moves into Realm of Voices and Smaller Groups." Billboard 86:34, June 29, 1974.

8102 Morgan, A. J. "Quincy Jones: A Man in Love." Soul 9:8-9, July 8, 1974.

8103 "Brain Surgery Saves Life of Quincy Jones." Billboard 86:14, August 24, 1974.

8104 "Quincy Jones Faces Additional Surgery." Billboard 86:4, September 7, 1974.

8105 "Quincy Jones 'Doing Well' After Surgery." Soul 9:1, September 30, 1974.

8106 "Quincy Marries Actress Peggy." Soul 9:6, November 11, 1974.

8107 Rubine, N. "Quincy Jones: Music's Living Legend." Soul 9:2-3, December 9, 1974.

8108 "Concert Reviews." Variety 277:34, December 25, 1974.

8109 "Records: Body Heat." Rolling Stone no. 177:64, January 2, 1975.

8110 Brown, G. F. "To Quincy Jones with Love Is Theme of Warm Tribute to Composer." Jet 47:60-63, January 16, 1975.

8111 "Quincy Jones to Be Saluted." Soul 9:4, January 20, 1975. The Brotherhood Crusade will honor Jones.

8112 Ruffin, W. D. "Stars Galore Turn Out to Salute 'Q.'" Soul 9:7, February 17, 1975.

8113 Tiegel, E. "Odd Concept for Jones Band." Billboard 87:43, February 22, 1975.

8114 "Caught." down beat 42:28, March 27, 1975. Jones is honored at a Los Angeles concert.

8115 Fridlund, H. "Quincy Jones--Hollywoods Guidgosse--Troett paa Film, Turnerar Igen." Orkester Journalen 43:10-12, September 1975.

8116   Lake, S. "Funk? We Used to Play That in Church." Melody Maker 50:14-15, September 27, 1975.

8117   Underwood, L. "Q. Lives." down beat 42:13-15, October 23, 1975.

8118   Gloster, D. "Quincy's Jones." Essence 6:36, December 1975.

8119   "Record Reviews: Mellow Madness." down beat 42:26, December 18, 1975.

8120   "Quincy Jones Talks About Life and Death." Ebony 31:132-136, March 1976.

8121   Hafferkamp, J. "Quincy's Biggest Score Yet: The History of Black Music." Rolling Stone no. 216:17, July 1, 1976.

8122   "Concert Reviews." Variety 284:58, September 1, 1976.

8123   "Non-Pros Assisted at Workshop; Quincy Jones Serves up 'Alternative _ Information.'" Billboard 88:39, September 25, 1976.

8124   "Talent in Action." Billboard 88:47, September 25, 1976.

8125   "Jazz Albums: At Basin Street East." Melody Maker 51:25, November 6, 1976.

8126   "Record Reviews: I Heard That!" down beat 44:20, January 13, 1977.

8127   Williams, J. "Soul Sauce: Workshop Showcases 40 in L.A." Billboard 89:66, October 15, 1977.

8128   _____. "Soul Sauce: Jones Nets Results at Workshop." Billboard 89:36, November 5, 1977.

8129   Harrison, E. "A Day in the Life of Quincy Jones." Billboard 90:75, July 15, 1978.

8130   Jacobs, I. "Symposium with Duke Ellington." Cadence 4:6-14, September 1978.

8131   "Records: Sounds ... and Stuff like That!!" Rolling Stone no. 274:68, September 21, 1978.

8132   Hoare, I. "Quincy Jones: Funk for All Seasons." Melody Maker 53:37, October 7, 1978.

8133   "Duke Ellington Symposium." Cadence 4:14-20, November 1978.

8134   Gilmore, M. "Quincy Jones: The Wizard of Funk." Rolling Stone no. 277:24, November 2, 1978.

JOPLIN, SCOTT, 1868-1917.

8135   Carew, R. J., and D. E. Fowler. "Scott Joplin: Overlooked Genius." Record Changer p. 12-14, September 1944; p. 10-12, October 1944; p. 10-11, December 1944.

8136 Thompson, K. C. "Reminiscing in Ragtime." Jazz Journal 3:4-5,
      April 1950.

8137 _____. "Lottie Joplin; Scott's Widow Reminisces on the Ragtime
      King." Record Changer 9:8, October 1950.

8138 "King of the Ragtimers." Time 56:48, October 30, 1950.

8139 Traill, S. "Jig-Piano or Ragtime--It Still Has a Beat." Melody
      Maker 26:9, December 23, 1950.

8140 Campbell, B. "More on Ragtime." Jazz Journal 4:4, May 1951.

8141 Hoefer, G. "Missouri Group Honors Memory of Scott Joplin." down
      beat 19:9, January 25, 1952.

8142 Waterman, G. "A Survey of Ragtime." Record Changer 14:8, no.
      7, 1955.

8143 _____. "Joplin's Late Rags: An Analysis." Record Changer
      14:5-8, no. 8, 1956.

8144 Ellsworth, R. "Americans on Microgroove; A Discography." High
      Fidelity/Musical America 6:69, July 1956.

8145 Montgomery, M. "Scott Joplin Rollography." Record Research no.
      22:2, April-May 1959.

8146 Testoni, G. "Gli Autori dei Temi." Musica Jazz 15:37, December
      1959.

8147 Morath, M. "Any Rags Today?" Music Journal 18:76-77, October
      1960.

8148 Charters, A. "The First Negro Folk Opera: 'Treemonisha.'" Jazz
      Monthly 8:6-11, August 1962.

8149 "Sedalia, Mo., Stakes Claim as Birthplace of Ragtime; Pitches for
      Historic Status." Variety 240:1, November 10, 1965.

8150 Raben, E. "Quincy Jones Diskografi." Orkester Journalen 34:32,
      November 1966.

8151 Campbell, S. B. "From Rags to Ragtime; A Eulogy." Jazz Report
      5:5-6, no. 5, 1967.

8152 Yuhasz, Sister M. J. "Black Composers and Their Piano Music."
      American Music Teacher 19:29, no. 5, 1970.

8153 Levin, F. "Brun Campbell--the Original Ragtime Kid of the 1890s."
      Jazz Journal 23:26-27, December 1970.

8154 "Scott Joplin--1916 Classic Rolls Played by the King of Ragtime Writ-
      ers & Others from Rare Piano Rolls." Jazz Report 7:17-18, no.
      6, 1971.

8155 Schonberg, H. C. "Scholars, Get Busy on Scott Joplin." Jazz Re-
      port 7:11-13, no. 6, 1971. Reprinted from New York Times, Jan-
      uary 24, 1971.

8156   "Piano Rags by Scott Joplin." American Record Guide 37:354-355,
       February 1971.

8157   Hitchcock, H. W. "Ragtime of the Higher Class." Stereo Review
       26:84, April 1971.

8158   Lipskin, M. "Record Reviews: Scott Joplin Piano Rags." Jazz and
       Pop 10:50, April 1971.

8159   "The Collected Works of Scott Joplin." Ragtimer p. 12, July-August
       1971. Discussion of the collection which is the first in the New
       York Public Library's American Historical Music Series.

8160   Scott, P. "Treasures of Two Ragtime Composers Are Preserved on
       Record." Ragtimer p. 11-12, September-October 1971.

8161   Wilson, J. S. "Fans of Ragtime Repay a Big Debt." Jazz Report
       8:7-8, no. 4, 1973. Review of a concert of Joplin's ragtime re-
       printed from the New York Times, October 25, 1971.

8162   Saal, H. "King of Rag." Newsweek 78:97-98, November 1, 1971.

8163   Williams, M. "Scott Joplin: Genius Rediscovered." down beat
       38:16, November 25, 1971.

8164   Bolcom, W. "Ragtime Revival: The Collected Works of Scott Jop-
       lin." Yearbook for Inter-American Musical Research 8:147-161,
       1972.

8165   "Complete Joplin Works Published by New York Public Library."
       ASCAP Today 5:35, no. 3, 1972.

8166   Dykstra, B. "Should Your Foot Tap at a Piano Recital?" Clavier
       11:18-20, no. 9, 1972.

8167   "Max Morath Plays the Best of Scott Joplin." Jazz Report 8:17, no.
       2, 1072.

8168   "Piano Rags by Scott Joplin--Joshua Rifkin." Jazz Report 8:20-21,
       no. 2, 1972.

8169   "Record Reviews: They All Played 'The Maple Leaf Rag.'" Coda
       10:27, no. 6, 1972; Sing Out 21:38, no. 2, 1972.

8170   Schonberg, H. C. "Music: 'Treemonisha.'" Jazz Report 8:6-7, no.
       4, 1973. Reprinted from the New York Times, January 30, 1972.

8171   Klee, J. "They All Played 'Maple Leaf Rag.'" Record Research
       no. 115:5, February 1972.

8172   Kunstadt, L. "Scott Joplin Has Arisen." Record Research no. 115:3-
       5, February 1972.

8173   "From Rags to Rags." Time 99:89-90, February 7, 1972. Review
       of Joplin's "Treemonisha."

8174   "Ragtime Opera." Newsweek 79:46, February 7, 1972. Discussion
       of "Treemonisha."

8175 Wilson, J. S. "Rifkin Plays Rags, Varied in Melody, by Scott Joplin." Jazz Report 8:8, no. 4, 1973. Reprinted from the New York Times, March 21, 1972.

8176 Sargeant, W. "Musical Events: Concert of S. Joplin's Works at Columbia University." New Yorker 48:110-112, March 25, 1972.

8177 "Atlanta Premiere." BMI p. 14-15, April 1972.

8178 "Joplin: Professional Genius of Frontier Saloons, Brothels." Ebony 27:90-91, April 1972.

8179 "An Old Ragtime Piano Man Goes to the Opera." Ebony 27:84-91, April 1972.

8180 Kolodin, I. "Second Coming of Scott Joplin." Saturday Review 55:18, April 1, 1972.

8181 "Scott Joplin Rediscovered." Ragtimer p. 13-16, May-June 1972.

8182 Lawrence, V. B. "Scott Joplin's Treemonisha." High Fidelity/Musical America 11:MA10-12, May 1972.

8183 Landry, R. J. "Wolf Trap's Pre-1916 All-Black Opera; Also Continues Mixed-Race Company." Variety 267:67, May 17, 1972.

8184 Hankins, R. "Sounds Familiar." Ragtimer p. 13-15, July-August 1972.

8185 Michie, L. "'Treemonisha' at Wolf Trap." Variety 268:60, August 16, 1972.

8186 "The Scott Joplin Opera." Arts Reporting Service 2:2, August 21, 1972.

8187 Ralston, J. L. "A Limited Edition of the Music of Scott Joplin in Stereo." Ragtimer p. 21-22, September-October 1972.

8188 "Scott Joplin Rediscovered." Ragtimer p. 20-21, September-October 1972.

8189 Kolodin, I. "Carry Me Back to 'Treemonisha.'" Saturday Review 55:62, September 2, 1972.

8190 Freed, R. "More on the Joplin Renascence." Stereo Review 29:108, October 1972.

8191 Gilmore, M. S. "Vienna, Va./Bel Air, Md." Opera News 37:29, October 1972.

8192 Shaw, A. "Scott Joplin Renaissance." High Fidelity/Musical America 22:81-83, October 1972.

8193 Jahant, C. "Washington." Opera 23:1006-1008, November 1972.

8194 "New Operas and Premieres." Central Opera Service Bulletin 14:1, Winter 1972.

8195 Gilmore, M. S. "King of Ragtime." Sepia 21:7-74, December 1972.

8196   "Record Reviews: Piano Rags by Scott Joplin." Footnote 4:31-32,
        no. 4, 1973.

8197   Reed, Addison Walker. "The Life and Works of Scott Joplin." (Ph.D.
        Dissertation, University of North Carolina, 1973).

8198   "Scott Joplin Rediscovered." Ragtimer p. 12-13, January-February
        1973.

8199   Fox, C. "Ragtime Revisited." Jazz & Blues 2:4-5, January 1973.

8200   "Record Reviews: Piano Rags by Scott Joplin, Vol. One and Two."
        Jazz & Blues 2:32-33, January 1973.

8201   "Scott Joplin Rediscovered." Ragtimer p. 11-14, March-April 1973.

8202   Bessom, M. E. "From Piano Thumping to the Concert Stage--the
        Rise of Ragtime." Music Educators' Journal 59:53-56, April 1973.

8203   Rusch, R. D. "Rusch on Ragtime." Jazz Journal 26:22-23, April
        1973.

8204   Drimmer, M. "Treemonisha." Phylon 34:197-202, June 1973.

8205   Offergeld, R. "Scott Joplin's Orchestrated Ragtime." Stereo Review
        30:116-117, June 1973.

8206   "Scott Joplin Rediscovered." Ragtimer p. 6-10, July-August 1973.

8207   "Records: Scott Joplin: The Red Back Book." Rolling Stone no.
        142:78, August 30, 1973.

8208   "Scott Joplin Rediscovered." Ragtimer p. 4-8, September-October
        1973.

8209   Atkins, J. L. "Heard and Seen: Scott Joplin Festival--Sedalia,
        Missouri." Coda 11:34-35, no. 12, 1974.

8210   Caldwell, Hansonia Laverne. "Black Idioms in Opera as Reflected in
        the Works of Six Afro-American Composers." (Ph.D. Dissertation,
        University of Southern California, 1974). Includes Joplin, William
        Grant Still, Clarence Cameron White, Arthur Cunningham, Mark
        Fox, and Ulysses Kay.

8211   Goodwin, N. "Ragtime Reckoning." About the House 4:12-17, no.
        7, 1974.

8212   "Record Reviews." Sing Out 23:43-46, no. 3, 1974.

8213   "Record Reviews: An Evening with Scott Joplin." Coda 11:19-20, no.
        5, 1974.

8214   Rogers, L. "Joplin Honored as Black Forerunner." Songwriters' Re-
        view 29:6, no. 5, 1974.

8215   "Scott Joplin Forgotten." Ragtimer p. 14-15, January-February 1974.
        Joplin is buried in an unmarked grave.

8216   Rowley-Rotunno, V. "Scott Joplin: Renascence of a Black Composer of Ragtime and Grand Opera." Negro History Bulletin 37:188-193, January 1974.

8217 Dallas, K. "Rag, Mama, Rag." Melody Maker 49:28, January 5, 1974.

8218 Pleasants, H. "Joshua Rifkin, Ragtime Ambassador." Stereo Review 32:52, April 1974.

8219 Dickie, N. "The Rag Trade." Melody Maker 49:46, April 20, 1974.

8220 Hayes, C. "Joplin Boosts Piano Sales." Melody Maker 49:47, April 20, 1974.

8221 "Turn-of-Century 'Rock and Roll' Makes It as a Hit in 1974." Ragtimer p. 8-9, May-June 1974. Discussion of Joplin's "The Entertainer" reprinted from Broadcasting, April 1, 1974.

8222 Wilford, C. "Ragtime; The Astonishing Boom." Jazz Journal 27:4-6, May 1974.

8223 Freedland, N. "Joplin's Rags Rule Roost in May with Popular 'Sting.'" Billboard 86:6, May 18, 1974.

8224 "Joplin to Be Cited." Billboard 86:34, May 18, 1974.

8225 Horowitz, I. "Max Morath: Story of Rags to 'Riches.'" Billboard 86:8, May 25, 1974.

8226 Marranca, B. "The Compleat Scott Joplin, If Rag Is Your Bag." Crawdaddy no. 37:82-84, June 1974. Includes discography.

8227 Terry, D. "Sedalia! An Old Railroad Town with a Somewhat Shady Past." Ragtimer p. 11-16, July-August 1974. A four-day Joplin music festival is planned for Sedalia, Mo. Reprinted from the Midwest Motorist, June 1974.

8228 "Prodigal Song." Melody Maker 49:66, June 22, 1974.

8229 Rich, A. "Rags to Rip-Offs--Scott Joplin's Music." Ragtimer p. 9-11, July-August 1974.

8230 "Ragtime Buffs to Salute Joplin." Variety 275:93, July 17, 1974.

8231 West, R. "The Scott Joplin Ragtime Festival, Sedalia, Missouri." Ragtimer p. 12, September-October 1974. Reprinted from Tailgate Ramblings, August 1974.

8232 Saal, H. "Glad Rags." Newsweek 84:60, August 5, 1974.

8233 West, R. "The Scott Joplin Ragtime Festival." Second Line 26:36, Fall 1974.

8234 Bell-Smith, P. "The Scott Joplin Ragtime Festival, Sedalia, Missouri--July 25th-28, 1974." Ragtimer p. 10-11, September-October 1974.

8235 Williams, M. "Scott Joplin, the Ragtime King, Rules Once More." Smithsonian 5:108-112, October 1974.

8236 "ASCAP Salutes Joplin." Variety 276:63, October 16, 1974.

8237 Freeman, J. W. "Dagli Stali Uniti." Rivista Italiana di Musicologia
      9:645, no. 4, 1975.

8238 Gammond, Peter. Scott Joplin and the Ragtime Era. New York:
      St. Martin's Press, 1975. A study of the great influence Joplin
      had on ragtime. Includes bibliography and discography plus a list
      of his works.

8239 Hayakawa, S. I. "The Saga of Scott Joplin." Jazz Report 8:7-9, no.
      6, 1975.

8240 Reed, A. W. "Scott Joplin, Pioneer." Black Perspectives in Music
      3:45-52, no. a, 1975.

8241 Schoep, A. "Houston." Opera Canada 16:37-38, no. 3, 1975.

8242 Anderson, W. "Animal, Vegetable or Classical?" Stereo Review
      34:6, February 1975.

8243 Fox, C. "The Story of Ragtime." Music and Musicians 23:24-25,
      February 1975.

8244 "Sue Joplin Trust on 'Treemonisha.'" Billboard 87:94, April 12, 1975.

8245 "Scott Joplin Rediscovered." Ragtimer p. 9-11, May-June 1975.

8246 "Periman Plays Joplin." Music and Musicians 23:22, May 1975. Re-
      view of Periman's recording "The Easy Winners."

8247 Sandner, W. "Ragtime--zur Geschichte einer Nationalen Amerikan-
      sichen Musik." Hifi-Stereophonie 14:482, May 1975.

8248 "Joplin Trust Counter Sues." Billboard 87:50, May 10, 1975.

8249 Current, G. B. "Scott Joplin." Crisis 82:219:221, June-July 1975.

8250 Blesh, R. "Scott Joplin." American Heritage 26:26-32, June 1975.

8251 "School Named for Scott Joplin." Ragtimer p. 14, July-August 1975.
      Joplin's name is given to a Chicago School in his honor.

8252 "Scott Joplin Rediscovered." Ragtimer p. 4-5, July-August 1975.

8253 Schulman, M. "Scott Joplin Shares the Spotlight with William Shake-
      speare." Ragtimer p. 11-13, July-August 1975. Discussion of the
      part Joplin's music will play in the 23rd Stratford Festival in On-
      tario. Reprinted from the Globe and Mail (Toronto), July 14, 1975.

8254 "Ragtime Opera." BMI p. 30-31, Fall 1975.

8255 "Scott Joplin Rediscovered." Ragtimer p. 11-12, September-October
      1975.

8256 Fleming, S. "Scott Joplin's 'Treemonisha.'" High Fidelity/Musical
      America 25:MA32-33, September 1975.

8257   Jones, R. "'Treemonisha'; Scott Joplin's Ragtime Opera Struts Its
       Stuff on Broadway." Opera News 40:12-15, September 1975.

8258   "Treemonisha." High Fidelity/Musical America 25:MA32-33, Septem-
       ber 1975; Newsweek 86:62-63, September 22, 1975.

8259   "Shows Out of Town." Variety 280:82, September 24, 1975.

8260   "Treemonisha." Ms. 4:40-41, October 1975.

8261   "'Treemonisha' Case Vs. AFM, Local 16." Variety 280:73, October
       8, 1975.

8262   "Shows on Broadway." Variety 280:71-72, October 29, 1975.

8263   "Record Reviews: Scott Joplin: His Complete Works." Coda no.
       143:19, November 1975.

8264   Taylor, P. "Opera and Ballet in London." Musical Opinion 99:63,
       November 1975.

8265   Sobel, R. "'Treemonisha' Noble, but Fails After Bright Start."
       Billboard 87:15, November 15, 1975.

8266   "Treemonisha." New Republic 173:22-23, November 15, 1975.

8267   Smith, P. J. "New York." Music Teacher 116:1084, December
       1975. Review of "Treemonisha."

8268   Jacobson, R. "New York." Opera News 40:39-40, December 6,
       1975.

8269   Davis, C. "Treemonisha." Encore 4:34, December 8, 1975.

8270   "Performance." Rolling Stone no. 202:110, December 18, 1975. Re-
       view of Joplin's opera "Treemonisha."

8271   Herbert, Rubye Nell. "A Study of the Composition and Performance
       of Scott Joplin's Opera 'Treemonisha.'" (D. M. A. Dissertation,
       Ohio State University, 1976).

8272   Van Diest, Norman Henry. "The Rhythms of Ragtime: An Operational
       Analysis of the Music of Turpin, Joplin, Scott, and Lamb." (Ed. D.
       Dissertation, Columbia University Teachers College, 1976).

8273   "Treemonisha." National Review 28:39, January 23, 1976.

8274   Kovner, B. "Ragtime Revival." Commentary 61:57-60, March 1976.

8275   "A Rewrite of History." Ragtimer p. 9, March-April 1976. Re-
       printed from the Toronto Star, March 12, 1976.

8276   "'Scott Joplin' as NBC 2-Hr. Spec." Variety 282:97, March 31, 1976.

8277   Lawrence, V. B. "Scott Joplin." BMI p. 38-39, Spring 1976.

8278   Harris, D. "New York." Music and Musicians 24:39-40, April 1976.

8279   Horowitz, I.   "Joplin LP on Way to Crossover."   Billboard 88:3,
       April 24, 1976.

8280   Schulz, R. E.   "Rites in Ragtime."   Music Ministry 8:2-4, May
       1976.

8281   "Joplin Wins Pulitzer Prize That Ducked Duke in 1965."   Jet 50:53,
       May 20, 1976.

8282   Lucas, J.   "Bicentennial Canticles."   Second Line 28:6-7, Summer
       1976.

8283   Sandner, W.   "Ragtime--zur Geschichte einer Nationalen Amerikan-
       ischen Musik."   Musik und Bildung 8:314-320, June 1976.

8284   Fleming, S.   "Joplin's 'Treemonisha': A Patchwork of Styles, Touch-
       ing and Trying."   High Fidelity/Musical America 26:72-73, July
       1976.

8285   "Record Reviews: Elite Syncopations; The Entertainer."   Coda 149:17-
       18, July 1976.

8286   Haskins, James, and Kathleen Benson.   Scott Joplin.   Garden City,
       N.Y.: Doubleday, 1978.

JUDKINS, STEPHEN D. see WONDER, STEVIE

KING, B. B. (Riley B.; Blues Boy), 1925- .

8287   "New Acts."   Variety 194:54, June 2, 1954.

8288   Demetre, J., and M. Chauvard.   "Voyage au Pays du Blues."   Jazz
       Hot 25:16-19, February 1960.

8289   _____.   "Land of the Blues."   Jazz Journal 13:5-8, July 1960.
       Translation of "Voyage au Pays du Blues" in Jazz Hot 25:16-19,
       February 1960.

8290   Welding, P.   "The Blues Are Brewing."   Saturday Review 43:45,
       July 30, 1960.

8291   "King of the Blues."   Sepia 10:63-66, September 1961.

8292   "Apollo, N.Y."   Variety 225:58, January 24, 1962.

8293   Chauvard, M., and J. Demetre.   "Les Jeunes du Blues."   Jazz Hot
       no. 174:24-25, March 1962.

8294   "Why I'll Always Sing the Blues."   Ebony 17:94-96, April 1962.

8295   "Bios for Deejays."   Cash Box 25:25, March 28, 1964.

8296   Glover, T.   "R&B."   Sing Out 15:11-12, no. 2, 1965.

8297   Dance, S.   "The King of the Blues, B. B. King."   Jazz 6:14-15,
       February 1967.

8298 "Gazzari's, L. A." Variety 245:53, February 15, 1967.

8299 "B. B. King." BMI p. 20, June 1967.

8300 Bourne, J. R. "The Anatomy of B. B. King." down beat 34:17,
      July 27, 1967.

8301 "King, Lucille und Lu--Zur Tournee von B. B. King." Musikalische
      Jugend 17:20, no. 1, 1968.

8302 Hofstein, F. "Le B. B. Roi." Jazz Magazine no. 150:32-35, Jan-
      uary 1968.

8303 Jones, M. "Magnificent Seven." Melody Maker 43:9, January 13,
      1968.

8304 Hofstein, F. "B. B. King Parle." Jazz Magazine no. 151:19-20,
      February 1968.

8305 _____. "Le Chaud King." Jazz Magazine no. 151:14-15, Febru-
      ary 1968.

8306 Korner, A. "A Guide to Blues Guitar." Melody Maker 43:17, Feb-
      ruary 17, 1968.

8307 "New Acts." Variety 250:63, April 19, 1968.

8308 "B. B. King, Holding Co. Winning Double Play." Billboard 80:16,
      April 13, 1968.

8309 Pekar, H. "From Rock to ???" down beat 35:20, May 2, 1968.

8310 "New Blues: B. B. King; Junior Wells; Buddy Guy." Newsweek
      71:112, June 24, 1968.

8311 Rivelli, P. "B. B. King." Jazz and Pop 7:18-22, July 1968.

8312 "Central Park, N.Y." Variety 251:46, August 7, 1968.

8313 "The New Blues." BMI p. 8-9, October 1968.

8314 Goldstein, R. "B. B. King, Father of Honkey Blues." Vogue 152:62,
      October 15, 1968.

8315 Von Hoffman, A. "B. B. King and the Blues: An Appreciation."
      down beat 35:16-17, October 31, 1968.

8316 Niquet, B. "L'Idole de la Nouvelle Generation: B. B. King." Jazz
      Hot no. 244:246, November 1968.

8317 "Village Gate, N.Y." Variety 253:47, January 1, 1969.

8318 Jones, M. "The Men Who Make the Blues." Melody Maker 44:12,
      January 4, 1969.

8319 Welding, P. "Records." Rolling Stone no. 25:28, January 4, 1969.

8320 "Blues Boy." Time 93:42-43, January 10, 1969.

8321 Gleason, R. J. "Like a Rolling Stone." Jazz and Pop 8:14, March
      1969.

8322 Traill, S. "Editorial." Jazz Journal 22:1, May 1969.

8323 Heineman, A. "Caught in the Act." down beat 36:36, May 1, 1969.

8324 Jones, M. "B. B. Brings the Story of Lucille to the Rescue." Mel-
      ody Maker 44:8, May 3, 1969.

8325 _____. "B. B. King Spells Out the Blues." Melody Maker 44:6,
      May 3, 1969.

8326 "A Gallery of the Greats." BMI p. 30, Summer 1969.

8327 "Great Guitars." Blues Unlimited 63:29, June 1969.

8328 Hackenbush, J. F. "B. B. King." Jazz Hot no. 251:9, June 1969.

8329 Hofstein, F. "Un Plaisir Royal." Jazz Magazine no. 167:7, June
      1969.

8330 Joe, R. "B. B. King Sings Tales of Love, Life and the Pursuit."
      Billboard 81:22, June 14, 1969.

8331 "Village Gate, N.Y." Variety 255:62, June 18, 1969.

8332 Cohn, L. "B. B. King." Jazz and Pop 8:20-21, July 1969.

8333 Comforti, J. M. "A Sociologist Talks to B. B. King." Blues no.
      64:4-6, July 1969.

8334 Powell, J. "The B. B. King Experience." down beat 36:14-15,
      August 7, 1969.

8335 Jones, M. "The Men Who Make the Blues." Melody Maker 44:16,
      August 16, 1969.

8336 Shaw, A. "The Rhythm & Blues Revival No White Gloved, Black
      Hits." Billboard 81:S3, August 16, 1969.

8337 Kirby, F. "Who, B. B. King, Airplane Soar." Billboard 81:19,
      August 23, 1969.

8338 Comforti, Joseph M. "A Sociologist Talks to B. B. King." Blues
      Unlimited 65:11-12, September 1969.

8339 Berton, R. "Caught in the Act." down beat 36:24, October 2, 1969.
      Review of King's performance at the Rutgers Jazz Festival.

8340 Morgenstern, D. "The Blues Comes to Ann Arbor." down beat
      36:15, October 2, 1969.

8341 Comforti, Joseph M. "A Sociologist Talks to B. B. King." Blues
      Unlimited 66:17-18, October 1969.

8342 Kofsky, F. "T-Bone Walker & B. B. King." Jazz and Pop 8:15-20,
      October 1969.

8343 Garland, P. "Bossman of the Blues." Ebony 25:54-56, November 1969.

8344 Goldman, A. "Rebirth of B. B. King." Life 67:16, December 12, 1969.

8345 "La Chronique des Disques." Jazz Hot no. 259:35-36, March 1970.

8346 Stewart-Baxter, D. "Blues and News." Jazz Journal 23:7, March 1970.

8347 "B. B. King Asks $2-Mil in Infringement Suit." Variety 258:55, April 22, 1970.

8348 "Caesars Palace, L.V." Variety 258:87, April 22, 1970.

8349 "Disques du Mois: Confessin' the Blues; Lucille, Mr. Blues." Jazz Magazine no. 177:37-38, April 1970.

8350 Oliver, P. "Record Review: B. B. King's Greatest Hits." Jazz Monthly no. 182:24, April 1970.

8351 Davis, L. "The Thrill Ain't Gone: B. B. King." Soul 4:12-13, April 6, 1970.

8352 "Record Reviews: Completely Well." Jazz and Pop 9:57-58, May 1970.

8353 Russell, T. "Record Review: Live and Well." Jazz Monthly no. 183:20-21, May 1970.

8354 Feather, L. "B. B. King Arrives After 27 Years." Melody Maker 45:18, May 9, 1970.

8355 Carroll, J. "Is His Name Really Riley B. King?" Rolling Stone no. 58:16, May 14, 1970.

8356 "Talent in Action." Billboard 82:21, May 16, 1970.

8357 "Americana, N.Y." Variety 259:58, June 10, 1970.

8358 "B. B. and Carla." New Yorker 46:25-26, June 13, 1970.

8359 "Talent in Action." Billboard 82:17, June 13, 1970.

8360 Harris, S. "Carnegie Hall, New York." Jazz and Pop 9:48-49, July 1970.

8361 Albertson, C. "Caught in the Act." down beat 37:30-31, August 6, 1970. Review of King's performance at Carnegie Hall.

8362 King, B. B. "Notice More Black Youth in My Audience." Billboard 82:16, August 22, 1970.

8363 "Record Reviews: Completely Well." Jazz Monthly no. 188:15, October 1970.

8364 "Concert Reviews." Variety 260:42, October 21, 1970.

8365   Greenwald, J. "BB." Rolling Stone no. 69:36-38, October 29, 1970.

8366   "Five Happy Moments." Esquire 74:139, December 1970.

8367   "Talent in Action." Billboard 82:28, December 5, 1970.

8368   Palmer, B. "All My Lungs and All My Body." Rolling Stone no. 73:10, December 24, 1970.

8369   Davis, L. "B. B. King." Soul 3:30-33, no. a, 1971.

8370   "Recordings: Indianola, Mississippi." Soul 3:15, no. 1, 1971.

8371   "Record Reviews: Indianola Mississippi Seeds." Jazz Journal 24:32, January 1971.

8372   Gibbs, V. "B. B. Bringing the Blues Back Home." Senior Scholastic 97:23-25, January 18, 1971.

8373   "Record Reviews: Indianola Mississippi Seeds." Jazz and Pop 10:40-41, February 1971.

8374   Feather, L. "BB--25 Years a King." Melody Maker 46:35, February 20, 1971.

8375   "ASCAP Dissidents Ride Again; Push Hans Lengsfelder for a Seat on Bd." Variety 262:53, March 3, 1971.

8376   Landau, J. "Records: Live in Cook County Jail." Rolling Stone no. 78:41, March 18, 1971.

8377   Chango. "Record Reviews: B. B. King Live in Cook County." Jazz and Pop 10:47, April 1971.

8378   Fiofori, T. "King's Head." Melody Maker 46:15, April 24, 1971.

8379   "Disques du Mois: Live in Cook County Jail." Jazz Magazine no. 190:40, June-July 1971.

8380   Jones, M. "The Blues Boy in London." Melody Maker 46:15, June 19, 1971.

8381   "Concert Reviews." Variety 263:51, June 30, 1971.

8382   Fiofori, T. "'Jag aer Blues' B. B. King." Orkester Journalen 39:6-7, July-August 1971.

8383   Willis, E. "Rock, etc. Concert at the Fillmore East a Week Before Closing, with B. B. King and Moby Grape Band." New Yorker 47:58, July 10, 1971.

8384   Brown, R. "Record Reviews: Take a Swing with Me." Jazz Journal 24:32, August 1971.

8385   Kofsky, F., and R. Urbino. "B. B. King." Black Lines 2:31-38, Fall 1971.

8386   Broven, J. J. "A Year in the Life of B. B. King." Blues Unlimited no. 85:15-17, October 1971.

8387 "B. B. King Digs Campus Freedom; 'Feel Alive' When Doing Concert." Billboard 83:34, October 30, 1971.

8388 Jones, M. "The Thrill Ain't Gone." Melody Maker 46:24, November 27, 1971.

8389 "Stargazing." Essence 2:24-39, December 1971.

8390 "Flamingo, Las Vegas." Variety 265:57, December 22, 1971.

8391 Cullaz, M. "Les Blues de B. B. King." Jazz Hot no. 279:4-7, January 1972.

8392 "Paris." Jazz Magazine no. 196:34, January 1972.

8393 Yates, B. "In Person: The B. B. King Show." Jazz & Blues 1:14, January 1972.

8394 Chance, J. T. "Records: B. B. King in London." Rolling Stone no. 99:64, January 6, 1972.

8395 Feather, L. "King of the Road." Melody Maker 47:25, January 8, 1972.

8396 Tiegel, E. "B. B.'s Travels Bridge the Past with the Present." Billboard 84:32, January 29, 1972.

8397 Leadbitter, M. "Take a Swing with Me." Blues Unlimited no. 89:4-6, February-March 1972.

8398 "Disques du Mois: The Very Best of B. B. King." Jazz Magazine no. 197:36, February 1972.

8399 Mayer, U. "Blues Giant: B. B. King." Jazz Podium 21:77-78, March 1972.

8400 "Caught in the Act." Melody Maker 47:22, March 11, 1972.

8401 Siders, H. "Talking with a King." down beat 39:14-15, March 30, 1972.

8402 Bastin, B. "The Blues Is Alive and Well?" Blues Unlimited no. 90:17, April 1972.

8403 "Record Reviews: B. B. King in London." Jazz & Blues 2:26-27, April 1972.

8404 "B. B. King, F. Lee Bailey Join to Aid Prisoners." down beat 39:10, April 13, 1972.

8405 "Albums: L.A. Midnight." Melody Maker 47:18, April 15, 1972.

8406 Blanc-Francard, P. "B. B. King: 'Bad Luck Sou.'" Jazz Magazine no. 200:16-17, May 1972.

8407 "RecWords: L.A. Midnight." Crawdaddy no. 11:19, May 14, 1972.

8408 "Record Reviews: L.A. Midnight." down beat 39:22, May 25, 1972.

8409 "Caught in the Act." down beat 39:30, June 8, 1972.

8410   St. Pierre, R. "The Cost of Being the Boss." Jazz & Blues 2:18-
       20, July 1972.

8411   Gest, D. "B. B. King Goes to Jail." Soul 7:4, July 3, 1972.

8412   "Record Reviews: L.A. Midnight." Jazz & Blues 2:30, July 30,
       1972.

8413   "B. B. King--Blues in Dartmoor." Melody Maker 47:7, September
       30, 1972.

8414   Lucas, B. "World's First Blues Superstar." Sepia 21:64-66, Oc-
       tober 1972.

8415   "B. B. King Hurt: Misses Show." Melody Maker 47:5, October 28,
       1972.

8416   "Caught in the Act." Melody Maker 47:51, November 4, 1972.

8417   Jones, M. "Slim King." Melody Maker 47:17, November 4, 1972.

8418   "Records: Guess Who." Rolling Stone no. 121:64, November 9,
       1972.

8419   "B. B. King Gives Show for Atlanta Inmates." Variety 269:65, No-
       vember 15, 1972.

8420   "Albums: Guess Who." Melody Maker 47:30, November 25, 1972.

8421   "Caught in the Act." Melody Maker 47:39, December 23, 1972.

8422   "A Gallery of the Greats." BMI no. 1:4-13, 1973.   A survey of 60
       years of rhythm and blues musicians.

8423   "The Blues in Belgium." Blues Unlimited no. 99:16, February-
       March 1973.

8424   "Records: Back in the Alley: The Classic Blues of B. B. King;
       The Best of B. B. King." Rolling Stone no. 131:58, March 29,
       1973.

8425   "B. B. King, Merman to Get B'nai B'rith Citations." Billboard
       84:63, May 26, 1973.

8426   "Caught in the Act." Melody Maker 48:62, May 26, 1973.

8427   "B. B. King Reveals." down beat 40:11-12, June 21, 1973.

8428   "It's Dr. B. B. King." Variety 271:93, July 18, 1973.

8429   "Caught in the Act." Melody Maker 48:48, August 25, 1973.

8430   "Live Blues." Living Blues no. 14:31, Autumn 1973.

8431   "B. B. King's Degree." Variety 272:38, October 3, 1973.

8432   "Degree for B. B. King." Billboard 85:24, October 6, 1973.

8433   "Records: To Know You Is to Love You." Rolling Stone no. 147:72,
       November 8, 1973.

8434   "B. B. King: The King of the Blues." Soul 8:11, November 26,
       1973.

8435   Cullaz, M. "Concerts." Jazz Hot no. 300:223, December 1973.

8436   "Concert Reviews." Variety 273:48, December 12, 1973.

8437   Wilmer, V. "B. B. Goes 'Home.'" Melody Maker 48:50, Decem-
       ber 15, 1973.

8438   Balagri, D., et al. "Trois Jours sans Surprises." Jazz Magazine
       no. 218:20-21, January 1974.

8439   "Talent in Action." Billboard 86:29, January 19, 1974.

8440   Wilmer, V. "Quand le Blues se Rappelle à l'Afrique." Jazz Mag-
       azine no. 219:12-13, February 1974.

8441   "Caught in the Act." Melody Maker 49:31, April 6, 1974.

8442   Fishel, J. "B. B. King Crusading for More TV, Radio Time for
       Blues Artists." Billboard 86:26, July 20, 1974.

8443   Stiff, J. "B. B. King." Jazz Journal 27:16-17, August 1974.

8444   "Caught in the Act Extra." Melody Maker 49:56, August 10, 1974.

8445   "Talent in Action." Billboard 86:22, August 17, 1974.

8446   Gibbs, V. "Soul, Man." Crawdaddy no. 42:14, November 1974.

8447   Litke, J. "B. B., Bobby Bland: 'Live' in the Studio." Rolling Stone
       no. 175:14, December 5, 1974.

8448   "B. B. King Awarded Fifth Time." Soul 9:1, January 6, 1975.

8449   "Hilton, Las Vegas." Variety 277:83, January 22, 1975.

8450   "Records: Together for the First Time ... Live." Crawdaddy no.
       45:78-79, February 1975.

8451   King, B. B., and J. Crockett. "My 10 Favorite Guitarists." Gui-
       tar Player 9:22-23, March 1975.

8452   "Mister Kelly's, Chi." Variety 278:75, March 19, 1975.

8453   "Talent in Action." Billboard 87:20, March 29, 1975.

8454   King, B. B. "Tips from GP's Advisory Board; How I Play the
       Blues." Guitar Player 9:48, April 1975.

8455   Modzelewski, J. "'An Entertainer's Life Is Lonely': B. B. King."
       Soul 9:14, April 14, 1975.

8456   "Concert Reviews." Variety 280:58, August 20, 1975.

8457 "Hilton, Las Vegas." Variety 280:68, October 15, 1975.

8458 "Records: Lucille Talks Back." Rolling Stone no. 206:92-93, February 12, 1976.

8459 "Concert Reviews." Variety 282:72, March 24, 1976.

8460 "Talent in Action." Billboard 88:28, April 10, 1976.

8461 "B. B. King a Nitery Operator; A New Policy for Wonder Garden in Atlantic City." Billboard 88:54, May 1, 1976.

8462 "Concert Reviews." Variety 283:52, July 21, 1976.

8463 "Talent in Action." Billboard 88:42, July 24, 1976.

8464 "Records: Together Again ... Live." Rolling Stone no. 220:65, August 26, 1976.

8465 "LP's: Bobby Bland and B. B. King Together Again ... Live." Living Blues no. 30:34, November-December 1976.

8466 "Stardust, Las Vegas." Variety 285:87, January 26, 1977.

8467 Sheridan, K., and P. Sheridan. "T-Bone Walker: Father of the Electric Blues." Guitar Player 11:22, March 1977.

8468 "Caught in the Act." Melody Maker 52:18, October 15, 1977.

8469 Dallas, K. "B. B.--High on Blues." Melody Maker 52:47, October 22, 1977.

8470 "LP's: King Size." Living Blues no. 35:28, November-December 1977.

8471 "Concert Reviews." Variety 288:74, November 2, 1977.

8472 "En Direct." Jazz Magazine no. 260:12, December 1977.

8473 "Talent in Action." Billboard 89:52, December 17, 1977.

8474 Davis, C. "B. B. King of the Blues." Encore 6:31-32, December 27, 1977.

8475 Williams, J. "Soul Sauce: B. B. King Returns to Seidenberg." Billboard 90:50, March 4, 1978.

8476 "Record Reviews: King Albert." down beat 45:28, March 9, 1978.

8477 "Talent in Action." Billboard 90:86, August 26, 1978.

8478 McEwen, J. "Riffs: B. B. King Sustains." Village Voice 23:93, September 25, 1978.

8479 "Concert Reviews." Variety 292:84, September 27, 1978.

8480 Welding, P. "B. B. King: The Mississippi Giant." down beat 45:20-22, October 5, 1978; 45:17, October 19, 1978.

8481   "Caught in the Act." Melody Maker 53:28, October 21, 1978.

8482   Ferdinand, V. "B. B. King: King of the Blues." Black Collegian
        8:44, November-December 1978.

KITT, EARTHA, 1928- .

8483   "Josh White Taught Her the Blues." Melody Maker 27:6, January 20,
        1951.

8484   "La Vie en Rose, New York." Billboard 63:9, December 29, 1951.

8485   "Forecasts and Side Glances." Theatre Arts 36:16, April 1952.

8486   "Eartha Kitt, the Bedroom Voice." Our World 7:45-47, May 1952.

8487   "Eartha Kitt; Ex-Dunham Dancer Is Singing Sensation of Two Contin-
        ents with Daring and Gusto on Stage." Ebony 7:60-64, June 1952.

8488   "Salty Eartha." Time 59:61-62, June 9, 1952.

8489   "New Faces." Theatre Arts 36:20, August 1952.

8490   "Eartha Kitt." Life 33:45-48, August 4, 1952.

8491   "Caught in the Act." down beat 19:16, August 13, 1952.

8492   "Most Exciting Men in My Life." Ebony 8:26-28, January 1953.

8493   "Off Stage with Eartha Kitt." Our World 8:44-45, January 1953.

8494   Pease, S. A. "Wallington One of Initial Pianists in Bop Movement."
        down beat 20:19, January 28, 1953.

8495   "Pix and TV Hot Shots N. S. H. on Wax; Eartha Kitt's Caboodle on Vic-
        tor." Variety 191:43, July 22, 1953.

8496   Powers, C. "Eartha Kitt Talks Turkey." down beat 20:3, July 29,
        1953.

8497   "Portrait of an Actress." Look 17:72-73, October 6, 1953.

8498   "Caught in the Act." down beat 20:4, December 16, 1953.

8499   "Box-Office Hits of 1953." Billboard 65:22, December 19, 1953.

8500   Holly, H. "How L.A. Mayor Set Off Eartha Quake in Calif." down
        beat 20:5, December 30, 1953.

8501   "New Faces; Sultry Eartha Kitt Makes Cinema Bow in Hollywood Ver-
        sion of Broadway Hit." Ebony 9:30-34, May 1954.

8502   "Caught in the Act." down beat 21:4, May 19, 1954.

8503   "Latin Quarter, Boston." Variety 194:60, May 19, 1954.

8504   "La Vie en Rose, N.Y." Variety 194:50, June 2, 1954.

8505   Donovan, R. "Eartha Kitt, Fire in Ice." Collier's 133:92-94, June
       11, 1954.

8506   "Recording Artists' Roster." down beat 21:109, June 30, 1954.

8507   "Kitt Digs Dixie, Sinatra, Calls Bop Uncomfortable." down beat
       21:21, July 14, 1954.

8508   Hepburn, D. "How Evil Is Eartha?" Our World 9:9-15, September
       1954.

8509   "Diva to Duse." Newsweek 44:60, November 1, 1954.

8510   "Acting the Part." Theatre Arts 38:13, December 1954.

8511   "Why Negroes Don't Like Eartha Kitt." Ebony 10:29-30, December
       1954.

8512   "Baby--It's Cold Outside." Melody Maker 30:1, December 18, 1954
       Supplement.

8513   "Copacabana, N.Y." Variety 198:60, April 27, 1955.

8514   Francis, B. "Kitt Condescension Ain't Copa-cetic." Billboard 67:16,
       April 30, 1955.

8515   "Two for the Show." Time 65:42, May 2, 1955.

8516   "Caught in the Act." down beat 22:8, June 1, 1955.

8517   Howard, J. R. "Cover." Negro History Bulletin 19:10, October
       1955.

8518   "El Rancho, Las Vegas." Variety 200:60, October 5, 1955.

8519   "Song Birds Doff Duds." Life 39:157, October 17, 1955.

8520   "What Makes Eartha Kitt a 'Bad Girl'?" Color 10:21-23, November
       1955.

8521   Willard, B. "Caught in the Act." down beat 22:16, November 2,
       1955.

8522   Kitt, Eartha. Thursday's Child. New York: Duell, Sloan and
       Pearce, 1956. Autobiographical.

8523   "Third Time Famous!" Melody Maker 31:11, January 7, 1956.

8524   "Blinstrub's, Boston." Variety 201:61, February 29, 1956.

8525   "Eartha Kitt Takes Off." Ebony 11:24, March 1956.

8526   "El Rancho, Las Vegas." Variety 202:64, March 28, 1956.

8527   "Cafe de Paris, London." Variety 202:53, May 9, 1956.

8528   "Eartha Kitt Raffinerad." Orkester Journalen 24:6, July 1956.

8529   "El Rancho, Las Vegas." Variety 204:60, September 12, 1956.

8530 "Eartha Kitt's Search for Love." Ebony 12:83-84, November 1956.

8531 Churchill, A. "Eartha's Tale." Saturday Review 39:34, November 3, 1956.

8532 "Miss Kitt." New Yorker 32:42-44, November 17, 1956.

8533 "James Dean I Knew." Ebony 12:104-106, January 1957.

8534 "Great Eartha Kitt." Melody Maker 32:9, January 19, 1957.

8535 "Shinbone Alley." Newsweek 49:69-70, April 22, 1957.

8536 "Cat-Like Miss Kitt." Ebony 12:24-26, July 1957.

8537 "Elmwood, Windsor." Variety 208:55, September 18, 1957.

8538 "El Rancho, Las Vegas." Variety 208:65, October 23, 1957.

8539 "Fame Can Be Lonely." Ebony 13:83-86, December 1957.

8540 "Americana, Miami B." Variety 209:56, December 18, 1957.

8541 "El Morocco, Montreal." Variety 209:66, January 15, 1958.

8542 "Fairmont Hotel, S.F." Variety 211:57, July 23, 1958.

8543 Dawbarn, B. "Eartha Purrs Her Way to Success." Melody Maker 33:9, November 8, 1958.

8544 "Cocoanut Grove, L.A." Variety 212:68, November 26, 1958.

8545 "Americana, Miami B." Variety 213:68, December 20, 1958.

8546 "Waldorf-Astoria, N.Y." Variety 213:45, December 31, 1958.

8547 "Eartha's Weekend Blinstrub's Exit." Variety 214:51, March 4, 1959.

8548 "Eden Roc, Miami Beach." Variety 214:61, April 1, 1959.

8549 Bradley, B. "Why Eartha Kitt Refuses to Get Married." Sepia 7:16-19, September 1959.

8550 "Latin Quarter, N.Y." Variety 218:68, March 9, 1960.

8551 "Eartha Kitt to Marry White Businessman William McDonald of Los Angeles, Calif." Jet p. 60, May 26, 1960.

8552 "Eartha Kitt Marries William McDonald; White Realtor in Calif." Jet p. 59, June 23, 1960.

8553 "Eartha Kitt Awarded the 1960 Merit and Honorary Fellowship Award." Jet p. 60, August 11, 1960. This award, from the George Washington Carver Memorial Institute, honored her contribution to mankind.

8554 "Marriage of Eartha Kitt." Ebony 15:37-42, September 1960.

8555 "Hotel Plaza, N.Y." Variety 222:68, April 19, 1961.

8556 "Chi Chi, Palm Springs." Variety 225:66, January 17, 1962.

8557 "Eartha and Ella." Melody Maker 37:9, February 24, 1962.

8558 Young, A. S. "Kitt, Eartha, Tells ... 'What I Want for My Baby.'"
      Sepia 11:43-45, March 1962.

8559 "Talk of Town, London." Variety 226:65, March 14, 1962.

8560 "Hotel Plaza, N.Y." Variety 227:62, May 30, 1962.

8561 "Mister Kelly's, Chi." Variety 227:68, July 11, 1962.

8562 "My Baby Travels with Me." Ebony 18:93-94, January 1963.

8563 "El Morocco, Mont'l." Variety 230:75, March 20, 1963.

8564 "Hotel Plaza, N.Y." Variety 230:61, April 17, 1963.

8565 "Apollo, N.Y." Variety 230:71, May 15, 1963.

8566 "Palmer House, Chi." Variety 231:50, June 5, 1963.

8567 "Cave, Vancouver." Variety 232:67, November 20, 1963.

8568 "Chi Chi, Palm Springs." Variety 234:59, May 13, 1964.

8569 "Hotel Plaza, N.Y." Variety 235:59, May 27, 1964.

8570 "Palmer House, Chi." Variety 237:59, December 9, 1964.

8571 "Caught in the Act." Melody Maker 40:4, February 27, 1965.

8572 "Talk of Town, London." Variety 238:66, March 3, 1965.

8573 "Hotel Plaza, N.Y." Variety 238:197, May 12, 1965.

8574 "Cave, Vancouver." Variety 243:61, June 22, 1966.

8575 "Century Plaza, L.A." Variety 244:59, September 28, 1966.

8576 "Hotel Plaza, N.Y." Variety 246:69, May 10, 1967.

8577 Carpenter, L. "White House Slant on Eartha." Variety 249:2, Jan-
      uary 24, 1968.

8578 "Down to Eartha." Time 91:14, January 26, 1968.

8579 "Peaceful White House Lunch, and Then--." U.S. News & World Re-
      port 64:13, January 29, 1968.

8580 "Word from Miss Kitt." Newsweek 71:23-24, January 29, 1968.

8581 "Question of Empathy." Commonweal 87:552-553, February 9, 1968.

8582 "Eartha Kitt's White House Spectacular." Christianity Today 12:28,
      February 16, 1968.

5883 "'No Regrets,' Says Eartha Kitt." Sepia 17:78-79, March 1968.

8584 "Caesars Palace, L.V." Variety 250:67, March 6, 1968.

8585 "Plaza Hotel, N.Y." Variety 251:52, June 12, 1968.

8586 "Tooters Tap Eartha 'Woman of the Year.'" Variety 251:2, July 31, 1968.

8587 "Royal York Hotel, Tor." Variety 253:58, December 11, 1968.

8588 "Hotel Plaza, N.Y." Variety 256:117, September 10, 1969.

8589 "Westside Room, L.A." Variety 257:44, December 24, 1969.

8590 "Eartha Kitt to Star in Swedish Made Film." Jet 39:56, March 18, 1971.

8591 "Eartha Kitt Says Africans Must See Other Than 'Soul.'" Jet 41:22-23, November 11, 1971.

8592 "C'est si Bon." Newsweek 78:61-62, November 22, 1971.

8593 Dawson, J. "Caught in the Act." Melody Maker 46:16, December 25, 1971.

8594 "Eartha Kitt." Music and Musicians 20:14, May 1972.

8595 "Eartha Kitt Is Barred from S. African Show." Jet 42:56, May 4, 1972.

8596 Levison, E. "Eartha Kitt Role in South Africa's Color Break-Thru." Variety 267:1, May 31, 1972.

8597 "Eartha Kitt as an Honorary White." Life 72:85, June 2, 1972.

8598 "South Africans Query Apartheid Inconsistency to Black Stars from U.S." Variety 267:1, June 14, 1972.

8599 Feldman, P. "Kitt Forms Fund in South Africa." Billboard 84:1, June 24, 1972.

8600 "S. African Leader Recalls Racism Against Eartha Kitt." Jet 43:57, December 14, 1972.

8601 Jack, A. "Eartha and Cleo." Music and Musicians 21:66, June 1973.

8602 Johnson, R. E. "Eartha Kitt Observes Seventh Year with Black Ghetto School." Jet 44:56-61, June 14, 1973.

8603 Lane, L. "American Women Can Save Us, Says Eartha." Soul 9:17, August 19, 1974.

8604 "Marc Plaza, Milwaukee." Variety 277:57, November 13, 1974.

8605 Kitt, Eartha. Alone with Me. Chicago: H. Regnery Co., 1975. Autobiographical.

8606 "Eartha Kitt Slaps CIA Report Linked to Her Viet Views." Jet 47:12-14, January 23, 1975.

8607   "Hotel Plaza, N.Y." Variety 281:103, January 21, 1976.

8608   Buckley, W. F. "Strenuous Life." National Review 28:971, September 3, 1976.

8609   "Stardust, Las Vegas." Variety 285:119, November 24, 1976.

8610   Lamb, P. "Eartha Kitt: The Rough Road up from Nowhere." Working Woman 3:74-77, April 1978.

8611   "Concert Reviews." Variety 291:192, May 10, 1978.

8612   Ebert, A. "Eartha!" Essence 9:68-71, June 1978.

8613   "Kitt Sizzles on Broadway." Jet 54:22-24, August 31, 1978.

LABELLE   (including Patti LaBelle, Sarah Dash, and Nona Hendryx).

8614   "Concert Reviews." Variety 263:43, August 4, 1971.

8615   Dove, I. "Talent in Action." Billboard 83:18, August 14, 1971.

8616   Aletti, V. "Records: LaBelle." Rolling Stone no. 93:52, October 14, 1971.

8617   _____. "No Walking Alone for Patti LaBelle." Rolling Stone no. 96:28, November 25, 1971.

8618   Freedland, N. "Talent in Action." Billboard 84:20, February 5, 1972.

8619   "RecWords: Gonna Take a Miracle." Crawdaddy no. 5:15, February 20, 1972.

8620   "Labelle; A New Beginning." Soul 7:10-11, August 28, 1972.

8621   "New Acts." Variety 268:54, September 27, 1972.

8622   "Records: Moonshadow." Rolling Stone no. 119:70, October 12, 1972.

8623   Alterman, L. "Rock and Roll Women." Melody Maker 47:51, October 14, 1972.

8624   "Concert Reviews." Variety 271:64, May 23, 1973.

8625   "Talent in Action." Billboard 85:20, June 2, 1973.

8626   "Caught in the Act." Melody Maker 48:52, June 9, 1973.

8627   "Labelle--a Musical Experience." Soul 8:13, October 29, 1973.

8628   "Records: Pressure Cookin'." Rolling Stone no. 147:75, November 8, 1973.

8629 Milton, D. "Labelle Cookin'." Melody Maker 48:52, November 17, 1973.

8630 "Records: Pressure Cookin'." Crawdaddy no. 31:73, December 1973.

8631 "Concert Reviews." Variety 275:48, July 3, 1974; 276:58, October 9, 1974.

8632 Jefferson, M. "Belles of the Ball." Newsweek 84:113, October 21, 1974.

8633 Johnson, H. "From Bluebells to Labelle of New York." Rolling Stone no. 172:17-18, October 24, 1974.

8634 Watts, M. "Life with Elton." Melody Maker 49:22-23, November 9, 1974.

8635 Smith, R. "Labelle." Crawdaddy no. 44:54-56, January 1975.

8636 Murphy, F. D. "Labelle: Metamorphosis of the Sweethearts of the Apollo." Encore 4:27-30, January 6, 1975.

8637 Gibbs, V. "Labelle Survives." Essence 5:81, February 1975.

8638 "Patti Labelle." Jazz Hot no. 313:21, February 1975.

8639 Lake, S. "Labelle--Wow!" Melody Maker 50:36-38, March 1, 1975. Review of their European performances.

8640 Ivy, A. "Stop the Train; Ride LaBelle." Soul 9:2-3, March 3, 1975.

8641 "Labelle, First Black Rock Act at Met, Will Do Same at Harkness Theatre, N.Y." Variety 278:62, March 5, 1975.

8642 Twonley, R. "Singles: A Marmalade Lady Rings Labelle." Rolling Stone no. 182:16, March 13, 1975.

8643 "Caught in the Act." Melody Maker 50:59, March 15, 1975.

8644 Williams, J. "Trio Labelle; Patti, Sarah and Nona Favor Revolutionary Songs, Attire." Billboard 87:33, March 29, 1975.

8645 "Concert Reviews." Variety 279:148, May 14, 1975.

8646 "Records: Nightbirds." Rolling Stone no. 187:63-64, May 22, 1975.

8647 "Caught in the Act America." Melody Maker 50:34, May 24, 1975.

8648 "Talent in Action." Billboard 87:26, May 24, 1975.

8649 Edwards, H. "The Street People Have Taken over the Discotheques!" High Fidelity/Musical America 25:56-58, July 1975.

8650 Harris, A. "Oh Baby It's Labelle." Rolling Stone no. 190:42-46, July 3, 1975.

8651 Kincaid, J. "Labelle Hustle." Ms. 4:34-35, September 1975.

8652   "Concert Reviews." Variety 280:1-6, October 1, 1975.

8653   "Records: Phoenix." Rolling Stone no. 198:65, October 23, 1975.

8654   "Performance." Rolling Stone no. 199:102, November 6, 1975.

8655   "Caught in the Act America." Melody Maker 50:48, November 15, 1975.

8656   Charlesworth, C. "Foxy Ladies." Melody Maker 50:21, November 22, 1975.

8657   "Records: Phoenix." Creem 7:67, December 1975.

8658   Salvo, P. "Sexiest Singers in Show Business." Sepia 25:44-48, March 1976.

8659   Weston, M. "Labelle." Ebony 31:100-102, May 1976.

8660   "Talent in Action." Billboard 88:42, July 24, 1976.

8661   Sako, T., and T. White. "For Whom Labelle Tolls: Glitter-Weary Chameleons Moving On." Crawdaddy no. 63:18, August 1976.

8662   "Records: Chameleon." Rolling Stone no. 223:70, October 7, 1976.

8663   "Soul Albums: Chameleon." Melody Maker 51:26, October 16, 1976.

8664   "Making Waves." Melody Maker 51:34, October 23, 1976.

8665   "Talent in Action." Billboard 88:36, December 18, 1976.

8666   "Pop Scene $\frac{1}{2}$1." BMI no. 4:12-13, 1977.

8667   Murphy, F. D. "Labelle and Their Latest Chance." Encore 6:28-31, February 7, 1977.

8668   "Records: Patti Labelle." Crawdaddy no. 77:72, October 1977.

8669   "Albums: Patti Labelle." Melody Maker 52:23, October 15, 1977.

8670   "Records: Patti Labelle." High Fidelity/Musical America 27:157, November 1977.

8671   "Concert Reviews." Variety 288:68, November 2, 1977.

8672   "Aladdin, Las Vegas." Variety 289:61, November 9, 1977.

8673   "Talent in Action." Billboard 89:59, November 19, 1977.

8674   Christgau, G. "Riffs: Labelles: Three Notes." Village Voice 22:64, November 28, 1977. Discusses careers of Patti Labelle, Sarah Dash and Nona Hendryx after the breakup of the group.

8675   Ebert, A. "After 16 Years a Trio Breaks Up: Labelle--a Whodunit." Essence 8:72-74, February 1978.

8676   "Concert Reviews." Variety 289:84, February 1, 1978; 291:74, June

28, 1978. Patti Labelle performs on her own after the Labelle group split.

8677   Sanders, C. L. "Patti Labelle: On Her Own and Doing Great." Ebony 33:162-164, September 1978.

8678   "Concert Reviews." Variety 292:84, September 27, 1978.

8679   "Talent in Action." Billboard 90:46, October 14, 1978.

LADY DAY   see   HOLIDAY, BILLIE

LEADBELLY   see   LEDBETTER, HUDDIE WILLIAM

LEDBETTER, HUDDIE WILLIAM (Leadbelly), 1885?-1949.

8680   Engel, C. "Views and Reviews; Negro Folk Songs as Sung by Lead Belly." Musical Quarterly 23:388-395, July 1937.

8681   "Lead Belly." Time 33:76-77, May 15, 1939.

8682   A Tribute to Huddie Ledbetter. General editors: Max Jones and Albert McCarthy. London: Jazz Music Books, 1949.

8683   Jones, M., and S. Traill. "Lead Belly Stages Folk-Song Counter-Attraction." Melody Maker 25:5, May 14, 1949.

8684   "First British Lead Belly Release." Melody Maker 25:6, June 4, 1949.

8685   Jones, M. "A Perfect Vintage Ledbetter." Melody Maker 25:3, July 30, 1949.

8686   "Lead Belly Perfects." Melody Maker 25:11, August 6, 1949.

8687   Jones, M. "Dynamic, Almost Hypnotic Magnetism." Melody Maker 25:4, December 3, 1949.

8688   ["Obituary."] Variety 177:63, December 14, 1949; Billboard 61:49, December 17, 1949; Newsweek 34:53, December 19, 1949; Time 54:71, December 19, 1949.

8689   "'Lead Belly' Dies in N.Y. Hospital." Melody Maker 25:1, December 24, 1949.

8690   Jones, M., and S. Traill. "'Lead Belly' and the Record Companies." Melody Maker 25:2, December 31, 1949.

8691   Grut, H. "Leadbelly Dod." Orkester Journalen 18:9, January 1950.

8692   ["Obituary."] Musical America 70:26, January 1, 1950; down beat 17:10, January 13, 1950.

8693   Jones, M. "King of the 12-String Guitar; An Appreciation of Huddie Ledbetter." Melody Maker 26:9, January 14, 1950.

8694   Ramsey, F. "Leadbelly's Legacy." Saturday Review of Literature
        33:60-61, January 28, 1950.

8695   _____. "'Take This Hammer'--Leadbelly's Song." Playback
        3:3-4, March 1950.

8696   "Good Night, Irene." Time 56:38, August 14, 1950.

8697   Finkelstein, S. "Some Folk Song Releases." American Record Guide
        17:119-121, December 1950.

8698   Lee, H. "Leadbelly's 'Frankie and Albert.'" Journal of American
        Folklore 64:314-317, 1951.

8699   "Unconventional Music by Huddie and Sonny." Melody Maker 27:9,
        April 21, 1951.

8700   Brown, D. "Leadbelly Land." Negro Digest 9:6-9, May 1951.

8701   Jones, M. "Lead Belly and the High Voltage Voice." Melody Maker
        29:13, October 31, 1953.

8702   Ramsey, F. "Leadbelly's Last Sessions." High Fidelity 3:49-51,
        November-December 1953.

8703   Hobson, W. "Blue, Turning Gay; Recordings." Saturday Review
        37:44, January 30, 1954.

8704   Holzman, J. "Leadbelly on Record." Record Changer 13:7, June
        1954; 13:27-28, Summer 1954; 13:7, December 1954.

8705   Jepsen, J. G. "Jazzens Instrumentalister: Manliga Vokalister."
        Orkester Journalen 24:12, April 1956.

8706   Oliver, P. "Blind Lemon Jefferson." Jazz Review 2:9-12, August
        1959.

8707   Ramsey, F. "The Lyre of Leadbelly and Django." Saturday Review
        42:56-57, December 5, 1959.

8708   Yurchenco, H. "Three Giants of Folk Music." Sing Out 12:57, no.
        3, 1962.

8709   "Leadbelly's 'Cottonfields' Hits Charts and Cues Unique Copyright
        Angles." Variety 226:51, March 21, 1962.

8710   Price, C. "Leadbelly." Negro Digest 11:20-29, April 1962.

8711   Lee, H. "Notes & Queries: Some Notes on Lead Belly." Journal
        of American Folklore 76:135-140, no. 300, 1963.

8712   "Legend of Leadbelly." Negro Digest 12:62-63, October 1963.

8713   Oliver, P. "Blues and the Folk Revival." International Musician
        62:12-13, April 1964.

8714   Ortiz Oderigo, N. R. "Ricordo di Leadbelly." Musica Jazz 20:43-
        44, May 1964.

8715 Lambert, G. E. "Leadbelly the Demoniac." Jazz Journal 17:22-23,
      July 1964.

8716 Ramsey, F. "Leadbelly; Plastic & Otherwise." Jazz Monthly 10:11,
      December 1964.

8717 Affeldt, P. E. "King of the 12-String, Huddie 'Leadbelly' Ledbet-
      ter." Jazz Report 4:5, no. 5, 1965.

8718 Famsey, F. "Leadbelly: A Great Long Time." Sing Out 15:6-11,
      no. 1, 1965.

8719 Testoni, G. C. "Il Mondo del Blues." Musica Jazz 21:26-30, March
      1965.

8720 "Victoria Spivey Cleffed 'T. B. Blues,' Not Leadbelly, Tune Detec-
      tives Discover." Variety 242:55, April 13, 1966.

8721 Hentoff, N. "The Leadbelly Legend Splendidly Documented." HiFi/
      Stereo Review 17:108, October 1966. The Library of Congress re-
      cordings have been released by Elektra.

8722 Yurchenco, H. "Leadbelly." American Record Guide 34:776-779,
      May 1968.

8723 Wilson, T. "The Folk Heroes." Melody Maker 43:11, October 26,
      1968.

8724 Leroux, B. "Blues Rural." Jazz Hot no. 247:35, February 1969.

8725 "A Gallery of the Greats." BMI p. 24, Summer 1969.

8726 Lambert, E. "Leadbelly's Last Sessions." Jazz Monthly no. 171[i.e.,
      no. 176]:11-4, June 1969.

8727 _____. "Leadbelly--in the Evening When the Sun Goes Down."
      Jazz Monthly no. 176:20, October 1969.

8728 "Record Reviews." Jazz Journal 22:32, October 1969.

8729 Russell, R. "Illuminating the Leadbelly Legend." down beat 37:12-
      14, August 6, 1970.

8730 Goodwin, M. "Records: Leadbelly." Rolling Stone no. 72:48, De-
      cember 2, 1970.

8731 Garvin, Richard M., and Edmond G. Addeo. The Midnight Special:
      The Legend of Leadbelly. New York: B. Geis Associates, 1971.

8732 Oliver, P. "Record Reviews: Leadbelly." Jazz Journal 24:37,
      March 1971.

8733 Marine, G. "Guerrilla Minstrel." Rolling Stone no. 106:45, April
      13, 1972.

8734 Carles, P. "Pourquoi le Blues?" Jazz Magazine no. 200:2, May
      1972.

8735   "A Gallery of the Greats." BMI no. 1:4-13, 1973. Sixty years of
       the foremost musicians in rhythm and blues.

8736   "Record Reviews: Leadbelly." Sing Out 22:49, no. 4, 1973.

8737   Gleason, R. J. "Perspectives: The Presence of Legends in a Funky
       Hall." Rolling Stone no. 140:7, August 2, 1973.

8738   "Album: Leadbelly." Melody Maker 48:35, September 1, 1973.

8739   "Records: Leadbelly Live." Crawdaddy no. 29:82, October 1973.

8740   "Records: Leadbelly." Rolling Stone no. 146:66, October 25, 1973.

8741   "Record Reviews: Leadbelly." Jazz Journal 27:44, January 1974.

8742   "Leadbelly's Legacy: 'New Iberia.'" Sing Out 23:9, no. 6, 1975.

8743   "Ain't No Grave Gonna Hold My Body Down; Texans Want Body of
       Louisiana Singer." Living Blues no. 19:32, January-February 1975.

8744   "Film Reviews." Variety 282:21, March 3, 1976.

8745   Flippo, C. "American Grandstand: Will the Real Huddie Ledbetter
       Please Stand Up." Rolling Stone no. 211:24, April 22, 1976.

8746   Verrill, A. "Par Rebuts Parks' 'Diller Bias' Crack; Big Who's
       Liable Tiff Re 'Leadbelly.'" Variety 282:5, April 28, 1976.

8747   Crist, J. "The Movies." Saturday Review 3:48, May 29, 1976.

8748   "Ledbetter Family Sues Paramount." Variety 283:5, June 2, 1976.

8749   Jones, M. "Leadbelly's Film Bio." Melody Maker 51:41, June 12,
       1976.

8750   "LP's: Original Sound Track from the Motion Picture Leadbelly."
       Living Blues no. 28:37-38, July-August 1976.

8751   "Films." Living Blues no. 30:27, November-December 1976.

8752   Gebhard, H. "March of Time 1935: Leadbelly." Living Blues no.
       30:26, November-December 1976.

LEE, MRS. R. EDWARD see ALLEN, BETTY

LE MENTHE, FERDINAND JOSEPH see MORTON, FERDINAND JOSEPH
(Jelly Roll)

LEON, MRS. ROBERT A. DE see CARROLL, DIAHANN

LISTON, MELBA DORETTA, 1926- .

8753   "The New Melba." Melody Maker 31:5, July 7, 1956.

8754 Feather, L. "This Melba Is a Peach." down beat 23:26, September
        19, 1956.

8755 Tenot, F. "Quincy Jones Face à Son Destin." Jazz Magazine 6:19-
        24, February 1960.

8756 Page, B. S. "A Toast to Melba." down beat 28:18-19, January 5,
        1961.

8757 "Whatever Happened to Melba Liston?" Ebony 32:122, June 1977.

MCADOO, BILL.

8758 Hentoff, N. "A Long Way from Houston." Reporter 23:65, Decem-
        ber 8, 1960.

8759 Welding, P. J. "Sing a Song of Segregation." Saturday Review
        44:42, April 29, 1961.

MCKAY, ELEANOR GOUGH see HOLIDAY, BILLIE

MCPHATTER, CLYDE L., 1931-1972.

8760 "Atlantic Record Artists." Billboard 70:40, January 13, 1958.

8761 Rolontz, B. "Clyde Hot--with Right Songs." Billboard 71:10, Feb-
        ruary 23, 1959.

8762 Grevatt, R. "Rock Will Leave Its Mark." Melody Maker 35:5,
        March 19, 1960.

8763 Tomlyn, T. "McPhatter, Clyde; Greatest Success Around the Cor-
        ner." Sepia 11:68, January 1962.

8764 "Apollo, N.Y." Variety 226:72, May 9, 1962.

8765 "Bios." Cash Box 23:20, July 14, 1962.

8766 "Today's Top Record Talent." Billboard 74:61, September 22, 1962.

8767 ["Obituary."] Variety 267:71, June 21, 1972.

8768 "McPhatter Dies at Age of 41." Billboard 84:4, June 24, 1972.

8769 Williams, R. "A Tribute to Clyde." Melody Maker 47:4, June 24,
        1972.

8770 ["Obituary."] Jet 42:53, June 29, 1972.

8771 Fong-Torres, B. "Clyde McPhatter Dead at 38." Rolling Stone no.
        113:12, July 20, 1972.

8772 Wexler, J. "Clyde McPhatter & the Drifter Years." Rolling Stone
        no. 113:14, July 20, 1972.

8773 ["Obituary."] Jazz Magazine no. 203:36, August-September 1972.

8774 Leadbitter, M. "Blue Ghost Blues." Jazz & Blues 2:16, August
      1972. McPhatter's obituary.

8775 ["Obituary."] Crawdaddy no. 15:4, August 1972; down beat 39:11,
      August 17, 1972.

8776 "Clyde McPhatter, 1933-1972." Blues Unlimited no. 94:17, Septem-
      ber 1972.

8777 "On Record: A Tribute to Clyde McPhatter." Jazz & Blues 3:21,
      July 1973.

8778 McCutcheon, L. "Clyde McPhatter: Epitome of a Musical Era."
      Negro History Bulletin 37:200-202, January 1974.

8779 Giddins, G. "Weatherbird: Placing the Dominoes." Village Voice
      22:65, November 2, 1977.

MCRAE, CARMEN, 1922- .

8780 Simon, B. "Miss McRae and Mr. Elgart." Saturday Review 36:62,
      December 26, 1953.

8781 "Caught in the Act." down beat 21:6, January 13, 1954.

8782 "'Recording Artists' Roster." down beat 21:114, June 30, 1954.

8783 "Carmen McRae." Metronome 70:17, December 1954.

8784 "Carmen McRae Looks Back on Her First Big Year." down beat
      22:17, January 12, 1955.

8785 Feather, L. "Carmen Blanches on Hearing R&B." down beat 22:25,
      May 18, 1955.

8786 Dean, N. "Boston--Symphony Hall." Metronome 72:11-12, January
      1956.

8787 "Carmen McRae; New Singer Challenges Ella, Sarah for Jazz Suprem-
      acy." Ebony 11:67-70, February 1956.

8788 Howard, J. "Introducing Miss Carmen McRae." Negro History Bul-
      letin 19:125, March 1956.

8789 Feather, L. "Carmen McRae." Melody Maker 31:5, August 25, 1956.

8790 "Mr. Kelly's, Chi." Variety 204:77, October 3, 1956.

8791 "Caught in the Act." down beat 23:19, October 31, 1956; 24:10, April
      4, 1957.

8792 "Kai Winding at Ridgecrest Inn." Metronome 74:11, July 1957.

8793 "Carmen McRae." down beat 24:41-42, November 28, 1957.

8794 "Village Vanguard, N.Y." Variety 211:67, July 9, 1958.

8795 "The Subtle Art of Carmen McRae." Billboard 70:5, July 14, 1958.

8796 "Village Vanguard, N.Y." Variety 212:68, October 8, 1958.

8797 "It's Been a Long Road for Carmen." Melody Maker 34:5, March
      28, 1959.

8798 "Cloister, Chi." Variety 215:76, July 15, 1959.

8799 "Arpeggio, N.Y." Variety 217:73, January 20, 1960.

8800 "Slate Bros., H'wood." Variety 220:62, October 12, 1960.

8801 Dawbarn, B. "Carmen's OK." Melody Maker 35:9, October 29,
      1960.

8802 "Neve, San Francisco." Variety 222:66, April 5, 1961.

8803 "Slate Bros., L.A." Variety 222:68, April 19, 1961.

8804 Gleason, R. "Perspectives." down beat 28:46, June 8, 1961.

8805 Hentoff, N. "Notes Between Sets." Metronome 78:29, October 1961.

8806 "Black Hawk, S.F." Variety 224:61, October 18, 1961.

8807 Lees, G. "Caught in the Act." down beat 29:38, February 15, 1962.

8808 Gardner, B. "On the Threshold; Singer's Singer, Carmen McRae."
      down beat 29:19-21, September 13, 1962.

8809 "Sugar Hill, S.F." Variety 228:44, October 17, 1962.

8810 Feather, L. "Blindfold Test." down beat 31:32, January 2, 1964.

8811 Nahman, P. "Il Est Difficile de se Faire Entendre." Jazz Hot no.
      196:20-21, March 1964.

8812 Tynan, J. A. "Caught in the Act." down beat 31:36, September 10,
      1964.

8813 "Basin Street East, N.Y." Variety 237:50, December 16, 1964.

8814 "The Losers, L.A." Variety 238:89, March 17, 1965.

8815 "Wonder Gardens, A.C." Variety 239:58, July 21, 1965.

8816 Hentoff, N. "Two Vocalists of Uncommon Talent--Mabel and Car-
      men." down beat 33:14, January 27, 1966.

8817 Gerber, A. "A la Recherche de Carmen." Jazz Magazine no. 135:30-
      35, October 1966.

8818 Korall, B. "McRae, Maye, and Lee." Saturday Review 50:76-77,
      April 29, 1967.

8819 "Americana, N.Y." Variety 247:54, July 12, 1967.

8820   "Mister Kelly's, Chi." Variety 248:100, October 11, 1967.

8821   Reed, R. "Something Very Special from Carmen McRae." HiFi/
       Stereo Review 19:89-90, November 1967.

8822   Tiegel, E. "Jazz Beat." Billboard 79:14, November 18, 1967.

8823   "Aladdin, L.V." Variety 249:52, December 13, 1967.

8824   "Caught in the Act." down beat 35:37, January 11, 1968; Melody
       Maker 43:4, February 3, 1968.

8825   "Playboy Club, London." Variety 249:60, February 7, 1968.

8826   "Mister Kelly's, Chi." Variety 252:47, September 4, 1968.

8827   "Ballad for the Sad Café Singer." Time 92:55, September 13, 1968.

8828   Mitchell, S. "The Magic of Carmen McRae." down beat 35:18, De-
       cember 12, 1968.

8829   "Hong Kong Bar, L.A." Variety 253:47, December 25, 1968.

8830   "Rainbow Grill, N.Y." Variety 254:61, February 19, 1969.

8831   Dove, I. "Carmen McRae Gives Solid Back-to-Back Performance."
       Billboard 81:12, February 22, 1969.

8832   Williams, M. "Mostly Modernists." Saturday Review 52:69, Febru-
       ary 22, 1969.

8833   Reed, R. "Carmen McRae Overachieves Again: 'Sound of Silence,'
       Her Latest Atlantic Album, Proves that She Is Still Ahead of the
       Game." Stereo Review 22:87, March 1969.

8834   "Harrah's, Reno." Variety 254:101, March 19, 1969.

8835   Albertson, C., et al. "Record Reviews." down beat 36:24, March
       29, 1969.

8836   "Copacabana, N.Y." Variety 254:69, April 2, 1969.

8837   "Sherman House, Chi." Variety 256:61, August 20, 1969.

8838   Jones, M. "Carmen and the Things of Today." Melody Maker 45:10,
       February 21, 1970.

8839   "Rainbow Grill, N.Y." Variety 259:52, June 17, 1970.

8840   Dove, I. "Talent in Action." Billboard 82:22, June 20, 1970.

8841   "P. J.'s, Los Angeles." Variety 259:47, July 15, 1970.

8842   "Recordings: Just a Little Loving." Soul 3:15, no. 1, 1971.

8843   "P. J.'s, L.A." Variety 261:64, January 13, 1971.

8844   "Talent in Action." Billboard 83:24, January 23, 1971.

8845 "Rainbow Grill, N.Y." Variety 262:53, February 24, 1971.

8846 "Talent in Action." Billboard 83:20, February 27, 1971.

8847 Feather, L. "Carmen Presque Africaine." Jazz Magazine no. 188:10-
      11, April 1971.

8848 Tolnay, T. "Caught in the Act." down beat 38:27-28, May 13, 1971.

8849 "Concert Reviews." Variety 263:40, June 2, 1971.

8850 Bennett, R. R. "Technique of the Jazz Singer." Music and Musi-
      cians 20:30-32, February 1972.

8851 "Record Reviews: Carmen McRae; Carmen's Gold." down beat 39:23-
      24, February 3, 1972.

8852 "Mister Kelly's, Chi." Variety 266:63, February 23, 1972.

8853 Szantor, J. "Windy City Wails with Getz, Carmen, et al." down
      beat 39:12, March 30, 1972.

8854 "Rainbow Grill, N.Y." Variety 268:87, September 13, 1972.

8855 Bennett, R. R. "Technique of the Jazz Singer." Educator 5:2-4,
      no. 3, 1973.

8856 "Concert Reviews." Variety 270:63, March 28, 1973.

8857 "Rainbow Grill, N.Y." Variety 271:99, July 18, 1973.

8858 "Talent in Action." Billboard 85:16, July 28, 1973.

8859 Smoker, P. "Australia: Big Bands Coming Back." Jazz Forum no.
      24:14-15, August 1973.

8860 Feather, L. "Blindfold Test." down beat 40:32, November 8, 1973.

8861 "Presentacion de Carmen McRae." Revista Musical Chilena 28:128,
      no. 126-127, 1974.

8862 "Record Reviews: The Great American Songbook." Coda 11:20, no.
      5, 1974.

8863 "MGM Grand, Las Vegas." Variety 273:55, February 6, 1974.

8864 "Concert Reviews." Variety 274:62, March 13, 1974.

8865 "London House, Chi." Variety 274:69, March 27, 1974.

8866 "Caught in the Act." Melody Maker 49:35, November 16, 1974.

8867 Jones, M. "Carmen: All I Have to Offer Is Myself." Melody Maker
      49:58, November 30, 1974.

8868 "London House, Chi." Variety 277:69, December 18, 1974.

8869 Gleason, Ralph J. Celebrating the Duke, and Louis, Bessie, Billie,

Bird, Carmen, Miles, Dizzy, and Other Heroes. Boston: Little, Brown, 1975.

8870 "Jazz in Britain." Jazz Journal 28:19, January 1975.

8871 Connolly, R. "Cabaret!" Stereo Review 34:70-75, February 1975.

8872 "Concert Reviews." Variety 278:60, March 12, 1975.

8873 "Buddy's Place, N.Y." Variety 278:63, April 30, 1975.

8874 "Carmen McRae paa Atlantic." Musikern no. 6:18, June 1975.

8875 Dahlgren, R. "Carmen McRae en av de Stora." Orkester Journalen 43:7, June 1975.

8876 Endress, G. "Carmen McRae: Telling a Story." Jazz Forum no. 41:41-44, 1976.

8877 _____. "Carmen McRae." Jazz Podium 25:3-6, January 1976.

8878 "Record Reviews: I Am Music." down beat 43:28, February 12, 1976.

8879 Hentoff, N. Indigenous Music." Nation 223:154-155, August 28, 1976.

8880 Reilly, P. "Singular Gifts and Considerable Art: Carmen McRae Gets Through." Stereo Review 37:98-9, December 1976.

8881 "Albums: Can't Hide Love." Melody Maker 52:23, January 22, 1977.

8882 Holmberg, G. "Stort Artisteri av Carmen McRae." Orkester Journalen 45:11, April 1977.

8883 "Record Reviews: Live at the Planetarium." Coda no. 155:16, May-June 1977.

8884 Voce, S. "It Don't Mean a Thing." Jazz Journal International 30:16-18, May 1977.

8885 "Record Reviews: As Time Goes By." down beat 44:28, May 19, 1977.

8886 "Caught in the Act." Melody Maker 52:16, July 9, 1977.

8887 "Talent in Action." Billboard 89:42, August 27, 1977.

8888 "Concert Reviews." Variety 288:88, September 7, 1977.

8889 "Waxing On: The Greatest." down beat 44:36, October 6, 1977.

8890 "Lainie's Room, L.A." Variety 289:99, February 1, 1978.

8891 "Mocambo, S.F." Variety 290:131, April 19, 1978.

8892 "Jazz Albums: Ronnie Scotts Presents Carmen McRae Live." Melody Maker 53:28, July 15, 1978.

8893 "Record Reviews: Carmen McRae at the Great American Music Hall."
      Radio Free Jazz 19:21-22, September 1978.

8894 Siegel, J. E. "Carmen Talk." Radio Free Jazz 19:6-7, October
      1978; 19:8-10, November 1978.

8895 "Record Reviews: Blue Note Meets the L.A. Philharmonic." down
      beat 45:28, November 16, 1978.

MARTELL, LINDA.

8896 "Singleton Inks Black Gal Country Singer." Billboard 81:46, July 5,
      1969.

8897 "Country Music Gets Soul." Ebony 25:66-68, March 1970.

MATHIS, JOHNNY, 1935- .

8898 "New Acts." Variety 202:60, March 28, 1956.

8899 "Pop Hopefuls." Time 70:43, September 2, 1957.

8900 Maher, J. "The Johnny Mathis Story." Metronome 74:18-19, Novem-
      ber 1957.

8901 "Johnny Mathis." Melody Maker 32:13, November 16, 1957.

8902 "Boy with the Golden Voice; Young Johnny Mathis Sings Way to $100,000-
      a-Year Success." Ebony 13:28-30, December 1957.

8903 "Town Casino, Buffalo." Variety 209:70, December 4, 1957.

8904 "Black Orchid, Chi." Variety 209:71, December 11, 1957.

8905 "Hometown Boy Makes Good with Money; Johnny Mathis Foots 50% of
      Frisco Hoopla." Variety 209:37, December 25, 1957.

8906 "Crescendo, Hollywood." Variety 209:70, February 5, 1958.

8907 "Mathis Means Money." down beat 25:13, February 6, 1958.

8908 "Mathis Tabs Early--Sinatra Appeal." Billboard 70:12, February 17,
      1958.

8909 "Fairmont Hotel, S. F." Variety 210:70, March 5, 1958.

8910 "Vegas & All." Time 71:39, March 10, 1958.

8911 "Big Jump for Johnny." Life 44:76, March 31, 1958.

8912 "Chase Club, St. Louis." Variety 210:110, April 9, 1958.

8913 "Copacabana, N.Y." Variety 210:53, May 14, 1958.

8914 Cook, H. "Mathis Makes Smooth Copa Debut." Billboard 70:7, May
      19, 1958.

8915 "Sands, Las Vegas." Variety 211:57, July 23, 1958.

8916 Itria, H. "Johnny Mathis." Coronet 44:40-44, October 1958.

8917 "Johnny Mathis: He Doesn't Need Rock'n'Roll." Look 22:111-113,
      October 28, 1958.

8918 "Black Orchid, Chi." Variety 213:69, December 10, 1958.

8919 "Mathematics on Mathis." Variety 213:37, December 24, 1958.

8920 Grevatt, R. "The Problem of Being a Star." Melody Maker 34:3,
      January 17, 1959.

8921 "Cocoanut Grove, L.A." Variety 213:76, January 21, 1959.

8922 "Mathis Wows at Cocoanut Grove." Billboard 71:16, January 26,
      1959.

8923 "Copacabana, N.Y." Variety 213:70, February 11, 1959.

8924 Lucraft, H. "Johnny Mathis." Music U.S.A. 76:11, March 1959.

8925 "Sands, Las Vegas." Variety 214:85, March 18, 1959.

8926 "Chez Paree, Chi." Variety 214:68, May 13, 1959.

8927 "Mathis to Thespis." down beat 26:10, May 14, 1959.

8928 "Birthday Fortune." down beat 26:13-14, November 26, 1959.

8929 "Johnny Mathis." down beat 26:35, November 26, 1959.

8930 "Cocoanut Grove, L.A." Variety 217:73, January 20, 1960.

8931 "Copacabana, N.Y." Variety 218:64, April 27, 1960.

8932 "Mathis' 3 Golden LP's." Variety 218:55, April 27, 1960.

8933 King, G. "The Lonely Mr. Mathis." Melody Maker 35:3, April 30,
      1960.

8934 "Johnny Mathis on 'Rexall TV Special,' May 1st." Jet p. 66, May
      5, 1960.

8935 "Twin Coaches, Pitt." Variety 219:55, June 22, 1960.

8936 Tubbs, V. "Johnny Mathis: Year's Best Stage Attraction." Sepia
      8:28-33, December 1960.

8937 "Sahara, Las Vegas." Variety 221:54, January 11, 1961.

8938 "Latin Casino, Camden." Variety 222:66, March 8, 1961.

8939 "Eden Roc, Miami Beach." Variety 222:53, March 29, 1961.

8940 "Tahoe, Harrah's." Variety 222:68, April 19, 1961.

8941 "Copacabana, N.Y." Variety 222:76, May 3, 1961.

8942 Brown, T. "Mathis Wows His First-Night Audience." Melody Maker
      36:8, June 22, 1961.

8943 "Jazz? Not Yet, Says Johnny Mathis." Melody Maker 36:8, July 1,
      1961.

8944 "Cocoanut Grove, L.A." Variety 224:62, September 27, 1961.

8945 "Johnny Mathis Answers Teen Questions." Sepia 10:71, November
      1961.

8946 Thompson, J. "Hear Your Heroes." Seventeen 21:76, January 1962.

8947 Shefrin, G. "Johnny Mathis Goes on the Road." Sepia 11:48-49,
      February 1962.

8948 "Johnny Mathis Tour Is Cancelled." Melody Maker 37:5, February
      10, 1962.

8949 "Today's Top Record Talent." Billboard 74:64, April 7, 1962.

8950 "Eden Roc, Miami Beach." Variety 226:53, April 25, 1962.

8951 "Johnny Mathis Answers Teen Questions." Sepia 11:70, July 1962.

8952 "Fan-fare!" America 107:709, September 15, 1962.

8953 "I Like to See the Money Rolling In! Says Johnny Mathis." Melody
      Maker 37:5, September 15, 1962.

8954 "Bios for Deejays." Cash Box 24:34, October 27, 1962.

8955 "Oh! Johnny! No!" Melody Maker 38:8-9, January 5, 1963.

8956 "Johnny Mathis and Mimi Dillard; The Newest Coosome Twosome."
      Sepia 12:73-76, February 1963.

8957 "Copacabana, N.Y." Variety 229:56, February 13, 1963.

8958 "Riviera, Las Vegas." Variety 230:67, March 13, 1963.

8959 "Cocoanut Grove, L.A." Variety 231:55, May 29, 1963.

8960 "Singers Pledge Money for Civil-Rights Struggle." down beat 30:11,
      August 15, 1963.

8961 "Cocoanut Grove, L.A." Variety 233:84, January 22, 1964.

8962 Tiegel, E. "Johnny Mathis' Voice a Grabber." Billboard 76:14,
      February 1, 1964.

8963 "Nugget, Sparks." Variety 236:54, October 28, 1964.

8964 "Mathis Forms Co. to Handle Himself as He Sues to Void Noga's Mgt.
      Pact." Variety 236:51, November 18, 1964.

8965 "Helen Noga Fights Mathis Suit; Files Counterclaim." Billboard
      76:4, December 19, 1964.

8966 Robinson, L. "Johnny Mathis: Millionaire with Problems." Ebony
      20:99-102, March 1965.

8967 "Talk of Town, London." Variety 243:60, August 3, 1966.

8968 "Copacabana, N.Y." Variety 246:57, March 8, 1967.

8969 "Johnny Mathis Near SRO at Bash in Forest Hills; Young Generation
      Clicks." Variety 247:53, July 12, 1967.

8970 "Palace West, Phoenix." Variety 254:75, March 5, 1969.

8971 "Waldorf-Astoria, N.Y." Variety 256:75, November 12, 1969.

8972 Sobel, R. "Mathis Exciting Performer--with Quality to Match."
      Billboard 81:26, November 15, 1969.

8973 "Concert Reviews." Variety 257:38, December 31, 1969.

8974 "Latin Casino, N.Y." Variety 257:55, February 11, 1970.

8975 "Now Grove, L.A." Variety 260:43, September 9, 1970.

8976 "Talent in Action." Billboard 82:29, September 12, 1970; 82:24,
      November 21, 1970.

8977 "Caesars Palace, L.V." Variety 261:52, December 9, 1970.

8978 Pearson, S. "Caught in the Act Extra." Melody Maker 46:44, Feb-
      ruary 27, 1971.

8979 "Talent in Action." Billboard 83:26, May 29, 1971.

8980 "Mathis, J." Billboard 83:M1-6, July 17, 1971.

8981 "Sahara, Las Vegas." Variety 264:51, September 29, 1971.

8982 "Mathis Plans Concerts with Symphonies; Cincinnati Set." Billboard
      83:8, October 16, 1971.

8983 "Talent in Action." Billboard 83:14, October 16, 1971.

8984 "Waldorf-Astoria, N.Y." Variety 264:47, November 10, 1971.

8985 Meyers, R. "Mister Wonderful Johnny Mathis." Rolling Stone no.
      97:16, December 9, 1971.

8986 "Col. Acts at Garden--a Way to Fill Gap." Billboard 84:6, January
      1, 1972.

8987 "Sahara, L.V." Variety 265:60, January 12, 1972.

8988 "Concert Reviews." Variety 267:44, July 5, 1972.

8989 "The Johnny Mathis Mystique." Soul 7:10, July 31, 1972.

8990 Watts, M. "Caught in the Act." Melody Maker 47:34, September
      2, 1972.

8991 "Sahara, L.V." Variety 268:63, October 11, 1972.

8992 "Waldorf-Astoria, N.Y." Variety 268:49, November 8, 1972.

8993 "Concert Reviews." Variety 271:112, May 16, 1973.

8994 "Even 25 G Waldorf Salary No Match for Concert Coin: Mathis,
      Bassey." Variety 271:113, May 16, 1973.

8995 Tiegel, E. "Mathis Goes to 'Original' Tunes." Billboard 85:14,
      June 9, 1973.

8996 "Concert Reviews." Variety 271:42, August 1, 1973.

8997 "Caught in the Act." Melody Maker 48:43, August 25, 1973.

8998 "Mathis Mastery." Melody Maker 48:40, September 15, 1973.

8999 Stevens, A. "Johnny Mathis." Crescendo International 12:2, Decem-
      ber 1973.

9000 Ebert, A. "Mathis: Singing Was Always Like Standing on Stage
      Naked, Nerve Endings and All." Essence 4:60-61, January 1974.

9001 Berry, W. E. "Millionaire Mathis Comes Home to Black Music."
      Jet 45:56-58, January 10, 1974.

9002 "Concert Reviews." Variety 273:48, January 30, 1974.

9003 "Talent in Action." Billboard 86:16, February 23, 1974.

9004 "Beverly Hilton, L.A." Variety 274:68, March 13, 1974.

9005 Beauford, F. "Johnny Mathis; Change Is the Essence." Music Jour-
      nal 32:20, May 1974.

9006 "Sahara, Las Vegas." Variety 274:279, May 8, 1974.

9007 Beauford, F. "Johnny Mathis: Changing but Staying the Same."
      Soul 9:8-9, May 13, 1974.

9008 "Concert Reviews." Variety 275:46, July 31, 1974.

9009 Henshaw, L. "Diplomatic Mathis." Melody Maker 49:44, September
      21, 1974.

9010 "Caught in the Act." Melody Maker 49:22, September 28, 1974.

9011 Atlas, J. "Mathis: Wearing Sinatra's Crown." Melody Maker 49:47,
      November 30, 1974.

9012 "Talent in Action." Billboard 86:23, December 7, 1974.

9013 "Concert Reviews." Variety 282:108, February 18, 1976.

9014 "Johnny Mathis: His Own Man Now." Ebony 31:44-48, March 1976.

9015 "Concert Reviews." Variety 282:62, March 10, 1976.

9016 "Talent in Action." Billboard 88:34, March 13, 1976.

9017 "Caught in the Act." Melody Maker 51:20, April 10, 1976.

9018 "Talent in Action." Billboard 88:43, September 4, 1976.

9019 "Mathis Battles Apartheid." Billboard 89:79, February 26, 1977.

9020 "Concert Reviews." Variety 286:108, April 6, 1977.

9021 "Caught in the Act." Melody Maker 52:42, May 21, 1977.

9022 "Talent in Action." Billboard 89:44, May 28, 1977.

9023 "Albums: The Mathis Collection." Melody Maker 52:14, July 30,
      1977.

9024 "Talent in Action." Billboard 89:104-105, December 24, 1977.

9025 Williams, J. "Mathis Goes R&B with Williams." Billboard 90:69,
      May 20, 1978.

9026 Grein, P. "Producer Shapes a New Mathis; An Ailing Jack Gold
      Makes Singer Bigger than Ever." Billboard 90:6, June 24, 1978.

9027 "Talent in Action." Billboard 90:42, July 29, 1978.

9028 "Caught in the Act." Melody Maker 53:62, October 21, 1978.

9029 Windeler, R. "Happy." People 10:67, October 23, 1978.

9030 "Concert Reviews." Variety 292:66, October 25, 1978.

9031 Garland, P. "Mathis & Williams, Inc." Stereo Review 41:149, No-
      vember 1978. Deniece Williams and Mathis have made a recording
      "That's What Friends Are For."

9032 "Talent in Action." Billboard 90:60, November 11, 1978.

MAYNOR, DOROTHY (Mrs. Shelby Albright Rooks), 1910- .

9033 "Native Flagstad?" Newsweek 14:26-27, August 21, 1939.

9034 "Salt at Stockbridge." Time 34:45, August 21, 1939.

9035 "Black Diva." Time 34:58, November 27, 1939.

9036 "Debut." Newsweek 14:25, November 27, 1939.

9037 Arthur, J. K. "Women of 1939." Independent Woman 19:4, January
      1940.

9038 "Debut Recital." Etude 58:75, February 1940.

9039   Taubman, H. "Million-Dollar Voice." Collier's 105:11-12, March
       2, 1940.

9040   Thomajan, P. K. "Temportrait." Musician 45:87, May 1940.

9041   "Maynor's Year." Time 36:58, November 4, 1940.

9042   "Not by the Pound." Time 53:39, June 27, 1949.

9043   "Dorothy Maynor." Music News 41:33, December 1949.

9044   "Maynor Makes First Tour of Australia." Musical America 72:20,
       June 1952.

9045   "Dorothy Maynor." Canon 6:33-34, August 1952; 6:68, September
       1952.

9046   "Five American Artists Heard in Recent Australian Tours." Musical
       America 72:25, November 15, 1952.

9047   "Biographical Note." Musical America 73:15, April 1, 1953.

9048   Dowdy, D. , and R. Devries. "Chicago." Musical Courier 151:27,
       April 1955.

9049   "Dorothy Maynor." Musical Courier 152:14-15, November 15, 1955.

9050   "Town Hall Recital." Musical America 75:22, November 15, 1955.

9051   "Dorothy Maynor." Pan Pipes 48:20, May 1956.

9052   Milburn, F. "Dorothy Maynor--a Singer Who Has Happily Combined
       Her Home Life with a Career." Musical America 76:16-17, May
       1956.

9053   "Little Orchestra Society." Variety 212:70, October 15, 1958.

9054   "Scherman Launches Season with 'Comus.'" Musical America 78:16,
       November 1, 1958.

9055   "Dorothy Maynor." Variety 216:71, November 25, 1959; Musical
       Courier 160:17, December 1959; Musical America 79:24, December
       15, 1959.

9056   Rogers, E. B. "High Honors." Musical America 81:184, January
       1961.

9057   "Fine Arts School." Ebony 21:80-82, May 1966.

9058   Fisher, M. M. "Community Concerts to Community Service." Mu-
       sic Journal 24:38-39, November 1966.

9059   Evans, O. "Making Friends with Music." Opera News 31:15-17, No-
       vember 5, 1966.

9060   Soria, D. J. "Artist Life." High Fidelity/Musical America 17:MA3-
       4, August 1967.

9061   Maynor, D.   "Arts in the Ghetto."   Music Educator's Journal 54:39-
       40, March 1968.

9062   Russcol, H.   "Can the Negro Overcome the Classical Music Estab-
       lishment?"   High Fidelity/Musical America 18:46, August 1968.

9063   Seward, W.   "Whatever Became of Dorothy Maynor?"   Stereo Review
       22:69-72, January 1969.

9064   Maynor, D.   "Why Should Whitey Care About the Ghetto?"   Music
       Educator's Journal 55:60-62, April 1969.

9065   Miller, P. L.   "Ever-Fresh Art of Dorothy Maynor."   American
       Record Guide 35:1111, August 1969.

9066   Ferguson, C. W.   "Dorothy Maynor."   PTA Magazine 64:10-12, No-
       vember 1969.

9067   Maynor, D.   "Looking Back Without Anger, Looking Forward to
       Change."   Symphony News 22:17, no. 4, 1971.

9068   Kolodin, I.   "Spirituals Spiritualized."   Stereo Review 33:98-99, July
       1974.

9069   Diedrichs, G.   "A Respect for Talent."   Opera News 39:39-42, October
       1974.

9070   Maynor, D.   "The Spiritual as Soul Music."   Saturday Review 3:38,
       September 4, 1976.

9071   _____.   "Remarks."   National Music Council Bulletin 36:7-8, no.
       2, 1977.   Remembrances of Nathaniel Dett's contributions to music.

9072   Peterson, M.   "Dorothy Maynor: The Musical Wiz of Harlem."   Es-
       sence 8:56, December 1977.

MENTHE, FERDINAND JOSEPH LE   see   MORTON, FERDINAND JOSEPH
(Jelly Roll)

MILLS, STEPHANIE.

9073   Wolff, A.   "Miss Stephanie Mills Vs. Motherhood."   Look 34:58-59,
       April 21, 1970.

9074   Nikolaieff, G.   "Stephanie Mills."   Senior Scholastic 105:36-37, Sep-
       tember 26, 1974.

9075   "Music People."   Seventeen 34:38, January 1975.

9076   Weinstein, B.   "'The Wiz' Has Its Own Whiz."   Rolling Stone no.
       177:20, January 2, 1975.

9077   Delaunoy, D.   "Stephanie Mills: 'Everybody Can Be a Dorothy.'"
       Soul 10:6, July 7, 1975.

9078   "New Acts."   Variety 285:86, February 2, 1977.

9079   Mitz, R.   "Pop Rotogravure." Stereo Review 39:96, August 1977.

9080   "Talent in Action." Billboard 89:46, August 6, 1977.

9081   Webster, I.   "Two from 'The Wiz' Ease on Down the Cabaret Cir-
       cuit." Encore 7:26-30, December 4, 1978.

MONK, THELONIOUS SPHERE, 1920- .

9082   Bacon, P.   "The High Priest of Be-Bop, the Inimitable Mr. Monk."
       Record Changer 8:9-11, November 1949.

9083   "Thelonius Monk Arrested on Drug Charge." Melody Maker 27:7,
       August 25, 1951.

9084   Wiedemann, E.   "Thelonius Monk; Bebopens Oversteprast." Orkester
       Journalen 20:12-13, April 1952.

9085   Williams, M. L.   "Then Came Zombie Music." Melody Maker 30:11,
       May 8, 1954.

9086   _____.   "The Mad Monk." Melody Maker 30:11, May 22, 1954.

9087   Nevard, M.   "Mulligan, Monk--and Then a French Surprise." Mel-
       ody Maker 30:8-9, June 5, 1954.

9088   "'Recording Artists' Roster." down beat 21:115, June 30, 1954.

9089   Dahlgren, C.   "Glimtar om Glimtar." Orkester Journalen 22:23,
       December 1954.

9090   Jepsen, J. G.   "Jazzens Instrumentalister: Pianot." Orkester Jour-
       nalen 23:13, September 1955.

9091   Dahlgren, C.   "Monk Komiker i Town Hall." Orkester Journalen
       24:6-7, May 1956.

9092   Hentoff, N.   "Just Call Him Thelonious." down beat 23:15-16, July
       25, 1956.

9093   "Ira Gitler Interviews Thelonious Monk." Metronome 74:19-20, March
       1957.

9094   "Thelonious Monk Quartet." down beat 24:33, September 5, 1957.

9095   Balliett, W.   "Jazz Records." New Yorker 34:110, March 15, 1958.

9096   Brown, F. L.   "More Man than Myth, Monk Has Emerged from the
       Shadows." down beat 25:13-16, October 30, 1958.

9097   Schuller, G.   "Reviews: Recordings." Jazz Review 1:22-27, Novem-
       ber 1958.

9098   Coulter, G.   "Clark Terry with Thelonious Monk: In Orbit." Jazz
       Review 2:37-38, January 1959.

9099   McKinney, J.   "Giants in Jazz." Music U.S.A. 76:21, January 1959.

9100 Balliett, W. "Jazz Concerts." New Yorker 35:153-156, March 7,
      1959.

9101 Rolontz, B. "Much Town Hall--Too Little Monk." Billboard 71:10,
      March 9, 1959.

9102 "Apollo, N.Y." Variety 214:87, March 18, 1959.

9103 "Tristano and Monk." Music U.S.A. 76:33, April 1959.

9104 "Magnificent Monk of Music." Ebony 14:120-122, May 1959.

9105 Schuller, G. "Thelonious Monk at Town Hall." Jazz Review 2:6-8,
      June 1959.

9106 Wellstood, D. "Monk's Music." Jazz Review 2:32, July 1959.

9107 Morgenstern, D. "Newport '59." Jazz Journal 12:4, August 1959.

9108 "A Night of Thelonious." Music U.S.A. 76:18-19, August 1959.

9109 Gaspard, J. J. "Thelonious Monk." Musica no. 67:30, October
      1959.

9110 "Monk et les 'Liaisons Dangereuses.'" Jazz Magazine 5:20-24, Oc-
      tober 1959.

9111 Lyttelton, H. "Monk ... Genius in a Straw Hat." Melody Maker
      34:13, October 10, 1959.

9112 _____. "That Hat Again." Melody Maker 34:3, October 17, 1959.

9113 Sales, G. "'I Wanted to Make It Better'; Monk at the Black Hawk."
      Jazz no. 5:31-41, 1960.

9114 "L'Oeuvre Enregistre de Thelonious Monk." Jazz Hot 26:16-21, Jan-
      uary 1960.

9115 Gibson, M. "Modern Jazz Piano." Jazz Journal 13:9, February
      1960.

9116 Balliett, W. "Jazz Concerts." New Yorker 36:134, February 20,
      1960.

9117 Testoni, G. "Gli Autori dei Temi." Musica Jazz 16:39, April 1960.

9118 Morgenstern, D. "An Evening with Monk." Jazz Journal 13:2-3,
      May 1960.

9119 Arrigoni, A. "Qualcosa sat Cambiando." Musica Jazz 16:17-21,
      June 1960.

9120 Guastone, G. "Quattro Chiacchiere con Enrico Intra su Cinque Pian-
      isti." Musica Jazz 16:29, July 1960.

9121 "United Nations Jazz." Metronome 77:8, August 1960.

9122 Jelmini, G. "Thelonious Monk e l'Arte Informale." Musica Jazz
      16:13-17, October 1960.

9123 "Monk, Thelonious." Metronome 77:39, October 1960.

9124 Jalard, M. C. "Trois Apotres du Discontinu." Jazz Magazine 6:42-
      47, December 1960.

9125 Williams, M. "Some Achievements of a Decade Past." Metronome
      78:23-24, January 1961.

9126 "Thelonious Monk Has a Fire." down beat 28:11, March 16, 1961.

9127 Lyttelton, H. "Monk--Joker or Genius." Melody Maker 36:5, April
      29, 1961.

9128 Arrigoni, A. "Il Piano Dopo Monk." Musica Jazz 17:17-19, May
      1961.

9129 Tronchot, J. "Trop Courte Prestation du Quartette de Monk." Jazz
      Hot no. 165:20-21, May 1961.

9130 Dawbarn, B. "The Greatest Show in Jazz." Melody Maker 36:3,
      May 6, 1961. Monk performs at the Royal Festival Hall.

9131 Harrison, M. "Concert Reviews." Jazz Journal 14:9-10, June 1961.

9132 Mouly, R., and J. R. Masson. "Monk, Newport, Cannonball, Ma-
      halia." Jazz Magazine 7:22-27, June 1961.

9133 Polillo, A. "Thelonious e Bud Insieme." Musica Jazz 17:12-14,
      June 1961.

9134 Atkins, R. "Thelonious Monk." Jazz Monthly 7:15-16, July 1961.

9135 Kotlowitz, R. "Monk Talk." Harper's Magazine 223:21-23, Septem-
      ber 1961.

9136 "Village Vanguard, N.Y." Variety 224:58, November 15, 1961.

9137 Testoni, G. "L'Eredita dei Compositori di Jazz." Musica Jazz
      18:31-33, February 1962.

9138 Williams, M. "Jazz Composition; What Is It?" down beat 29:20-23,
      February 15, 1962.

9139 Cooke, J. "Better Times Ahead." Jazz Monthly 8:3-5, January 1963.

9140 Östberg, L. "Monk i Högform." Orkester Journalen 31:14, March 1963.

9141 "Une Retrospective Monkienne." Jazz Hot no. 185:6, March 1963.

9142 Bens, J. "Monk l'Explorateur." Jazz Magazine 9:37-38, April 1963.

9143 Clouzet, J., and M. Delorme. "L'Amertume du Prophete." Jazz
      Magazine 9:38-41, April 1963.

9144 Postif, F. "'Round 'bout Sphere." Jazz Hot no. 186:22-25, April
      1963.

9145 Rouse, C. "Monk, un Classique Moderne." Jazz Hot no. 186:6-8,
      April 1963.

9146   Williams, M.   "Thelonious Monk; Arrival Without Departure."   Satur-
       day Review 46:32-33, April 13, 1963.

9147   "Five-Spot, N.Y."   Variety 231:63, June 19, 1963.

9148   Astrup, O. J.   "Musikern a Kring Monk."   Orkester Journalen 31:10-
       11, July-August 1963.

9149   Balliett, W.   "Musical Events."   New Yorker 39:89, July 20, 1963.

9150   "The Land of Monk."   down beat 30:14-15, October 20, 1963.

9151   "Annuaire Biographique du Piano."   Jazz Magazine 9:30, November
       1963.

9152   Balliett, W.   "Jazz Concerts."   New Yorker 39:92-93, January 11,
       1964.

9153   "Caught in the Act."   down beat 31:34-35, February 27, 1964.

9154   Jones, L.   "The Acceptance of Monk."   down beat 31:20-22, Febru-
       ary 27, 1964.

9155   "Loneliest Monk."   Time 83:84-88, February 28, 1964.

9156   Ostberg, L. , and L. Werner.   "Kontrasterna Bilk och Monk."   Or-
       kester Journalen 32:17, March 1964.

9157   Testoni, G. , and A. Polillo.   "Incontro con Thelonious Monk."   Mu-
       sica Jazz 20:8-10, March 1964.

9158   Gaspard, J. , and M. Delorme.   "En Butte à Monk."   Jazz Hot no.
       197:18-22, April 1964.

9159   Jalard, M. C.   "Thelonious Monk à l'Heure du Simulacre!"   Jazz
       Magazine no. 105:26-31, April 1964.

9160   Koechlin, P.   "L'Original et Inquietant: Thelonious Monk."   Musica
       no. 121:28-30, April 1964.

9161   Welles, C.   "Rewarding Workouts by Monk and Mingus."   Life 56:15,
       April 10, 1964.

9162   Lapham, L. H.   "Monk; High Priest of Jazz."   Saturday Evening Post
       237:70, April 11, 1964.

9163   Feather, L.   "Feather's Nest."   down beat 31:39, April 23, 1964.

9164   Williams, M.   "Bigger Monk and Bigger Duke."   Saturday Review
       47:63-64, May 16, 1964.

9165   Fox, C.   "Thelonious Monk: Still a Legend but Very Much Alive."
       Philips p. 20-21, Summer 1964.

9166   "Caught in the Act."   down beat 31:17, July 30, 1964.

9167   Williams, M.   "Rehearsing with Monk."   down beat 31:14-16, July
       30, 1964.

9168 _____ . "Thelonious Monk: Arrival Without Departure." Jazz Journal 17:12-14, August 1964.

9169 _____ . "Thelonious Monk: Prelude to Success." Jazz 3:8-10, October 1964.

9170 Lucraft, H. "Monk and Mingus Masterpieces Steal the Top Honours." Melody Maker 39:15, October 10, 1964.

9171 "Monterey and All that Jazz." Ebony 20:55-62, December 1964.

9172 Hennessey, M. "Monk's Moods." Melody Maker 40:9, March 20, 1965.

9173 "Jazzmen of the Year." BMI p. 12, April 1965.

9174 Lascelles, G. "Thelonious Monk." Jazz Journal 18:10-12, April 1965.

9175 Lenissois, C. "Monk Toujours." Jazz Hot no. 208:3, April 1965.

9176 Traill, S. "Thelonious Monk at the Festival Hall." Jazz Journal 18:12, April 1965.

9177 Wilmer, V. "Monk on Monk." down beat 32:20-22, June 3, 1965.

9178 Noames, J. L. "Jazz à New York." Jazz Magazine no. 123:19-20, October 1965.

9179 De Toledano, R. "Thelonious Monk and Some Others." National Review 17:940-942, October 19, 1965.

9180 Noames, J. L. "Monk Entre Deux Sommes." Jazz Magazine no. 124:46-49, November 1965.

9181 "Thelonious Monk." Ruch Muzyczny 10:9-10, no. 10, 1966.

9182 Williams, M. "Yesterday's Monk Again: New Record Release." Saturday Review 49:60-61, January 29, 1966.

9183 Feather, L. "Blindfold Test." down beat 33:39, April 21, 1966.

9184 Bird, C. "Monk Is Now Instant Creation Twice Nightly." Melody Maker 41:6, April 30, 1966.

9185 Gerber, A. "Monk à la Mutualite." Jazz Magazine no. 130:17, May 1966.

9186 Lattes, P. "Quelle Palette!" Jazz Hot no. 220:5-6, May 1966.

9187 Östberg, L. "Tre Pianokonserter." Orkester Journalen 34:12, May 1966.

9188 Hogarth, A. D. "Monk--in Europe." Jazz Journal 19:23, June 1966.

9189 Carr, I. "Monk in Perspective." Jazz Journal 20:4-6, January 1967.

9190 Houston, B. "Great Jazz Solo." Melody Maker 42:8, February 11, 1967.

9191   Williams, M. "Mostly Monk." Saturday Review 50:91, June 10,
       1967.

9192   Priestley, B. "Thelonious Monk and Herbie Mann." Jazz Monthly
       13:12-13, December 1967.

9193   Shera, M. "Monk/Mann." Jazz Journal 20:10-11, December 1967.

9194   Feather, L. "Notes from All Over." down beat 35:15, March 21,
       1968.

9195   Franksen, J. "Jazz Record Reviews." Jazz and Pop 7:57-58, Sep-
       tember 1968.

9196   Jepsen, Jorgen Grunnet. A Discography of Thelonious Monk and Bud
       Powell. Copenhagen NV: Karl Emil Knudsen, 1969.

9197   Arvanitas, G., et al. "Panorama des Pianistes." Jazz Hot no.
       247:37, February 1969.

9198   McRae, B. "A B Basics; A Column for the Newcomer to Jazz."
       Jazz Journal 22:37, May 1969.

9199   Albertson, C., et al. "Record Reviews." down beat 36:23-24, Au-
       gust 7, 1969.

9200   "The Duke in Berlin." American Musical Digest 1:40, no. 4, 1970.
       Translated from the Frankfurter Neue Press November 11, 1969.

9201   Henshaw, L. "Caught in the Act." Melody Maker 44:6, November
       15, 1969.

9202   Hentoff, N. "Thelonious Monk." BMI p. 18, December 1969.

9203   Arnoldi, N. "Thelonious Monk à Pleyel." Jazz Hot no. 257:7, Jan-
       uary 1970.

9204   Locke, D. "Record Reviews: The Thelonious Monk Orchestra in
       Concert." Jazz Monthly no. 179:21, January 1970.

9205   "La Chronique des Disques." Jazz Hot no. 260:41, April 1970.

9206   Langford, J. "Monk's Horns." Jazz Journal 23:2-6, November 1970.

9207   Voce, S. "It Don't Mean a Thing." Jazz Journal 23:7, November
       1970.

9208   Elder, G. "Well, You Needn't." Journal of Pop Culture 4:850-862,
       no. 4, 1971.

9209   Langford, J. "Monk's Horns." Jazz Journal 24:7-8, January 1971;
       24:3-4, February 1971.

9210   Tepperman, B. "Record Reviews: Reflections, Volume 1." Coda
       9:20, no. 12, 1971.

9211   Feather, L. "Caught in the Act Extra." Melody Maker 46:45, Jan-
       uary 30, 1971.

9212 "Caught in the Act." down beat 38:31, March 4, 1971.

9213 Feather, L. "Monk au Point Mort." Jazz Magazine no. 188:5, April 1971.

9214 "Concert Reviews." Variety 263:43, August 4, 1971.

9215 Gonzalez, P. "Monk Talk." down beat 38:12-13, October 28, 1971.

9216 Williams, R. "The Giants of Jazz." Melody Maker 46:12, November 13, 1971.

9217 Gerber, A. "Giants of Jazz." Jazz Magazine no. 195:22-24, December 1971.

9218 "Caught in the Act." down beat 38:27-28, December 9, 1971.

9219 "Record Reviews: Blue Monk, Vol. 2." Coda 10:19, no. 6, 1972.

9220 "La Chronique des Disques: Monk's Music." Jazz Hot no. 279:33, January 1972.

9221 "Chronique des Disques: Little Rootie Tootie." Jazz Hot no. 284:38, June 1972.

9222 Priestley, B. "Monk in the Studio." Melody Maker 47:30, July 22, 1972. Discussion of Monk's recent recording "Something in Blue."

9223 "Record Reviews: Something in Blue." Jazz & Blues 2:28, September 1972.

9224 "Chronique des Disques: Jazz Connection." Jazz Hot no. 287:25, October 1972.

9225 Keating, L. "Coleman Hawkins on Record." Jazz & Blues 2:23, October 1972.

9226 "Jazz Records: Thelonious Monk." Melody Maker 48:46, November 18, 1972.

9227 Piazza, T. "Caught in the Act." down beat 39:26, December 7, 1972.

9228 Taylor, J. R. "The Prestige 24000 Series." Journal of Jazz Studies 1:90-110, no. 1, 1973. Discussion of Prestige's reissues of recordings.

9229 "Record Reviews: Thelonious Monk Quintet; Trio." Jazz & Blues 2:30-31, January 1973.

9230 "On Record: Art Blakey's Jazz Messengers with Thelonious Monk." Jazz & Blues 2:11, February 1973.

9231 "Record Reviews: Family." down beat 40:22, April 26, 1973.

9232 Dutilh, A., and M. Lequime. "Thelonious Monk; ou, Comment Bougent les Pierres." Jazz Hot no. 306:6-9, June 1974.

9233 "Caught." down beat 41:37-38, July 18, 1974.

9234   Rosenthal, A. "Music of Thelonious Monk." Nation 219:247-250,
       September 21, 1974.

9235   "Record Reviews: Something in Blue." Coda 12:20, no. 6, 1975.

9236   "Records: Brilliance." Jazz Forum no. 37:62, 1975.

9237   Williams, M. "And What Might a Jazz Composer Do?" Music Edu-
       cator's Journal 61:24-31, January 1975.

9238   "Record Reviews: Who's Afraid of the Big Band Monk?" Coda no.
       140:18-19, August 1975.

9239   Paihle, J. "Piano Miles." Jazz Hot no. 323:9-15, January 1976.

9240   Gitler, I. "Thelonious Monk Returns to Carnegie Hall." Radio Free
       Jazz 17:10, May 1976.

9241   Balliett, W. "Jazz: New York Notes." New Yorker 52:85, July 19,
       1976.

9242   Ruppli, M. "Discographie de Thelonious Monk." Jazz Hot no. 331:225,
       October 1976.

9243   Lake, S. "Piano Giants." Melody Maker 51:44-45, October 2, 1976.

9244   Goodman, A. "Thelonious Gestalt: Monk Disrobed." Crawdaddy no.
       66:72, November 1976. Monk's influence on other musicians, such
       as Archie Shepp, is discussed.

9245   "Record Reviews: In Person." Jazz Journal 29:34, November 1976.

9246   "Records: The Complete Genius." Creem 8:59-60, November 1976.

9247   "Waxing On: In Person." down beat 44:27-30, February 10, 1977.

9248   "Waxing On: The Complete Genius." down beat 44:32, August 11,
       1977.

9249   Groves, A. "The Loneliest Monk." Jazz Journal International 30:10-
       13, November 1977.

9250   "A Tribute to Monk and Bird." Jazz Magazine (U.S.) 3:63, no. 1,
       1978.

9251   Buhles, G. "Thelonious Monk Jazz Composer." Jazz Podium 27:4-
       9, March 1978; 27:11-13, April 1978.

9252   "Waxing On: At the Five Spot." down beat 45:27-28, May 4, 1978.

9253   "Thelonious Monk." Jazz Journal International 31:17, June 1978.

9254   "Prez Awards." Jazz Journal International 31:36, August 1978.

9255   Priestley, B. "Thelonious Monk." Melody Maker 53:18, August 19,
       1978.

MONTGOMERY, TAMMY see TERRELL, TAMMI

MOORE, CARMAN.

9256 "Music." Vogue 155:58, April 15, 1970; 156:38, August 15, 1970.

9257 "Soul at the Center." Saturday Review 55:68, August 26, 1972.

9258 Moore, Carman. "International Carnival of Experimental Sound."
      Saturday Review 55:64-66, November 4, 1972.

9259 Breuer, R. "New York: Breit Aufgefaechertes Neuheiten-Quintett."
      Melos, Neue Zeitschrift für Musik 1:218-220, no. 3, 1975.

9260 "Premieres." Symphony News 26:26, no. 2, 1975.

9261 "Wildfires and Field Songs." Lincoln Center p. 17, January 23-28,
      1975.

9262 Michener, C. "Double Header." Newsweek 85:71, February 3, 1975.

9263 "Premieres." Music Journal 33:38, March 1975. Moore's composi-
      tion "Gospel Fuse" is reviewed.

9264 DeRhen, A. "N.Y. Phil. Moore Premiere." High Fidelity/Musi-
      cal America 25:MA29-30, May 1975.

9265 "Premieres." Music Educator's Journal 61:14, May 1975.

9266 Southern, E. "America's Black Composers of Classical Music."
      Music Educator's Journal 62:46-59, November 1975.

9267 "Premieres." Symphony News 27:31, no. 2, 1976. Moore's "Four
      Movements for a Fashionable Five-Toed Dragon" is reviewed.

9268 Rouse, C. "New American Music in Cross Section." Stereo Review
      37:126-127, September 1976.

9269 Moses, K. "Essence Men: Carman Moore." Essence 8:8, Decem-
      ber 1977.

MORRIS, STEVELAND JUDKINS see WONDER, STEVIE

MORTON, FERDINAND JOSEPH (Jelly Roll; Ferdinand Joseph LeMenthe),
1885-1941.

9270 Anderson, J. L. "Evolution of Jazz." down beat 16:11, November
      18, 1942; 16:11, December 2, 1942; 16:11, December 16, 1942.

9271 Morton, Ferdinand Joseph. "A Fragment of an Autobiography."
      Record Changer p. 15-16, March 1944.

9272 De Toledano, R. "Autobiography in Tone: F. Morton's Recordings."
      Saturday Review 31:47, January 31, 1948.

9273 Thompson, K. C. "Rag-time and Jelly Roll." Record Changer 8:8,
      April 1949.

9274   Smith, C. E. "From Jelly Roll to Bop." Record Changer 8:13-14,
       September 1949.

9275   Jones, M. "Morton's 'Spanish Tinge.'" Melody Maker 25:5, Sep-
       tember 10, 1949.

9276   Preston, S. D. "Notes on Morton's 'New Orleans Jays.'" Melody
       Maker 25:11, September 17, 1949.

9277   Hulsizer, K. "That's When Jelly Fell Out." Playback 2:3-4, De-
       cember 1949.

9278   Hobson, W. "New Orleans Jazz Professor." Saturday Review 33:14,
       May 13, 1950.

9279   "Mister Jelly Roll." Time 55:52, June 19, 1950.

9280   Moon, B. "Mr. Jelly Roll." Record Changer 9:5, September 1950.

9281   Ramsey, F. "Contraband Jelly Roll." Saturday Review 33:64, Sep-
       tember 30, 1950.

9282   Hoefer, G. "Rare Morton Piano Roll Discovered in Junk Shop."
       down beat 17:7, November 17, 1950.

9283   Hobson, W. "Hits and Misses." Saturday Review 34:60, January
       27, 1951.

9284   Grut, H., L. Feather, and E. Borneman. "Three Famous Interna-
       tional Critics Look at 'Mr. Jelly Roll.'" Melody Maker 27:3, Feb-
       ruary 10, 1951.

9285   Lucas, J. "Notes on Bunk and Jelly Roll." Record Changer 10:5,
       April 1951.

9286   Kay, G. W. "Basin Street Stroller; Washington, D.C. and Jelly
       Roll Morton." Jazz Journal 4:1-2, July-August 1951.

9287   Levin, F. "The American Jazz Scene." Jazz Journal 4:4-5, July-
       August 1951.

9288   Kay, G. W. "Basin Street Stroller; Washington, D.C. and Jelly
       Roll Morton." Jazz Journal 4:1-2, September 1951.

9289   Levin, F. "The American Jazz Scene." Jazz Journal 4:6, Septem-
       ber 1951.

9290   _____. "The Spikes Brothers--a Los Angeles Saga." Jazz Jour-
       nal 4:12-14, December 1951.

9291   Hobson, W. "Monuments of the Great." Saturday Review 35:44-45,
       January 26, 1952.

9292   Jones, M. "Of Course Jelly Arranged His Jazz--but So Did Arm-
       strong and Oliver." Melody Maker 28:9, June 14, 1952.

9293   Postgate, J. "Does He Really Deserve All This Purist Esteem?"
       Melody Maker 28:9, June 14, 1952.

9294 Jones, M. "Six Solo Sides of Jelly Roll." Melody Maker 28:9, July 12, 1952.

9295 McKenzie, M. "If You Think Morton Was an 'Amateur' Pianist-- Try Playing His Music!" Melody Maker 28:9, July 12, 1952.

9296 Rust, B. "The Jelly Roll Morton Discography." Melody Maker 28:9, August 16, 1952.

9297 Carew, R. "Remember Ferd Morton Was His Own Press Agent!" Melody Maker 28:9, August 30, 1952.

9298 _____. "Let Jelly Roll Speak for Himself." Record Changer 2:7-9, December 1952.

9299 Souchon, E. "Doctor Bites Doctor Jazz." Record Changer 12:6, February 1953.

9300 Durgnat, R. E. "Jelly Roll Morton's New Orleans Jazz Men; A Critical Revaluation." Jazz Journal 6:2-3, November 1953.

9301 Williams, M. L. "A Diamond Mouthful." Melody Maker 30:5, April 10, 1954.

9302 Daniel, K. K. "The Strange Case of the Victor Houseman." Jazz Journal 7:8-9, May 1954.

9303 Stewart-Baxter, D. "Jelly Roll Morton Plays and Sings." Jazz Journal 7:26-27, July 1954.

9304 Jepsen, J. G. "Jazzens Instrumentalister: Pianot." Orkester Journalen 23:12, September 1955.

9305 Gara, L. "The Baby Dodds Story." Jazz Journal 8:26-27, October 1955.

9306 "The Jelly Roll Morton Piano-Rollography." Record Changer 1:11-12, December 1955.

9307 Carew, R. "Jelly Roll Morton." Melody Maker 31:5, January 21, 1956.

9308 Wilson, J. S. "New Orleans Jazz." High Fidelity/Musical America 6:82, June 1956.

9309 Balliett, W. "Billie, Big Bill, and Jelly Roll." Saturday Review 39:32-33, July 14, 1956.

9310 Smith, H. "The 'Fablelous' Jelly Roll." Record Research 2:9, January-February 1957.

9311 _____. "Debunking Jelly Roll." Record Research 3:5, June-July 1957.

9312 Wilson, J. S. "Jazz Pianists, a Discography." High Fidelity/Musical America 7:67, August 1957.

9313 Cerulli, D. "Charivari." down beat 24:40-42, November 14, 1957.

9314   Carew, R. "Of This and That and Jelly Roll." Jazz Journal 10:10-
       12, December 1957.

9315   Merriam, A. P. "Jelly Roll Morton: A Review Article." Midwest
       Folklore 8:217-221, 1958.

9316   Wilson, J. S. "Jelly Roll Morton & All That Jazz." High Fidelity/
       Musical America 8:46-47, March 1958.

9317   Balliett, W. "This Whiskey Is Lovely." New Yorker 34:137-138,
       March 22, 1958. Some of Morton's works are being produced on
       Library of Congress recordings.

9318   Waterman, G. "New Orleans Memories." Jazz Review 1:35-38, De-
       cember 1958.

9319   Jepsen, Jorgen Grunnet. Discography of Jelly Roll Morton. Brande,
       Denmark: Debut Records, 1959. Volume 1 covers the years 1922-
       1929.

9320   Hadlock, R. "Morton's Library of Congress Albums." Jazz no.
       2:133-137, Spring 1959.

9321   Barker, D. "Jelly Roll Morton in New York." Jazz Review 2:12-
       14, May 1959.

9322   Locke, D. "The Importance of Jelly Roll Morton." Jazz Journal
       12:2-4, June 1959.

9323   Davin, T. "Conversations with James P. Johnson." Jazz Review
       2:15, August 1959.

9324   "Ferdinand 'Jelly Roll' Morton's Red Hot Peppers." Jazz Magazine
       6:30-31, December 1959.

9325   "Discografia di J. R. Morton." Jazz di Ieri e di Oggi 11:19-23,
       January-February 1960.

9326   Suriani, E. "Doctor Jazz; Vita di Jelly Roll Morton." Jazz di Ieri
       e di Oggi 11:8-23, January-February 1960.

9327   Locke, D. "Jelly Roll Morton--the Library of Congress Recordings."
       Jazz Journal 13:15-18, January 1960.

9328   Postgate, J. "Between You and Me." Jazz Monthly 6:16, February
       1960.

9329   Williams, M. "Jelly Roll Morton and the Library of Congress Rec-
       ords." Jazz Monthly 6:4-7, March 1960.

9330   Testoni, G. "Gli Autori dei Temi." Musica Jazz 16:39, April 1960.

9331   Williams, M. "Jelly Roll Morton and the Library of Congress Rec-
       ords." Jazz Monthly 6:8-9, May 1960.

9332   Smith, H. "Some Jelly Roll Morton Vignettes." Record Research
       no. 30:6, October 1960.

9333 Kramer, K. "Jelly Roll in Chicago." Second Line no. 1-2:1, 1961;
      no. 3-4:19-22, 1961.

9334 "Jelly Roll Morton on LP." Jazz Monthly 6:27-28, January 1961.

9335 Smith, H. "Jelly Roll's Strange Will." Record Research no. 38:1,
      October 1961.

9336 _____. "Malice in Blunderland." Record Research no. 40:11,
      January 1962.

9337 Williams, M. "Jazz Composition; What Is It?" down beat 29:20-23,
      February 15, 1962.

9338 Carey, D., F. Dutton, and G. Hulme. "Jelly Roll's Victor Jazz."
      Jazz Journal 15:8-10, June 1962.

9339 Littler, F. "Palms Down." Jazz Monthly 8:5, September 1962.

9340 "Some Morton Piano Solos." Jazz Monthly 8:7-8, September 1962.

9341 Williams, Martin T. Jelly Roll Morton. New York: A. S. Barnes,
      1963.

9342 Montgomery, M. "More Rolls by Morton!" Record Research no.
      49:6-7, March 1963.

9343 "Annuaire Biographique du Piano." Jazz Magazine 9:30, November
      1963.

9344 "Mr. Jelly Roll; un Extrait du Remarquable Ouvrage Recemment
      Paru." Jazz Hot no. 203:9-10, November 1964.

9345 Testoni, G. "Il Mondo del Blues." Musica Jazz 20:30-33, Novem-
      ber 1964.

9346 Destombes, A. "Mysterieux Mister Morton." Jazz Magazine no.
      114:38-40, January 1965.

9347 Koechlin, P. "L'Inventeur du Jazz: Jelly Roll Morton." Musica
      no. 130:60-61, January 1965.

9348 "La Lettre de Jelly." Jazz Magazine no. 117:26-27, April 1965.

9349 Lucas, J. "Lord and Lion: Let the Records Set the Record Straight."
      Second Line 16:61-64, May-June 1965.

9350 Chase, Gilbert. The American Composer Speaks: A Historical An-
      thology, 1770-1965. Baton Rouge: Louisiana State University Press
      1966. Morton is the only black musician discussed. Included is
      an excerpt from Alan Lomax's book Mister Jelly Roll.

9351 Williams, M. "Mostly About Pianists." Saturday Review 49:130,
      March 12, 1966.

9352 McRae, B. "A B Basics; A Column for the Newcomer to Jazz."
      Jazz Journal 20:9, November 1967.

9353   Shera, M. "Monk/Mann." Jazz Journal 20:10-11, December 1967.

9354   Davies, John R. T., and Laurie Wright. Morton's Music. Dagen-
       heim, Essex, Eng: Storyville Publications, 1968.

9355   Carew, R. J. "A Tribute to Roy Carew." Jazz Journal 21:22-23,
       May 1968.

9356   Shivers, G. "Correspondence: Jelly Roll in Washington, D.C."
       Record Research no. 90:10, May 1968.

9357   "Morton's Music: Addenda." Storyville no. 17:29-30, June-July 1968.

9358   Franksen, J. "Jazz Record Reviews." Jazz and Pop 7:57-58, Sep-
       tember 1968.

9359   Kay, G. W. "Final Years of Frustration (1939-1941) as Told by
       Jelly Roll Morton in His Letters to Roy J. Carew." Jazz Journal
       21:2-5, November 1968; 21:8-9, December 1968.

9360   Arvanitas, G., et al. "Panorama des Pianistes." Jazz Hot no.
       246:26, January 1969.

9361   Dallas, K. "20 Dollars a Side--and No Thoughts of Posterity."
       Melody Maker 44:18, March 1, 1969.

9362   Smith, H. "The Strange Case of Jelly's Will as Told to Bob Kumm."
       Storyville no. 25:8-9, October-November 1969.

9363   Kumm, B. "Record Reviews: Jelly Roll Morton--Piano Rolls."
       Storyville no. 32:76-77, December 1970-January 1971.

9364   Spear, H. L. "Jelly Rolls." Storyville no. 32:47-50, December
       1970-January 1971.

9365   "Reeditions: Jelly Roll Morton and His Red Hot Peppers (1926-1939)--
       Volume II." Jazz Magazine no. 180:48, July-August 1970.

9366   Sherrer, M. "Jazz Menu: Jelly Roll and Peppers." Music Journal
       28:26-27, October 1970.

9367   McRae, B. "Record Reviews: Blues and Stomps from Rare Piano
       Rolls." Jazz Journal 23:31, December 1970.

9368   "Blues & Stomps from Rare Piano Rolls--Jelly Roll Morton." Jazz
       Report 7:17, no. 6, 1971.

9369   Mitchell, B. "Vinyl Highlight: The Complete Piano Works of Jelly
       Roll Morton Played by John W. 'Knocky' Parker." Jazz Report
       7:15-16, no. 5, 1971.

9370   "Record Reviews: The Immortal J. R. Morton." Footnote 3:26, no.
       1, 1971.

9371   Spear, H. L. "Some Notes on Jelly Roll." Storyville no. 33:88-89,
       February 1971.

9372   Williams, R. "Jazz Records: Jelly Roll Morton." Melody Maker
       46:32, February 20, 1971.

9373 Bevan, R. V. "Which Tiger Is It?" Ragtimer p. 13-14, March-
April 1971. Discussion of Morton's "Tiger Rag."

9374 Traill, S. "Editorial." Jazz Journal 24:1, March 1971.

9375 _____. "Record Reviews: Doc Cooke and His Dreamland Or-
chestra/Johnny Dunn and His Band with Jelly Roll Morton." Jazz
Journal 24:35, March 1971.

9376 "Jelly Roll Morton on Library of Congress." Matrix no. 92:13-14,
April 1971.

9377 Morel, M. "Il y a Trente Ans Mourait: Jelly Roll Morton." Jazz
Hot no. 274:10-13, July 1971; no. 275:28-30, September 1971.

9378 Richard, R. "Aimer le Jazz: Jelly Roll Morton." Points du Jazz
no. 5:41-48, September 1971.

9379 Morel, M. "Il y a Trente Ans Mourait: Jelly Roll Morton." Jazz
Hot no. 276:20-21, October 1971.

9380 Ahlstroem, T. "Jazzdiskoteket: Jelly Roll Morton." Musikrevy
27:206-210, no. 4, 1972.

9381 Barrell, A. "Morton's Red Hot Peppers and Orchestra, Dec. 1928-
30." Footnote 3:2-6, no. 4, 1972.

9382 "Record Reviews: Jelly Roll Morton." Footnote 3:26, no. 4, 1972.

9383 "Record Reviews: Jelly Roll Morton, Vols. 1, 2, and 3." Coda
10:25, no. 9, 1972.

9384 "Record Reviews: The Library of Congress Recordings, Vol. 1."
Coda 10:21, No. 6, 1972.

9385 "Record Reviews: Archive of Jazz, Vol. 30." Jazz & Blues 2:30,
June 1972.

9386 Goines, L. "Traditional Jazz." Allegro p. 4, July 1972. Louis
Armstrong and Morton are examined.

9387 Jones, M. "Blowing with Jelly Roll." Melody Maker 47:32, July
22, 1972.

9388 Richard, R. "Jelly Roll News." Points du Jazz no. 7:159-160, October 1972.

9389 "Schallplattenbesprechungen; Jelly Roll Morton and His Red Hot Peppers, Vol. 3." Jazz Podium 21:35, November 1972.

9390 "Jelly Roll Morton--the Library of Congress Recordings Classic Jazz
Masters." Footnote 5:28-29, no. 2, 1973-1974.

9391 Lomax, Alan. Mister Jelly Roll; The Fortunes of Jelly Roll Morton,
New Orleans Creole and Inventor of Jazz. 2d ed. Berkeley: University of California Press, 1973. Includes discography and a
chronological list of Morton's works.

9392 "Record Reviews: Jelly Roll Morton Rarities." Jazz & Blues 2:31-
32, January 1973.

9393 Richard, R. "Jelly Roll News." Points du Jazz no. 8:120-122, April 1973.

9394 "On Record: Jelly Roll Morton and His Orchestra; Piano Solo, Vol. 5." Jazz & Blues 3:28, July 1973.

9395 Richard, R. "Jelly Roll News." Points du Jazz no. 9:121-123, December 1973.

9396 Wilson, J. S. "He'll Give Us Lots of His Jelly Roll." Jazz Report 8:5-6, no. 5, 1974.

9397 Feather, L. "Jelly Roll Erkaend som Klassisk Musiker." Orkester Journalen 42:6, February 1974.

9398 "'World of Jelly Roll Morton,' Alice Tully Hall." Jazz Digest 3:17, February 1974.

9399 Wilson, J. S. "Bob Greene's Jelly Roll Morton Concert." Second Line 26:11, Spring 1974. Reprinted from the New York Times, February 18, 1974.

9400 "Quelques Grands Pianistes." Jazz Hot no. 305:10, May 1974.

9401 Goodfriend, J. "The Triumphant, if Slightly Overdue, Return of Mr. Jelly Lord." Stereo Review 32:110-111, June 1974.

9402 "Duke, Jelly Roll Due for Revivals in Ragtime Wake." Variety 275:1, June 5, 1974.

9403 Klee, J. H. "Jelly Rolls Again." Record Research no. 129-130:1, October-November 1974.

9404 Richard, R. "Jelly Roll News." Points du Jazz no. 10:97-99, October 1974.

9405 Greene, B. "Concert Reviews." Variety 277:64, December 18, 1974.

9406 "Record Reviews: New Orleans Memories and Last Band Dates." Coda 12-14, no. 3, 1975.

9407 Williams, M. "And What Might a Jazz Composer Do?" Music Educator's Journal 61:24-31, January 1975.

9408 Richard, R. "Jelly Roll Morton et l'Opera." Points du Jazz no. 11:89-92, June 1975.

9409 "Piano Music of Ferdinand 'Jelly Roll' Morton." Jazz Magazine (U.S.) 1:48, no. 2, 1976.

9410 Lucas, J. "Bicentennial Canticles." Second Line 28:8, Summer 1976.

9411 "Record Reviews: Jelly Roll Morton, Vol. 7--1929-30." Coda no. 150:22, August-September 1976.

9412 Newberger, E. H. "The Development of New Orleans and Stride Piano Styles." Journal of Jazz Studies 4:43-45, no. 2, 1977.

9413 "The Music of Jelly Roll Morton Is Revived." International Musician

75:7, March 1977. A performance of Morton's music is given at New York's Carnegie Hall.

9414 Richard, R. "Jelly Roll News." Points du Jazz no. 13:132-134, June 1977.

9415 Russell, W. "Albert Nicholas Talks About Jelly Roll." Second Line 30:3-10, Spring 1978.

9416 Erskine, G. M. "Movie Review: Pretty Baby." Second Line 30:40-41, Summer 1978.

9417 Berry, J. "Jazz Literature: Through a Rhythm, Joyously." Village Voice 23:61, May 8, 1978. Examines autobiographies of Morton, Louis Armstrong, Bunk Johnson, and Sidney Bechet.

9418 Russell, W. "Albert Nicholas Talks About Jelly Roll." Second Line 30:34-36, Winter 1978.

MWANDISHI see HANCOCK, HERBIE

NELSON, OLIVER EDWARD, 1932-1975.

9419 Goldberg, J. "Focus on Oliver Nelson." down beat 29:17, February 15, 1962.

9420 "Des 'Sketches' Signes Nelson." Jazz Magazine 8:15, March 1962.

9421 Cooke, J. "Better Times Ahead." Jazz Monthly 8:4-5, January 1963.

9422 Wilson, J. S. "Jazz 1962." International Musician 61:12, January 1963.

9423 Schiozzi, B. "Oliver Nelson." Musica Jazz 19:28, March 1963.

9424 Feather, L. "Blindfold Test." down beat 31:32, June 4, 1964.

9425 "Tangents." down beat 31:14-17, June 18, 1964.

9426 "Oliver Nelson Leads New Breed--Musicians with Wide Portfolios." Billboard 77:26, March 20, 1965.

9427 "At Home with Oliver Nelson." Jazz 5:15-18, no. 7, 1966.

9428 Harman, C. "Old Blues Dressed Up Fit to Kill." Life 60:10, March 11, 1966.

9429 "At Home." BMI p. 20, October 1966.

9430 Williams, R. "Straight Ahead--the Early Work of Oliver Nelson & Eric Dolphy." Jazz Journal 20:4-6, July 1967.

9431 Feather, L. "Blindfold Test." down beat 34:35, September 7, 1967.

9432 "Premieres." BMI p. 23-24, October 1967. Premiere of Nelson's "Concerto for Xylophone, Marimba and Vibraphone."

9433 "The Commercial Composer Enters the School Music Field--a Phenomenon of Our Times." Instrumentalist 22:88, November 1967.

9434 Dance, S. "Premieres." Music Journal 25:65, November 1967; BMI p. 7-8, December 1967.

9435 Ginibre, J. L. "Los Angeles 68 de A à Z." Jazz Magazine no. 156-157:27, July-August 1968.

9436 Feather, L. "From Pen to Screen." International Musician 67:14, July 1968.

9437 Weisenberg, C. M. "The State of Jazz Education." down beat 35:16-17, September 19, 1968. Interview with Nelson.

9438 Garland, P. "Many Bags of Oliver Nelson." Ebony 24:108-110, November 1968.

9439 "In the Press." BMI p. 8-9, January 1969.

9440 Woods, P. "La Musique d'Oliver Nelson." Jazz Magazine no. 164:36-39, March 1969.

9441 "Oliver Nelson Tours Africa for State Dept." down beat 36:12, April 3, 1969.

9442 Feather, L. "Saxophone and Septet Through Darkest Africa." Melody Maker 44:8, June 28, 1969.

9443 Rivelli, P. "Oliver Nelson's African Tour." Jazz and Pop 8:46-50, July 1969.

9444 "Record Reviews." down beat 36:23-24, August 7, 1969.

9445 "Premieres." BMI p. 26, October 1969. Discussion of Nelson's "Piece for Orchestra."

9446 "Record Reviews." Jazz Journal 22:33, November 1969.

9447 Bourne, M. "Record Reviews: Black, Brown, and Beautiful." down beat 37:26-27, July 9, 1970.

9448 Siders, H. "Oliver's New Twist." down beat 37:17, July 23, 1970.

9449 Smith, W. "Record Reviews: 3 Shades of Blue." Jazz and Pop 9:49, November 1970.

9450 Simmonds, R. "Oliver Nelson in Berlin." Crescendo International 9:26-27, January 1971.

9451 Lacombe, A. "Retour sur Nelson." Jazz Magazine no. 190:46-47, June-July 1971.

9452 Kimball, G. "Records: Leon Thomas in Berlin with Oliver Nelson." Rolling Stone no. 89:39, August 19, 1971.

9453 Storb, I. "Eindruecke vom 5. Internationalen Jazz-Festival in Montreux." Musik und Bildung 3:441, September 1971.

9454 "Disques du Mois: Black, Brown and Beautiful." Jazz Magazine no. 193:48, October 1971.

9455 Klee, J. H. "Record Reviews: Berlin Dialogue for Orchestra." down beat 38:16, November 11, 1971.

9456 "Record Reviews: Berlin Dialogue for Orchestra." Coda 10:21-22, no. 7, 1972.

9457 "Record Reviews: Black, Brown and Beautiful." Coda 10:21, no. 6, 1972.

9458 "The Score: The Writers in Profile." BMI no. 1:27, 1974.

9459 Fowler, W. L. "Oliver Nelson: New Hope for the Abstract Truth." down beat 42:10, April 24, 1975.

9460 "How to Produce a Recording ... Oliver Nelson Style." down beat 42:40, April 24, 1975.

9461 Nelson, Oliver. "Improvisation Patterns." down beat 42:41, April 24, 1975. An excerpt from Nelson's book Patterns for Improvisation.

9462 Dexter, D. "Donald Byrd & Oliver Nelson: 2 Arrangers with a Knack for Breaking Pop." Billboard 87:28, June 28, 1975.

9463 "Talent in Action." Billboard 87:54, July 19, 1975.

9464 "Caught." down beat 42:37-38, October 23, 1975.

9465 ["Obituary."] Variety 280:86, November 5, 1975.

9566 "Oliver Nelson Dies Suddenly." Billboard 87:55, November 8, 1975.

9467 ["Obituary."] Jet 49:55, November 13, 1975; Jazz Magazine no. 239:6, December 1975; International Musician 74:15, December 1975; Jazz Podium 24:28, December 1975.

9468 Feather, L. "Saxophonist Oliver Nelson Dead at 43." Rolling Stone no. 202:23, December 18, 1975.

9469 Fowler, B. ["Obituary."] down beat 42:11, December 18, 1975.

9470 ["Obituary."] Jazz Forum no. 39:17, 1976; Music Educator's Journal 62:109, January 1976.

9471 "Les Faces de Nelson--Discographie Selective du Saxophoniste et Compositeur Oliver Nelson." Jazz Magazine no. 242:14, March 1976.

9472 ["Obituary."] Coda no. 145:32, March 1976.

9473 "Waxing On: Images." down beat 43:34, October 21, 1976.

9474 "Record Reviews: A Dream Deferred." down beat 43:18-19, December 2, 1976.

9475   Bacsik, E. "A Tribute to Oliver Nelson." Educator 9:42-43, no. 3,
       1977.

NOVOSEL, MRS. STEPHEN see FLACK, ROBERTA

OLIVER, JOE (Joseph; King), 1885-1938.

9476   Thompson, K. C. "Improvisation: The Fact and the Fable." Record
       Changer 8:5, June 1949.

9477   Baker, J. H. "Discology: Personnel-ities in the Williams Discog-
       raphy--I. King Oliver." Playback 2:22-23, August 1949.

9478   Anderson, J. L. "Evolution of Jazz." down beat 17:11, March 10,
       1950.

9479   Tanner, P. "Oh, Didn't They Ramble." Melody Maker 26:9, April
       29, 1950.

9480   Armstrong, L. "Joe Oliver Is Still King." Record Changer 9:10-11,
       July-August 1950.

9481   Ulanov, B. "A History of Jazz." Metronome 66:14-15, August 1950.

9482   Anderson, J. L. "Evolution of Jazz." down beat 19:18, March 7,
       1952.

9483   Armstrong, L. "A Toast to Mezzrow and Joe Oliver." Melody Mak-
       er 29:3, January 10, 1953.

9484   Allen, W. C. "The King's Saxophone: Paul Barnes." Record Chang-
       er 12:5, April 1953.

9485   "King Oliver in the Archives." Jazz Journal 7:8-9, July 1954.

9486   Jepsen, J. G. "Jazzens Instrumentalister: Trumpeten." Orkester
       Journalen 23:10, February 1955.

9487   Gara, L. "The Baby Dodds Story." Jazz Journal 8:8-10, July 1955.

9488   Panassie, H. "The First Giant, King Oliver." Melody Maker 31:7,
       December 3, 1955.

9489   Ramsey, F. "King Oliver in Savannah." Saturday Review 39:30-31,
       March 17, 1956.

9490   Allen, W. C. "On the Trail of the King." Jazz Journal 9:8, April
       1956.

9491   Wilson, J. S. "New Orleans Jazz." High Fidelity/Musical America
       6:83, June 1956.

9492   "King Oliver Will Be First Again." down beat 23:30, June 13, 1956.
       The Dictionary of American Biography included Oliver as its first
       jazz musician.

9493 Wood, B. "George Orendorf--Quality Serenader." Jazz Journal
      10:4-6, January 1957.

9494 Allen, Walter C., and Brian A. L. Rust. King Joe Oliver. London:
      Sidgwick and Jackson, 1958.

9495 "Joe 'King' Oliver's Savannah Syncopaters." Jazz Magazine 6:32-33,
      December 1959.

9496 Williams, Martin T. King Oliver. London: Cassell, 1960.

9497 Souchon, E. "King Oliver, a Very Personal Memoir." Jazz Review
      3:6-11, no. 4, 1960. Souchon relates Oliver's influence on his
      own life.

9498 Dance, S. "Utmost." Jazz Journal 13:22-23, February 1960.

9499 "MCA Booked Oliver in 1924." Second Line no. 11-12:13, 1961.

9500 Williams, M. "When the Big Bands Played Swing." High Fidelity/
      Musical America 12:49-51, April 1962.

9501 "King Oliver, Pere du Jazz Moderne?" Jazz Hot no. 182:39-43, De-
      cember 1962.

9502 Malson, L., and C. Bellest. "Gravures Celebres." Jazz Magazine
      9:35-36, April 1963. Examines Oliver's "Sugar Foot Stomp" on
      the Fletcher Henderson 1925 recording.

9503 "King Oliver's Creole Jazz Band 1923." Orkester Journalen 33:2,
      May 1965.

9504 Sjögren, R. "King Oliver 1923." Orkester Journalen 33:8-9, May
      1965.

9505 McRae, B. "A B Basics; A Column for the Newcomer to Jazz."
      Jazz Journal 20:16, March 1967.

9506 Spivey, V. "The King and I." Record Research no. 87:3, Decem-
      ber 1967. An excerpt from Spivey's autobiography about Oliver.

9507 Kumm, B. "Louis Armstrong; Reflections on King Oliver and the
      Cotton Club." Storyville no. 19:9-11, October-November 1968.

9508 Larson, P. A. "King Oliver-Lizzie Miles Date." Jazz Report 7:7,
      no. 2, 1970.

9509 _____. "Filling in the Gaps: King Oliver--Lizzie Miles Record
      Date." Second Line 23:284-285, January-February 1970.

9510 Lambert, E. "Record Review: The Immortal King Oliver." Jazz
      Monthly no. 182:26, April 1970.

9511 Kay, G. W. "The Johnny Wiggs Story." Jazz Journal 23:12-13,
      January 1970.

9512 Goddet, L. "La Chronique des Disques: Papa Joe." Jazz Hot no.
      263:46-47, Summer 1970.

9513   "Reeditions: Papa Joe." Jazz Magazine no. 181:53, September 1970.

9514   Hillman, C. "King Oliver and the Dixie Syncopators." Footnote
       2:2-6, no. 4, 1971.

9515   Jones, W. "Record Reviews: Creole Jazz Band, 1923." Coda 9:21-
       22, no. 12, 1971.

9516   "Record Reviews: New Orleans Shout." Footnote 3:24-25, no. 2,
       1971.

9517   Ahlstroem, T. "Jazzdiskoteket: Joe 'King' Oliver." Musikrevy
       27:135-138, no. 3, 1972.

9518   Moore, F. "King Oliver's Last Tour." Footnote 4:20-24, no. 6,
       1973.

9519   "Record Reviews: King Oliver's Dixie Syncopators." Jazz Journal
       26:32, February 1973.

9520   "Record Reviews: The Great 1923 Gennets." Footnote 5:29-30, no.
       5, 1974.

9521   Nevers, D. "Autour d'un Disque: King Oliver." Jazz Hot no. 312:18-
       19, January 1975.

9522   "Records: The Great 1923 Gennets." Crawdaddy no. 44:78-79, Jan-
       uary 1975.

9523   "Schallplatten-Besprechungen: King Oliver's Dixie Syncopators."
       Jazz Podium 24:33, January 1975.

9524   Dalziel, J. M. "Memories of King Oliver." Second Line 27:36-38,
       Fall 1975.

9525   Daubresse, J. P., and D. Nevers. "Chicago." Jazz Hot no. 322:22-
       23, December 1975.

9526   Koch, L. O. "Structural Aspects of King Oliver's 1923 Okeh Re-
       cordings." Journal of Jazz Studies 3:36-46, no. 2, 1976.

9527   Wilson, J. S. "From the Smithsonian: Perspective on King Oliver,
       Hines, & Satchmo." High Fidelity/Musical America 26:140, April
       1976.

9528   "Record Reviews: King Oliver's Jazz Band, 1923." down beat 43:30-
       31, May 20, 1976.

9529   "Record Reviews: The Great 1923 Gennets." Coda no. 151:12, Oc-
       tober-November 1976.

9530   Nevers, D. "Discographie de King Oliver." Jazz Hot no. 333:36-
       39, December 1976.

9531   "Record Reviews: King Oliver Vol. 1." Jazz Journal 29:34-35, De-
       cember 1976.

9532   Wiggs, J. "Wiggs--Self-Explained." Second Line 30:4, Spring 1977.

9533 Balliett, W. "Jazz." New Yorker 53:94-98, April 25, 1977.

9534 "Record Reviews: King Oliver's Jazz Band 1923." Coda no. 156:21-
      22, July-August 1977.

9535 "Reissues: Volume One." Coda no. 157:23, September-October 1977.

9536 "Jazz Albums: King Oliver's Creole Jazz Band." Melody Maker
      52:32, September 24, 1977.

9537 "Record Reviews: King Oliver's Creole Jazz Band." Jazz Journal
      International 30:48, October 1977.

9538 Erskine, G. M. "The Question of King Oliver's Birth Date." Second
      Line 30:49-51, Winter 1978.

PARKER, CHARLES CHRISTOPHER (Charlie; Bird; Yardbird), 1920-1955.

9539 "Charlie Parker." Metronome 65:18, January 1949.

9540 "When Yardbird Turned His Back." Melody Maker 25:2, March 19,
      1949.

9541 Levin, M., and J. S. Wilson. "No Bop Roots in Jazz: Parker."
      down beat 16:1, September 9, 1949.

9542 "Bird Wrong; Bop Must Get a Beat: Diz." down beat 16:1, October
      7, 1949.

9543 "Charlie Parker." Metronome 66:16, January 1950.

9544 Russo, B., and L. Lifton. "Jazz Off the Record." down beat 17:12,
      March 10, 1950; 17:12, April 7, 1950.

9545 "Birdland, New York." Billboard 62:43, July 22, 1950.

9546 "In Person." Metronome 66:19, August 1950.

9547 "Bird, Backed by Strings, Disappoints at Birdland." down beat 17:4,
      August 25, 1950.

9548 Stewart-Baxter, D. "Anti-Bopper's Attitude to Charlie Parker."
      Jazz Journal 3:6, November 1950.

9549 "En Natt med Charlie Parker." Orkester Journalen 18:18, December
      1950.

9550 Lindgren, C. E. "Charlie Parker, Storst av Dem Alla." Orkester
      Journalen 18:16-17, December 1950.

9551 "Charlie Parker to Play at Paris Salon du Jazz." Melody Maker
      26:1, December 2, 1950.

9552 Kaye, C. "When Bird Flew Out of the West." Melody Maker 26:3,
      December 2, 1950.

9553   "The Incredible Story of Parker in Paris." Melody Maker 26:1, December 9, 1950.

9554   "All Stars." Metronome 67:14, February 1951.

9555   Parker, C. "My Best on Wax." down beat 18:15, June 29, 1951.

9556   "Charlie Parker School." Metronome 67:11-12, September 1951.

9557   "Charlie Parker's Discography." Metronome 67:12, September 1951.

9558   Lindgren, C. E. "Mina Sex Stora Jazzminnen." Orkester Journalen 19:26-27, December 1951.

9559   Dankworth, J. "The Man in the Faded Suit." Melody Maker 27:4, December 8, 1951.

9560   "From the 'Bird's' Mouth; Quotes from Parker." Melody Maker 27:4, December 8, 1951.

9561   Wiedemann, E. "Charlie Parker Discography." Melody Maker 27:4, December 8, 1951.

9562   Morgan, A. "'White Christmas' from the Bird in the Roost: Parker's Better-Known Transcriptions." Melody Maker 27:4, December 15, 1951.

9563   Wiedemann, E. "Charlie Parker Discography." Melody Maker 27:4, December 15, 1951; 27:4, December 22, 1951; 27:4, December 29, 1951; 28:4, January 5, 1952; 28:4, January 12, 1952; 28:4, January 19, 1952; 28:4, February 2, 1952.

9564   Callender, R. "Bop Is Just Everybody Playing Like Diz or Bird." Melody Maker 28:4, May 10, 1952.

9565   Nevard, M. "'Well, I Don't Know' Says Charlie Parker." Melody Maker 28:4, June 28, 1952.

9566   Morgan, A. "Retrospection." Jazz Journal 5:6, August 1952.

9567   Nevard, M. "The Man Who Stopped Recording as Bird Began to Blow." Melody Maker 28:5, November 1, 1952.

9568   Hentoff, N. "Counterpoint." down beat 20:15, January 28, 1953.

9569   Wells, G. "Charlie Parker--the 'Bird.'" Jazz Journal 6:1-2, June 1953.

9570   Simon, G. T. "Winding-Parker at Birdland." Metronome 69:18-19, July 1953.

9571   "New Society Concert Held at Massey Hall, Toronto, Canada." Metronome 69:30, August 1953.

9572   Nevard, M. "Is Parker Washed Up?" Melody Maker 29:3, December 26, 1953.

9573   Morgan, A. "The Parkerless Quintet." Jazz Journal 7:5, January 1954.

9574 "Parker." Melody Maker 30:3, January 2, 1954.

9575 Ulanov, B. "Bird on the Run." Metronome 70:34, March 1954.

9576 "'Recording Artists' Roster." down beat 21:118, June 30, 1954.

9577 Eckstine, B. "Bird Blew in His Socks!" Melody Maker 30:3, August 14, 1954.

9678 "Charlie Parker Booked to Play in Britain." Melody Maker 30:1, September 4, 1954.

9579 Eckstine, B. "Dizzy, Bird and the Birth of Bop." Melody Maker 30:5, September 4, 1954.

9580 "'Bird' Attempts Suicide on Eve of Tour." Melody Maker 30:1, September 18, 1954.

9581 Kahn, H. "Death of Parker Rumours Began as Joke in Paris Club." Melody Maker 31:20, January 29, 1955.

9582 "Charlie Parker, Founder of Modern Jazz School, Dies of Heart Attack." Variety 198:50, March 16, 1955.

9583 Nevard, M. "Fallen Bird." Melody Maker 31:3, March 19, 1955.

9584 "Sudden Death of Charlie Parker." Melody Maker 31:1, March 19, 1955.

9585 Simon, B. "Charlie Parker a Jazz Great." Billboard 67:19, March 26, 1955.

9586 "Troubled Genius." Melody Maker 31:3, March 26, 1955.

9587 "Top Jazz Names Set Memorial for Parker." Variety 198:51, March 30, 1955.

9588 Coss, B. "Bop 1955, a Summing Up." Metronome 71:20-21, April 1955.

9589 Dahlgren, C. "Minneskonsert för Parker." Orkester Journalen 23:12-13, April 1955.

9590 "Den Störste är Borta." Orkester Journalen 23:8-9, April 1955.

9591 Jepsen, J. G. "Charlie Parker Diskografi." Orkester Journalen 23:10, April 1955.

9592 Lindgren, C. E. "Att Vila i Frid." Orkester Journalen 23:3, April 1955.

9593 "Minneskonsert för Charlie Parker." Orkester Journalen 23:4, April 1955.

9594 "Farewell to the Bird." Melody Maker 31:9, April 2, 1955.

9595 Feather, L. "Parker Finally Finds Peace." down beat 22:6, April 20, 1955.

9596   "Jazz World Mourns Loss of Charlie Parker." down beat 22:5, April 20, 1955.

9597   Hobson, W. "Farewell to the Bird." Saturday Review 38:54-55, April 30, 1955.

9598   "Charlie Parker, 1920-1955." Metronome 71:6, May 1955.

9599   Dahlgren, C. "Mäktigt Carnegie-uppbad för Parker." Orkester Journalen 23:10-22, May 1955.

9600   Jepsen, J. G. "Charlie Parker Diskografi." Orkester Journalen 23:35, May 1955.

9601   _____. "Jazzens Instrumentalister: Altsaxen." Orkester Journalen 23:14-15, May 1955.

9602   "Simon Says...." Metronome 71:54, May 1955.

9603   "Bird Memorial Jams Carnegie." down beat 22:4, May 4, 1955.

9604   "Record Firms Rush to Release Charlie Parker Memorial Sets." down beat 22:4, 1955.

9605   Ulanov, B. "Charlie Parker: A New Legend Born." down beat 22:22, May 4, 1955.

9606   Feather, L. "The Parker Memorial Concert." Melody Maker 31:5, May 7, 1955.

9607   Ramey, G. "My Memories of Bird Parker." Melody Maker 31:5, May 28, 1955.

9608   Jepsen, J. G. "Charlie Parker Diskografi." Orkester Journalen 23:39, June 1955.

9609   "Memorial." Jazz Journal 8:28, June 1955.

9610   Wiedemann, E. "Charlie Parker: An Appreciation and Additions to Bird Discography." Melody Maker 31:5, June 25, 1955.

9611   Coss, B. "The Pleasure Is Yours: King Pleasure Sings Bird Requiem as Memorial Albums Begin to Appear." Metronome 71:30, July 1955.

9612   Jepsen, J. G. "Charlie Parker Diskografi." Orkester Journalen 23:34-35, July 1955.

9613   "Sad Case of Charlie Parker." Our World 10:9-12, July 1955.

9614   Wood, B. "That's the Blues, Old Man." Jazz Journal 8:1-2, July 1955.

9615   "Parker Discography Concluding Erik Wiedemann's Addenda." Melody Maker 31:6, July 2, 1955.

9616   Dunn, R. "Anecdotes About Charlie Parker." Record Research 1:14, August 1955.

9617 Jepsen, J. G. "Charlie Parker Diskografi." Orkester Journalen
      23:34-35, August 1955.

9618 Feather, L. "Feather's Nest." down beat 22:37-38, August 10,
      1955.

9619 "Jazz Photos." down beat 22:38-39, August 10, 1955.

9620 "Parker Concert Raised $10,000." down beat 22:6, August 10, 1955.

9621 "Bird of Paradise." Metronome 71:6, September 1955.

9622 "Readers Name Charlie Parker Fourth Hall of Fame Member." down
      beat 22:7, December 28, 1955.

9623 "Concert Loot Will Benefit Bird's Children." down beat 23:9, Jan-
      uary 25, 1956.

9624 Balliett, W. "The Measure of 'Bird.'" Saturday Review 39:33-34,
      March 17, 1956.

9625 Nevard, M. "Charlie Parker." Melody Maker 31:17, April 7, 1956.

9626 Dunn, R. "Charlie Parker Airshots." Record Research 2:24, May-
      June 1956.

9627 Lindgren, C. E. "Konserten Som Aldrig tog Slut." Orkester Jour-
      nalen 24:8-9, January 1956.

9628 Hoefer, G. "The Hot Box." down beat 23:38, August 22, 1956.

9629 Brown, T. "The Truth About Charlie Parker; Last Days of Parker's
      Life Told by the Baroness de Koenigswarter-Rothschild." Melody
      Maker 32:4-5, February 16, 1957.

9630 Balliett, W. "The Measure of 'Bird.'" Jazz Journal 10:3-4, May
      1957.

9631 Horricks, R. "Parker Revisited." Melody Maker 32:15, July 20,
      1957.

9632 Robertson, C. A. "Knocky Parker: Old Rags." Audio 42:44, Feb-
      ruary 1958.

9633 Mehegan, J. "The 'Parker Story.'" Saturday Review 41:43-44, Feb-
      ruary 8, 1958.

9634 Gold, D. "Tangents." down beat 25:60, April 17, 1958.

9635 Race, S. "Immortal Charlie Parker." Melody Maker 33:4, June 21,
      1958; 33:10, June 28, 1958; 33:4, July 5, 1958.

9636 _____. "Blue Bird." Melody Maker 33:5, December 13, 1958.

9637 Schmidt-Joos, Siegfried. Charlie Parker; Ein Porträt. Wetzlar:
      Pegasus Verlag, 1959.

9638 Harrison, M. "Charlie Parker on Savoy." Jazz Monthly 4:7-10, Jan-
      uary 1959.

9639   Morgenstern, D. "The Charlie Parker Message." Jazz Journal
       12:31-32, January 1959.

9640   Shih, H. W. "King Pleasure: Parker's Mood; Annie Ross: Twisted."
       Jazz Review 2:42-43, January 1959.

9641   Wiedemann, E. "Charlie Parker, Diskografiskt Sedd." Orkester
       Journalen 27:10-11, January 1959.

9642   Hakim, S. "The Charlie Parker 'Koko' Date." Jazz Review 2:11,
       February 1959.

9643   Tomkins, L. "There's No Successor to Bird." Melody Maker 34:16,
       May 16, 1959.

9644   Malson, L. "Quatre Ans Apres Sa Mort Charlie Parker Demeure le
       Plus Vivant des Modernes." Jazz Magazine 5:29-21, June 1959.

9645   "Ornithologically Speaking." Jazz Review 2:42, June 1959.

9646   "Charlie Parker Wins: Modern Stars Score High in All-Time Poll."
       Music U.S.A. 76:12-14, August 1959.

9647   Gaspard, J. J. "Charlie Parker." Musica no. 67:27, October 1959.

9648   Harrison, Max. Charlie Parker. New York: Barnes, 1961, c1960.

9649   Bagnoli, C. "Album di Charlie Parker." Jazz di Ieri e di Oggi
       11:29-44, January-February 1960.

9650   "Stitt, Parker, and the Question of Influence." Jazz Monthly 5:9-10,
       January 1960.

9651   Gazzaway, D. "Conversations with Buster Smith." Jazz Review
       3:12-16, February 1960.

9652   Gillespie, D. "Charlie Parker Tel que Je l'Ai." Jazz Hot 26:38-39,
       March 1960.

9653   Prevignano, D. I. "Nota su Parker." Musica Jazz 16:21-23, March
       1960.

9654   Reisner, B. "Bird; A Biography in Interviews." Jazz Review 3:7-
       15, September-October 1960.

9655   Hadlock, D. "Earl Hines on Bird." Jazz Review 3:12-13, November
       1960.

9656   Reisner, B. "Bird; A Biography in Interviews." Jazz Review 3:8-
       11, November 1960.

9657   Russell, R. "Record Reviews." Jazz Review 3:21-23, November
       1960.

9658   "U.S. Disc Chief Unearths Jazz Treasure." Melody Maker 35:8, No-
       vember 5, 1960.

9659   Manskleid, N. "Diz on Bird." Jazz Review 4:11-13, January 1961.

9660 Reisner, B., A. Blakey, and O. Pettiford. "Bird; Interviews." Jazz Review 4:9-10, January 1961.

9661 "Set Up Disk, Publishing Firms for Billie Holiday, Parker; Seek Royalties." Variety 221:55, February 22, 1961.

9662 Mortara, A. "Coltrane (e Altri); La Crisi del Parkerismo." Musica Jazz 17:18-22, March 1961.

9663 "Two Estates Seek Royalties." down beat 28:15, April 13, 1961.

9664 "Carlton Snares Parker Material in Jazz Coup." Billboard 73:3, April 17, 1961.

9665 "Carlton Swings into Jazz with Parker Estate." Variety 222:57, April 19, 1961.

9666 Lyttelton, H. "Bird Was Anything but Cool." Melody Maker 36:5, May 6, 1961.

9667 "A Charlie Parker Record Company." down beat 28:11, May 25, 1961.

9668 Lees, G. "The Years with 'Yard': Interview with Dizzy Gillespie." down beat 28:22, May 25, 1961.

9669 "Des Inedits de Bird." Jazz Magazine 7:18, June 1961.

9670 Lees, G. "Bird et Diz." Jazz Magazine 7:29-31, August 1961.

9671 Bennett, L. "Charlie Parker--Madman or Genius?" Negro Digest 10:70-75, September 1961.

9672 Testoni, G. "L'Eredita dei Compositori di Jazz." Musica Jazz 17:17-19, September 1961; 17:30-31, October 1961.

9673 Welding, P. J. "Charlie Parker as Composer." HiFi/Stereo Review 7:70-71, October 1961.

9674 Cooke, J. "The Blithe Spirit." Jazz Monthly 7:14-15, November 1961.

9675 Hentoff, N. "The Soft Mythology of Jazz." Show 1:40-41, November 1961.

9676 "Blues for Bird in Kansas City." down beat 28:11, November 9, 1961.

9677 Green, Benny. The Reluctant Art: The Growth of Jazz. Plainview, New York: Books for Libraries Press, 1975. Reprint of the 1962 edition published by MacGibbon & Kee in London which examines Bix Beiderbecke, Benny Goodman, Lester Young, Billie Holiday, and Parker.

9678 Reisner, Robert George. Bird: The Legend of Charlie Parker. New York: Citadel Press, 1962.

9679 Gazzaway, D. "Before Bird--Buster." Jazz Monthly 7:7-8, January 1962. Discussion of Buster Smith's influence on Parker.

9680   Masson, J. R. "Il y a Sept Ans." Jazz Magazine 8:20-24, March 1962.

9681   Postif, F. "Gene Ramey: Une Interview." Jazz Hot no. 174:20-23, March 1962.

9682   Hoefer, G. "Hot Box." down beat 29:41, April 12, 1962.

9683   Woo, W. F. "Jazz in K.C." High Fidelity/Musical America 82:8-9, May 1962.

9684   Wiedemann, E. "Chords and Discords; Discographical Disclaimer." down beat 29:6, July 5, 1962.

9685   Morgan, A. "Bird & the 'Lover Man' Session." Jazz Monthly 8:3-6, August 1962.

9686   Williams, M. "Gillespie in Concert." Saturday Review 45:41, August 25, 1962.

9687   Leonard, N. "Bop Brotherhood." New Republic 147:24-25, October 8, 1962.

9688   James, M. "Jazz at Massey Hall." Jazz Monthly 8:25-26, February 1963.

9689   Morgan, A. "Le Commencement de la Fin." Jazz Magazine 9:32-35, April 1963.

9690   Hoefer, G. "Earl Hines in the 1940s." down beat 30:25, April 25, 1963.

9691   Williams, M. "In the Wake of Parker." Saturday Review 46:71, May 11, 1963.

9692   "Lorna Music's Paramor Gets 24 LPs, 350 Tunes of Late Charlie Parker." Variety 230:51, May 22, 1963.

9693   "Charlie Parker Memorial Concert." down beat 30:36, May 23, 1963.

9694   Dance, S. "The Happy Bird." Jazz 2:10, June 1963.

9695   "Parker Memorial Fund Set Up by Jazz Arts Society." down beat 30:13, June 20, 1963.

9696   "The 'Bird.'" Melody Maker 38:7, August 31, 1963. Remembrances of Parker by several who knew him well.

9697   Koechlin, P. "L'Ombre de Coltrane sous le Soleil de Parker." Jazz Hot no. 194:10, January 1964.

9698   Garner, M., and F. Gibson. "A Discography of the Studio Recordings of Charlie Parker." Jazz Journal 17:26-27, May 1964.

9699   _____. "A Discography of the 'Live' Recordings of Charlie Parker." Jazz Journal 17:29, June 1964.

9700 "Les Paroles du Bird." Jazz Hot no. 200:24-26, July-August 1964.
An interview Mark Gardner had with Parker in 1950.

9701 Gardner, M., and F. Gibson. "A Discography of the 'Live' Recordings of Charlie Parker." Jazz Journal 17:25, July 1964.

9702 Gitler, I. "Bird and the Forties." down beat 31:32-36, July 2,
1964.

9703 "Dick Gregory Possible Lead in Parker Movie." down beat 31:10,
October 22, 1964.

9704 Schmidt-Joos, S. "Bird: The Genius of Charles Parker." Jazz
4:8-9, no. 6, 1965.

9705 Schiozzi, B. "L'Evoluzione del Sax Alto." Musica Jazz 21:15-17,
February 1965.

9706 Dahlgren, R. "Parker i Sverige." Orkester Journalen 33:16-17,
March 1965.

9707 Delorme, M. "Discographie Commentee des Enregistrements Publics
de Charlie Parker." Jazz Hot no. 207:30-35, March 1965.

9708 Glanzelius, I. "Charlie Parker, den Siste Individualisten." Orkester Journalen 33:12-13, March 1965.

9709 "Il Etait une Fois un Oiseau." Jazz Hot no. 207:23-29, March 1965.

9710 Lemery, D. "Les Enfants du Bird." Jazz Magazine no. 116:16-27,
March 1965.

9711 Testoni, G. C. "Bird: In Memoriam." Musica Jazz 21:10-12,
March 1965.

9712 Weck, L. "Arvet Fraan Parker." Orkester Journalen 33:5, March
1965.

9713 Werner, L. "Parkers Privatinspelningar." Orkester Journalen 33:15,
March 1965.

9714 Wiedemann, E. "Myten om Charlie Parker." Orkester Journalen
33:14-15, March 1965.

9715 Cohen, M. T. "With Care and Love." down beat 32:19-20, March
11, 1965.

9716 Feather, L. "Blindfold Test." down beat 32:32, March 11, 1965.
Discussion of an interview with Parker in 1948.

9717 _____. "A Fist at the World." down beat 32:15-18, March 11,
1965.

9718 Heckman, D. "Bird in Flight; Parker the Improviser." down beat
32:22-24, March 11, 1965.

9719 Levin, M., and J. S. Wilson. "The Chili Parlor Interview." down
beat 32:13-15, March 11, 1965. Refers to a 1949 interview with
Parker.

9720   Segal, J.   "Bird in Chicago."   down beat 32:18-19, March 11, 1965.

9721   Williams, M.   "The Listener's Legacy."   down beat 32:20-21, March
       11, 1965.

9722   Balliett, W.   "Jazz Concerts; Performance in His Memory at Car-
       negie Hall."   New Yorker 41:116-118, April 10, 1965.

9723   DeMicheal, D.   "Charlie Parker."   BMI p. 20, June 1965.

9724   "Jazz Opera Dedicated to Late Charlie Parker Bows March 26 in
       K.C."   Variety 242:1, March 23, 1966.

9725   "Charlie Byrd's Good Fri. Service with Rev. Boyd."   Variety 242:1,
       April 6, 1966.

9726   "Un Opera pour l'Oiseau."   Jazz Magazine no. 130:14, May 1966.

9727   Chesmore, R.   "An Opera for the Bird."   down beat 33:13, May 5,
       1966.

9728   "Seven Steps to Jazz."   Melody Maker 41:8, May 7, 1966.

9729   Quinn, B.   "Caught in the Act."   down beat 33:22-23, October 20,
       1966.   Review of a Parker Memorial Concert in Chicago.

9730   "Dictionnaire de l'Alto."   Jazz Magazine no. 137:47, December 1966.

9731   Tirro, F.   "The Silent Theme Tradition in Jazz."   Musical Quarter-
       ly 53:316, no. 3, 1967.

9732   Gardner, M.   "Bargain Bird."   Jazz Journal 20:8-11, June 1967.
       Lists Parker records available at cut-rate.

9733   "Jay McShann ou la Legende de K. C. B. Niquet."   Jazz Hot no.
       235:23-25, October 1967.

9734   Jepsen, Jorgen Grunnet.   A Discography of Charlie Parker.   Copen-
       hagen NV: Karl Emil Knudsen, 1968.

9735   Voce, S.   "We the People Bop."   Jazz Journal 21:9, August 1968.

9736   Hodeir, A.   "Ceci N'est Pas le Jazz."   Jazz Hot no. 243:6-7, Oc-
       tober 1968.

9737   Houston, B.   "Second Opinion."   Melody Maker 43:10, October 26,
       1968; 43:8, November 2, 1968; 43:8, November 9, 1968; 43:12,
       November 16, 1968; 43:8, November 23, 1968.

9738   McRae, B.   "A B Basics; A Column for the Newcomer to Jazz."
       Jazz Journal 22:17, April 1969.

9739   Dawbarn, B.   "Saxists--Always the Innovators."   Melody Maker 44:16,
       June 14, 1969.

9740   Burns, J.   "Bird in California."   Jazz Journal 22:10, July 1969.

9741   Williams, T.   "Charlie Parker Discography."   Disco Forum no. 13:13-
       17, July 1969.

9742   "Record Reviews." Jazz Journal 22:33, October 1969.

9743   Russell, R.   "Yardbird in Lotus Land, les Souvenirs de Ross Russell
       sur Charlie Parker." Jazz Hot no. 255:22-25, November 1969.

9744   _____. "Yardbird in Lotusland." Orkester Journalen 37:8-9, De-
       cember 1969; Jazz Hot no. 257:15-17, January 1970; Orkester Jour-
       nalen 38:8-9, January 1970.

9745   Williams, T. "Charlie Parker Discography." Disco Forum no.
       16:15-18, January 1970.

9746   Russell, R.   "Yardbird in Lotus Land." Jazz Hot no. 258:18-20,
       February 1970; Orkester Journalen 38:10-11, February 1970; Jazz
       Hot no. 259:26-28, March 1970; Orkester Journalen 38:12-13, March
       1970.

9747   Peterson, O. "The Massey Hall Concert." Jazz Journal 23:8-10,
       March 1970. Discussion of a Parker recording made at Massey
       Hall, May 15, 1963.

9748   Russell, R.   "Yardbird in Lotus Land." Jazz Hot no. 260:26-28,
       April 1970; Orkester Journalen 38:10-11, April 1970.

9749   Gitler, I. "Bird Still Lives." down beat 37:16-17, April 2, 1970.

9750   Paris, C. "Charlie Parker in Time." Jazz Hot no. 261:16-19, May
       1970.

9751   "Record Reviews: Bird at St. Nick's." Jazz Journal 23:30, May
       1970.

9752   "Reeditions: The Bird on Savoy." Jazz Magazine no. 178:51, May
       1970.

9753   Russell, R.   "Yardbird in Lotus Land." Jazz Hot no. 262:16-17,
       June 1970; Orkester Journalen 38:10-11, June 1970; 38:10-11, July-
       August 1970.

9754   Burks, J. "Records: Bird on 52nd Street." Rolling Stone no. 62:39-
       40, July 9, 1970.

9755   Amram, D. "Bird in Washington." Jazz Journal 23:4-5, August
       1970. An excerpt from Amram's book Vibrations.

9756   Gardner, M. "Charlie Parker." Jazz Journal 23:2-3, August 1970.

9757   West, H. E. "The Neglected Memory of Charlie Parker." Jazz
       Forum no. 11:83, Spring 1971. Reprinted from the International
       Herald Tribune, August 28, 1970.

9758   "Charlie Parker Memorial Concerts." Jazz and Pop 9:12, September
       1970.

9759   Russell, R.   "Yardbird in Lotus Land." Jazz Hot no. 264:24-25,
       September 1970.

9760   "Bird Month in Chicago Honors Jazz Immortal." down beat 37:7,
       September 3, 1970.

9761 "'Bird' Lives." BMI p. 14-15, November 1970.

9762 Gardner, M. "Norman Simmons." Jazz Monthly no. 189:3-5, November 1970.

9763 "Bird Lives: K.C. Plans Art Center, Memorial." down beat 38:11, January 21, 1971.

9764 "Charlie Parker Memorial." Jazz Magazine no. 186:15, February 1971.

9765 Levin, J. "Reeditions: The Complete Charlie Parker." Jazz Magazine no. 187:43, March 1971.

9766 "Bird." BMI p. 19, April 1971.

9767 Peterson, O. "Early Bird." Jazz Journal 24:34-36, April 1971. Examination of Parker's early recordings.

9768 Sherrer, M. "Kansas City's Jazz Ambassador--Yardbird." Music Journal 29:22-23, May 1971.

9769 Raeftegaard, B. "Parker paa Dial." Orkester Journalen 39:14-17, July-August 1971.

9770 Williams, R. "Jazz Records: Charlie Parker Vol. 2." Melody Maker 46:28, July 17, 1971.

9771 "Handful of Records: Charlie Parker on Dial--Vol. 5." Points du Jazz no. 5:130-132, September 1971.

9772 "K.C. Honors Parker in Graveside Ceremony." down beat 38:8, November 11, 1971.

9773 "Bird Lives." BMI no. 5:36-37, 1972. The influence and contributions of Parker are examined.

9774 Lightfoot, W. E. "Charlie Parker: A Contemporary Folk Hero." Keystone Folklore Quarterly 17:51-62, 1972.

9775 "Record Reviews: Lullaby in Rhythm." Coda 10:22, no. 6, 1972.

9776 Burns, J. "The Charlie Parker 'Ko Ko' Date." Jazz & Blues 1:10, January 1972.

9777 "Record Reviews: A Musical Tribute to Charlie Parker on His Fiftieth Birthday Anniversary." Jazz & Blues 1:24-25, January 1972.

9778 Russell, R. "Yardbird in Lotus Land." Jazz Hot no. 280:8-9, February 1972; no. 281:10-11, March 1972.

9779 "Charlie Parker auf Dial." Jazz Podium 21:150-151, March 1972.

9780 "Kansas City: Coping with Modern-Day Urban Dilemmas Sobers Once Bawdy Missouri Blues Town." Black Enterprise 2:45-49, June 1972.

9781 "Jazz Records: Pensive Bird." Melody Maker 47:36, June 10, 1972.

9782 Morgenstern, Dan, Ira Gitler, and Jack Bradley. Bird & Diz: A
      Bibliography. New York: New York Jazz Museum, 1973.

9783 Russell, Ross. Bird Lives: The High Life and Hard Times of
      Charlie (Yardbird) Parker. New York: Charterhouse, 1973.

9784 Taylor, J. R. "The Prestige 24000 Series." Journal of Jazz Studies
      1:90-110, no. 1, 1973. Discussion of a series of recording reis-
      sues.

9785 Wang, R. "Jazz Circa 1945: A Confluence of Styles." Musical
      Quarterly 59:532, no. 4, 1973.

9786 Lees, G. "Bird in the Band; Influence of Charlie Bird Parker."
      High Fidelity/Musical America 23:24, February 1973.

9787 Albertson, C. "Gillespie and Parker: An Important Reissue--'the
      Greatest Jazz Concert Ever.'" Stereo Review 30:84-85, June 1973.

9788 Koster, Piet, and Dick M. Bakker. Charlie Parker: [Discography].
      Alphen aan den Rijn, Holland: Micrography, 1974-1976. Four
      volumes: V. 1. 1940-1947; V. 2. 1948-1950; V. 3. 1951-1954;
      V. 4. 1940-1955.

9789 Davis, Nathan Tate. "Charlie Parker's Kansas City Environment
      and Its Effect on His Later Life." (Ph.D. Dissertation, Wesleyan
      University, 1974).

9790 Koch, L. O. "Ornithology: A Study of Charlie Parker's Music."
      Journal of Jazz Studies 2:60-87, no. 1, 1974.

9791 Owens, Thomas. "Charlie Parker: Techniques of Improvisation."
      (Ph.D. Dissertation, University of California, Los Angeles, 1974).

9792 "Record Reviews: Broadcast Performances 1948-49." Jazz Journal
      27:46, January 1974.

9793 Esposito, B. "Homage to Bird." Jazz Journal 27:4-5, March 1974.

9794 "Jazz Records: Immortal Sessions, Volumes 1-6." Melody Maker
      49:64, March 2, 1974.

9795 "Records: The Comprehensive Charlie Parker--Live Performances,
      2 V." Rolling Stone no. 156:64-65, March 14, 1974.

9796 Hawes, H., and D. Asher. "Remembering Billie and Bird." Har-
      per's Magazine 248:44, June 1974. An excerpt from Hawes' and
      Asher's Raise Up off Me.

9797 Palmer, B. "Charlie Parker: Post-Flight." Rolling Stone no.
      164:22, July 4, 1974.

9798 McDonough, J. "Bird Rediscovered--Spotlite's Six-Disc Series Re-
      stores Charlie Parker's Vital Dial Recordings to Circulation."
      High Fidelity/Musical America 24:95-96, November 1974.

9799 Townley, R., and T. Hogan. "Supersax; The Genius of Bird X Five."
      down beat 41:13-15, November 21, 1974.

9800 Carriere, C. "Tribute to Charlie Parker." Jazz Hot no. 311:23,
      December 1974.

9801 Olsson, J. "Konsert til Parkers Aera." Orkester Journalen 42:18,
      December 1974.

9802 Sullivan, P. "Charlie Parker on Dial-Spotlite Set." Jazz Forum
      no. 32:61, December 1974.

9803 "Charlie Parker Discography." Jazz Forum no. 37:58-61, 1975.

9804 Cholinski, H. "Charlie Parker on LP: Live Recordings." Jazz
      Forum no. 37:56-58, 1975.

9805 Evans, T. "Jazz from the Forties on Onyx Records." Journal of
      Jazz Studies 2:96-103, no. 2, 1975.

9806 Gleason, Ralph J. Celebrating the Duke, and Louis, Bessie, Billie,
      Bird, Carmen, Miles, Dizzy, and Other Heroes. Boston: Little,
      Brown, 1975.

9807 "Heard and Seen." Coda 12:35-36, no. 4, 1975.

9808 Koch, L. O. "A Numerical Listing of Charlie Parker's Recordings."
      Journal of Jazz Studies 2:86-95, no. 2, 1975.

9809 _____. "Ornithology: A Study of Charlie Parker's Music." Jour-
      nal of Jazz Studies 2:61-85, no. 2, 1975.

9810 "Muenchen." Oper und Konzert 13:25, no. 4, 1975.

9811 Patrick, J. "Charlie Parker and Harmonic Sources of Bebop Compo-
      sition: Thoughts on the Repertory of New Jazz in the 1940s." Jour-
      nal of Jazz Studies 2:3-23, no. 2, 1975.

9812 "Record Reviews: Broadcast Performances 1948-1949, Vol. 2."
      Coda 12:18, no. 5, 1975.

9813 "Charlie Parker, Diskographie." Hifi-Stereophonie 14:136, February
      1975.

9814 Panke, W. "Jazzportraet: Charlie Parker." Hifi-Stereophonie
      14:130, February 1975.

9815 Gardner, M. "Bird: Twenty Years After." Jazz Journal 28:4-5,
      March 1975.

9816 Sheridan, C. "Chasin' the Bird." Jazz Journal 28:6, March 1975.

9817 Welch, C. "Bird Lives On!" Melody Maker 50:51, March 15, 1975.
      Notes that Parker died twenty years ago.

9818 "Charlie Parker Discography." Jazz Forum no. 35:52-54, June 1975.

9819 Cholinski, H. "Charlie Parker on LP: Studio Recordings." Jazz
      Forum no. 35:52-54, June 1975.

9820 "Charlie Parker Discography." Jazz Forum no. 36:51-53, August
      1975.

9821 Cholinski, H. "Charlie Parker on LP: Studio Recordings." Jazz Forum no. 36:49-51, August 1975.

9822 "Charlie Parker Fans Get the Bird as Row Cancels N.Y. Concert." Variety 280:47, August 27, 1975.

9823 Goddet, L. "Le Be-Bop." Jazz Hot no. 322:30-31, December 1975.

9824 Stites, T. "Memorial for Bird." Jazz Magazine (U.S.) 1:15, no. 1, 1976.

9825 Strommen, C. "Bird's Oboe Player Remembers the Man." Jazz Magazine (U.S.) 1:30-31, no. 1, 1976.

9826 Owens, T. "Parker at the Tradewinds--Bootleg Jazz." Jazz Journal 29:7, January 1976.

9827 Albertson, C. "Charlie Parker on Dial." Stereo Review 36:94, February 1976.

9828 Balliett, W. "Jazz." New Yorker 52:80-84, March 1, 1976.

9829 Dexter, D. "Bird Lives: Music Bigger than Ever." Billboard 88:31, April 3, 1976.

9830 "Record Reviews: Bird in Sweden." Jazz Journal 29:33, May 1976.

9831 Buhles, G. "Charlie Parker, Ornette Coleman--Vergleich und Deutung." Hifi-Stereophonie 15:628-631, June 1976.

9832 Carriere, C. "Parker en Verve." Jazz Hot no. 328:34, June 1976.

9833 "Record Reviews: Bird's Nest." Jazz Journal 29:36-37, July 1976.

9834 "Jazz Albums: Jazz at the Philharmonic 1944-1946." Melody Maker 51:24, July 10, 1976.

9835 "Jazz Albums: Bird's Nest." Melody Maker 51:20, August 21, 1976.

9836 "Records: Bird/the Savoy Recordings." Creem 8:60-61, September 1976.

9837 "Records: The Verve Years." Creem 8:60-61, September 1976.

9838 "Records: Bird/the Savoy Recordings." Rolling Stone no. 221:51-52, September 9, 1976.

9839 "Records: The Verve Years." Rolling Stone no. 221:51-52, September 9, 1976.

9840 "Jazz Albums: Concert Carnegie Hall." Melody Maker 51:31, November 13, 1976.

9841 "Jazz Albums: Jazz at the Philharmonic 1946, Vol. 2." Melody Maker 51:30, November 20, 1976.

9842 Buhles, G. "Bebop und die Folgen--Avant Gardisten von Heute vor dem Hintergrund der Modernen Jazztradition." Jazz Podium 25:12-14, December 1976.

9843 "Record Reviews: Bird/the Savoy Recordings." Jazz Journal 29:35, December 1976.

9844 "Record Reviews: Charlie Parker/Miles Davis/Dizzy Gillespie." Jazz Journal 29:35-36, December 1976.

9845 "A 10-Year-Old Wins Parker Award in K.C." Variety 285:74, December 8, 1976.

9846 Kjellberg, E. "Charlie Parkers Improvisationsteknik Kartlagd." Nutida Musik 21:22-30, no. 1, 1977-1978.

9847 Zumbrunn, K. F. "Charlie Parker: Stylistic Features of His Blues." Educator 9:6-8, no. 4, 1977.

9848 "Gallery." Jazz Magazine (U.S.) 1:39-41, no. 4, 1977.

9849 Johnson, S. "Bird Lives." Jazz Magazine (U.S.) 1:21, no. 4, 1977.

9850 Greenberg, R. "Parker: A Great Man to Be With." Crescendo International 15:20-22, February 1977.

9851 "Jazz Albums: Yardbird in Lotus Land." Melody Maker 52:32, March 5, 1977.

9852 "Record Reviews: Early Bird." Jazz Journal 30:33, April 1977.

9853 "Dispute on Bird Tapes." Billboard 89:104, June 11, 1977.

9854 Glaser, M. "How Garner Tried to Provide a 'Nest' Egg for Bird." Jazz Journal International 30:34, July 1977.

9855 "Record Reviews: Encores." Jazz Journal International 30:49, July 1977.

9856 Tomkins, L. "Guitar Special: The Thoughts of Jimmy Raney." Crescendo International 15:6-7, July 1977.

9857 "Waxing On: Jazz at the Philharmonic--Bird and Pres: The '46 Concerts; The Verve Years." down beat 44:45-47, July 14, 1977.

9858 "Record Reviews: At the Pershing Ballroom." Jazz Journal International 30:38, August 1977.

9859 Rosenblum, B. "Chet Baker." Coda no. 157:6-7, September-October 1977.

9860 "Waxing On: Encores." down beat 44:39, September 8, 1977.

9861 "Record Reviews: Bird at the Roost." Jazz Journal International 39:48, October 1977.

9862 "Waxing On: Apartment Jam Sessions." down beat 44:37, October 6, 1977.

9863 "Waxing On: At the Pershing Ballroom." down beat 44:37, October 6, 1977.

9864 "Capsule Reviews: Afro-Cuban Jazz." Crawdaddy no. 78:109-110,
      November 1977.

9865 "Charlie Parker--the Legendary Dials." Swinging Newsletter 8:1,
      no. 37, 1978.

9866 "Reviews: Contemporary Masters on Columbia." Jazz Magazine
      (U.S.) 2:71, no. 3, 1978.

9867 "A Tribute to Monk and Bird." Jazz Magazine (U.S.) 3:63, no. 1,
      1978.

9868 "Waxing On: Afro-Cuban Jazz; Bird at the Roost." down beat 45:34,
      January 12, 1978.

9869 "Records: Summit Meeting at Birdland." High Fidelity/Musical
      America 28:119, February 1978.

9870 Wilson, J. S. "Contemporary Masters Series: Davis, Mulligan,
      Parker, Young." High Fidelity/Musical America 28:118-119, Feb-
      ruary 1978.

9871 "Record Reviews: Bird with Strings; One Night at Birdland; Summit
      Meeting at Birdland." down beat 45:27, February 23, 1978.

9872 Boecker, I. "Charlie Parker's 'Barbados.'" Musikern no. 3:10-11,
      March 1978.

9873 Goldberg, J. "Going Legit." Creem 9:63, March 1978. Discussion
      of reissues of Parker's music by Columbia Records.

9874 Albertson, C. "Calling All Fans: More Charlie Parker." Stereo
      Review 40:120, April 1978.

9875 "Records: Bird with Strings; One Night in Birdland; Summit Meeting
      at Birdland." Crawdaddy no. 83:84, April 1978.

9876 Giddins, G. "Weather Bird: Bugs Throws Bird a Carrot." Village
      Voice 23:67, May 22, 1978. Review of "The Very Best of Bird."

9877 Dexter, D. "WB Goes All-Out of Jazzman Parker; Movie and a
      6-LP Set." Billboard 90:46, May 27, 1978.

9878 Williams, L. "Summit Meeting at Birdland." Black Scholar 9:51-
      52, July-August 1978.

9879 "Recordings: The Very Best of Bird." Rolling Stone no. 269:51-52,
      July 13, 1978.

9880 "Prez Awards." Jazz Journal International 31:36, August 1978.

9881 "Records: Charlie Parker." High Fidelity/Musical America 28:113-
      114, August 1978.

9882 Kessel, B. "Recording with Charlie Parker." Guitar Player 12:16,
      September 1978.

9883 "Charlie Parker: The Very Best of Bird." New Leader 61:26, Sep-
      tember 11, 1978.

9884   "Jazz Albums: One Night at Birdland." Melody Maker 53:22, Sep-
       tember 16, 1978.

9885   Fremer, B. "The Beautiful Dream that Came True." Jazz Journal
       International 31:33, November 1978.

9886   "Record Reviews: One Night at Birdland." Jazz Journal Internation-
       al 31:44, December 1978; Radio Free Jazz 19:15-16, December
       1978.

9887   "Record Reviews: Summit Meeting at Birdland." Radio Free Jazz
       19:15-16, December 1978.

PEAY, BENJAMIN FRANKLIN see BENTON, BROOK

PENDERGRASS, TEDDY (Theodore; Teddy Bear).

9888   Sako, T. "No More 'Blue' Notes for Harold & Friends." Soul 8:8,
       January 21, 1974.

9889   "Talent in Action." Billboard 88:59, February 7, 1976.

9890   Vickers, T. "Break Up Everybody: The Blue Notes Split." Rolling
       Stone no. 209:18, March 25, 1976.

9891   Williams, J. "Sues Former Bluenotes for $624,000." Billboard
       88:3, May 22, 1976.

9892   "Making Waves." Melody Maker 52:44, February 26, 1977.

9893   Williams, J. "New Career for Former Blue Note." Billboard 89:36,
       March 5, 1977.

9894   Maslin, J. "Teddy Bear." Newsweek 89:86, March 7, 1977.

9895   "Albums: Teddy Pendergrass." Melody Maker 52:20, April 2, 1977.

9896   "Concert Reviews." Variety 286:66, April 27, 1977.

9897   Ferdinand, V. "Teddy Bear." Black Collegian 7:42, May-June 1977.

9898   "Records: Teddy Pendergrass." Rolling Stone no. 238:66, May 5,
       1977.

9899   "New on the Charts." Billboard 89:42, May 28, 1977.

9900   "Singer Sues Philly for $1-Mil; Alleges Police Brutality." Variety
       287:66, June 15, 1977.

9901   Lear, L. "Teddy Bear: New Superstar in the Making." Sepia 26:72-
       76, July 1977.

9902   "Talent in Action." Billboard 89:40, July 9, 1977.

9903   "Concert Reviews." Variety 288:60, August 31, 1977.

9904 "Talent in Action." Billboard 89:58, October 1, 1977.

9905 Adderton, D. "Teddy Pendergrass Won't Let Tragedy Change His
      Style." Jet 54:58-60, July 20, 1978.

9906 "Records: Life Is a Song Worth Singing." Rolling Stone no. 272:53,
      August 24, 1978.

9907 McKenna, K. "Sex and the Solo Blue Note." Rolling Stone 273:18,
      September 1978.

9908 Guzman, P. "Riffs: This Teddy Bear Burns." Village Voice 23:93,
      September 18, 1978.

9909 Farber, J. "Oooooh! It's Teddy Bear." Crawdaddy no. 90:22, No-
      vember 1978.

9910 Maslin, J. "Teddy Pendergrass: The Ladies' Choice; Avery Fisher
      Hall Concert." Rolling Stone no. 277:74, November 2, 1978.

9911 Lane, B. "Teddy Pendergrass Sings for Women Only." Sepia 27:39-
      45, December 1978.

9912 Rein, R. K. "On the Move." People 10:77-78, December 4, 1978.

PICKETT, WILSON, 1941- .

9913 "Artists' Biographies." Billboard 75:12, May 4, 1963.

9914 Grevatt, R. "Wilson Pickett Is 'In' at the 'Innest' Places." Melody
      Maker 40:7, October 2, 1965.

9915 "In the Press." BMI p. 20, February 1967.

9916 Landau, J. "Wilson Pickett." Crawdaddy no. 13:30-32, February
      1968.

9917 Llorens, D. "Soulin' with 'Wicket Pickett.'" Ebony 23:130-138, Oc-
      tober 1968.

9918 "Soul's Shock Troopers." Melody Maker 44:11, January 25, 1969.

9919 "Pickett Date Cancelled!" Melody Maker 44:1, February 8, 1969.

9920 "Why Wilson Dropped the 'La-la-la' Bit." Melody Maker 44:11, Feb-
      ruary 15, 1969.

9921 Eldridge, R. "Magnificent Seven of Soul." Melody Maker 44:10, July
      26, 1969.

9922 "Wilson Keeps on Travelling." Melody Maker 44:10, September 6,
      1969.

9923 "Caught in the Act." Melody Maker 44:15, September 27, 1969; down
      beat 36:26-27, November 13, 1969.

9924 "Don't Let the Short Hair Fool You!" <u>Melody Maker</u> 45:11, February
      21, 1970.

9925 John, W. "Records: Wilson Pickett in Philadelphia." <u>Rolling Stone</u>
      no. 71:34, November 26, 1970.

9926 Reilly, P. "Wilson Pickett Sings for Geraldine." <u>Stereo Review</u>
      26:77, January 1971.

9927 "New Pop Albums: In Philadelphia." <u>Melody Maker</u> 46:28, January
      23, 1971.

9928 "Concert Reviews." <u>Variety</u> 265:80, November 17, 1971.

9929 "Copacabana, N.Y." <u>Variety</u> 266:61, February 16, 1972.

9930 "Records: Don't Knock My Love." <u>Rolling Stone</u> no. 102:49, Febru-
      ary 17, 1972.

9931 Ochs, E. "Talent in Action." <u>Billboard</u> 84:15, February 26, 1972.

9932 "RecWords: Don't Knock My Love." <u>Crawdaddy</u> no. 6:17, March 5,
      1972.

9933 Fuchs, A. "Pickett at the Copa; Soul Under Glass." <u>Crawdaddy</u> no.
      10:38-40, April 30, 1972.

9934 Browne, T. "Caught in the Act." <u>Melody Maker</u> 47:58, May 13,
      1972.

9935 "Pickett Pulls Out: Jerry Lee Walks Off." <u>Melody Maker</u> 47:5, May
      13, 1972.

9936 Guild, H. "Pickett Draws 2,000 in Air Force W. German Hangar."
      <u>Variety</u> 267:59, May 17, 1972.

9937 Lewis, A. "Pickett--Better than We Deserve." <u>Melody Maker</u> 47:44,
      May 20, 1972.

9938 "Hilton, Las Vegas." <u>Variety</u> 269:69, November 15, 1972.

9939 "Concert Reviews." <u>Variety</u> 269:48, December 13, 1972.

9940 Joe, R. "Talent in Action." <u>Billboard</u> 85:18, January 20, 1973.

9941 "Records: Mr. Magic Man." <u>Rolling Stone</u> no. 134:62, May 10,
      1973.

9942 "Records: Greatest Hits." <u>Crawdaddy</u> no. 25:78-80, June 1973.

9943 "Concert Reviews." <u>Variety</u> 271:64, June 27, 1973.

9944 "The Soul Report." <u>Melody Maker</u> 49:28-29, January 12, 1974.

9945 "Hilton, Las Vegas." <u>Variety</u> 277:69, December 18, 1974.

9946 "Wilson Pickett; His Popularity Is World-Wide." <u>Soul</u> 9:10, March
      3, 1975.

9947 Fong-Torres, B. "Mr. Pickett Goes to Vegas: A Mustang Rally."
      Rolling Stone no. 201:20, December 4, 1975.

9948 "Records: Chocolate Mountain." Rolling Stone no. 219:68, August
      12, 1976.

9949 Williams, J. "New Label, Single Teed by Pickett." Billboard 89:50,
      June 25, 1977.

9950 "Pickett Forms Diskery." Variety 287:55, July 13, 1977.

POWELL, MRS. ADAM CLAYTON see SCOTT, HAZEL

PRICE, LEONTYNE (Mrs. William Warfield), 1927- .

9951 Rosenfield, J. "A New 'Porgy' in Dallas." Saturday Review 35:44,
      June 28, 1952.

9952 "Leontyne Price." Musical Courier 150:36, November 1, 1954; 150:19-
      20, December 1, 1954.

9953 "Town Hall Debut." Musical America 74:26, December 1, 1954.

9954 "Leontyne Price's 2-Hour 'Tosca' Registers a Major First for TV."
      Variety 197:31, January 26, 1955.

9955 "TV Tosca." Time 65:68, January 31, 1955.

9956 "Soprano's Dream." Newsweek 45:81, January 31, 1955.

9957 "Leontyne Price Heard in NBC-TV Tosca." Musical America 75:23,
      February 1, 1955.

9958 Kolodin, I. " 'Tosca' on TV, etc." Saturday Review 38:27, February
      5, 1955.

9959 "Inimitable Warfields." Our World 10:31-37, April 1955.

9960 "Integrated Love Meets Dixie Test; North Raises Greatest Protest as
      Leontyne Price Sings Lead Role in TV Opera Tosca." Ebony 10:32-
      34, May 1955.

9961 Reisfeld, B. "Amerika Braucht ein Kultusministerium." Musica
      9:238-239, May 1955.

9962 Sargent, M. "Leontyne Price Talent, Voice Draw Raves from Coun-
      try's Top Critics." down beat 22:14, October 5, 1955.

9963 Waldrop, G. "A Dazzling Career." Musical Courier 154:7, Decem-
      ber 1, 1956.

9964 Johnen, L. J. "Cincinnati." Musical Courier 155:35, April 1957.

9965 Wagner, W. "Sidney." Canon 10:375, June 1957.

9966 "Concert Reviews." Canon 10:405, July 1957.

9967   Briggs, E. "Brisbane." Canon 11:48, September 1957.

9968   "Aida." Musical Times 99:437, August 1958.

9969   "Covent Garden Opera." Musical Opinion 81:697, August 1958.

9970   "Covent Garden." Opera 9:540, August 1958.

9971   "Leontyne Price." Pan Pipes 51:39, January 1959.

9972   Hughes, A. "Leontyne Price." Musical America 79:10-11, May
       1959.

9973   "Covent Garden." Opera 10:474, July 1959.

9974   Dragadze, P. "Verona Arena." Musical America 79:6, September
       1959.

9975   "Biographical Sketch." Musical America 79:4, October 1959.

9976   "Leontyne Price Soloist in Barber Work." Musical America 79:37-
       38, December 1, 1959.

9977   "Leontyne Price Engaged for 'Met' Next Season." Musical Courier
       161:19, February 1960.

9978   Wolf, A. W. "Los Angeles." Musical Courier 161:30, March 1960.

9979   "Leontyne's Latest." Time 77:83, April 7, 1960.

9980   "Leontyne Price Has a Leading Role in NBC Opera Co.'s 'Don Gio-
       vanni.'" Jet p. 66, April 14, 1960.

9981   "Leontyne Price Will Make Her Debut at Metropolitan Opera Co., in
       Jan. 1961." Jet p. 60, April 28, 1960.

9982   Gilbert, E. "Detroit." Musical Courier 161:31, May 1960.

9983   "Leontyne Price: As Donna Anna in Mazart's 'Don Giovanni.'" Jet
       p. 62, May 19, 1960.

9984   "Mistress of Stage and Score." Time 75:35, May 30, 1960.

9985   "Makes Triumphant Debut in Title Role of Verdi's 'Aida' at La Scala,
       Milan, Italy." Jet p. 62, June 9, 1960.

9986   Dragadze, P. "Price Conquers La Scala." Musical America 80:17,
       July 1960.

9987   Hoffer, P. "Welshman at La Scala." Music and Musicians 8:26,
       July 1960.

9988   Wechsberg, J. "The 50th Salzburg Festival." Opera 11:50, Autumn
       1960.

9989   "Tony and Cleo." Newsweek 68:98, September 26, 1960.

9990   Brunner, G. "American Artists Score at Berlin Festival." Musical
       Courier 162:31, December 1960.

9991   Von Mittag, E. "Vienna Splendor." Opera News 25:29, December
       10, 1960.

9992   De Schauensee, M. "Price as Aida." Musical America 81:182,
       January 1961.

9993   Devries, D. "Chicago Opera Series Ends Triumphantly." Musical
       Courier 163:29, January 1961.

9994   Goldberg, A. "Solti Opens Season." Musical America 81:156, Jan-
       uary 1961.

9995   Schickel, R. "Leontyne Price: From Mississippi to the Met."
       Look 25:88-90, January 17, 1961.

9996   Kolodin, I. "Price-Warren-Tucker-Tozzi-Elias Trovatore." Sat-
       urday Review 44:39, January 28, 1961.

9997   Dettmer, R. "Chicago." Opera 12:115, February 1961.

9998   Sabin, R. "Leontyne Price Triumphs in Debut in 'Trovatore.'"
       Musical America 81:30, February 1961.

9999   "Skylark & Golden Calves." Time 77:45, February 3, 1961.

10000 Sargeant, W. "Musical Events; Role of Leonora." New Yorker
       36:100-101, February 4, 1961.

10001 "Il Trovatore." Variety 221:96, February 8, 1961.

10002 "Critics Hail Her Debut at Metropolitan Opera in Verdi's 'Il Trova-
       tore.'" Jet 19:56, February 9, 1961.

10003 "Met Triumph for Leontyne." Life 50:107-110, February 10, 1961.

10004 Fitzgerald, G. "Heroine at Home." Opera News 25:14-15, Febru-
       ary 14, 1961.

10005 Murphy, R. "On Stage: Leontyne Price." Horizon 3:72-73, March
       1961.

10006 "Price and Corelli in 'Trovatore.'" Musical Courier 163:12, March
       1961.

10007 "Voice Like a Banner Flying." Time 77:58-60, March 10, 1961.

10008 Kolodin, I. "Music to My Ears; First Aida." Saturday Review
       44:91, March 11, 1961.

10009 "Sings 'Madam Butterfly' at Metropolitan." Jet 19:61, March 16,
       1961.

10010 Kolodin, I. "Music to My Ears; Price's Butterfly." Saturday Re-
       view 44:39-40, March 18, 1961.

10011 "Aida." Musical Courier 162:9, April 1961.

10012 "Made Debut at New York Metropolitan Opera." Journal of Negro
       History 46:131, April 1961.

10013 "Prima Donna from Mississippi." Ebony 16:96-98, April 1961.

10014 RePass, R. "New York." Opera 12:252, April 1961.

10015 Sabin, R. "Leontyne Price Is Magnificent as Aida." Musical America 81:56, April 1961.

10016 _____. "Price Heard as Cio-Cio-San." Musical America 81:57-58, April 1961.

10017 "Metropolitan Soprano." Jet 19:66, April 6, 1961.

10018 Kolodin, I. "Music to My Ears." Saturday Review 44:42, April 8, 1961.

10019 RePass, R. "New York." Opera 12:321, May 1961.

10020 Sabin, R. "Price Triumphs as Donna Anna." Musical America 81:33, May 1961.

10021 Stevens, D. "New York." Musical Courier 163:15, May 1961.

10022 "What Price Leontyne?" Variety 222:2, May 24, 1961.

10023 "Voice Like a Banner Flying." Reader's Digest 78:152-156, June 1961.

10024 Hepburn, D. "Leontyne Price; Rare Magic in Opera Roles." Sepia 10:42-47, July 1961.

10025 Witeschnik, A. "Die Opernpremieren der Wiener Festwochen." Osterreichische Autorenzeitung 16:381, August 1961.

10026 Marcus, M. "Salzburg Success with New 'Simon Boccanegra.'" Music and Musicians 10:35, October 1961.

10027 Landry, R. J. "Negro Soprano & Sec'y of Labor Star as Harassed Met Opens 77th." Variety 224:1, October 25, 1961.

10028 Bloomfield, A. "'Blood Moon' Premiere." Musical America 81:16, November 1961.

10029 "A Job Well Done." Crisis 68:619, November 1961.

10030 Sheean, V. "Leontyne Price Onstage." Show 1:98-100, November 1961.

10031 Stevens, D. "New York: Met Opens." Music Magazine 163:28, November 1961.

10032 Kolodin, I. "Music to My Ears." Saturday Review 44:31, November 4, 1961.

10033 "Opens Metropolitan Opera's 1961 Season in Leading Role of Opera 'The Girl of the Golden West.'" Jet 21:60-61, November 9, 1961.

10034 RePass, R. "New York." Opera 12:788-789, December 1961.

10035 Sabin, R. "Price Soloist with Berlin Philharmonic." Musical America 81:61-62, December 1961.

10036 _____. "Price, Tucker and Colzani Star in Puccini Revival." Musical America 81:28, December 1961.

10037 "To Sing 'Tosca' at Metropolitan Opera." Jet 21:62, December 28, 1961.

10038 Ruchs, H. "At the Metropolitan." Musical Leader 94:11, January 1962.

10039 Todd, A. "Leontyne Price: The Voice of the Century." Musical America 82:12-15, January 1962.

10040 Dennis, P. "Leontyne Price: Praise and Plaudits at the Met." Sepia 11:46-47, February 1962.

10041 Casale, G. "Five of the World's Leading Singers of Opera." Look 26:39, February 27, 1962.

10042 Kolodin, I. "Price as Tosca." Saturday Review 45:29, April 14, 1962.

10043 "Leontyne Price: A Superbly Complete Interpretation." American Record Guide 28:739-740, May 1962.

10044 Helm, E. "Tosca." Musical America 82:38, June 1962.

10045 Widder, R. "Cleveland: Met: 'St. John'; Two Serkins." Music Magazine 164:30, June 1962.

10046 "Leontyne Price: Great Lady of Opera." Negro Digest 11:3-9, August 1962.

10047 "Yet Another 'Aida.'" Opera 13:627-628, September 1962.

10048 Faulkner, M. "Salzburg Has More Spectacle than Substance." Music Magazine 164:39, October 1962.

10049 Marcus, M. "Meccano for Mozart." Music and Musicians 11:14, October 1962.

10050 Barrow, W. "Five Fabulous Females." Negro Digest 12:78-83, July 1963.

10051 Miller, P. L. "Leontyne Price as Tosca." American Record Guide 30:92094, October 1963.

10052 Bloomfield, A. "California." Musical America 84:22, January 1964.

10053 Greenfield, E. "Opera on the Gramophone: 'Tosca.'" Opera 15:6-15, January 1964.

10054 Harrison, J. S. "The New York Music Scene." Musical America 84:34, January 1964.

10055 "Star-Besetzungen in der Wiener Staatsoper." Österreichische Autorenzeitung 17:489-490, October 1962.

10056   Thomas, E.   "Teurer Verdi, Billiger Mozart; die Neuinszenierungen
        der Festspiele 1962."   Neue Zeitschrift für Musik 123:463, Oc-
        tober 1962.

10057   Sargeant, W.   "Musical Events."   New Yorker 38:177-178, October
        27, 1962.

10058   "People Are Talking About...."   Vogue 140:108-109, November 1,
        1962.

10059   Helm, E.   "Opera in New York."   Musical America 82:22, Decem-
        ber 1962.

10060   Wechsberg, J.   "Vienna."   Opera 13:813, December 1962.

10061   "The Cast."   Opera News 27:21, December 1, 1962.

10062   Wechsberg, J.   "Vienna Nights."   Opera News 27:32, December 15,
        1962.

10063   Brozen, M.   "Opera in New York."   Musical America 83:25, Feb-
        ruary 1963.

10064   Miller, P. L.   "Leontyne Price as Tosca."   American Record
        Guide 30:92-94, October 1963.

10065   Chotzinoff, S.   "Conversation with Leontyne Price."   Holiday 35:103-
        104, March 1964.

10066   Harrison, J. S.   "The New York Music Scene."   Musical America
        84:28, March 1964.

10067   Sheean, V.   "Spiritual Ground."   Opera News 28:22-23, March 28,
        1964.

10068   Maclain, J.   "Completely Dissimilar; Price and Crespin Sing 'Nuits
        d'Ete'."   American Record Guide 30:672-673, April 1964.

10069   "Editorial Delights in Leontyne Price as Token of a 'Liberalized'
        Atlanta."   Variety 235:67, May 27, 1964.

10070   "Maria Callas, Leontyne Price Running Note 'n' Note in Operatic
        Role Race."   Variety 235:73, July 22, 1964.

10071   Miller, P. L.   "Leontyne Price as Carmen."   American Record
        Guide 31:10-12, September 1964.

10072   Osborne, C. L.   "The Best Grand-Opera 'Carmen' on Records."
        High Fidelity/Musical America 14:63-64, September 1964.

10073   "Price's 'Carmen.'"   Musical America 84:50, September 1964.

10074   Sheean, V.   "A Great 'Carmen.'"   Show 4:79, September 1964.

10075   Thomas, C. W.   "Three Negroes Receive 1964 Presidential Freedom
        Medal."   Negro History Bulletin 28:58-59, December 1964.

10076   "Back in the U.S."   Cash Box 26:12, December 5, 1964.

10077 Kolodin, I. "Music to My Ears." Saturday Review 48:34, Febru-
       ary 13, 1965.

10078 "Leontyne Price Keeps Her LBJ Act to 12 Minutes." Variety 238:1,
       April 28, 1965.

10079 Miller, P. L. "Beyond Any Doubt or Peradventure, the Finest
       Recorded Performance of 'La Forza del Destino.'" American
       Record Guide 31:798-799, May 1965.

10080 "50th Spingarn Medalist." Crisis 72:378, June-July 1965.

10081 "Leontyne Price Closes Old Met and Reopens New." Variety 240:1,
       September 22, 1965.

10082 Bloomfield, A. "San Francisco." Opera 17:138, February 1966.

10083 Dettmer, R. "Chicago." Opera 17:116, February 1966.

10084 "50th Spingarn Medalist." Crisis 75:129, February 1966.

10085 "The Stars at Home." Opera News 30:14-16, February 12, 1966.

10086 Ardoin, J. "New York." Opera 17:288, April 1966.

10087 Mayer, M. "Price's 'Ballo,' Grist and Lorengar Debuts." High
       Fidelity/Musical America 16:134, May 1966.

10088 "Diva Sang for the Old Met Ghosts." Life 61:38-39, September 30,
       1966.

10089 Kolodin, I. "Music to My Ears." Saturday Review 49:35-36, Oc-
       tober 1, 1966.

10090 Osborne, C. L. "Summer Opera, New and Nervy." High Fidelity/
       Musical America 16:MA16, November 1966.

10091 "Diva's Date with Destiny." Ebony 22:184-186, December 1966.

10092 "Lovely Leontyne Price." Sepia 15:81, December 1966.

10093 Soria, D. J. "Artist Life." High Fidelity/Musical America 16:MA5,
       December 1966.

10094 Tiegel, E. "Price and Previn Form a Team." High Fidelity/Mu-
       sical America 17:18, August 1967.

10095 Kolodin, I. "Music to My Ears: Lustrous Leonora." Saturday Re-
       view 50:106, October 14, 1967.

10096 Mayer, G. L. "Prima Donna: Price." American Record Guide
       34:188-189, November 1967.

10097 Wimbush, R. "And at Walthamstow." Gramophone 45:255, Novem-
       ber 1967.

10098 Kolodin, I. "Music to My Ears." Saturday Review 50:49-50, No-
       vember 4, 1967.

10099   "Leontyne Price." Opera News 32:30, November 4, 1967.

10100   Movshon, G. "The Metropolitan Opera." High Fidelity/Musical America 17:MA8, December 1967.

10101   Weinstock, H. "New York." Opera 18:1001, December 1967.

10102   Ward, H. "Listening In." Music and Artists 1:8, no. 2, 1968.

10103   Jellinck, G. "Leontyne Price: A Prima Donna Revisited--Her Second Volume of Operatic Repertoire for RCA Victor Is Magnificent from Start to Finish." HiFi/Stereo Review 20:86-87, January 1968.

10104   Kolodin, I. "This Price Isn't Right." Saturday Review 51:61, January 27, 1968.

10105   Mayer, M. "Recordings." Esquire 69:18, April 1968.

10106   Movshon, G. "Verdi's Hot-Blooded 'Ernani,' Now Complete and in Stereo." High Fidelity/Musical America 18:71-72, April 1968.

10107   Kessler, G. "Primadonnenglanz in der Scala." Opern Welt no. 7:24-25, July 1968.

10108   Barker, F. G. "Outstanding Soprano." Music and Musicians 16:38, August 1968.

10109   Duras, M. "La Voce." Vogue 152:136-137, September 15, 1968.

10110   Rockwell, J. "Kein Glaenzender Auftakt." Opern Welt no. 11:32, November 1968.

10111   Franze, J. P. "Teatro Colon: 'El Trovador.'" Buenos Aires Musicale 24:1, no. 396, 1969.

10112   "New York, N.Y." Music and Artists 2:30, no. 2, 1969.

10113   Stevanovitch, E. A. "Un Momento con Leontyne Price." Buenos Aires Musicale 24:1, no. 396, 1969.

10114   Movshon, G. "Mozart's 'Cosi'; Truly Complete and Sumptuously Cast." High Fidelity/Musical America 19:78-79, January 1969.

10115   "Recordings in Review." Saturday Review 52:52, March 29, 1969.

10116   Harewood, Lord. "A Week in New York." Opera 20:398, May 1969.

10117   "The Metropolitan Opera." High Fidelity/Musical America 19:MA12-13, May 1969.

10118   "Speaking of Records." High Fidelity/Musical America 19:28, May 1969.

10119   Kohn, R. "Letters to the Recording Editor." Saturday Review 52:58, May 31, 1969.

10120   Flanagan, W. "Samuel Barber's Best--'Knoxville: Summer of 1915.'" Stereo Review 22:75-76, June 1969.

10121 Oppens, K. "Verdi und Seine Interpreten." Opern Welt no. 6:24,
       June 1969.

10122 Diggs, P. V. "Letters to the Editor: Price Preceded by Williams."
       Saturday Review 52:25, June 14, 1969.

10123 ["Recital, New York."] High Fidelity/Musical America 19:MA22-23,
       July 1969.

10124 Figueroa, O. "Buenos Aires." Opera 20:801, September 1969.

10125 "Mozart Arias." Opera News 34:36, January 10, 1970.

10126 Oppens, K. "Spaete Einigung; Die Met Eroeffnete Endlich mit
       'Aida.'" Opern Welt no. 2:37-38, February 1970.

10127 Campbell, M. "Leontyne Price: Portrait of a Prima Donna."
       Music Journal 28:38-39, March 1970.

10128 "The Metropolitan Opera." High Fidelity/Musical America 20:13,
       March 1970, Section 2.

10129 "Leontyne Price Cuts a Benefit LP in Nashville." Billboard 82:98,
       May 9, 1970.

10130 "Il Trovatore." American Record Guide 36:792-794, June 1970.

10131 Reynolds, M. "The Rise of Price." Music and Musicians 19:52,
       October 1970.

10132 "Covent Garden Opera." Musical Opinion 94:121, December 1970.

10133 Rosenthal, H. "London Opera Diary." Opera 21:1158-1159, De-
       cember 1970.

10134 "Il Trovatore." Music and Musicians 19:77-78, December 1970;
       Musical Times 111:1241, December 1970.

10135 Barker, F. G. "London." Opera News 35:31, December 5, 1970.

10136 Botsford, W. "About Baseball Giants, and the Great Leontyne
       Price." American Record Guide 37:296-297, January 1971.

10137 Schreiber, U. "Oper als Gala-Repraesentation--'Aida' und 'Salome'
       in der Hamburgischen Staatsoper." Hifi-Stereophonie 10:16, Jan-
       uary 1971.

10138 "Names, Dates and Places." Opera News 35:5, February 13, 1971.

10139 "Das Portraet: Leontyne Price." Opern Welt no. 5:40-42, May
       1971.

10140 Smith, P. J. "Minnesota Orchestra, Price." High Fidelity/Musical
       America 21:MA26, June 1971.

10141 Blyth, A. "Leontyne Price." Gramophone 49:303, August 1971.

10142 Movshon, G. "Milestone 'Aida'; Leontyne Price and RCA Celebrate the Opera's Centenary with a Splendid New Recording." High Fidelity/Musical America 21:57-58, August 1971.

10143   Bloomfield, A. "San Francisco." Opera 23:131, February 1972.

10144   Jenkins, S. "Today's Price." Opera News 36:14-16, February 12, 1972.

10145   "Blacks Win 17 Grammy Awards, but Miles Davis, Motown Exec. Walk Out." Jet 42:58, March 3, 1972.

10146   "Il Tabbaro." American Record Guide 38:351, April 1972.

10147   ["Recital, New York."] High Fidelity/Musical America 22:MA23, June 1972.

10148   Wells, W. H. "USA." Music and Musicians 20:73, June 1972.

10149   Botsford, W. "A Pair of Aidas in a Trio of Recordings: Price (Twice) and Milanov." American Record Guide 35:548-551, July 1972.

10150   Kolodin, I. "Leontyne Price: I Love Opera, But...." Saturday Review 55:31-34, September 9, 1972.

10151   "London." Oper und Konzert 11:32-33, no. 6, 1973.

10152   Lyon, Hugh Lee. Leontyne Price: Highlights of a Prima Donna. New York: Vantage Press, 1973.

10153   Sargeant, Winthrop. Divas. New York: Coward, McCann & Geoghegan, 1973. Six great singers are included: Joan Sutherland, Marilyn Horne, Beverly Sills, Birgit Nilsson, Eileen Farrell, and Leontyne Price.

10154   "A Gala and Then Some." Opera News 37:6-7, April 7, 1973.

10155   Barker, F. G. "Aida." Music and Musicians 21:66, May 1973.

10156   Loppert, M. "'Aida': Royal Opera, Covent Garden." Opera 24:468-469, May 1973.

10157   Movshon, G. "New York." Opera 24:443-445, May 1973.

10158   Petrobelli, P. "Music in London." Musical Trades 114:508, May 1973.

10159   "Covent Garden: Garden Revivals." Musical Events 28:23-24, July 1973.

10160   "Names, Dates and Places." Opera News 38:8-9, July 1973.

10161   Jellinek, G. "The Essential 'Tosca.'" Stereo Review 32:82-83, February 1974.

10162   Daniels, R. D. "Loved and Lost." Opera News 38:19, April 13, 1974.

10163   "Names, Dates and Places." Opera News 38:8-9, June 1974.

10164   Lawrence, R. "The Metropolitan Opera." High Fidelity/Musical
        America 24:MA32-34, July 1974.

10165   Bloomfield, A. "San Francisco: 'Salome' and 'Parsifal.'" Opera
        25:993-994, November 1974.

10166   Von Buchau, S. "San Francisco." Opera News 39:51-52, Novem-
        ber 1974.

10167   Ebert, A. "Leontyne--the Price of Being." Essence 5:64-67, Feb-
        ruary 1975.

10168   Jellinek, G. "Two Complementary Readings of Richard Strauss'
        'Four Last Songs.'" Stereo Review 34:70-71, March 1975.

10169   Kolodin, I. "The Operatic Career and How It Prospers (or Doesn't)."
        Saturday Review 2:37-38, April 5, 1975.

10170   Jacobson, R. "New York." Opera News 39:44, April 19, 1975.

10171   Lawrence, R. "The Metropolitan Opera: 'Manon Lescaut.'" High
        Fidelity/Musical America 25:MA16-17, June 1975.

10172   "Muenchen." Oper und Konzert 14:29-30, no. 1, 1976.

10173   Hemming, R. "Leontyne Price." Stereo Review 36:62-64, January
        1976.

10174   "4-Star New Met 'Aida'; McCracken Takes Tumble, Steps on Price's
        Train." Variety 282:84, February 11, 1976.

10175   Rubin, S. E. "Price on Price." Opera News 40:16-20, March 6,
        1976.

10176   Wadsworth, S. "Victors and Vanquished." Opera News 40:29, March
        6, 1976.

10177   Movshon, G. "The Metropolitan Opera: 'Aida.'" High Fidelity/
        Musical America 26:MA20-21, May 1976.

10178   "Concert Reviews." Variety 283:68, May 26, 1976.

10179   "Leontyne Price Benefit." Crisis 83:208, June-July 1976.

10180   Schaumkell, C. D. "Met-Stars von Vorgestern, Gestern und Haute--
        Wiederveroeffentlichungen und Neuerscheinungen." Opernwelt no.
        10:53-55, October 1976.

10181   Wortham, J. "Shoot the Piano Player and the Cellist, the Oboist
        and the Drummer: Blacks in the World of Orchestras." Black
        Enterprise 7:31-32, December 1976.

10182   Limmert, E. "Levine als Verdi-Dirigent--'Die Macht des Schick-
        sals' mit Price und Domingo." Opernwelt 18:58, no. 12, 1977.

10183   Lipton, G. "Pawns of Fate." Opera News 41:27, March 12, 1977.

10184   Sterritt, D. "Two Great Sopranos Tackle Their Roles: Leontyne

Price's Passion as Leonora; Sills' Liberated Louise." Christian Science Monitor 69:31, March 24, 1977.

10185 "America: To Leontyne Price, Opportunities Are Growing." U.S. News and World Report 82:56, March 28, 1977.

10186 Arthur, D. "Something to Savor." American Record Guide 40:47-48, June 1977. Review of the recording "La Forza del Destino."

10187 Leslie, M. "Salzburg: Karajan's 'Trovatore.'" Opera 28:558, June 1977.

10188 Furie, K. "In the Opera House: How Much Does Neatness Count?" High Fidelity/Musical America 27:71-74, August 1977.

10189 "Names, Dates and Places." Opera News 42:12-13, August 1977.

10190 "20 Year Medal; Leontyne Price Hailed by San Francisco Opera." Variety 288:86, November 2, 1977.

10191 Von Buchau, S. "San Francisco." Opera News 42:34, December 17, 1977.

10192 Bloomfield, A. "San Francisco." Opera 29:47-48, January 1978.

10193 "Leontyne Price Receives San Francisco Opera Medal." Opera 29:21, January 1978.

10194 Harris, D. "San Francisco." Music and Musicians 26:44-45, February 1978.

10195 Jellinck, G. "Leontyne Price: Prima Donna--Volume 4; RCA Recording." Stereo Review 41:142-143, November 1978.

PRIDE, CHARLEY, 1938- .

10196 "They Call Him Country Charley." Ebony 22:60-62, March 1967.

10197 "New Acts." Variety 249:69, June 31, 1968.

10198 Williams, B. "Country Music Now Interracial." Billboard 80:1, August 17, 1968.

10199 "Country Music's Pride." Sepia 17:28-33, October 1968.

10200 "Cash Picks Up New Gold Disk for Col LP: Pride Album Cops Goldie." Variety 257:51, February 4, 1970.

10201 "Black Pride." Newsweek 76:82, August 17, 1970.

10202 "Black C&W Artist Has Golden Touch." Variety 262:1, March 24, 1971.

10203 Metcalfe, R. H. "Charley Pride--Sweet Sound of $ucce$$." Jet 4:56, April 29, 1971.

10204 "This Pitcher Won't Make It." Ebony 26:45-46, May 1971.

10205   Burton, C.   "Charley Pride."   Rolling Stone no. 83:52, May 27,
        1971.

10206   "Pride at Bat."   BMI p. 6, June 1971.

10207   "Charley Pride Captures Dual Awards on '71 CMA TV Hour."   Bill-
        board 83:36, October 23, 1971.

10208   Windeler, R.   "Charley Pride, a Casual Perfectionist."   Stereo Re-
        view 28:69-70, January 1972.

10209   Freedland, N.   "The Jackie Robinson of Country Music: Charley
        Pride."   Billboard 84:50-51, January 29, 1972.

10210   "... And Living in Dallas."   BMI p. 15, March 1972.

10211   "Blacks Win 17 Grammy Awards, but Miles Davis, Motown Exec.
        Walk Out."   Jet 42:58, March 3, 1972.

10212   Preece, H.   "No. 1 Country Singer."   Sepia 21:35-36, May 1972.

10213   Brack, R.   "Talent in Action."   Billboard 84:14, May 13, 1972.

10214   Chalker, B.   "Pride and Prejudice."   Melody Maker 47:19, May 27,
        1972.

10215   _____.   "Caught in the Act."   Melody Maker 47:50, June 17,
        1972.

10216   "Hilton, Las Vegas."   Variety 267:53, July 26, 1972.

10217   Littleton, B.   "Charley Pride."   International Musician 72:6, Oc-
        tober 1973.

10218   Williams, B.   "Pride's '73 $4 Mil Tops Country Mark."   Billboard
        85:1, October 13, 1973.

10219   Barclay, Pamela.   Charley Pride.   Mankato, Minn.: Creative Ed-
        ucation; Distributed by Childrens Press, Chicago, 1974, c1975.
        Juvenile literature about Pride who was the first black to become
        prominent in country music.

10220   "Black Star of White Soul."   Time 103:52, May 6, 1974.

10221   "Hilton, Las Vegas."   Variety 275:55, May 29, 1974.

10222   "Current Swamp Opera Trail Blazers."   High Fidelity/Musical Amer-
        ica 24:38-41, June 1974.

10223   "Concert Reviews."   Variety 276:60, October 9, 1974.

10224   "Pride Sees Barriers Still to Be Broken."   Billboard 86:18, October
        26, 1974.

10225   "Caught in the Act."   Melody Maker 50:51, February 1, 1975.

10226   Chalker, B.   "Pride and Joy."   Melody Maker 50:35, February 15,
        1975.

10227 "Concert Reviews." Variety 281:52, November 12, 1975.

10228 "Talent in Action." Billboard 87:39, November 29, 1975.

10229 Davis, C. "Charley Pride, Country's Darling." Encore 5:22-24,
       January 5, 1976.

10230 "Concert Reviews." Variety 282:92, April 21, 1976.

10231 "Popularity Abroad Spurs Still Another Pride Tour." Billboard
       88:93, May 8, 1976.

10232 "Pride Troupe Big Winner in Australia." Billboard 88:71, August
       28, 1976.

10233 "Caught in the Act." Melody Maker 51:20, November 13, 1976.

10234 "Charley Pride Stays on Top as Only Black Country and Western
       Music Star." Jet 53:82, November 24, 1977.

10235 "Albums: The Hits of Charley Pride." Melody Maker 53:25, July
       15, 1978.

10236 "Harrah's, Reno." Variety 293:121, November 22, 1978.

PRIDGETT, GERTRUDE MALISSA NIX see RAINEY, GERTRUDE MA

RAINEY, GERTRUDE MA (Gertrude Malissa Nix Pridgett; Mrs. William Pa
Rainey), 1886-1939.

10237 Jones, M. "She Jest Catch Hold of Us." Melody Maker 25:5, Sep-
       tember 24, 1949.

10238 Smith, C. E. "The Making of a King." Record Changer 9:19-21,
       July-August 1950.

10239 Traill, S. "Jazz on Brunswick 04516." Melody Maker 26:9, July
       15, 1950.

10240 Schuler, V. "The Mystery of the Two Ma Raineys." Melody Maker
       27:9, October 13, 1951.

10241 Turner-Towles, N. "The Paramount Wildcat." Jazz Journal 7:2-3,
       March 1954.

10242 Smith, C. E. "Ma Rainey and the Minstrels." Record Changer
       14:5-6, no. 6, 1955.

10243 Fulbright, T. "Ma Rainey and I." Jazz Journal 9:1-2, March 1956.

10244 McRae, B. "The Ma Rainey and Bessie Smith Accompaniments."
       Jazz Journal 14:6-8, March 1961.

10245 Oliver, P. "Ma Rainey Was Here." Jazz Monthly 11:21-23, March
       1965.

10246   Steiner, J. "Beyond the Impression." Record Research no. 67:11-
        12, April 1965.

10247   Williams, M. "Mostly Modernists." Saturday Review 50:25, July
        29, 1967.

10248   "Record Reviews." Jazz Journal 22:35, October 1969; down beat
        36:32, December 25, 1969.

10249   "Oh My Babe Blues--Ma Rainey's Georgia Jazz Band." Jazz Report
        7:12, no. 3, 1970.

10250   Stewart-Baxter, Derrick. Ma Rainey and the Classic Blues Singers.
        New York: Stein and Day, 1970.

10251   Godrich, J. "Ma Rainey." Storyville 35:173-175, June-July 1971.

10252   "Record Reviews: Queen of the Blues, Vol. 3." Jazz Journal
        24:37, December 1971.

10253   "Record Reviews: Queen of the Blues." Journal of American Folk-
        lore 86:415, no. 342, 1973.

10254   Russell, R. "Master Drummer; Jesse Price." Jazz & Blues 3:14-
        15, July 1973.

10255   Stewart-Baxter, D. "Blues Digest." Jazz Journal 26:22-23, July
        1973.

10256   Jones, Hettie. Big Star Fallin' Mama; Five Women in Black Music.
        New York: Viking Press, 1974. The women musicians discussed
        are Bessie Smith, Mahalia Jackson, Billie Holiday, Aretha Frank-
        lin, and Ma Rainey. Juvenile literature.

10257   "Chroniques des Disques: Ma Rainey." Jazz Hot no. 312:34, Jan-
        uary 1975.

10258   O'Neal, J., and A. O'Neal. "Living Blues Interview: Georgia Tom
        Dorsey." Living Blues no. 20:21-23, March-April 1975.

10259   Lieb, Sandra Robin. "The Message of Ma Rainey's Blues: A Bi-
        ographical and Critical Study of America's First Woman Blues
        Singers." (Ph.D. Dissertation, Stanford University, 1976).

10260   Bentley, J. "I Remember Bessie--Art Hodes Plays Bessie Smith
        and Ma Rainey." Jazz Report 9:12, no. 4, 1977.

RAZAF, ANDY (Andreamentania Paul Razafin-keriefo), 1895-1973.

10261   "Andy Razaf, Collaborator with 'Fats' Waller in Many of His Compo-
        sitions." Jazz Journal 3:1, May 1950.

10262   "Do You Remember Andy Razaf?" Negro Digest 9:11-12, October
        1951.

10263   Levin, F. "Andy Razaf--the Melody Man." Jazz Journal 4:1-2,
        October 1951.

10264 "Andy Razaf Honoured by Howard University." Jazz Journal 5:4,
       September 1952.

10265 Levin, F. "The American Jazz Scene." Jazz Journal 6:2, March
       1953.

10266 "Mr. Tin Pan Alley." Our World 8:38-39, July 1953.

10267 "Know Thyself; Poem." Negro History Bulletin 18:169, April 1955.

10268 "Time Out for Thinking." Negro History Bulletin 18:167, April
       1955.

10269 Cartwright, M. "Andy Razaf." Negro History Bulletin 19:82-83,
       January 1956.

10270 "Time Out for Thinking." Negro History Bulletin 19:83, January
       1956.

10271 "Maxine to Record Tribute to Razaf." down beat 23:11, September
       19, 1956.

10272 "Man-Made Madness; Poem." Negro History Bulletin 20:61, Decem-
       ber 1956.

10273 "Wheel Chair Composer." Ebony 13:73-74, March 1958.

10274 Razaf, Andy. "Passing Years." Negro History Bulletin 22:93-94,
       January 1959.

10275 Brackney, B. "Songwriting's Forgotten Master, Andy Razaf." Jazz
       Report 2:1-3, November 1961.

10276 "Held Notes." down beat 29:51, February 15, 1962.

10277 Feather, L. "Lonely Wait of Andy Razaf." Negro Digest 11:75-77,
       March 1962.

10278 "Tunesmith Andy Razaf Caps 27-Yr. Romance in Valentine Day
       Nuptials." Variety 230:52, February 27, 1963.

10279 "No Rock 'n' Roll for Me." Sepia 12:61-64, May 1963.

10280 Affeldt, P. E. ["Obituary."] Jazz Report 8:32, no. 3, 1973.

10281 ["Obituary."] Black Perspectives in Music 1:199, no. 2, 1973;
       Coda 10:39, no. 12, 1973; IAJRC Journal 6:24, no. 2, 1973.

10282 "Whatever Happened to Andy Razaf?" Ebony 28:122, January 1973.

10283 "Songwriter Razaf Dies." Melody Maker 48:4, February 17, 1973.

10284 ["Obituary."] Jet 43:33, February 22, 1973; down beat 40:12, March
       29, 1973; Jazz & Blues 3:30, April 1973; Jazz Magazine no. 210:8,
       April 1973; Crisis 80:175, May 1973; Jazz Forum no. 23:37, Au-
       gust 1973.

10285 Brackney, R. L. "Musical Legacy of Andy Razaf." Jazz Report
       8:7-9, no. 5, 1974.

10286 Cayer, D. A. "Black and Blue and Black Again: Three Stages of Racial Imagery in Jazz Lyrics." Journal of Jazz Studies 2:38-71, no. 1, 1974.

RAZAFIN-KERIEFO, ANDREAMENTANIA PAUL see RAZAF, ANDY

REED, MRS. WAYMON see VAUGHAN, SARAH LOIS

RIPERTON, MINNIE, 1947-1979.

10287 Robinson, L. "Superstars of Future Need Break." Billboard 87:20, January 11, 1974.

10288 Ivy, A. "Minnie Smashed Black Tie Audience." Soul 9:8, December 23, 1974.

10289 Rudis, A. "Perfect Angel." Melody Maker 49:30, July 20, 1974.

10290 Rensin, D. "Riperton: s'Wonderlove." Rolling Stone no. 171:18, October 10, 1974.

10291 Charlesworth, C. "Minnie Ha Ha!" Melody Maker 50:25, April 12, 1975.

10292 "Concert Reviews." Variety 278:50, April 23, 1975.

10293 "Caught in the Act America." Melody Maker 50:34, May 24, 1975.

10294 "Talent in Action." Billboard 87:48, May 24, 1975.

10295 "Records: Adventures in Paradise." Rolling Stone no. 190:56, July 3, 1975.

10296 "Concert Reviews." Variety 279:100, July 16, 1975.

10297 "Caught in the Act America." Melody Maker 50:40, July 19, 1975.

10298 "Talent in Action." Billboard 87:28, July 19, 1975.

10299 Jefferson, M. "Stevie's Angel." Newsweek 86:71, July 28, 1975.

10300 Ivy, A. "Minnie Riperton Gave Up $500,000 to Remain a Singer." Soul 10:2-3, September 1, 1975.

10301 "Performances." Soul 10:12, September 1, 1975.

10302 "Riviera, Las Vegas." Variety 282:85, March 3, 1976.

10303 "Talent in Action." Billboard 88:28, March 6, 1976.

10304 Lucas, B. "Minnie Riperton Reveals How Breast Removal Affects Her New Life." Jet 50:58-59, September 9, 1976.

10305 _____. "Minnie Riperton and Husband: A Musical Team." Jet 51:56-60, October 28, 1976.

10306 _____. "Minnie Riperton." Ebony 32:33-34, December 1976.

10307 Rankin, Edwina L. "Pleased with Outcome of First Lady's Operation, Riperton Sends Telegram." Jet 52:22-23, May 19, 1977.

10308 Ferdinand, V. "Positive Personality of Minnie Riperton." Black
Collegian 8:43-44, September-October 1977.

10309 Lucas, B. "Minnie Riperton Makes New Music and New Lifestyle."
Jet 54:54-56, June 1, 1978.

ROBINSON, RAY CHARLES see CHARLES, RAY

ROOKS, MRS. SHELBY ALBRIGHT see MAYNOR, DOROTHY

ROSS, DIANA (Mrs. Robert Ellis Silberstein), 1944- .

10310 "Toting for Tamla." Melody Maker 40·3, October 16, 1965.

10311 Miller, E. "Off the Record with the Supremes." Seventeen 25:280-
281, August 1966.

10312 Walton, D. "Diana Ross and the Supremes' Greatest Hits." Journal
of Pop Culture 1:291-295, no. 3, 1967.

10313 Landau, J. "A Whiter Shade of Black." Crawdaddy no. 11:35-36,
September-October 1967.

10314 Tiegel, E. "Sound Flunks Out at UCLA's Supremes, Masekela Concert." Billboard 79:24, November 18, 1967.

10315 "Deauville, M. B." Variety 249:44, December 27, 1967.

10316 "Supremes on Palladium TV." Melody Maker 43:1, January 6, 1968.

10317 Hennessey, M. "With Their Looks, the Supremes Don't Even Have
to Sing!" Melody Maker 43:11, January 20, 1968.

10318 Hutton, J. "Stars Come Out for the Supremes." Melody Maker
43:4, January 27, 1968.

10319 "Talk of Town, London." Variety 249:68, January 31, 1968.

10320 Dawbarn, B. "At the Shrine of the Supremes." Melody Maker 43:5,
February 3, 1968.

10321 Hennessey, M. "Supremes Capture MIDEM Show with Swinging
Tunes." Billboard 80:45, February 3, 1968.

10322 "Supremes Invited to Return Visit at Talk." Melody Maker 43:4,
February 10, 1968.

10323 Landergren, C. "Supremes pa Berns." Orkester Journalen 36:9,
March 1968.

10324 Wilmer, V. "Caught in the Act." down beat 35:40, March 21, 1968.

10325 "Copacabana, N.Y." Variety 250:69, April 3, 1968.

10326 Sternfield, A. "Diana Ross & Supremes in Flawless & Polished Act." Billboard 80:16, April 13, 1968.

10327 "Frontier, Las Vegas." Variety 251:43, July 10, 1968.

10328 "Cocoanut Grove, L.A." Variety 253:55, October 9, 1968.

10329 Mulligan, B. "Diana Ross & Supremes' Racial Song Punctuates Royal Variety Show." Variety 253:1, November 27, 1968.

10330 Welch, C. "How Diana Ross Became a Talking, Instead of Just a Walking, Doll." Melody Maker 43:16-17, November 30, 1968.

10331 "Concert Reviews." Variety 253:54, December 4, 1968.

10332 "Frontier, Las Vegas." Variety 253:63, February 5, 1969.

10333 "Waldorf-Astoria, N.Y." Variety 255:63, May 21, 1969.

10334 Dove, I. "For Diana & Supremes, It's Swinging at Its Supreme." Billboard 81:8, May 24, 1969.

10335 "Why the Supremes Must Split." Melody Maker 44:5, May 31, 1969.

10336 "Is Diana Ross Leaving the Supremes?" Sepia 18:46-49, June 1969.

10337 Eldridge, R. "Britain Turns Down Diana, Temptations." Melody Maker 44:7, July 5, 1969.

10338 "Supremes' Walkout from Latin Casino Cues Lotsa Action in Union and Courts." Variety 255:53, August 13, 1969.

10339 "J. Brown, Aretha, Sly, Supremes Win 'Mikes.'" Billboard 81:34, August 30, 1969.

10340 Hamilton, J. "Supreme Supreme: Diana Ross." Look 33:68-74, September 23, 1969.

10341 "Motown Gets 2 Acts from Supremes; Spin Off Diana Ross as Single in Feb." Variety 256:59, October 15, 1969.

10342 "Diana Ross to Quit Supremes for Solo Route." Billboard 81:3, November 8, 1969.

10343 "Diana Will Split Supremes--Honest." Rolling Stone no. 47:12, November 29, 1969.

10344 "Diana's Dogs Offed: She Sues Casino." Rolling Stone no. 47:12, November 29, 1969.

10345 "Frontier, Las Vegas." Variety 257:41, December 31, 1969.

10346 "An Emotional Farewell from Diana in Vegas." Melody Maker 45:6, January 31, 1970.

10347   Robinson, L. "Why Diana Ross Left the Supremes." Ebony 25:120-
        126, February 1970.

10348   Farrell, B. "Farewell, More or Less, to the Supremes." Life
        68:188, February 13, 1970.

10349   "New Acts." Variety 258:64, March 18, 1970.

10350   "Harrah's, Reno." Variety 258:115, April 8, 1970.

10351   "Random Notes." Rolling Stone no. 57:6, April 30, 1970.

10352   "Frontier, Las Vegas." Variety 259:55, May 20, 1970.

10353   Watts, M. "I'm Only Here for the Tennis." Melody Maker 45:7,
        July 4, 1970.

10354   "Now Grove, L.A." Variety 259:53, August 5, 1970.

10355   "Talent in Action." Billboard 82:26, August 15, 1970.

10356   "Baby, Baby, Where Did Diana Go?" Time 96:30-31, August 17,
        1970.

10357   "Diana Ross: Still Supreme Without the Supremes." Sepia 19:58-
        60, September 1970.

10358   "Waldorf-Astoria, N.Y. Variety 260:80, September 16, 1970.

10359   "Talent in Action." Billboard 82:20, September 19, 1970.

10360   Winters-Rosen Sues to Block Motown's Diana Ross Special." Variety
        261:30, December 16, 1970.

10361   "Diana Ross TVer Bows Motown $15 Mil Project." Billboard 82:3,
        December 19, 1970.

10362   "Judge Denies Injunction Against 'Diana' Special." Jet 39:6, Jan-
        uary 7, 1971.

10363   "Diana Ross in Surprise Rites Weds White Businessman." Jet 39:53,
        February 4, 1971.

10364   Landau, J. "Singles: 'Remember Me.'" Rolling Stone no. 76:56,
        February 18, 1971.

10365   "Diana Ross as Holiday for Motown; Diana Sands Ditts for Ossie
        Davis." Variety 262:2, March 31, 1971.

10366   "Ross Rage." Harper's Bazaar 104:84-89, April 1971.

10367   Goodwin, R. "The New Diana." Jet 4:56-58, April 8, 1971.

10368   Siders, H. "Diana Ross to Star in Billie Holiday Movie." down
        beat 38:10, June 10, 1971.

10369   Gersten, R. "Records: Surrender." Rolling Stone no. 94:52, Oc-
        tober 28, 1971.

10370 Knight, A. "Two Educations." Saturday Review 55:81, no. 46, 1972.

10371 "Waldorf-Astoria, N.Y." Variety 266:94, April 12, 1972.

10372 Taras, J. "Talent in Action." Billboard 84:20, April 22, 1972.

10373 Bartley, G. F. "The Lady Sings at N.Y.'s Waldorf." Soul 7:13, May 22, 1972.

10374 Peterson, M. "Diana, Diana." Essence 3:34-35, June 1972.

10375 "Caesars Palace, L.V." Variety 267:55, June 28, 1972.

10376 Westin, K. Otto. "Filmen om Billie Holiday Klar." Orkester Journalen 40:7, July-August 1972.

10377 Abrams, M. "Lady Sings the Blues." Jazz Digest 1:41, September-October 1972.

10378 Miller, E. "Spotlight." Seventeen 31:82, September 1972.

10379 Berry, W. E. "Diana Ross Brings Back Billie Holiday in New Movie." Jet 43:56-61, October 19, 1972.

10380 Robinson, L. "Lady Sings the Blues." Ebony 28:37-46, November 6, 1972.

10381 Cocks, J. "Holiday on Ice." Time 100:86-88, November 6, 1972.

10382 Bates, J. "La Ross Piques Holiday Movie." Billboard 84:4, November 11, 1972.

10383 Watts, M. "Diana Triumphs as Billie." Melody Maker 47:38, November 11, 1972.

10384 Nickerson, R. "The Lady Sings the Blues." Soul 7:1-3, November 20, 1972.

10385 Gleason, R. J. "Perspectives: Diana Ross Is Billie Holiday." Rolling Stone no. 122:22, November 23, 1972.

10386 Morgenstern, D. "Diana Ross Almost Saves Billie 'Bio.'" down beat 39:11, November 23, 1972.

10387 "Berry Gordy Raps on His 'Lady.'" Soul 7:8-9, December 4, 1972.

10388 "New Day for Diana." Life 73:42-45, December 8, 1972.

10389 "Billie Holiday Film, Star Gets NAACP Image Award." Jet 43:56, December 14, 1972.

10390 Walling, W., and R. Shatzkin. "'It Ain't the Blues': Billie Holiday, Sidney J. Furie, and Kitsch." Journal of Jazz Studies 1:21-33, no. 1, 1973. The accuracy of Holiday's life as shown in the film is questioned.

10391 Comas, B. "Black Films: Is Quality Coming?" Soul 7:3, January 1, 1973.

10392   "Diana Ross Named Golden Apple Winner." Soul 7:1, January 29, 1973.

10393   Batten, J. "On Screen." Jazz & Blues 2:30, February 1973.

10394   Thomas, M. "Diana Ross Goes from Riches to Rags." Rolling Stone no. 127:28-31, February 1, 1973.

10395   "Caesars Palace, L. V." Variety 270:83, February 14, 1973.

10396   "Four Blacks Are Honored with Golden Globe Awards." Jet 43:58, February 15, 1973.

10397   Deni, L. "Talent in Action." Billboard 85:18, February 24, 1973.

10398   Duhé, C. "Diana Ross." Vogue 161:142-145, March 1973.

10399   "It's Back to Las Vegas for Diana." Soul 7:1, March 12, 1973.

10400   "Records: Lady Sings the Blues." Rolling Stone no. 130:54-55, March 15, 1973.

10401   "Diana Sings Billie." Melody Maker 48:33, March 17, 1973.

10402   Jones, M. "The Legend of Lady Day." Melody Maker 48:33-34, March 17, 1973.

10403   Bell, J. N. "Diana Ross Grows Up." Good Housekeeping 176:92-93, April 1973.

10404   Jones, M. "Lady Ross." Melody Maker 48:3, April 14, 1973.

10405   Brown, M. L. "Diana Ross--Film Actress 1972." Soul 7:28, April 23, 1973.

10406   Ivy, A. "Lady Sings the Blues--Film of 1972." Soul 7:26, April 23, 1973.

10407   Keating, L. "On Screen: Lady Sings the Blues." Jazz & Blues 3:16-17, June 1973.

10408   Massaquoi, H. "There's No Place Like Home for Diana Ross." Ebony 28:100-104, July 1973.

10409   Stewart-Baxter, D. "Blues Digest." Jazz Journal 26:22-23, July 1973.

10410   Wilson, G. M. "Diana Ross." Ebony 28:99, July 1973.

10411   Jones, M. "Cannes Film Festival and Hollywood Reporter Give Highest Honors to 'Lady' Diana." Soul 8:1, July 9, 1973. Reprinted from Hollywood Reporter.

10412   "One-Man Shows." Variety 271:46, August 1, 1973.

10413   Charles, R. "That Skinny Kid Wows 'em Again." Soul 8:14, August 6, 1973.

10414   "Invited to the Palace--Diana Honored by Japanese." Soul 8:2-3,
        September 3, 1973.

10415   "Caught in the Act." Melody Maker 48:23, September 22, 1973;
        48:27, September 29, 1973.

10416   "Ross Ingen Holiday." Orkester Journalen 41:10, October 1973.

10417   "Concert Reviews." Variety 272:38, October 3, 1973.

10418   Reilly, P. "Diana Ross, Lady of the Theater--Motown's New 'Touch
        Me in the Morning' Captures Her Elusive Live-Performance."
        Stereo Review 31:75-76, November 1973.

10419   Gambaccini, P. "Singles: You're a Special Part of Me." Rolling
        Stone no. 149:26, December 6, 1973.

10420   "Albums: Diana and Marvin." Melody Maker 48:37, December 15,
        1973.

10421   Itzkowitz, Leonore K. Diana Ross. New York: Random House,
        1974. Juvenile literature.

10422   "The Soul Report." Melody Maker 49:28-29, January 12, 1974.

10423   Spiegelman, J. "From Sequins to Wedding Bells and Babies; The
        Supremes Still Sparkle." Soul 8:2-3, January 21, 1974.

10424   "Caesars Palace, L.V." Variety 274:89, February 13, 1974.

10425   "Sahara-Tahoe." Variety 275:55, July 3, 1974.

10426   Stewart, T. "What Next for Diana Ross." Sepia 23:44-48, August
        1974.

10427   Palmer, B. "Newport." Rolling Stone no. 167:23, August 15, 1974.

10428   "Diana Gives Greatest Concert." Soul 9:2, September 2, 1974.

10429   Eldred, Patricia Mulrooney. Diana Ross. Mankato, Minn.: Cre-
        ative Education; Distributed by Childrens Press, Chicago, 1975.
        Juvenile literature.

10430   "Performances." Soul 10:6, June 9, 1975.

10431   "Spectacular New Film for Diana Ross: Mahogany." Ebony 30:144-
        146, October 1975.

10432   Brown, G. F. "Ghetto Experience Makes 'Mahogany' a Get Down
        Movie." Jet 49:58-61, October 9, 1975.

10433   Black, D. "Diana Ross' Big Gamble: Can Star Switch from Singing
        to Acting." Sepia 24:34-46, December 1975.

10434   Windeler, R. "Mr. & Mrs. Diana Ross? No Way, Says Her Hus-
        band of Five Years." People 5:22-26, January 26, 1976.

10435   "Caught in the Act." Melody Maker 51:27, March 20, 1976.

10436 "Diana." Billboard 88:D1, March 20, 1976.

10437 "Discography: Diana Ross and the Supremes." Billboard 88:D62-63,
       March 20, 1976.

10438 Jones, M. "Diana: The Lady Knows Where She's Going." Melody
       Maker 51:32, March 20, 1976.

10439 "Review Section." Melody Maker 51:26, March 27, 1976.

10440 "Concert Reviews." Variety 282:110, March 31, 1976.

10441 "Caught in the Act." Melody Maker 51:21, April 24, 1976.

10442 "Jazz en Direct." Jazz Magazine no. 244:8, May 1976.

10443 "Records: Diana Ross." Rolling Stone no. 212:65, May 6, 1976.

10444 "Caesars Palace, L. V." Variety 283:119, May 19, 1976.

10445 "Talent in Action." Billboard 88:35, May 29, 1976.

10446 Lucas, B. "Diana Ross Goes to Broadway with Show that Sizzles."
       Jet 50:56-60, June 10, 1976.

10447 "One Woman Show." Variety 232:66, June 16, 1976.

10448 Beaufort, J. "Diana Ross's Broadway Debut: Exotic Yet Real."
       Christian Science Monitor 68:23, June 21, 1976.

10449 "Talent in Action." Billboard 88:32, June 26, 1976.

10450 Orth, M. "Boss Lady." Newsweek 87:61, June 28, 1976.

10451 Wiseman, R. "Singles; 'Love Hangover' a Ballad Hit, a Disco Hit,
       Two Hits in One." Rolling Stone no. 216:17, July 1, 1976.

10452 Davis, C. "Rhinestone Ross." Encore 5:23, August 2, 1976.

10453 "Performance." Rolling Stone no. 219:78, August 12, 1976.

10454 "Sahara Tahoe." Variety 284:67, September 1, 1976.

10455 "Concert Reviews." Variety 284:62, October 6, 1976.

10456 "Diana Ross: A Quartet of Superstars." Ebony 32:156-158, March
       1977.

10457 "Diana Ross Weaves Musical Magic in New TV Special." Jet 51:60-
       64, March 10, 1977.

10458 "Albums: An Evening with Diana Ross." Melody Maker 52:22,
       April 2, 1977.

10459 Ebert, A. "Diana." Essence 8:70-71, May 1977.

10460 Reilly, P. "A Glittering Evening with Diana Ross: Teasing Messages from the Chiffon Beyond." Stereo Review 39:88-89, July 1977.

10461 "Concert Reviews." Variety 287:58, July 27, 1977.

10462 "Caught in the Act." Melody Maker 52:12, August 6, 1977.

10463 Driscoll, O. "Diana: An Encounter in Three Scenes." Rolling Stone no. 245:35, August 11, 1977.

10464 Davis, C. "Diana Ross--from Rhinestones to Diamonds." Encore 6:34, September 12, 1977.

10465 Kisner, R. E. "Is There Room at the Top for Big Three of Songs." Jet 52:58-60, September 15, 1977.

10466 "Albums: Baby It's Me." Melody Maker 52:22, November 5, 1977.

10467 "Records: Baby It's Me." High Fidelity/Musical America 27:140, December 1977; Rolling Stone no. 253:78, December 1, 1977.

10468 Berman, Connie. Diana Ross: Supreme Lady. New York: Popular Library, 1978.

10469 "Caesars Palace, L.V." Variety 290:85, May 3, 1978.

10470 "Caught in the Act." Melody Maker 53:14, May 13, 1978.

10471 "Concert Reviews." Variety 291:446, May 17, 1978.

10472 Lucas, B. "Diana Ross Does It Best." Jet 54:58-61, May 18, 1978.

10473 Tiegel, E. "New Diana Ross Show a Dazzler." Billboard 90:36, September 30, 1978.

10474 Bell, J. N. "I Love Being Diana Ross." McCall's 106:122, October 1978.

10475 "Music Hall, N.Y." Variety 292:177, October 11, 1978.

10476 Boyd, B. M. "Riffs: Diana Ross's Stairway to Heaven." Village Voice 23:87, October 16, 1978. Review of a concert held at Radio City Music Hall.

10477 Mieses, S. "Ross No Wiz." Melody Maker 53:5, October 21, 1978.

10478 "Sneak Preview of Diana Ross with 'Wiz' Stars." Jet 55:20-23, October 26, 1978.

10479 "Diana Ross in the Wiz." Ebony 34:112-116, November 1978.

10480 Schoen, E. "Diana Ross: The Lady Doesn't Sing the Blues." Ladies' Home Journal 95:36, November 1978.

10481 Reilly, P. "Diana Ross Is Dorothy." Stereo Review 41:127, December 1978.

10482 "Albums: Diana." Melody Maker 53:43, December 9, 1978.

10483 McMurran, K. "Screen." People 11:32-34, January 15, 1979.

SAMPSON, SAMMY see BROONZY, BIG BILL

SASSY see VAUGHAN, SARAH LOIS

SATCHMO see ARMSTRONG, LOUIS

SCOTT, HAZEL (Mrs. Adam Clayton Powell), 1920- .

10484 Davis, L., and J. Cleveland. "Hi, Hazel!" Collier's 109:16, April
       18, 1942.

10485 "Hot Classicist." Time 40:88, October 5, 1942.

10486 "Hep Hazel." Newsweek 22:71, November 29, 1943.

10487 Bontemps, A. "Pianist with a Mind of Her Own." Scholastic 46:13-
       14, March 5, 1945.

10488 "Powell Weds Scott." Life 19:30-31, August 13, 1945.

10489 "Help from the D.A.R." Time 46:22, October 22, 1945. Scott
       planned to give a concert in Washington's Constitution Hall, but
       the Daughters of the American Revolution would permit only white
       artists.

10490 "Tea for Fifty Ladies." Newsweek 26:36, October 22, 1945.

10491 "Hazel Scott." Musical News 41:11, February 1949.

10492 "Hazel Scott's 75 Concert Dates to Gross $120,000." Variety 173:49,
       February 2, 1949.

10493 "Hazel Scott, Husband File 50 G Suit Vs. Eatery for Discrimination."
       Variety 173:44, February 23, 1949.

10494 "Hazel Scott Awarded $250 in Discrimination Suit." Variety 178:55,
       April 26, 1950.

10495 "Hazel Crashes TV." Our World 5:60-61, June 1950.

10496 "Hazel Scott Collects Damages from Suit." down beat 17:11, June 2,
       1950.

10497 "Biz Sees Red, Fights Back." Billboard 62:3, September 23, 1950.

10498 "Hazel Scott's Anti-Communist Statement." Billboard 62:4, Septem-
       ber 23, 1950.

10499 "Hazel Scott." Musical America 71:20, June 1951.

10500 Jones, M. "I Never De-compose the Composers!" Melody Maker
       27:3, September 29, 1951.

10501 "Hazel Scott--Parant Barpianist." Orkester Journalen 19:10, December 1951.

10502 "Hazel Scott Scores in 10-Concert Israel Tour." Variety 185:55, January 9, 1952.

10503 "Hazel Scott Walks Out on Memphis Because $1,000 Guarantee Isn't Ante'd Up." Variety 194:43, April 7, 1954.

10504 "'Recording Artists' Roster." down beat 21:123, June 30, 1954.

10505 "Embers, N.Y." Variety 196:61, November 10, 1954.

10506 "Great Scott: Says Hazel of Holiday." down beat 22:19, May 4, 1955.

10507 "Hazel Scott." Musical Courier 15:51, June 1955.

10508 Feather, L. "'Come Back to My Place' Said Hazel--and They Came and Blew." Melody Maker 31:6, August 20, 1955.

10509 "Latin Quarter, N.Y." Variety 201:62, December 14, 1955.

10510 Francis, B. "Whatever Became of Miss Scott?" Billboard 67:38, December 17, 1955.

10511 "Hazel Scott to Keep Jazz After-bit at Recitals." Variety 202:72, March 28, 1956.

10512 "Cameo, N.Y." Variety 202:69, April 25, 1956.

10513 "Caught in the Act." down beat 23:8, June 13, 1956.

10514 "Latin Quarter, N.Y." Variety 203:52, July 4, 1956.

10515 "Mister Kelly's, Chi." Variety 218:53, March 23, 1960.

10516 "The Trials of Hazel Scott and Her Adam Powell." Jet p. 58-60, March 31, 1960.

10517 "Finds Happiness and a New Phase of Her Career." Jet 20:60-61, May 25, 1961.

10518 Robinson, L. "Hazel Scott Comes Home to the Action." Ebony 23:96-98, March 1968.

10519 "What Paris Means to Me." Negro Digest 11:60-62, November 1961.

10520 "Living Room, N.Y." Variety 245:69, January 11, 1967.

10521 "L'Intrigue, N.Y." Variety 246:50, May 17, 1967.

10522 "Playboy Club, L.A." Variety 249:60, February 7, 1968.

10523 Robinson, L. "Hazel Scott Comes Home to the Action." Ebony 23:96-98, March 1968.

10524 Feather, L. "Caught in the Act." down beat 35:42-43, March 21, 1968.

10525   "Plaza 9, N.Y." Variety 253:55, January 22, 1969.

10526   Dove, I. "Hazel Scott Puts Bounce Back in Oldie Tunes." Billboard 81:11, January 25, 1969.

10527   "Rainbow Grill, N.Y." Variety 262:229, May 12, 1971.

10528   Thompson, T. "Hazel Weaves a New Black Magic." Life 70:14, June 18, 1971.

10529   "Hotel St. Regis, N.Y." Variety 267:95, July 19, 1972.

10530   "Jimmy Weston's, N.Y." Variety 271:53, July 11, 1973.

10531   Jefferson, M. "Great (Hazel) Scott!" Ms. 3:25-26, November 1973.

10532   Davis, C. "Hazel Scott: Deeper Now." Encore 4:36-37, August 18, 1975.

10533   Darden, N. J. "Hazel Scott." Essence 9:76-78, November 1978.

SHIRLEY, GEORGE, 1934- .

10534   Selden-Goth, G. "Young American Singers Bow in Florence Opera." Musical Courier 162:41-42, November 1960.

10535   "Awards and Honors." Musical Courier 162:41, December 1961.

10536   Confalonieri, G. "Contests and Concerts." Musical America 81:149, January 1961.

10537   Locklair, W. "Amato Opera." Musical America 81:61, April 1961.

10538   "Shirley, George (Tenor) ... Among 6 Winners of Opera Auditions Sponsored by Metropolitan Opera in N.Y.C." Jet 19:62, April 20, 1961.

10539   Kolodin, I. "Music to My Ears." Saturday Review 44:30, April 22, 1961.

10540   "The Final Round." Opera News 25:20-21, April 29, 1961.

10541   "Audition Winners." Musical America 81:29-30, May 1961.

10542   "George Shirley Met Auditions Winner." Musical Courier 163:8, May 1961.

10543   "George Shirley Winner of Met Opera Audition." Music of the West 16:3, May 1961.

10544   Herst, E. "Plaudits Given to Jack Benny and Others for Musical Feats." Music of the West 16:13, May 1961.

10545   Bloomfield, A. "Spring Opera Debut." Musical America 81:37, July 1961.

10546   Weaver, W. "Spoleto." Opera 12:47, Autumn 1961.

10547   Glass, H. "La Boheme." Musical America 81:27, November 1961.

10548   Ardoin, J. "George Shirley: 2 Years to the Met." Musical America 81:48, December 1961.

10549   Sabin, R. "Stich-Randall Bows in 'Cosi Fan Tutte.'" Musical America 81:28-29, December 1961.

10550   Stevens, D. "New York." Music Magazine 163:42, December 1961.

10551   Ardoin, J. "Madama Butterfly." Musical America 82:208, January 1962.

10552   Brozen, M. "La Traviata." Musical America 82:227, January 1962.

10553   Repass, R. "New York." Opera 13:27, January 1962.

10554   "Shirley, George, Negro Tenor Sings a Leading Role in Mozart's Opera 'Cosi Fan Tutte.'" Interracial Review 35:30, January 1962.

10555   "Washington Honors." Opera News 26:34, February 24, 1962.

10556   Crowder, C. "Brightness and Starkness." Musical America 82:17, March 1962.

10557   Stevenson, F. "Pride of Detroit." Opera News 26:15, April 14, 1962.

10558   "Slated for Success--Nine Young Artists." Musical America 82:11, July 1962.

10559   Bright, R. "New Mexico; The Sixth Season." Musical America 82:18-19, October 1962.

10560   "The Cast." Opera News 27:21, December 8, 1962.

10561   Uebel, R. "Don Giovanni." Musical America 84:37, January 1964.

10562   Brozen, M. "Opera in New York." Musical America 83:25, February 1963.

10563   Martin, G. "'Lulu' Arrives." Opera News 28:12, September 28, 1963.

10564   Ardoin, J. "Manon." Musical America 83:252, December 1963.

10565   ["Recital, New York."] Musical America 84:194, December 1964.

10566   Brown, P. "Detached Mourning." Music and Musicians 13:45, July 1965.

10567   "Tenor in Whiteface." Time 86:54, August 13, 1965.

10568   Ward, H. "Opera/Concert Talk." Music Journal 23:16, October 1965.

10569   "Leading Man at the Met." Ebony 21:84-86, January 1966.

10570   "Negro Tenor Coming to Glyndebourne." Musical Events 21:8, June
        1966.

10571   Montagu, G.   "Glyndebourne Festival."   Musical Opinion 89:653, Au-
        gust 1966.

10572   Greenfield, E.   "London Report: Festival in the Ancient City."   High
        Fidelity/Musical America 16:MA26-27, October 1966.

10573   Syer, W. B.   "'Magic Flute,' Almost All-American."   High Fidelity/
        Musical America 16MA15, November 1966.

10574   Mason, E.   "Cool Thinker."   Music and Musicians 15:34-35, June
        1967.

10575   Rosenthal, H.   "To Scotland for Operatic Tonic."   Opera 18:594-595,
        July 1967.

10576   "'Don Giovanni' Revived."   Musical Events 22:32, August 1967.

10577   "Don Giovanni."   Opera 18:769, September 1967.

10578   Chiusano, M.   "Carnegie Hall."   Music and Artists 1:42, no. 1,
        1968.

10579   Movshon, G.   "And We Quote...."   High Fidelity/Musical America
        18:MA21, January 1968.

10580   "Names, Dates and Places."   Opera News 33:5, December 7, 1968.

10581   Fuchs, H.   "M & A Reviews: Opera and Concert."   Music and Art-
        ists 2:34, no. 1, 1969.

10582   Schonberg, H. C., and H. Johnson.   "M & A Reviews: The Press."
        Music and Artists 2:44, no. 1, 1969.

10583   Movshon, G.   "Mozart's 'Cosi'; Truly Complete and Sumptuously
        Cast."   High Fidelity/Musical America 19:78-79, January 1969.

10584   Mayer, M.   "Simon Boccanegra."   High Fidelity/Musical America
        19:MA11, February 1969.

10585   "The Musical Whirl."   High Fidelity/Musical America 19:MA14-15,
        February 1969.

10586   Goodwin, N.   "Guildmen at the Garden."   Music and Musicians 17:26,
        March 1969.

10587   "London Opera Diary."   Opera 20:259, March 1969.

10588   Natan, A.   "Reizt zu Zustimmung, Widerspruch und Nachdenken."
        Opern Welt no. 3:27, March 1969.

10589   Barker, F. G.   "London."   Opera News 33:32-33, March 1, 1969.

10590   "Names, Dates and Places."   Opera News 34:5, December 6, 1969.

10591   "Spotlight."   Music and Artists 3:55, no. 1, 1970.

10592 Chapman, E. "'Pelleas' at Covent Garden." Musical Events 25:11, January 1970.

10593 Wocker, K. H. "London: 'Pelleas und Melisande.'" Orchester 18:126-128, March 1970.

10594 "The Musical Whirl." High Fidelity/Musical America 20:23, May 1970, Section 2.

10595 "Names, Dates and Places." Opera News 35:5, September 5, 1970.

10596 Gould, B. "A Series of Met Firsts." Music Journal 28:24, November 1970.

10597 Shirley, G. "Black Performer; From the Minstrels to the Met." Opera News 35:6-13, January 30, 1971.

10598 "The Black Performer." Opera 22:858-867, October 1971.

10599 Mayer, M. "Recordings." Esquire 76:72, December 1971.

10600 Blyth, A. "'Pelleas et Melisande'; Royal Opera, Covent Garden." Opera 23:273, March 1972.

10601 Crichton, R. "Recitals." Musical Times 113:283-284, March 1972.

10602 Simmons, D. "London Music." Musical Opinion 95:288, March 1972.

10603 Turner, G. "Singers." Music and Musicians, 20:78, May 1972.

10604 "Names, Dates and Places." Opera News 37:6-7, February 3, 1973.

10605 Jahant, C. "Washington." Opera 24:447-448, May 1973.

10606 Wimbush, R. "Here and There." Gramophone 51:1363, January 1974.

10607 "Names, Dates and Places." Opera News 38:8-9, June 1974.

10608 Rosenthal, H. "'Idomeneo' at Glyndebourne." Opera 25:585-586, July 1974.

10609 Donington, R. "'Das Rheingold,' 'Die Walkuere.'" Musical Times 115:962, November 1972.

10610 "Names, Dates and Places." Opera News 41:6-7, December 18, 1976.

10611 Lucano, R. V. "Haydn's Mad Knight." American Record Guide 41:16-17, November 1977.

SILBERSTEIN, MRS. ROBERT ELLIS see ROSS, DIANA

SIMONE, NINA (Eunice Waymon), 1933- .

10612   "Nina Loves Porgy; Gershwin Tune Makes Singer-Pianist a Star."
        Ebony 15:169-170, December 1959.

10613   "Nina Simone." Musica Jazz 16:17, April 1960.

10614   "The Rareness of Nina Simone." Metronome 77:30, June 1960.

10615   Hepburn, D. "Little Girl Blue; Nina Simone." Sepia 8:28-31, Oc-
        tober 1960.

10616   Dutton, F. "Odds and Soda-Mints." Jazz Journal 13:27, November
        1960.

10617   "Songstress Won't Tell If She Has Card in New Test of N.Y. Police
        Authority." Variety 221:50, December 14, 1960.

10618   "Village Vanguard, N.Y." Variety 221:54, January 25, 1961.

10619   "Nina's Style Is Rooted in the Blues." Melody Maker 36:7, Febru-
        ary 4, 1961.

10620   Lucas, B. "Simone, Nina." Negro Digest 11:22-25, February 1962.

10621   "Caught in the Act." down beat 30:34, April 11, 1963.

10622   "Simmering Down." Newsweek 62:82, September 30, 1963.

10623   Williams, M. "Mostly About Pianists." Saturday Review 49:130,
        March 12, 1966.

10624   "Nina Simone's '4 Women' Getting Stations' Snubs; Similar Cases Re-
        called." Variety 244:1, September 14, 1966.

10625   Tiegel, E. "Nina Simone Keeps Patrons in the Right Mood: Loose."
        Billboard 79:32, February 4, 1967.

10626   "Nina Simone; Angry Woman of Jazz." Sepia 16:60-64, March 1967.

10627   Feather, L. "Nina High Priestess of Soul Heads for Vegas." Mel-
        ody Maker 42:13, March 11, 1967.

10628   Didymus, G. "Caught in the Act." Melody Maker 42:6, April 22,
        1967.

10629   Tiegel, E. "Jazz Beat." Billboard 79:14, August 5, 1967.

10630   "Nina Simone Pulls SRO $11,000 in Swinging Bash at Carnegie Hall,
        N.Y." Variety 249:51, January 10, 1968.

10631   Zwerin, M. "The Real Nina Simone." down beat 35:16-17, January
        11, 1968.

10632   Ochs, E. "Loyal Subjects Hail Queen Nina at Carnegie Concert."
        Billboard 80:16, January 20, 1968.

10633   "Troubadour, L.A." Variety 250:66, March 20, 1968.

10634 Lees, G. "A Jazz Celebration at Montreux." High Fidelity/Musical America 18:104, September 1968.

10635 Walsh, A. "Nina Hits with 'Hair.'" Melody Maker 43:14, November 23, 1968.

10636 Smith, M. "The Other (More Serious) Side of Nina." Melody Maker 43:7, December 7, 1968.

10636a Walsh, A. "The Fantasy World of Nina Simone." Melody Maker 43:13, December 21, 1968.

10637 "Caught in the Act." down beat 36:34-35, January 23, 1969.

10638 "More than an Entertainer." Time 93:63, February 21, 1969.

10639 Wilson, J. S. "Nina Simone." International Musician 67:8, April 1969.

10640 Eldridge, R. "Nina's the Medium for the Message." Melody Maker 44:5, April 19, 1969.

10641 Cullaz, M. "Un Divine Nina." Jazz Hot no. 250:7, May 1969.

10642 Hofstein, F. "Nina: Back to Black." Jazz Magazine no. 166:13, May 1969.

10643 "Caught in the Act." down beat 36:36, May 1, 1969; 36:28, July 24, 1969.

10644 Garland, P. "Nina Simone, High Priestess of Soul." Ebony 24:156-159, August 1969. An excerpt from Garland's The Sound of Soul: The Music and Its Meaning.

·10645 Cullaz, M. "Antibes." Jazz Hot no. 253:41, September 1969.

10646 _____. "Nina Simone." Jazz Hot no. 253:23, September 1969.

10647 Gerber, A. "Antibes an 10." Jazz Magazine no. 169-170:61-62, September 1969.

10648 Reilly, P. "Nina Simone; The Tigress Learns to Purr." Stereo Review 23:94, September 1969.

10649 "Concert Reviews." Variety 256:60, October 29, 1969.

10650 Ehrlich, N. "Nina Simone in Prize-Winning Form in Concert." Billboard 81:22, November 8, 1969.

10651/2 "Caught in the Act." Melody Maker 29:6, November 22, 1969; Variety 257:52, December 17, 1969.

10653 Dahlgren, R. "Nina Simone Artisteri av Hoegsta Klass." Orkester Journalen 38:12, January 1970.

10654 "Disques du Mois: 'Heart and Soul.'" Jazz Magazine no. 179:41-42, June 1970.

10655 "Concert Reviews." Variety 259:46, June 3, 1970.

10656   Smith, W. "Record Reviews: To Love Somebody." Jazz and Pop
        9:42, July 1970.

10657   Cullaz, M. "La Chronique des Disques." Jazz Hot no. 264:44-45,
        September 1970.

10658   Feather, L. "Newport sans Grise." Jazz Magazine no. 181:12,
        September 1970.

10659   Goldman, A. "Return of the Queen of Shebang." Life 69:11, Oc-
        tober 2, 1970. After studying at Juilliard, Simone found jazz to
        be a more profitable way to use her musical talent.

10660   Angelou, M. "Nina Simone: High Priestess of Soul." Redbook
        136:77, November 1970.

10661   "The Best of Nina Simone." Stereo Review 26:105, January 1971.

10662   "Pop Albums: Black Gold." Melody Maker 46:23, January 30, 1971.

10663   Traill, S. "Record Reviews: Black God." Jazz Journal 24:38,
        March 1971.

10664   Feather, L. "Caught in the Act." Melody Maker 46:32, May 8,
        1971.

10665   _____. "Los Angeles." Jazz Magazine no. 189:11, May 1971.

10666   Joe, R. "Talent in Action." Billboard 83:22, May 22, 1971.

10667   Wickham, V. "Nina the Leader." Melody Maker 46:8, May 22,
        1971.

10668   Stewart-Baxter, D. "Record Reviews: Heart and Soul." Jazz
        Journal 24:40, June 1971.

10669   Crouse, T. "Records: Here Comes the Sun." Rolling Stone no.
        88:45, August 5, 1971.

10670   "Concert Reviews." Variety 264:50, October 20, 1971.

10671   Joe, R. "Talent in Action." Billboard 83:14, October 23, 1971.

10672   Bartley, G. F. "Nina Simone Ripped-Off in New York." Soul 6:4,
        January 31, 1972.

10673   "Concert Reviews." Variety 267:44, July 5, 1972.

10674   "Nina Simone Sees 'Bias' Vs. Black Songstresses; Sez 'Kill the
        Pushers.'" Variety 267:1, July 26, 1972.

10675   "Records: Emergency Ward!" Rolling Stone no. 121:62, November
        9, 1972.

10676   Merla, P. The Merging of Pop and Rock." Saturday Review 1:54,
        January 6, 1973.

10677   Rockwell, J. "New York." Opera News 37:25, March 3, 1973.

10678 Watts, M. "Return of the Priestess." <u>Melody Maker</u> 48:24, May 12, 1973.

10679 "Concert Reviews." <u>Variety</u> 271:34, August 8, 1973.

10680 "Three Music Names that Spell Greatness." <u>Soul</u> 8:10-11, October 1, 1973.

10681 "Soul Reviews." <u>Soul</u> 8:6, November 26, 1973.

10682 Korall, B. "The Pop and Jazz Scene." <u>International Musician</u> 73:7, July 1974.

10683 "Records: It Is Finished." <u>Crawdaddy</u> no. 43:80-81, December 1974.

10684 Reilly, P. "Nina Simone Has Only Just Begun." <u>Stereo Review</u> 33:98, December 1974. Review of Simone's recording "It Is Finished."

10685 "An Often Misunderstood Lady." <u>Soul</u> 10:11, July 7, 1975.

10686 "Record Reviews: The Finest of Nina Simone: I Loves You Porgy." <u>down beat</u> 43:34, July 15, 1976.

10687 "Nina Simone Takes a Grand Slam at Music Industry." <u>Variety</u> 285:2, January 26, 1977.

10688 "Simone: Don't Let Me Be Misunderstood." <u>Melody Maker</u> 52:24, February 5, 1977.

10689 Siders, H. "Perfectionist Carmen McRae." <u>Jazz Magazine</u> (U.S.) 3:34-37, no. 1, 1978.

10690 Ferdinand, V. "Baltimore." <u>Black Collegian</u> 8:65, May-June 1978.

10691 "Albums: Baltimore." <u>Melody Maker</u> 53:20, July 1, 1978.

10692 "Caught in the Act." <u>Melody Maker</u> 53:14, July 29, 1978.

10693 "Records: Baltimore." <u>Rolling Stone</u> no. 271:54, August 10, 1978.

10694 Garland, P. "Well Worth a Four-Year Wait: A Fresh Release from Nina Simone." <u>Stereo Review</u> 41:99-100, September 1978.

10695 Mieses, S. "Nina and Courage Bring Me to Tears." <u>Melody Maker</u> 53:4, December 30, 1978.

SMITH, BESSIE, 1898?-1937.

10696 "Bessie's Blues." <u>Time</u> 30:38, November 22, 1937.

10697 Thompson, K. C. "An Interview with Sidney Bechet." <u>Record Changer</u> 8:9-10, July 1949.

10698 Moon, B. "The Horn Behind the Blues." <u>Record Changer</u> 9:14, July-August 1950.

10699 Stevens, A., and H. Giltrap. "Good Queen Bess." Jazz Journal 3:17, September 1950.

10700 Dahlgren, C. "Amerikanskt Stjarnalbum--Bessie Smith." Orkester Journalen 18:5, October 1950.

10701 Emge, C. "Showing of Jazz Movies Arouses Big Storm in L.A." down beat 17:9, November 17, 1950.

10702 "Bessie Smith in 'St. Louis Blues.'" Jazz Journal 4:4, January 1951.

10703 "Bessie Smith--Supreme Jazz Artist." Melody Maker 27:9, January 29, 1951.

10704 Borneman, E. "The Difference Between Concert Music and Folk Music." Melody Maker 27:2, April 21, 1951.

10705 Webman, H. "Bessie Smith Lives Again on Disks, Bringing Back Her Rich, Hot Blues." Billboard 63:3, December 15, 1951.

10706 "Forty-Seven of Bessie's Songs--on Four Discs!" Melody Maker 27:9, December 22, 1951.

10707 Hobson, W. "Jewels of the Empress: Bessie Smith." Saturday Review of Literature 34:33, December 29, 1951.

10708 Levin, F. "The American Jazz Scene." Jazz Journal 5:4-5, January 1952.

10709 Staley, R., and G. H. Boas. "In Memoriam--Bessie Smith." Jazz Journal 5:12-13, September 1952.

10710 "Bessie Smith Songs on Sale." Billboard 64:1, October 18, 1952.

10711 Liden, R. "Bessie Smith." Orkester Journalen 21:10-11, July 1953.

10712 "An Unusual Photograph of Bessie Smith as a Young Girl." Jazz Journal 7:11, September 1954.

10713 Stewart-Baxter, D. "The Bessie Smith Story." Jazz Journal 8:27-28, April 1955.

10714 "The Legendary Recordings of Bessie Smith." Record Research 1:5, June 1955.

10715 Melly, G. "The Bessie Smith Story." Melody Maker 31:4, December 3, 1955.

10716 Jepsen, J. G. "Kvinnliga Vokalister." Orkester Journalen 24:14, February 1956.

10717 Kunstadt, L. "From the Archives." Record Research 2:2, May-June 1956.

10718 Preston, D. "Blue Yodel No. 9." Melody Maker 32:6, May 11, 1957.

10719 Hoefer, G. "The Hot Box." down beat 24:6, October 17, 1957.

10720 "Bessie Redivivus in Three Thoughtful Tries." High Fidelity/Musical America 8:68, June 1958.

10721 Oliver, Paul. Bessie Smith. New York: Barnes, 1961, c1959.

10722 "'Empress of the Blues' Died 21 Years Ago Beside Dark Highway, North of Clarksdale." Second Line 10:9-11, July-August 1959.

10723 Tamony, P. "Bessie: Documentary." Jazz no. 4:280-285, Fall 1959.

10724 "The True Story of Bessie Smith's Death." Second Line 10:9-10, September-October 1959.

10725 Tenot, F. "L'Imperatrice du Blues." Jazz Magazine 6:44-49, December 1959.

10726 "A Short Play, 'The Death of Bessie Smith' Written by Edward Albee About the Death of the Blues Singer." Jet p. 62, May 5, 1960.

10727 McRae, B. "The Ma Rainey and Bessie Smith Accompaniments." Jazz Journal 14:6-8, March 1961.

10728 Lyttelton, H. "She Sold over Eight Million Jazz Discs." Melody Maker 36:3, March 4, 1961.

10729 De Toledano, R. "Empress of the Blues." National Review 10:426-427, July 1, 1961.

10730 Testoni, G. "Gli Autori dei Temi." Musica Jazz 18:34, January 1962.

10731 Spivey, V. "Blues Is My Business." Record Research no. 44:7, July 1962.

10732 "Bessie Smith Story Readied for Movies." down beat 30:12, October 10, 1963.

10733 Allen, W. C. "Hendersonia." Record Research no. 56:12, November 1963.

10734 "Frank Walker Finds Bessie Smith." Billboard 75:43, November 2, 1963 Supplement.

10735 Jones, M. "Great Jazz Solos." Melody Maker 41:6, September 3, 1966.

10736 Shaw, A. "100 Years of the Blues." Billboard 79:10, June 24, 1967 Supplement.

10737 Morgenstern, D. "Hall of Fame Winner Bessie Smith: Empress of the Blues." down beat 34:22-23, August 24, 1967.

10738 McRae, B. "A B Basics." Jazz Journal 21:5, January 1968.

10739 Jones, M. "Magnificent Seven." Melody Maker 43:8, January 13, 1968.

10740   Moore, Carman. Somebody's Angel Child; The Story of Bessie
        Smith. New York: Crowell, 1969. Juvenile literature.

10741   Polillo, A. "Bessie the Great." Jazz Journal 22:6-8, April 1969.

10742   Grimes, S. "True Death of Bessie Smith." Esquire 71:112-113,
        June 1969. Several accounts of Smith's car accident and death
        are related.

10743   Worsfold, S. A. "Empress of the Blues." Storyville no. 25:28-31,
        October-November 1969.

10744   Affeldt, P. E. "After Thirty Years, a Marker Is Put on Bessie
        Smith's Grave." Jazz Report 7:4, no. 3, 1970.

10745   "Bessie Smith--the World's Greatest Blues Singer." Jazz Report
        7:11, no. 3, 1970.

10746   "Put It Right Here or Keep It Out There." Black Scholar 1:46, Jan-
        uary-February 1970.

10747   Dance, S. "The Empire of the Empress." Jazz Journal 23:6, May
        1970.

10748   Ackerman, P. "Historic Bessie Smith Set Aimed at Youth Market."
        Billboard 82:1, May 30, 1970.

10749   "Columbia Records to Release Entire Bessie Smith Catalog." Jazz
        and Pop 9:10, June 1970.

10750   Dance, S. "Jazz." Music Journal 28:18, June 1970.

10751   "Bessie Smith Grave No Longer Unmarked." Second Line 23:370,
        July-August 1970.

10752   "Les Integrales de Bessie." Jazz Magazine no. 180:13, July-August
        1970.

10753   "Record Reviews: The World's Greatest Blues Singer." Storyville
        no. 30:236, August-September 1970.

10754   "Miss Bessie's Blues." Time 96:40, August 3, 1970.

10755   Dance, S. "The Empress Still Reigns." Saturday Review 53:41, Au-
        gust 29, 1970. Columbia is releasing a collection of all of Smith's
        blues recordings.

10756   "Dave Oxley Tells His Story." Second Line 23:388-389, September-
        October 1970. Oxley's version of Smith's fatal car accident.

10757   "Record Reviews: The World's Greatest Blues Singer." Jazz and
        Pop 9:62-63, September 1970.

10758   "Bessie Smith's Grave Gets Stone Dedication." Billboard 82:77,
        September 5, 1970.

10759   "Bessie Smith's Belated Gift." Rolling Stone no. 66:18, September
        17, 1970.

10760 "A Stone for Bessie's Grave--33 Years Late." down beat 37:8, September 17, 1970.

10761 "Graveyard Blues." Melody Maker 45:5, September 26, 1970.

10762 Dance, S. "Lightly & Politely." Jazz Journal 23:8, October 1970.

10763 Feather, L. "Aentligen Gravsten foer Bessie Smith." Orkester Journalen 38:6-7, October 1970.

10764 Ames, M. "First Lady of the Blues; The Initial Installment of Columbia's Complete Bessie Smith Recordings." High Fidelity/Musical America 20:86-87, October 1970.

10765 Jones, M. "Jazz Records: The World's Greatest Blues Singer." Melody Maker 45:34, October 24, 1970.

10766 "Record Reviews: The World's Greatest Blues Singer." down beat 37:21-22, October 29, 1970.

10767 "Tribute to Bessie Smith." Jazz and Pop 9:10, November 1970.

10768 Schuller, G. "Bessie Smith." down beat 37:37-38, November 12, 1970. An excerpt from Schuller's book Early Jazz.

10769 Noel, G. "La Chronique des Disques: The World's Greatest Blues Singer." Jazz Hot no. 267:48, December 1970.

10770 "Record Reviews: The World's Greatest Blues Singer." Rolling Stone no. 72:48, December 2, 1970.

10771 "Bessie Smith--the Empress." Jazz Report 7:23, no. 6, 1971.

10772 Mitchell, B. "Vinyl Highlights: Empty Bed Blues." Jazz Report 7:16-17, no. 5, 1971.

10773 "Record Reviews: The World's Greatest Blues Singer." Footnote 2:26-27, no. 3, 1971.

10774 Cullaz, M. "La Chronique des Disques: Any Woman's Blues." Jazz Hot no. 268:38, January 1971.

10775 "Reeditions: The World's Greatest Blues Singer." Jazz Magazine no. 185:45, January 1971.

10776 Voce, S. "Record Reviews: The World's Greatest Blues Singer." Jazz Journal 24:35, January 1971.

10777 Gerber, L. "The Complete Bessie Smith." American Record Guide 37:340-342, February 1971.

10778 Saal, H. "Bessie's Blues." Newsweek 77:44-45, February 1, 1971.

10779 "Bessie Smith." Billboard 83:8, February 13, 1971.

10780 Jones, M. "Jazz Records: Any Woman's Blues." Melody Maker 46:32, February 20, 1971.

10781   Crais, B.   "The Taping of Bessie Smith."   Second Line 25:49-50,
        Spring 1971.

10782   "Record Reviews: Any Woman's Blues."   Jazz Journal 24:38, March
        1971.

10783   "Any Woman's Blues."   Blues Unlimited no. 81:23, April 1971.

10784   Pleasants, H.   "Bessie Smith--World's Greatest Blues Singer."
        Stereo Review 26:100-101, April 1971.

10785   "Reeditions: Any Woman's Blues."   Jazz Magazine no. 188:45-46,
        April 1971.

10786   McMillan, L. K.   "Sounds."   Essence 2:78, May 1971.

10787   Jones, M.   "Jazz Records: Empty Bed Blues."   Melody Maker 46:26,
        June 12, 1971.

10788   Gleason, R.   "Records: Bessie Smith--World's Greatest Blues Sing-
        er; Any Woman's Blues; Empty Bed Blues."   Rolling Stone no.
        85:48, June 24, 1971.

10789   Traill, S.   "Record Reviews: Empty Bed Blues."   Jazz Journal
        24:34, August 1971.

10790   Balliett, W.   "Jazz Records; B. Smith Reissue Project."   New
        Yorker 47:160-166, November 6, 1971.

10791   Albertson, Chris.   Bessie.   New York: Stein and Day, 1972.   A
        definitive biography of Smith.

10792   _____.   "In Search of the Real Bessie Smith."   Jazz Report
        8:3-4, no. 2, 1972.

10793   "Die 'Niemand Kennt Dich'--Legende."   Neue Musikzeitung 21:11, no.
        2, 1972.

10794   "Record Reviews: Empty Bed Blues; The Empress."   Coda 10:18-19,
        no. 5, 1972.

10795   "Jazz Records: The Empress."   Melody Maker 47:34, January 15,
        1972.

10796   Albertson, C.   "In Search of the Real Bessie Smith."   Saturday Re-
        view 55:56, February 26, 1972.

10797   "Schallplattenbesprechungen: The Empress."   Jazz Podium 21:87,
        March 1972.

10798   "Disques du Mois: The Empress."   Jazz Magazine no. 199:44, April
        1972.

10799   Balliett, W.   "Bessie Smith Plain."   New Yorker 49:128-129, Feb-
        ruary 24, 1973.

10800   Boas, G.   "Bessie Smith: Empress of the Blues."   Jazz Podium
        22:16-18, March 1973.

10801   Stewart-Baxter, D. "Blues and Views." Jazz Journal 26:2, March
        1973.

10802   "Jazz Records: Nobody's Blues but Mine." Melody Maker 48:50,
        March 10, 1973.

10803   "Records: Nobody's Blues but Mine." Crawdaddy no. 23:78-79,
        April 1973.

10804   Stewart-Baxter, D. "Blues and Views." Jazz Journal 26:12, April
        1973. Review of the second issue of a five volume set of Smith's
        works.

10805   "Rights to Biopic of Bessie Smith Stalling Filming." Variety 270:1,
        April 11, 1973.

10806   Maranca, B. "Bessie Smith Story." Jazz Magazine no. 211:12-13,
        May 1973.

10807   Stewart-Baxter, D. "Blues and Views." Jazz Journal 26:53-54,
        May 1973; 26:2, June 1973.

10808   Dance, S. "Bessie Again." Jazz Journal 26:18-19, July 1973.

10809   "On Record: Nobody's Blues but Mine." Jazz & Blues 3:26, Sep-
        tember 1973.

10810   "W. C. Handy, Bessie Smith Honored." down beat 40:10, December
        20, 1973.

10811   Dugan, J., and J. Hammond. "An Early Black-Music Concert 'From
        Spirituals to Swing.'" Black Perspectives in Music 2:196-206, no.
        2, 1974. Discussion of a Carnegie Hall concert held December 23,
        1938.

10812   Jones, Hettie. Big Star Fallin' Mama; Five Women in Black Music.
        New York: Viking Press, 1974. Juvenile literature about Ma
        Rainey, Mahalia Jackson, Billie Holiday, Aretha Franklin, and
        Bessie Smith.

10813   Gleason, Ralph J. Celebrating the Duke, and Louis, Bessie, Billie,
        Bird, Carmen, Miles, Dizzy, and Other Heroes. Boston: Little,
        Brown, 1975.

10814   Lees, G. "Linda as Bessie: One of the Most Exciting Theater
        Pieces in Years." High Fidelity/Musical America 24:14-15, May
        1975.

10815   Williams, J. "Linda Hopkins Feels Role of Bessie Smith in Play."
        Billboard 87:37, June 7, 1975. Discussion of "Me and Bessie."

10816   "Bessie Smith 'Heir' Sues for Royalties." Variety 279:99, July 16,
        1975.

10817   "Shows on Broadway: 'Me and Bessie.'" Variety 280:72, October
        29, 1975.

10818   Joe, R. "Linda Hopkins Resembles Blues Queen Bessie Smith."
        Billboard 87:32, November 1, 1975.

10819 Davis, C. "Me and Bessie." Encore 4:34, December 8, 1975.

10820 "'Me and Bessie' Hits Broadway." down beat 42:10, December 18,
       1975.

10821 "Linda Hopkins Outside of Bessie Smith." Encore 4:29, December
       22, 1975.

10822 "Members in Profile." Sacred Music 103:32, no. 3, 1976.

10823 "Bessie Smith Suit Vs. CBS Tests Flat-Fee Disk Pacts." Variety
       285:59, December 1, 1976.

10824 "Bessie Smith Heirs Sue CBS: Say Discrimination." Billboard 88:67,
       December 11, 1976.

10825 Bentley, J. "I Remember Bessie--Art Hodes Plays Bessie Smith
       and Ma Rainey." Jazz Report 9:12, no. 4, 1977.

10826 Lear, L. "Lawsuit for What's Owed Bessie Smith." Sepia 26:65-69,
       September 1977.

10827 "John Hammond." Jazz Magazine (U.S.) 2:33, no. 2, 1978. An ex-
       cerpt from John Hammond on Record: An Autobiography which in-
       cludes information on Billie Holiday and Bessie Smith.

10828 Moss, G. "I Remember Bessie Smith." Essence 9:66-67, Decem-
       ber 1978.

SMITH, MAMIE (Trixie), 1883-1946.

10829 Spencer, O. "First Blues Disc Was Made by Mamie Smith." down
       beat 8:8, no. 12, 1941.

10830 "Mamie Smith; A Very Tentative Discography of Her Okeh Record-
       ings, with Rega Orchestra." Jazz Journal 3:20, December 1950.

10831 Tanner, P. "Oh, Didn't They Ramble!" Melody Maker 26:9, De-
       cember 23, 1950.

10832 Kunstadt, L., and B. Colton. "Mamie Smith, 'The First Lady of
       the Blues.'" Record Research no. 31:6-7, November 1960.

10833 "Mamie Smith; A Provisional Discography." Record Research no.
       57:8-12, January 1964. Reprinted from Discophile, November
       1961.

10834 Smith, E. R. "The Film Career of Mamie Smith." Record Research
       no. 65:3, December 1964.

SMITH, WILLIE THE LION (William Henry Joseph Berthol Bonaparte Berth-
oloff), 1897-1973.

10835 "The Lion: Willie Smith." Time 34:64, October 2, 1939.

10836   Goepfert, A. "The 'Lion' and Others in Switzerland." Jazz Journal
        3:5, May 1950.

10837   Decker, D. "Lion on the Loose." Negro Digest 9:69-74, July 1951.

10838   Jepsen, J. G. "Jazzens Instrumentalister: Altsaxen." Orkester
        Journalen 23:14, May 1955.

10839   "The Lion to Roar 40th Year of Jazz." down beat 23:11, November
        28, 1956.

10840   Smith, E. R. "The Lion Roars." Record Research 2:2, January-
        February 1957.

10841   "From Muggs to Diz, They Honor the Lion." down beat 24:11, Jan-
        uary 9, 1957.

10842   Feather, L. "The Lion Roars." down beat 25:39, April 17, 1958.

10843   Waterman, G. "The Lion Roars." Jazz Review 1:39, December
        1958.

10844   Davin, T. "Conversations with James P. Johnson." Jazz Review
        2:13-14, August 1959.

10845   "Piccola Enciclopedia del Curioso." Musica Jazz 16:43, June 1960.

10846   Testoni, G. "Gli Autori dei Temi." Musica Jazz 18:34, January
        1962.

10847   Rosenkrantz, T. "Reflections: Willie the Lion." down beat 30:21,
        February 14, 1963.

10848   "Annuaire Biographique du Piano." Jazz Magazine 9:36-37, Novem-
        ber 1963.

10849   Smith, Willie, and George Hoefer. Music on My Mind: The Mem-
        oirs of an American Pianist. New York: Da Capo Press, 1978.
        Reprint of the 1964 edition published by Doubleday, New York.

10850   "Willie 'the Alto' Smith Rides Again." Jazz 4:23, no. 11, 1965.

10851   Lucas, J. "Lord and Lion: Let the Records Set the Record
        Straight." Second Line 16:61-64, May-June 1965.

10852   "The Lion: Digging the Local Vibrations." Melody Maker 40:7, No-
        vember 13, 1965.

10853   Ellington, D. "The Most Essential Instrument." Jazz Journal 18:14-
        15, December 1965.

10854   Traill, S. "Editorial." Jazz Journal 18:5, December 1965.

10855   "Le Lion à Paris." Jazz Magazine no. 126:13-14, January 1966.

10856   Niquet, B. "Un Lion Salle Corot." Jazz Hot no. 216:9, January
        1966.

10857   Traill, S. "In My Opinion." Jazz Journal 19:7-8, July 1966.

10858   "Still Roaring." Time 90:38, July 28, 1967.

10859   Hentoff, N. "A Happy Meeting with Willie 'the Lion' Smith--Don
        Ewell and 'the Lion' Collaborate in a Robust Four-Hand Tribute
        to the Stride Piano Style." HiFi/Stereo Review 19:80, September 1967.

10860   "Tooters Help Willie Smith Mark His 70th Milestone." Variety
        249:45, November 22, 1967.

10861   Arvanitas, G., et al. "Panorama des Pianistes." Jazz Hot no.
        246:28, January 1969.

10862   Russell, R. "Jazz Record Review." Jazz and Pop 8:52-53, January
        1969.

10863   Norris, J. "Rowntowner (Montecello) Motor Inn." Coda 10:45-46,
        no. 2, 1971.

10864   Crouse, T. "How Willie the Lion Won the War." Rolling Stone no.
        80:12, April 15, 1971.

10865   Goddet, L. "La Chronique des Disques: Original Piano Solo." Jazz
        Hot no. 276:34, October 1971.

10866   "Record Reviews: Grand Piano." Jazz Journal 24:37-38, December 1971.

10867   "Record Reviews: Grand Piano, Willie 'the Lion' Smith/Don Ewell."
        Footnote 3:34, no. 5, 1972.

10868   "Record Reviews: Grand Piano." Jazz & Blues 1:24, January 1972.

10869   "Record Reviews: California Here I Come." down beat 39:21, Feb-
        ruary 17, 1972.

10870   Dance, S. "Jazz." Music Journal 30:22, June 1972.

10871   "Chronique des Disques: Pork and Beans." Jazz Hot no. 287:30,
        October 1972.

10872   Simmen, J. "Trois Gentlemen qui Firent Tanguer le Zuercher Ton-
        halle." Points du Jazz no. 7:80-104, October 1972.

10873   Affeldt, P. E. ["Obituary."] Jazz Report 8:32, no. 3, 1973.

10874   ["Obituary."] Black Perspectives in Music 1:200, no. 2, 1973; Foot-
        note 4:14, no. 5, 1973; IAJRC Journal 6:24, no. 2, 1973.

10875   "Record Reviews: Live at Blues Alley." down beat 40:25, March
        15, 1973.

10876   ["Obituary."] Variety 270:63, April 25, 1973; International Musician
        71:28, May 1973; Jazz Podium 22:6, May 1973.

10877   "Portrait of the Lion." Jazz Magazine no. 211:9-10, May 1973.

10878   Jones, M. "The Lion Sleeps." Melody Maker 48:24, May 5, 1973.

10879   Gleason, R. J. "Perspectives: Willie the Lion Had a Mighty Roar."
        Rolling Stone no. 135:7, May 24, 1973.

10880 ["Obituary."] Second Line 25:33, Summer 1973; Jazz Journal 26:1,
       June 1973.

10881 Von Konow, A. ["Obituary."] Orkester Journalen 41:5, June 1973.

10882 ["Obituary."] down beat 40:11, June 7, 1973.

10883 "Willie (the Lion) Smith, 1897-1973." Ragtimer p. 15-16, July-
       August 1973.

10884 ["Obituary."] Crawdaddy no. 26:21, July 1973.

10885 Stewart-Baxter, D. ["Obituary."] Jazz Journal 26:23, July 1973.

10886 "The Lion Strides Off." Jazz Forum no. 24:27, August 1973.

10887 "Quelques Grands Pianistes." Jazz Hot no. 305:10, May 1974.

10888 "Record Reviews: Memorial." Jazz Journal 27:43, December 1974.

10889 Newberger, E. H. "The Transition from Ragtime to Improvised
       Piano Style." Journal of Jazz Studies 3:16-17, no. 2, 1976.

10890 _____. "The Development of New Orleans and Stride Piano
       Styles." Journal of Jazz Studies 4:59-60, no. 1977.

10891 "Records in Brief--Reissues: Black and White Masters." Coda no.
       156:24, July-August 1977.

10892 Feather, L. "Piano Giants of Jazz: Willie 'the Lion' Smith."
       Contemporary Keyboard 3:55, October 1977.

10893 Russell, W. "Albert Nicholas Talks About Jelly Roll." Second Line
       30:5-6, Spring 1978. Interview with Nicholas in which he remin-
       isces about Morton and Smith.

10894 Doerschuk, B. "Ellington Protege--Brooks Kerr." Contemporary
       Keyboard 4:41, November 1978.

10895 "Record Reviews: Cliff Jackson--Willie 'the Lion' Smith--Don
       Frye." Jazz Journal International 31:40, December 1978.

SOMMER, MRS. HELMUT see SUMMER, DONNA

STILL, WILLIAM GRANT, 1895-1978.

10896 "Jazz Symphony." Time 30:44-45, December 20, 1937.

10897 Arvey, V., and W. G. Still. "Negro Music in the Americas."
       La Revue Internationale de Musique 2:7-8, May-June 1938.

10898 Arvey, V. William Grant Still. New York: Fischer, 1939.

10899 Embree, Edwin Rogers. 13 Against the Odds. Port Washington,
       N.Y.: Kennikat Press, 1968. Reprint of the 1944 edition which
       has biographies of 13 blacks including the musician W. G. Still.

10900   Pilcher, J. M.   "Negro Spiritual, Lively Leaven in the American
        Way of Life."   Etude 64:194, April 1946.

10901   "Blues in California."   Time   51:55, June 7, 1948.

10902   Gehrkens, K. W.   "How About William Grant Still?"   Etude 66:478,
        August 1948.

10903   "William Grant Still."   Music Journal 7:21, January-February 1949.

10904   West, S.   "Composer Needs Determination and Faith."   Etude 67:7-8,
        January 1949.

10905   "Troubled Island."   Musical America 69:5, April 1, 1949; Newsweek
        33:86, April 11, 1949; Time 53:71, April 11, 1949.

10906   Still, W. G.   "The Structure of Music."   Etude 68:17, March 1950.

10907   _____.   "Negrene i Amerikansk Musik."   Dansk Musiktidsskrift
        26:91-96, no. 5, 1951.

10908   Goss, Madeleine Binkley.   Modern Music-Makers, Contemporary
        American Composers.   New York: Dutton, 1952.   Grant is the
        only black musician included.

10909   "William Grant Still."   Pan Pipes 44:45, January 1952; 45:67-68,
        January 1953.

10910   Kyle, M. K.   "AmerAllegro."   Pan Pipes 46:62, January 1954.

10911   "William Grant Still."   Pan Pipes 47:68-69, January 1955.

10912   Still, W. G.   "Serious Music: New Field for the Negro."   Variety
        197:227, January 5, 1955.

10913   Kyle, M. K.   "AmerAllegro."   Pan Pipes 48:74, January 1956;
        49:70, January 1957; 50:73-74, January 1958.

10914   "To You, America; for Band."   Music Library Association Notes
        16:144, December 1958.

10915   "William Grant Still."   Composers of the Americas 5:85-97, 1959.

10916   Kyle, M. K.   "AmerAllegro."   Pan Pipes 51:86, January 1959.

10917   "William Grant Still Classified Chronological Catalog of Works by the
        United States Composer."   Inter-American Music Bulletin 14:18-29,
        November 1959.

10918   Sargeant, W.   "Musical Events."   New Yorker 35:201, November 21,
        1959.   Review of Still's "In Memoriam: the Colored Soldiers Who
        Died for Democracy."

10919   Kyle, M. K.   "AmerAllegro."   Pan Pipes 52:73, no. 2, 1960; 53:77,
        no. 2, 1961.

10920   Morgan, L. M.   "An Interview with William Grant Still."   Pan Pipes
        53:35, no. 2, 1961.

10921 "The Peaceful Land." Showcase 41:6, no. 1, 1961.

10922 Still, W. G., and V. Arvey. "Our American Musical Resources."
       Showcase 41:7-9, 1961.

10923 "Hollywood Symphony Closes Season with World Premiere." Music
       of the West 16:14, June 1961. Still's "Patterns" is presented.

10924 Still, W. G. "The Composer's Creed." Music of the West 17:13-
       15, October 1961.

10925 "William Grant Still Given National Federation Award." Music of
       the West 17:9, October 1961.

10926 "Composer Wins $1,500 for an Orchestral Work, 'The Peaceful Land,'
       Written for National Federation of Music Clubs Contest of Compo-
       sitions." Jet 20:61, October 5, 1961.

10927 "Premieres." International Musician 60:14, December 1961. Still's
       "The Peaceful Land" is dedicated to the U. N.

10928 Reno, D. "Miami." Music Magazine 163:66, December 1961.

10929 Kyle, M. K. "AmerAllegro." Pan Pipes 54:72-73, no. 2, 1962.

10930 "University of Miami Symphony Chosen to Premiere 'The Peaceful
       Land' by William Grant Still." Symphony News 13:14, no. 2,
       1962.

10931 "William Grant Still's Composition Wins Aeolian Music Foundation
       Award." Musical Leader 94:14, January 1962.

10932 Kyle, M. K. "AmerAllegro." Pan Pipes 55:71, no. 2, 1963.

10933 "Nueva Opera en Miami." Buenos Aires Musical 18:6, no. 291,
       1963. Still's opera, "Highway 1, U.S.A." opened in Miami.

10934 Arvey, V. "With His Roots in the Soil." International Musician
       62:20-21, July 1963.

10935 "Miami." Opera 14:462, July 1963.

10936 "New Still Opera Premiered in Miami." Musical Leader 95:23, July
       1963.

10937 "William Grant Still Opera Premiers in Miami." Music and Dance
       54:15, August 1963.

10938 Reno, D. "Miami Medley." Opera News 28:28, September 28, 1963.

10939 Lippey, J., and W. E. Muns. "William Grant Still." Music Jour-
       nal 21:34, November 1963.

10940 Kyle, M. K. "AmerAllegro." Pan Pipes 56:81, no. 2, 1964.

10941 Simpson, Ralph Ricardo. "William Grant Still: The Man and His
       Music." (Ph.D. Dissertation, Michigan State University, 1964).

10942 Robinson, L. "Thirty-Eight Years of Serious Music." Ebony 19:102-106, February 1964.

10943 Kyle, M. K. "AmerAllegro." Pan Pipes 57:80-81, no. 2, 1965; 58:86, no. 2, 1966.

10944 Still, W. G., and V. Arvey. "The Lost Audience for New Music." Music Journal Annual p. 38-39, 1966.

10945 Thompson, Leon Everette. "A Historical and Stylistic Analysis of the Music of William Grant Still and a Thematic Catalog of His Work." (Ph.D. Dissertation, University of Southern California, 1966).

10946 Harvey, J. "What Is There to Say?" Storyville no. 3:15, February 1966.

10947 Kyle, M. K. "AmerAllegro." Pan Pipes 59:97, no. 2, 1967; 61:77-78, no. 2, 1967.

10948 Waters, E. N. "Harvest of the Year: Selected Acquisitions of the Music Division." Quarterly Journal of the Library of Congress 24:62, no. 1, 1967.

10949 Kyle, M. K. "AmerAllegro." Pan Pipes 60:94, no. 2, 1968.

10950 Arvey, V. "Afro-American Music Memo." Music Journal 27:36, November 1969.

10951 "Composers." Music and Artists 3:39, no. 4, 1970.

10952 Kyle, M. K. "AmerAllegro." Pan Pipes 62:84, no. 2, 1970.

10953 Yuhasz, Sister M. J. "Black Composers and Their Piano Music." American Music Teacher 19:28, no. 5, 1970.

10954 Still, W. G. "The Negro Musician in America." Music Educator's Journal 56:100-101, January 1970.

10955 Ardoin, J. "A Black Composers Concert." American Musical Digest 1:5-6, no. 5, 1970. Reprinted from the Dallas Morning News, January 31, 1970.

10956 Yancy, H. M. "The Contribution of the American Negro to the Music Culture of the Country." School Musician 41:62-63, April 1970.

10957 "Estrenos." Inter-American Music Bulletin no. 78:99, July-October 1970. Review of Still's "Symphony No. 5 (Western Hemisphere)."

10958 "News Nuggets." International Musician 69:17, December 1970.

10959 Kyle, M. K. "AmerAllegro." Pan Pipes 63:79-80, no. 2, 1971.

10960 "Premieres." Music Journal 29:63, February 1971.

10961 Haas, Robert Bartlett. William Grant Still and the Fusion of Cultures in American Music. Los Angeles: Black Sparrow Press, 1972.

10962 Kyle, M. K. "AmerAllegro." Pan Pipes 64:80, no. 2, 1972.

10963 "Highway 1, U.S.A." Newsweek 80:68, December 4, 1972.

10964 King, B. "Eubie Blake; A Legend in His Own Lifetime." Black
       Perspectives in Music 1:151-156, no. 2, 1973.

10965 Kyle, M. K. "AmerAllegro." Pan Pipes 65:74, no. 2, 1973.

10966 "Ulysses Kay's Juggler of Our Lady and William Grant Still's High-
       way 1, U.S.A." Opera News 37:23, January 13, 1973.

10967 Hains, F. "Opera/South: All-Black and Hopeful." High Fidelity/
       Musical America 23:MA23, May 1973. Opera/South is a black
       opera company which performed Still's "Highway 1, U.S.A."

10968 Caldwell, Hansonia Laverne. "Black Idioms in Opera as Reflected
       in the Works of Six Afro-American Composers." (Ph.D. Disser-
       tation, University of Southern California, 1974). The composers
       include Scott Joplin and William Grant Still.

10969 "'Deep River' Popularizes a Composer." Black Perspectives in Mu-
       sic 2:75-79, no. 1, 1974.

10970 Douglass, F. H. "A Tribute to William Grant Still." Black Per-
       spectives in Music 2:51-53, no. 1, 1974. This talk was presented
       on the occasion of the Treble Clef Club of Washington Sixtieth An-
       niversary.

10971 Harris, C. G. "Three Schools of Black Choral Composers and Ar-
       rangers 1900-1970." Choral Journal 14:11-18, no. 8, 1974.

10972 Kyle, M. K. "AmerAllegro." Pan Pipes 66:74, no. 2, 1974.

10973 Still, W. G., and V. Arvey. "On Composing for the Harp." Amer-
       ican Harp Journal 4:32-33, no. 4, 1974.

10974 Arvey, V. "Symphonies in Black." Music Journal 32:28-29, April
       1974.

10975 "Music Journal Adds Eight New Members to Its Advisory Council."
       Music Journal 32:10-11, July 1974.

10976 "Bayou Legend." Time 104:84, November 25, 1974.

10977 Kyle, M. K. "AmerAllegro." Pan Pipes 67:74, no. 2, 1975.

10978 Southern, E. "Reviews of Records: Black Composers Series."
       Musical Quarterly 61:645-650, no. 4, 1975.

10979 "William Grant Still Honored." Pan Pipes 68:20, no. 1, 1975.

10980 "William Grant Still Honored on Birthday." Triangle 69:8, no. 4,
       1975.

10981 "Jackson, Miss." Music Journal 33:46, January 1975. Still's opera
       "A Bayou Legend" is presented by Opera/South.

10982 "Premieres." Music Educator's Journal 61:84, January 1975.

10983 Eggler, B. "Opera South's William Grant Still's Highway 1, U.S.A.
       and Ulysses Kay's Juggler of Our Lady and World Premier of Still's
       Bayou Legend." Opera News 39:33, January 11, 1975.

10984 Hains, F. "William Grant Still--an American Composer Who Hap-
       pens to Be Black." High Fidelity/Musical America 25MA27, March
       1975.

10985 Durrett, C. W. "Jackson, Mississippi." Opera 26:381-382, April
       1975.

10986 A Birthday Offering to William Grant Still: Upon the Occasion of
       His Eightieth Anniversary. Cambria Heights, N.Y.: Foundation
       for Research in the Afro-American Creative Arts, 1975. A 240
       page special issue of Black Perspectives in Music, vol. 3, no. 2,
       May 1975.

10987 Southern, E. "America's Black Composers of Classical Music."
       Music Educator's Journal 62:48-49, November 1975.

10988 Kyle, M. K. "AmerAllegro." Pan Pipes 68:74-75, no. 2, 1976.

10989 Cariaga, D. "Los Angeles." Opera News 40:38, April 17, 1976.
       Still's opera "A Bayou Legend" is performed.

10990 Kyle, M. K. "AmerAllegro." Pan Pipes 69:73-74, no. 2, 1977.

10991 Spence, Martha Ellen Blanding. "Selected Song Cycles of Three
       Contemporary Black American Composers: William Grant Still,
       John Duncan, and Hale Smith." (Ph.D. Dissertation, University
       of Southern Mississippi, 1977).

10992 "Citations Honor Fiedler, Fromm, and Still." Triangle 72:4, no. 1,
       1978. These honors were presented by Mu Phi Epsilon.

10993 Kyle, M. K. "AmerAllegro." Pan Pipes 70:64-65, no. 2, 1978.

10994 ["Obituary."] Variety 293:111, December 13, 1978; Billboard 90:83,
       December 16, 1978; Jet 55:29, December 28, 1978.

SUMMER, DONNA (Donna Gaines; Mrs. Helmut Sommer).

10995 "Concert Reviews." Variety 282:64, February 25, 1976.

10996 "Caught in the Act." Melody Maker 51:26, March 6, 1976.

10997 "Talent in Action." Billboard 88:64, March 13, 1976.

10998 Cromelin, R. "Donna Summer: Love on the Road." Rolling Stone
       no. 209:18, March 25, 1976. Review of Summer's "Love to Love
       You Baby."

10999 Tiegel, E. "Close-Up." Billboard 88:102, March 27, 1976. Re-
       view of Summer's album "A Love Trilogy."

11000 "Making Waves: Oh, Oh Donna." Melody Maker 51:24, April 3,
       1976.

11001   "Donna Summer Jams Roseland in One-Niter; It's a NSG Showcase."
        Variety 284:64, November 3, 1976.

11002   "Talent in Action." Billboard 88:38, November 6, 1976.

11003   Lucas, B. "Donna Summer Rises to Top on Sexy Songs." Jet 51:52-
        55, December 9, 1976.

11004   "Records: Four Seasons of Love." Rolling Stone no. 231:68, Jan-
        uary 27, 1977.

11005   "Records: I Remember Yesterday." Rolling Stone no. 245:63, Au-
        gust 11, 1977.

11006   "Records: The Deep." Crawdaddy no. 77:73, October 1977.

11007   Sanders, C. L. "Donna Summer." Ebony 32:33-36, October 1977.

11008   Irwin, C. "Summer in the City." Melody Maker 52:44, October 15,
        1977.

11009   "Concert Reviews." Variety 288:68, November 2, 1977.

11010   "Caught in the Act." Melody Maker 52:66, November 5, 1977.

11011   Goldman, A. "Disco Fever." Esquire 88:60, December 1977.

11012   "Closeup." Billboard 89:75, December 3, 1977. Review of Sum-
        mer's "Once upon a Time."

11013   "Talent in Action." Billboard 90:34, January 7, 1978.

11014   Holden, S. "Donna Summer's Sexy Cinderella; Once upon a Time."
        Rolling Stone p. 54, January 12, 1978.

11015   "Riffs: Donna Summer Plays Around." Village Voice 23:41, January
        30, 1978.

11016   "Sahara Tahoe." Variety 290:67, February 8, 1978.

11017   "Hilton, Las Vegas." Variety 290:77, February 15, 1978.

11018   "Talent in Action." Billboard 90:46, February 25, 1978.

11019   Buxbaum, E. "Donna Summer: Disco Breakthrough." Stereo Re-
        view 40:128, March 1978. Review of "Once upon a Time."

11020   Gilmore, M. "Donna Summer: Is There Life after Disco?" Rolling
        Stone no. 261:11, March 23, 1978.

11021   Lucas, B. "Donna Summer Makes Acting Debut in Hot Disco Movie."
        Jet 54:56-59, March 23, 1978.

11022   "Talent in Action." Billboard 90:57, July 1, 1978.

11023   Cocks, J. "Gaudy Reign of the Disco Queen." Time 112:93, De-
        cember 4, 1978.

11024 "Records: Live and More." Rolling Stone no. 280:86, December
       14, 1978.

11025 "Queen of Disco Is Softening Her Act." People 10:112-113, Decem-
       ber 25, 1978.

TATUM, ART (Arthur), 1910-1956.

11026 "Solo Man." Time 54:56, December 5, 1949; Negro Digest 8:7,
       March 1950.

11027 "In Person." Metronome 67:15, May 1951.

11028 Ulanov, B. "History of Jazz; Pianists." Metronome 67:14-15, Au-
       gust 1951.

11029 Sharon, R. "Tatum." Melody Maker 27:4, August 18, 1951.

11030 "Tatum Is Still the Greatest of Jazz Pianists, States Feather." down
       beat 18:2, December 28, 1951.

11031 "Jazz Package." Time 59:53, May 19, 1952. Jazz pianists Johnson,
       Garner, Lewis, and Tatum are discussed.

11032 "Art Tatum." Ebony 7:67-71, August 1952; Metronome 68:14, Oc-
       tober 1952.

11033 "Caught in the Act." down beat 20:8, January 14, 1953.

11034 Morgan, A. "Retrospection." Jazz Journal 6:16, February 1953.

11035 Turner, J. "The Pianists in My Life." Melody Maker 29:2, May
       2, 1953.

11036 Feather, L. "'Fatha' Digs Tatum, Nixes Brubeck." down beat
       20:19, September 23, 1953.

11037 "'Recording Artists' Roster." down beat 21:130 June 30, 1954.

11038 "Socko Packaged Jazz Sets by Tatum, Getz, Satchmo, Mezz, Hamp,
       Others." Variety 195:42, July 7, 1954.

11039 "Tatum LP's Capture His Real Genius." Billboard 66:15, July 10,
       1954.

11040 "Art Tatum." Jazz Journal 7:26, August 1954.

11041 "The 'Autobiography' of Art Tatum: Chapters 1-5." High Fidelity
       4:53, August 1954.

11042 Simon, B. "Brown, Brubeck, Tatum." Saturday Review 37:59, Au-
       gust 28, 1954.

11043 "A Monumental Offering of Art." Metronome 70:24, September 1954.

11044 Granz, N. "The Story Behind the Records." Melody Maker 31:3,
       January 8, 1955.

11045   Thompson, E. "The Genius of Tatum." Melody Maker 31:3, Jan-
        uary 8, 1955.

11046   "Med Tatum pa Grammis." Orkester Journalen 23:16, March 1955.

11047   Hodeir, A. "Art Tatum; A French Jazz Critic Evaluates the Music
        of a Great Pianist." down beat 22:9-10, August 10, 1955.

11048   Jepsen, J. G. "Jazzens Instrumentalister: Pianot." Orkester Jour-
        nalen 23:12, September 1955.

11049   Wiedemann, E. "Tatum-Myten." Orkester Journalen 23:10-11, Sep-
        tember 1955.

11050   "Tatum-Myten Obefintlig: Tva Bemötanden till Erik Wiedemanns Ta-
        tum-Artikel." Orkester Journalen 23:20-21, October 1955.

11051   Race, S. "Tatum." Melody Maker 31:9, October 15, 1955.

11052   Balliett, W. "Art, and Tatum." Saturday Review 38:44, October
        29, 1955.

11053   Hodeir, A. "Critic's Reply to Billy Taylor." down beat 22:34, No-
        vember 2, 1955.

11054   "Caught in the Act." down beat 23:8, January 25, 1956.

11055   "Art Tatum to Swing with Longhair Groups." Variety 202:45, April
        11, 1956.

11056   "Tatum Seriously Ill." Melody Maker 31:4, July 21, 1956.

11057   Barksdale, E. "Tatum." Melody Maker 31:3, August 11, 1956.

11058   "Tatum Död." Orkester Journalen 24:7, November 1956.

11059   ["Obituary."] Variety 204:54, November 7, 1956.

11060   "Art Tatum the Great Is Dead." Melody Maker 31:1, November 10,
        1956.

11061   "Tribute to Tatum." Melody Maker 31:8, November 10, 1956.

11062   Aldam, J. "Collectors' Corner." Melody Maker 31:6, November
        17, 1956.

11063   ["Obituary."] Time 68:94, November 19, 1956.

11064   "Music Figures Fall Before Grim Reaper." Billboard 68:15, Novem-
        ber 24, 1956.

11065   "All Over." International Musician 55:35, December 1956.

11066   "All Too Soon." Jazz Journal 9:35-36, December 1956.

11067   "Jazz World Mourns Art Tatum." Jazz Today 1:30, December 1956.

11068   Gleason, R. J. "Perspectives." down beat 23:49, December 12,
        1956.

11069 Mehegan, J. "In Memoriam." down beat 23:15, December 12, 1956.

11070 "Tatum Death Brings Flood of Tributes from Jazzmen." down beat
       23:9, December 12, 1956.

11071 "Tribute to Tatum to be Rebroadcast." down beat 23:7, December
       26, 1956.

11072 "Rest in Peace." Metronome 74:42, January 1957.

11073 "Barry Ulanov." down beat 24:35-36, January 9, 1957.

11074 Hoefer, G. "The Hot Box." down beat 24:29, January 9, 1957.

11075 Lascelles, G. "The Genius of Art Tatum." Jazz Journal 10:7, Feb-
       ruary 1957.

11076 Balliett, W. "P Is for Pianists." Saturday Review 40:36, March
       16, 1957.

11077 _____. "Jazz Records." New Yorker 33:77, July 13, 1957.

11078 Wilson, J. S. "Jazz Pianists; A Discography." High Fidelity/Mu-
       sical America 7:67-68, August 1957.

11079 Edey, M. "Art Tatum." Jazz Review 2:28-29, June 1959.

11080 Katz, D. "Record Reviews." Jazz Review 2:28-30, September 1959.

11081 Edey, M. "Tatum, the Last Years." Jazz Review 3:4-5, August
       1960.

11082 Gibson, M. "The Paradox of Art Tatum." Jazz Journal 13:3-4, Oc-
       tober 1960.

11083 Jepsen, Jorgen Grunnet. Discography of Art Tatum and Bud Powell.
       Brande, Denmark: Debut Records, 1961.

11084 Coss, B. "Jazz Piano--Three Fountainheads." down beat 28:16-17,
       October 26, 1961.

11085 "New Art Tatum Material Found." down beat 29:13-14, May 24,
       1962.

11086 Rosenkrantz, T. "Reflections on Art." down beat 29:15, July 5,
       1962.

11087 Hoefer, G. "Tatum." down beat 30:24, October 24, 1963.

11088 "Annuaire Biographique du Piano." Jazz Magazine 9:37, November
       1963.

11089 Wilson, T., O. Peterson, and D. Moore. "Three Pianists Discuss
       Art Tatum." Jazz Journal 16:22-24, November 1963.

11090 Entremont, P., et al. "Admirable Tatum." Jazz Magazine no.
       126:36-38, January 1966.

11091 Reda, J. "Ode à Tatum." Jazz Magazine no. 126:26-29, January
       1966.

11092 Spencer, R. "Art Tatum; An Appreciation." Jazz Journal 19:6-10,
       August 1966; 19:11-16, September 1966.

11093 McRae, B. "Tatum, the Clef Recordings." Jazz Journal 19:11-12,
       October 1966.

11094 Spencer, R. "Art Tatum; An Appreciation." Jazz Journal 19:13-16,
       October 1966.

11095 Stewart, R. "Genius in Retrospect; Art Tatum." down beat 33:17-
       19, October 20, 1966.

11096 Schnore, L. F. "The Legacy of Tatum's Art." Journal of Pop Cul-
       ture 2:98-105, no. 1, 1968.

11097 Hennessey, M. "When Oscar and Art Played Together." Melody
       Maker 43:10, March 2, 1968.

11098 Balliett, W. "Jazz Records." New Yorker 44:104, September 7,
       1968.

11099 Korall, B. "Tatum Like the Wind." Saturday Review 51:67, Oc-
       tober 12, 1968.

11100 Arvanitas, G., et al. "Panorama des Pianistes." Jazz Hot no.
       246:30, January 1969.

11101 Jones, M. "Tatum--the World's Greatest Bluesman Says Jan Mc-
       Shann." Melody Maker 44:10, November 15, 1969.

11102 "La Chronique des Disques: The Art of Tatum." Jazz Hot no.
       262:38, June 1970.

11103 "Reeditions: The Art of Tatum--Piano Solo." Jazz Magazine no.
       180:46, July-August 1970.

11104 Brown, R. "Record Reviews: The Art of Tatum." Jazz Journal
       24:40-41, April 1971.

11105 Jones, M. "Jazz Records: The Art of Tatum." Melody Maker
       46:24, April 3, 1971.

11106 "Record Reviews: Capitol Jazz Classics, Vols. 1-10." Coda 10:15-
       16, no. 10, 1972.

11107 "Chroniques des Disques: Willow Weep for Me." Jazz Hot no.
       281:30, March 1972.

11108 "Jazz Records: Art Tatum and His Friends." Melody Maker 47:52,
       April 22, 1972.

11109 "Disques du Mois: Solo Piano." Jazz Magazine no. 200:54, May
       1972.

11110 "Classics on Capitol: Capitol Jazz Classics, Vol. 3." Jazz &
       Blues 2:8, June 1972.

11111   "Record Reviews: The Genius." Jazz & Blues 2:31-32, November
        1972.

11112   "Record Reviews: God Is in the House!" down beat 40:24, June 7,
        1973.

11113   Albertson, C. "Art Tatum: Buried Treasure--Some Previously Un-
        released Revelations from One of the Greats of Jazz Piano." Ster-
        eo Review 31:81-82, September 1973.

11114   Tiegel, E. "Leonard Feather's MCA's Nest with Nat, Duke, Tatum
        Vintages." Billboard 85:15, October 20, 1973.

11115   "Quelques Grands Pianistes." Jazz Hot no. 305:11, May 1974.

11116   "Jazz Records: Art Tatum." Melody Maker 49:66, November 9,
        1974.

11117   Evans, T. "Jazz from the Forties on Onyx Records." Journal of
        Jazz Studies 2:96-103, no. 2, 1975.

11118   "Chroniques des Disques: The Art Tatum Trio." Jazz Hot no.
        312:35, January 1975.

11119   "Reedition d'Art." Jazz Magazine no. 233:26-29, May-June 1975.

11120   Endress, G. "Sammy Price--Über die Musik mit den Menschen in
        Kontakt Kommen." Jazz Podium 24:7-9, September 1975.

11121   Kolodin, I. "Art Tatum Plain and Fancy." Stereo Review 35:104-
        105, September 1975.

11122   "The Tatum Solo Masterpieces." Jazz Journal 28:27, November
        1975.

11123   Larrabee, E. "Recordings/Jazz: The Tatum Magic." Saturday Re-
        view 3:44-45, November 1, 1975.

11124   "Record Reviews: Art Tatum--Solo Piano." Jazz Journal 28:38-39,
        December 1975.

11125   Albertson, C. "Art Tatum and Company." Stereo Review 36:98,
        January 1976.

11126   "Record Reviews: Song of the Vagabonds." Jazz Journal 29:38, Sep-
        tember 1976.

11127   "Record Reviews: Masterpieces." Coda no. 151:23, October-Novem-
        ber 1976.

11128   "Jazz Albums: The Tatum Group Masterpieces." Melody Maker
        51:32, November 27, 1976.

11129   "Record Reviews: Art Tatum/Buddy DeFranco." Coda no. 152:12,
        December 1976.

11130   "Record Reviews: Group Masterpieces." Jazz Journal 29:36, De-
        cember 1976.

11131 Newberger, E. H. "The Development of New Orleans and Stride Piano Styles." Journal of Jazz Studies 4:63-66, no. 2, 1977.

11132 Morgan, A. "Art Tatum--the Group Masterpieces." Jazz Journal 30:39-40, January 1977.

11133 Colombe, G. "Side by Side." Jazz Journal 30:26-27, April 1977. Earl Hines and Tatum are compared as jazz pianists.

11134 "Record Reviews: Get Happy." Jazz Journal International 30:51, September 1977.

11135 "Jazz Albums: The Tatum Group Masterpieces." Melody Maker 52:29, September 19, 1977.

11136 "Waxing On: Masterpieces, Vol. 2." down beat 44:35-36, October 6, 1977.

11137 "Waxing On: The Keystone Sessions." down beat 44:36, October 6, 1977.

11138 "Jazz Albums: The Tatum Group Masterpieces." Melody Maker 52:36, October 8, 1977.

11139 "Albums Reviews: The Tatum Group Masterpieces, Vol. 2." Crescendo International 16:27, April 1978.

11140 "Prez Awards." Jazz Journal International 31:36, August 1978.

11141 Ullman, M. A. "Jazz." New Republic 179:18-19, September 16, 1978.

TEDDY BEAR see PENDERGRASS, TEDDY

TERRELL, TAMMI (Tammy Montgomery), d. 1970.

11142 Peters, A. "Ordeal of Tammi Terrell." Ebony 25:94-96, November 1969.

11143 ["Obituary."] Variety 258:71, March 18, 1970.

11144 "Tammi Terrell Dies--Brain Tumor?" Rolling Stone no. 56:9, April 16, 1970.

11145 "Tammi Terrell Dies." Melody Maker 45:4, March 28, 1970.

TURMAN, MRS. GLYNN see FRANKLIN, ARETHA LOUISE

TURNER, IKE AND TINA (Ike Turner, 1934- ; Mrs. Ike Turner; Aillene Bullock, 1941-).

11146 "Bios." Cash Box 23:18, March 31, 1962.

11147 "Today's Top Recorded Talent." Billboard 74:69, April 7, 1962.

11148 Grevatt, R. "Ike and Tina--and the Spirit of St. Louis." Melody Maker 41:8, July 9, 1966.

11149 Jones, M. "Ike and Tina Show Comes to Town--All Nineteen of Them." Melody Maker 41:8-9, October 1, 1966.

11150 "Blind Date." Melody Maker 41:10, October 22, 1966.

11151 Walsh, A. "Race Riots Drive Ike & Tina to Britain." Melody Maker 43:11, April 27, 1968.

11152 "Ike Turner." Blues Unlimited no. 56:8, September 1968.

11153 Niquet, B. "Deux Pionniers Meconnus: Ike et Tina Turner." Jazz Hot no. 243:14-16, October 1968.

11154 Kudlacek, K., and D. Sax. "The Ike Turner Blues Story." Blues Unlimited no. 57:4-6, November 1968.

11155 Sander, E. "Cussin', Cryin', Gettin' It On." Saturday Review 52:43, August 30, 1969.

11156 Albertson, C., et al. "Record Reviews." down beat 36:20, October 2, 1969.

11157 "Ike & Tina Strive to Soulfulize Vegas Hearts." Billboard 81:SC7, October 4, 1969.

11158 "Turning On." Newsweek 74:92-93, November 3, 1969.

11159 Welding, P. "Records: The Hunter." Rolling Stone no. 46:33, November 15, 1969.

11160 "Concert Reviews." Variety 257:50, November 19, 1969.

11161 Dove, I. "Turner Revue Stages Soul Show That Grabs Audience." Billboard 81:22, December 6, 1969.

11162 "A New Start for the Ike and Tina Turner Man." Melody Maker 44:22, December 13, 1969.

11163 "In the Press." BMI p. 18, January 1970.

11164 "Concert Reviews." Variety 257:70, January 14, 1970.

11165 Tiegel, E. "International Hotel, Las Vegas." Billboard 82:27, January 31, 1970.

11166 "International, Las Vegas." Variety 257:59, February 4, 1970.

11167 Siders, H. "Straight Ahead with Ike and Tina." down beat 37:16-17, April 30, 1970.

11168 Von Tersch, G. "Records: Ooh-Poo-Pah-Doo." Rolling Stone no. 62:40, July 9, 1970.

11169 "Concert Reviews." Variety 259:50, July 22, 1970.

11170   Kaye, L. "Record Reviews: Come Together." Jazz and Pop 9:60, August 1970.

11171   Reilly, P. "Try a Little Togetherness with Ike & Tina Turner." Stereo Review 25:73-74, August 1970.

11172   "International, Las Vegas." Variety 259:47, August 12, 1970.

11173   Feather, L. "Newport Sans Grise." Jazz Magazine no. 181:12, September 1970.

11174   Dunbar, E. "Ike and Tina Turner; They're Too Much." Look 34:62-64, September 8, 1970.

11175   Reilly, P. "Our Man in the Catskills Talks to Ike and Tina Turner." Stereo Review 25:124-125, October 1970.

11176   "Tina Turns On." Life 69:57-61, December 18, 1970.

11177   Landau, J. "Records: Workin' Together." Rolling Stone no. 73:51, December 24, 1970.

11178   Spiegelman, J. "The Soul-Mama: Tina Turner." Soul Illustrated 3:46-47, no. 3, 1971.

11179   Lentz, P. R. "Caught in the Act: Soul Bowl '70." down beat 38:30, January 21, 1971.

11180   "Turners Turn 'em On." Melody Maker 46:6, January 30, 1971.

11181   "Pop Albums: Workin' Together." Melody Maker 46:20, February 20, 1971.

11182   Williams, R. "Is Tina All Sex and No Soul?" Melody Maker 46:18, February 20, 1971.

11183   Perin, J. "Comme une Tornade Noire." Jazz Magazine no. 187:9-10, March 1971.

11184   Postif, F. "Ike & Tina." Jazz Hot no. 270:6-11, March 1971.

11185   Berg, G. "Ike and Tina at Grossinger's." Jazz and Pop 10:26, April 1971.

11186   "Talent in Action." Billboard 83:20, April 17, 1971.

11187   "Ike & Tina Turner." Ebony 26:88-90, May 1971.

11188   "Talent in Action." Billboard 83:26, May 29, 1971.

11189   Szyfmanowicz, R. "La Chronique des Disques: Live in Paris." Jazz Hot no. 273:37-38, June 1971.

11190   Aronowitz, A. "Likeable Ike." Melody Maker 46:31, June 12, 1971.

11191   Noel, G. "La Chronique des Disques: Outta Season." Jazz Hot no. 274:34, July 1971.

11192   "Concert Reviews." Variety 263:49, July 14, 1971.

11193 Kimball, G. "Records: What You Hear Is What You Get." Rolling
        Stone no. 88:45, August 5, 1971.

11194 Higgins, C. "Torrid Theatrics Take Tina Turner to the Top." Jet
        41:6-63, September 3, 1971.

11195 Fong-Torres, B. "The World's Greatest Heartbreaker." Rolling
        Stone no. 93:36-40, October 14, 1971.

11196 "Talent in Action." Billboard 83:14, October 16, 1971.

11197 Reilly, P. "One More Time with Tina Turner." Stereo Review
        27:97-98, November 1971.

11198 Trachtman, P. "Ike and Tina." Essence 2:50-51, November 1971.

11199 "Concert Reviews." Variety 265:46, December 1, 1971.

11200 "La Chronique des Disques: 'Nuff Said." Jazz Hot no. 279:34, Jan-
        uary 1972.

11201 Gersten, R. "Records: 'Nuff Said." Rolling Stone no. 99:66, Jan-
        uary 6, 1972.

11202 "RecWords: 'Nuff Said." Crawdaddy no. 4:16, January 30, 1972.

11203 "The Turner 'Explosion.'" BMI p. 21-22, February 1972.

11204 Fonteyne, A. "A Propos d'une Interview d'Ike et Tina Turner."
        Points du Jazz no. 6:90-94, March 1972.

11205 "Ike & Tina Turner Open New Recording Studios." Jet 41:57, March
        23, 1972.

11206 "Records: Blues Roots." Rolling Stone no. 116:37, August 31,
        1972.

11207 Balliett, W. "Jazz Records." New Yorker 48:62-64, August 19,
        1972.

11208 Leadbitter, M. "A Fresh Look at Ike Turner's Early Years." Blues
        Unlimited no. 95:4-5, October 1972.

11209 Stevenson, S. "Tina Turner: 'Ike Only Loved Stallions.'" Craw-
        daddy no. 17:45-50, October 1972.

11210 "Concert Reviews." Variety 268:57, October 11, 1972.

11211 "Records: Feel Good." Crawdaddy no. 18:80-81, November 1972.

11212 Brown, G. "A Question of Taste." Melody Maker 47:52, November
        11, 1972.

11213 Sandner, W. "Frankfurt A.M.: Soul-Gruppen 'Jackson-Five,' 'Ike
        & Tina Turner' und 'The Four Tops' in Deutschland." Neue Zeit-
        schrift für Musik 134:37-38, no. 1, 1973.

11214 "Ike & Tina." Blues Unlimited no. 98:21, January 1973.

11215 Olsson, O. T. "Ike & Tina Jobbade Haart." Orkester Journalen 41:16, January 1973.

11216 "Records: Blues Roots." Crawdaddy no. 20:84-85, January 1973.

11217 Lucas, B. "Two Worlds of Ike and Tina Turner." Sepia 22:22-28, February 1973.

11218 "Ike Turner, Black Panthers Scuffle at Show." Rolling Stone no. 142:20, August 30, 1973.

11219 Milton, D. "How Tina Found Her Limits." Melody Maker 48:47, September 29, 1973.

11220 "Caught in the Act." Melody Maker 48:24, December 1, 1973.

11221 Hansen, H. "Mit Show-Erotik zum Erfolg--Ike und Tina Turner Show in Frankfurt." Neue Zeitschrift für Musik 23:12, no. 6, 1974.

11222 Sandner, W. "Frankfurt/Main: Chanson--Rock--Soul." Neue Zeitschrift für Musik 135:46-47, no. 1, 1974.

11223 "Hilton, Las Vegas." Variety 273:37, January 2, 1974.

11224 "The Soul Report." Melody Maker 49:28-29, January 12, 1974.

11225 "How Ike and Tina Keep Turning 'em On." Soul 8:11, February 18, 1974.

11226 "Ike Turner Bust: Phone 'Fraud.'" Rolling Stone no. 160:18, May 9, 1974.

11227 Haynes, H. "Gospel According to Ike and Tina." Sepia 23:60-62, June 1974.

11228 Jones, M. "Exciting Tina." Melody Maker 49:32, October 26, 1974.

11229 "Bookers Seek Damages in Suits Against the Turners." Billboard 86:14, November 9, 1974.

11230 "Sex und Seifenblassen die Ike und Tina Turner Show in Frankfurt." Jazz Podium 23:23, December 1974.

11231 "Ike & Tina Turner Show." Musikern no. 1:15, January 1975.

11232 "Ike and Tina Turner Awarded European Gold." Soul 9:1, January 20, 1975. The Turners received the European Record Award.

11233 "Talent in Action." Billboard 87:26, January 25, 1975.

11234 Brown, G. F. "Tina Turner Talks About Ike and 'Tommy.'" Jet 48:60-63, April 24, 1975.

11235 "Hilton, Las Vegas." Variety 279:56, June 4, 1975.

11236 "Caught in the Act America." Melody Maker 50:27, July 26, 1975.

11237 Kubernik, H. "Acid Queen." Melody Maker 50:26-27, October 11, 1975.

11238 "Caught in the Act." Melody Maker 60:28, November 1, 1975.

11239 "Records: Acid Queen." Rolling Stone no. 199:68, November 6, 1975.

11240 "Concert Reviews." Variety 281:52, November 12, 1975.

11241 Reilly, P. "Until You Get It from Tina Turner, You Just Haven't Gotten the Message." Stereo Review 36:76-77, January 1976.

11242 "Waldorf-Astoria, N.Y." Variety 282:78, March 24, 1976.

11243 "Ike & Tina's Tour Trouble: Last Plane to Hong Kong." Rolling Stone no. 210:20, April 8, 1976.

11244 "Hilton, Las Vegas." Variety 282:86, April 14, 1976.

11245 Thompson, M. C. "Trouble Trails Tina Turner." Jet 50:58-61, April 15, 1976.

11246 "Talent in Action." Billboard 88:37-38, May 1, 1976.

11247 Ebert, A. "Strange and Stormy Love of Tina Turner." Sepia 25:56-62, December 1976.

11248 Lucas, B. "Trials and Triumphs Test Tina Turner." Jet 52:58-60, July 28, 1977.

11249 "New Acts." Variety 287:70, August 3, 1977.

11250 "Concert Reviews." Variety 288:97, September 14, 1977.

11251 Lucas, B. "New Year, New Tina, New Title." Jet 53:20-24, January 5, 1978.

11252 Jones, A. "Tina Just Porn in the Game." Melody Maker 53:3, February 18, 1978.

11253 "Talent in Action." Billboard 90:45, July 22, 1978.

UGGAMS, LESLIE, 1943- .

11254 "New Acts." Variety 187:118, July 16, 1952.

11255 "Leslie Uggams Clicks Via 'One More Sunrise.'" Billboard 71:41, September 21, 1959.

11256 "Child Star Grows Up." Ebony 15:115-120, December 1959.

11257 "Eden Roc, M.B." Variety 242:61, April 6, 1960.

11258 "Leslie Uggams Is Guest Singer on Ford Startime." Jet p. 66, May 26, 1960.

11259 "Leslie Uggams Makes 3rd Appearance as Guest on 'Sing Along with Mitch.'" Jet 19:66, March 2, 1961.

11260 "She Sings Along with Mitch." Ebony 17:40-42, March 1962.

11261 "Holiday House, Pitt." Variety 227:98, July 25, 1962.

11262 Mendlowitz, L. "Leslie Uggams Belts Five in Pitt." Billboard 74:12, August 4, 1962.

11263 "Leslie Uggam's Glory Road." Sepia 11:33, December 1962.

11264 "Lacely Ugigimous." Time 80:66, December 7, 1962.

11265 "Gallery of Easter Fashions." Ebony 18:126-129, March 1963.

11266 "Flamingo, Las Vegas." Variety 231:63, July 10, 1963.

11267 "Bishop College Adopts Leslie Uggams." Sepia 12:76-77, December 1963.

11268 "Hotel Plaza, N.Y." Variety 233:39, December 25, 1963.

11269 "Growing Up." Newsweek 62:59, December 30, 1963.

11270 "Flamingo, Las Vegas." Variety 235:60, May 24, 1964.

11271 "Nugget, Sparks, Nev." Variety 235:63, June 24, 1964.

11272 Astor, G. "The Little Girl Grows Up." Look 28:42-44, June 30, 1964.

11273 "Cocoanut Grove, L.A." Variety 235:57, August 19, 1964.

11274 Tiegel, E. "Leslie Uggams a Show-Stopper." Billboard 76:10, August 29, 1964.

11275 "Waldorf-Astoria, N.Y." Variety 236:54, October 28, 1964.

11276 "Leslie Uggams Visits Australia." Sepia 13:46-50, November 1964.

11277 "Fairmont Hotel, S.F." Variety 238:67, February 24: 1965.

11278 "Flamingo, Las Vegas." Variety 238:58, April 7, 1965.

11279 "Copacabana, N.Y." Variety 238:59, April 28, 1965.

11280 "Cocoanut Grove, L.A." Variety 239:42, August 11, 1965.

11281 Tiegel, E. "Leslie Uggams Delightful Treat at Cocoanut Grove." Billboard 77:16, August 21, 1965.

11282 "Copacabana, N.Y." Variety 242:62, April 20, 1966.

11283 "Roostertail, Detroit." Variety 243:56, August 10, 1966.

11284 "Club Harlem, A.C." Variety 244:60, August 24, 1966.

11285 "Harrah's, Reno." Variety 244:63-64, September 14, 1966.

11286   Curnow, H.   "Why I Married an Australian."   Ebony 22:140-142,
         May 1967.

11287   "Hallelujah, Baby."   Variety 246:68, May 3, 1967.

11288   Prideaux, T.   "Leslie, a Cool Bombshell."   Life 62:88-90, June
         23, 1967.

11289   "Hallelujah, Baby!"   Sepia 16:58-62, July 1967.

11290   "People Are Talking About ..."   Vogue 150:78-79, July 1967.

11291   "Leslie Uggams, Star in a New Galaxy."   Newsweek 70:63-67, July
         17, 1968.

11292   "Flamingo, Las Vegas."   Variety 249:58, February 14, 1968.

11293   Reed, R.   "Leslie Uggams Polishes up Her New Image."   Good
         Housekeeping 166:50, April 1968.

11294   Watt, D.   "Popular Records."   New Yorker 44:186, December 14,
         1968.

11295   "Sands, Las Vegas."   Variety 253:82, January 15, 1969.

11296   "Leslie Uggams' Secret."   Harper's Bazaar 102:150-151, February
         1969.

11297   "Copacabana, N.Y."   Variety 254:61, February 19, 1969.

11298   "Civil Rights Leaders Protest Cancellation of Her TV Show."   Jet
         37:68-69, November 20, 1969.

11299   Sohigian, K.   "Leslie Uggams."   House Beautiful 112:68-69, Febru-
         ary 1970.

11300   "Americana, N.Y."   Variety 258:66, February 18, 1970.

11301   Gross, M.   "Talent in Action."   Billboard 82:24, February 21, 1970.

11302   "Leslie Uggams; Down but Not Out."   Sepia 19:26, June 1970.

11303   "International, Las Vegas."   Variety 262:61, May 5, 1971.

11304   Deni, L.   "Talent in Action."   Billboard 83:31, May 15, 1971.

11305   "Elmwood, Windsor, Ont."   Variety 265:53, November 24, 1971.

11306   "Harrah's, Tahoe."   Variety 266:247, May 3, 1972.

11307   "Flamingo, Las Vegas."   Variety 268:53, September 20, 1972.

11308   "Waldorf-Astoria, N.Y."   Variety 269:61, December 6, 1972.

11309   Spiegelman, J.   "A Black Woman Trying to Lose a White Image."
         Soul 7:8, January 1, 1973.

11310   "Thunderbird, Las Vegas."   Variety 271:99, July 18, 1973.

11311 "Waldorf-Astoria, N.Y." Variety 272:41, October 17, 1973.

11312 Gant, L. "Beauty Talk with the Stars." Essence 4:38-39, January
       1974.

11313 "Hilton, Las Vegas." Variety 274:47, February 20, 1974.

11314 "Flamingo, Hilton, L.V." Variety 274:85, April 17, 1974.

11315 "Flamingo, Las Vegas." Variety 275:55, July 3, 1974.

11316 Williams, J. "Uggams Aims at R & B and Disco Crowd." Bill-
       board 87:40, December 13, 1975.

11317 "Sahara, Las Vegas." Variety 281:61, February 4, 1976.

11318 "Pfister Hotel, Milwaukee." Variety 283:119, May 19, 1976.

11319 "Sahara, Las Vegas." Variety 285:97, December 22, 1976.

11320 Ebert, A. "Leslie Uggams: Coming to Terms." Essence 8:84-85,
       March 1978.

VAUGHAN, SARAH LOIS (Sassy; Mrs. Marshall Fisher; Mrs. Waymon Reed),
1924- .

11321 "Sugar and Spice." Time 55:53, January 16, 1950.

11322 "Sarah Vaughan Fixed for London Concert." Melody Maker 26:1,
       January 21, 1950.

11323 "Capsule Comments." down beat 17:2, February 10, 1950.

11324 "Great Sarah Vaughan." Our World 5:24-27, May 1950.

11325 "Sugar and Spice." Negro Digest 8:41-42, June 1950.

11326 "Voices and Modern Jazz." Metronome 66:20, June 1950.

11327 "Birdland, New York." Variety 180:51, November 22, 1950; Bill-
       board 62:39, December 2, 1950.

11328 Vaughan, S. "Man Behind Me." Our World 6:15-19, March 1951.

11329 "Sarah's Singing 'Superb' in Carnegie Hall Concert." down beat 18:1,
       April 6, 1951.

11330 "Ellington-Vaughan-Cole in Sock $4.80-Top Show at N.Y.'s Carnegie
       Hall." Variety 184:52, October 3, 1951.

11331 "Sarah's Answer to Critics: Sing Best Way I Know How." down
       beat 19:3, April 4, 1952.

11332 "Birthday for Sarah." Ebony 7:108-110, July 1952.

11333 Brown, T. "Even Sarah Vaughan Can Be Scared Stiff!" Melody
       Maker 29:3, January 24, 1953.

11334   Leslie, P.   "They Call Her the Musical Miracle."   Melody Maker
        29:3, January 24, 1953.

11335   Nevard, M.   "Summing up Sarah."   Melody Maker 29:5, February
        7, 1953.

11336   "Sarah Vaughan Clicks in First London Date."   Variety 189:47, Feb-
        ruary 11, 1953.

11337   "Sarah Vaughan--the New Sound."   Jazz Journal 6:1, March 1953.

11338   "Caught in the Act."   down beat 20:4, May 6, 1953.

11339   "Birdland, N.Y."   Variety 194:61, March 31, 1954.

11340   "The Stormy Love Life of Sarah Vaughan."   Ebony 9:95-96, June
        1954.

11341   "'Recording Artists' Roster."   down beat 21:132, June 30, 1954.

11342   Eckstine, B.   "When Sarah Vaughan Began to Sing."   Melody Maker
        30:5, August 21, 1954.

11343   Lindgren, C. E.   "Den Gudomliga Sarah."   Orkester Journalen
        22:10-11, September 1954.

11344   "Vaughan Pkge. Scores in Berlin; Hopped-up Paris."   Variety 196:126,
        October 20, 1954.

11345   "Basie, Sarah Wail, But Some Others Suffer an Off Night."   down
        beat 21:20, November 3, 1954.

11346   "Caught in the Act."   down beat 22:4, February 23, 1955.

11347   "Blue Note, Chi."   Variety 199:61, June 22, 1955.

11348   "One of 2 Record Pacts 'for Me,' Asserts Sarah."   down beat 22:2,
        January 26, 1955.

11349   "Here Are EmArcy Jazz Stars' Bios."   down beat 23:13, January 25,
        1956.

11350   Jepsen, J. G.   "Kvinnliga Vokalister."   Orkester Journalen 24:15,
        February 1956.

11351   "Sarah Vaughan."   down beat 23:8, May 2, 1956.

11352   "Sarah Signs New Contract."   down beat 23:9, June 27, 1956.

11353   "Fontainebleau, M. B'ch."   Variety 203:53, July 18, 1956.

11354   Dahlgren, C.   "Sarah och Ella med Basie."   Orkester Journalen
        25:6-7, January 1957.

11355   Gold, D.   "Soulful Sarah."   down beat 24:13, May 30, 1957.

11356   "The Two-Sided Sarah Vaughan."   Jazz Today 2:11, June 1957.

11357   "Waldorf-Astoria, N.Y."   Variety 207:57, June 5, 1957.

11358 "Wows at the Waldorf." Newsweek 50:66, July 1, 1957.

11359 "Mr. Kelly's, Chi." Variety 207:57, August 7, 1957.

11360 "Sarah Vaughan." down beat 24:33-34, September 5, 1957.

11361 "Mr. Kelly's, Chi." Variety 210:71, March 5, 1958.

11362 Gold, D. "Sarah Vaughan." down beat 25:20, April 3, 1958.

11363 Burman, M. "I Love--Yes Love--Mr. B." Melody Maker 33:7,
       April 19, 1958.

11364 "Sarah on Sinatra." Melody Maker 33:6, April 26, 1958.

11365 "Mister Kelly's, Chi." Variety 214:61, April 1, 1959.

11366 "La Vaughan a Winner at Waldorf." Billboard 71:28, December 21,
       1959.

11367 "Waldorf-Astoria, N.Y." Variety 217:55, December 23, 1959.

11368 Dawbarn, B. "Sarah Is an Object Lesson to All Singers." Melody
       Maker 35:3, January 30, 1960.

11369 Jones, M. "'Please Don't Type Me,' Interview with Sarah Vaughan."
       Melody Maker 35:2-3, January 30, 1960.

11370 "Chez Paree, Chi." Variety 218:67, March 16, 1960.

11371 "Cloister, H'wood." Variety 220:69, October 5, 1960.

11372 Leydi, Roberto. Sarah Vaughan. Milano: Ricordi, 1961.

11373 Rolontz, B. "Sarah Stresses Jazz at Basin St." Billboard 73:6,
       January 9, 1961.

11374 "Basin St. East, N.Y." Variety 221:54, January 11, 1961.

11375 Gardner, B. "Sarah." down beat 28:18-21, March 2, 1961.

11376 "Cloister, Hollywood." Variety 222:65, March 15, 1961.

11377 Rolontz, B. "Basin Street Magic for Sarah." Billboard 73:5, May
       15, 1961.

11378 Gardner, B. "Plain Girls Can Make It Too." Negro Digest 10:10-
       15, June 1961.

11379 Morrison, A. "Sarah Vaughan Adopts a Baby." Ebony 16:88-92,
       September 1961.

11380 Hentoff, N. "Sarah Vaughan Emancipated." High Fidelity/Musical
       America 8:63, January 1962.

11381 Zylberstein, J. C. "Les Girls." Jazz Magazine 8:32-33, May
       1962.

11382 "Crescendo, L.A." Variety 227:52, August 8, 1962.

11383 "Sarah se Fache." Jazz Magazine 8:20, December 1962.

11384 Hoefer, G. "Earl Hines in the 1940s." down beat 30:25, April 25,
       1963.

11385 Ioakimidis, D. "Sarah la Plus Caline des Trois." Jazz Hot no.
       189:18-20, July-August 1963.

11386 Kopelowicz, G. "Tendre et Divine Sarah." Jazz Magazine 9:25-27,
       July 1963.

11387 "Edgewater Beach, Chi." Variety 231:62, July 10, 1963.

11388 Dawbarn, B. "Basie's Back--Sarah Too!" Melody Maker 38:8-9,
       September 7, 1963.

11389 Jones, M. "Madame Butterfly." Melody Maker 38:9, September
       21, 1963.

11390 Jones, Q. "Sarah Makes It All Worth While." Melody Maker 38:12,
       October 12, 1963.

11391 "Count Basie and Sarah Vaughan." Jazz Monthly 9:6-9, November
       1963.

11392 "Barclay Hotel, Toronto." Variety 235:60, June 10, 1964.

11393 "Basin St. East, N.Y." Variety 237:57, November 4, 1964.

11394 "Menzies & Savoy Plaza, Melbourne." Variety 239:69, June 23,
       1965.

11395 "Sarah Vaughan Works Good Gig on Pennsylvania Ave." down beat
       32:12-13, February 25, 1965.

11396 Gardner, M. "Sarah Vaughan Bargains." Jazz Journal 20:8-10,
       January 1967. Cheap label discographies of Vaughan's works are
       available.

11397 "Chateau Madrid, Ft. L." Variety 245:69, February 1, 1967.

11398 Quinn, B. "Sassy '67." down beat 34:18-20, July 27, 1967.

11399 Williams, M. "Words for Sarah Vaughan." Saturday Review 50:81,
       August 26, 1967.

11400 Locke, D. "The Jazz Vocal." Jazz Monthly 13:11, September 1967.

11401 Dawbarn, B. "Sarah--Jazz Singer Unique." Melody Maker 42:18,
       October 14, 1967.

11402 Vacher, A. "Duke et Sarah à Montreal." Jazz Magazine no. 148:12,
       November 1967.

11403 "Mister Kelly's, Chi." Variety 251:52, June 26, 1968.

11404 Williams, M. "Sarah Vaughan." Jazz Journal 21:36-37, July 1968.

11405 "Rainbow Grill, N.Y." Variety 252:96, September 11, 1968.

11406 Ochs, E. "Sarah Vaughan Soars to New Heights at Rooftop Nightery." Billboard 80:14, September 21, 1968.

11407 "Westside Room, L.A." Variety 252:50, October 23, 1968.

11408 Feather, L. "Time for the Recording Famine to Come to an End." Melody Maker 43:10, December 7, 1968.

11409 "Caesars Palace, L.V." Variety 254:88, March 26, 1969.

11410 "Strange Story of 'Passing Strangers.'" Melody Maker 44:6, April 26, 1969.

11411 Feather, L. "TV Soundings." down beat 36:13, May 15, 1969.

11412 "Moon, Hazel Pk., Mich." Variety 255:69, May 28, 1969.

11413 "Bonanza, Las Vegas." Variety 255:60, June 25, 1969.

11414 Feather, L. "Blindfold Test." Opera 20:641-642, July 1969.

11415 Gerber, A. "Sarah Encore et Toujours." Jazz Magazine no. 172:30-33, November 1969.

11416 Jones, M. "Why Miss Vaughan Isn't Recording." Melody Maker 44:8, November 1, 1969.

11417 "Disques du Mois." Jazz Magazine no. 176:36, March 1970.

11418 "Kings Castle, Tahoe." Variety 259:55, July 22, 1970.

11419 Feather, L. "Sassy, le Genius et Compagnie." Jazz Magazine no. 182:11, October 1970.

11420 "Mister Kelly's, Chi." Variety 260:48, October 7, 1970.

11421 Feather, L. "Caught in the Act." Melody Maker 45:38, October 10, 1970.

11422 Jones, M. "Jazz Records: Back to Back." Melody Maker 45:38, October 10, 1970.

11423 Brown, R. "Record Reviews: Back to Back." Jazz Journal 24:39, April 1971.

11424 "Westside Room, L.A." Variety 262:87, April 14, 1971.

11425 Feather, L. "Sarah--Better than Ever." Melody Maker 46:43, April 17, 1971.

11426 "Regency, Hyatt Hse, Chi." Variety 263:53, June 16, 1971.

11427 "Lat Bastile, Houston." Variety 264:47, August 25, 1971.

11428 Deni, L. "Talent in Action." Billboard 83:14, October 16, 1971.

11429 "Hilton Intl., Las Vegas." Variety 265:32, December 29, 1971.

11430   "Buenos Aires, Tiempo y Espacio; Balance de una Temporada."
        Buenos Aires Musical 27:3, no. 443, 1972.

11431   Deni, L. "Talent in Action." Billboard 84:16, January 15, 1972.

11432   Jones, M. "Caught in the Act." Melody Maker 47:22, February 5,
        1972.

11433   "Record Reviews: A Time in My Life." down beat 39:24, March
        30, 1972.

11434   "Disques du Mois: Sweet and Sultry: A Time in My Life." Jazz
        Magazine no. 200:56, May 1972.

11435   "Rainbow Grill, N.Y." Variety 266:247, May 3, 1972.

11436   Tiegel, E. "Sarah Vaughan, Michel Legrand Mainstream's New Jazz
        Team." Billboard 84:3, May 27, 1972.

11437   "Recording of Special Merit: A Time in My Life." Stereo Review
        28:103, June 1972.

11438   Thompson, T. "Almost Nobody's as Classy as Sassy." Life 72:27,
        June 16, 1972.

11439   "Sweet Sarah." Melody Maker 47:48, October 14, 1972.

11440   "Record Reviews: Sarah Vaughan." down beat 39:22, November 23,
        1972.

11441   "Fairmont-R'velt, N.O." Variety 269:55, December 13, 1972.

11442   "On Record: On the Swingin' Side; The Intimate Sarah Vaughan."
        Jazz & Blues 2:21-22, February 1973.

11443   "Sarah Vaughan: Riding the Rainbow of Sound." Soul 7:10, February
        26, 1973.

11444   "Copacabana, N.Y." Variety 270:85, March 21, 1973.

11445   "Thunderbird, L.A." Variety 271:117, May 16, 1973.

11446   Suber, C. "The First Chorus." down beat 43:4, June 7, 1973.

11447   "Caught in the Act." Melody Maker 48:36-37, August 11, 1973.

11448   "Concert Reviews." Variety 272:34, August 15, 1973.

11449   Tercinet, A., and M. Cullza. "Antibes." Jazz Hot no. 297:26,
        September 1973.

11450   "Concert Reviews." Crescendo International 12:15, November 1973.

11451   "Caught in the Act." Melody Maker 48:26, November 3, 1973.

11452   Jones, M. "Sarah: Searching for That Natural Sound." Melody
        Maker 48:52, November 17, 1973.

11453   Goddet, L. "Concerts." Jazz Hot no. 300:22, December 1973.

11454   Balagri, D., et al. "Trois Jour sans Surprises." Jazz Magazine
         no. 218:20-21, January 1974.

11455   "Talent in Action." Billboard 86:13, February 16, 1974.

11456   "Caught." down beat 41:25-26, February 28, 1974.

11457   "Sarah Casts Her Magic Spell." Soul 8:17, April 15, 1974.

11458   "Mister Kelly's, Chi." Variety 274:84, April 17, 1974.

11459   "Capitol Gold for Sassy." down beat 41:11, April 25, 1974.

11460   Ebert, A. "Still Sassy: Sarah Vaughan Never Felt Better." Es-
         sence 5:42-43, October 1974.

11461   "St. Regis, N.Y." Variety 277:67, January 29, 1975.

11462   "Sarah Vaughan Asks $200,000." Billboard 87:65, March 22, 1975.

11463   Robinson, L. "Divine Sarah." Ebony 30:94-96, April 1975.

11464   Williams, J. "Sarah Vaughan in a Resurgence; She Credits Switch
         to 'General' Music from Jazz." Billboard 87:31, April 5, 1975.

11465   "Berusande Saang." Orkester Journalen 43:13, September 1975.

11466   "Heard and Seen." Coda no. 141:36, September 1975.

11467   "Concert Reviews." Variety 281:52, November 19, 1975.

11468   Tomkins, L., and J. Carter. "Sinatra at the Palladium." Crescen-
         do International 14:25, December 1975.

11469   "Talent in Action." Billboard 88:35, March 20, 1976.

11470   "Concert Reviews." Variety 282:66, March 24, 1976.

11471   "Record Reviews: More Sarah Vaughan from Japan Live." down
         beat 43:33, March 25, 1976.

11472   Kolodin, I. "'Ellington Is Forever,' Likewise Mozart." Saturday
         Review 3:51-52, June 12, 1976.

11473   Feather, L. "Blindfold Test." down beat 43:33, June 17, 1976.

11474   Balliett, W. "Jazz: New York Notes." New Yorker 52:86, July 19,
         1976. Review of the Newport Jazz Festival and Vaughan's performance.

11475   Jones, M. "Symphonies for Sarah." Melody Maker 51:47, August
         14, 1976.

11476   "Record Reviews: Tenderly." Jazz Journal 29:40, September 1976.

11477   Von Know, A. "Raffig Sarah paa Atlantic." Orkester Journalen
         44:8, September 1976.

11478   "Jazz Albums: Tenderly." Melody Maker 51:30, October 16, 1976.

11479   "Jazz Albums: Sarah Vaughan." Melody Maker 51:25, November 6,
        1976.

11480   Chase, M. "Sarah Vaughan Sings the Beatles--'for Posterity.'"
        Rolling Stone no. 228:21, December 16, 1976.

11481   "Condado Inn, P.R." Variety 286:69, March 2, 1977.

11482   "Concert Reviews." Variety 286:64, March 9, 1977.

11483   Smith, A. J. "Sarah Vaughan: Never Ending Melody." down beat
        44:16-17, May 5, 1977.

11484   "Caught in the Act." Melody Maker 52:18, June 4, 1977.

11485   Carter, J. "The Magnificent Sarah Is Reviewed." Crescendo Inter-
        national 15:23, July 1977.

11486   "Jazz Live!" Jazz Journal International 30:20, July 1977.

11487   Tomkins, L. "Jazz Singer Supreme: Sarah Vaughan." Crescendo
        International 15:20-23, July 1977.

11488   Balliett, W. "Jazz: New York Notes." New Yorker 53:80, July 18,
        1977.

11489   "Marshall Fisher." Crescendo International 16:24, August 1977.

11490   Morgenstern, D. "Report from Newport--Sarah and Ornette Take
        the Honors." Jazz Journal International 30:26-27, August 1977.

11491   Tomkins, L. "Sarah Vaughan." Crescendo International 16:22-23,
        August 1977.

11492   "Talent in Action." Billboard 89:42, August 17, 1977.

11493   "Concert Reviews." Variety 288:88, September 7, 1977.

11494   "Talent in Action." Billboard 89:54, November 26, 1977.

11495   "Harrah's Tahoe." Variety 289:80, December 7, 1977.

11496   Siedell, M. "Gallery: Sarah Vaughan." Jazz Magazine (U.S.) 3:41-
        43, no. 1, 1978.

11497   "Concert Reviews." Variety 289:72, January 25, 1978.

11498   "Jazz Albums: Golden Hour Presents." Melody Maker 53:23, Feb-
        ruary 4, 1978.

11499   "Caught!" down beat 45:42, February 23, 1978.

11500   "Talent in Action." Billboard 90:69, March 18, 1978.

11501   "Album Reviews: Two Sounds." Crescendo International 16:29,
        April 1978.

11502   "Sarah Vaughan Awarded Berklee Degree." Crescendo International
        16:1, June 1978.

11503 "Reviews." Crescendo International 16:10, July 1978. Vaughan performs at the Valley Forge Music Fair.

11504 "Prez Awards." Jazz Journal International 31:36, August 1978.

11505 "Caught in the Act." Melody Maker 53:28, November 18, 1978.

11506 Tiegel, E. "Closeup." Billboard 90:82, December 9, 1978. Review of "How Long Has This Been Going On."

11507 "Jazz Albums: How Long Has This Been Going On." Melody Maker 53:33, December 16, 1978.

WALLER, FATS (Thomas Wright), 1904-1943.

11508 "How Tom Is Doin'." Time 42:55, August 9, 1943.

11509 ["Obituary."] Time 42:70, December 27, 1943.

11510 Jones, M., and L. Henshaw. "'Man, Fetch Me My Liquid Ham and Eggs,' Said Fats." Melody Maker 25:3, September 17, 1949.

11511 "Andy Razaf, Collaborator with 'Fats' Waller in Many of His Compositions." Jazz Journal 3:1, May 1950.

11512 "National Memorial Week of the Music of Thomas 'Fats' Waller." Jazz Journal 3:1, May 1950.

11513 Whiteman, P. "A Legendary Figure." Jazz Journal 3:1, May 1950.

11514 Burton, J. "Honor Roll of Popular Songwriters; No. 59--Thomas (Fats) Waller." Billboard 62:45, May 6, 1950.

11515 Traill, S. "Fats Waller." Melody Maker 26:9, May 20, 1950.

11516 Jones, M., and S. Traill. "'Fats' Waller's Six Pieces Depicting the City of London." Melody Maker 26:9, August 5, 1950.

11517 Schiedt, D. "Fats Waller; From a Biographer's Notebook." Record Changer 9:7, September 1950.

11518 "The Great Songwriters and Records of Their Greatest Songs." Billboard 62:93-94, October 7, 1950 Supplement.

11519 Schiedt, D. "Fats in Retrospect." Record Changer 9:7, December 1950.

11520 Davies, John R. T. The Music of Thomas "Fats" Waller with Complete Discography. London: J. J. Publications, 1951? A 26-page discography which was first published in Jazz Journal.

11521 "Oh, Didn't They Ramble." Melody Maker 27:9, January 20, 1951.

11522 "Editorial: Thomas 'Fats' Waller." Jazz Journal 4:7, May 1951.

11523 Levin, F. "The American Jazz Scene." Jazz Journal 4:3, May

1951. Waller is discussed as the musician who bridges jazz and popular music.

11524 Thompson, K. C. "'Fats' Waller in a Moon River Phase." Jazz Journal 4:1-2, May 1951.

11525 "Waller." Jazz Journal 4:16, May 1951.

11526 Traill, S. "Delicate Fats--and Don't Expect Any Fireworks!" Melody Maker 27:9, May 12, 1951.

11527 Ulanov, B. "History of Jazz; Pianists." Metronome 67:14-15, August 1951.

11528 "Hazel, Deeps Remember 'Fats.'" Melody Maker 27:6, September 15, 1951.

11529 Levin, F. "Andy Razaf--the Melody Man." Jazz Journal 4:1-2, October 1951.

11530 RCA to Cut Long-Lost Waller Solos." Billboard 63:20, November 10, 1951.

11531 Cooke, R. "The Genius of Thomas Fats Waller." Jazz Journal 5:13, May 1952.

11532 "Fats Says a Mouthful." Jazz Journal 5:12, May 1952.

11533 Levin, F. "The American Jazz Scene." Jazz Journal 5:4-5, May 1952.

11534 "One in a Million." Jazz Journal 5:20, May 1952.

11535 Paine, B. "That Lovable Guy; Memories of Fats Waller." Jazz Journal 5:1, May 1952.

11536 Parry-Jones, J. C. "A Nostalgic Note." Jazz Journal 5:13, May 1952.

11537 Ulanov, B. "Nostalgia." Metronome 68:34, December 1952.

11538 "Milan Fans Honor Fats, Form Club." Billboard 65:18, February 7, 1953.

11539 Mezzrow, M. "Memories of 'Fats.'" Jazz Journal 6:21-22, May 1953.

11540 Panassie, H. "A Critic Looks at 'Fats' Waller." Jazz Journal 6:14-16, May 1953.

11541 "Mr. Tin Pan Alley." Our World 8:38-39, July 1953.

11542 Davies, J. R. "The Music of Thomas 'Fats' Waller." Melody Maker 29:13, September 19, 1953; Jazz Journal 6:22, November 1953.

11543 Stewart-Baxter, D. "Thanks Mr. Kirkeby!" Jazz Journal 6:5-6, December 1953.

11544 Williams, M. L. "A Diamond Mouthful." Melody Maker 30:5, April 10, 1954.

11545 Sedric, G. "Talking About 'Fats' Waller." Jazz Journal 7:1-2, May 1954.

11546 "Fats' Pianist Son Favors Bud Powell but Cites Dad's 'Overpowering' Ability." down beat 21:6, June 16, 1954.

11547 Wilson, J. S. "A Lot of Waller Goes a Little Way." High Fidelity 4:84, December 1954.

11548 Kirkeby, E. "Fats." Melody Maker 31:3, March 5, 1955; 31:9, March 12, 1955; 31:7, March 26, 1955.

11549 "Waller Leaves Confusion as Songs Near Renewal." Billboard 67:25, September 17, 1955.

11550 Smith, H. "Walleresque." Record Research 1:8, October 1955.

11551 Flakser, H. "Continental Jazz Disc-ology; The English Recording of Thomas 'Fats' Waller, 1938-1939." Record Research 1:13-14, December 1955.

11552 Coss, B. "Jazz Pianists and the Jazz Piano." Jazz Today 2:20, March 1957.

11553 Wilson, J. S. "Jazz Pianists; A Discography." High Fidelity/Musical America 7:67, August 1957.

11554 "Piano--Rollography." Record Research 3:11, July-August 1958.

11555 Fox, Charles. Fats Waller. New York: A. S. Barnes, 1961, c1960.

11556 Wellstood, D. "Waller to Wellstood to Chaos." Jazz Research 3:10-11, August 1960.

11557 "Fats Waller's Son Goes to Court over Father's Musical Copyrights." Billboard 73:5, April 24, 1961.

11558 "Fats Waller Renewal Suit Going to Federal Courts; Illegitimate Sons an Issue." Variety 222:75, May 10, 1961.

11559 Balliett, W. "Jazz Concerts." New Yorker 37:157-158, September 30, 1961.

11560 Coss, B. "Jazz Piano--Three Fountainheads." down beat 28:16-17, October 26, 1961.

11561 Seeger, P. "Johnny Appleseed, Jr." Sing Out 12:66-67, no. 3, 1962.

11562 Dance, S. "Al Casey Back on the Scene." down beat 29:22, July 19, 1962.

11563 Rosenkrantz, T. "Fats Waller." down beat 29:35, August 30, 1962.

11564   Testoni, G. "Gli Autori dei Temi." Musica Jazz 18:42, October
        1962.

11565   Flasker, H. "Chords and Discords; Setting Records Straight." down
        beat 25:10, October 25, 1962.

11566   Fayenz, F. "Thomas 'Fats' Waller." Musica Jazz 19:11-16, Sep-
        tember 1963.

11567   Laverdure, M. "Portrait: Fats Waller." Jazz Magazine 9:40-44,
        November 1963.

11568   Feather, L. "Over My Jazz Shoulder." Melody Maker 39:9, Jan-
        uary 18, 1964.

11569   Barazzella, G. "Rulli di Pianola di Fats Waller." Musica Jazz
        20:41, November 1964.

11570   Feather, L. "Life with Feather." down beat 32:25, February 25,
        1965.

11571   Davies, J. R. "The Music of Thomas 'Fats' Waller." Storyville no.
        2:5-8, December 1965.

11572   Kumm, B. "Reflections on Fats." Storyville no. 2:2-4, December
        1965.

11573   Kirkeby, W. T. E., Duncan F. Schiedt, and Sinclair Traill. Ain't
        Misbehavin': The Story of Fats Waller. New York: Da Capo
        Press, 1975. Reprint of the 1966 edition published by Dodd,
        Mead, New York.

11574   Davies, J. R. "The Music of Thomas 'Fats' Waller." Storyville
        no. 3:6-10, February 1966; no. 5:25-27, June 1966; no. 6:9-10,
        August-September 1966.

11575   Kumm, B. "Kumm Let Us Waller; Reflections on Fats." Storyville
        no. 6:4-8, August-September 1966.

11576   Davies, J. R. "The Music of Thomas 'Fats' Waller." Storyville
        no. 7:14-16, October-November 1966.

11577   Linderoth, L. "Fats Waller; En Stor Spelman och Glaedjespridare
        som Aater Blivit Aktuell." Orkester Journalen 34:10-11, Decem-
        ber 1966.

11578   _____. "Fats Waller; En Stor Spelman och Skämtare." Orkester
        Journalen 35:10-11, January 1967; 35:10-11, February 1967.

11579   Davies, J. R. "The Music of Thomas 'Fats' Waller." Storyville
        no. 9:9-13, February-March 1967; no. 10-28-30, April-May, 1967;
        no. 11:13-18, June-July 1967; no. 12-36-37, August-September
        1967.

11580   Cooper, R. "The Immortal Fats Waller." Jazz Journal 20:24-25,
        December 1967.

11581   Dubois, P., et al. "Fats Waller." Jazz Hot no. 245:30-32, De-
        cember 1968.

11582 Laverdure, M. "Fats Waller: Vingt-Cinq Ans apres Tounours
       Vingt Ans!" Jazz Magazine no. 161:32-33, December 1968.

11583 Kumm, B. "Further Facets of Fats." Storyville no. 23:179-183,
       June-July 1969.

11584 "Record Reviews." Jazz Journal 22:36, November 1969.

11585 "Disques du Mois: Earl Hines Plays Fats Waller." Jazz Magazine
       no. 177:42, April 1970.

11586 "Record Reviews: Rare Fats Waller." Storyville no. 29:195-196,
       June-July 1970.

11587 "Fats Waller Honored with Commemorative Medal." Jazz and Pop
       9:11, July 1970.

11588 "La Chronique des Disques: Earl Hines Plays Fats Waller." Jazz
       Hot no. 264:40, September 1970.

11589 McCarthy, A. "Record Reviews: Ain't Misbehavin': Fats Waller
       and His Buddies." Jazz Monthly no. 189:21, November 1970.

11590 Kumm, B. "Record Reviews: Thomas 'Fats' Waller--Piano Rolls."
       Storyville no. 32:76-77, December 1970-January 1971.

11591 Voce, S. "Record Reviews: Parlour Piano Solos from Rare Piano
       Rolls." Jazz Journal 23:36-37, December 1970.

11592 "Parlor Piano Solos from Rare Piano Rolls--Thomas 'Fats' Waller."
       Jazz Report 7:17, no. 6, 1971.

11593 Goddet, L. "Chronique des Disques: Fats Waller Vol. 1 and 2."
       Jazz Hot no. 269:39, February 1971.

11594 Kumm, B. "Record Reviews." Storyville no. 33:116, February
       1971.

11595 Reda, J. "Reeditions: Fats Waller: Vol. 1 et 2." Jazz Magazine
       no. 187:45, March 1971.

11596 Stewart-Baxter, D. "Record Reviews: Fats Waller on the Air."
       Jazz Journal 24:41, June 1971.

11597 Traill, S. "Record Reviews: Piano Rolls 1924-31." Jazz Journal
       24:35, August 1971.

11598 Goddet, L. "La Chronique des Disques: Fats Waller Memorial
       No. 2." Jazz Hot no. 278:38, December 1971.

11599 Laverdure, M., et al. "Remember Fats." Jazz Magazine no.
       195:32-35, December 1971.

11600 Kumm, B. "Fats Waller on the Radio." IAJRC Journal 5:13-15,
       no. 2, 1972.

11601 "Disques du Mois: Memorial Album No. 2." Jazz Magazine no.
       196:31, January 1972.

11602   Terjanian, L. "Handful of Records: Memorial No. 2." Points du
        Jazz no. 6:140-144, March 1972.

11603   Berger, M. "Fats Waller: The Outside Insider." Journal of Jazz
        Studies 1:3-20, no. 1, 1973.

11604   Kumm, B. "Fats Waller in 1943." IAJRC Journal 6:14-15, no. 4,
        1973.

11605   "Record Reviews: Rare Fats Waller." Coda 10:26-27, no. 12, 1973.

11606   "Jazz Records: The Joint Is Jumpin'." Melody Maker 48:47, March
        24, 1973.

11607   "On Record: The Vocal Fats Waller." Jazz & Blues 3:26, Septem-
        ber 1973.

11608   Laverdure, M. "N'Oublions pas Fats." Jazz Magazine no. 217:6,
        December 1973.

11609   Brackney R. L. "Musical Legacy of Andy Razaf." Jazz Report
        8:7-9, no. 5, 1974.

11610   Cayer, D. A. "Black and Blue and Black Again: Three Stages of
        Racial Imagery in Jazz Lyrics." Journal of Jazz Studies 1:38-71,
        no. 1, 1974.

11611   "Record Reviews: The Rhythmakers, Eddie Condon, Fats Waller,
        Joe Sullivan." Coda 11:21, no. 6, 1974.

11612   Balliett, W. "Simplicity." New Yorker 50:117-118, March 25, 1974.

11613   Byard, J. "Around About Fats." Jazz Hot no. 305:12-13, May 1974.

11614   "Quelques Grands Pianists." Jazz Hot no. 305:10, May 1974.

11615   Berendt, J. E. "Organs, Keyboards and Synthesizer in Jazz." Jazz
        Forum no. 32:30-34, December 1974. An excerpt from Berendt's
        The Jazz Book: From Rag to Rock.

11616   Magnusson, T., and B. Bonner. "The Piano Rolls by Thomas Wal-
        ler and by 'Fats' Waller." Matrix no. 106:3-8, February 1975.

11617   Sundin, B. "Fats Waller: Complete Recordings." Orkester Jour-
        nalen 43:14-15, March 1975.

11618   Francis, H. "Jazz Development in Britain 1924-1974." Crescendo
        International 13:12, May 1975. Discusses the influence of Amer-
        ican jazz musicians such as Waller.

11619   Sundin, B. "Fats Waller; Complete Recordings 6-12." Orkester
        Journalen 43:14-15, July-August 1975.

11620   Magnusson, T. "Fats Waller with Gene Austin on the Record."
        Journal of Jazz Studies 4:75-83, no. 1, 1976.

11621   "Records: The Complete Fats Waller Vol. 1, 1934-35." Creem
        7:61, March 1976.

11622   Vance, J. "The Complete Fats Waller." Stereo Review 37:98, July
        1976.

11623   "Record Reviews: Fats Waller and His Rhythm: Vol. 17." Jazz
        Journal 29:40, September 1976.

11624   Newberger, E. H. "The Development of New Orleans and Stride
        Piano Styles." Journal of Jazz Studies 4:59, no. 2, 1977.

11625   Vance, Joel. Fats Waller, His Life and Times. Chicago: Con-
        temporary Books, 1977.

11626   Waller, Maurice, and Anthony Calabrese. Fats Waller. New York:
        Schirmer Books, 1977.

11627   "Record Reviews: Fractious Fingering." Jazz Journal 30:37-38,
        April 1977.

11628   Laverdure, M. "Fats Waller Memorial." Points du Jazz no. 13:62-
        68, June 1977.

11629   "Reissues: Piano Solos." Coda no. 157:23, September-October
        1977.

11630   "Broadway Jazz." Swinging Newsletter 8:5, no. 36, 1978.

11631   Dobie, W. "An Interview with Maurice Waller." Jazz Forum no.
        53:52-53, 1978.

11632   Johnson, S. "Ain't Misbehavin'." Jazz Magazine (U.S.) 2:20, no.
        4, 1978.

11633   "Fats Waller; Piano Solos, 1929-1941." Stereo Review 40:141, Feb-
        ruary 1978.

11634   "Record Review: Piano Solos/1929-1941." Radio Free Jazz 19:19,
        February 1978.

11635   Vance, J. "Stride Pianist Fats Waller: Dee-licious." Stereo Re-
        view 40:140-141, February 1978.

11636   Balliett, W. "Jazz." New Yorker 54:110-112, April 10, 1978.

11637   "Harlem's Sultan of Stride." Time 111:70, June 5, 1978.

11638   Kolodin, I. "The Mirth, Girth and Worth of 'Fats' Waller." Satur-
        day Review 5:40, August 1978.

11639   Sundin, B. "Fats Lever." Orkester Journalen 46:5, September
        1978.

11640   Weiss, P. "Wallermania." Stereo Review 41:72-73, September
        1978.

11641   Vance, J. "Ain't Misbehavin'." Stereo Review 41:180-181, Novem-
        ber 1978.

11642   "Fats' Fun Pure Broadway." down beat 45:14, November 2, 1978.
        Review of "Ain't Misbehavin'."

11643 Gottfried, M. "Theater: Openings in the Non-News Vacuum." Sat-
       urday Review 5:54, November 25, 1978.

11644 Hentoff, N. "Indigenous Music." Nation 227:589-590, November 25,
       1978.

WARFIELD, MRS. WILLIAM see PRICE, LEONTYNE

WARWICK, DIONNE (Marie Dionne Warwicke), 1941- .

11645 "Artists' Biographies." Billboard 74:12, December 29, 1962.

11646 Mourichon, E. "Stevie Wonder et Dionne Warwick: Le Jazz Cache."
       Jazz Hot no. 194:10-11, January 1964.

11647 Dawbarn, B. "Dionne Kills War Rumours." Melody Maker 39:7,
       May 30, 1964.

11648 _____. "Dionne Drops In." Melody Maker 39:7, September 26,
       1964.

11649 "New Acts." Variety 236:56, October 28, 1964.

11650 Hennessey, M. "Dionne Defiant." Melody Maker 41:8-9, February
       5, 1966.

11651 "New Acts." Variety 242:68, April 27, 1966.

11652 "Caribe Hilton, San Juan." Variety 243:38, July 13, 1966.

11653 "Sweet Smell of Success for Dionne Warwick." Sepia 15:12-15, Au-
       gust 1966.

11654 Saal, H. "Gospel Girl; Philharmonic Hall Concert." Newsweek
       68:101-102, October 10, 1966.

11655 "Copacabana, N.Y." Variety 246:66, May 3, 1967.

11656 "Dionne Warwick's What the Nightclub World Needs Now." Billboard
       79:6, May 6, 1967.

11657 "Spreading the Faith." Time 90:75, July 14, 1967.

11658 "Westside Room, L.A." Variety 247:51, July 19, 1967.

11659 "Mister Kelly's, Chi." Variety 249:52, December 6, 1967.

11660 "Dionne Weaves Magic Blues Spell at Apollo." Billboard 80:22,
       March 23, 1968.

11661 "Presenting Dionne Warwick ... 100 Per Cent." Sepia 17:72-73,
       April 1968.

11662 "Diplomat, H'wood, Fla." Variety 250:54, April 17, 1968.

11663 Smith, M. "Dionne, the Universal Warwick." Ebony 23:36-38, May
       1968.

11664 "Copacabana, N.Y." Variety 250:69, May 15, 1968.

11665 Henshaw, L. "Dionne." Melody Maker 43:10, June 15, 1968.

11666 "Dionne Warwick Ghetto Work Reflects New Mood of Negro Show
       Bizites." Variety 251:1, July 17, 1968.

11667 "Westside Room, L.A." Variety 253:56, December 4, 1968.

11668 Tiegel, E. "Dionne Warwick Displays Much Heart and Soul." Bill-
       board 80:15, December 14, 1968.

11669 Feather, L. "Blindfold Test." down beat 36:30, February 6, 1969.

11670 "Copacabana, N.Y." Variety 254:77, May 14, 1969.

11671 Dove, I. "Dionne Warwick in Poised and Polished Performance."
       Billboard 81:10, May 17, 1969.

11672 "Concert Reviews." Variety 255:50, July 23, 1969.

11673 "Sands, Las Vegas." Variety 255:51, August 6, 1969.

11674 "'I've Gotta Be Me' Attitude Wins for Dionne Warwick." Billboard
       81:SC25, October 4, 1969.

11675 "Sands, Las Vegas." Variety 257:60, January 21, 1970.

11676 "Diplomat, H'wood, Fla." Variety 258:83, April 1, 1970.

11677 Eldridge, R. "Caught in the Act." Melody Maker 45:12, April 18,
       1970.

11678 "Concert Reviews." Variety 258:56, April 22, 1970.

11679 Eldridge, R. "Dionne Warwick--the Ability to Communicate an Emo-
       tion." Melody Maker 45:5, April 25, 1970.

11680 "Copacabana, N.Y." Variety 258:95, May 6, 1970.

11681 "Talent in Action." Billboard 82:18, May 16, 1970.

11682 "Harrah's, Reno." Variety 259:53, June 3, 1970.

11683 "Miss Warwick Forms Labels." Billboard 82:14, July 18, 1970.

11684 "Talent in Action." Billboard 82:25, September 5, 1970.

11685 "Sands, Las Vegas." Variety 260:43, September 9, 1970.

11686 "Lifestyle." American Home 73:8, October 1970.

11687 "Dionne's Sweetest Years." Sepia 19:74-77, December 1970.

11688 "Now Grove, L.A." Variety 262:69, March 17, 1971.

11689   "Scepter, Blue Jac in Unsettled Settlement." Billboard 83:3, March 20, 1971.

11690   Feather, L. "Caught in the Act." Melody Maker 46:18, March 27, 1971.

11691   "Scepter Scores Blue Jac's Attorney for 'Leaking' Story." Billboard 83:3, March 27, 1971.

11692   "Talent in Action." Billboard 83:36, April 3, 1971.

11693   Feather, L. "Los Angeles." Jazz Magazine no. 189:9, May 1971.

11694   "Dionne Warwicke, Hayes, Cropper Take Top Memphis Music Awards." Billboard 83:3-4, June 5, 1971.

11695   "Harrah's, Reno." Variety 263:53, June 16, 1971.

11696   Wickham, V. "Dionne Today." Melody Maker 46:13, July 17, 1971.

11697   "Sands, Las Vegas." Variety 263:37, July 28, 1971.

11698   Feather, L. "Too Much Perfection from Dionne." Melody Maker 46:26, August 21, 1971.

11699   Moore, B. "Dionne Warwick on the Fears and Worries of a Star." Sepia 20:36-40, September 1971.

11700   "Copacabana, N.Y." Variety 264:47, October 13, 1971.

11701   "Talent in Action." Billboard 83:62, October 23, 1971.

11702   "Sands, Las Vegas." Variety 265:32, December 29, 1971.

11703   Deni, L. "Talent in Action." Billboard 84:12, January 8, 1972.

11704   Watts, M. "Dionne." Melody Maker 47:25, January 29, 1972.

11705   "Records: Dionne." Rolling Stone no. 102:48, February 17, 1972.

11706   "Grove, L.A." Variety 266:100, April 5, 1972.

11707   "Riviera, Las Vegas." Variety 267:63, May 17, 1972; 267:46, August 2, 1972.

11708   "Harrah's Tahoe." Variety 268:54, October 4, 1972.

11709   Alterman, L. "Miss Warwicke, Just Being Herself." Melody Maker 48:40, March 3, 1973.

11710   "Records: Just Being Myself." Rolling Stone no. 131:60, March 29, 1973.

11711   "Concert Reviews." Variety 271:94, July 18, 1973.

11712   "Harrah's, Reno." Variety 271:99, July 18, 1973.

11713   "Exhausted Warwicke Cancels Buffalo Perf." Variety 272:36, August 15, 1973.

11714 "Riviera, Las Vegas." Variety 272:41, October 17, 1973.

11715 "Caught in the Act." Melody Maker 48:70, November 24, 1973; 48:19, December 8, 1973.

11716 "Riviera, Las Vegas." Variety 274:61, February 27, 1974.

11717 "Harrah's, Reno." Variety 274:53, May 1, 1974.

11718 "Riviera, Las Vegas." Variety 275:55, May 29, 1974.

11719 Ebert, A. "Bill and Dionne." Essence 5:38-39, June 1974.

11720 Windeler, R. "Dionne Warwicke." Stereo Review 32:78-79, June 1974.

11721 "Concert Reviews." Variety 275:48, July 3, 1974.

11722 "Starlight Theatre, K.C." Variety 276:54, August 21, 1974.

11723 Dove, I. "Singles: Dionne: Winner with Spinners." Rolling Stone no. 169:27, September 12, 1974.

11724 "Harrah's, Reno." Variety 277:85, January 15, 1975.

11725 "Riviera, Las Vegas." Variety 278:79, February 12, 1975.

11726 "Caught in the Act." Melody Maker 50:16, March 1, 1975.

11727 "Talent in Action." Billboard 87:36, March 8, 1975.

11728 "Records: Then Came You." Rolling Stone no. 185:60, April 24, 1975.

11729 "Caught in the Act." Melody Maker 50:24, June 14, 1975.

11730 "Cunard Int'l, London." Variety 279:70, June 25, 1975.

11731 "Caught in the Act." Melody Maker 50:21, June 28, 1975.

11732 "Riviera, Las Vegas." Variety 279:67, July 2, 1975.

11733 "Warwicke Sues Bacharach and David for $6,000,000." Variety 279:45, August 6, 1975.

11734 "Harrah's, Reno." Variety 280:68, October 15, 1975.

11735 "Records: Track of the Cat." Rolling Stone no. 205:51, January 29, 1976.

11736 "Concert Reviews." Variety 282:74, March 3, 1976.

11737 "Talent in Action." Billboard 88:36, March 13, 1976.

11738 "Diplomat, H'wood, Fla." Variety 282:93, March 17, 1976.

11739 Burgess, A. A. "Dionne and Isaac Sizzle on Stage with Sexy Songs." Jet 49:58-62, March 18, 1976.

11740   "Performance." Rolling Stone no. 211:94, April 22, 1976.

11741   "Concert Reviews." Variety 283:68, May 26, 1976.

11742   "Talent in Action." Billboard 88:38, June 5, 1976.

11743   "Concert Reviews." Variety 283:44, August 4, 1976.

11744   Horowitz, I. "Scepter Warwick Tapes Awarded." Billboard 88:14,
        December 18, 1976.

11745   Williams, R. "Dionne Warwick Is Never Less Than Perfect--Al-
        ways Incapable of Awkwardness." Melody Maker 52:10, January
        15, 1977.

11746   "Bacharach & David Sue Springboard for $19-Mil over Warwick Mas-
        ters." Variety 285:77, February 2, 1977.

11747   "Diplomat, H'wood, Fla." Variety 278:64, March 5, 1975.

11748   Winters, J. "New Career for Dionne Warwick." Sepia 26:42-46,
        July 1977.

11749   "Concert Reviews." Variety 288:46, August 17, 1977.

11750   "Sands, Las Vegas." Variety 288:71, August 31, 1977.

11751   "Albums: Love at First Sight." Melody Maker 52:23, November 12,
        1977.

11752   "Sands, Las Vegas." Variety 289:89, November 16, 1977.

11753   "Records: Love at First Sight." High Fidelity/Musical America
        28:133, January 1978.

WATERS, ETHEL, 1900-1977.

11754   "Singing for Your Supper." Independent Woman 15:106-108, April 1936.

11755   "Ethel Waters Conquers the Devil in Cabin in the Sky." Life 9:63,
        December 9, 1940.

11756   "Portrait as Hager in Mamba's Daughters." Theatre Arts 25:752,
        October 1941.

11757   Davies, R., et al. "The Records of Ethel Waters." Playback 2:26-
        29, June 1949.

11758   Morrison, A. "Ethel Waters Comes Back to Broadway." Negro Di-
        gest 8:6-10, April 1950.

11759   Waters, Ethel, and Charles Samuels. His Eye Is on the Sparrow:
        An Autobiography. Westport, Conn.: Greenwood Press, 1978.
        Reprint of the 1951 edition published by Doubleday.

11760   _____. "Mamba's Daughter." Atlantic 187:31-36, March 1951.
        Excerpt from His Eye Is on the Sparrow.

11761 "Stormy Weather." Newsweek 37:92-93, March 5, 1951.

11762 "Where the Blues Began." Time 57:104, March 12, 1951.

11763 Smith, H. "It Had God in It." Saturday Review of Literature 34:18, March 24, 1951.

11764 Ramsey, F. "Lonely Life." Nation 172:303-304, March 31, 1951.

11765 "Ethel Waters in Symphonic Bow." Musical Courier 144:20, December 1, 1951.

11766 "Men in My Life." Ebony 7:24-32, January 1952.

11767 " 'I'm Just Old, Human, and Tired,' Says Ethel Waters." down beat 19:6, April 4, 1952.

11768 "Apollo, N.Y." Variety 188:55, November 5, 1952.

11769 "Member of the Wedding." Ebony 8:47-51, December 1952. Waters plays the part of the cook, Bernice, in the film version of this Broadway hit.

11770 "Still Waters." Saturday Review 36:30-32, October 10, 1953.

11771 "Caught in the Act." down beat 20:2, November 4, 1953.

11772 Kunstadt, L. "From the Archives." Record Research 1:10, April 1955.

11773 "The Black Swan Story." Record Research 1:4, August 1955.

11774 "Boulevard, Queens, N.Y." Variety 202:53, May 16, 1956.

11775 "Le Ruban Bleu, N.Y." Variety 204:53, November 7, 1956.

11776 "Miss Waters Regrets." Ebony 12:56-60, February 1957.

11777 Hentoff, N. "Garvin Bushell and New York Jazz in the 1920's." Jazz Review 2:16-17, April 1959.

11778 Malcolm, D. F. "Off Broadway." New Yorker 35:81, April 18, 1959.

11779 "Jazzmen to Take Ride on 'Route 66.'" down beat 28:12, September 28, 1961.

11780 Young, A. S. "Private Life of Ethel Waters." Sepia 11:55-58, January 1962.

11781 Ames, M. "Ethel Waters: Clearly One of the Greatest." High Fidelity/Musical America 18:108, August 1968.

11782 Reilly, P. "Ethel Waters: Unique and Indispensable." High Fidelity/Musical America 21:73-74, August 1968. Review of her recording "On Stage and Screen 1925-1940."

11783 Ellis, C. "Ethel Waters--Jazz Singer." Storyville no. 22:128-130, April-May 1969.

11784 "Cast in Marna Cooper as Segment of NBC-TV's Daniel Boone Series." Jet 37:53, December 18, 1969.

11785 "Chicago's Own Tonys: One to Ethel Waters." Variety 260:73, September 23, 1970.

11786 Jones, M. "Jazz Records: Jazzin' Babies Blues--1921-1927, Vol. 2." Melody Maker 46:22, April 24, 1971.

11787 Stewart-Baxter, D. "Record Reviews: Jazzin' Babies Blues--1924-1927, Vol. 2." Jazz Journal 24:35, May 1971.

11788 Dobrin, Arnold. Voices of Joy, Voices of Freedom: Ethel Waters, Sammy Davis, Jr., Marian Anderson, Paul Robeson, Lena Horne. New York: Coward, McCann & Geoghegan, 1972.

11789 "Record Reviews: Jazzin' Babies Blues 1921-1927." Coda 10:17, no. 5, 1972.

11790 Waters, Ethel. To Me It's Wonderful. New York: Harper & Row, 1972. Autobiography.

11791 Niquet, B. "Ethel Waters." Points du Jazz no. 6:5-18, March 1972.

11792 Rankin, A. "Three Lives of Ethel Waters." Reader's Digest 101:81-85, December 1972.

11793 Pleasants, H. "Bel Canto in Jazz and Pop Singing." Music Educator's Journal 59:54-59, May 1973.

11794 "On Record: Ethel Waters." Jazz & Blues 3:30, July 1973.

11795 "Records: Ethel Waters Greatest Hits." Crawdaddy no. 26:91, July 1973.

11796 "Record Reviews: Ethel Waters--1938-1939." Coda 11:15-16, no. 7, 1974.

11797 "Happy Birthday, Ethel Waters." Stereo Review 37:119, October 1976.

11798 ["Obituary."] Jazz Forum no. 49:18, 1977; Neue Zeitschrift für Musik 3:541, no. 6, 1977; Nuova Rivista Musicale Italiana 11:530-531, no. 3, 1977; Coda no. 157:31, September-October 1977.

11799 "Ethel Waters Dies at 80." Variety 288:2, September 7, 1977.

11800 "Ethel Waters, 76, Dies in California." Billboard 89:74, September 10, 1977.

11801 Dahlgren, R. ["Obituary."] Orkester Journalen 45:5, October 1977.

11802 ["Obituary."] Jazz Magazine no. 258:50, October 1977; Jazz Podium 26:27, October 1977.

11803 Giddins, G. "Weatherbird: Ethel Waters: Mother of Us All." Village Voice 22:63, October 10, 1977.

11804 Kunstadt, L. "Ethel Waters, Vocal Pioneer, 1896-1977." Rolling
       Stone no. 25:26, October 20, 1977.

11805 Gillespie, M. A. "Ethel Waters." Essence 8:63, November 1977.

11806 Stewart-Baxter, D. ["Obituary."] Jazz Journal International 30:33,
       November 1977.

11807 ["Obituary."] down beat 44:12, November 3, 1977; Crescendo Inter-
       national 16:37, December 1977.

11808 DeKorte, Juliann. Finally Home. Old Tappan, N.J.: F. H. Revell
       Co., 1978. A biography of Waters written by the nurse who cared
       for her in her later years.

11809 Knaack, Twila. Ethel Waters: I Touched a Sparrow. Waco, Texas:
       Word Books, 1978. Biographical work by a friend during her last
       years.

11810 Nevers, D. "Ethel Waters." Jazz Hot no. 346:42-45, February
       1978.

11811 "Ethel Waters." Music Educator's Journal 64:64-65, March 1978.

11812 "Records: A Tribute to Ethel Waters." High Fidelity/Musical Amer-
       ica 28:170-171, October 1978.

11813 Kresh, P. "Diahann Carroll Sings for Ethel Waters." Stereo Re-
       view 41:107, December 1978.

WATTS, ANDRE, 1946- .

11814 "Nowojorski Debiut Andre Wattsa." Ruch Muzyczny 7:4, no. 11,
       1963.

11815 "Col. Hopes It Has Another Cliburn in Andre Watts." Variety
       229:49, February 6, 1963.

11816 "Giant & a Prince." Time 81:60, February 8, 1963.

11817 "Real Pro." Newsweek 61:58, February 11, 1963.

11818 "A Teen-ager Rocks Hall of Great Music." Life 54:30, February 15,
       1963.

11819 Kolodin, I. "Music to My Ears; Rising Star of A. Watts." Saturday
       Review 46:53-54, February 16, 1963.

11820 Ardoin, J. "Debut of Andre Watts." High Fidelity/Musical America
       83:45-46, April 1963.

11821 _____. "Orchestras." High Fidelity/Musical America 83:33,
       April 1963.

11822 "Virtuoso on the Rise." Ebony 18:124-126, April 1963.

11823 "The High-Voltage Mr. Watts." American Record Guide 29:718, May
       1963.

11824 Jacobson, R. "Lewisohn Stadium." High Fidelity/Musical America
       83:6, August 1963.

11825 "Andre Watts: Prodigious Talent; An Interview." Clavier 3:18-19,
       no. 1, 1964.

11826 "What Music Means to Me." Seventeen 23:22, January 1964.

11827 Mayer, M. "Prodigies." Esquire 61:106-107, May 1964.

11828 Walsh, S. "Dead Easy." Music and Musicians 14:39, August 1966.

11829 Russell, F. "Andre Watts Interview." Piano Quarterly no. 57:16-
       21, Fall 1966.

11830 Sargeant, W. "Musical Events; Recital in Philharmonic Hall." New
       Yorker 42:234, November 5, 1966.

11831 Watts, A. "Recordings Vs. Live Performances?" Symphony News
       18:11, no. 3, 1967.

11832 Diamond, R. "Rochester, N.Y." Musical Leader 99:4, January
       1967.

11833 "January's Guest Artists." San Francisco Symphony Program Notes
       p. 13, January 1967.

11834 ["Recital, New York."] High Fidelity/Musical America 17:MA15,
       January 1967.

11835 Rich, A. "Young Excitement in Music." House Beautiful 109:102-
       103, July 1967.

11836 Soria, D. J. "People and Places." High Fidelity/Musical America
       17:MA5, September 1967.

11837 Karp, V. "Master Watts Comes of Age." Music and Artists 1:30-
       31, no. 2, 1968.

11838 Saal, H. "Beautiful Innocence." Newsweek 71:81, January 29, 1968.

11839 Fleming, S. "And We Quote." High Fidelity/Musical America
       18:MA19, February 1968.

11840 Sargeant, W. "Musical Events." New Yorker 43:94, February 3,
       1968.

11841 "May's Guest Artists." San Francisco Symphony Program Notes p.
       11, May 1968.

11842 Schonberg, H. C. "M & A Reviews: The Press." Music and Art-
       ists 2:48, no. 1, 1969.

11843 Crichton, R. "Music in London." Musical Times 110:46, January
       1969.

11844 Mason, E. "Young Lion." Music and Musicians 17:40-41, January 1969.

11845 Wimbush, R. "Here and There." Gramophone 46:989, January 1969.

11846 Blyth, A. "The Form of the 'Hero.'" Music and Musicians 17:53, February 1969.

11847 Kirby, F. "Watt's Glowing Performance Lights Up Hall." Billboard 81:13, February 1, 1969.

11848 Cusumano, R. "The Prep Schools Days of Andre Watts." International Musician 67:5, April 1969.

11849 Satz, A. "Boston Symphony, Watts." High Fidelity/Musical America 19:MA16, April 1969.

11850 Massaquoi, H. J. "André Watts, a Giant Among Giants at Age Twenty-Two." Ebony 24:90-91, May 1969.

11851 Romadinova, D. "Concert Problems in America." American Musical Digest 1:43-44, October 1969. Translation of "Muzyka i Muzykantz Ameriki" in Sovetskaya Muzyka 33:140-149, May 1969.

11852 Darden, N. "My Man Andre." Saturday Review 52:43-45, July 26, 1969.

11853 "The Musical Whirl." High Fidelity/Musical America 19:MA14-15, October 1969.

11854 Gyongy, P. "Watts Stars in Budapest." Billboard 81:86, November 8, 1969.

11855 "Concert Notes." Strad 80:383, December 1969.

11856 "Jekyll and Hyde Out West." American Musical Digest 1:14, December 1969.

11857 Pandi, M. "Kuelfoeldi Muveszek Hangversenyei." Muzsika 12:26-28, December 1969.

11858 Jarocinski, S. "BEMUS: Belgradzki Festiwal Muzyczny." Ruch Muzyczny 14:14, no. 1, 1970.

11859 Chamfray, C. "Andre Watts." Journal Musical Francais no. 188:36, January 1970.

11860 Simmons, D. "London Music." Musical Opinion 93:183, January 1970.

11861 ["Recital, New York."] High Fidelity/Musical America 20:24-25, June 1970, Section 2.

11862 Chanan, M. "A Mild 'Spring.'" Music and Musicians 19:60, November 1970.

11863 "Muenchner Konzerte." Oper und Konzert 8:34-35, November 1970.

11864 Pandi, M. "Koncertkronika." Muzsika 14:35, January 1971.

11865   "The Musical Whirl."   High Fidelity/Musical America 21:MA12-13,
        October 1971.

11866   Cemino, R.   "Filarmonica de Buenos Aires."   Buenos Aires Mu-
        sical 27:2, no. 441, 1972.

11867   Dresskell, N.   "1972 Portland Convention Evening Programs."   Amer-
        ican Music Teacher 21:25, no. 3, 1972.

11868   Fahrer, A.   "An Interview with Andre Watts."   American Music
        Teacher 21:18-19, no. 5, 1972.

11869   Black, D.   "Andre Watts: World's No. 1 Black Concert Pianist."
        Sepia 21:2-26, March 1972.

11870   Simmons, D.   "London Music."   Musical Opinion 95:568, August
        1972.

11871   "Ten Outstanding Single Men."   Ebony 27:88-96, August 1972.

11872   Bredemann, D., and G. Ackerman.   "'The Point Is to Make Music';
        an Interview with Andre Watts."   Piano Quarterly 21:12-15, no.
        81, 1973.

11873   "Herkulessaal: Klavierabend Andre Watts."   Oper und Konzert 11:31,
        no. 1, 1973.

11874   Hermann, I.   "Mainz: Leinsdorf, Watts und die Wiener Symphon-
        iker."   Neue Zeitschrift für Musik 134:373-374, no. 6, 1973.

11875   "Konzerte."   Oper und Konzert 11:25-31, no. 7, 1973.

11876   Hamburger, K.   "Koncertkronika."   Muzsika 16:35-42, January 1973.

11877   Kolodin, I.   "A Weekend Chez Boulez."   Saturday Review 1:78, Jan-
        uary 27, 1973.

11878   Hiemenz, J.   "Musician of the Month: Andre Watts."   High Fidel-
        ity/Musical America 23:MA4-5, February 1973.

11879   Kolodin, I.   "Destiny Has No Prejudice."   Saturday Review 1:52,
        February 1973.

11880   "Pittsburgh Sym.; Watts."   High Fidelity/Musical America 23:MA24,
        February 1973.

11881   Smith, P. J.   "N.Y. Phil.: Schumann."   High Fidelity/Musical
        America 23:MA20, April 1973.

11882   "Spotlight."   Music Journal 31:33, April 1973.

11883   "Leinsdorf, Watts und die Wiener Symphoniker--Konzert in der Main-
        zer Rheingoldhalle."   Orchester 21:433, July-August 1973.

11884   "The Musical Whirl."   High Fidelity/Musical America 23:MA18-19,
        September 1973.

11885   Ginzburg, L.   "Orkestr iz San-Frantsisko."   Sovetskaya Muzyka
        37:72-78, November 1973.

11886 "Muenchen." Opera und Konzert 12:33, no. 7, 1974.

11887 Watts, A. "How About a Truth-in-Recordings Movement?" High Fidelity/Musical America 24:16, January 1974.

11888 "Andre Watts: A Universe of Music." Sepia 23:48-50, March 1974.

11889 "Concert Reviews." Variety 276:46, September 25, 1974.

11890 Hall, D. "Andre Watts at the Piano--Four Times." Stereo Review 34:108, March 1975.

11891 Wallgruen, H. "Hamburg: Erich Leinsdorf, Andre Watts und die NDR-Sinfoniker." Orchester 23:109, March 1975.

11892 "Liszt Award to 'Todtentanz [sic].'" Billboard 87:34, November 29, 1975.

11893 Moor, P. "Festival de Berlin, 1970." Buenos Aires Musical 25:5, no. 422, 1976.

11894 Morrison, B. "American Piano Music." Music and Musicians 25:30-32, November 1976.

11895 "Concert Reviews." Variety 284:64, November 3, 1976.

11896 Watt, D. "Popular Records." New Yorker 52:166-168, December 13, 1976.

11897 Berg, G. "Andre Watts: A Promise Fulfilled." Encore 6:32-34, May 9, 1977.

11898 Watts, A. "Music, Youth, Racial Equality: Views of Pianist André Watts." U.S. News & World Report 82:69, June 6, 1977.

11899 Doerschuk, B. "Andre Watts." Contemporary Keyboard 3:12-14, December 1977.

11900 Gaines, J. R. "Bio." People 9:48-50, June 26, 1978.

11901 Morriwon, B. "Andre Watts." Music and Musicians 26:34, August 1978.

11902 Thackeray, R. "Orchestral." Musical Times 119:700, August 1978.

11903 Phillips, H. E. "Musician of the Month: André Watts." High Fidelity/Musical America 28:MA4-5, December 1978.

WAYMON, EUNICE see SIMONE, NINA

WEATHERS, FELICIA.

11904 Limmert, E. "Scherzo mit Tödlichem Ausgang; Neuinszenierung von 'Salome' im Opernhaus." Neue Zeitschrift für Musik 125:201, no. 5, 1964.

11905 McCredie, A. D. "Hanover." Opera 15:406, June 1964.

11906 Welsh, C. N. "Graz." Opera 15:49, Autumn 1964.

11907 Barnes, C. "Boris in Caledonia." Music and Musicians 13:32, July
       1965.

11908 Porter, A. "Glasgow." Musical Times 106:530, July 1965.

11909 "Scottish Opera." Opera 16:538, July 1965.

11910 Koegler, H. "Cologne." Opera 16:826, November 1965.

11911 Kolodin, I. "Music to My Ears." Saturday Review 48:47, Novem-
       ber 6, 1965.

11912 Koegler, H. "Cologne." Opera 17:950, December 1966; Opera News
       31:30, December 10, 1966.

11913 Hoffman, R. L. "Wednesday Nights at the Lyric." Musical Leader
       99:3, January 1967.

11914 Steadman, J. W., and G. McElroy. "Chicago." Opera News 31:30,
       January 21, 1967.

11915 Marsh, R. C. "Lyric Opera and Mary Garden's Shadow." High Fi-
       delity/Musical America 17:MA29, February 1967.

11916 Spingel, H. O. "Felicia Weathers." Opern Welt no. 2:35-37, Feb-
       ruary 1967.

11917 Eaton, Q. "Winner; Interview." Opera News 31:13, June 10, 1967.

11918 Koegler, H. "Cologne." Opera 18:920, November 1967.

11919 _____. "Köln: Balladeske Tabieaux Vivants." Opern Welt no.
       11:42, November 1967.

11920 Desick, S. A. "San Diego." Opera News 32:28, December 23, 1967.

11921 "Information im Bild." Musikalische Jugend 17:12, no. 5, 1968.

11922 "M & A Reviews: Festivals." Music and Artists 1:44, no. 3, 1968.

11923 Fossum, K. "Oslo." Opera 19:62-63, January 1968.

11924 Bernheimer, M. "San Diego." Opera 19:145, February 1968.

11925 Katona, P. M. "Berlin." Opera 19:121, February 1968.

11926 Abody, B. "Tito Gobbi es Felicia Weathers." Muzsika 11:32, April
       1968.

11927 Holmes, A. "Houston." Opera News 32:25, May 18, 1968.

11928 Gualerzi, G. "Bologna." Opera 19:490, June 1968.

11929 Wilson, C. "Scottish Opera Season." Opera 19:678, August 1968.

11930 "'Don Carlos'; Covent Garden Opera at the Royal Albert Hall." Opera 19:768-769, September 1968.

11931 O'Daniel, H. "At Zoo Opera: The Stars Return." High Fidelity/Musical America 18:MA25, September 1968.

11932 Crankshaw, G. "Proms: Audible Drama." Music and Musicians 17:45, October 1968.

11933 Stedman, J. W., and G. McElroy. "Chicago." Opera News 33:24, November 23, 1968.

11934 Dettmer, R. "Resumption in Chicago." Opera 19:966-967, December 1968.

11935 Matzner, J. "Simone Boccanegra." Musica 23:257, no. 3, 1969.

11936 Jacobson, B. "Lyric Opera--a Happy Return." High Fidelity/Musical America 19:MA20-21, January 1969.

11937 Holmes, A. "Houston." Opera News 33:34, January 25, 1969.

11938 Spingel, H. O. "Ein Hoehepunkt der Saison." Opern Welt no. 6:15, June 1969.

11939 "Names, Dates and Places." Opera News 34:4, November 22, 1969.

11940 Stedman, J., and G. McElroy. "Chicago." Opera News 34:24, December 13, 1969.

11941 "Hartford." Opera News 34:32-33, January 31, 1970; Opera 21:219, March 1970.

11942 Bims, H. "Felicia Weathers: Dauntless Diva." Ebony 25:52-56, May 1970.

11943 Grier, C. "Sore Throat Defeats Aida." Music and Musicians 19:50, September 1970.

11944 Osborn, C. "London Opera Diary." Opera 21:885, September 1970.

11945 "Names, Dates and Places." Opera News 35:5, September 19, 1970.

11946 Humphreys, H. S. "Cincinnati: Zoo Opera Going Strong." High Fidelity/Musical America 20:MA22-23, October 1970.

11947 Fierz, G. "Auf Schweizer Buehnen." Opernwelt no. 7:40-41, July 1976.

11948 Schaumkell, C. D. "Met-Stars von Vorgestern, Gestern und Heute." Opernwelt no. 10:54-55, October 1976.

11949 Neubauer, S. "Konzentriert auf ein Familiendrama--Strauss' 'Salome' in Bremen." Opernwelt 18:40, no. 10, 1977.

11950 Rasponi, L. "Rome." Opera News 41:39-40, June 1977.

11951 Bellingardi, L. "Rome." Opera 28:892-895, September 1977.

WEBB, CHICK (William), 1925- .

11952   Noonan, J. P.   "The Secrets of Chick Webb's Drumming Technique."
        down beat 39:26, July 20, 1972.   Reprinted from down beat, Sep-
        tember 1938.

11953   Tanner, P.   "Oh, Didn't They Ramble."   Melody Maker 26:9, July
        1, 1950.

11954   Staley, R.   "Stomping at the Savoy, a Tribute to the Late Chick
        Webb."   Jazz Journal 4:1-2, April 1951.

11955   Lucas, J.   "Wild Drummers I Have Known."   Jazz Journal 8:4-5,
        March 1955.

11956   Balliett, W.   "Drums, Now and Then."   Saturday Review 38:50-51,
        May 28, 1955.

11957   Jepsen, J. G.   "Jazzens Instrumentalister: Trummor."   Orkester
        Journalen 23:24, December 1955.

11958   DeMicheal, D.   "Evolution of the Drum Solo."   down beat 28:23-24,
        March 30, 1961.

11959   Dance, H.   "Drum Mad and Lightening Fast."   Saturday Review
        46:52-53, June 15, 1963.

11960   Barazzetta, G.   "La 'Jungle Band,' Chick Webb o Fletcher Hender-
        son?"   Musica Jazz 20:21, April 1964.

11961   Hoefer, G.   "History of the Drum in Jazz."   Jazz 4:14, no. 10, 1965.

11962   Schiozzi, B.   "L'Evoluzione della Batteria."   Musica Jazz 21:12,
        July 1965.

11963   Ioakimidis, D.   "Chick Webb, le Coeur, l'Esprit et les Drums."
        Jazz Hot no. 230:18-21, April 1967.

11964   Korall, B.   "King of the Savoy."   Saturday Review 50:51, December
        30, 1967.

11965   Williams, R.   "It All Began with Chick Webb."   Melody Maker 45:26,
        March 14, 1970.

11966   McRae, B.   "A B Basics, a Column for the Newcomer to Jazz."
        Jazz Journal 23:13, October 1970.

11967   Cullaz, M.   "La Chronique des Disques: A Legend; King of the Sa-
        voy."   Jazz Hot no. 268:38, January 1971.

11968   Allen, W. C.   "Random Notes on Some Big Band Personnels."   Ma-
        trix no. 91:5, February 1971.

11969   "Handful of Records: Chick Webb and His Orchestra Featuring Ella
        Fitzgerald."   Points du Jazz no. 5:133-134, September 1971.

11970   "Disques du Mois: Chick Webb 'a Legend'."   Jazz Magazine no.
        204:48, October 1972.

11971 Cressant, P., and D. Humair. "50 Ans de Batterie." Jazz Hot no. 291:11, February 1973.

11972 "Petite Encyclopedie des Drummers." Jazz Hot no. 291:33, February 1973.

11973 Simmen, J. "Crystal Clear." Coda no. 143:25-26, November 1975.

11974 "Drum Beat." Melody Maker 51:30, April 24, 1976.

11975 Hillary, R. "The Legendary Chick Webb--a Profile in Courage." Modern Drum 1:22-23, no. 3, 1977.

11976 "Reviews: The Best of Chick Webb and His Orchestra.; Bronzeville Stomp." IAJRC Journal 10:18-19, no. 2, 1977.

11977 "Michael's Pub, N.Y." Variety 292:77, September 6, 1978. A performance in honor of Webb.

11978 Giddins, G. "Weatherbird: Chick's Web Revisited." Village Voice 23:100, September 11, 1978.

WONDER, STEVIE (Steveland Judkins Morris; Steveland Judkins Hardaway; Stephen D. Judkins), 1950?- .

11979 "Little Stevie Wonder." Sepia 11:39-41, August 1962.

11980 "Wonderful World of Stevie Wonder." Ebony 18:99-100, July 1963.

11981 Mourichon, E. "Stevie Wonder et Dionne Warwick: Le Jazz Cache." Jazz Hot no. 194:10-11, January 1964.

11982 "Jazz Soul of Little Stevie Wonder." Sepia 13:21-25, April 1964.

11983 "Mr. Harmonica Man." Melody Maker 41:13, January 29, 1966.

11984 Jones, M. "It's Not Such a Drag Being Blind." Melody Maker 42:11, October 14, 1967.

11985 Landau, J. "A Whiter Shade of Black." Crawdaddy no. 11:35-40, September-October 1967.

11986 "Steve Talk." Melody Maker 42:5, September 2, 1967.

11987 "Marty's on Hill, L.A." Variety 251:51, May 29, 1968.

11988 "Stevie's Story." MBI p. 32, November-December 1968.

11989 "Soul's Shock Troopers." Melody Maker 44:11, January 25, 1969.

11990 Eldridge, R. "What Makes Stevie So Wonderful." Melody Maker 44:5, February 1, 1969.

11991 _____. "Funkedelic!" Melody Maker 44:7, March 15, 1969.

11992 _____. "Stevie's a Big Star Now." Melody Maker 44:6, March 15, 1969.

11993 _____ . "Will Stevie Wonder Become Another Sammy Davis?"
Melody Maker 44:7, April 5, 1969.

11994 "Stevie Wonder's Award." Variety 254:61, April 23, 1969.

11995 "Apollo, N.Y." Variety 255:60, June 4, 1969.

11996 Joe, R. "Wonder a Wonder in Hot Concert; Masekela Clicks, Too."
Billboard 81:26, October 11, 1969.

11997 Eldridge, R. "Stevie Gets His Number 1." Melody Maker 44:7, December 20, 1969.

11998 "Concert Reviews." Variety 257:38, December 24, 1969.

11999 Oberbeck, S. K. "Big Stevie." Newsweek 75:65, January 12, 1970.

12000 "Copacabana, N.Y." Variety 258:55, March 25, 1970.

12001 Joe, R. "Talent in Action." Billboard 82:20, April 4, 1970.

12002 Lewis, A. "Caught in the Act." Melody Maker 45:8, July 4, 1970.

12003 Plummer, M. "The Boy Wonder." Melody Maker 45:7, July 18,
1970.

12004 Aletti, V. "Records: Signed, Sealed & Delivered." Rolling Stone
no. 74:48, January 21, 1971.

12005 Graves, R. "Caught in the Act." Melody Maker 46:14, January 30,
1971.

12006 "Stevie Freaks Out." Melody Maker 46:7, January 30, 1971.

12007 "Talent in Action." Billboard 83:20, March 20, 1971.

12008 "Pop Albums: Where I'm Coming From." Melody Maker 46:40,
June 19, 1971.

12009 Aletti, V. "Records: Where I'm Coming From." Rolling Stone
no. 88:43-44, August 5, 1971.

12010 Clark, S. C. "Steve Wonder Gets Good and Pissed." Rolling Stone
no. 92:12, September 30, 1971.

12011 "Talent in Action." Billboard 83:13, December 4, 1971.

12012 Gibbs, V. "Stevie Wonder." Essence 3:23, November 1972.

12013 "Records: Talking Book." Rolling Stone no. 125:61-62, January 4,
1973.

12014 Welch, C. "Hah--the Boy Is Getting Militant!" Melody Maker 48:17,
February 10, 1973.

12015 "Concert Reviews." Variety 270:76, February 14, 1973.

12016 Wickham, V. "Caught in the Act." Melody Maker 48:47, February
17, 1973.

12017   Aletti, V. "Stevie Wonder." Senior Scholastic 102:20-24, March
        26, 1973.

12018   Fong-Torres, B. "The Formerly Little Stevie Wonder." Rolling
        Stone no. 133:48-50, April 26, 1973.

12019   Howard, N. "New York pour Vous." Jazz Hot no. 295:16-17, June
        1973.

12020   Tolces, T. "Wonder's Weekend." Melody Maker 48:48, July 14,
        1973.

12021   Vance, J. "Stevie Wonder." Stereo Review 31:60-62, August 1973.

12022   Welch, C. "Stevie: Not Quite Outta Sight." Melody Maker 48:9,
        August 11, 1973. Wonder's upcoming album, "Innervisions," is
        reviewed.

12023   "Stevie Wonder Hospitalized After Car-Truck Collision." Jet 44:56,
        August 23, 1973.

12024   "Stevie Wonder Recupes; Back to Work Next Year." Variety 272:35,
        August 1973.

12025   Gaer, E. "The Renaissance of Little Stevie Wonder." down beat
        40:13, September 13, 1973.

12026   Werbin, S. "Stevie Wonder's Auto Accident: He's Recovering."
        Rolling Stone no. 143:14, September 13, 1973.

12027   "Stevie Wonder Injured in Auto Crash." Soul 8:1, September 17,
        1973.

12028   "Wonder, Much Improved to Return to Concerts." Variety 272:37,
        September 19, 1973.

12029   Wickham, V. "Wonder Bounces Back." Melody Maker 48:3, Sep-
        tember 22, 1973.

12030   "Wonder Halts Further Work." Billboard 85:12, September 22, 1973.

12031   "Records: Innervisions." Rolling Stone no. 144:98, September 27,
        1973.

12032   "Stevie Wonder Discusses Car Crash." Rolling Stone no. 144:14,
        September 27, 1973.

12033   "Records: Innervisions." Crawdaddy no. 29:67-68, October 1973.

12034   Salvo, P., and W. Salvo. "Stevie Wonder: His Tragedies and Tri-
        umphs." Sepia 22:16-21, November 1973.

12035   "Stevie Wonder's Friends Rally to Support Shaw U." Jet 45:25, De-
        cember 13, 1973.

12036   Hasegawa, Sam. Stevie Wonder. Mankato, Minn.: Creative Educa-
        tion; Distributed by Childrens Press, Chicago, 1974, c1975. Ju-
        venile literature.

12037   Snider, B. "Hey, Stevie Wonder, How's Your Bad Self?" Esquire
        81:100-102, April 1974.

12038   "Caught in the Act." Melody Maker 49:31, April 6, 1974.

12039   "Black, Blind and on Top of Pop." Time 103:50-52, April 8, 1974.

12040   Brown, C. "Stevie Wonder: Musical Giant with View from the Top."
        Jet 46:58-62, May 9, 1974.

12041   Brown, G. "Rock Giants from A-Z; Stevie Wonder: The New Sound
        of Soul." Melody Maker 49:31-32, June 22, 1974.

12042   Hilburn, R. "Wonder--I've Never Liked Follow-ups." Melody Maker
        49:3, August 3, 1974.

12043   Underwood, L. "Boy Wonder Grows Up." down beat 41:14-15, Sep-
        tember 12, 1974.

12044   "Records: Fulfillingness' First Finale." Rolling Stone no. 170:98,
        September 26, 1974.

12045   Orth, M. "Stevie the Wonder Man." Newsweek 84:59-62, October
        28, 1974.

12046   Goddet, L. "Higher Ground." Jazz Hot no. 310:5-9, November
        1974.

12047   "Concert Reviews." Variety 277:44, December 11, 1974.

12048   Willis, E. "Rock, etc.: The Importance of Stevie Wonder." New
        Yorker 50:56-57, December 30, 1974.

12049   Ebert, A. "Stevie's World." Essence 5:70-71, January 1975.

12050   "Elton John, Wonder, White & Olivia Top NARM Awards." Variety
        278:61, March 12, 1975.

12051   "Wonder, Hamlisch Dominate NARA Awards." Billboard 87:26,
        March 15, 1975. The National Academy of Record Artists recog-
        nized Wonder.

12052   Weinstein, R. "Wonder of Steve." Senior Scholastic 106:23-25,
        April 24, 1975.

12053   Kirsch, B. "Wonder-ful New $13 Mil Contract an Industry High."
        Billboard 87:1, August 16, 1975.

12054   Sims, J. "Stevie's $13 Mil Contract an Industry High." Billboard
        87:1, August 16, 1975.

12055   "Stevie Has Contributed in 15 Years What Usually Takes a Lifetime."
        Soul 10:4-5, September 15, 1975.

12056   "Stevie Wonder Stays at Motown for $13,000,000." Soul 10:1, Sep-
        tember 15, 1975.

12057   Davis, C. "Music's Pied Piper: Stevie Wonder." Encore 4:32-36,
        September 22, 1975.

12058   Ward, E. "Jamaican 'Dream' Show: Will Wonder Never Cease?"
        Rolling Stone no. 200:12, November 20, 1975.

12059   Haskins, James. The Story of Stevie Wonder. New York: Lothrop,
        Lee & Shepard Co., 1976. Juvenile literature.

12060   Jacobs, Linda. Stevie Wonder: Sunshine in the Shadow. St. Paul:
        EMC Corp., 1976. Juvenile literature.

12061   Williams, J. "Stevie Wonder $13 Mil Contract Finally Executed."
        Billboard 88:6, April 24, 1976.

12062   "Wonder Asks $1.5-Mil in Truck Crash Suit." Variety 284:66, Au-
        gust 18, 1976.

12063   "New Albums: Songs in the Key of Life." Melody Maker 51:33, Oc-
        tober 9, 1976.

12064   Freedland, N. "Close-Up." Billboard 88:81, October 23, 1976. Re-
        view of "Songs in the Key of Life."

12065   Lucas, B. "Inside Wonder's New Wonderful World of Music." Jet
        51:60-63, November 18, 1976.

12066   Dragonwagon, Crescent. Stevie Wonder. New York: Flash Books,
        1977.

12067   Elsner, Constanze. Stevie Wonder. London: Everest, 1977.

12068   Slater, J. "Stevie Wonder: The Genius of the Man and His Music."
        Ebony 32:29-32, January 1977.

12069   "Stevie Wonder Says It All; Songs in the Key of Life." High Fi-
        delity/Musical America 27:141-142, February 1977.

12070   Evearitt, D. J. "Key of Stevie Wonder." Christianity Today 21:30,
        February 18, 1977.

12071   "Wonder Leads in NARM Nominating." Billboard 89:3, February 19,
        1977. The National Association of Record Merchandisers is pre-
        paring to give awards.

12072   Lucas, B. "Aretha, Stevie Chosen SBT 20 Queen, King." Jet 53:78-
        80, November 24, 1977.

12073   "Albums: Anthology." Melody Maker 52:23, December 17, 1977.

12074   Haskins, James and Kathleen Benson. The Stevie Wonder Scrapbook.
        New York: Grosset & Dunlop, 1978.

12075   Gersten, R. "Looking Back to When Stevie Was Little." Village
        Voice 23:49, February 6, 1978. Review of "Looking Back."

12076   "Records: Looking Back." High Fidelity/Musical America 28:129-
        130, March 1978.

12077   "Break Through: Stevie Wonder." Crawdaddy no. 83:27, April
        1978.

12078 "Talent in Action." Billboard 90:65, April 22, 1978.

12079 Wilson, Beth P. Stevie Wonder. New York: Putnam, 1979. Juven-
       ile literature.

YANCY, MRS. MARVIN see COLE, NATALIE

YARDBIRD see PARKER, CHARLES CHRISTOPHER

12080 Hatfield, Edwin Francis, comp. Freedom's Lyre; Or, Psalms,
       Hymns, and Sacred Songs for the Slave and His Friends. New
       York: S. W. Benedict, 1840; Miami, Fla.: Mnemosyne Pub. Co.,
       1969. "Selection of hymns undertaken at the request of the Ex-
       ecutive Committee of the American Anti-slavery Society." No mu-
       sic or historical background is included.

12081 The Negro Singer's Own Book: Containing Every Negro Song That
       Has Ever Been Sung or Printed. Philadelphia, New York: Turner
       & Fisher, 1846? Text of the songs only; some tunes are indicated
       by the title. Caption title is "Popular Negro Songs."

12082 Christy's Panorama Songster; Containing the Songs as Sung by the
       Christy, Campbell, Pierce's Minstrells, and Sable Brothers. New
       York: W. H. Murphy, 185-. Black songs and songs used in min-
       strel shows; text of the songs only.

12083 "Songs of the Blacks." Dwight's Journal of Music 9:51-52, Novem-
       ber 15, 1856. A contrast of songs by blacks and whites, illustrat-
       ing the "artistic nature" of the former.

12084 Dwight, J. S. "The Spiritual Worth of Music." Dwight's Journal of
       Music 11:197-199, September 19, 1857.

12085 McKim, J. "Negro Songs." Dwight's Journal of Music 21:148-149,
       August 9, 1862.

12086 Higginson, T. W. "Negro Spirituals." Atlantic Monthly 19:685-694,
       June 1867.

12087 Brown, J. M. "Songs of the Slave." Lippincott's Magazine 2:617-
       619, 1868.

12088 "Literature of the Day: Slave Songs of the United States." Lippin-
       cott's Magazine 1:341-343, March 1868. A view of songs of the
       slave as poor quality music.

12089 Barrett, W. A. "Negro Hymnology." Musical Times 15:559-561,
       1871-1873. Discussion of the elements of spirituals and the way
       they are sung.

12090 Pike, Gustavus D. The Jubilee Singers, and Their Campaign for
       Twenty Thousand Dollars. Boston: Lee and Shepard, 1873; New
       York: AMS Press, 1974. An account of a singing group from

Fisk University, Nashville, who traveled extensively to raise money for their school by singing songs related to black culture.

12091 _____. The Singing Campaign for Ten Thousand Pounds. Freeport, N.Y.: Books for Libraries Press, 1971. Reprint of the 1875 edition which was also entitled The Jubilee Singers in Great Britain.

12092 Marsh, J. B. T. The Story of the Jubilee Singers; With Their Songs. Revised edition. New York: AMS Press, 1971. Reprint of the 1881 edition which is similar to Pike's books with a history and the same songs sung by the Jubilee Singers of Fisk University, Nashville.

12093 Trotter, James M. Music and Some Highly Musical People. Chicago: Afro-Am Press, 1969. Reprint of the 1881 edition which gives "... sketches of the lives of remarkable musicians of the colored race, with portraits, and an appendix containing copies of music composed by colored men."

12094 Griffin, G. H. "Slave Music of the South." American Missionary 36:70-72, 1882.

12095 Harris, J. C. "Plantation Music." Critic 3:505-506, 1883. Banjo playing among blacks on plantations is examined.

12096 "Negro Minstrels." Saturday Review p. 739-740, June 7, 1884. Discussion of instruments which were used by blacks and the possible origin of minstrel music.

12097 Hutton, L. "The Negro on the Stage." Harper's Magazine p. 131-145, June 1889.

12098 Hopkins, P. E. "Famous Women of the Negro Race as Phenomenal Vocalists." Colored American Magazine 4:45, 1891.

12099 Ryder, C. J. "The Theology of Plantation Songs." American Missionary 45:123-124, 1891; 46:9-16, 1892.

12100 Tonsor, J. "Negro Music." Music 3:119-122, 1892-1893. Examintion of the elements of spirituals.

12101 Nathanson, Y. S. "Negro Melodies and National Music." Music Review 2:514-516, 1893.

12102 Rathburn, F. G. "The Negro Music of the South." Southern Workman 22: 174, 1893.

12103 Wallaschek, Richard. Primitive Music; An Inquiry into the Origin and Development of the Music, Songs, Instruments, Dances, and Pantomimes of Savage Races. London: Longmans, 1893. Includes a discussion of black folk music which Wallaschek feels was derived from Europe.

12104 Bedford, Rev. "Another Tribute to the Negro Melodies." Southern Workman 23:45, 1894.

12104a Christensen, A. M. H. "Spirituals and Shouts of Southern Negroes." Journal of the American Folklore Society 7:154-155, 1894.

12105   "Negroes and Negro Melodies; The Real Negro Music Is to Be Found
        at a Camp Meeting or Revival." American Art Journal 62:477-
        478, 1894.

12106   Backus, E. M. "Negro Hymns from Georgia." Journal of the Amer-
        ican Folklore Society 10:202, 1897; 11:22, 1898.

12107   _____. "Negro Songs from North Carolina." Journal of the
        American Folklore Society 11:60, 1898.

12108   Barton, William Eleazar. Old Plantation Hymns. New York: AMS
        Press, 1972. Reprint of the 1899 edition which states that it is
        "a collection of hitherto unpublished melodies of the slave and the
        freeman, with historical and descriptive notes."

12109   _____. "Hymns of the Negro." New England Magazine 19:609-
        624, January 1899.

12110   Haskell, M. A. "Negro Spirituals." Century Magazine 58:577-581,
        August 1899.

12111   Murphy, J. R. "The Survival of African Music in America." Popu-
        lar Science Monthly 55:660-672, September 1899.

                                1900-1919

12112   Kirby, P. R. "A Study of Negro Harmony." Musical Quarterly
        16:404-414, 1900. An examination of spirituals to illustrate that
        they have been influenced by European harmony.

12113   Weeden, H. "Bandanna Ballads." Ladies' Home Journal 17:9, April
        1900.

12114   Sherlock, C. R. "From Breakdown to Rag-time." Ragtimer p. 13-
        16, May-June 1977; p. 10-12, July-August 1977. Reprinted from
        Cosmopolitan October 1901.

12115   "Chance for Colored Composers." Cadenza 9:14, September 1902.

12116   "Eleven Negro Songs; Poems." Century Magazine 67:263-270, De-
        cember 1903.

12117   Murphy, Jeannette Robinson. Southern Thoughts for Northern Think-
        ers. New York: Bandanna Pub. Co., 1904. Sections include
        "African Music in America," "Slave Spirituals," and "Two Imita-
        tion Negro Songs."

12118   "What Is American Music?" Music Trade Review 38:8, no. 14,
        1904. C. von Sternberg argues that plantation songs are not Af-
        rican but American.

12119   Peabody, C. "Notes on Negro Music." Southern Workman 33:305-
        309, May 1904. Discussion of black music in Mississippi and how
        Peabody collected information on this music.

12120   Murphy, J. R. "Must the True Negro Music Become Obsolete?"
        Kunkel's Musical Review 30:10, no. 305, 1905.

12121   Johnson, J. W. "Negro of To-day in Music." Charities and the
        Commons 15:58-59, October 7, 1905.

12122   Ferrero, F. "La Musica dei Negri Americani." Rivista Musicale
        Italiana 13:393-436, 1906.

12123   Read, A. M. "Negro Melodies Not American Music." Musical
        America 4:2, no. 13, 1906; 4:13, no. 20, 1906.

12124   Von Ende, A. "Die Musik der Amerikanischen Neger." Musik
        5:368-375, no. 24, 1906.

12125   Wilson, H. J. "The Negro and Music." Outlook 84:823-826, 1906.
        The harmony of the spiritual "Let My People Go" is examined.

12126   Proctor, H. H. "The Theology of the Songs of the Southern Slave."
        Southern Workman 36:584-592, November-December 1907.

12127   Odum, Howard Washington. Religious Folk-Songs of the Southern
        Negroes. Worcester, Mass.: s.n. 1909? Based on his disser-
        tation, Clark University, and reprinted from the American Journal
        of Religious Psychology and Education 3:265-365, July 1909.

12128   "Syncopated Melody Not Negro Music." Music Trade Review 48:15,
        February 20, 1909.

12129   Speers, M. W. F. "Negro Songs and Folk-lore." Journal of the
        American Folklore Society 23:435-439, October 1910.

12130   Odum, H. W. "Folk Song and Folk Poetry as Found in the Secular
        Songs of the Southern Negroes." Journal of the American Folklore
        Society 24:255-294, 1911. Odum examines 115 texts.

12131   Barrett, Harris. Negro Folk Songs. Hampton, Va.: Press of the
        Hampton Normal and Agricultural Institute, 1912. Reprinted from
        Southern Workman 41:238-245, April 1912. Separates the various
        songs into categories such as freedom songs, labor songs, and
        game songs.

12132   "Negro Spirituals." Living Age 309:38-41, 1912. Discussion of the
        style and origin of spirituals.

12133   "Indian and Negro in Music." Literary Digest 44:1346-1347, June
        29, 1912.

12134   "Higher Music of Negroes." Literary Digest 45:565, October 5,
        1912.

12135   Smith, C. A. "The Negro and the Ballad." University of Virginia
        Alumni Bulletin Series 3:88, 1913. Suggests that black revival
        songs evolved into ballads.

12136   Burlin, N. C. "Negro's Contribution to the Music of America."
        Craftsman 23:660-669, March 1913.

12137   "Legitimizing the Music of the Negro." Current Opinion 54:384-385,
        May 1913.

12138   Krehbiel, Henry Edward. Afro-American Folksongs: A Study in

Racial and National Music. 4th Edition. Portland, Me.: Long-
wood Press, 1976. Reprint of the 1914 edition published by G.
Schirmer, New York. An analysis of the elements of black music.

12139 "A Notable Negro Concert." Southern Workman 43:381-383, 1914.

12140 Odum, H. W. "Religious Folk Songs of the Southern Negros."
American Journal of Religious Psychology and Education 3:328,
1914.

12141 "Negro Music in the Land of Freedom." Outlook 106:611-612, March
21, 1914.

12142 Adams, E. L. "The Negro Music School Settlement. Southern
Workman 44:161-165, 1915.

12143 Charlton, Melville. The Evolution of Negro Music. New York:
National Negro Exposition, New York Commission, 1915?

12144 Moton, R. R. "Negro Folk Music." Southern Workman 44:329-
350, June 1915.

12145 "Tribute to the Music of the American Negro." Current Opinion
59:100-101, August 1915.

12146 Diton, C. R. "Present Status of Negro-American Musical Endeav-
or." Musician 20:689, November 1915.

12147 Bruce, J. E. "A History of Negro Musicians." Southern Workman
10:569-573, 1916.

12148 Dett, N. "Folk Song of the American Negro." Southern Workman
45:125-126, 1916.

12149 "Canning Negro Melodies." Literary Digest 52:1556, May 27, 1916.

12150 "Objecting to the Negro Dialect." Literary Digest 53:1253, November 11, 1916.

12151 "Black Music--and Its Future Transmutation into Real Art." Current Opinion 63:26-27, July 1917.

12152 Lomax, J. A. "Self-pity in Negro Folk-songs." Nation 105:141-
145, August 9, 1917.

12153 Modernwell, H. K. "Epic of the Black Man." New Republic 12:154-
155, September 8, 1917.

12154 "Negro's Contribution to American Art." Literary Digest 55:26-27,
October 20, 1917.

12155 Burlin, N. C. "Again the Negro." Poetry 11:147-151, December
1917.

12156 Lemmermann, K. "Improvised Negro Songs." New Republic 13:214-
215, December 22, 1917.

12157   Dett, N. "The Emancipation of Negro Music." <u>Southern Workman</u>
        47:176-186, 1918.

12158   _____. "Negro Music of the Present." <u>Southern Workman</u>
        47:243-247, 1918.

12159   Gaul, H. B. "Negro Spirituals." <u>New Music Review</u> 17:147-151,
        1918.

12160   Goldenstein, W. "The Natural Harmonic and Rhythmic Sense of the
        Negro." <u>National Association of Music Teachers Proceedings</u>
        12:29-30, 1918.

12161   Mason, D. G. "Folk-song and American Music." <u>Musical Quarter-
        ly</u> 4:323-332, 1918.

12162   Pound, Louise. "The Ancestry of a 'Negro Spiritual.'" <u>Modern
        Language Notes</u> 33:442-444, 1918. "Weeping Mary" is the spir-
        itual examined.

12163   Williams, E. H. "The Emancipation of Negro Music." <u>Musical
        America</u> 27:48, January 5, 1918.

12164   White, C. C. "Negro Music a Contribution to the National Music
        of America." <u>Musical Observer</u> 18:18-19, no. 11, 1919.

12165   Burlin, N. C. "Negro Music at Birth." <u>Musical Quarterly</u> 5:86-
        89, January 1919.

12166   Grant, F. "Negro Patriotism and Negro Music." <u>Outlook</u> 121:343-
        347, February 26, 1919.

12167   Burlin, N. C. "How Negro Folk-Songs are 'Born.'" <u>Current Opin-
        ion</u> 66:165-166, March 1919.

12168   Howard, J. T. "Capturing the Spirit of the Real Negro Music."
        <u>Musician</u> 24:13, March 1919.

12169   Burlin, N. C. "Negro Music at Birth." <u>Current Opinion</u> 66:165-
        166, March 1919.

12170   "A Negro Explains Jazz." <u>Literary Digest</u> 61:28-29, April 26, 1919.
        Interview with James Reese Europe which appeared in the <u>New
        York Tribune</u>.

12171   "Stale Bread's Sadness Gave Jazz to the World." <u>Literary Digest</u>
        61:47-48, April 26, 1919. Suggests that Stale Bread's Spasm
        Band in New Orleans may have been the first to play jazz.

12172   Barstow, M. "Singers in a Weary Lan'." <u>World Outlook</u> 5:22, Oc-
        tober 1919.

12173   Burlin, N. C. "Black Singers and Players." <u>Musical Quarterly</u>
        5:499-504, October 1919.

1920-1929

12174   Burlin, N. C. "A Plea for Our Native Art." Musical Quarterly
        6:175-178, 1920.

12175   _____. "Recognition of Negro Music." Southern Workman 49:6-
        7, 1920.

12176   Hare, M. C. "Folk Music of the Creoles." Musical Observer
        19:16-18, no. 9-10, 1920; 19:12-14, no. 11, 1920.

12177   White, C. C. "Negro Music a Contribution to the National Music
        of America." Musical Observer 19:16-17, no. 1, 1920; 19:50-
        52, no. 2, 1920; 19:13, no. 3, 1920.

12178   "Racial Traits in the Negro Song." Sewanee Review 28:396-404,
        July-September 1920.

12179   Blades, William C. Negro Poems, Melodies, Plantation Pieces,
        Camp Meeting Songs, etc. Boston: R. G. Badger, 1921. In-
        cludes songs without music.

12180   Kerlin, R. T. "Canticles of Love and Woe: Negro Spirituals."
        Southern Workman 50:62-64, 1921.

12181   Lovinggood, Penman. Famous Modern Negro Musicians. New York:
        Da Capo Press, 1978. Reprint of the 1921 edition published by
        Press Forum Co., Brooklyn.

12182   Owen, M. W. "Negro Spirituals: Their Origin, Development and
        Place in American Folk-Song." Musical Observer 19:12-13, 1921.

12183   "Negro Spirituals." Living Age 309:38-41, April 2, 1921.

12184   Cameron, I. "Negro Songs." Musical Times 63:431-432, 1922.

12185   Graham, A. "Original Plantation Melodies as One Rarely Hears
        Them." Etude 40:74, 1922. Review of singing heard at Colum-
        bus, Mississippi.

12186   Grant, F. R. "Respect Spirit of Negro Song Is a Plea of Fisk
        Leader." Musical America 36:9, no. 12, 1922.

12187   Parsons, E. C. "From 'Spiritual' to Vaudeville." Journal of the
        American Folklore Society 35:331, 1922.

12188   Talley, Thomas Washington, comp. Negro Folk Rhymes, Wise and
        Otherwise, with a Study. Port Washington, N.Y.: Kennikat
        Press, 1968, c1922. Includes texts and melodies.

12189   Garnett, L. A. "Spirituals." Outlook 130:589, April 12, 1922.

12190   Talbot, E. A. "True Religion in Negro Hymns." Southern Work-
        man 51:213, May-July 1922.

12191   Ballanta-Taylor, N. G. J. "Jazz Music and Its Relation to African

Music." Musical Courier 84:7, June 1, 1922. Examples of how rhythms derived from Africa appear in jazz.

12192   Perkins, A. E. "Negro Spirituals from the Far South." Journal of the American Folklore Society 35:223-249, July 1922.

12193   Howe, R. W. "The Negro and His Songs." Southern Workman 51:381, August 1922.

12194   "Desecration of 'Spirituals.'" Southern Workman 51:501, November 1922.

12195   Clark, Francis A. The Black Music Master. Philadelphia, Pa.: F. A. Clark, 1923. "A fascinating, but truthful setting forth of facts, giving indisputable evidence that the primitive black peoples were the first natural musicians."

12196   McAdams, Nettie Fitzgerald. Folk-Songs of the American Negro; A Collection of Unprinted Texts Preceded by a General Survey of the Traits of Negro Song. [n.p.] 1923. Based on the author's thesis, University of California.

12197   Webb, W. P. "Miscellany of Texas Folklore: Negro Songs and Stories." Texas Folklore Society Publications no. 2:45-49, 1923.

12198   Kennedy, R. E. "Poetic and Melodic Gifts of the Negro." Etude 41:149-160, March 1923.

12199   Chotzinoff, S. "Jazz: A Brief History." Vanity Fair 20:69, June 1923.

12200   "Modern Negro's Contribution to the Musical Art." Playground 17:219, July 1923.

12201   "Negro Folk-Song." Opportunity; Journal of Negro Life 1:292-294, October 1923.

12202   Kennedy, Robert Emmet. Black Cameos. Freeport, N.Y.: Books for Libraries Press, 1970, c1924. Includes 17 songs from southern Louisiana.

12203   White, C. C. "The Story of the Negro Spiritual: 'Nobody Knows the Trouble I've Seen.'" Musical Observer 23:29, no. 6, 1924.

12204   Wood, M. T. "Community Preservation of Negro Music." Southern Workman 53:60, February 1924.

12205   Smith, J. H. "Folk Songs of the American Negro." Sewanee Review 32:206-224, April 1924.

12206   White, C. C. "Musical Genius of the American Negro." Etude 42:305-306, May 1924.

12207   "Black Voices." Nation 119:278, September 17, 1924.

12208   "Negro Spiritual." Etude 42:678, October 1924.

12209   Milhaud, D. "The Jazz Band and Negro Music." Living Age 323:169-173, October 18, 1924.

12210 Kennedy, Robert Emmet. Mellows, a Chronicle of Unknown Singers.
       New York: Boni, 1925. Work songs, street cries, and spirituals
       from Louisiana with background information on this literature.

12211 Odum, Howard Washington, and Guy B. Johnson. The Negro and
       His Songs: A Study of Typical Negro Songs in the South. New
       York: Negro Universities Press, 1968, c1925. Text of 205
       songs with historical information.

12212 Locke, Alain. "Negro Folk Songs." Southern Workman 54:533,
       1925.

12213 White, Lorenzo. "The Negro and His Songs." Southern Workman
       54:527-528, 1925.

12214 Rogers, J. A. "Jazz at Home; One Part American and Three Parts
       American Negro." Survey 53:665-667, March 1, 1925.

12215 "Association of Negro Musicians." Southern Workman 54:388, Sep-
       tember 1925.

12216 "Art from the Cabin Door." Outlook 141:268-269, October 21, 1925.
       Schools, such as Fisk University, attempted to preserve Negro
       spirituals.

12217 Carlisle, N. T. "Old Time Darkey Plantation Melodies." Texas
       Folklore Society Publications 5:137-143, 1926.

12218 Chatterton, J. "Concerning Negro Spirituals and Songs." Musical
       Standard 28:41-42, 1926.

12219 Harrison, R. C. "The Negro as Interpretor of His Own Folk Songs."
       Texas Folklore Society Publications 5:144-153, 1926.

12220 Odum, Howard Washington, and Guy B. Johnson. Negro Workaday
       Songs. New York: Negro Universities Press, 1969. Reprint of
       the 1926 edition which is a compilation of songs and their history.

12221 "Popularity of the Spirituals." Southern Workman 55:149-150, 1926.

12222 Schaeffner, A. "Notes sur la Musique des Afro-Américains."
       Ménéstrel 88:297, 1926.

12223 "A Tribute to Negro Spirituals." Southern Workman 55:397, 1926.

12224 Niles, A. "Blue Notes." New Republic 45:292-293, February 3,
       1926.

12225 Mencken, H. L. "Songs of the American Negro." World Review
       1:279, February 8, 1926.

12226 Buermeyer, L. "The Negro Spirituals and American Art." Oppor-
       tunity; Journal of Negro Life 4:158-159, May 1926.

12227 "Negro Spiritual Contest in Columbus, Ga." Playground 20:90-92,
       May 1926.

12228 Johnson, G. B. "Recent Contributions to the Study of Negro Songs."
       Social Forces 14:788-792, June 1926.

12229   Johnson, J. W. "How to Understand and Enjoy Negro Spirituals."
        Flutist 7:141-145, June 1926.

12230   Seitz, D. C. "Ballads of the Bad; Colored Chain Gang Chansons."
        Outlook 143:478, August 4, 1926.

12231   Ballanta-Taylor, N. G. J. "American Jazz Is Not African." Met-
        ronome 42:21, October 1, 1926. Reprinted from the New York
        Times, September 29, 1926.

12232   Von Hornbostel, E. M. "American Negro Songs." International Re-
        view of Missions 15:748-753, October 1926.

12233   Bennett, G. "The Ebony Flute." Opportunity; Journal of Negro
        Life 4:356-358, November 1926.

12234   Niles, A. "Rediscovering the Spirituals." Nation 123:598-600, De-
        cember 8, 1926.

12235   Norman, H. D. "Native Wood Notes." Atlantic Monthly 138:771-
        775, December 1926.

12236   White, C. C. "The Labor Motif in Negro Music." Modern Quarter-
        ly 4:79-81, 1927-1928.

12237   Bartholomew, M. "Your Own Music." Southern Workman 56:398,
        1927.

12238   Garbett, A. S. "Blues!" Etude 45:434, 1927. Taken from Negro
        Workaday Songs by Odum and Johnson.

12239   "Hampton Institute Choir." Southern Workman 56:53-54, 1927.

12240   Von Hornbostel, E. M. "Ethnologisches zu Jazz." Neue Zeitschrift
        für Musik 6:510-512, 1927.

12241   Johnson, Guy Benton. "A Study of the Musical Talent of the Amer-
        ican Negro." (Ph.D. Dissertation, University of North Carolina,
        1927).

12242   Moton, R. R. "Universal Language." Southern Workman 56:349-
        351, 1927. Asserts that folk songs of the slaves were the only
        truly American folk songs.

12243   Phenix, G. P. "Religious Folksongs of the Negro." Southern Work-
        man 56:151-152, 1927.

12244   "A Tribute to Hampton Choir." Southern Workman 56:506, 1927.

12245   Botkin, B. A. "Self-Portraiture and Social Criticism in Negro
        Folksong." Opportunity; Journal of Negro Life 5:38-42, February
        1927.

12246   "Negro Spirituals Again in Columbus, Ga." Playground 20:605-606,
        February 1927.

12247   Williams, Alberta. "A Race History Told in Song." World Review
        4:30, February 14, 1927.

12248 Johnson, G. B. "Double Meaning in the Popular Negro Blues."
Journal of Abnormal Psychology 22:12-20, April 1927.

12249 Allen, C. G. "Negro's Contribution to American Music." Current
History 26:245-249, May 1927.

12250 Johnson, G. B. "The Negro and Musical Talent." Southern Workman 56:339-444, October 1927.

12251 Niles, J. J. "Singing Soldiers." Scribner's Magazine 81:90-95,
January 1927.

12252 Arrowwood, M. D., and T. F. Hamilton. "New Negro Spirituals
from Lower South Carolina." Journal of the American Folklore
Society 41:579-582, 1928.

12253 Cohen, Lily Young. Lost Spirituals. New York: W. Neale, 1928.
"This book ... is intended to ... embrace the soul of the Negro
as found in its highest expression ... in his melodies and in his
lyrics...."

12254 Metfessel, Milton Franklin. Phonophotography in Folk Music; American Negro Songs in New Notation. Chapel Hill: University of
North Carolina Press, 1928.

12255 "Putting a Ban on Spirituals." Southern Workman 52:384, 1928.
A movement was growing against permitting spirituals to be sung
in theaters and other places of amusement.

12256 Niles, J. J. "In Defense of Backwoods." Scribner's Magazine
83:738-745, 1928. Black music of Kentucky is examined.

12257 White, New Ivey. American Negro Folk-songs. Hatboro, Pa.:
Folklore Associates, 1965. "Reprinted in facsimile from the
original edition of 1928." Includes bibliography and unaccompanied
melodies.

12258 Chirgwin, A. M. "Vogue of the Negro Spiritual." Edinburgh Review 247:57-74, January 1928.

12259 Gilbert, A. K. "Aunt Sukey's Apocalypse." Literary Digest 96:32,
March 31, 1928.

12260 Niles, A. "Ballads, Songs and Snatches; Columbia Race Records."
Bookman 67:422-424, June 1928.

12261 Kerby, M. "Warning Against Over-Refinement of the Negro Spiritual." Musician 33:9, July 1928.

12262 Gordon, R. W. "Lyrics Collected from the Folk-songs of Georgia
Negroes." Golden Book 8:194-196, August 1928.

12263 "Negro Spiritual." Literary Digest 98:34, September 22, 1928.

12264 Nathanson, Y. S. "Musical Ability of the Negro." Annals of the
American Academy of Political and Social Science 140:186-190,
1928.

12265 Seashore, C. E. "Three New Approaches to the Study of Negro Music." Annals of the American Academy of Political and Social Science 140:191-192, 1928. The tonal, temporal, and dynamic elements of black music are examined.

12266 "Hampton Institute Choir." Southern Workman 58:158-160, 1929.

12267 Johnson, Guy Benton. John Henry: Tracking Down a Negro Legend. New York: AMS Press, 1969. Reprint of the 1929 edition which is a thorough examination of the legend of the steel driver, John Henry.

12268 White, N. I. "The White Man in the Woodpile: Some Influences on Negro Secular Folk Songs." American Speech 4:207-215, 1929. Discussion of black songs which appear to have been influenced by white minstrel songs.

12269 Johnson, J. W. "Negro Folk Songs and Spirituals." Mentor 17:50-52, February 1929.

12270 "Folk-songs in the Making." Literary Digest 101:27, April 13, 1929.

12271 Gordon, R. W. "Palmettos; Folk-songs of Georgia Negroes." Golden Book 9:76-77, May 1929.

12272 Johnson, J. W. "Negro Anthem: Lift Ev'ry Voice and Sing." World Tomorrow 12:257, June 1929.

12273 "Preserving the Negro Spiritual." Musician 34:13, June 1929.

12274 Young, S. "Shoat." New Republic 59:153-154, June 26, 1929.

12275 "Negro Music in America." Playground 23:234-235, July 1929.

12276 Kempf, P. "Striking the Blue Note in Music." Musician 34:29, August 1929.

1930-1939

12277 Emerson, William Canfield. Stories and Spirituals of the Negro Slave. Boston: R. G. Badger, 1930.

12278 Gehring, Carl E. "The Western Dance of Death." Modern Quarterly 5:492-503, 1930. Black folk music as it relates to jazz.

12279 Grissom, Mary Allen, comp. The Negro Sings a New Heaven. New York: AMS Press, 1973. Reprint of the 1930 edition which concentrates on songs from Kentucky.

12280 Johnson, Guy Benton. Folk Culture on St. Helena Island, South Carolina. Hatboro, Pa.: Folklore Associates, 1968, c1930.

12281 Terrell, C. S. "Spirituals from Alabama." Journal of the American Folklore Society 43:322-324, 1930.

12282 Furness, C. J. "Communal Music Among Arabians and Negroes." Musical Quarterly 16:38-51, January 1930.

12283 Moreland, J. R. "Doomsday: Negro Spiritual." Catholic World 130:438, January 1930.

12284 Diton, C. "Struggle of the Negro Musician." Etude 48:89-90, February 1930.

12285 Murphy, E. F. "Black Music." Catholic World 130:687-692, March 1930.

12286 "Blight of Jazz and the Spirituals." Literary Digest 105:20, April 12, 1930.

12287 Howe, M. A. D. "Song of Charleston." Atlantic Monthly 146:108-111, July 1930.

12288 Kirby, P. R. "Study of Negro Harmony." Musical Quarterly 16:404-414, July 1930.

12289 Laubenstein, P. F. "Race Values in Aframerican Music." Musical Quarterly 16:378-403, July 1930.

12290 "In the Driftway." Nation 131:245, September 3, 1930.

12291 Niles, J. J. "Shout, Coon, Shout!" Musical Quarterly 16:516-530, October 1930.

12292 Allen, C. G. "The Negro and His Songs." Musical Courier 103:7, 1931.

12293 Beckman, A. S. "The Psychology of Negro Spirituals." Southern Workman 60:391-394, 1931. Asserts that spirituals appeal to the emotions.

12294 Johnson, G. B. "The Negro Spiritual, a Problem in Anthropology." American Anthropologist 33:157-171, 1931.

12295 Sargent, N., and T. Sargent. "Negro American Music or the Origin of Jazz." Musical Times 72:653-655, 1931. Discussion of the origin of jazz and its development.

12296 Ketcham, G. F. "Hampton Choir and Quartette." Southern Workman 60:51-59, 1931.

12297 Society for the Preservation of Spirituals. The Carolina Low-Country. By Augustine T. Smythe, et al. New York: Macmillan Co., 1931. Describes life in South Carolina with information on black music.

12298 Barragan, M. "Putting the Spirit into Spirituals." Etude 49:95, February 1931.

12299 Kerby, M. "Recapturing America's Folk Music." Theatre Magazine 53:44, February 1931.

12300 "Spirituals and Race Relations." Christian Century 48:230-231, February 18, 1931.

12301   Moreland, J. R.   "De Promise Lan'."   Catholic World 133:435,
        July 1931.

12302   Turner, L. P.   "Negro Spirituals in the Making."   Musical Quarter-
        ly 17:480-485, October 1931.

12303   Ashbury, S. E., and H. E. Meyer.   "Old-Time White Camp-Meeting
        Spiritual."   Texas Folklore Society Publications no. 10:169-185,
        1932.   These white spirituals are contrasted with Negro spirituals.

12304   Dawson, W.   "Le Caractère Spécial de la Musique Negre en Amér-
        ique."   Société des Américanistes Journal, new series 24:273-
        286, 1932.

12305   Goffin, Robert.   Aux Frontières du Jazz.   Deuxième edition.   Paris:
        Editions du Sagittaire, 1932.   Examines music in the United States
        (especially jazz).

12306   Hitchens, W.   "Music, a Triumph of African Art."   Art and Archae-
        ology 33:36-41, January 1932.

12307   Niles, J. J.   "White Pioneers and Black."   Musical Quarterly 18:60-
        75, January 1932.

12308   Jackson, G. P.   "Genesis of the Negro Spiritual."   American Mer-
        cury 26:243-248, June 1932.

12309   Carlson, A. D.   "Negro Spirituals at Our Own Firesides."   Better
        Homes and Gardens 10:16, July 1932.

12310   Fisher, W. A.   "Swing Low, Sweet Chariot: The Romance of a
        Famous Spiritual."   Etude 50:536, August 1932.

12311   White, C. G.   "The Musical Genius of the American Negro."   South-
        ern Workman 62:108-117, 1933.

12312   "Negro Music."   Commonweal 17:396-397, February 8, 1933.

12313   "First Negro Symphony."   Literary Digest 115:20, March 4, 1933.

12314   Brawley, B.   "The Singing of Spirituals."   Southern Workman
        63:209-213, 1934.

12315   Damon, S. F.   "The Negro in Early American Songsters."   Bibli-
        ographical Society of America Papers 28:132-163, 1934.   A his-
        tory of black music in America from the late 1700's to the early
        1900's with a bibliography of songsters.

12316   Lee, George William.   Beale Street, Where the Blues Began.   Col-
        lege Park, Md.: McGrath Pub. Co., 1969, c1934.   Information
        on music and the general street life in Memphis, Tennessee in
        the early 20th century.

12317   Mary, Sister Esther.   "Spirituals in the Church."   Southern Work-
        man 63:308-314, 1934.

12318   Lomax, A.   "Sinful Songs of the Southern Negro."   Southwest Re-
        view 19:53-68, January 1934.

12319   Dett, R. N. "From Bell Stand to Throne Room." Etude 52:79-80, February 1934. Autobiographical.

12320   Lomax, A. "Sinful Songs of the Southern Negro." Musical Quarterly 20:177-187, April 1934.

12321   Hawkins, W. E. "Debunking the Spirituals." Challenge 1:13-14, September 1934. Asserts that spirituals are of poor musical quality.

12322   "From Jim Crow to Jazz." British Musician and Musical News 10:223-225, October 1934.

12323   Locke, A. "Toward a Critique of Negro Music." Opportunity; Journal of Negro Life 12:328-331, November-December 1934.

12324   "'The Spiritual,' Its Public Debut." British Musician and Musical News 10:225-254, November 1934.

12325   Parrish, L. "Plantation Songs of Our Old Negro Slaves." Country Life p. 68-70, 1935.

12326   Grew, S. "Random Notes on the Spirituals." Music and Letters 16:96-109, April 1935.

12327   "Singin' High, Singin' Low, Strugglin' for Success." Newsweek 5:34-35, May 4, 1935.

12328   Gehrkens, K. W. "Negro in Various Fields of Music." Etude 53:375, June 1935.

12329   Harth, L. H. "Negro Musicians and Their Music." Journal of Negro History 20:428-432, October 1935.

12330   Hare, Maud Cuney. Negro Musicians and Their Music. New York: Da Capo Press, 1974. Reprint of the first edition, 1936, published by Associated Publishers, Washington, D.C. A history including biographical sketches.

12331   Locke, Alain LeRoy. The Negro and His Music; Negro Art: Past and Present. New York: Arno Press, 1969. Reprints of editions published 1936 on both music and art.

12332   Panassie, Hugues. Hot Jazz; The Guide to Swing Music. Revised for the English edition. Westport, Conn.: Negro Universities Press, 1970. Reprint of the 1936 edition. This study of jazz devotes a chapter each to Duke Ellington and Louis Armstrong.

12333   Spaeth, S. "Dixie, Harlem, and Tin Pan Alley; Who Writes Negro Music, and How?" Scribner's Magazine 99:23, January 1936.

12334   Hilarian, Sister Mary. "Negro Spiritual." Catholic World 143:80-84, April 1936.

12335   Johnson, J. W. "National Negro Anthem." Missionary Review of the World 59:300, June 1936.

12336   "Songs of Protest." Time 27:51, June 15, 1936.

12337   Graham, S. "Spirituals to Symphonies." Etude 54:691-692, November 1936.

12338   Brawley, Benjamin Griffith. The Negro Genius; A New Appraisal of the Achievement of the American Negro in Literature and the Fine Arts. New York: Biblo and Tannen, 1966, c1937. Three chapters cover musicians from around 1865-1935, such as the Fisk Jubilee Singers and William Grant Still.

12339   Tupper, V. G. "Plantation Echoes, a Negro Folk Music--Drama as Given Each Year in Charleston, S. C." Etude 55:153-154, March 1937.

12340   Arvey, V., and W. G. Still. "Negro Music in the Americas." Revue Internationale de Musique 1:280-288, 1938.

12341   Handy, William Christopher. Negro Authors and Composers of the United States. New York: AMS Press, 1976. Reprint of the 1938? edition published by Handy Bros. Music Co., New York. Biographical.

12342   Whiting, Helen Adele Johnson. Negro Art, Music and Rhyme for Young Folks. Washington, D.C.: Associated Publishers, 1967, c1938. Teaching material suitable for elementary school grades.

12343   Crichton, K. "Thar's Gold in Them Hillbillies; Recording Hillbilly and Race Music." Collier's 101:24, April 30, 1938.

12344   Taubman, H. H. "Negro Music Given at Carnegie Hall." Black Perspectives in Music 2:207-208, no. 2, 1974. Reprinted from the New York Times 24, December 1938.

12345   Gordon, Robert Winslow. Folk-songs of America. Sponsored by Joint Committee on Folk Arts W.P.A., Issued by Folk-song and Folklore Dept., Herbert Halpert Supervisor. New York: National Service Bureau, 1939. A compilation of articles including black music which first appeared in the New York Times.

12346   Hobson, Wilder. American Jazz Music. New York: Da Capo Press, 1976. Reprint of the 1939 edition published by Norton, New York.

12347   Longini, M. D. "Folksongs of Chicago Negroes." Journal of the American Folklore Society 52:96-111, 1939.

12348   Lovell, J. "The Social Implications of the Negro Spiritual." Journal of Negro Education 8:634-642, 1939.

12349   Stokes, Anson Phelps. Art and the Color Line. Washington, D.C.: [n.p.] 1939. "An appeal made May 31, 1939 to the president general and other officers of the Daughters of the American Revolution to modify their rules so as to permit distinguished Negro artists such as Miss Marian Anderson to be heard in Constitution Hall."

12350   Thurman, H. "Religious Ideas in Negro Spirituals." Christendom 4:515-528, 1939.

12351   "Spirituals to Swing." Time 33:23, January 2, 1939.

12352   Arvey, V. "Worth While Music in the Movies; Much Choral Work Done by Negro Organizations." Etude 57:152, March 1939.

12353   "Tomtom Beat in Harlem: Mwalimu Festival Chorus Revives the Negro's African Heritage." Newsweek 13:37, April 3, 1939.

12354   Wooding, S. "Eight Years Abroad with a Jazz Band." Etude 57:233-234, April 1939.

12355   Hilarian, Sister Mary. "Negro Spiritual." Catholic World 145:82-84, April 1939.

12356   Logan, W. A. "Song Gleaning Among the Cabins; Collecting Negro Spirituals." Musician 44:122, July 1939.

12357   Campbell, E. S. "Blues Are the Negroes' Lament." Esquire 7:100, December 1939.

1940-1949

12358   Hershovits, Melville Jean. Patterns of Negro Music. [n. p., 194-?].

12359   Clark, Edgar Rogie. Moment Musical; Ten Selected Newspaper Articles. Fort Valley, Ga.: Fort Valley State College Department of Music, 1940.

12360   _____. "Music Education in the Negro Schools and Colleges." Journal of Negro Education 9:580-590, 1940.

12361   "Wings over Jordan Program Fulfills Negro Preacher's Dream." Newsweek 15:38, March 4, 1940.

12362   MacTaggart, E. "I Saw a Spiritual Born." Etude 58:236, April 1940.

12363   "Wings over Jordan." Time 35:69, June 10, 1940.

12364   Greene, M. "The Background of the Beale Street Blues." Tennessee Folklore Society Bulletin 7:1-11, 1941.

12365   Ortiz Oderigo, N. R. "El Negro Norteamericano y sus Cantos de Labor." Sustancia; Revista de Cultura Superior 2:552-560, 1941.

12366   Sears, W. P. "Negro Spiritual, America's Folk Music." Education 61:274-277, January 1941.

12367   Work, J. W. "Planatation Meistersinger: Alabama State Sacred Harp Shape-Note Singing Convention." Musical Quarterly 27:97-106, January 1941.

12368   "Golden Gate Quartet in Washington." Time 37:50, January 27, 1941.

12369   Ferguson, O. "Spirits: 100 Proof." New Republic 104:143-144, February 3, 1941.

12370   "Blow! Joshua! Blow! The American People Do Not Enjoy Having Their

Beloved Melodies and Spirituals Caricatured." Etude 59:221, April 1941.

12371   Zolotow, M. "Harlem's Great White Father: Moe Gale." Saturday Evening Post 214:37, September 27, 1941.

12372   "Negro Opera Company Launched." Musician 46:176, November 1941.

12373   Arvey, V. "Outstanding Achievements of Negro Composers." Etude 60:171, March 1942.

12374   "Great Godamighty." Saturday Review of Literature 25:7, May 16, 1942.

12375   McDermott, W. F. "Wings over Jordan." Reader's Digest 41:96-99, September 1942.

12376   "Song of Faith: Lift Every Voice and Sing." Time 40:63, September 14, 1942.

12377   Sass, H. R. "I Can't Help from Cryin'; Negro Spiritual in Danger of Extinction." Saturday Evening Post 215:16-17, October 3, 1942.

12378   Jackson, George Pullen. White and Negro Spirituals, Their Life Span and Kinship: Tracing 200 Years of Untrammeled Song Making and Singing Among Our Country Folk: With 116 Songs as Sung by Both Races. New York: Da Capo Press, 1975. Reprint of the 1943 edition published by J. J. Augustin, New York.

12379   Ames, R. "Art in Negro Folksong." Journal of the American Folklore Society 56:241-254, 1943.

12380   Elzy, R. "Spirit of the Spirituals." Etude 61:495-496, August 1943.

12381   Gillum, R. H. "The Negro Folksong in the American Culture." Journal of Negro History 12:173-180, 1943.

12382   Slotkin, J. S. "Jazz and Its Forerunners as an Example of Acculturation." American Sociological Review 8:570-576, 1943. Aspects of black music which evolved into jazz.

12383   Crite, Allan Rohan. Were You There When They Crucified My Lord; A Negro Spiritual in Illustrations. Cambridge, Mass.: Harvard University Press, 1944. An illustration accompanies each phrase of the spiritual.

12384   Ewen, David. Men of Popular Music. Freeport, N.Y.: Books for Libraries Press, 1972. Reprint of the 1944 edition published by Ziff, Davis Pub. Co., Chicago which includes biographies of jazz musicians.

12385   Ortiz Oderigo, Néstor R. Panorama de la Musica Afroamericana. Buenos Aires: Editorial Claridad, 1944.

12386   Ewen, D. "American Song from the Negro." Common Ground 5:76-83, 1945.

12387   Gilbert, Will G. Rumbamuziek, Volksmuziek van de Midden-Amer-
        ikaansche Negers. 's-Gravenhage: J. P. Kruseman, 1945?

12388   Goffin, Robert. Histoire du Jazz. Montreal: L. Parizeau, 1945.

12389   Thurman, Howard. Deep River and the Negro Spiritual Speaks of
        Life and Death. Richmond, Ind.: Friends United Press, 1975.
        "Originally separate books, but now in a single volume, Deep
        River was copyrighted in 1945 and 1955, and The Negro Spiritual
        Speaks of Life and Death in 1947."

12390   Preston, D., and A. McCarthy. "Poetry of Afro-American Folk-
        song; The Impact of Christianity." Folk p. 22-26, 1945.

12391   "Spirituals Go to War; Wings over Jordon Chorus Headed for a 26-
        Week Battlefront Tour." Time 45:93, March 12, 1945.

12392   "Jungle Band; Army's Hottest Negro Musicians Come Home." Life
        19:134, November 5, 1945.

12393   Borneman, Ernest. A Critic Looks at Jazz. London: Jazz Music
        Books, 1946. "Originally published in the Record Changer in
        serial form under the title "Anthropologist Looks at Jazz."

12394   Dexter, Dave. Jazz Cavalcade: The Inside Story of Jazz. New
        York: Da Capo Press, 1977. Reprint of the 1946 edition pub-
        lished by Criterion in New York.

12395   Goffin, Robert. Jazz, from Congo to Swing. London: Musicians
        Press, 1946. First published as Jazz, from the Congo to the
        Metropolitan.

12396   _____. La Nouvelle-Orléans, Capitale du Jazz. New York:
        Editions de la Maison Française, 1946.

12397   Höweler, Caspar. "De Beeldspraak van de Negro-Spirituals."
        Mensche en Melodie 1:33, 1946.

12398   Parrish, C. "Music in the Negro Colleges." Saturday Review of
        Literature 29:10-11, January 26, 1946.

12399   "Crucifixion; Spiritual." Scholastic 48:15, April 8, 1946.

12400   Pilcher, J. M. "Negro Spiritual, Lively Leaven in the American
        Way of Life." Etude 64:194, April 1946.

12401   Bentham, A. T. "Bland Memorial Dedicated; Negro Minstrel Who
        Wrote Carry Me Back to Old Virginny." Etude 64:553-554, Oc-
        tober 1946.

12402   "In Egypt Land." Time 48:59-60, December 30, 1946.

12403   Berger, M. "Jazz: Resistance to the Diffusion of a Culture Pat-
        tern." Journal of Negro History 32:461-494, 1947.

12404   Condon, Eddie. We Called It Music; A Generation of Jazz. West-
        port, Conn.: Greenwood Press, 1970. Reprint of the 1947 edi-

tion published by Holt, Rinehart & Winston, New York. Condon, the dance band leader, recalls individuals who played jazz with him, such as Louis Armstrong and Fats Waller.

12405 Duncan, J. "Negro Spirituals--Once More." Negro History Bulletin 10:80-82, 1947. A short history of spirituals.

12406 Ewen, David. Songs of America; A Cavalcade of Popular Songs, with Commentaries. Chicago: Ziff-Davis Pub. Co., 1947. Two short chapters give some historical information on "The Songs of the Negro."

12407 Friedel, L. M. The Bible and the Negro Spirituals. Bay St. Louis, Miss.: St. Augustine Seminary, 1947.

12408 Jones, Max. Jazz Photo Album. London: British Yearbooks, 1947. "A history of jazz in pictures."

12409 Ruspoli, Mario. Blues: Poésia de l'Amérique Noire. Paris: Publications Techniques et Artistiques, 1947.

12410 Kendall, J. S. "New Orleans' Negro Minstrels." Louisiana Historical Quarterly p. 128-148, January 1947.

12411 Callista, Sister Mary. "Negro Folk Songs." Catholic World 164:537-540, March 1947.

12412 "Ya Ess Goony Gress; The Three Flames." Time 50:56, July 28, 1947.

12413 Cook, W. M. "Cloundy, the Origin of the Cakewalk; How the First All-Negro Show Landed on Broadway in 1898." Theatre Arts 31:61-65, September 1947.

12414 "We Sing to Life; Echoes of Eden Choir." Time 50:52, December 22, 1947.

12415 Borneman, E. "Les Racines de la Musique Américaine Noire." Présence Africaine 4:576-589, 1948. Discusses West African music's influence in the United States.

12416 Crite, Allan Rohan. Three Spirituals from Earth to Heaven. Cambridge: Harvard University Press, 1948. Each phrase of these spirituals is illustrated. An unaccompanied melody is provided for each: "Nobody Knows the Trouble I See," "Swing Low, Sweet Chariot," and "Heaven."

12417 Finkelstein, Sidney Walter. Jazz, a People's Music. New York: Da Capo Press, 1975. Reprint of the 1948 edition published by Citadel Press, New York.

12418 Gilbert Will G., and C. Poustochkine. Jazzmuziek, Inleiding tot de Volksmuziek der Noord-Amerikaanse Negers. Den Haag: J. P. Kruseman, 1948?

12419 Goffin, Robert. Nouvelle Histoire du Jazz, du Congo, au Bebop. Bruxelles: L'Ecran du Monde, 1948.

12420 Waterman, Richard A. "'Hot' Rhythm in Negro Music." American
       Musicological Society Journal 1:24-28, Spring, 1948.

12421 Feather, Leonard G. Inside Be-bop. New York: J. J. Robbins,
       1949. A brief history of be-bop beginning about 1940 with infor-
       mation on the principal bands including singers such as Sarah
       Vaughan.

12422 Fisher, Miles M. "The Evolution of Slave Songs of the United
       States." (Ph.D. Dissertation, University of Chicago, 1949).

12423 "Downbeat in Philadelphia Raided Again." down beat 16:20, January
       14, 1949.

12424 "1st Miami Beach Negro Show Set for Paddock." Billboard 61:3,
       February 5, 1949.

12425 Preston, S. D. "Bop: The Music of a Social Revolution." Melody
       Maker 25:3, March 12, 1949.

12426 Ortiz Oderigo, Néstor R. "Una Expresión Genuina del Folklore
       Negro: Los Blues." Vea y Lea 4:41-43, March 17, 1949.

12427 Work, J. W. "Changing Patterns in Negro Folk Songs." Journal
       of the American Folklore Society 62:136-144, April-June 1949.

12428 "Miami Area Colored Policy Succeeds." down beat 16:3, April 8,
       1949.

12429 Ulanov, B. "Crow Jim." Metronome 65:42, May 1949.

12430 Lee, A. "Figs Might Do Well to Take a Hint from Bop--Make New
       Dixie Sounds." down beat 16:2, May 6, 1949.

12431 "Costanzo Blocked Out of Cole Trio in South." Variety 175:39, June
       29, 1949.

12432 Clark, E. R. "Folk Music Confusion." Music Journal 7:10, July-
       August 1949.

12433 Simon, G. T. "Words, Action, and Arthur Godfrey." Metronome
       65:34, July 1949.

12434 "Godfrey Blasts DAR Jim Crow." down beat 16:1, July 1, 1949.

12435 "RCA Hires Exploiteer to Plug Negro Artists." Variety 175:37,
       August 3, 1949.

12436 Levin, M. "Night Clubs in New York's Harlem." down beat 16:9,
       August 26, 1949.

12437 Anderson, J. L. "Evolution of Jazz." down beat 16:14, September
       9, 1949.

12438 "Battle Jim Crow in Miami Locals." down beat 16:1, September 23,
       1949.

12439 "Let's Get Rid of That Minority Tag." down beat 16:10, October 21,
       1949.

12440   Emge, C. "L.A. Council Votes Down Anti-Discrimination Law."
        down beat 16:3, November 4, 1949.

12441   "Jim Crow Halts Granz Date in New Orleans." down beat 16:2,
        November 18, 1949.

12442   Muddel, J. "Coloured Players Were the Pioneers Who Initiated
        Bop Bass Trends." Melody Maker 25:8, December 17, 1949.

                            1950-1959

12443   Vidossiche, Edoardo. O Negro e a Música. São Paulo? 195-.

12444   Davis, Henderson. "The Religious Experience Underlying the Negro
        Spiritual." (Ph.D. Dissertation, Boston University, 1950).

12445   Henry, L. "Is Jazz an Art?" Canon 3:353-355, January 1950.

12446   "GI Chorus; De Paur's Infantry Chorus." Newsweek 35:74-75, Jan-
        uary 23, 1950.

12447   Brubeck, D. "Jazz' Evolvement as Art Form." down beat 17:12,
        January 27, 1950.

12448   "It's a Matter of Wanting to Live." down beat 17:10, January 27,
        1950.

12449   Stevens, A., and H. Giltrap. "Drums." Jazz Journal 3:2-3, March
        1950.

12450   "Ten Most Promising Crooners." Ebony 5:20-26, March 1950.

12451   Hoefer, G. "Jazzmen--Past, Present--Share All-Time Honors."
        down beat 16:11, March 11, 1949.

12452   "Last Hired, First Fired, Negroes in Economic Twist." Billboard
        62:3, April 1, 1950.

12453   Duncan, T. "South African Songs and Negro Spirituals." Music
        Journal 8:19, May-June 1950.

12454   Nettl, B. "Die Negro-Spirituals." Musica 4:197-199, May-June
        1950.

12455   "Symphony Sid, Disc Jockey Who Plugged Bop Music and Negro Mu-
        sicians to Fame." Our World 5:54-57, May 1950.

12456   Feather, L. "Jim Crow Versus 'Crow Jim.'" Melody Maker 26:3,
        May 13, 1950.

12457   Ames, R. "Protest and Irony in Negro Folksong." Science and So-
        ciety 14:193-213, Summer 1950.

12458   Gleason, R. J. "Frisco Dancery Sets Up Two-Way Jim Crow Pol-
        icy." down beat 17:18, June 30, 1950.

12459 Smith, C. E. "Folk Music, the Roots of Jazz." Saturday Review 33:35-36, July 29, 1950.

12460 "Blues Singer; Their Popularity Is at Peak in Nation's Negro Night Clubs." Ebony 5:35-39, August 1950.

12461 Morriwon, A. "Who Will Be First to Crack Met Opera?" Negro Digest 8:52-56, September 1950.

12462 "Unique and Unfortunate Birth of Crow Jim." Jazz Journal 3:4, September 1950.

12463 Eldridge, R. "Jim Crow Is Killing Jazz." Negro Digest 8:44-49, October 1950.

12464 Race, S. "The Other Side of the Picture." Jazz Journal 3:3, October 1950.

12465 Nettl, B. "Über Neger-Musiker." Musica 4:423-426, November 1950.

12466 "Beach Clubs in Miami Book Negro Artists for Season." Billboard 62:42, November 18, 1950.

12467 "Gospel Singers." Ebony p. 91-95, December 1950.

12468 Ames, R. "Implications of Negro Folk Song." Science and Society 15:163-173, 1951.

12469 Clark, E. R. "Negro Folk Music in America." Journal of the American Folklore Society 64:281-287, 1951. A discussion of the conditions which contributed to the development of black folk music.

12470 Fonollosa, J. M. Breve Antología de los Cantos Spirituals Negros. Barcelona: Cobalto, 1951.

12471 Powell, A. C. "Rocking the Gospel Train." Negro Digest 9:10-13, 1951.

12472 Still, W. G. "Negrene i Amerikansk Musik." Dansk Musiklids-skrift 26:91-96, no. 5, 1951.

12473 Waterman, R. A. "Gospel Hymns of a Negro Church in Chicago." International Folk Music Council Journal 3:87-93, 1951.

12474 Race, S. "The Other Side of the Picture." Jazz Journal 4:3, January 1951.

12475 "The Colour-Bar." Melody Maker 27:2, January 20, 1951.

12476 "Top Talent Bears Brunt of Virginia Segregation Law." Variety 181:35, January 31, 1951.

12477 Race, S. "The Other Side of the Picture." Jazz Journal 4:5-6, February 1951.

12478 Thompson, K. C. "The American Negro in the Field of Popular Music." Jazz Journal 4:1-2, February 1951.

12479   "Whites Who Sing Like Negroes." Ebony 6:49-54, February 1951.

12480   "Separate-Seat Idea Cuts Take; Promoters Hit." Billboard 63:3,
        February 24, 1951.

12481   "Crow Jim as Bad as Jim Crow." down beat 18:10, March 9, 1951.

12482   Roth, R. "The Saxophone; An Analysis." Record Changer 10:13-14,
        April 1951.

12483   Jones, M. "When the Blind Men Stood on the Corner; Blind Men
        Who Sang the Blues." Melody Maker 27:9, April 7, 1951.

12484   Eldridge, R. "Not All Honey--But a Lovely Place to Live In!"
        Melody Maker 27:3, April 14, 1951.

12485   "Spotlight on American Jazzmen in Europe." Melody Maker 27:3,
        April 14, 1951.

12486   Quay, R. "Worksongs and Religion." Jazz Journal 4:5, May 1951.

12487   "Easing of Race Barriers Helps Dates for Negro Bands in South--
        Hampton." Variety 182:1, May 16, 1951.

12488   Feather, L. "No More White Bands for Me, Says Little Jazz."
        down beat 18:1, May 18, 1951.

12489   Emge, C. "Move Grows to Scrap L.A.'s Jim Crow Union." down
        beat 18:1, June 15, 1951.

12490   "Harlem Piano." Record Changer 10:37, July-August 1951.

12491   Stewart-Baxter, D. "Painted Jazz; A Record-Collector Looks at
        Russell Quay's Jazz Pictures." Jazz Journal 4:6-7, July-August
        1951.

12492   Gilbert, W. G. "Buiten-Europese Muziek." Mens en Melodie 6:223,
        July 1951.

12493   Holzfeind, F. "Roy Wasn't on Soap Box, Says Club Op." down beat
        18:7, July 13, 1951.

12494   Borneman, E. "A Letter from the Days When Jass Was King."
        Melody Maker 27:3, August 11, 1951.

12495   Grut, H. "Church Rock." Melody Maker 27:9, August 25, 1951.

12496   "DAR Willing to Drop Color Bar but Won't Be Pushed." Variety
        183:58, August 29, 1951.

12497   Thomas, B. K. "The Thomas Negro Composers Study Group."
        Hymn 2:21-23, October 1951.

12498   "1st Negro at Met; Legit Spotlighted in New Roster." Variety 184:1,
        October 3, 1951.

12499   Borneman, E. "One Night Stand." Melody Maker 27:2, November
        17, 1951.

12500 Bruynoghe, Y. "Mezzrow Talks About the Old Jim Crow." Melody
       Maker 27:9, November 17, 1951.

12501 Roth, R. "Drums." Record Changer 10:7-8, December 1951.

12502 Braithwaite, Coleridge. "A Survey of the Lives and Creative Ac-
       tivities of Some Negro Composers." (Ph.D. Dissertation, Colum-
       bia University, 1952).

12503 Ulanov, Barry. A History of Jazz in America. New York: Da
       Capo Press, 1972. Reprint of the 1952 edition published by Vik-
       ing Press, New York.

12504 Douglas, V. C. "Music as a Cultural Force in the Development of
       the Negro Race." Negro History Bulletin 15:87, February 1952.

12505 Oliver, P. H. "Give Me That Old-Time Religion." Jazz Journal
       5:1-2, February 1952.

12506 Thompson, Kay C. "Early Cakewalks--the Roots of Ragtime."
       Jazz Journal 5:14-15, March 1952.

12507 Hentoff, N. "Classical Color Line?" down beat 19:1, March 7,
       1952.

12508 Freeman, D. "Jazz Knows No Racial Lines, Says Louie Bellson."
       down beat 19:1, April 4, 1952.

12509 "Negro Talent Now Rating Better Reception, More Play in Dixie--
       Eckstine." Variety 186:1, April 23, 1952.

12510 "Only 13 Negroes Had B'way Parts over 6½ Month Period; Mostly
       Bits." Variety 186:56, May 28, 1952.

12511 Cagle, C. "The Wilbur De Paris Band." Record Changer 11:9-10,
       June 1952.

12512 Nathan, H. "The First Negro Minstrel Band and Its Origins."
       Southern Folklore Quarterly 16:132-144, June 1952.

12513 "Spreading the Word." Time 60:81, July 21, 1952.

12514 Csida, J. "Billboard Backstage." Billboard 64:2, July 26, 1952.

12515 Borneman, E. "The Anthropologist Looks at Jazz." Record Chang-
       er 11:10, August-September 1952.

12516 Keepnews, O. "Jazz and America." Record Changer 11:31-34,
       August-September 1952.

12517 "Los Angeles to Have Negro Symphony Group." Music of the West
       8:13, October 1952.

12518 Whitton, D. "Inside 'Rhythm and Blues.'" Jazz Journal 5:1-2,
       October 1952.

12519 Merriam, A. "The African Background: An Answer to Barry
       Ulanov." Record Changer 11:7-8, November 1952.

12520   Stewart-Baxter, D. "Preachin' the Blues." Jazz Journal 5:15-16,
        November 1952; 5:4, December 1952.

12521   "MU to Investigate Conditions at American Camp." Melody Maker
        28:12, December 6, 1952.

12522   Dehn, M. "Eye-Witness Account of a Service in a Harlem Church."
        Melody Maker 28:6, December 13, 1952; 28:5, December 20, 1952;
        28:4, December 27, 1952.

12523   Brown, S. "Negro Folk Expression: Spirituals, Seculars, Ballads
        and Work Songs." Phylon 14:45-61, no. 1, 1953.

12524   Fisher, Miles Mark. Negro Slave Songs in the United States. New
        York: Russell & Russell, 1968, c1953. A study of slave song
        texts as a history.

12525   Grimes, A. "Possible Relationships Between 'Jump Jim Crow' and
        Shaker Songs." Midwest Folklore 3:47-57, 1953.

12526   Strider, R. H. "The Negro's Contribution to Music Education."
        Music Educator's Journal 39:27-28, February-March 1953.

12527   Ray, J. "Negroes Taught Me to Sing." Ebony 8:48-50, March
        1953.

12528   "NBC's 'Talent Has No Color' Projects Negro Contribs to New High
        in '52." Variety 190:1, March 18, 1953.

12529   "Moslem Musicians." Ebony 8:104, April 1953.

12530   Borneman, E. "A Break in the Racial Barriers." Melody Maker
        29:4, April 4, 1953.

12531   Eckstine, B. "South May Be Ready for Mixed Acts in Five Years,
        Sez Billy." Variety 190:48, April 22, 1953.

12532   Oliver, P. H. "Jazz in Negro Literature." Jazz Journal 6:19-20,
        May 1953.

12533   Borneman, E. "Background of Bop." Melody Maker 29:5, May 23,
        1953.

12534   Thompson, R. L. "Ethnic Music and Jazz Roots." Record Changer
        12:17-18, June 1953.

12535   Borneman, E. "Music and the Negro." Melody Maker 29:4, June
        6, 1953.

12536   Ramsey, F. "A Photographic Documentary of Jazz and Folk Back-
        grounds." Record Changer 12:23-47, July-August 1953.

12537   "Jubilee Singers." Our World 8:24-27, July 1953.

12538   "Negro ASA to Aid Young Talent." Variety 192:57, September 23,
        1953.

12539   Taubman, H. "12 Most Promising Negro Singers." Ebony 8:48-52,
        October 1953.

12540   "Celebrities' Cavalcade at ASA Shindig." Billboard 65:19, October
        17, 1953.

12541   Gleason, R. J. "Have Racial Lines in Jazz Disappeared?" down
        beat 20:4, December 30, 1953.

12542   Claxton, William. Jazz West Coast; A Portfolio of Photographs.
        Hollywood, Calif.: Linear Productions, 1955, c1954.

12543   Fletcher, Tom. 100 Years of the Negro in Show Business; The Tom
        Fletcher Story. New York: Burdge, 1954. Background of early
        musicians with information on ragtime, blues and ragtime.

12544   Vam Dam, T. "The Influence of the West African Songs of Derision
        in the New World." African Music 1:53-56, 1954.

12545   Wilgus, D. K. "A History of Anglo-African Ballad Scholarship
        Since 1989." (Ph. D. Dissertation, Ohio State University, 1954).

12546   Clark, E. R. "Negro Composer: A Mid-Century Review." Negro
        History Bulletin 17:132-133, March 1954.

12547   Chandler, B. "WLIB's All-Negro Music & Drama Gotham Festival
        in Socko Bow." Variety 193:39, March 3, 1954.

12548   Cook, M. "The Negro Spiritual Goes to France." Music Educator's
        Journal 40:42, April-May 1954.

12549   Roth, R. "The Esthetics of Jazz; Between the Piano and the Voice."
        Record Changer 13:3, July 1954.

12550   Stoddard, H. "Music in Pennsylvania." International Musician
        53:10, July 1954.

12551   Clapham, J. "Dvorak and the Impact of America." Music Review
        15:203-211, August 1954.

12552   "Negro Musicians Group Meets in New Orleans." Musical America
        74:14, September 1954.

12553   "Opera's Gain." Newsweek 44:96, October 18, 1954. The Metro-
        politan Opera breaks tradition by hiring a black performer.

12554   "Music in South Carolina." International Musician 53:14-15, Novem-
        ber 1954.

12555   "Barrier Is Broken." Musical America 74:4, November 1, 1954.

12556   Dodge, R. P. "Jazz: Its Rise and Decline." Record Changer 14:5-
        11, no. 3, 1955.

12557   Hughes, Langston. Famous Negro Music Makers. New York: Dodd,
        Mead, 1955. Juvenile literature.

12558   "The Romance of the Negro Folk Cry in America." Phylon 16:15-30,
        no. 1, 1955.

12559   Shapiro, Nat, and Nat Hentoff. Hear Me Talkin' to Ya; The Story
        of Jazz as Told by the Men Who Made It. New York: Dover Pub-

lications, 1966. Reprint of the 1955 edition published by Rinehart and Company in which musicians reminisce about blues and
ragtime in New Orleans around 1900.

12560 "Absent Friend." Musical America 75:9, January 15, 1955.

12561 Brown, T. "Film Notes." Melody Maker 31:17, January 29, 1955.

12562 Ford, E. C. "Negro Singers I Have Heard." Negro History Bulletin 18:122, February 1955.

12563 Feather, L. "Feathers' Nest." down beat 22:12, February 9, 1955.
Observation that few black jazz musicians reside and perform in
California.

12564 Bronson, A. "Interracial Opera Co., First of Kind, Pays Off in
'Salome' Southern Tours." Variety 197:1, February 16, 1955.

12565 "'Carmen Jones' Boxoffice Click Improves Negro Casting Chances."
Variety 197:3, February 23, 1955.

12566 Jackson, M. Y. "Folklore in Slave Narratives Before the Civil
War." New York Folklore Quarterly 11:14-19, Spring 1955.

12567 Dawson, W. L. "Interpretation of the Religious Folk-songs of the
American Negro." Etude 73:11, March 1955.

12568 "Negro D. J. Raps Spread of 'Filth' via R & B Disks." Variety
198:1, March 23, 1955.

12569 "Freed Breaks Record; Jive Big in Harlem." Billboard 67:28,
April 23, 1955.

12570 Merrifield, N. L. "Spiritual Distortion." Music Educator's Journal
41:44-46, June-July 1955.

12571 Dance, S. "Rhythm and Blues--an Assessment." Melody Maker
31:3, June 18, 1955.

12572 Ramsey, F. "The Singing Horns." Saturday Review 38:31-32, June
25, 1955. Discussion of brass bands in America's musical development.

12573 "Negro Role in Music Lauded in Congress." Variety 199:42, June
29, 1955.

12574 "R & B Cracking Racial Barriers in Southwest Where It's Bigger'n
Ever." Variety 199:43, July 6, 1955.

12575 "Negro Artists Rise as Solid Pops Sellers." Billboard 67:18, July
23, 1955.

12576 "That Hollywood Question." Metronome 71:50, November 1955. Few
blacks are in the musicians' union.

12577 Pleasants, H. "What Is This Thing Called Jazz?" High Fidelity
5:50-52, December 1955.

12578 Achille, L. T. "Les Negro-Spirituals et l'Expansion de la Culture

Noire." Présence Africaine 8-10:227-237, 1956. The development of spirituals in the United States, and other areas.

12579 Grossman, William Leonard, and Jack W. Farrell. The Heart of Jazz. New York: Da Capo Press, 1976, c1956. Reprint of the 1956 edition published by New York University Press.

12580 Hansen, Chadwick Clarke. "The Ages of Jazz: A Study of Jazz in Its Cultural Context." (Ph.D. Dissertation, University of Minnesota, 1956).

12581 Hodeir, André. Jazz, Its Evolution and Essence. New York: Da Capo Press, 1975. Reprint of the 1956 edition published by Grove Press, New York; translation of Hommes et Problèmes du Jazz.

12582 Kurath, G. "Rhapsodies of Salvation; Negro Responsory Hymns." Southern Folklore Quarterly 23:178-182, 1956.

12583 Ortiz Oderigo, N. R. "Negro Rhythm in the Americas." African Music 1:68-69, no. 3, 1956.

12584 Stearns, Marshall Winslow. The Story of Jazz. New York: Oxford University Press, 1956. A history of jazz with an extensive bibliography.

12585 Cohen, J. "Show Biz Long Proved There's No Frontier on Talent; Negro Artists' Great Progress." Variety 201:414, January 4, 1956.

12586 Oliver, P. H. "Shoutin' Home to Glory." Jazz Journal 9:1-2, February 1956.

12587 Friedman, J. "Spirituals Maintain Stabilizing Status." Billboard 68:55, February 4, 1956.

12588 Hentoff, N. "The Vanishing Female Jazz-Singer." Saturday Review 39:32-33, March 17, 1956.

12589 Boatfield, G. "Skiffle Artificial." Jazz Journal 9:2, April 1956. The Negro skiffle is being copied by white musicians.

12590 Wood, B. "Racial Prejudice." Jazz Journal 9:25-26, April 1956.

12591 "Segregationists Would Ban All Rock, Roll Hits." Billboard 68:130, April 7, 1956.

12592 "Let's Move." Jazz Journal 9:4, May 1956. A discussion of jazz, race and blues recordings.

12593 Banks, D. "Groups Seeks to Remove R & B Discs from Boxes." down beat 23:7, May 2, 1956.

12594 "Jim Crow Chief Hits at Rock and Roll." Melody Maker 31:7, May 12, 1956.

12595 "Negroes in Musical Careers." America 95:152, May 12, 1956.

12596 "Negro Opera: Ouanga." Variety 202:60, May 30, 1956. Presented by the National Negro Opera Foundation.

12597 "Rock 'n' Roll Helping Race Relations, Platters Contend." <u>down</u>
       <u>beat</u> 23:14, May 30, 1956.

12598 Randall, F. "Jim Crow Nearly Spoiled Our U.S. Trip." <u>Melody</u>
       <u>Maker</u> 31:3, June 16, 1956.

12599 Stewart-Baxter, D. "Big Band Jazz." <u>Jazz Journal</u> 9:9, July 1956.
       Negro bands are becoming popular again.

12600 Landry, R. J. "Sepia Yanks Hit Operatic Gravy Train--in Europe."
       <u>Variety</u> 203:1, July 18, 1956.

12601 "Near-Riot in Houston as Police Nix Dancing by Negroes at R &
       R'er." <u>Variety</u> 203:1, August 15, 1956.

12602 Hentoff, N. "Counterpoint." <u>down beat</u> 23:31-32, August 22, 1956.

12603 Ramsey, F. "A Study of the Afro-American Music of Alabama,
       Louisiana, and Mississippi, 1860-1900." <u>Ethnomusicology</u> no.
       8:28-31, September 1956.

12604 "Jim Crow Shadow Hovers over Vegas Jazz Efforts." <u>down beat</u>
       23:11, September 5, 1956.

12605 Cohen, J. "Desegregation in Show Biz." <u>Variety</u> 204:1, September
       26, 1956.

12606 Nathan, H. "Early Banjo Tunes and American Syncopation." <u>Mu</u>-
       <u>sical Quarterly</u> 42:455-472, October 1956.

12607 "Teen-age Singers; Negro Youths Highest Paid in Junior Rock 'n
       Roll Biz." <u>Ebony</u> 12:76, November 1956.

12608 "Frisco Columnist Raps White Tooters for Nixing Merger with Ne-
       gro Local." <u>Variety</u> 205:58, December 19, 1956.

12609 "Musician Group to Battle Bias." <u>down beat</u> 23:9, December 26,
       1956.

12610 Anderson, Edison Holmes. "The Historical Development of Music
       in the Negro Secondary Schools of Oklahoma and at Langston Uni-
       versity." (Ph.D. Dissertation, State University of Iowa, 1957).

12611 Canziani, W. "Negro Spirituals." <u>Jazz Podium</u> 6:12-13, no. 12,
       1957.

12612 Ewen, David. <u>Panorama of American Popular Music; The Story of</u>
       <u>Our National Ballads and Folk Songs, the Songs of Tin Pan Alley,</u>
       <u>Broadway and Hollywood, New Orleans Jazz, Swing, and Symphon-</u>
       <u>ic Jazz.</u> Englewood Cliffs, N.J.: Prentice-Hall, 1957. Includes
       a chapter "Gonna Sing All over God's Heaven--the Songs of the
       Negro."

12613 Hadlock, D. "An Open Letter to <u>Ebony</u>." <u>Record Changer</u> 15:5, no.
       2, 1957.

12614 Lucas, John. <u>The Great Revival on Long Play.</u> Northfield, Minn.:
       Carleton Jazz Club, Carleton College, 1957.

12615 Paul, Elliot Harold. That Crazy American Music. Indianapolis:
       Bobbs-Merrill, 1957. Discussion of Dixieland jazz including mu-
       sicians such as Joe Oliver and Louis Armstrong.

12616 Shapiro, Nat, and Nat Hentoff. The Jazz Makers. Westport, Conn.:
       Greenwood Press, 1975. Reprint of the 1957 edition published by
       Rinehart, New York; includes biographies of 21 jazz musicians
       such as Billie Holiday.

12617 Traill, Sinclair, and Gerald Lascelles. Just Jazz. London: P.
       Davies, 1957.

12618 _____. Just Jazz 3. London: Landsborough Publications, 1957.

12619 Ulanov, Barry. A Handbook of Jazz. Westport, Conn.: Green-
       wood Press, 1977. Reprint of the 1957 edition published by Vik-
       ing Press, New York.

12620 Smith, C. E. "The Moment of Truth." Record Changer 14:7-8,
       January 1957. Examines jazz development in New Orleans as it relates
       to segregation.

12621 "Blues from Dixieland." Nation 184:1-2, January 5, 1957.

12622 Moskowitz, G. "American Negroes' Impact on Parisian Show Biz."
       Variety 205:204, January 9, 1957.

12623 King, G. "Rhythm and Blues--an Apologia." Jazz Journal 10:9,
       February 1957.

12624 Kramer, G. "On the Beat." Billboard 69:26, March 9, 1957.
       Rhythm and blues records are being sold on white and black mar-
       kets.

12625 Wood, B. "Are Negroes Ashamed of the Blues?" Ebony 12:64-68,
       May 1957.

12626 Bruynoghe, Y., and S. Dance. "Perennial Blues." Saturday Re-
       view 40:34-35, May 11, 1957.

12627 "Inte Bara Blues." Orkester Journalen 25:3, July-August 1957.

12628 Feather, L. "Feather's Nest." down beat 24:7, July 11, 1957.
       Feather's comments on an article "Are Negroes Ashamed of the
       Blues."

12629 Wood, B. "Who's St. Cyr?" Jazz Journal 10:9-10, August 1957.

12630 Tallmadge, W. "Afro-American Music." Music Educator's Journal
       44:37-39, September-October 1957.

12631 Ramsey, F. "Lines from Buckner's Alley." Saturday Review 40:61,
       September 14, 1957.

12632 "Jazz Shows Nix Texas Dates, Want 'Integrated' Auds." Variety
       208:1, September 18, 1957.

12633 "Local 47 Bids Petrillo Support Resolution Entered Vs. Race Bias."
       Variety 208:50, October 9, 1957.

12634   "The Walls Came Tumbling Down." Woodwind World 1:2, Novem-
        ber 1957. A black musician is hired by the Boston Symphony
        Orchestra.

12635   Deuchar, P. "Jim Crow in New Orleans." Melody Maker 32:6,
        November 9, 1957.

12636   "Decline of Negro in Jazz Cued by Growth of Integration: Fr.
        O'Connor." Variety 208:65, November 20, 1957.

12637   Drexler, G. "Letters to the Editor." Woodwind World 1:7, De-
        cember 1957. Los Angeles Philharmonic hires a black musician.

12638   "AFM Going over Petrillo's Head on Segregated Locals." Variety
        209:43, December 18, 1957.

12639   Achille, L. T. "Die 'Negro Spirituals' als Geistliche Volkmusik."
        Music und Altar 2:64-70, 1958.

12640   _____. "Les Negro-Spirituals, Musique Populaire Sacree." Re-
        vue Musicale no. 239-240:239-245, 1958.

12641   Bird, Brian. Skiffle; The Story of Folk-song with a Jazz Beat.
        London: Hale, 1958. One chapter deals with Afro-American folk
        songs.

12642   Blesh, Rudi. Shining Trumpets: A History of Jazz. 2d ed., rev.
        and enl. New York: Da Capo Press, 1975. Reprint of the 1958
        edition published by Knopf, New York.

12643   Chase, G. "A Note on Negro Spirituals." Civil War History 4:261-
        267, 1958.

12644   Correa de Azevedo, L. H. "L'Heritage Africain dans la Musique
        du Nouveau Monde." Revue Musicale no. 242:109-112, 1958.

12645   Dauer, Alfons M. Der Jazz, Seine Ursprünge und Seine Entwicklung.
        Eisenach: E. Röth-Verlag, 1958. Includes information on black
        music in the United States.

12646   Gammond, Peter. The Decca Book of Jazz. London: F. Muller,
        1958.

12647   Phillips, W. B. "Negro Spirituals in Retrospect." Negro History
        Bulletin 22:51-53, 1958.

12648   Ramsey, F. "Elder Songsters." Jazz Monthly 3:6-8, 1958. Ex-
        amines early black folk music and its possible influence on jazz.

12649   Mehegan, J. "Jazz Creator as Performer." Saturday Review 41:79-
        80, January 11, 1958.

12650   "Headaches for Caesar." down beat 25:8-9, January 23, 1958.

12651   "B'way Legit for Integration but Jobs Are Still Scarce for Negroes."
        Variety 209:65, January 29, 1958.

12652   "Double Launching." Time 71:46, February 24, 1958.

12653 Harris, L. R. "Songs of the Negro Railroader." Music Journal
       16:44, March 1958.

12654 Smith, W. R. "Hepcats to Hipsters." New Republic 138:18-20,
       April 21, 1958.

12655 Ackerman, P. "What Has Happened to Popular Music?" High Fi-
       delity/Musical America 8:35-37, June 1958.

12656 "Disappearing Shadow." down beat 25:11, June 12, 1958.

12657 Hanft, W. "Theologie und Schwarze Kunst." Musik und Kirche
       28:160-168, July-August 1958.

12658 Gehman, R. "God's Singing Messengers; Ward Singers." Coronet
       44:112-116, July 1958.

12659 "Best of the Blues." Time 72:39, September 1, 1958.

12660 Jones, M. "Stars Combine to Fight Race Bias." Melody Maker
       33:11, September 13, 1958.

12661 Sinatra, F. "Jazz Has No Colour Bar!" Melody Maker 33:2-3,
       October 18, 1958.

12662 Martin, D. "The Negro in Popular Song." Music Journal 16:54-56,
       November-December 1958.

12663 Clar, M. "The Negro Church: Its Influence on Modern Jazz."
       Jazz Review 1:16-18, November 1958; 1:21-23, December 1958.

12664 Phillips, W. B. "Negro Spirituals in Retrospect." Negro History
       Bulletin 22:51-53, December 1958.

12665 Steif, B. "L.A. Local 47 Set to Perch on Chair of Gov.-Elect
       Brown in Pressure Vs. Intra-Union Race Bias." Variety 231:36,
       December 24, 1958.

12666 Feather, L. "Jazz Gives Jim Crow a Beating." Melody Maker
       33:3, December 27, 1958.

12667 Charters, Samuel Barclay. The Country Blues. New York: Da
       Capo Press, 1975. Reprint of the 1959 edition published by Rine-
       hart, New York.

12668 Hentoff, Nat, and Albert J. McCarthy. Jazz; New Perspectives on
       the History of Jazz by Twelve of the World's Foremost Jazz Crit-
       ics and Scholars. New York: Da Capo Press, 1974. Reprint of
       the 1959 edition published by Rinehart, New York which includes
       chapters on musicians such as Jelly Roll Morton, Charlie Parker,
       and Duke Ellington.

12669 Horricks, Raymond, et al. These Jazzmen of Our Time. London:
       Gollancz, 1959. Biographical information on prominent jazz mu-
       sicians such as Miles Davis and Quincy Jones.

12670 Ramsey, Frederic, and Charles Edward Smith. Jazzmen. New
       York: Harcourt Brace Jovanovich, 1977. Reprint of the 1959

edition published by Harcourt, Brace, New York which is filled
with contributions of black musicians to jazz.

12671   Williams, Martin T.   The Art of Jazz: Essays on the Nature and
        Development of Jazz. New York: Da Capo Press, 1979. Re-
        print of the 1959 edition published by Oxford University Press,
        New York.

12672   Borneman, E. "Ashamed of Race." Jazz Monthly 4:28, January
        1959.

12673   Clar, M. "The Negro Church: Its Influence on Modern Jazz."
        Jazz Review 2:22-24, January 1959.

12674   _____. "Negro Folk Elements in the Garner Style." Jazz Re-
        view 2:9-10, January 1959.

12675   "WLIB Set for Another Negro Music Festival." Variety 213:40,
        January 28, 1959.

12676   Clar, M. "The Negro Church: Its Influence on Modern Jazz."
        Jazz Review 2:28-29, February 1959.

12677   Oliver, P. "Special Agents; An Introduction to the Recording of
        Folk Blues in the Twenties." Jazz Review 2:20-25, February
        1959.

12678   "Another Iron Curtain." down beat 26:9, February 5, 1959. Dis-
        cussion of discrimination in symphony orchestras in New York.

12679   McCarthy, A. J. "Comment." Jazz Monthly 5:1, March 1959. Dis-
        crimination black musicians face in New Orleans.

12680   "No Bigotry in the Arts, Notes Richard Rodgers; Gets Tolerance
        Award." Variety 214:57, March 4, 1959.

12681   "U. of Ga. Nixes Brubeck but OK at Atlanta 'Race' Spot." Variety
        214:49, March 4, 1959. Brubeck group had a black bassist.

12682   "Urban League Totes Up 11 Negro Tooters Integrated in 'Class'
        Orchs." Variety 214:49, March 4, 1959.

12683   "'A Deathblow to Jim Crow'; AFL-CIO, NAACP's Music 'Summit'."
        Variety 214:49, April 1, 1959.

12684   "Brubeck Stands Fast." down beat 26:9, April 2, 1959. Brubeck's
        jazz group has been denied admittance to some stages in the South
        because of their black bass player.

12685   Hentoff, N. "The Strange Case of the Missing Musicians." Re-
        porter 20:25-27, May 28, 1959.

12686   _____. "Race Prejudice in Jazz: It Works Both Ways." Har-
        per's Magazine 218:72-77, June 1959.

12687   "Negro Makes It Longhair." Variety 215:99, June 24, 1959.

12688   "Ömsesidiga fördomar." Orkester Journalen 27:3, July-August

1959. A response to Hentoff's "Race Prejudice in Jazz" which appeared in the June 1959 issue of Harper's Magazine.

12689 "Jog Symphonies Re Race Bias." Variety 215:56, July 1, 1959.

12690 Stearns, M. "If You Want to Go to Heaven Shout." High Fidelity/ Musical America 9:36-38, August 1959.

12691 Cohen, J. "Negro Acts Dominate Vaude." Variety 215:1, August 5, 1959.

12692 Landry, R. J. "ASCAP, NAACP Patrons of Orchestra of America Using All-Native Music." Variety 215:43, August 26, 1959.

12693 Wayland, C. "A Super Race?" Jazz Monthly 5:27-28, September 1959.

12694 Dawbarn, B. "Jazz from Clayton to Dizzy." Melody Maker 34:2-4, September 19, 1959.

12695 Sargent, C. J. "Statement of Concern; Negro Spirituals." Christian Century 76:1090, September 23, 1959.

12696 Cooke, J. "Lessons in Jazz--a Review." Jazz Monthly 5:30-31, October 1959.

12697 McCarthy, A. J. "Newport Jazz Stars." Jazz Monthly 5:29-30, November 1959.

12698 Steif, B. "Calif. Atty. General's Merger Order to White & Negro Frisco AFM Locals." Variety 216:59, November 4, 1959.

12699 "Merger of White-Negro AFM Locals in Frisco Shapes as Odds-on Bet." Variety 216:60, November 18, 1959.

12700 "Broken Color Line." down beat 26:11, November 26, 1959.

12701 Steif, B. "Calif. Atty. Gen.'s 'Reasonable Time' Stance on White-Negro AFM Merger." Variety 217:57-58, December 2, 1959.

12702 Gleason, R. J. "A Blow to Jim Crow." down beat 26:14-15, December 10, 1959.

1960-1969

12703 Achille, L. T. "Les Negro Spirituals." Le Monde Réligieux 28:526-532, 1960-1961.

12704 Blesh, Rudi. O Susanna; Samples of the Riches of American Folk Music. New York: Grove Press, 1960. Includes jazz, blues, and spirituals.

12705 Bluestein, Eugene. "The Background and Sources of an American Folksong Tradition." (Ph.D. Dissertation, University of Minnesota, 1960).

12706   Carawan, G.   "Spiritual Singing in the South Carolina Sea Islands."
        Caravan no. 20:20-25, 1960.

12707   Francis, André.   Jazz.   Translated and Revised by Martin Williams.
        New York: Da Capo Press, 1976.   Reprint of the 1960 edition
        published by Grove, New York.

12708   Hansen, C.   "Social Influences on Jazz Style, Chicago, 1920-1930."
        American Quarterly 12:493-507, 1960.

12709   Harris, Rex.   The Story of Jazz.   New York: Grosset & Dunlap,
        1960.

12710   Leonard, Neil.   "The Acceptance of Jazz by Whites in the United
        States, 1918-1942."   (Ph.D. Dissertation, Harvard University,
        1960).

12711   Ostransky, Leroy.   The Anatomy of Jazz.   Westport, Conn.: Green-
        wood Press, 1973.   Reprint of the 1960 edition published by the
        University of Washington Press, Seattle.

12712   Panassie, Hugues.   The Real Jazz.   Revised and Enlarged Edition.
        New York: Barnes, 1960.   Translation of Histoire du Vrai Jazz
        which is an examination of jazz in New Orleans up to the 1950's.

12713   Ramsey, Frederic.   Been Here and Gone.   New Brunswick, N.J.:
        Rutgers University Press, 1960.   Compiled from photos taken on
        his trips through the South 1951-1957 to tape black music.

12714   Reisner, Robert George.   The Jazz Titans, Including "The Parlance
        of Hip."   New York: Da Capo Press, 1977.   Reprint of the 1960
        edition published by Doubleday, Garden City, N.Y.   Includes bi-
        ographies and discographies of jazz musicians plus a slang glos-
        sary.

12715   Ricks, George Robinson.   Some Aspects of the Religious Music of
        the United States Negro: An Ethnomusicological Study with Special
        Emphasis on the Gospel Tradition.   New York: Arno Press, 1977.
        Author's Ph.D. dissertation, Northwestern University, 1960.

12716   Rookmaaker, Hendrik Roelof.   Jazz, Blues, Spirituals.   Wageningen:
        Gebr. Zomer & Keuning, 1960.

12717   Runmark, A.   "Negerspiritualens Rötter."   Musikrevy 15:41-43, no.
        2, 1960.

12718   Schickel, Richard.   The World of Carnegie Hall.   Westport, Conn.:
        Greenwood Press, 1973.   Reprint of the 1960 edition published
        by Messner, New York.   The chapter on jazz discusses and il-
        lustrates a large number of black musicians who performed there,
        such as W. C. Handy.

12719   Stock, Dennis.   Jazz Street.   Garden City, New York: Doubleday,
        1960.

12720   Thieme, D. L.   "Negro Folksong Scholarship in the United States."
        African Music 2:67-72, no. 3, 1960.

12721 "Spadework on Desegregation of Locals Preceding L. A. -S. F. Quiz by U. S. Body." Variety 217:209, January 6, 1960.

12722 "Finds Europeans Kind to U. S. Negroes." Variety 217:51, January 13, 1960.

12723 Lucchese, S. E. "Brubeck's 'No Play sans Negro Bassist' Cues Shutout at Dixie U." Variety 217:63, January 20, 1960.

12724 "Rap 46 'Jim Crow' AFM Locals." Variety 217:63, January 20, 1960.

12725 "Granz Blasts TV Discrimination." down beat 27:12-13, February 4, 1960.

12726 Lees, G. "Afterthoughts." down beat 27:19-20, February 4, 1960.

12727 "Work Upbeat for Negro Musicians in Symph, Legit, TV." Variety 217:57, February 10, 1960.

12728 "S. F. Locals Head Toward Merger via AFM Nudge." Variety 217:45, February 17, 1960.

12729 Gleason, R. J. "An Appeal from Dave Brubeck." down beat 27:12-13, February 18, 1960. Brubeck's group was denied admission to many southern stages because his bassist was black.

12730 "SF Tooters Break Down Barriers via Merger of White & Negro Locals." Variety 217:91, February 24, 1960.

12731 Gleason, R. J. "Perspectives." down beat 27:43, March 17, 1960. Comments of Brubeck's tour of the South which was cancelled.

12732 Grunfeld, F. "The Great American Opera." Opera News 24:6-9, March 19, 1960.

12733 "End of a Friction." down beat 27:16, March 31, 1960.

12734 Gleason, R. J. "Don't Snow the Press." down beat 27:16, March 31, 1960.

12735 Mortara, A. "Un Aspetto della Condizione dei Negri d'America." Musica Jazz 16:18-19, April 1960.

12736 Testoni, G. "Lo Spettacolo Negro e Il Jazz." Musica Jazz 16:14-17, April 1960.

12737 "Stations in South Reject NBC Opera with Negro Star." Variety 218:1, April 13, 1960.

12738 Tynan, J. "Take 5." down beat 27:45-46, April 14, 1960.

12739 "U. S. Negro College Books Integrated Brubeck 4 but Lebanese Said Nix." Variety 218:141, April 20, 1960.

12740 Testoni, G. "Lo Spettacolo Negro e Il Jazz." Musica Jazz 16:25-27, May 1960.

12741   "First American Negro on Yearly Contract in O'seas Opera: Reri
        Grist." Variety 218:1, May 25, 1960.

12742   Demetre, J., and M. Chauvard.   "Holy Spirit!" Jazz Hot 26:22-25,
        June 1960.

12743   Testoni, G.   "Lo Spettacolo Negro e Il Jazz." Musica Jazz 16:26-
        28, June 1960.

12744   "Negro AME Zion Church Bishop Raps Jazz Versions of Traditional
        Spirituals." Variety 219:44, June 22, 1960.

12745   LaRocca, N.   "Jazz Began with Us!" Melody Maker 35:5, June 25,
        1960.

12746   Demetre, J., and M. Chauvard.   "Land of the Blues." Jazz Journal
        13:5-8, July 1960.

12747   Testoni, G.   "Lo Spettacolo Negro e Il Jazz." Musica Jazz 16:13-
        14, July 1960.

12748   Lyttelton, H.   "Another White Revival?" Melody Maker 35:4, July
        2, 1960.

12749   Feather, L.   "Feather's Nest." down beat 27:57, July 21, 1960.

12750   Granz, N.   "The Brubeck Stand; A Divergent View." down beat
        27:24, July 21, 1960.

12751   Demetre, J., and M. Chauvard.   "Land of the Blues." Jazz Jour-
        nal 13:17-19, August 1960.

12752   "Increasing Number of Negro Singers in Opera." World of Music
        no. 4:77, August 1960.

12753   Shih, H. W.   "Jazz in Print." Jazz Review 3:32-35, August 1960.

12754   Testoni, G.   "Lo Spettacolo Negro e Il Jazz." Musica Jazz 16:12-
        14, August-September 1960.

12755   Demetre, J., and M. Chauvard.   "Land of the Blues." Jazz Jour-
        nal 13:9-11, September 1960.

12756   Fox, C.   "Blues and the White Musicians." Jazz Monthly 6:8-10,
        September 1960.

12757   Feather, L.   "Feather's Nest." down beat 27:43-44, September 1,
        1960.

12758   Brown, G. M.   "Whither Jazz?" Jazz Journal 13:25, October 1960.

12759   Dehn, M.   "A Propos d'un Film sur la Danse des Noirs Americains."
        Jazz Hot 26:16-19, October 1960.

12760   Manheim, H. L., and A. Cummins.   "Selected Musical Traits
        Among Spanish, Negro, and Anglo-American Girls." Sociology
        and Social Research 45:56-64, October 1960.

12761 Pavlakis, C. "A Boys Choir in the Congo." School Musician 32:46-47, October 1960.

12762 Dehn, M. "Night Life in Georgia." Jazz Monthly 6:11-12, November 1960.

12763 Gruver, R. "The Origin of the Blues." Jazz Report 1:7-8, November 1960.

12764 Testoni, G. "Lo Spettacolo Negro e Il Jazz." Musica Jazz 16:20-22, November 1960.

12765 "Funk, Groove, Soul." down beat 27:18-19, November 24, 1960.

12766 Testoni, G. "Lo Spettacolo Negro e Il Jazz." Musica Jazz 16:20-22, December 1960.

12767 Rossac, G. "El Negro Spiritual." Boletín de Programas 20:24-28, no. 209, 1961-1962.

12768 Adams, Rosemary Frayser. "A Study of Community Services as Professional Laboratory Experiences in the Preservice Preparation of Teacher in Music at Knoxville College, Tennessee." (Ph.D. Dissertation, New York University, 1961).

12769 Berendt, Joachim Ernst, and William Claxton. Jazz Life, auf den Spuren des Jazz. Offenburg: Burda Druck und Verlag, 1961. An examination of jazz, chiefly in the United States, with many informal photographs of musicians such as Duke Ellington.

12770 Boeringer, J. "Recordings of Spirituals." Hymn 12:125-126, no. 4, 1961.

12771 Charters, A. R. "Negro Folk Elements in Classic Ragtime." Ethnomusicology 5:174-183, no. 3, 1961.

12772 Cray, E. "An Acculturative Continuum for Negro Folk Song in the United States." Ethnomusicology 5:10-15, no. 1, 1961.

12773 Dance, Stanley. Jazz Era; The 'Forties. London: Macgibbon & Kee, 1961.

12774 Dauer, Alfons M. Jazz, die Magische Musik; Ein Leitfaden Durch den Jazz. Bremen: C. Schünemann, 1961.

12775 Ewen, David. History of Popular Music. New York: Barnes & Noble, 1961. Includes chapters on jazz, ragtime, and blues.

12776 Hubert, Gadus Johnson. "An Examination of the Music Programs of Four Selected Negro Colleges in the Atlanta University Center with Recommendations for Morris Brown College." (Ph.D. Dissertation, Columbia University, 1961).

12777 Jeffreys, M. D. "Negro Influences on Indonesia." African Music 2:10-16, no. 4, 1961.

12778 Kinney, S. "The E. Azalia Hackley Collection." Ethnomusicology 5:202-203, no. 3, 1961.

12779   Landeck, Beatrice. Echoes of Africa in Folk Songs of the Americas.
        New York: McKay, 1961.

12780   Lehmann, T. "Die Bedeutung der Negro Spirituals für Unseren
        Kirchengesang." Zeichen der Zeit 15:28-30, 1961.

12781   Lilje, Hanns, Kurt Heinrich Hansen, und Siegfried Schmidt-Joos.
        Das Buch der Spirituals und Gospel Songs. Hamburg: Furch-
        Verlag, 1961. This history of spirituals and gospel songs in-
        cludes bibliography, discography, and a recording.

12782   Oliver, Paul. Blues Fell This Morning; The Meaning of the Blues.
        New York: Horizon Press, 1961. History of blues and analysis
        of 350 texts of blues.

12783   Patterson, Cecil Lloyd. "A Different Drum: The Image of the
        Negro in the Nineteenth Century Popular Song Book." (Ph.D.
        Dissertation, University of Pennsylvania, 1961).

12784   "Some Negro Folk Singers." Western Folklore 29:292-296, no. 4,
        1961.

12785   Terpilowski, L. "Negro Spirituals a Jazzologiczna Semantyka."
        Ruch Muzyczny 5:20-21, no. 4, 1961.

12786   Thieme, D. L. "Negro Folksong Scholarship in the United States."
        African Music 2:67-72, no. 3, 1961.

12787   Ortiz Oderigo, N. R. "La Musica Negra nel Cinema." Musica
        Jazz 17:21-23, January 1961.

12788   Williams, J. "Le Blues est Notre Historie." Jazz Magazine 7:32-
        35, January 1961.

12789   Hull, D. "The Authentic Voice of the Southland in Stereo." HiFi/
        Stereo Review 6:48-49, February 1961.

12790   Smith, C. E. "Cross-Seeding in Southern Songs." Saturday Review
        44:74, February 11, 1961.

12791   "Negro Acts Big on Japan Junkets." Variety 221:62, February 15,
        1961.

12792   Welding, P. J. "Holy Blues." Saturday Review 44:52-53, February
        25, 1961.

12793   Jones, L. "Blues, Black & White America." Metronome 78:11-15,
        March 1961.

12794   Ressac, G. "Le Negro Spiritual, Creation Spontanee des Noirs
        Americans." Musica no. 84:4-7, March 1961.

12795   Tenot, F. "Black, Brown and Beige." Jazz Magazine 7:19, March
        1961.

12796   Hentoff, N. "Jazz and Jim Crow." Commonweal 73:656-658, March
        24, 1961.

12797 Jalard, M. C. "La Recherche du 'Soul.'" Jazz Magazine 7:28-33,
       April 1961.

12798 Welding, P. J. "Sing a Song of Segregation." Saturday Review
       44:42, April 29, 1961.

12799 "First Festival." Metronome 78:6, May 1961. Discussion of the
       Harlem Jazz Festival.

12800 Whent, C. "The Phenomenon of Jazz." Jazz Monthly 7:13-14, May
       1961.

12801 "Hold Downfront Tickets, but 4 Negroes See Met Opera in Atlanta
       Balcony." Variety 222:88, May 10, 1961.

12802 "Inside Stuff--Music." Variety 222:45, May 24, 1961. Discussion
       of orchestral members of the National Symphony Orchestra of
       Washington, D.C. who are all white.

12803 Larrabee, E. "Throwback." Harper's Magazine 223:104, July 1961.

12804 Hobson, W. "Reflections on the Blues." Saturday Review 44:41,
       July 15, 1961.

12805 "Negro Bassist Charges Dayton Agency, Hotel Kayoed His Band
       Date." Variety 223:43, August 16, 1961.

12806 Hentoff, N. "New Faces of Jazz." Reporter 25:50-52, August 17,
       1961.

12807 Asman, J. "The Living Legends of New Orleans." Jazz Journal
       14:2-3, September 1961.

12808 "Dayton, O., Hotel Mgr. Can't Explain Why No Negro Played Inn
       Since '42." Variety 224:50, September 20, 1961.

12809 "Cincy AFM Locals Fight State Rap of Segregation." Variety 224:55,
       September 27, 1961.

12810 Bryant, L. C. "Status of Music in the Negro High Schools in South
       Carolina." Negro Educational Review 12:141-147, October 1961.

12811 Welding, P. J. "Blues from Texas." Saturday Review 44:86-87,
       October 14, 1961.

12812 Hentoff, N. "The Soft Mythology of Jazz." Show 1:39-47, Novem-
       ber 1961.

12813 "AFM, Agencies Back Granz Plan for Jazzmen's Non-Segregation
       Clause." Variety 224:55, November 8, 1961.

12814 Bennett, L. "Soul of Soul." Ebony 17:111-112, December 1961.

12815 "Voices of Hope." Sepia 10:76-78, December 1961.

12816 "Strong Action Against Jim Crow." down beat 28:13, December 7,
       1961. Discussion of the Granz plan for non-discrimination.

12817   "Ohio Civil Rights Examiner Finds for Negro Musician in Dayton
        Bias Case." Variety 225:49, December 13, 1961.

12818   Balliett, Whitney. Dinosaurs in the Morning; 41 Pieces on Jazz.
        Philadelphia: Lippincott, 1962. Essays which first appeared in
        the New Yorker 1957-1962 including writings on Charles Mingus,
        Billie Holiday, and Thelonious Monk.

12819   Bryant, Lawrence Chesterfield. A Study of Music Programs in Pri-
        vate Negro Colleges. Orangeburg, S.C.: South Carolina State
        College, 1962.

12820   _____. A Study of Music Programs in Public Negro Colleges.
        Orangeburg, S.C.: South Carolina State College, 1962.

12821   Charters, Samuel Barclay and Leonard Kunstadt. Jazz; A History
        of the New York Scene. Garden City, N.Y.: Doubleday, 1962.
        The book focuses on jazz history in New York from brass bands
        through Dixieland.

12822   De Toledano, Ralph. Frontiers of Jazz. 2d ed. New York: F.
        Ungar Pub. Co., 1962.

12823   Ewen, David. Popular American Composers from Revolutionary
        Times to the Present; A Biographical and Critical Guide. New
        York: H. W. Wilson Co., 1962. A few black composers such
        as Ellington and Waller are included.

12824   Grafman, Howard, and B. T. Manning. Folk Music U.S.A. New
        York: Citadel Press, 1962. Chiefly photographs and biographical
        sketches of American folk singers such as Mahalia Jackson.

12825   Hentoff, Nat. The Jazz Life. New York: Da Capo Press, 1975.
        Reprint of the 1962 edition published by P. Davies, London.

12826   Jazz Review. Jazz Panorama, from the Pages of Jazz Review.
        Edited by Martin Williams. New York: Collier Books, 1967,
        c1962. Much information on black jazz musicians.

12827   Leonard, Neil. Jazz and the White Americans: The Acceptance of
        a New Art Form. Chicago: University of Chicago Press, 1962.
        Discussion of the impact jazz had on the American musical scene.
        Includes charts which analyze the songs of Bessie Smith, Louis
        Armstrong, and Billie Holiday.

12828   Oster, H. "Negro French Spirituals of Louisiana." International
        Folk Music Council Journal 14:166-67, 1962.

12829   Ortiz Oderigo, Néstor R. La Música Afronorteamericana. Buenos
        Aires: Editorial Universitaria de Buenos Aires, 1963, c1962.

12830   Pyke, Launcelot Allen. "Jazz, 1920 to 1927: An Analytical Study."
        (Ph.D. Dissertation, University of Iowa, 1962).

12831   Zimmermann, H. W. "Neue Musik und Neues Kirchenlied." Musik
        und Gottesdienst 16:149-163, no. 6, 1962. Discussion of the use
        of Negro spirituals in the church music of Lutherans.

12832   Riedel, J. "Let Us Break Bread Together." Music Ministry 3:12-
        13, February 1962.

12833   Sinatra, F. "Musicians Must Fight Prejudice." Music Journal
        20:20-21, February 1962.

12834   "Jazz Benefit for Negro Pianist Refutes Charge that Dixieland's
        Dead." Variety 225:51, February 21, 1962.

12835   Brown, C. "Best of the Blues." Redbook 118:116, March 1962.

12836   Holder, G. "The Awful Afro Trend." Show 2:94-95, March 1962.

12837   "Racial Prejudice in Jazz." down beat 29:20-26, March 15, 1962.

12838   "The Fight for Equality: A Reply to G. E. Lambert." Jazz Month-
        ly 8:26, April 1962.

12839   Fumex, G. "Un Soir à Harlem." Jazz Magazine 8:30-31, April
        1962.

12840   "Tough Times for Mixed Band in Los Angeles." down beat 29:13,
        April 26, 1962.

12841   Conley, D. L. "Origin of the Negro Spirituals." Negro History
        Bulletin 25:179-180, May 1962.

12842   "Chords and Discords; 'Racial Prejudice in Jazz.'" down beat
        29:5-6, May 19, 1962.

12843   Alilunas, L. J. "Negro Music in American Culture." Human Re-
        lations Journal 10:474-479, Summer 1962.

12844   "Gospelers; Gospel Songs at Washington's International Jazz Festi-
        val." Time 79:64, June 15, 1962.

12845   "Gospel to Pop to Gospel; Meditation Singers." Ebony 17:107-108,
        July 1962.

12846   Cohn, L. "Recordings Reports: Folk and Blues LPs." Saturday
        Review 45:60, July 28, 1962.

12847   "Crow Jim." Time 80:58-60, October 19, 1962.

12848   Cohn, L. "Recordings Reports: Folk and Blues LPs." Saturday
        Review 45:58, November 10, 1962.

12849   Tenot, F. "La Boite de l'Oncle Tom." Jazz Magazine 8:21, De-
        cember 1962.

12850   Bradford, A. "Gospel Music." Jazz Journal 16:13-14, no. 7, 1963.

12851   Buszin, W. E. "Church Music in the Lutheran Churches of the
        U.S.A." Response 5:61-62, no. 2, 1963. Discussion of the
        spirituals in the Lutheran Church.

12852   Charters, Samuel Barclay. The Poetry of the Blues. New York:

Oak Publications, 1963. The social content of blues poetry is examined.

12853 Courlander, Harold. Negro Folk Music, U.S.A. New York: Columbia University Press, 1963. A history of the development of Negro folk music with bibliography and discography. Also includes some melodies with text.

12854 Dennison, Tim. The American Negro and His Amazing Music. New York: Vantage Press, 1963. A brief study of jazz, blues, and spirituals.

12855 Ehmann, W. "Negergottesdienst und Jazz." Musik und Gottesdienst 17:12-16, no. 1, 1963.

12856 Feather, Leonard G., and Jack Tracy. Laughter from the Hip; The Lighter Side of Jazz. New York: Da Capo Press, 1979. Reprint of the 1963 edition published by Horizon Press, New York, which includes reminiscences of famous jazzmen such as Count Basie.

12857 Goines, Leonard. "Music and Music Education in Predominantly Negro Colleges and Universities Offering a Four-Year-Program of Music Study Terminating in a Degree." (Ph.D. Dissertation, Columbia University, 1963).

12858 Jones, LeRoi. Blues People; Negro Music in White America. New York: W. Morrow, 1963. Jones discusses the roots of the music of the black man plus its influence on other American music.

12859 Jones, R. P. Jazz. London: Methuen, 1963. An overview of the history of jazz which includes information on musicians such as Muddy Waters and Louis Armstrong.

12860 Kmen, H. A. "Old Corn Meal; A Forgotten Urban Negro Folksinger." Second Line 14:15-20, no. 1-2, 1963.

12861 McLaughlin, W. B. "Symbolism and Mysticism in the Spirituals." Phylon 24:69-77, 1963.

12862 "Negro Spirituals im Gottesdienst--Ja oder Nein?" Evangelische Kirchenchor 63:62-63, no. 5, 1963.

12863 "New Trend?" Second Line 14:10, no. 11-12, 1963. Examination of the trend toward using jazz in church music.

12864 Posell, Elsa Z. American Composers. Boston: Houghton Mifflin, 1963. Includes biographies of Ulysses Kay and William Grant Still.

12865 Scarborough, Dorothy. On the Trail of Negro Folk-songs. Hatboro, Pa.: Folklore Associates, 1963.

12866 Schimmel, Johannes C. Spirituals & Gospelsongs. Gelnhausen: Burckhardthaus-Verlag, 1963. A short history of black music.

12867 Walker, W. T. "The Soulful Journey of the Negro Spiritual." Negro Digest 12:84-95, 1963.

12868 Waterman, R. A. "On Flogging a Dead Horse; Lessons Learned from the Africanisms Controversy." Ethnomusicology 7:83-87, no. 2, 1963.

12869 Bryant, L. C. "Music Programs in Public Negro Colleges." Negro Educational Review 14:39-46, January 1963.

12870 Perry, C. "The Spiritual and Jazz." International Musician 61:32, January 1963.

12871 Shelton, R. "Theatre; Black Nativity at Philharmonic Hall." Nation 196:20, January 5, 1963.

12872 Cohn, L. "Blues at a Bargain." Saturday Review 46:79, January 12, 1963.

12873 Suber, C. "Preservation Hall; New Orleans Rebirth." down beat 30:18, January 17, 1963.

12874 Hayes, R. "Music of Aframerica; My Songs." Music Journal 21:20-21, February 1963.

12875 "Batoneer of Chi Suburb Symph Quits over Hiring Ban on Negro Violinist." Variety 229:2, February 13, 1963.

12876 Berendt, J. E. "Americans in Europe." Jazz 2:20-21, March 1963.

12877 Cohn, L. "Blues: Three of a Kind." Saturday Review 46:97, March 16, 1963.

12878 Roth, M. "60 Yrs. of Segregation Ends in Chi as Negro Tooters Join White Local." Variety 230:53, March 27, 1963.

12879 Robinson, L. "Blues Becomes Big Business." Ebony 18:34-41, April 1963.

12880 "The Need for Racial Unity in Jazz; A Panel Discussion." down beat 30:16-21, April 11, 1963.

12881 "Coup Dur pour Jim Crow." Jazz Magazine 9:13-14, May 1963.

12882 Matteson, L. "Harlem; Mellan Himmel och Helvete." Orkester Journalen 31:8-9, May 1963.

12883 "Young Troupers Make Hit Debut." Ebony 18:156-158, May 1963.

12884 "Gospel Singers: Pop Up, Sweet Chariot." Time 81:48, May 24, 1963. Gospel singers are moving into nightclubs and other commercialism.

12885 "Now Hear the Word: Sweet Chariot Nite Club." Newsweek 61:94, May 27, 1963.

12886 Brown, C. "True Gospel Singing." Redbook 121:15, June 1963.

12887 "Negro Spirituals, Uninhibited Works of Art." Choir 54:97-98, June 1963.

12888 "Holy War; Gospel-Singing in Nightclubs." Newsweek 61:70, June
       24, 1963.

12889 Demetre, J. "Les Sortileges du Gospel." Jazz Hot no. 189:26-29,
       July-August 1963.

12890 "Capital Music Maker; Bethesda, Md. Congregational Church Choir."
       Ebony 18:91-92, July 1963.

12891 "Prexy Kenin Hits 3 Negro Tooters' Bias Charges Vs. AFM as 'In-
       famous.'" Variety 231:65, July 17, 1963.

12892 Shelton, R. "Freedom Songs." Nation 197:57-58, July 27, 1963.

12893 Roth, M. "Chi Tooters' Racial Discord; Negro Local 208 Won't In-
       tegrate." Variety 231:95-96, July 31, 1963.

12894 Pereverzev, L. "Rabochie Pesni Negrityanskogo Naroda." Sovets-
       kaya Muzyka 27:125-128, August 1963.

12895 Wagner, J. "Du Folklore à l'Ecriture." Jazz Magazine 9:28-30,
       August 1963.

12896 "Break Color Line; WBBM Signs Lurlean Hunter to Live Show."
       Billboard 75:39-40, August 3, 1963.

12897 "Battle Hymn of the Integrationists; We Shall Overcome." U.S. News
       & World Report 55:8, August 5, 1963.

12898 "Suburban Chi Symph Solves Audition 'Bias.'" Variety 231:53, Au-
       gust 7, 1963.

12899 Hentoff, N. "Gospel as Gimmick; Sweet Chariot Night Club." Re-
       porter 29:46-47, August 15, 1963.

12900 Jones, L. "Jazz and the White Critic; A Provocative Essay on the
       Situation of Jazz Criticism." down beat 30:16-17, August 15,
       1963.

12901 "Buck Clayton on 'Crow Jim' in Jazz." Variety 231:45, August 21,
       1963.

12902 "Chi Negro Musicians Local Resists Integration; CORE Urges AFM
       Action." Variety 232:1, August 28, 1963.

12903 Williams, M. "Gospel at the Box Office." Saturday Review 46:41,
       August 31, 1963.

12904 Cumming, R. "Editorially Speaking." Music Journal 21:19, Sep-
       tember 1963. Discussion of the contributions of black Americans
       to music.

12905 Wilson, J. S. "A Real New Orleans Sound; The Story of Preserva-
       tion Hall and Its Ancient Jazzmen." High Fidelity/Musical Amer-
       ica 13:59-63, September 1963.

12906 "AFM Prexy Kenin Orders Fast Merger of White & Negro Chi Tooter
       Locals." Variety 232:41, September 4, 1963.

12907 Sherman, R. "Sing a Song of Freedom." Saturday Review 46:65-67, September 28, 1963.

12908 Demetre, J. "Les Sortileges du Gospel." Jazz Hot no. 191:19-21, October 1963.

12909 Paige, E. D. "The Race Record." Music Journal 21:44, October 1963.

12910 Reda, J. "De Jelly-Roll Morton à Monk." Jazz Magazine 9:20-23, November 1963.

12911 Charosh, P. "Slander in Song." Listen 1:3-7, December 1963. Discussion of coon songs.

12912 Molleson, J. "Negro in Music." High Fidelity/Musical America 83:24-25, December 1963.

12913 Postgate, J. "Jazz and Race." Jazz Monthly 9:2-4, December 1963.

12914 Allen, W. C. "Another New Orleans First." Second Line 15:7-9, no. 5-6, 1964. Comments on the first live radio broadcast of jazz played by black musicians.

12915 Bryant, L. C., and J. H. Deloach. "The Status of Music in the Negro High Schools in South Carolina." Journal of Research in Music Education 12:177-179, no. 2, 1964.

12916 Dexter, Dave. The Jazz Story, from the '90s to the '60s. Englewood Cliffs, N.J.: Prentice-Hall, 1964.

12917 Ewen, David. The Life and Death of Tin Pan Alley; The Golden Age of American Popular Music. New York: Funk and Wagnalls Co., 1964.

12918 Hansen, B. "The Gospel Revival: Is God on Their Side?" Sing Out no. 1:25-27, 1964. Traces the development of gospel music.

12919 Lester, J. "Country Blues Comes to Town? The View from the Other Side of the Tracks." Sing Out 14:37-39, no. 4, 1964.

12920 McKinney, H. "Negro Music; A Definitive American Expression." Negro History Bulletin 27:120-121, no. 5, 1964.

12921 Myrus, Donald. I Like Jazz. New York: Macmillan Co., 1964. A history of jazz with many photographs and biographical sketches of jazz musicians.

12922 Ortiz Oderigo, Néstor R. Rostros de Bronce; Musicos Negros de Ayer y de Hoy. n.p., 1964.

12923 Patterson, C. L. "A Different Drum: The Image of the Negro in the Nineteenth-Century Songster." College Language Association Journal 8:44-50, 1964.

12924 Washington, J. R. "Negro Spirituals." Hymn 15:101-110, no. 4, 1964. An excerpt from his book Black Religion.

12925 "Noir sur Blanc." Jazz Magazine no. 104:17, March 1964. Comments on Ebony which has not listed great jazz musicians.

12926 Williams, M. "The Bystander." down beat 31:39, March 12, 1964. Additional notes on Ebony's failure to cite outstanding black musicians.

12927 "Musicians and Segregation." High Fidelity/Musical America 84:20, April 1964.

12928 Roth, M. "'Black Bottom' Negro Hitting America's Cultural Top, Asserts Oscar Brown Jr." Variety 234:2, April 8, 1964.

12929 McCarthy, A. J. "Jazz at Preservation Hall." Jazz Monthly 10:26-27, May 1964.

12930 Anderson, O. "Negro Music Imports Surge." Billboard 76:4, May 16, 1964.

12931 "'Soul' Disks Sell." Cash Box 25:3, May 16, 1964.

12932 "'The Magnificent' Puts Soul Behind His Work." Billboard 76:14, May 23, 1964.

12933 Balliett, W. "Jazz Concerts; Deep-Country Blues Singers at Hunter College." New Yorker 40:133-135, May 30, 1964.

12934 "Fisk Jubilee Singers." Sepia 13:24-27, July 1964.

12935 Conners, J. "Negroes' Contribution to Theatre Praised, Recounted by Fred O'Neal." Variety 235:59, August 19, 1964.

12936 "Without These Songs; Freedom Music." Newsweek 64:74, August 31, 1964.

12937 Dance, S. "Harlem Yesterdays." Saturday Review 47:74-75, September 26, 1964.

12938 Jones, M. "Singin' the Blues with the Third American Negro Blues Festival." Melody Maker 39:6, October 17, 1964.

12939 Feather, L. "From Willie the Lion to Monk." Melody Maker 39:6, October 31, 1964.

12940 Greeley, B. "Negroes 'Rock' TV Barriers; Top Disk Names on Major Shows." Variety 236:1, November 18, 1964.

12941 Rookmaker, H. "From Eliza to Odetta." Philips p. 17-20, Winter 1964-1965.

12942 "U.S. Again Sets Pop Pace in Britain as 'Colored Sound' Grooves Trend." Variety 237:45, December 2, 1964.

12943 Hentoff, N. "Harlem Sounds." Reporter 31:41-42, December 3, 1964.

12944 Bradford, Perry. Born with the Blues; Perry Bradford's Own Story; The True Story of the Pioneering Blues Singers and Musicians in the Early Days of Jazz. New York: Oak Publications, 1965.

12945 Cohen, J. "The Folk Music Interchange: Negro and White." Sing
       Out 14:42-45, no. 6, 1965.

12946 Dane, B. "The Chambers Brothers Do That Real Thing." Sing Out
       15:22-24, no. 4, 1965.

12947 Dunson, J. "Blues on the South Side." Sing Out 15:16-20, 1965.
       Examines blues found in south Chicago.

12948 _____. Freedom in the Air; Song Movements of the Sixties.
       New York: International Publishers, 1965. Includes history of
       the development of civil rights songs of the South.

12949 Glover, T. "R & B." Sing Out 15:6-13, no. 2, 1965.

12950 Hadlock, Richard. Jazz Masters of the Twenties. New York: Mac-
       millan, 1965. A major portion of this book examines black mu-
       sicians such as Louis Armstrong and Bessie Smith.

12951 Howard, John Tasker. Our American Music; A Comprehensive His-
       tory from 1620 to the Present. 4th ed. New York: T. Y. Cro-
       well Co., 1965. A short section on "Negro Folk Music" is in-
       cluded plus information and bibliographies of prominent musicians
       such as Marian Anderson and Louis Armstrong.

12952 Kofsky, F. "Jazz Mailbox: A Reply to My Critics." Jazz 4:4-7,
       no. 11, 1965.

12953 Lehmann, Theo. Negro Spirituals; Geschichte und Theologie. Witten
       u. Berlin: Eskart-Verlag, 1965.

12954 Longstreet, Stephen. Sportin' House; A History of the New Orleans
       Sinners and the Birth of Jazz. Los Angeles: Sherbourne Press,
       1965. Discussion of jazz musicians in general in regard to New
       Orleans' houses of prostitution.

12955 Merriam, A. P. "The African Idiom in Music." Journal of the
       American Folklore Society 75:120-132, 1965.

12956 Miller, William Robert. The World of Pop Music and Jazz. St.
       Louis: Concordia Pub. House, 1965. Some information on the
       part that black musicians played in the development of jazz and
       other popular music.

12957 O'Connor, N. J. "Editorial." Jazz 4:5, no. 9, 1965. Examination
       of the black musicians' passive attitude to jazz.

12958 Oliver, Paul. Conversation with the Blues. New York: Horizon
       Press, 1965. Interviews with many blues musicians.

12959 Hentoff, N. "Jazz and Race." Commonweal 81:4820484, January 8,
       1965.

12960 Williams, M. "Bystander." down beat 32:35, January 14, 1965.
       Examines the "natural rhythm" of black musicians.

12961 Benzo, P. "Ce Soir-la, Dieu Etait Noir." Jazz Hot no. 206:3-4,
       February 1965.

12962   "Savoy Cites Wherefores of Spiritual Disk Doom." Billboard 77:34,
        February 27, 1965.

12963   Hentoff, N. "Filling Holes in the Soul: Blues Singers." Reporter
        32:44, March 11, 1965.

12964   Cohn, L. "Recordings Reports: Folk and Blues LPs." Saturday
        Review 48:134, Marcy 13, 1965.

12965   "U.S. Negro Conducting Sydney Symph Regularly." Variety 238:2,
        March 24, 1965.

12966   "Moment of History; Development of We Shall Overcome." New
        Yorker 41:37-38, March 27, 1965.

12967   "Two Coloured Prima Donnas." Record Research no. 67:5, April
        1965.

12968   "Preservation Hall; New Orleans." Ebony 20:64-66, May 1965.

12969   Hentoff, N. "Second Chorus." down beat 32:38, May 6, 1965;
        32:41, June 3, 1965. Treats the sociological aspects of blues
        and bop in black life.

12970   "Set Negro Song Fest in Miss. Delta." Variety 239:92, July 28,
        1965.

12971   "Does the Colour Bar Creep into Popland?" Melody Maker 40:3,
        August 14: 1965.

12972   Hodes, A. "Sittin' In." down beat 32:18, August 26, 1965.

12973   "Jazz Musicians Tour Harlem by Truck." down beat 32:15, August
        26, 1965.

12974   "Jester Hairston and His Chorus." Choral & Organ Guide 18:24,
        September 1965.

12975   "On Preserving Our National Culture, Heritages and Treasured Art
        Forms." Choral & Organ Guide 18:9, September 1965.

12976   Hall, C. "Negro Gospel; No Other Musical Form Is Quite Like It."
        Billboard 77:71, October 23, 1965 Supplement.

12977   "Negro Gospel Music Makes Cultural Heritage Contribution." Bill-
        board 77:78, October 23, 1965 Supplement.

12978   Doig, I. "Music Hope for the Ghetto." Music Journal 23:43, No-
        vember 1965.

12979   Santamaria, F. "Afro Jazz à New York." Jazz Magazine no. 124:60-
        61, November 1965.

12980   Cohn, L. "Recordings Reports; Folk and Blues LPs." Saturday Re-
        view 51:86, November 30, 1968.

12981   Capel, M. "The Blessing of the Damned." Jazz Monthly 11:13-16,
        December 1965.

12982 Hall, C. "NARA Backs War on Bias." Billboard 77:1, December 18, 1965. Discrimination is examined by the National Association of Radio Announcers.

12983 Blesh, Rudi, and Harriet Janis. They All Played Ragtime. Rev. New York: Oak Publications, 1966. A detailed study of ragtime and extensive material on Scott Joplin.

12984 Carawan, Guy, and Candie Carawan. Ain't You Got a Right to the Tree of Life? The People of Johns Island, South Carolina, Their Songs. New York: Simon and Schuster, 1967, c1966. Includes melodies with texts.

12985 Chase, Gilbert. America's Music, from the Pilgrims to the Present. Rev. 2d ed. New York: McGraw-Hill Book Co., 1966. Includes an examination of spirituals, jazz, and blues.

12986 Cron, Theodore O., and Burt Goldblatt. Portrait of Carnegie Hall; A Nostalgic Portrait in Pictures and Words of America's Greatest Stage and the Artists Who Performed There. New York: Macmillan, 1966. Black musicians who have performed at Carnegie Hall are noted chiefly in the chapters "Jazz" and "Ballads and Folk Songs."

12987 Curnow, W. "Jazz and the American Negro." Comment 7:17-23, no. 2, 1966.

12988 Gammond, Peter, and Peter Clayton. Fourteen Miles on a Clear Night: An Irreverent, Sceptical, and Affectionate Book About Jazz Records. Westport, Conn.: Greenwood Press, 1978. Reprint of the 1966 edition published by Owne, London.

12989 Garrett, R. B. "African Survivals in American Culture." Journal of Negro History 51:239-245, no. 4, 1966.

12990 Gitler, Ira. Jazz Masters of the Forties. New York: Macmillan Co., 1966. Discussion of developments in jazz during the decade of the 1940's with information on black musicians such as Sarah Vaughan.

12991 Golos, J. "Wklad Murzynow w Kulture obu Ameryk." Ruch Muzyczny 10:18, no. 4, 1966.

12992 Hagen, R. A. "'Deutsche Spirituals' und Jazzmesse; Eine Untersuchung über die Verwendung Afroamerikanischer Musik im Katholischen Gottesdienst." Musik und Kirche 36:69-74, no. 2, 1966.

12993 Hill, A. "Send Money." Jazz 5:11, no. 8, 1966.

12994 "Jazz and Revolutionary Black Nationalism." Jazz 5:28-30, no. 4, 1966; 5:27-29, no. 5, 1966; 5:28-30, no. 6, 1966; 5:34-35, no. 7, 1966; 5:28-29, no. 8, 1966; 5:29-30, no. 9, 1966; 5:39-41, no. 10, 1966; 5:37-38, no. 11, 1966; 5:43-45, no. 12, 1966.

12995 Keepnews, Orrin, and Bill Grauer. A Pictoral History of Jazz; People and Places from New Orleans to Modern Jazz. New ed. rev. New York: Crown Publishers, 1966.

12996 Keil, Charles. Urban Blues. Chicago: University of Chicago Press,

1966. An examination of blues styles and development with a chapter on "Afro-American Music."

12997 Kmen, Henry A. Music in New Orleans: The Formative Years, 1791-1841. Baton Rouge: Louisiana State University Press, 1966. One chapter, "Negro Music," examines folklore and music styles.

12998 Kofsky, F. "The Avant-Garde Revolution: Origins and Directions." Jazz 5:14-19, no. 1, 1966.

12999 Lehmann, Theo. Blues and Trouble. Berlin: Henschel, 1966.

13000 Lester, J. "The Angry Children of Malcolm X." Sing Out 16:20-25, no. 5, 1966.

13001 Simms, D. M. "The Negro Spiritual: Origins and Themes." Journal of Negro Education 35:35-41, 1966.

13002 Stearns, M., and J. Stearns. "Vernacular Dance in Musical Comedy; Harlem Takes the Lead." New York Folklore Quarterly 22:251-256, no. 4, 1966.

13003 Szwed, J. F. "The Joyful Noise." Jazz 5:29, no. 2, 1966; 5:27, no. 4, 1966.

13004 Wilgus, D. K. "Gospel Songs." Journal of the American Folklore Society 79:510-515, 1966.

13005 Wilson, John Steuart. Jazz: The Transition Years, 1940-1960. New York: Appleton-Century-Crofts, 1966.

13006 Yourcenar, Marguerite. Fleuve Profond, Sombre Rivière: Les Negro Spirituals. Paris: Gallimard, 1966. Includes texts without music.

13007 "American Negro Acts Cashing in on U.K. Mkt. as British Rockers Plug 'em." Variety 241:2, January 26, 1966.

13008 Oliver, P. "Literature on Negro Folk Song." Jazz Monthly 11:29-30, February 1966.

13009 Jones, L. "Apple Cores: Strong Voices in Today's Black Music." down beat 33:15, February 20, 1966.

13010 Wachsmann, K. P. "Negritude in Music." Composer no. 19:12-16, Spring 1966.

13011 Leiser, W. "The Negro Spiritual and Gospel Festival of 1966." Gospel News Journal 2:1-5, March 1966.

13012 Jones, L. "New Voices in Newark." down beat 33:13, March 10, 1966.

13013 "Jazz and Watts Youth." down beat 33:12-13, April 7, 1966.

13014 Matzorkis, G. "Down Where We All Live." down beat 33:21-22, April 7, 1966.

13015   "Groups Boycott Colour Bar Midland Club." Melody Maker 41:5,
        April 9, 1966.

13016   "Disk Bias Charge by Negro Batoneer Dean Dixon Brings Quick De-
        nials." Variety 242:1, April 20, 1966.

13017   Matzorkis, G. "Down Where We All Live." down beat 33:17-18,
        April 21, 1966.

13018   Comolli, J. L. "Les Conquerants d'un Nouveau Monde." Jazz Mag-
        azine no. 131:30-35, June 1966.

13019   Johnson, B. "Toms and Tomming: A Contemporary Report." down
        beat 33:24, June 16, 1966.

13020   Feather, L. "Jim Crow; Things Ain't What They Used to Be in
        Atlanta." Melody Maker 41:6, June 25, 1966.

13021   King, B. "Introducing the High-Life." Jazz Monthly 12:3-8, July 1966.

13022   "Woodfin and Inevitability." Jazz Journal 19:13-14, July 1966. The
        black community strongly supports jazz musicians.

13023   "Blues Is How It Is; Chicago's Eminence." Time 88:53, September
        2, 1966.

13024   Feather, L. "Watts Apres la Crise." Jazz Magazine no. 135:15-16,
        October 1966.

13025   Szwed, J. F. "Music Style and Racial Conflict." Phylon 27:358-
        366, Winter 1966.

13026   Berger, D. "Harlem on la Terre Promise." Jazz Hot no. 226:11-
        16, December 1966.

13027   Borris, S. "Jazz--Wesen und Werden." Musik im Unterrecht
        58:113-116, 1967.

13028   Charters, Samuel Barclay. The Bluesmen; The Story and the Music
        of the Men Who Made the Blues. New York: Oak Publications,
        1967-1977. Vol. 1: The singers and the styles from Mississippi,
        Alabama, and Texas up to the Second World War, with a brief
        consideration of some of the traceable relationships between the
        blues and African song. Vol. 2: Sweet as the showers of rain.

13029   Dixon, Christa. Wesen und Wandel Geistlicher Volkslieder. Negro
        Spirituals. Wuppertal: Jugenddienst-Verlag, 1967. A history of
        spirituals issued originally as the author's thesis.

13030   Hagen, R. A. "Negro Spirituals im Kirchenchor." Der Kirchen-
        chor 27:73-74, no. 5, 1967.

13031   _____. "Das Spiritual--Versuche zu Seiner Erforschung." Mu-
        sica 21:58-61, no. 2, 1967.

13032   Hansen, Barret Eugene. Negro Popular Music, 1945-1953. Los
        Angeles: Hansen, 1967. A history of black music during these
        years emphasizing jazz.

13033 Henderson, S. E. "Blues for the Young Blackman." Negro Digest
       16:10-17, no. 10, 1967.

13034 Hughes, Langston, and Milton Meltzer. Black Magic; A Pictorial
       History of the Negro in American Entertainment. Englewood
       Cliffs, N.J.: Prentice-Hall, 1967. A pictorial work covering
       a wide range of black culture including music.

13035 Jackson, Bruce. The Negro and His Folklore in Nineteenth Century
       Periodicals. Austin: University of Texas Press, 1967. Includes
       reprints of articles such as "Songs of the Slave" and "The Sur-
       vival of African Music in America."

13036 _____. "What Happened to Jody." Journal of the American Folk-
       lore Society 80:387-396, 1967. Brief history of "Jody" songs
       which blacks sang while in prison and in the army.

13037 Jones, LeRoi. Black Music. New York: W. Morrow, 1967. Es-
       says on black music and reviews of various black musicians.

13038 King, B. "The Formative Years." Jazz Monthly 13:5-7, no. 4,
       1967. African influence on American jazz.

13039 McRae, Barry. The Jazz Cataclysm. South Brunswick, N.J.: A.
       S. Barnes, 1967.

13040 Nagy, B. C. "Afroamerikai Nepzene." Magyar Zene 8:574-591,
       no. 6, 1967.

13041 Rout, L. B. "AACM: New Music (!) New Ideas (?)." Journal of
       Popular Culture 1:28-140, no. 2, 1967.

13042 Rublowsky, John. Popular Music. New York: Basic Books, 1967.
       Chapters on jazz and rock and roll discuss the influence of black
       musicians in these fields.

13043 Wallagh, Constant. Spiritual en Gospel. Van Plantage tot Concert-
       podium. Amsterdam: Koninginneweg, 1967.

13044 Wilgus, D. K. "From the Record Review Editor: Negro Music."
       Journal of the American Folklore Society 80:104-109, 1967.

13045 Williams, Martin T. Jazz Masters of New Orleans. New York:
       Da Capo Press, 1978. Reprint of the 1967 edition published by
       Macmillan, New York which consists of chapters on eleven im-
       portant jazz musicians, including Louis Armstrong and Jelly Roll
       Morton.

13046 Zenetti, Lothar. Peitsche & Psalm; Geschichte und Glaube, Spir-
       ituals und Gospelsongs der Neger Nordamerikas. 2., Verb. Aufl.
       München: Pfeiffer, 1967.

13047 "Jazz and Revolutionary Black Nationalism." Jazz 6:38, January
       1967.

13048 Balliett, W. "Jazz Concerts: Spirituals to Swing--1967." New
       Yorker 42:109-111, January 28, 1967.

13049 Feather, L. "Black Blues in Studios." down beat 34:13, February
9, 1967. Black musicians face discrimination at Hollywood studios.

13050 "Lesson of Experience; Members of Symphony of the New World."
Newsweek 69:102, February 20, 1967.

13051 Le Bris, M. "L'Artiste Vole par Son Art." Jazz Hot no. 229:16-
19, March 1967.

13052 Neal, L. P. "The Black Musician in White America." Negro Digest 16:53-57, March 1967.

13053 "Donaly Byrd Writing Negro History Musical." down beat 34:14,
March 23, 1967. Musical is to be presented at Expo 67 in Montreal.

13054 Shank, B. "A Reply to Leonard Feather." down beat 34:6, March
23, 1967. Comments on Feather's article "Black Blues in Studios"
which appeared in the February 9, 1967 issue of down beat.

13055 Schwartz, J. "Black Power & 'Soul' Music." Broadside no. 80:20,
April-May 1967.

13056 "Jazz and Revolutionary Black Nationalism." Jazz 6:30, April 1967.

13057 Kofsky, F. "The Jazz Scene." Jazz 6:20-24, April 1967.

13058 Hentoff, N. "Roots." down beat 34:15, April 6, 1967. Discussion
of the musical being prepared for Expo 67, Montreal.

13059 Kofsky, F. "The Jazz Scene." Jazz 6:26, May 1967.

13060 Kopelowicz, G. "Le Nouveau Jazz et la Realite Americaine." Jazz
Hot no. 231:18-23, May 1967.

13061 Garland, P. "In Groups of the Big Beat." Ebony 22:38, June 1967.

13062 "Jazz and Revolutionary Black Nationalism." Jazz 6:30, June 1967.

13063 "5 Yank Negro Troupes Currently on Tours in Europe, Mostly Longhair." Variety 247:1, June 14, 1967.

13064 "Jazz and Revolutionary Black Nationalism." Jazz 6:37-38, July
1967.

13065 Eldridge, R. "Magnificent Seven of Soul." Melody Maker 44:10,
July 26, 1967.

13066 Adams, A. "Africa Revisited." High Fidelity/Musical America
17:MA26-27, August 1967.

13067 Henderson, S. E. "Blues for the Young Blackman." Negro Digest
16:10-17, August 1967.

13068 Schoenfeld, H. "Negro Ghettos May Be Aflame but R & B Songs
Fail to Mirror Plight." Variety 247:1, August 2, 1967.

13069 Landau, J. "A Whiter Shade of Black." <u>Crawdaddy</u> no. 11:34-40,
       September-October 1967.

13070 Williams, M. "The Same Old Story." <u>down beat</u> 34:14, September
       7, 1967.

13071 Christgau, R. "Secular Music; Soul Music." <u>Esquire</u> 68:54, Oc-
       tober 1967.

13072 "Le Jazz, Musique de Negres?" <u>Jazz Magazine</u> no. 147:23-29, Oc-
       tober 1967.

13073 Carles, P. "Noir sur Blanc." <u>Jazz Magazine</u> no. 149:17, Decem-
       ber 1967.

13074 "More Negroes in Grand Opera." <u>Variety</u> 249:48, December 27,
       1967.

13075 Boeckman, Charles. <u>Cool, Hot and Blue; A History of Jazz for
       Young People</u>. Washington: R. B. Luce, 1968. An introduction
       to the origins of jazz; lists many black musicians such as Louis
       Armstrong and Duke Ellington.

13076 Crawford, P. N. "A Study of Negro Folk Songs from Greensboro,
       North Carolina and Surrounding Towns." <u>North Carolina Folk-
       lore</u> 16:69-139, 1968.

13077 Dankworth, Avril. <u>Jazz: An Introduction to Its Musical Basis</u>.
       New York: Oxford University Press, 1968. An introduction to
       jazz styles including representative musicians.

13078 Daughtry, Willa Estelle. "Sissieretta Jones: A Study of the Ne-
       gro's Contribution to Nineteenth Century American Concert and
       Theatrical Life." (Ph.D. Dissertation, Syracuse University,
       1968).

13079 Dorigné, Michel. <u>Jazz 1; Les Origines du Jazz, le Style Nouvelle
       Orléans et Ses Prolongements</u>. Paris: l'Ecole des Loisirs, 1968.

13080 Foreman, R. C. "Jazz and Race Records, 1920-32; Their Origins
       and Their Significance for the Record Industry and Society." (Ph.D.
       Dissertation, University of Illinois, 1968).

13081 French, R. F. "Choral Music in the Liturgy; A Celebration of the
       Life of Malcolm X." <u>American Choral Review</u> 10:79-85, no. 2,
       1968.

13082 "Ghetto Song." <u>Sing Out</u> 17:52-53, no. 4, 1967.

13083 Jackson, Clyde Owen. <u>The Songs of Our Years; A Study of Negro
       Folk Music</u>. New York: Exposition Press, 1968.

13084 Krähenbühl, Peter. <u>Der Jazz und Seine Menshen: Eine Soziologische
       Studie</u>. Bern: München: Francke, 1963.

13085 Leadbitter, Mike. <u>Crowley, Louisiana Blues</u>. Bexhill-on-Sea, Sus-
       sex, Eng.: Blues Unlimited, 1968.

13086 _____. Delta Country Blues. Bexhill-on-Sea, Sussex, Eng.: Blues Unlimited, 1968.

13087 Malone, Bill C. Country Music U.S.A. Austin: Published for the American Folklore Society by the University of Texas Press, 1968. Black musicians are included with a discussion of their musical styles.

13088 Oliver, Paul. Screening the Blues: Aspects of the Blues Tradition. London: Cassell, 1968. A history of blues with many lyrics illustrating the various styles. The U.S. edition in 1970 was entitled Aspects of the Blues Tradition, published by Oak Publications, New York.

13089 "The Power of Gospel Music." Gospel News Journal 5:4, 1968.

13090 Rockmore, Noel. Preservation Hall Portraits. Text by Larry Borenstein, and Bill Russell. Baton Rouge: Louisiana State University Press, 1968. Pictures and biographical sketches of many black jazz musicians of New Orleans.

13091 Schuller, Gunther. The History of Jazz. New York: Oxford University Press, 1968. Vol. 1: Early Jazz: Its Roots and Musical Development.

13092 Stevenson, R. "The Afro-American Musical Legacy to 1800." Musical Quarterly 54:476-502, no. 4, 1968.

13093 Tallmadge, W. H. "The Responsorial and Antiphonal Practice in Gospel Song." Ethnomusicology 12:219-238, no. 2, 1968.

13094 Wilgus, D. K. "From the Record Review Editor: Negro Music." Journal of the American Folklore Society 81:89-94, 1968; 81:276-280, 1968.

13095 "Black America." Jazz 6:20-25, January 1967.

13096 "Black Power et New Thing." Jazz Magazine no. 150:19, January 1968.

13097 Hentoff, N. "Soundings." Jazz and Pop 7:13, January 1968.

13098 Goodman, J. "Looking for the Black Message." New Leader 51:26-28, January 1, 1968.

13099 Drushler, P. "Integration and Instrumental Music--a Case Study." Instrument 22:30, March 1968.

13100 Maynor, D. "Arts in the Ghetto." Music Educator's Journal 54:39-40, March 1968.

13101 Duncan, J. "Art Music by Negro Composers on Record." Negro History Bulletin 31:6-8, April 1968.

13102 "Souls Forgotten Gleam." Negro History Bulletin 31:4-5, April 1968.

13103 "Sammy Davis Deplores Lack of Negro Openings." Billboard 80:8, April 27, 1968.

13104   Oppens, K. "Kafka Oper in Kafka Architektur." Opern Welt no.
        5:29, May 1968.

13105   Spellman, A. B. "Deeper Than Jazz; Afro-American Music." New
        Republic 158:37-38, May 11, 1968.

13106   Dane, B. "Black Music Today." Guardian p. 34, May 25, 1968.

13107   Feather, L. "Jim Crow Flies West." down beat 35:14, May 30,
        1968.

13108   James, M. "New Ebb, Old Flow." Jazz Monthly 14:7-8, June 1968.

13109   Ianni, F. A. "Cultivating the Arts of Poverty." Saturday Review
        50:60-61, June 17, 1967.

13110   Gleason, R. "Can the White Man Sing the Blues?" Jazz and Pop
        7:28-29, August 1968.

13111   Russcol, H. "Can the Negro Overcome the Classical Music Estab-
        lishment?" High Fidelity/Musical America 18:42-46, August 1968.

13112   Brack, R. "New Market for Black Blues." Billboard 80:28, August
        17, 1968 Supplement.

13113   Shaw, A. "Blue-Eyed Soul." Billboard 80:34-35, August 17, 1968
        Supplement.

13114   _____. "Choreography & Soul." Billboard 80:42-49, August 17,
        1968 Supplement.

13115   Bennett, M. "Negro Promoter Teddy Powell's View of Racial Show
        Biz Responsibilities." Variety 252:45, August 21, 1968.

13116   Tiegel, E. "TV Showcasing Black Artists." Billboard 80:1, August
        24, 1968.

13117   White, K. "The Palace of Soul." Billboard 80:16-18, August 31,
        1968 Supplement. Discussion of the Apollo Theatre, N.Y. where
        many black musicians performed.

13118   Ekkens, T. A. "Earliest Folkers on Disc?" Record Research no.
        92:4, September 1968.

13119   Gleason, R. "Anthem of the Black Revolution." Jazz and Pop 7:11,
        September 1968.

13120   Bennett, M. "Black-and-White Duos on Disks Reflect New Inter-
        racial Stance." Variety 252:1, September 4, 1968.

13121   Korall, B. "At the Roots." Saturday Review 51:128-129, Septem-
        ber 14, 1968.

13122   "Donald Byrd Conducts N.C. College Seminar." down beat 35:13,
        September 19, 1968.

13123   "Black Artists Finally Get Television Shows." Rolling Stone no.
        18:4, September 28, 1968.

13124 Crawford, P. N. "A Study of Negro Folk Songs from Greensboro, North Carolina and Surrounding Towns." North Carolina Folklore 16:65-139, October 1968.

13125 Stevenson, R. "The Afro-American Legacy (to 1800)." Musical Quarterly 54:475-502, October 1968.

13126 Albright, T. "Visuals; Black Art." Rolling Stone no. 19:20, October 12, 1968.

13127 Shaw, A. "Country Music and the Negro." Billboard 79:82-83, October 28, 1968 Supplement.

13128 Schoenfeld, H. "802 Backs Blacks on Jobs; Tells Batoners to Share Work." Variety 253:73, November 20, 1968.

13129 Ochs, E. "R & B Comes of Age as Musical Culture." Billboard 80:34, December 14, 1968.

13130 Tiegel, E. "R & B Disks Swing to 'Black Hope' Tunes." Billboard 80:1, December 14, 1968.

13131 "Baltimore Brings Jazz to Black Youngsters." down beat 35:13, December 26, 1968.

13132 De Lerma, D. "Black-American Music Viewed from Europe." Your Music Cue 6:22-24, no. 3, 1969-1970.

13133 "Black Music Seminar at Indiana University." ASCAP Today 3:24, no. 2, 1969.

13134 Braun, D. Duane. Toward a Theory of Popular Culture: The Sociology and History of American Music and Dance, 1920-1968. Ann Arbor, Mich.: Ann Arbor Publishers, 1969. Examines the beginnings of jazz through rock and roll with discussions of many black musicians.

13135 "Broadcast Music, Inc." National Music Council Bulletin 29:29-30, no. 3, 1969.

13136 Chametzky, Jules, and Sidney Kaplan. Black and White in American Culture. Amherst, Mass.: University of Massachusetts Press, 1969. Includes many articles printed from the Massachusetts Review on jazz and blues.

13137 Conforti, J. M. "Racism in Music Education." Musart 22:28, no. 1, 1969.

13138 "Einheimischer Theologe Rechnet mit Missionsgesangbuch Ab." Musik und Gottesdienst 23:137-138, no. 5, 1969.

13139 Garland, Phyl. The Sound of Soul. Chicago: H. Regnery Co., 1969. Traces the development of soul music and examines musicians such as Chuck Berry and Aretha Franklin.

13140 Katz, Bernard. The Social Implications of Early Negro Music in the United States; With Over 150 of the Songs, Many of Them with Their Music. New York: Arno Press, 1969. Reprints many periodical articles from the nineteenth century.

13141 Layng, J. "Black Images in Opera." Opera Journal 2:28-32, no. 1, 1969.

13142 Leadbitter, Mike and Eddie Shuler. From the Bayou; The Story of Goldband Records. Bexhill-on-Sea, Sussex, Eng.: Blues Unlimited, 1969.

13143 Lee, R. C. "The American Negro Work Songs." Jazz Forum no. 6:63-64, 1969.

13144 Lomax, Alan. Black Musical Style. New York: Cantometrics Project, 1969.

13145 Lovell, J. "Reflections on the Origins of the Negro Spirituals." Negro American Literature Forum 3:91-97, no. 3, 1969.

13146 Memphis Housing Authority. Beale Street, U.S.A.: Where the Blues Began. Bexhill-on-Sea, Sussex, Eng.: Blues Unlimited, 1969. "This booklet is a replica of one prepared by the City of Memphis Housing Authority in consideration of Beale Street as an Urban Redevelopment Scheme."

13147 Oliver, Paul. The Story of the Blues. Philadelphia: Chilton Book Co., 1969. A history of blues, with information on musicians such as Bessie Smith.

13148 Oster, Harry. Living Country Blues. Detroit: Folklore Associates, 1969. Includes texts of many blues with historical information.

13149 Patterson, Lindsay. The Negro in Music and Art. 2d. ed., rev. New York: Publishers Co., 1969.

13150 Portelli, Alessandro. Veleno di Piombo sul Muro; Le Canzoni del Black Power. Bari: Laterza, 1969. A history of black songs in both English and Italian.

13151 Schaeffner, A. "La Musique Noire d'un Continent à un Autre." Musique dans la Vie 2:7-23, 1969.

13152 "School of Music Awarded Grant for Black Music Research." Your Music Cue 5:22, no. 6, 1969.

13153 Shaw, Arnold. The Rock Revolution. New York: Crowell-Collier Press, 1969. A study of the development of rock music with one chapter on black music: "Where It Started; Blues, Race, and Rhythm and Blues."

13154 Spearman, R. "Music and Black Culture." Musart 22:30-31, no. 1, 1969.

13155 Surge, Frank. Singers of the Blues. Minneapolis: Lerner Publications, 1969. Juvenile literature.

13156 Tallmadge, William H. Afro-American Music. Rev. ed. Buffalo, N.Y.: College Bookstore, State University College, 1969. A 16-page history.

13157 Trippin': A Need for Change. Jones, LeRoi, Larry Neal, and A. B. Spellman. New Ark: Cricket? 1969. A study of black music.

13158 Turner, F. W. "Black Jazz Artists: The Dark Side of Horatio Alger." Massachusetts Review 10:341-353, no. 2, 1969.

13159 Williams, Martin T. Where's the Melody? A Listener's Introduction to Jazz. Rev. ed. New York: Pantheon Books, 1969. Discusses the modern development of jazz with an examination of some musicians such as Billie Holiday and Thelonious Monk.

13160 Work, John Wesley. Folk Song of the American Negro. New York: Negro Universities Press, 1969.

13161 Leroux, B. "Blues Rural." Jazz Hot no. 246:31-33, January 1969.

13162 "AFM Negotiators Ask Equality for Blacks." down beat 36:10, January 9, 1969.

13163 Mulligan, B. "Soul Oldies' British Payoff; Diskeries Score in Growing Mkt." Variety 253:47, January 22, 1969.

13164 "Phil Morre Urges Aid for Young Negro Artists with Untapped Pop Talent." Variety 253:62, January 29, 1969.

13165 Comolli, J. L. "Loin de Gunther Schuller, Pres de LeRoi Jones." Jazz Magazine no. 163:47-49, February 1969.

13166 Pleasants, H. "The Afro-American Epoch." Stereo Review 22:55-59, February 1969.

13167 Rout, L. B. "Reflections on the Evolution of Post-War Jazz." Negro Digest 18:32-34, February 1969.

13168 Wilson, J. S. "Preservation Hall." International Musician 67:10, February 1969.

13169 Booth, S. "Rebirth of the Blues: Soul." Saturday Evening Post 242:26-31, February 8, 1969.

13170 Burns, J. "Turning East." Jazz Journal 22:2-4, March 1969.

13171 Gleason, R. J. "Minority Music into an Art." Jazz and Pop 8:7, March 1969.

13172 "Grant for Black Musicians." Music Educator's Journal 55:3, January 1969.

13173 Heckman, D. "Here, There & Everywhere." Jazz and Pop 8:46, January 1969.

13174 Hentoff, N. "Soundings." Jazz and Pop 8:15, March 1969.

13175 Ochs, E. "'Blues Power' in Comeback." Billboard 81:1, March 29, 1969.

13176 Szwed, J. F. "Musical Adaptation Among Afro-Americans." Journal of the American Folklore Society 82:112-121, April-June 1969.

13177 "Crowder Gives Foundation His 'Paper' on Negroes' Influences." Billboard 81:65, April 19, 1969.

13178 Pleasants, H. "Re-birth of the Blues." Music and Musicians 17:36-
       37, May 1969.

13179 Weinstein, R. V. "Black 'n Blues." Negro History Bulletin 32:13-
       15, May 1969.

13180 Suber, C. "The First Chorus." down beat 36:4, May 1, 1969.

13181 "Gospel-Spiritual Influence Marking Pop Music as Names Go Re-
       ligioso." Variety 254:68, May 14, 1969.

13182 Eldridge, R. "The Sound That Survived." Melody Maker 44:13,
       May 17, 1969.

13183 Gross, M. "Rock Stations Dial R & B as Black Artists Win Air-
       play." Billboard 81:1, May 17, 1969.

13184 Lewis, T. "Trumpets of the Lord; Soulfest of Negro Spirituals."
       America 120:599, May 17, 1969.

13185 "Beat of Love; Gospel Song 'Oh Happy Day.'" Newsweek 73:117,
       May 19, 1969.

13186 "Soul Music--a Long Time Arriving in Canada." Billboard 81:C12,
       May 24, 1969.

13187 Heckman, D. "Five Decades of Rhythm and Blues." BMI p. 4-21,
       Summer 1969.

13188 "Concert Music: In the News." BMI p. 21, June 1969.

13189 Feather, L. "In Memoriam." Jazz Magazine no. 167:11-12, June
       1969. A tribute to Martin Luther King in Los Angeles.

13190 Skoog, L. "The Negro in America: His Life & Times." Blues
       no. 63:4-7, June 1969.

13191 Weingarten, S. L. "Soul Music Panorama." Audio 53:66-67, June
       1969.

13192 Wilmer, V. "'Bout Soul." Melody Maker 44:11, June 21, 1969.

13193 "Harlem Jazzmobile Rolls with Expanded Series of Ghetto Musical
       Programs." Variety 255:51, June 25, 1969.

13194 Douglas, F. "The Negro in America: His Life & Times, Blues
       1860? as a Slave Saw It." Blues no. 64:7-8, July 1969.

13195 Hentoff, N. "Soundings." Jazz and Pop 8:18, July 1969.

13196 Hammond, J. "Seminar Spotlights Black Music." Billboard 81:6,
       July 5, 1969.

13197 Goldman, A. "Detroit Retools Its Rock; The Motown Comeback."
       Life 67:12, July 25, 1969.

13198 Giraudo, P. "Bringing It All Back Home." Rolling Stone no. 38:26-
       28, July 26, 1969.

13199 Pines, M. "Brotherhood and Racial Equality Keynote New Disk Crop of Pops." Variety 225:1, July 30, 1969.

13200 Spellman, A. B. "Revolution in Sound: Black Genius Creates a New Music in Western World." Ebony 24:84-89, August 1969.

13201 Feather, L. "End of Brainwash Era." down beat 36:11, August 7, 1969.

13202 Clark, S. C. "Soul Sounds in the Mass Marketplace." Billboard 81:S6, August 16, 1969.

13203 "A Dominating Trend--Soul in Poland." Billboard 81:S20, August 16, 1969.

13204 Helopaltio, K. "Soul Artists Steady Sales in Finland." Billboard 81:S23, August 16, 1969.

13205 Messina, M. "For Italians, Soul Replaces U.K. Beat." Billboard 81:S22, August 16, 1969.

13206 Robinson, R. "The Dilemma of the Soul Producer." Billboard 81:S24, August 16, 1969.

13207 _____. "Small Soul Labels Have an Advantage." Billboard 81:S14, August 16, 1969.

13208 _____. "Soul Music and Social Change." Billboard 81:S12, August 16, 1969.

13209 Shaw, A. "Flipside Blacks Sing Country Music." Billboard 81:S5, August 16, 1969.

13210 _____. "The Rhythm & Blues Revival No White Gloved, Black Hits." Billboard 81:S3, August 16, 1969.

13211 Sigg, B. "Soul Sells Well in Switzerland." Billboard 81:S22, August 16, 1969.

13212 "Soul Radio Stations." Billboard 81:S30, August 16, 1969.

13213 Stewart, K. "Soul Package Needed for Irish Scene." Billboard 81:S23, August 16, 1969.

13214 "Top 50 Soul Albums." Billboard 81:77, August 16, 1969.

13215 "Top 100 Soul Albums." Billboard 81:78, August 16, 1969.

13216 Trachter, I. "Soul Trends--the Widening of Its Audience into Pop." Billboard 81:S8, August 16, 1969.

13217 "World of Soul." Billboard 81:S30, August 16, 1969.

13218 "Black and White Notes; Discrimination Charge Against New York Philharmonic by Two Black Musicians." Newsweek 74:82, August 18, 1969.

13219 Tiegel, E. "Vault Springs LP by Black Panther." Billboard 81:1, August 23, 1969.

13220 "Macon's Soul Fest No Woodstock; Problems Minute in Comparison."
        Variety 256:53, August 27, 1969.

13221 Kostik, B. "Soul Is Still Clicking Its Heels in Yugo; Blame Folk."
        Billboard 81:64, August 30, 1969.

13222 Ochs, E. "Tomorrow." Billboard 81:6, August 30, 1969.

13223 Revert, R. "Soul Sales Level Off in Spain; 'Loyalists' Buy." Bill-
        board 81:64, August 30, 1969.

13224 "U. S. Labels Spurring Soul Most in Denmark, Norway." Billboard
        81:64, August 30, 1969.

13225 Alessandrini, P. "L'Amerique Noire au Festival d'Alger." Jazz
        Magazine no. 169-170:16-17, September 1969.

13226 Constant, D. "Cinema Afro-Americain." Jazz Magazine no. 169-
        170:16-17, September 1969.

13227 Sauvaget, D. "Alger: Le Grand Retour." Jazz Hot no. 253:30-33,
        September 1969.

13228 "Black Music Pub Firm Floats 100,000 Shares." Variety 256:109,
        September 10, 1969.

13229 "Black Culture in Spotlight at K. C. Oct. Arts Festival." Variety
        256:50, September 17, 1969.

13230 Bourne, M. "Defining Black Music." down beat 36:14-15, Septem-
        ber 18, 1969. David Baker discusses black music.

13231 "Cleaver Writes Notes for Black Panther LP." Variety 256:54, Sep-
        tember 24, 1969.

13232 Goodman, J. "Cultural Kissoff." New Leader 53:25-26, September
        29, 1969.

13233 Caswell, A. B. "What Is Black Music." Music Journal 27:31, Oc-
        tober 1969.

13234 Fuchs, A. "Inner-City Soul." Crawdaddy no. 117:83-85, October
        1972.

13235 "Ragtime Revisited." BMI p. 13, October 1969.

13236 "The Return of the Native." American Musical Digest 1:31-32, Oc-
        tober 1969.

13237 Frederick, R. B. "N. Y. Philharmonic Rolls New Season with
        'Bias' & Acoustics Still Unsolved." Variety 256:57, October
        1, 1969.

13238 Tiegel, E. , and G. Link. "Black Gold Sparkles in Vegas, Reno,
        Tahoe." Billboard 81:SC2-SC3, October 4, 1969.

13239 Joe, R. "Harlem to Get Cultural Site." Billboard 81:1, October
        11, 1969.

13240 Tiegel, E. "Black Panthers Helping Prepare 'Time' on Vault." Billboard 81:98, October 11, 1969.

13241 Ochs, E. "Tomorrow." Billboard 81:12, October 25, 1969.

13242 Arvey, V. "Afro-American Music Memo." Music Journal 27:36, November 1969.

13243 De Lerma, D. R. "Black Music; What Is It? Where Is It?" High Fidelity/Musical America 19:MA16-17, November 1969.

13244 Gibbs, V. "Soul, Man." Crawdaddy no. 18:12-13, November 1972.

13245 Lena, A. "Derriere le Sourire du Jazz Nori." Jazz Magazine no. 172:15, November, 1969.

13246 Peterson, O. "Random Reflections on Race." Jazz Monthly no. 177:17-18, November 1969.

13247 "New World Symph One-Third Negro." Variety 256:53, November 5, 1969.

13248 Hall, C. "Black Jobs Spurting as Radiomen Step Up Hunt." Billboard 81:1, November 8, 1969.

13249 Tiegel, E. "Blunt Music from a Black Panther." Rolling Stone no. 46:8, November 15, 1969.

13250 "The Sound of Harlem." Jazz Monthly no. 178:12-14, December 1969.

13251 Standifer, J. A. "Choosing an Approach to Black Studies in Music." School Musician 41:60-62, December 1969.

13252 Hall, C. "'Backlash' Cuts Soul on Top 40 Radio." Billboard 81:1, December 6, 1969.

13253 "Bell to Tell NARM of Negro Mkt.'s Importance Variety 257:39, December 24, 1969.

13254 "Black Acts Posing as Name Talent Spark Lotsa Complaints in Britain." Variety 257:2, December 24, 1969.

13255 Tiegel, E. "Radio Geared to Blacks Only Seen at End of Line in 5 Yrs." Billboard 81:22, December 27, 1969.

1970-1979

13256 Appleton, Clyde Robert. "The Comparative Preferential Response of Black and White College Students to Black and White Folk and Popular Musical Styles." (Ph.D. Dissertation, New York University, 1970).

13257 Borneman, E. "Black Light and White Shadow; Notes for a History of American Negro Music." Jazz Research 2:54-70, 1970.

13258 Boyd, J. D. "Judge Jackson: Black Giant of White Spirituals."

Journal of the American Folklore Society 83:446-451, 1970. Examines Jackson's The Colored Sacred Harp.

13259 Brooks, T. "The Black Musician in American Society." Missouri Journal of Research in Music Education 2:18-28, no. 4, 1970.

13260 De Lerma, Dominique-René. Black Music in Our Culture; Curricular Ideas on the Subjects, Materials and Problems. Kent, Ohio: Kent State University Press, 1970. Most of the material was drawn from a seminar held at Indiana University, June 18-21, 1969: "Black Music in College and University Curricula."

13261 Dixon, Robert M. W., and John Godrich. Recording the Blues. New York: Stein and Day, 1970.

13262 Evans, D. "Afro-American One-Stringed Instruments." Western Folklore 29:229-245, no. 4, 1970.

13263 _____. "Black Religious Music." Journal of the American Folklore Society 83:472-480, 1970.

13264 Fernett, Gene. Swing Out; Great Negro Dance Bands. Midland, Mich.: Pendell Pub. Co., 1970. Many photographs and much information on bands such as Count Basie's and Cab Calloway's.

13265 Ferris, W. R. "Racial Repertoires Among Blues Performers." Ethnomusicology 14:439-449, no. 3, 1970.

13266 Gilmore, M. S. "Blues with Blacks & Whites." Jazz Report 7:5-6, no. 4, 1970.

13267 Gruver, R. "The Blues as Dramatic Monologues." JEMF Quarterly 6:28-31, pt. 1, 1970.

13268 Herrema, R. D. "Choral Music by Black Composers." Choral Journal 10:15-17, no. 4, 1970.

13269 Kofsky, Frank. Black Nationalism and the Revolution in Music. New York: Pathfinder Press, 1970. Based on the author's thesis, University of Pittsburgh. A sociological analysis of black music plus interviews with many musicians.

13270 Ladner, R. "Folk Music, Pholk Music and the Angry Children of Malcolm X." Southern Folklore Quarterly 34:131-135, no. 2, 1970.

13271 Larkin, Philip. All What Jazz; A Record Diary, 1961-68. New York: St. Martin's Press, 1970. Reprints of articles which originally appeared in the Daily Telegraph. Many black musicians are discussed, such as Billie Holiday and Duke Ellington.

13272 Larkin, Rochelle. Soul Music: [The Sound, the Stars, the Story]. New York: Lancer Books, 1970.

13273 McBrier, V. F. "The Inner City Child and His Need for an Image: Challenge to the Music Educator." Musart 22:14-15, no. 3, 1970.

13274 Marsh, J., and J. Fitch. "The Effect of Singing on the Speech

Articulation of Negro Disadvantaged Children." Journal of Music Therapy 7:88-94, no. 3, 1970.

13275   Miller, M. "'Bitches Brew' und das Neue Afrika." Neue Musik-zeitung 19:9, no. 4, 1970.

13276   Mullen, P. B. "A Negro Street Performer: Tradition and Innovation." Western Folklore 29:91-103, no. 2, 1970.

13277   Oliver, Paul. Savannah Syncopators; African Retentions in the Blues. New York: Stein and Day, 1970. Chiefly describes the musical styles of various African tribes, however, some material is devoted to the musical links between African music and the music of America.

13278   Olsson, Bengt. Memphis Blues and Jug Bands. London: Studio Vista, 1970. Traces the background of black musicians of Memphis including musicians such as W. C. Handy and Sleepy John Estes.

13279   Pleasants, H. "The Afro-American Epoch." Educator 2:4-5, no. 4, 1970.

13280   Ramsey, Frederic. Where the Music Started: A Photographic Essay. New Brunswick, N.J.: Rutgers University Institute of Jazz Studies, 1970. A descriptive guide for an exhibit of photographs taken in the South, 1951-1960.

13281   Rivelli, Pauline, and Robert Levin. The Black Giants. New York: World Pub. Co., 1970. Interviews with black musicians such as John Coltrane and Ornette Coleman.

13282   Russell, Tony. Blacks, Whites, and Blues. New York: Stein and Day, 1970. A study of how the early blues evolved as sung by both black and white musicians.

13283   Ryder, Georgia Atkins. "Melodic and Rhythmic Elements of American Negro Folk Songs as Employed in Cantatas by Selected American Composers Between 1932 and 1967." (Ph.D. Dissertation, New York University, 1970).

13284   Seeger, P. "Johnny Appleseed, Jr." Sing Out 29:36-37, no. 1, 1970.

13285   Shaw, Arnold. The World of Soul; Black America's Contribution to the Pop Music Scene. New York: Crowles Book Co., 1970.

13286   Stockholm, G. "Dean Dixon; A Return with Laurels." Music and Artists 3:7, no. 3, 1970.

13287   Webster, D. "One for Philadelphia." American Musical Digest 1:10-11, no. 5, 1970. Renard Edwards is a black violist who joined the Philadelphia Orchestra.

13288   Whitten, Norman E., and John F. Szwed. Afro-American Anthropology; Contemporary Perspectives. New York: Free Press, 1970. Includes chapters such as "The Homogeneity of Afro-American Musical Style" and "Afro-American Musical Adaptations."

13289 Williams, M. D. "Indiana University Black Music Project." Current Musicology no. 10:8-10, 1970.

13290 Williams, Martin T. Jazz Masters in Transition, 1957-69. New York: Macmillan Co., 1970.

13291 _____. The Jazz Tradition. New York: Oxford University Press, 1970. Consists of chapters examining important jazz musicians, such as Louis Armstrong and Miles Davis.

13292 Yuhasz, Sister M. J. "Black Composers and Their Piano Music." American Music Teacher 19:24-26, no. 4, 1970; 29:28-29, no. 5, 1970.

13293 "Black Music." BMI p. 19, January 1970.

13294 "Blacks Rap 'Today' Jazz." Variety 257:30, January 21, 1970.

13295 De Lerma, D. R. "Ghettos and Cultural Centers: How Far Apart?" American Musical Digest 1:4-5, no. 5, 1970. An excerpt taken from Your Musical Cue, January 1970.

13296 Reeder, B. "Afro Music: As Tough as a Mozart Quartet." Music Educator's Journal 56:88-90, January 1970.

13297 Reimer, B. "General Music for the Black Ghetto Child." Music Educator's Journal 56:94-97, January 1970.

13298 Yancy, H. M. "The Contribution of the American Negro to the Music Culture of the Country." School Musician 41:55-57, January 1970.

13299 Ardoin, J. "A Black Composers' Concert." American Musical Digest 1:5-6, no. 5, 1970.

13300 Yancy, H. M. "The Contribution of the American Negro to the Music Culture of the Country." School Musician 41:60-62, February 1970.

13301 Tiegel, E. "Cap in Soul Market Drive." Billboard 82:1, February 21, 1970.

13302 Green, A. W. C. "'Jim Crow,' 'Zip Coon': The Northern Origins of Negro Minstrelsy." Massachusetts Review 11:385-397, Spring 1970.

13303 Harris, S. "Super Black Blues." Jazz and Pop 9:54-5, March 1970.

13304 Jones, S., and P. Tanner. "Afro-American Music: Black Moans." Music Journal 28:36-37, March 1970.

13305 Levin, R. "Editorial." Jazz and Pop 9:7, March 1970.

13306 Yancy, H. M. "The Contribution of the American Negro to the Music Culture of the Country." School Musician 41:60-61, March 1970.

13307 "Rock Rocks South; Soul Off." Billboard 82:38, March 21, 1970.

13308 Yuhasz, Sister M. J. "Black Composers and Their Piano Music."
       American Music Teacher 19:28-29, April-May 1970.

13309 Kofsky, F. "Record Reviews: The Giant Is Awakened." Jazz and
       Pop 9:44-45, April 1970.

13310 Niquet, B. "R 'n' B ou New Thing." Jazz Hot no. 260:24-25, April
       1970.

13311 Yancy, H. M. "The Contribution of the American Negro to the Mu-
       sic Culture of the Country." School Musician 41:62-63, April
       1970.

13312 "Black Impact Is Cited by Al Bell." Billboard 82:8, April 4, 1970.

13313 "New Thing." Time 95:87-88, April 6, 1970.

13314 Samuels, J. "Black Artists Do Own Disk Thing." Variety 258:1,
       April 8, 1970.

13315 Tiegel, E. "Muntz Co. Teams to Open Business Doors to Blacks."
       Billboard 82:1, April 18, 1970.

13316 "A Black Anthem?" Variety 258:2, April 22, 1970.

13317 Prideaux, T. "Three Times Round and Still Victorious." Life
       68:18, April 24, 1970.

13318 "Pride, SCLC Drive for a Black National Anthem." Billboard 82:78,
       April 25, 1970.

13319 Cotler, G. "Preservation Hall." Holiday 47:54-55, May 1970.

13320 Farmer, J. "People Have to Be What They Are." Music Educa-
       tor's Journal 56:38-41, May 1970.

13321 King, H. "Hair; Controversial Musical Is Biggest Outlet for Black
       Actors in U.S. Stage History." Ebony 25:120-122, May 1970.

13322 Noel, G. "Au Confluent des Musiques Nouvelles." Jazz Hot no.
       261:8-10, May 1970.

13323 "Soul History." Music Educator's Journal 56:104, May 1970.

13324 "Black Musicians in H'wood Pitch for a 25 Percent Quota." Variety
       258:53, May 13, 1970.

13325 "Local Rejects MBA on Racial Quotas." Billboard 82:3, May 23,
       1970.

13326 "Eddie Harris Protests L.A. Police Incident." down beat 37:11,
       May 28, 1970.

13327 "Come On, Nigger, Get It On!" Rolling Stone no. 59:8, May 28,
       1970.

13328 "Unseen Black Pickets Rub Glamor Off Oscar." down beat 37:11,
       May 28, 1970.

13329 Goldman, A. "Return of a Good Four-Letter Favorite." Life 68:12, May 29, 1970.

13330 Joe, R. "FORE Maps Black Role." Billboard 82:1, May 30, 1970.

13331 Metcalf, R. H. "The Western African Roots of Afro-American Music." Black Scholar 1:16-25, June 1970.

13332 Russell, T. "Key to the Bushes." Blues Unlimited no. 73:18, June 1970. Discussion of the black Holiness Church music.

13333 "Black National Anthem Drive Backed by SCLC." down beat 37:8, June 25, 1970.

13334 Baumel, R. B. "Integrated Trio Goes South: Baumel-Booth-Smith Trio's Southern Tour." High Fidelity/Musical America 20:26-27, Section II, July 1970.

13335 Guild, H. "Black Talent & Integrated GI Clubs Primed to Ease Tensions O'seas." Variety 259:1, July 1, 1970.

13336 "Black Musicians Blast L. A. Studio Policies." down beat 37:11, July 9, 1970.

13337 "The New Black Voices." Melody Maker 45:20, July 11, 1970.

13338 Bushnell, D. D. "Black Arts for Black Youth." Saturday Review 53:43-46, July 18, 1970.

13339 "Technology and the Urban Arts." Saturday Review 53:44, July 18, 1970.

13340 Wilmer, V. "Great Black Music." Melody Maker 45:12, July 18, 1970.

13341 Oberbeck, S. K. "Southern Comfort; New Orleans Jazz at New York's Philharmonic Hall." Newsweek 76:86, July 20, 1970.

13342 Thornton, C. "Caught in the Act: Black Solidarity Festival." down beat 37:30, July 23, 1970.

13343 Hentoff, N. "Soundings." Jazz and Pop 9:18, August 1970.

13344 Kofsky, F. "Black Music in the Service of Imperialism: The Case of Willis Conover." Jazz and Pop 9:35-37, August 1970.

13345 Sinclair, J. "Self-Determination Music." Jazz and Pop 9:51-52, August 1970.

13346 "Soul Sounds Without Words." Sepia 19:12-15, August 1970.

13347 Butler, J. "Black Music Is Getting Intellectually Involved." Billboard 82:18, August 22, 1970.

13348 "Chicago--to Build a Creative Soul Center." Billboard 82:20, August 22, 1970.

13349 "Desto to Release Boxes of Music by Black Composers." Billboard 82:63, August 22, 1970.

13350   Garnett, B. E. "Soul Radio Must Serve Community Needs." Bill-
        board 82:14, August 22, 1970.

13351   King, B. B. "Notice More Black Youth in My Audience." Bill-
        board 82:16, August 22, 1970.

13352   "Soul Spoken Here!" Billboard 82:28, August 22, 1970.

13353   Tiegel, E. "Who Will Own the Soul 70's?" Billboard 82:24, Au-
        gust 22, 1970.

13354   "Top Soul Records, Artists and Labels." Billboard 82:13, August
        22, 1970.

13355   Williams, R. "The Black Pride of 13 Hip Kids." Melody Maker
        45:23, August 22, 1970.

13356   Hankins, R. "Sounds Familiar: Those Bill Bailey Songs." Rag-
        timer p. 10-14, September-October 1970.

13357   Pleasants, H. "Afro-American Epoch Emergence of a New Idiom."
        Music Educator's Journal 57:33-35, September 1970.

13358   "All Black Co. Formed to Produce Country Blues." Billboard 82:64,
        September 5, 1970.

13359   "Black Jazzmen Set Equality Sights at TV." Billboard 82:70, Sep-
        tember 12, 1970.

13360   Williams, R. "Give Soul a Chance." Melody Maker 45:37, Septem-
        ber 12, 1970.

13361   Jones, M. "Preservation Hall Goes Stomping On." Melody Maker
        45:14, September 19, 1970.

13362   Glassenburg, B. "Black Acts Gain on Campus as White Bookings
        Slide." Billboard 82:1, September 19, 1970.

13363   Bruer, J. "Musikerprotest mot USA TV." Orkester Journalen
        38:8-9, October 1970.

13364   Mims, A. G. "Soul: The Black Man and His Music." Negro His-
        tory Bulletin 33:141-146, October 1970.

13365   Russell, T. "Blues Masters of the 30s." Jazz Monthly no. 188:23,
        October 1970.

13366   "Grass Roots Jazz Protest Hits TV." down beat 37:12, October 15,
        1970.

13367   Hankins, R. "Sounds Familiar: Those Bill Bailey Songs." Rag-
        timer p. 5-10, November-December 1970.

13368   "Black Music Center." Music Educator's Journal 57:81, November
        1970.

13369   De Lerma, D. R. "Black Music Now!" Music Educator's Journal
        57:25-29, November 1970.

13370 Fox, C. "Record Reviews: Blacks, Whites and Blues." Jazz Monthly no. 189:14-15, November 1970.

13371 Oliver, P. "Record Reviews: Ten Years of Black Country Religion 1926-1936." Jazz Journal 23:36-37, November 1970.

13372 "Tucker Talks." BMI p. 17, November 1970.

13373 "1st Black-Produced Blues Fest in D.C. Set." Billboard 82:4, November 7, 1970.

13374 "Jazz & Peoples Movement Promised NBC Action." down beat 37:11, November 12, 1970.

13375 "Jazz Avant Garde Wants on Tube." Rolling Stone no. 71:8, November 26, 1970.

13376 "Jazz Protesters Do Cavett Show, Push On." down beat 37:8, November 26, 1970.

13377 Dance, S. "Lightly & Politely." Jazz Journal 23:8-9, December 1970.

13378 Harris, S. "Editorial." Jazz and Pop 9:7, December 1970.

13379 "The Jazz Protest." BMI p. 15, December 1970.

13380 Postgate, J. "The Black and White Show, 1970-80: A Speculation on the Future of Jazz." Jazz Monthly no. 190:2-6, December 1970.

13381 Sinclair, J. "Motor City Music." Jazz and Pop 9:52, December 1970.

13382 Landau, J. "Rock 1970: It's Too Late to Stop Now." Rolling Stone no. 72:40-44, December 2, 1970.

13383 West, H. I. "A Blues Festival for Black People." Rolling Stone no. 72:8, December 2, 1970.

13384 "Booker of A. C.'s Club Harlem Charges Black Stars with 'Bias' Against Spot." Variety 261:49, December 9, 1970.

13385 Morgenstern, D. "It Don't Mean a Thing." down beat 37:13, December 10, 1970. Discussion of Jazz and the Peoples Movement.

13386 Jones, Q. "The Institute of Black American Music." down beat 37:14, December 24, 1970.

13387 Kolodin, I. "The Racial Bias in Music." Saturday Review 53:43, December 26, 1970.

13388 Riedel, J. "'Soul' Music and Church Music." Student Musicologists at Minnesota 5:220-249, 1971-1972.

13389 "Additions to Blues & Gospel Records 1902-1942." JEMF Quarterly 7:142, pt. 3, 1971.

13390 Adkins, Aldrich Wendell. "The Development of Black Art Song."
       (D. M. A. Dissertation, University of Texas at Austin, 1971).

13391 Balliett, Whitney. Ecstasy at the Onion; Thirty-One Pieces on Jazz.
       Indianapolis: Bobbs-Merrill, 1971. A collection of articles which
       first appeared in the New Yorker. Black musicians examined in-
       clude Duke Ellington and Bessie Smith.

13392 Baskerville, D. "Black Music, Pop and Rock Vs. Our Obsolete
       Curricula." Educator 3:5-7, no. 4, 1971.

13393 Bastin, Bruce. Crying for the Carolines. London: Studio Vista,
       1971. Blues of North and South Carolina, Georgia, and Virginia
       are analyzed. Black musicians such as Blind Boy Fuller are in-
       cluded.

13394 Chase, G. "Editor's Outlook: Afro-American Anthropology and
       Black Music." Inter-American Musical Research Yearbook 7:117-
       124, 1971.

13395 De Lerma, Dominique-René. Explorations in Black Music; The Sem-
       inar Program. Bloomington: Indiana University, Black Music
       Center, 1971.

13396 _____. "Foundations for the Study of Black Music." Musart
       23:4-5, no. 6, 1971.

13397 Dunham, B. "New York Philharmonic Gives Workshop for Minority
       Players." Symphony News 22:12-14, no. 5, 1971.

13398 Durgnat, R. "Rock, Rhythm and Dance." British Journal of Aes-
       thetics 11:28-47, no. 1, 1971.

13399 Ferris, W. R. "The Blues: Africa to America." Close Up 6:14-
       15, no. 10, 1971.

13400 Fishwick, M. "Black Popular Culture." Journal of Popular Culture
       4:637-645, no. 3, 1971.

13401 Gayle, Addison. The Black Aesthetic. Garden City, N.Y.: Double-
       day, 1971. Includes chapters examining black music, such as "In-
       troduction to Black Aesthetics in Music."

13402 Glass, Paul. Songs and Stories of Afro-Americans. New York:
       Grosset and Dunlap, 1971. A 61-page book which includes some
       music.

13403 Goldman, Albert Harry. Freakshow; The Rocksoulbluesjazzsickjew-
       blackhumorsexpoppsych Gig and Other Scenes from the Counter-
       Culture. New York: Atheneum, 1971. An examination of popular
       culture in regard to music, including material on musicians such
       as B. B. King and Aretha Franklin.

13404 Groom, Bob. The Blues Revival. London: Studio Vista, 1971.
       This history of blues includes material on Son House and Sleepy
       John Estes.

13405 Gruver, R. "Sex, Sound, Cows and the Blues." JEMF Quarterly
       7:37-39, pt. 1, 1971.

13406 Guralnick, Peter. Feel Like Going Home; Portraits in Blues &
       Rock 'n' Roll. New York: Outerbridge & Dienstfrey, 1971. A
       history and profiles of blues and rock musicians such as Muddy
       Waters and Howlin' Wolf.

13407 Heilbut, Tony. The Gospel Sound: Good News and Bad Times.
       New York: Simon and Schuster, 1971.

13408 Höweler, Casper. Negro Spirituals en Hun Beeldspraak. Bussum:
       De Haan, 1971.

13409 Keil, C. "Record Reviews." Ethnomusicology 15:161-164, no. 1,
       1971.

13410 Kofsky, F. "The Big Rip-Off." Soul Illustrated 3:30-33, no. 2,
       1971. An excerpt from Kofsky's book Black Nationalism and the
       Revolution in Music.

13411 Leadbitter, Mike. Nothing but the Blues: An Illustrated Documen-
       tary. London: Hanover Books, Ltd, 1971. Articles which were
       originally published in Blues Unlimited. Chiefly examines black
       blues musicians and the development of blues.

13412 Lee, R. C. "The Afro-American Foundations of the Jazz Idiom."
       Jazz Forum no. 11:68-79, 1971; no. 12:68-81, 1971; no. 13-14:86-
       93, 1971.

13413 Lindemann, B. "An Introduction to Black Gospel Music." Living
       Blues 2:21-22, 1971.

13414 McCutcheon, Lynn Ellis. Rhythm and Blues; An Experience and Ad-
       venture in Its Origin and Development. Arlington, Va.: Beatty,
       1971. A history of rhythm and blues with discographies and pho-
       tographs including several sections on soul music.

13415 Martinez, Raymond Joseph. Portraits of New Orleans Jazz; Its
       Peoples and Places. New Orleans: Hope Publications, 1971.

13416 Maynor, D. "Looking Back Without Anger, Looking Forward to
       Change." Symphony News 22:17, no. 4, 1971.

13417 Minelli, Maria Gioia. Canto Populare Negro-Americano. Ivrea:
       Cardinale, 1971.

13418 Minne, Pierre. "Une Resurgence de la Mentalité Africaine aux
       U.S.A.: La Musique de Jazz de la Nouvelle-Orleans." Présence
       Africaine 77:109-130, 1971.

13419 Mitchell, George. Blow My Blues Away. Baton Rouge: Louisiana
       State University Press, 1971. Biographical sketches and inter-
       views with blues musicians from the Mississippi Delta.

13420 Morse, David. Motown & the Arrival of Black Music. London:
       Studio Vista, 1971. A history of black music and Motown Record
       Corporation (Detroit).

13421 National Portrait Gallery. A Glimmer of Their Own Beauty: Black
       Sounds of the Twenties. Washington, D.C.: Smithsonian Insti-

tution, 1971. Concentrates on black jazz musicians from the 1920s, as Bessie Smith.

13422 Nicholas, A. X. The Poetry of Soul. New York: Bantam Books, 1971. Includes texts of songs by writers such as Nina Simone and B. B. King.

13423 Somma, Robert. No One Waved Good-bye; A Casualty Report on Rock and Roll. New York: Outerbridge & Dienstfrey, 1971. A survey of rock musicians who met early, often violent, deaths, such as Jimi Hendrix.

13424 "Orchestra USA." Music and Artists 3:25, no. 5, 1971.

13425 Owens, James Garfield. All God's Chillun; Meditations on Negro Spirituals. Nashville: Abingdon Press, 1971. Essays on selected spirituals plus the text to these spirituals, such as "We Are Climbin' Jacob's Ladder."

13426 Porter, T. J. "The Social Roots of Afro-American Music." Freedomways 2:264-271, no. 3, 1971.

13427 "Record Reviews: Black Bands, 1927-1934." Hip 9:13, no. 4, 1971.

13428 "Record Reviews: Black Religious Music." Journal of the American Folklore Society 84:472-480, no. 334, 1971.

13429 The Rolling Stone Interviews. Compiled by the Editors of Rolling Stone. New York: Paperback Library, 1971. Among those interviewed are Little Richard and Chuck Berry.

13430 Rublowsky, John. Black Music in America. New York: Basic Books, 1971. Traces the development of black music from Africa to soul and pop.

13431 Russell, T. "Clarkside Piccolo Blues: Jukebox Hits in Black Taverns Thirty Years Ago." Jazz & Blues 1:30, no. 7, 1971.

13432 Schiffman, Jack. Uptown: The Story of Harlem's Apollo Theatre. New York: Cowles Book Co., 1971. The Apollo was a prominent place of entertainment beginning in the 1930s.

13433 Shaun, J. "Can Blacks Make It Alone?" Soul Illustrated 3:37-38, no. 2, 1971.

13434 Shaw, Arnold. The Street That Never Slept; New York's Fabled 52d St. New York: Coward, McCann & Geoghegan, 1971. Reprinted in 1977 by Da Capo Press, New York, as The Street That Never Slept. Examines jazz music performed between Fifth and Sixth Avenues on 52d Street.

13435 Sidran, Ben. Black Talk. New York: Holt, Rinehart and Winston, 1971. Subtitle: "How the Music of Black America Created a Radical Alternative to the Values of Western Literary Tradition."

13436 Simon, George Thomas. Simon Says; The Sights and Sounds of the Swing Era, 1935-1955. New Rochelle, N.Y.: Arlington House

1971. Includes material on the bands of Lionel Hampton, Cab Calloway, and Duke Ellington.

13437   Sinclair, John, and Robert Levin. Music & Politics. New York: World Pub. Co., 1971. Articles originally published in Jazz and Pop. Included are musicians such as Archie Shepp and Anthony Braxton.

13438   Southern, Eileen. The Music of Black Americans: A History. New York: W. W. Norton, 1971.

13439   _____. Readings in Black American Music. New York: W. W. Norton, 1972, c1971. An anthology of articles.

13440   Spiegelman, J., and M. L. Brown. "The Whites Behind the Blacks." Soul Illustrated 3:24-29, no. 2, 1971.

13441   Suthern, O. C. "Minstrelsy and Popular Culture." Journal of Popular Culture 4:658-673, no. 3, 1971.

13442   Taylor, John Earl. "The Sociological and Psychological Implications of the Texts of the Antebellum Negro Spirituals." (Ed.D. Dissertation, University of Northern Colorado, 1971).

13443   Titon, Jeff Todd. "Ethnomusicology of Downhome Blues Phonograph Records, 1926-1930." (Ph.D. Dissertation, University of Minnesota, 1971).

13444   Toll, R. C. "From Folktype to Stereotype: Images of Slaves in Antebellum Minstrelsy." Folklore Institute Journal 8:38-47, no. 1, 1971.

13445   Walker, C. "Making the American Symphony Orchestra Truly American." Symphony News 22:13, no. 4, 1971.

13446   Wilgus, D. K. "Record Reviews: Afro-American Tradition." Journal of the American Folklore Society 84:264-271, no. 332, 1971.

13447   Wilson, Burton. Burton's Book of the Blues. Austin, Texas: Speleo Press, 1971. Chiefly portraits of blues musicians.

13448   Hankins, R. "Sounds Familiar: Those Bill Bailey Songs." Ragtimer p. 7-11, January-February 1971.

13449   Novak, B. J. "Opening Doors in Music." Negro History Bulletin 34:10-14, January 1971.

13450   Palmer, C. "Delius and Folksong." Musical Times 112:24-25, January 1971.

13451   Cyrille, A., and D. Morgenstern. "Jazz, Cavett & the JPM: An Exchange." down beat 38:13, January 21, 1971.

13452   "Back to the Apollo; Soul Acts at Harlem Theatre." New Yorker 46:24-26, January 23, 1971.

13453   "Black Musicians Rap Alleged 'Bias' in Mpls." Variety 261:1, January 27, 1971.

13454   Feather, L. "Donald Byrd, MA--Ethnomusicologist." Melody Maker 46:12, January 30, 1971.

13455   Shirley, G. "The Black Performer." Opera News 35:6-13, January 30, 1971.

13456   Noel, G. "Regards sur l'Histoire de la Musique Afro-Americaine." Jazz Hot no. 269:18-21, February 1971.

13457   "Bias Vs. Black Tooters Still Practiced by U.S. Symphs, Dixon Asserts." Variety 261:53, February 3, 1971.

13458   "'White Control' Scored by Sonderling Exec." Billboard 83:41, February 6, 1971.

13459   "White Mpls. Execs Nix Black Tooters' Complaints of Bias." Variety 262:58, February 17, 1971.

13460   Lee, R. C. "The African Beat; Introduction." Jazz Forum no. 11:69-79, Spring 1971.

13461   _____. "The Afro-American Foundations of the Jazz Idiom." Jazz Forum no. 11:68, Spring 1971.

13462   "Blues Like Showers of Rain." Jazz Journal 24:24-25, March 1971. Pictures taken from the film "Blues Like Showers of Rain."

13463   "Lettre de Caen." Jazz Magazine no. 187:16, March 1971.

13464   Moore, L. "The Spiritual: Soul of Black Religion." Church History 40:79-81, March 1971.

13465   "Rev. Jackson Cites Need for More Blacks." Billboard 83:70, March 13, 1971.

13466   Dixon, D. "Mirrors of Our Time; Black Conductors in Europe and the US." Senior Scholastic 98:17, March 22, 1971.

13467   "Black C&W Artist Has Golden Touch." Variety 262:1, March 24, 1971.

13468   "Opera-South's 'Aida.'" Variety 262:2, March 24, 1971.

13469   "Black Music Institute." BMI p. 19, April 1971.

13470   Dance, S. "Lightly and Politely." Jazz Journal 24:27, April 1971.

13471   Gerber, L. "In Two Desto Albums, Music by a Dozen Black Composers." American Record Guide 37:476-479, April 1971.

13472   Fisher, M. "Orch for Academy Awards Show Has More Black Tooters & a New Sound." Variety 262:81, April 14, 1971.

13473   Higgins, C. "What's Ahead for Blacks in Music." Jet 4:58-61, April 22, 1971.

13474   Hankins, R. "Sounds Familiar: Those Bill Bailey Songs." Ragtimer p. 4-12, May-June 1971.

13475 Noel, G. "Des Demons d'Hodeir au Monde du Jazz." Jazz Hot no.
       272:14-15, May 1971.

13476 "Charge Black Music Brushed Off by White Radio Stations & Rack-
       jobbers." Variety 262:51, May 5, 1971.

13477 Landau, J. "The Motown Story." Rolling Stone no. 82:42-43, May
       13, 1971.

13478 "Guggenheim to Mingus; Protest at Foundation." down beat 38:8,
       May 27, 1971.

13479 Maremaa, T. "Berkeley Jazz: Black & Rootsy." Rolling Stone
       no. 83:16, May 27, 1971.

13480 Wilmer, V. "Cyrille-ism." Melody Maker 46:16, May 29, 1971.

13481 Levin, R. "The Third World." Jazz and Pop 10:10-11, June 1971.
       The Guggenheim Foundation is receiving demands from the Black
       Artists for Community Action.

13482 Wilmer, V. "One Sweet Letter from You." Jazz Journal 24:15,
       June 1971.

13483 Stenbeck, L. "Negro Spirituals i Jakobs Kyrka." Orkester Jour-
       nalen 39:11, July-August 1971.

13484 "Black Members a Must for American Symphony Boards." Music
       Trades 119:26, July 1971.

13485 Goines, L. "Early Afro-American Music in the United States--
       Sacred and Secular." Allegro p. 11, July 1971.

13486 Jones, L. "The Ban on Black Music." Black World 2:4-11, July
       1971.

13487 Ochs, E., and D. Ovens. "Soul Hot on Top 40 Despite Chill."
       Billboard 83:1, July 3, 1971.

13488 Williams, R. "Black People Have Always Been Militant." Melody
       Maker 46:12, July 3, 1971.

13489 "Paula Stone Forms Unit to Aid Blacks." Variety 263:1, July 7,
       1971.

13490 Goines, L. "Afro-American Music: The Spiritual." Allegro p. 4,
       August 1971.

13491 Hentoff, N. "Soundings." Jazz and Pop 10:10-11, August 1971.

13492 Zimmermann, K. R. "Saints Preserved; Preservation Hall Con-
       certs." National Review 23:882, August 10, 1971.

13493 Tiegel, E. "Black Music Maintains Its Identity." Billboard 83:30,
       August 14, 1971.

13494 "Music News." Arts Reporting Service no. 26:2, August 23, 1971.

13495 Paige, E. "NATRA's '71 Convention Sparks Soul Searching in Black

Radio." Billboard 83:34, August 28, 1971. Report on the National Association of TV and Radio Announcers' meeting.

13496 Evans, D. "Africa and the Blues." Living Blues no. 10:27-29, Autumn 1971.

13497 Summers, L. S. "African Influence and the Blues; An Interview with Richard A. Waterman." Living Blues no. 6:30-36, Autumn 1971.

13498 Wilcos, R. "Further Ado About Negro Music Ability." Journal of Negro Education 4:361-364, Fall 1971.

13499 Goines, L. "Gospel Music." Allegro p. 4, September 1971.

13500 "'Soul to Soul' Breaks Ground; U.S. Blacks Spark Concert." Billboard 83:3, September 4, 1971.

13501 Wickham, V. "Soul Goes Back to the Roots." Melody Maker 46:6, September 4, 1971.

13502 Fager, C. E. "Dance, Saith the Lord; The Motown Story." Christian Century 88:1094, September 15, 1971.

13503 Utts, T. "Soul Music for Seoul." Music Journal 29:30-31, October 1971.

13504 "Top Black Performers at Posh Spots Fail to Crack B. O. Color Barrier." Variety 264:66, October 27, 1971.

13505 Blondell, B. "Drums Talk at Howard." Music Educator's Journal 58:46-49, November 1971.

13506 Morgan, H. "Music--a Life Force in the Black Community." Music Educator's Journal 58:34-37, November 1971.

13507 "Overcoming Cultural Racism; Profile of a Black Community Arts Center." Music Educator's Journal 58:42-45, November 1971.

13508 Simmons, O. D. "Musical Nourishment for Ghetto Youth; Reach the Bedrock of Student Interest." Music Educator's Journal 58:38-41, November 1971.

13509 "There's a New World Comin'." Music Educator's Journal 58:11, November 1971.

13510 Williams, B. "Integrated Atlanta Meeting Forming Black Gospel Association." Billboard 83:1-3, November 13, 1971.

13511 Goines, L. "The Classic Blues." Allegro p. 7, December 1971.

13512 Cole, B. "The New Music." down beat 38:11, December 23, 1971.

13513 Millroth, T. "Great Black Music." Nutida Musik 16:43-50, no. 2, 1972-1973.

13514 "Additions to Blues & Gospel Records 1902-1942." JEMF Quarterly 8:7 pt. 1, 1972.

13515   Boeckman, Charles.   And the Beat Goes On; A Survey of Pop Mu-
        sic in America.   Washington: R. B. Luce, 1972.   Two chapters
        deal extensively with black music: "Singing the Blues" and "The
        Blues Gets Rhythm and Soul."

13516   Borroff, E.   "Black Musicians in the United States."   American Mu-
        sic Teacher 22:30-31, no. 2, 1972.

13517   Brooks, T.   "The Black Musician in American Society."   Monthly
        Journal of Research in Music Education 2:18-28, no. 4, 1970.

13518   _____. "A Historical Study of the Negro Composer and His Role
        in American Society: A Source Book for Teachers." (Ed. D. Dis-
        sertation, Washington University, 1972).

13519   Carles, Philippe, and Comolli, Jean-Louis.   Free Jazz, Black Pow-
        er.   Paris: Union Générale d'Editions, 1972.

13520   Cone, James H.   The Spirituals and the Blues: An Interpretation.
        New York: Seabury Press, 1972.   Examines the political and
        theological implications of spirituals and blues.

13521   Denisoff, R. Serge.   Sing a Song of Social Significance.   Bowling
        Green, Ohio: Bowling Green University Popular Press, 1972.
        Includes some information on spirituals and civil rights freedom
        songs.

13522   Evans, Arthur Lee.   "The Development of the Negro Spiritual as
        Choral Art Music by Afro-American Composers with Annotated
        Guide to the Performance of Selected Spirituals." (Ph. D. Dis-
        sertation, University of Miami, 1972).

13523   Evans, D.   "Africa and the Blues."   Living Blues no. 10:27-29,
        1972.

13524   _____. "Black Fife and Drum Music in Mississippi."   Mississippi
        Folklore Register 6:94-107, 1972.

13525   Ewen, David.   Great Men of American Popular Song; The History of
        the American Popular Song Told Through the Lives, Careers,
        Achievements, and Personalities of Its Foremost Composers and
        Lyricists.   Rev. and enl. ed. Englewood Cliffs, N. J.: Prentice-
        Hall, 1972.   Includes historical information on black music of the
        past beginning with spirituals.

13526   Feather, Leonard G.   From Satchmo to Miles.   New York: Stein
        and Day, 1972.   A critical history of jazz musicians.

13527   Fox, Charles.   The Jazz Scene.   New York: Hamlyn, 1972.

13528   Goines, L.   "Ragtime."   Allegro p. 7, March 1972.

13529   Harris, Carl Gordon.   "A Study of Characteristic Stylistic Trends
        Found in the Choral Works of a Selected Group of Afro-American
        Composers and Arrangers." (D. M. A. Dissertation, University of
        Missouri, 1972).

13530   Hirshowitz, B.   "The Old Testament in Negro Spirituals."   Tatzlil
        no. 12:52, 1972.

13531 Jones, Bessie, and Bess Lomax Hawes. Step It Down; Games,
       Plays, Songs, and Stories from the Afro-American Heritage.
       New York: Harper and Row, 1972.

13532 _____. "Teach In: Children's Game." Sing Out 21:12-13, no.
       4, 1972.

13533 Jones, Thomas Marshall. "The Development and Evaluation of a
       Black Music Syllabus for Elementary Music Education." (D. Mus.
       Ed. Dissertation, University of Oklahoma, 1972).

13534 Kamin, J. "Taking the Roll Out of Rock 'n' Roll: Reverse Ac-
       culturation." Popular Music and Society 2:1-17, no. 1, 1972.

13535 Kebede, A. "La Musique Africaine dans l'Hemisphere Occidental:
       La Musique Noire des Ameriques." Revue Musicale no. 288-
       289:129-134, 1972.

13536 Lee, Edward. Jazz: An Introduction. New York: Crescendo Pub-
       lishing Co., 1977. Reprint of the 1972 edition published by Kahn
       & Averill, London.

13537 Lee, R. C. "The Afro-American Foundations of the Jazz Idiom."
       Jazz Forum no. 15:84-86, 1972; no. 16:74-77, 1972.

13538 Leipold, L. E. Famous American Musicians. Minneapolis: T. S.
       Denison, 1972. Included are Louis Armstrong, Marian Anderson,
       and Lena Horne. Juvenile literature.

13539 Lovell, John. Black Song: The Forge and the Flame; The Story of
       How the Afro-American Spiritual Was Hammered Out. New York:
       Macmillan, 1972. Traces the development of spirituals from Af-
       rica and Europe.

13540 McCarroll, J. C. "Black Influence on Southern White Protestant
       Church Music During Slavery." (Ed. D. Dissertation, Columbia
       University, 1972).

13541 McNeil, W. K. "Syncopated Slander: The 'Coon Song,' 1890-1900."
       Kentucky Folklore Quarterly 17:63-82, 1972.

13542 Mauro, Walter. Jazz e Universo Negro. Milano: Rizzoli, 1972.

13543 Middleton, Richard. Pop Music and the Blues; A Study of the Re-
       lationship and Its Significance. London: Gollancz, 1972.

13544 Nanry, Charles. American Music: From Storyville to Woodstock.
       New Brunswick, N.J.: Transaction Books, Distributed by E. P.
       Dutton, 1972.

13545 Oliver, Paul. The Meaning of the Blues. New York: Collier Books,
       1972. Originally published as Blues Fell This Morning, 1961.

13546 Otto, J. S., and A. M. Burns. "The Use of Race and Hillbilly Re-
       cordings as Sources for Historical Research; The Problem of Col-
       or Hierarchy Among Afro-Americans in the Early Twentieth Cen-
       tury." Journal of the American Folklore Society 85:344-355, no.
       338, 1972.

13547 Patterson, E. "Our Own Thing." Journal of Music Therapy 9:119-
       122, no. 3, 1972. Description of the program developed to en-
       courage black children in the arts in Ann Arbor, Michigan.

13548 Ramsey, F. "Where the Music Started; Home-Made String Bass."
       Probas 1:5, no. 1, 1972. Reprinted from Where the Music Start-
       ed.

13549 "Record Reviews: African Rhythm and American Jazz; Music His-
       torians Explore the African Origins of Jazz." Ethnomusicology
       16:558-560, no. 3, 1972.

13550 "Record Reviews: Afro-American Music; A Demonstration Record-
       ing." Journal of the American Folklore Society 85:99, no. 335,
       1972.

13551 Rhinehart, Charles P. "Effecting Attitude Change Through Music
       Presented by an Integrative Black Studies Approach." (Ed. D.
       Dissertation, University of Houston, 1972).

13552 Roberts, John S. Black Music of Two Worlds. New York: Praeger,
       1972.

13553 Stewart, Tex William. Jazz Masters of the Thirties. New York:
       Macmillan Co., 1972. Discussion of many jazz musicians prom-
       inent during the 1930s, such as Louis Armstrong and Duke El-
       lington.

13554 Thomas, F. W. "A Seat in a Symphony Orchestra." Symphony
       News 23:11-12, no. 2, 1972.

13555 Turner, Richard Martin. "An Analysis of the Qualifications of Mu-
       sic Graduates of Black Private and Church-Related Colleges upon
       Entrance into Graduate Music Programs in Major American Uni-
       versities." (Mus. Ed. D. Dissertation, Indiana University, 1972).

13556 Uya, O. E. "The Mind of Slaves as Revealed in Their Songs: An
       Interpretative Essay." Current Bibliography of African Affairs
       5:3-11, 1972.

13557 Walton, Ortiz. Music: Black, White & Blue; A Sociological Survey
       of the Use and Misuse of Afro-American Music. New York: W.
       Morrow, 1972.

13558 Wilgus, D. K. "Afro-American Tradition." Journal of the Amer-
       ican Folklore Society 85:99-107, 1972.

13559 Williams, Willie Lee. "Curriculum for Teaching the Black Exper-
       ience Through Music and Dramatic History." (Ed. D. Dissertation,
       University of Massachusetts, 1972).

13560 Wolfe, C. K. "Where the Blues Is At; A Survey of Recent Research."
       Popular Music and Society 1:152-166, no. 3, 1972.

13561 Young, A. "Black Folk Music." Mississippi Folklore Register
       6:1-4, 1972.

13562 Watts, S. "First Annual Black Jazz Festival Held." Soul 6:4, Jan-
       uary 17, 1972. Festival was held in Los Angeles.

13563 "Artists Are Color Blind When Looking at Copyrights." Billboard
       84:40, January 29, 1972.

13564 Deni, L. "Vegas Hotels Seek a Soulful Crowd for the Black Art-
       ists." Billboard 84:43, January 29, 1972.

13565 Ovens, D. "Oh Happy Day! Everybody's Listening to Soul Music."
       Billboard 84:31, January 29, 1972.

13566 Paige, E. "Black Artists Find a Home on Jukeboxes in White Neigh-
       borhoods." Billboard 84:42, January 29, 1972.

13567 Davis, L. "Soul Train." Soul 6:12-13, February 14, 1972.

13568 "Soul to Soul Wins Ethiopian Film Fest." Soul 6:1, February 14,
       1972.

13569 Meadow, E. "Harlem Music Center: More Than a Dream." down
       beat 39:10, February 17, 1972.

13570 Williams, B. "First Integrated Gospel Act." Billboard 84:3-4,
       February 26, 1972.

13571 Gibbs, V. "Progressive Soul." Senior Scholastic 100:25-27, Feb-
       ruary 28, 1972.

13572 Oliver, P. "African Influence and the Blues." Living Blues no.
       8:13-17, Spring 1972.

13573 Fonteyne, A. "Brian Rust, 'Jazz Records 1897-1942': Quelques
       Corrections et Additions." Points du Jazz no. 6:106-110, March
       1972.

13574 "A Black Unit from U.S. Wins 'Honorary Whites' Status in South
       Africa." Variety 266:1, March 8, 1972.

13575 "White Groups Add Black Musicians & Even Gospel Combos Join
       Trend." Variety 266:55, March 8, 1972.

13576 "The Ethnic Market: Small, Lean But Very Soulful." Billboard
       84:24, March 25, 1972 Supplement.

13577 "Musicians Purchase Black Radio Station." down beat 39:12-13,
       March 30, 1972.

13578 Pearson, W. D. "Going Down to the Crossroads: The Bluesmen
       and Religion." Jazz & Blues 2:13-15, April 1972.

13579 Secca, J. "Afrikas Musik in den USA." Instrumentenbau-Zeitschrift
       26:289-90, April 1972.

13580 "AFM In Las Vegas Denies Charges of Bias Vs. Blacks in Major
       Hotels." Variety 266:85, April 12, 1972.

13581 "N.Y. Concerts Reveal Black Music Spectrum." down beat 39:10,
       April 13, 1972.

13582 Tiegel, E. "KJLH Offers Soft Jazz as Its Program Specialty."
       Billboard 84:27, April 22, 1972.

13583 "Blacks Discovered Me First, Says Hayes as He Wins Hollywood Os-
       car." Jet 42:58, April 27, 1972.

13584 Banks, L. J. "Gospel Music: A Shout of Black Joy." Ebony 27:161-
       165, May 1972.

13585 Palmer, C. "Delius's Negro Opera." Opera 23:403-407, May 1972.

13586 Redwood, C. "The First Negro Opera?" Musical Opinion 95:407,
       May 1972.

13587 "Black Acts Need More Label Help." Billboard 84:1, May 6, 1972.

13588 Sippel, J. "Columbia Fortifies Black Artists Roster & Promotion."
       Billboard 84:1, May 20, 1972.

13589 Ackerman, P. "Blacks Sizzling on the Hot 100." Billboard 84:1,
       May 27, 1972.

13590 Byrd, D. "The Meaning of Black Music." Black Scholar 3:28-31,
       Summer 1972.

13591 Roach, M. "What 'Jazz' Means to Me." Black Scholar 3:2-6, Sum-
       mer 1972.

13592 Southern, E. "An Origin for the Negro Spiritual." Black Scholar
       3:8-13, Summer 1972.

13593 Tyler, R. "The Musical Culture of Afro-America." Black Scholar
       3:22-27, Summer 1972.

13594 Walters, H. "Black Music and the Black University." Black Scholar
       3:14-21, Summer 1972.

13595 Easter, G. "So, What Is Jazz? A Mainstream View of the Avant-
       Garde." Jazz & Blues 2:25, June 1972.

13596 Konen, W. "Die Bedeutung der Aussereuropaeischen Kulturen für
       die Komponistenschulen des 20. Jahrhunderts." Kunst und Litera-
       tur 20:643-670, June 1972. An excerpt from Konen's book Die
       Musik des Zwanzigsten Jahrhunderts.

13597 "South Africans Query Apartheid Inconsistency to Black Stars from
       U.S." Variety 267:1, June 14, 1972.

13598 Joe, R. "FORE Acts to Spur 'Black Experience.'" Billboard 84:1,
       June 17, 1972.

13599 "Group Formed to Protect Black Music via Copyright." Billboard
       84:3, June 24, 1972.

13600 Cullaz, M. "Psychologie de Fossoyeur et d'Ed Cercueil." Jazz Hot
       no. 285:13-14, July-August 1972.

13601 "CBA Conference Seeks Unity of Black Artists." down beat 39:10-11,
       July 20, 1972.

13602 Cordle, O. "The Soprano Saxophone: From Bechet to Coltrane to
       Shorter." down beat 39:14-15, July 20, 1972.

13603   Patridge, R. "Soul Surge in U.K. as 10 Make Top 50." Billboard
        84:1, July 15, 1972.

13604   "Black Disk Artists Extend Impact from Singles to Album Market."
        Variety 267:47, July 26, 1972.

13605   Monson, K. "'Tribute to Black Music'--All-Purpose Mishmash?"
        High Fidelity/Musical America 22:MA16, August 1972. Review of
        concert given by the Los Angeles Philharmonic.

13606   "'Soul at Lincoln Center' Shaping OK for First Year Despite 70 G
        Deficit." Variety 267:41, August 2, 1972.

13607   "Black Development Pilot Firm Sets Up Varied Music Complex."
        Billboard 84:3, August 5, 1972.

13608   Paige, E. "Black Firms in Unifying Effort." Billboard 84:1, Au-
        gust 12, 1972.

13609   Moore, C. "Soul at the Center; Lincoln Center." Saturday Review
        55:68, August 26, 1972.

13610   Sippel, J. "'Soul Train's' 45-Mkt. $1 Mil Backing." Billboard
        84:4, August 26, 1972.

13611   Byrd, D. "The Meaning of Black Music." Black Scholar 3:28-31,
        September 1972.

13612   Dance, S. "Our Adversaries." Jazz Journal 25:19, September 1972.

13613   Hiemenz, J. "N.Y. Philharmonic Reaches Out for Black Players."
        High Fidelity/Musical America 22:MA18, September 1972.

13614   Trick [sic], B., i.e., Truck, B. "Second Line Jump; Looks at
        R 'n' B in New Orleans." Jazz & Blues 2:10-13, September
        1972.

13615   "National Black Gospel Meet Draws 8,000; D. J.'s Active." Bill-
        board 84:1, September 2, 1972.

13616   "Dearth of Black Conductors Puts 'Purlie' in Pickle." Variety
        268:89, September 13, 1972.

13617   Berry, W. E. "How Watts Festival Renews Black Unity." Jet 42:52-
        55, September 14, 1972.

13618   Cole, B. "Caught in the Act." down beat 39:36-37, September 14,
        1972. Report of an African-American Cultural Festival in Walla
        Walla, Washington.

13619   Grant, C. D. "Beginnings: The Harlem Music Center." Essence
        3:36-37, October 1972.

13620   Obatala, J. K. "Soul in Africa; Black Africans' Belief in the Myth
        of Afro-American Influence." Ramparts 11:45-46, October 1972.

13621   Reeder, B. "Getting Involved in Shaping the Sounds of Black Music."
        Music Educator's Journal 59:80-84, October 1972.

13622   Truck, B.   "Second Line Jump; Reelin' and Rockin' Down in New
        Orleans."   Jazz & Blues 2:8-14, October 1972.

13623   "Ex-Beatle Tells How Black Stars Changed His Life."   Jet 43:6-62,
        October 26, 1972.

13624   Borroff, E.   "Black Musicians in the United States."   American Mu-
        sic Teacher 22:30-31, November-December 1972.

13625   "Music of Black Americans, New U of Texas Course."   School Mu-
        sician 44:27, November 1972.

13626   Peterson, O.   "Why Bother About Soul Music?"   Jazz & Blues 2:4-
        7, November 1972.

13627   "Week of Gospel Happiness; Annual Convention of the Gospel Music
        Workshop of America."   Ebony 28:86-92, November 1972.

13628   Joe, R.   "Blacks Find Difficulty in Establishing City One-Stops."
        Billboard 84:3, November 25, 1972.

13629   "As If Bereav'd of Light."   Jazz Journal 25:12-13, December 1972.

13630   Peterson, O.   "The Soul Question."   Jazz & Blues 2:4-7, December
        1972.

13631   "Yale's Ellington Fellowship Program to Preserve Black Musical
        Legacy."   School Musician 44:61, December 1972.

13632   "Divas in Dixie."   Newsweek 80:67-68, December 4, 1972.   Opera/
        South is an opera company composed of black musicians.

13633   Lucraft, H.   "Black Artists Insist Diskers Brush Them Off."   Va-
        riety 269:1, December 6, 1972.

13634   Morgenstern, D.   "Yale's Conservatory Without Walls."   down beat
        39:11, December 7, 1972.

13635   Freeman, P.   "Black Symphonic Music Will Now Be Heard."   Sym-
        phony News 24:7-10, no. 6, 1973-1974.

13636   Abrahams, R. D.   "Christmas Mummings on Nevis."   North Carolina
        Folklore 21:120-131, no. 3, 1973.

13637   Adams, C. G.   "Some Aspects of Black Worship."   Church Music
        15:2-9, 1973.

13638   Alkire, Stephen Robert.   "The Development and Treatment of the
        Negro Character as Presented in American Musical Theatre 1927-
        1968."   (Ph.D. Dissertation, Michigan State University, 1972).

13639   Allen, W. D.   "Musings of a Music Columnist."   Black Perspectives
        in Music 1:107-114, no. 2, 1973.

13640   Boyer, Horace Clarence.   "An Analysis of Black Church Music, with
        Examples Drawn from Services in Rochester, New York."   (Ph.D.
        Dissertation, University of Rochester, 1973).

13641 Buerkle, Jack V., and Danny Barker. Bourbon Street Black: The New Orleans Black Jazzman. New York: Oxford University Press, 1973.

13642 Cane, Giampiero. Canto Nero; Il Free Jazz Degli anni Sessanta. Rimini: Guaraldi, 1973.

13643 Carter, W. L. "Music in the Black Studies Program." Black Perspectives in Music 1:147-150, no. 2, 1973.

13644 De Lerma, D. R. "Dett and Engel." Black Perspectives in Music 1:70-72, 1973.

13645 _____. Reflections on Afro-American Music. Kent, Ohio: Kent State University Press, 1973. Chiefly consists of essays, such as "Black Music in the Undergraduate Curriculum," by different contributing authors.

13646 Dundes, Alan. Mother Wit from the Laughing Barrel; Readings in the Interpretation of Afro-American Folklore. Englewood Cliffs, N.J.: Prentice-Hall, 1973. An anthology of black folklore with considerable information on black music.

13647 Ennett, Dorothy Maxine. "An Analysis and Comparison of Selected Piano Sonatas by Three Contemporary Black Composers: George Walker, Howard Swanson, and Roque Cordero." (Ph.D. Dissertation, New York University, 1973).

13648 Epstein, D. "The Search for Black Music's African Roots." University of Chicago Magazine 66:18-22, 1973.

13649 Evans, D. "An Interview with H. C. Speir." JEMF Quarterly 8:117-121, pt. 3, 1972. Speir worked with black musicians in the South in the early twentieth century.

13650 _____. "Record Reviews: Black Religious Music." Journal of the American Folklore Society 86:82-86, 1973.

13651 Harris, C. "The Negro Spiritual: Stylistic Development Through Performance Practices." Choral Journal 13:15-16, no. 9, 1973.

13652 Hennessey, Thomas J. "From Jazz to Swing: Black Jazz Musicians and Their Music, 1917-1935." (Ph.D. Dissertation, Northwestern University, 1973).

13653 Hofmann, Heinz P. Beat: Rock, Rhythm & Blues, Soul. Berlin: Lied der Zeit, Musikverlag, 1973.

13654 Jackson, Raymond Thompson. "The Piano Music of Twentieth-Century Black Americans as Illustrated Mainly in the Works of Three Composers." (Ph.D. Dissertation, Juilliard School of Music, 1973). Analysis of the works of R. Nathaniel Dett, Howard Swanson, and George Walker.

13655 Jahn, Mike. Rock; From Elvis Presley to the Rolling Stones. New York: Quadrangle, 1973. Includes many black musicians, such as Chuck Berry, Chubby Checker, and Fats Domino.

13656   Jost, E. "Zum Problem des Politischen Engagements im Jazz."
        Jazz Research 5:33-43, 1973.

13657   Kofsky, Frank Joseph. "Black Nationalism and the Revolution in
        Music: Social Change and Stylistic Development in the Art of
        John Coltrane and Others, 1954-1967." (Ph.D. Dissertation, Uni-
        versity of Pittsburgh, 1973).

13658   Kwabena Nketia, J. H. "The Study of African and Afro-American
        Music." Black Perspectives in Music 1:7-15, no. 1, 1973.

13659   Lewis, G. H. "Social Protest and Self Awareness in Black Popular
        Music." Popular Music and Society 2:327-333, no. 4, 1973.

13660   Miller, S. D., and K. Muckelroy. "Let's Put Soul in Your Class-
        room Listening Lesson." Educator 6:2-4, no. 1, 1973.

13661   "New Books." Black Perspectives in Music 1:93-95, no. 1, 1973.

13662   "New Music." Black Perspectives in Music 1:97-100, no. 1, 1973.

13663   "New Recordings." Black Perspectives in Music 1:101-102, no. 1,
        1973.

13664   Nicholas, A. X. Woke Up This Mornin'; Poetry of the Blues. New
        York: Bantam, 1973.

13665   Paul, June Dolores Brooks. "Music in Culture: Black Sacred Song
        Style in Slidell, Louisiana and Chicago, Illinois." (Ph.D. Disser-
        tation, Northwestern University, 1973).

13666   "Record Reviews: Black Religious Music." Journal of the American
        Folklore Society 86:82-86, no. 339, 1973.

13667   "Record Reviews: Roots of Black Music in America; Some Corre-
        spondences Between the Music of the Slave Areas of Africa and
        the Music of the United States and the Caribbean." Ed. by S.
        Charters. Black Perspectives in Music 1:90-92, no. 1, 1973.

13668   "Report on the 1972 Symposium on African and Afro-American Mu-
        sic." Black Perspectives in Music 1:5-6, no. 1, 1973.

13669   "Reports from Member Organizations." National Music Council Bul-
        letin 33:9, no. 3, 1973.

13670   Rhinehart, C. "The Black Impact upon American Music." South-
        Western Musician 42:12-13, 1973.

13671   Robinson, Marie Hadley. "The Negro Spiritual: An Examination of
        the Texts, and Their Relationship to Musical Performance Prac-
        tice." (Ph.D. Dissertation, Florida State University, 1973).

13672   Roffeni, Alessandro. Il Blues; Saggio Critico e Raccolta di Lirich
        della Più Importante Froma di Canto Afro-Americana. Milano:
        Accademia, 1973.

13673   Schafer, William John, and Johannes Riedel. The Art of Ragtime:
        Form and Meaning of an Original Black American Art. New York:

Da Capo Press, 1977. Reprint of the 1973 edition published by
Louisiana State University Press, Baton Rouge.

13674 Southern, E. "Afro-American Musical Materials." Black Perspectives in Music 1:24-32, no. 1, 1973.

13675 _____. "Needs for Research in Black-American Music." College
Music Symposium 13:43-52, 1973.

13676 Stagg, Tom, and Charlie Crump. New Orleans, the Revival: A
Tape and Discography of Negro Traditional Jazz Recorded in New
Orleans Bands, 1937-1972. Dublin: Bashall Eaves Publication,
1973.

13677 Stanley, M. "R. N. Dett of Hampton Institute Helping to Lay Foundation for Negro Music of Future." Black Perspectives in Music
1:64-69, no. 1, 1973.

13678 Starks, George Leroy. "Black Music in the Sea Islands of South
Carolina: Its Cultural Context--Continuity and Change." (Ph. D.
Dissertation, Wesleyan University, 1973).

13679 Stevenson, R. "America's First Black Music Historian." American
Musicological Society Journal 26:383-404, no. 3, 1973.

13680 Vacha, J. E. "Black Man on the Great White Way." Journal of
Popular Culture 7:288-301, no. 2, 1973.

13681 White, C. "Check Yourself!" Black Perspectives in Music 1:129-
35, no. 2, 1973. Reprinted from Charles Nanry's book, American Music: From Storyville to Woodstock.

13682 Williams, Robert. "Preservation of the Oral Tradition of Singing
Hymns in Negro Religious Music." (Ph. D. Dissertation, Florida
State University, 1973).

13683 Wilson, O. "The Black-American Composer." Black Perspectives
in Music 1:33-36, no. 1, 1973.

13684 Yestadt, Sister Marie. "Song Literature for the 70's: A Socio-
Musical Approach." NATS Bulletin 29:22-27, no. 4, 1973.

13685 Gibbs, V. "Soul, Man." Crawdaddy no. 20:16, January 1973.

13686 Jefferson, M. "Ripping Off Black Music; From Thomas 'Daddy'
Rice to Jimi Hendrix." Harper's Magazine 246:40, January 1973.

13687 McCutcheon, L. "Unsung Heroes Who Also Sang; Soul Singers."
Negro History Bulletin 36:9-11, January 1973.

13688 Phillips, R. E. "White Racism in Black Church Music." Negro
History Bulletin 36:17-20, January 1973.

13689 "Two Gatherings: Party Celebrating Free the Black Man's Chains,
First Black Rock Opera." New Yorker 48:22-23, January 13,
1973.

13690 Thompson, M. C. "What's Ahead for Soul Music in 1973." Jet
43:58-62, January 25, 1973.

13691   Black, D. "How Black Churches Became a School for Singing Stars."
        Sepia 22:70-74, February 1973.

13692   Gibbs, V. "Soul, Man." Crawdaddy no. 22:16, March 1973.

13693   "On Record: Black and White Ragtime." Jazz & Blues 2:22-23,
        March 1973.

13694   Thacker, E. "Gottschalk and a Prelude to Jazz." Composer no.
        50:19-22, Winter 1973-1974. Reprinted from Jazz & Blues, March
        1973.

13695   Knight, A. "Film: Facing Reality." Saturday Review 1:71-72,
        March 10, 1973.

13696   "Pop-Rock Artists Gain Recognition." Soul 7:1, March 12, 1973.

13697   "Blacks Take Top Pop and Rhythm Grammy Awards." Jet 43:58-59,
        March 22, 1973.

13698   Tepper, R. "Black Music: Sought After but Like Other Gems, It's
        Often Hard to Buy." Billboard 85:59, March 31, 1973 Supplement.

13699   "Major Diskers Step Up Ethnic Accent on Blacks." Variety 270:2,
        April 4, 1973.

13700   "Paul Robeson Annual Award via Equity." Variety 270:2, April 18,
        1973.

13701   Tanter, L. "Jazz in Transition: Black Music." Soul 7:32, April
        23, 1973.

13702   Joans, T. "Jazz Is My Religion." Jazz Magazine no. 211:18-21,
        May 1973.

13703   "New 'Soul-Blues' Awards as Black Slap at Grammys." Variety
        270:1, May 2, 1973.

13704   Hunt, J. "Conversation with Thomas J. Anderson: Blacks and the
        Classics." Black Perspectives in Music 1:157-165, no. 2, 1973.
        Reprinted from Real Paper p. 26-32, May 16, 1973.

13705   Garon, P. "Editorial." Living Blues no. 13:3, Summer 1973. Dis-
        cussion of blues in everyday life.

13706   Oliver, P. "Echoes of the Jungle?" Living Blues no. 13:29-32,
        Summer 1973.

13707   Reitman, D. "Jazz: An Hysterical Introduction." Crawdaddy no.
        25:32-34, June 1973.

13708   "Valerie Wilmer's Exhibition at Victoria and Albert Museum." Jazz
        Forum no. 23:23, June 1973.

13709   Wilmer, V. "New York Is Alive!" Jazz Forum no. 23:47-49, June 1973.

13710   Fong-Torres, B. "'Soul Train' Vs. Dick Clark: Battle of the Band-
        stands." Rolling Stone no. 136:8, June 7, 1973.

13711 Joe, R. "NATRA's Cordell Attacks News Reports of Payola." Billboard 85:1, June 16, 1973.

13712 Aletti, V. "Soul Train--the Gang That Couldn't Dance Straight." Rolling Stone no. 137:28-29, June 21, 1973.

13713 Alexander, T. "In Memory of Malcolm X." Soul 8:6, July 9, 1973. A concert in Hollywood is reviewed.

13714 "Col. to Showcase Black Composers." Variety 271:1, July 18, 1973.

13715 Tiegel, E. "Soft Sounds Spell Success for Today." Billboard 85:26, July 21, 1973.

13716 "Columbia Will Record Black Symphony Writers." Billboard 85:40, August 11, 1973.

13717 Locke, D. "U.S. Notebook No. 3." Jazz & Blues 3:13, August 1973.

13718 McRae, B. "Black Call." Jazz Journal 26:39, August 1973.

13719 Kirby, F. "Black-Angled 'Soul at the Center '73' Way Ahead of Last Year in B. O. Impact." Variety 271:34, August 8, 1973.

13720 _____. "'Soul' Series Top Last Year's Biz But Lincoln Ctr. Looks 100 G in Red." Variety 272:33, August 15, 1973.

13721 "A Festival of Soulful Jazz." Soul 8:12, August 20, 1973. The Hollywood Bowl in Los Angeles is the site of the Newport West Jazz Festival.

13722 Kirby, F. "Lincoln Ctr. Seeks Bankroller for 'Soul' Series in '74; $100,000 in Red." Variety 272:37, August 22, 1973.

13723 "Black Gospel Music Proves Vitality on Radio & Adv." Billboard 85:4, August 25, 1973.

13724 Joe, R. "CORE to Organize Music Biz Blacks." Billboard 85:1, August 25, 1973.

13725 Robinson, L. "'Soul Train' & 'Omnibus' Lift Soul TV Hopes." Billboard 85:20, August 25, 1973.

13726 Brown, R. "Jazz Seen: The Face of Black Music." Jazz Journal 26:6-7, September 1973. Discussion of Valerie Wilmer's exhibit: "The Face of Black Music" on display at the Victoria & Albert Museum.

13727 Carles, P., and F. Marmande. "Les Contradictions du Festival." Jazz Magazine no. 215:10-12, September 1973.

13728 "Jazz Records: Jazz Anthology." Melody Maker 48:56, September 29, 1973.

13729 "First Annual Ebony Black Music Poll." Ebony 28:143-164, October 1973.

13730 Gibbs, V. "Soul, Man." Crawdaddy no. 29:18, October 1973.

13731 "Lauds Labels' Boost for PUSH." Billboard 85:3, October 6, 1973.

13732 Robinson, L. "Contributors Keep Soul's Soul Alive." Billboard
       85:27, October 6, 1973.

13733 "A Trouble-Plagued Black Expo '73." Rolling Stone no. 145:16, Oc-
       tober 11, 1973.

13734 Aletti, V. "Paar-ty! at the Lincoln Center: Beige Is Beautiful."
       Rolling Stone no. 146:20, October 25, 1973.

13735 "Black Music Center." Instrumentalist 28:34, November 1973. A
       black music center is created at Indiana University.

13736 Boyer, H. C. "Gospel Music Comes of Age." Black World 33:42-
       48, November 1973.

13737 Brown, M. "Improvisation and the Aural Tradition in Afro-American
       Music." Black World 23:14-19, November 1973.

13738 Goines, L. "The Blues as Black Therapy." Black World 23:28-40,
       November 1973.

13739 Parks, C. A. "Self-Determination and the Black Aesthetic: An In-
       terview with Max Roach." Black World 23:62-71, November 1973.

13740 Southern, E. "Some Guidelines; Music Research and the Black Aes-
       thetic." Black World 23:4-13, November 1973.

13741 Thacker, E. "Ragtime Roots: The Classical Succession." Jazz &
       Blues 3:6-7, November 1973.

13742 Walton, O. "Some Implications for Afro-American Culture: Ration-
       alism and Western Music." Black World 23:54-56, November
       1973.

13743 Proctor, D. "Bill Withers Shares His Views on Hollywood and So-
       cial Rituals." Rolling Stone no. 147:18, November 8, 1973.

13744 "Six Nashville Gospel Groups Band to Improve Conditions." Bill-
       board 85:6, November 10, 1973.

13745 "Det. Symphony to Cut Black Composers LPs; 1st Waxing in 10
       Years." Variety 273:67, November 21, 1973.

13746 Phillips, R. E. "Black Folk Music: Setting the Record Straight."
       Music Educator's Journal 60:41-45, December 1973.

13747 "Spotlight." Music Journal 31:12-15, December 1973.

13748 Thacker, E. "Ragtime Roots: African and American Minstrels."
       Jazz & Blues 3:4-6, December 1973.

13749 Robinson, L. "Blacks Wait for Yule Yield." Billboard 85:32, De-
       cember 22, 1973.

13750 Ferris, W. R. "Black Prose Narrative from the Mississippi Delta."
       Jazz Research 6-7:9-138, 1974-1975.

13751 Abdul, Raoul. Famous Black Entertainers of Today. New York: Dodd, Mead, 1974. Juvenile literature.

13752 "The Afro-American Music Opportunities Association." Black Perspectives in Music 2:106-107, no. 1, 1974.

13753 Anderson, H. "Some Negro Slave Songs from an 1856 Novel." Mississippi Folklore Register 8:221-226, 1974.

13754 "The Black Composers Series." Black Perspectives in Music 2:231, 1974.

13755 Blum, M. "Black Music: Pathmaker of the Harlem Renaissance." Missouri Journal of Research in Music Education 3:72-79, no. 3, 1974.

13756 Brown, Marian Tally. "A Resource Manual on the Music of the Southern Fundamentalist Black Church." (Ed.D. Dissertation, Indiana University, 1974).

13757 Buckner, Reginald Tyrone. "A History of Music Education in the Black Community of Kansas City, Kansas, 1905-1954." (Ph.D. Dissertation, University of Minnesota, 1974).

13758 Carter, Ann Louise. "An Analysis of the Use of Contemporary Black Literature and Music and Its Effects upon Self-Concept in Group Counseling Procedures." (Ph.D. Dissertation, Purdue University, 1974).

13759 Cayer, D. A. "Black and Blue and Black Again: Three Stages of Racial Imagery in Jazz Lyrics." Journal of Jazz Studies 1:38-71, no. 1, 1974.

13760 "Commentary: Strings and Strings." Black Perspectives in Music 2:104-106, no. 1, 1974.

13761 Dugan, J., and J. Hammond. "An Early Black-Music Concert, 'From Spirituals to Swing.'" Black Perspectives in Music 2:191-207, no. 2, 1974. Discussion of the concert held December 23, 1938 in Carnegie Hall.

13762 Ekwueme, L. "African Music Retentions in the New World." Black Perspectives in Music 2:128-144, 1974.

13763 Evans, D. "Techniques of Blues Composition Among Black Folksingers." Journal of the American Folklore Society 87:240-249, no. 345, 1974.

13764 Ferris, W. "Blue Roots and Development." Black Perspectives in Music 2:122-127, no. 2, 1974.

13765 Floyd, S. A. "Black Music in the Driscoll Collection." Black Perspectives in Music 2:158-171, no. 2, 1974.

13766 Fortunato, Joanne Alba. "Major Influences Affecting the Development of Jazz Dance, 1950-1971." (Ph.D. Dissertation, University of Southern California, 1974).

13767 Giddins, Gary, Peter Keepnews, and Dan Morgenstern. The Sax
       Section: Biographical Sketches. New York: New York Jazz Mu-
       seum, 1974.

13768 Green, R. A. "Report from Bloomington: The Black Music Center
       at Indiana University." Current Musicology no. 18:35-36, 1974.

13769 Groia, Philip. They All Sang on the Corner; New York City's
       Rhythm and Blues Vocal Groups of the 1950's. Rev. ed. Setauket,
       N.Y.: Edmond Pub. Co., 1974.

13770 Handy, D. Antoinette. Black Music: Opinions & Reviews. Ettrick,
       Va.: BM & M, 1974. A compilation of articles written by Handy
       in the Richmond Afro-American.

13771 Haralambos, Michael. Right On: From Blues to Soul in Black Amer-
       ica. New York: Da Capo Press, 1979. Reprint of the 1974
       edition published by Eddison Press, London.

13772 Harris, C. G. "Three Schools of Black Choral Composers and Ar-
       rangers 1900-1970." Choral Journal 14:11-18, no. 8, 1974.

13773 Hennessey, T. J. "The Black Chicago Establishment 1919-1930."
       Journal of Jazz Studies 2:15-45, no. 1, 1974.

13774 Hill, R. "Fannie Douglas's Reminiscences of Yesteryear." Black
       Perspectives in Music 2:54-62, no. 1, 1974. Douglas recalls mu-
       sicians she has known, such as Marian Anderson.

13775 Hitchcock, Hugh Wiley. Music in the United States: A Historical
       Introduction. Englewood Cliffs, N.J.: Prentice-Hall, 1974. Sev-
       eral sections treat the subject of black music, especially rhythm
       and blues as a forerunner of rock and roll.

13776 Hoffmann, R. "Black-Music: Vom Altar zum Alltag." Neue Mu-
       sikzeitung 23:9, no. 5, 1974.

13777 Hunt, D. C. "Black Voice Lost in White Superstructure." Coda
       11:12-14, no. 6, 1974.

13778 Jackson, Irene Viola. "Afro-American Gospel Music and Its Social
       Setting with Special Attention to Roberta Martin." (Ph.D. Disser-
       tation, Wesleyan University, 1974).

13779 Lax, J. "Chicago's Black Jazz Musicians in the Twenties: Portrait
       of an Era." Journal of Jazz Studies 1:107-127, no. 2, 1974.

13780 Lee, H. "Swing Low, Sweet Chariot." Black Perspectives in Mu-
       sic 2:84-86, no. 1, 1974.

13781 Maultsby, Portia Katrenia. "Afro-American Religious Music: 1619-
       1861." (Ph.D. Dissertation, University of Wisconsin, 1974).

13782 Patterson, C. L. "A Different Drum: The Image of the Negro in
       the Nineteenth Century Songster." Canadian Library Association
       Journal 8:44-50, 1974.

13783 Petrie, Gavin. Black Music. London: Hamlyn, 1974. Essays on

black music with biographical sketches of musicians such as Ray
Charles and Smokey Robinson.

13784 Pleasants, Henry. The Great American Popular Singers. New York:
       Simon and Schuster, 1974. Many chapters are devoted to indi-
       vidual black singers, such as Bessie Smith, Mahalia Jackson,
       and B. B. King.

13785 "Record Reviews: John's Island, South Carolina: Its People and
       Songs." Ethnomusicology 18:181-183, no. 1, 1974.

13786 Redd, Lawrence N. Rock Is Rhythm and Blues; The Impact of Mass
       Media. East Lansing: Michigan State University Press, 1974.
       Blues development is traced as it proceeded through radio, motion
       pictures, and television.

13787 "Reports from Member Organizations." National Music Council Bul-
       letin 34:8, no. 2, 1974.

13788 Shaw, Arnold. The Rockin' '50s; The Decade That Transformed the
       Pop Music Scene. New York: Hawthorn Books, 1974. Many
       black groups are included in this examination of rock music.

13789 Simon, George Thomas. The Big Bands. Rev. ed. New York:
       Macmillan, 1974. A history of the rise and decline of the big
       band sound, with a large section "Inside the Big Bands" which
       examines bands of Count Basie, Duke Ellington, and others.

13790 Smith, L. "American Music." Black Perspectives in Music 2:111-
       116, no. 2, 1974.

13791 Southall, G. "Black Composers and Religious Music." Black Per-
       spectives in Music 2:45-50, no. 1, 1974.

13792 Stearne, J. B. The Grand Tradition; Seventy Years of Singing on
       Record. New York: C. Scribner's Sons, 1974. Discussion of
       singers, principally in opera, and their recordings, including
       Marian Anderson and Leontyne Price.

13793 Taubman, H. "Negro Music Given at Carnegie Hall." Black Per-
       spectives in Music 2:207-208, no. 2, 1974.

13794 Toll, Robert C. Blacking Up: The Minstrel Show in Nineteenth
       Century America. New York: Oxford University Press, 1974.
       A history of the minstrels, with one chapter on "Black Men Take
       the Stage."

13795 "The Use of Music from Other Cultures in Music Courses for Gen-
       eral Students." College Music Symposium 14:138-146, 1974.

13796 Walling, W. "The Politics of Jazz: Some Preliminary Notes."
       Journal of Jazz Studies 2:46-60, no. 1, 1974.

13797 Wilson, O. "The Significance of the Relationship Between Afro-
       American Music and West African Music." Black Perspectives in
       Music 2:3-22, no. 1, 1974.

13798 Robinson, L. "1974 Looms Bleak for Soul Music." Billboard 86:13,
       January 5, 1974.

13799 "Black Music Collection Given to U. of Michigan." Diapason 65:14, February 1974.

13800 "Ebony Black Music Poll: Winners for 1974." Ebony 29:44, February 1974.

13801 McNeil, A. J. "The Social Foundations of the Music of Black Americans." Music Educator's Journal 60:43-46, February 1974.

13802 "The Music as Institution--from Joplin to Coltrane." down beat 41:9, February 14, 1974. The Smithsonian Institution has a collection of jazz available.

13803 Simmons, O. D. "Teaching the Arts in a Black Institution; Active Participation Made This Institute Work." Music Educator's Journal 60:47-49, February 1974.

13804 Feather, L. "Do You Have to Be Black to Play Jazz?" Melody Maker 49:55, February 16, 1974.

13805 Robinson, L. "Acts Unaware of Values of PR and Promotion." Billboard 86:28, February 23, 1974.

13806 Keepnews, P. "What Is the CBAE?" down beat 41:10, February 28, 1974. CBAE is the Collective Black Artists Ensemble.

13807 LeBlanc, L. "Black Artists Crave Opportunities for Free Expression." Music Scene no. 276:4-6, March-April 1974.

13808 Bretschneider, K. "Harlem Jazz 1921." Jazz Podium 23:16-19, March 1974.

13809 Dance, S. "Lightly & Politely." Jazz Journal 27:6-8, March 1974.

13810 Gibbs, V. "Soul, Man." Crawdaddy no. 34:12-13, March 1974.

13811 Brown, G., and D. Milton. "Black Power!" Melody Maker 49:34-35, March 2, 1974.

13812 Robinson, L. "Black Flacks Seek Acts for PR Campaign." Billboard 86:20, March 2, 1974.

13813 _____. "Internecine Department Tiff Hurts." Billboard 86:28, March 9, 1974.

13814 "Record Reviews: Masekela: Introducing Hedzoleh Soundz." down beat 41:20, March 14, 1974.

13815 Arvey, V. "Symphonies in Black." Music Journal 32:28-29, April 1974.

13816 "Music Still Sweet, but Beat New." Billboard 86:34, April 13, 1974.

13817 Saal, H. "Black Composers." Newsweek 83:82, April 15, 1974.

13818 Eckstine, E. "Yesterday's Stars: Some Still Glitter While Many Have Lost Their Shine." Soul 9:1-4, April 29, 1974.

13819   Ivy, A. "Yes! 'Jazz' Is Dead--but Long Live Jazz." Soul 9:28,
        April 29, 1974.

13820   Ruffin, W. D. "Top Black Musicians Set Disc World in a Spin."
        Soul 9:12, April 29, 1974.

13821   Atkins, C. "Afro-American Music Mixes." Music Journal 32:43,
        May 1974.

13822   Carriere, C. "Autour d'un Disque." Jazz Hot no. 305:29, May
        1974.

13823   Demetre, J. "Blues & Boogie." Jazz Hot no. 305:7-9, May 1974.

13824   "Quelques Grands Pianistes." Jazz Hot no. 305:10-11, May 1974.

13825   Feather, L. "Jazz: Goodwill Ambassador Overseas; Fighter Against
        Jim Crow in the U. S." Billboard 86:N10, May 4, 1974.

13826   Beaupre, L. "White Showmen See Black Life 'All Babes, Needles,
        and Jive'; Black Intellectuals Hate It." Variety 275:3, May 15,
        1974.

13827   "Pitt's Black Tooters Suing AFM over Bias." Variety 275:93, May
        15, 1974.

13828   Furie, K. "Columbia's Black Composers Series." High Fidelity/
        Musical America 24:71-73, June 1974.

13829   Robinson, L. "Lull in Soul Means No 'Leadership.'" Billboard
        86:34, June 15, 1974.

13830   _____. "Indies Aid Musicians' A&R Goals." Billboard 86:36,
        June 22, 1974.

13831   Evans, D. "Techniques of Blues Composition Among Black Folk-
        singers." Journal of the American Folklore Society 87:240-249,
        July-September 1974.

13832   Roberts, J. S. "Columbia Launches Its Black Composers Series."
        Stereo Review 33:104-105, July 1974.

13833   Whalum, W. P. "The Spiritual as Mature Choral Composition."
        Black World 23:34-39, July 1974.

13834   Robinson, L. "Youth Puts His Faith in Black Music." Billboard
        86:27, July 6, 1974.

13835   "Finally, Black Composers Get the Recognition They Deserve."
        Soul 9:17, July 8, 1974.

13836   Lake, S. "Newport: from Boredom to Black Power." Melody Maker
        49:14, July 13, 1974.

13837   "Black Musicians Sue AFM in Pitt, Claiming Color Bias." Variety
        276:44, August 14, 1974.

13838   "Watergate Cop at Last, Wins Recognition from Black B'casters'
        Outfit." Variety 276:2, August 14, 1974.

13839   Robinson, L. "NATRA Conclave a Time for Sharing." Billboard
        86:3, August 17, 1974.

13840   "Gospel Workshop Looks to New Talent Era." Billboard 86:18, Au-
        gust 31, 1974.

13841   Commanday, R. "San Francisco: The Symphony Scandal." High
        Fidelity/Musical America 24:MA28-29, September 1974.

13842   Fine, M. "Jazz: Emergence as an International Art Form." Jazz
        Journal 27:16, September 1974.

13843   Wilson, W. G. "Black Classical Musicians: Their Struggle to the
        Top." Essence 5:58-59, September 1974.

13844   Burrell, W. "Watts Festival a Pathetic Flop." Soul 9:5, September
        3, 1974.

13845   Runcie, J. "American Negro Music Is Very Political, Whites Don't
        Want to Accept This." Melody Maker 40:30, September 21, 1974.

13846   Gleason, R. J. "Perspectives: Some Great Black Bands." Rolling
        Stone no. 170:30, September 26, 1974.

13847   "Second Annual Ebony Black Music Poll." Ebony 29:59-62, October
        1974.

13848   "Record Reviews: Black Composers Series." down beat 41:26, Oc-
        tober 10, 1974.

13849   Harris, C. G. "Three Schools of Black Choral Composers and Ar-
        rangers." School Music News 38:33-39, December 1974.

13850   Otto, J. S., and A. M. Burns. "Black and White Cultural Inter-
        action in the Early Twentieth Century South: Race and Hillbilly
        Music." Phylon 35:407-417, December 1974.

13851   Ardoyno, D. "Opera/South: Witness for the Defense." Opera Jour-
        nal 8:19-26, no. 4, 1975.

13852   Bartis, P. T. "An Examination of the Holler in North Carolina
        White Tradition." Southern Folklore Quarterly 39:209-217, no.
        3, 1975.

13853   "Black Musicians and Early Ethiopian Minstrelsy." Black Perspec-
        tives in Music 3:77-99, no. 1, 1975.

13854   Boyer, H. C. "An Analysis of Black Church Music with Examples
        Drawn from Services in Rochester, New York." Choral Journal
        16:23-24, no. 3, 1975.

13855   Branch, London Grigsby. "Jazz Education in Predominantly Black
        Colleges." (Ph.D. Dissertation, Southern Illinois University,
        1975).

13856   Brooks, T. "A Historical Study of Black Music and Selected Twen-
        tieth Century Black Composers and Their Role in American So-
        ciety." Choral Journal 16:24, no. 3, 1975.

13857 _____. "Why Study Black Music?" Musart 27:21-24, no. 3, 1975.

13858 Charters, Samuel Barclay. The Legacy of the Blues; A Glimpse in- to the Art and the Lives of 12 Great Bluesmen: An Informal Study. New York: Da Capo Press, 1977. Reprint of the 1975 edition published by Calder & Boyers, London. Blues musicians such as Memphis Slim and Lightnin' Hopkins are examined.

13859 Cohen, N. "Folk Music on Records." Western Folklore 34:350- 353, no. 4, 1975.

13860 Cummings, T. "Soul City, U.S.A." Melody Maker 50:18-19, Oc- tober 18, 1975. An excerpt from his book, The Sound of Phila- delphia.

13861 _____. The Sound of Philadelphia. London: Methuen, 1975. A history of black music and musicians in Philadelphia.

13862 Erlich, Lillian. What Jazz Is All About. Rev. ed. New York: J. Messner, 1975. Juvenile literature which is an introduction to jazz and includes biographical sketches of musicians such as Count Basie.

13863 Esquire. Esquire's World of Jazz. New York: Thomas Y. Crowell, 1975.

13864 "Film Reviews: Dry Wood and Hot Pepper." Ethnomusicology 19:339-341, no. 2, 1975.

13865 Floyd, S. A. "The Great Lakes Experience: 1942-45." Black Per- spectives in Music 3:17-24, no. 1, 1975.

13866 Garon, Paul. Blues & the Poetic Spirit. London: Eddison Press, 1975. An examination of blues in the U.S.

13867 Green, Mildred Benby. "A Study of the Lives and Works of Five Black Women Composers in America." (D. Mus.E. Dissertation, University of Oklahoma, 1975). Includes Florence B. Price, Mar- garet Bonds, Evelyn Pittman, Julia Perry, and Lena McLin.

13868 Guitar Notables: Brief Interviews from Guitar Player Magazine's "Pro's Reply" Column. Saratoga, Calif.: Guitar Player Produc- tions, 1975. Includes photographs and short interviews with gui- tarists such as Bo Diddley and Grant Green.

13869 Harris, C. G. "A Study of Characteristic Stylistic Trends Found in the Choral Works of a Selected Group of Afro-American Compos- ers and Arrangers." Choral Journal 16:22-23, no. 3, 1975.

13870 "In Retrospect--a Pictorial Survey." Black Perspectives in Music 3:207-234, no. 2, 1975.

13871 Jazz Guitarists: Collected Interviews from Guitar Player Magazine. Saratoga, Calif.: Guitar Player Productions, 1975. A few black musicians are interviewed, such as George Benson and Grant Green.

13872 Johnson, Theodore Wallace. "Black Images in American Popular
       Song, 1840-1910." (Ph.D. Dissertation, Northwestern University,
       1975).

13873 Kamin, J. "Music Culture and Perceptual Learning in the Populariza-
       tion of Black Music." Journal of Jazz Studies 3:54-65, no. 1,
       1975.

13874 _____. "The White R & B Audience and the Music Industry,
       1952-1956." Popular Music and Society 4:170-187, no. 3, 1975.

13875 Leonard, N. "Some Further Thoughts on Jazzmen as Romantic Out-
       siders." Journal of Jazz Studies 2:42-52, no. 2, 1975.

13876 Lornell, C. "Pre-Blues Black Music in Piedmont, North Carolina."
       North Carolina Folklore 23:26-32, no. 1, 1975.

13877 McNeill, Willie. "Verbal and Creative Responses by Fifth-Grade
       Children to Three Types of Black American Folk Music." (D. Ed.
       Dissertation, Pennsylvania State University, 1975).

13878 Maultsby, P. K. "Music of Northern Independent Black Churches
       During the Ante-bellum Period." Ethnomusicology 19:401-420,
       no. 3, 1975.

13879 Michaelis, A. "Still Music on the Western Air." Black Perspec-
       tives in Music 3:177-189, no. 2, 1975.

13880 Mitchell, Joseph Thurman. "Black Music in the University System
       of North Carolina: 1960-1974." (Ed.D. Dissertation, University
       of North Carolina at Greensboro, 1975).

13881 Morgenstern, D. "Notes and Comments: The 'Chicago Establish-
       ment' and Its Recordings." Journal of Jazz Studies 2:111-114,
       no. 2, 1975.

13882 Neff, Robert, and Anthony Connor. Blues. Boston: D. R. Godine,
       1975. Interviews with blues musicians.

13883 Olivier, C. "The End of the Old Sound." Jazz Report 8:13-14, no.
       6, 1975. Jazz in New Orleans is changing.

13884 Pinkston, Alfred Adolphus. "Lined Hymns, Spirituals, and the As-
       sociated Lifestyle of Rural Black People in the United States."
       (Ph.D. Dissertation, University of Miami, 1975).

13885 Raichelson, Richard M. "Black Religious Folksong: A Study in
       Generic and Social Change." (Ph.D. Dissertation, University of
       Pennsylvania, 1975).

13886 Reagen, Bernice Johnson. "Songs of the Civil Rights Movement,
       1955-1965: A Study in Culture History." (Ph.D. Dissertation,
       Howard University, 1975).

13887 "Record Reviews: Sorrow Come Pass Me Around: A Survey of
       Rural Black Religious Music." Ethnomusicology 19:500, no. 3,
       1975.

13888 Rehin, G. F. "Harlequin Jim Crow: Continuity and Convergence in Blackface Clowning." Journal of Popular Culture 9:682-701, no. 3, 1975.

13889 "Reports from Member Organizations." National Music Council Bulletin 34:8, no. 3, 1975; 38:12, no. 1, 1975. Reports from the Afro-American Music Opportunities Association.

13890 Reyes-Schramm, Adelaida. "The Role of Music in the Interaction of Black Americans and Hispanos in New York City's East Harlem." (Ph.D. Dissertation, Columbia University, 1975).

13891 Riedel, Johannes. Soul Music Black & White: The Influence of Black Music on the Churches. Minneapolis: Augsburg Pub. House, 1975.

13892 Rowe, Mike. Chicago Breakdown. New York: Drake Publishers, 1975. A history of black music and the blues.

13893 Ryder, G. A. "Another Look at Some American Cantatas." Black Perspectives in Music 3:135-40, no. 2, 1975.

13894 Sargeant, Winthrop. Jazz, Hot and Hybrid 3d ed., enl. New York: Da Capo Press, 1975. A thorough analysis of jazz which includes an examination of Bessie Smith's style as part of this study of the theory of jazz.

13895 Simosko, V. "Cross Cultures." Coda 12:2-5, no. 5, 1975.

13896 The Soul Book. Edited by Ian Hoare. London: E. Methuen, 1975. A history of black popular music in the U.S.

13897 Stevenson, G. "Race Records; Victims of Benign Neglect in Libraries." Wilson Library Bulletin 50:224-232, 1975.

13898 Taylor, J. E. "Somethin' on My Mind: A Cultural and Historical Interpretation of Spiritual Texts." Ethnomusicology 19:387-399, no. 3, 1975.

13899 Terkel, Studs. Giants of Jazz. Rev. ed. New York: Crowell, 1975. Examines 13 musicians, including Joe Oliver and Duke Ellington.

13900 Thompson, L. "The Black Performing Artist and Achievement." Black Perspectives in Music 3:160-164, no. 2, 1975.

13901 Vidossich, Edoardo. Sincretismos na Música Afro-Americana. São Paulo: Edições Quíron, 1975.

13902 Williams, Robert Caroll. "A Study of Religious Language: Analysis/Interpretation of Selected Afro-American Spirituals, with Reference to Black Religious Philosophy." (Ph.D. Dissertation, Columbia University, 1975).

13903 Williams-Jones, P. "Afro-American Gospel Music: A Crystallization of the Black Aesthetic." Ethnomusicology 19:373-385, no. 3, 1975.

13904 Campbell, D. "Black Musicians in Symphony Orchestras: A Bad Scene." Crisis 82:12-17, January 1975.

13905 Cummingham, C. "How Black Is Black? Black Composers Gather
       for Symposium and Performance Sessions." High Fidelity/Musical
       America 25:MA24-26, January 1975.

13906 Robinson, L. "'75 Can Be Better Year for Blacks." Billboard
       87:38, January 4, 1975.

13907 Tiegel, E. "Soul Community Picks Up Jazz Despite Sparse Play
       on Radio." Billboard 87:3, January 11, 1975.

13908 Tesser, N. "Jazzscene: Mingus Moves On." Melody Maker 50:32,
       January 25, 1975.

13909 Garland, P. "Ebony Black Music Poll: The Winners for 1975."
       Ebony 30:114-115, February 1975.

13910 Tiegel, E. "The Synthesizer; Improvising Requires Special Care
       Claims Herbie Hancock." Billboard 87:30, February 8, 1975.

13911 Palmer, B. "Perspective; What Is American Music?" down beat
       42:11, February 27, 1975.

13912 Welding, P. "Afro Mud: A Personalized History of the Blues."
       down beat 42:17-18, February 27, 1975.

13913 Cullaz, M. "Spirituals, Gospel, Blues, R'n'B, Soul Music et Jazz."
       Jazz Hot no. 314:24-26, March 1975.

13914 Melhuish, M. "Motown's Newman Views Involvement in Canada."
       Billboard 87:46, March 29, 1975.

13915 "Black Press Raps Cafe; Stars Who Never Return Home Again."
       Variety 278:62, April 9, 1975.

13916 Williams, J. "Soul of Chicago: Base for PUSH, NATRA Organiza-
       tions." Billboard 87:C14, April 19, 1975.

13917 "Talent in Action." Billboard 87:46, April 12, 1975. Review of
       the Black Classical Music Society.

13918 Ferdinand, V. "Expressions: A National Review of the Black Arts."
       Black Collegian 5:42-44, May-June 1975.

13919 "Soft-Soul Artists Finding U.K. Filled with Crossover Success."
       Billboard 87:53, May 17, 1975.

13920 "The Great Evolution of the Soul Revolution!" Soul 10:1-4, May 26,
       1975.

13921 "Stage Is a Style Show Where Anything Goes!" Soul 10:22, May 26,
       1975.

13922 Ross, L. "Black Talent Blooming in Country Mart." Billboard
       87:6, May 31, 1975.

13923 Goldstein, R. "Disco Soul: Melancholy Which Moves." Mademoi-
       selle 81:32, June 1975.

13924 "Record Reviews: Prison Worksongs." down beat 42:22-23, June 5, 1975.

13925 Schoenfeld, H. "Black Artists Surging Ahead in Disk Field." Variety 279:1, June 11, 1975.

13926 "Isolation of Black Music Spurs Debate." Billboard 87:16, June 14, 1975.

13927 "Motown LPs Herald Beat of Major Catalog Artists." Billboard 87:43, June 21, 1975.

13928 Williams, J. "Blacks Are Buying More Music." Billboard 87:43, June 21, 1975.

13929 "D.C. Solon-Artist Calls for Probe of Bias in Disk Biz." Variety 279:1, June 25, 1975.

13930 Brooks, T. "The Black Musician in American Society." Music Journal 33:40-45, July 1975.

13931 "Soul Explosion Rocks Land of Rising Sun." Ebony 30:42-44, July 1975.

13932 Hall, M. "IRS Admits Probing Disk Industry Taxes." Billboard 87:1, July 5, 1975.

13933 Underwood, L., and C. Kirk. "Black Recording Artists: No Longer Second Class." Soul 10:14, July 7, 1975.

13934 _____. "Music Industry: Black Money Is Black Power." Soul 10:16-17, July 21, 1975.

13935 Durrett, C. W. "Jackson." Opera 26:754-755, August 1975. Review of Opera South's production of the "Flying Dutchman."

13936 "Opera/South: 'Flying Dutchman.'" High Fidelity/Musical America 25:MA22-23, August 1975.

13937 "Ebony Black Music Poll." Ebony 30:64-68, October 1975.

13938 Frankenstein, A. "Columbia's Black Composers Series." High Fidelity/Musical America 25:65-66, October 1975.

13939 Southern, E. "Reviews of Records: Black Composers Series." Musical Quarterly 61:645-650, October 1975.

13940 "White Acts Breaking Black Radio's Color Barrier; Scot Combo Scores." Variety 280:107, October 1, 1975.

13941 "Records: Traveling Through the Jungle." Rolling Stone no. 198:71, October 23, 1975.

13942 Southern, E. "America's Black Composers of Classical Music." Music Educator's Journal 62:46-59, November 1975.

13943 Moss, R. F. "The Arts in Black America." Saturday Review 3:12-19, November 15, 1975.

13944   Cullaz, M. "La Voix dans la Musique Negro-Americaine." Jazz
        Hot no. 322:16-19, December 1975.

13945   Gleason, R. J. "Jazz Discography." Atlantic 236:110-111, Decem-
        ber 1975. An excerpt from J. Lyon's book, Celebrating the Duke
        and Louis, Bessie, Billie, Bird, Carmen, Miles, Dizzy and Other
        Heroes.

13946   Kirsch, B. "Black Gospel Changing." Billboard 87:3, December 6,
        1975.

13947   Williams, J. "Black Music Gets Break in Pictures." Billboard
        87:36, December 6, 1975.

13948   Brown, G. "White Leads Disco Overkill: Soul '75." Melody Maker
        50:21-22, December 27, 1975.

13949   Meyer, F. "Black Execs Moving from R&B Areas into Wider Re-
        sponsibility." Variety 281:1, December 31, 1975.

13950   Wheaton, J. "The Technological and Sociological Influences on Jazz
        as an American Art Form: The Impact of African Musical Cul-
        ture in America." Educator 9:6-9, no. 2, 1976-1977.

13951   Allen, W. F. "From the Preface to Slave Songs of the United States."
        Choral Journal 17:25-27, no. 2, 1976.

13952   Aning, B. A., et al. "Musical Behaviour and Music Education in
        Different Musical Settings, with Special Reference to the Back-
        grounds of Jazz." Jazz Research 8:137-157, 1976.

13953   Austin, Bill Joe. The Beat Goes On and On and On. Erwin, N.C.:
        Carolina Arts and Pub. House, 1976. Includes biographies of
        jazz musicians in the U.S.

13954   Beasley, Cecily Reeves. "Creole and Afro-Creole Music of Louisi-
        ana: Its Origin and Influence." (Ph.D. Dissertation, Florida
        State University, 1976).

13955   Berlin, Edward Alan. "Piano Ragtime: A Musical and Cultural
        Study." (Ph.D. Dissertation, City University of New York, 1976).

13956   Brask, Ole, and Dan Morgenstern. Jazz People. New York: H.
        N. Abrams, 1976.

13957   Burgett, Paul Joseph. "Aesthetics of the Music of Afro-Americans;
        A Critical Analysis of the Writings of Selected Black Scholars
        with Implications for Black Music Studies and for Music Educa-
        tion." (Ph.D. Dissertation, University of Rochester, Eastman
        School of Music, 1976).

13958   Dexter, Dave. Playback: A Newsman-Record Producers' Hits and
        Misses from the Thirties to the Seventies. New York: Billboard
        Publications, 1976.

13959   Dixon, Christa. Negro Spirituals: From Bible to Folk Song. Phil-
        adelphia: Fortress Press, 1976. A history of spirituals.

13960   Emerson, Lucy. The Gold Record. New York: Fountain Pub. Co.,

1976. Contains biographies of rock musicians, such as Gladys Knight and the Pips.

13961 Eppstein, D. J. "Documenting the History of Black Folk Music in the United States: A Librarian's Odyssey." Fontes Artis Musicae 23:151-157, no. 4, 1976.

13962 Evans, D. "Notes & Queries: The Singing-Stammerer Motif in Black Tradition." Western Folklore 35:157-160, no. 2, 1976.

13963 _____. "The Roots of Afro-American Gospel Music." Jazz Research 8:119-135, 1976.

13964 Eyle, Wim van. Jazz Pearls. Oudkarspel: W. van Eyle, 1976.

13965 Feather, Leonard G. The Book of Jazz, from Then till Now. Rev. New York: Dell, 1976.

13966 _____. The Pleasures of Jazz: Leading Performers on Their Lives, Their Music, Their Contemporaries. New York: Horizon Press, 1976.

13967 Franklin, Jacquelyn C. "Relationship Between Teacher Viewpoints Towards a Culturally Oriented Music Program and Black Pupils' Achievement and Viewpoints Towards the Program." (Ph.D. Dissertation, Purdue University, 1976).

13968 Gillett, Charlie, and Stephen Nugent. Rock Almanac: Top 20 Singles, 1955-73, and Top 20 Albums, 1964/73. New York: Doubleday, 1976.

13969 Goines, Leonard. "Walk Over; Music in the Slave Narratives." Sing Out 24:6-11, 1976.

13970 Grame, Theodore C. America's Ethnic Music. Tarpon Springs, Fla.: Cultural Maintenance Associates, 1976.

13971 Harrison, Max. A Jazz Retrospect. Newton Abbot, Eng.: David & Charles; Boston: Crescendo Pub. Co., 1976.

13972 Hentoff, N. "The Political Economy of Jazz." Social Policy 6:53-56, no. 5, 1976.

13973 Horne, Aaron. "A Comprehensive Performance Project in Clarinet Literature with an Essay on Solo and Chamber Music for Woodwinds by Black Composers Composed from 1893-1976." (D.M.A. Dissertation, University of Iowa, 1976).

13974 Hughes, Langston. The First Book of Jazz. Updated ed. New York: F. Watts, 1976. An introduction of the study of jazz with an emphasis on Louis Armstrong and Duke Ellington.

13975 Hunkemoeller, J. "Studien zur Idiomatik Afroamerikanischer Instrumentalmusik." Jazz Research 8:41-65, 1976.

13976 Jackson, I. V. "Afro-American Sacred Song in the Nineteenth Century: A Survey of a Neglected Source." Black Perspectives in Music 4:22-38, 1976.

13977 _____. "Black Women and Afro-American Song Tradition." Sing
         Out 25:10-13, no. 2, 1976.

13978 James, Janice Leggette. "The Music of Afro-Americans in Elem-
         entary Music Series Books; An Investigation of Changing Textbook
         Content, 1864 to 1970." (Ph.D. Dissertation, University of South-
         ern Mississippi, 1976).

13979 Kamin, Jonathan Liff. "Rhythm & Blues in White America: Rock
         and Roll as Acculturation and Perceptual Learning." (Ph.D. Dis-
         sertation, Princeton University, 1976).

13980 Kaslow, A., et al. "Jazz: Sounds of Survival." Sing Out 24:24-
         25, no. 6, 1976.

13981 Lampkins, Ernest Harold. "The Understanding and Teaching of Af-
         ro-American Music; 'A Case Study of the Lakeside School of Mu-
         sic.'" (Ph.D. Dissertation, University of Pittsburgh, 1976).

13982 Lee, A. "Black Music Study Traces Origin of Spirituals." Educator
         8:10, no. 4, 1976.

13983 Levy, Louis Herman. "The Formalization of New Orleans Jazz Mu-
         sicians; A Case Study of Organizational Change." (Ph.D. Disser-
         tation, Virginia Polytechnic Institute and State University, 1976).

13984 McClendon, W. H. "Black Music: Sound and Feeling for Black
         Liberation." Black Scholar 7:20-25, 1976.

13985 Malson, Lucien. Histoire du Jazz et de la Musique Afro-Améri-
         caine. Paris: Union Générale d'Editions, 1976.

13986 Maultsby, P. K. "Black Spirituals: An Analysis of Textual Forms
         and Structures." Black Perspectives in Music 4:54-69, 1976.

13987 Murray, Albert. Stomping the Blues. New York: McGraw-Hill,
         1976. A history of the blues from around the time of Bessie
         Smith (1920's) to the 1970's.

13988 Oakley, Giles. The Devil's Music: A History of the Blues. New
         York: Taplinger Pub. Co., 1977, c1976. Almost entirely devoted
         to black musicians and their lives.

13989 Reagon, B. "In Our Hands; Thoughts on Black Music." Sing Out
         24:1-2, no. 6, 1976.

13990 "Reports from Member Organizations." National Music Council Bul-
         letin 35:27, no. 2, 1976. Report of the National Association of
         Negro Musicians Incorporated.

13991 Roach, Hildred. Black American Music, Past and Present. Rev.
         ed. New York: Crescendo Pub. Co., 1976.

13992 Roberts, John Willie. "The Uses and Function of Afro-American
         Folk and Popular Music in the Literature of James Baldwin."
         (Ph.D. Dissertation, Ohio State University, 1976).

13993 Smith, Lamar. "A Study of the Historical Development of Selected
         Black College and University Bands as a Curricular and Aesthetic

Entity, 1867-1975." (Ph.D. Dissertation, Kansas State University, 1976).

13994 Taylor, John Armstead. "The Emergence of the Black Performing Musician in the American Symphony Orchestra." (Mus. Ed. D. Dissertation, Indiana University, 1976).

13995 Waldo, Terry. This Is Ragtime. New York: Hawthorn Books, 1976.

13996 Watkins, Clifford Edward. "The Works of Three Selected Band Directors in Predominantly-Black American Colleges and Universities." (Ph.D. Dissertation, Southern Illinois University, 1976).

13997 Wheaton, Jack William. "The Technological and Sociological Influences of Jazz as an Art Form in America." (Ed. D. Dissertation, University of Northern Colorado, 1976).

13998 Wilmer, Valerie. The Face of Black Music; Photographs. New York: Da Capo Press, 1976.

13999 McClendon, W. H. "Black Music: Sound and Feeling for Black Liberation." Black Scholar 7:20-25, January-February 1976.

14000 Pleasants, H. "Die Afro-Amerikanische Epoch in der Entwicklungsgeschichte Abendlaendischer Musik." Jazz Podium 25:6-8, January 1976.

14001 Rosemont, F., et al. "Surrealism & Blues." Living Blues 25:19-34, January-February 1976.

14002 "Tops in Pop." International Musician 74:9, January 1976. Overview of black music's evolution.

14003 Brown, G. "Can Whites Sing Soul?" Melody Maker 51:3, January 3, 1976.

14004 Williams, J. "Changes on the Way for Black Radio." Billboard 88:22-23, January 3, 1976.

14005 Masekela, H. "Black U.S. Stars Should Give More to S. African Blacks." Jet 49:44-45, January 15, 1976.

14006 Williams, J. "Black Is Beautiful." Billboard 88:40, January 31, 1976.

14007 Joyner, J. "Black Music in a White Church." Music Ministry 8:2-5, February 1976.

14008 "Black-Favoring Image Awards." Variety 282:28, February 11, 1976.

14009 "Black Acts Cut Full B. O. Share on Concert Trail." Variety 282:107, February 18, 1976.

14010 Brown, G. "Soul Searching Dialogue." Melody Maker 51:32-34, February 28, 1976.

14011 "Black Composers Prestige Concert." Variety 282:76, March 3, 1976.

14012 White, A. "Soul Music Hot in U.K." Billboard 88:6, March 13,
       1976.

14013 "1776-1976--It Happened." down beat 43:44, April 8, 1976.

14014 Hudgins, Stewart. "Jazz Musicians in Sketches." Black Scholar
       7:48-51, May 1976.

14015 Ryder, G. A. "Black Women in Song; Some Socio-Cultural Images;
       Address, October 1975." Negro History Bulletin 39:601-603, May
       1976.

14016 King, M. "Beale Street Urban Renewal Blues." Encore 5:16-18,
       May 3, 1976.

14017 Melanson, J. "Black Music Blossoms at CBS; May Account for 35-
       40% Sales." Billboard 88:45, May 15, 1976.

14018 "Music and Dance Celebrated at N.Y. 'All American Day Celebra-
       tion.'" Billboard 88:56, May 29, 1976.

14019 "Harvard U. Band Records Black American Composers Music for
       Voice of America." School Musician 47:20, June-July 1976.

14020 De Schauensee, M. "Philadelphia." Opera News 40:39-40, June
       1976. National Opera Ebony performs "Aida."

14021 Garland, P. "Ebony Music Poll: The Winners for 1976." Ebony
       31:62-64, June 1976.

14022 Rivers, C. J. "Black Culture in the Ecumenical Movement." Mu-
       sic Ministry 8:2-5, June 1976.

14023 Tusher, W. "Dismantle Entertainment Checks on Minority Hiring
       Practices." Variety 283:28, June 2, 1976.

14024 Freedland, N. "WB's All-Out Campaign Moves Black Talent into
       Prominence." Billboard 88:33, June 5, 1976.

14025 Williams, J. "Conference Pulls 200 to Detroit." Billboard 88:54,
       June 12, 1976.

14026 _____. "Put Black Back into Black Radio Is Group's Goal."
       Billboard 88:39, June 12, 1976.

14027 Douglas, C. C. "Spinners." Ebony 31:40-41, July 1976.

14028 "Best of Soul: Albums." Billboard 88:MR120, July 4, 1976. List
       of the best soul albums each year 1966-1975.

14029 "Best of Soul: Artists." Billboard 88:MR126, July 4, 1976. List
       of artists 1946-1975.

14030 "Best of Soul: Singles." Billboard 88:MR118, July 4, 1976. List
       of single hits yearly 1946-1963, 1965-1975.

14031 Lewis, G. H. "Protest and Social Change in Black American Popu-
       lar Music." Billboard 88:MR147, July 4, 1976.

14032   Green, P.   "Black Now Beautiful to Majors; Col, Cap & WB Gain
        Understanding with the Years."   Billboard 88:6, July 24, 1976.

14033   Locke, T. A.   "Forgotten Sacred Harp."   Negro History Bulletin
        39:6190621, September 1976.

14034   Maynor, D.   "The Spiritual as Soul Music."   Saturday Review 3:38,
        September 4, 1976.

14035   Morrison, H.   "See Politics in N. Y.   Charge of Legit Tooter Hiring
        Bias."   Variety 284:85, September 29, 1976.

14036   Garland, P.   "Fourth Annual Ebony Black Music Poll."   Ebony
        31:178, October 1976.

14037   Houlihan, B.   "How Harlem Captured Broadway."   Sepia 25:34-38,
        October 1976.

14038   "Stars Join Ebony in Salute to Black Music."   Ebony 31:176-177,
        October 1976.

14039   Freedland, N.   "Biggest Concert Tour for Black Acts Tees."   Bill-
        board 88:1, October 2, 1976.

14040   Gravett, J.   "Black Musicals: A White Opinion."   Encore 5:27-28,
        October 4, 1976.

14041   "Black Press First Bias Charge Vs. Hub Nitery; Liquor in Jeopardy."
        Variety 284:79, October 27, 1976.

14042   Adderton, D.   "Jazz Artists Reflect on 25 Years of Black Music."
        Jet 51:124, November 11, 1976.

14043   Graves, E. A.   "A Gift of Music."   Black Enterprise 7:7, Decem-
        ber 1976.

14044   King, A.   "Black Music History: Who, What, Where."   Essence
        4:34, December 1976.

14045   Weathers, D.   "Managing the Muses; The Business Side of Black
        Music."   Black Enterprise 7:21-27, December 1976.

14046   Wortham, J.   "Blacks in the World of Orchestras."   Black Enter-
        prise 7:31-32, December 1976.

14047   "Blacks in Push Against 'Sex Rock'; Say Song Lyrics Promote Il-
        legitimacy."   Variety 285:1, December 1, 1976.

14048   "Suspend Boston Disco for Bias Against Blacks; Warn Area Clubs."
        Variety 285:65, December 1, 1976.

14049   Abdul, Raoul.   Blacks in Classical Music: A Personal History.
        New York: Dodd, Mead, 1977.   Organized into sections by types
        of musicians, as composers, singers, and instrumentalists.

14050   Allen, H. T.   "Is There an American 'Shape of the Liturgy'?   Re-
        sponse 17:7-27, no. 2, 1977.

14051   Balliett, Whitney.   Improvising: Sixteen Jazz Musicians and Their

Art. New York: Oxford University Press, 1977. Includes discussion of Joe Oliver and Earl Hines.

14052   Berry, Peter E. "... and the Hits Just Keep on Comin." Syracuse, N.Y.: Syracuse University Press, 1977. A chronological history of popular music, 1955-76, with information on black musicians such as Ray Charles and Aretha Franklin.

14053   Broven, John. Walking to New Orleans: The Story of New Orleans Rhythm & Blues. 2d ed. Bexhill-on-Sea, England: Flyright, 1977. Covers 1946-1973 with extensive listings of musicians and their recordings.

14054   Cole, M. S. "Afrika Singt: Austro-German Echoes of the Harlem Renaissance." Journal of the American Musicological Society 30:72-95, no. 1, 1977.

14055   Dufour, Barry. The World of Pop and Rock. London: Macdonald Educational, 1977.

14056   Dyen, D. J. "The Role of Shape-Note Singing in the Musical Culture of Black Communities in Southeast Alabama." (Ph.D. Dissertation, University of Illinois at Urbana Champaign, 1977).

14057   Epstein, Dena J. Sinful Tunes and Spirituals: Black Folk Music to the Civil War. Urbana: University of Illinois Press, 1977.

14058   Ewen, David. All the Years of American Popular Music. Englewood Cliffs, N.J.: Prentice-Hall, 1977.

14059   Goldblatt, Burt. Newport Jazz Festival: The Illustrated History. New York: Dial Press, 1977. Highlights of each festival held since 1954.

14060   Grobman, N. R. "The Role of Popular Nineteenth-Century Periodical Literature in Shaping Afro-American Religious Folksong Scholarship." New York Folklore 2:43-59, no. 3-4, 1977.

14061   Haskins, James. The Cotton Club. New York: Random House, 1977. A story of this nightclub in Harlem and many of the performers who began their careers in show business there.

14062   Humanities Through the Black Experience. By David N. Baker, et al. Dubuque, Iowa: Kendall/Hunt Pub. Co., 1977.

14063   Hunkemoeller, J. "Zur Terminologie Afro-Amerikanischer Musik." Jazz Research 9:69-88, 1977.

14064   Lamaison, Jean Louis. Soul Music. Paris: A. Michel, 1977.

14065   Lemmon, A. E. "Los Jesuitas y la Musica de los Negros." Heterofonia 10:5-9, no. 57, 1977.

14066   McCall, M. "Afro-American Music: Let Americans Be Proud of Their Musical Heritage." Freeing the Spirit 5:6-9, 1977.

14067   Marshall, Ammie Theresa Hooper. "An Analysis of Music Curricula and Its Relationship to the Self-Image of Urban Black Middle-

School Age Children." (Ph.D. Dissertation, Rutgers University, 1977).

14068 Mauro, Walter. Il Blues e l'America Nera. Milano: Garzanti, 1977.

14069 Moore, Marvelene Clarisa. "Multicultural Music Education: An Analysis of Afro-American and Native American Folk Songs in Selected Elementary Music Textbooks of the Periods 1928-1955 and 1965-1975." (Ph.D. Dissertation, University of Michigan, 1977).

14070 Music in American Society, 1776-1976: From Puritan Hymn to Synthesizer. Edited by George McCue. New Brunswick, N.J.: Transaction Books, 1977. Includes a chapter by E. Southern: "The History of Black Music."

14071 Pickett, Andrew Morris. "The Use of Black American Slave Folk Songs in the Social Studies Curriculum." (Ph.D. Dissertation, University of Illinois at Urbana-Champaign, 1977).

14072 "Problems of Black Composers Faced by MECA Symposium." Symphony News 28:7, no. 1, 1977.

14073 Rivers, C. J. "Should a White Parish Sing Black Music?" Pastoral Music 1:10-12, no. 5, 1977.

14074 Schafer, William John, and Richard B. Allen. Brass Bands and New Orleans Jazz. Baton Rouge: Louisiana State University Press, 1977.

14075 Selections from the Gutter: Jazz Portraits from "The Jazz Record." Edited by Art Hodes, and Chadwick Hansen. Berkeley: University of California Press, 1977. Information on jazz musicians such as Louis Armstrong and Sidney Bechet.

14076 Solothurnmann, J. "Insights and Views of the Art Ensemble of Chicago." Jazz Forum no. 49:28-33, 1977.

14077 _____. "Zur Aesthetik der Afro-Amerikanischen Musik: Timbre-Geraeusch-Emotion." Jazz Research 9:49-68, 1977.

14078 Southern, E. "Musical Practices in Black Churches of Philadelphia and New York, ca. 1800-1844." Journal of the American Musicological Society 30:296-312, no. 2, 1977.

14079 Taft, Michael Ernest. "The Lyrics of Race Record Blues, 1920-1942: A Semantic Approach to the Structural Analysis of a Formulaic System." (Ph.D. Dissertation, Memorial University of Newfoundland, Canada, 1977).

14080 Tanner, Paul, and Maurice Gerow. A Study of Jazz. 3d ed. Dubuque, Iowa: W. C. Brown, 1977. A survey of jazz in which the contributions of many black musicians are noted.

14081 Tirro, Frank. Jazz: A History. New York: Norton, 1977.

14082 Titon, Jeff Todd. Early Downhome Blues: A Musical and Cultural

Analysis. Urbana: University of Illinois Press, 1977. An examination of the music and culture of blues musicians.

14083 Warrick, Mancel, Joan R. Hillsman, and Anthony Manno. The Progress of Gospel Music: From Spirituals to Contemporary Gospel. New York: Vantage Press, 1977. A short history of gospel music in the U.S. with many references to black musicians and their contributions.

14084 Wilmer, Valerie. As Serious as Your Life: The Story of the New Jazz. New York: Quartet Books, 1977.

14085 _____. Jazz People. 3d ed. London: Allison & Busby Ltd., 1977. This book is based on interviews with fourteen jazz musicians including Thelonious Monk.

14086 Williams, J. "Old Strategies Revamped by Black Industry Execs." Billboard 89:8, January 8, 1977.

14087 "Jazzmobile Expands School Projects for Ghetto Children." Variety 286:61, February 23, 1977.

14088 Milner, A. "Life from the Library; Program of the Free Library of Philadelphia's Fleisher Collection." American Libraries 8:75-76, February 1977.

14089 Price, A. F. "Younger Elementary Music." Music Ministry 9:24-25, February 1977. Discussion of spirituals which elementary school children sing.

14090 Williams, J. "Blacks Draw a Blank in Symphonies." Billboard 89:1, February 12, 1977.

14091 "Duke Scholarship to N.Y. Musician Residing in L.A." Billboard 89:53, February 19, 1977. The Jazz Heritage Foundation awards Duke Ellington Composer/Arranger Scholarship.

14092 Lees, G. "At a Nation's Heart; Ethnicity of Sounds in Jazz." High Fidelity/Musical America 27:22, March 1977.

14093 "Black Promoter Raps Cut-ins by Disk Jocks at FCC Payola Probe." Variety 286:2, March 2, 1977.

14094 "NARM Seminar Goes to Roots of Black Music Role in Disk Biz." Variety 286:65-66, March 9, 1977.

14095 Williams, J. "Black AM Audiences Lured by FM Sound." Billboard 89:1, March 12, 1977.

14096 "'Soul Amba' Blends Black Sound with Native Brazilian Music." Variety 286:78, April 6, 1977.

14097 Williams, J. "Byrd Organizes Talent to Aid Black Colleges." Billboard 89:1, April 23, 1977.

14098 "Claim Prejudice by Establishment in Broadcasting Curbs Minorities." Variety 286:1, May 4, 1977.

14099 "Waxing On: Detroit Ghetto Blues." down beat 44:28-32, May 5, 1977.

14100 Williams, J. "Black Music Trend: Soft & Mellow." Billboard
       89:1, May 7, 1977.

14101 Lees, G. "Mu$ic U.$.A.; Jazz: Music of Exile." High Fidelity/
       Musical America 27:19-20, June 1977.

14102 Godwin, H. E. "Listen! Hear That Original Memphis Sound?"
       Second Line 29:36-37, Summer 1977. Discussion of early Beale
       Street blues.

14103 De Schauensee, M. "Philadelphia." Opera News 41:36, June 1977.
       National Opera Ebony presents "Faust" in Philadelphia.

14104 "700 Tradesters Show for Black Radio-Music Event." Billboard
       89:75, June 11, 1977.

14105 "Boston Blacks Win Important Victory in Disco Bias Case." Variety
       287:73, June 15, 1977.

14106 Williams, J. "Atlanta Confab Tees Soul Caucus; Rapper 'Affair'
       Sees Execs Focus on Black Industry." Billboard 89:51, June 25,
       1977.

14107 "Black-Owned Stations Form Industry Group." Variety 287:1, June
       29, 1977.

14108 "Ebony Music Poll: The Winners for 1977." Ebony 32:83-84, July
       1977.

14109 Storb, I. "Jazz und Afro-Amerikanistik." Jazz Podium 26:21-22,
       July 1977.

14110 Williams, J. "3 Confabs 2 Too Many, Critics Say." Billboard
       89:36-37, July 2, 1977.

14111 "New Studies Explore Black American Music." School Musician
       49:20, August-September 1977.

14112 Flores, A. "Authorities Act, Make It Easier to Be Admitted to
       N.Y. Clubs." Billboard 89:48, September 3, 1977.

14113 Kerner, L. "The Whiter Half of a Black Heritage." Village Voice
       22:71-72, September 19, 1977.

14114 Gillespie, M. A. "Black Music." Essence 8:59, October 1977.

14115 Hentoff, N. "My Life in Country Music." Village Voice 22:37-38,
       October 3, 1977.

14116 Williams, J. "L.A. Small Labels Walk Pickets; Independents Ac-
       cuse Radio of Major Label Favoritism." Billboard 89:46, October
       8, 1977.

14117 Kolodin, I. "Music to My Ears: Convocation at the Philharmonic."
       Saturday Review 5:42-43, October 15, 1977. The Philharmonic
       Symphony Orchestra hold a "Celebration of Black Composers."

14118   "Black Tooter Sues AFM, Vegas Hotel for Racial Firing."   Variety
        288:73, October 26, 1977.

14119   "LP's: If Beale St. Could Talk; A Selection of Pre-War Memphis
        Blues Favorites 1928-1939."   Living Blues no. 35:31, November-
        December 1977.

14120   Armstrong, R.   "Blacks and Bluegrass: A Study in Musical Inte-
        gration."   Bluegrass 12:22-24, November 1977.

14121   Haskins, J.   "Cotton Club."   Essence 8:64-69, November 1977.

14122   "Musexpo Report: Black Crossover Spotlighted."   Billboard 89:40,
        November 12, 1977.

14123   Farrell, D.   "Canadian Airwaves Lack Soul."   Billboard 89:3, No-
        vember 19, 1977.

14124   Adderton, D.   "Jazz Giants Help Turn Black Music Classical."   Jet
        53:18-19, November 24, 1977.

14125   "10 Years of Top Soul Music Stars."   Jet 53:61-63, November 24,
        1977.

14126   Leibow, L. A., and A. Slovin.   "Music in America."   Strad 88:767,
        December 1977.

14127   Lane, S.   "Black Radio Today: Difficult to Program."   Billboard
        89:32, December 10, 1977.

14128   "Jazz Albums: Black California."   Melody Maker 52:24, December
        17, 1977.

14129   Gallagher, B.   "The Year of Soul."   Melody Maker 52:24, Decem-
        ber 31, 1977.

14130   The Afro-American in Music and Art.   Edited by Lindsay Patterson.
        1979 ed. Cornwells Heights, Pa.: Publishers Agency, 1978.
        Earlier editions published as The Negro in Music and Art.

14131   Bastin, B.   "Flyright Records: Aims and Objectives of a Small
        Documentary Concern."   JEMF Quarterly 14:75-77, no. 50, 1978.

14132   The Black Composer Speaks.   Edited by David N. Baker, Lida M.
        Belt, and Herman C. Hudson.   Metuchen, N.J.: Scarecrow Press,
        1978.   "A project of the Afro-American Arts Institute, Indiana
        University."   Fifteen composers give their views of black music.

14133   Budds, Michael J.   Jazz in the Sixties: The Expansion of Musical
        Resources and Techniques.   Iowa City: University of Iowa Press,
        1978.   An examination of factors which influenced the styles of
        the 1960's.

14134   Collier, James Lincoln.   The Making of Jazz: A Comprehensive
        History.   Boston: Houghton Mifflin, 1978.   Examines the chron-
        ological development of jazz from its "African Roots" to "The
        Future," and includes materials on the contributions of prominent
        black jazz musicians.

14135   Coryell, Julie, and Laura Friedman. Jazz-Rock Fusion: The Peo-
        ple, the Music. New York: Delacorte Press, 1978. Includes
        photograph, biography, and interview with over fifty jazz and rock
        musicians such as Miles Davis.

14136   Csida, Joseph, and June Bundy Csida. American Entertainment; A
        Unique History of Popular Show Business. New York: Watson-
        Guptill, 1978. Traces the history of popular entertainment, ex-
        cluding classical forms. Much of the materials is reprinted from
        Billboard and one section is entitled "A Breakthrough for Blacks."

14137   Craig, Warren. Sweet and Lowdown: America's Popular Song Writ-
        ers. Metuchen, N.J.: Scarecrow Press, 1978. Includes bio-
        graphical sketches of song writers plus lists of their works.

14138   Girard, H. A. "Hundert Jahre Negro Spirituals in de Schweiz."
        Musik und Gottesdienst 32:90-96, no. 3, 1978.

14139   Green, A. "Graphics: Miguel Covarrubias' Jazz and Blues Mu-
        sicians." JEMF Quarterly 13:183-195, no. 48, 1977.

14140   Gridley, Mark C. Jazz Styles. Englewood Cliffs, N.J.: Prentice-
        Hall, 1978. Musical styles of musicians such as Miles Davis and
        Ornette Coleman are examined.

14141   Jasen, David A., and Trebor Jay Tichenor. Rags and Ragtime: A
        Musical History. New York: Seabury Press, 1978. Short biog-
        raphies of black musicians such as Scott Joplin and Jelly Roll
        Morton are included.

14142   Kings of Jazz. Edited by Stanley Green. Rev. South Brunswick,
        N.J.: A. S. Barnes, 1978. Biographies of eleven jazz musicians,
        originally published separately. Louis Armstrong, Charlie Parker,
        and Bessie Smith are among those discussed.

14143   Lyons, Jimmy, and Ira Kamin. Dizzy, Duke, the Count and Me:
        The Story of the Monterey Jazz Festival. San Francisco: Calif-
        ornia Living Book, 1978. Photographs and information covering
        the festival from 1958-1977.

14144   "New Orleans Jazz Museum and Jazz Hall of Fame to Be Established
        at the State Museum." Swinging Newsletter 8:3, no. 35, 1978.

14145   Ostransky, Leroy. Jazz City: The Impact of Our Cities on the De-
        velopment of Jazz. Englewood Cliffs, N.J.: Prentice-Hall, 1978.
        Examination of the influence of various cities, as New Orleans,
        Chicago, and New York, on the development of jazz. Musicians
        such as Count Basie and Duke Ellington are discussed.

14146   Pearson, Barry Lee. "The Life Story of the Blues Musician: An
        Analysis of the Traditions of Oral Self-Portrayal." (Ph.D. Dis-
        sertation, Indiana University, 1978).

14147   Reagon, B. "Sanctuary of Black Song: Creating the Georgia Sea
        Island Festival." Sing Out 26:22-29, no. 4, 1978.

14148   Rose, A., and Edmond Souchon. New Orleans Jazz: A Family Al-
        bum. Rev. Baton Rouge: Louisiana State University Press, 1978.

14149   Shaw, Arnold.   Honkers and Shouters: The Golden Years of Rhythm
        and Blues.   New York: Macmillan, 1978.   Rhythm and blues re-
        placed "race" music, and this work concentrates on a fifteen-year
        period of recordings, 1945-1960.

14150   Stevenson, R.   "El Elemento Negro en los Albores de la Musica
        del Nuevo Mundo."   Heterofonia 11:4-9, no. 59, 1978.

14151   The Story of Jazz: From New Orleans to Rock Jazz.   Edited by
        Joachim-Ernest Berendt.   Englewood Cliffs, N.J.:   Prentice-Hall,
        1978.

14152   Giddins, G.   "Weatherbird: American Money for American Music."
        Village Voice 23:62, January 2, 1978.

14153   Ford, R.   "Boom Proves Boon for Blacks; Artists, Producers, Song-
        writers Busily Meet Demand."   Billboard 90:73, January 14, 1978.

14154   "Black Acts Use Staging Savvy to Enhance Live Concert Dates."
        Variety 289:84, January 18, 1978.

14155   Cullaz, M.   "La Voix dans la Musique Negro-Americaine."   Jazz
        Hot no. 346:12-19, February 1978.

14156   Demetre, J.   "Evenements & Figures Historiques à Travers les
        Chants Populaires Noirs."   Jazz Hot no. 346:20-25, February
        1978.

14157   "Music in the Black Church."   Journal of Church Music 20:2-6, Feb-
        ruary 1978.

14158   Wiesmann, C.   "Jazz im Unterricht."   Musikerziehung 31:161-166,
        February 1978.

14159   Williams, J.   "4 L.A. Black Stations Cite Music over DJ."   Bill-
        board 90:28, February 18, 1978.

14160   Cooper, B. L.   "Record Revivals as Barometers of Social Change:
        The Historical Use of Contemporary Audio Resources."   JEMF
        Quarterly 14:38-44, Spring 1978.

14161   Thornton, C.   "Nouvelle Musique, Nouvelle Conscience."   Jazz Mag-
        azine no. 263:34-35, March-April 1978.

14162   Demetre, J.   "Evenements & Figures Historiques à Travers les
        Chants Populaires Noirs."   Jazz Hot no. 347:20-23, March 1978.

14163   "Blacks Organize Own Association."   Billboard 90:26, March 4,
        1978.   The Black Music Association of America is established.

14164   Goldstein, R.   "Artbreaks: For Colored Folks Who Have Considered
        Censorship."   Village Voice 23:44, March 13, 1978.

14165   Williams, J.   "Black Music Assn. Succeeds NATRA."   Billboard
        90:1, March 18, 1978.

14166   Kozak, R.   "CBS Hikes Community Relations; Black Marketing Head
        Claims 25% of Ethnic Sales Pie."   Billboard 90:6, March 25, 1978.

14167   Demetre, J. "Evenements & Figures Historiques à Travers." Jazz
        Hot no. 348:14-17, April 1978.

14168   Haas, C. "Rhythm Without Blues; New Soul." New Times 10:62-
        66, April 17, 1978.

14169   "All Black Symphony to Preem in Phillu." Variety 290:2, April 19,
        1978.

14170   Williams, J. "New Black Assn. Asks Industry Funding." Billboard
        90:6, April 29, 1978.

14171   "Record Reviews: The Changing Face of Harlem, Vol. II." Radio
        Free Jazz 19:27, May 1978.

14172   Orodenker, M. "All-Black Symphony for Philly." Billboard 90:51,
        May 6, 1978. The National Afro-American Philharmonic Orches-
        tra is founded in Philadelphia.

14173   "Black Is Black, White Is White, but Things Sometimes Look Alike."
        Variety 291:448, May 17, 1978.

14174   Williams, J. "Soul Sauce: L.A. Births Classic Tie to Church."
        Billboard 90:68-69, May 20, 1978.

14175   "New Black Music Assn. Debuts with Malamud in Philly." Billboard
        90:3, May 27, 1978.

14176   "Black Music Assn. Formed in Philly with Ethnic Aims." Variety
        291:79, May 31, 1978.

14177   Freis, R. "Jackson, Miss." Opera News 42:34, June 1978. Opera/
        South performs in Jackson.

14178   Evensmo, J. "Jazz Solographies." Coda no. 161:16, June 1, 1978.

14179   Williams, J. "Blacks Question Malamud's Post; Wonder Why a
        White Heads New Black Music Assn." Billboard 90:59, June 3,
        1978. Jules Malamud is in charge of the Black Music Associa-
        tion of America.

14180   Williams, J. "78 Image Awards Snake-Bitten." Billboard 90:61,
        June 10, 1978.

14181   _____. "Black Music: New Association Progressing Well as
        Labels Donate Substantial $$." Billboard 90:81, June 17, 1978.

14182   Ford, R. "Black Patrons Significant in Club Activities." Billboard
        90:59, June 24, 1978.

14183   Williams, J. "Meeting of Blacks Brings Plea to Train Youngsters."
        Billboard 90:4, June 24, 1978.

14184   _____. "Soul Sauce: Poor Image by NAACP at Awards." Bill-
        board 90:48, June 24, 1978.

14185   Phillips, W. "The Therapeutics of the Blues." Cadence 4:17-19,
        July 1978.

14186 Betts, G. "Heart and Soul." Melody Maker 53:26-27, July 1, 1978.
       Discussion of the ways black musicians strive to help solve social
       problems.

14187 Williams, J. "Black Industry Issues Probed at Jack the Rapper's
       Confab." Billboard 90:47, July 1, 1978.

14188 _____. "Soul Sauce: Good & Bad at Atlanta Convention." Bill-
       board 90:46-47, July 1, 1978.

14189 _____. "Soul Sauce: The Rapper Owes 1 to 'The Hawk.'" Bill-
       board 90:34-35, July 8, 1978.

14190 _____. "Southern DJs: New Assn. Organized to Assist Blacks;
       Medlin Named Chief." Billboard 90:37, July 15, 1978.

14191 Grein, P. "Twist to an L.A. Awards Dinner." Billboard 90:57,
       August 5, 1978.

14192 Meyer, F. "WEA Cultivating Minority Retailer in Push to Build
       Black Product." Variety 292:49, August 9, 1978.

14193 Williams, J. "NARM Beefs Up Pursuit of Black Dealer in Meets."
       Billboard 90:3, August 12, 1978.

14194 _____. "Soul Sauce: Image Fete Flops, Axed by NAACP." Bill-
       board 90:60, August 12, 1978.

14195 "Far Out Prods. Toppers Analyze Disk Biz Music 'Color' Problems."
       Variety 292:64-65, August 16, 1978.

14196 Feather, L. "Where Have All the Young Men Gone?" Melody Mak-
       er 53:28, August 26, 1978. Fewer blacks are becoming jazz mu-
       sicians it appears.

14197 Williams, J. "Soul Sauce: NARM Gets 30% Blacks in Detroit."
       Billboard 90:40, August 26, 1978.

14198 Orton, R. "Black Folk Entertainments and the Evolution of American
       Minstrelsy." Negro History Bulletin 41:885-887, September 1978.

14199 Kirk, C. "PUSH Pushing for Black Radio Ban of Rolling Stones'
       Hit Album." Variety 292:1, September 6, 1978.

14200 "Black Music Assn. Gets Heavy Disk Biz Backing at L.A. Launch."
       Variety 292:103, September 13, 1978.

14201 Kubernik, H. "Moves to Black Stones' Girls LP." Melody Maker
       53:5, September 16, 1978.

14202 Williams, J. "Soul Sauce: PUSH Hot to Boycott Stones' Cut." Bill-
       board 90:52, September 16, 1978.

14203 Grein, P. "Black Music Assn. Firms Heads, Bylaws." Billboard
       90:3, September 23, 1978.

14204 "Black Music in Nevada Classes." Billboard 90:38, September 30,
       1978.

14205 Dixon, C. K. "Negro Spirituals from Bible to Folksong." Journal of Church Music 20:11, October 1978.

14206 "Nat. Afro-American Philharmonic." High Fidelity/Musical America 28:MA40-41, October 1978.

14207 Rozek, M. "What Is Funk?" High Fidelity/Musical America 28:160-162, October 1978.

14208 "Motown Finally Seeing Evidence That Black Music Can Sell Well in Canada." Billboard 90:76, October 7, 1978.

14209 "Lots of Reasons for Black Tooters to Live in Europe." Variety 292:2, October 18, 1978.

14210 "Black Representation Increased." International Musician 77:4, November 1978.

14211 Wilmer, V. "Music as an Escape from the Ghetto." Jazz Journal International 31:8, November 1978.

14212 Betts, G. "The Motown Machine--from Detroit to L.A." Melody Maker 53:39-41, November 18, 1978.

14213 Williams, J. "Cornelius Urges Acts to Use TV." Billboard 90:36, November 18, 1978.

14214 "Black Music Association Asks Bigger Ethnic Piece of the Disk Action." Variety 293:116, November 22, 1978.

14215 Salaam, A. "Money, Management, and All That Jazz; Collective Black Artists, Inc." Black Enterprise 9:45-47, December 1978.

14216 Ford, R. "Black Music Assn. Discloses Goals at Implementation Meet." Billboard 90:47, December 2, 1978.

14217 Norman, P. "Ol' Black Rock: A Short Story." Melody Maker 53:19-20, December 23, 1978.

14218 Balliett, Whitney. American Singers. New York: Oxford University Press, 1979. Profiles of jazz singers such as Billie Holiday and Alberta Hunter.

14219 Berendt, Joachim Ernst. Jazz, a Photo History. New York: Schirmer Books, 1979. Traces the development of jazz from New Orleans to the present.

14220 Hamm, Charles E. Yesterdays: Popular Song in America. New York: Norton, 1979. Includes information on black singers such as Johnny Mathis and Ray Charles.

14221 Lyttelton, Humphrey. The Best of Jazz: Basin Street to Harlem: Jazz Masters and Masterpieces, 1917-1930. Examines jazz music and musicians of the 1920's. Louis Armstrong and Bessie Smith are among the musicians discussed.

14222 Palmer, Robert. A Tale of Two Cities: Memphis Rock and New Orleans Roll. Brooklyn: Brooklyn College of the City University of New York, 1979. A brief survey of rock music's history in two cities including many black musicians.

14223   Rosenberg, Deena, and Bernard Rosenberg. The Music Makers. New York: Columbia University Press, 1979. One section is "Music of the Inner City" and includes an interview with Dorothy Maynor.

14224   Tudor, Dean, and Nancy Tudor. Black Music. Littleton, Colo.: Libraries Unlimited, 1979.

14225   _____. Jazz. Littleton, Colo.: Libraries Unlimited, 1979.

III.   REFERENCE WORKS

14226 "Bibliography of Negro Folk Songs." Journal of the American Folklore Society 24:393-394, 1911.

14227 New York Public Library. The Folk Music of the Western Hemisphere; A List of References in the New York Public Library. Compiled by Julius Mattfeld. New York: Public Library, 1925. Reprinted, with additions, from the Bulletin of the New York Public Library, November-December 1924. Includes bibliographical references on black music in the U.S.

14228 Becker, M. L. "Reader's Guide." Saturday Review of Literature 8:497, January 30, 1932.

14229 Cleveland. Public Library. Index to Negro Spirituals. Cleveland: Cleveland Public Library, 1937.

14230 Smith, Charles Edward, et al. The Jazz Record Book. New York: Smith & Durrell, 1942. A discography of jazz records which includes an "Index of bands and other recording units."

14231 Pensoneault, Ken, and Carl Sarles. Jazz Discography: Additions and Corrections. New York: Dart Press, 1944.

14232 Merriam, Alan P. "An Annotated Bibliography of African & African-Derived Music Since 1936." Africa 21:319-330, October 1951.

14233 Lucas, John. Basic Jazz on Long Play; The Great Soloists: Ragtime, Folksong, Blues, Jazz, Swing, and the Great Bands: New Orleans, Swing, Dixieland. Northfield, Minn.: Carleton Jazz Club, Carleton College, 1954.

14234 George, Zelma Watson. "A Guide to Negro Music: An Annotated Bibliography of Negro Folk Music, and Art Music by Negro Composers or Based on Negro Thematic Material." (Ph.D. Dissertation, New York University, 1954).

14235 Merriam, Alan P. A Bibliography of Jazz. New York: Da Capo, 1970. Reprint of the 1954 edition published by the American Folklore Society, Philadelphia. Contains over 3000 entries.

14236 Ramsey, Frederic. A Guide to Longplay Jazz Records. New York: Da Capo, 1977. Reprint of the 1954 edition published by Long Player, New York.

14237 Reisner, Robert George. The Literature of Jazz, a Preliminary Bibliography. New York: New York Public Library, 1954. Reprinted from the Bulletin of the New York Public Library, March-May 1954.

14238 American Music Center, New York. American Music on Records;
       A Catalogue of Recorded American Music Currently Available.
       New York: American Music Center, 1956.

14239 Harris, Rex, and Brian Rust. Recorded Jazz; A Critical Guide.
       Harmondsworth, Middlesex: Penguin Books, 1958.

14240 Reisner, Robert George. The Literature of Jazz, a Selective Bib-
       liography. 2d ed. rev. and enl. New York: New York Public
       Library, 1959.

14241 Fox, Charles, Peter Gammond, and Alun Morgan. Jazz on Record,
       A Critical Guide. Westport, Conn.: Greenwood Press, 1978. Re-
       print of the 1960 edition published by Hutchinson, London.

14242 Gammond, Peter, and Peter Clayton. Dictionary of Popular Music.
       New York: Philosophical Library, 1961.

14243 Mercury Records Corporation. Mercury Catalog of Popular Jazz
       [and] Classical Long Playing Albums [n.p.], 1961.

14244 Burton, Jack. The Blue Book of Tin Pan Alley, a Human Interest
       Encyclopedia [of] American Popular Music. Watkins Glen, N.Y.:
       Century House, 1962-1965. Vol. 1. 1776-1910. --Vol. 2. 1910-
       1950; 1950-1965 Supplement.

14245 Gammond, Peter, and Burnett James. Music on Record: A Critical
       Guide. Westport, Conn.: Greenwood Press, 1978. Reprint of
       the 1962 edition published by Hutchinson, London. Vol. 1. Or-
       chestral Music, A-L. --Vol. 2. Orchestral Music, M-Z. --Vol. 3.
       Chamber and Instrumental Music, with Supplements to Vols. 1 &
       2. --Vol. 4. Opera and Vocal Music, with Supplements to Vols.
       1-3.

14246 Charters, Samuel Barclay. Jazz: New Orleans, 1885-1963; An In-
       dex to the Negro Musicians of New Orleans. Rev. ed. New York:
       Oak Publications, 1963.

14247 Epstein, D. "Slave Music in the United States Before 1860; A Sur-
       vey of Sources." Music Library Association Notes 20:195-219,
       Spring 1963; 20:377-390, Summer 1963.

14248 Jepsen, Jorgen Grunnet. Jazz Records, 1942-1965--1942-1969: A
       Discography. Holte, Denmark: K. E. Knudsen, 1964-1970. Elev-
       en volumes.

14249 Lawless, Ray McKinley. Folksingers and Folksongs in America; A
       Handbook of Biography, Bibliography, and Discography. Rev. ed.
       New York: Duell, Sloan and Pearce, 1965. Includes black mu-
       sicians such as Harry Belafonte.

14250 Stambler, Irwin. Encyclopedia of Popular Music. New York: St.
       Martin's Press, 1965.

14251 Gillis, Frank, and Alan P. Merriam. Ethnomusicology and Folk
       Music; An International Bibliography of Dissertations and Theses.
       Middletown, Conn.: Published for the Society for Ethnomusicology
       by the Wesleyan University Press, 1966.

14252 Bruyninckx, Walter. 50 Years of Recorded Jazz, 1917-1967. Meche-len, Belgium: Bruyninckx, 1967?

14253 Ferris, W. R. "Discography of Mississippi Negro Folk Music." Mississippi Folklore Register 2:51-54, no. 2, 1968.

14254 Jazz on Record: A Critical Guide to the First 50 Years: 1917-1967. By Albert McCarthy, et al. New York: Oak Publications, 1968.

14255 Lawrenz, Marguerite Martha. Bibliography and Index of Negro Music. Detroit: Board of Education, Detroit, 1968.

14256 Leadbitter, Mike, and Neil Slaven. Blues Records, January 1943 to December 1966. London: Hanover Books, 1968.

14257 Carl Gregor, Duke of Mecklenburg. International Jazz Bibliography; Jazz Books from 1919 to 1968. Strasbourg, France: P. H. Heitz, 1969.

14258 Dance, S. "A Selective Jazz Discography, 1968-69." Music Journal Annual p. 14, 1969.

14259 De Lerma, Dominique-René. The Black American Musical Heritage; A Preliminary Bibliography. Kent, Ohio: Music Library Association, Midwest Chapter, 1969.

14260 Godrich, John, and Robert M. Dixon. Blues & Gospel Records, 1902-1942. London: Storyville Publications, 1969. They " ... attempted to list every distinctly Negroid folk music record made up to the end of 1942."

14261 Irvine, Betty Jo, and Jane A. McCabe. Fine Arts and the Black American and Music and the Black American. Bloomington: Indiana University Libraries and Focus: Black America, 1969.

14262 McCabe, Jane Ann. Black Entertainers and the Entertainment Industry. Bloomington: Indiana University Libraries and Focus: Black America, 1969.

14263 Sjolund, James, and Warren Burton. The American Negro; A Selected Bibliography of Materials Including Children's Books, Reference Books, Collections and Anthologies, Recordings, Films and Filmstrips. Olympia, Washington, [n.p.], 1969.

14264 "Bibliographie." Musik und Bildung 2:290, June 1970.

14265 Indiana University. Archives of Traditional Music. Catalog of Afro-American Music and Oral Data Holdings. Compiled by Philip M. Peek. Bloomington: Indiana University, 1970.

14266 Rohde, H. Kandy. The Gold of Rock & Roll, 1955-1967. New York: Arbor House, 1970. Lists top records by year and includes many black musicians.

14267 Allen, W. C. Studies in Jazz Discography. Westport, Conn.: Greenwood Press, 1978. Reprint of the 1971 edition published by the Institute of Jazz Studies, Rutgers University, New Brunswick, N.J.

14268 Cullaz, Maurice. Guide des Disques de Jazz; Les 1,000 Meilleurs
       Disques de Spirituals, Gospel Songs, Blues, Rhytm [sic] and
       Blues, Jazz et Leur Histoire. Paris: Buchet/Chastel, 1971.

14269 Ferris, William R. Mississippi Black Folklore; A Research Bib-
       liography and Discography. Hattiesburg: University and College
       Press of Mississippi, 1971.

14270 Kennington, Donald. The Literature of Jazz: A Critical Guide.
       Chicago: American Library Association, 1971.

14271 Ploski, Harry A., Otto J. Lindenmeyer, and Ernest Kaiser. Ref-
       erence Library of Black America. New York: Bellwether Pub.
       Co. for exclusive distribution by Afro-American Press, 1971.
       Vol. 3 of this 5-vol. set contains "The Black Entertainer in the
       Performing Arts" and "The Jazz Scene."

14272 Wood, Graham. An A-Z of Rock and Roll. London: Studio Vista,
       1971. Short biographies of English and U.S. rock musicians in-
       cluding many black performers.

14273 "Selected Resources for Black Studies in Music." Music Educator's
       Journal 58:56, November 1971.

14274 Bogaert, Karel. Blues Lexicon; Blues Cajun, Boogie Woogie, Gos-
       pel. Antwerpen: Standaard, 1972.

14275 Chilton, John. Who's Who of Jazz! Storyville to Swing Street.
       Philadelphia: Chilton Book Co., 1972.

14276 De Lerma, D. R. "A Selective List of Choral Music by Black Com-
       posers." Choral Journal 12:5-6, no. 8, 1972.

14277 Moon, Pete. A Bibliography of Jazz Discographies Published Since
       1960. 3rd ed. South Harrow, Eng.: British Institute of Jazz
       Studies, 1972.

14278 Panzeri, Louis. Louisiana Composers. New Orleans, La.: Din-
       stuhl Print. and Pub., 1972. Includes "Biographies of the Negro
       in Louisiana" and a bibliography of "Negro Spirituals, Work Songs,
       and Stories of Louisiana."

14279 Standifer, James A., and Barbara Reeder. Source Book of African
       and Afro-American Materials for Music Educators. Washington:
       Music Educator's National Conference, 1972.

14280 De Lerma, Dominique-René. A Discography of Concert Music by
       Black Composers. Minneapolis: AAMOA Press, 1973.

14281 _____. A Name List of Black Composers. Minneapolis: AAMOA
       Press, 1973.

14282 _____. "The Teacher's Guide to Recent Recordings of Music by
       Black Composers." College Music Symposium 13:114-119, 1973.

14283 Jackson, Richard. United States Music; Sources of Bibliography and
       Collective Biography. Brooklyn: Brooklyn College of the City
       University of New York, 1973. Includes sections on "Black Music

as a Genre" and "Blues, Ragtime, Jazz" which contain annotated lists of bibliographical sources.

14284 Jasen, David A. Recorded Ragtime, 1897-1958. Hamden, Conn.: Archon Books, 1973. A discography of ragtime.

14285 Johnson, James Peter. Bibliographic Guide to the Study of Afro-American Music. Washington: Howard University Libraries, 1973.

14286 Rust, Brian A. L., and Allen G. Debus. The Complete Entertainment Discography, from the Mid-1890s to 1942. New Rochelle, N.Y.: Arlington House, 1973. Jazz and blues musicians are excluded, but other fields of music list musicians such as Andy Razaf and Paul Robeson.

14287 Whitburn, Joel. Top Rhythm & Blues Records, 1949-1971. Menomonee Falls, Wis.: Record Research, 1973. Kept up-to-date by supplements.

14288 "Bibliographie: Jazz--Blues--Worksong--Spiritual--Gospelsong." Musik und Bildung 5:198-202, April 1973.

14289 Garcia, W. B. "Church Music by Black Composers: A Bibliography of Choral Music." Black Perspectives in Music 2:145-157, no. 2, 1974.

14290 Kinkle, Roger D. The Complete Encyclopedia of Popular Music and Jazz, 1900-1950. New Rochelle, N.Y.: Arlington House, 1974. Vol. 1. Music Year by Year, 1900-1950.--Vol. 2. Biographies, A Through K.--Vol. 3. Biographies, L Through Z.--Vol. 4. Indexes & Appendices.

14291 Nite, Norm N. Rock On; The Illustrated Encyclopedia of Rock n' Roll: The Solid Gold Years. New York: T. Y. Crowell Co., 1974.

14292 Propes, Steve. Golden Oldies; A Guide to 60's Record Collecting. Radnor, Pa.: Chilton Book Co., 1974. Prominent singles are listed along with many black performers such as the Motown groups.

14293 Stambler, Irwin. Encyclopedia of Pop, Rock and Soul. New York: St. Martin's Press, 1974.

14294 Laade, W. "Bibliographie: Von Country & Western zum Hard Rock --eine Bibliographie der Pop-Musik und Ihres Soziokulturellen Hintergrunds." Music und Bildung 6:322-329, May 1974.

14295 Garcia, W. "Church Music by Black Composers: A Bibliography of Choral Music." Black Perspectives in Music 2:145-157, Fall 1974.

14296 Arkansas Arts Center, Little Rock. Catalog of the John D. Reid Collection of Early American Jazz. Compiled by Meredith McCoy and Barbara Parker. Little Rock: Arkansas Arts Center, 1975.

14297 Cooper, David Edwin. International Bibliography of Discographies: Classical Music and Jazz & Blues, 1962-1972: A Reference Book

for Record Collectors, Dealers, and Libraries. Littleton, Colo.:
Libraries Unlimited, 1975.

14298 De Lerma, Dominique-René. Black Concert and Recital Music, a
       Provisional Repertoire List. Bloomington: Afro-American Music
       Opportunities Assn., 1975.

14299 Modern Jazz: The Essential Records: A Critical Selection. By
       Max Harrison, et al. London: Aquarius Books, 1975. An an-
       notated list of important recordings in jazz, many by black mu-
       sicians.

14300 Voigt, John, and Randall Kane. Jazz Music in Print. Winthrop,
       Mass.: Flat Nine Music, 1975.

14301 White, Evelyn Davidson. Selected Bibliography of Published Choral
       Music by Black Composers. Washington?: White, 1975.

14302 Brown, Ernest James. "An Annotated Bibliography of Selected Solo
       Music Written for the Piano by Black Composers." (D.M.A. Dis-
       sertation, University of Maryland, 1976).

14303 The Encyclopedia of Rock. Edited by Phil Hardy, and Dave Laing.
       St. Albans, Eng.: Panther, 1976.

14304 Feather, Leonard G., and Ira Gitler. The Encyclopedia of Jazz in
       the Seventies. New York: Horizon Press, 1976.

14305 Ferlingere, Robert D. A Discography of Rhythm & Blues and Rock
       'n Roll Vocal Groups, 1945 to 1965. Pittsburg, Calif.: Ferlingere,
       1976.

14306 Townley, Eric. Tell Your Story: A Dictionary of Jazz and Blues
       Recordings 1917-1950. Chigwell, Eng.: Storyville Pub., 1976.

14307 Goldstein, Stewart, and Alan Jacobson. Oldies but Goodies: The
       Rock 'n' Roll Years. New York: Mason/Charter, 1977. Dis-
       cography of rock music by year, 1955-1965, including musicians
       such as Nat King Cole and Little Richard.

14308 Gonzalez, Fernando L. Disco-file: The Discographical Catalog of
       American Rock & Roll and Rhythm & Blues Vocal Harmony Groups:
       Race, Rhythm & Blues, Rock & Roll, Soul: 1902-1976. 2nd ed.
       Flushing, N.Y.: Gonzalez, 1977.

14309 Jones, W. J. "Music Materials for Instructional Use from the Eth-
       nic American Art Slide Library of the University of South Ala-
       bama." College Music Symposium 17:102-119, no. 1, 1977.

14310 Phillips, Linda Nell. "Piano Music by Black Composers: A Com-
       puter Based Bibliography." (D.M.A. Dissertation, Ohio State Uni-
       versity, 1977).

14311 Turner, Patricia. Afro-American Singers: An Index and Preliminary
       Discography of Long-Playing Recordings of Opera, Choral Music,
       and Song. Minneapolis: Challenge Productions, 1977.

14312 Case, Brian, and Stan Britt. The Illustrated Encyclopedia of Jazz.
       New York: Harmony Books, 1978.

14313 Mapp, Edward. Directory of Blacks in the Performing Arts. Me-
       tuchen, N.J.: Scarecrow Press, 1978. Opera, jazz, and class-
       ical music are among the areas covered.

14314 Roxon, Lillian. Lillian Roxon's Rock Encyclopedia. Compiled by
       Ed Naha. Rev. ed. New York: Grosset & Dunlap, 1978.

14315 Rust, Brian A. L. Jazz Records, 1897-1942. 4th rev. and enl. ed.
       New Rochelle, N.Y.: Arlington House Pub., 1978. A 2-volume
       discography with an index by artist and by song titles.

14316 Walker, Leo. The Big Band Almanac. Pasadena, CA: Ward Ritchie
       Press, 1978. A synopsis of dance bands from before the 1920's
       to the 1950's. Includes some black bands such as those of Louis
       Armstrong and Lionel Hampton.

14317 Williams, Ora. American Black Women in the Arts and Social Sci-
       ences: A Bibliographic Survey. Rev. and expanded ed. Metuchen,
       N.J.: Scarecrow Press, 1978. Contains a section listing ar-
       rangers, composers, and lyricists.

14318 Harris, Sheldon. Blues Who's Who. New Rochelle: Arlington
       House, 1979.

14319 Jackson, Irene V. Afro-American Religious Music: A Bibliography
       and a Catalogue of Gospel Music. Westport, Conn.: Greenwood
       Press, 1979.

Aasland, Benny H. 4564, 4614, 4624, 5462
Abdul, Raoul 13751, 14049
Abel, B. 3370
Abody, B. 11926
Abrahams, R. D. 13636
Abrans, M. 10377
Achille, L. T. 12578, 12639-12640, 12703
Ackerman, G. 11872
Ackerman, P. 406, 2118, 3174, 5022, 10748, 12655, 13589
Adams, A. 13066
Adams, C. G. 13637
Adams, E. L. 12142
Adams, Rosemary Frayser 12768
Addeo, Edmond G. 8731
Adderley, J. 3358
Adderton, D. 1997, 2021, 9905, 14042, 14124
Adkins, Aldrich Wendell 13390
Adler, P. 753
Affeldt, P. E. 200, 865, 2122, 2153, 7654, 7715, 8717, 10280, 10744, 10873
Ahlstroem, T. 1765, 9380, 9517
Aikin, J. 1572, 6849
Ainslie, P. 7413
Albertson, Chris 208, 773, 1071, 1406, 1945, 2121, 2274, 2281, 2332, 3904, 4166, 4179, 4220, 4262, 4400, 4414, 5621, 5937, 6558, 6562, 6628, 6854, 6870, 7092, 7877, 7880, 7924, 7931, 8010, 8361, 8835, 9199, 9787, 9827, 9874, 10791-10792, 10796, 11113, 11125, 11156
Albright, T. 13126
Albus, Harry James 60
Adam, J. 11062
Alessandrini, P. 2213, 4192, 5144, 13225
Aletti, V. 2646, 2651, 4198, 6097, 6209, 6218, 6316, 7777, 7783, 8616-8617, 12004, 12009, 12017, 13712, 13734
Alexander, T. 13713

Alilunas, L. J. 12843
Alkire, Stephen Robert 13638
Allan, J. W. 5197
Allan, L. 7294
Allen, Betty 13-14
Allen, C. G. 12249, 12292
Allen, H. T. 14050
Allen, Richard B. 14074
Allen, S. 6379
Allen, Walter C. 859, 1040, 6894, 9484, 9490, 9494, 10733, 11968, 12914, 14267
Allen, W. D. 13639
Allen, W. F. 13951
Almquist, D. Idestam see Idestam-Almquest, D.
Alterman, L. 6257, 7800, 8623, 11709
Amatneedk, B. 6205
American Music Center, New York 14238
Ames, M. 10764, 11781
Ames, R. 12379, 12457, 12468
Ammann, B. 1144
Amram, D. 9755
Anders, J. 3567, 7921, 7942
Anderson, Edison Holmes 355, 396, 12610
Anderson, H. 13753
Anderson, J. L. 340, 343, 345, 1620, 1643, 4015, 9270, 9478, 9482, 12437
Anderson, L. 1245, 1709, 4625, 4749, 4764, 4771, 4806, 4825, 4907, 5082, 5463
Anderson, Marian 108, 112, 142
Anderson, O. 12930
Anderson, W. 8242
Andre, J. 3438
Angelou, M. 10660
Aning, B. A. 13952
Antcliffe, H. 3607
Antoine, R. 3338
Antrim, Doron Kemp 4440
Appleton, Clyde Robert 13256
Ardoin, J. 2496, 10086, 10548, 10551, 10564, 10955, 11820-

Ellis, G. 7303
Ellison, R. 7639
Ellsworth, R. 8144
Elsdon, A. 925
Elsner, Constanze 12067
Elsner, J. 721
Elzy, R. 12380
Embree, Edwin Rogers 10899
Emerson, Lucy 13960
Emerson, William Canfield
  12277
Emery, J. 2470
Emge, C. 335, 3055, 10701,
  12440, 12489
Ende, A. Von see Von Ende, A.
Endress, G. 1579, 1776, 1950,
  4383, 6033, 8876-8877, 11120
Engel, C. 8680
Englin, M. 1733
Englund, B. 212, 1051, 1751
Eniss, J. 4232
Ennett, Dorothy Maxine 13647
Entremont, P. 11090
Epstein, D. 13648, 14247
Epstein, Dena J. 13961,
  14057
Erlich, Lillian 13862
Erskine, G. M. 1057, 1074,
  7006, 9416, 9538
Esposito, B. 9793
Esquire 13863
Evans, Arthur Lee 13522
Evans, D. 13262-13263, 13496,
  13523-13524, 13649-13650,
  13763, 13831, 13962-13963
Evans, O. 9059
Evans, T. 9805, 11117
Evearitt, D. J. 12070
Evensmo, J. 14178
Everett, T. 1157, 6052
Evers, Mrs. M. W. 2763
Ewen, David 12384, 12386,
  12406, 12612, 12775, 12823,
  12917, 13525, 14058
Eyer, R. 91
Eyle, Wim van 13964

Faber, Anne 1096
Fabio, S. W. 4214
Fagan, Eleanora see Holi-
  iday, Billie
Fager, C. E. 13502
Fahrer, A. 11868
Failows, J. R. 727
Falk, R. 1874
Falls, M. 7761
Farber, J. 9909
Farmer, A. 3344

Farmer, J. 13320
Farrell, B. 10348
Farrell, D. 14123
Farrell, Jack W. 12579
Fatha see Hines, Earl Kenneth
Faulkner, M. 10048
Fayenz, F. 1738, 6481, 11566
Feather, Leonard G. 225, 231,
  235, 392, 397, 411-412, 524,
  539, 581, 584, 634, 638, 640,
  681, 684, 694, 698, 731, 775,
  783, 786, 827, 833, 845, 850,
  855, 944, 968, 1061, 1072-1073,
  1076, 1179, 1198, 1210, 1306,
  1363, 1365-1366, 1384, 1394,
  1408, 1413, 1415, 1459-1460,
  1599, 1736, 1946, 1975, 1977,
  1983, 1986, 2008, 2010, 2012,
  2120, 2161, 2425, 2860, 2876,
  2929, 2945-2946, 2966, 2969,
  2977, 3075, 3122, 3140, 3204,
  3226, 3235, 3255, 3284, 3349,
  3388, 3405, 3623, 3751, 3784,
  3801, 3988, 3997, 4008, 4014,
  4024, 4058, 4094, 4098-4099,
  4122-4125, 4127, 4149-4152,
  4219, 4222, 4224, 4244, 4319,
  4477, 4490, 4493, 4497, 4512,
  4538, 4560, 4566, 4582, 4589,
  4597, 4600, 4627, 4631, 4643,
  4649, 4660, 4673, 4692, 4716,
  4727, 4786, 4906, 4942, 4979,
  4998, 5013, 5047-5048, 5085,
  5103-5104, 5159, 5203, 5205,
  5207, 5239, 5340, 5443, 5466,
  5502, 5517, 5659, 5678-5679,
  5700, 5708, 5758, 5774, 5857,
  5889, 5926, 5951, 5954, 5979,
  6067, 6069, 6072, 6099, 6155,
  6201, 6225, 6237, 6414, 6441,
  6448, 6450, 6470, 6472, 6504,
  6507, 6544, 6546, 6556, 6566,
  6568, 6598, 6646, 6648, 6679,
  6739, 6740-6741, 6743, 6755,
  6773, 6837, 6979, 7022, 7066,
  7153, 7190, 7209, 7216, 7262,
  7277, 7291, 7323, 7349, 7356,
  7453, 7491, 7530, 7567-7569,
  7682, 7701, 7709-7710, 8015,
  8019, 8037, 8039, 8050, 8062-
  8063, 8070, 8094, 8354, 8374,
  8395, 8754, 8785, 8789, 8810,
  8847, 8860, 9163, 9183, 9194,
  9211, 9213, 9284, 9397, 9424,
  9431, 9436, 9442, 9468, 9595,
  9606, 9618, 9716-1917, 10277,
  10508, 10524, 10627, 10658,
  10664-10665, 10763, 10842,
  10892, 11036, 11173, 11408,

11411, 11414, 11419,
11421, 11425, 11473,
11568, 11570, 11669, 11690,
11693, 11698, 12421, 12456,
12488, 12563, 12628, 12666,
12749, 12757, 12856, 12939,
13020, 13024, 13049, 13107,
13189, 13201, 13454, 13526,
13804, 13825, 13965-13966,
14196, 14304
Feda, J. 6709
Feinstein, H. 7511
Feldman, P. 8599
Fellowes, M. H. 6874
Ferdinand, V. 6821, 8482,
9897, 10308, 10690, 13918
Ferguson, C. W. 9066
Ferguson, O. 12369
Ferlingere, Robert D. 14305
Fernett, Gene 13264
Ferrara, D. 4001, 6440
Ferrero, F. 12122
Ferris, W. 13764
Ferris, William R. 13265,
13399, 13750, 14253, 14269
Fierz, G. 11947
Figueroa, O. 10124
Fine, M. 13842
Finkelstein, S. 8697
Finkelstein, Sidney Walter
12417
Finola, G. 5116
Fiofori, T. 6597, 6611, 8378, 8382
Fischer-Williams, B. 2621
Fishel, J. 8442
Fisher, Mrs. Marshall see
Vaughan, Sarah Lois
Fisher, Miles Mark 6669,
9058, 12422, 12524, 13472
Fisher, W. A. 12310
Fishwick, M. 13400
Fitch, J. 13274
Fitzgerald, G. 2581-2582,
10004
Flakser, H. 1732, 4651, 4932,
11551, 11565
Flanagan, W. 10120
Fleming, R. 4361
Fleming, S. 26, 8256, 8284,
11839
Fletcher, Tom 12543
Flicker, C. 7902
Flippo, C. 2956, 8078, 8745
Flores, A. 14112
Floyd, S. A. 13765, 13865
Flückiger, O. 2698, 3040
Fong-Torres, B. 2980, 7098,
7326, 7781, 8771, 9947,

11195, 12018, 13710
Fonollosa, J. M. 12470
Fonteyne, A. 7319, 11204, 13573
Ford, E. C. 12562
Ford, R. 14153, 14182, 14216
Foreman, R. C. 13080
Fortunato, Jeanne Alba 13766
Fossum, K. 11923
Fowler, B. 9469
Fowler, D. E. 8135
Fowler, W. L. 1149, 1524, 9459
Fox, Charles 2051, 2432, 8199,
8243, 9165, 11555, 12756,
13370, 13527, 14241
Fox, H. 5688
Fox, T. C. 2204
Francard, P. Blanc see Blanc-
Francard, P.
Francis, André 12707
Francis, B. 2690, 3105, 3110,
8514, 10510
Francis, H. 1547, 1780, 5470,
11618
Frankenstein, A. 2526, 13938
Franklin, Jacquelyn C. 13967
Franksen, J. 9195, 9358
Franze, J. P. 10111
Frazier, G. 4992
Frederick, R. B. 13237
Freed, R. 8190
Freedland, N. 6797, 8223, 8618,
10209, 12064, 14024, 14039
Freeman, D. 327, 341, 820, 1230,
1796, 3069, 3079, 3111, 4514,
4555, 4607, 6971, 12508
Freeman, J. W. 8237
Freeman, P. 13635
Freis, R. 14177
Fremer, B. 3618, 6420, 9885
French, R. F. 13081
Fresia, E. 3781, 4722, 4837
Freyse, R. 2498
Fridlund, H. 8115
Fried, A. G. 2137
Friedel, L. M. 12407
Friedlander, W. 388
Friedli, H. 3554
Friedman, J. 1811, 12587
Friedman, Laura 14135
Friend, R. 6078
Frost, H. 4005
Fuchs, A. 9933, 13234
Fuchs, H. 10581
Fulbright, T. 461, 10243
Fumex, G. 12839
Furie, K. 10188, 13828
Furness, C. J. 12282

Harrison, R. C. 12219
Hasegawa, Sam 12036
Haskell, M. A. 12110
Haskins, James 8286, 12059,
  12074, 14061, 14121
Harth, L. H. 12329
Harvey, J. 10946
Hatfield, Edwin Francis 12080
Hawes, Bess Lomax 13531-
  13532
Hawes, H. 7382, 9796
Hawkins, W. 158, 161
Hawkins, W. E. 12321
Hayakawa, S. I. 8239
Hayes, C. 8220
Hayes, C. J. 7688, 7690
Hayes, R. 12874
Haynes, H. 2603, 6123, 11227
Hayton, Mrs. Lennie see
  Horne, Lena
Heckman, D. 1987, 3397,
  3409, 3412, 3427, 3436,
  3456, 3479, 3811, 3845,
  3948, 4104, 4190, 4350,
  5062, 6730, 6742, 7531,
  9718, 13173, 13187
Hegedüs, L. 5916
Heilbut, Tony 13407
Heineman, A. 8323
Helander, O. 8031
Helm, E. 10044
Helopaltio, K. 13204
Hemming, Roy 18, 131, 10173
Henderson, F. 281
Henderson, S. E. 13033,
  13067
Hennessey, M. 741, 747, 3437,
  3790-3791, 4985, 5899, 5930,
  6090, 6216, 7875, 8040, 9172,
  10317, 13021, 11097, 11650
Hennessey, Thomas J. 13652,
  13773
Henricksson, S. A. 1942
Henry, L. 12445
Henschen, R. 8003
Henshaw, L. 1955, 2064, 4804-
  4805, 5108, 5946, 6170, 8083,
  9009, 9201, 11510, 11665
Hentoff, Nat 525, 603, 1099,
  1293, 1311, 1344, 1564, 1660,
  1856, 2391, 2394, 2888, 3382,
  3756, 3998, 4018, 4041, 4077,
  4132, 4141, 4619, 4628, 4630,
  4671, 4762, 4883, 4890, 5538,
  5555, 5594, 5608, 5637, 5658,
  5765, 5857, 6412, 6557, 6692,
  6891, 7042, 7214, 7274, 7296,
  7392, 7394, 7631, 7636, 8013,

8048, 8051, 8721, 8758, 8805,
8816, 8879, 9092, 9202, 9568,
9675, 10859, 11380, 11644,
11777, 12507, 12559, 12588,
12602, 12616, 12668, 12685-
12686, 12796, 12806, 12812,
12825, 12899, 12943, 12959,
12963, 12969, 13058, 13097,
13174, 13195, 13343, 13491,
13972, 14115
Hepburn, D. 1883, 2028, 7505,
  8508, 10024, 10615
Herbert, Rubye Nell 8271
Heribel, S. 3045
Hermann, I. 11874
Herrema, R. D. 13268
Hershovits, Melville Jean 12358
Herst, E. 10544
Hess, J. B. 4237
Hetherington, B. 7798
Heughan, G. W. 4799
Heylbut, R. 52
Hickman, C. S. 111
Hiemenz, J. 3973, 11878, 13613
Higgins, C. 7718, 7726, 11194,
  13473
Higginson, T. W. 12086
Hilarian, Sister Mary 12334,
  12355
Hilbert, B. 682, 695
Hilburn, R. 2101, 12042
Hildebrand, B. J. 715
Hill, A. 12993
Hill, R. 180, 13774
Hillary, R. 11975
Hillman, C. 9514
Hillsman, Joan R. 14083
Hines, Earl Kenneth (Fatha) 6977-
  6978, 6992, 7052
Hinton, J. 101
Hippenmeyer, J. R. 2709, 5329
Hirshowitz, B. 13530
Hitchcock, Hugh Wiley 8157, 13775
Hitchens, W. 12306
Hoare, I. 8132
Hoberman, J. 1104, 2712
Hobson, C. 7699
Hobson, W. 298, 324, 421, 1206,
  1661, 3739, 6967, 7009, 7566,
  7590, 8703, 9278, 9283, 9291,
  9597, 10707, 12346, 12804
Hodara, M. 5506
Hodeir, André 1281, 4745, 9736,
  11047, 11053, 12581
Hodenfield, C. 6269
Hodes, A. 201, 1735, 2392, 12972
Hodgkins, B. 4518
Hoefer, George 299-300, 311, 314,